MW00627591

"Fr. Réginald Garrigou-Lagrange, O.P., was and is the greatest theologian of the twentieth century. Recognizing this fact is not to diminish other theologians of the postconciliar period who were lionized for lesser talents, but only to understand why his work is now experiencing an extraordinary and welcome revival among a new generation that is looking for a more stable footing. It's easy to understand his attraction when you begin to inhabit the comprehensive scope, coherence, and power of his thought, so well communicated here and throughout his corpus. We owe a great debt to Matthew Minerd for so masterfully translating Garrigou-Lagrange's monumental two-volume work on divine Revelation—a work of such exquisite depth and wisdom that one could confidently rebuild and refresh the entirety of Catholic theological education upon these forgotten and fecund foundations. We see here in these volumes, as if held high in a magnificent monstrance, the triumph of truth itself."

CHAD PECKNOLD
Associate Professor of Systematic Theology
The Catholic University of America, Washington, DC

"Whether one agrees or disagrees with him, Garrigou-Lagrange's treatise on divine Revelation is one of the most important and influential texts of twentieth century apologetics. It sets forth the common position of classical Thomism on issues such as the preambles and mysteries of faith, the nature of divine Revelation and faith, the motives of credibility, and related topics. A great deal of theology both before and after this text is a reaction to the principles and positions set forth here."

FR. JAMES BRENT, O.P.
Assistant Professor of Philosophy
Pontifical Faculty of the Immaculate Conception at the Dominican House of Studies, Washington, DC

"It is impossible to grasp what was going on in theology, whether Catholic or not, in the first half of the twentieth century without appreciating how central to it were the debates around divine Revelation, the act of faith, and apologetics. Even those Catholics who parted ways with neo-Scholasticism cannot be properly understood without a sense of the balanced and intricate account honed by such significant and influential figures as Fr. Réginald Garrigou-Lagrange, O.P. Combining linguistic skill with extensive knowledge of the Thomist tradition, Dr. Matthew Minerd has put a wider theological public in his debt by making available this fine and accurate translation of Garrigou-Lagrange's *De Revelatione*. A broader readership can now begin to rediscover not only the importance of this text as a point of reference for the history of theology but also its insights for the theological task today."

FR. SIMON FRANCIS GAINE, O.P.
Pinckaers Professor in Theological Anthropology and Ethics
Pontifical University of St. Thomas (Angelicum), Rome

"One does not have to be a Thomist to appreciate the brilliance and perspicacity of these tomes. They are among the timeless classics of a *faith seeking understanding* and will still shine brightly when many other works have been forgotten."

ULRICH LEHNER
William K. Warren Professor of Theology
University of Notre Dame, Notre Dame, IN

"We theologians today often fancy ourselves sophisticated, learned, and subtle. But how can we be so if we ignore the great theologians of the early twentieth century and eschew the scholastic tradition that they furthered? Garrigou-Lagrange's text *De Revelatione* is a treasure that, until the publication of this splendid translation, few could access. We have much to learn from this master, much to emulate, even if we take issue with him here or there. He defines his terms, establishes his starting claims, and clearly argues his case. If we today juggle two or three concepts about some topic, Garrigou-Lagrange works with not a few more, both distinguishing and uniting. Nor does he simply entrap us in a labyrinth. By his manifold consideration of each topic and his global vision of the whole, he presents to us a grand example of theological wisdom. This text, challenging and rewarding, promises abundant fruit for those who labor in its field. Dr. Minerd has done a great service in rendering this tome into clear and articulate English. Let us hope that young scholars and seminarians pick it up and read."

CHRISTOPHER J. MALLOY
Associate Professor of Theology
The University of Dallas, Dallas, TX

"Though published nearly a century ago, the relevance of Fr. Garrigou-Lagrange's *De Revelatione* perdures. In the work, Fr. Garrigou-Lagrange masterfully lays out the first principles of the defensive branch of fundamental theology called apologetics and proceeds to give an account of how one ought to consider the very possibility of revelation. Far from a topical handbook with *ad hoc* replies to various and sundry objections to the faith, the work attempts to provide a speculative account of apologetics, understood as a part of sacred theology. In this regard, it is not only important as an introduction to the understanding of the faith, that is, for beginners, but also for advanced students in theology. Aside from delineating the important role that prophecy and miracles play as extrinsic motives of credibility (often considered passé in our times), Fr. Garrigou-Lagrange emphasizes the properly supernatural character of faith, which requires an elevation through grace that perfects, without destroying, the deepest longings of the human heart. In providing us with a careful translation of Fr. Réginald Garrigou-Lagrange's *De Revelatione*, Matthew Minerd has performed an important service for the Church and for contemporary Catholic theology."

JOSHUA LIM
Tutor in Theology
Thomas Aquinas College, Santa Paula, CA

"This is a monumental effort of making Garrigou-Lagrange's fundamental theology more accessible to students and scholars alike. Garrigou-Lagrange upholds what so much of theology has abandoned over many decades: an understanding of revelation as divine speech, *locutio Dei*. These two volumes are valuable complements to other fundamental theologies, which, together and in dialogue with each other, can offer a more holistic understanding of divine Revelation, its possibility and credibility. In addition, the translation and re-publication of this masterpiece, along with other works by Garrigou-Lagrange, will undoubtedly affect the dynamics of twentieth-century Catholic historiography for the better: the Dominican master cannot be caricatured, ignored, or dismissed as a relic from a bygone era. He continues to teach today!"

ANDREW MESZAROS
Professor of Systematic Theology
Pontifical University, St. Patrick's College, Maynooth, Ireland

ON DIVINE
REVELATION

VOLUME ONE

ON DIVINE REVELATION

The Teaching *of the* Catholic Faith

FR. RÉGINALD GARRIGOU-LAGRANGE, O.P.

Translated by Matthew K. Minerd

EMMAUS
ACADEMIC

Steubenville, Ohio
www.emmausacademic.com

EMMAUS
A C A D E M I C

Steubenville, Ohio
www.emmausacademic.com
A Division of The St. Paul Center for Biblical Theology
Editor-in-Chief: Scott Hahn
1468 Parkview Circle
Steubenville, Ohio 43952

The original French *De revelatione per ecclesiam Catholicam proposita*, 5th edition, was published in Rome in 1950 by Desclée et Socii.

Library of Congress Cataloging-in-Publication Data applied for
ISBN hardcover 978-1-64585-154-7 / paperback 978-1-64585-155-4 /
ebook 978-1-64585-156-1

Cover image: Guido Reni, *Moses with the Tables of the Law* (1624), Galleria Borghese, Rome.
Cover design by Allison Merrick
Layout by Emily Demary

Table of Contents

INTRODUCTION BY CAJETAN CUDDY, O.P.   1

TRANSLATOR'S INTRODUCTION   45

ORIGINAL PREFACE BY POPE BENEDICT XV   57

AUTHOR'S PREFACE   59

DIVISION OF THE ENTIRE WORK   65

VOLUME I

PROLEGOMENA CONCERNING FUNDAMENTAL THEOLOGY,
    IN PARTICULAR ITS APOLOGETIC PORTION   69

CHAPTER ONE: WHAT IS SACRED THEOLOGY?   79

    ART. 1: THE DEFINITION OF SACRED THEOLOGY   79

       §1. The nominal definition of sacred theology   80

       §2. The necessity of sacred theology, taken from its end   80

       §3. The real definition of sacred theology   81

       §4. The Integral Definition of Sacred Theology   95

       §5. Corollaries concerning the Relations of Sacred
         Theology to Faith, to the Knowledge of God,
         to the Gift of Wisdom, and to the Sciences of
         the Natural Order   96

       §6. Whether the Aforementioned Notion of Theology
         Is Found, at Least Implicitly, in Sacred Scripture and
         in the Councils   106

    ART. 2: THE DIVISION AND UNITY OF SACRED THEOLOGY   112

       §1. Division of Sacred Theology   112

       §2. The Unity of Sacred Theology   117

    ART. 3: ON THE METHODOLOGY EMPLOYED   120
    IN SACRED THEOLOGY

       §1. The Methodology Employed in Sacred Theology
         Is Principally a Method from Authority   120

       §2. On the Basis of These Authorities, the Doctrinal
         Body Is Constructed through an Analytic-Synthetic
         Methodology, Which Is Set Forth in the Treatise on
         Theological Sources   124

CHAPTER TWO: CONCERNING FUNDAMENTAL THEOLOGY,
APOLOGETICS IN PARTICULAR   127
    ART. 1: THE DEFINITION AND DIVISION OF FUNDAMENTAL
    THEOLOGY, IN PARTICULAR THAT OF APOLOGETICS   127
       §1. The Nominal Definition of Fundamental Theology
          and Apologetics   127
       §2. The Necessity of Apologetics   129
       §3. The Real Definition of Apologetics   130
       §4. The Division of Apologetics   136
       §5. Whether Apologetics Is a Science, Properly Speaking,
          or at Least Part of a Science   142
    ART. 2: THE RELATIONS OF APOLOGETICS TO SACRED
    THEOLOGY AND TO SCIENCES OF THE NATURAL ORDER   143
       §1. Whether Apologetics Is Specifically Distinct from
          Sacred Theology   143
       §2. Whether Apologetics Is Rightly Said to Be a Part of
          Fundamental Theology   161
       §3 The Relation of Apologetics to the Natural Sciences
          That It Presupposes   162

CHAPTER THREE: ON THE METHODOLOGY OF APOLOGETICS   165
    ART. 1: HOW THIS METHODOLOGY IS TO BE DETERMINED   165
       §1. In Relation to the Methodology Used in Sacred Theology   165
       §2. The Methodology of Apologetics Is Analytic-Synthetic,
          Especially an External One, but Also an Internal One   167
    ART. 2: WHAT THE CHURCH TEACHES ABOUT THE TRUE
    METHOD OF APOLOGETICS   172
       §1. The Church Proposes and Defends a Determinate
          Method for the Defense of the Faith   172
       §2. The Church Condemns the Methodology of Protestants
          (Especially Liberal Protestants) and Modernists   174
    ART. 3: HISTORICAL OVERVIEW OF APOLOGETICS
    FROM THE PERSPECTIVE OF METHODOLOGY   183
       §1. Terminology Regarding Apologetic Methodology   184
       §2. How Did the Prophets Prove Their Divine Mission?   187
       §3. What Was the Via / Way (or Methodology) Used by
          Christ (and, Afterwards, by His Apostles)?   189
       §4. The Apologetic Methodology of the Fathers of
          the Church   197
       §5. The Apologetic Methodology of the Scholastic
          Theologians   202

§6. Apologetic Methodology after the Rise of Protestantism   210

§7. Following the Appearance of Kantianism, Apologetic
   Methodology according to Protestants and Catholics   210

BOOK ONE:

ON THE NOTION, POSSIBILITY, NECESSITY,

AND DISCERNIBILITY OF REVELATION.   249

INTRODUCTORY REMARKS   249

SECTION I: ON THE NOTION OF SUPERNATURAL REVELATION

PROLOGUE   249

CHAPTER FOUR: THE DEFINITION AND DIVISION OF

REVELATION   255

ART. 1: THE CATHOLIC NOTION OF REVELATION AND

HETERODOX NOTIONS THEREOF   255

§1. The Nominal Definition of Revelation   256

§2. The More Explicit Definition Proposed by the
   Catholic Church   257

§3. Heterodox Notions of Revelation   266

ART. 2: THEOLOGICAL EXPLICATION AND DEFENSE OF THE

CATHOLIC NOTION OF REVELATION   271

§1. The formal constitutive of revelation must be
   determined analogically   271

§2. Divine Revelation Is Formally the Speech of God to
   Men after the Manner of a Teaching Authority   274

§3. What Does This Divine Speech Involve?   276

ART. 3: THE DIVISION OF REVELATION   289

§1. This Division Is to Be Taken according to the
   Four Causes   289

§2. Explanation of This Division   290

CHAPTER FIVE: ON THE NOTIONS OF MYSTERY AND

OF DOGMA   297

ART. 1: THE CATHOLIC NOTIONS OF MYSTERY AND

OF DOGMA; HETERODOX NOTIONS   297

§1. The Catholic Notion of Mystery   297

§2. Heterodox Notions of Mystery and of Dogma   300

ART. 2: THEOLOGICAL EXPLICATION OF THE CATHOLIC
NOTIONS OF MYSTERY AND OF DOGMA   304
  §1. Definition of Mystery in General and Its Division   305
  §2. On the Intelligibility of the Mysteries and on Their
      Interconnection   310
  §3. Explanation of the Notion of Dogma   317
  §4. On the Immutability of Dogma and on Its
      Progressive Understanding   320

CHAPTER SIX: ON THE NOTION OF SUPERNATURALITY   327
  ART. 1: THE CATHOLIC NOTION AND HETERODOX
  NOTIONS OF SUPERNATURALITY   327
    §1. (A) The State of the Question and (B) the Nominal
        Definition of Supernaturality   327
    §2. The Catholic Notion of Supernaturality and of the
        Supernatural Order   329
    §3. Heterodox Notions of Supernaturality   332
  ART. 2: THEOLOGICAL EXPLICATION OF THE CATHOLIC
  NOTION OF SUPERNATURALITY   334
    §1. Definition of Supernaturality   335
    §2. Division of Supernaturality   341
    §3. What the Natural and Supernatural Orders Are   353
    §4. Resolution of Objections against the Division of
        Supernaturality Discussed Above   357

SECTION II: ON THE POSSIBILITY OF REVELATION   365
PART ONE: NEGATIVE DEFENSE: AN EXAMINATION OF
THE PRINCIPLES OF RATIONALISM   367

CHAPTER SEVEN: ON RATIONALISM / NATURALISM IN
GENERAL   369
  SINGLE ART: DEFINITION AND DIVISION OF RATIONALISM   369
    §1. The Definition of Rationalism   369
    §2. What the Foundation of Rationalism (or the Claim
        That Reason Is Absolutely Autonomous) Is   370
    §3. The Consequences of Naturalism and Rationalism   373
    §4. On the Spirit of Rationalism, according to the Church 377
    §5. Division of Systems of Rationalism and Naturalism   384

CHAPTER EIGHT: EXAMINATION OF PANTHEISTIC
EVOLUTIONISM, INASMUCH AS IT DENIES THE
POSSIBILITY OF SUPERNATURAL REVELATION
FROM THE PERSPECTIVE OF THE OBJECT 389
ART. 1: EXPOSITION OF PANTHEISTIC EVOLUTIONISM
IN ITS MATERIALISTIC AND IDEALISTIC FORMS 389
§1. What Is Pantheistic Evolutionism in General? 390
§2. Materialistic or Empiricist Evolutionism 392
§3. Idealistic Evolutionism 396
ART. 2: CRITIQUE: PANTHEISTIC EVOLUTIONISM
ULTIMATELY MUST DENY THE FIRST PRINCIPLES
OF REASON 413
§1. What Are the First Principles of Reason and
How Are They Subordinated? 413
§2. Pantheistic Evolutionism Must Deny the First
Principles of Reason 422
§3. Resolution of Objections 429

CHAPTER NINE: EXAMINATION OF AGNOSTICISM,
INASMUCH AS IT DENIES THE POSSIBILITY OF
SUPERNATURAL REVELATION FROM THE
PERSPECTIVE OF THE SUBJECT (I.E., MAN) 445
ART. 1: EXPOSITION OF EMPIRICAL AGNOSTICISM
AND IDEALISTIC AGNOSTICISM 445
§1. Agnosticism in General 445
§2. Empiricist Agnosticism 448
§3. Idealist Agnosticism 454
ART. 2: CRITICISM OF AGNOSTICISM THROUGH A
REDUCTIO AD ABSURDUM 465
§1. Defense of the Ontological Value of the First Notions
and Principles of Reason 466
§2. Defense of the Transcendent Value of the Same Notions
and Principles of Reason 477
§3. Resolution of Objections Raised by Agnostics against the
Ontological and Transcendent Value of the First
Notions and Principles of Our Reason 488

PART TWO: POSITIVE DEFENSE OF THE POSSIBILITY OF
REVELATION 503
PROLOGUE 503

CHAPTER 10: ON THE POSSIBILITY OF SUPERNATURAL
REVELATION IN GENERAL AND SPECIFICALLY
THE POSSIBILITY OF REVELATION OF THE NATURAL
TRUTHS OF RELIGION   507
ART. 1: ON THE POSSIBILITY OF IMMEDIATE REVELATION   507
§1. Reason Alone Can Prove the Possibility of Immediate
Revelation of the Natural Truths of Religion   507
§2. Resolution of Objections   513
ART. 2: ON THE POSSIBILITY OF MEDIATE REVELATION   522
§1. The Possibility of Mediate Revelation Can Be Proven by
Reason Alone   522
§2. Resolution of Objections   524

CHAPTER ELEVEN: ON THE POSSIBILITY OF THE REVELATION
OF SUPERNATURAL MYSTERIES, CONSIDERED FROM
THE PERSPECTIVE OF THE OBJECT   529
SINGLE ART: PROOF FOR THE EXISTENCE OF A
SUPERNATURAL ORDER OF LIFE AND TRUTH IN GOD
(I.E., THE EXISTENCE OF THE ORDER OF SUPERNATURAL
MYSTERIES)   529
§1. Heterodox Doctrines and the Doctrine of the Church   530
§2. On the Demonstrability of the Existence of a
Supernatural Order of Truth and Life in God   534
§3. Demonstration of the Existence of a Supernatural
Order *Objectively* Exceeding the Natural Powers of
the Created Intellect   543
§4. First Corollary: The Supernatural Order Even
Subjectively Exceeds the Power of Whatsoever
Created Intellect   552
§5. Second Corollary: Moreover, the Supernatural
Order Exceeds the *Exigencies* of Whatsoever
Created Intellect   553
§6. Third Corollary: There Cannot Be Disagreement nor
Confusion between Natural Truths and Supernatural
Truths. Rather, They Exist in *Harmony*   555
§7. Resolution of Objections Raised by Semi-rationalists
and Those Coming from Scotus   558
§8. Examination of Ontologism, as well as a Resolution
of the Objections Raised by Ontologists   567

CHAPTER TWELVE: ON THE POSSIBILITY OF REVELATION
OF SUPERNATURAL MYSTERIES, CONSIDERED FROM
THE PERSPECTIVE OF THE AGENT AND SUBJECT   573
SINGLE ART: A DEFENSE IS OFFERED FOR THIS POSSIBILITY
AND ESPECIALLY FOR THE EXISTENCE OF THE OBEDIENTIAL
OR ELEVABLE CAPACITY OF OUR NATURE IN RELATION
TO THE SUPERNATURAL ORDER   573
    §1. State of the Question   573
    §2. This Possibility Cannot Be Disproven   575
    §3. We Can Persuasively Argue That Our Nature Has
       an Obediential Capacity to Be Elevated to the
       Supernatural Order, Arguing from a Consideration
       of the Adequate Object of Our Intellect   580
    §4. The Existence of an Obediential or Elevable Capacity
       for Supernatural Life Can Be Persuasively Argued
       for from a Consideration of Our Natural Desire to
       See God through His Essence   591
    §5. Resolution of Objections   610

SECTION III: ON THE BEFITTINGNESS AND NECESSITY OF
REVELATION   617

CHAPTER THIRTEEN: ON THE BEFITTINGNESS AND
NECESSITY OF REVELATION   619
ART. 1: HETERODOX DOCTRINES AND THE CHURCH'S
DOCTRINE ON THE BEFITTINGNESS AND NECESSITY OF
REVELATION   619
    §1. Heterodox Doctrines   619
    §2. Doctrine of the Church   622
ART. 2: RATIONAL DEFENSE OF THE CHURCH'S DOCTRINE
CONCERNING THE BEFITTINGNESS AND NECESSITY OF
REVELATION   624
    §1. Revelation Is Indeed Morally Necessary So That Men
       May Know Certain Natural Truths about God   624
    §2. Revelation of the Full Array of the Natural Truths of
       Religion Is Morally Necessary   628
    §3. Revelation of Supernatural Mysteries Is Hypothetically,
       but Strictly, Necessary   633
    §4. A Persuasive Argument Can Be Made for the Befittingness
       of the Gratuitous Ordering of Mankind to the
       Supernatural End   635

§5. A Doubt: Whether in the State of Pure Nature
the Revelation of the Full Array of Natural
Truths of Religion Would Have Been Morally
Necessary   638

§6. Resolution of Objections   640

SECTION IV: ON THE CREDIBILITY OF THE MYSTERIES
OF THE FAITH: THE KNOWABILITY OF THE FACT OF
REVELATION   649

PROLOGUE: STATE OF THE QUESTION AND ITS DIVISION   650

CHAPTER FOURTEEN: ON THE ACT OF FAITH IN RELATION
TO CREDIBILITY   655

ART. 1: THE CATHOLIC NOTION OF FAITH AND
HETERODOX NOTIONS THEREOF   655

§1. The Catholic Notion of Faith and of the Act of Faith   655

§2. Heterodox Notions of Faith   659

ART. 2: THEOLOGICAL EXPLANATION OF THE CATHOLIC
NOTION OF FAITH (I.E., AN ANALYSIS OF THE ACT OF FAITH
CONSIDERED FROM THE PERSPECTIVE OF THE OBJECT AND
FROM THE PERSPECTIVE OF THE SUBJECT)   665

§1. Explanation of the Act of Faith from the Perspective
of the Object   666

§2. Explanation of Faith and the Act of Faith from
the Perspective of the Subject   674

ART. 3: HOW REVELATION MUST BE KNOWN PRECISELY
AS THE FORMAL MOTIVE OF INFUSED FAITH (THAT IS,
ON SUPERNATURAL OR [VEL] INTRINSIC CREDIBILITY)   694

§1. The State of the Question and the Difficulty Involved
in It   694

§2. What Do Sacred Scripture and Tradition Say about
This Matter?   699

§3. What Did the Medieval Theologians before
St. Thomas Teach?   707

§4. What Does St. Thomas Teach in These Matters?   711

§5. Historical Exposition of the Opposition between the
Thomists and Suarez on the One Hand and the Scotists,
Nominalists, Molina, Lugo, and a Number of Modern
Thinkers on the Other   727

§6. Proof of the Thomist Position   753

§7. Resolution of Objections   761

§8. Appendix: Corollaries of the Thomistic Thesis
concerning the Supernaturality of Faith and
Our Manner of Knowing the Formal Motive of Faith   771

CHAPTER FIFTEEN: ON THE NOTION OF RATIONAL
CREDIBILITY AND ITS NECESSITY FOR THE ACT OF FAITH   777

ART. 1: THE NATURE OF RATIONAL CREDIBILITY   777

§1. The Catholic Notion of Credibility   777

§2. Heterodox Notions of Credibility   781

§3. Theological Explanation of the Catholic
Notion of Credibility   785

ART. 2: THE NECESSITY OF CERTAIN, RATIONAL
CREDIBILITY, AT LEAST WITH MORAL CERTITUDE   787

§1. The Difficulty of This Question   788

§2. What Do Sacred Scripture and the Doctors
of the Church Say?   788

§3. We Stand in Need of Certain Rational Knowledge
of the Fact of Revelation   790

§4. Moral Certitude Suffices   795

§5. This Moral Certitude Can Be Had by All Men,
at Least with the Aid of Grace, Although Grace
Is Not Absolutely Necessary for Having It   800

ART. 3: ON THE OFFICE OF THE JUDGMENT OF CREDIBILITY
IN THE GENESIS OF THE ACT OF FAITH   807

§1. The Acts That Dispose to the Act of Faith   807

§2. The Distinction between the Judgment of Credibility
and the Judgment of Credentity   810

ART. 4: RESOLUTION OF OBJECTIONS (THE RECONCILIATION
OF THE RATIONAL OBEDIENCE OF FAITH WITH THE
OBSCURITY, FREEDOM, AND SUPERNATURALITY OF FAITH)   812

§1 Objection: Probability of the Fact of Revelation
Suffices for Having Rational Credibility   812

§2. Evident Credibility Is Reconciled with the Freedom
of the Act of Faith   818

§3. Evident Credibility Can Be Reconciled with the
Obscurity of Faith   820

§4 Evident Credibility Is Reconciled with the
Supernaturality of Faith   821

CHAPTER SIXTEEN: ON THE DEMONSTRABILITY OF
CREDIBILITY ON THE BASIS OF THE MOTIVES OF
CREDIBILITY   825

SINGLE ART.   825

   §1. The Necessity of This Demonstration for the Faith
       of the Church as a Whole   825
   §2. The Possibility of This Demonstration   826
   §3. The Notion of a Motive of Credibility   830
   §4. The Division of the Motives of Credibility   831

Introduction

GARRIGOU-LAGRANGE AND THE
RENEWAL OF CATHOLIC THEOLOGY

Cajetan Cuddy, O.P.

Even those who possess only a modicum of familiarity with Réginald Garrigou-Lagrange, O.P., associate him and his work with Thomas Aquinas. Aquinas and his interpreters have played key roles in the history of Catholic theology.[1] The Catholic Church has bestowed upon Thomas Aquinas the titles of (among others) "Common Doctor," "Angelic Doctor," and "Doctor of Humanity."[2] Why has Aquinas been found worthy of such honor? Some may cite the hundreds of places in her magisterial teaching where the Church cites Aquinas with approval. Others may trace historical contingencies and show how Aquinas and his interpreters served as key instruments in the Church's exposition of her teaching.[3] Still others may cite the inspiring

---

[1] For an introductory survey of the ways in which Aquinas and his interpreters have served the Church, see Romanus Cessario, O.P., and Cajetan Cuddy, O.P., *Thomas and the Thomists: The Achievement of Thomas Aquinas and His Interpreters* (Minneapolis, MN: Fortress Press, 2017). See also *The Life of Saint Thomas Aquinas: Biographical Documents*, trans. Kenelm Foster, O.P., (Baltimore: Helicon Press, 1959); James A. Weisheipl, O.P., *Friar Thomas D'Aquino: His Life, Thought, and Works* (Washington, DC: The Catholic University of America Press, 1983); Frederick J. Roensch, *Early Thomistic School* (Dubuque, IA: The Priory Press, 1964); Jean-Pierre Torrell, O.P., *Aquinas's Summa: Background, Structure, and Reception*, trans. Benedict M. Guevin, O.S.B. (Washington, DC: The Catholic University of America Press, 2005).

[2] Even in the thirteenth century, Aquinas was referred to as the *Doctor eximius* and as *Venerabilis doctor, vir, pater, magister* (see Jean-Pierre Torrell, O.P., *Saint Thomas Aquinas*, vol. 1, *The Person and His Work* [Washington, DC: The Catholic University of America Press, 1996], 325). See also Pierre Mandonnet, O.P., "Les titres doctoraux de saint Thomas d'Aquin," *Revue Thomiste* 17 (1909): 597–608; Francis Cardinal George, O.M.I., "St. Thomas: Timeless and Timely" (keynote lecture, Pontifical Academy of St. Thomas Aquinas, October 18, 2013, University of St. Thomas, Houston, Texas).

[3] Ulrich Horst, O.P., *The Dominicans and the Pope: Papal Teaching Authority in the Medieval and Early Modern Thomist Tradition*, trans. James D. Mixson (Notre Dame, IN: University of Notre Dame Press, 2006).

examples of priests and bishops who effectively employed Saint Thomas's account of theology in their pastoral work.[4]

In a word, the Catholic Church has recognized in Aquinas's thought a uniquely faithful, clear, and comprehensive account of sacred theology grounded in the *depositum fidei* Christ entrusted to his bride, the Church.[5] With regard to this point, Leo XIII's encyclical letter *Aeterni Patris* comes to mind: "Among the Scholastic Doctors, the chief and master of all towers Thomas Aquinas, who, as Cajetan observes, because 'he most venerated the ancient doctors of the Church, in a certain way seems to have inherited the intellect of all.'"[6] One observes here the invocation of the most famous of all Thomistic "commentators" (Cardinal Cajetan) along with the venerable Saint Thomas. The Church has historically expressed appreciation for both Thomas and the Thomists. Finally, with an eye to more recent ecclesial pronouncements, consulting the documents of the Second Vatican Council (e.g., *Optatam Totius*) and the *Catechism of the Catholic Church* reveals that the Church continues to favor and to rely upon Saint Thomas Aquinas.[7]

Admittedly, the pontificate of Pope Leo XIII and the nineteenth century "Leonine revival of Thomism" are long past. Ours is a different day of a different age. Moreover, many contemporary Catholic theologians—from roughly the mid-twentieth century until our present moment—have argued that Thomas and the Thomists ought *not* to be accredited central place in the modern period. We can summarize the various steps away from Thomas and the Thomists in the modern epoch according to two movements: (1) In the period that directly preceded and immediately followed

---

[4] For a concise account of one such pastoral Thomist, see Steven M. Avella, "John T. McNicholas in The Age of Practical Thomism," *Records of the American Catholic Historical Society of Philadelphia* 97, no. 1/4 (1986): 15–25.

[5] "Guarding the deposit of faith is the mission which the Lord has entrusted to his Church and which she fulfills in every age" (John Paul II, Apostolic Constitution on the Publication of the Catechism of the Catholic Church *Fidei Depositum* [October 11, 1992]), §I; First Vatican Council, Dogmatic Constitution on the Catholic Faith *Dei Filius* (April 24, 1870), c. 4; Second Vatican Council, Dogmatic Constitution on Divine Revelation *Dei Verbum* (November 18, 1965), §10. See also Santiago Ramirez, O.P., "The Authority of St. Thomas Aquinas," *The Thomist* 15, no. 1 (1952): 1–109.

[6] Leo XIII, *Aeterni Patris* (August 4, 1879), §17.

[7] "[Clerical] students [of theology] should learn to penetrate them more deeply with the help of speculation, under the guidance of St. Thomas, and to perceive their interconnections. They should be taught to recognize these same mysteries as present and working in liturgical actions and in the entire life of the Church. They should learn to seek the solutions to human problems under the light of revelation, to apply the eternal truths of revelation to the changeable conditions of human affairs and to communicate them in a way suited to men of our day" (Second Vatican Council, *Optatam Totius*, §16).

the Second Vatican Council, there was a decided movement away from Thomas *because* of the Thomists. Charges of "dry" and "arid" "manualism" and "neo-scholasticism" were often leveled against Thomistically inspired authors and their writings. (2) After the Council, we have witnessed efforts to recover Thomas *without* the Thomists.[8] Many of the writings about Aquinas published today would fall within this category. Rigorous historical-critical scholarship into the person and work of Aquinas as well as the distinction between *Thomasienne* (sometimes translated as *Thomasian* or *Thomanian*) and *Thomist* come to mind here.[9]

And yet, after all of that, there is renewed interest in Thomas *and* the Thomists. New books on the reception of Aquinas's thought and the practice of commenting on the *Summa Theologiae* continue to appear.[10] Classical

---

[8] On March 14, 1965, the renowned Dominican historian, philosopher, and theologian James Athanasius Weisheipl, O.P., delivered a lecture titled "Thomism as a Perennial Philosophy" (James A. Weisheipl, O.P., "Thomism as a Perennial Philosophy" [Chaplain's Day Address, Cardinal Stritch College, Milwaukee, WI, March 14, 1965]). One notes that this date was only a few months prior to the formal close of the Second Vatican Council (December 8, 1965). Clearly, the conciliar moment in the Vatican II renewal provided the context for his reflections on the history and situation of Thomas and the Thomists. The lecture attracted the attention of ecclesial thinkers, and the following year Fr. Weisheipl was invited to give a version of this "brief and important history of Thomism" at a conference on "Philosophy in an Age of Christian Renewal" at the University of Notre Dame (September 1966) (this version of his lecture was published as "The Revival of Thomism as a Christian Philosophy" in *New Themes in Christian Philosophy*, ed. Ralph M. McInerny [Notre Dame, IN: University of Notre Dame Press, 1968], 164–185). In his lecture, Weisheipl remarks: "A distinction must be made between Thomanian doctrine and Thomistic doctrines. Thomanian, to coin an adjective, refers to a doctrine as understood and intended by St. Thomas himself. Thomistic, on the other hand, refers to doctrines as understood, applied, and developed by those who claim to follow the teaching of St. Thomas. In this paper we are not concerned with Thomanian doctrine, but with Thomism" (Weisheipl, "Revival of Thomism," 171). Fr. Weisheipl later observes that "many reactions to Thomism in the past half-century have been, in fact, to a pseudo-Thomanianism and a half-understood Thomism" (184). It is interesting to note that Weisheipl does not invoke the distinction between Thomanian and Thomistic doctrines in the original (1965) version of his essay.

[9] "Since around 1950 it [the adjective 'Thomist'] has been in competition with a new word, 'Thomasian,' although this coinage has not been accepted everywhere or by everyone. 'Thomasian' is sometimes used to refer to what relates directly to Aquinas, and the literal exegesis of what he wrote, while 'Thomist' and 'Thomism' are used to refer to his followers" (Jean-Pierre Torrell, "Thomism," in *Encyclopedia of Christian Theology*, ed. Jean-Yves Lacoste, vol. 3 P-Z (New York: Routledge, 2005), 1578.

[10] To cite but only two recent examples: Matthew Levering and Marcus Plested, eds., *The Oxford Handbook of the Reception of Aquinas* (Oxford: Oxford, 2021); Lidia Lazana and Marco Toste, eds., *Summistae: The Commentary Tradition on Thomas Aquinas' "Summa Theologiae" from the 15th to the 17th Centuries* (Leuven: Leuven University Press, 2021).

figures like Capreolus, Dominic of Flanders, Cajetan, Bañez, the Salmanti-censes, and John of St. Thomas have begun to receive renewed attention.[11] The thought and writings of Réginald Garrigou-Lagrange, O.P., too, have once again attracted the interest of philosophers, theologians, and histo-rians.[12] Several of his books have recently been translated into English for the first time.[13] One could argue, however, that this translation of Garrig-ou's *De Revelatione* (hereafter referred to as *On Divine Revelation*) stands at the forefront of this list of recent publications. Garrigou-Lagrange is a big-picture thinker. In each of his books (and even in his essays) Garrigou deliberately draws out the universal implications of each of the matters he treats. In *On Divine Revelation*, however, our author formally addresses a topic that touches on every part of the *sacra doctrina*: divine revelation itself. This particular work has unique importance for Catholic theology as a whole.

---

[11] For example, see Domenic D'Ettore, *Analogy after Aquinas: Logical Problems, Thomis-tic Answers* (Washington, DC: The Catholic University of America Press, 2019); Michael O'Connor, *Cajetan's Biblical Commentaries: Motive and Method* (Leiden: Brill, 2017); Hier-omonk Gregory Hrynkiw, *Cajetan on Sacred Doctrine* (Washington, DC: The Catholic University of America Press, 2020); Dylan Schrader, *A Thomistic Christocentrism: Recovering the Carmelites of Salamanca and the Logic of the Incarnation* (Washington, DC: The Catholic University of America Press, 2021).

[12] For example: Richard A. Peddicord, O.P., "Another Look at the Theological Enterprise of Réginald Garrigou-Lagrange, O.P.," *Angelicum* 82, no. 4 (2005): 835–848; Richard Peddi-cord, O.P., *The Sacred Monster of Thomism: An Introduction to the Life and Legacy of Réginald Garrigou-Lagrange, O.P.* (South Bend, IN: St. Augustine's Press, 2005); Michael Kerlin, "Réginald Garrigou-Lagrange: Defending the Faith from *Pascendi dominici gregis* to *Humani Generis*," *U.S. Catholic Historian* 25, no. 1 (2007): 97–113; Aidan Nichols, O.P., *Reason with Piety: Garrigou-Lagrange in the Service of Catholic Thought* (Ave Maria, FL: Sapientia Press, 2008); Anthony Daum, "St. Thomas Aquinas and Fr. Réginald Garrigou-Lagrange on Wonder and the Division of the Sciences," *Studia Gilsoniana* 8, no. 2 (2019): 249–276; Taylor Patrick O'Neill, *Grace, Predestination, and the Permission of Sin: A Thomistic Analysis* (Wash-ington, DC: The Catholic University of America Press, 2019).

[13] This is due, in large part, to the remarkable industry of Matthew K. Minerd who has translated the following works by Garrigou-Lagrange: *The Sense of Mystery: Clarity and Obscurity in the Intellectual Life* (Steubenville, OH: Emmaus Academic, 2017); *Philosophizing in Faith: Essays on the Beginning and End of Wisdom* (Providence, RI: Cluny Media, 2019); *The Order of Things: The Realism of the Principle of Finality* (Steubenville, OH: Emmaus Academic, 2020); *Thomistic Common Sense: The Philosophy of Being and the Development of Doctrine* (Steuben-ville, OH: Emmaus Academic, 2021).

On Divine Revelation: Garrigou-Lagrange's Objective Fundamental Theology

In his preface to *On Divine Revelation*, Garrigou-Lagrange explains that this work "contains the whole of apologetics—namely, the defense of the divine origin of Christianity and of the divine institution of the Catholic Church for preserving and infallibly proposing revelation."[14] This explains the length of the project. Addressing the whole of apologetics—classically understood—is no mean task. It requires familiarity with the nature, limits, and range of natural reason; the divine origin and nature of faith; as well as the interplay between the two. We also observe that Garrigou-Lagrange places within apologetical defense both the divine origin of Christianity itself and the divine institution of the Catholic Church. The Christian religion itself and the Catholic Church both enjoy divine origin. They share the same divine principle. Therefore, their consideration cannot be separated.

Lest any ambiguities linger, however, Garrigou continues to clarify exactly how he understands his task. "In this book, apologetics is not considered as being a science specifically distinct from sacred theology but, rather, is held to be one of its particular offices, one that is rational and defensive, for apologetics does argue *from reason*, though *under the direction of faith*."[15] *On Divine Revelation*, thus, is a book of apologetics. And because apologetics is not a discipline distinct from sacred theology, this work represents a project of *sacra doctrina*. Thus, the *theological* question that both unifies and shapes *On Divine Revelation* is this: "How is revelation to be recognized as the formal motive of infused faith?"[16] Hence, formally, this question is "the same as the question concerning the ultimate resolution of the supernatural certitude of faith, which is commonly set forth in the treatise on faith."[17] Consequently, Garrigou contextualizes his *On Divine Revelation* among the themes treated in the "*Secunda secundae* in the *Summa theologiae* after the questions on grace and before the articles on hope, charity, and the other vir-

---

[14] Réginald Garrigou-Lagrange, O.P., *On Divine Revelation: The Teaching of the Catholic Faith* (Steubenville, OH: Emmaus Academic, 2022), I, 15.

[15] Ibid. Emphasis original. See also Réginald Garrigou-Lagrange, O.P., "L'apologétique et la théologie fondamentale," *Revue des sciences philosophique et théologiques* 9, no. 3 (1902): 352–59; Réginald Garrigou-Lagrange, "Apologetics Directed by Faith," in *Philosophizing in Faith: Essays on the Beginning and End of Wisdom*, ed. and trans. Matthew K. Minerd (Providence, RI: Cluny Media, 2019), 399–420. For more on Garrigou's apologetic work, see S. Giuliani, O.P., "P. R. Garrigou-Lagrange Apologeta," *Angelicum* 42, no. 1/2 (1965): 117–136.

[16] Garrigou-Lagrange, *On Divine Revelation*, I, 16.

[17] Ibid.

tues."[18] Aquinas's examination of revelation lies squarely within the formal boundaries of sacred theology. Therefore, Garrigou is not *per se* concerned with the extrinsic probability of faith and its articles. Rather, his focus is on the *intrinsic* nature of faith itself: As ought to be done in fundamental theology, the first words of the Apostolic Creed: *I believe*" capture his focus in *On Divine Revelation*.[19] Hence, *On Divine Revelation* is also "conceived as being a work on *fundamental theology*—that is, theology concerned with the foundations of faith."[20]

This formal theological characterization of apologetics may surprise contemporary students of theology. Apologetics is frequently associated with those topics that lie outside—and before the threshold—of the *sacra doctrina*. "Apologetics" can strike contemporary readers as something that is propaedeutic to theology rather than as something included under its disciplinary jurisdiction. Indeed, some regard apologetics with suspicion.[21] Garrigou invites his readers to reconsider these impressions. He explains that "never did the doctors of the Church consider apologetics as being a science distinct from sacred theology." Moreover, "apologetics is ultimately part of sacred theology, inasmuch as sacred theology, as *a supreme science* (or wisdom), defends its faith-received principles, as well as faith itself, against those who deny them."[22] The teacher of apologetics (the "apologete"), classically understood, "does not present himself as though he were lacking faith

---

18 Ibid., I, 17.

19 Ibid.

20 *On Divine Revelation*, I, 15, emphasis original. "The scientific consideration of the foundations of faith is rightly called the first part of fundamental theology. The term 'theology' is used inasmuch as it is a part of theology, the supreme science, as was said above; and it is 'fundamental' (or 'general') inasmuch as it is concerned with the foundations of faith—that is, with revelation itself, credibility, and the proximate rule of faith, or with revealed data in general. However, it is not called 'fundamental' in the sense that apologetic argumentation would be the source or principle from which theology would proceed in its particular considerations. In reality, *apologetic argumentation is only an aid by whose help revelation and Christian faith are defended, and properly speaking, faith is the source and principle of theology properly so-called*" (ibid., I, 117–118).

21 As Avery Cardinal Dulles observes: "In the minds of many Christians today the term 'apologetics' carries unpleasant connotations. The apologist is regarded as an aggressive, opportunistic person who tries, by fair means or foul, to argue people into joining the Church. Numerous charges are laid at the door of apologetics: its neglect of grace, of prayer, and of the life-giving power of the word of God; its tendency to oversimply and syllogize the approach to the faith; its dilution of the scandal of the Christian message; and its implied presupposition that God's word should be judged by the norm of fallible, not to say fallen, human reason" (*A History of Apologetics* [San Francisco: Ignatius Press, 2005], xix).

22 *On Divine Revelation*, I, 30, emphasis original. See *ST* I, q. 1, a. 8.

and investigating into it like a mere seeker." Rather, "whatever he may prudently do *per accidens* in order to convince this or that nonbeliever who is lacking in faith, nonetheless, *per se* and *normally*, he presents himself as the Apostles and the Fathers did—namely, as a member or minister of the Catholic Church—so that he may manifest to unbelievers *the rational value* of the very apologetics that is proposed by the very magisterium of the Church."[23]

Garrigou-Lagrange divides *On Divine Revelation* into two parts: "The first of which is concerned with the possibility, befittingness, and knowability of revelation, whereas the other part is concerned with the existence of revelation, historically considered."[24] The former proceeds according to the intrinsic nature of revelation itself. The latter presents an extrinsic presentation of the revelation as a reality situated in the domain of historical contingency. He also notes that the matters contained under the heading of "fundamental theology" can receive profitable treatment at the beginning and at the end of a student's theological formation—and that it should be treated "integrally."[25]

The first chapter of *On Divine Revelation* considers the nature of sacred theology. In many ways, this is the heart of the work. The intrinsic form and proper method of sacred theology govern and direct Fr. Garrigou's presentation of apologetics, divine revelation, the mysteries of faith, and motives of credibility. Unlike natural theology (*"which is concerned with God known in light of things that are naturally knowable"*), sacred or "supernatural theology" is a *"science concerning God, proceeding from revelation* (or science concerning the divine mysteries revealed and accepted through faith)."[26]

With great care, Garrigou-Lagrange explains that "the formal object that is known" (*obiectum formale quod*) of sacred theology is God considered under the aspect of *deity*. The emphasis upon deity is absolutely critical, for this emphasis essentially distinguishes the science of sacred theology from the highest philosophical science (i.e., metaphysics). Additionally, he establishes sacred theology's "formal principle or motive by which" (*principium formale quo*) as "revelation as virtually containing conclusions that can be

---

[23] Ibid., 29, emphasis original.

[24] *On Divine Revelation*, I, 18.

[25] "Generally speaking, fundamental theology is difficult enough if it is treated deeply and integrally. Indeed, we find ourselves here concerned with the remote and proximate foundations of the supernatural certitude of faith. And therefore, it is not surprising if all these matters are thoroughly understood only after a complete study of sacred theology, even though they are necessary for an initial understanding of this subject, at least in the elementary manner" (ibid.).

[26] Ibid., I, 36.

deduced through rational discourse."[27] He concludes to the "real definition of sacred theology—namely, science concerning God, considered from the perspective of the Deity, inasmuch as he falls under virtual revelation (or science concerned with God from the perspective of the Deity, proceeding from revelation [*sic*])."[28] Consequently, sacred theology is *distinguished* from divine faith, but it also *presupposes* divine faith.

Garrigou-Lagrange argues that sacred theology is *integrally one science*. Each of the "parts" of sacred theology (i.e., "systematic or scholastic" and "positive" theology) are *integral parts* of the single scientific whole that is *sacred theology*—the unified undertaking seeking to arrive at *aliqua mysteriorum fidei intelligentia*, some understanding of the mysteries of faith.[29] The relationship between positive theology and systematic theology, Garrigou explains, is one of "scientific matter and scientific form. Indeed, positive theology, as it were, materially collects all the revealed matters that are the material object[s] of sacred doctrine. However, systematic theology formally orders all revealed matters according to their relation to God, considered from the perspective of the Deity, which is formally considered object and principle for the ordering of the entire edifice of theological doctrine."[30]

Positive theology proceeds according to an "analytic" or inductive method. Systematic theology follows a "synthetic" or deductive method.[31] Garrigou-Lagrange reminds his readers that "analytic (or inductive) methodology ascends from composite things to simple ones, from particulars to universals, all the way to the most universal and first intelligible things." In contrast, "*synthetic* (or deductive) methodology descends from simple things to composite ones, from more universal things to less universal ones."[32] Con-

---

[27] Ibid., I, 42.

[28] Ibid., I, 43.

[29] "Positive theology and systematic theology seem to be integral parts of sacred theology, parts that necessarily concur for perfection. However, the applications of moral theology . . . seem to be power parts inasmuch as they are applications to a specific matter. However, in theology there are no parts that are specifically distinct as diverse sciences" (ibid., I, 75n82). For a concise breakdown of different kinds of wholes and parts (i.e., integral, subjective, and power/potential), Garrigou points his readers to *ST* II-II, q. 48, a. 1. Some modern Thomists have argued that sacred theology, itself, is a "power whole" (i.e., a potential whole) rather than an integral whole. For an interesting argument in defense of this position, see Francisco P. Muñiz, O.P., *The Work of Theology* (Washington, DC: The Thomist Press, 1953). See also Reinhard Hütter, *Dust Bound for Heaven: Explorations in the Theology of Thomas Aquinas* (Grand Rapids, MI: William B. Eerdmans Publishing Company, 2012), 331–346.

[30] *On Divine Revelation*, I, 74.

[31] Ibid., I, 80.

[32] Ibid., I, 77, emphasis original. "Thus, we ascend from the object of experience that is first

sequently, *positive theology* "(whether biblical, patristic, or symbolic) strives to uncover the individual truth to be believed from the sources of revelation." And its specific scientific *regulae* receive treatment in the treatise on *theological sources* (i.e., *de locis theologicis* or *de fontibus theologicis*).[33] The synthetic method of *systematic theology* follows the deductive method. "It first speculatively defends the authority of divine revelation against those who deny it, then speculatively explains and considers revealed truths, draws conclusions from them, and orders all things synthetically *by proceeding* from what is simpler and loftier—namely, *from the One and Triune God to creatures* in general and in particular—then to actions of creatures as ordered to God."[34]

Garrigou-Lagrange thus summarizes the relationship between the treatise on theological sources and fundamental theology:

> Therefore, the treatise on theological sources [*tractatus de locis*] contains the methodology belonging to the whole of theology and, likewise, positively presupposes divine faith concerning the mission of Christ and the infallibility of the Church in proposing revelation. This treatise is placed among the propaedeutic instructions for sacred theology. However, it is the final part of fundamental theology and already, like theology properly speaking, *argues from revelation.*[35]

The source considerations contained in the *tractatus de locis* stand in continuity with sacred theology because both presuppose divine faith and argue from revelation. A consideration of theological sources is critical for sacred theology because of their *propaedeutic* relationship to sacred theology.[36] The-

---

known (from our perspective) to the first notions and first principles or even to the first causes that are first known in themselves, and from principles and supreme causes by the deductive *via*, the notions and causes of the object of experience are assigned, thus making the latter more intelligible to us. In this way science (or knowledge of things through causes) comes to be constructed" (ibid.).

[33] Ibid., I, 80.

[34] Ibid., I, 81, emphasis original.

[35] Ibid., I, 82.

[36] Garrigou explains that "This treatise [on theological sources, *de locis theologicis*] positively presupposes revelation and, under the light of faith, explains: (1) *the rules for discerning the literal sense of Sacred Scripture* 'from which alone can an argument be brought forth' [*ST* I, q. 1, a. 10, a. 1]; (2) the rules for discerning, among traditions, *divine tradition*, which also contains the revealed data [*revelata*], as well as the rules for determining its true sense; (3) the rules for discerning what *authority* is held by *the doctrines of the Fathers,* or *that of the theologians,* the *decisions of* [the *Roman*] *congregations,* and *that of particular Councils,* as well as the rules for

ological sources are not ends in themselves. God—the principle of the divine revelation—is the end. Nonetheless, theological sources—as theological—stand within the formal objectivity of sacred theology: supernatural faith. And it is because of the formal objectivity of faith that theological sources have their theological value.

Because the treatise on theological sources resides within the domain of fundamental theology or apologetics, Garrigou-Lagrange proceeds to define what, exactly, fundamental theology is: "'Fundamental theology' signifies the theology that is concerned with *the foundations* of divine faith."[37] Specifically, "apologetics" denotes "the universal defense of faith both from the perspective of the object and from the perspective of the manner of defending."[38] The "perspective of the object" refers to "the whole Christian religion in general" (and not merely to a particular mystery of the Christian religion singly considered or all the mysteries collectively considered). The "perspective of the manner" refers to the universality of apologetics' argumentation: "Its defensive argumentation does not depend on the circumstances of a given time or place but instead has an absolute value inasmuch as it is founded both on the most certain principles of natural reason (or of metaphysics) and on historical testimonies that are certain."[39]

> Hence, we can see here the difference between apologetics, theology properly speaking, and philosophy. *Sacred theology argues from faith* by deducing theological conclusions from revealed premises. *Philosophy argues from reason alone, not contradicting faith*, inasmuch as reason by its own power [i.e., middle term] for proving its theses, and is directed by faith as by a negative norm. *Apologetics argues from reason under the positive direction of faith*, for reason does not by its own power discover the motives of credibility but only judges concerning the value of those things that are proposed by God, who reveals, and by his ministers.[40]

---

determining the exact way that we must understand *the solemn definitions* of the Church or the propositions that she has condemned, along with their various notes; (4) finally, the treatise on theological sources sets forth the rules governing positive theology's use of history" (ibid., I, 80–81).

[37] Ibid., I, 83. Emphasis original. Here Garrigou cites Vatican I's *Dei Filius*, ch. 4: "Faith and reason also support each other, since right reason demonstrates the foundations of faith and, illuminated by its light, pursues the science of divine things."

[38] Ibid., I, 84–85.

[39] Ibid., I, 85.

[40] Ibid., I, 90.

Therefore, Garrigou-Lagrange structures his fundamental theology in *On Divine Revelation* according to "the traditional way of proceeding" reflected in the First Vatican Council's dogmatic constitution *Dei Filius*. "The defense of revelation and the defense of the true Church of Christ who proposes such revelation can be exposited in a unified manner."[41] In this way, he dissents from his contemporaries who "divide fundamental theology (or apologetics) into two parts": (1) the defense of Christian revelation itself (against the rationalists), and (2) the defense of the infallibility of the Catholic Church (against the Protestants and schismatics).[42] By rejecting this artificial bifurcation of the apologetical discipline, Garrigou maintains the univocity of Christianity and Catholicism. The defense of divine revelation's existence ultimately and necessarily terminates in Christ's Catholic Church. The "apologete" cannot separate the fact of divine revelation from the Church to whom Christ has entrusted his divine revelation. "True Christianity is nothing other than Catholicism; hence, true and complete demonstration of Christianity already contains the demonstration of Catholicism."[43]

The structure of *On Divine Revelation*, therefore, comprises a theoretical part and a positive part: (I) The *theoretical part* defends (against philosophical rationalism) (1) the possibility of revelation, (2) the befittingness and necessity of revelation, and (3) the knowability of revelation from certain signs. (II) The *positive part* defends (against biblical rationalism) (1) "Christ's own historical testimony concerning his divine mission and concerning the institution of the Church for proposing revelation infallibly set forth," (2) the fact that "this testimony is confirmed by the miraculous fulfillment of our aspirations by the Church's sublimity of the doctrine and life," (3) the fact that this testimony "is confirmed by miracles and prophesies," (4) Christianity's veracity against the truth claims of other religions, and (5) "the obligation of embracing the Catholic religion."[44]

Lest readers interpret this division of *On Divine Revelation* as reflect-

---

[41] Ibid., I, 93.

[42] Ibid., I, 92.

[43] Ibid., I, 94.

[44] Ibid., I, 94–95. Garrigou notes that "afterwards comes the properly theological treatise on the Church (namely, on the intimate constitution of the Church, her properties, her twofold power, the value of [doctrinal] definitions and [various] declarations taken in particular), as well as the treatise on other theological sources [*locis*] (namely, on Sacred Scripture, Tradition, etc.) in which one determines the intimate nature, authority, and use of the various sources used in sacred theology. These theological treatises already positively argue from faith, just as do the treatises on the Trinity or the Incarnation" (ibid., I, 95).

ing an *intrinsically polemical nature*, Garrigou clarifies: "Even if there were no adversaries, the obedience of our faith would need to be rational." Fundamental theology or apologetics is only polemical *per accidens*. It is *per se* scientific, however, because of the intelligibility of faith's foundations and of the human mind's scientific relation to intelligible objects. Indeed, "although all the faithful do not need a scientific demonstration of the foundations of faith, nevertheless, for theologians there is a place for scientific inquiry concerning revelation before coming to the particular treatises of theology." Why? "The scientific proof of credibility pertains to the integrity of sacred theology (or the science of faith), after the manner of an introduction or a critical reflection."[45]

The importance of this latter point is difficult to overestimate. Of course, no human person can *exhaust* the divine mysteries. But all human persons who receive the mysteries of the faith seek to understand the mysteries. The mysteries of the faith do not lack intelligibility. Rather, they are super-intelligible. Thus, the theologian does not err in pursuing the intelligibility of the mysteries. Rather, the science of sacred theology compels the theologian to scrutinize—under the light of faith—the mysteries in their full super-intelligibility. A rational agent cannot come to true and certain knowledge about any real object without some conformity (deliberate or not) to the form and method of *scientia*.

A divine objectivity (*deity*) informs every step of Garrigou-Lagrange's scientific and sapiential study of theology in *On Divine Revelation*. The very structure of *On Divine Revelation* reveals its Godward orientation. Fr. Garrigou sees with great clarity that the end of the *sacra doctrina*—and of fundamental theology and apologetics—is the union of the human person to God. And because the human person is essentially rational, such a union will necessarily include an objective formality. Although reason cannot prove the articles of the faith, a human person who has truly received the grace of divine faith will always be inclined to—and actively pursue some—understanding of the revealed mysteries.

Faith does not do away with reason. Reason is always perfected in the mysteries of the faith. These foundational convictions clearly inspired and informed Garrigou-Lagrange's massive work, *On Divine Revelation*.

Catholic Theology after Vatican II (and Garrigou-Lagrange)

Many things have changed, however, since the final edition of Garrigou's *On*

---

[45] Ibid., I, 117.

Divine Revelation was published in 1950 (let alone since the first edition in 1918).[46] Few would dispute the claim that "the Second Vatican Council stands out as one of the most important religious and ecclesial events in the twentieth century."[47] The legacy of the Council continues to enjoy a prominent place in the life and thought of the Catholic faithful of the present day. The Council's attention to the vitality of ecclesial life in general and of Christian life in particular remains a notable influence on the contemporary Christian experience.

Yves Congar, O.P., was one of the most significant theological influences at and interpreters of Vatican II. Indeed, his theological contributions to the deliberations surrounding the Council are difficult to overestimate. Avery Dulles, S.J., once observed that "Vatican II could almost be called Congar's Council."[48] In the same vein, church historian John W. O'Malley, S.J., summarizes Congar's significance during the pre-conciliar deliberations: "[Congar] was brought to Rome by John XXIII for the preparatory work for the council. Once the council got under way, he became an almost ubiquitously influential *peritus*. He was sought for his opinion on almost every major issue before the assembly."[49] Thus, Congar was a central figure in the event of Vatican II and its continued legacy—particularly with regard to the pre-conciliar and post-conciliar efforts of theological renewal.[50]

---

[46] For a bibliography of Garrigou's writings published shortly after his death, see Benedetto Zorcolo, O.P., "Bibliografia del P. Garrigou-Lagrange," *Angelicum* 42 (1965): 200–272. Although Garrigou's *De Revelatione* later underwent abridgment in some subsequent editions, the 1950 edition contains the full and complete text.

[47] Matthew L. Lamb and Matthew Levering, introduction to *Vatican II: Renewal within Tradition*, ed. Matthew L. Lamb and Matthew Levering (Oxford: Oxford University Press, 2008), 3. See also Gerald O'Collins, S.J., *The Second Vatican Council: Message and Meaning* (Collegeville, MN: Liturgical Press, 2014), vii.

[48] Avery Dulles, S.J., "Yves Congar: In Appreciation," *America* 173 (July 15, 1995): 6–7; as cited in Mathew Levering, *An Introduction to Vatican II as an Ongoing Theological Event* (Washington, DC: The Catholic University of America Press, 2017), 86. "Careful study of [Congar's] contribution to Church reform shows him to be an architect of the contemporary church" (Gabriel Flynn, "Introduction: The Twentieth-Century Renaissance in Catholic Theology," in *Ressourcement: A Movement for Renewal in Twentieth-Century Catholic Theology*, ed. Gabriel Flynn and Paul D. Murray, with the assistance of Patricia Kelly [Oxford: Oxford University Press, 2012], 7).

[49] John W. O'Malley, *What Happened at Vatican II* (Cambridge, MA: The Belknap Press, 2008), 120. Congar's own detailed record of his involvement at the Council was published (in 2002) after his death (and in English translation in 2012): Yves Congar, O.P., *My Journal of the Council*, trans. Mary John Ronayne, O.P., and Mary Cecily Boulding, O.P., ed. Denis Minns, O.P. (Collegeville, MN: Liturgical Press, 2012).

[50] For a historical consideration of Congar's influence on the preparatory phase of the Council,

Before the Council—in what some have called his "most original book and the most important"[51]—Congar lamented the status of Catholic theology with regard to Christian vitality: "Theologians have only studied the *structure* of the church, so to speak, not its actual *life*. Naturally, the church has a structure deriving from its constitutive elements, but with this structure it *lives*, and the faithful within it live in unity. The church is not just a framework, however, not just a mechanism or an institution; it is a communion."[52] He goes on to express chagrin over the estimation that "Catholic theology has devoted little study to the life of the church," especially in light of the fact that "reform represents an ongoing feature in the life of the church." Indeed, "theologians could only give up studying the reality of 'reforms' if they were first to abandon investigating the life of the church theologically."[53] To Congar's mind, an ongoing spirit of reform is an essential component of the life of the Church. And this component represents something akin to a principle of theological vitality—particularly with regard to Catholic theology faithfully practiced within the Church.

Congar did not think that his convictions reflected anything revolutionary in nature. Rather, he argues that "the church has always tried to reform itself."[54] With historical examples, he defends his point: "At least since the end of the classical period, when the first great councils, the writings of the Fathers, and the development of a fixed liturgy more or less defined the

---

see Michael Quisinsky, "Vers un Concile pastorale? La réception (ou non-réception) de la théologie de Chenu et de Congar au cours de la phase préparatoire du Concile," in *La théologie catholique entre intransigeance et renouveau: La réception des mouvements préconciliaires à Vatican II*, ed. Gilles Routhier, Philippe J. Roy, and Karim Schelkens (Louvain-la-Neuve, Leuven: Brepols, 2011), 145–178.

[51] Jean-Pierre Jossua, O.P., personal letter to Gabriel Flynn (Gabriel Flynn, "Yves Congar and Catholic Church Reform: A Renewal of the Spirit," in *Yves Congar: Theologian of the Church*, ed. Gabriel Flynn [Leuven: Peeters, 2005], 133n113). See also Levering, *Introduction to Vatican II*, 82.

[52] Yves Congar, O.P., *True and False Reform in the Church*, trans. Paul Philibert, O.P. (Collegeville, MN: Liturgical Press, 2011), 9. Emphasis original. For another, similar, vision of the reform of the Church presented at the close of the Second Vatican Council, see George H. Tavard, *The Church Tomorrow* (New York, NY: Herder and Herder, 1965).

[53] Congar, *True and False Reform*, 9. He continues: "Sometimes people are frightened by the word 'reform' because, unfortunately, history has associated this term with revolutions as such. A sort of curse seems to hang over the word. Admittedly the term is a bit vague and can designate equally well either the simple determination to go back to following one's principles (in this sense, we ought to reform ourselves daily) or the great upheavals that destroy more than they create. We are well aware that there are *inauthentic* reforms. But, all things considered, reform refers only to what is normal and even ordinary" (ibid., 13), emphasis original.

[54] Ibid., 19.

church's nature, its history has been marked by periods of reform."[55] He observes that the various reform movements identifiable throughout the history of the Church have emerged from various origins:

> Sometimes the reform movement has been the result of religious orders correcting their own failings or returning to a more exact expression of their original inspiration. . . . At other times the popes undertook a general reform of abuses or addressed moments of crisis (Gregory VII, Innocent III). . . . Sometimes an evangelical spirit, an apostolic "yeast," developed, touching people's hearts, as was the case throughout the twelfth century, finding expression in the mendicant orders of St. Dominic and St. Francis. At other times, it was church councils which addressed themselves to needed reforms.[56]

The final type of movement represents, in Congar's estimation, the type of reform that the Second Vatican Council effected. He wrote these words in 1950. One could, however, read the analysis he offered in *True and False Reform in the Truth* as providing rather direct inspiration for the renewal efforts of Vatican II.[57] From a post-conciliar vantage point, Congar later opined:

> I had wondered if John XXIII had ever read *Vraie et fausse réforme*. I got the answer one day from a missionary who willingly told me the following story: In 1952, while he was visiting Archbishop Roncalli at the nunciature in Paris, he found him in the midst of reading this book, in the margins of which he had been writing in pencil (this copy still exists somewhere, no doubt). Archbishop Roncalli said to his visitor, "A reform of the church, is such a thing possible?"[58]

Although Congar, in the first edition of *True and False Reform*, "had intentionally refrained from proposing or even suggesting a concrete program of

---

[55] Ibid.

[56] Ibid., 19–20.

[57] For more on the dating and the chronology of redaction and publication that Congar's *True and False Reform* saw, see Paul Philibert, O.P., "Translator's Introduction," in *True and False Reform*, xi–xvi, as well as Congar's own preface to his book's second ("revised and corrected") edition (ibid., 1–8).

[58] Ibid., 2n2.

reforms so as to remain on the level of a theological study,"[59] he would later observe that "the cautious suggestions for reform mentioned in my text of 1950 have been surpassed by far."[60] Indeed, Congar suggests that what he observed "happening right now [in 1967], insofar as it is positive, is certainly in line with what [he] had intended, yet it goes a great deal further, well beyond what one could have hoped for in 1950."[61]

Congar framed his renewal prognosis in light of a prior, communal work of ecclesial self-evaluation. As already noted, he did not think that reforms of various degrees and diverse kinds were essentially abnormal ecclesial phenomena. "I could never completely enumerate the countless partial reforms, reformist texts, or the historical studies dedicated to reform movements in the church." Even without the formal appellations of "reform" or of "renewal," one can "still allude to the many different activities which, without being called reformist, nonetheless actually represented a movement toward reform in the life of the church."[62] The perennial process of self-criticism, as Congar expresses it, does not bear a primarily negative connotation. Acts of ecclesial self-critique inspire movements of renewal because such acts always occur within the context of the Church's life. The vitality of the Church engenders a self-reflective criticality that animates and engenders movements of vital renewal. "Every spiritual organization that is really alive must encourage genuine critique."[63]

Such critiques proceed from the inextricable nature of the Church

---

[59] Ibid., 2n3.

[60] Ibid., 2.

[61] Ibid.

[62] Ibid., 21.

[63] Ibid., 33. In some ways, Joseph Ratzinger echoes Congar's analysis on this point: "The [Second Vatican] Council understood itself as a great examination of conscience by the Catholic Church; it wanted ultimately to be an act of penance, of conversion. This is apparent in the confessions of guilt, in the intensity of the self-accusations that were not only directed to the more sensitive areas, such as the Reformation and the trial of Galileo, but were also heightened into the concept of a Church that was sinful in a general and fundamental way and that feared as triumphalism whatever might be interpreted as satisfaction with what she had become or what she still was" (*Principles of Catholic Theology: Building Stones for a Fundamental Theology*, trans. Sister Mary Frances McCarthy, S.N.D. [San Francisco, CA: Ignatius Press, 1987], 371). Ratzinger continues, however, to explain that "true penance leads to the gospel, that is, to joy—even to joy in oneself. The kind of self-accusation at which the Council arrived with respect to the Church's own history was not sufficiently aware of this fact and so expressed itself in ways that can only be called neurotic. It was both necessary and good for the Council to put an end to the false forms of the tendency to defend her past history, to eliminate her false justification of self. But it is time now to reawaken our joy in the reality of an unbroken community of faith in Jesus Christ" (ibid., 373).

to live united to Christ and to share his life with the world. Because the identity of the Church and her mission of evangelization are inseparable, critical reflection on both (and their continued integration with each other) remains constant in her life and activity. As Congar wrote in 1937:

> The church is constantly reforming itself; it can really live only by doing so, and the intensity of its effort to reform itself measures at any given moment the health of its muscle tone (*tonus vital*). Don't be fooled: Pius X's initiative, which found its formula in his motto *Instaurare omnia in Christo* (Renew all things in Christ), an initiative diminished somewhat by the war, but not extinguished, is a true movement of reform.[64]

The Church's Christological nature (as the Bride of Christ) and mystical identity remain the impetus and the explanation for her openness to continual reform.[65] Recent studies of Vatican II have continued to echo this point. Matthew Levering adumbrates "the very heart of the Council's dogmatic and pastoral contributions" as an "insistence upon the centrality of Jesus Christ within the modern pluralistic, technologically advancing, and historically conscious world."[66] Levering suggests that "renewal (or true reform) must steer between two poles: an ahistorical extrinsicism, for which no reform is ever needed in the Church, and an atheological historicism, for which reform is merely a matter of adjudicating power within ever-changing human constructs."[67] Overly static or overly political conceptions of the Church and her

---

[64] Ibid., 21. Congar is citing his earlier book, *Chrétiens désunis* (Paris: Cerf, 1937), 339–340.

[65] For a summary of Congar's ecclesiology, see Yves Congar, *The Mystery of the Church*, trans. A. V. Littledale (Baltimore, MD: Helicon Press, 1960).

[66] Levering, *Introduction to Vatican II*, 11. Levering links this résumé of the Council to the central documents in this manner: "Put succinctly: We can encounter Christ personally and know him cognitively (propositionally) as our Savior today, two thousand years after his Pasch (*Dei Verbum*). We are called to actively participate liturgically in Christ's holy self-offering on the Cross to the Father through the Holy Spirit (*Sacrosanctum Concilium*). As members of Christ's eschatological people and his mystical Body, we receive the holy gifts of Christ's teaching, sacraments, and hierarchical order that enable us, in a manner that is ever in need of renewal and reform, to share in his priestly, prophetic, and royal mission (*Lumen Gentium*). Lastly, in the midst of the unique pastoral developments, challenges, and opportunities of the modern world, we attain in Jesus Christ to the graced fulfillment of the world's highest aspirations (*Gaudium et Spes*)" (ibid.).

[67] Ibid. See also Maurice Blondel, *History and Dogma*, trans. Alexander Dru, in Maurice Blondel, *The Letter on Apologetics and History and Dogma* (Grand Rapids, MI: Eerdmans, 1994), 221–287.

life do not accurately reflect her reality. The saving dynamism of the Word of God—both Incarnate and written—lies as the unifying center of any efforts of "true reform" or authentic "renewal."

The Project of "Theological Renewal"

Although many theologians were enthusiastic about the project of renewal in Catholic life and thought, the exact contours, range, and limits of the prospective renewal eluded easy identification. Cardinal Paul-Émile Léger offered the following observations about the nature of renewal itself:

> Renewal is not easy to define. Not all change is renewal: a thing can change for better or for worse; one can even, in changing alter the essentials or damage forms which have an abiding usefulness, which are, indeed, indispensable. Renewal demands that we respect what is unalterable and that we cooperate in the unfolding of the true tradition. Nonetheless, renewal is not simply a return to forms and customs of the past. It is rather what in French we call a *ressource-ment*, a return to the sources in the sense that the life which gave birth to the Church must spring up ever more vigorously without endangering her own proper and unalterable nature.[68]

This passage carefully distinguishes renewal from mere change. Change can be either good or bad. Renewal is something profoundly good—a bridge between that which is constant and that which develops in the Church's tradition. "Renewal tries to understand better God's revelation given once and for all to the Church, in order to put it into terms which are meaningful for the past and the present. It is a more faithful listening to the word in order that it may be proclaimed more effectively."[69] And as Léger says, this articulation of the dynamics of renewal resonates deeply with the inclinations and methods of *ressourcement* theology.[70]

---

[68] Paul-Émile Cardinal Léger, "Introduction: Theology of the Renewal of the Church," in *Renewal of Religious Thought: Proceedings of the Congress on the Theology of the Renewal of the Church, Centenary of Canada, 1867–1967*, vol. 1, ed. L. K. Shook, C.S.B. (Montreal: Palm Publishers, 1968), 20.

[69] Ibid.

[70] "Enriching the work and achievements of the Second Vatican Council (1962–5), various elements of *ressourcement* theology, concerned to rediscover forgotten or neglected dimensions of the great tradition found in the scriptures, the Fathers of the church, and the liturgy, flowed together: for instance, in the biblical movement, the ecumenical movement, the litur-

In addition to the reorientation of theology around Christ, the Church, and sacred sources, others have identified in the project of theological renewal the presence of an *aggiornamento* openness to engagement with the priorities and concerns of the modern world. Catholic life and thought are not insular realities.[71] Bernard Lonergan, S.J., for example, offered the following explanation of the Council's renewal intentions: "Usually in Catholic circles 'renewal' has meant a return to the olden times of pristine virtue and deep wisdom. But good Pope John [XXIII] has made 'renewal' mean '*aggiornamento*,' 'bringing things up to date.'"[72] Lonergan goes on to develop his analysis according to what a "bringing things up to date" presupposes and implies in a period of Vatican II renewal: "Obviously, if theology is to be brought up to date, it must have fallen behind the times. Again, if we are to know what is to be done to bring theology up to date, we must ascertain when it began to fall behind the times, in what respects it got out of touch, in what ways it failed to meet the issues and effect the developments that long ago were due and now are long overdue."[73] Specifically, he identifies the moment at which theology fell behind the times as "the end of the seventeenth century and, more precisely, to the year 1680." This, he explains, "was the time of the great beginning": "Then it was that Herbert Butterfield placed the origins of modern science, then that Paul Hazard placed the beginning of the Enlightenment, then that Yves Congar placed the beginning of dogmatic theology. When modern science began, when the Enlightenment began, then the theologians began to reassure one another about their certainties."[74]

---

gical renewal, the patristic renewal (championed, in particular, by those who had launched the *Sources chrétiennes* series), and the renewal of Thomism" (Gerald O'Collins, S.J., "*Ressourcement* and Vatican II," in *Ressourcement: A Movement for Renewal in Twentieth-Century Catholic Theology*, ed. Gabriel Flynn and Paul D. Murray, with the assistance of Patricia Kelly [Oxford: Oxford University Press, 2012], 372). This text from O'Collins also appeared in his *The Second Vatican Council: Message and Meaning* (Collegeville, MN: Liturgical Press, 2014), 1–24.

[71] Michael Bredeck, *Das Zweite Vatikanum als Konzil des Aggiornamento: Zur hermeneutischen Grundlegung einer theologischen Konzilsinterpretation* (Paderborn: Schöningh, 2007); Karim Schelkens, John A. Dick, and Jürgen Mettepenningen, *Aggiornamento? Catholicism from Gregory XVI to Benedict XVI* (Leiden: Brill, 2013).

[72] Bernard Lonergan, S.J., "Theology in Its New Context," in *Renewal of Religious Thought: Proceedings of the Congress on the Theology of the Renewal of the Church, Centenary of Canada, 1867–1967*, vol. 1, ed. L. K. Shook, C.S.B. (Montreal: Palm Publishers, 1968), 34. This text was later republished in *The Lonergan Reader*, ed. Mark D. Morelli and Elizabeth A. Morelli (Toronto: University of Toronto Press, 1997), 408–419.

[73] Ibid. For a description of the *ressourcement* and *aggiornamento* movements and their effect at Vatican II, see Marcellino D'Ambrosio, "*Ressourcement* Theology, *Aggiornamento*, and the Hermeneutics of Tradition," *Communio* 18 (1991): 530–555.

[74] Ibid.

With regard to the rise of modern science, Lonergan notes that But-terfield "by no means meant to deny that from the year 1300 on numerous discoveries were made that since have been included within modern science and integrated with it."[75] Rather, in light of the fact that "the dominant cultural context was Aristotelian, and the discoverers themselves had Aris-totelian background . . . there existed a conflict between the new ideas and the old doctrines, and this conflict existed not merely between an old guard of Aristotelians and a new breed of scientists but, far more gravely, within the minds of the new scientists."[76] Otherwise put, the lingering Aristotelian legacy itself hindered the development of modern thought after the Enlight-enment—particularly in the Church. And the apparent division between the Stagirite's teaching and the conviction of modern science continued to become more apparent as the world transitioned into the twentieth century. "Before these new ideas could be formulated accurately, coherently, cogently, they had to multiply, cumulate, coalesce to bring forth a new system of con-cepts and a new body of doctrine that was somehow comparable in extent to the Aristotelian and so capable of replacing it."[77] Discrete and new scientific ideas alone were inadequate to replace classical *scientia*. Only a completely new whole—a new system of concepts and of doctrine—could displace Aristotle and replace his influence.

Reference to the historical influence of Aristotelianism in Catholic thought provokes an examination of the nature of theology in general and of dogmatic theology in particular. Scholasticism and neo-scholasticism both reflected Aristotle's method of dialectic and *scientia*.[78] Lonergan observes

---

[75] Ibid., 35. The work on which Lonergan depends throughout his analysis is Herbert Butter-field, *The Origins of Modern Science, 1300–1800* (New York, NY: The Macmillan Company, 1959).

[76] Ibid. For a contemporary attempt to reconcile Aristotelian *scientia* and modern science, see Benedict M. Ashley, O.P., *The Way Toward Wisdom: An Interdisciplinary and Intercultural Introduction to Metaphysics* (Notre Dame, IN: University of Notre Dame Press, 2006).

[77] Ibid.

[78] "Some version of scholasticism had held the field in Catholic thought for some eight centuries. . . . Regrettably, neo-scholasticism came to epitomize the weakness more than the glory of scholasticism: a penchant for ahistorical orthodoxy, abstractness, antiquated science; a pre-dilection for logic over discovery, proof over understanding; a posture of defense rather than creativity. . . . A tendency to sacralize Aristotelian philosophy and science, antique cosmology, and particular cultural and political forms contributed to the scandal of faith and the empow-erment of secularists. . . . When Vatican II finally took the lid off the pot, it boiled over with a vengeance because positive solutions were long overdue" (Jeremey D. Wilkins, *Before Truth: Lonergan, Aquinas, and the Problem of Wisdom* [Washington, DC: The Catholic Univer-sity of America Press, 2018], 50–51). See also Thomas F. O'Meara, "Thomas Aquinas and German Intellectuals: Neoscholasticism and Modernity in the Late 19th Century," *Gregoria-*

that it was the theologians of the seventeenth century who "introduced 'dogmatic' theology" as a discrete discipline.[79]

> It is true that the word "dogmatic" had been previously applied to theology. But then it was used to denote a distinction from moral, or ethical, or historical theology. Now it was employed in a new sense, in opposition to scholastic theology. It replaced the inquiry of the *quaestio* by the pedagogy of the thesis. It demoted the quest of faith for understanding to be a desirable, but secondary, and indeed, optional goal. It gave basic and central significance to the certitudes of faith, their presuppositions, and their consequences. It owed its mode of proof to Melchior Cano and, as the theologian was also a bishop and an inquisitor, so the new dogmatic theology not only proved its theses, but also was supported by the teaching and the sanctions of the Church.[80]

This "conception of theology," he remarks, "survived right into the twentieth century, and even today in some circles it is the only conception that is understood."[81] Nonetheless, "among theologians its limitations and defects have been becoming more and more apparent, especially since the 1890s."[82] And this awareness brings one to the genesis of the Second Vatican Council: "During the last seventy years, efforts to find remedies and to implement

---

num 68 (1987): 719–736; Philip Gleason, "Neoscholasticism as Preconciliar Ideology," *U.S. Catholic Historian* 7 (1988): 401–411; Walter Kasper, "Introduction: Systematic Theology Today and the Tasks Before It," in *Theology and Church*, trans. Margaret Kohl (London: SCM Press, 1989), 1–16; Thomas G. Guarino, *Revelation and Truth: Unity and Plurality in Contemporary Theology* (Scranton, PA: University of Scranton Press, 1993), 81–113; Fergus Kerr, "A Different World: Neoscholasticism and its Discontents," *International Journal of Systematic Theology* 8 (2006): 128–148.

[79] Lonergan, "Theology in Its New Context," 36.

[80] Ibid. Lonergan here relies upon Congar's *DTC* article: "*Théologie*" (XV, cols. 398–502). For more on the modern division of theology into various departments of specialization, see Edward Farley, *Theologia: The Fragmentation and Unity of Theological Education* (Philadelphia, PA: Fortress Press, 1983). For a study of Melchior Cano's influence on the study of theology, see Albert Lang, *Die Loci Theologici des Melchior Cano und die Methode des dogmatischen Beweises: Ein Beitrag zur theologischen Methodologie und ihrer Geschichte* (Munich: Kösel und Pustet, 1925); Eugène Marcotte, O.M.I., *La nature de la théologie d'après Melchior Cano* (Ottawa: Universitas Catholica Ottaviensis, 1949).

[81] Ibid., 36. For a representative example of an older conception of theology, in addition to that of Garrigou-Lagrange, see Joseph Clifford Fenton, *What Is Sacred Theology?*, ed. Cajetan Cuddy, O.P. (Providence, RI: Cluny Media, 2018).

[82] Ibid., 36.

them have been going forward steadily, if unobtrusively. The measure of their success is the radically new situation brought to light by the Second Vatican Council."[83]

In order to protect his readers from misunderstanding him, however, Lonergan clarifies his point with precision: "There is, perhaps, no need for me here to insist that the novelty resides not in a new revelation or a new faith, but in a new cultural context."[84] He argues that newness of any renewal emerges from the freshness of the modern "cultural context" in which theologians undertake their work. Both the internal structure of the discipline itself and the external context of the contemporary period shape theology's actual (and efficacious) practice.

> For a theology is a product not only of the religion it investigates and expounds, but also of the cultural ideals and norms that set its problems and direct its solutions. Just as theology in the thirteenth century followed its age by assimilating Aristotle, just as theology of the seventeenth century resisted its age by retiring into a dogmatic corner, so theology today is locked in an encounter with its age. Whether it will grow and triumph, or whether it will wither to insignificance, in no small measure depends on the clarity and the accuracy of its grasp of the external cultural factors that undermine its past achievements and challenge it to new endeavors.[85]

By way of summary, Lonergan draws attention to a series of distinct contrasts between the practice of theology before and after the commencement of the modern period.[86] Formerly "theology was a deductive [sic], and it has become largely an empirical science."[87] He explains that the deductive exercise of theology operated according to a manualist method in which "theses were conclusions to be proven from the premises provided by Scripture and Tradition."[88] The intellectual orientation of doctrinal manualism tended to operate on the level of the *a priori* and the abstract. At the time of the Second Vatican Council, however, Catholic thinkers proposed alternatives

---

[83] Ibid., 36–37.

[84] Ibid. 37.

[85] Ibid.

[86] For a recent consideration of Catholic thought in the early-Modern period, see Ulrich L. Lehner, *The Catholic Enlightenment: The Forgotten History of a Global Movement* (Oxford: Oxford University Press, 2016).

[87] Lonergan, "Theology in Its New Context," 37.

[88] Ibid., 37.

to this method that facilitated a greater appreciation for the human person and for historical development.[89]

Lonergan praises the fact that the theology of renewal "has become an empirical science in the sense that Scripture and Tradition now supply not premises, but data . . . viewed in its historical perspective."[90] This historical perspective—which profits from "the light of contemporary techniques and procedures"—changed the tenor of theology's practice: "Where before the step from premises to conclusions was brief, simple, and certain, today the steps from data to interpretation are long, arduous, and, at best, probable."[91] With the displacement of the scholastic method of theology by a more historically informed approach to sacred sources, Neo-Scholastic theses also gave way to dialectical engagement with those outside of the mainstream Catholic intellectual tradition.[92] In this sense, modern theology benefits from the epistemological dividends of modern science: "An empirical science does not demonstrate. It accumulates information, develops understanding, masters ever more of its materials, but it does not preclude the uncovering of further relevant data, the emergence of new insights, the attainment of a more comprehensive view."[93] This investigative approach to sacred knowledge appears to reflect the inclinations of the theologians who influenced Vatican II. It is here that

---

[89] Here some have suggested certain similarities between Enlightenment and neo-scholastic priorities: "The Enlightenment ideal was to attain timeless, universal and objective conclusions by exercising a unitary and ahistorical form of reasoning. Similarly, neoscholastic theology 'identified truth and life with immutability and rationality; it opposed being to history and ignored concreteness in human life and in the economy of salvation.' For neothomists, as for Enlightenment philosophers, appealing to experience, tradition and historical studies was the wrong way to get to truth" (Fergus Kerr, O.P., *Twentieth-Century Catholic Theologians: From Neoscholasticism to Nuptial Mysticism* [Oxford: Blackwell Publishing, 2007], 2).

[90] Lonergan, "Theology in Its New Context," 37.

[91] Ibid., 37–38.

[92] Nonetheless, Lonergan does believe that theology ought to be swallowed up by mere conjecture: "If we are to revise scholastic categories and make our own the concepts worked out in historicist, personalist, phenomenological, and existentialist circles, then we must be able to distinguish tinsel and silver, gilt and gold. No less important than a critique of notions and conclusions is a critique of methods. The new largely empirical approach to theology can too easily be made into a device for reducing doctrines to probable opinions. A hermeneutics [*sic*] can pretend to philosophic neutrality yet force the conclusion that the content of revelation is mostly myth. Scientific history can be so conceived that a study of the narrative of salvation will strip it of matters of fact. If our renewed theology is not to be the dupe of every fashion, it needs a firm basis and a critical stance" (ibid., 42).

[93] Ibid., 38.

the vitality of renewal meets *aggiornamento*.[94] And it is also here that the former ways of theological method appeared to be insufficient. "The old dogmatic theology had misconceived history on a classicist model . . . It thought not in terms of evolution and development, but of universality and permanence."[95]

Significantly, Lonergan argues that the example of Thomas Aquinas (and of the medieval period) continues to bear much value for those participating in the renewal of theology. Contrary to the abstract aridity of manualism, Lonergan suggests that Aquinas's thought intrinsically reflected—and historically anticipated—the dynamism of both *ressourcement* and *aggiornamento*.[96]

> In the medieval period theology became the queen of the sciences. But in the practice of Aquinas it was also the principle for the moulding and transforming of a culture. He was not content to write his systematic works, his commentaries on Scripture and on such Christian writers as the Pseudo-Dionysius and Boethius. At a time when Arabic and Greek thought were penetrating the whole of Western culture, he wrote extensive commentaries on numerous works of Aristotle to fit a pagan's science within a Christian context and to construct a world view that underpinned Dante's *Divine Comedy*. To this paradigm theology today must look if it is to achieve its *aggiornamento*. Its task is not limited to investigating, ordering, expounding, communicating divine revelation. All that is needed, but more must be done. For revelation is God's entry into man's making of man, and so theology not only has to reflect on revelation, but also it has somehow to mediate God's meaning into the whole of human affairs.[97]

---

[94] "The first step to what later came be known as *aggiornamento* had to be *ressourcement*—a rediscovery of the riches of the Church's two-thousand-year treasury, a return to the very headwaters of the Christian tradition" (D'Ambrosio, "*Ressourcement* Theology," 532).

[95] Ibid.

[96] For more on the link between *aggiornamento* and *ressourcement*, see Ormond Rush, "Toward a Comprehensive Interpretation of the Council and Its Documents," in *Probing the Riches of Vatican II*, ed. David G. Schultenover, S.J. (Collegeville, MN: Liturgical Press, 2015), 35–60; Ormond Rush, "Principle 4: *Ressourcement/Aggiornamento*," in *The Vision of Vatican II: Its Fundamental Principles* (Collegeville, MN: Liturgical Press Academic, 2019), 17–21.

[97] Lonergan, "Theology in Its New Context," 40–41.

Lonergan summarizes: "My reflections have come full circle. Not only does the cultural context influence theology to undo its past achievements, but theology is also called upon to influence the cultural context, to translate the word of God and so project it into new mentalities and new situations."[98] This characterization of the work of renewal suggests that the task of theology is one of communication ("to translate the word of God"). And the particular type of communication that Lonergan envisions is one leading to universal religious conversion. A communication-focused theology, then, would facilitate a renewal that was even evangelical in nature. In this way, historical awareness, personalist emphases, and sacred sources would find a sanctifying integration:

> It follows that theology will be reflection on conversion. But conversion is fundamental to religion. It follows that reflection on conversion can supply theology with its foundation and, indeed, with a foundation that is concrete, dynamic, personal, communal, and historical. Just as reflection on the operations of the scientist brings to light the real foundation of the science, so too reflection on the ongoing process of conversion may bring to light the real foundation of a renewed theology.[99]

Bernard Lonergan articulates the renewal of theology as ordered to "a total transformation of dogmatic theology."[100] The project of renewal will penetrate even to the core of theology: "So great a transformation needs a renewed foundation." Indeed, he argues, "The needed renewal is the introduction of a new type of foundation." What does this new foundation look like? He explains that the new type of theological foundation "is to consist not in objective statements, but in subjective reality. The objective statements of a *de vera religione, de Christo legato, de ecclesia, de inspiratione scripturae, de locis theologicis*, are as much in need of a foundation as are those of other tracts."[101] A radically renewed theology requires a new appreciation for the foundations of theology—and this new fundamental theology will bear a greater appreciation for the subjective and the dynamics of conversion. The

---

[98] Ibid., 41.

[99] Ibid., 45.

[100] Ibid.

[101] Ibid., 46. He continues: "But behind all statements is the stating subject. What is normative and foundational for subjects stating theology is to be found, I have suggested, in reflection on conversion, where conversion is taken as an ongoing process, concrete and dynamic, personal, communal, and historical."

formulation of a new fundamental theology was seen as an essential part of the broader project of renewal in Catholic thought and life.

With regard to theology's "tasks after Vatican II," Yves Congar echoes much of Lonergan's analysis, and he speaks of the project of renewal in Catholic thought as grounded in the mysteries of the faith. "Surely, there is every reason for theological renewal. But this novelty will be such in a relative sense only. The aspect of continuity, and even of identity, is incomparably weightier. The task of theology remains what it always has been. It is still a reflection on the mysteries of faith."[102] Because of his emphasis on the task of theology as "a reflection on the faith," Congar defends the claim that theology "has value in itself, independently of any 'usefulness.' But theology has also a function in the service of the people of God, in the historical situation in which this people now finds itself."[103] Thus, Congar suggests that in a renewed theology "two lines" of theological reflection can be identified: "In the first we reflect on the various articles comprised in faith; in the second on the overall situation of faith, that is, on how faith and the act of believing as such are possible, appropriate, and fitting."[104] This proposal would imply that "in the first case we have the theology of the different theological matters; in the second we have fundamental theology or, as Karl Rahner says, formal dogmatics."[105] "Whichever the case may be," he concludes, "theology today simply must develop the reference to man."[106]

---

[102] Yves Marie-Joseph Congar, O.P., "Theology's Tasks after Vatican II," in *Renewal of Religious Thought: Proceedings of the Congress on the Theology of the Renewal of the Church, Centenary of Canada, 1867–1967*, vol. 1, ed. L. K. Shook, C.S.B. (Montreal: Palm Publishers, 1968), 59.

[103] Ibid., 60.

[104] Ibid.

[105] Ibid.

[106] Ibid. This anthropological focus characterizes numerous considerations of the nature of fundamental theology. For example, see Claude Geffré, O.P., "Recent Developments in Fundamental Theology: An Interpretation," *The Development of Fundamental Theology*, ed. Johannes B. Metz, *Concilium*, vol. 46 (New York, NY: Paulist Press, 1969), 5–27. "When we try to explain the development that has taken place in fundamental theology during the last thirty years, we realize that it fits in with the urge to overcome the intellectualist and objectivist way in which neo-Thomism saw the problems. We can no longer rest content with the analysis of a purely rational credibility because this no longer corresponds to our modern frame of mind. If fundamental theology aims at 'justifying' the faith in the eyes of both the believer and the unbeliever, it has to take into account the philosophical and cultural situation which conditions our mind. Therefore, the best students of fundamental theology will take note of the changes that have affected human understanding since Kant; they will take man's historicity much more seriously, and they will not overlook the fact that today we have reached the age of criticism, or, rather, of hermeneutics. This is the background to that 'anthropocentric' concern which is evident in so much work in fundamental theology today" (ibid., 15).

The need for some "reference to man" in the renewal of theology does not mean, according to Congar, that man is "the center and measure of everything." He cautions that a "conversion" to "pure humanism cannot be the program of theology."[107] And yet the fact remains: "The God of revelation" proper to theology "is the God of grace, a God for men, the Creator of man made to his image."[108] Hence, "the true content of revelation, its *objectum formale quod*, is the truth of the religious relation, covenant, and filial adoption, which God proposes to conclude with men in Jesus Christ. This is the reason why revelation speaks jointly of God *and* man. They are the very terms of the religious relation."[109] Of course, these themes bear continuity with Congar's analysis in his earlier *True and False Reform*.[110] Concretely and with an eye to the future, he suggests that a theological renewal in which a "reflection on the faith . . . investigat[es] with particular care its relation to man as he endeavors to understand himself" could proceed "alongside of a theology of the traditional plan and structure which will continue to follow the ancient pattern, namely, exhaustive examination of the datum in Scripture, Tradition, and the magisterium."[111] Here and elsewhere throughout his academic career, Congar maintained that "a synthesis of these two types" of theology was "desirable but difficult."[112]

"Anything and Everything": The New Fundamental Theology and the Project of Renewal

Founded in 1965, the theological journal *Concilium* was, from the begin-

---

[107] Ibid.

[108] Ibid., 61.

[109] Ibid., emphasis original.

[110] "We also need to rethink and reformulate what we mean by Christian reality, in response to the claim that now nothing else exists but a world where human beings are the center and master of everything" (Congar, *True and False Reform*, 5).

[111] Congar, "Theology's Tasks," 63–64.

[112] Ibid., 64. Congar refers his readers to his article "Théologie" in the *DTC* (XV, cols. 398–502) and to his book *La foi et la théologie* (Paris: Desclée, 1962). For an English translation of the *DTC* article in its entirety, see Yves Congar, O.P., *A History of Theology*, trans. Hunter Guthrie, S.J. (Hindmarsh: ATF Press, 2019). In his preface to this work, Congar explains that "this book substantially reproduces the article entitled 'Théologie' which appeared in the *Dictionnaire de Théologie Catholique* published in Paris in 1938–39. My manuscript was sent to the editor, Msgr. Amann, on the second of September 1939, just as I was preparing to leave for the general mobilization prior to World War II. Returning from the war at the end of May 1939, I was surprised to see that the editor had discarded about two-fifths of my text. . . . The present text is more complete than that published in the *Dictionnaire*" (ibid., 25).

ning, a publication noted for its interest in furthering the renewal and the reform of the Church and of her theology.[113] The project of renewal gave unifying shape to *Concilium*'s conception. During the first year of its existence, the journal devoted an issue to fundamental theology. In his preface to the volume, Johannes Baptist Metz observed that "Vatican Council II has brought into the limelight the constantly 'exposed flank' of the Church and of her theology in its commitment to the world." Consequently, the journal's contributors were intent to focus on "those borderline questions on the frontiers of theology."[114] Metz located questions such as these within "the scope" of fundamental theology—because of its "engagement in an unceasing dialogue with the world of our time."[115] Indeed, he suggests that fundamental theology "perhaps more than any other [theological discipline] is seeking a new understanding of itself and of its genuine theological character so that it can be faithful to its responsibility for Christian hope."[116]

This desired new understanding of fundamental theology was not easy to achieve.[117] Four years later, *Concilium* devoted another of its issues

---

[113] As is well known, its founders include: Hans Urs von Balthasar, Anton van den Boogaard, Paul Brand, Yves Congar, Hans Küng, Henri de Lubac, Johann-Baptist Metz, Karl Rahner, and Edward Schillebeeckx. Balthasar and de Lubac later broke with the journal and worked with theologians like Louis Bouyer, Walter Kasper, Marc Ouellet, and Joseph Ratzinger to found the journal *Communio*. *Communio* theologian Tracey Rowland explains: "At the time of the Second Vatican Council all the leading *Periti* who were later to split into the different *Concilium* and *Communio* camps were in agreement that Catholic intellectual life operated too much in a ghetto. There was an almost universal desire to break free of the neo-scholastic straitjacket and to enter into serious intellectual engagements with non-Catholic scholars.... Underneath all the many fault lines one can enumerate, which distinguish the *Communio* from the *Concilium* approaches to Catholic theology, perhaps the most fundamental is a different attitude to issues in eschatology" (*Catholic Theology* [London: Bloomsbury, 2017], 165).

[114] Johannes B. Metz, preface to *Fundamental Theology: The Church and the World*, Concilium, vol. 6 (New York, NY: Paulist Press, 1969), 1. He explains that this initiative of the journal "will deal with the very foundations of a deeper understanding and of a more effective proclamation of our faith in its *confrontation* with contemporary philosophical and theological problems.... In this confrontation, theology should serve the hope of contemporary man not only by giving answers, but also by listening and learning, and even often perhaps by re-learning" (emphasis original).

[115] Ibid.

[116] Ibid.

[117] "The assertion has been made many times concerning preconciliar fundamental theology that it was searching for its identity: its object, method, structure and limits. In the aftermath of Vatican Council II when ecclesiastical studies are being restructured in three cycles, the crisis—far from being resolved—seems to be aggravated" (René Latourelle, S.J., "Dismemberment or Renewal of Fundamental Theology?," *The Development of Fundamental Theology*, ed. Johannes B. Metz, Concilium, vol. 46 [New York: Paulist Press, 1969], 29).

to the questions of fundamental theology. The discipline's search for its theological character continued. Its editors explained that "in this [1969] volume, which deals explicitly with fundamental theology, the purpose is to give the reader an insight into the general situation of fundamental theology rather than to deal with specific questions."[118] The 1965 volume had identified the importance of a renewed understanding of theology and of its fundamentals. It had not, however, formally or fully articulated the specifics that this renewed understanding would (or ought) to comprise.[119]

In the 1969 volume of *Concilium*, the French theologian, Claude Geffré, O.P., contributed the opening essay, titled "Recent Developments in Fundamental Theology: An Interpretation."[120] Geffré begins by observing that, "in contrast with the other theological disciplines, the nature of fundamental theology is still hotly debated among theologians."[121] "Uncertainty" continued to characterize the discipline and to frustrate its renewed realization. "The most common definitions [of 'fundamental theology'] today betray a definite uncertainty about the epistemology of a discipline which wants to fulfill at the same time the function of the old apologetics—i.e., that of providing a rational justification of the Christian faith—and exercise the critical function inherent in all science—i.e., that of explaining the basis and method of the science of theology."[122]

Geffré cautions against any attempts to situate fundamental theology within a preconceived disciplinary framework. He explains that "the meaning of fundamental theology is therefore somewhat variable, and this should make us beware of pinning it down to a too rigid definition as if it were once and for all perfectly clear about its object, its themes and its method."[123] Fundamental theology's essential litheness originates from "its specific function," which "is to explain Christianity to the human mind." And as the questions and conditions of human cognition are subject to var-

---

[118] Johannes B. Metz, Werner Bröker, Willi Oelmuller, preface to *The Development of Fundamental Theology*, ed. Johannes B. Metz, *Concilium*, vol. 46 (New York, NY: Paulist Press, 1969), 1.

[119] Jean-Pierre Torrell points out this lacuna in his 1982 essay, "New Trends in Fundamental Theology in the Postconciliar Period," in *Problems and Perspectives of Fundamental Theology*, ed. René Latourelle and Gerald O'Collins, trans. Matthew J. O'Connell (New York: Paulist Press, 1982), 14–15.

[120] Claude Geffré, O.P., "Recent Developments in Fundamental Theology: An Interpretation," *The Development of Fundamental Theology*, ed. Johannes B. Metz, *Concilium*, vol. 46 (New York, NY: Paulist Press, 1969), 5–27. This essay was later included in Geffré's book: *A New Age in Theology* (New York: Paulist Press, 1974), 11–30.

[121] Ibid., 5.

[122] Ibid.

[123] Ibid., 6.

iation, so fundamental theology's "set of subjects and even its method" will naturally "develop according to the historical development of the mind." Indeed, he continues, "we shall thus have to allow even more room for historical relativity in the structure and practice of fundamental theology than in the other sectors of theology."[124]

The interpretation of contemporary fundamental theology that Geffré proposes consists of three parts.[125] The first part outlines the "collapse of apologetics as an objective science to the benefit of a fundamental theology." The second looks at the "anthropocentric view which inspires most modern works on fundamental theology." Finally, the third part summarizes the "tendency which is beginning to take shape today and which reaches beyond objectivism and anthropocentrism to the social and political existence of modern man."[126]

In his summary of "the failure of apologetics as an objective science," Geffré expressly cites Garrigou-Lagrange's *On Divine Revelation* as what he believes to be an example of this gravely limited, traditional apologetics.[127] He suggests that "during the last thirty years we have become far more aware of the grave limitations of the traditional apologetics of the textbooks, particularly with regard to its concept of *revelation*."[128] He argues that "one of the great weaknesses of apologetics as an objective science lay in thinking that credibility was a characteristic that extended equally to all dogma without having theologically and critically examined the key dogma of revelation itself."[129] Because revelation is a "transcendental theological category," proponents of the new fundamental theology do "not proceed, as the old treatises on apologetics did, by asking ourselves the questions of the possibility, fittingness and need of revelation." Rather, he exhorts his colleagues "to start straightaway with the event of revelation as recorded in Scripture and then try to disentangle its overall significance for the believer and for man in general in a given cultural situation."[130] And it is here, Geffré indicates, that one can recognize the demise of the former discipline of the "old apologetics" and the rise of the term "fundamental theology" as the preferred

---

[124] Ibid.

[125] With regard to the history of fundamental theology, Geffré "believe[s] that we can discern three main tendencies which followed each other chronologically, and this with a certain historical logic" (ibid., 6–7).

[126] Ibid., 7.

[127] Ibid., 9.

[128] Ibid., 10, emphasis original.

[129] Ibid., 10.

[130] Ibid.

"science of the dogma of revelation itself."[131] Indeed, Geffré concludes his presentation of "the new kind of fundamental theology" by pointing to its main goals. Among these goals, he says: "It seems right to say that the most active research into fundamental theology is trying to reach beyond the objectivism of neo-Scholastic theology."[132]

Nineteen years later, in 1980, Jean-Pierre Torrell, O.P., gave another look to the state of fundamental theology in the post-conciliar period. Interestingly, he observes that a noteworthy "uncertainty" still characterized publications that examined the nature of fundamental theology: "Anyone who casts an eye over recent work in fundamental theology must be struck by the persistent recurrence of questions about its identity, object and method." Indeed, he suggests that one can "discern a real uncertainty with regard to the concept behind the term 'fundamental theology.'"[133] Theologians extolled the importance of the new fundamental theology. But they found it difficult to articulate, clearly and precisely, its exact form and method.

Torrell offers a very concise history of the ongoing effort to renew fundamental theology: "From the beginning, therefore, we can see, on the one hand, a certain practical confusion about the precise boundaries of the area covered by fundamental theology, and, on the other hand, some theoretical difficulty in defining the proper object of this discipline."[134] Torrell is very measured in his engagement with the new fundamental theologians and the lack of clarity about exact identity, object, and method. Nonetheless, he reminds his readers that "fundamental theology cannot deal with anything and everything without losing its identity."[135]

---

[131] Ibid., 11. "Because of the *a priori* method used by the old apologetics, one can understand that the expression 'apologetics' is being rejected more and more widely, and that the term 'fundamental theology' is preferred as the science of the foundation of the faith (and hence of theology)—that is, the science of the dogma of revelation itself" (ibid., 10–11).

[132] Ibid., 27.

[133] Jean-Pierre Torrell, "New Trends in Fundamental Theology in the Postconciliar Period," in *Problems and Perspectives of Fundamental Theology*, ed. René Latourelle and Gerald O'Collins, trans. Matthew J. O'Connell (New York, NY: Paulist Press, 1982), 13. This volume was originally published in Italian under the title: *Problemi e prospettive di teologia fondamentale* (Rome: Editrice Queriniana, 1980). Torrell observes that, in addition to the journal *Concilium*, the journal *Gregorianum* in 1969 also "published the papers of a meeting of several professors at the Gregorian University who were in search of this discipline's [i.e., fundamental theology's] lost identity." In spite of "the relative agreement among the participants in the meeting," however, "in the papers of this meeting as in those published by *Concilium*, we can discern a real uncertainty with regard to the concept behind the term 'fundamental theology'" (Torrell, "New Trends in Fundamental Theology," 13).

[134] Torrell, "New Trends in Fundamental Theology," 14–15.

[135] Ibid., 15. Torrell continues: "Lacking a sufficiently clear and exclusive choice at the very outset,

The quest for the specific nature and method of fundamental theology has continued. Many theologians have attempted to clarify its precise object. Ultimately, however, consensus has not been reached. The new fundamental theology still struggles to distinguish itself from philosophy, apologetics, and dogmatic theology.[136] It shares something in common with all of these disciplines but claims a fresh—even if elusive—specificity.[137] Like the project of renewal in Catholic theology more generally, the formulation of a new fundamental theology remains unfinished.

"Fragmentation": Contemporary Catholic Theology

In a 1978 article titled "L'Église catholique en crise" ("The Catholic Church in Crisis"), Louis Bouyer describes a dinner party to which he was invited by Cardinal Jean Daniélou. Cardinal Daniélou "hosted a dinner for a leading member of the French episcopacy, also a cardinal, and certain French theologians, all members of the International Theological Commission."[138] As

---

the theologian will be constantly tempted to include in fundamental theology a number of subjects which seem to have in common only the fact that they have no specific place elsewhere in theology."

[136] For examples of significant subsequent works on fundamental theology, see Gerald O'Collins, S.J., *Fundamental Theology* (New York, NY: Paulist Press, 1981); Francis Schüssler Fiorenza, *Foundational Theology: Jesus and the Church* (New York, NY: Crossroad, 1984); Randy L. Maddox, *Toward an Ecumenical Fundamental Theology* (Chico, CA: Scholars Press, 1984); Gerald O'Collins, S.J., *Retrieving Fundamental Theology: The Three Styles of Contemporary Theology* (New York, NY: Paulist Press, 1993); René Latourelle and Rino Fisichella, *Dictionary of Fundamental Theology* (New York, NY: Crossroad Publishing Company, 1994); Gerald O'Collins, S.J., *Rethinking Fundamental Theology: Toward a New Fundamental Theology* (Oxford: Oxford University Press, 2011); Gilbert Narcisse, O.P., *Premiers pas en théologie* (Paris: Parole et Silence, 2005); Fernando Ocáriz and Arturo Blanco, *Fundamental Theology* (Downers Grove, IL: Midwest Theological Forum, 2009); Matthew L. Becker, *Fundamental Theology: A Protestant Perspective* (London: Bloomsbury, 2015); Neil Ormerod and Christiaan Jacobs-Vandegeer, *Foundational Theology* (Minneapolis, MN: Fortress Press, 2015); Lawrence Feingold, *Faith Comes from What Is Heard: An Introduction to Fundamental Theology* (Steubenville, OH: Emmaus Academic, 2016); Guy Mansini, O.S.B., *Fundamental Theology* (Washington, DC: The Catholic University of America Press, 2018); Hans Waldenfels, *Contextual Fundamental Theology*, trans. Susan Johnson (Leiden: Ferdinand Schöningh, 2018).

[137] See René Latourelle, S.J., "Spécificité de la théologie fondamentale," in *Interpréter: Hommage amical à Claude Geffré*, ed. Jean-Pierre Jossua and Nicolas-Jean Sed (Paris: Cerf, 1992): 103–122; Edwin Diniz, "The Point of Departure of Fundamental Theology," *Teresianum* 45, no. 2 (1994): 439–455; Claude Geffré, O.P., "La leçon toujours actuelle d'Henri Bouillard," *Recherches de science religieuse* 97, no. 2 (2009): 211–222.

[138] These details and those which follow are taken from the closing pages of Jon Kirwan's fascinating and significant book: *An Avant-garde Theological Generation: The* Nouvelle Théologie *and*

is well known, theologians like the Jesuits Daniélou and Henri de Lubac and the Dominicans Marie-Dominique Chenu and Yves Congar emerged as a response to the dry and arid scholasticism of the "Thomists" who had dominated the pre-conciliar area. These "*ressourcement*" theologians were associated with what many considered to be a fresh Catholic project—a project that would return Catholic theology and Catholic life to the revered "sources" included in the patrimony of the Church (in particular, the Sacred Scriptures, the Fathers of the Church, and the holy liturgy) as well as engage in a more sympathetic manner the concerns and preoccupations of the twentieth century (ecumenism, contemporary philosophy, and so forth). Although there are many and varied figures associated with what some considered a "new theology" (*la nouvelle théologie*), they all held one fundamental conviction in common: Previous forms of neo-scholasticism and, especially, neo-Thomism propagated by Thomists had to be retired—for the good of theology, evangelization, and, indeed, the Church herself.[139] Unfortunately, Pius XII's 1950 encyclical *Humani Generis* explicitly condemned any "new theology."[140] Thus, controversy followed over what, exactly, the "new theology" was and who, exactly, the "*nouveaux théologiens*" were. Although in the years immediately following *Humani Generis* those suspected of theological novelty were reassigned from their academic teaching posts and/or silenced, their vindication seemed to come with the Second Vatican Council. Their critics (theologians like Marie-Michel Labourdette, O.P., Charles Boyer, S.J., Raymond Bruckberger, O.P., Marie-Joseph Nicolas, O.P., and especially Garrigou-Lagrange) were largely forgotten. And, to the delight of all, the formerly suspect, newer theologians Hans Urs von Balthasar, Congar, Jean Daniélou, Henri de Lubac, and (later) Joseph Ratzinger were all elevated to the cardinalate—and, in the latter's case, eventually to the papacy.

---

the *French Crisis of Modernity* (Oxford: Oxford University Press, 2018), 277. With meticulous scholarship, Kirwan presents the most important examination, to date, on this significant period in modern Catholic history.

[139] Of course, the appellation *la nouvelle théologie* carried polemical connotations. Although the infamous essay "La nouvelle théologie où va-t-elle?" (*Angelicum* 23 [1946]: 126–145 / in English translation: Réginald Garrigou-Lagrange, O.P., "Where is the New Theology Leading Us?" *Josephinum Journal of Theology* 18, no. 1 [2011]: 63–78) by Réginald Garrigou-Lagrange, O.P., is frequently associated with this title, the term was first used four years earlier in the Vatican newspaper *L'Osservatore Romano* by theologian Pietro Parente ("Nuove tendenze teologiche," *L'Osservatore Romano* [9–10 February 1942]: 1).

[140] See Joseph A. Komonchak, "Thomism and the Second Vatican Council," in *Continuity and Plurality in Catholic Theology: Essays in Honor of Gerald A. McCool, S.J.* (Fairfield, CT: Sacred Heart University Press, 1998), 53–73; Aidan Nichols, O.P., "Thomism and the *Nouvelle Théologie*," *The Thomist* 64 (2000): 1–19.

No one would describe the spirit of Vatican II as a specter of scholasticism (neo- or otherwise). The style, tone, and method of the Second Vatican Council and its theologians signaled a preferential option for the sources and for the theologians who championed the sources during the mid-twentieth century (largely French-Catholic) disputes. Again, this project promised the renewal of Catholic life, a rediscovery of authentic spirituality, a deeper appreciation for a personal union with Christ, through the rejection of artificial scholastic categories.

All is well, yes?

Not exactly. And this is what makes Fr. Bouyer's account of this dinner gathering at Cardinal Daniélou's home so interesting. (Of course, Bouyer was, himself, a theological *peritus* at Vatican II and a renowned expert on the liturgy).[141] Things, it seems, were not all well. The Second Vatican Council was now over. And yet, tranquility and order did not characterize the Catholic atmosphere. Although strategies of *ressourcement* renewal had been prominent during the Council, "the project of *ressourcement* was simply dismissed by many intellectuals after the Council by a hermeneutic that interpreted it as merely a first step in a larger liberalizing process that ultimately sought to reinterpret Catholic thought along modern more progressive lines."[142] It was an agitated time. Efforts that took the form of revision rather than renewal continued to spread (in the area of moral theology particularly). This is something that Joseph Ratzinger would later describe as "something unexpected."[143] *Ressourcement* hopes were now ceding to revisionist movements. Bouyer explains that Daniélou hosted this dinner as a way to provide "a calm environment in which to discuss the problems raised by the 'pastoral' policies of the French episcopate."[144]

---

[141] For Bouyer's own account of his life and work, see Louis Bouyer, *Memoirs* (San Francisco, CA: Ignatius Press, 2015).

[142] Kirwan, *Avant-garde Theological Generation*, 277. See also Joseph Komonchak, "Interpreting the Council: Catholic Attitudes toward Vatican II," in *Being Right: Conservative Catholics in America*, eds. Scott Applebee and Mary Jo Weaver (Bloomington, IN: Indiana University Press, 1995), 17–37. Kirwan helpfully invokes this text from Komonchak in his *Avant-garde Theological Generation*.

[143] Joseph Cardinal Ratzinger, "The Renewal of Moral Theology: Perspectives of Vatican II and *Veritatis Splendor*," *Communio: International Catholic Review* 32, no. 2 (2005): 357–368. For my analysis of this fascinating essay from Ratzinger, see "Thomas Aquinas on the Bible and Morality: The Sacred Scriptures, the Natural Law, and the Hermeneutic of Continuity," in *Towards a Biblical Thomism: Thomas Aquinas and the Renewal of Biblical Theology*, eds. Piotr Roszak and Jörgen Vijgen (Pamplona: Ediciones Universidad de Navarra, S.A., 2018), 173–196.

[144] Kirwan, *Avant-garde Theological Generation*, 277. Kirwan observes that the quotation-marked

Bouyer recounts with disbelief—while insisting that his quote is verbatim—that one of the cardinals [present at Daniélou's dinner] exclaimed: "It is true, we bishops did bet on the 'progressives' after the Council. It may well be that we were wrong! Well, in that case, then, we'll fall back on the '*intégristes*'!" These words had been addressed to an unnamed theologian who sounds suspiciously like de Lubac—Bouyer describes [him] as "the most impressive [theologian among those gathered], on account of his age and venerable personality." The theologian replied: "'But, Your Eminence, isn't the problem, rather, one of recovering the pure and authentic sources of Christianity so as to express it and in practice translate it in such a way that it makes sense to our contemporaries?' 'Oh!', the Cardinal replied quite simply, 'that's just the intellectuals talking!'"[145]

Whether or not the revered theologian was actually Henri de Lubac is not of ultimate importance here. What does elicit our interest is the obvious concession by conciliar fathers that the *ressourcement* motivations and emphases present at and around the Second Vatican Council were not coming to fruition as originally planned. Moreover, in a well-intentioned effort to bolster and sustain the *ressourcement* élan after the Council, the bishops had consciously placed their support behind the vision of implementation championed by progressive theologians during and after the Council. In some ways, this is consistent with the subtle, yet profound influence theologians exercised at the Council. Some of those present at the Council itself admit that Vatican II was a notably theologian-led council.[146] As members

---

word *pastoral* comes from the pen of Bouyer himself (ibid., 277n103).

[145] Kirwan, *Avant-garde Theological Generation*, 277. He is providing a translation of Bouyer's "L'Église catholique en crise," 24.

[146] Marie-Dominique Chenu offers the following candid reflections on the influence theologians exercised in Vatican II: "There is some gossip that claims that it was the theologians who led the Council, and this is not entirely false. I remember a very small but very revealing episode [during the Council]. During the discussion surrounding the Decree on the Laity [*Apostolicam Actuositatem*], I noticed a paragraph still permeated by the very dualistic notion of a 'mandate' given by the hierarchy to the laity: on one side the world, on the other the Church. Another French expert and I agreed that this was bad, but it had already been adopted by the commission and was therefore impossible to change. So we drafted an additional text that corrected it, a second paragraph that said pretty much the opposite [of this 'dualistic notion of a "mandate"']. The former admitted to a kind of dualism, and the second insisted that the action of the Church must surpass this. It was the French bishops who presented our new text, and it was adopted" (*Jacques Duquesne interroge le père Chenu: Un théologien en liberté* [Paris: Le Centurion, 1975], 17). This translation of Chenu's remark comes from Kirwan, *Avant-garde*

of the hierarchy began to second-guess the wisdom of their wager with the progressives, clearly some took consolation from the fact that the conservative *intégristes* were possible allies should things spiral too far out of control. This statement betrays a surprising optimism on the part of the bishop who thought a quick change in allegiance from progressive to conservative could correct any of the nascent confusions (particularly in light of the dramatic ecclesial and political events that took place in the decades immediately following the Council).[147]

Finally, and of greatest significance, was the mysterious theologian's insistence that any correctives to revisionist excess ought to be affected by "recovering the pure and authentic sources of Christianity." If this theologian was indeed de Lubac, we can understand his frustration. Praised during the Council, de Lubac himself began to be marginalized after the Council more and more with each passing year. De Lubac was greatly disturbed by what he understood to be a hijacking of *ressourcement* momentum. The momentum he and his allies fostered in their movement of renewal was now being expended in revisionist projects. De Lubac wanted a return of the momentum to the original source of the momentum: *ressourcement*. And it is here that, perhaps, de Lubac himself is slightly (though understandably) naive. This is something that the Cardinal puts his finger on with the directness that only a practical churchman can: "That's just the intellectuals talking!" One is led to wonder, then: If the *ressourcement* project, ultimately, was just a lot of "intellectual talk" after the Council, what made it more than "intellectual talk" before and during the Council? What, if anything, had changed?

De Lubac probably saw only faint signs of ecclesial stabilization during the remaining years of his life. Sadly, the vision that he and Daniélou shared did not come to fruition. And even though, at the time of the dinner party, Daniélou had already been elevated to the cardinalate and de Lubac would be elevated to the cardinalate in 1983, other theologians seemed to think that their original instinct had outgrown the figures who stood at its

---

Theological Generation, 265.

[147] Bouyer, again, gives us a snapshot of the spirit that dominated the 1970s particularly: "[As the] months and years passed, it turned out that in France in particular, the 'New Pentecost,' greeted with confidence by the good Pope John [XXIII], turned out to be a 'New Babel' in every ecclesiastical domain: after the seminaries, it was catechesis, *Action catholique*, and especially that which is most visible to the faithful rank-and-file, Sunday worship, which degenerated into novelty, anarchy, and even more, left-wing politicization, while mere carelessness was pompously called 'desacralization'" ("L'Église catholique en crise," 21, as translated by Kirwan, *Avant-garde Theological Generation*, 273).

historical point of origin.[148] It was only through the "hermeneutic of continuity" proposed by their junior colleague, Joseph Ratzinger, that something approximating a *ressourcement* solution to a *ressourcement* problem came to the fore.[149] Like de Lubac, Ratzinger wanted to remain faithful to the original project of ressourcement theology. This also appears to be the inspiration behind his "hermeneutic of continuity"—the affirmation that later ecclesial sources not just proceed from but perpetually depend on and presuppose the prior sources of the Christian faith. No legitimate Catholic theology, Ratzinger argued, can countenance essential change in Church teaching on matters of faith and morals. The hermeneutic of continuity is, fundamentally, a *ressourcement* tool whose continuity is founded upon an intrinsic harmony of the documents to proceed from the magisterium of the Church. This, it appears, is where he believes revisionist theologians went astray in their application of the *ressourcement* priorities: They started with sources but then abandoned the sources!

Although it has been criticized by the inheritors of progressivistic ideologies, Ratzinger's *ressourcement* solution to the crisis of Vatican II has largely dominated theological discourse since he first proposed it. During the pontificate of Saint John Paul II and, later, during Benedict's own pontificate, theologians felt compelled to follow, to varying degrees, this hermeneutic. The period that has followed Saint John Paul II and Benedict XVI, however, has seen a different movement. Theologians have begun to wonder if the hermeneutic of continuity has merely served as an artificial corrective that has impeded the full flowering of the Spirit's work at Vatican II.[150] In other words, the hermeneutic of continuity has been criticized as artificial, as frustrating the progress of the Church in much the same way that Thomas and the Thomists had been criticized.

One would imagine that, were he still alive today, Cardinal de Lubac would be no less surprised than he was in the post-Vatican II period by the

---

[148] It is worth noting that although de Lubac and Daniélou were ignored in the latter parts of their life, Chenu and Congar continued to receive a lot of attention and approbation for their work. Although these Jesuit and Dominican theologians had started on much the same page of the same project, their final days were spent producing pages of consciously opposed *ressourcement* application. Here, we recall the history and origins of the journals *Concilium* and *Communio*, and the role these Jesuit and Dominican theologians played in their deployment.

[149] Cf. Benedict XVI's first statement as pope on April 20, 2005 (available at http://www.vatican.va/holy_father/benedict_xvi/messages/pont-messages/2005/documents/hf_ben-xvi_mes_20050420_missa-pro-ecclesia_en.html).

[150] For an example, see John Dadosky, "Has Vatican II been *Hermeneutered*? Recovering and Developing its Theological Achievements following Rahner and Lonergan," *Irish Theological Quarterly* 79, no. 4 (2014): 327–349.

currents and discussions presently at the fore of theological discussion in the twenty-first century. We can also wonder if he would still maintain that *ressourcement* solutions (like the hermeneutic of continuity) are adequate correctives in today's Church to the problems that emerged through his *ressourcement* movement. The phenomenon of "intellectuals talking" has not saved Catholic theology from a rather penurious condition. One formally studies texts (i.e., sources and authors of texts) through a hermeneutic. One formally studies God according to the structures of a science—a science unified by revealed *deitas*. Even with the hermeneutic of continuity, theologians can identify what the International Theological Commission has called the "fragmentation of theology."[151] In our post-*ressourcement* period, the study of theology has largely fallen into a loose collection of isolated areas of specialization that often lack an explicit and formal integration into the unified and saving *sacra doctrina*.

In previous ages, theologians from different schools shared a common intellectual goal, culture, and language that enabled them to interact precisely as theologians from different schools. The speculative differences between members of the doctrinal schools associated with the Franciscans, the Dominicans, and the Jesuits, for example, did not inhibit their real engagement of one with another. A common theological language and culture facilitated profitable discussions among theologians who adhered to different accounts of the *sacra doctrina*. What is more, they shared a desire to arrive at a real resolution in sacred truth. They did not consider the omnipresence of refutational arguments in theological writings as a negative attribute. If one schoolman definitively refuted another in a doctrinal dispute, the theological culture regarded this as a great gain for the Church. The truth was now clearer than before. And the theologians of these earlier periods universally understood their vocations in relation to ecclesial service. Theirs was a vocation in pursuit of divine truth in union with the mind of the Church.

The schoolmen were, ultimately, churchmen. The ambience of this

---

[151] In the 2011 document *Theology Today: Perspectives, Principles, and Criteria*, the International Theological Commission observed: "The years following the Second Vatican Council have been extremely productive for Catholic theology. . . . However, this period has also seen a certain fragmentation of theology, and in the dialogue just mentioned theology always faces the challenge of maintaining its own true identity. The question arises, therefore, as to what characterises Catholic theology and gives it, in and through its many forms, a clear sense of identity in its engagement with the world of today" (§1). See also, from a Protestant perspective, Edward Farley, *Theologia: The Fragmentation and Unity of Theological Education* (Philadelphia, PA: Fortress Press, 1983).

commonly shared goal, culture, and language seems less pronounced in contemporary theology. The more contemporary a particular group of theologians is, the more frequently they appear to talk past each other. With the loss of a commonly shared and mutually understood language, a dialectical vacuum, of sorts, has taken its place. A common language had facilitated serious theological exchange for generations prior. The subsequent vacuum stands as a grave impediment to the continuation of the fruitful interschool debates that had marked previous generations. One cannot dispute, refute, or persuade a colleague if both parties lack a common language that has the durability to support serious dialectical engagement.

Beyond the question of a robust common language, something else—something even more alarming to a student searching for divine truth—also taints the theological writings of the modern period: Contemporary authors appear either to lack interest in actually resolving theological disputes or to despair that such resolutions are realistic. Here we might call attention to the inception of autonomous "styles" of theology. As the influence of theological schools declined, a proclivity for theological styles surfaced. A particular theologian's prior, subjective-personal identity (and even political convictions) now gives defining shape to theological discourse. In other words, theology now receives a new mission and identity—a mission and identity derived from the theologian himself or herself. As each theologian has a unique personality and history of experiences, so each style of theology has a unique configuration and set of priorities. *Theology now seems to be identified with the theologian.* Theology now receives its primary orientation from the theologian as source (or "re-sourcer") rather than from God as end. Within this structure, one can understand how interest in the actual resolution of theological disputes has waned. If God is the end, then theologians of even varying schools can dispute and discuss with a common goal before them. They are moving in the same direction. God is able to be the end, equally, of all theologians. The individual style of a particular theologian, however, is not so easily shared or jointly pursued. Unsurprisingly, then, there appears to be an eclipse of theological science by a seemingly new academic discipline: comparative "theologian-ology." Compare-and-contrast studies of various theologians—at times stunning in their degree of erudition—have displaced the properly theological objective that the schools once shared. Many theologians still find the objectivity of the Thomas and the Thomists excessively arid and elusive—out of touch with contemporary needs and priorities. Moreover, when Thomas and the Thomists do receive attention, it is according to the compare-and-contrast model or style of analysis. In other words, they are examined as anachronistically marked vestiges of intellectual history. They are like relics to be observed as one would museum pieces, witnesses to past debates. The resolution of legitimate controversies as the ultimate goal of theology is largely forgotten.

Finally, by résumé and extension: On the one hand, if theologians now exercise a certain sovereignty over their discipline, and on the other, if they study other theologians according to a compare-and-contrast method that does not necessarily pursue doctrinal resolution, then one could only expect that this compare-and-contrast model would morph into a method applicable not just to theologians but also to theological doctrines themselves. In other words, a lack of a common intellectual language and culture, combined with skepticism about the possibility of arriving at true theological resolution, results in the gradual isolation of theological figures. Theologians begin to be identified, more and more, as creators of their own particular, abstract, intellectual structures and priorities. Common efforts toward real consensus and truthful resolution become increasingly difficult. The contrastive diversity of theologians has inspired an individuated formality within theological inquiry itself. The doctrinal parts of a particular theologian's theology begin to reflect the radical individuality of the theologian himself or herself. This movement finds expression in the hyper-specialization most young theologians are encouraged to pursue. Specialization itself, of course, does not signify a negative thing. Each theologian naturally enjoys a greater facility with some doctrines than with others. We can observe, however, that doctrinal accounts—and not just theologians—are becoming so specialized that they, themselves, are becoming isolated. And this evidently reflects changes in the conception of theological science itself. Theologians of earlier periods understood that each doctrine served as part of a greater whole—the *sacra doctrina*. Contemporary theological texts can, at times, serve as chronicles of the gradual disintegration of theological science and its ever-growing fragmentation. And this fragmentation can, inadvertently, impede the sacred and ecclesial nature of the theologian's sacred vocation: "Theology has importance for the Church in every age so that it can respond to the plan of God 'who desires all men to be saved and to come to the knowledge of the truth' (1 Tim 2:4)."[152]

A lack of clarity about the nature of theology is alarming for many reasons. Something far more important (and troubling) than solely academic considerations is involved: Human salvation is frustrated by theological fragmentation. If theology is the study of the *sacra doctrina*, and if the *sacra*

---

[152] Cf. Congregation for the Doctrine of the Faith, *Donum Veritatis*, "On the Ecclesial Vocation of the Theologian," (May 24, 1990), §1.

doctrina is revealed by God for the salvation of humanity, then the fragmentation of theology results in the frustration of any attempt to bring Christ's "holy teaching" to a humanity in dire need of his mercy and grace—a mercy and grace that transforms the human person. *All of the human person.*

To be clear, we ought to attribute all responsibility to the *ressourcement* theologians of the twentieth century for the balkanizing infelicities that afflict the practice of Catholic theology in the twenty-first century. Nor ought we to discount immediately the efforts of some theologians to renew the life of the Church through the formulation of a new fundamental theology built upon textual sources and human experience. Many of these theologians were admirably earnest and exemplarily industrious in their sincere efforts to serve the Church during the cultural and political complexities of the previous century. No authentic theologian wants their sacred discipline to suffer. All Catholics desire the salvation of souls.

Nonetheless, a survey of theology in our post-*ressourcement* period reveals an alarming scene. Does *theology* even still exist (in practice)? It seems that the multiplication of disparate *theologies* is now the norm—and not just the norm, but the ideal.

Conclusion: On Divine Revelation and the Future of Catholic Theology

During the time of the Second Vatican Council, theologians were convinced that their sacred discipline required reformulation and renewal. Consequently, Garrigou-Lagrange and the objective approach to theology he exemplifies in *On Divine Revelation* fell out of favor in the academy.

In an effort to facilitate the renewal of Catholic theology, Catholic theologians began to rethink the practice of theology in the modern world. This engendered a new approach to theology—a new fundamental theology. This new approach to the foundations of theology, however, eluded its very proponents. In spite of the best efforts of theologians after Garrigou-Lagrange, it seems that the "whole territory of Catholic theology is highly fragmented and there is little agreement about methodological principles and issues that are classified as central to the subject of 'Fundamental Theology.'"[153] The new fundamental theology was expected to captain the renewal of Catholic theology. But Catholic theology now bears the stamp of the very uncertainty and confusion that marked the (still?) "new fundamental theology."

---

[153] Rowland, *Catholic Theology*, 2.

Ironically, perhaps, Réginald Garrigou-Lagrange's *On Divine Revelation* can serve the ongoing project of theological renewal in the life of the Church. Admittedly, Garrigou-Lagrange is an insufficient resource vis-à-vis the needs of the twenty-first century. He was a philosopher and a theologian of a former time characterized by its own peculiar complications. The questions and problems of our period do not, exactly, match the questions and problems of his. Nonetheless, the foundational principles that Garrigou-Lagrange magisterially expounds in *On Divine Revelation* have a timeless—even perennial—quality such that they can aid Catholic theologians in their ongoing quest for disciplinary renewal.

Garrigou-Lagrange's presentation of divine revelation in this book is built upon truth's renewal of the human person. The unifying theme found (at least implicitly) on every page of these two volumes is this: Real truth about the real God really transforms human persons. The human person is transformed by the renewal of the mind (Rom 12:2). And it is here that the scientific precision of *On Divine Revelation* emerges as not just intellectually stimulating but spiritually sanctifying. Even skeptics cannot remain completely unaffected when placed in contact with the Catholic proposition of divine truth.

God is real. He has really revealed his mysteries. He really imparts divine faith. He really established the Catholic Church. And there are real motives of credibility that human rationality—even without faith—cannot help but recognize as real motives.

With regard to the discipline of sacred theology, *On Divine Revelation* manifests with remarkable precision the division and method of this sacred discipline. Theology is a specific science. It has a precise and supernatural formal *objectivity*. Nonetheless, theology's scientific nature is such that each of its integral (and power) parts has a proper identity, dignity, value, and use—all within a sublime unity. Although Garrigou-Lagrange carefully parses the various distinctions that reside within sacred theology, these distinctions illumine its fundamental objective unity. *On Divine Revelation* masterfully shows how sacred theology is eminently one—and how it retains its eminent unity even in its various offices and discrete extensions. Moreover, Garrigou-Lagrange illustrates how supernatural principles and objects sapientially govern the theologian's use of reason, sources, and even historical analysis.

To conclude: *On Divine Revelation*—as its title states—expounds the nature of divine revelation. It elucidates how revelation is the formal motive of infused faith. And, in the process, its author provides its readers with a pellucid presentation of the unified nature of sacred theology through its exposition of the dynamics of reason and faith in fundamental theology and apologetics. Garrigou-Lagrange demonstrates why all authentic theologians require faith. Additionally, he explains why no theologian can theologize without reason. *On Divine Revelation*—in its whole and in its integral parts—is a stunning work of inestimable value. No other subsequent work on this topic has come close to meeting it (much less surpassing it).

For, as careful readers will discover in the pages that follow, *On Divine Revelation* explains, with the utmost clarity, how reason and faith, principles and objects can serve the salvific union of man to God. And this salvific union, all can agree, is what authentic Catholic renewal is all about.

Translator's Introduction

The substance of the *Tractatus de revelatione*, with its importance for the substance of theological reflection, has been excellently treated by Fr. Cuddy in his foreword. I turn the reader's attention to his remarks. In this brief translator's introduction, I merely wish to register a few words as I draw to a close my time working as a translator of Fr. Garrigou-Lagrange's works. In particular, I wish to reflect on the question, "Why read his *De revelatione* today?"

Clarity is important, and one fact is very clear: When it comes to the seemingly pugilistic term "apologetics," great care is needed. From the earliest days of the Gospel message, Christians have felt the need to make a humble defense of the belief and hope that we have through the message of Christ's Paschal Mystery (cf. 1 Pet 3:15–16). Turning to those who do not yet believe—or, as the case may be, turning to that part of our own soul that still retains some questioning alongside the unshaken certitude of faith—Christians have taken up a whole host of genres while responding to pagans and barbarians, whether ancient or modern.[1] The Christian faith is a supernatural gift, but it also is the most rational of messages, at once fulfilling the loftiest aspirations of human reason, culture, art, and morality, and yet doing so in a way that is infinitely beyond the hopes of "mere human nature." Christians have always felt ready to defend the mysteries of faith against those who would deny them as irrational. In response, we must always be ready to say: These supernatural mysteries are eminently rational, true, beautiful, good, and beyond your wildest hopes!

However, all too often, the task of apologetics can sink down into a sort of constant occupation with *particular defenses*: a defense of the Trinity against those who believe it to be an irrational dogma; a defense of the historical claims of the Church in union with Rome; a defense of the perpetual virginity of Mary; and so forth. And all of these topics—along with many

---

[1] For a detailed but accessible history, see Cardinal Avery Dulles, *A History of Apologetics* (San Francisco, CA: Ignatius Press, 2005).

others—are pivotally important! Yet, behind these *particular "apologies,"* these particular *defenses*, which should in fact be peppered throughout the various particular treatises of theology, there is a great question: What about the very possibility of *supernatural* revelation that is made to *natural* reason? The discussion of this general issue is of great fruit for the theologian and for the philosopher.

Theology is a science, yes. But it is more than a mere science, drawing conclusion after conclusion in light of first principles. It is eminently science, precisely because it is a form of wisdom.[2] According to the broadly Aristotelian epistemological schema, a given intellectual perfection is a form of "wisdom" when, beyond the sure drawing of conclusions *per se* connected to principles, one is also enabled to judge the very principles of a discourse and to set other disciplines in order in relation to the concerns of this "sapiential" discussion. Therefore, acquired, discursive theological wisdom must enable its practitioner to reflect on its principles, show the profound meaning of the revealed truths, and defend the faith against those who would deny its possibility. In other words, in addition to the ostensive tasks of such theology, it must also become both reflective and *critical*.

Because faith is a freely given supernatural light that elevates the human intellect and will so that we might assent to truths beyond the scope of natural reason, we must consider the nature of the "receptive subject" of faith—namely, the heights of the human intellect in the spiritual peak of the soul, as well as the judgments of which it is capable.[3] What can *natural* human reason affirm concerning the *supernatural* truths of faith? In what way can we say that such *natural* human reason is open to the gift of *supernatural* faith? How is this possible? These questions, and others in the same vein, are the ones at the root of the *Tractatus de revelatione*. Because it deals with such preliminary questions concerning the very possibility of faith, it came to be placed at the head of theology. This state of affairs is quite understandable, in particular, in the climate of a post-Enlightenment world, in which the supernaturality of faith is denied. Before taking up those tasks of theology that unpack the meaning and implications of the revealed truths, one must engage in the theological defense of faith in the face of the objections raised by those who would misrepresent the relationship between reason and faith.

---

[2] Regarding this point, reflected on along lines drawn from Fr. Garrigou-Lagrange, see Matthew K. Minerd, "Wisdom Be Attentive: On the Noetic Structure of Sapiential Knowledge," *Nova et Vetera* (English ed.) 18, no. 4 (2020): 1103–1146.

[3] For related reflections on this topic, see Ambroise Gardeil, *La structure de l'âme et l'expérience mystique,* 3rd ed., vol. 2 (Paris: Gabalda, 1927), 1–352.

This also provides the theologian with a ready understanding of the essential supernaturality of the faith that he presupposes.[4] Because external critique is often most profitably engaged in *after* undertaking direct and ostensive practice of one's own discipline, the theologian can also profitably revisit these topics after the course of full study of theological subjects. Such is the helicoidal discursion of theological contemplation, forever aware of its unity as the reflection, in faith, on the mysteries revealed about God and his providential economy.

However, given that the *Tractatus de revelatione* is concerned with faith-directed reasoning concerning reason's own grandeur and limitations, the philosopher will find much of interest herein as well. In apologetics, the furthest reaches of reason's quest for the truth are laid out before reason itself, though by a higher light, the light of theology, conducting its sapiential inquiries in the light of faith. There are many places within the treatises of theology in which reason feels the higher light of faith illuminating its concepts, carrying them aloft by the superanalogy of faith:[5] the notion of *personality* applied to the mysteries of the Trinity and the Redemptive Incar-

---

4   The traditional Thomistic approach to theological explanation places the detailed discussion of the theological virtue of faith in the context of *ST* II-II, which came to be known as *Theologia moralis specialis*. There, the object, nature, and properties of faith are discussed at much greater length, in connection with the other mysteries as well. Fr. Garrigou-Lagrange himself takes up this discussion in his commentary on the *Tractatus de fide* in Garrigou-Lagrange, *The Theological Virtues*, vol. 1, *On Faith*, trans. Thomas à Kempis Reilly (St. Louis, MO: Herder, 1965). Note, however, that this translation contains certain idiosyncratic characteristics, as the translator has restructured certain sections, though on the whole without substantially changing the meaning of the text. In harmony with Fr. Garrigou-Lagrange, see Michel Labourdette, *Grand cours de théologie morale*, vol. 8, *La foi* (Paris: Parole et Silence Editions, 2015); also see Iacobus M. Ramirez, *Opera omnia*, vol. 10, *De fide divina: In II-II Summae theologiae divi Thomae expositio q. 1–7* (Madrid: Instituto de Filosofia Luis Vives, 1970).

5   On the superanalogy of faith (a topic deserving of several dissertations and books), see J.-H. Nicolas, *Dieu connu comme inconnu: Essai d'une critique de la connaissance théologique* (Paris: Desclée de Brouwer, 1966), 237–316; Jacques Maritain, *Degrees of Knowledge*, trans. Gerald B. Phelan et al. (Notre Dame, IN: University of Notre Dame Press, 1995), 256–59; Charles Journet, *The Dark Knowledge of God*, trans. James F. Anderson (London: Sheed and Ward, 1948), 61–64 and 69n20; idem., *The Wisdom of Faith*, trans. R. F. Smith (Westminster, MD: Newman Press, 1952), 14–32. The examples used here are drawn from page 16, where Journet cites a perceptive remark in Gardeil's *Le donné révélé et la théologie*, 2nd ed. (Paris: Cerf, 1932). Also, for an older treatment, see Édouard Hugon, "Quels concepts avons-nous des vérités surnaturelles?" *Revue Thomiste*, New Series, 6 (1906): 413–429; "Foi et Révélation" and "Les Concepts Dogmatiques" in *Réponses théologiques à quelques questions d'actualité* (Paris: Téqui, 1908), 91–182; and in sum *Cursus philosophiae Thomisticae*, vol. 3, *Metaphysica*, 136–137 ("De cognitione rerum supernaturalium, seu de natura specierum ad illam requisitarum" and "De verbo, seu conceptu, requisito ad cognitionem supernaturalem").

nation; the notion of *relation* in the discussion of the Trinity; the notion of *practical signification* in the treatise on the sacraments; the notion of *society* in the discussion of the Church as a supernatural sacrament-society, the Mystical Body of Christ; the notion of *experiential knowledge* in mystical theology; and so forth for many notions. The light of faith illuminates, from within, the analogical "instruments" that it takes up for the sake of expressing revealed truths, and theology often draws further connections between such conceptual instruments and their broader philosophical domains.[6] For this reason, a Christian who philosophizes cannot help but realize that he knows of many things that he must strive to connect to purely philosophical argumentation. To put it briefly, "Christian philosophy is intrinsically Christian, on account of the objective assistance that it receives from theologically explicated revelation."[7]

All such uses of reason by faith and theological discursion illuminate reason from within, also elevating its notions.[8] Such illumination is much more "down-to-earth" in the *Tractatus de revelatione* as the theologian deploys reason so as to show reason the latter's own lofty heights, considering the supernatural action of God through his miracles, shining forth in

---

[6] Important distinctions must be made concerning how philosophical reasoning is and is not used in statements of faith and theology. For Fr. Garrigou-Lagrange's position concerning this question, see *Thomistic Common Sense: The Philosophy of Being and the Development of Doctrine*, trans. Matthew K. Minerd (Steubenville, OH: Emmaus Academic, 2021). For recent, well-informed critical reflections on this topic, see Guy Mansini, O.S.B., "The Historicity of Dogma and Common Sense: Ambroise Gardeil, Réginald Garrigou-Lagrange, Yves Congar, and the Modern Magisterium," *Nova et Vetera* (English ed.) 18, no. 1 (2020): 111–38. For indications concerning a way to retain the main lines of Fr. Garrigou-Lagrange's own position, see my remarks in *Thomistic Common Sense*, 8n17.

[7] This position, which may seem striking to some readers, is that of Fr. Garrigou-Lagrange, who ultimately finds himself profoundly in agreement (explicitly) with Jacques Maritain concerning the notion of "Christian philosophy" as well as (implicitly) with the main lines of the position held by Étienne Gilson, who on many points stands outside of the *schola Thomae*, strictly so called. See Réginald Garrigou-Lagrange, "On the Relationship between Philosophy and Religion," *Philosophizing in Faith: Essays on the Beginning and End of Wisdom*, ed. and trans. Matthew K. Minerd (Providence, RI: Cluny Media, 2019), 361–398. For the general outlines of the Francophone debates over Christian philosophy, see *Reason Fulfilled by Revelation: The 1930s Christian Philosophy Debates in France*, ed. and trans. Gregory B. Sadler (Washington, DC: The Catholic University of America Press, 2011), 1–98.

[8] In such cases, one senses the way that the notions used for enunciating supernatural truths are elevated, in the course of their use in the judgments of faith and theology, in line with their own objective obediential potency. Thus, the notion of *practical signification* is not opposed to being used as it is in sacramental theology, and *relatio secundum esse* is not opposed to being substantial, as is the case in the Trinitarian relations. For the appropriate precisions on this topic, see note 5 above.

the miraculous life of the Church, and the amazing way that the revealed message, proposed by the Church, universally fulfills the aspirations of the human spirit, while in fact presenting a religious, moral, cultural, and intellectual vocation that far exceeds every other religion. By showing the rational credibility of the supernatural mysteries of faith, the theologian allows reason itself to see its own glory, expressed in the reasonable obedience of faith.

We live in an era that risks crowding out these notions of faith and reason, and all philosophers and theologians of "good faith" should join together where there is agreement—no matter the differences of methodology. Fr. Garrigou-Lagrange's concerns are highly philosophical and are marked by the relevant concerns that arose in the wake of the modernist controversy at the turn of the twentieth century. He writes here on the borders of faith and reason, above all taking care to allow faith to illuminate reason so that the latter may know its own ability to acknowledge the eminent reasonability of faith, which itself nonetheless infinitely outstrips reason's grasp. By his own admission, these lengthy pages are nothing but a kind of reflection and commentary on one single syllogistic inference: "Whatever God reveals is rationally credible; now, God revealed the Christian doctrine, as is clear from the signs by which it is confirmed; therefore, this doctrine is rationally credible." The conclusion is not supernatural, but it stands at the door of reason's obediential potency for the supernatural order. It represents the loftiest of judgments that we can form by reason alone, one that calls for one further attitude: prayer, the opening of the hand in order to await from God what he alone can give—namely, the gift of faith.

A few translation-specific remarks are in order as well.

I cannot help but register one brief word regarding the fact that I am an Eastern (Ruthenian) Catholic, a fact that on occasion has affected my translation work on Fr. Garrigou-Lagrange. In *Thomistic Common Sense*, I added a somewhat lengthy footnote regarding an unmeasured remark he made concerning the *filioque*. Here, in *De revelatione*, his occasional *identification* of Catholicism with *Roman* Catholicism stood out as a particular vexation. In several places, I have noted the fact that such words are *his*, especially when on occasion he refers to the Church as *the Roman Catholic Church*. Such vocabulary is an inexact way of expressing the interrelationship between sister Churches within the one Catholic Church.[9] But it would be

---

9 To this end, the precisions offered by Cardinal Ratzinger in 2000 animate my own sensitivities as an Eastern Catholic, aware of the need to be careful with this language while nonetheless recognizing its ancient use in understanding the nature of the One Church.

all too unfortunate if such historically dated Latin-Catholic language were to obscure the profound truths communicated by this great theologian of the previous century. Similarly, I note the unfortunate Roman chauvinism in Fr. Garrigou-Lagrange's language concerning the Orthodox Churches (which he refers to quite inexactly as "Photian") and their saints (whose sanctity he seems to doubt). In any case, of all the traditional *scholae* in Latin Scholasticism, the Thomist school is the jealous guardian of the essential supernaturality of faith. The communication of the uncreated life of God through grace buds forth in the apprehension of supernatural mysteries, which are so lofty that this gift intrinsically calls for the loftiest of apophatic mysticism, purifying faith's apprehension through the activity of the gifts of the Holy Spirit.[10] I remain of the opinion that much of Thomist mystical theology is susceptible to rich dialogue with the mystical theology of the various Eastern Churches,[11] and this is also true in other treatises as well.[12]

The two volumes of *De revelatione* are massive works, incorporating

---

Congregation for the Doctrine of the Faith, "Note on the Expression 'Sister Churches'" June 30, 2000, http://www.vatican.va/roman_curia/congregations/cfaith/documents/rc_con_cfaith_doc_20000630_chiese-sorelle_en.html.

[10] For a masterful treatment of these themes, see John of St. Thomas, *The Gifts of the Holy Spirit*, ed. Cajetan Cuddy, trans. Dominic Hughes (Providence, RI: Cluny Media, 2016), especially chs. 3 ("The Gift of Understanding") and 4 ("The Gifts of Wisdom and Knowledge"), 103–204.

[11] I outline themes of contact on this point in Matthew Minerd, "The Ontology of the Divine Indwelling: A Hard-Headed Thomist Meets with Palamas," to be published in 2022–2023 in the annual *American Maritain Association* volume by The Catholic University of America Press. In relation to Palamism as well, see the appreciative article by Charles Journet, "Palamisme et Thomisme, À propos d'un livre récent," *Revue Thomiste* 60 (1960): 429–52. More broadly, as regards points of connection with Patristic themes of divinization, see the work of Fr. Juan Arintero, who was of great influence on Fr. Garrigou-Lagrange. See Juan G. Arintero, *The Mystical Evolution in the Development and Vitality of the Church*, trans. Jordan Aumann (St. Louis, MO: B. Herder, 1949 / 1951); *Cuestiones místicas, o sea las alturas de la contemplacion accesibles a todos*, 2nd ed. (Salamanca: Calatrava, 1920). For Fr. Garrigou-Lagrange's works on spiritual theology see *The Three Ages of the Interior Life: Prelude to Eternal Life*, trans. Sister M. Timothea Doyle (St. Louis, MO: B. Herder, 1947 / 1948); *Love of God and the Cross of Jesus*, trans. Jeanne Marie, vols. 1 and 2 (St. Louis, MO: B. Herder, 1948 / 1951). For a profound and brief discussion of divinization and the Christian life from a Thomist perspective, see Ambroise Gardeil, "The Fundamental Idea of the Christian Life," in *The True Christian Life: Thomistic Reflections on Divinization, Prudence, Religion, Prayer*, trans. Matthew K. Minerd (Washington, DC: The Catholic University of America Press, 2021).

[12] Here, I echo the sentiments deeply held by the Orthodox theologian Marcus Plested, as expressed in "Reconfiguring East and West in Byzantine and Modern Orthodox Theology" in *Never the Twain Shall Meet? Latins and Greeks Learning from Each Other in Byzantium*, ed. Denis Searby (Berlin: De Gruyter, 2017), 21–45.

texts from Scripture, the Fathers, the Councils, the magisterium, and a whole variety of Scholastic theologians. For this reason, a number of decisions needed to be made concerning when to align various translational choices and when not to. (One good example of this is my use of "religious sentiment" for "religiosus sensus," a translation choice I made so as to remain in line with the Vatican translation of *Pascendi dominici gregis*.) Moreover, given my familiarity with Fr. Garrigou-Lagrange's French style, it was clear to my eye that he is primarily thinking in French while writing in Latin. This fact is reflected in his word order and, at times, his very choice of phrases. Thus, his language weaves in and out of dry scholastic Latinity to certain warmer phrases marked by his own pedagogical broad-mindedness. I have attempted to sail between the scholastic Scylla and a more colloquial Charybdis in order to make this book sufficiently technical while also, at times, expanding the text for the sake of readability. (On the whole, the importance of notional clarity has led me to retain no small amount of scholastic rigidity, but one will particularly sense my expansions in the objection-response sections, where I felt the need to significantly extend Fr. Garrigou-Lagrange's scholastic shorthand.)

In general, all lengthy citations from Scripture in this volume are taken from the Douay-Rheims, Challoner edition of the Bible. This is not my preferred translation, given its often-clunky, literalistic Latinate literalness. However, since Fr. Garrigou-Lagrange uses the Vulgate in his own citations, I thought it best to retain an official scriptural translation that reflects the Roman Church's ancient received scriptural text.

All citations from Denzinger are amended to follow the numeration and translations from Ignatius Press's 43rd edition of the text. In almost all cases, I follow the translations in that edition, even where the translational style might differ from my own.

Throughout my translation, I have included some pedagogical footnotes. In these, I have tried to provide the reader with remarks concerning points that may well be opaque, often citing the works of Thomists in the same tradition as that of Fr. Garrigou-Lagrange. However, given the scope and size of this project, I have been less detailed with such notes in comparison with my other translations of Fr. Garrigou-Lagrange's works. I refer my reader to these other volumes, also from Emmaus Academic,[13] as well as

---

[13] See Réginald Garrigou-Lagrange, *The Sense of Mystery: Clarity and Obscurity in the Intellectual Life*, trans. Matthew K. Minerd (Steubenville, OH: Emmaus Academic, 2017); *The Order of Things: The Realism of the Principle of Finality*, trans. Matthew K. Minerd (Steubenville, OH: Emmaus Academic, 2020); *Thomistic Common Sense: The Philosophy of Being and the Development of Doctrine*, trans. Matthew K. Minerd (Steubenville, OH: Emmaus Academic, 2021).

to the volume *Philosophizing in Faith*, which gathers together many important philosophical essays by Fr. Garrigou-Lagrange concerning a number of topics discussed herein.[14]

Throughout the text, bibliographical references required expansion, as Fr. Garrigou-Lagrange often did not provide complete reference information in his citations. Unless otherwise noted, when possible, I have chosen to cite the relevant pages of the English translations of Fr. Garrigou-Lagrange's works, as this will be more useful for English readers than would be French citations.

No book comes to press without the involvement of many hands. I owe a debt of the greatest gratitude to Chris Erickson for shepherding this project throughout its process of publication. All you who read this book and draw wisdom from it owe Chris an immense debt for his long-suffering—through all the numerous tasks involved in bringing my various volumes of Fr. Garrigou-Lagrange to publication with Emmaus Academic, and through years of dealing with my own idiosyncrasies—doing so with the greatest of grace. *Mnohaya lita!* May God grant him many blessed years!

Similar gratitude is owed to Dr. Scott Hahn, who has given such support to this project as one of the many good works he has done on behalf of the Church whom he loves. So many of us owe a great debt to him for his long witness and teaching. Here, I wish to express my *sincerest* and humble thanks to be able to bring the great twentieth-century theologian to the readers of the twenty-first century. I write this not merely as a translator but as a Catholic who wishes Fr. Garrigou-Lagrange had been widely available and acceptable during the post-conciliar period. But, at the very least, let us thank Dr. Hahn for this great gift to the English-speaking Church today.

Likewise, I owe a great debt of thanks to the two men who expended much labor reviewing my translation: Dr. Luke Deweese and Rev. Dr. Christiaan Kappes. In his great providential humor, God sent me two men with Scotist orientations to be my translation reviewers. They were an immense help respectively reviewing volumes 1 and 2 of the work. The weaknesses of the translation are my own; its strengths owe a great deal to their devoted work looking over these sizeable tomes. Both are graced with insightful knowledge of scholasticism and of Latinity. I pray that they may both have many years of joyful service to the Truth.

Many kind remarks and words of encouragement have been given to me during this extensive project. To those persons (here unnamed for fear

---

[14] See Réginald Garrigou-Lagrange, *Philosophizing in Faith: Essays on the Beginning and End of Wisdom*, ed. and trans. Matthew K. Minerd (Providence, RI: Cluny Media, 2019).

of forgetting someone) who provided such kind emotional and intellectual support: thank you.

Finally, but most certainly not least of all, I should like to thank Emily Demary, Patty Borgman, and Caroline Rock for their excellent design and proofing work with this volume. The layout of a text of this length and complexity requires a great deal of skill, which has been brought to bear on this project. All of us who will refer to these volumes thank you for making it easy on the eyes! Lastly, may God's face shine eternally on the patient, talented, and diligent Rachael Clements, who copyedited both volumes, working with ready joy and patience as we made our way toward the final layout version of this very lengthy text.

As an act of intellectual-filial piety, I dedicate these two extensive volumes to the man who has become a beloved teacher to me these past five years: Fr. Garrigou-Lagrange. May he rest in peace, and if perhaps he is indeed in heaven, may he be canonized a saint, to be a public and illustrious example of the theological task of faith seeking understanding.

With the greatest of pleasure, and as a sign of gratitude and of filial obedience, the author dedicates this book to the Blessed Virgin Mary, the Mother of God, the Queen of teachers and of those who have full knowledge, she who sweetly and profoundly instructs little ones in the revealed mysteries.

Original Preface by Pope Benedict XV

To Our Beloved Son
Réginald Garrigou-Lagrange,
Decurial Doctor in the *Collegium Anglicum Urbis*
For the Handing on of Sacred Theology
Pope Benedict XV

{{vii}} *Beloved son,*
Greetings and apostolic benediction,

In your recently published book, *De revelatione*, whose exemplar you piously gave to Us as a gift, it is wondrously manifest that Aquinas is a strong support not only for the illumination of Christian wisdom but also in its defense. In it, explaining what pertains to fundamental theology (which is, as is commonly said, a part of theology), you so make use of the discipline and reasoning of St. Thomas that you admirably overcome not only the ancient adversaries of the Christian faith but also more recent ones. Indeed, since the errors of our own days ultimately flow from principles which are utterly opposed to the philosophy received by the Church, as well as by her Fathers and Doctors, you rightly set this philosophy in opposition to them, calling forth the leader of the School himself, the Angelic Doctor, refuting them with invincible strength. Moreover, you take up many other topics as well, drawing from the various sources of theology in your discussions and disposing all things fittingly and ingeniously in order to establish a full and valid defense of the truth, which has been divinely handed on to us. Thus, you have constructed a work which is held in no small esteem by experts in these matters, and We desire that it may be of use especially for young men studying for the priesthood so that they may be able to preserve and defend those things which are above nature, a task of importance today. We affectionately bestow the apostolic blessing upon you, beloved son, the pledge of heavenly gifts, and a witness of our special benevolence for you.

Given at Rome, at St. Peter's, the 15th day of February, 1919, in the fifth year of Our Pontificate.

Author's Preface

{{ix}} 1. This treatise *On Revelation, Proposed by the Catholic Church*, contains the whole of apologetics—namely, the defense of the divine origin of Christianity and of the divine institution of the Catholic Church for preserving and infallibly proposing revelation. These two forms of defense were considered together by the third session of the [First] Vatican Council.[1] Thus, the apologetic part of the treatise on the Church is connected with the treatise on revelation (or on the true religion). However, this is not the place for considering the intimate constitution of the Church, nor theological sources [*locis theologicis*], both of which must be treated later on in a properly theological manner—namely, by arguing from revelation itself, already infallibly proposed by the Catholic Church.[2] (Nay, the treatise on the intimate constitution of the Church logically ought to be treated only after the treatise on the Incarnate Word and Redeemer, following the rightful order of the Apostolic Creed, although, for the sake of convenience and in order to avoid repetitions, the exposition of this Constitution [*sic*] may be placed after the apologetic proof of the Church's divine authority.)

2. In this book, apologetics is not considered as being a science specifically distinct from sacred theology but, rather, is held to be one of its particular offices, one that is rational and defensive, for apologetics does indeed argue *from reason*, though *under the direction of faith*, as we will explain more fully in the Prologue below. Hence, this work is conceived as being a work on *fundamental theology*—that is, theology concerned with the foundations of faith (or, to put it another way, as a critical reflection

---

[1] See [First] Vatican Council, sess. 3, *Constitutio de fide catholica* [*Dei filius*], ch. 2 *De revelatione*, ch. 3 *De fide*, and ch. 4 *De fide et ratione*. See Denzinger, nos. 3004–3020. [Trans. note: I have extended the citation from Denzinger, as Fr. Garrigou-Lagrange only cites up to no. 3014, the end of the third chapter.]

[2] Thus, the [First] Vatican Council, after the aforementioned Constitution on the Catholic Faith, set forth, in session 4, the particular *Constitutionem de ecclesia Christi* [*Pastor aeternus*], ch. 1 *De Apostolici primatus . . . institutione*, ch. 2 *De primatus perpetuitate*, ch. 3 *De primate Romani Pontificis*, ch. 4 *De Romani Pontificis infallibili magisterio*. See Denzinger, nos. 3050–3075.

on the value of the supernatural knowledge of faith). However, in order for fundamental theology to be complete, it must include not only the whole of apologetics but also the treatise on theological sources [*de Locis seu fontibus theologicis*], especially on Sacred Scripture, Divine Tradition, and the magisterium of the Church.[3] Hence, we have given the following title to this work: {{x}} *Fundamental Theology: Apologetic Part*. We added "according to St. Thomas's doctrine," because the texts of St. Thomas pertaining to the matter at hand are carefully chosen and explained for each question at hand. In this way, one will come to have a true introduction to a study of Aquinas's *Summa theologiae*.

3. In this, our critique of the value of the supernatural knowledge of faith, especially in the speculative part of our work, will develop its arguments in opposition to philosophical rationalism. This is so because lengthier arguments against biblical rationalism by rights fall to an introduction to Sacred Scripture and exegesis. Therefore, to accomplish our own end here, we will treat at length of the notions of revelation, mysteries, dogmas, the supernaturality of faith, and the notion of credibility by comparing Catholic notions of all these various matters with heterodox notions of them. Some readers will perhaps think that our treatment is longer than is necessary for beginners. Nevertheless, in the course of teaching this subject for eight years, we have noted that nearly all students, especially the most talented of them, need all these explanations for the resolution of naturalistic thinkers' objections, which today especially are concerned with the very foundations of faith and are cited by all. In addition, we wanted to pay heed to what would be useful for students (and even for professors) by making clear how the foundations that we treat herein are connected with the various problems of theology.

4. Among the questions occurring in the treatise *On Revelation*, one is of the greatest importance: How is revelation to be recognized as the formal motive of infused faith? This problem is the same as the question concerning the ultimate resolution of the supernatural certitude of faith, which is commonly set forth in the treatise on faith. However, many other contemporary authors settle these matters immediately after their lectures on revelation, the Church, and theological sources, doing so before their lectures on the

---

[3]   However, when, in our Prologue, we say at times, "fundamental theology or [*vel*] apologetics," such an expression is not used so as to restrict the scope of fundamental theology but instead is used so as to speak more briefly about those things being considered concerning its apologetic part. Nevertheless, in reality, as we will say, beyond the apologetic demonstration of the divine origin of Christianity and of the divine institution of the Church, fundamental theology is also concerned with theological sources. The reader needs to keep this in mind so as to avoid confusions, as we will indicate again in the first two headings of the topical index.

One and Triune God. By contrast, and according to the tradition of the scholastics, the true location of the treatise on faith was placed by St. Thomas at the beginning of the *Secunda secundae* in the *Summa theologiae* after the questions on grace and before the articles on hope, charity, and the other virtues. Now, here in the treatise *On Revelation*, treating of its knowability, as well as of the credibility of the mysteries of faith, we will inquire into how revelation may be known, not only from an external perspective, inasmuch as it is confirmed in an utterly certain manner by naturally knowable miracles, but moreover from the intimate and most lofty perspective—namely, inasmuch as it is the formal motive of infused faith. Thus, we will explain, as ought to be done in fundamental theology, the first words of the Apostolic Creed: *I believe.*

However, in order to resolve this important question, we will at length set forth the opinions of various theologians, especially those of St. Thomas and his disciples, concerning the grace needed for the beginning of faith, as well as for adhering to its formal motive. According to these illustrious authors, supernatural faith is not discursive and is not formally and intrinsically founded on natural certitude regarding the fact of revelation known on the basis of miracles but instead is founded on supernatural revelation itself, which, under the infused light of faith, is simultaneously that *by which* what is believed is believed and *that which* is believed (or that which is entrusted to the mysteries [*concreditur mysteriis*]). {{xi}} Indeed, the apologetic demonstration [*concerning the rational credibility of revelation*] has the character of being only a support (or a disposition of an inferior order) for the supernatural act of faith.

Some theologians will perhaps be surprised at our insistence upon the importance of this chapter of doctrine.[4] Nevertheless, we believe it is absolutely necessary that there be a defense of the essential supernaturality of infused faith, which requires a formal motive exceeding that of natural faith such as is found, for example, in the demons—a motive, I say, which *a fortiori* exceeds that of the opinion that a formal heretic can preserve concerning the truth of the mystery of the Incarnation. Indeed, St. Thomas says, "The species of any given *habitus* depends on the formal character of its object, without which the species of the *habitus* cannot remain. Now,

---

4   Fr. Ambroise Gardeil, O.P., our master, who taught us many things concerning this topic, indeed with great profundity, thus notes in his book *La crédibilité et l'apologétique*, 2nd ed. (Paris: Gabalda, 1902), xvii: "We are accustomed to confining ourselves within the material and narrow theories of positive faith, forgetful of the great and vast outlooks articulated by the Council of Orange, St. Augustine, and by St. Thomas himself concerning the *intitium fidei*."

the formal object (or motive) of faith is the First Truth as manifested in the Sacred Scriptures and the Church's doctrine, which proceeds from the First Truth. . . . And therefore, whoever fails in achieving this mean is totally lacking in faith."[5]

This chapter concerning the mode of our knowledge of revelation, as it is the formal motive of infused faith, will perhaps be more difficult for students beginning a course of studies in sacred theology. However, for their greater benefit, we will summarize it more clearly in a concluding section so that they will not need to read through those things that are set forth in smaller typeset concerning this matter. Later on, in the course of their theological studies, they will perceive the importance of this conclusion.

5. Generally speaking, fundamental theology is difficult enough if it is treated deeply and integrally. Indeed, we find ourselves here concerned with the remote and proximate foundations of the supernatural certitude of faith. And therefore, it is not surprising if all these matters are thoroughly understood only after a complete study of sacred theology, even though they are necessary for an initial understanding of this subject, at least in an elementary manner. Thus, according to Aristotle and St. Thomas, "Metaphysics (whose critical portion is concerned with the value of intellectual knowledge) must be taught last among all the parts of philosophy,"[6] even though, at the start, it is necessary that we have a natural and vague [*confusa*] knowledge of those things that are considered in general metaphysics.

Hence, the study of fundamental theology can be profitably taken up again at the end of a course in sacred theology, and in this way, one can thereby undertake a critical reflection after having direct knowledge of theology. In fact, we gave these lectures *De revelatione*, in accord with the scholastic program of studies, through several years in two forms—namely, in an elementary fashion for beginning students, though in a more rigorous and detailed form in a course for students in the more advanced studies [*in cursu superiori*]. Therefore, note well that we have written out in smaller type those things that are not necessary for beginners, though they nevertheless are of use for more diligent readers.

We have divided the whole treatise into two books, the first of which is {{xii}} concerned with the possibility, befittingness, and knowability of revelation, whereas the other part is concerned with the existence of revelation, historically considered.

---

[5]   *Summa theologiae* [hereafter cited as *ST*] II–II, q. 5, a. 3c and ad 2.

[6]   See *Summa contra gentiles* [hereafter cited as *SCG*] I, ch. 4 and *In De Trinitate Boetii*, q. 5, a. 1 and q. 6, a. 1, ad 3.

With the exception of its final section, the first book is contained[7] in the first volume. This final section, which is concerned with the value of the motives of credibility, especially concerning the value of miracles, is found, along with book two, in the second volume.

As regards our use of Latin in writing this text, we often use scholastic expressions, which are of greatest use in understanding theological concepts, although they are not conducive to elegant prose.

We express our gratitude to the Reverend Father B[enedict] Lemeer, O.P., professor of apologetics at the Angelicum, who prepared this new edition with us by suggesting many additions.

Rome, at the *Collegium Angelicum*, on the Solemnity of the Most Holy Rosary of the Blessed Virgin Mary, in the year 1944.[8]

Fr. Réginald Garrigou-Lagrange, O.P.

---

7   [Trans. note: Reading *continetur* for *continentur*.]

8   In 1925, a third edition of this work was published in the form of a compendium for the use of students; however, since many professors from various regions asked for a new edition of the whole work, it is again committed to print, as it was in prior editions, with due emendations.—7 March, 1944, Fr. Réginald Garrigou-Lagrange.

Division of the Entire Work

{{xiii}} VOLUME I
Prolegomena concerning Fundamental Theology,
in Particular Its Apologetic Portion

Ch. 1.   What Is Sacred Theology?
Ch. 2.   Concerning Fundamental Theology, Apologetics in Particular
Ch. 3   On the Methodology of Apologetics

BOOK I
On the Notion, Possibility, Necessity, and Discernibility of Revelation

Section I. — On the Notion of Supernatural Revelation
   Ch. 4.   The Definition and Division of Revelation
   Ch. 5.   On the Notions of Mystery and of Dogma
   Ch. 6.   On the Notion of Supernaturality

Section II. — On the Possibility of Revelation
Part 1. Negative Defense: An Examination of the Principles of Rationalism
   Ch. 7.   On Rationalism / Naturalism in General
   Ch. 8.   Examination of Pantheistic Evolutionism, Inasmuch as
                 It Denies the Possibility of Supernatural Revelation from
                 the Perspective of the Object
   Ch. 9.   Examination of Agnosticism, Inasmuch as It Denies the
                 Possibility of Supernatural Revelation from the Perspective
                 of the Subject (i.e., Man)

Part 2. Positive Defense of the Possibility of Revelation
   Ch. 10.   On the Possibility of Supernatural Revelation in General
                 and Specifically the Possibility of Revelation of the
                 Natural Truths of Religion
   Ch. 11.   On the Possibility of the Revelation of Supernatural
                 Mysteries, Considered from the Perspective of the Object

Ch. 12.   On the Possibility of Revelation of Supernatural Mysteries,
            Considered from the Perspective of the Agent and Subject

Section III. — On the Befittingness and Necessity of Revelation
Ch. 13.   [On the Befittingness and Necessity of Revelation]

{{xiv}} *Section IV. — On the Credibility of the Mysteries of the Faith: The
Knowability of the Fact of Revelation*
Ch. 14.   On the Act of Faith in Relation to Credibility
Ch. 15.   On the Notion of Rational Credibility and Its Necessity
            for the Act of Faith
Ch. 16.   On the Demonstrability of Credibility on the Basis of
the   Motives of Credibility

VOLUME II

*Section V. — On the Value of the Motives of Credibility Considered Each in
Particular*
Ch. 17.   On the Value of the Motives of Credibility That Are
            Internal to Us
Ch. 18.   On the Value of External Motives That Are Intrinsic to
            Religion
Ch. 19.   On the Value of Miracles
Ch. 20.   On the Value of Prophecy

Book II
On the Existence of Revelation

Introduction
Ch. 1.   On the Methodology and Division of This Part of
            Apologetics
Ch. 2.   On the Historical Authority of the Four Gospels

Section I. — Jesus Christ's Testimony
Ch. 3.   Jesus Christ's Testimony concerning His Divine Mission
Ch. 4.   Christ's Testimony concerning the Mysteries to Be
            Believed and the Precepts to Be Kept
Ch. 5.   Christ's Testimony concerning the Establishment of the
            Church in Order for Revelation to Be Guarded and
            Infallibly Proposed until the End of the World

Ch. 6.   In View of His Wisdom and Holiness, Christ's Testimony concerning Himself Is Deserving of Faith

Section II. — Confirmation of Christ's Testimony through Motives That Are Internal to Us, as well as by Motives That Are Intrinsic to Religion
Ch. 7.   Confirmation of Christ's Testimony through the Way That Christianity Miraculously Fulfills Human Aspirations
Ch. 8.   Confirmation of Christ's Testimony through the Sublimity of His Doctrine
Ch. 9.   Confirmation of Christ's Testimony through the Church's Miraculous Life

Section III. — Confirmation of Christ's Testimony through Miracles and Prophecies
Ch. 10.   On Christ's Miracles
Ch. 11.   On Christ's Prophecies
Ch. 12.   On the Messianic Prophecies

Section IV. — Comparison of Christianity with the Mosaic Religion and with Other Religions
Ch. 13.   Comparison of Christianity with the Mosaic Religion, with a Defense of Its Divine Origin
Ch. 14.   The Divinity of Christianity Is Confirmed through a Comparison with Other Religions

Conclusion: On the Duty to Receive the Divine Revelation Proposed by the Catholic Church
Ch. 15.   On the Duty of Receiving Divine Revelation after It Has Been Proposed by the Church

Prolegomena concerning Fundamental Theology, in Particular Its Apologetic Portion

{{1}}

Ch. 1. What Is Sacred Theology?
     Art. 1.   Definition of Sacred Theology
     Art. 2.   Division and Unity of Sacred Theology
     Art. 3.   Methodology of Sacred Theology

Ch. 2. Concerning Fundamental Theology, Apologetics in Particular
     Art. 1.   Definition and Division of Apologetics
     Art. 2.   Its Relations with Theology Itself and with the Natural
              Sciences Which It Presupposes

Ch. 3. On the Methodology of Apologetics
     Art. 1.   How This Methodology Is to Be Determined
     Art. 2.   What the Church Teaches concerning the Methodology
              of Apologetics
     Art. 3.   Historical Overview of Apologetics, Considered in
              Relation to Methodology

STATE OF THE QUESTION

As all admit, in the treatise *On Divine Revelation* (or on the divine origin of the Christian religion), one is concerned with the possibility, befittingness, knowability, and existence of revelation, which are denied by rationalists (or naturalists). Normally, difficulties are not raised concerning the nature of the subject matter to be discussed in this treatise. However, disputations do indeed arise concerning the nature of the discipline itself (that is, that to which it formally pertains), which is variously called either fundamental (or general) theology or apologetics (i.e., the defense of the faith).

Therefore, by way of introduction, we must discuss fundamental theology itself and, in particular, apologetics, which represents, according to many thinkers, the first part of fundamental theology, although some hold that it is a distinct science.

We must start by considering the nominal meaning of terms.

"Theology" commonly signifies a science concerning God and is designated as being natural or supernatural. "Natural theology" designates a science concerning God, known on the basis of his naturally knowable effects, whereas "supernatural theology" designates a science concerning divine mysteries that are supernaturally revealed and accepted through faith. Generally, "fundamental theology" is said to belong to this supernatural theology. Now, the former receives its name from the fact that it treats of *the foundations* and rules of *faith itself,* such as revelation, the infallibility of the Church, and the authority of Sacred Scripture, as well as that of Tradition. However, "apologetics" literally means "the defense (ἀπολογία) of the Christian faith."

{{2}} According to many authors,[1] *apologetics* is *the first part of fundamental theology,* for this must treat of the foundations and rules of Christian and Catholic faith—namely, first *of Christian revelation,* then *of Christ's Church, Sacred Scripture, Divine Tradition,* as well as the other theological sources (e.g., of the authority of the Fathers of the Church, the authority of theologians, etc.)—before the theologian is then concerned in particular with the various mysteries and precepts revealed and proposed by the Church, namely, those concerning the One and Triune God, the Incarnate Word and Redeemer, and so forth.

On the other hand, according to certain more recent thinkers, *apologetics* stands at the summit of Christian philosophy, like a *philosophy of religion,* which after demonstrating God's existence as well as the spirituality and

---

[1] This is what is commonly written by those authors who treat of apologetics under the title *Fundamental* (or general) *Theology*: Ehrlich, Knoll, Reinerding [*Reinegding*], Schwetz, Hettinger, Jansen, Sprinzl, Stadler, Kuhn, Hagemann, Jungmann, Ottiger, Stummer, Jules Didiot (*Logique surnaturelle objective,* v–vi, 4), and Maisonneuve (*Dictionnaire théologie catholique,* article "Apologétique," col. 1512).

Among these authors, we must cite Fr. Ambroise Gardeil, O.P., *La crédibilité et l'apologetique,* 2nd ed. (Paris: Gabalda, 1912), xi and 246–251. Better than the preceding authors, he notes that fundamental theology is not the wellspring of theology in its concern with particular topics [*fontem theologiae specialis*] but, instead, is concerned with the foundation of faith and of theology, which foundation is divine revelation proposed through the Catholic Church. This is so because, as we will discuss below, supernatural faith and sacred theology are not formally founded on an apologetic, rational demonstration, which is only an aid and a way by which one is led by the hand to faith [*est solum subsidium et manuductio ad fidem*]. See our discussion below in vol. 1, ch. 19, a. 3.

immortality of the soul, would, without any superior direction, prove in a merely rational manner the divine origin of Christianity and of the Catholic Church.

Therefore, in this question, we are concerned not only *with the possibility of choosing* one or the other consideration of the same matter but, moreover, are concerned *with the very nature* of apologetics (or the defense of Christian faith). Indeed, we here presuppose that apologetics, which has always existed in the Church, has a determinate nature, just as philosophy and theology have their own proper natures. Therefore, the question facing us is the following: Does apologetics pertain, as something [purely] rational, to philosophy as its final part, following upon natural theology, or rather, is it the beginning of supernatural theology (that is, the science concerned with truths that are revealed and accepted through faith)?

So that the difficulty of this question may be more clearly evident, the reasons for the two opposed opinions must be laid out before we set forth the resolution to the problem at hand.

(1) Let us consider the more recent thinkers who were mentioned above.[2] According to them, apologetics is a science that is specifically distinct from supernatural theology, for apologetics precedes faith (to which it leads) and proceeds *solely under the light of reason*. Thus, it is, as it were, a philosophy of religion, whereas, by contrast, sacred theology presupposes faith and argues from truths of faith so as to deduce theological conclusions.

Hence, according to this opinion, apologetics *is not under the direction of faith* except in an extrinsic manner, as is the case for philosophy, which has faith only as an infallible rule and negative norm related to it in an external manner inasmuch as philosophy must not contradict revealed doctrine.

Thus, apologetics *would not, properly speaking, make use* of philosophy, for only a superior makes use of an inferior. Instead, it would be *under the direction of philosophy and subordinated to it*. Likewise, the apologete[3] would speak as though he did not have faith. He would inquire, as it were, alongside men who do not yet believe in the true religion and {{3}} would consider Christianity and Catholicism only from the outside, as something like Buddhism or Islam. He would be a *seeker* [*investigator*] rather than a teacher [*doctor*].

---

2 For example, see Fr. Ambroise de Poulpiquet, O.P., *L'objet intégral de l'apologetique* (Paris: Bloud et Cie, 1912), 499–534; Fr. le Bachelet in his article "Apologétique" in the *Dictionnaire apologétique de la foi catholique*.

3 [Trans. note: This term is being reserved for the person who teaches apologetics as such, as opposed to the apologist who defends particular contested revealed data. The distinction is mentioned by Fr. Garrigou-Lagrange in a footnote below.]

(2) Other authors say, however, that the aforementioned manner of proceeding is indeed of value for the Christian *philosopher* or *historian* who wishes to write philosophical and historical works about the origin and value of Christianity and of the Church.

These works are all the more useful inasmuch as they are rigorously conceived according to the method of rational and historical criticism. The apologete himself ought to make use of such works and can propose them, with great fruit, to nonbelievers to be converted. Nay, on the basis of these philosophical and historical works, we can already have a kind of imperfect apologetics, one that is indeed efficacious inasmuch as it is a historical and philosophical defense of traditional apologetics itself, an apologetics proposed by Christ in the Gospel, by the apostles in their letters, and by the Church thereafter.[4] However, *traditional and classical apologetics itself*, considered in itself as it appears in the evangelical preaching and later in a more explicit manner in the works of the great doctors of the Church (e.g., St. Justin, St. Irenaeus, St. Augustine, St. Thomas, et al.), is more than a juxtaposition (or collection) of philosophical-historical arguments proving the credibility of Christ's preaching. Indeed, it has its order, unity, loftiness, profundity, and integrity, and it does not enjoy these perfections, *which de iure* belong to it except inasmuch as *it is positively directed* from on high to its superior end *by faith itself*, thus *making use* of philosophy and history as inferior disciplines for the rational defense of faith. Indeed, the order of agents (or of what directs) must correspond to the order of ends, as St. Thomas often says,[5] and, as a rule, in order to arrive at a superior end, a proportion-

---

[4] Thus, Fr. Ambroise Gardeil (in *Le crédibilité et l'apologétique*, 231) concedes that one can establish a kind of (philosophico-historical) apologetic science specifically distinct from sacred theology, although he reduces apologetics adequately conceived to fundamental theology. According to him, this latter represents a theological epistemology and criteriology: "This seems to me to be the most exact notion that we can form concerning apologetics, a notion that is most adequate to its object. Indeed, it seems to be the conception of apologetics that will endure into the future" (Gardeil, xi).

    Cf. Gardeil, 246–251: "Without a doubt, this notion of apologetics represents the most adequate one that could be formulated. Credibility is formally a property of a supernatural object. We are occupied with a property of the object of faith in the same order of knowledge as the science that is occupied with that very object. Therefore, not only does the study of credibility fall by rights to theology but, moreover, theology must be concerned with the question of the real existence of credibility, as well as the defense of this existence against external adversaries."

    Likewise, see our article, "L'apologétique dirigée par la foi," *Revue Thomiste* 24, New Series, 2 (1919): 193–213.

[5] See *ST* I–II, q. 109, a. 6. Likewise, he frequently says wisdom *directs* the other intellectual virtues. See *ST* I–II, q. 57, a. 2; q. 66, a. 5.

    However, if the order, unity, profundity, and integrity of apologetics is not sought from this

ate, lofty direction is required. The apologete's superior end is the evident credibility of the mysteries of Christianity, a credibility which not only corresponds to the demands of reason but also to the demands of the certitude of faith. Therefore, in order to constitute an apologetics, one at least stands in need of exact knowledge of the analysis of the act of divine faith, not as the foundation for the proof being set forward but, rather, as providing it with its positive direction.

Thus, according to the traditional conception [of apologetics], the apologete does not present himself {{4}} as though he were lacking faith and investigating into it like a mere seeker. Instead, as the name "apologete" implies, he is a defender of the faith (ἀπολογία, defense). Therefore, whatever he may prudently need to do *per accidens* in order to convince this or that nonbeliever who is lacking in faith, nonetheless, *per se* and *normally*, he presents himself as the apostles and Fathers did—namely, as a member or minister of the Catholic Church—so that he may manifest to nonbelievers *the rational value* of the very apologetics that is proposed by the very magisterium of the Church. Indeed, he can avoid speaking about this superior direction, but nevertheless, he in fact must positively follow it if he wishes to proceed in a correct and perfect manner. Not only does he not turn himself away from it, but moreover, he is inspired by it as regards the end to be achieved and the means to be employed; nay, he finds in it the true *spirit* of Catholic apologetics.

Therefore, such authors hold that apologetics represents the first part of fundamental theology, which, under the direction of faith itself, must treat of Revelation itself before theology may discuss Christ's Church, Sacred Scripture, Tradition, and the other theological sources [*de locis theologicis*]. However, all Catholic authors admit that the treatise on theological sources [*de fontibus seu locis theologicis*], inasmuch as it is concerned with the Church, Sacred Scripture, Tradition, and so forth, already belongs to sacred theology; however, if this is so, it is not clear why the treatise on revelation should, *per se*, be diminished to the status of being an inferior science.

This conclusion [*sententia*] can be defended in three ways: (a) on the basis of the authority of the doctors of the Church; (b) on the basis of the nature of sacred theology; (c) on the basis of the nature of apologetics.

(a) Never did the doctors of the Church consider apologetics as being a

---

direction, these perfections are often sought out in the natural aspirations of man. In that case, the loftiness of traditional apologetics is lacking, and frequently, the supernaturality of Christianity comes to be diminished. See the article "Immanence (Méthode d')" in *Dictionnaire apologetique de la foi catholique*, col. 605, 611.

science distinct from sacred theology. Nay, [according to them,] the defense of the faith pertains to the evangelical preaching just as does the exposition of the mysteries. Thus, before the end of the nineteenth century, no theologians conceived of apologetics as a science distinct [from sacred theology].

(b) Apologetics is ultimately part of sacred theology, inasmuch as sacred theology, as *a supreme science* (or wisdom), defends its faith-received principles, as well as faith itself, against those who deny them, as St. Thomas says in *ST* I, q. 1, a. 8. Indeed, as is explained in the same place, *the supreme science cannot relinquish the defense of its principles to an inferior science.* Thus, metaphysics, as the supreme science of the natural order, defends the real value of the first principles of reason, as well as reason itself, against skeptics, as Aristotle does in the fourth book of the *Metaphysics*, before treating of being in itself and of God, considered from the formal perspective of being. To this end, metaphysics makes use of logic without, however, being subordinated to it. Similarly, for the defense of the faith, theology apologetically *makes use* of natural reason, philosophy, and history, all of which are placed among the external [*extraneos*] theological sources [*locos*], but is not[6] subordinated to them.[7] However, as the [First] Vatican Council says, these disciplines (namely, philosophy and history) "[each] in its own domain should make use of their own principles and the method proper to it."[8] Thus, in no way is their "rightful freedom" diminished, as the Council says in the same place.

(c) Apologetics rationally defends the faith *under the direction of faith itself*—namely, through the motives of credibility, which are not discovered by our reason[9] but, rather, are handed on by God, who reveals, and are proposed by the Church as naturally knowable signs of revelation. Thus, apologetics normally presupposes faith, certainly not in the listener or reader but, rather, in the apologete himself. In reality, he is positively under the direction of faith, not indeed arguing from faith but, rather, by receiving from God, who reveals the notions and theses to be defended (e.g., the notions of revelation, {{5}} of faith, and so forth), as well as the means (e.g., miracles) for defending revelation rationally. Indeed, God himself, while teaching the obscure mysteries to be believed, simultaneously taught the right way to defend the faith inasmuch as he gave sensible testimony to the prophets and to the Church, especially miracles and prophecies, so as to confirm the testimony of his invisible revelation. Thus, God himself

---

6   [Trans. note: This "not" is missing in the original, but the context demands it.]

7   See ch. 1, a. 3 below.

8   [First] Vatican Council, *Dei filius*, ch. 4 (Denzinger, 3019).

9   [Trans. note: Reading *ratione* for *natione*.]

through the prophets, Christ, and the apostles, is the teacher of apologetes, just as he is the teacher of theologians. Therefore, the apologetic ladder must not be erected from the earth to heaven like a tower (Gen 11:4) but instead descends from heaven to earth like the ladder that Jacob saw in his sleep: "And he saw in his sleep a ladder standing upon the earth, and the top thereof touching heaven: the angels also of God ascending and descending by it. And the Lord leaning upon the ladder, saying to him: 'I am the Lord God of Abraham thy father, and the God of Isaac'" (Gen 28:12–13, DR).

This metaphor sensibly expresses the truth contained in the principles of causality and of finality themselves—namely, just as the supreme science cannot relinquish the defense of its principles to inferior sciences, so too inferior sciences, such as philosophy and history, cannot, as a rule, defend the principles of faith and of theology, as well as faith itself, without the superior direction of faith itself and of theology. To this end, theology, as a form of wisdom, orders and directs inferior disciplines.[10] Indeed, this point can be confirmed in virtue of the *principle of causality*: The inferior cannot of itself do something positively concerning that which is superior to it but [can do so] only from the influence or positive direction of this very superior.[11]

More recent authors object: If this defense of the faith is already under the direction of faith, then there is a vicious circle involved in such a defense. Or there is at least the danger of fideism (that is, of the condemned error holding that human reason cannot, before having received faith, know the fact of revelation with certainty).

Others respond: This defense does not argue from faith but instead argues from reason under the direction of faith; and its probative strength can be known by reason alone with certainty. Thus, the prophet, under the direction of faith, proposes naturally knowable signs of revelation. Nor is it necessary to confuse the rational approach toward faith with the rational defense of faith, nor him who listens to evangelical or apologetic preaching with the apologete himself. For the apologete, precisely as an apologete, does not arrive at faith but instead does so precisely as a hearer of apologetic preaching. Afterwards, under the direction of faith, he teaches, just as the prophets taught, the rational path to faith and defends it, for no one defends something unless he already possesses it. Thus, man arrives at life inasmuch as he is begotten by his father, but that person begets inasmuch as he is already a man and not inasmuch as he is begotten (for the child does not beget). Likewise, the student does not teach; the teacher does. Nor is it of little importance in the exposition of a given science to proceed according to the way of discovery or according to the way of formally teaching the doctrine in question [*secundum viam inventionis aut secundum viam doctrinae*], [especially] when this doctrine comes from God

---

[10] See *ST* I–II, q. 66, a. 5.
[11] This will be taken up in greater detail later in ch. 2, a. 2.

himself and was not contrived by men themselves. However, God taught not only the obscure mysteries of faith but also taught the way that faith should be rationally defended, by which signs and arguments.

Therefore, we are faced with the following question: Is apologetics a rational and defensive office of sacred theology, or is it a science that is specifically distinct from sacred theology, one that would rightly be called the philosophy of religion?

This question is not of small import, as is clear {{6}} if it is expressed in other words: Must the rational defense of faith come into being from on high, or from below? *From on high*: namely, as it were, from the citadel of divine faith, under its direction, descending to those who seek a rational pathway to faith or against those who oppose faith. Such was the approach taken, in faith, by the prophets, apostles, and preachers. Or, on the contrary, *from below*: against the objections raised by adversaries, ascending from reason to faith, with those seeking the faith akin to philosophers who as yet do not believe. Is the rational defense of the faith the same as the rational approach to the faith, teaching the same as investigation, the teacher the same as the seeker? Did God teach—and we are speaking here *per se* and not *per accidens*—the right way for rationally arriving at the obedience of faith, or did he leave that to be discovered by our inquiry? These questions coincide with the aforementioned one—namely, is apologetics part of fundamental theology, or is it rather (as liberal Protestants frequently say) the philosophy of religion,[12] a philosophical investigation concerning religion (Essays on Religion[13])?

In order to resolve this difficulty and determine the real definition of our discipline, in whatever manner it may be said, we must state more explicitly what sacred theology is. Indeed, all Catholic authors agree on the nature of theology itself,[14] properly so-called, and admit that apologetics is related to the principles of sacred theology as the pathway is related to its terminus.[15]

---

[12] [Trans. note: Eliminating the comma in "philosophia, religionis."]

[13] [Trans. note: In this parenthetical note, it seems that Fr. Garrigou-Lagrange is referring to the basic genre of purely philosophical essays on the phenomenon of religion, not any particular publication.]

[14] [Trans. note: This is a bit of a simplification, even for Fr. Garrigou-Lagrange's time—indeed, a simplification that he himself had to have been aware of, given the centuries of disputation among the various *scholae* concerning the nature of theology. A comment like this bears witness to the fact that this is a textbook, as well as to the fact that he did not wish to raise controversies unnecessarily.]

[15] However, nonbelievers can read this introduction as a simple *exposition* of the conception that theologians have concerning their own science. Afterwards, the possibility and existence of revelation, on which theology is founded, will be defended.

However, the nature of what is directed to the end [i.e., the nature of the means] is determined by the end.

Therefore, there are three chapters in this introduction:

1) What is sacred theology (its definition, division, and method)?
2) What is fundamental theology (and, in particular, apologetics)?
3) What is the methodology employed in apologetics?

CHAPTER ONE

What Is Sacred Theology?

{{7}} This chapter is comprised of three articles: (1) the definition of theology; (2) the division thereof; and (3) its methodology.

One must proceed from the nominal definition to the real definition, which for any science whatsoever is taken from its formal object and from the formal notion under which the scientifically knowable thing [*scibile*][1] is an object. Afterwards, on the basis of the object, we will then deduce the divisions of the science, inasmuch as the distribution of the whole through its parts follows the definition of the whole. Then, from the object we will determine the methodology to be used therein, for the methodology or efficacious way of demonstrating in a given science depends on the object to be known, just as that which is ordered to the end [i.e., the *means*] depends upon the end, and as motion depends upon the terminus toward which it tends.

In this first chapter, we will gather together, under these three divisions, what is said by St. Thomas concerning sacred doctrine in *ST* I, q. 1.

ART. 1: THE DEFINITION OF SACRED THEOLOGY

§1. The nominal definition of sacred theology
§2. The necessity of sacred theology, taken from its end
§3. The real definition of sacred theology
    1) Objectively
        A) From the *formal object that is known* (*obiectum formale quod*)

---

[1] [Trans. note: Concerning *scibile*, see Ioannis a Sancto Thoma, *Ars Logica*, p.2, q.27, a.1 (823a:15–22): "To be scientifically knowable [*scibile*] adds beyond being intelligible a given mode of knowing, namely that something is understood not in a simple manner but in an inferential manner [*modo illativo*], from causes or premises proceeding to conclusions; for to know scientifically [*scire*] is to know [*cognoscere*] the cause, on account of which the thing is, etc."]

B) From the *principle by which* one knows (*principium quo*)

C) The *per accidens* object

2) Subjectively

A) Whether it is a science, *properly speaking*

B) Whether it is *a wisdom*; also, concerning its *extension* inasmuch as it is a form of wisdom

C) Whether it is an entitatively supernatural *habitus*

§4. *The integral definition* of sacred theology

§5. Corollaries *concerning the relations* of sacred theology to faith, to God's knowledge [*scientiam Dei*], the gift of wisdom, and to sciences of the natural order

§6. Whether the aforementioned notion of sacred theology is found at least implicitly in Sacred Scripture and in the Councils

§1. Nominal Definition

The term "theology" signifies *science concerning God*, θεολογία = θεός λόγος.[2] Among the Greeks, those who sang of the origin and history of the gods were called θεολόγοι (e.g., Orpheus, Hesiod, and Homer). According to Aristotle, speculative philosophy is threefold: {{8}} mathematics, physics, and theology (φιλοσοφία Θεολογική).[3] According to the Fathers of the Church, theology is a science concerned with God and especially with the Divine Trinity. Sometimes, among the Fathers, οἰκονομία (or *dispensatio*), which treats of the dispensation of salvation through the Incarnation and the Redemption, is distinguished from theology, which considers the Trinity.

As is well known, Aristotle spoke of *natural theology*, which is *concerned with God known in light of things that are naturally knowable*. However, the Fathers speak of *supernatural theology*, which can be given the nominal definition: *science concerning God, proceeding from revelation* (or science concerning the divine mysteries revealed and accepted through faith).

§2. The Necessity of Sacred Theology

Presupposing revelation, whose befittingness and existence will be defended below, and likewise presupposing the acceptance of revelation through faith, some science of faith is necessary:

1) *In order to defend faith itself* against adversaries.

---

[2] See Plato, *Republic*, 379. Aristotle, *Metaphysics*, bk. 4, ch. 1, no.7; bk. 9, ch. 7, no. 7.
[3] See Aristotle, *Metaphysics*, 4.1, no. 7.

2) *In order to have some understanding of the mysteries of the faith*, as regards their interconnection as well as their harmony with naturally knowable truths.

3) *In order to infer truths* that are contained virtually in the revealed mysteries and in order to refute errors opposed to them.[4] Hence, St. Augustine says:[5] "To this knowledge [*scientiae*] is attributed only that by which that most wholesome faith is begotten,[6] nourished, defended, and strengthened."

The reason for this necessity is found in the fact that man, inasmuch as he is a rational being, cannot accept revelation through faith without in some manner engaging in reasoning concerning it. Thus, one necessarily sees that there is a science of faith (or a science concerning the mysteries revealed by God), although it is not necessary that any given, particular member of the faithful be a theologian. Thus, theology is necessary not for anyone in particular but, rather, for the society of believers, which is called the Church.

§3. The Real Definition of Sacred Theology

From the nominal definition and from the end for which sacred theology is necessary, we must proceed now to its real definition, which expresses the essence of the thing. However, any given knowledge can be considered: (1) from the perspective of its object, and (2) from the perspective of its subject [i.e., the supposit in which the science inheres qualitatively], inasmuch as it is a *habitus* or an act of the mind. The essence of knowledge is determined by the object known and especially from the formal principle under which the object is known, for things do not specify knowledge inasmuch as they exist in themselves but, rather, inasmuch as they are scientifically knowable [*scibiles*]—that is, under the formal notion by which they are scientifically knowable (thus, there can be a number of sciences concerning one and the same thing understood from various perspectives).[7]

---

4 See *ST* I, q. 1, a. 1, and Jean Baptiste Gonet, *Clypeus theologiae Thomisticae*, disp. proem., a.10.

5 See Augustine, *De Trinitate*, bk. 14, ch. 1.

6 St. Thomas says in *ST* II–II, q. 6, a. 1, ad 1: "Through science faith *is begotten* and *nourished* by way of external persuasion, which is brought about by a given science; however, the principle and proper cause of faith is that which interiorly moves one to assent." Through sacred science, faith is begotten not in the theologian but in those who come unto faith from nonbelief.

7 See Zigliara, *Summa philosophica, Critica*, bk. 4, c. 2, a. 1, no. 7. [Trans. note: As noted above but worth repeating, the term "scibile" is of importance here, for in denoting the *scientific knowability* of something, it expresses something different than mere *knowability*. Moreover,

Therefore, in order to determine the real definition of sacred theology, it must be considered:

1) *Objectively*
   A) With regard to the formal object *that* is known (*obiectum formale quod*)
   B) With regard to the formal principle by which one knows it (*principium formale quo*)
2) *Subjectively*
   A) Whether it is a *science*, properly speaking
   B) Whether it is a form of *wisdom* (as well as concerning its *extension* inasmuch as it is a form of wisdom)
   C) Whether it is a *supernatural habitus* [, entitatively speaking]

1. Theology Objectively Considered

{{9}} As we have already said, this doctrine is nominally defined, "science concerning those things that are divinely revealed by God," and already from this nominal definition it is clear that God is the material object of this science. However, God is also the object of natural theology. Thus, we must determine what in this material object is primarily and essentially [*primo et per se*] attained by sacred theology— in other words, its formal object *that* is known (*obiectum formale quod*), as well as the formal character under which it is considered (i.e., its *obiectum formale quo*), or the motive by which it is known (*motivum quo*).[8]

---

what he is saying here implies the important distinction between thing and object, something found in Aquinas but developed by the later school. See Réginald Garrigou-Lagrange, *The Sense of Mystery: Clarity and Obscurity in the Intellectual Life*, trans. Matthew K. Minerd (Steubenville, OH: Emmaus Academic, 2017), 126n9; Jacques Maritain, *Degrees of Knowledge*, trans. Gerald Phelan et al. (Notre Dame, IN: University of Notre Dame Press, 2002), 96–107, 127–36; and John C. Cahalan, "The Problem of Thing and Object in Maritain," *The Thomist* 59, no. 1 (1995): 21–46. Also see the wealth of texts from Aquinas found in L. M. Régis, Epistemology, trans. Imelda Choquette Byrne (New York: Macmillan, 1959), 177–93. On the prehistory of the notion of object, see also Lawrence Dewan, "'Obiectum': Notes on the Invention of a Word" in *Wisdom, Law, and Virtue: Essays in Thomistic Ethics* (New York: Fordham University Press, 2008), 403–43.]

8   See *ST* I, q. 1, a. 1, ad 2: "A diversity in formal perspective [*ratio cognoscibilis*] leads to a diversity of sciences. For instance, the astronomer and the natural philosopher demonstrate the same conclusion (for example, that the earth is round), but the astronomer does so through a mathematical middle term that is abstracted from matter, whereas, the natural philosopher does so through a middle term including matter in it [*per medium circa materiam consideratum*]. Whence, nothing prevents it from being the case that, concerning things treated by the philosophical disciplines inasmuch as they are knowable by the light of natural reason, such things may also be treated of by another science inasmuch as they are known by the light of

It is to be noted, as Capreolus remarks,[9] that in a given science, the *subject* and *object* somewhat differ from each other. Indeed, an object of a science is a conclusion demonstrated in it; however, its subject is that which stands as the subject in the conclusions and concerning which certain predicates are demonstrated. Nonetheless, according to the common use of terminology by theologians, "subject" and "object" are understood as having the same meaning, such that the object would be reduced to the subject and not *vice versa*, for the subject exists outside the mind, while, by contrast, the conclusion is, formally speaking [i.e., precisely as a conclusion], in the mind, and sciences (except for logic) are concerned with things existing outside the soul.[10]

St. Thomas determines the subject (or object) of sacred theology in *ST* I, q. 1, a. 7: "Whether God[11] is the subject of sacred doctrine." However, the Holy Doctor's position is commonly proposed thus:[12] *The formal and specificative object of sacred theology is God, known from the perspective of the Deity, as it falls under virtual revelation.*[13] In this proposition, the Deity itself is the formal notion *that* is considered, while virtual divine revelation is the formal notion *under which* (i.e., the medium or principle) *by which* the Deity is known. However, the secondary object of sacred theology is created

---

divine revelation. Thus, theology, which pertains to sacred doctrine, differs in kind from the theology that is a part of philosophy." See Cajetan's commentary on this article as well.

9   See Capreolus, *In Sent.*, prol., q. 4, a. 1, c.1.

10   [Trans. note: Fr. Garrigou-Lagrange almost certainly is implying that mathematics is *solely* a science of real quantity, a position often held by Thomists in his day. Moreover, logic, as a science of second intentions, would include, for him, the content of Aristotle's *Rhetoric* and *Poetics*, following in the wake of certain Arabic commentators' influence on medieval thinkers concerning the division of the logical disciplines.

For an overview of different Thomistic opinions regarding mathematics, see Armand Maurer, "Thomists and Thomas Aquinas on the Foundation of Mathematics," *The Review of Metaphysics* 47, no. 1 (Sept. 1993): 43–61. Also, for particular views, see Yves R. Simon, "Nature and the Process of Mathematical Abstraction," in *Philosopher at Work*, ed. Anthony O. Simon (Lanham, MD: Rowman and Littlefield Publishers, 1999), 113–133; Vincent E. Smith, *St. Thomas on the Object of Geometry* (Milwaukee: Marquette University Press, 1954).

Regarding issues related to logic, see Deborah Black, *Logic and Aristotle's Rhetoric and Poetics in Medieval Arabic Philosophy* (Leiden: Brill, 1990); Matthew K. Minerd, "Thomism and the Formal Object of Logic," *American Catholic Philosophical Quarterly* 93, no. 3 (2019): 411–444.]

11   [Trans. note: *Deus* is missing from the Latin here.]

12   See, for example, Gonet in his *Clypeus theologiae Thomisticae.*

13   [Trans. note: For an outline of the point of terminology, "virtual revelation," see Réginald Garrigou-Lagrange, "Remarks Concerning the Metaphysical Character of St. Thomas's Moral Theology, in Particular as It Is Related to Prudence and Conscience," trans. Matthew K. Minerd, *Nova et Vetera* 17, no. 1 (2019): 261–266 ("Translator's Appendix 1: Concerning the Formal Object of Acquired Theology"); also see the further points of explanation offered in Matthew K. Minerd, "Wisdom Be Attentive: The Noetic Structure of Sapiential Knowledge," *Nova et Vetera* 18, no. 4 (2020): 1120–1125 (esp. 1108n13).]

reality, in relation to God, from the perspective of the Deity. This must be explained in parts.

A. GOD, CONSIDERED FROM THE PERSPECTIVE OF THE DEITY, IS THE FORMAL OBJECT THAT IS KNOWN (*OBIECTUM FORMALE QUOD*) OF SACRED THEOLOGY

This is the first part of St. Thomas's position concerning these matters. [It is argued for syllogistically as follows.]

Any given science's formal object that is known (or [*vel*] subject) is that which this science essentially and primarily considers and under whose notion it knows all other things.

Now, God, considered from the perspective of the Deity, is what sacred theology considers essentially and primarily and under whose notion it knows all other things.

Therefore, God, known from the perspective of the Deity, is the formal object (or subject) that is known (*obiectum formale quod*) by sacred theology.

The *major premise* is obvious. It represents the very definition of the formal object that is known (*obiectum formale quod*)—namely, {{10}} that which is formally set before a power [*obiicitur*] and considered. For example, the colored is called the *obiectum formale quod* of sight because it is that which is *essentially and primarily* (i.e., necessarily and immediately) attained by sight and is the reason on account of which other things are visible—namely, magnitude, figure, and so forth. Likewise, in the sciences, being insofar as it is being is called the *objectum formale quod* of metaphysics because it is that which metaphysics essentially and primarily considers and is that under whose notion it knows all other things—namely, God, the soul, and the world. So too, for the same reason, quantity is designated as the object of mathematics, and health the object of medicine.

However, the minor premise is proven as follows by St. Thomas in *ST* I, q. 1, a. 7: "All things are discussed in sacred doctrine from *the perspective of God*, either because they are God Himself, or because they are ordered to God as to their principle and their end." Indeed, whatever is considered by theology either is God himself (his essence, attributes, or persons) or something pertaining to him as an effect proceeding from him (such as creatures) or as a means leading toward him and ordered to him (such as human acts, laws, grace, the virtues, the Incarnation, the Redemption, and the sacraments). Thus, all the treatises of sacred theology are concerned with God: concerning the One and Triune God in himself; concerning God as creating and elevating [to the supernatural order]; concerning God the Ultimate

End; concerning God the Lawgiver, the first rule of human life; concerning God the principle of grace and the virtues; concerning God Incarnate and the Redeemer; concerning God the Just Judge [at the end of time].

But why do we say, "God, from the perspective of the Deity"? Because, as St. Thomas notes in *ST* I, q. 1, a. 6: "Sacred doctrine *most properly* makes determinations concerning God . . . because it does so not only with regard to that which is knowable by way of creatures (which the philosophers knew . . .) but also *with regard to that which is known by Him alone about Himself,* and by others through revelation that has been communicated to them."

In other words, supernatural theology not only considers God, just as metaphysics does, *from the common notion of being,* as he is the first and most perfect being, the First Cause and Ultimate End of every being in the natural order, but rather considers him from a loftier perspective. Thus, in metaphysics, the consideration of creatures comes first, and God is known only on the basis of our knowledge of creatures, by way of notions that are analogically and evidently common to both him and created things—namely, from the perspective of being, unity, truth, goodness, intelligence, wisdom, and so forth. By contrast, in supernatural theology, the consideration of God is prior to consideration of creatures, and God is considered according to what is most proper to him—namely, according to his *Deity,* which in its hidden eminence is naturally unknowable, uniting together in itself all the perfections that are analogically common to him and to creatures. In other words, sacred theology considers God *according to the mystery of his intimate life and inasmuch as he is the Author of the supernatural order.*[14] Thus, all the divine attributes are considered as being expressions of God's intimate life,[15] {{11}} which is manifested to us to a greater extent in the mystery of the Holy Trinity. Likewise, when we speak about God Incarnate, we are not concerned with the Incarnation of the First Being precisely as a being, but rather with the Incarnation of the Word, the Second Person of the Trinity. Now, the greatest difference separates knowing God externally and knowing even his

---

[14]   See Jean Baptiste Gonet, *Clypeus,* disputatio prooemialis, a. 3, no. 26.

[15]   Hence, in the *Summa theologiae,* St. Thomas treats, for example, of the supernatural providence to which predestination pertains, and not only of the providence of God the Author of nature, which is already considered by the philosopher.

Philosophy considers God from the common notion *of being,* whereas sacred theology considers him from the proper and loftiest notion *of the Deity:*

Deity

True   Being   Wisdom   Will   Justice

secret, intimate life, just as the greatest difference separates seeing a man externally and penetrating the secrets of his heart.

Indeed, supernatural theology treats *of creatures* but does so *secondarily* and *inasmuch as they are related to God, considered from the perspective of the Deity*. For just as psychology, which is the science of the soul, also considers human languages, not in themselves (as does linguistics) but, rather, inasmuch as they are related to the soul, which is expressed in them (i.e., inasmuch as they are in some manner a "thing of the soul"), so too supernatural theology undertakes discussions concerning creatures inasmuch as they are, in some manner, a "thing of God"[16]—namely, effects of God in which God is expressed as in an image or a footprint—and inasmuch as they are referred to God (understood from the perspective of the Deity) as to an end—namely, inasmuch as they can be (and indeed are) elevated to the supernatural order. Thus, it deals with grace, justification, supernatural merit, the supernatural theological virtues, which have as their object God from the perspective of the Deity, as well as the supernatural [infused] moral virtues that are essentially ordered to the theological virtues as means to an end.

The first part of our conclusion is confirmed, as St. Thomas says, "From this science's principles, which are the articles of faith, which is concerned with God. However, the subject of the principles and of the whole science is the same since the whole science is virtually contained in its principles."[17]

Hence, just as the formal subject or object of metaphysics is being qua being and the formal object of mathematics is quantity and the object of medicine is health, so too is the subject of sacred theology God, considered from the perspective of the Deity.

B. VIRTUAL REVELATION IS THE FORMAL PRINCIPLE OR MOTIVE BY WHICH (*PRINCIPIUM FORMALE QUO*) OF SACRED THEOLOGY

This is the second part of our position being discussed here. However, virtual revelation is revelation as virtually containing conclusions that can be deduced from it through rational discourse.[18]

This second part of our conclusion is made manifest like the first by beginning with theology's nominal definition. And indeed, according to this

---

[16] A remark made by Cajetan. See St. Thomas, *SCG* II, ch. 4 (*that the philosopher considers creatures in one way, while the theologian another*).

[17] *ST* I, q. 1, a. 7.

[18] [Trans. note: On this topic, see the articles cited in note 13 above.]

definition, sacred theology is distinguished from divine faith and from metaphysics, as well as the other natural sciences, truly standing, as it were, like a kind of middle point between. Now, it cannot be distinguished from them, nor be a midpoint between them, unless it has virtual revelation as its formal motive. Indeed, if its formal motive were formal revelation, it would be the same thing as faith, which depends immediately on divine revelation, inasmuch as we believe in supernatural mysteries because they are expressly and formally revealed by God. However, if it were not to depend on revelation and were to proceed from principles known under a solely natural light, it would not be distinguished from natural sciences, especially from metaphysics, which considers God, as he is knowable from creatures under the light of natural reason.[19] Thus, we must say that the formal means or motive of sacred theology {{12}} is the light of revelation together with the light of reason, or *the light of reason illuminated by faith*, which is called virtual revelation—that is, revelation as virtually containing conclusions that can be deduced through rational discourse. Thus, for example, from the formally revealed mystery of the Incarnation, theology deduces the infallibility of Christ's human understanding, and this theological conclusion is said to be virtually revealed.

Hence, on the basis of both of these formal objects (*quod and quo*), we have the real definition of sacred theology—namely, science concerning God, considered from the perspective of the Deity, inasmuch as he falls under virtual revelation (or science concerned with God from the perspective of the Deity, proceeding from revelation [*sic*]).

Indeed, the subject and the object of this science could be distinguished,[20] but this is of little importance, for they are commonly understood

---

[19] See John of St. Thomas, *In ST* I, q. 1, disp. 2, a. 7, no. 11 and 12. See *ST* I, q. 1, a. 3.

[20] If we do indeed distinguish the subject and the object, the following points must be made: (1) *The material subject* of sacred theology is *God and the works of God*—namely, creatures not only according to their supernatural perfections but also according to their natures. For all these things are treated in sacred theology, and it is not only a question of the created order concerning grace and the infused virtues, but also of human or angelic nature, which is made in the image of God and is capable of grace and of the natural virtues, which serve the supernatural virtues, just as reason serves faith. (2) *The formal subject* is *God alone, considered from the perspective of the Deity inasmuch as he falls under virtual revelation*, for all things are treated in sacred theology inasmuch as they are ordered to God, considered from the perspective of the Deity. (3) *The material object*, inasmuch as it is distinguished from the material subject, is nothing other than the conclusions that are demonstrated in theology concerning God and his works. (4) *The formal object that is known* (*obiectum formale quod*) is the objective coordination of theological conclusions that are concerned with God from the perspective of the Deity inasmuch as he falls under virtual revelation; however, the conclusions that are already formally revealed are the object, improperly speaking. (5) *The formal object by which* (*obiectum formale quo*), or the medium by which / motive, is virtual revelation. See R. M. Martin,

as being the same.

As regards how virtually revealed theological conclusions are related to faith, see §5, corollary, below.

C. CONCERNING THE *PER ACCIDENS* OBJECT OF SACRED THEOLOGY

Sacred theology, just like divine faith, has, besides its primary, essential object (namely, God, known from the perspective of the Deity) and its secondary object (namely, creation in relation to the Deity), a *per accidens* object— namely, *naturally knowable conclusions concerning God*, which *per se* pertain to natural theology. Thus, St. Thomas says in *ST* I q. 2, a. 2, ad 1:

> God's existence and other things of this sort, which can be known through natural reason concerning God, as is said in the first chapter of the letter to the Romans, are not articles of faith but, rather, are preambles to the articles. Indeed, in this way, faith presupposes natural knowledge, just as grace presupposes nature and a perfection presupposes that which is perfectible. Still, nothing prevents that which of itself is demonstrable and knowable [*scibile*] from being accepted as something believable by someone who does not grasp the demonstration.[21]

Therefore, the demonstrations concerning God that are made in sacred theology from two natural premises, or [*vel*] from premises that are *per accidens* revealed, pertain *per se* to natural theology and *per accidens* to sacred theology. Nevertheless, these truths, not formally as conclusions but as truths, are considered *per se* by sacred theology relative to supernatural mysteries, for it is impossible to treat of God's intimate life, the Trinity, without considering the Divine Unity, or to treat of grace without considering nature.

2. Theology Subjectively Considered

A. Whether theology is a science, properly speaking {{13}}
B. Whether it is a form of wisdom
C. Whether it is an entitatively supernatural *habitus*

"L'objet intégrale de la théologie," *Revue Thomiste* 20 (1912): 12–21.

[21] See also *ST* I, q. 1, a. 1 and *ST* II–II, q. 2, a. 5 and a. 6, ad 1.

A. Is theology a science, properly speaking?

Now that we have considered both formal objects of sacred theology, we must consider it subjectively—that is, inasmuch as it is a *habitus* of the mind, [a consideration] which always pertains to its real definition. However, at first glance, sacred theology does not seem to be a science, properly speaking, given its lack of evidential knowledge, for it proceeds from principles that are not evident—namely, from the articles of faith. For this reason, some[22] say that theology is, in fact, an unnamed *habitus* between science and faith. The nominalists or [*vel*] empiricists, for whom metaphysics is not a science but a collection of hypotheses, *a fortiori* do not wish to admit that sacred theology is a science but, rather, hold that it is only a collection of thoughts or [*seu*] opinions.

Certain semi-rationalists, by contrast, wish to demonstrate the mysteries of faith and to reduce sacred theology to the natural sciences—namely, to philosophy and history.[23] This is a heretical claim.

St. Thomas responds to this question by making three points: (a) Sacred theology is a science; (b) however, it is a subalternate science; (c) and in us wayfarers it exists in an imperfect state.

(a) *It is a science.* Indeed, science is "knowledge through the cause on account of which a thing is and cannot be otherwise"[24]—namely, through a necessary cause. Science differs from common knowledge inasmuch as it not only knows things but also knows the reasons or causes of things, not only the *per accidens* causes but the *per se* and proper causes. Now, in theology, theological conclusions are deduced from principles of faith necessarily and with certitude and not only as opinions in a contingent and probable manner. For example, from the fact that Christ is at one and the same time both God and man, we can deduce necessarily and with certitude that he has human freedom and not only divine freedom. In order to deny that theology

---

[22] For example, [Gregory of] Valentia, [Gabriel] Vasquez, and other modern thinkers.

[23] Thus, Günther, Hermes, Frohschammer, and, in a certain manner, Rosmini. See Denzinger, nos. 2738, 2829, 2854, and 3225. [Trans. note: Bl. Antonio Rosmini-Serbati (1797–1855) had his work *Delle Cinque Piaghe della Santa Chiesa* placed on the index during his lifetime. After his death, forty propositions taken from his works were condemned. He was later rehabilitated and beatified for his heroic virtue in 2007. Details on his rehabilitation should be interpreted in light of the 2001 decree by then Cardinal Ratzinger, "Note on the Force of the Doctrinal Decrees concerning the Thought and Work of Fr. Antonio Rosmini Serbati," promulgated July 1, 2001. *Rosmini* was rehabilitated, not the conclusions that might be drawn from his works by those who are not careful.]

[24] See Aristotle, *Posterior analytics*, bk. 1. *In* I *Post. An.*, lect. 4.

is a science, we would need to deny the necessity and certitude of all theological conclusions and to reduce them to mere opinions. Indeed, there are theological opinions that are more or less probable, but above them theological science exists, situated immediately below divine faith.

(b) *It is a science subalternate to God's knowledge* [*scientia*]. St. Thomas says in *ST* I, q. 1, a. 2:

> It must be known that the genus of sciences is twofold. Indeed, certain ones proceed from principles known by the natural light of the intellect, such as arithmetic, geometry, and other such things. However, there are others that proceed from principles known by the light of a superior science, just as perspective (i.e., optics) proceeds from principles known through geometry, and music (or harmony) from principles known through arithmetic. And, in this way, sacred doctrine is a science, for it proceeds from principles known in the light of a superior science, which, in fact, is the knowledge [*scientiae*] had by God and the blessed. Whence, just as music believes the principles given to it by arithmetic, so too does sacred doctrine believe the principles revealed to it by God.

Therefore, sacred theology is *per se* a true science, subalternated to God's knowledge [*scientiae Dei*], for by its nature it is conjoined with God's knowledge [*scientiae Dei*] in which evidential knowledge of the articles of faith is had.

{{14}} (c) *However, in us wayfarers, theology exists in an imperfect state,* just as perspective (i.e., optics) exists in an imperfect state in him who only believes but does not know the principles given to him by geometry. Thus, a boy is *per se* substantially a man, but in an imperfect state, inasmuch as he lacks the use of reason and the exercise of freedom. But when the theologian arrives at the Beatific Vision in heaven, he will then possess theology in a perfect state.

B. WHETHER SACRED THEOLOGY IS A FORM OF WISDOM, AND CONCERNING ITS EXTENSION INASMUCH AS IT IS A FORM OF WISDOM (*ST* I, Q. 1, A. 6)

Wisdom differs from science inasmuch as it is knowledge of things not only through inferior causes but through the highest causes.[25] Now, sacred theo-

---

[25] See Aristotle, *Metaphysics,* bk. 1. *In* I *Meta.*, lect. 1. Aristotle, *Nicomachean Ethics*, bk. 6, ch. 4.

logy "considers, without qualification, the universe's highest cause, God."[26] Nay, rather, it is wisdom in the greatest sense—namely, much more than natural theology. Indeed, in this supreme part of philosophy, whatever is known concerning God is had as a conclusion and not as a principle, for we cannot rise up to God except from creatures. Christian theology, by contrast, treats of God in such a way that it knows him according to his Deity or intimate life, taking as its principles not creatures but, rather, God himself. Thus, it is maximally a form of wisdom (that is, knowledge through the highest causes and supreme reasons of things).

In order to determine later what fundamental theology is, we must note that a particular property pertains *per se* to theology inasmuch as it is not only a form of science but also is a form of wisdom, for wisdom as a *habitus* perfecting the intellect is specifically distinguished from mere science.[27] *Wisdom has a special eminence inasmuch as it orders and judges all things, even concerning its own principles, doing so by defending and explaining them.* Thus, it is a kind of rule and measure perfecting the remaining sciences.

St. Thomas lucidly explains what the *extension* of sacred theology as a wisdom is in *ST* I, q. 1, a. 8:

> Just as other sciences do not argue in proof of their principles but, instead, argue from their principles so as to show other things in these sciences, so too this (sacred) doctrine does not argue in *proof* of its principles, which are the articles of faith, but from these it proceeds to something to be made manifest, just as the Apostle, on the basis of the resurrection of Christ, argues in proof of the general resurrection (1 Cor 15). Nonetheless, one must consider the fact that, in the philosophical sciences, the inferior sciences neither prove their principles nor dispute against those who deny them, but instead leave this to a superior science. Now, the supreme science among them, namely metaphysics, disputes against those who deny its principles, if the adversary concedes something; however, if he concedes nothing, it cannot dispute with him but nevertheless can answer his objections.

---

[26] *ST* I, q. 1, a. 6.

[27] See *ST* I–II, q. 57, a. 2, ad 1, and John of St. Thomas, *In ST* I–II, disp. 16, a. 3, q. 1. [Trans. note: For a discussion of important historical ambiguities surrounding the distinction of science and wisdom, see Minerd, "Wisdom Be Attentive: The Noetic Structure of Sapiential Knowledge," *Nova et Vetera* 18, no. 4 (2020): 1103–1146; Tomáš Machula, "Theology as Wisdom: Renaissance and Modern Scholastic Commentaries on Aquinas," *American Catholic Philosophical Quarterly* 93, no. 2 (2019): 211-225.]

Hence, *sacred doctrine, since it has no superior, disputes with those who deny its principles,* by arguing indeed, if the adversary concedes something from among those things that are had through divine revelation, just as, through the authorities of sacred doctrine, we dispute against heretics and, against those who deny one article of faith, we can argue from another. However, if an adversary believes none of those things that are divinely revealed, there no longer remains a way for proving the articles of faith by reasoning. Instead, one can only resolve his objections against the faith, {{15}} if he has any such objections. For since faith rests on the infallible truth, and it is impossible that the contrary of a truth be demonstrated, it is quite clear that the proofs that are brought against the faith are not demonstrations but, instead, objections that can be resolved.[28]

This requires an explanation. St. Thomas compares sacred theology and metaphysics inasmuch as they are supreme sciences in different orders. He says that because in the natural order metaphysics is not only a science but a supreme science, or wisdom, it not only deduces conclusions from its principles but also "disputes with those denying its principles." Thus, it defends against skeptics the ontological value of the first principles of reason, as well as the real value of the supreme criterion or motive of natural knowledge—namely, objective evidence. Consequently, Aristotle in the fourth[29] book of the *Metaphysics* defends in particular the real value of the supreme principle of reason—namely, the principle of contradiction—by resolving the objections of those who deny it—namely, Heraclitus and the Sophists. Hence, this supreme principle stands forth not only as the logical rule of our reason but also as the ontological rule of extramental being itself, which is the object of metaphysics.

This defensive part of metaphysics can be called critical metaphysics or epistemology

---

[28] Likewise, in *In De Trinitate Boetii*, q. 2, a. 3, St. Thomas asks whether in the science of the faith, which is about God, it is permitted for one to make use of philosophical reasonings. And he concludes: "*In sacred doctrine we can make use of philosophy in three ways.* First, *to demonstrate* those things that are *preambles of faith*, which are necessary in the science of faith, such as those things that are proven about God by natural reasonings, such as that God exists and other things of this sort, whether concerning God or concerning creatures, that are proven in philosophy which faith presupposes. Second, *for making known through certain likenesses those things that are of faith*, just as Augustine in his *De trinitate* makes use of many likenesses taken from philosophical doctrines so as to manifest the Trinity. Third, *to resist those things that are said against the faith*, either by showing that they are *false* or *are not necessary*." Also, in Quod. IV, q. 9 a. 3: "If adversaries receive no authority (of sacred doctrine), it is necessary to have recourse to natural reasonings so as to convince them [of their error]." Also see *SCG* II, chs. 2, 8, and 9.

[29] [Trans. note: Reading IV for IX.]

(ἐπιστήμη, science; λόγος, discourse)—that is, the science concerning the real value of our scientific knowledge. This critique, which is frequently set forth at the end of logic, is thus transferred from logic to ontology, and since it now treats not only of *ens rationis*, which is the subject of logic,[30] but [rather] of extramental being inasmuch as it is knowable by us, it now pertains *per se* to metaphysics, which is the science of being. Hence, Aristotle treated of it not in logic but in the fourth book of the *Metaphysics*. Critical metaphysics indeed *uses* logic in order to defend the ontological value of our natural knowledge—but now in relation to extramental being. Hence, it can be called fundamental philosophy because it treats of the objective foundation of our natural certitude. Thus, the defense of the first principles *per se* pertains to metaphysics inasmuch as it is not only science but is the supreme science. I say *per se* and not only *per accidens*, for even if nobody happened to deny them—namely, the skeptics—it would be necessary to scientifically determine the objective foundation or ultimate resolution of our natural certitude.

Similarly, according to St. Thomas, in the supernatural order, sacred theology is not only a science but the supreme science, and from this perspective it pertains *per se* to it not, indeed, to prove the principles of faith but, rather, to defend them against those who deny them. In this way, it resolves the objections of naturalists against the mysteries of the Trinity or of the Incarnation by showing their inefficacy. This defense pertains *per se* to theology, for even if no adversaries to the faith existed, such a defense would be useful for having a certain understanding of the mysteries, in order to show forth their befittingness or, at least, the fact that they are not opposed to reason.

{{16}} "And if it is insisted," says Cajetan, "that a solution of this sort does not belong to the theologian qua theologian because it is not from the principles of theology, the assumption should be denied, for *theology not only enjoys its own activities but also makes external [sciences] its own when, for its own defense, it* MAKES USE *of propositions from the other sciences, on account of us [propter nos]*, as was touched on in a. 5 ad 2 [i.e., as regards the deficiency in our own manner of knowing]."[31]

Thus, this defense of the principles of faith does not fall to sacred theology only in a *per accidens* manner, as do the natural conclusions concerning God that are *per se* demonstrated in natural theology. Indeed, this natural theology neither *per se* nor *per accidens* intends to defend the principles of the Catholic faith, for example, to resolve objections against the possibility of God being triune.

If, however, as St. Thomas teaches, sacred theology, inasmuch as it is the supreme science, must defend the principles of faith and likewise treat of faith itself as well as the assent of faith that is in consonance with reason, why could it not *extend* itself to a defense of the foundations of faith against

---

[30] [Trans. Note: More exactly, the particular *ens rationis* that is treated in logic, namely, the *relationes rationis* naturally formed by the intellect and which are called also *second intentions*.]

[31] *In ST* I, q. 1, a. 8, no. 4.

the rationalists or naturalists—namely, by resolving objections against the possibility, befittingness, knowability, and existence of Revelation, as well as those raised against the infallibility of the Catholic Church, who proposes what has been revealed? Thus, fundamental theology or apologetics would be a defensive office of sacred theology. However, it is not a specifically distinct science and is related to theology, properly speaking, just as critical metaphysics, in its defense of the ontological value of our natural cognition, is related to ontology. Thus, the supreme science would have, properly speaking, a reflection on its own principles, as well as on the foundation of its certitude. In this way, we have a verification for the general law holding that "Human reasoning, according to the way of acquisition (or discovery) proceeds from certain simply known things that are its first principles. And in turn, in the way of judgment, by way of resolution, it returns to the first principles in whose light it examines what it has found."[32] However, the proper nature of fundamental theology (or apologetics) must be determined in chapter 2.

C. WHETHER SACRED THEOLOGY IS A SUPERNATURAL *HABITUS*

Some, such as Conteson, hold that sacred theology is an entitatively supernatural *habitus* because it essentially proceeds from supernatural faith and is specified by a supernatural object. Others say, by contrast, that sacred theology can remain even when faith dies away when the theologian becomes a formal heretic, thus meaning that it is a merely natural *habitus*.

Generally speaking, the Thomists distance themselves from these opposed extremes and teach that sacred theology is a not a *habitus* that is entitatively and intrinsically supernatural but, rather, is one that is supernatural in its root [*radicaliter*], thus depending on faith in such a way that it is lost when faith is destroyed.[33]

(a) *Sacred theology is not an entitatively or intrinsically supernatural habitus*, for "it is acquired by human study," as St. Thomas says in *ST* II-II, q. 45, a. 1, ad 2 and *ST* I, q. 1, a. 6, ad 3. Thus, it differs from the gift of wisdom, which is given by the Holy Spirit through infusion. However, no intrinsically and entitatively supernatural *habitus* is acquired through human study, through the exercise of reason, but instead *per se* requires a supernatural cause.

---

[32] *ST* I, q. 79, a. 8.

[33] Thus, John of St. Thomas in *ST* I, q. 1, disp. 2, a. 2 ("Whether supernatural faith is required for Theology"). So too Jean Baptiste Gonet, Charles René Billuart, etc.

{{17}} (b) *Nevertheless, sacred theology is a habitus that is originatively supernatural in its root* because it is concerned with conclusions that can be deduced from the principles of faith and essentially depends on the supernatural *habitus* of faith in which it is contained as in its root. Therefore, the theology of heretics is not a true form of theology and is specifically distinct from Catholic theology because it does not have the same formal motive—namely, virtual revelation.

Indeed, a formal heretic does not deduce conclusions from principles believed by divine faith, for when he pertinaciously rejects the authority of God and of the Church concerning one article, he does not preserve divine faith concerning the other articles but instead retains only a human faith or opinion founded on his own judgment and his own will.[34] Hence, when faith perishes, sacred theology necessarily is destroyed as a *habitus*. Certainly, the heretical theologian retains a kind of material coordination of theological concepts; however, this coordination lacks the light of faith which enables them to be formally connected. It is akin to how once the soul leaves the body the parts of the human body remain materially ordered in the corpse for a time, even though it is no longer a human body (for it lacks its substantial form). Therefore, formal heretics can only retain a corpse of sacred theology, or better, a sophistical dialectic concerning divine things jumbled up among themselves, for having rejected the external authority of God and the Church and having lost the internal light of faith, heretics lack the cognitive rule and principle for rightly judging concerning things of faith. Therefore, they often confuse supernatural things with natural ones and frequently fall into error.[35] Hence, it is not surprising that they say theology is not a science but, rather, a collection of opinions, for their theology in fact is nothing other than that.

§4. The Integral Definition of Sacred Theology

An integral definition differs from a real, essential definition, just as the integrity that a given perfection adds to the essence is distinguished from said essence. (For example, the blind man preserves the essence of humanity but not its integrity.) Therefore, the integral definition is taken from all those things involved in theology—namely, *it is a science that defends the*

---

[34] *ST* II–II, q. 5, a. 3.

[35] Even if the formal heretic sometimes can arrive at true theological conclusions and write about them without error, nonetheless, he knows these conclusions only in a material manner and not in the same way that they are known by Catholic theologians. For in a theological conclusion, the formal connection between the subject and the predicate depends on the light of revelation proposed by the Church and upon the internal light of faith. However, the formal heretic has lost the light of faith and believes only the dogmas that are pleasing to him by means of his own judgment and will.

principles of faith against those who deny them, seeks a degree of understanding concerning these principles, and deduces conclusions from them.[36] Or, as St. Augustine says in the aforementioned text from *De Trinitate* 14.1: "To this knowledge [*scientiae*] is attributed only that by which that most wholesome faith is begotten, nourished, defended, and strengthened"—namely, begotten in those who do not have faith, though in teachers this science essentially *presupposes* the faith that it defends and sets forth.

Hence, theology does three things. (1) *It defends* the principles of faith against those who deny them, and it does this in two ways: positively and negatively. It does so *positively* by showing adversaries who admit revelation that the mysteries of faith are in the deposit of revelation—namely, in Sacred Scripture or in Tradition—and against those who reject revelation, it does so by manifesting the signs of revelation. It performs its defense *negatively* by resolving the objections of those who deny them, by showing that these objections are false or at least not necessary, as St. Thomas says in *Quodlibet* IV, q. 9, a. 3. {{18}} (2) Sacred theology seeks *some degree of understanding* of the mysteries of faith, not only through analogies on the basis of things that we naturally know but also through the connection of the mysteries among themselves and with man's final end. (3) From the principles of faith, *it deduces theological conclusions*. In this way, theology comes to be constituted in its integrity.

§5. Corollaries concerning the Relations of Sacred Theology to Faith, to the Knowledge of God, to the Gift of Wisdom, and to the Sciences of the Natural Order

A. IN RELATION TO FAITH

Sacred theology is essentially *distinguished from divine faith* from the perspective of the formal motive, for the formal motive of faith is the authority of God who reveals (or formal revelation), whereas the formal motive or medium by which theological knowledge is known is virtual revelation. However, sacred theology *essentially presupposes the faith* in which it is contained in root, just as knowledge of the conclusions essentially presupposes knowledge of the principles from which the conclusions are drawn. Thus, as has been said, the heretic's theology is not true theology but instead is specifically distinct from Catholic theology because it

---

[36] See St. Thomas, *In De Trinitate Boetii*, q. 2, a. 3, *Quod.* IV, q. 9, a. 3.

does not have the same formal motive—namely, virtual revelation.

For this reason, in his encyclical *Providentissimus Deus,* Pope Leo XIII says concerning studies of Sacred Scripture:

> But it is most unbecoming to pass by, in ignorance or contempt, the excellent work which Catholics have left in abundance, and to have recourse to the *works of non-Catholics* [*heterodoxorum libros*]—and to seek in them, to the detriment of sound doctrine and often to the peril of faith, the explanation of passages on which Catholics long ago have successfully employed their talent and their labour. For although the studies of non-Catholics [*heterodoxorum studiis*], used with prudence, may sometimes be of use to the Catholic student, he should, nevertheless, bear well in mind—as the Fathers also teach in numerous passages—*that the sense of Holy Scripture* can nowhere be found *incorrupt* outside of the Church [*incorruptum sacrarum Litterarum sensum extra Ecclesiam neutiquam reperiri*], and cannot be expected to be found in writers who, being without the true faith, only gnaw the bark of the Sacred Scripture, and never attain its pith.[37]

As regards the relation of theological conclusions to faith, several things must be noted. A proposition of faith is that which, in the written Word of God or in Tradition, is formally and immediately revealed and proposed by the Catholic Church as being revealed: For if this second condition is lacking, even though the first remains, it will indeed be of faith *in itself* [*quoad se*], but not *from our perspective* [*quoad nos*]. This is so because the Church alone is the infallible rule in distinguishing what is revealed from what is not revealed, as will be explained below.

A theological conclusion is what is deduced through a natural [rational] discourse either from two *de fide* premises or from one *de fide* premise and another that is naturally certain.

A theological conclusion, *strictly speaking*, is reached through [objectively] illative discourse[38] and is contained only *virtually in a connected manner* [*virtualiter connexive*] in revelation—namely, by reason of a natural connection. This is either as a property in an essence or as an effect in a cause. For example, every man is capable of laughter. Now, by faith, we know

---

37 [Trans. note: Taken from the official translation, noting several original Latin words that are necessary to understand Fr. Garrigou-Lagrange's point more clearly. The English emphasis reflects emphasis that Fr. Garrigou-Lagrange placed in the selection.]

38 [Trans. note: That is, through a discourse of reason by which a new truth is reached by means of a discourse through a middle term. This is in contrast to a merely explicative discourse, which exposits the same truth but only in a clearer manner.]

Christ is a true man. Therefore, Christ is capable of laughter. These conclusions are only *virtually* (or *mediately*) *revealed*.[39]

A theological conclusion *improperly speaking* is reached not through an [objectively] illative discourse but, rather, through a simple explication of a truth of faith. Hence, it is {{19}} said to be *formally or immediately revealed, though implicitly*,[40] that is, vaguely (from our perspective) [*confuse quoad nos*]. Indeed, these conclusions are in the revealed truths either as a part in a whole, or as a singular in a universal, or as the implicit is in the explicit, expressed in equivalent terms. For example: Christ died for all of us; therefore, he died for me.

Four things follow from this:

1) A proposition that is deduced from at least one expressly revealed premise not through an illative discourse *but through an explanatory discourse* and that, hence, is formally-implicitly revealed (or revealed in itself [*quoad se*] and not from our perspective [*quoad nos*]) can, according to the judgment of the Church, be defined as a dogma on the authority of God who reveals what is to be believed. And, when the faithful assent to this truth as defined by the Church, they do not assent on the strength of a theological discourse but, rather, on account of Divine testimony, because the Holy Spirit is thus seen to be assisting the Church. In such a case, the discourse explains only the subject or the predicate of an expressly revealed proposition and does not produce a new notion. For example, it has been revealed that Christ is true God and true man. Now, for true humanity, a rational soul is essentially required. Therefore, Christ had a rational soul, as was defined against Apollinarius.[41]

---

[39] See John of St. Thomas in *ST* I, disp. 2, a. 4; Charles René Billuart, *Cursus theol.*, diss. prooem, a. 7.

[40] Some say, "*virtually inclusively*," but it seems better to say, "*formally implicitly*," because a new notion is not added in this theological conclusion; instead, only the notions that are in a premise of faith are explained.

On this matter, see "*Explicite et implicite*," in *Dictionnaire de théologie catholique*, vol. 5, col. 1860–1870; and in Francisco Marín-Sola, "Melchior Cano et la conclusion théologique," *Revue Thomiste* 9 (1920): 1–13, 101–115, in which it is shown that the opinion of Melchior Cano agrees with the opinion of other Thomists and differs, whatever may be commonly said, from the opinion of Vasquez and Vega. See Cano, *De locis theologicis*, 12.2, near the end.

We defend, against the modernists who diminish the value of theology, the homogeneity of theology with faith, nonetheless preserving the specific difference between both of them. Their homogeneity is not absolute, but it is relative, inasmuch as theology is in faith as in a root.

[Trans. note: The citation for the articles from Fr. Marín-Sola are a bit garbled. The original text has Jan. 1420 and p. 1914.]

[41] See John of St. Thomas, on *ST* I q. 1, disp. 2, a. 4, no. 16.

2) *Particular* propositions included in an expressly revealed universal proposition are *de fide*. For example, that Abraham contracted original sin is contained under that general proposition: "In Adam, all have sinned." This assertion is common among theologians. The reason for this fact is that these particular propositions are formally-implicitly revealed, for a universal proposition has [logical] equivalence [*aequivalet*] to all the particular propositions that are included under it.

3) To the extent that a proposition immediately deduced through discourse, properly so called, *from two premises* expressly revealed *by faith*, is obtained from them by the power of drawing a conclusion and of illation, that proposition is a theological conclusion, even though specificatively it is *de fide*. Thus, we can assent to it as much through faith as through theology. This is how the *Salmanticenses*[42] reduce to appropriate concord the discord of many theologians. Why are such propositions, considered specificatively, *de fide*? They are so because they are implicitly revealed, for nothing can be found in these conclusions that was not posited as being expressly revealed in the premises; they do not bring forth a new notion, and the connection between the predicate and the subject can be affirmed on account of formal revelation.

4) By contrast, a proposition that is deduced from one expressly revealed premise and from another natural premise *by an* [objectively] *illative discourse*—and, hence, is only *virtually connectively revealed* (namely, revealed in its adequate or inadequate cause)—is only a theological conclusion and is not *de fide*. For example: The soul of Christ always had {{20}} infused knowledge; this is the position expressed by the *Salmanticenses*,[43] who cite illustrious Thomists in support of the same opinion: Capreolus, Cajetan, Bañez, John of St. Thomas, and so forth, against Vega and Vasquez. Indeed, in this case, such discourse is, properly speaking, [objectively] illative, and a new notion is brought forward in the naturally known premise and not only an explanation of the subject or of the predicate of an expressly revealed proposition.[44] And therefore, in

---

[42] *Salmanticenses, Cursus theologicus, De fide*, disp. 1, dub. 4, no. 127.

[43] Ibid. no. 124.

[44] This is particularly clear if the major premise is natural but the minor premise is *de fide*, because the principle is expressed in the major premise. For example, man is capable of laughter; now, according to faith, Christ is a true man; therefore, Christ is capable of laughter. Similarly, in *ST* III, q. 9, a. 3, St. Thomas proves that Christ always had an *infused knowledge* because this knowledge was necessary so that his human intellect would not remain imperfect and would actually know all intelligible things to which it was in potency. This conclusion is not revealed, nor can it be defined by the Church.

However, if the major premise is *de fide* and the minor premise natural, then often the discourse can be reduced to an explanation of the major, inasmuch as the minor explains the predicate of the major or attributes it to some individual. For example, Christ constituted

the conclusion, the connection between the subject and the predicate is not reached formally in the light of formal revelation but, rather, in the light of virtual revelation. Therefore, this proposition cannot be known from the formal perspective of faith but can only be known from the formal perspective of theology. Hence it pertains *per se* to theology and not to faith. Such propositions (if they are not elsewhere revealed in an equivalent manner in Sacred Scripture or Tradition) are not defined by the Church. Nonetheless, the Church can infallibly condemn as erroneous opinions which deny such certain theological conclusions. See what is said below in chapter 5, article 2 concerning the progressive understanding of dogma.

B. In relation to God's knowledge

Since sacred theology by its very essence presupposes faith, it is said to be a *science subalternated to God's knowledge [scientia] and that of the blessed.* Indeed, as St. Thomas says in *ST* I, q. 1, a. 2: "Sacred doctrine is a science because it proceeds from principles known in the light of a superior science, namely, God's knowledge [*scientia*] and that of the blessed. Thus, just as music believes the principles given to it by arithmetic, so too does sacred doctrine believe the principles revealed to it by God." And therefore, in a. 3, ad 2, St. Thomas says that "*sacred doctrine is, as it were, a kind of impression of the divine knowledge [scientia]*" in us. Jean Baptiste Gonet says, "This is the Christian Minerva, fully armed, who proceeds not from the skull of Jove but from the mind of God; for it is, as it were, a kind of effusion from the divine knowledge [*scientia*] and a kind of emanation of the splendor of almighty God, as is said in Wisdom 7."[45]

This subalternation is the reason why sacred theology is truly and properly a science in an essential manner [*quoad substantiam*] (that is, an intellectual virtue infallibly inclining one to the truth to be known through discursive knowledge). Nonetheless, as was said above, in us wayfarers, it is an imperfect science as regards its state, due to the fact that the evidence for its principles falls short here below *in via*. It will be in a perfect state *in patria* when we see God face to face.[46]

Peter as the unfailing foundation of the teaching Church; now, the unfailing foundation of the teaching Church must be infallible; therefore, Christ gave Peter infallibility for handing on the doctrine for the salvation of all to the Church.

[45] Gonet, *Clypeus*, vol. 1, *De natura theologiae*, a. 12.

[46] See John of St. Thomas, *Cursus theologicus, In ST* I, q. 1, disp. 2, a. 5.

C. IN RELATION TO THE GIFT OF WISDOM

Nonetheless, however much it may be a wisdom proceeding from divine revelation, *sacred theology is distinct from the gift of wisdom*, as St. Thomas shows in *ST* I, q. 1, a. 6, ad 3:

> Since judgment pertains to wisdom, there are two kinds of wisdom, in accord with the two ways that one can {{21}} judge. Indeed, in one way, it happens that one judges *in an inclinational manner*, just as the person having the *habitus* of virtue rightly judges concerning those things that are to be done in accord with virtue inasmuch as he is inclined to them. Whence, in *Nicomachean Ethics* 10.5 it is said that "the virtuous man is the measure and rule of human acts." In another way, one judges *in a cognitional manner*, as someone instructed in moral science can judge concerning virtuous acts even though he may not have the virtue in question. Therefore, the first way of judging concerning divine things pertains to wisdom that is considered a gift of the Holy Spirit, in accord with what is said in 1 Cor 15: "The spiritual man judges all things," etc.; and [Ps.-]Dionysius says in *De divinis nominibus*, ch. 2, "Hierotheus was taught not only by learning but also through suffering divine things." However, the second manner of judging pertains to this doctrine on account of the fact that it is acquired through study, although its principles are acquired through revelation.

Similarly, St. Thomas says in *ST* II-II, q. 45, a. 1, ad 2: "The wisdom that is numbered among the gifts of the Holy Spirit differs from that which is an acquired intellectual virtue, for the latter *is acquired through human study*, whereas the former '*is that which descends from on high*' as is said in James 3:15." In the subsequent article, St. Thomas notes: "To have right judgment concerning divine things, *through reason's own inquiry (or according to the perfect use of reason)* pertains to that wisdom which is an intellectual virtue; however, to have right judgment concerning those things *according to a kind of connaturality* with them pertains to the wisdom that is a gift of the Holy Spirit. . . . Now, a sympathy of this kind, or a connaturality for divine things, takes place through charity, which unites us to God, as is said in 1 Cor 6:17: 'He who clings to God is one spirit [with him].'" Therefore, the gift of wisdom "presupposes charity and cannot exist alongside mortal sin," while, on the contrary, sacred theology does not necessarily presuppose charity but only has need of faith as a presupposition.

Thus, philosophical contemplation, theological contemplation, and infused contemplation that proceeds from the gift of wisdom in prayer all specifically differ from each other.

This distinction notwithstanding, there are *the mutual relations* between sacred theology and the gift of wisdom, as is obvious in great theologians in particular. St. Thomas excelled in every kind of wisdom, as much in experiential (or mystical) wisdom as in speculative wisdom. Sacred theology receives great assistance from the gift of wisdom—namely, the perfection of the very Spirit of the Lord, or the Sense of Christ, which informs and vivifies sacred theology as its soul so that it may have a kind of understanding of the mysteries and so that it may avoid errors in difficult matters, such as questions concerning predestination and grace.[47] And, in turn, sacred theology, by removing deceits of the imagination, rightly disposes one to supernatural and affective contemplation of the mysteries of the faith. Indeed, all theological conclusions are ordered to a more profound knowledge of its subject—namely, God, understood from the perspective of his intimate life. And this knowledge is all the more savory to the degree that it proceeds from love of God and not only from love of knowledge. Indeed, many love knowledge, even theological knowledge, on account of the intellectual joy they experience and because they wish to be called masters, without, however, sufficiently loving God himself, who is to be known in theology. However, the contemplative life is founded in charity—namely, in the love of God (*ST* II-II q. 180 a. 1). Hence, in order that one be declared a doctor of the Church, exceptional sanctity of life is required, nay, canonization [*sic*].

D. The relations that sacred theology has to sciences of the natural order

{{22}} Concerning this question, there are two extreme positions condemned by the Church.

Semi-rationalists, such as Günther, Frohschammer, and Hermes subordinated sacred theology to sciences of the natural order, especially the sciences of philosophy and history, as is obvious from their theses condemned in the Syllabus of Errors of Pius IX, namely: "Since human reason is on par with religion itself, theological disciplines have to be handled in the same manner as the philosophical ones.—Human reason with only historical training can, by means of its natural powers and principles, come to a true understanding of all, even the more obscure, dogmas, provided only that such dogmas be proposed to reason as its object.—Philosophy is to be treated without any regard to supernatural revelation.—As there is a distinction between the philosopher and his philosophy, he has the right and the duty to submit himself to the authority he acknowledges as legitimate; but philosophy neither can nor must submit to any authority."[48] Like-

---

[47] Thus, Vatican I, *Dei filius*, ch. 4 (Denzinger, no. 3016) says: "Nevertheless, if reason illuminated by faith inquires in an earnest, *pious*, and sober manner, it attains *by God's grace* [*Deo dante*] a certain understanding of the mysteries."

[48] Pius IX, *Syllabus of Errors*, nos. 8, 9, 14, and 10 (Denzinger, nos. 2908, 2909, 2914, 1910).

wise, the following thesis of the semi-rationalists was condemned by the [First] Vatican Council as a heresy: "As science progresses, at times, a sense is to be given to dogmas proposed by the Church different from the one that the Church has understood and understands."[49] Therefore, semi-rationalism must be rejected, not only theoretically but also in practice (e.g., in the manner of judging the books of semi-rationalists). A number of more recent thinkers, drawing more or less close to modernism, do not sufficiently heed this [condemnation].[50]

On the other hand, *fideists* such as Bautain and Bonnetty do not acknowledge well enough the usefulness of philosophy for theology. Hence, the Sacred Congregation of the Index declared against them: "The method that St. Thomas and St. Bonaventure and other Scholastics after them used does not lead to rationalism, nor has it been the reason why philosophy in today's schools tends toward naturalism and pantheism."[51]

On the basis of these condemnations, we thus know that *philosophy must be distinct but not separated from sacred theology*, just as the State is distinct but not separated from the Church.

However, *Catholic theologians* avoid these two aforementioned, opposed excesses that diminish the dignity of sacred theology in different ways.[52] They commonly teach *sacred theology has no subalternation to natural sciences and is more certain than they are; however, it does make use of them as inferiors.*

In fact, the science that is subalternated to God's knowledge [*scientia Dei*] is *nobler* than all the natural sciences, both with regard to its certitude and with regard to the dignity of its subject matter, as St. Thomas says in

---

[49] [First] Vatican Council, *Dei filius*, can. 4.2 (Denzinger, no. 3043).

[50] Pius X, *Pascendi*, no. 18 (Old Denzinger, no. 2086) as well as the formula of the anti-modernist oath, in the *Motu proprio, Sacrorum antistitum*, Sept. 1, 1910.

   Against this, Cardinal Billot said, "This represents the laicization of the divine things themselves. It is *the laicization of exegesis*, which is reduced to a method of interpreting sacred texts solely according to the rules which are now customarily applied to all human texts, with no other view than that which is expressed by the movement of contemporary thought in the philosophical order. It likewise represents *the laicization of theology*, which no longer will be what St. Anselm defined as faith seeking understanding: the understanding of the mysteries of God, of their supernatural beauties, and of their admirable meaning. Instead, it will become nothing more nor anything less than the history of systems, the counting of opinions, the nomenclature of theories imagined by man in connection with them. In brief, it will become *the study of man's thought with regard to the truth of God*—which is yet another manner of substituting man for God and of setting man in the place of God. It represents the laicization of Christian morality, etc. . . . " (*Eloge du Card. Pie*).

[51] Decree of the Sacred Congregation of the Index, June 11, 1855 (Denzinger, no. 2814).

[52] Frequently, as we will often say in this work, truth appears as being at once a *mean* and a *peak* between two opposed, extreme errors. It is, as it were, the mountain peak above the wandering paths of error, which proceeds from an inferior and imperfect knowledge of things.

ST I, q. 1, a. 5: *"With regard to certitude,* indeed, {{23}} for other sciences have certitude from the light of human reason, which can err, whereas this science has certitude from the light of divine knowledge, which cannot be deceived. *So too with regard to the dignity of the subject matter,* for this science is principally concerned with those things that, through their sublimity, transcend reason, whereas other sciences consider only those things that fall under reason." However, if one were to object that theology is less certain because it does not have evidence of its principles, the Holy Doctor responds: *"Nothing prohibits that which is more certain in itself from being less certain from our perspective"*[53] on account of the weakness of our intellect, "which is related to the most manifest things of nature in a way that is akin to how the eye of the owl is related to the light of the sun," as is said in *Metaphysics* 2.1.

And the Thomists commonly teach that, on account of its formal motive, theology is *more certain* than any given natural science not only *of itself* but also *in us* (for it produces its formal effect in us), even though it is *less certain from our perspective* on account of the weakness of our intellect, whose connatural mode is not as proportioned to the object of theology as it is to the object of the natural sciences. For example, a theological conclusion concerning Christ's inability to sin is more certain in itself and in us than is the law of universal attraction, but from our perspective, we come to know it with greater difficulty. Thus, in the student receiving and understanding a metaphysical proposition such as "every agent acts on account of an end," this metaphysically certain proposition is more certain in itself and also in the student than that which is only physically certain through sensation; however, from the perspective of the weak subject in which this proposition is found, it is less certain than sensation. This student perhaps does not know how to respond to objections against finality. Likewise, St. Paul says grace and charity are nobler and firmer than nature and the natural virtues: "However, we have this treasure in earthen vessels, that the excellency may be of the power of God and not of us" (2 Cor 4:7, DR). Thus, sacred theology is more certain in itself and in us than the natural sciences; however, we have it in earthen vessels—namely, in a weak intellect whose connatural mode of knowing is more proportioned to sensible and rational things than to supernatural ones.

Moreover, *sacred theology makes use of the natural sciences,* and this use is explained by St. Thomas in *ST* I, q. 1, a. 5, ad 2:

> This science can receive something from philosophical disciplines, not that it needs them of necessity, but, rather, receives something from them in order to manifest more clearly those things that are

---

[53] *ST* I, q. 1, a. 5.

handed on in this science. For it does not take its principles from the other sciences but, rather, immediately from God through revelation. And therefore, it does not receive something from the other sciences as though from superiors, but, instead, *makes use of them as inferiors* and handmaidens, just as the master craft makes use of those that minister under it and as the civic order makes use of the military.

Hence, sacred theology in no way is subordinated to the lower sciences as optics is to geometry, but, on the contrary, sacred theology *makes use* of them according to the proper meaning of the word "use." That is, it subordinates them to its own end. For we only speak of "using" with regard to the way a superior is related to an inferior. But this subordination does not diminish the dignity of the natural sciences. On the contrary, what is nobler for them than to serve supernatural truth? For example, what is nobler for Aristotle's philosophy than for it to serve in explaining the Word of God? Similarly, metaphysics makes use of physics and accepts from it, indeed, not its principles but, rather, the matter to be understood under the light of its own principles. Nay, as St. Thomas notes in the same place:

> The fact that theology thus makes {{24}} use of the philosophical sciences is not on account of a defect and insufficiency in it but, rather, is on account of a defect in our intellect, which is led more easily from those things that are known through natural reason (from which the other sciences proceed) to those things that are above reason, which are handed on in this science.

So too, the teacher of philosophy makes use of examples in order to explain a metaphysical principle (for example, the principle of causality). However, this indeed is not on account of some kind of shortcoming in a self- [*per se*] evident principle but, rather, is on account of some shortcoming in his students' intellects—namely, so that they may perceive more clearly in these examples the meaning of the subject and the predicate of the principle to be accepted.

Hence, before sacred theology makes use of a given natural proposition that it accepts from a given natural science, *it judges* that proposition under the light of revelation. Indeed, as St. Thomas says in *ST* I, q. 1, a. 6, ad 2: "It does not fall to it to prove the principles of the other sciences but, rather, only to judge concerning them, for whatever in other sciences is found to contradict the truth of this science is wholly condemned as false."[54] For it is the privilege of wisdom to make use not only of its own principles but also those of the other sciences and to judge concerning them.[55] Therefore, "It depends on them as subjected to a superior light and as corrected and approved by it, which means that one formally depends only on the superior and sapiential light," as John of St. Thomas notes.[56] Hence, when sacred theology takes up a natural premise so as to infer its conclusions, such a *natural premise* does not concur as the principal cause of assent and as providing the formal reason but, rather, concurs *ministerially*, as *elevated*, and *approved* by a supernatural principle.[57] Thus, a theological conclusion is more certain than a natural proposition (for the instrument, in virtue of the higher cause, produces an effect exceeding the instrument's own power). However, it is less certain than a *de fide* premise, for such a conclusion involves the lower degree of certitude involved in the natural proposition that is instrumentally used.[58]

These are the principle relations that sacred theology has with faith, God's knowledge, the gift of wisdom, and the natural sciences.

§6. Whether the Aforementioned Notion of Theology Is Found, at Least Implicitly, in Sacred Scripture and in the Councils

Now, in the rational defense of the faith, we do not argue from the Councils

---

[54] But in this the theologian must proceed cautiously, prudently, and humbly as the minister of divine truth, and not tenaciously adhere to his own erroneous prejudices. For, as the [First] Vatican Council states in *Dei filius*, ch. 4: "The deceptive appearance of such a contradiction is mainly due to the fact that either the *dogmas of faith have not been understood and expounded according to the mind of the Church* or *fanciful conjectures are taken for verdicts of reason*" (Denzinger, no. 3017).

[55] See *ST* I–II, q. 57, a. 2, ad 1.

[56] See John of St. Thomas, *Cursus theologicus, In ST* I, q. 1, disp. 2, a. 6, no. 7.

[57] See ibid. For the instrument not only *is applied* in order for the act to be performed [*ad agendum*] but *is elevated* and applied simultaneously. Thus, in moving the lyre, the musician elevates and animates it.

[58] [Trans. note: For explanatory reasons, I have slightly expanded the text, "sic intelligitur eam sequi, peiorem partem." This seems to come from a rule of Aristotelian modal logic: "Peiorem sequitur semper conclusio partem; the conclusion always follows the weaker part [of the argument]." It seems to have originated in a dictum by Theophrastus (ca. 371–287 BC). For some discussion and bibliography, see Nicholas Rescher, "Three Post-Aristotelian Concepts of Syllogistic Logic," in *Essays in Philosophical Analysis* (Pittsburgh: University of Pittsburgh Press, 1969), 64; Rescher, *On Rules and Principles* (Berlin: Walter de Gruyter, 2010), 133; Charles A. Dubray, *Introduction to Philosophy: A Textbook for Colleges and High School Students* (New York: Longmans, Green, and Co., 1912), 229–230; Kevin L. Flannery, *Ways into the Logic of Alexander of Aphrodisias* (Leiden: Brill, 1995), 54.]

that propose revelation. However, the doctrine of the Councils must be set forth here, for apologetics must defend religious faith precisely as it is conceived of by the Catholic Church, not as it is conceived of by heretics.

A. *With regard to the Councils and declarations of the Church*, see Denzinger, *Enchiridion definitionum*, 10th edition, Systematic Index I and II h ("The mutual relationship between revelation and reason").[59]

Reason explains, protects, and defends revealed truths (nos. 2775ff, 2814, and 3019). *But revelation frees reason from errors, illuminates it, and confirms it* (nos. 3019 and 3027). It fosters the certitude and purity {{25}} of natural knowledge (no. 3005); it is the infallible guide of philosophy (nos. 2829 and 2877) and its negative norm (no. 2914). Not only the philosopher but also philosophy itself is placed under the magisterium of faith (nos. 2858, 2878, 2910; 3476, 3486ff) and it ought to be the handmaid of theology (nos. 824ff, 2829, 2910, 3487). Hence, errors of reason are rightly and usefully proscribed by the Church (nos. 2858ff, 2911, 3018, 2093 (old)), to whose judgment it must acquiesce even with regard to things that have not yet been defined, (no. 2880).

Theology must be treated in a different manner than natural science (nos. 824ff, 1642 (old), 28829, 1666 (old), 2853ff, 2877, 2908, 3015, 3028, 2104 (old)). The method and principles of scholastic theology are not to be rejected (nos. 2876, 2913). All speculation concerning revealed truth must rest upon the doctrine of the Church and of the Fathers (nos. 625, 2732, 2738, 2830, 2086 (old)). And even in one's words, the sound form [of expression] is to be retained and the commonly received terminology preserved (nos. 791ff, 2831, 3020).

The written wellspring of revelation are the *canonical books of both Testaments* (nos. 1501). These books are to be received in full, with all their parts, as holy and canonical as though from God, who is the Author of both Testaments, inspired and as such handed on to the Church (nos. 1502, 3006) . . . and are to be interpreted in accord with the unanimous consent of the Fathers and the sense of the Church, according to sound exegetical principles (nos. 1506 . . . 3286 . . . 3397 . . .).

The other wellspring of revelation is *ecclesiastical tradition* (nos. 265, 352, 212 old, 609, 1501, 1863, 3011). The authority of the Fathers in matters of faith and morals is the highest (nos. 517 . . . 3007, 2083), as well as the commonly held doctrines of the theologians (nos. 1179, 2814, 2830, 2876). Modern authors are not to be preferred heedlessly (no. 2042). The Church's custom is the norm of believing (nos. 247, 863). "The law of praying establishes the law of believing" (no. 246).

The direction of theological study belongs to the functions of the ecclesiastical jurisdiction (nos. 824, 1666 old . . . 2933, 2946, 3121ff).

Among all these testimonies, it suffices to cite the text of the [First]

---

[59] [Trans. note: No such heading is found in this section of the systematic index in the current edition. But where possible, all numbers are taken from the 43rd edition.]

Vatican Council in which a kind of definition of sacred theology is found:

> Nevertheless, if reason illumined by faith inquires in an earnest, pious, and sober manner, it attains by God's grace a certain understanding of the mysteries, which is most fruitful, both from the analogy with the objects of its natural knowledge and from the connection of these mysteries with one another and with man's ultimate end. But it never becomes capable of understanding them in the way it does truths that constitute its proper object. For divine mysteries by their very nature so exceed the created intellect that, even when they have been communicated in revelation and received by faith, they remain covered by the veil of faith itself and shrouded, as it were, in darkness as long as in this mortal life "we are away from the Lord; for we walk by faith, not by sight." . . .

> Not only can there be no conflict between faith and reason, they also support each other since right reason demonstrates the foundation of faith and, illumined by its light, pursues the science of divine things, while faith frees and protects reason from errors and provides it with manifold insights. . . .

> Nor does the Church in any way forbid that these sciences, each in its own domain, should make use of their own principles and of the method proper to them. While, however, acknowledging this just freedom, she seriously warns lest they fall into error by going contrary to the divine doctrine or, stepping beyond their own limits, enter into the sphere of faith and create confusion.[60]

---

[60] [First] Vatican Council, *Dei filius*, ch. 4 (Denzinger, nos. 3016, 3019). Also see the letter concerning the terminology and theological tradition to be preserved, "Tacti dolore" of Gregory IX to the Parisian theologians, July 7, 1228 (Denzinger, no. 824). The brief *Eximiam tuam* of Pius IX (June 15, 1857) to the Archbishop of Cologne against Günther declared, "Human reason and philosophy, which in religious matters should not dominate but rather remain completely subservient" (Denzinger, no. 2829). Likewise, see the section of Pius IX's Syllabus of Errors against semi-rationalism [*rationalismum moderatum*]: "Theological disciplines have to be handled in the same manner as the philosophical ones.—Philosophy neither can nor must submit to any authority.—The Method and principles according to which the ancient Scholastic Doctors treated theology are by no means suited to the necessities of our times and to the progress of the sciences.—Philosophy is to be treated without any regard to supernatural revelation" (Denzinger, nos. 2908, 2910, 2913, 2914). Finally, see nos. 3486, 2086 (old), and 2104 (old) from Pius X's encyclical *Pascendi* against the errors of the modernists, who contend "That science is to be entirely independent of faith . . . that faith must be subject

{{26}} B. *However, throughout Sacred Scripture* we find express affirmation of the essential distinction between natural knowledge concerning God and supernatural knowledge concerning the divine mysteries. This distinction can be reduced to four heads: (a) as regards the object of knowledge; (b) as regards its motive; (c) as regards the possibility or ease [*facilitatem*] of knowledge; (d) as regards the effects of knowledge.

(a) *The object* of natural knowledge concerning God is what is knowable [about him] from creatures. As St. Paul writes to the Romans: "Because that which is known of God is manifest in them (namely, the Gentiles). For God hath manifested it unto them. For the invisible things of him, from the creation of the world, are clearly seen, being understood by the things that are made; his eternal power also, and divinity: so that they are inexcusable. Because that, when they knew God, they have not glorified him as God, or given thanks; but became vain in their thoughts, and their foolish heart was darkened" (Rom 1:19–21, DR).

By contrast, the object of supernatural knowledge concerning God is the intimate life of God (or the Deity considered from the formal perspective of the Deity [*sub ratione Deitatis*]), for "no man hath seen God at any time: the only begotten Son who is in the bosom of the Father, he hath declared him" (John 1:18, DR). "The mystery which hath been hidden from ages and generations, but now is manifested . . ." (Col 1:26). Hence, as the [First] Vatican Council says,[61] the Apostle, who testifies that God is known "through those things that have been made," nonetheless, in speaking concerning the grace and truth that is given through Jesus, pronounces: "But we speak the wisdom of God in a mystery, a wisdom which is hidden, which God ordained before the world, unto our glory: which none of the princes of this world knew. . . . But to us God hath revealed them by his Spirit. For

---

to science. . . . In the same way, they draw their distinctions between theological and pastoral exegesis and scientific and historical exegesis" (nos. 7 and 18, official translation).

However, as regards the common doctrines of theologians, Pius IX wrote in his letter *Tuas libenter* to the Archbishop of Munich-Freising (December 21, 1863): "Nor are We unaware that in Germany also there prevailed a false opinion *against the old school* and against the teaching of those eminent Doctors whom the universal Church venerates because of their admirable wisdom and sanctity of life. By this false opinion, the authority of the Church herself is called into doubt, especially since the Church herself not only, through so many continuous centuries, has permitted that theological science be cultivated according to the method of these same Doctors and according to the principles established by the *common consent of all Catholic schools*, but she [the Church] also very often extolled their theological doctrine with the highest praises and emphatically recommended it as a most strong rampart of the faith and a formidable weapon against its enemies" (Denzinger, no. 2876).

61 *Dei filius*, ch. 4 (Denzinger, no. 3015).

the Spirit searcheth all things, yea, the deep things of God, *profunda Dei*, τα βάθη του Θεού. For what man knoweth the things of a man, but the spirit of a man that is in him? So the things also that are of God, no man knoweth, but the Spirit of God" (1 Cor 2:7–11, DR). Natural knowledge concerning God in the mirror of creatures remains external; only supernatural knowledge [of him] is an utterly intimate form of knowledge of him.

{{27}} (b) *The motive* or light of natural knowledge concerning God is the light of reason, which reasons from those things that are made to the Creator: "For the invisible things of him from the creation of the world are clearly seen, being understood by the things that are made" (Rom 1:20, DR).

Whereas, by contrast, the motive of supernatural knowledge concerning God is divine revelation and not the discourse of natural reason. Thus, it is said, "So the things also that are of God, no man knoweth, but the Spirit of God. . . . But to us God hath revealed (ἀπεκάλυψεν) them by his Spirit" (1 Cor 2:11, 10, DR). And the Unbegotten One himself bore witness to the Father, "Because He has hidden these things from the wise and from the prudent and has revealed them to these little ones" (Matt 11:25). Therefore, St. Paul says in 1 Corinthians 2:4–5 (DR): "My speech and my preaching was not in the persuasive words of human wisdom but in shewing of the Spirit and power: that your faith might not stand on the wisdom of men, but on the power of God."

(c) *With regard to its possibility*, natural knowledge concerning the existence of God and his primary attributes is not only possible but, moreover, is easy for all; hence, it is said concerning the Gentiles: "That they are inexcusable. Because that, when they knew God, they have not glorified him as God or given thanks: but became vain in their thoughts" (Rom 1:20–21, DR).

By contrast, supernatural knowledge is absolutely inaccessible to the natural powers of a created intellect, and divine faith is a gift from God. Hence, it is said concerning the hidden wisdom of God: "Which none of the princes of this world knew" (1 Cor 2:8, DR); "seeing that in the wisdom of God, the world, by wisdom, knew not God, it pleased God, by the foolishness of our preaching, to save them that believe" (1 Cor 1:21, DR). "For we walk by faith and not by sight" (2 Cor 5:7, DR),[62] "bringing into captivity every understanding unto the obedience of Christ" (2 Cor 10:5, DR).

(d) *Finally, with regard to the effect of knowledge*, natural knowledge, even about God, of itself only produces the natural man, whom the Apostle

---

[62] [Trans. note: Fr. Garrigou-Lagrange incorrectly has Hebr 11:1.]

calls the "sensual [*animalis*] man, ψυχικός ἄνθρωπος": "But the sensual man perceiveth not these things that are of the Spirit of God. For it is foolishness to him: and he cannot understand [it]" (1 Cor 2:14, DR). "Greeks seek after wisdom. But we preach Christ crucified: unto the Jews indeed a stumbling block, and unto the Gentiles foolishness" (1 Cor 1:22–23, DR). Thus, the Deists highly praised the speculations of Plato and Aristotle concerning God but rejected the supernatural mysteries as fables.

By contrast, the spiritual man, πνευματικός ἄνθρωπος, is brought into existence [*efficitur*] through supernatural knowledge concerning God, in accord with the words of St. Paul:

> Now we have received not the spirit of this world, but the Spirit that is of God: that we may know the things that are given us from God. Which things also we speak: not in the learned words of human wisdom, but in the doctrine of the Spirit, comparing spiritual things with spiritual. But the sensual man perceiveth not these things that are of the Spirit of God. . . . But the spiritual man judgeth all things: and he himself is judged of no man. For who hath known the mind of the Lord, that he may instruct him? But we have the mind of Christ. (1 Cor 2:12–16, DR)

All these points are gathered together in this declaration of the [First] Vatican Council:

> The perpetual common belief of the Catholic Church has held and holds also this: there is a *twofold order of knowledge*, distinct not only in its *principle* but also in its *object*; in its principle, because in the one we know by natural reason, in the other by divine faith; in its object, because {{28}} apart from what natural reason can attain, there are proposed to our belief *mysteries* that are hidden in God that can never be known unless they are revealed by God.[63]

These points suffice as regards the notion of sacred theology. See the objections in the text of St. Thomas in *ST* I, q. 1; likewise, see the commentators on this text.

---

[63] *Dei filius*, ch. 4 (Denzinger, no. 3015). Likewise, see the canon 4 (Denzinger, no. 3041ff).

Art. 2: The Division and Unity of Sacred Theology

§1. Division of Sacred Theology

The distribution of a whole through its parts follows upon the definition of the whole. Hence, the division of sacred theology is taken from its definition. Now, as we have said, it is formally defined as being that science which is concerned with God, considered from the formal perspective of the Deity, proceeding from revelation, and it is defined integrally: the science that defends the principles of faith against those denying them, seeks a kind of understanding concerning these principles, and deduces conclusions therefrom. From this definition follows the commonly admitted division:

We will see later the place to be assigned to fundamental theology. There, we will say that it is the general and defensive part of positive theology as well as of systematic dogmatic theology.

Right now, we must explain what these various parts of theology are in particular. On this basis, it will be quite clear that they are not different sciences but instead are *integral parts* of sacred theology, inasmuch as all of them are required for its perfection. Indeed, presupposing revelation and the fact that it has been infallibly proposed, we still must defend the principles of faith by showing that those things are in the deposit of faith. This is the work of *positive theology*, which uncovers the individual truths to be believed from the sources of revelation. Then, having gathered together the body of sacred doctrine concerning the mysteries of the faith, theology seeks a kind of understanding of them and also deduces theological conclusions from them. This is the work of *systematic (or scholastic) theology*.

A. **Positive theology** presupposes revelation and faith concerning the Church's infallible magisterium, as well as concerning the inspiration of Sacred Scripture. It performs its scientific work by determining how this or that proposition is contained in the deposit of Revelation or how it falls under the Church's own infallibility.

This positive theology is subdivided into three parts: (1) *biblical theology*, (2) *patristic theology*, and (3) *symbolic [/ creedal] theology*.

Biblical theology critically determines as much as is possible the propositions {{29}} that can be gathered from the literal sense of the various books of Sacred Scripture. It is above all an ordered collection of dogmatic texts, as well as the exegesis and defense of them, as is obvious in many gleanings [*spicilegiis*] and in works of biblical theology concerning each Testament.[64]

Patristic theology sets forth the doctrine of the Fathers, whose authority in matters of faith and morals is of the greatest importance, and whose unanimous consent shows the theologian that an argument is certain.[65] The *Enchiridion Patristicum* by Fr. Roüet de Journel, S.J., is a compendium of this part of theology.

Symbolic[66] theology establishes a critical assessment of the symbols of the faith, of the definitions and declarations of the Church concerning matters of faith and morals, and likewise, of propositions which have been condemned (along with their various notes—namely, heretical, erroneous, rash, scandalous, and so forth). Thus, Denzinger's *Enchiridion Symbolorum definitionum et declarationum de rebus fidei et morum* is, as it were, a synopsis of the collections of the Sacred Councils, among which we must cite the "new and most full collection" (*Sacrorum conciliorum nova et amplissima collectio*) begun by Giovanni Domenico Mansi.

The Fathers cultivated this positive theology against the heretics rising up in their times—for example: St. Irenaeus against the Gnostics, St. Athanasius against the Arians, St. Cyril of Alexandria against the Nestorians, and so forth. Against the Protestants, a good number of theologians have exposited this part of theology as well, among whom Petavius (Denis

---

[64] For example, see the three-volume work of Franciscus Ceuppens, *Theologia biblica* (Rome, 1938–1939).

    In a second way and legitimately, after the establishment of systematic theology as well, biblical theology also can be conceived as a theological reflection upon the sacred source—that is, upon the Word of God contained in Sacred Scripture. Thus, St. Thomas, in his commentaries on the Book of John and upon the Letters of St. Paul sets forth how heresies have defiled the sacred page, what the Fathers said, and finally what is the fullness of the dogmatic sense of these texts composed under the inspiration of the Holy Spirit.

[65] See Denzinger, nos. 517, 3007.

[66] [Trans. note: On multiple occasions, I considered translating this as "creedal" or something similar. However, given that this expression can be found, at times, in scholastic texts, I have retained the somewhat awkward and ambiguous "symbolic," taken from the Greek "Symbolon."]

Pétau, S.J., 1583–1652) and Thomassinus (Louis Tomassin, C.O., 1619–1695) are preeminent.

It must be noted that because biblical theology is truly theology, like patristic theology, and therefore presupposes faith, it does not make use of rational hermeneutics or rational heuristics that consider Sacred Scripture as being a book written by a human author but, [rather], makes use of a Christian and Catholic heuristic that accepts Sacred Scripture as an inspired book, handed on to the Catholic Church to be cared for and exposited.[67]

Positive theology is not, properly speaking, history but instead is theology. It does indeed *make use of history*, but it is not subordinated to it—just as scholastic theology makes use of metaphysics, [philosophical] psychology, and ethics as inferior sciences, judging them, as was said above, under the light of revelation. This is the privilege of wisdom.[68] Hence, positive theology must not make use of history in the way that we find it used in the writings of rationalists[69] but, rather, must use history as do those who acknowledge the historical signs[70] of revelation and of the Church's infallibility.[71]

---

[67] See Vincenz Zapletal, *Hermenutica Biblica* (Freiburg, 1908), whose heuristic is divided into rational, Christian, and Catholic heuristic. Nevertheless, there is no truly Christian heuristic which is not, at the same time, Catholic, for Christianity is not true unless it is Catholic, whatever the Protestants may say. Hence, in the *formula of the anti-modernist oath* one reads: "Likewise, I reject that manner of judging and interpreting Sacred Scripture that, departing from the Church's tradition, the analogy of faith, and the norms of the Apostolic See, adheres to the fabrications of the *rationalists*, embracing, rashly and without restraint, textual criticism as the sole and supreme rule."

[68] *ST* I, q. 1, a. 6, ad 2.

[69] See Pius X, *Pascendi*, no. 9 (Denzinger, 3479).

[70] [Trans. note: Reading *historia signa* as *historica signa*.]

[71] Hence, in the *formula of the anti-modernist oath* we find: "Furthermore, I reject the opinion of those who hold that it is necessary for the teacher of the discipline of theological history to be handed on, or for the person writing upon the same things, first to set aside any *preconceived opinion* whether about the supernatural origin of Catholic tradition or regarding the divinely promised aid in the perpetual preservation of every revealed truth whatsoever; thence, the writings of the Fathers must be interpreted solely through the principles of science, excluding any sacred authority whatsoever, indeed, with the same freedom of judgment as that by which any profane record is customarily investigated." For this reason, we can see well that *the history of the Church and the history of dogmas essentially [per se] and formally cannot be known or written except by a Catholic.* He who lacks infused faith knows the supernatural life of the Church and her doctrine only *in a material manner*—namely, from the perspective of material signs, not from the perspective of what is formally signified. Thus, he who does not have an ear for music only materially hears one of Beethoven's symphonies. Indeed, he perceives all the sounds; however, he does not perceive the form of the symphony. See what must be said below concerning the intelligibility of the mysteries of faith and concerning the formal effect of infused faith.

{{30}} B. *Systematic (or scholastic) theology* is the part of theology that speculatively defends the principles of faith against those who deny them by resolving the objections registered against the possibility of the mysteries. It also seeks a kind of understanding about these mysteries by way of analogy with natural things and by considering how the mysteries are themselves interconnected. Finally, it deduces theological conclusions from these mysteries. In this way, the doctrinal edifice concerning matters of faith and morals comes to be fully constructed. This part of theology is altogether necessary, for the various propositions of the faith may indeed have been collected together, but when they are so collected, they have not yet been ordered. Without such ordering, theology would propose those matters that pertain to the intimate nature of God (those that pertain to the loftiest mystery of the Trinity) as though they were on equal footing with those pertaining to the sacrament of matrimony or of penance. It is the mark of the wise man to order, and *sacred theology, inasmuch as it is wisdom, must order all things that are to be believed and are connected with faith under those things that are essentially and primarily concerned with God considered from the formal perspective of the Deity.* Thus, the principle of the whole ordering (or systematization)[72] of theology is the true revealed notion of God himself, which is like the sun that illuminates sacred theology, with the various notions concerning him being akin to the rays of this sun. *Hence, among various theological systems, such as Thomism, Scotism, and Molinism, that system is loftiest which takes as the principle of the whole doctrinal ordering the highest and truest notion of God* so that it judges all other questions in accord with it, not that system which considers all things in relation to a given particular problem, such as, for example, the problem of human freedom. Finally, among the loftier and more universal systems, the system that draws more closely to the perfection of theological science is that which is essentially and primarily concerned with *God in himself* (or the intimate mystery of the Supreme *Being*), as we find in St. Thomas, and not only *God relative to us*, as the [supreme] *Good* and our ultimate end, as we find in Augustinians and Scotus.[73]

This *systematic* (or *scholastic*) *theology* is subdivided into *dogmatic* and *moral theology.* Dogmatic theology is concerned with things to be believed concerning God, the divine attributes, the Trinity, that which pertains to the mysteries of Creation, the Incarnation, the Redemption, and the sac-

---

[72] [Trans. note: He explicitly translates *ordinationis* to the French *systématisation.*]

[73] See Ambroise Gardeil, *Le donné révélé et la théologie* (Paris: Lecoffre, 1910), 246–279 ("Theological science; theological systems"). See *ST* I, 1. 5, a. 2, ad 1: *Being,* according to its notion is, simply speaking, prior to *good.*

raments, which do not tend directly toward praxis but, rather, draw us to contemplation of these mysteries, thereby bringing the mind to its rest.[74] Moral theology, however, is concerned with matters pertaining to morals—namely, human acts, laws, grace, the virtues, the gifts of the Holy Spirit, sins, and the Christian life, both active and contemplative.[75] {{31}} All of these matters are treated as ordered to God, considering Him from the formal aspect of the Deity, and they are considered by moral theology, properly speaking, in themselves and systematically.

However, casuistic theology, like ascetic and mystical theology, are all applications of moral theology. *Casuistic* theology is the application of moral theology to the resolution of cases of conscience.[76] *Ascetic* theology teaches the way of Christian perfection to beginners and proficients. That is, it proposes the practical motives and means for the active purification from sin and progress in the virtues. *Mystical* theology[77] teaches how one is to arrive at the unitive life and to make progress therein, especially through passive purification and under the influence of the gifts of the Holy Spirit. It also treats, secondarily, of extraordinary graces that frequently accompany the loftiest kinds of contemplative union. Thus, leading one to the perfection of charity and of contemplation of the mysteries, moral theology attains at

---

[74] Thus, see St. Thomas in *ST* I and III. [Trans. note: It is interesting to note, however, that at the time of the writing of *De revelatione*, it was normal to include treatment of the sacraments in moral theology as well, seeing the topic of the sacraments as being partly speculative and partly practical in content, as is evidenced, for example in the once well-known manuals of Benoît-Marie Merkelbach and Dominic Prümmer. Likewise, the master sacramental theologian (and student of Fr. Garrigou-Lagrange) Emmanuel Doronzo notes the practical and speculative importance of the treatise on the sacraments. See Emmanuel Doronzo, *De sacramentis in genere* (Milwaukee: Bruce, 1946), xvi. However, Doronzo's own methodology makes it clear that the sacraments must also be considered wholly *in themselves*. Indeed, his many lengthy volumes show that this intrinsic consideration by itself is no small task.]

[75] Thus, see St. Thomas in the whole of *ST* II.

[Trans. note: For some reason, he leaves out the treatise on beatitude, though one is well aware from reading his commentary on this section of the *Summa theologiae* that he holds it as being pivotally important to moral theology.]

[76] Some modern manuals of moral theology contain almost nothing other than casuistic theology, and in them moral theology appears like a science of grave and minor sins to be avoided rather than a science concerning virtues to be perfected. Likewise, many modern treatises of ascetic theology and mystical theology do not proceed fully enough from the rightful foundation of moral theology concerning the nature and progress of the infused virtues and of the gifts of the Holy Spirit. Thus, they come to be constructed in too empirical a fashion and are lacking in doctrinal value. Ultimately, these defects lead to the diminution of the notion of the eminent unity of sacred theology.

[77] This mystical theology which is acquired through human study is called speculative, in contrast to the experiential wisdom that is the infused gift of the Holy Spirit.

its end the object of dogmatic theology and the marrow of Sacred Scripture and Tradition—that is, the Word of God, from whom all theology proceeds. And so we see how the principle and the end coincide, bringing the circle of sacred doctrine to its perfection.

§2. *The Unity of Sacred Theology*

Notwithstanding the aforementioned division into positive and systematic theology (the latter itself being divided into dogmatic and moral theology), *sacred theology remains one single science with a specific unity, as a lowest species* [i.e., not as an intermediate genus-species that would be susceptible to further specific division].

A. ***This is proven*** by St. Thomas in *ST* I, q. 1, a. 3 on the basis of the unity of sacred theology's formal object:

> For the unity of a power and of a *habitus* must be considered in accord with its object (not materially, indeed, but rather, according to the formal notion of the object). For example, man, donkey, and stone agree in one formal notion of being colored, which is the object of sight. Therefore, since sacred doctrine considers any given thing from the perspective of what is divinely revealed, according to what we have said, *all things whatsoever that are divinely revealable agree in the one formal character* [ratione formali] *of the object of this science*. And therefore, they are included under sacred doctrine as under one science.[78]

Here we have the unity of its formal object *quo*—namely, virtual revelation.

In the response to the first objection in the same article, St. Thomas also notes the unity of the science from the perspective of the formal object *quod*, which is what is formally considered in that science [*ex parte obiecti quod formaliter consideratur*]: "Sacred doctrine does not determine matters concerning God and concerning creatures in the same way. Rather, it primarily determines matters concerning God and determines those concerning creatures only inasmuch as they are referred to God as their principle and end. Whence the unity of the science is not obstructed [by these two kinds of objects]."

B. *Confirmation*. This unity is not destroyed through the distinction between *positive* theology and *systematic* theology, because these two parts are related as scientific

---

[78] See also John of St. Thomas, *Cursus theologicus, In ST* I, q. 1, disp. 2, a. 7.

matter and scientific form. Indeed, positive theology, as it were, materially collects all the revealed matters that are the material object[s] of sacred doctrine. However, systematic theology formally orders all revealed matters according to their relation to God, considered {{32}} from the perspective of the Deity, which is the formally considered object and principle for the ordering of the entire edifice of theological doctrine.

C. *Another confirmation*. Nor is the unity of theology destroyed through its division into *dogmatic* and *moral* theology, for as St. Thomas says in *ST* I, q. 1, a. 4:

> Sacred doctrine extends itself as one [science] to those things that belong to different philosophical sciences on account of the formal notion that it heeds in those various things, namely, *inasmuch as they are knowable by the divine light*. Thus, although in the philosophical sciences some are speculative and others practical, nevertheless sacred doctrine embraces both under itself, just as by the same knowledge [*scientia*] God knows Himself and the things that He brings about. However, sacred doctrine is more speculative than practical because it is more principally concerned with divine matters than with human acts, about which it is concerned inasmuch as through them man is ordered to perfect knowledge of God, wherein man finds his eternal beatitude.

Hence, the Thomists commonly teach that *theology is formally-eminently speculative and practical*, although it is more speculative in character.[79] They hold this position in contrast to a number of more recent authors who hold that theology is partly speculative and partly practical according to different partial *habitus* [pl.], which they believe are brought together into a composition making up the whole of theology.

This opinion expressed by more recent authors does not acknowledge well enough the eminence of theology: *Those things that are dispersed in inferior things are united in superior ones*, as [Ps.-]Dionysius teaches. Hence, St. Thomas says in *ST* I, q. 1, a. 3, ad 2:

> Nothing forbids inferior powers or *habitus* from being diversified concerning those matters that in general fall under one superior power or *habitus*, for the superior or *habitus* considers the object from a more universal formal perspective—just as the object of the common sense (or, the internal senses) is a sensible that embraces under itself the visible and the audible. Whence, since the common sense is one power, it extends to all the objects of the five senses. And similarly, sacred doctrine, remaining indeed as one doctrine, can consider those things that are treated in the various philosophical sciences from one formal perspective, namely inasmuch as they are *divinely revealable*, so that sacred doctrine is a kind of impression of the divine knowledge

---

[79] See Cajetan, *In ST* I, q. 1, a. 4. Likewise, John of St. Thomas, Gonet, and other Thomists.

[*scientia*], which is one and simple, yet extending to all things.

This also is evident from the formal object *quod* considered in sacred theology—namely, God considered from the formal perspective of the Deity—for in its eminence, *the Deity* reduces to identity the formal notion of *being* that metaphysics considers in God and the formal notion of *the good* that is considered by ethics. For metaphysics does not consider God from the formal perspective of the Deity but, rather, as the First Being, abstracting from all matter.[80] Moreover, sacred theology has its roots in faith, which is formally-eminently speculative and practical[81] like the Spirit's gifts of wisdom, understanding, and knowledge.

The unity of sacred doctrine is marvelously preserved inasmuch as mystical contemplation, to which moral theology leads, returns to the loftiest mysteries that are speculatively considered in dogmatic theology, as well as to the most intimate truths communicated in Sacred Scripture and Tradition, on which truths the entire science of faith is based.

Hence, someone cannot profoundly know moral theology or mystical theology without also profoundly knowing dogmatic theology, as is clear in the questions concerning predestination and grace. The training afforded by particular study (specialization) is of great use in inferior sciences, such as mathematics, physics, and biology. However, it is less useful in the supreme science, which is maximally unified. The parts of theology are related to each other as are the parts of physics (namely, mechanics, hydrostatics, hydrodynamics, acoustics, optics, thermodynamics, etc.); nay, the parts of theology are much more united than they are.

From all that we have said, it is quite clear that the various parts of sacred theology are not {{33}} subjective parts (as the species are parts of a genus) but, rather, are *integral parts* or branches of the same science.[82] And already from this altitude and extension of

---

[80] See Gonet, *Clypeus theologiae Thomisticae, In ST* I, q. 1, a. 4, no. 4. [Trans. note: This paragraph numeration does not match every modern edition. He seems to be referring to the response to the first objection to the 4th article.]

[81] See *ST* II–II, q. 9, a. 3.

[82] In *ST* II–II, q. 48, a. 1, St. Thomas says: "'Part' is understood in three ways: (1) *integral* parts such as the wall, roof, and foundation are parts of the house; (2) *subjective* parts, just as ox and lion are subjective parts of [the genus] animal; and *power parts* [*potentialis*], as the nutritive and sensitive powers are parts of the soul. Therefore, in these three modes can the parts of a given virtue be assigned. (The same can be said concerning a scientific *habitus*.)"

"In one manner, it can be done through likeness to integral parts, namely just as those virtues *that must of necessity concur for the perfect act of a given virtue* are said to be *integral parts* of that virtue. . . . And thus memory, reason, understanding, docility, and shrewdness pertain to prudence and, from another perspective, foresight, circumspection, and caution. . . ."

"However, the various species of a virtue are called its *subjective parts*. . . . Thus are distinguished individual prudence and the prudence by which one governs the multitude, the latter

sacred theology is it quite clear that apologetics (or the defense of the faith) is not a specifically distinct science but instead is an initial, general, and defensive part of positive
theology and of dogmatic, systematic theology, as will be shown below.

ART. 3: ON THE METHODOLOGY EMPLOYED IN SACRED THEOLOGY

§1. The methodology of sacred theology is principally a method from
authority.

§2. On the basis of these authorities, the doctrinal body is constructed
through an analytic-synthetic methodology, which is set forth in
the treatise on theological sources [de locis theologicis].

§1. The Methodology Employed in Sacred Theology Is Principally a Method from Authority

By the term "method" [or "methodology"], we mean to indicate the right
way that one travels toward knowledge of the truth (μετά, with; ὁδός,
way). We must briefly consider the reason for the variety of methodologies
employed in the various sciences so that the nature of sacred theology's own
proper methodology may be made clear, as well as, later on, the methodology employed in fundamental theology or apologetics.

In order for there to be a right way toward knowledge of the truth,
methodology in general must proceed from what is more known, step by step.
Likewise, the same certitude should not be required in all sciences.

Now, methodologies are first divided into *analytic and synthetic* ones.
Analytic (or inductive) methodology ascends from composite things to
simple ones, from particulars to universals, all the way to the most universal

---

being subdivided into economic, military, and political prudence...."

"*Finally, the power parts* of a given virtue are those *virtues that are adjoined to it*, being
ordered to certain secondary acts or matters, as it were, not having the full power of the principle virtue. In this way does one provide a place for parts of prudence [such as] *euboulia*,
which is concerned with counsel, *synesis*, which is concerned with judgment concerning those
things that are to be done in accord with common rules, and *gnome*, which is concerned with
judgment concerning those things in which it is sometimes necessary to withdraw from the
common law. Prudence, however, concerned with the principal act, which is to command."

Hence, positive theology and systematic theology seem to be integral parts of sacred
theology, parts that necessarily concur for its perfection. However, the applications of moral
theology (i.e., casuistic, ascetic, and mystical theology) seem to be power parts inasmuch as
they are applications to a specific matter. However, in theology there are no parts that are
specifically distinct as diverse sciences.

and first intelligible things. However, *synthetic* (or deductive) methodology descends from simple things to composite ones, from more universal things to less universal ones. Thus, we ascend from the object of experience {{34}} that is first known (from our perspective) to the first notions and first principles or even to the first causes that are first known in themselves, and from principles and supreme causes, by the deductive *via*, the notions and causes of the object of experience are assigned, thus making the latter more intelligible for us. In this way science (or knowledge of things through causes) comes to be constructed.[83]

However, the *specific method* of a given science is determined on the basis of the object to be known and on the basis of the formal perspective under which it is known, just as motion is specified by the terminus toward which it tends. Thus, physics' methodology is more experimental (or inductive) than is that of mathematics, given that the object of physics is less abstracted from sensible things.

Moreover, as regards the diversity of methodologies one must distinguish, with St. Thomas, *two genera of sciences*—namely, *subalternated sciences* and *subalternating sciences*, as was said above:

> Indeed, certain ones proceed from principles known by the natural light of the intellect, such as arithmetic, geometry, and other such things. However, there are others that proceed from principles known by the light of a superior science, just as perspective (i.e., optics) proceeds from principles known through geometry, and music (or harmony) from principles known through arithmetic.[84]

Now, as we said above, *sacred theology is subalternated to God's knowledge [scientiae Dei],* by the mediation of divine faith, for "just as music believes the principles handed on to it from arithmetic, so too does sacred doctrine *believe* the principles revealed to it by God."[85] Hence, the methodology of sacred theology is said to be principally a methodology that is based on

---

[83] See *ST* I, q. 79, a. 9: "According to the way of discovery [*viam inventionis*], we arrive at knowledge of eternal things through temporal ones.... But in the way of discovery [*via iudicii*] we judge concerning temporal things through eternal ones that are now known." [Trans. note: One should also consult Réginald Garrigou-Lagrange, "On the Twofold *Via inventionis* and the Twofold *Via iudicii* According to St. Thomas," in *Philosophizing in Faith: Essays on the Beginning and End of Wisdom*, trans. Matthew K. Minerd (Providence, RI: Cluny Media, 2019), 11–20.]

[84] *ST* I, q. 1, a. 2.

[85] *ST* I, q. 1, a. 2.

authority, *for it argues principally from the authority of God who reveals.* However, sacred theology makes use of other arguments *instrumentally*, as a superior makes use of an inferior.

This is explained by St. Thomas in *ST* I, q. 1, a. 8, ad 2:

> *To argue from authority* is especially proper to this doctrine, for the principles of this doctrine are obtained through revelation. And thus, it must be believed upon the authority of those by whom revelation has been made. Nor does this take away from the dignity of this doctrine, for although an argument from authority [*locus ab auctoritate*] that is founded on human reason is the weakest kind of argument, nevertheless, an argument from authority that is founded on divine revelation is most efficacious.

> *However, sacred doctrine also makes use of human reason*—indeed, not so as to prove faith (because this would lead to the loss of the merit of faith) but, rather, so as to manifest some other things that are handed on in this doctrine. Therefore, since grace does not destroy nature but instead perfects it, natural reason must minister to faith just as the natural inclination of the will yields to charity. Hence, also, the Apostle says in 2 Corinthians 10:5: "Bringing into captivity every understanding unto the obedience of Christ."

> And for this reason, *sacred doctrine makes use even of the authorities of the philosophers* in those matters where they were able to have knowledge through natural reason, as St. Paul expresses in the words of Aratus, "Just as some of your poets said, 'We are God's offspring.'" But, nevertheless, sacred doctrine makes use of authorities of this kind *as extrinsic and probable arguments.*

> *However, it makes use of the authorities of the canon of Scripture properly as necessary arguments* [*ex necessitate argumendo*].

> *And it makes use of authorities from other doctors of the Church,* as it were, by arguing *from proper but* {{35}} *probable* [*principles*]. For our faith rests on the revelation made to the Apostles and the Prophets, who wrote the canonical books, and not upon revelation—if there were such—made to other doctors.

Likewise, see no. 6 of Cajetan's commentary on *ST* I, q. 1, a. 8. Summarizing what Cajetan says in this text, theology argues:

1. *From the divine authorities* of Sacred Scripture and of divine tradition, as *from proper* and *necessary* [*principles*]

2. *From the authority of the Holy Doctors as from proper and probable* [*principles*]

3. *From natural or metaphysical resons* {
    as *from extraneous* and *probable* [*principles*], if considered unqualifiedly [*simpliciter*]

    as *from proper* and sometimes *necessary* [*principles*] (1*), if considered as they are handmaidens of theology (2*)
}

4. *From the authorities of the philosophers*, as *extraneous* and *probable* [*principles*]

(1*) That is, for drawing a theological conclusion, but not for demonstrating the intrinsic possibility and existence of supernatural mysteries.

(2*) For natural reason as a handmaiden of theology, is elevated and illuminated by the supernatural light of faith under which theology proceeds.

Thus, the method of sacred theology is principally based on authority, though theology makes use of reason for explaining, defending, giving order to, and deducing conclusions from authority.[86]

---

[86] Hence, theological sources are generally divided thus:

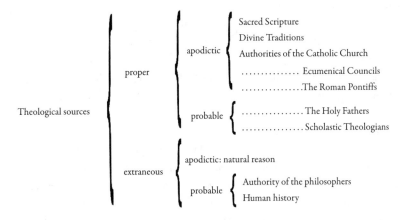

Theological sources
- proper
  - apodictic
    - Sacred Scripture
    - Divine Traditions
    - Authorities of the Catholic Church
      - . . . . Ecumenical Councils
      - . . . . .The Roman Pontiffs
  - probable
    - . . . . The Holy Fathers
    - . . . . Scholastic Theologians
- extraneous
  - apodictic: natural reason
  - probable
    - Authority of the philosophers
    - Human history

As regards history, if all esteemed and weighty historians agree about the same thing that has occurred, then a certain argument is drawn from their authority. See Melchior Cano, *De locis theologicis*, 11.4. [Trans. note: As regards a complete scholastic treatment of the treatise *De locis theologicis*, Fr. Garrigou-Lagrange elsewhere cites Joachim Joseph Berthier, *Tractatus de locis theologicis* (Turin: Marietti, 1888). He also cites the section dealing with this in Reginald Schultes, *De ecclesia catholica praelectiones apologeticae* (Paris: Lethielleux, 1925), 512–742. Likewise, J. M. Hervé, *Manuale theologiae dogmaticae*, vol. 1, *De vera religione, De ecclesia Christi, De fontibus revelationis* (Paris: Berche et Pagis, 1929), 525–600. To this end, one should also consult Ambroise Gardeil, *La notion du lieu théologique* (Paris: Gabalda, 1908). For a more recent treatment by a student of Fr. Garrigou-Lagrange, see Emmanuel Doronzo,

§2. On the Basis of These Authorities, the Doctrinal Body Is Constructed through an Analytic-Synthetic Methodology, Which Is Set Forth in the Treatise on Theological Sources

In order to argue rightly from divine authority, sacred theology must *defend* this authority against the objections of adversaries, *explain* the notions of what is revealed, *order* the various revealed truths, and *deduce conclusions* from them. In this way, the theological, doctrinal body comes to be constructed, and in this work, theology makes use of an analytic-synthetic method. *For positive theology in particular makes use of an inductive or analytic method*, proceeding step by step from composite things to simple ones, from less universal things to more universal ones, whereas *systematic theology especially makes use of a deductive and synthetic methodology.*

Indeed, **positive theology** (whether biblical, patristic, or symbolic) strives to uncover the individual truth to be believed from the sources of revelation. {{36}} Hence, it inductively or *analytically* gathers from various texts of Sacred Scripture and documents of Tradition the dogmatic propositions which bear evident witness that the mysteries of the Holy Trinity, the Incarnation, the Redemption, the Eucharist, and so forth, have been revealed by God himself. However, the particular rules falling to the methodology to be practiced in positive theology are contained in the treatise *on theological sources* [*De locis theologicis, seu de fontibus theologicis*]. This treatise positively presupposes revelation and, under the light of faith, explains: (1) *the rules for discerning the literal sense of Sacred Scripture* "from which alone can an argument be brought forth";[87] (2) the rules for discerning, among traditions, *divine tradition*, which also contains revealed data [*revelata*], as well as the rules for determining its true sense; (3) the rules for discerning what *authority* is held by *the doctrines of the Fathers*, or *that of the theologians*, the *decisions of* [the *Roman*] *congregations*, and *that of particular Councils*, as well as the rules for determining the exact way that we must understand *the solemn definitions* of the Church or the propositions that she has condemned, along with their various notes; (4) finally, the treatise on theological sources sets forth the rules governing positive theology's use of history.

However, **systematic theology** makes use of *a synthetic* (or deductive) methodology in particular, proceeding from simple and more universal

---

Theologia dogmatica, vol. 1 (Washington, DC: Catholic University of America, 1966), 399–544. Regarding the relationship between authority and argument in theology, see Michel Labourdette, "Ferme propos," *Revue Thomiste* 47 (1947): 5–19.]

[87] *ST* I, q. 1, a. 10, ad 1.

things to composite and particular ones, from principles to conclusions. Thus, it first speculatively defends the authority of divine revelation against those who deny it, then speculatively explains and considers revealed truths, draws conclusions from them, and orders all things synthetically *by proceeding* from what is simpler and loftier—namely, *from the One and Triune God to creatures* in general and in particular—then to actions of creatures as ordered to God. Thus, it considers all things inasmuch as they proceed from God and are ordered to him.

By contrast, metaphysics considers creatures before it considers God, gradually ascending from sensible things to spiritual ones and, at last, to the First Cause. Hence the *Physics* of Aristotle is the pathway to the metaphysical consideration of God, which is found at the end of the *Metaphysics*. Therefore, in order to write an account of Thomistic philosophy, one must not proceed according to the order found in the *Summa theologiae* but, rather, must proceed according to the order followed in St. Thomas's various commentaries on the philosophical works of Aristotle.[88]

Indeed, before deducing its conclusions, systematic theology also makes use of *analysis* in the explication and defense of the notions of revealed matters, as when it determines, for example, what a divine person [*persona in divinis*] is (in matters pertaining to the Trinity and the Incarnation), what the real presence of the Body of Christ in the Eucharist is, as well as what revelation, inspiration, faith, hope, charity, and so forth all are. However, this *theological analysis* itself proceeds according to a particular method— namely, the *method of analogy*, which attributes to God and his supernatural gifts the perfections participated in by created natures, while removing [any] imperfections from them, as St. Thomas explains in *ST* I, q. 13.[89] Thus, Divine Wisdom is known {{37}} by way of analogy with created wisdom, Providence from its likeness with our prudence, the Trinity from the analogical notion of relation, and likewise, infused charity is conceived by way of analogy as being a form of friendship between God and the soul. And thus,

---

[88] Hence, to write a Thomistic [philosophical] psychology, the matter must be set forth not according to the order of the theological treatise *On Man*, which is found in the *Summa theologiae*, but, rather, according to the order of Aristotle's treatise *On the Soul*, by gradually ascending from vegetative and sensitive life to intellective life before the spirituality and immortality of the soul is proven. [Trans. note: See Réginald Garrigou-Lagrange, "The Order of the Philosophical Sciences," in *The Order of Things: The Realism of the Principle of Finality*, trans. Matthew K. Minerd (Steubenville, OH: Emmaus Academic, 2020), 225–250.]

[89] St. Thomas explains the mode of cognition only here in the 13th question and not at the beginning of the *Prima pars* because he proceeds synthetically in his *Summa theologiae*. Hence, he considers God in himself first and only afterwards considers how he is known by us.

through analogy, systematic theology arrives at some understanding of the mysteries before deducing theological conclusions. *However, the particular laws for the right theological use of natural reason and the authority of philosophers is explained in the treatise on theological sources.*[90]

Therefore, the treatise on theological sources [*tractatus de locis*] contains the methodology belonging to the whole of theology and, likewise, positively presupposes divine faith concerning the divine mission of Christ and the infallibility of the Church in proposing revelation. This treatise is placed among the propaedeutic instructions for sacred theology. However, it is the final part of fundamental theology and already, like theology properly speaking, *argues from revelation.*

Nevertheless, the first parts of fundamental theology, which are also called *apologetics*, defend the existence of revelation itself and the infallibility of the Catholic Church. Therefore, they cannot argue positively from the Catholic faith. We must now consider how these apologetics are related to sacred theology, properly speaking.

---

[90] See the 8th and 9th *loci* in Melchior Cano's *De locis theologicis.*

CHAPTER TWO

Concerning Fundamental Theology, Apologetics in Particular

{{38}}This chapter is divided into two articles. The first is concerned with the definition and division of fundamental theology. The second is concerned with its relation to theology properly speaking (i.e., considering whether apologetics is distinct from it) and to the natural forms of scientific knowledge [*ad scientias naturales*].

ART. 1: THE DEFINITION AND DIVISION OF FUNDAMENTAL THEOLOGY, IN PARTICULAR THAT OF APOLOGETICS

§1. The nominal definition of fundamental theology and apologetics

§2. The necessity of apologetics

§3. Its real definition taken from its object and end

§4. Its division

§5. Whether it is a science, properly speaking, or at least a part of a science

§1. The Nominal Definition of Fundamental Theology and Apologetics

"Fundamental theology" signifies the theology that is concerned with *the foundations* of divine faith.[1] That is, as will be said below, it is concerned with revelation, which is the formal motive of faith, as well as with the infallible proposal of this revelation by the Church instituted by Christ, a

---

[1] Thus, the [First] Vatican Council says in *Dei filius*, ch. 4: "Faith and reason also support each other, since right reason demonstrates the foundations of faith and, illuminated by its light, pursues the science of divine things" (Denzinger, no. 3019).

proposal that represents a *sine qua non* condition for our faith. In addition, fundamental theology is concerned with the various *sources of theology [locos theologicos]*, as was said in the preceding chapter.[2]

It is also called "general theology" inasmuch as it is concerned with what is revealed in general, precisely as revealed, or with dogma in general, and not with particular revealed dogmas—namely, of the Trinity, the Incarnation, and the Redemption. In this way, the general defense of the faith is distinguished from a particular branch of theology.

According to its nominal definition, "apologetics" seems to coincide with the first part of fundamental theology. Indeed, the term "apologetics" comes from the Greek ἀπολογία, whose meaning is "defense." Thus, {{39}} "apologetics" signifies the defense of the faith. And it must be distinguished from an "apology."[3] *For an apology is a defense that is particular*, either *from the perspective of the object to be defended*, or *at least from the perspective of the manner of defending*, whereas, on the contrary, apologetics is the universal defense of the faith both from the perspective of the object and the manner [of making its defense]. Hence, apologies are called defenses of a given particular doctrine (e.g., a defense of the infallibility of the Roman Pontiff, or a defense of ecclesiastical celibacy) or the defense of a given saint, doctor, or pope. In antiquity, Plato wrote the *Apology* in defense of Socrates. There are also certain apologies concerning the whole of the Christian religion, but, at least in their manner of defending, they do not arrive at the universal because their argumentation depends on the circumstances of time and place in which they are conceived. Frequently, such arguments do not have an absolute value but have only a value that is relative to the men of a given time. And because science is not concerned with particulars, such apologies do not constitute a given science or part of a science.[4]

By contrast, "apologetics" means "the universal defense of the faith both

---

[2] [Trans. note: As noted above, this fact is attested to in the fact that the manual *De ecclesia catholica praelectiones apologeticae* by Schultes represented the course following Garrigou-Lagrange's *De revelatione* in the sequence of studies at the Angelicum in the first quarter of the twentieth century. It also indicates that the treatment of the Church in that manual is primarily taken from the perspective of apologetics and not as a unique treatise on the nature of the Church such as one would find, for instance, in the work of Charles Cardinal Journet. This situation is similar to something noted above regarding the sacraments—namely, that moral and juridical discussions of the sacraments (both necessary and worthwhile endeavors) are not the same as the inquiry into the sacraments taken in themselves, such as one would find, for example, in the works of Fr. Emmanuel Doronzo, O.M.I.]

[3] See Maisonneuve's article "Apologétique" in the *Dictionnaire de théologie catholique*.

[4] Similarly, he who writes an apology is "an apologist," and he who teaches apologetics is called "an apologete."

from the perspective of the object and from the perspective of the manner of defending." From the perspective of the object, this is indeed clear, for it is a defense not of a given person or mystery, nor of all the mysteries in particular, but of the whole Christian religion in general, given that it intends to show that this religion is revealed by God. From the perspective of the manner [of defending the faith], apologetics is universal because its defensive argumentation does not depend on the circumstances of a given time or place but instead has an absolute value inasmuch as it is founded both on the most certain principles of natural reason (or of metaphysics) and on historical testimonies that are certain. Thus, as much from its object as in its manner [of defending], apologetics, if it can so proceed, will merit the name of science (or, at least, that of being a part of a science).

Consequently, *fundamental theology* and *apologetics* denote the same thing, at least if they are considered as being defensive parts of fundamental theology and not the methodological part of it (namely, the treatise on theological sources, which positively argues from faith). However, we must soon determine whether apologetics in reality is the first part of fundamental theology.[5] Still, before we come to that, we must treat of its necessity, which belongs to the question concerning "whether it is" [*an sit*], which must be decided upon before discussing the question "what it is" [*quid sit*].

§2. *The Necessity of Apologetics*

As we said in the previous chapter, sacred theology presupposes supernatural faith, whose formal motive is divine revelation, which properly manifests to us truths of the supernatural order. However, this sacred theology cannot, without falling into a vicious circle, prove from its proper formal perspective (namely, from virtual revelation) the existence of its object, nor the existence of revelation, for this would be to prove the same through the same. And, thus, no science proves directly and *per se*, from its proper formal perspective, the existence of its object. Mathematics presupposes the existence of quantity and does not prove it, just as physics presupposes the existence of the sensible world and does not defend it. It sets aside this defense, leaving it to metaphysics.

Nevertheless, because the fact of revelation is not immediately evident to us, as is the existence of the sensible world, this fact requires proof and a defense. And since rationalists deny not only the existence of revelation but

---

[5] [Trans. note: Reading *pars prima theologiae fundamentalis* for *pars prima theologia fundamentalis*.]

also {{40}} its possibility (inasmuch as they reject the existence of a super-natural order that is manifested through revelation), we must set up a first treatise in defense of the existence of revelation and, before this, of its possibility, befittingness, and knowability.

This defense of the foundations of faith is the proper end of apologetics. Thus, the necessity of this discipline is clear.

§3. The Real Definition of Apologetics

As we said above in the first chapter, the real definition of a given science must be taken from both its formal objects *quod* and *quo*.[6] Now, the object of apologetics is easily determined on the basis of its nominal definition and on the basis of the end for which it is necessary. Let us now consider (A) its formal object *quod* and (B) the light under which [it scrutinizes what is known].

A. **The formal object quod** of a given science is what is primarily and essentially considered by this science, that under whose notion everything else is treated in that science, just as, for example, the object of metaphysics is being inasmuch as it is being and the object of sacred theology is God considered from the formal perspective of the Deity.

Now, what is considered primarily and essentially by apologetics, the notion that guides the consideration of everything else treated therein?

Many, treating of these matters under the title "On the True Religion" or "On Revealed Religion," say the object of apologetics is *revealed religion considered in general*, before one treats of particular revealed mysteries and precepts.

Others, considering this object in a more formal manner, say it is *the rational credibility* of the true religion, for apologetics formally intends to prove the evident credibility of the mysteries of faith taken in general.[7]

These two opinions can be easily reconciled, for the first assigns the subject of apologetics, while the second assigns the formal notion that apologetics considers in this subject—namely, that which it intends to make manifest in particular.

Hence, it is rightly said that the formal object *quod* (or the subject) of apologetics is *revealed religion considered from the formal perspective of evident credibility*, just as it is said that the subject of sacred theology is God considered from the formal perspective of the Deity.

However, as will be discussed more below, because revealed religion is rationally and

---

[6] [Trans. note: I am retaining "formal object *quod*" and "formal object *quo*" as technical terms, rather than directly translating them or expanding them.]

[7] For example, see Gardeil, *La crédibilité et l'apologetique*, 210.

evidently credible to us only inasmuch as it is evident to our reason, on the basis of certain signs, as being truly revealed by God himself, it is more briefly and rightly said that the object of apologetics is *divine revelation,* as many authors say under this title, treating of the possibility, befittingness, knowability, and existence of revelation.

This is clear from the very doctrine of St. Thomas.

The formal notion that apologetics considers in revealed religion is its rational credibility, for as St. Thomas says in *ST* II-II, q. 1, a. 4 ad 2:

> Those things that fall under faith can be considered in two ways. In one way, they can be considered in particular, and in this way they cannot be seen and believed at the same time, as was said above.[8] In another way, they can be considered in general, namely, *under the common notion of credibility,* and thus they are *seen* by the believer. *For he would not believe unless he saw that they ought to be believed,* either on account of the evidence of signs or on account of something of this sort.

What does it mean to say the mysteries of the Catholic faith are seen under the common notion of credibility? It is to say that all the mysteries can be seen, not in themselves, but inasmuch as they are evidently credible, or evidently deserving of faith, nay, that they must be believed [*imo credenda*]. (*Credentity* signifies an obligation to believe).[9] In order that they be evidently deserving, not only of {{41}} whatsoever human and mutable faith but of divine and immutable faith, they must appear to our reason, on the basis of certain signs, as being revealed by God. Therefore, to prove the evident credibility of all the mysteries of faith is to prove that they are *de facto* revealed God, who can neither deceive nor be deceived.

This will be the final conclusion to which all of apologetics is ordered. However, in order to rightly and integrally defend this evident credibility, we must treat not only of the existence of revelation but also of its possibility, befittingness, and knowability, which are denied by rationalists. Now, all these are more briefly expressed under one title: *On Divine Revelation.* In other words, the various revealed mysteries pertain to the same subject, as we said in assigning the subject of theology and of faith—namely, God, considered from the perspective of the hidden formal character of the Deity. Hence, it must be said that the subject of apologetics is the mystery of the Deity inasmuch as it is rationally credible. However, because this mystery is thus credible only as it appears as being revealed by God, it must be said more briefly: The subject of apologetics is God as revealed by himself, or God who reveals himself. Hence, apologetics is called *"On Divine Revelation"* or "On God

---

[8] As, for example, the mystery of the Trinity or the Incarnation, considered in particular, is believed and not seen.

[9] See our discussion later on in vol. 1, ch. 15, a. 3, no. 2.

Who Reveals." Under this title, "*De revelatione*," the [First] Vatican Council[10] gathers its various definitions pertaining to this question. Similarly, positive symbolic theology[11] unites under the word "revelation" (and not under the title "credibility") all those things that pertain to our treatise (the nature and character of revelation; the particular objects of revelation, or the mysteries; acceptance of revelation; the powers, offices, and limits of reason; the mutual relationship between revelation and reason; the sources of revelation). Likewise, Journel's *Enchiridion Patristicum* begins, in its index, with revelation. In all these, credibility has the character of being [*se habet*] the ultimate conclusion.

Hence, it must be said that the subject of apologetics is revealed religion from the formal perspective of evident credibility. More briefly stated, its subject is revelation. Often, the title "On the True Religion" is proposed for this treatise, but it is better to say, "On Divine Revelation," for in this treatise, religion is considered only in relation to revelation (that is [*seu*], inasmuch as it is revealed). Indeed, in this treatise one is not concerned with the various duties pertaining to the virtue of religion (e.g., prayer, and the offering of sacrifice).

B. *What the formal object quo (or the light) of apologetics is.* From the nominal definition and from the end of this discipline, it is clear that this light is *the natural light of reason, under the direction of faith, so as to rationally defend faith itself.* This will be explained through the parts [of this assertion].

(a) *It is the light of reason*: For we wish to manifest the rational credibility of the mysteries of faith. However, in order for the obedience of faith to be rational, we must be able, in the light of reason itself, to prove the fact of revelation and also defend the infallibility of the Church proposing revelation. This defense cannot be made by the light of faith arguing from faith, for in that case, there would be a vicious circle in our argumentation. Thus, in the critical part of metaphysics, there would be a vicious circle if one were to prove the ontological value of the first principles of reason while already presupposing this value.

(b) *It is not the light of reason inasmuch as it totally abstracts from faith*, as, for example, in natural theology. Indeed, natural theology considers neither revelation nor faith but instead considers God as he is naturally knowable from natural things. Hence, it is not directed by faith except in an exter-

---

[10] [First] Vatican Council, *Dei filius*, chs. 2 and 3 (Denzinger, nos. 3004–3009). [Trans. note: Fr. Garrigou-Lagrange has an error in the numeration, writing "1885" where he clearly means "1785" according to the older Denzinger numeration. Technically, the second chapter *De revelatione* of *Dei filius* ends at 3008, but I am following his citation, which passes over to the first paragraph of the third chapter.]

[11] See the index of Denzinger's *Enchiridion definitionum*.

nal manner as a negative norm—that is, inasmuch as it must not contradict faith.

The case is different for apologetics, which aims to defend faith itself {{42}} and to manifest its credibility, which is the sufficient condition for divine faith; for this credibility is measured not only according to the requirements of reason but also according to the requirements of divine faith, which must be not only prudent but also utterly firm and irrevocable.

(c) *It is the light of reason under the direction of faith.* Indeed, it is the light of reason as it *serves under* faith so as to rationally defend it. Now, reason serves under faith by being *directed* by it, for to direct is to determine in advance the end to be pursued and to indicate the means that are apt for attaining that end. However, faith determines in advance *the end to be sought* by apologetics inasmuch as it itself is to be defended. And since the end is prior in intention, this defense presupposes a correct consideration of the faith to be defended as well as the correct notion of the credibility to be obtained, and this notion depends on legitimate notions of divine faith, revelation, and the supernatural order. However, these subordinate notions are not handed on by natural reason, nor by philosophy, but instead by revelation itself and are adulterated by rationalists.

Moreover, God who reveals *taught* us the rationally knowable and efficacious *means* for the defense of faith. God has not left these means to be discovered by our investigation, but instead he himself freely gave sensible testimony to the prophets and the Church, especially miracles, and revealed to the prophets how *this* miracle to be performed is connected with *this* revelation to be confirmed. Otherwise, there would be confusion. Indeed, mere reason is not the source for this major premise: "In order for revealed religion to be credible, it must be confirmed by miracles." Nor does one discover from reason alone this minor premise: "This revelation must be confirmed by this miracle." It is declared by the prophet under the direction of revelation itself and of faith, but the hearers can know, by reason alone, the probative strength of the miracle thus proposed. Thus, revelation and faith direct their self-defense inasmuch as they indicate both the end to be attained (credibility) and the rationally knowable efficacious means for attaining it.

Therefore, these means (namely [*seu*], the motives of credibility) can be considered from two perspectives: (1) from on high, inasmuch as they are freely proposed by God, who revealed their probative strength (thus, apologetics, *in proposing*, is directed by faith); and (2) from below, inasmuch as their probative strength is knowable by reason alone by the hearers of the argument to whom [these means] are proposed. (Thus, apologetics, *in proving*, rationally defends faith).[12]

Hence, we can see here the difference between apologetics, theology properly speaking, and philosophy. *Sacred theology argues from faith* by deducing theological conclusions from revealed premises. *Philosophy argues from reason alone, not contradicting faith*, inasmuch as reason by its own power [i.e., middle term] for proving its theses, and is directed by faith as by a negative norm. *Apologetics argues from reason under the positive direction of faith*, for reason does not by its own power discover the due motives of credibility but only judges concerning the value of those things that are proposed by God, who reveals, and by his ministers.

Adversaries[13] indeed object: Then the apologete does not proceed in a scientific manner because, under the direction of faith, he is already certain concerning the conclusion to be reached. Response: I concede that he does not proceed scientifically in the manner of physics {{43}} or metaphysics. However, he proceeds in a rational and sapiential manner, like the prophets and apostles who were the first apologetes and presented themselves not as seekers but as defenders of the truth of faith. Nor does the direction of faith diminish the rationality of the defense, if the probative strength of the motives proposed by God can be defended by reason alone.[14]

First confirmation. If, on the contrary, the defense of faith were not established under the direction of faith, then the end to be sought—namely, the credibility to be proven—is not rightly known. Without faith, one would not know whether it is credibility as it is conceived by the Catholic doctors, leading to true divine faith, or whether

---

[12] In this way, we see verified for the motives of credibility what the semi-rationalists wrongly said about supernatural mysteries—namely: they are *proposed* by God who reveals but are then *demonstrated by reason.*

[13] [Trans. note: Reading *adversarii* for *adversariis.*]

[14] The apologete must say what Léon Ollé-Laprune says in his book, *Le prix de la vie*, 345–357: "Intellectual honesty [*loyauté*] obliges us to declare all that is of Christian origin in our preoccupations, in our very questions, in our investigations, and in our philosophical theories. . . . Such a solution as we have proposed comes from positive religion. In a sense, this solution is very philosophical since it was accepted by reason and proven by reasoning [*par des raisons*]. But reason left to itself would not have discovered it. . . . There is more. We must say that reason alone could not have posed such a question, nor could have suspected it. . . . Yes, in these investigations, where I have had the most and best possible use of my mind, methodically, according to the laws of reason, I often had a light that is not a natural light." [Trans. note: It is not clear what edition he is citing.]

Likewise, in the historical order one finds Fr. Lemonnyer, O.P., writing in Wilhelm Schmidt and Antoine Lemonnyer, *La révélation primitive et les données actuelles de la science* (Paris: Lecoffre-Gabalda, 1914): "This little book is an apologetic work, and it is openly so, which is the frankest and the best manner for it to present itself. It is also, so it is believed, a work of solid and honest science."

it is credibility as it is conceived by liberal Protestants, leading only to a kind of religious experience. Likewise, as regards the means to be used in this defense, an apologetics that is not directed by faith only accepts, in an accidental manner, the means proposed by God himself, while often choosing more human means that are not adapted to the end. Thus, it comes to argue, for example, solely from how the mysteries of faith are conformed to our nature. However, this does not lead to proof that the mysteries are revealed by God, nor hence, that they are most firmly and irrevocably credible. And therefore, as we will say, the Catholic Church has defined many things as being revealed by God concerning the methodology of apologetics and the motives of credibility.

In other words, the Christian faith to be defended itself reveals the means that are efficacious for its rational defense. God reveals not only the obscure mysteries to be believed, such as the Trinity and the Incarnation, but also the fact that miracles are the most certain signs of revelation so that our obedience of faith may be rational. God himself defends his revelation and does not abandon it to a merely philosophical defense.

Second confirmation. Similarly, as was said above, *in critical metaphysics*, the defense of the ontological value of the first notions and first principles of reason is not performed solely under the light of logic, inasmuch as it abstracts from extramental being. Instead, critical metaphysics accepts from natural reason and from metaphysics the right notion of their ontological value and then defends it logically by reducing its adversaries to absurdity. By contrast, if critical metaphysics is instituted in a merely logical and subjective manner, as we see in subjectivist philosophers, it does not arrive *per se* at extramental being.

Objection: Although, in many cases, reason alone, inasmuch as it abstracts from the direction of faith, does not arrive at true credibility, nevertheless, *per se* it can arrive at such credibility because this object is not supernatural.

Response: I concede that, indeed, *per se* reason can *know* credibility by examining the motives of credibility proposed by God himself and by his ministers, as happens for those who hear apologetic preaching. However, in order to *establish* apologetics and {{44}} to *propose* [credibility] to those who do not believe, one must have, under the direction of faith, a true notion of credibility and choose motives of credibility proposed as most certain signs of revelation by God himself revealing. Hence, the apologete himself must already have faith, for one only defends what one already possesses. Thus, he can efficaciously lead unbelievers to faith. An unbelieving philosopher cannot, properly speaking, establish an apologetics of the Christian religion. This does not fall to him but, rather, to teachers of the faith.

Therefore, on the basis of its formal object *quod* and *quo*, we have *the real definition of apologetics*—namely: "Apologetics is *the rational defense of divine revelation.*" It is a *rational defense* (ἀπολογία) because it is performed under the light of reason. Indeed, it is a defense *of divine revelation*: This is the subject or object that is formally considered. However, the word "defense" indicates that apologetics already acknowledges the truth of revelation, for one only defends what one thinks is certain.

§4. The Division of Apologetics

(1) First, we will lay out the division proposed by many present-day authors. (2) Then we will lay out the division that is more conformed to tradition and to the [First] Vatican Council.

(1) **Many present-day authors** divide fundamental theology (or apologetics) into two parts. First, against the rationalists, it defends *Christian revelation* itself, and is called "the Christian demonstration." Second, against Protestants and schismatics, it defends *the infallibility of the Catholic Church* inasmuch as it was historically instituted by Christ in order to preserve and infallibly propose divine revelation. This defense is called "the Catholic demonstration" and represents the apologetic part of the treatise on the Church.

The first part—namely, that on revelation—is subdivided into two sections: theoretical and historical.

The theoretical section, against rationalists, defends the possibility of revelation, its befittingness and knowability on the basis of certain signs, and the moral obligation of receiving divine revelation when sufficiently proposed.

The historical section, against rationalists, defends the existence of divine revelation handed on to us by Christ and, by a regressive methodology, defends the existence of the Mosaic revelation and of primitive revelation. However, some authors proceed according to a progressive methodology, passing from the earlier documents of the Old Testament to the New. Nonetheless, it is better to begin from times that are more familiar to us—namely, from more recent times.

The second part—namely, *on the Church*, apologetically considered—historically defends:

(a) That Christ, who was sent by God, instituted the Church as a visible society that is knowable from the marks [*notis*] inhering in her, as well as the fact that he conferred infallibility upon her for proposing revelation.

(b) That the marks [*notas*] of the Church instituted by Christ are found only in the Roman-Catholic Church [*sic*].[15]

This division can be admitted, for in following this program, the foundations of faith are rationally defended: (1) the formal motive of Catholic

---

[15] [Trans. note: The current translator, a member of the *sui iuris* Ruthenian Catholic Church feels the need to note, with a critical eye, this dated manner of speaking of the Church, while obviously himself professing the prerogatives of the Roman Pontiff.]

faith (namely, divine revelation); and (2) the *sine qua non* condition of Catholic faith (namely, the infallible proposition of revelation by the Catholic Church). Likewise, this way of proceeding distinguishes between controversies that arise in response to Protestants and those that arise in response to rationalists.

(2) ***Nevertheless, according to the traditional way of proceeding***, which was preserved by *the [First] Vatican Council, the defense of revelation and the defense of the true Church of Christ* {{45}} who proposes such revelation can be exposited *in a unified manner*. Indeed, in the Dogmatic Constitution on the Catholic Faith, *Dei filius*, ch. 3 (on faith), the [First] Vatican Council gathers all the motives of credibility in confirmation of revelation, among which is placed the miraculous [*mirabilis*] life of the Church, along with its marks [*notis*].[16] Moreover, later in the other constitution—namely, *Pastor aeternus* on the Church of Christ[17]— there are set forth those things that pertain to the intimate constitution of the Church, its hierarchy, and the primacy of the Roman Pontiff, all of which are the object of the properly theological treatise on the Church, in which one then argues positively from revelation infallibly proposed by the Catholic Church. Indeed, the Church, already apologetically defended, is manifested by herself, without a vicious circle, in a manner akin to how light manifests itself: To see light, we do not need to kindle another light.

Hence, following the way set forth by the [First] Vatican Council, in the historical part of the treatise on revelation, the apologete can set forth those things that pertain to the rational or historical defense of the true Church of Christ. And thus, the defense of Christian revelation itself is most fully corroborated.

Therefore, to prove the existence of divine revelation handed on to us by Christ, the apologete can begin from the very historical testimony of Christ concerning his divine mission and concerning the institution of the Church to propose revelation infallibly. Then he can set forth how this twofold testimony of Christ is confirmed by all the motives of credibility taken together—namely, miracles, prophesies, the miraculous [*mirabili*] fulfillment of all human aspirations, the miraculous propagation of the Church, and the marks [*notis*] of the Catholic Church, especially her unity, catholicity, holiness, and fecundity in all good things. Otherwise, the treatise on revelation would come to argue too exclusively from extrinsic signs and past events (namely, miracles and prophecies) and would not argue enough from

---

[16] See Denzinger, no. 3014.

[17] See Denzinger, no. 3051.

the intrinsic signs that remain in our time and are easily knowable by all.[18]

In this way, we have a clearer expression of the unity of apologetics, and the external motives of credibility, such as miracles, are gathered more closely together to the motives intrinsic to religion, such as its miraculous life. In addition, the demonstration of Christianity is only *per accidens* and *ad hominem* and must be distinguished from the demonstration of Catholicism, for the distinction between Christianity and Catholicism comes from Protestants, who wish to be called Christians and nonetheless fight against the true Church of Christ. On the contrary, according to Tradition, true Christianity is nothing other than Catholicism; hence, the true and complete demonstration of Christianity already contains the demonstration of Catholicism.[19]

Hence, the treatise *On Divine Revelation* can contain the whole of apologetics and thus can be divided into two parts:

1) *The theoretical part* against philosophical rationalism defends
   a) the possibility of revelation;
   b) the befittingness and necessity of revelation;
   c) the knowability of revelation from certain signs.

2) {{46}} *The positive part* against biblical rationalism defends the existence of divine revelation handed on by Christ and proposed by the Catholic Church:
   a) Christ's own historical testimony concerning his divine mission and concerning the institution of the Church for proposing revelation infallibly is set forth.
   b) This testimony is confirmed by the miraculous fulfillment of our aspirations by the Church's sublimity of the doctrine and life.[20]
   c) It is confirmed by miracles and prophesies.
   d) True Christianity is compared with the Mosaic religion (whose divine origin is proven) and with other religions.

---

[18] See Allo, "'Extrinsécisme' et 'historicisme,'" *Revue Thomiste* 12 (1904): 437–465. Poulpiquet, *L'objet intégrale de l'apologetique*, pt. 1, ch. 5.

[19] Thus did Fr. Lacordaire proceed in the first volume of his *Conférences*, as did Cardinal Victor Augustin Isidore Dechamps (*Oeuvres*, vol. 1), Jules Didiot (*Logique surnaturelle*, no. 317), and also Cardinal Tommaso Maria Zigliara, in *Propaedeutica ad sacram theologiam in usum scholarum seu tractatus de ordine supernaturali*, 5th ed. (Rome, 1903), bk. 4, treated simultaneously of Christian religion and the Catholic Church.

[20] The internal motives from the miraculous fulfillment of human aspirations can be exposited first, for thus is the man who does not yet believe disposed to consider the other signs [of revelation]. Then one can proceed from present-day and more known signs (namely, from the miraculous life of the Church) to ones that are in the past (namely, to miracles and prophesies).

e) Conclusion: The obligation of embracing the Catholic religion that has been sufficiently proposed.

Afterwards comes the properly theological treatise on the Church[21] (namely, on the intimate constitution of the Church, her properties, her twofold power, the value of [doctrinal] definitions and [various] declarations taken in particular[22]), as well as the treatise on other theological sources [*locis*] (namely, on Sacred Scripture, Tradition, etc.) in which one determines the intimate nature, authority, and use of the various sources used in sacred theology. These theological treatises already positively argue from faith, just as do the treatises on the Trinity or the Incarnation.[23]

As regards the theoretical part of the treatise on revelation, one must note that frequently, in theological manuals, this part is reduced to a brief prologue concerning the possibility of revelation and of the miracles by which revelation can be known. Such a prologue hardly suffices for the defense of revelation against rationalists. Indeed, they begin from the denial of the supernatural order and set up naturalism as a fundamental principle in accord with which the true historical methodology must be instituted. Such a methodology excludes all supernatural facts from the history of Christianity, and also from the history of all other religions, because [they hold that] the supernatural order is *a priori* impossible.

Therefore, at the beginning of the treatise on revelation we must defend the existence of the supernatural order, which we will do when we treat of the possibility of supernatural revelation from the perspective of the object and of the agent.[24]

---

[21] [Trans. note: Recall, however, that according to Fr. Garrigou-Lagrange (and other eminent theologians), the proper location for discussion of the Church is to be placed after that concerning the Incarnate Word.]

[22] In this theological treatise on the Church, one is also concerned with the marks [*notis*] of the Church, but then they are not only considered in an external manner, as in apologetics, but instead are considered as they proceed from what is interior—namely, from the essence of the Church, as its properties. Generally, our knowledge proceeds inductively from marks, the exteriors of things, to the essences of things, and afterward deductively from the known essence are its properties (or marks [*notae*]) deduced, which are thus made intelligible. See *ST* I, q. 85, a. 5.

[23] Thus does one now find the index ordered in Denzinger's *Enchiridion symbolorum et definitionum ecclesiae* and in Fr. Roüet de Journel's *Enchiridion patristicum*. [Trans. note: Fr. Garrigou-Lagrange is referring to the 10th edition of Denzinger.]

[24] Cardinal Zigliara, O.P., in his *Propaedeutica ad sacram theologiam* establishes a first book: on the nature and existence of the supernatural order, before the question concerned with the possibility of revelation, which is the manifestation of this order. From the perspective of the thing itself, Cardinal Zigliara rightly indeed proceeds to establish a complete apologetics that would be efficacious as much against philosophical objections as against historical objections of rationalists. Nevertheless, from the perspective of the disposition of the matter, the unity of

{{47}} Thus, the rational defense of divine revelation will be complete from a theoretical perspective, opening the way for a historical defense.

This division of apologetics is the correct one, for it is drawn in accord with the formal notion of the whole to be divided—namely, of the rational defense of the foundations of the Catholic faith—and it adequately contains whatever necessarily and immediately pertains to this defense.

Corollaries. Consequently, apologetics (or the general defense of the foundations of faith) formally, as such, must not set up a treatise concerning the existence of God, concerning religion, concerning the divinity of Christ, concerning the intimate constitution of Christ's Church, or concerning theological sources.[25] This is easily explained in parts.

(a) The existence of God is expressly proven in philosophy—namely, in natural theology. For example, see the twelfth book of Aristotle's *Metaphysics*.

(b) Apologetics must not establish a treatise *on religion* considered in itself either objectively (as the complex of religious truths and duties) or subjectively (as a virtue). Indeed, natural religion is treated of objectively in natural theology and subjectively in natural ethics; supernatural religion is discussed objectively in the whole of dogmatic and moral theology and is discussed subjectively especially in the theological treatise concerning the virtue of religion in relation to God,[26] wherein the internal and external acts of religion (e.g., prayer, adoration, oblation, and sacrifice) are determined.

Nevertheless, apologetics must treat of religion as ordered to revelation and the credibility of the mysteries of faith. Thus, the true notion of religion is useful for manifesting the credibility of Catholicism on the basis of intrinsic criteria, inasmuch as Catholicism shows itself to be the most perfect and superhuman religion.[27]

---

the whole treatise is not clear enough. And in order to avoid this unsuitable situation, it is easy to place under the title "On the Possibility of Revelation" a defense of the supernatural order; for here the supernatural order in our treatise is considered only in relation to revelation and not in itself as in the treatises on the Trinity, on grace, and on glory.

[25] See Gardeil, *La crédibilité et l'apologetique*, 210.

[26] See *ST* II-II, q. 81. [Trans. note: Fr. Garrigou-Lagrange has "q. 81 ad 1." The whole of this question is concerned with the moral virtue of religion.]

[27] On this pretext, one must not follow authors who, under the title "apologetics," treat of nearly all the philosophical and theological questions concerning God's existence, the soul's immortality, the Incarnation, the Redemption, and so forth. These books are more apologetic defenses on behalf of the principal truths of Christianity taken in isolation than *apologetics*, which considers a determinate object. Often, in these works, philosophy and theology are not distinguished well enough, to the detriment of these sciences. Hence, certain more rigid traditional theologians have said about apologetics conceived along these lines: it is the theology of those who blush with shame concerning their faith, and fear to assert dogmas as to be believed on the authority of God who reveals, writing as though every dogma whatsoever were in need of a specific rational apologetic defense and on account of this would be admitted as a philosophical opinion. In reality, the befittingness of the particular mysteries is expressly exposited in theology, properly speaking, and not in apologetics.

(c) Similarly, apologetics must not establish a treatise *On the Divinity of Christ* but, rather, defends the credibility of this and the other mysteries. Indeed, the treatise on the Incarnation of the Word belongs to a particular treatise in dogmatic theology. Apologetics essentially and properly must treat not of the Incarnate Word but, rather, of *Christ sent by God* to hand on the final revelation. At the same time, however, it shows that Christ called himself the Son of God and true God, for if Christ is the true God and not only someone sent by God, then for all the more reason does he infallibly transmit to us the final divine word (that is, the fullness of revelation).

(d) Likewise, apologetics formally as such must not establish a treatise *on the Church's intimate constitution*, which is essentially supernatural and is {{48}} an object of faith. However, of its own nature [*per se*] apologetics must show historically that Christ, having been sent by God, established the Church as a visible society that is knowable by certain marks [*notis*] and gave it infallibility for proposing revelation, likewise showing that the marks of this Church are found solely in the Roman-Catholic Church [*sic*]. Thus, the marks are considered here only in an external manner, and the Church is discussed only in relation to revelation, as is befitting in the treatise on revelation.

However, to treat of the instituting of the Church not only historically but also in a properly theological manner (and this is true too when one treats of the institution of the Eucharist), discussions concerning the intimate constitution of the Church, of her hierarchy, of her marks known from within as properties flowing from the essence of the Church, of the Roman Pontiff, of the congregations, and so forth all already pertain partly to theology properly speaking, which argues from faith, and partly to canon law.

By proceeding in this way, the apologete avoids making many demonstrations that indeed have a properly theological and canonical value but not, perhaps, an apologetic value, because they presuppose many other things that, properly speaking, are certain solely because they have been declared by the Church, who is infallible. Moreover, one must not confuse apologetics, which remains general, with an apologetic defense on behalf of the Church.

(e) Finally, apologetics formally as such must be distinguished from the treatise on theological sources [*De locis theologicis*], which already presupposes faith concerning revelation and the infallibility of the Church, arguing from faith in order to establish the intrinsic method of theology itself, properly speaking.[28] On the contrary, apologetics does not argue from faith but rationally shows the credibility of truths revealed by God through Christ and proposed by the Church.

Thus, we can clearly see that our division of apologetics is necessary and adequate.

---

[28] See Ambroise Gardeil, *La crédibilité et l'apologetique*; and the short work by the same author, entitled, *La notion de lieu théologique* (Paris: Gabalda, 1908).

§5. *Whether Apologetics Is a Science, Properly Speaking, or at Least Part of a Science*

Science is certain knowledge through the causes that explain why a thing is what it is and cannot be itself otherwise, as Aristotle shows in the first book of the *Posterior Analytics*.[29] This is knowledge *a priori* through a cause. Science also proves *a posteriori* the existence of the cause through its proper effect or at least from a sign, but science from a sign is an imperfect kind of science. Hence, if apologetics can supply certain knowledge through the causes that explain why the mysteries of faith are rationally knowable and cannot be otherwise, it will deserve the name of science. However, as we will see in the course of this treatise, apologetics indeed assigns this cause by proving the fact of revelation and reducing its adversaries to absurdity. However, it does not prove this fact from its cause, nor from its proper effect, but instead from signs. Hence, apologetics is imperfectly a science—namely, a defensive science from signs, or rather, as we will say, the defensive part of a given supreme science (or wisdom)—that is, of sacred theology.

Objection: Science is not concerned with singulars. Now, apologetics is concerned with a given singular fact—namely, the fact of revelation through Christ. Therefore, it is neither a science nor a part of a science.

{{49}} *Response*: I deny that apologetics is concerned with a given singular fact formally inasmuch as that fact is singular. I concede that it is so concerned with a given singular fact inasmuch as it is considered according to its essence. Thus, it is concerned not only with the fact of revelation but, rather, with the notion of revelation, its possibility, befittingness, and knowability. Thus, astronomy could treat of the sun even if the nature of the sun were found only in one singular existent. Likewise, sacred theology treats of the one Incarnation and Redemption by considering what is essential in them.

First counterpoint: But apologetics does not arrive at universality, at least from the perspective of its manner of arguing, and it seems to be an art rather than a science. Indeed, art is right reason regarding things to be made (or the right ordering of reason to some particular work to be made). And, in fact, apologetics is only the right ordination of arguments for showing the credibility of Christianity, which is manifested variously according to the various dispositions of men, all depending on circumstances of time and place.

Response: As was said above, apologetics is different from an apology. Indeed, because an apology depends upon particular circumstances, it is an art, just as is the art of oratory. Apologetics, by contrast, abstracts from particular circumstances, argues from most certain principles of natural reason and from historically certain facts, and thus is a

---

[29] Also see St. Thomas, *In* I *Post. An.*, lect. 4.

science or at least part of a science. However, it can be said that apologetics, like logic too, is a science in itself and an art in its application, for logic is a science insofar as it assigns in a universal manner the cause explaining why our knowledge is right and necessary; and logic is an art inasmuch as it directs reason in knowing the truth. Likewise, apologetics is a science assigning the cause of the credibility of the mysteries of faith, and simultaneously directs reason in the manifesting of this credibility in practice.

Second counterpoint: Even if it proceeds in a universal manner, apologetics is not a science. Indeed, no science is merely defensive, [arguing] by an extrinsic demonstration from signs. Instead, every science treats of its object positively and intrinsically. However, apologetics is merely defensive and demonstrates the credibility of the mysteries only in an extrinsic manner—namely, from signs that confirm revelation.

Response: First, there is no difficulty if apologetics (or the defense of the faith) is only the defensive part of sacred theology, just as critical metaphysics is the defensive part of metaphysics. However, it can also be said that apologetics treats positively of revelation and of credibility, assigning the proper cause explaining why the mysteries of the faith are credible—namely, because they have been revealed by God.

ART. 2: THE RELATIONS OF APOLOGETICS TO SACRED THEOLOGY AND TO SCIENCES OF THE NATURAL ORDER

§1. Whether it is specifically distinct from sacred theology
§2. Whether it is rightly said to be the first part of fundamental theology
§3. Its relation to the sciences of the natural order that it presupposes

§1. Whether Apologetics Is Specifically Distinct from Sacred Theology

It is indeed evident that *philosophy and history*, which already provide scientific works of much use in apologetics, are specifically distinct from sacred theology. Nay, as we said above, there is a kind of imperfect apologetics that is indeed efficacious inasmuch as it is the historical and philosophical defense of traditional apologetics itself, proposed by Christ {{50}} in the Gospel, by the apostles in their letters, and by the Church over the course of time. However, here we are concerned *with traditional (or classic) apologetics itself, rightly ordered and complete*, according to its *due* amplitude, profundity, and loftiness, as it appears in the great doctors of the Church.

It is certain that *in a qualified sense [secundum quid]* apologetics is distinguished from theology properly speaking, inasmuch as it argues from principles of natural reason and not from the authority of God who reveals, so as to know a conclusion naturally. However, above we noted that dogmatic theology and moral theology are distinguished in a qualified sense but not, however, as two *habitus* (i.e., not as two specifically distinct sciences). According to St. Thomas in *ST* I, q. 1, a. 3 and 4, they belong to the same eminent science, which is simultaneously speculative and practical and, nevertheless, simply speaking, one lowest species [i.e., not as an intermediate genus-species that could be further divided specifically].

Therefore, the question is whether, not only in a qualified sense, but *simply speaking*, apologetics of its very nature is a distinct *habitus* (or a science specifically distinct from sacred theology) or, rather, only a function (or rational, defensive office) of sacred theology, which would be distinguished from its expositive and deductive office, somewhat like how in one and the same science (e.g., in psychology) inductive experimental work and the rational deductive work are distinguished or, rather, as critical (or defensive) metaphysics is distinguished from metaphysics properly speaking (that is [*seu*] ontology).[30]

Certain thinkers,[31] as we already noted, affirm a specific distinction [between apologetics and theology properly speaking] because sciences are specifically distinct by their object and the principle by which they make their demonstrations [*principio quo*]. Now, theology has for its object the revealed mysteries taken in particular, and for the principle by which it makes its demonstrations it has virtual revelation, which is received from divine faith. Apologetics, by contrast, has for its object the preambles of faith and the very truths of faith considered under the common formal notion of credibility, and for the principle by which it makes its demonstrations it has the natural light of reason. These authors concede, however, that apologetics is essentially ordered to the principles of faith and of theology to be admitted, and this end is not only the personal end of him who acts [*finis operantis*]—namely, the apologete—but, rather, is the end of the work itself [*finis operis*]—namely, the end of apologetics as a discipline.

Other thinkers, however,[32] who call the defense of faith "fundamental theology" say:

---

30 [Trans. note: Fr. Garrigou-Lagrange at times uses the anachronistic terminology of later scholasticism regarding the division of sciences, not because he takes up the post-Wolffian division of philosophy but, rather, because of the customs of ecclesiastical faculties in his days. See Réginald Garrigou-Lagrange, *The Order of Things: The Realism of the Principle of Finality*, trans. Matthew K. Minerd (Steubenville, OH: Emmaus Academic, 2020), 225–250.]

31 See De Poulpiquet, *L'objet integral de l'apologétique*, 499–534. Also see Le Bachelet's article "Apologétique" in *Dictionnaire apologétique de la foi catholique*.

32 See Maisonneuve's article "Apologétique," in *Dictionnaire théologie catholique*. Gardeil, *La crédibilité et l'apologétique*, 2nd ed., xi and 246–351. Thus also write authors who treat of apologetics under the title *fundamental theology* such as Schwetz, Hettinger, Jansen, Ottiger, Stummer, Didiot (*Logique surnaturelle obiective*, v–vi and 4). This opinion, which is traditional, is proposed explicitly by John of St. Thomas in *Cursus theologicus, In ST* I, disp. 2, a. 12, no. 4.

Concerning the exposition of each opinion, see Michel's article "Fondamentale (Théologie)" in *Dictionnaire théologie catholique*, col. 519, and our article "L'apologétique dirigée par la foi" in *Revue Thomiste* 24, New Series, 2 (1919): 193–213.

Inasmuch as it is a supreme science (or wisdom), *theology by extension becomes apologetics*, and the proper object of apologetics pertains to[33] the extensive object of sacred theology, which, inasmuch as it is the science of faith, defends the foundations of faith, and in this work, it makes use of the light of natural reason inasmuch as it serves under faith. Hence, apologetics and sacred theology are not two specifically distinct scientific *habitus*. Rather, sacred theology by extension becomes apologetics, just as the speculative intellect by extension becomes practical,[34] or just as metaphysics, which is concerned with being, extensively and by way of resolution becomes critical metaphysics, which is concerned with the ontological value of our natural knowledge.

This second opinion can be proven in five ways:[35] (1) from the need to have a given theological treatise on revelation itself; (2) from the nature {{51}} of sacred theology; (3) from the nature of apologetics; (4) from the traditional usage of the doctors of the Church; and (5) from the resolution of the objections presented by the opposed positions.

Our thesis is: Apologetics is the rational office of sacred theology, though not a specifically distinct science.

(1) ***From the necessity to have a given theological treatise on revelation***. Indeed, sacred theology must treat of all those things that are matters of faith. Now, there are many matters of faith that are defined concerning revelation itself. Therefore, sacred theology must establish a treatise on revelation.

The major premise is had from the definition of sacred theology, which is the science of faith.

The minor premise is also certain. God, in revealing the obscure mysteries to be believed, simultaneously taught the prophets and apostles what divine faith is, as well as its formal motive, and as we said above, he also taught them the right way to propose revelation rationally to other men, as well as the right way to defend it. Not only did God give the prophets and the Church a sensible testimony, especially miracles, as a sign of revelation, but he also revealed *per se* (and not *per accidens*) to a given prophet the connection of this revelation with this particular miracle to be performed. Otherwise, the prophet could not have announced this sign as being a confirmation of this revelation.[36] Hence, the Church accepted from God himself the motives of credibility, as well as her firm certitude concerning their efficacy. Therefore,

---

[33] [Trans. note: Reading *ad* for *ab*.]
[34] See *ST* I, q. 79, a. 11.
[35] [Trans. note: Reading *quinqupliciter* for *quadrupliciter*.]
[36] For example, in Exodus 4:1–19, 29–31; 7:3–5; 1 Kings 13:1–6; Isaiah 38:7. Likewise, Jesus Christ announced the signs by which revelation is confirmed, especially his Resurrection.

she has defined many things concerning these matters *as things revealed by God* and not as discovered by reason.

The [First] Vatican Council in particular defined many things against the rationalists concerning the nature of revelation, concerning its possibility, necessity, and knowability, concerning the motive of credibility in general, and in particular concerning miracles, concerning prophecies, concerning the miraculous life of the Church, and concerning the very fact of revelation proven by these signs, as well as concerning the infallible proposition of revealed things by the Roman-Catholic Church [*sic*].[37]

Symbolic positive theology collects these definitions and declarations under the title *De revelatione*.[38]

However, all these defined matters not only must be treated in positive theology but also stand in need of systematic (or speculative) theological exposition, one that deserves to be called "fundamental theology," for it is concerned with the foundations of faith. In this treatise, the definitions and declarations of the Church should be set forth, indeed inasmuch as they have infallible authority for the faithful, though properly speaking inasmuch as they are to be defended through reason against rationalists. However, some of these matters are defended by way of demonstration, while others only persuade in a probable manner from befittingness and by way of resolving objections raised against what is proposed. Thus, we will say that the possibility of the supernatural revelation of the natural truths of religion is demonstrated, but the possibility of the supernatural revelation of truths that are, strictly speaking, supernatural, {{52}} at least from man's perspective, only persuades in a probable manner and is defended by the resolution of objections.

Confirmation:

This treatise on revelation is already found in a nearly integral manner in St. Thomas's *Summa theologiae*, though spread throughout the work, because in the thirteenth century the denials made by rationalists did not yet demand a general, preliminary defense of faith. Thus, the possibility of revelation is treated in the treatise on prophetic revelation (*ST* II-II, q. 171–175); the necessity of revelation in *ST* I, q. 1, a. 1, and in

---

[37] See [First] Vatican Council, Dogmatic Constitution on the Catholic Faith (*Dei filius*), ch. 2, *De revelation*; ch. 3, *De fide*; ch. 4, *de fide et ratione*. Likewise see the Dogmatic Constitution on the Church of Christ, *Pastor aeternus*.

[38] For example, see Denzinger, *Enchiridion definitionum ecclesiae* [10th ed.] Index: *Revelationis natura et indoles*; *Revelationis objecta praecipua (Mysteria)*; *Revelationis acceptatio (Fides)*; *Rationis vires, officia, limites*; *Mutua inter revelationem et rationem relation*; *Revelationis fontes*. Then see *Ecclesia*; *Romanus pontifex*; *De Deo uno*; and so forth. Likewise, see the index to Roüet de Journel's *Enchiridion patristicum*.

the treatise on faith *ST* II-II, q. 2, a. 3–5. Likewise, credibility in general and credentity (or the obligation of believing) were treated in the treatise on faith (e.g., *ST* II-II, q. 1, a. 4; q. 2, a. 9, ad 3; a. 10, etc.), and the commentators on this treatise exposit and resolve various questions concerning credibility (cf. John of St. Thomas, Jean-Baptiste Gonet, the *Salmanticenses*, etc.). St. Thomas also treated of the motives of credibility, in particular of miracles. He considered them from the perspective of their possibility in *ST* I, q. 105, a. 6 and 7, q. 110. In *ST* I, q. 105, a. 8, he presented their division. And he discussed the befittingness of miracles for confirming revelation in *ST* II-II, q. 178 (on the grace of miracles) and in *ST* III, q. 43 (whether Christ ought to have performed miracles). Likewise, he treats of prophecy in *ST* II-II, q. 171–175. However, he treats of the motives of credibility that are intrinsic to the revealed doctrine (namely, concerning the harmony or fittingness [or befittingness] of the mysteries with natural truths and with the aspirations of our nature) in regard to the befittingness of each mystery in particular (e.g., the befittingness of our elevation to a supernatural end in *ST* I, q. 12 and *ST* I-II, q. 2 and 3, the befittingness of the Trinity, of the Incarnation, of the Redemption, of the Eucharist, etc.). Properly speaking, all such discussions belong to theology, properly so-called. However, concerning the "interior impulse of God attracting [us]" to faith or confirming faith, see *ST* II-II, q. 2, a. 9, ad 3, and in questions devoted to the gifts of the Holy Spirit. Finally, he treats of the motives of credibility inasmuch as they confirm *de facto* and historically the existence of revelation in *ST* III, q. 43 and 44 (on the miracles of Christ in general and in particular, whether they had been true miracles, and what was their probative strength) and in *ST* III, q. 55 (on the manifestation of Christ's Resurrection and on the sufficiency of the arguments by which this Resurrection is proven).

However, if all these questions pertain to theology, the consideration of all of them together is not extraneous to theology. To say, "Theology, which is concerned with what is revealed, should not itself contain a treatise on revelation," is like saying, "Our vocabulary should not include the word 'word.'"

Objection: However, the *Summa theologiae* also contains many philosophical questions, and nevertheless, philosophy is specifically distinct from sacred theology.

Response: These questions are treated by way of recollection concerning those things that are proven *per se* in philosophy; by contrast, sacred theology treats *per se* of revelation and of its notes.

Another objection: In that case, we would need to establish a theological treatise on revelation and another apologetic treatise pertaining to a specifically distinct science.

Response: There can be two kinds of consideration of revelation, one that is properly theological and the other apologetic.[39] Now, the theological consideration itself,

---

[39] Thus is the matter expressed in Vicenz de Groot, *Summa apologetic de ecclesia catholica ad mentem S. Thomae Aquinatis* (Paris: Ratisbon, 1890). Also see Fr. De Poulpiquet's *Objet integral de l'apologétique.*

inasmuch as it is not only positive but also speculative, must already speculatively and rationally defend revelation, and for this defense, theology apologetically *makes use*[40] of philosophy and history. {{53}} However, it does not make use of a new, intermediate natural science that would be apologetics. Otherwise, the speculative and defensive part of the theological treatise on revelation would merely repeat the apologetic treatise.

(2) ***From the nature of theology.*** Sacred theology, *inasmuch as it is* [*the*] *supreme science*, must defend the principles of faith and the motive of faith. Now, this defense of the motive of faith is the proper work of apologetics. Therefore, apologetics is a defensive office (or function) of sacred theology. This is the way this matter is explained by John of St. Thomas.[41]

The minor premise is taken from the definition of apologetics. (See above.)

The major premise is from St. Thomas as regards the defense of the principles of faith. Indeed, he says this in the text already cited[42]—namely, *ST* I, q. 1, a. 8:

> However, one must consider in the philosophical sciences, that the inferior sciences neither prove their principles nor dispute against those who deny them, but instead leave this to a superior science. Now, the supreme science

---

[40] Thus, see Fr. Gardeil, *La crédibilité et l'apologétique*, 1st ed., 183; 2nd ed., 246.

[41] John of St. Thomas, *Cursus theologicus*, q. 1 (On sacred doctrine), disp. 2, a. 12, no. 4 says: "*Can the credibility of faith be exhibited by theology in an evident manner?* Some thinkers deny that it can, such as Arrubal in disp. 7, ch. 3. However, one of the evidences of faith's credibility is that *it can resolve, in an evident manner, all the reasons given against it*; for whatever is greatly credible can be shown by no reasoning to be opposed to the truth; if, therefore, theology can show that the reasons [against it] may be resolved in an evident manner, it can also show evidently that what it proposes is credible.

"And hence, because although theology cannot, when faith is first acquired in a subject, demonstrate the credibility of faith to itself because this precedes, *in a given subject*, faith—and consequently theology, which is generated from faith—nevertheless it is not contradictory that theology would demonstrate *to another person* the credibility of faith, so that the other person would be converted to faith or confirmed in it, as Augustine says here, in article 2 as cited by St. Thomas, 'that through theology a most wholesome faith is begotten, nourished, and defended.' And theologians accumulate many reasons for exhibiting this credibility of faith in an evident manner, as we also brought forth in the preceding disputation.

"*And therefore, this is because theology, since it is a form of wisdom, can reflect upon its principles so as to defend and explicate them, just as Metaphysics does* with respect to its principles. Thus also, the theologian can exhibit for himself this evidence concerning credibility, for although he proceeds from premises coming from faith and consequently subjectively presupposes credibility concerning it, nevertheless he can more fully set it forth by connecting to premises taken from faith certain other principles that are naturally known, or through experience, and thus can prove credibility."

[42] Likewise, see *In III Met.*, lect. 5; *In IV Met.*, lect. 1; *In II Post Anal.*, lect. 20 and 21.

among them, namely metaphysics, disputes against those who deny its principles, if the adversary concedes something; however, if he concedes nothing, one
cannot dispute with him but nevertheless can resolve his objections. Whence,
sacred doctrine, since it has no superior to itself, disputes with those who deny
its principles, by arguing indeed, if the adversary concedes something from
among those things that are had through divine revelation, just as, through the
authorities of sacred doctrine, we dispute against heretics and, against those
who deny one article of faith, we can argue from another. But if the adversary
believes none of those things that are divinely revealed, there no longer remains
a way for proving the articles of faith by reasoning. Instead one can only resolve
his objections against the faith, if he has any such objections.

Hence, before sacred theology deduces conclusions from principles of faith concerning
the Trinity or the Incarnation, it resolves arguments against the possibility of these mysteries "either by showing that (they) are false, or by showing that (they) are not necessary,"
as St. Thomas says in *In De Trinitate Boetii*, q. 2, a. 3.

Thus, it is evident that sacred theology must defend, and in fact does defend, its
principles against those who deny them. As to the question regarding whether or not it
also must defend the *preambles of faith*, St. Thomas responds in the same text from *In De
Trinitate Boetii*: "In sacred doctrine, we can make use of philosophy {{54}} in three ways.
First, we can make use of it in order to demonstrate those things that are preambles of
the faith, which are necessary in the science of faith, such as those things that are proven
about God through natural reasoning. Second, we can make use of philosophy in making
known those things that are of faith by using certain likenesses. . . . Third, we can make
use of it by resisting those who speak against the faith."

Therefore, if adversaries not only deny the principles of faith (namely,
the primary revealed mysteries) but also the motive of faith (namely, the fact
of revelation) and the [*sine qua non*] condition of faith (i.e., infallible proposition by the Church), sacred theology, inasmuch as it is a form of wisdom
and the science of faith, must defend faith itself and thus, by extension,
becomes apologetics.[43]

Hence, *natural reason* and *history*, from which apologetics argues, are
ordinarily placed among the theological sources [*locos*].[44]

---

[43] Cf. St. Thomas, *In I Sent.*, prol., q. 1, a. 5.

[44] Therefore, the principle of this proof is: *it pertains to the supreme science to defend its principles*;
for it cannot *leave this defense to an inferior science*, but instead *makes use* of inferior sciences.
This principle is founded on the principle of causality, in virtue of which, *that which is inferior
cannot positively do something concerning that which is superior except under the positive influence of the superior thing itself*. Hence, the apologetic demonstration must be made by reason
under the direction of faith. Nay, if some unbeliever, on account of mere philosophical curi-

Objection: But natural theology demonstrates the preambles of faith (e.g., the existence of God) and nevertheless is distinct from sacred theology.

Response: I concede that natural theology demonstrates the preambles of faith that do not depend on the fact of revelation and that do not properly pertain to it. By contrast, apologetics defends the preambles of faith that are foundations of faith—namely, the fact of revelation and the proposing of revelation. Hence, natural theology could be established, as is found in the 12th book of Aristotle's *Metaphysics*, even if there had been no supernatural revelation. On the other hand, apologetics is nothing other than the defense of revelation under the direction of faith.

(3) ***Proof based on the nature of apologetics.*** Through the means given by God himself, who reveals, apologetics must defend the evident credibility of the mysteries of faith, and this credibility is the condition for faith (or the disposition to faith). Now, one and the same science considers the end and those things that are directed to the end (i.e., the means) because the notion of a means (or of a condition) is taken from the end. Therefore, apologetics is not a science that is specifically distinct from the science of faith—namely, sacred theology.

The major premise is had from the definition of apologetics.[45]

---

osity, were to prove the rational credibility of Christianity in a merely rational and historical way, even he would stand under the direction of a superior doctrine inasmuch as knowledge of the faith in which he ought to be instructed would propose to him that whose rationality he would have shown. However, in this case, the influence of preconceived faith would be merely material. Nevertheless, for true and perfect apologetics the formal direction of faith is required. But this is not required for philosophy and history, of which apologetics ought *to make use* as inferior disciplines.

[45] The apologete says with St. Paul, "I believed, for which cause I have spoken" (2 Cor 4:13, DR).

See Lacordaire's fourteenth conference at Notre-Dame: "The chief design of a doctrine . . . is to conquer minds. . . . The aim of doctrine, then, is to govern minds: this it does not hide; and me, living doctrine, to whom it has been said in the persons of my ancestors, '*Go and teach all nations,*'' me . . . why should you wish me to hide my ambition from you? My ambition does not have limits; my ambition is wider than the seas: my desire for domination over every creature capable of understanding the divine word is, as St. Paul said, 'To take captive every intellect, every height that raises itself,' by the power of the doctrine that comes from God. Thus, we have a great ambition, and if you have a doctrine, this ambition is also yours. Let us not dissemble; let us say that we are men who wish to conquer all things, to possess minds, to govern them. Why? Is it from an egoistic desire for preeminence? No, good sirs, it is because the truth is also charity. . . . *This certitude* which is so difficult for all . . . this certitude, which has only enemies, *we possess it*. We have it . . . my brothers and I. . . . Behold us, certain of ourselves and of our doctrine!" [Trans. note: This passage was translated with an eye to the excellent translation of Henry Langdon. See Jean-Baptiste Henri Lacordaire, *Conferences Delivered in the Cathedral of Notre Dame in Paris*, trans. Henry Langdon (London: Thomas Richardson, 1853), 190–194.]

{{55}} The minor premise is drawn from Aristotle and St. Thomas:[46] "It falls to the same science to consider the end and those things that are directed to the end, and this is because the reason for those things that are directed to the end is taken from the end." The application of this to credibility is obvious: *What must evident credibility be* so that it may be a true and legitimate condition, not of any faith whatsoever but of divine and immutable faith? This must be determined not only according to the requirements of reason, which desires evidence, but also *according to the requirements of the firmness of a faith* that is not human and mutable but instead is divine, *a faith that must never be revoked in doubt*, such that it would be necessary to undergo martyrdom rather than deliberately doubt the truth of faith. And this is the reason why God himself, in revealing the mysteries of the faith to the prophets, Christ, and the apostles, gave them signs (or motives) of credibility so that revelation may be rationally proposed to men and defended—namely, so that "the obedience of our faith may be in harmony with reason" (cf. Rom 12:1), and the mysteries may be evidently credible.

Likewise, for this reason the Church has declared that in order to have evident knowledge of credibility, *it does not suffice to have a great probability* concerning the fact of revelation, a point that is especially clear if we read the letters of Pius IX against the doctrines of Georg Hermes.[47] And as one who is taught by God, the Church defined the value of the motives[48] of credibility.[49]

Finally, in its analysis of the act of faith, sacred theology determines in what manner this act, as regards its supernatural essence [*substantiam*], must be in harmony with reason, and what credibility's evidence precisely is. Indeed, the true notion of credibility quite clearly depends on the revealed notion of divine faith. Moreover, the notion of divine faith depends on the true notion of supernatural revelation, which is the motive of faith, and the notion of revelation depends on the prior notion of the order of supernatural truth itself. Therefore, if the apologete does not have a true, theological notion of the exceeding and lofty nature of the order of supernatural truth but instead has a more or less rationalistic notion of it (as did the semi-rationalists Hermes and Günther), then he will form false notions of revelation, of supernatural faith, and of credibility, consequently coming to form a false notion of the efficacious methodology to be used in proving credibility. Thus, it is clear why God himself taught the right way for ration-

---

[46] See Aquinas, *In* II *Phys.*, ch. 2, lect. 4.

[47] See Denzinger, nos. 2775ff.

[48] [Trans. note: Reading *valorem motivorum* for *valerem motivonem*.]

[49] See [First] Vatican Council, *Dei filius*, can. 3.4 (Denzinger, no. 3034).

ally defending revelation. Hence, we said above: Apologetics argues from reason, though under the direction of faith. *In addition, apologetics must treat of the obligation to believe* and, hence, must say something *about the grace needed for faith, nay, for the beginning of faith.* Therefore, apologetics reductively pertains to the science of faith.[50]

{{56}} *First confirmation.* If apologetics[51] were considered as a merely rational science to be established before theology, many incongruities would emerge.

Proceeding thus, certain apologetes intended to determine by reason alone what credibility is required for believing by divine faith, and many affirmed that it sufficed to have a great probability without true certitude regarding the fact of revelation. Others, however, timidly and without security, proposed the traditional motives of credibility, which were firmly proposed by the apostles and doctors of the Church and were judged by the Church to be most certain. Others said nearly nothing about the concurrence of grace needed for faith, as though the act of divine faith were the conclusion of an apologetic syllogism. Finally, some have argued from a kind of natural, efficacious desire for supernatural religion; however, this efficacious (or [naturally] demanded) desire has been rejected by sacred theology and by the declaration of the Church herself against Michael Baius and the modernists.[52]

Therefore, the apologete must be a theologian in order to treat rightly and integrally of the object of apologetics. And apologetics itself depends in a certain way upon theology properly speaking in the determination of its object and, consequently, of its method. Hence, it is a preliminary part of sacred theology (or theology that makes use of philosophy and history so as to defend the foundations of faith.)[53]

---

[50] Indeed, as we said above, the apologete, in practice, as regards a given distrusting unbeliever to be convinced, can prudently *not speak about this superior direction of faith*, especially in the beginning. Nay, the Christian philosopher or historian, without this positive direction, can write philosophical and historical works that are quite useful for apologetics, nay, efficacious for it inasmuch as they defend the traditional apologetics proposed by Christ, the apostles, and the Church. However, this does not mean that traditional apologetics would thereby be constituted in whole (no less lofty as it is profound) as it appears in the great apologetes, such as St. Justin, St. Irenaeus, St. Augustine, St. Thomas, Bossuet, et al. Nay, if some philosopher or historian were to believe himself able to convince nonbelievers more efficaciously *by abstracting totally from the direction of faith*, nonetheless he would be directed by apologetics itself, which is found in the Gospel and in tradition and which he would defend philosophically and historically.

[51] [Trans. note: Reading *apologetica* for *apostolica*.]

[52] See Pius X, *Pascendi dominici gregis*, no. 37 (Denzinger, nos. 1921 and 2103, old numbering).

[53] See Joseph Huby et al., *Christus: Manuel d'histoire des religions*, 5th ed. (Paris: Beauchesne, 1913), 966: "If the brilliant dawn (of the nineteenth century) was not followed by a beautiful day, the principal cause of this was (not only in France, but everywhere) found in the superficial character of philosophical and theological studies. *One allowed oneself to be blinded* by immediate needs, which were pressing, *by topicality.* One did not go to the source of the

Second confirmation. Evident credibility not only is a prerequisite condition and mark [*nota*] of the true faith but also, after the infusion of faith, remains *as a property of the object of faith.*[54] Now, theology (or the science of faith) *per se* must treat of the properties of faith. Therefore, [it must treat of the evident credibility of faith as a property thereof.] Indeed, that which appears first in the inductive order (the way of discovery), as we noted earlier, appears afterwards in the deductive order (the way of judgment) as a property. Thus, faith presupposing evident credibility has for its property the fact that it is in harmony with reason. So, too, the true Church of Christ is inductively discerned from her marks, and afterwards, from the true Church's intimate essence, we come to deduce the properties that coincide with her marks. (However, they are called marks when considered externally and properties as proceeding from what is interior [i.e., from the essential nature of the Church]). {{57}} Nonetheless, it falls to the same science, according to a twofold inductive and deductive method, to treat of the marks by which a given essence is discerned and of the properties of this essence. They are two scientific tasks, not two scientific *habitus.* Therefore, the science of faith necessarily must treat of the property of the object of faith—namely, credibility.

Third confirmation. No science is solely defensive but instead also is expositive and deductive in nature. Nor does external demonstration from signs suffice for constituting

---

evil. One did not think to confront modern thought with the traditional theology that the masters then knew only slightly or understood poorly. *In order to be efficacious, apologetics should have flourished, from overflow of an assured religious philosophy, from a theology renewed at the sources of faith, from a knowledge of history acquired by a long and methodical effort.* But, then, one cultivated this dangerous genre on one's own [*pour lui-même*]. One had to hide the irreparable lacunae as best as one could, by the eloquence of words, by the divination of genius, by the uncertain brilliance of improvised theories. The best apologists were laymen and priests insufficiently initiated in ecclesiastical science or thrown ahead of time into discussions for which zeal does not suffice as a supplement for everything. Talent can suffice for the pioneer to form a group of disciples for himself and to trace, through the silt of free thought, original derivations. It does not suffice for him who must *rally minds to an established doctrine, defend an authoritative religion, and clear or enlarge the riverbed of the great, traditional river.*" See in the same work what is said concerning the historical method and of the comparative and evolutionistic method in the history of religions on 2, 35, 165, 589, and 591. [Trans. note: Slight emendations had to be made to this based upon the original text. Also, Fr. Garrigou-Lagrange cites 900 instead of 966.]

[54] This is how matters stand in the order of cognition, just as they do in the order of nature; in the process of [substantial] generation, the [preceding accidental] disposition precedes the [new substantial] form, and [following upon substantial change] naturally follows the form as a property, just as heat is a disposition toward the form of fire and, afterwards, a property of fire. See *ST* III, q. 7, a. 13, ad 2. Also see the end of *De veritate*, q. 28, a. 2. The disposition precedes in the order of material causality but follows in the order of formal causality, as causes are causes of each other. See *ST* I-II, q. 113, a. 8. [Trans. note: See also, Réginald Garrigou-Lagrange, *The Order of Things: The Realism of the Principle of Finality*, trans. Matthew K. Minerd (Steubenville, OH: Emmaus Academic, 2020), 319–347.]

a science. Instead, such demonstrations only can constitute a part of a science.

(4) *From the traditional custom of the doctors of the Church*, it is clear that apologetics is not, according to them, a science that is specifically distinct from theology. Commonly, theologians, with St. Thomas,[55] refer to the aforementioned definition of sacred theology handed on by St. Augustine in his *De trinitate*, bk. 14, ch. 1: "To this knowledge [*scientiae*] is attributed only that by which that most wholesome faith is begotten, nourished, defended, and strengthened." However, that by which such most wholesome faith is begotten[56] and defended *per se* pertains to apologetics, which defends the foundations of faith. And that by which divine faith is nourished and strengthened pertains to theology in its specific discussions (or theology properly speaking), which sets forth the connection of the mysteries among themselves and with man's ultimate end, and also deduces the conclusions of the articles of faith. Hence, all these things pertain to the same science.

De facto, as regards the credibility of the mysteries of the faith, [medieval and later] scholastics never instituted a science specifically distinct from sacred theology but, rather, generally treated of it in the treatise on faith, inasmuch as evident credibility is a *sine qua non* condition for divine faith. However, regarding the other parts of apologetics—namely, concerning revelation, prophecy, the possibility, knowability, and probative strength of miracles—such questions were treated either in the treatise on prophetic revelation,[57] in the treatise on divine governance,[58] or in the treatise on Christ.[59]

However, in the eighteenth and nineteenth centuries, the denials proclaimed by the rationalists led to the need to respond to them by establishing a separate treatise on *revelation* (or on the true revealed religion) and *the true Church of Christ*. Now, in this defense of faith, one proceeded by arguing not from revelation but from reason and history. In this way, apologetics came to be constituted as something that can indeed be called a scientific task distinct from theology properly speaking; however, it is not a scientific *habitus* (or [*seu*] science) *per se* distinct from sacred theology. In reality, it is its *initial* part, just as in many sciences the inductive part that ascends to the principles

---

[55] See *ST* I, q. 1, a. 2.

[56] St. Thomas says in *ST* II-II, q. 6, a. 1, ad 1: "Through science faith *is begotten* and *nourished* by way of external persuasion, which is done by a given science; but the principle and proper cause of faith is that which interiorly moves one to assent." And through sacred science, faith is begotten not in the theologian, nor in the apologete, as is obvious, but in those who come to faith from nonbelief.

[57] See *ST* II-II, q. 171. [Trans. note: Again, as above, he has "q. 171, ad 1."]

[58] See *ST* I, q. 105 on miracles.

[59] See *ST* III, q. 43 and 44 on the miracles of Christ; q. 53–55 on the Resurrection of Christ.

precedes the deductive part. Nevertheless, as a critical reflection, *it is perfected* only after the progressive constituting of the science, just as reflective knowledge [*reflexio*] in general presupposes direct knowledge of reality.[60]

Therefore, apologetics is not a new science that was unknown by the ancient theologians and is now in need of being established. So too critical philosophy [*critica*] is not a new science unknown by traditional philosophers and discovered in the nineteenth century for refuting subjectivists {{58}} but instead is the defensive part of general metaphysics by which the transition from logic to ontology properly speaking is made, although it is perfected only after ontology is established.

Note well: Some, considering the aforementioned reasons, concede the necessity of apologetic (or fundamental) theology but wish that it be distinguished from apologetic science (or apologetics) and from the art of apologetics (or from apologetic preaching).[61] Hence, according to them, by means of a regressive method [*via regressiva*] (i.e., in a resolutive manner), *apologetic theology* would set forth those things that are revealed about revelation itself and about the foundations of faith and from these revealed data would deduce theological conclusions. *Apologetic science* would be a rational science that theoretically and historically would show the evident credibility of the mysteries of faith and the obligation for one to believe. *However, apologetic art* would lead unbelievers to faith in particular matters (and not in general), doing so in a practical manner, and would dispose not only their intellect through exposition of the motives of credibility but also their will by making clear that it is good to believe by proposing revealed religion not only as true but also as good, worthy of love, and necessary for achieving our life's ultimate end.

To this claim, we must respond as follows. These three undertakings indeed constitute *distinct tasks* but not essentially distinct *scientific habitus* [pl.]. However, many today judge that a diversity of sciences exists merely on account of the phenomenal diversity of scientific tasks and do not judge profoundly according to the ontological distinction of *habitus* [pl.], as St. Thomas does, who reduces speculative and practical (or moral) theology to one and the same science,[62] just as he does positive theology and systematic theology.[63]

Therefore, the following must be said. Positive theology must manifest the nature of revelation based on the very sources of revelation—that is, from Sacred Scripture and Tradition. However, concerning revelation itself, systematic theology must not only deduce

---

[60] [Trans. note: On this, see John of St. Thomas, *The Material Logic of John of St. Thomas: Basic Treatises*, trans. Yves R. Simon, John J. Glanville, G. Donald Hollenhorst (Chicago: University of Chicago Press, 1955), q. 23, a. 3 (421–428).]

[61] See Pinard, S. J., *Recherches de science religieuse* 4 (July-Oct. 1913). [Trans. note: This appears to be referring to his "Bulletin d'apologétique" in this issue.]

[62] See *ST* I, q. 1, a. 4.

[63] See *ST* I, q. 1, a. 8.

theological conclusions from revealed data but first must show, against the objections raised by rationalists, that revelation is not impossible, unbefitting, and unknowable but instead is knowable, on the basis of divine signs, and that the mysteries of faith are rationally credible. Hence, fundamental theology cannot be specifically distinguished from apologetic science, for otherwise, the systematic part of fundamental theology would be destroyed or would be a mere reiteration of apologetic science. To put it another way, systematic theology, which rationally defends the various mysteries of faith (e.g., the Trinity, the Beatific Vision, the Incarnation, the Redemption, the Eucharist, and so forth) against the objections of rationalists, must rationally defend the mystery of revelation itself. Indeed, the science of faith looks into the very foundation of faith before it considers its particular articles and draws theological conclusions.[64] Nor is apologetic science distinguished from the art of apologetics any more than is logic as a science distinct from the art of syllogistic reasoning.

{{59}} (5) *Resolution of objections*

First objection: Sacred theology and apologetics are distinguished specifically as sciences and not only as offices of the same science.

Indeed, sciences are specifically distinguished according to their objects. Now, apologetics and theology have diverse objects, for the object of apologetics is naturally knowable credibility, whereas the object of theology is that which is deduced from

---

[64] See Gardeil, *La crédibilité et l'apologétique*, xi and 247–251: "The apologetic function of theology is deduced from its supernatural, metaphysical character.

"Rational metaphysics, as the supreme science in the natural order, defends its proper principles and, among these latter, the principles that provide the foundation for human knowledge itself. In this way, we come to form at the head of metaphysics a general and fundamental doctrine that is called epistemology (critical metaphysics), or the doctrine concerning the possibility of true, certain, and scientific knowledge.

"To this doctrine is joined ... criteriology, or the treatise concerned with the signs by which certain knowledge is recognized. The motive for connecting these fundamental disciplines to metaphysics is the same as that which St. Thomas gives: given that it is the supreme science, it must offer its own self-defense.

"In a parallel manner, therefore, supernatural metaphysics will need to possess a critique or defense of the supernatural knowledge of the faith, of its possibility, of its legitimacy, a supernatural epistemology, and a supernatural criteriology. Now, one defends the possibility of supernatural knowledge by theses concerned with the possibility of revelation, of miracles, of prophecy, and so forth. One defends its legitimacy by establishing the signs by which the true revelation is recognized, as well as the effective intervention of these signs in support of Christian revelation. But all this is nothing other than apologetics, properly speaking.

"Without a doubt, this notion of apologetics represents the most adequate one that could be formulated. Credibility is formally a property of a supernatural object. Therefore, we are occupied with a property of the object of faith in the same order of knowledge as the science that is occupied with that very object. . . . This manner of understanding apologetics is, moreover, that of the ancients, who connected apologetics to the theology of the object of faith. In the end, it is the perspective of the *Summa contra gentiles*."

revealed truths. Therefore, apologetics and theology are specifically distinct.

Response: I make a distinction regarding the major premise. I concede that sciences are specifically distinguished according to their specifically distinct formal objects. However, I deny that sciences are specifically distinguished according to a diversity that exists between the *proper object* and the *extensive object* of the same consideration. I contradistinguish the minor premise. I concede that apologetics and theology have different objects in terms of the proper object and the extensive object of the same consideration. However, I deny that they have diverse objects as specifically distinct formal objects.

Indeed, outside its proper object, the supreme science can have an extensive object to which it is extended—just as, according to Aristotle,[65] metaphysics, which has for its proper object being inasmuch as it is being, existing outside the soul, extends itself, as the supreme natural science, to the defense of the ontological value of the first principles of reason that are concerned with being; and in this defense, metaphysics makes use of middle terms drawn from logic [*utitur mediis logicis*].[66]

Thus, sacred theology, which has as its proper object God understood from the formal perspective of the Deity known by revelation, extends itself, as the supreme science, to the defense of revelation itself by means of rational middle terms [*per media rationalia*].

First counterpoint: Nevertheless, apologetics and theology have specifically distinct formal objects.

Means of cognition (or lights) of different orders constitute diverse formal objects. Now, theology proceeds under the supernatural light of revelation and not under the natural light of reason, as does apologetics. Therefore, theology and apologetics have different formal objects.

Response: I make a distinction regarding the major premise. I concede that ostensive middle terms of different orders constitute different formal objects. However, I deny that *the ostensive middle term* and the *defensive middle term* of the same object *of the supreme science* [constitute different formal objects]. I contradistinguish the minor premise. I concede that theology does not proceed under the natural light of reason in setting forth its own object; however, I deny that it does not do so in order *to defend* it. Indeed, it does this inasmuch as it is the supreme science, for the supreme science must {{60}} defend the credibility of the mysteries of faith, since this credibility is a *sine qua non* condition of faith itself and a property of the objects of faith.

Second counterpoint: Nevertheless, theology and apologetics do not defend revelation and credibility in the same manner. Therefore, the difficulty remains.

Indeed, theology defends revelation by arguing only from the sources of revelation. Now, apologetics defends revelation by arguing only from reason. Therefore, theology and apologetics do not defend revelation in the same manner. Hence, apologetic theology

---

[65] See Aristotle, *Metaphysics*, bk. 4.
[66] [Trans. note: Or, perhaps, "middle terms drawn from logic" (*utitur mediis logicis*).]

is specifically distinguished from apologetic science.

Response: I make a distinction regarding the minor premise. I concede that *positive* theology defends revelation by arguing solely from the sources of revelation—namely, from Sacred Scripture and Tradition—in order to manifest authoritatively what revelation is and how it was given and transmitted. However, I deny that *systematic* theology defends revelation from the sources of theology alone. Instead, it defends revelation by reason by manifesting against rationalists that revelation is not impossible or unbefitting but instead is befitting and knowable on the basis of divine signs. I concede the minor premise. I make a distinction regarding the conclusion. I concede that theology and apologetics do not defend revelation in the same way, if we are concerned with positive theology alone. I deny this if we are concerned with systematic theology.

Third counterpoint: But no science proves its formal object. Now, according to the previous response, sacred theology would prove its formal object *quo*—namely, revelation itself. Therefore, the response is false.

Response: I make a distinction with regard to the major premise. I concede that no science proves its formal object from its proper formal perspective [*ex sua propria ratione formali*], for then there would be a vicious circle. However, I deny that no science proves its formal object from reasons borrowed from another science. I contradistinguish the minor premise. I deny that theology would prove revelation from revelation. I concede that theology defends revelation and the credibility of the mysteries from reasons borrowed from metaphysics and history. Likewise, critical metaphysics proves the value of the first principles of reason concerning extramental being by reducing skeptics to absurdity through logical means.[67] Thus, as it is the supreme science,[68] metaphysics makes use of logic for the defense of itself; theology likewise makes use of metaphysics and history for the defense of faith.

Fourth counterpoint: What depends on faith in an essential manner cannot defend the foundations of faith without falling into a vicious circle. Now, sacred theology depends on faith in an essential manner. Therefore, sacred theology cannot defend the very foundations of faith against rationalists without falling into a vicious circle.

Response: I make a distinction with regard to the major premise. I concede the point *as regards its manner of arguing from faith*; however, I deny it as regards its *making use* of rational sciences under the direction of faith. I concede the conclusion. I contradistinguish the conclusion. I concede that sacred theology cannot defend the foundations of faith against rationalists by arguing from faith. However, I deny that it cannot defend the foundations of faith against the rationalists by arguing from reason inasmuch as, under the direction of faith, it makes use of inferior sciences.[69]

---

[67] [Trans. note: Or, as above: middle terms drawn from logic.]

[68] [Trans. note: I am reading a comma here where there is a period.]

[69] See below, ch. 3, a. 1, about the methodology of apologetics in relation to the methodology of

Fifth counterpoint: However, the rational defense of faith cannot be directed by faith itself without danger of fideism (that is [*seu*], a diminution of the powers of reason).

Response: This defense is directed by faith from the perspective of *the reception of the notions* of revelation and of divine faith and from the perspective of *the proposition* of the particular motives of credibility, but it *proves* the value of these motives in a merely rational manner. And in this there is no risk of fideism.

Sixth counterpoint: Theology cannot efficaciously defend the credibility of the mysteries of faith. Hence another science is required.

Indeed, in defending the mysteries, theology does not prove them but instead only resolves the objections of adversaries. Now, in order to defend the credibility of revealed data, one must not only {{61}} resolve objections but also prove the very fact of revelation. Therefore, theology cannot efficaciously defend the credibility of revealed data.

Response: I make a distinction regarding the major premise. I concede that it cannot do so by defending the mysteries *taken in particular*. However, I deny that it cannot do so in defending the mysteries *from the common formal perspective of credibility* because, from this general perspective, the mysteries are seen on account of the divine signs by which they are confirmed. I concede the minor premise. I contradistinguish the conclusion. I concede the point if there were a parity between the common credibility of the mysteries and the mysteries in particular; otherwise, I deny it.

Seventh counterpoint: A given man not yet having faith (and hence, no theology) can establish an apologetics for arriving at faith. Therefore, theology and apologetics are distinct since one can exist without the other.

Response: I will let the antecedent pass. I make a distinction regarding the consequent. I concede that theology and apologetics are distinguished as parts of one science. However, I deny that they are distinguished as two sciences. Indeed, someone can, in some way, know one part of a science and not another, like the critical philosophers who establish critical metaphysics but never arrive at ontology. Likewise, a given unbeliever, thinking that Christianity is useful to society, can write a book for showing that the very mysteries of Christianity, taken individually, are not absurd but are worthy opinions [*sed opinabilia*].

Note that I said that I would let the antecedent "pass"; however, I did not say, "I concede it." Indeed, someone not yet having faith cannot, properly speaking, establish apologetics for arriving at faith, for apologetics is not, properly speaking, the *approach* to faith but instead is the rational *defense* of faith; and nobody, properly speaking, defends something unless he already possesses it. However, a given man who does not yet believe obviously can *read the Gospel and ecclesiastical history, which contain a kind of demonstrative apologetics*. However, the apologete, like the prophets and apostles, who were the first apologetes, is not ascending toward faith but instead already possesses it and, as it were,

---

theology properly speaking.

descends from on high to those who seek the rational way of faith or object against faith.

Eighth counterpoint: But the obedience of faith in the apologete himself must be rational, even from the beginning. Now, it would not be so if the apologete were to proceed from on high (i.e., from faith) in constituting apologetics. Therefore, apologetics is not constituted in this way but instead is constituted by reason alone, as a merely rational science—that is, as a *philosophy of religion*—and not as fundamental theology.

The response to this is twofold. (1) If the apologete thus were to proceed from on high such that he would defend faith from faith, the rationality of the obedience of faith would not be preserved in his apologetic exposition; however, things are quite different if he defends faith by reason from on high—that is, under the direction of faith.

(2) The apologete *himself* arrives rationally at the act of faith not as an apologete but, rather, as a *hearer* of evangelical and apologetic preaching; nor does this involve an infinite regress into the past, for the first apologetes were Christ and the prophets who, under the prophetic light, received from God himself the signs of revelation and knowledge of how such signs are connected with the revelation to be confirmed by miracles. In other words, the right way for proposing and defending revelation rationally was not invented by men, like a philosophy, but instead was handed on by God, although it is made more explicit through the work of reason. Thus, those who have not yet arrived at faith cannot defend it efficaciously, just as a child cannot yet beget. Finally, *the proximate end of a course of fundamental theology is to form apologetes rather than to lead unbelievers to faith.*

Ninth counterpoint: Apologetics is not a preliminary part of theology nor an introduction to theology but, rather, the way to faith that precedes theology. Therefore, it is distinguished from theology. Indeed, many desire to know the motives of credibility but do not thereafter study theology; faith suffices for them.

Response: I make a distinction regarding the antecedent. I will let pass the claim that apologetics according to common understanding [*sensum commune*m] is only a way to simply received faith. However, apologetics scientifically considered {{62}} is the way to faith scientifically[70] considered—namely, to theology. Thus, the examination and refutation of rationalism in general precedes the refutation of the objections of rationalists against the mysteries taken individually.

The final objection: In Pius X's encyclical *Communium rerum* (Apr. 21, 1909), we read: "The chief office, therefore, of philosophy is to show us the reasonableness of our faith and the consequent obligation of believing (that is, the credibility of the mysteries).... Far different is the proper function of Christian theology."[71]

Response: This text is not assigning an office that is *per se* and immediately suitable for philosophy, for philosophy could exist without our elevation to the supernatural

---

[70] [Trans. note: Reading *scientifice* for *scientiae*.]

[71] Denzinger, no. 2120 (old numbering). [Trans. note: Translation taken from official version.]

order and without divine revelation. Instead, it is concerned with an office of philosophy inasmuch as it serves under faith—namely, inasmuch as theology itself makes use of philosophy to manifest the credibility of the mysteries of faith. However, the proper office of theology is to exposit and guard [*tueri*] the revealed mysteries and to deduce theological conclusions. This proper office does not prevent theology from becoming apologetics by extension so as to defend revelation itself. Nay, this defense pertains *per se* to theology inasmuch as it is the supreme science, which in no manner can be subordinated to rational science. Indeed, the supreme science of the supernatural order is subordinated only to God's knowledge [*scientiae*] and that of the blessed, and itself defends from on high (and not only from below) its principles, as well as the credibility of the mysteries against those who deny them. Hence, as we have said, the first apologetes[72] were not philosophers but the prophets, Christ, and the apostles.

§2. Whether Apologetics Is Rightly Said to Be a Part of Fundamental Theology

In relation to the rationalists, the term "apologetics" seems more suitable, for ἀπολογία in Greek means *defense*, and in fact, in this treatise, the divine origin of the doctrine of Christ and of the Roman-Catholic Church [*sic*] is defended against adversaries.

However, even if there were no adversaries, the obedience of our faith would need to be rational,[73] and although all the faithful do not need a scientific demonstration of the foundations of faith, nevertheless, for theologians there is a place for scientific inquiry concerning revelation before coming to the particular treatises of theology. Thus, just as evident credibility is a *sine qua non* condition for divine faith, so too *the scientific proof of credibility pertains to the integrity of sacred theology (or the science of faith)*, after the manner of an introduction or a critical reflection.

However, this scientific consideration of the foundations of faith is rightly called the first part of fundamental theology.[74] The term "theology" is used inasmuch as it is a part of theology, the supreme science, as was said above; and it is "fundamental" (or "general") inasmuch as it is concerned with the foundations of faith—that is, with revelation itself, credibility, and the proximate rule of faith, or with revealed data in general. However, it is not called "fundamental" in the sense that apologetic argumentation would

---

[72] [Trans. note: Reading *apologetae* for *Apologetate*.]

[73] In such a case, apologetics would in no way be polemical but would only be irenic.

[74] This name is taken as legitimate by Ottiger, S.J., in *Theologia fundamentalis*, vol. 1, p. 2, by Ehrlich, Knoll, Reinerding [*Krinerding*], Schwetz, Hettinger, Jansen, Stadler, etc.

be the source or principle from which theology would proceed in its particular considerations. In reality, *apologetic argumentation is only an aid by whose help revelation and Christian faith are defended, and properly speaking, faith is the source and principle of theology properly so-called.*[75] Thus, the natural light of reason is the {{63}} source of metaphysics, although critical metaphysics could be called "fundamental metaphysics" inasmuch as it is concerned with the value of the light of reason and defends it against those who deny it. The natural light of reason is loftier than critical metaphysics, just as the supernatural light of revelation and of faith is loftier than fundamental theology, which is concerned with the same [i.e., with faith].

This first part of fundamental theology, which precedes the treatise *on theological sources*, is also rightly called "apologetic theology," for apologetics can be taken either adjectivally or substantively, as is true of the term "dogmatics."[76]

§3. The Relation of Apologetics to the Natural Sciences That It Presupposes

Apologetics presupposes *philosophy*, especially general metaphysics, natural theology, philosophical psychology [*psychologiam rationalem*], and cosmology.[77] Thus, it gathers together what is proven in sound philosophy against phenomenalism, agnosticism, and immanentism concerning the ontological and transcendent value of the first notions and principles of reason. However, it does this only insofar as it is necessary to its own end—namely, for the defense of revelation. Likewise, against absolute evolutionism, it presupposes the philosophical demonstration of God's existence, of providence, and the true notion of the natural law that can be abrogated because of the extraordinary power of God. These things are treated in philosophy and taken up by fundamental theology as ordered to the defense of revelation, just as moral theology takes up those things that are proven by moral phi-

---

[75] Thus, writes Joseph Kleutgen, S.J., in the final volume of his *Theologie der Vorzeit*, 553, 850. Also see Gardeil, *La crédibilité et l'apologétique*, 247–251.

[76] [Trans. note: The text also includes "mystica", but there is no correlative substantive readily of use in English. For this reason, the term is often translated above as "mystical theology," and even "dogmatica" is translated as "dogmatic theology" in place of "dogmatics."]

[77] [Trans. note: Though using this kind of post-Wolffian terminology, which was regularly found in the ecclesiastical faculties of his days (in part because of certain requirements of canon and particular law), Fr. Garrigou-Lagrange was a proponent of the traditional Aristotelian distinction and ordering of the philosophical disciplines. On this, see Réginald Garrigou-Lagrange, *The Order of Things: The Realism of the Principle of Finality*, 225–250.]

losophy concerning the natural virtues and orders them to the supernatural end.

Similarly, apologetics presupposes critical *history* and the rational exegesis of Sacred Scripture, not inasmuch as Sacred Scripture is a divine book, but as it is a historical book written by some truthful human author. Hence, apologetics does not need to discuss at length the many questions concerning the genuineness and integrity of the Gospels, questions that are treated expressly in the historical part of an introductory course on Sacred Scripture [*cursus introductionis ad Sacram Scripturam*]. However, concerning these matters, it must be noted that history is not to be understood in the restrictive form that we find in the writings of agnostics. As is said in the encyclical *Pascendi* of Pius X, "Agnosticism tells us that history, like every other science, deals entirely with phenomena, and the consequence is that God, and every intervention of God in human affairs, is to be relegated to the domain of faith belonging to it alone (according to the agnostics)." For thus, the rational knowability of the miracles by which revelation is confirmed would be ruled out *a priori*.[78] History is to be understood as it is conceived by natural reason and by sound philosophy.

Would apologetics be subordinated to these presupposed natural sciences? The semi-rationalists and modernists respond affirmatively.

By contrast, traditional theologians respond: It is not subordinated to them but instead makes use of them. The reason for this is that apologetics is the defensive office of sacred theology and not a merely rational science that is distinct from theology. If it were a merely rational science, it would rightly be called "religious philosophy" or "the philosophy of religion" (an expression used, in particular, by liberal Protestants) and, hence, would be subalternated to philosophy in general and would choose the great philosophers as its principal leaders and not Christ, the prophets, and the apostles.

However, in reality, apologetics is a defensive office of sacred theology {{64}} and is related to the sciences of the natural order as critical metaphysics is related to the logic that it utilizes.

Indeed, metaphysics, which is the supreme science of the natural order, is not subalternated [*subordinatur*] to logic, even though *it makes use* of logic for metaphysics' own self-defense. That is, metaphysics takes its object, extramental being, from the natural light of reason and not from logic; being is not demonstrated but instead is immediately grasped by the intellect as color is by sight. Nonetheless, metaphysics makes use of logic so as to defend the real value of the first principles of reason and the light of reason

---

[78] Denzinger, no. 3495. See also Denzinger, nos. 3496–3497 and 3499.

by logically leading its adversaries to absurdity—that is, to illogicality.

Similarly, fundamental theology, which is a defensive office of the supreme science of a loftier order, is not subordinated to natural [philosophical and historical] sciences but instead *makes use* of them as aids. It is subordinated only to divine faith and, hence, to God's knowledge [*scientiae*] and that of the blessed, from which revelation proceeds. Indeed, Christ himself, as well as the apostles, gave the true notions of revelation, faith, credibility, and the Church's infallibility, and presented the signs for the defense of the faith. As a kind of minister of Christ and the Church, apologetics accepts all these things handed on by the Church's magisterium and rationally defends them by showing that those who deny or place in doubt the fact of revelation must necessarily deny (or place in doubt) what is held as certain in metaphysics, cosmology, or in history (e.g., the existence of God, his providence, the possibility of miracles, and the utterly certain historical testimony concerning the existence of miracles). And before making use of a philosophical or historical argument, even fundamental theology judges it, at least negatively under the superior light of revelation and of faith inasmuch as that argument is not opposed to revealed data but, on the contrary, agrees with them. This is the privilege of the supreme science, which defends itself, as well as the stronghold of faith, from on high. However, the theologian must not tenaciously adhere to his erroneous prejudices but should acknowledge whatever is demonstrated with certainty in the natural sciences.[79] However, what is more noble for these sciences than for them to serve supernatural truth (that is [*seu*], the Word of God)?

---

[79] The theologian who would reject, for example, what is certain in modern astronomy, and would adhere to the theories of the ancients, would subordinate theology to ancient physics. And in reality, at the time of Galileo, many theologians forgot what St. Thomas profoundly had said in the thirteenth century in *ST* I, q. 32, a. 1, ad 2: "In two ways can reason be persuaded regarding a particular thing. In one way, it can be used to prove sufficiently some root [of the matter], just as in natural science there is adduced a reason that is sufficient to proving that the movement of the heaven is always of a uniform velocity. In another way is there adduced a reason that does not sufficiently proof the root [of the matter] but that shows that an already posited root [principle] is congruous with effects that follow upon it—just as in astronomy one posits the notions [*ratio*] of eccentrics and epicycles from the fact that *by means of this positing can the sensible appearances of heavenly movements be explained* [*salvari*]. However, this reason is not sufficiently proven, for perhaps it is also the case that the facts could be explained by some other posited explanation.*" Likewise, see *In* I *De caelo*, lect. 3; *In* XII *Meta.*, lect. 10.

CHAPTER THREE

On the Methodology of Apologetics

{{65}} There are three articles in this chapter:

Art. 1. How this methodology is to be determined

Art. 2. What the Church teaches about the methodology of apologetics

Art. 3. A historical overview of apologetics, considered from the perspective of its methodology

ART. 1: HOW THIS METHODOLOGY IS TO BE DETERMINED

§1. It is determined in relation to the methodology from authority of which theology makes use.

§2. It is determined in itself, as an analytic-synthetic method, especially an external one, but also an internal one.

§1. In Relation to the Methodology Used in Sacred Theology

The methodology (or the way) for demonstrating in this or that science must be determined from the object to be known and from the formal perspective under which it is known, just as motion is specified by the terminus toward which it tends. Thus, the methodology of apologetics must be determined from the conclusion that apologetics aims at—namely, the mysteries of faith are rationally credible and must be believed with the firmest faith, as revealed by God. However, quite clearly, this conclusion to be proven is *not* expressed against the rationalists *on the basis of the authority of divine revelation* (for then there would be a vicious circle) but instead is expressed against them in a rational manner.

Hence, it is already manifestly clear that the proper methodology in apologetics is not the method [of arguing] from authority. However, a new counterargument arises against the preceding thesis that, notwithstanding this diversity of methods, apologetics is not a science that is specifically distinct from theology.

To resolve this difficulty, two points must be recalled.

(1) As was said above, theology properly speaking does indeed argue *principally* from the authority of God who reveals, and accepts its principles—namely, the articles of faith—from God. However, *secondarily* and ministerially, sacred theology argues from principles of reason, not only in drawing theological conclusions but also for defending particular mysteries themselves. Therefore, it is not astonishing that sacred theology, in its general defense of faith, makes use of principles of reason and proceeds in light of them.

{{66}} (2) Apologetics is part of theology properly speaking inasmuch as it accepts from God who reveals the *notions* to be defended (those of revelation itself and of divine faith), as well as the efficacious means for defending credibility rationally (especially miracles and prophecies). Thus, *under the direction of God who reveals,* it *proposes* these means and then *rationally* defends them.

Therefore, the Church herself, taught by God, like the prophets, is most firmly certain concerning her divine origin, even if apologetics were not yet established in a properly scientific manner. In addition, common sense can certainly know the motives of credibility before critically and scientifically expositing them in response to objections raised by rationalists, just as common knowledge of the will's capacity for free choice is certain even for those who are not aware of the [philosophico-]scientific refutation of determinism. Hence, at the [First] Vatican Council, the Church defined, against the semi-rationalist Hermes, that "Catholics cannot[1] have a just reason for suspending their judgment and calling into question the faith that they have already received under the teaching authority of the Church *until they have completed a scientific demonstration of the credibility and truth of their faith.*"[2] This definition must be handed on expressly at the beginning of a course of apologetics; however, if apologetics were a merely rational science, it would not be necessary to refer to this declaration *expressly,* nor to exposit what the Church teaches about the method of apologetics.

---

[1] [Trans. note: Fr. Garrigou-Lagrange negates the sense of the anathema to make it express the Church's positive teaching on this manner. This *non* is not in the original, which expresses the position to be condemned.]

[2] The [First] Vatican Council, *Dei filius*, can. 3.6 (Denzinger, no. 3036).

§2. The Methodology of Apologetics Is Analytic-Synthetic, Especially an External One, but Also an Internal One

We will consider the methodology of apologetics (A) generically, then (B) specifically.

A. *Generically*, the methodology of apologetics, like that of theology properly speaking, is *analytico-synthetic*. As was said above, gathering its principles from divine authorities, theology constructs its body of doctrine analytically and synthetically. It *inductively* gathers revealed truths from Scripture and Tradition, establishes an analysis of the ultimate notions and principles of faith concerning God himself, and *synthetically* descends from God to creatures and from the principles of faith to theological conclusions. Likewise, fundamental theology accepts from revelation (i.e., from Sacred Scripture and Tradition) the foundational notions it uses: supernatural mystery, revelation itself, divine faith, due credibility, and so forth. It explains these notions *analytically*, defends them against the adulterations of adversaries, and *synthetically* orders them by descending from the supreme, simpler, and more universal notion of supernatural revelation itself to the subordinate notions of faith and credibility, and finally to the motives of credibility, by which the fact of revelation is proven.

This methodology is determined on the basis of the object to be known, that is, from the conclusion to be proven—namely, the mysteries of the Catholic faith, as manifestly revealed by God, are evidently credible and to be believed. Indeed, in order to prove this proposition, we first must know what exactly is signified by the *subject* and *predicate* of the proposition, and we must determine the *principle* or means by which the attribution of the predicate is inferred as necessarily belonging to the subject. Hence, Aristotle says in his theory of demonstration that three things must be first known for a demonstration: the subject, the predicate, and the principle whereby the conclusion is inferred.[3] Thus, every science proceeds from prior knowledge of notions and principles.

Therefore, to inferentially draw this apologetic conclusion [*conclusionem apologeticae*], we stand in need of (1) the true notion of both *the mystery* of the Catholic faith and of divine *revelation* itself, (2) the true notion of *credibility*, and (3) the cognitional *principle* [*cognoscere principium*] {{67}} by which the fact of revelation (and, hence, the credibility of the mysteries) could be proven—that is, the *value of the motives of credibility*.

The reason for the subordination of the aforementioned notions was

---

3   See Aristotle, *Posterior Analytics*, bk. 1, ch. 1 and 2.

already made clear. Indeed, the notion of *credibility* depends on the notion of *divine faith* (or the act of believing), for that which is credible is that which can legitimately be believed. However, the notion of divine faith depends upon the notion of *divine revelation,* which is the motive of faith. Finally, this final notion of supernatural revelation depends *a priori* upon the notion of *supernatural mysteries* and the notion of *the supernatural order* itself. And therefore, if there are two opposed notions concerning the supernatural order, one orthodox and the other heterodox, there will consequently be[4] two opposed notions of revelation, two opposed notions of faith, and hence, two opposed notions of credibility, and finally, two methodologies for proving credibility. Therefore, apologetics must defend the true notions handed on by revelation itself, establishing an analysis of them and synthetically ordering them from the more universal to the less universal. Hence, its method, generically considered, is analytic-synthetic.

B. However, **specifically** considered, this method is said to be *above all external,* although it is, at the same time, *secondarily internal.* This is clear in light of how the Catholic notions of the supernatural order, revelation, faith, and credibility differ from the adulterated notions of the same things that are proposed by liberal Protestants or rationalists.

This opposition is made manifest in the following synopsis:

[Catholic Notions]	[Liberal Protestant / Rationalist Notions]
Absolutely supernatural mysteries	*Non-supernatural* mysteries
|	|
External divine revelation	Revelation that is *immanent* (from the subconscious)
|	|
Faith on account of the *authority* of God who reveals. The mysteries are credible as being manifestly *revealed by God.* |	Religious sentiment and *religious experience.* The mysteries are credible as being *conformed to our aspirations.*
	|
Motives of credibility that are above all *external.* |	Motives of credibility that are above all or only *internal.* |
Thus, religion is, properly speaking, *divine* and *supernatural,* as in the Catholic Church.	Thus, religion is predominantly *human* and *natural* as in the liberal Christianity of liberal Protestants.

In this synopsis, we have a verification of the adage, "The corruption of the best

---

4   [Trans. note: Reading *erunt* for *erunti*.]

is the worst," for it is the corruption of the loftiest notions and the denial of God's supernaturality.

(a) Indeed, in reality, there are two opposed notions of the supernatural order and supernatural mysteries. The Catholic Church conceives of this order as being simply and *absolutely supernatural*—that is, absolutely exceeding all the natural powers and exigencies of any created nature whatsoever, and not only of human nature, no matter how much the latter might progressively develop / evolve, meaning that the created intellectual nature only contains a passive capacity and befittingness {{68}} for being elevated to the supernatural order but not an active capacity, nor a[n] [efficacious] demand [*exigentia*] for it.[5]

However, rationalists deny the existence of a supernatural order so defined, or at least the possibility or befittingness of the revelation of this order. And if certain rationalists verbally admit that something supernatural exists, this is only a *wholly relative supernatural* that is not yet scientifically explained but later on will appear, simply speaking, as being something natural, understood through the progress of our reason and our sciences. Semi-rationalists, however, admit that divine revelation exists, but they wish to demonstrate by natural reason all the revealed mysteries.[6]

(b) Consequently, the Catholic Church conceives of divine revelation as something *external*—that is, coming from God himself, who is essentially distinct from the world, in order to manifest properly supernatural mysteries. However, if rationalists happen to retain the term "revelation," they conceive of it as *internal* or *immanent*—that is, proceeding from our vital immanence or subconscious according to the evolution of religious sentiment and of reason. Among the errors of the modernists, this proposition has been condemned: "Revelation could be nothing else than the consciousness acquired by man of his relation to God."[7]

(c) Hence, the Catholic Church conceives of *divine faith* as *the supernatural adherence of our intellect to the external testimony of God* on account of *the authority* of God who reveals. By contrast, our enemies have conceived of religious faith as "*a religious sentiment* springing forth from hidden places of the subconscious, under the impulse of the heart and of the bent of a

---

[5] See Pius V, *Ex omnibus afflictionibus*, (Denzinger, nos. 1921–1923). [First] Vatican Council, *Dei filius*, can. 2.3 (Denzinger, no. 3028). Pius X, *Pascendi dominici gregis*, no. 37 (Denzinger, 2103, old numbering).

[6] [First] Vatican Council, *Dei filius*, can. 4.1 (Denzinger, no. 3041).

[7] Pius X, *Lamentabili*, no. 20 (Denzinger, no. 3420). Also see [First] Vatican Council, *Dei filius*, can. 2.2–3 (Denzinger, nos. 3027–3028).

morally informed will";[8] thus the act of faith is reduced to the religious experience of those things that proceed from our vital immanence.[9]

(d) Consequently, the Catholic Church conceives of the *credibility* of the mysteries of faith as their aptitude for being believed inasmuch as they appear as being *revealed by God*. Our enemies, on the contrary, conceive of the credibility of the mysteries of faith, if they retain any [such credibility], as their aptitude for being believed, inasmuch as they appear *conformed to our reason and to the aspirations* of religious sentiment.[10]

(e) Hence, in the end, according to the Catholic Church, *the method for proving the credibility of the mysteries* is especially *external*—namely, from external signs of revelation, which can be produced by God alone—such as miracles, prophecies, and the miraculous life of the Church. On the other hand, the methodology of our enemies is above all *internal*; that is, it argues especially from the aspirations of religious sentiment. According to the Church, these internal motives are not to be held in scorn, though they remain secondary.

Between absolute rationalists and Catholics there are also intermediaries to be noted: liberal Protestants, semi-rationalists, modernists, and so forth, according to whom Christianity is not a supernatural religion but only a superior form of natural religious evolution, something that is forever changeable and perfectible. However, if supernatural life, uncreated [in itself] and participated in by us [through grace], is thus the best, such that nothing could be better, the corruption of its notion is the worst of all things, {{69}} indeed, much more dangerous than its open denial, for an error is all the more condemnable the more it makes use of the truth in recommending itself. Thus, the idealistic rationalism of Kant or Hegel is much more condemnable than materialism, whose absurdity is more evident.[11]

Hence, apologetics must first determine the true notions of *supernatural mystery* and *the supernatural order*, the true notions of *revelation* and *credibility*, and then the very method to be used in proving credibility. Therefore, the true principle to be first known so as to infer the apologetic conclusion

---

[8] See the *Anti-Modernist Oath* (Pius X, motu proprio, *Sacrorum antistitum*, Sept. 1910). Also see Denzinger, nos. 3437ff.

[9] See [First] Vatican Council, *Dei filius*, can. 3.1–2 (Denzinger, nos. 3031–3032).

[10] See ibid., ch. 3 (Denzinger, no. 3009) and can. 3.3–4 (Denzinger, nos. 3033 and 3034).

[11] Hence, L[ouis] Veuillot, while reading Calvin, was impatient when he found the best sort of doctrine on certain pages, for these good pages were directed to the commendation [*sic*] of blasphemies. Indeed, in these books, truth does not exist as the soul of the doctrine but as a servant of error. [Trans. note: Reading *ad blasphemarium commendationem* for *ab blasphemarium commendationem* above.]

[*conclusionem apologeticam*] will be the value of the signs of revelation. Thus, the fact of revelation will be proven *a posteriori* from divine signs, and the mysteries of faith will stand forth as something rationally credible by the firmest of faith, as being manifestly revealed by God himself.

And therefore, the apologetic treatise on revelation accepts from the magisterium of the Church its *primary notions* of revelation, divine faith, and legitimate credibility, rationally explicating and defending them analytically and synthetically by making use of metaphysics and [philosophical] psychology. Afterwards, it exposits and defends *the demonstrative principle*—namely, the rational value of the motives of credibility proposed by Christ and the Church, especially the probative force of miracles and prophecies. Finally, it historically proves the existence of these signs and arrives at its conclusion. Thus, it makes use of a methodology that is analytic-synthetic, and, in particular, external, in arguing from reason under the direction of faith (or [*seu*] the magisterium of the Church).

From this, we can more clearly see the reason for the way the apologetic treatise on revelation is divided and why the theoretical part must be exposited before its historical part (or why philosophical rationalism must be refuted before biblical rationalism, which proceeds from the former).

I. *Indeed, in the theoretical part,* the following must be defended:

1. The possibility of supernatural revelation
   - *a)* from the perspective of the object: *the existence of the order of supernatural truth in God* is defended
   - *b)* from the perspective of the subject: *the obediential potency (or, elevability) of our nature to the supernatural order* is defended

2. The suitability of revelation
   - *a)* from the perspective of God
   - *b)* from the perspective of man

(In this way, we will thus come to have the true notion of the subject of the conclusion of apologetics: "Revealed supernatural mysteries.")

3. *The knowability of the fact of revelation and the credibility of the mysteries*

(In this way, we will thus come to have the notion of the predicate of the conclusion of apologetics—namely, "credible"—and the principle from which the conclusion is inferred is established—namely, *the value of the motives of credibility*.)

II. *The historical part* defends the existence of divine revelation handed on by Christ and proposed by the Catholic Church, as we said above.

ART. 2: WHAT THE CHURCH TEACHES ABOUT THE TRUE METHOD OF APOLOGETICS

{{70}} §1. The Church proposes and defends a determinate method for the defense of the faith.

§2. The Church condemns the methods of Protestants, especially liberal Protestants, and modernists.

§1. The Church Proposes and Defends a Determinate Method for the Defense of the Faith

This is found especially in the [First] Vatican Council's Dogmatic Constitution on the Catholic Faith, *Dei filius*, under the headings *De revelatione* and *De fide*. This way of rationally defending the faith is defined by the Church as something that is handed on by God himself who reveals, and not as being discovered by reason. We must defend three things: (1) the possibility of revelation, (2) its knowability, and (3) its existence.

(1) **The Church defends the possibility of revelation** by proposing the true notions of revelation and of the supernatural order. Indeed, under the heading "*De revelatione*," the [First] Vatican Council defines:

- in the first canon of this section, that existence of the true God can be known with certainty by the natural light of reason;[12]
- in its second canon, the possibility of divine revelation considered in general;[13]
- in its third canon, against absolute evolutionism, the possibility, from the perspective of the object, of some revelation *of mysteries that are, strictly speaking, supernatural*, and the true notion of the supernatural order of truth;[14]

---

[12] See [First] Vatican Council, *Dei filius*, can. 2.1 (Denzinger, no. 3026): "If anyone says that the one true God, our Creator and Lord, cannot be known with certainty [by] the natural light of human reason through the things that are created, let him be anathema." The demonstration of the existence of God is presupposed in our treatise, as pertaining to natural theology, whereas agnosticism will be refuted.

[13] See ibid., can. 2.2 (Denzinger, no. 3027): "If anyone says that it is impossible or useless for man to be taught *through divine revelation* about God and the worship to be rendered Him, let him be anathema."

[14] See ibid., can. 2.3 (Denzinger, no. 3028): "If anyone says that man cannot be *called by God*

- finally, in the first canon on faith, the possibility of revelation is defined from the perspective of the subject (i.e., from man's perspective) and the rationalistic *principle asserting the absolute autonomy of reason* is condemned.[15]

Along with the possibility of revelation, the [First] Vatican Council defines its *befittingness*, as is clear in the second canon on revelation and in the corresponding chapter.[16] Indeed, the Council declares that the revelation of the natural truths of religion is morally necessary, whereas the revelation of supernatural mysteries is strictly necessary so that man may arrive at the supernatural end to which he has been gratuitously ordered.

(2) *The Church defends the knowability of the fact of revelation* (that is, the credibility of the mysteries of faith) and at the same time the value of the motives of credibility. Indeed, under the heading "*De fide*":

- In the second canon, there is a definition of *the true notion of faith*, on which *the true notion of credibility* depends.[17]
- In the third canon, the *credibility* of the mysteries of faith is defended inasmuch as it is founded *on external signs* and not {{71}} only in internal experience. In this way, the method of liberal Protestants (e.g., that of Schleiermacher) is condemned.[18] Now, according to the Council, these external signs are *miracles, prophecies*, and *the [miraculous] life of the Church*.[19]
- In the fourth canon are defined the *possibility of miracles, their knowability, and their probative force*.[20]
- Finally, in the fifth and sixth canons it is declared that the super-

---

to a knowledge and perfection that surpasses the natural but that he can and must by himself, through constant progress, finally arrive at the possession of all that is true and good, let him be anathema."

[15] See ibid., can. 3.1 (Denzinger, no. 3031): "If anyone says that *human reason is so independent* that faith cannot be enjoined upon it by God, let him be anathema."

[16] See ibid., ch. 2 (Denzinger, no. 3005).

[17] Ibid., can. 3.2 (Denzinger, no. 3032): "If anyone says that divine faith is not distinct from the natural theology of God and of moral truths; that, therefore, for divine faith it is not necessary that the revealed truth be believed *on the authority of God who reveals it*, let him be anathema."

[18] Ibid., can. 3.3 (Denzinger, no. 3033): "If anyone says *divine revelation cannot be made credible by outward signs* and that, therefore, men ought to be moved to faith solely by each one's inner experience or by personal inspiration, let him be anathema."

[19] See ibid., ch. 3 (Denzinger, nos. 3009 and 3014).

[20] See ibid., can. 3.4 (Denzinger, no. 3034): "If anyone says that *no miracles are possible* and that, therefore, all accounts of them are to be dismissed as fable and myths; or that miracles *can never be recognized with certainty* and *that the divine origin of the Christian religion cannot be legitimately proved by them*, let him be anathema."

natural *act of faith* is nonetheless *free*, even after the consideration of the motives of credibility, although it must never be called into doubt.[21]

(3) *The Church defends the existence of revelation*, as duly proven by historically certain miracles.[22]

All these points are opposed to rationalism. After this, against semi-rationalism, the Council treats, in particular, the relations between faith and reason and defines:

- that supernatural mysteries certainly cannot be demonstrated following upon revelation;
- that assertions opposed to dogmas are not true;
- that the sense of the dogmas revealed by God is immutable, notwithstanding the progress of human science.

In our treatise, this response to semi-rationalism will be found in the chapter concerning the notion of supernatural mysteries.

After this dogmatic constitution on the Catholic faith, the [First] Vatican Council passed on to the dogmatic constitution on Christ's Church, which infallibly guards and proposes the deposit of revelation.

Hence, it is clear that the [First] Vatican Council defends a determinate method for the defense of the faith, a method that is said to be traditional. And therefore, in our treatise, we will follow exactly the order of the canons of the [First] Vatican Council in refuting philosophical rationalism before biblical rationalism.

§2. The Church Condemns the Methodology of Protestants (Especially Liberal Protestants) and Modernists

(1) *The first Protestants* admitted [the existence of] an external revelation confirmed by miracles, but they rejected the infallibility of the Church proposing revelation. In place of the Church's role in proposing this truth, they placed a private instinct. Hence, Leo X condemned this

---

[21] See ibid., can. 3.5 (Denzinger, no. 3035): "If anyone says that the *assent to the Christian faith* is not *free* but is produced with necessity by arguments of human reason; or that the grace of God is necessary only for that living faith which works by love, let him be anathema."

Also, ibid., can. 3.6 (Denzinger, no. 3036): "If anyone says that *the condition of the faithful* and of those who have not yet attained to the only true faith is the *same*, so that Catholics could have a just reason for suspending their judgment and calling into question the faith that they have already received under the teaching authority of the Church until they have completed a *scientific demonstration of the credibility* and truth of their faith, let him be anathema."

[22] See ibid., can. 3.4 (Denzinger, no. 3034).

proposition from Luther: "It is certain that it is not the power of the Church or the pope to decide upon the articles of faith, and much less concerning the laws for morals or for good works."[23] Thus, we can see the need to inquire into the marks of the true Church.

(2) *Liberal Protestants* indeed do not admit an external revelation or, at least, its knowability, retaining only religious truths that appear to be conformed to the aspirations of our nature's religious sentiment. {{72}} Hence, according to liberal[24] Protestants, the methodology of apologetics is primarily an internal methodology (or even exclusively so). This was condemned by the [First] Vatican Council: "If anyone says *divine revelation cannot be made credible by outward signs* and that, therefore, men ought to be moved to faith solely by each one's inner experience or by personal inspiration, let him be anathema."[25]

(3) *Modernists* proposed a methodology of apologetics that has significant affinities with the methodology of liberal Protestants, which is condemned by Pius X in his encyclical *Pascendi*.[26]

Regarding this matter, the aforementioned encyclical addresses three points:

A. It sets forth and condemns *the foundations* of this new method—namely, agnosticism and evolutionistic immanentism (or the doctrine of immanence).

B. It condemns *the objective (or historical) methodology*, understood in the agnostic way that it is used by the modernists.

C. It condemns *the methodology of immanence*, inasmuch as this methodology, proceeding from immanence, presupposes that our nature either embryonically contains the Catholic faith or makes a

---

23 Leo X, *Exsurge Domine*, no. 27 (Denzinger, no. 1477).

24 [Trans. note: Reading *liberales* for *liberalis*.]

25 [First] Vatican Council, *Dei filius*, can. 3.3 (Denzinger, no. 3033). We read in the schema proposed for the examination of the fathers of the [First] Vatican Council: "Indeed, if rejecting extrinsic criteria or stripping them of their value, by which God rendered His revelation knowable as by divine signs, one reduces all things to 'internal experience' and 'internal sentiment,' there no longer would be a certain way for discerning true revelation from fictitious revelation. Indeed, according to the ordinary course of divine providence, the aforementioned [internal] sentiment is not based on experience precisely qua supernatural [*non subset experientiae sub formali ratione, quatenus sit supernaturalis*], and if it is separated from extrinsic criteria, is open to the gravest of illusions. Whence also, we see men, on behalf of false religion and manifest errors, call upon 'experience and an internal sentiment' which they attribute to the Holy Spirit." See Jean-Michel-Alfred Vacant, *Études théologiques sur les constitutions du Concile du Vatican d'après les actes du concile*, vol. 1 (Paris: Delhomme et Briguet, 1895), 594.

26 See Denzinger, nos. 3475, 2103 (old numbering; official English paragraph no. 37).

demand [*exigentiam*] for it.

A. The foundations of the methodology of the modernists are condemned: (a) the primary and negative foundation, namely, agnosticism; (b) the positive foundation, namely, evolutionistic immanentism (or the doctrine of immanence).

(a) Concerning the primary and negative foundation, the encyclical states:

> We begin, then, with the philosopher. Modernists place the foundation of religious philosophy in that doctrine which is usually called *Agnosticism*. According to this teaching human reason is confined entirely within the field of *phenomena*, that is to say, to things that are perceptible to the senses, and in the manner in which they are perceptible; it has no right and no power to transgress these limits. Hence it is incapable of lifting itself up to God, and of recognizing His existence, even by means of visible things. From this it is inferred that God can never be the direct object of science, and that, as regards history, He must not be considered as an historical subject. Given these premises, all will readily perceive what becomes of *Natural Theology*, of the *motives of credibility*, of *external revelation*. The Modernists simply make away with them altogether; they include them in *Intellectualism*, which they call a ridiculous and long ago defunct system. Nor does the fact that the Church has formally condemned these portentous errors exercise the slightest restraint upon them. Yet the Vatican Council has defined, "If anyone says that the one true God, our Creator and Lord, cannot be known with certainty by the natural light of human reason by means of the things that are made, let him be anathema" (*De Revel.*, can. I); and also: "If anyone says that it is not possible or not expedient that man be taught, through the medium of divine revelation, about God and the worship to be paid Him, let him be anathema" (*Ibid.*, can. 2); and finally, "If anyone says that divine revelation cannot be made credible by external signs, and that therefore men should be drawn to the faith only by their personal internal experience or by private inspiration, let him be anathema" (*De Fide*, can. 3).[27]

Indeed, according to *philosophical agnosticism*, the principle of causality holds only for phenomena and is formulated, {{73}} "Any given phenomenon presupposes a preceding phenomenon." Hence, in virtue of this principle, it is impossible to prove the existence of the First Supra-phenomenal Cause. Likewise, it is impossible to assert that a given phenomenon, even if it is utterly extraordinary, is a miracle (i.e., a fact immediately produced by God outside the order of nature). For, in virtue of the principle of causality, a

---

[27] See Denzinger, no. 3475. [Trans. note: Taken from official English translation, no. 6.]

given phenomenon proceeds from an antecedent phenomenon, but if the proportion between the antecedent and consequent phenomenon is not clear, it is merely said that this fact is not yet explained, due to the current state of science and philosophy.

Therefore, the modernists pass over from agnosticism to *scientific and historical atheism*:[28]

As the encyclical notes:

> Yet it is a fixed and established principle among them that both science and history must be atheistic: and within their boundaries there is room for *nothing but phenomena*; God and all that is divine are utterly excluded. . . . However, this *Agnosticism* is only the negative part of the system of the Modernist.[29]

(b) However, it is easy to transition to the positive foundation of the methodology of the modernists, as the encyclical shows:

> The positive side of it (the doctrine of the modernists) consists in what they call *vital immanence*. This is how they advance from one (part) to the other.— Religion, whether natural or supernatural, must, like every other fact, admit of some explanation. But when Natural theology has been destroyed, the road to revelation closed through the rejection of the arguments of credibility, and all external revelation absolutely denied, it is clear that this explanation will be sought in vain outside man himself. It must, therefore, be looked for in man; and since religion is a form of life, the explanation must certainly be found in the life of man. Hence the *principle of religious immanence* is formulated. . . . (Hence), we must conclude that *faith*, which is the basis and the foundation of all religion, *consists in a sentiment which originates from a need of the divine*. This need of the divine . . . is at first latent within [*infra*] the consciousness, or, to borrow a term from modern philosophy, in the *subconsciousness*, where also its roots lies hidden and undetected.[30]

Thus, divine faith comes to be identified with our natural religious sentiment and the

---

[28] They do not admit *philosophical atheism*, properly speaking—that is, they do not, properly speaking, deny God's existence but remain in doubt concerning it. Nevertheless, according to them, science and history ought to be atheist, inasmuch as no intervention by God in the world can be scientifically or historically certain.

[29] See Denzinger, nos. 3475–3476. [Trans. note: Taken from no. 6 and 7 of the official translation.]

[30] See Denzinger, no. 2074 (old numbering). [Trans. note: Taken from no. 7 of the official translation.]

act of faith with the religious experience of those things that proceed from our subconscious. This identification represents the denial of the supernatural order (or, in other words, is naturalism, properly speaking) expressed using the terms "immanence" and "evolutionism": All religions would be nothing other than moments in the evolution of human nature's religious sentiments; Christianity would only be a loftier form of religious evolution.

Now, according to the modernists, how does the transition from this twofold foundation (namely, from agnosticism and immanentism) to the method of apologetics take place? In short, it takes place by considering the end aimed at by modernist apologetics, as is explained in the encyclical: "The aim he sets before himself is to make the nonbeliever attain that *experience* of the Catholic religion which, according to the system, is the basis of faith."[31] Hence, the modernist apologete does not intend to show that the mysteries of Christianity are deserving of immutable faith as being manifestly revealed by God but instead only intends to show that these mysteries are worthy of religious experience, which is forever {{74}} mutable and perfectible. Therefore, the end aimed at by apologetics is to lead the not-yet-believing person to the experience of Christianity. However, to achieve this end, its methodology is twofold—namely, objective and subjective or [that] of immanence—as the encyclical notes in the same place: "There are two ways open to him, the objective and the subjective."

B. **The objective (or historical) methodology used by the modernists in an agnostic manner is condemned.** Indeed, this methodology shows not that Christianity has been revealed by God but instead that *something unknown remains hidden in* Christianity, especially in Catholicism, something which cannot be scientifically explained and, hence, remains as an object of faith (that is [*seu*], of religious experience).

This is explained in the encyclical in a clear manner:

> The first (path) proceeds from agnosticism. It tends to show that religion, and especially the Catholic religion, is endowed with such *vitality* [*vitalem virtutem*] as to compel every psychologist and historian of good faith to recognize that its history hides some *unknown* element. To this end it is necessary to prove that this religion [*catholicam religionem*] ... is that which was founded by Jesus Christ; that is to say, that it is the product of the progressive development of the germ which He brought into the world.... Christ announced the coming of the kingdom of God, which was to be realized within a brief lapse of time....

---

[31] See Denzinger, no. 3499. [Trans. note: Taken from no. 35 of the official translation.]

Then it must be shown how this germ, always immanent and permanent in the bosom of the Church, has gone on slowly developing in the course of history, adapting itself successively to the different mediums through which it has passed, borrowing from them by *vital* assimilation all the dogmatic, cultural, ecclesiastical forms that served its purpose; whilst, on the other hand, it surmounted all obstacles, vanquished all enemies, and survived all assaults and all combats. Anybody who well and duly considers this mass of obstacles, adversaries, attacks, combats, and the vitality and fecundity which the Church has shown throughout them all, must admit that if the laws of evolution are visible in her life they fail to explain the whole of her history - the *unknown* rises forth from it and presents itself before us.[32]

According to them, this unknown is a *natural mystery* rather than a supernatural one, like the mystery of the universal unfolding of evolution.

Modernists also concede to the rationalists "that there are many distasteful things in it. Nay, they admit openly, and with ill-concealed satisfaction, that they have found that even its dogma is not exempt from errors and contradictions. They add also that this is not only excusable but—curiously enough—even right and proper. . . . [For] life has its own truth and its own logic, belonging as they do to a different order."[33]

Therefore, the objective (or historical[34]) method of the modernists does not show that the Catholic religion has been revealed by God but instead that something unknown lies hidden within it. However, their apologetic work is brought to completion through the methodology of immanence.

C. **Inasmuch as it presupposes that our nature either embryonically contains the Catholic faith or makes a demand for it, the methodology of immanence is condemned.** This methodology is derived from immanentism, just as the preceding methodology is {{75}} derived from agnosticism. It intends to show the *unknown* hidden in Christianity is desirable, good, and best for us inasmuch as it corresponds to our nature's

---

[32] Denzinger, no. 3500. [Trans. note: Taken from no. 35 of the official translation.]

[33] Denzinger, no. 2102 (old numbering). [Trans. note: Taken from no. 36 of the official translation.]

This is founded on the evolutionistic doctrine of Hegel, holding that the principle of contradiction is only a *logical law* of inferior reason (or of discursive reason [*ratiocinatus*]), which makes use of immobilities, but not a *law of reality* which is in a perpetual flux and in whose evolution contraries and contradictories are identified just as in becoming itself being and non-being are identified.

Thus, supernatural mysteries are reduced to natural evolution, which is alleged as being a natural mystery but in reality is a radical absurdity, an identification of contraries.

[34] [Trans. note: Reading *historica* for *historia*.]

aspirations and even to its exigencies. And hence, *the mysteries of Christianity* are credible only in the sense that *they deserve* not, indeed, divine and immutable faith but, rather, *religious experience*. In other words, they are *the legitimate object of religious experience*.

This subjective methodology is set forth in the encyclical *Pascendi*:

> But it is not solely by *objective* arguments that the non-believer may be disposed to faith. There are also *subjective* ones at the disposal of the Modernists, and for those they return to their doctrine of immanence. They endeavour, in fact, to persuade their non-believer that down in the very deeps of his nature and his life lie the need and the desire for religion, and this not a religion of any kind, but the specific religion known as Catholicism, which, they say, is absolutely *postulated* by the perfect development of life. And here We cannot but deplore once more, and grievously, that there are Catholics who, while rejecting *immanence* as a doctrine, employ it as a method of apologetics, and who do this so imprudently that they seem to admit that there is in human nature a true and rigorous *necessity* [*exigentiam*] with regard to the supernatural order—and not merely a capacity and a befittingness for the supernatural, order—and not merely a capacity and a befittingness for the supernatural, such as has at all times been emphasized by Catholic apologists. Truth to tell it is only the moderate Modernists who make this appeal to an *exigency* [*exigentia*] *for the Catholic religion*. As for the others, who might be called intergralists, they would show to the non-believer, hidden away in the very depths of his being, the very *germ* which Christ Himself bore in His conscience, and which He bequeathed to the world.[35]

Whence, *the mystery* of Christianity would only be *natural*, like the mystery of the universal unfolding of evolution.

"Such, Venerable Brethren," concludes Pius X in this part of the encyclical, "is a summary description of the apologetic method of the Modernists, in perfect harmony, as you may see, with their doctrines - methods and doctrines brimming over with errors, made not for edification but for destruction, not for the formation of Catholics but for the plunging of Catholics into heresy; methods and doctrines that would be fatal to any religion."

From this methodology, two things follow in particular: (a) The immutability and absolute truth of dogmas are denied; (b) religious faith is made subject to human science.

---

[35] Denzinger, no. 2103 (old numbering). [Trans. note: Taken from no. 37 of the official translation.]

(a) Indeed, the methodology of the modernists does not prove that the Catholic religion is deserving of immutable faith as being something revealed by God but instead only that this religion is a legitimate object of religious experience, which is ever mutable and perfectible according to the progress of humanity. What indeed is the value of the dogmas that are defended by this methodology? As the encyclical *Pascendi* sets forth:

> Hence (according to the modernists) it is quite impossible to maintain that they (i.e., *dogmatic formulas*) express absolute truth: for, in so far as they are symbols, they are the images of truth, and so must be adapted to the religious sentiment in its relation to man. . . . But the object of the religious sentiment, since it embraces that absolute, possesses an infinite variety of aspects of which now one, now another, may present itself. In like manner, he who believes may pass through different phases. Consequently, the formulae too, which we call dogmas, must be subject to these vicissitudes, and are, therefore, liable to change. Thus the way is open to the intrinsic evolution of dogma. . . .[36] {{76}} First of all they lay down the general principle that in a living religion everything is subject to change.[37]

For example, under the influence of fear, men conceive of God as being frightful and angry; then, later, under the influence of love, they conceive of him as being a Father. However, this latter conception, like the preceding one, is only symbolic and expresses our religious sentiment rather than God himself, in whom there is not, properly speaking, paternity, just as wrath also is not found in him. So [think] the modernists, who hold that dogmatic formulas are not absolutely true because the concepts from which they are constructed do not have, from their agnostic outlook, an ontological and transcendent value but instead only have a phenomenal value.

(b) Finally, in this dogmatic evolution, *religious faith is made subject to human science*, for according to the modernists, whereas the object of religious experience remains unknown in itself, nevertheless: "The religious formulas[38] of it, belongs to the sphere of phenomena and therefore falls under the control of science." The encyclical continues, "It is therefore the right of philosophy and of science to form conclusions concerning the idea of God, to direct it in its evolution, and to purify it of any extraneous elements that may become confused with it. From this, there follows the axiom of the modernists: *Religious evolution ought to be brought into accord with moral and intellectual evolution;*

---

[36] Denzinger, no. 3483. [Trans. note: Taken from no. 13 of the official translation.]

[37] Denzinger, no. 3493. [Trans. note: Taken from no. 26 of the official translation.]

[38] [Trans. note: Fr. Garrigou-Lagrange has *formulae dogmaticae*, whereas the original has *religiosas formulas*.]

that is, as one of their teachers puts it, it should be *subordinated to [them]*."[39] For example, as they say, "The divinity of Christ is not proven from Gospels but instead is a dogma that Christian awareness [*conscientia*] deduced from the notion of Messiah,"[40] and it was indeed legitimate at the time of the Council of Nicaea for Christian awareness to conceive of Christ as being consubstantial with the Father. Indeed, this conception was true at its time, with a relative truth value—namely, one in accord with the state of this era's philosophy. Indeed, it corresponded to the notions of nature, substance, and person, which were discovered by Greek philosophers, especially Aristotle and Plato. Moreover, in the Middle Ages, the scholastics who accepted Aristotle's philosophy were able to retain this conception of Christ's personhood [*personalitatis*] and defined Christ's personhood in terms of the subsistence or divine hypostasis of the divine word. This was true in a relative manner in the Middle Ages because, at this moment of [dogmatic] evolution, critical philosophy was not yet a possibility, and the realism of common sense was admitted as being philosophically true. Now, however, with the progress of critical philosophy, personhood [*personalitas*] can no longer be defined ontologically in terms of subsistence or hypostasis, but instead is to be defined only in a psychological manner in terms of self-awareness. And therefore, in our own era, religious experience (or Christian awareness), according to the new requirements of philosophy and critical reflection, must conceive of Christ as indeed being [a] son of God, though only in the sense that in comparison to all others, Jesus had the greatest possible awareness of his intimate dependence upon God and union with him.

In this way, dogmatic formulas vary in accord with the progress of science. Nevertheless, something remains—namely, something unknown that is hidden in Christ's life. This is the object of Christian experience, which is a livelier form of religious experience than the other various forms of religious experience.

It is quite clear that this methodology of the modernists' apologetics proceeds from naturalism and leads to a merely natural interpretation of Christianity. In place of external revelation, it posits the subconscious (or vital immanence) with all its natural demands. Hence, in place of divine and supernatural faith, it posits a natural religious sentiment. Finally, in place of the supernatural act of faith, it posits natural religious experience. Clearly, if our nature[41] embryonically contains the Catholic faith or makes a demand for it, the Catholic religion will no longer be supernatural but instead will be only a natural form of religious evolution. Moreover, whatever mystery

---

[39] Denzinger, no. 3486. [Trans. note: This text was taken from Denzinger, as the official English of no. 17 is significantly truncated at an important part of this quote.]

[40] See Pius X, *Lamentabili*, no. 27 (Denzinger, no. 3427) and no. 31 (Denzinger, no. 3431).

[41] [Trans. note: This "nature" is supplied. Fr. Garrigou-Lagrange only has "nostra" as the subject of the clause.]

{{77}} remains in it will be only natural, like the mystery of vital activity in plants and animals.

Hence, we can quite clearly see the infinite abyss that separates the methodology of the modernists' apologetics from that which is defended by the Church itself. In order to make this difference even more manifest, it is useful to briefly set forth the history of apologetics from the perspective of methodology.

ART. 3: HISTORICAL OVERVIEW OF APOLOGETICS FROM THE PERSPECTIVE OF METHODOLOGY

In this overview, we will see how the traditional methodology of apologetics[42] was constituted from the beginning [of Christianity], whereas, by contrast, the method of immanence finds its beginnings in the Lutheran notion of faith, which already gradually reduced faith to a form of faith-confidence and to a given individual experience. Later, under the influence of Kant, liberal Protestants reduced divine faith to natural religious experience. However, once the notion of faith changes, the notion of credibility likewise changes, as well as the method for proving credibility.

This article is subdivided into seven sections:

§1. Terminology regarding apologetic methodology.

§2. How did the prophets prove their divine mission?

§3. What was the *via* / way (or methodology) used by Christ (and, afterwards, by his apostles)?

§4. The apologetic methodology of the Fathers of the Church.

§5. The apologetic methodology of the scholastic theologians.

§6. Following the appearance of Protestantism, apologetic methodology according to Protestants and Catholics.

§7. After the appearance of Kantianism, apologetic methodology according to Protestants and Catholics.

---

[42] See the first part of Fr. le Bachelet's article "Apologétique" in the 4th edition (1909) of the *Dictionnaire apologétique de la foi catholique* wherein he provides an overall exposition of historical development of apologetics (in the first five centuries, in the middle ages, in modern times, in the nineteenth century). Also see Jules Martin, *L'apologétique traditonelle* (Paris: Lethielleux, 1905). Also see the section on credibility in the Fathers and in the scholastic theologians in Fr. Ambroise Gardeil's article "Crédibilité" in the *Dictionnaire de théologie catholique*.

§1. Terminology Regarding Apologetic Methodology

In order to facilitate greater ease in understanding the history of apologetics, we must first fix our terminology. Indeed, frequently, in historical exposition of this kind, the internal methodology is often not distinguished clearly enough from the external-intrinsic methodology. In order to avoid confusions, we must consider from the start the exact meaning of our terms. Now, the methodology of apologetics is called external or internal, and the external is subdivided into intrinsic and extrinsic, as is more clearly expressed in the following division of the motives of credibility: {{78}}

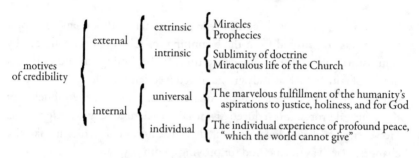

An *external methodology* is that which makes use of motives of credibility existing *outside of the awareness* of the nonbeliever—namely, of miracles, prophecies, and the miraculous life of the Church. *The internal methodology*, on the contrary, proceeds from a consideration of the aspirations that are already an object of the awareness of the nonbeliever.

This first division is indicated by the [First] Vatican Council when it defined: "If anyone says that divine revelation cannot be made credible by outward [*externis*] signs and that, therefore, men ought to be moved by faith solely by each one's inner experience or by personal inspiration, let him be anathema."[43]

However, external methodology is subdivided into intrinsic and extrinsic.

External-extrinsic methodology makes use of motives external to awareness that likewise are extrinsic to the doctrine and life of Christianity, as is the case for the majority of the physical miracles and prophecies that confirm revelation.[44]

Hence, the [First] Vatican Council places among "*external* arguments for

---

[43] [First] Vatican Council, *Dei filius*, can. 3.3 (Denzinger, 3033).

[44] Certain miracles, such as Christ's conception and Resurrection, are intrinsic to Christianity; however, the majority, such as the multiplication of loaves and the healing of the man born blind, are extrinsic.

revelation, namely divine facts," "especially miracles and prophecies, which since they manifestly display the omnipotence and infinite knowledge of God are the most certain signs of the divine revelation, adapted to the intelligence of all men."[45] These signs are rejected by liberal Protestants and by modernists inasmuch as, according to their agnosticism, reason cannot discern whether a given extraordinary fact is, in reality, produced by God outside of the order of nature.

External-intrinsic methodology makes use of motives that are external to awareness but intrinsic to the Christian religion. That is, they are taken from the sublimity of its doctrine and its moral effects (namely, from the miraculous life of the Church). These motives of credibility are recommended by the [First] Vatican Council when it says:

> In fact, it is to the Catholic Church alone that belong all those signs that are so numerous and so wonderfully arranged by God to make evident the credibility of the Christian faith. In fact, the Church by herself, with her marvelous propagation, eminent holiness, and inexhaustible fruitfulness in everything that is good, with her catholic unity and invincible stability, is a great and perpetual motive of credibility and {{79}} an irrefutable testimony of her divine mission. Thus, like a standard lifted up among the nations (cf. *Isa* 11:12), she invites to herself those who do not believe and at the same time gives greater assurance to her children that the faith that they profess rests on solid grounds.[46]

Modernists corrupt this methodology, as is obvious in their historical or objective methodology, which only shows that something unknown is hidden in the history of the Church, but not some miraculous intervention (or moral miracle) brought about by God. However, certain Catholic apologists, as it were, timidly propose these external-intrinsic motives because they do not distinguish them well enough from internal motives or because they leave a complete demonstration of them to "the demonstration of Catholicism" presented after "the demonstration of Christianity" and thereby distinguish too much these two parts of apologetics.

Internal methodology proceeds from a consideration of the aspirations that are already an object of the internal experience of the person who does not yet believe. However, these aspirations proceed either from our nature alone or also unconsciously from actual prevenient grace stirring the nonbeliever to faith and conversion. The motives of credibility of this order

---

45 [First] Vatican Council, *Dei filius*, ch. 3 (Denzinger, 3009). [Trans. note: Fr. Garrigou-Lagrange has slightly ellipsed the passage for emphasis, as will be evident from a citation below.]

46 Ibid. (Denzinger, nos. 3013 and 3014).

are either universal or individual. They are *universal* if it is made manifest that only in Christianity does one find the fulfillment of all of the legitimate (and, especially, supreme) aspirations of our nature to truth, justice, fortitude, sanctity, to God and the future life, and so forth. A motive is *individual* if it is concerned with the individual experience of this fulfillment or the profound peace that seems to come from a supernatural intervention by God.

These aspirations exist before the acceptance of revelation. Nay, *the fulfillment* of them is known *inchoately* before the acceptance of faith by men of good will to whom the religion to be believed is proposed, but it exists *consummatively* (in the manner of a confirmation) together with the living faith that acts in charity.

The value of this internal methodology is exaggerated by liberal Protestants and modernists, who consider it either as being the only efficacious methodology or, at least, as being the primary one, which is so necessary that the other methodologies would remain inefficacious without it. Hence, liberal Protestants and modernists retain from Christianity only the truths that evidently appear as being conformed to our natural aspirations, and they admit them on account of this conformity and not on account of the authority of God who reveals. However, they reject or symbolically interpret the properly supernatural mysteries of the Trinity, the Incarnation, the Redemption, the Eucharist, grace, glory, and eternal damnation.

In contrast, the Church has defined that by itself, an internal methodology is not efficacious. However, she does not rule out its use. One reads in the [First] Vatican Council's declaration *Dei filius*: "However, in order that the obedience of our faith be nevertheless in harmony with reason, God willed that exterior proofs of his revelation, viz., divine facts, especially miracles and prophecies, should be joined to the *interior* helps of the Holy Spirit"[47] Likewise: "If anyone says that divine revelation cannot be made by outward signs and that, therefore, men ought to be moved to faith *solely* by each one's inner experience or by personal inspiration, let him be anathema."[48] Therefore, according to the Church, the internal motives are indeed not to be held in scorn. However, in order for them to be sufficient of themselves and without others, it would not suffice to argue from the conformity of Christianity with our soul's aspirations, for this conformity already would exist if Christianity were only the most perfect natural religion and a superior form of religious evolution; in reality, we would need to argue, from *so great a* conformity and from *such a miraculous* and profound fulfillment {{80}} of our aspirations, that [Christianity] would seem to arise from a supernatural intervention of God: inas-

---

[47] Ibid. (Denzinger, no. 3009).
[48] Ibid., can. 3.3 (Denzinger, no. 3033).

much as God alone can thus know and satiate the human heart.

As will be shown below, when they are understood in this manner, *universal* internal motives, taken together and known by common experience, offer moral certitude regarding the divine origin of Christianity.

However, *individual* internal motives can manifest that the credibility of the mysteries of faith is probable, but essentially [*per se*] and ordinarily they do not suffice for proving credibility.[49]

This sufficiently fixes our terminology related to the various kinds of apologetic methodology. Let us now historically look into how the defenders of the faith proceeded.

§2. How Did the Prophets Prove Their Divine Mission?

In the *Old Testament*, it is said that the prophets proved their divine mission in three principal ways: (a) by miracles, (b) by the fulfillment of the prophecies, and (c) by the excellency of their religious preaching.

(a) *By miracles.* In many places in the Old Testament we read that God himself gave the prophets the power of performing miracles so as to confirm their divine mission.

For example, in *Exodus* 4:1–5 (DR):

> Moses answered and said: They will not believe me, nor hear my voice, but they will say: The Lord hath not appeared to thee. Then He said to him: What is that thou holdest in thy hand? He answered: A rod. And the Lord said: Cast it down upon the ground. He cast it down, and it was turned into a serpent, so that Moses fled from it. And the Lord said: Put out thy hand and take it by the tail. He put forth his hand, and took hold of it, and it was turned into a rod. That they may believe, saith he, that the Lord God of their fathers . . . hath appeared to thee.[50]

---

49 The pre-conciliar schema of the [First] Vatican Council notes: "Indeed, according to the ordinary course of divine providence, the aforementioned [internal] sentiment, is not based on experience precisely qua supernatural [*non subset experientiae sub formali ratione, quatenus sit supernaturalis*], and if it is separated from extrinsic criteria, is open to the gravest of illusions. Whence also, we see men, on behalf of false religion and manifest errors, call upon 'experience and an internal sentiment' which they attribute to the Holy Spirit. Equally consistent with this confidence in 'internal sentiment' and with a rejection of the motives of credibility is another error at our time spread among many, by which they dare to affirm that it is sometimes divinely ordained that one defect from the Catholic religion to another, if it is discovered that it does not satisfy one's internal experience and religious sentiment." See Jean-Michel-Alfred Vacant, *Études théologiques sur les constitutions du Concile du Vatican d'après les actes du concile*, vol. 1 (Paris: Delhomme et Briguet, 1895), 504.

50 [Trans. note: Fr. Garrigou-Lagrange cites Exodus 4:1–19.]

Thus, in the name of God, Moses, with rod in hand, accomplished many miracles or changed the water into blood (Exod 4:1–19, 29–31; 7:3–5). Likewise, in 1 Kgs 13:1–6, a prophet sent from Judah to Jeroboam prophesied and gave "a sign, that the Lord hath spoken: Behold the altar shall be rent, and the ashes that are upon it shall be poured out" (1 Kgs 13:3, DR). Similarly, in 1 Kings 17: 23–24 we read concerning the resurrection of the son of the widow from Sarephta by Elijah: "And the woman said to [Elijah]: Now by this I know that thou art a man of God, and the word of the Lord in thy mouth is true" (DR). Similarly, after another of Elijah's miracles, "[all the people] fell on their faces, and they said: The Lord, he is God; the Lord, he is God" (1 Kgs. 18:39). Isaiah also accomplished many miracles in confirmation of the truth of his prophecies. See in *Isaiah* 8:7–12, 38:5–8 God himself says to him: "And this shall be a sign to thee from the Lord, that the Lord will do this word which he hath spoken: [etc.]" (DR).

(b) *The fulfillment of the prophecies* is the principal sign for distinguishing true prophets from false ones.

{{81}} God himself revealed this to Moses in Deuteronomy 18:20–22 (DR):

> But the prophet, who being corrupted with pride, shall speak in my name things that I did not command him to say, or in the name of strange gods, shall be slain. And if in silent thought thou answer: How shall I know the word that the Lord hath not spoken? Thou shalt have this sign: Whatsoever that same prophet foretelleth in the name of the Lord, and it cometh not to pass: that thing the Lord hath not spoken, but the prophet hath forged it by the pride of his mind: and therefore thou shalt not fear him.

In many places in the Old Testament, we read that the fulfillment of prophecies was accomplished not long after the [prophet's] preaching. See 1 Kings 18:1–4; 22:25–28, 29–40; 2 Kings 6:31–38; 7:1–2, 16–20; 8:13–15; 12:14–19, 25; 19:20–35; 24:2; *Amos* 7:17; *Jeremiah* 28:8–9, 15–17.

But many prophecies were not fulfilled in the eyes of those hearing them, and for this reason many exclaimed and scoffed about them. Hence, we read in *Amos* 5:18: "Woe to those scoffing at the day of the Lord."[51] Likewise in *Amos* 9:10 and *Ezekiel* 12:21–28. Nay, because the prophets foretold future evils to the sinful people, they were therefore persecuted (see Matt 5:12; Acts 7:52).

(c) Finally, the preaching of the true prophet is confirmed by its own *excellence*, its *moral end*, and its religious effects.

By contrast, we read in the Old Testament that the false prophets prophesied for

---

51 [Trans. note: Fr. Garrigou-Lagrange has "vae deridentibus diem Domini" rather than the Vulgate's original "vae desiderantibus diem Domini": "Woe to them that desire the day of the Lord" (DR).]

money, motivated by greed or ambition. See Micah 3, Jeremiah 23:14–15, and so forth.

§3. What Was the Via / Way (or Methodology) Used by Christ (and, Afterwards, by His Apostles)?

(1) **Christ.** *A priori*, as it were, it is clear from Christ's teaching what sort of methodology should be used. Indeed, the right way or methodology for proposing a given teaching depends upon *the object* of this teaching and upon *the motive* on account of which it ought to be admitted. Now, the teaching that Christ proposed is, as he himself said, a teaching that is, properly speaking, divine and hidden, to be admitted most firmly on account of the authority of God who reveals. Thus, the right way for proposing this teaching was necessary to lead men to acknowledge its divine origin; and such was, in fact, the way Christ proceeded in handing on his teaching. Both this reason and this fact must be explained from the Gospel.

The object. Indeed, it is clear that Christ did not propose a philosophical teaching, to be accepted on account of its conformity with our reason, or only a moral doctrine (or moral precepts) as liberal Protestants claim, but instead proposed *mysteries which are hidden from human reason.* See Matthew 11:25–27 (DR):

> I confess to thee, O Father, Lord of Heaven and earth, because thou hast hid these things from the wise and prudent, and hast revealed them to little ones. Yea, Father: for so hath it seemed good in thy sight. All things are delivered to me by my Father. And no one knoweth the Son but the Father: neither doth any one know the Father, but the Son, and he to whom it shall please the Son to reveal him.

Likewise, in John 1:18 (DR): "No man hath seen God at any time: the only begotten Son who is in the Bosom of the Father, he hath declared him." Also, St. Paul in 1 Corinthians 2:4–8 (DR) says:

> And my speech and my preaching was not in the persuasive words of human wisdom, but in shewing of the Spirit and power, that your faith might not stand on the wisdom of men, but on the power of God. . . . But we speak the wisdom of God in a mystery, a wisdom which is hidden, {{82}} which God ordained before the world, unto our glory: [a mystery] which none of the princes of this world knew.

Therefore, Christ's teaching is proposed as divine and hidden from human reason.

The motive. On account of what motive is this preaching to be accepted? Not on account of human reasons, for Christ did not demonstrate "by persuasive words of human wisdom," by showing in particular the conformity of his doctrine with our nature. Instead, Christ's words were to be admitted on account of the authority of God who reveals. And therefore, Christ taught "As one having power, and not as the scribes" (Mark 1:22, DR). "And the Jews wondered, saying: How doth this man know letters, having never learned? Jesus answered them and said: *My doctrine is not mine, but his that sent me*" (John 7:15–16). Therefore, he preached with the greatest humility and, at the same time, with the greatest authority. Hence, Christ demanded absolute *and utterly firm adherence* to his words and to the incomprehensible revealed mysteries. However, *faith-confidence* [*fiducia*] or *sympathy* does not suffice, as liberal Protestants wish to be the case. Nor did he only proclaim the mysteries as though they were a *theme* of a given variable *religious experience*, as the modernists wish. Instead, he commands that this divine teaching must be preached to all the nations and believed under pain of eternal damnation, such that one would be bound to prefer martyrdom to denying the faith. Hence, it is said in Mark 16:16 (DR): "He that believeth and is baptized shall be saved: but he that believeth not shall be condemned." Likewise, in Matthew 10:28–32 (DR): "And fear ye not them that kill the body, and are not able to kill the soul. . . . Everyone therefore that shall confess me before men, I will also confess him before my Father who is in heaven." Also, Matthew 24:35 (DR): "Heaven and earth shall pass, but my words shall not pass."

Therefore, the right way for proposing this teaching needed to lead men to acknowledge its divine origin so that the divine mysteries might be believed with utter firmness.

However, how did Christ manifest the divine origin of his teaching? In short, (A) by external-extrinsic motives; (B) by external-intrinsic motives; and (C) by internal motives.

A. **Above all, Christ invoked his miracles and the prophesies of the Old Testament.** This is clear as much from the three Synoptic Gospels as from John's Gospel. See Matthew 11:3–6 (DR), when the disciples of John the Baptist asked Jesus:

> Art thou he that art to come, or look we for another? And Jesus making answer said to them: Go and relate to John what you have heard and seen. *The blind see, the lame walk, the lepers are cleansed, the deaf hear, the dead rise again, the poor have the gospel preached to*

them. And blessed is he that shall not be scandalized in me.

In Mark 2:10–12 (DR):

> *But that you may know that the Son of man hath power on earth to forgive sins, (he saith to the sick of the palsy,) I say to thee: Arise.* Take up thy bed and go into thy house. And immediately he arose and, taking up his bed, went his way in the sight of all: so that all wondered and glorified God, saying: We never saw the like.

Likewise, Matthew 9:6 and Luke 5:21. Again, in Mark 9:38 (DR), Jesus says, "For there is no man that doth a miracle in my name and can soon speak ill of me."

{{83}} The Gospels themselves are, as it were, a series of sermons by Christ, accompanied by narrations of his miracles confirming his preaching.[52]

Now, someone might say, "These sensible signs are indeed more suitable for the multitude who need sensible arguments, and therefore the Synoptic Gospels in particular report proofs from miracles. However, if the Gospel is considered in a more spiritual manner, miracles will seem to be of less importance."

The response to this is as follows: It is difficult to consider the Gospel in a more spiritual sense than it was considered by the author of the fourth Gospel. Now, in the fourth Gospel, miracles are often reported as being proper and irrefutable signs of revelation. See John 5:36 (DR): "But I have a greater testimony than that of John: *for the works which the Father hath given me to perfect, the works themselves which I do, give testimony of me, that the Father hath sent me.*" Later, in John 11:42, St. John tells us that Jesus prayed before the resurrection of Lazarus, saying, "because of the people who stand about have I said it, that they may believe that thou hast sent me," and in fact many Jews believed. Likewise, see John 2:11, 3:2, 7:31, and 20:30.[53]

---

[52] In Matthew 11:21 (DR): "[Jesus upbraids] the cities wherein were done the most of his miracles, for that they had not done penance. 'Woe to thee, Corozain . . .'"

In Matthew 14:33 (DR): After Peter, by the Lord's power, walked upon the waters, "they that were in the boat came and adored him, saying, 'Indeed thou art the Son of God.'"

Likewise, Luke 1:36 reports the sign announced to Mary by the angel: "And behold thy cousin Elizabeth . . . hath conceived a son in her old age."

In Luke 7:16 (DR), after the resurrection of the son of the widow of Nain, it is said, "They glorified God, saying, 'A great prophet is risen up among us: and, God hath visited his people.'"

[53] As regards the question of credibility and the probative force of miracles according to St. John, see Fr. Ambroise Gardeil's article "Crédibilité" in the *Dictionnaire théologie catholique,* col.

The Evangelists also note *that this methodology was in fact efficacious,* at least with respect to the many, and they explain why it was not efficacious for all. See John 2:11 (DR): "This beginning of miracles did Jesus in Cana of Galilee and manifested his glory. And his disciples believed in him." Likewise, see John 2:23 (DR):[54] "Now when He was at Jerusalem, at the pasch, upon the festival day, many believed in his name, seeing his signs which he did." John 3:2 (DR): "[Nicodemus] came to Jesus by night, and said to him: Rabbi, we know that thou art come a teacher from God; for no man can do these signs which thou dost, unless God be with him." John 7:31 (DR): "But of the people many believed in him and said: When the Christ cometh, shall he do more miracles than these which this man doth?" Finally, on many occasions Christ announces the *sign of his future Resurrection* (see Matt 12:39; 16:21; 17:22; 20:19; 27:63).

{{84}} Likewise, Jesus frequently[55] argued *from the prophecies* of the Old Testament. For example, John 5:39–46 (DR): "Search the scriptures . . . the same are they that give testimony of me. . . . For if you did believe Moses, you would perhaps believe me also: for he wrote of me." Christ also opened the prophecies to the disciples on the way to Emmaus: "O foolish and slow of heart to believe in all things which the prophets have spoken" (Luke 24:25, DR).

Why did not all believe? This is explained in the Gospel: not because miracles were insufficient signs, as liberal Protestants and modernists say, but because an evil disposition of soul can shut the mind's eyes even to the most manifestly visible miracles. Thus, it is said in Matthew 11:20–21 (DR): "Then [Jesus] began to upbraid the cities wherein were done the most of his miracles [*virtutes*],[56] for that they had not done penance. Woe thee,

---

2238. At the end of his Gospel, St. John wrote, "Many other signs also did Jesus in the sight of his disciples, which are not written in this book" (John 20:30, DR). Nevertheless, divine faith is not formally founded on the evidence of sensible signs, and Christ (see John 4:48, DR) as a reproach said, "Unless you see signs and wonders, you believe not," for as St. Thomas teaches in *ST* III, q. 43, a. 1, ad 3, "Miracles diminish the merit of faith insofar as those who are unwilling to believe those things that are proven by the divine scriptures unless [they are proven] through miracles are shown to be hard of heart. And, nevertheless, it is better for them that they be converted to faith even through miracles, than that they remain utterly unbelieving. Indeed, it is written in 1 Cor 14:22 that 'signs were given to unbelievers,' namely so that they may be converted to faith."

Hence, St. John indicates in many places that divine faith is a *gift from God.* See John 8:47 (DR): "He that is of God heareth the words of God. Therefore, you hear them not, because you are not of God." Likewise, see John 10:26, 12:37–43.

54 [Trans. note: Replacing "John 5:23" with "John 2:23."]
55 [Trans. note: Reading *frequenter* for *frequienter.*]
56 Discussing the grace of miracles in *ST* II-II, q. 178, a. 1, ad 3, St. Thomas observes, with regard to the various names by which miracles are designated: "In miracles, two things can be paid heed to. One indeed is what is done, which is indeed something exceeding the power [*facultatem*] of nature, and on account of this, miracles are called 'powers' [*virtutes*]. The other is that on account of which the miracles are performed, namely for manifesting something

Corozain, woe to thee, Bethsaida, for if in Tyre and Sidon had been wrought the miracles that have been wrought in you, they had long ago done penance in sackcloth and ashes." Likewise, in John 5:40, 8:47, 9:41, and 15:24 (DR): *"If I had not done among them the works that no other man hath done, they would not have sin: but now they have both seen and hated both me and my Father."*

Nay, the Pharisees said:

This man casteth not out devils but by Beelzebub the prince of the devils. And Jesus knowing their thoughts, said to them: . . . If Satan cast out Satan, he is divided against himself: how then shall his kingdom stand? . . . But if I by the Spirit of God cast out devils, then is the kingdom of God come upon you. . . . Therefore I say to you: Every sin and blasphemy shall be forgiven men, but the blasphemy of the Spirit shall not be forgiven. (Matt 12:24–31, DR)

This is the sin against the Holy Spirit and against his manifest intervention. Thus, the miracle was not an insufficient argument. Instead, the unbelief of the Jews came from their perversity, by which they resisted the grace of faith. Hence, it is said, "[These] give testimony of me. But you do not believe, because you are not of my sheep. My sheep hear my voice" (John 10:25–27, DR). In this, we can clearly see the supernaturality of faith. Likewise, John 8:47 (DR): *"He that is of God heareth the words of God. Therefore you hear them not, because you are not of God."* Also, Acts 13:48 (DR): "And as many as were ordained to life everlasting believed."

Hence, Christ frequently argued from his miracles to prove the divine origin of his teaching.

B. **Christ also argued from motives intrinsic to his teaching or to his life.** Indeed, Christ's doctrine concerning himself attracted men of good will, as is obvious from the beginning of Jesus's ministry, when he pronounced the Sermon on the Mount, beginning with the beatitudes: "Blessed are the poor in spirit. . . . Blessed are the meek. . . . Blessed are those who hunger and thirst for justice. . . . Blessed are the pure of heart. . . . Blessed are those who suffer persecution on account of justice. . . . Blessed are the peacemakers . . . (and so forth). . . . You are the light of the world. . . . Unless your justice abounds beyond that of the Scribes and the Pharisees, you will not enter the kingdom of heaven." In this sermon, Christ proposes the evangelical law in its perfection, the love of God and of neighbor, and teaches the best manner of praying. And, at the end of the sermon, as St. Matthew writes in 7:28–29

---

supernatural, and on account of this, they are commonly called 'signs.' However, on account of their excellence they are called 'wonders' [*portenta*] or 'prodigies' [*prodigia*], as it were displaying something far off."

(DR), "when Jesus had fully ended {{85}} these words, *the people* [*turbae*] *were in admiration at his doctrine*, for he was teaching them as one having power, and not as the scribes and Pharisees." These crowds [*turbae*] had not yet seen Christ's miracles but had already discovered a particular motive of credibility in the excellence of his doctrine. Indeed, to men of good will, this preaching appears sublime and above nature. For example, the beatitude "blessed are those who suffer persecution" is so elevated above nature that even those who already believe, when persecution comes, do not immediately understand the beatitude [or bliss] to be found in it. Indeed, this beatitude can only be known and preached supernaturally. Thus, believers already have a motive of credibility in Christ's very teaching.

Nay, later on, at the end of an enumeration of miracles, Christ himself says, "The blind see, the lame walk, . . . the dead rise again," and adds, as a sign of his divine mission, *"the poor have the gospel preached to them"* (Matt 11:5, DR). Likewise, he argued from his holiness in John 8:29–47 (DR):

> And he that sent me is with me: and he hath not left me alone. For I do always the things that please him. . . . But if I say the truth, you believe me not. *Which of you shall convince me of sin?* If I say the truth to you, why do you not believe me? He that is of God heareth the words of God. Therefore you hear them not, because you are not of God.

Similarly, he argued *from the fruits of his teaching* and, on the other hand, from the fruits of the teaching of false prophets. See Matthew 7:15–17 (DR): "Beware of false prophets, who come to you in the clothing of sheep, but inwardly they are ravening wolves. By their fruits you shall know them. . . . Even so every good tree bringeth forth good fruit, and the evil tree bringeth forth evil fruit." Thus, even the very ministers of the Pharisees confessed, *"Never did man speak like this man"* (John 7:46, DR).

C. **Finally, Christ did, in a way, make use of internal motives, not separately but together with the others.** It is said in John 7:17 (DR): "If any man will do the will of him (i.e., of the Father), he shall know of the doctrine, whether it be of God, or whether I speak of myself." Here Christ speaks also about the moral dispositions that remove impediments to knowledge of the truth for the man of good will and about the moral effects of his charity in those who already have arrived at faith. Among these effects, there is profound peace, which comes only from God: *"Peace I leave with you: my peace I give unto you: not as the world giveth, do I give unto you. Let not your heart be troubled: nor let it be afraid"* (John 14:27, DR). "He that shall drink of the water that I will give him shall *not thirst for ever*" (John 4:13, DR). Likewise, the disciples, going to the town named Emmaus, not only heard from Christ an explanation of the prophets but "said one to the other: *Was not our heart burning within us, whilst he spoke in this way and opened to us the Scriptures?*" (Luke 24:32, DR). Similarly, Christ "*interiorly drew Mary Magdalene*," as St. Thomas notes.[57] We also read in the Acts of the Apostles, 16:14: "*The Lord opened the heart of Lydia to hear those things that were being said by Paul.*" However, we cannot always easily discern ordinary grace from extraordinary grace in these internal aids.

{{86}} Thus, in his preaching, Christ made use of all the motives of credibility—namely, external and internal motives—not only to show the conformity of his doctrine with our nature's aspirations but also to manifest its divine origin.

(2) *The apostles* proved the divine origin of Christ's teaching in the same manner.

A. **Among the miracles, they especially argued from Christ's Resurrection.** In the first two sermons to the Jews related in the Acts of the Apostles, St. Peter thus proves the divine authority of Jesus Christ:

> Ye men of Israel, hear these words: *Jesus of Nazareth, a man approved of God among you by miracles and wonders and signs, which God did by him, in the midst of you*, as you also know: This same being delivered up, by the determinate counsel and foreknowledge of God, you by the hands of wicked men have crucified and slain. (Acts 2:22–23, DR)

Likewise, in 3:14–16 (DR):

> But you denied the Holy One and the Just: and desired a murderer to be granted unto you. *But the author of life you killed, whom God hath raised from the dead: of which we are witnesses.* And in the faith of his name, this man (lame since birth), whom you have seen and known, hath his name strengthened. *And the faith which is by him hath given this perfect soundness in the sight of you all.*

---

[57] St. Thomas, *Quodlibet* II, q. 4, a. 1, ad 1: "Among those works that Christ did among men, there ought also to be numbered the interior calling by which he attracted certain people. As Gregory says in a given homily, Christ, who through his external clemency received Mary Magdalen, through mercy interiorly drew her."

Many believed, as we are told in Acts 4; however, the elders, scribes, and priests, who "could say nothing against it," said, "What shall we do to these men? For indeed a miracle hath been done by them, known to all the inhabitants of Jerusalem. It is manifest: and we cannot deny it. But that it may be no farther spread among the people, let us threaten them that they speak no more in this name to any man" (Acts 4:16–17, DR).

Likewise, St. Paul (Acts 28:23–31 and especially in 1 Cor 15:4–58) proves the Gospel's divine authority on the basis of Christ's Resurrection:

> That Christ rose again on the third day according to the scriptures (which is simultaneously a miracle and fulfillment of the prophecies), and that he was seen by Cephas, and after that by the eleven. Then was He seen by more than five hundred brethren at once: of whom many remain until this present, and some are fallen asleep. After that, he was seen by James: then by all the apostles. And last of all, he was seen also by me, as by one born out of due time (1 Cor 15:4–8, DR).

Likewise, in the Synoptic Gospels, St. Matthew, St. Luke, and St. Mark argue from miracles and prophecies. Similarly, St. Philip (Acts 8:35-40) explains to the Eunuch of Queen Candace the prophecy of Isaiah (Isa 53:7): "He was led as a sheep to the slaughter: and like a lamb without voice before his shearer, so openeth he not his mouth. In humility his judgment was taken away" (Acts 8:32–33, DR). St. John also says at the end of his Gospel in 20:30–31 (DR): "Many other signs also did Jesus in the sight of his disciples, which are not written in this book. But these are written, that you may believe that Jesus is the Christ, the Son of God: and that believing, you may have life in his name."

Indeed, by means of new miracles, God confirmed the apostles' own preaching, as is said in Mark 16:20 (DR): "But they going forth (after the Ascension) *preached everywhere: the Lord working withal, and confirming the word with signs that followed*" and in Hebrews 2:4 (DR): "God also bearing them witness by signs and wonders."

{{87}} B. **The apostles argued from motives intrinsic to Christian teaching and life.** This is clear especially in St. Paul's letters. For example, St. Paul says in 2 Corinthians 3:2–3 (DR): "*You are our epistle, written in our hearts, which is known and read by all men:* Being manifested, that you are the epistle of Christ, ministered by us, and written: not with ink but with the Spirit of the living God: not in tables of stone but in the fleshly tables of the heart." What is meant here is that the Christian life of the faithful is a sign confirming the teaching of the apostles. "Indeed, every good tree bears good fruit" (Matt 7:17).

C. **Likewise, the apostles also made use of internal motives simultaneously, not separately,** especially for those who already had faith and charity, for the fruits of charity in them were signs confirming the truth of the faith's teaching. In Romans 8:9–16 (DR): "But you are not in the flesh, but in the Spirit. . . . For you have not received the spirit of bondage again in fear: but you have received the spirit of adoption of sons, whereby we cry: Abba (Father). *For the Spirit himself giveth testimony to our spirit, that we are the sons of God.*" Likewise, in 1 John 2:27 (DR), it is said, "His unction teacheth you of all things." This is concerned with the gifts of the Holy Spirit, especially with the gift of wisdom.[58] Likewise, St. Paul enumerates in Galatians 5:19–23 (DR): "Now the works of the flesh are manifest: which are fornication, . . . idolatry, . . . enmities, contentions, . . . envies, murders, drunkenness," and in opposition, "*The fruit of the Spirit* is, charity, joy, peace, patience, . . . mildness, faith, modesty, continency, chastity." Likewise, in Philippians 4:7 (DR): "*[May] the peace of God, which surpasseth all understanding,* keep your hearts and minds in Christ Jesus." Indeed, this peace not only fulfills our natural aspirations but surpasses them; thus, it confirms all the other motives of credibility and guards our understanding, for we need the motives of credibility not only for arriving at faith but also for persevering in it.

Thus, the divine origin of Christ's teaching is made manifest through the various external and internal motives [of credibility].

§4. The Apologetic Methodology of the Fathers of the Church

(1) *The Apostolic Fathers*: St. Barnabas, St. Clement of Rome, St. Ignatius of Antioch, St. Polycarp, and Papias wrote, in particular, letters for moral exhortation, presenting the faithful with the excellence of salvation through the grace of Christ, as well as their duty to obey the bishops and reject heresies and schisms. In defense of the faith, the Apostolic Fathers argue from miracles but even more so from the prophecies of the Old Testament. This was more efficacious against the Jews who had not seen the miracles of Christ but knew the books of the Old Testament. However, the general defense of Christianity was not yet established during this era as an independent undertaking.

(2) *In the second century, the apologists appear*: Quadratus, Aristides,

---

[58] See St. Thomas, *ST* II-II, q. 45, a. 5.

St. Justin (who wrote two *Apologies* and the *Dialogue with Trypho*), Tatian, Athenagoras, Theophilus of Alexandria, Minutius Felix, *Tertullian* (*Apologetics*), Hermias, and *St. Irenaeus* against the Gnostics. These apologists (A) refuted the calumnies made against Christians; (B) showed the excellence of Christianity over paganism and Judaism; and (C) manifested the divine origin of Christ's teaching.

A. The apologists *repelled the calumnies* of the Jews and the Gentiles concerning the life of the Christians. Indeed, the Christians were accused of impiety, {{88}} incestuous relations, quasi-atheism (because they did not worship visible gods), of being violators of the laws, haters of mankind, eaters of the flesh of children, and so forth.

To repel these calumnies, the apologists *argued from the purity of the Christian life*: Christians are neither atheists, nor incestuous, nor dissolute, nor murderers of infants, but on the contrary, worship God in spirit and truth, are chaste, and practice charity toward their neighbors.

B. *They proved the excellence of Christianity* over paganism and Judaism *by means of the antiquity and purity of Christ's teaching*. The antiquity of the Christian religion is clear from the fact that Christ did not come to abolish the law of the Jews but, rather, to fulfill it. Indeed, he is announced by the entire Old Testament, and Moses is much more ancient than Homer.[59] However, the purity of Christ's teaching is manifested through the things that he taught concerning God, the rejection of idolatry, and the virtues (especially charity, beneficence, chastity, and penance). As much from the perspective of dogmas as from that of the precepts, this doctrine shows itself to be more excellent than the polytheism of the pagans and even than Moses's teaching. To prove this, it suffices to argue from motives intrinsic to Christian doctrine and the Christian life, and also from universal internal motives, as Tertullian did when he spoke in favor of Christianity by appealing to "the testimony of the naturally Christian soul,"[60] inasmuch as the human soul naturally admits the unity of God, the future life, and the existence of evil spirits. Tertullian did not wish to deny the supernaturality of Christianity. Rather, his intention was to manifest its conformity with our nature, for all the natural truths of religion are most perfectly proposed in Christ's teaching.

C. Finally, to prove not only the excellence but also *the divine origin* of Christianity, the apologists of this era refer to *miracles and prophecies*.

In chapter 32 of the first *Apology*, St. Justin broadly shows that the

---

[59] See, for example, Tatian, *Oratio*, ch. 31, 36, 41.

[60] Tertullian, *Apology*, ch. 1, and *On the Soul's Testimony*.

prophecies of the Old Testament were fulfilled in Christ. And he develops this argument more fully in his *Dialogue with Trypho*, in which (no. 69), he refers to the miracles and prophecies of Christ himself. Quadratus, St. Irenaeus, and Tertullian wrote similar sorts of apologies.

Finally, these apologists generally argue *from the conversion of the world*, notwithstanding the innumerable obstacles faced in this task, looking upon this conversion as a kind of moral miracle. They show that this conversion can only come from God. Now, it was brought about through Christ's teaching and power. Therefore, Christ's teaching and power is divine. For example, St. Justin wrote: "We who, once upon a time, delighted in sexual shame now only embrace chastity. We who also practiced magical arts, now have consecrated ourselves to the good and unbegotten God. We who once followed the universally time-honored ways regarding money and possessions now also gather together our possessions in common."[61] The apologists add an argument *based on the constancy of the martyrs*, inasmuch as this constancy, accompanied as it is with serenity and humility and lacking in fanaticism, seems to arise from God's supernatural aid.

We must, however, note that St. Justin does not seem at times to acknowledge well enough the infinite distance between the supernatural teaching of Christ and Plato's philosophy. However, in the end, he does not so much diminish the supernaturality of Christianity as he, instead, elevates Plato too much. Indeed, according to him, Plato and certain ancient philosophers {{89}} borrowed many truths from the sacred books of the Jews, or received a kind of quasi-obscure illumination from the divine word, lest the Gentiles would wholly lack the divine light.[62] On the contrary, Tertullian and [the Shepherd of] Hermas excessively ridicule the errors of the Greeks.[63]

At the same time, *St. Irenaeus*, bishop of Lyon, wrote *Against the Heresies* against the Gnostics who wished to conjoin Christ's revealed teaching with eastern systems, especially with Indian Brahmanism and Zoroastrian dualism, and to clothe that syncretism with a form of Greek philosophy. The general idea of Gnosticism is this: God never manifests himself nor does anything immediately in the world because this would take away from his perfections; instead, he acts through the power of divine spirits (Eons) born of him. One of these spirits is the Demiurge, the other is Christ. St. Irenaeus sets out the first of these systems in book 1 of his *Against the Heresies*; then, he refutes it by means of reason (book 2), by means of tradition

---

[61] St. Justin, *Apology*, I, ch. 14.

[62] Ibid., *Apology*, I, ch. 5, 10, 44, and 46; II, ch. 8, 10, and 13.

[63] Tertullian, *Apology*, ch. 46.

and the teaching of the apostles (book 3), by means of Christ's teaching and the prophecies of the Old Testament (book 4), and finally discusses man's ultimate end (book 5).

Therefore, the apologists made use of all the various kinds of motives, though especially miracles and prophecies, in proving the divine origin of Christ's teaching. They conveyed other motives more so as to manifest the purity and excellence of Christianity.

(3) *In the third century, Clement of Alexandria and Origen* stood out as apologetes in the school of Alexandria. Clement, in his *Exhortation to the Greeks* sets forth and refutes the superstition, disgracefulness, and impiety of paganism. In the *Paedagogus*, he shows that the truth is no longer to be found in the Greek poets but in Christ, the Word of God, for Christ is the pedagogue (or teacher) of men, who not only lavishes them with wisdom but also leads them to amend their lives. Finally, in the *Stromata*, Clement sets forth and defends Christian doctrine against pagan philosophy, especially against false *gnosis*. He does not reproach all of philosophy but, rather, only Epicurean and Stoic philosophy, for there are many truths in the pagans, especially in Plato. However, no philosophical school embraces the fullness of the true teaching, and to attain unto it, we need the divine revelation handed on to us by Christ and accepted through faith. Thus, Clement shows that only the Christian religion responds to the legitimate aspirations of our nature. However, to prove its divine origin and the divine filiation of Jesus Christ, he argues from the prophecies of the Old Testament and from the various testimonies and miracles that are related in the New Testament, especially from the prodigies accomplished after Christ's Ascension, and from the miraculous diffusion of the Christian religion.[64] Hence, Clement makes use of all the motives of credibility.

Origen wrote the apologetic work *Contra Celsum*. Celsus was an epicurean philosopher who depicted Christ as being an imposter and explained the miraculous diffusion of Christianity in a natural manner. Origen, on the other hand, showed the purity and extraordinary nature of Christ's virtues, manifested the purity and elevation of Christianity from intrinsic criteria, and proved its divine origin through prophecies and miracles, especially through Christ's Resurrection.[65]

{{90}} (4) *In the fourth and fifth centuries*, Lactantius (*The Divine Institutes*), Eusebius of Caesaria (*The Proof of the Gospel*), St. Cyril of Jerusalem, and St. John Chrysostom, like Christ himself, the apostles, and preceding

---

[64] See Clement, *Stromata*, bk. 6, ch. 15.

[65] See Origen, *Contra celsum*, bk. 1, ch. 2.

Fathers, noted that the only people who are moved by miracles and prophecies are those who seek the truth with a sincere and humble disposition.

St. Augustine, in the two short works *On the True Religion* and *On the Usefulness of Believing*, prepared the way for demonstrating the truth of the Christian faith. However, he set forth this proof in the book *The City of God*. In this great work, he does not consider the intrinsic and extrinsic motives of credibility separately but instead joins them all together in the miraculous life of the Church, or [*seu*] of the whole Christian religion, which appears as the City of God in opposition to paganism, wherein there is found, as he makes clear, the city of perdition (or of the devil). In this text, St. Augustine responded to the objections raised by the pagans, who attributed the fall of the Roman Empire to the abandonment of the old religion of the gods. And the Holy Doctor twisted the objection back at them, saying polytheism, on the contrary, was a religion entirely useless both for increasing temporal prosperity and for [obtaining] felicity in the future life, which many philosophers also promised. Therefore, polytheism of itself, as much in temporal matters as in future and eternal ones, leads to death and perdition and is the City of the Devil (or of Perdition). He proves this claim by making use of the history of paganism. By contrast, divine providence is clear in the history of Christianity, and St. Augustine shows the ways of providence successively by describing the appearance of the City of God alongside the City of the Devil, their progress before Christ, and the end toward which they tend—namely, eternal beatitude for the children of God and eternal reprobation for the children of the devil. Meanwhile in this age, the two cities are mixed together. In the end, they will be separated, but for now they are separate in men's hearts.

In this marvelous work by St. Augustine, the very life of the Church stands forth, as the [First] Vatican Council says, as "a great and perpetual motive of credibility and an irrefutable testimony of her divine mission." Indeed, it is the greatest of miracles, and at the same time, as St. Augustine says, "a sign of past things and a herald of things to come,"[66] inasmuch as the prophecies are fulfilled in her and those things that she now announces will in the end be brought to fulfillment.

Like all the Fathers, St. Augustine teaches that all these arguments are efficacious only for men who seek the truth with love and humility; however, he never says that these subjective dispositions bestow upon the arguments a value that they do not have in themselves. They only dispose men for per-

---

[66] Augustine, *De fide rerum quae non videntur*, no. 8.

ceiving the objective value of the signs.[67]

§5. The Apologetic Methodology of the Scholastic Theologians

{{91}} In the Middle Ages, the Christian religion was assailed especially by Jews and Muslims [*Mahumetanis*]. Arab philosophers such as Avicenna and Averroes set forth Aristotle's doctrine and interpreted it in a manner contrary to the Catholic faith. These philosophers externally professed Islam but, in reality, denied all revelation; nay, they rejected creation properly speaking and providence with regard to particulars, as well as the personal immortality of the soul.[68] Equally, in order to avoid persecution, they[69] taught that something is true according to philosophy but not according to faith. Already, like the rationalists after them, they affirmed, somewhat obscurely, the absolute autonomy of human reason.

Against the Jews and Muslims, *Raymond Martini*, O.P., wrote, from the school of St. Raymond of Peñafort, *The Dagger of the Faith Against the Moors and the Jews*. In this great and quite scientific work, he proves the divine origin of Christianity from the prophecies, which, with the help of the rabbinic interpretations, he excellently sets forth and explains.

St. Thomas, at the urgings of St. Raymond of Peñafort and Pope Urban IV, wrote the *Summa contra gentiles* (or *On the Truth of the Catholic Faith*) for use by those undertaking apostolic work for the conversion of the Moors.

This illustrious work was translated into Greek and Hebrew and was augmented by commentaries. It includes four books, and in this division, the dis-

---

[67] As regards the various texts of St. Augustine pertaining to the credibility of the mysteries of faith, see Fr. Ambroise Gardeil's article "Crédibilité" in the *Dictionnaire de théologie catholique*, col. 2254ff. He collects the principal texts from the *Confessions*, the *Sermons*, the *Treatise on Faith in Things That Are Not Seen*, *On Seeing God*, *The City of God*, his *Commentary on John*, and others. St. Augustine explicitly says, "Obviously nobody believes something unless he first thinks that it ought to be believed" (*On the Predestination of the Saints*, ch. 2, no. 5, ML, vol. 45, col. 963). And he defends the probative force of miracles especially in *On the Usefulness of Believing*, ch. 16, no. 34, ML, vol. 42, col. 89. "He who has called you so that you may believe has not abandoned you; although he may have ordered you to believe that which you cannot see, nevertheless he does not send you away seeing nothing, whence you can believe what you do not see.... Indeed, he came, he performed miracles" (*Sermon* 126, no. 5 in ML, vol. 38, col. 700). "Every man has eyes by which he can see that the dead arise" (*Sermon* 98, no. 1, ML, vol. 38, col. 591).

See the same article by Fr. Gardeil with regard to the doctrine concerning credibility in the Greek and Latin Fathers. The principal texts are cited there.

[68] [Trans. note: In the case of Averroes (Ibn Rushd), at least.]

[69] [Trans. note: Most famously, again, in the case of Averroes, at least in the popular telling.]

tinction of the natural order from the supernatural order is clearer than it was in preceding theologians.[70] Indeed, in the first three books, St. Thomas discusses, by considerations of reason alone, the truths of religion that can be demonstrated by reason. In the first book, he discusses the existence of God and his principal attributes. In the second book, he discusses creation and creatures. The third book is concerned with man's final end. Here he shows that the vision of God through his essence is above the natural power of any created intellect whatsoever. In the fourth book, he discusses properly supernatural truths, which cannot be demonstrated by reason—namely, the mysteries of the Holy Trinity, the Incarnation, Redemption, original sin, the sacraments, the resurrection, and the final judgment. Likewise, he defends these truths through the authority of Sacred Scripture and Tradition, simultaneously showing that they are not opposed to reason but are instead in conformity with it.

Therefore, this *Summa* is more a defense of the truths of our religion in particular than in general. Thus, it is not a work of apologetics[, strictly speaking],[71] for such a work only defends the foundation of faith. Rather, the *Summa contra gentiles* is an apology for all the truths of Christianity and differs from the *Summa theologiae* inasmuch as it is more a defense than an expositive and didactic presentation of theology. Hence, the former is called "Against the Gentiles."

In *SCG* I, ch. 4, St. Thomas proposed a kind of synopsis of the whole of apologetics. Indeed, he here intends to defend the very fact of revelation and conveys three arguments. These must be set forth as an example of the apologetics of the scholastics, for similar things are found in other Catholic teachers of this age. His argument is set forth on the basis of (1) Christ's own miracles, (2) the miraculous conversion of the entire world, and (3) the prophecies of the Old {{92}} Testament. These three arguments vigorously and clearly include the principal proofs offered by the Fathers, and in particular, make clear how they are connected to each other.

St. Thomas wishes to show "that to assent to those things that are of faith, is not foolishness, even though they are above reason."

(1) He *argues from miracles* and notes well the befittingness of this sign when he says:

Indeed, the Divine Wisdom itself, which most fully knows all things, has

---

[70] For example, St. Anselm wished to quasi-demonstrate the Trinity. St. Thomas shows that this demonstration is impossible in *ST* I, q. 32, a. 1 and in *SCG* I, ch. 9.

[71] Nor is it a philosophical summa because it is missing logic, general metaphysics, and cosmology; nay, it begins from God and not from creatures as metaphysics does. It is a theological work but in the form of a defense rather than that of an exposition.

deigned to reveal to men these *secrets* of the Divine Wisdom. This Wisdom *sets forth her own presence and the truth of her teaching and inspiration by means of suitable arguments, whereas to confirm those things that exceed natural knowledge, she visibly sets forth works that exceed the power of the whole of nature.*

This is the reason for the befittingness of miracles—namely, because they are sensible signs that can be produced by God alone, as is more fully explained in the *Summa theologiae*.[72] Then, St. Thomas enumerates the principal physical and intellectual miracles: "Namely, the miraculous curing of illnesses, the raising of the dead, the miraculous alterations of celestial bodies, and what *is more miraculous*,[73] the inspiration of human minds, so that unlettered and simple people, filled with the Holy Spirit, *instantaneously* acquired the heights of wisdom and eloquence."

(2) *St. Thomas likewise argues from the miraculous conversion of the world*, inasmuch as it is a moral and chief miracle, and simultaneously an effect of the aforementioned signs. Indeed, he says:

Having examined these signs, through the efficacy of the aforementioned proof, not the violence of arms, nor by the promise of pleasures, and (what is most miraculous of all) in the midst of the tyranny of persecutors, an innumerable host, not only of the simple but also of the wisest of men, flocked to the Christian faith. In this faith, things exceeding every human intellect are preached, the pleasures of the flesh are restrained, and it is taught that all things that are in the world are to be held in contempt. In order for the minds of

---

[72] See *ST* II-II, q. 178, a. 1 ("Whether there is some freely given grace for performing miracles?"): "It is necessary that the uttered word be confirmed so that it may be credible. However, this is brought about through the work of miracles, according to the words of Mark (16:20): 'And confirming the word with the signs that followed'—and reasonably so. For it is natural to man to arrive at intelligible truth through sensible effects. Whence, just as man, led by natural reason, can arrive at some knowledge of God through natural effects, so too through certain supernatural effects, which are called miracles, man is led to a kind of supernatural knowledge of things to be believed." Likewise, in *ST* III, q. 43, a. 1 ("Whether Christ should have performed miracles?"): "It is divinely permitted for man to perform miracles for two reasons. First, indeed, and principally, so as to confirm the truth that one teaches: for, because those things that are held on faith exceed human reason, they cannot be proven through human reasons but must be proven through *an argument of the divine power, so that when someone performs works that only God can do, one may believe those things that are said to be from God*, just as when someone delivers letters sealed by the king's ring, what is contained in them is believed to come from the will of the king. Secondly, [man is permitted to perform miracles] so as to show the presence of God in man through the grace of the Holy Spirit, namely so that when a man does the works of God, God is believed to dwell in him through grace."

[73] These miracles of the intellectual order are more miraculous in themselves and to the eyes of the wise, but perhaps not for all men because they are not as sensibly manifest.

mortals to assent to such things this involves both *the greatest of miracles* and a manifest work of divine inspiration so that, spurning visible things, men should only desire invisible ones.[74]

{{93}} (3) Similarly, St. Thomas argues *from prophesies* inasmuch as they were fulfilled in the aforementioned miracles and in the conversion of the world: "However, that this happened neither suddenly nor by accident but, instead, by divine arrangement was made manifest through the fact that beforehand, through many oracles of the prophets, God foretold that He would do this. The books of these prophets are held in veneration among us as bearing witness to our faith."

(4) Finally, by way of conclusion, St. Thomas shows *that the miraculous life of the Church* is now a sufficient motive of credibility for us, such that physical miracles are no longer necessary today:

> However, this *miraculous* conversion of the world to the Christian faith is the most certain evidence of the signs from the past, such that it is no longer nec-

---

[74] In *ST* I-II, q. 113, a. 10 ("Whether the justification of the ungodly [*impii*] is a miraculous work?"), St. Thomas says, "Sometimes it is miraculous and sometimes it is not. Indeed, it is the common and customary course of justification that by God moving the soul interiorly, man is converted to God, first indeed by an imperfect conversion, so that it may afterwards become perfect, for 'inchoate charity merits to be increased, and having been increased merits to be brought to perfection,' as St. Augustine says (*Tractates on the Epistle of John*, tract. 5). However, sometimes, God vehemently moves the soul so that a kind of perfection of justice follows, as was the case in St. Paul's conversion, which was also accompanied externally by a miraculous prostration, and therefore the conversion of Paul is solemnly commemorated in the Church as something miraculous."

Likewise, St. Thomas, in this passage from *SCG* I, ch. 6, shows how the conversion of the world was marvelous and miraculous, and to make this manifest he argues not indeed from the conformity of Christianity with the aspirations of our nature but, rather, from the impossibility of naturally embracing the Christian teaching and perfection, likewise from the impediments of the persecutors, from the simplicity and natural powerlessness of the apostles, and from the wisdom of many converts.

When he says that this conversion of the world is *the greatest of miracles*, he wishes to say this is so at least *in itself*, according to the judgment of the wise, though perhaps not according to the judgment of all men. Indeed, in itself, this miraculous conversion of the world is something greater than the resurrection of any given corpse, for it is a spiritual resurrection of souls; however, because the spiritual is also of higher order than the physical miracle, it is not as easily perceived by men who are in need of sensible signs. Aristotle often says (e.g., in *Metaphysics*, bk. 1, ch. 1) those things that are the most intelligible *in themselves*, such as spiritual things and the supreme causes, are less intelligible *to us* because they are most distant from the senses.

[Trans. note: This footnote is only found in the footnote section of this page of the original and is not attached to the text. The general point appears to be relevant to the matters here under discussion.]

essary that they be further repeated, since they are evidently apparent in their effect. Indeed, it would be *more miraculous than all signs* if the world were led by simple and humble men without miraculous signs to believe such difficulty things, to perform such difficult actions, and to have so lofty a hope. Nevertheless, even in our days, God does not cease to work miracles through his saints for the confirmation of the faith.

Thus, he provides an excellent exposition of how all the signs are interconnected.

Then St. Thomas argues against the divine origin of Islam because (1) Mohammed proposed a worldly and carnal ethics, and, as regards dogmas, proposed naturally knowable truths with many fables and utterly erroneous doctrines; (2) because miracles were wanting; (3) because the miraculous conversion of the world is lacking, but on the contrary, violence of arms was used to impose the faith of Islam; and (4) because prophecies are also lacking, nay, the true prophecies of Sacred Scripture are adulterated [by Islam].

Therefore, what is to be concluded concerning St. Thomas's thought regarding the methodology of apologetics? Two conclusions are sufficiently clear: (A) from the perspective of external motives and (B) from the perspective of internal motives.

A. *From the perspective of external motives*: St. *Thomas makes use of all the external motives*, not only those *extrinsic* to doctrine and the Christian life (as are the majority of sensible miracles) but also *those that are intrinsic* to our religion.

And these latter that are drawn from the sublime loftiness and the befittingness of the Christian life and teaching are developed in the whole of dogmatic and moral theology when one shows how given revealed mysteries (e.g., of the Trinity, the Incarnation, the Redemption, the Eucharist, and so forth, as also in any given Christian virtue of humility, virginity, fortitude {{94}} in martyrdom, faith, hope, and charity) supernaturally exceed our nature while, nonetheless, being maximally in conformity with it. None of the preceding theologians, nor of those that came after[75] St. Thomas, more exactly and profoundly distinguished the natural order from the supernatural order than he did, and nevertheless neither did any of them better show the harmony of these two orders according to the principle: "Grace presupposes nature as a perfection presupposes that which can be perfected."[76] Indeed, grace does not destroy what is right in nature. However, what is inordinate must be destroyed through mortification and the cross, and then the true harmony is clearly apparent; otherwise, there would be only a

---

[75] Indeed, afterward, Scotus, the nominalists, Molina, and Suarez diminish the distinction of the two orders, as we will see below when we discuss obediential potency (or the elevability of our nature to the supernatural order).

[76] *ST* I, q. 2, a. 2, ad 1.

false likeness of harmony (or the confusion which is practical naturalism)

B. *From the perspective of internal motives.* In many places throughout his works, St. Thomas spoke of internal motives when he was concerned with: (a) the instinct of the Holy Spirit leading one to faith,[77] (b) the influx of the very light of faith for confirming the judgment of credibility,[78] and (c) the experiential knowledge of divine things through the gift of wisdom for confirming the faith that one has already accepted.[79]

The Holy Doctor also asks in *Quodlibet* II, q. 4, a. 1, "Whether men would have been bound to believe in Christ were he not to have performed miracles?" And he responds, "*If Christ had not performed visible miracles, then other manners for attracting men to faith would have remained, by which men would have been bound to assent.* Indeed, men were bound to believe the Author of the Law and of the Prophets. *They were also bound not to resist the interior calling [that they received].*" And in ad 1: "Among those works that Christ did among men, [there ought also to be numbered the interior calling by which he attracted certain people], just as Gregory says in a given homily, that Christ, who through his external clemency received Mary Magdalen, through mercy inwardly drew her."[80] Likewise, in ad 3: "The interior instinct by which Christ could manifest Himself without exterior miracles, pertained to the power of the first truth, which inwardly illuminates and teaches man." Likewise, this is more briefly stated in *ST* III, q. 43, a. 1, ad 3.

---

77 See *ST* II-II, q. 2, a. 9, ad 3: "He who believes has a sufficient motive for believing, for he is influenced by the authority of the divine doctrine confirmed by miracles and, what is more, *by the interior instinct of God inviting* [him to faith]. Whence, he does not believe flippantly. Nevertheless, he does not have sufficient motive for knowing in a scientific manner, and therefore the notion of merit is not destroyed [for him]."

78 See *ST* II-II, q. 1, a. 4, ad 3: "The light of faith makes seen those things that are believed. Indeed, just as through the other *habitus* of the virtues man sees that which is befitting in accord with that *habitus*, so too through the habit of faith is the mind of man inclined to assent to those things that are befitting to right faith and not to others." Also see a. 5, ad 1: "The faithful have knowledge of those things that are held on faith, not in a quasi-demonstrative manner, but inasmuch as through the light of faith they see that they are to be believed in." See also *ST* II-II, q. 2, a. 3, ad 2.

79 See *ST* II-II, q. 8, a. 2: "(Through the gift of understanding), man understands that one is not to depart, on account of external appearances, from those things that are held on faith." Likewise, see a. 5. Hence it is said in John 8:12 (DR), "He that followeth me, walketh not in darkness," and in 1 John 2:27 (DR), "The unction [of the Holy Spirit] teacheth you of all things."

See also *ST* II-II, q. 45 on the gift of wisdom and *ST* I-II, q. 68 on the gifts [of the Holy Spirit] in general, q. 69 on the beatitudes, and q. 70 on the fruits of the Holy Spirit (charity, joy, peace, patience, kindness, goodness, longsuffering, meekness . . . chastity), which are opposed to the works of the flesh (fornication, . . . worship of idols, enmity, anger, dissensions, sects, hatred, murders, etc.).

80 [Trans. note: This quote was missing text near the beginning. The missing content has been supplied.]

Therefore, we must conclude: All the motives are noted by St. Thomas. However, according to him and all the scholastics, in order for a sign to be a motive of credibility, it does not suffice that it show that Christianity is conformed to {{95}} our natural aspirations. Beyond this, it must manifest the divine origin of Christ's doctrine or at least must concur in this manifestation.

Hence, in the aforementioned *SCG* I, ch. 6, the argument proceeds *not so much from the conformity of Christianity with our nature, as, on the contrary, from the impossibility of naturally embracing Christian teaching and perfection* "to believe such difficult things, to perform such difficult actions, and to have so lofty a hope." Likewise, when one alleges the aforementioned conformity of Christianity with our nature or the internal peace that it produces in us, according to St. Thomas's thought, one must argue *from such conformity and profound peace* so as to show that it can come from God alone, especially inasmuch as God alone can intimately join together these seemingly opposed *extremes: namely, the greatest conformity to nature and the greatest gratuity and sublimity,* as appears in the Incarnation and the Eucharist. On the one hand, judging this conformity in accord with the natural spirit, men deny the gratuity of God's gifts, thereby falling into naturalism. On the other hand, neglecting this conformity (as did the Montanists and the Jansenists after them), they arrogantly give in to a false and rigid supernaturalism, without simplicity [*simplicitate*], against nature. (Nay, they sometimes give in to the ravings of false mysticism.) However, this harmony of nature and grace stands forth in its miraculousness only after nature is profoundly purified through mortification and the Cross, as we see in the lives of the saints.

Thus, an abyss separates the methodology of apologetics conceived in line with St. Thomas's thought and that practiced by the modernists, although on both sides there are internal motives. Modernists present how Christianity contains a more perfect form of the development of natural religion; by contrast, St. Thomas discloses how they show that Christianity is the supernatural religion.

The other great scholastics argue in nearly the same manner.[81] They all admit the probative force of miracles, which they hold to be the most certain signs of divine revelation. *Richard of St. Victor* says, "Lord, if there is error, we were deceived by you yourself. Indeed, these things were confirmed among us by so many signs and prodigies of such a nature that they could only have been performed by you."[82]

---

[81] See Ambroise Gardeil, "Crédibilité" in *Dictionnaire théologie catholique*, col. 2259–2269 ("Crédibilité in chez les scolastiques"). [Trans. note: The reference has been corrected here. Fr. Garrigou-Lagrange has "col. 2259–2229."]

[82] Richard of St. Victor, *De Trinitate,* bk. 1, ch. 2. The Victorines differed from the other scholas-

{{96}} *In the fourteenth century*, there was no apologetic work deserving of particular comment. *Nominalists* like Ockham greatly reduced the powers of reason with regard to the knowability of God and of miracles and paved the way for the fideism of Luther, who was their disciple.[83]

In the fifteenth century, *Raymond of Sabunde* wrote a natural theology in which he defends the Catholic faith in a traditional manner by insisting on the harmony of the mysteries of faith with man's final end. At the same time, *Savonarola* wrote *The Triumph of the Cross Over the Wise of the Age* (1497). He first makes use of intrinsic motives—namely, showing the moral effects and practical value of Christianity—then afterwards argues from extrinsic signs.

At the time of the Renaissance [*Regenerationis*], or of the renovation of science, poetry [*poeseos*], and the arts that were cultivated in imitation of models derived from Greco-Roman antiquity, many apologetes proposed a

---

tics in a certain sense inasmuch as they placed the essence of faith in the affect and not in the intellect.

Hugh of St. Victor says in *De sacramentis*, bk. 1, pt. 10, ch. 3: "The substance of faith is found in the affect; its matter is found in knowledge."

By contrast, St. Thomas says in *ST* II-II, q. 2, a. 9: "However, belief itself is an act of the intellect assenting to the divine truth from the command of the will moved by God through grace."

But, in both cases, a certain judgment concerning the rational credibility of the mysteries of faith is prerequired.

It is also to be noted that the *Thomists* and the *Scotists* do not disagree as regards the approval of credibility, but only as regards the relation of the judgment of credibility to divine faith. And indeed, for the Thomists, divine faith is essentially supernatural and has a formal object and a formal motive that are supernatural and unattainable by the powers of reason alone. On the contrary, according to the Scotists, divine faith is only modally supernatural, for [according to them,] someone can see by reason alone from miracles that the mysteries of faith are revealed by God and can believe in them, naturally, as do the demons; however, [according to them] in order to have theological faith the advent of a supernatural modality is required. Luis de Molina, Juan de Lugo, Giles de Coninck, and many others more or less follow Scotus. According to the Thomists, this represents a grave diminution of the supernaturality of divine faith and, [ultimately,] the resolution of its supernatural certitude into the natural certitude of credibility. We need not dwell on this question now, for we will discuss it later in the chapter on credibility and its relation to faith. See the Salmanticenses, *Cursus theologicus*, *De gratia*, tr. 14, diss. 3, dub. 3. Cajetan, *In ST* II-II, q. 1, a. 1, no. 11. Billuart, *De gratia*, diss. 3, a. 2, §2. Likewise, Ambroise Gardeil, "Crédibilité" in *Dictionnaire théologie catholique*, col. 2278–2294 ("De la crédibilité chez Scot, Durand, J. de Lugo; la foi discursive et la crédibilité").

[83] [Tr. note: See Paul Hacker, *Faith in Luther: Martin Luther and the Origin of Anthropocentric Religion* (Steubenville, OH: Emmaus Academic, 2017). Also see Heiko Oberman, *The Dawn of the Reformation: Essays in Late Medieval and Early Reformation Thought* (Grand Rapids, MI: Eerdmans, 1992); *The Harvest of Medieval Theology: Gabriel Biel and Late Medieval Nominalism* (Grand Rapids, MI: Baker Academic, 2000).]

conception of Christianity that was more or less natural. Therefore, they primarily made use of an intrinsic methodology, and *Marsilius Ficinus*, in his book *On the Christian Religion and the Piety of Faith* mixed together the philosophy of Plato with the teaching of Christ so much that Plato appears to be the precursor to Christ. *Juan Luis [Ludovicus] Vivès*, in the five books of *On the Truth of the Christian Faith*, is more traditional and historically sets forth extrinsic and intrinsic arguments.

§6. Apologetic Methodology after the Rise of Protestantism

Here we will consider developments following the rise of Protestantism, specifically: (1) the adversaries of the Christian faith; (2) Protestant apologetics; (3) and Catholic apologetics.

(1) ***The adversaries of the Christian faith: the rationalists.*** At this time, from the very beginning of the practice of free inquiry brought about by Protestants, there arose rationalism (or naturalism). Its origin must be briefly set forth. Following this, we will then present its proper division.

A. *The origin of rationalism (or of naturalism)*: The pseudo-reformers denied neither the fact of revelation nor the inspiration of Sacred Scripture. However, for discerning the meaning of Scripture, they admitted *the principle of free inquiry*, having rejected the Church's authority. In virtue of this principle, certain Protestants, who were called *Socinianists*, already in the sixteenth century did not acknowledge anything as being true in Sacred Scripture except that which can be perceived by natural reason, and they rejected or symbolically interpreted the supernatural mysteries of the Holy Trinity, the Incarnation, the Redemption, and the Eucharist. Such errors are professed today by the *Unitarians*, who are so called because they acknowledge only one person in God. However, since many doubts and contradictions arise from the free interpretation of the Scriptures, they were more inclined to think that nothing can be known with certainty from revelation, that revelation is therefore not necessary, and that merely natural religion suffices. In England, such was the thought of *Edward Herbert Cherbury, Thomas Hobbes, Charles Blount, John Toland, Shaftsbury, Matthew Tindal, and David Hume*, who like[84] *Hobbes* professed skepticism. Likewise, in France, this outlook could be found in *Voltaire, Jean-Jacques Rousseau*, and the *Encyclopedists*, many of whom denied even the existence of God and the immortality of the soul. Likewise, in Holland, *Spinoza*, and in Germany, *Christian Wolff, Gotthold Ephraim Lessing*,

---

[84] [Trans. note: Reading *sicus* as *sicut*.]

Hermann Samuel Reimarus, and others professed similar errors.

{{97}} Thus, rationalism (i.e., the doctrine holding that human reason is absolutely independent and autonomous, the supreme judge in matters of religion) proceeds from the principle of free inquiry, by which the first Protestants rejected the authority of the Church. Indeed, Luther, fighting against philosophy and scholastic theology, reduced the powers of reason and, as a disciple of the nominalists, paved the way for philosophical skepticism and religious fideism. On the other hand, denying the very authority of the Church, he overly extolled the powers of individual sentiment and already posited the principle of rationalism, for from the denial of the authority of the Church, it is easy to make the transition to the denial of the very fact of revelation (or of the authority of God who reveals). However, rationalism is nothing other than the affirmation of the absolute autonomy of human reason and the denial of its subordination to the authority of God who reveals.[85]

B. *The division of rationalism (or naturalism)*. Henceforth, as regards the means that it uses, rationalism comes to be subdivided into *philosophical* rationalism, which proceeds in a theoretical manner, and *biblical* rationalism, which by way of a historical explanation or exegesis of Sacred Scripture rejects everything supernatural. In the order of discovery, the biblical semi-rationalism of the Socinians paved the way for philosophical rationalism. Afterwards, philosophical rationalism provided the *a priori* principles for biblical rationalism, as is obvious in the writings of Spinoza, who, on the basis of the philosophical denial of the supernatural order, the possibility of miracles, and revelation, deduced the rules of the rationalistic hermeneutics of Sacred Scripture.

(a) Now, *philosophical rationalism* appeared in two forms: (α) in a *spiritualistic* form in the writings of the Deists and Spinoza, and (β) in a *sensualistic or empiricist* form in the writings of Hobbes, Hume, and the French encyclopedists.

(α) *Spiritualistic rationalism* first appeared in the writings of the *Deists*. These philosophers are so called because they only admit God's existence as the foundation of religion and reject revelation. They differ from theistic philosophers inasmuch as they also deny, as did the Averroists, particular providence, as well as the possibility of miracles. According to the Deists, God does not have particular relations with men but only governs them through the universal laws of nature from which natural facts proceed in a necessary manner. Voltaire and Rousseau in particular held this doc-

---

[85] See [First] Vatican Council, *Dei filius*, can. 3.1 (Denzinger, no. 3031).

trine. *Voltaire* fought against Sacred Scripture with derision and sophisms, omitting or corrupting its words in order to make them appear laughable. *Jean-Jacques Rousseau* also rejected everything supernatural, fought against miracles, prophecies, and revelation, but nevertheless admitted the possibility of miracles[86] and sometimes extolled Christ and the Gospel with the greatest of praise.[87]

Spinoza also denied the real and essential distinction between God and the world, and taught absolute determinism, holding that all things proceed with mathematical necessity from the divine nature. Having thus denied God's freedom, the denial of the possibility of miracles and of supernatural revelation logically follows. Nay, the whole supernatural order is radically denied, even in God, because of the identification of the divine nature and created nature. Human nature cannot be elevated to supernatural life since it already is not really {{98}} distinct from the divine nature. This pantheistic doctrine is set forth in the *Ethics*. Moreover, in his *Theological-Political Treatise*, Spinoza deduces from his philosophical principles the rationalistic method of the exegesis of Sacred Scripture, according to which human reason is supreme and also the sole criterion for distinguishing what is *true* in Sacred Scripture from what is merely *allegorical and symbolic*. Thus, everything supernatural vanishes through an allegorical interpretation.

In Germany, *Christian Wolff* also taught rationalism and was called "the professor of mankind" by his disciples. He acknowledged the existence of God but held that revelation is useless. Likewise, he rejected everything that reason cannot evidently demonstrate through intrinsic arguments concerning God and morals.

(β) *Rationalism (or empiricist naturalism)* appeared in England especially[88] in the writings of *Hobbes* and *Hume*, who as sensualists and nominalists reduced all intellectual knowledge to sense knowledge, such that whatever exceeds the knowledge of the external or internal senses[89] would be declared to be verbal entities,[90] mere sounds. Hume especially denies the absolute necessity of the first principles of reason, which, according to empiricism, are nothing other than customs (or empirical laws of our knowledge). In this way, every form of metaphysics (or the value of any knowledge exceeding [sense] experience) is destroyed. Consequently, natural theology is likewise

---

[86] See Rousseau, *Lettres de la Montagne*, letter 3.

[87] See Rousseau, *Émile*, bk. 4 (Profession of Faith of the Savoyard Vicar).

[88] [Trans. note: Reading *praesertim* for *praesertiam*.]

[89] [Trans. note: Reading *sensuum* for *sensum*.]

[90] [Trans. note: Reading *entitates verbales* for *entitas verbales*.]

overthrown, and the proofs of the existence of God, of providence, and of the possibility of miracles are all brought to ruin, as is the knowability of miracles.[91]

Likewise, in France, *Diderot* denied all religion, even natural religion, like *d'Alembert* and the other Encyclopedists. Nay, through their thought, many fell into materialism, such as *d'Holbach*,[92] *Helvetius,* and *Lamettrie*, all of whom denied the existence of God and the immortality of the soul. Finally, *Dupuis*, in his work *The Origin of all Cults*, contended that all religions are forms of idolatry.

These represent the various forms of philosophical rationalism up to the end of the eighteenth century. At that time, Kant sought to reconcile them.

(b) *Biblical rationalism*. As we said above, *Spinoza* established a method of biblical rationalism. At nearly the same time, in England, *Anthony Ashley Cooper, Earl of Shaftsbury* and *Anthony Collins* attacked the prophecies, *Thomas Woolston* interpreted the miracles of Christ, even the Resurrection, allegorically, and *Henry Bolingbroke* derided the mysteries of the faith. In Germany, *Hermann von der Hardt* denied the authenticity of many of the books of the Old Testament and explained the miracles in an allegorical manner. *Lessing* and *Reimarus (Fragmenta Wolfenbüttel)* in particular attacked Christianity most bitterly, denying the authority of the Pentateuch, the other books of the Old {{99}} Testament, and even of the Gospels, not fearing to say that Moses and Christ were imposters.

All these rationalists were the principal adversaries of the Christian faith from the appearance of Protestantism up to the end of the eighteenth century.

(2) **Protestant apologetics**. Among the Protestant apologetes, many set forth not only internal arguments but also external arguments (whether intrinsic ones or extrinsic ones), as we find in *Du-Plessis-Mornay* in France (*On the Truth of the Christian Religion*, 1579–1581), *Hugo Grotius* (*On the Truth of the Christian Religion*, 1627), and *Charles Bonnet* (*Philosoph-*

---

[91] Thus did empiricist phenomenalism appear, which is psychologically opposed to rationalism (or idealism), inasmuch as it denies the essential superiority of reason, which it reduces to [sense-level] experience; however, from the perspective of religious questions, this empiricism is an inferior form of rationalism (or of naturalism) inasmuch as it declares empirical reason to be absolutely autonomous and the supreme judge of all things, even in matters of faith and morals. Thus, in order to fully avoid equivocation, it is better to call it "empiricist naturalism" than "empiricist rationalism."

[92] Against the materialist d'Holbach, Voltaire wrote: "Never perhaps did philosophy speak an absurdity more foolish, a falsity more notorious, even though she has been lying and absurd upon many other occasions" (Letter to Frederick [the Great], 16 Feb., 1773).

ical Investigations into the Proofs of Christianity, 1770). In England *Lardner* and *Paley* proceeded in like manner, as did *Leibnitz, Euler,* and *Haller* in Germany. Some also refuted biblical rationalism (e.g., *Lilienthal* and *Rosenmuller*).

But many other Protestants already favored internal motives. That is, they especially showed the conformity of Christianity with the legitimate aspirations of our nature so that Christianity would appear as being the principle of peace and the firm means for reconciliation with God. Such was the procedure followed by *John Locke, Clarke, Butler,* and *Jennings* in England, *Abbadie* in France, and *Ierusalem* and *Less* in Germany.

Now, why do many Protestants favor the internal methodology? In short, for two reasons.

A. Because they intended to refute the rationalists, many of whom also denied the natural truths of religion. Now, these truths, *setting metaphysics aside*, are more easily defended through an internal methodology inasmuch as the superior aspirations of our nature remain without a *raison d'être* once these truths have been rejected. For example, the pantheistic determinism of Spinoza must be rejected in order to preserve the notions of freedom and moral obligation.

B. *The internal methodology has greater affinity with the new notion of faith proposed by Luther and Calvin.* Indeed, this new conception is *more subjective* than the traditional definition of faith on four heads: (a) on account of the role played by private inspiration in order to discern what is to be believed; (b) on account of the so-called faith-confidence that leads to justification; (c) on account of Luther's philosophical skepticism; (d) on account of a kind of confusion between nature and original justice. All of these must be briefly explained, for the pseudo-reformation of apologetics proceeds from them.

(a) The first Protestants rejected the objective proximate rule of faith—namely, the infallible authority of the Church for proposing dogmas—and they did not admit any other rule of faith besides Sacred Scripture. However, they were accustomed to discern the genuine Word of God from its "relish" and "taste." Thus, they held that the Holy Spirit immediately testified in any given member of the faithful whatsoever.[93] The innovators and their disciples judge through *private inspiration* that any given article is revealed and to be believed. So too do they distinguish between true and false religion, excluding even signs and distinguishing notes of the true religion. Thus, faith takes on a more subjective and individual character, inasmuch as private spirit and private inspiration comes to replace the Church's objective and infallible proposal of the truths of faith. Already,

---

[93] Calvin, *Institutes,* I, ch. 7, nos. 1 and 5. Luther, *De instituendis ecclesiae ministris.*

in a way, faith is identified with religious experience. On the other hand, according to Catholic theologians, religious experience is either natural, proceeding from natural religious sentiment, and is thus essentially distinct from divine faith, or it is supernatural, thus presupposing {{100}} (and not constituting) faith, instead proceeding from the gifts of the Holy Spirit, according to the words of St. John: "The unction (of the Holy Spirit) teacheth you of all things."

Hence, Protestants generally say, "Faith, as it is conceived of by us, is more personal and pious, for it is our religious experience; whereas, on the contrary, the faith of Catholics proceeds from the authority of the Church, as it were, an external act of obedience."[94] (This is the origin of *pietism*, which, according to Catholic theologians,[95] represents a perversion of piety, just as the pessimism of the first Protestants represents the corruption of holy Christian sorrow.)

(b) Moreover, beyond this faith, which they call historical—namely, that by which we believe all things that are contained in the sacred texts—Lutherans admitted a faith that is even more subjective—namely, that by which any given person among the faithful believes or has certain confidence that his sins have been remitted on account of Christ's merits. According to them, this faith justifies even without works. (This doctrine is consistent with the Lutheran notion of predestination, which is the worst corruption of what is best, as is obvious from the words of the innovator: "Sin boldly [*forititer*] and believe even more boldly [*fortius*]". Thus, not only the proximate rule of faith is rejected but so too is the rule of morals. Indeed, the principle of absolute individualism and liberalism is thereby established.)

Protestants frequently call this justifying faith faith-confidence [*fiducia*]; whereas, on the contrary, according to Catholic theologians, faith-confidence pertains to hope and not faith.[96] However, Lutheran faith-confidence already is, in some manner, an individual religious experience, for its object is nowhere revealed objectively, neither in Sacred Scripture nor in tradition, but instead each particular person individually accepts from God this certitude about his own justification. It is to be noted that Protestants frequently make use of the word *faith-confidence* [*fiducia*], where Catholics say or write *faith* [*fides*]. In this way faith comes to be rendered increasingly subjective and individual.

(c) Moreover, Luther's *philosophical skepticism* renders the Lutheran conception of

---

94 See Jean Monod article "Foi" in the *Encyclopédie des sciences religieuses publiée sous la direction de Frederic Lichtenberger*, vol. 5 [Paris: Librairie Sandoz et Fischbacher, 1878], 7. Also, as regards the criticism of these conceptions, see Jean Vincent Bainvel article "Foi" in the *Dictionnaire apologétique de la foi catholique*, 35.

95 [Trans. note: Reading *catholicos theologos* for *cathologos*.]

96 See *ST* II-II, q. 129, a. 6: "Faith-confidence [*fiducia*] pertains to hope . . . and the name of faith-confidence seems principally to signify this, that a given person draws hope from the fact that he believes in the words of someone showing him help." In ad 2: "Faith-confidence conveys a kind of strength of hope."

faith more subjective than the Catholic one. He vehemently fought against scholastic philosophy and the metaphysics of Aristotle, which he said came from the inspiration of the devil. In place of the realism and intellectualism of the peripatetic scholastics, even before his apostasy he admitted the nominalism and empiricism of Ockham. However, according to this nominalism, the rational demonstrations of God's existence, of the divine infinity, of divine providence, and hence, of the possibility and discernibility of miracles, are all matters to be held in doubt. According to Ockham, all the truths that transcend experience are certain only by faith. This is a form of *fideism*. Thus, on account of his nominalism (or philosophical skepticism), Luther was not able to grant a great value to external extrinsic motives of credibility (e.g., miracles) and hence, greatly despising reason, fell into fideism, although on the other hand, by rejecting the authority of the Church, he already asserted the principle of rationalism.

(d) Finally, Protestants (like Michael Baius and Cornelius Jansen later on) said that the elevation of our nature to a share in the divine nature was *owed* to the integrity of man's primal condition and is to be called natural and not supernatural.[97] This ultimately leads to a form of *pseudo-supernaturalism* in which the revealed mysteries are not essentially supernatural and respond not only to our nature's *aspirations* but even to its *demands*. (In other words, they are claimed as being something intrinsic to our nature.) Thus, one has a *confusion* {{101}} *of the natural order with the supernatural order* in a mirror image of how such a confusion is arrived at by Pelagianism. In Pelagianism, this confusion came from the exaggeration of our natural *powers*; by contrast, in Protestantism and Jansenism, it comes from an exaggeration of our natural *needs* [*indigentarium*]. Thus, on the one hand, original sin comes to be denied (moderate optimism); on the other hand, the consequences of this sin come to be exaggerated (pessimism).

Thus, the notion of faith is radically altered on account of the notions of private inspiration,[98] justifying faith-confidence, and philosophical skepticism, as well as through the confusion of Adam's nature with original justice.

This new notion of faith (which, as is obvious, is more subjective than the traditional conception), leads to a new notion of credibility and, hence, to a new methodology for proving credibility. Indeed, already for the first Protestants something is divinely credible because it conforms to our religious sentiment, according to private inspiration.

(3) **Catholic apologetics.** Among Catholics, three apologetes from this era will be cited in particular: *Jacques-Bénigne Bossuet, Pierre-Daniel Huet, Blaise Pascal.*

Bossuet in the second part of his work *Discourse on Universal History* (1681), like St. Augustine in *The City of God*, simultaneously makes use of

---

[97] See Pius V, *Ex omnibus afflictionibus*, no. 21 (Denzinger, no. 1921).

[98] [Trans. note: Reading *inspirationis* for *ispirationis*.]

all the motives of credibility, especially external ones, whether extrinsic or intrinsic, though also of internal motives. All these motives are united in the miraculous life of the whole of the religion whose divine origin stands forth in its beginning, progress, and miraculous diffusion and perennial nature [*perennitate*]. The whole of the Old Testament appears as being a progressive prophecy of the New Testament, and he explains the prophecies in general and some of them in particular. Likewise, he makes manifest the probative force of Christ's miracles[99] and prophecies. At the same time, Bossuet insisted on the excellence and simplicity of Christ's teaching[100] and his utterly lofty and connatural holiness,[101] in which the loftiest dignity and humility are marvelously united, along with extraordinary sublimity and abundant meekness. He shows how the Christian life not only {{102}} fulfills but even exceeds our legitimate aspirations.[102] Finally, he sets forth

---

[99] Jacques-Bénigne Bossuet, *Discours sur l'histoire universelle*, pt. 2, ch. 19: "His miracles are of a particular order and of a new character. They are not 'signs in heaven' such as what the Jews asked for (Matt 16:1): He performed nearly all of them on men themselves and did so in order to heal their infirmities. All these miracles expressed goodness as much as they expressed power, and it is not surprising that they touch so many spectators in the depths of their hearts. He did them as one ruling; the demons and sicknesses obey him; at His word, those who were born blind receive sight, the dead come forth from the tombs, and sins are remitted. The principle of it is in Himself; they flow from the source: 'I feel,' he says, 'that a power has passed out of me' (cf. Luke 7:19, 8:46). Also, none had performed such great miracles nor so great a number of them; and nevertheless, He promises that His disciples will do in his name even greater things (John 14:12): so fruitful and inexhaustible is the virtue that he carries in Himself."

[100] Ibid.: "Who would not admire the condescension with which he tempers the loftiness of his doctrine? It is both milk for children and bread for the strong. One sees it as being full of the secrets of God; but one sees that He is not astonished by it, as other mortals to whom God communicates Himself: He speaks of it naturally as being born in this secret and in this glory: and *what He has without measure* (John 3:34), He spreads with measure so that our weakness can bear it."

[101] Ibid.: "The holiest and best of all men, holiness and goodness itself, becomes the most envied and the most hated. . . . The wisest of the philosophers (Socrates), while seeking after the idea of virtue, discovered that just as the most wicked of men would be he who covers his malice so well that he would pass as a good man and thereby enjoy all the credit virtue can give, so too the most virtuous man would be without question he who by his perfection attracts the jealousy of all men—such that he has for himself only his conscience, and that he would see himself exposed to all sorts of injuries, to the point of being placed upon the cross, without his virtue being able to give him this feeble aid in exempting him from such torment (Socrates in the writings of Plato, *Republic*, bk. 2). Does it not seem that God would have placed this marvelous idea of virtue in the mind of a philosopher only to render it effective in the person of His Son, and to make it clear that the just man has another glory, another repose, and finally, another happiness than that which one can have on earth?"

[102] Ibid.: "Jesus Christ fills our desires and surpasses our hopes. . . . Everything is ours by Jesus

the miraculous life of the Church in the midst of persecutions and heresies. Likewise, St. Robert Bellarmine (1541–1621) a little earlier defended traditional apologetics against the innovators.

Huet, in his work *The Evangelical Demonstration* [*Demonstratio evangelica*] (1679) developed the argument from prophecies in particular, on account of which he defended the historical authority of the books of Sacred Scripture, beginning with the New Testament and thence passing back to the Old Testament, and he shows that the whole history of Jesus Christ was predicted in advance. But he did not set forth the prophecies critically enough, nor did he acknowledge well enough the powers of natural reason, thus paving the way for fideism.

Pascal,[103] in a work that he was unable to complete, the *Pensées*, wished first to show, as he himself says,[104] that the religion that unbelievers fear, scorn, and even sometimes hate, is not contrary to reason but, rather, is deserving of veneration and love, and hence wished to arouse in the good the desire that it be good, ultimately proving that it is in fact true. Therefore, he begins with a consideration of our nature, and he shows in a quite lively manner that it contains a profound opposition—namely, between its nobility and wretchedness [*miseriae*]—such that man desires an explanation for this antinomy and a remedy for his own wretchedness. Now, this explication and this remedy is found in Christianity. Our nobility is explained by the doctrine of creation and of original justice, whereas our infirmity is explained in the doctrine of original sin. At the same time, the remedy is found in redemption through Christ; however, already the principal dogmas appear as being worthy of veneration and love. Pascal also insisted on the outstanding holiness of Christ, which manifestly exceeds all human genius and every natural virtue.[105] Next, Pascal wished to prove the truth and divine

---

Christ: grace, holiness, life, glory, beatitude. In short, the kingdom of the Son of God is our inheritance; there is nothing above us, provided that we do not debase ourselves."

[103] See Hyacinthe Petitot, *Pascal: Sa vie religieuse et son apologie du Christianisme* (Paris: Beauchesne, 1910).

[104] Blaise Pascal, *Pensées*, ed. Havet, 375: "Men have contempt for religion; they hate it and fear that it may be true. To remedy this, we must begin by showing that religion is not contrary to reason, that it is venerable and deserving of respect; then we must render it loveable, to make good men wish that it be true; and then, we must show that it is true. Venerable, because it indeed knows man; loveable because it promises the true good." [Trans. note: It is not completely clear what edition he is citing. Several editions by Ernest Havet were published in two volumes in the late nineteenth century in Paris by Libraire Ch. Delagrave. I only reproduce Fr. Garrigou-Lagrange's pagination.]

[105] See ibid 268: "The great geniuses have their rule, their glory, their grandeur, their victory, and their luster, and they have no need of carnal grandeurs, for which they have no affinity.

origin of {{103}} Christianity by way of external arguments, both intrinsic ones (the excellence and fecundity of its teaching) as well as extrinsic ones (prophecies and miracles). And already we find in this unfinished work many chapters concerning miracles and prophecies, as well as concerning their obscurity and clarity.[106]

However, Pascal in a certain manner falls into the excesses of the Jansenists when he sets forth the wretchedness of man, for he reduces the value of human nature and reason too much. Nor does he sufficiently acknowledge that our elevation to the supernatural order is entirely gratuitous and in no way necessary to man's natural perfection. Hence, he does not always distinguish well enough the natural and supernatural orders, although he wrote many profound things about this matter.[107] Consequently

---

They are seen not by eyes but by minds; this suffices. The saints have their rule, their glory, their grandeur, their victory, and their luster, and have need of neither carnal nor intellectual [spirituelles] grandeurs, for which they have no affinity, for they neither add anything to them nor take anything away from them. They are seen by God and the angels, and not by bodies, nor by curious minds [esprits]. God suffices for them.

"Archimedes, without much fuss [sans éclat], would receive the same veneration from them. He did not undertake battles for the sight of the eyes, but furnished his inventions for all minds. Oh! How radiant was he to minds!"

"Jesus Christ, without much and without external exhibition of science, is in His own order of holiness. He did not invent; He did not reign; but He was humble, patient, holy, holy to God, terrible to the demons, without any sin. Oh! He has come in great pomp and with a prodigious magnificence to the eyes of the heart, which sees Wisdom . . .

"It is most absurd to be scandalized at the lowliness of Jesus Christ, as though this lowliness were of the same order as that which He came to manifest. Would that one consider the grandeur of His life, His passion, His obscurity, His death, the choice of those who were His, their desertion, His secret resurrection, and of all the rest! One will see it to be so great that one will have no reason for being scandalized by a lowliness that is not there. But there are those who can admire only carnal grandeurs, as though intellectual [spirituelles] grandeurs did not exist; and there are others who admire intellectual grandeurs as though infinitely higher grandeurs in Wisdom did not exist."

[106] See ibid., 303: "God wished to appear openly to those who seek Him with all their heart, and to be hidden to those who flee Him with all their heart. He so tempers knowledge of Him in such a manner that He has given marks of Himself that are visible to those who seek Him and hidden to those who do not seek Him. *There is enough light for those who desire only to see, enough obscurity for those who have a contrary disposition.* There is enough brightness to illuminate the elect and enough obscurity to humble them. There is enough obscurity to blind the reprobate and enough brightness to condemn them and render them inexcusable."

[107] See ibid., 269: "All bodies, the firmament, the stars, the earth and its kingdoms—all these are not equal to the least of minds [esprits]; for it knows all of these and itself; and these bodies, nothing. All the bodies taken together, and all minds taken together, and all their productions, do not have the worth of the least movement of charity. This latter is of an

(in the argument, *The Wager*) he does not acknowledge well enough that something exists between the life of libertines and the Christian life, at least theoretically—namely, natural moral befittingness [*honestatem naturalem*]; however, this omission can be explained—namely, because Pascal considers human nature precisely in the form that it takes on after original sin and not in the abstract, precisely as a nature. Now, *de facto*, according to the Catholic faith, man cannot observe the whole natural law without healing grace, which proceeds from Christ the Redeemer. Moreover, *de facto*, every man is either in a state of grace or in a state of sin.

In the eighteenth century, there were many apologetes [*Apologeticae*], who wrote against the Deists and the Encyclopedists and set forth arguments that were both intrinsic and extrinsic. Among these authors, those who are worthy of praise include *Nicolas-Sylvestre Bergier, Valsecchi, Vincenzo Ludovico Gotti*, O.P. (*The Truth of the Christian Religion*, 1735–1740), *St. Alphonsus de Liguori* (*The Truth of the Faith . . .*), *Cardinal Hyacinthe Sigismond Gerdil*, and *Daniello Concina*, O.P. (*On Revealed Religion Against the Atheists, Deists, Materialists, and Indifferentists*). All these apologetes admitted the traditional notion of faith and of credibility, and intended {{104}} to prove the fact of revelation historically and especially by external-extrinsic means. Thus, at this time two new treatises came to be established in theology—namely, "On the True Religion" and "On Christ's Church." Hence, apologetics comes to be seen as a defensive undertaking distinct from theological reflection, properly so-called, although they are not two specifically distinct sciences.

§7. Following the Appearance of Kantianism, Apologetic Methodology according to Protestants and Catholics

Here we will consider developments following the appearance of Kantianism, specifically: (1) the adversaries of the Christian faith; (2) the apologetics of Protestants and of semi-rationalists; and (3) the apologetics of Catholics.

(1) *The adversaries of the Christian faith*. New forms of philosophical and biblical rationalism come to be opposed to Christianity during this time.

A. **Philosophical rationalism** appears at this time in either an idealistic form or an empiricist form.

---

infinitely more elevated order.

"From all bodies taken together, one cannot succeed at bringing forth one small thought: that is impossible, and is of another order. From all bodies and minds, one cannot draw a movement of true charity: that is impossible, and of another order, one that is supernatural."

Among the *idealists, Kant* intended to reconcile the empiricism of Hume and the spiritualism of Wolff. On the one hand, he admitted the subjective necessity of the first principles of speculative and practical reason, and on the other, he denied the possibility of theoretically certain knowledge concerning the existence of God, human freedom, and the immortality of the soul. However, he admitted these truths *by means of a kind of moral faith* as being postulates of practical reason. He rejected everything supernatural and retained only the natural truths pertaining to religion.

After Kant, many idealists, (e.g., Fichte, Schelling, and Hegel) professed pantheism. *Hegel* in particular taught absolute evolutionism and identified the divine essence with the essence of the very evolution of the world and of human reason. This represents a radical denial of the supernatural order, to which our nature cannot be elevated, for there is nothing over and above the world, which itself is God in the process of becoming.

At the same time, in France, the *Eclectics*—namely, Victor Cousin, Théodore Jouffroy, and Jules Simon—were Deists, though they frequently inclined toward pantheism. They rejected the idea that divine freedom would exercise particular interventions in the world and hence denied the possibility of miracles and of revelation, thinking that natural religion is completely sufficient.

Finally, the *positivists* admitted an agnostic empiricism—namely, human reason can know only external and internal phenomena, as well as their experimental laws. Such was the thought of Auguste Comte, Émile Littré, Hippolyte Taine, John Stuart Mill, and Herbert Spencer.

As regards the history of apologetics, among these various rationalistic theories we must note in particular *the Kantian notion of faith*,[108] which begot the new concept of credibility found in the writings of liberal Protestants and semi-rationalists, just as in the sixteenth century the Lutheran notion of faith already changed the methodology of apologetics in the writings of the reformers.

The Kantian theory concerning faith has a twofold foundation: (a) the agnosticism of speculative reason and (b) the autonomy of practical reason and of the will. These ultimately lead to (c) the Kantian notion of moral faith.

{{105}} (a) *The agnosticism of speculative reason.* According to Kant, we cannot have

---

[108] See Fr. Auguste Valensin's article "Criticisme Kantian" in *Dictionnaire apologétique de la foi catholique*. Also see Fr. Ambroise Gardeil's article "Crédibilité" in the *Dictionnaire de théologie catholique*, col. 2300.

certitude concerning the ontological value of the first principles of reason. For example, the principle of causality is only a subjectively necessary principle (a "synthetic a priori principle"). Hence, speculative reason can demonstrate neither God's existence, nor the immortality of the soul, nor man's free will, nor moral obligation.

(b) *The autonomy of practical reason and of the will.* According to Kant, practical reason knows moral obligation as a kind of internal fact that is not only experiential but rational, as a "fact of reason." That is, every sincere man finds in his own conscience a kind of imperative [*imperium*] that is not only hypothetical but categorical—namely, the command to act morally, which is formulated by Kant as follows: "Act such that the moral direction of your will could at the same time be the principle of common legislation"; in other words, do what you would will all men to do. This first principle of practical reason is not formulated as a foundation in an objective sense, as it is in traditional philosophy, "the good is to be done and evil avoided," such that the law would depend upon the nature of the fitting [*honesti*] good. Rather, it is only a *subjectively necessary formal law.* Nor, according to Kant, can we demonstrate that the foundation of moral obligation is found in God the Lawgiver and the ultimate end of man; nay, if an obligation were imposed upon us by God, our moral life would be a form of *servitude* and hence would not be, properly speaking, moral. In order for the human will to be truly rational, moral, and free, it must impose the categorical imperative upon itself, "a law unto itself" without undergoing servitude.[109] Thus, the human will remains *autonomous*—that is, independent from a law externally imposed by a superior. This is the fundamental principle simultaneously of rationalism and of individualism, because the individual himself, notwithstanding his egoism, must judge whether his action can be at the same time the principle of shared legislation. From this notion of the autonomy of the will proceeds the thesis that was

---

[109] See Kant, *Fondement de la métaphysique des moeurs* [*Groundwork of the Metaphysics of Morals*], ed. Victor Delbos, 170–175: "The autonomy of the will is the property that the will has of being a law for itself, independent of every property of the objects of the will.... When the will seeks its law above itself, a form of heteronomy always follows.... It is necessary that practical reason (the will) not be limited to administer to a foreign interest but that it manifests only its own imperative authority, as a supreme legislation....

"The concept of the divine will, taken from the attributes of love and glory and of dominion, linked to the redoubtable representations of power and of anger, could pose necessarily the foundation of a system of ethics, which would be the contrary of morality." In other words: If the moral law were imposed upon us from outside by God, the will could be submitted to it only out of fear, love, or interest, which would be foreign or contrary to morality.

Thus, as Victor Delbos notes in his introduction to this work by Kant, 46: "This principle (of the autonomy of the will) argues for a moral order that is based on a foundation akin to what Rousseau had held for the social order, according to which man ought to prescribe for himself the law that he obeys."

[Trans. note: These translations are taken from the French text cited by Fr. Garrigou-Lagrange. He does not cite the publication details. I have translated the passages in as direct a manner as possible.]

condemned as a heresy at the [First] Vatican Council: "Human reason is so independent that faith cannot be enjoined upon it by God,"[110] as though external obedience could be admitted but not "an obedience of the intellect." This is the same as what [Lucifer] first said in the spiritual order: "I will not serve."

(c) *The notion of moral faith*. However, the moral law can only subsist if it includes three postulates to be believed: man's freedom, the immortality of the soul, and the existence of God. Indeed, (1) man cannot fulfill his moral obligation unless he is free; therefore, morally speaking, we must admit the existence of *free will*, although it is speculatively indemonstrable. (2) The perfection prescribed by the categorical imperative cannot be obtained except by way of an infinite series of approximations; hence, there must be a continuation of never-ending life (or *a future life*). (3) The man who follows moral obligation in all things is {{106}} deserving of beatitude, but stable felicity is not found on this earth; Thus, morally speaking, we must admit *the existence of God the [Just] Rewarder*, inasmuch as God alone can, in the next life, join virtue and stable beatitude.

Therefore, the existence of free will, of God the [Just] Rewarder, and of the future life must all be admitted by a moral (or rational) faith, for it is rational and moral to believe these postulates. Now, according to Kant, the certitude of this faith is *subjectively and practically sufficient* because it is subjectively deduced from the categorical imperative. However, it is *objectively and theoretically insufficient* because a speculative demonstration founded in objective reality does not exist for these truths.

Therefore, *this moral and rational faith* is essentially *natural* and in no way supernatural, being founded not upon the authority of God who reveals but, rather, upon the requirements of our practical reason. Moreover, according to Kant, this faith believes that[111] the existence of the moral order *is completely sufficient*. Hence, the mysteries of the Trinity, the Incarnation, the Eucharist, and prayer itself, as well as the various forms of ritual, all must be rejected as superstitions or must be interpreted symbolically as imaginative expressions of truths of the moral order, to which the supernatural order is reduced.

Nor is one to argue from miracles, for according to Kant, miracles either do not exist or at least cannot be distinguished from natural facts. (In the end, this is indeed the legitimate consequence of agnosticism.) Hence, nobody can be certain concerning the fact of revelation, and therefore, every form of positive faith is rash and evil—in short, as Kant says, inciting one to lies and fraud.[112]

---

[110] [First] Vatican Council, can. 3.1 (Denzinger, no. 3031).

[111] [Trans. note: Reading "haec fides credit quod . . ." for "haec fides creditor . . .".]

[112] See Kant, *La religion dans les limits of reason* [*Religion Within the Bounds of Mere Reason*], pt.

Nevertheless, Kant retains the terminology of Christianity, though he gives its words a completely different meaning. For example, *original sin* is nothing other than the struggle between flesh and spirit (or between sensuality and reason). *Christ* is only the most perfectly wise person, the exemplar of the moral virtues. *Justification* (or regeneration) is nothing other than the domination of the reason and the will over the passions. *The Church* is only useful as the assembly of those who fight against sensuality so as to be more effectively obedient to the categorical imperative (and, thus, this imperative is substituted for the Holy Spirit). Neither worship nor ministers are required, except as instruments for better observing the moral law. The Church *militant* is the collection of churches fighting among themselves and the Church *triumphant* will be the reconciliation of the churches in a rational religion within the limits of reason.

In sum, Kant holds the following:

1) *Agnosticism* must be accepted as regards the capacities of speculative reason.

2) One must admit the autonomy of practical reason and of the will (or of conscience), whose requirements provide the foundation of religion (thus, religion is founded in ethics and not ethics in the teaching concerning God). This represents a form of *immanentism*.

3) He rejects everything supernatural and explains Christianity through the development [*evolutionem*] of religious awareness. This represents a form of *naturalism*.

This Kantian notion of faith proceeds from the Lutheran notion of faith, but the categorical imperative is posited in place of the private instinct of the Holy Spirit. {{107}} This new outlook appeared in various ways later on, in the writings of semi-rationalists like Hermes and the writings of the liberal Protestants and modernists.

Among the rationalists themselves, following upon Kant, *Fichte* reduced the supernatural order to the moral order, which he conceived of pantheistically. *Hegel* upheld pantheistic evolutionism.[113] According to him the three superior forms of evolution are art, religion, and philosophy, so that religion, understood as being moral, would be superior to art, and philosophy, understood as being speculative knowledge of the supreme reasons for things would be superior to religion, which only symbolically proposes philosophical truth. Thus, Hegelianism appears as being the perfect form

---

4, ch. 5 and 6: "Belief in revelation is the interior confession of its unshakeable certitude to our wishes. . . . But it is contrary to conscience to declare as being true that concerning which one cannot be convinced." Concerning the positive faith of the Church, Kant says: "It is an absurd and condemnable superstition as leading to fraud and treachery."

[113] [Trans. note: Here Fr. Garrigou-Lagrange writes, literally, "evolutionistic pantheism," though his customary expression is "pantheistic evolutionism".]

of absolute rationalism, in which reason in no way serves under faith but, on the contrary, judges religious faith from on high, and whatever in faith cannot be subordinated to the principles of reason must be rejected as being a myth or at least must be metaphorically interpreted.

These philosophical systems of Kant and Hegel, like the system of Spinoza before them, exerted great influence on the rationalistic exegesis of Sacred Scripture.

B. **Biblical rationalism** in the nineteenth and twentieth centuries appeared in various forms: mythicism, evolutionistic criticism,[114] and so forth.

(a) *Mythicism* is nothing other than the mythical interpretation or exegesis of Sacred Scripture, which *Wilhelm de Wette* (1780–1849) proposed for the Old Testament and *David Strauss* (1808–1874) for the New. Miraculous facts would be only more or less extraordinary natural facts, enlarged and adorned by the imagination. They would be myths just like the fables concerning Romulus and Remus. However, given that myths cannot be formed except after some time, mythicism contradicts certain facts of history and, therefore, has been rejected by most.

(b) *Evolutionistic criticism* then was proposed by *Ferdinand Christian Baur* (1792–1860), a master of the Tübingen School. Baur adapted Hegelian philosophy to the origins of Christianity, contending that Christianity is, as it were, the synthesis of two systems opposed to one another—namely, *Petrinism*, proceeding from St. Peter and more or less favoring the Jews, and *Paulinism*, propagated by St. Paul and accommodated to the Gentiles. According to the universal law set forth by Hegel, the thesis (Petrinism) and the antithesis (Paulinism) were resolved in a superior synthesis. After many conflicts, the reconciliation of them both appeared in the fourth Gospel, which was falsely attributed to John the Apostle. Indeed, the authenticity of the various books of the New Testament must be decided according to intrinsic notes, in accord with a Hegelian methodology, such that those books in which appear the vestiges of the division between thesis and antithesis are older, whereas those that manifest the synthesis or reconciliation [of thesis and antithesis] are more recent. Among the rationalist critics

---

[114] See Frédéric Lichtenberger, *Histoire des idées religieuses en allemagne depuis le milieu du XVIIIe siècle jusqu'à nos jours*, 2nd ed. (1888). Translated into English as *History of German Theology in the Nineteenth Century*, ed. and trans. William Hastie (Edinburgh: T & T Clark, 1889). Also see François-Marie Braun, O.P., *Où en est le problème de Jesus* (Bruxelles: Edition de la cité chrétienne, 1932). Also, Giuseppe Ricciotti, "Le interpretationi razionaliste dela vita di Gesù" in *Vita di Gesù Cristo* (Milan, 1941), 194–224. [Trans. note: Fr. Garrigou-Lagrange notes the English translation in his original.]

who made use of this method,[115] one can cite *Heinrich Ewald* (1803–1875), *Ferdinand Hitzig* (1807–1875), *August Knobel* (1807–1863), *Edouard Guillaume Eugène Reus* (1804–1891), and more recently *Julius Wellhausen* (1844–1918), who developed his system especially with regard to the books of the Old Testament.

(c) *Messianic explanation*: Wilhelm Wrede (1859–1906) swept away every supernatural matter in the Gospels; according to him the first Christians invented the notion that Christ is the *Messiah*. {{108}} Of greater influence was the explanation proposed by Johannes Weiss (1900), Albert Schweitzer (1901), and others: Christ did not wish to found any new religion, but adhering to the expectations of the messianic eschatology of his time (according to which the end of the world was desired along with the subsequent messianic kingdom, a kingdom of justice, peace, and felicity, in which God would destroy every evil), he announced that said kingdom was at hand. Hence, he also preached a provisional moral doctrine for the time of expectation. All things in the Gospels not in agreement with this explication were rejected as inventions of primitive Christianity falsely attributed to Christ. In France, this eschatological messianism was fought for by Loisy (1903). According to Robert Eisler (1930), Christ believed himself to be a political messiah.

(d) *The school of the comparative history of religions.* This school also *a priori* rejects everything supernatural in the Gospels. It interprets primitive Christianity as though it depended essentially upon the influence of other religions—namely, eastern religions (Franz-Valéry-Marie Cumont, 1906), the religions of the Greeks (Richard August Reitzenstein, 1906; Alfred Loisy, 1909), Gnosticism (Wilhelm Bousset, 1907; E. De Taye, 1913; Francis Crawford Burkitt, 1932), and so forth. Nay, such a method denies the historical existence of Christ, as was proposed in Germany by Andrew Drews (1919), in England by John Mackinnon Robertson (1902), in America by William Benjamin Smith (1906), in France by Paul-Louis Couchoud (1924), and in the Netherlands by Gustaaf Adolf van den Bergh van Eysinga (1930).

(e) *The historical-formal method (Formegeschichtliche Methode).* This modern, particularly German, school looks into the various literary forms with which the narrations about Christ in the oral tradition of primitive Christianity would have clothed themselves before they were fixed in the Gospels by an editor. In general, they admit the historical existence of Christ. However, the narrations of the Gospels are generally considered as

---

[115] [Trans. note: Reading "qui hac methodo usi sunt" for "qui hac methodou si sunt."]

being popular religious fabrications so that almost nothing is established concerning that historical Christ. As proponents of this outlook, we have the works of Karl Ludwig Schmidt (1919), Martin Dibelius (1919), Rudolf Bultmann (1921), Martin Albertz (1921), and Georg Bertram (1922).

These are the principal forms of rationalism (or of naturalism) propagated by the multiform sects *of the Masons* in various regions in the nineteenth and twentieth centuries, about whom Pope Leo XIII said: "Let no one be deceived by a pretense of honesty. It may seem to some that Freemasons demand nothing that is openly contrary to religion and morality; but, as the whole principle and object of the sect lies in what is vicious and criminal, to join with these men or in any way to help them cannot be lawful."[116] In reality, many Masons profess that God exists, calling him "the Great Architect," although most of them have a pantheistic conception of the divine nature. Many recognize some natural religion. Nay, some honor Christianity while, however, rejecting whatever is supernatural in the teaching of Christ and of the Church[117] (namely, the dogmas of original sin, the Incarnation, Redemption, etc.) and reducing the Christian virtues to merely human virtues, turning charity into philanthropy and tolerance. Thus, they defend liberalism, which is nothing other than a false, natural substitute for supernatural charity, a reverence for the opinions of men, {{109}} even perverse ones, and scorn for the divine word and the divine law. However, this half-denial is more damnable than open denial, for it [mis]uses the truth in praise of error.

(2) *Protestant and semi-rationalist apologetics in the nineteenth and twentieth centuries*

(A) **Protestant apologetes** increasingly came to make use of the internal method in particular. They are divided into conservatives and liberals.

Protestant conservatives, such as Tholuck, Delitzsch, Baumstark, and Ebrard indeed intended to save supernatural revelation in one way or another, and against rationalists they defended the authenticity and historical authority of the Gospels and of the books of the New Testament, though they principally argued from internal motives.

After Søren Kierkegaard (1813–1855), in recent times, in the "dialectic theology" of Protestants, Karl Barth awakened a storm against extreme biblical rationalism, along with Emile Brunner, Friedrich Gogarten, and

---

[116] Leo XIII, *Humanum genus*, no. 31. [Trans. note: Taken from the official Vatican translation. Fr. Garrigou-Lagrange cites Denzinger, no. 1854 (new, 3145), which is a citation of *Arcanum divinae sapientiae*. This passage is not in the current edition of Denzinger.]

[117] [Trans. note: Reading *Ecclesia* as *Ecclesiae*.]

others, although they disagreed among themselves in some ways.[118] Karl Barth, reverting to a form of Calvinistic orthodoxy declared that human nature is completely powerless for attaining knowledge of God, even natural knowledge. Thus, he admitted only faith in the Word of God actually and personally revealed to us. However, such faith required neither preparation nor defense, such that the motives of credibility were altogether rejected as being unnecessary.

However, liberal Protestants, as it were, make use of an exclusively internal method for two reasons. (A) They do so because they generally admitted the agnosticism of Kant or of the positivists, and therefore reject the possibility of natural theology and the traditional demonstrations of the possibility of miracles and their knowability, as well as the proofs of the fact of revelation. (B) Likewise, they do so because, under the influence of Kantianism and Hegelianism, liberal Protestants conceive of Christianity not as a supernatural religion but as a superior form of natural religion, which *must be believed*, not on account of the authority of God who reveals but *on account of its conformity with the aspirations* of our own consciousness; in other words, it is the object evidently worthy of religious experience. Hence, they either deny supernatural mysteries or interpret them as being symbols of natural truths. They maintain the words "revelation," "miracle," and "redemption," but they deny their very reality (or, at least, call it into doubt). Luther had rejected the infallible authority of the Church; without further ado, liberal Protestants rejected the very motive of faith: the authority of God who reveals.

Among them we must cite Friedrich Schleiermacher, Albrecht Ritschl, Adolf Harnack, and Ernst Troeltsch in Germany; Auguste Sabatier and Albert Réville in France; and Henry Drummond, Samuel[119] Harris, and William Hurrell Mallock in England.

Schleiermacher (1786–1834) admitted, with Kant, that speculative reason cannot demonstrate the existence of God and therefore made recourse to religious sentiment, which is nothing other than a natural sense or knowledge of our dependence upon God. Indeed, we do not know, said Schleiermacher, whether or not God is truly a person dis-

---

[118] Karl Barth, *Die christliche Dogmatik im Entwürf* (Munich, 1927); *Der Römerbrief* (Munich, 1929); *Die Kierchliche Dogmatik* (Munich, 1932); *Credo di Hauptprobleme der Dogmatik darge stellt im Anschluss an das apostlische Glaubensbekenntiss* (Munich, 1935). See Johannes Ries, O.M.I., *Die natürliche Gotteserkenntnis in der Theologie der Krisis im Zusammenhang mit dem Imagobegriff bei Calvin* (Bonn, 1939).

[119] [Trans. note: In this case in particular, I am not completely sure to whom Fr. Garrigou-Lagrange is referring. There was a nineteenth-century New England theologian by the name of Samuel Harris to whom he might be referring.]

tinct from the world, {{110}} but in practice this is of little importance, so long as we feel the Infinite in some manner and have a kind of communion with him. Hence, faith is not supported by external revelation and confirmed by miracles and prophecies but instead is reduced to the religious experience of each and every person. And therefore, according to Schleiermacher, *revelation* is nothing other than a new idea of the Infinite, which is conceived through the evolution of religious sentiment. (For example, Christians conceive of God as Father.) Likewise, we call a *miracle* whatever phenomenon that we ascribe to the Infinite. *The inspired books* are those that are aimed at exciting religious sentiments in our mind. *Christ* is called the Messiah and the Son of God because he was more conscious of the Infinite much more than are other men.[120]

Albrecht Ritschl (1822–1889)[121] attempted to perfect this system of liberal Christianity. With Kant, he professed that our rational concepts are merely subjective, and with Schleiermacher, he admitted that that religion is based upon religious sentiment, although he did not embrace pantheism. However, he differed from both inasmuch as he accepted Sacred Scripture, especially the New Testament, as being the historical foundation of religion. Nevertheless, according to him, it ultimately falls to human awareness (or religious sentiment) to judge concerning the inspiration of the books of Scripture, and those things in the Gospels that our religious sentiment approves are true.

By this method, Ritschl was led to a naturalistic interpretation of Christianity. That is, *Christ* is the Son of God because he was aware of his union with God in an altogether special manner. *Revelation* is a kind of education of Christian consciousness by God. *Miracles* are extraordinary events inasmuch as witnesses to the divine benevolence can be had: Thus, one and the same fact is natural from the perspective of science and preternatural from the perspective of faith. This distinction was admitted by the modernists, who more often than not follow the liberal Protestants. Finally, the *Church*, according to Ritschl, is the assembly of those who believe in Christ and act out of charity.

Ernst Troeltsch (1865–1923), on the basis of the teaching proposed by Albrecht Ritschl, applied a historical and philosophical methodology to religion: Religion rests upon internal religious sentiment by which God manifests himself. Because of the philosophical difficulties that would be involved, it cannot be dependent upon the absolute value of Christianity, nor upon external motives (namely, miracles proving its supernatural revelation), nor upon the argumentation of idealism, by which Christianity would be manifested as the loftiest concept of religion. Its value must be determined[122] from a religious and ethical perspective, which depends on the spiritual, social, and natural

---

[120] See Georges Goyau, *L'Allemagne religieuse: Le protestantisme* (Paris: Perrin, 1898).

[121] See Albrecht Ritschl, *Die Christliche Lehre von der Rechtfertigung und Versöhnung*, 3 vols. 1870–1874. Also see Henri Schoen, *Les origines historiques de la théologie de Ritschl* (Paris: Fischbacher, 1893).

[122] [Trans. note: Reading *determinandus* for *detrminandus*.]

condition of any given people. According to this norm, Christianity does not have an absolute value, although one may admit that in relation to the development [*evolutionem*] of the peoples of Europe it is the sole best religion.[123]

Louis Auguste Sabatier (1839–1901) disseminated the theories of Albrecht Ritschl in France, proposed a symbolic interpretation of Christianity, and also tended toward pantheism.[124] Later on, when we come to discuss the nature of revelation, we will explicitly see how he defined religion, revelation, inspiration, miracles, and dogma. *Revelation*, according to him, is nothing other than {{111}} the progressive knowledge of God manifesting himself within any given individual consciousness; however, this knowledge was much livelier in the prophets and especially in Christ. Hence, *the religious inspiration* of the books of Sacred Scripture did not seem to him to be psychologically distinct from poetic inspiration. *Miracles* cannot be scientifically demonstrated but, rather, are perceived by faith as being a divine answer to our prayer. *Prophecy* is not a miraculous foreknowledge and prediction of a future contingent but, rather, only a more perfect concept of the Godhead, justice, and charity, along with firm faith-confidence that the law and divine will be fulfilled. Modernists admitted nearly all of these doctrines.

Hence, quite clearly, internal methodology is, as it were, the exclusive apologetic methodology of liberal Protestants. All of this necessarily arises[125] from their conception of revelation and of faith, a conception that excludes everything supernatural, although it sometimes retains Christian terms.

(B) **The apologetics of the semi-rationalists.** The Catholic Church uses the term "semi-rationalism" for the doctrine of certain Catholics (e.g., Hermes, Günther, and Frohschammer), who under the influence of Kantianism and Hegelianism were inclined toward rationalism. Indeed, they did not deny the supernatural fact of revelation but instead said that no indemonstrable mysteries are contained in divine revelation and that the whole of the dogmas of the faith can be understood and demonstrated on the basis of natural principles by sufficiently developed reason, provided that these dogmas then will have been proposed to reason itself as objects.[126] Thus, the

---

[123] See Ernst Troeltsch, *Die Absolutheit des Christentuus und die Religionsgeschichte* (Tubingen, 1912); *Der Historismus und seine Uberwindung* (Berlin, 1924); *Glaubenslehre,* ed. M. Troeltsch (Munich, 1925). Cf. Emil Spiess, *Die Religionstheorie von Ernst Troeltsch* (1927). Jakob Fehr, "Der weg zur dialektische Theologie," *Divus Thomas* (Fribourg) 14 (1936): 163–180.

[124] In particular his works are Louis Auguste Sabatier, *Equisse d'une philosophie de la religion d'après la psychologie et l'histoire* (Paris: Fischbacher, 1897); *Les religions d'authorité et la religion de l'esprit* (Paris: Fischbacher, 1903).

[125] [Trans. note: Reading "proveniunt" for "provenint".]

[126] See Pius IX, *Syllabus,* nos. 9–14 and [First] Vatican Council, *Dei filius,* ch. 4. (Denzinger, 2909–2914, 3016.) [Trans. note: This required slight correction to the numbers provided by Fr. Garrigou-Lagrange, which read "1708–1814" instead of "1708–1714".]

mysteries of the Trinity and the Incarnation would not exceed the created intellect by their very natures, and all the dogmas of the Christian religion would indiscriminately be the object of natural science (or of philosophy). Hence, the semi-rationalists destroyed the essential supernaturality of faith.

From this alteration of the notion of faith *a new notion of credibility* followed, as is clear *especially* in Hermesianism. We must briefly speak about the way that Hermes presented his apologetics. This does not lack currency, for many apologetes who are more or less modernist, following the ways of Kant, have often spoken like Hermes.

Let us look into (a) the philosophical foundation of Hermesianism, and (b) the Hermesian theory of faith. (This is the same process as in the Kantian theory).

(a) *The philosophical foundation of Hermesianism* is twofold: negative and positive—namely, the agnosticism of speculative[127] reason and the autonomy of practical reason.

The agnosticism of speculative reason. Holding all the doctors of the Church in scorn, Hermes deemed that the whole of theology had hitherto lain in darkness and stood in need of a new foundation.[128]

The Hermesian method begins from *doubt* and remains in doubt for as long as reason is not impelled of necessity to remove it.[129] Therefore, it is not only a question of hypothetical {{112}} or methodical doubt but of true, absolute, and universal doubt, at least for some time. For example, according to Hermes, Catholics can have just cause to call into doubt, by way of a suspense of assent, the faith they have already received under the Church's magisterium, maintaining such doubt until they have completed a scientific demonstration of the credibility and truth of their faith—a position condemned as a heresy by the [First] Vatican Council.[130]

Therefore, beginning in this way with doubt, Hermes, after a long and subtle inquiry concludes, like Kant, that theoretical reason can only have *a merely subjective persuasion concerning objective reality,* which can in fact be only phenomenal and apparent. For all the more reason, according to Hermes, theoretical reason cannot demonstrate the absolute distinction of God from the world, nor the divine omnipotence, nor the possibility of miracles. This amounts to a form of agnosticism in the order of speculative reason.

However, as regards practical reason, Hermes establishes, in a Kantian manner, *that it is*

---

[127] [Trans. note: Reading *speculativae* for *speculative*.]

[128] His works are especially *A Philosophical Introduction to Christian Theology* and *Christian-Catholic Dogmatics*. See Vacant, *Études sur le Concile du Vatican*, vol. 1, 124–127, 594–596; vol. 2, 31, 67–76, 196.

[129] See Gregory XVI, *Dum acerbissimas* (Denzinger, no. 2738).

[130] See [First] Vatican Council, *Dei filius*, can. 3.6 (Denzinger, no. 3036). See also Vacant, *Études sur le Concile du Vatican*, vol. 2, 167 and 601.

autonomous (or is the Supreme Lawgiver, whose categorical imperative is "Purely produce and preserve human dignity in yourself and in others"). In virtue of this principle, practical reason imposes practical ends (or moral necessities) upon us. And to the degree that it imposes some duty upon us, so too does it thereby oblige us to everything necessary for fulfilling that obligation. Therefore, according to Hermes, there sometimes arises an obligation to admit as true, notwithstanding theoretical doubt, either the testimony of the external senses, or the experience and moral excellence [*honestem*] of [some] men, or the experience of others, whether they be contemporary or past, and hence the truth of history and of miracles. In these cases, although theoretical reason can forever remain in doubt, we must admit the truth of objective reality in virtue of practical reason. Thus, that which is speculatively dubious becomes practically certain; and *moral certitude*, which Hermes admits is not speculative moral certitude but instead only *practical* moral certitude—that is, for action and not for knowing the thing in itself. In short, one is to act *as if* the thing in question were objectively certain. Such is the philosophical foundation of Hermesianism.

(b) *The Hermesian theory of faith* follows from the aforementioned points. Indeed, these things having been posited, *the motives of credibility*, which are commonly proposed by the Church (i.e., miracles), are *only speculatively probable*. This was condemned in Pius IX's encyclical *Qui pluribus* against the Hermesians.[131] The Supreme Pontiff affirmed: "Right reason demonstrates the truth of the faith. . . . Indeed, human reason, lest it be deceived and err in a matter of so great importance, ought to investigate diligently the fact of divine revelation so that it can know with certainty that God has spoken,"[132] and at the [First] Vatican Council, the doctrine of those who say, "That the divine origin of the Christian religion cannot be legitimately proven by miracles[, which themselves are not possible]," was condemned as heretical.[133]

Therefore, what is the *formal motive of faith* according to Hermes, if the fact of revelation is not, properly speaking, certain? It is not the authority of God who reveals but instead a kind of *practical exigency*. As the pre-synodal schema of the [First] Vatican Council states:

Semi-rationalists deny that the authority of God speaking is the formal motive of faith by which we are called and are faithful. . . .

---

[131] See Vacant, *Études sur le Concile du Vatican*, vol. 2, 126 and 595 (The pre-conciliar schema for a dogmatic constitution on Catholic doctrine, no. 18).

[132] Pius IX, *Qui pluribus* (Denzinger, nos. 2776 and 2778). [Trans. note: The first number from Denzinger is not cited by Fr. Garrigou-Lagrange even though he cites the brief introductory text from that portion of the encyclical.]

[133] Cf. [First] Vatican Council, *Dei filius*, can. 3.4 (Denzinger, 3034).

Indeed, they teach that firm persuasion concerning God and divine things is the faith itself, properly speaking, by which the faithful are so named, even if the motive for embracing and {{113}} holding the truth is not God's authority, but the truth would be held only on account of the intrinsic perspective of the interconnection of ideas.

Hermes expressly said: "If authority is designated as the sole motive of faith and thus as its foundation, the intrinsic solidity of faith is thereby overthrown."[134] A little earlier he had said:

> If we wish to define faith, it must be said that faith is in us a state of certitude (or of persuasion) concerning the truth of the thing known. We are led to such a state [of certitude] through a necessary assent of theoretical reason or through a necessary consent of practical reason. This rational faith is the supreme end of all of philosophy, the sole true norm of man in this life, and the necessary condition of his elevation.[135]

Thus, divine faith is reduced to rational faith, which was been condemned as a heresy by the [First] Vatican Council.[136] Already, Innocent XI had condemned this proposition: "Faith in the broad sense, which is based upon the testimony of creatures or on a similar reason, is sufficient for justification."[137] Hence, Hermes enunciated a position that also was condemned as a heresy by the [First] Vatican Council: "The assent to the Christian faith is not free but is produced with necessity by arguments of human reason; [and] the grace of God is necessary only for that living faith which works by love."[138]

However, Hermes explained this doctrine in two different ways, one pertaining to the simple faithful and the other to philosophers.

According to him,[139] *the simple faithful* must believe the mysteries of Christianity on account of revelation and revelation itself on account of the obligation of admitting moral and religious truth, for without revelation this truth cannot be known, at least explicitly. By reason alone, they would not arrive at it. Hence, they are morally bound to

---

[134] Georg Hermes, *Philosophical Introduction to Theology*, 265.

[135] Ibid., 259.

[136] [First] Vatican Council, *Dei filius*, can. 3.2 (Denzinger, no. 3032).

[137] Sixty-Five Propositions Condemned in the Decree of the Holy Office, March 2, 1679, no. 23 (Denzinger, no. 2123).

[138] [First] Vatican Council, *Dei filius*, can. 3.5 (Denzinger, no. 3035).

[139] See Vacant, *Études sur le Concile du Vatican*, vol. 1, 126.

accept revelation. Therefore, according to Hermes, on account of this obligation they are certain concerning the truth of revelation.

However, *for philosophers*, revelation is not necessary for knowing religious and moral truth. They can arrive at it by considering the exigencies of practical reason, on account of which they must admit the mysteries (e.g., the mystery of the Redemption). And therefore, the Hermesians intended to demonstrate the dogmas [of the Christian faith], at least according to practical reason.[140] However, concerning the mysteries not yet demonstrated it was not necessary to have explicit faith. Nevertheless, Hermes added, although the philosophers themselves are not in need of revelation, they must admit the fact of revelation as something necessary for the simple faithful and as a condition for the first proposal of the mysteries, which subsequently are gradually and increasingly rendered intelligible, at last coming to be demonstrated by practical reason.

All these positions were condemned as heretical by the [First] Vatican Council when it defined against Hermes that the formal motive of faith is the authority of God who reveals.[141]

{{114}} What we have said suffices as regards the apologetic methodology found in the writings of the semi-rationalists. Certain apologetes who more or less follow the ways of Kant, admitting the primacy of practical reason and action, have proposed, as we will immediately discuss, a methodology that is not lacking in affinity with Hermesianism.[142]

Among the errors pertaining to apologetics in the nineteenth century, the Church also condemned the *fideism and traditionalism* of Louis Bautain and Augustin Bonnetty, which held that human reason cannot prove and know with certitude the fact of revelation—nay, not even the existence of God, the infinity of his perfections, and the spirituality and freedom of the rational soul. Bautain was required to subscribe to these propositions: "With regard to these various questions, *reason precedes faith*, and must lead us to them." "Although reason was rendered weak and obscure through original sin, there remained in it enough clarity and power so that it could lead us with certitude to (know) the existence of God, and to the fact of revelation made to the Jews through Moses and to the Christians through the God-Man who is worthy of adoration."[143]

---

[140] See Pius IX, *Qui pluribus* (Denzinger, no. 2777).

[141] See [First] Vatican Council, *Dei filius*, can. 3.2 (Denzinger, no. 3032). See Vacant, *Études sur le Concile du Vatican*, vol. 2, 196. Also, concerning Hermesianism, see Giovanni Perrone, *Praelectiones theologicae*, vol. 3 (*De locis theologicis*), pt. 3, sect. 1, 2, §3; and Jacques-Paul Migne, *Démonstrations évangéliques [de Tertullien, et al.]*, vol. 14 [Paris: Petit-Montrouge, 1843], col. 956. [Trans. note: The edition of Perrone is not cited.]

[142] See Pius X, *Pascendi*, no. 37 (Denzinger, no. 2103 [old numbering]).

[143] See Gregory XVI, "Theses Subscribed to by Louis-Eugène Bautain by Order of the Sacred

(3) *The apologetics of Catholics in the nineteenth century.* As regards apologetics in the nineteenth century among Catholics, three categories can be distinguished—namely, theologian-apologetes and several philosopher-apologetes who are subdivided into two classes.

A. The theologian-apologetes, on account of the supernaturality of the revealed mysteries, in particular made use of an external methodology (whether extrinsic or intrinsic), and secondarily made use of an internal methodology in the manner of a preparation and confirmation [for credibility known by using external methods]. Such thinkers generally conceived of apologetics as being fundamental theology.

B. Many philosopher-apologetes, such as Ollé-Laprune in France, who without qualification admitted the ontological value of speculative reason, chiefly made use of an internal methodology together with an intrinsic-external methodology and, as it were, secondarily made use of an extrinsic-external methodology—namely, by means of miracles.

C. Certain philosopher-apologetes, such as Blondel, who are partisans for a primacy of action and practical reason, defend the primacy of the methodology of immanence—that is, the primacy of an internal methodology—so that without it the other methods would remain inefficacious. From this perspective, apologetics is conceived as being a philosophy of religion and not as fundamental theology.

These positions must be explained briefly.

A. Theologian-Apologetes, among whom we may cite Denis-Luc Frayssinous, Rosaven, Jean-Baptiste Henri Lacordaire, Louis-Frédéric Brugère, Franz Hettinger, Giovanni Perrone, Ignaz Ottiger, Tommaso Maria Zigliara, Adolphe Tanquerey, and so forth, determined the methodology of apologetics by considering the end toward which it tends—namely, the supernatural mysteries to be most firmly believed on account of the authority of God who reveals. Hence, their methodology is principally external.

(a) They made use of *external-intrinsic criteria* so as to show the excellence of Christianity in itself and in relation to other religions. They insisted upon the purity, harmony, and sublimity of Christ's doctrine. Nay, they made clear that the miraculous life of the Church is a moral miracle that provides "an irrefutable testimony of her divine mission."[144]

In this way, Fr. Lacordaire, O.P., showed the excellence of Christian doctrine, its

---

Congregation of Bishops and Regulars, April 26, 1844" (Denzinger, nos. 2765–2769) and Pius IX, "Decree of the Sacred Congregation of the Index, June 11 (15), 1855" (Denzinger, nos. 2811–2814).

[144] [First] Vatican Council, *Dei filius*, ch. 3 (Denzinger, no. 3014).

harmony, firmness, and the illustrious virtues that are the privilege of Christianity, especially humility, chastity, and charity. Thus, he demonstrated the divinity of the religion of Christ from {{115}} the marvelous fruits that it brings forth in the social and moral order.[145] And because the miraculous life of the Church already stands forth as a moral miracle, it is easy to transition to a consideration of sensible miracles historically testified to.

(b) The theologian-apologetes made use of *extrinsic-external criteria*— that is, miracles of the physical order and prophecies—so as to prove properly not only the excellence but also the divine origin of Christianity, all of whose dogmas must be believed most firmly, even if some of them (such as the Trinity and eternal damnation) remain very obscure. In order to prove the divine origin of the whole doctrine of Christ, it adduces "miracles as a befitting testimony, as a visible action that can only be divine reveals an invisibly inspired teacher of the truth," as St. Thomas had said in *SCG* I, ch. 6.

In the nineteenth century, arguments from miracles were defended in particular among the traditional apologetes, Frayssinous, Nicolas, Brugère, and Hettinger, against philosophical rationalism, and against the biblical rationalism of de Valroger, H. Wallon, Vigouroux, and so forth.

(c) The theologian-apologetes also made use of *internal criteria*— namely, the legitimate aspirations of our nature—but did so secondarily in the manner of preparation and confirmation [of what was known by means of external criteria]. Indeed, they showed that the legitimate[146] aspirations of our nature, especially its superior aspirations, are fulfilled only in Christianity and not in other religions or in philosophical systems; nay, they showed that Christianity surpasses these natural aspirations (e.g., someone could desire the Incarnation or the Eucharist naturally; these supernatural gifts infinitely exceed our natural desire and nevertheless, in an utterly marvelous manner, are most profoundly conformed to our loftiest aspirations). These internal motives were set forth in preaching and in spiritual direction— that is, in practical apologetics rather than in the manuals of apologetics. However, the befittingness of the mysteries and the precepts is speculatively made clear in dogmatic and moral theology.

---

[145] See the 1835 *Conférences* of Lacordaire, first chapter on the necessity of a teaching church and on its distinctive character; those of 1843, *On the effects of Catholic doctrine upon the mind* [*esprit*] (the certitude that it produces and the extraordinary opposition that it produces; humility, chastity, charity, and the virtue of religion); also see his conferences from 1845, *On the effects of Catholic doctrine upon society* (from the intellectual point of view, as regards the principles of law, as regards property, family, authority, with respect to community of goods and of life); also, in 1846, *Jesus Christ* (on his intimate life, his public power, on his miracles, and on the establishment, perpetuity, and progress of the reign of Jesus Christ).

[146] [Trans. note: Reading *legitimas* for *legitimis*.]

These internal motives were used especially by *Chateaubriand* (*The Genius of Christianity*, 1802), *Lamennais* (*Essay on Indifference in the Matter of Religion*, 1817), *Lacordaire* (*Conférences*), *Bougaud* (*Christianity and the Present Times*, 8th edition in 1901). Likewise, *de Broglie* most excellently wrote about Christianity in comparison with other religions.

These authors generally set forth, as it were, in a unified manner both internal arguments (from the aspirations [of human nature]) and intrinsic-external arguments (from the excellence and fecundity of Christianity). {{116}} Hence, *Cardinal Dechamps*[147] established that the Christian-Catholic demonstration is supported by a twofold fact that is obvious to all, partly internal and partly external. The internal fact is our need for some authority in which we could have complete confidence regarding everything that concerns our final end. The external fact is the existence of the Church, which claims for herself infallible authority in religious matters and shows herself to be credible on account of her miraculous life and fecundity in the moral order. For more on this, read *Cardinal Newman*.[148]

Therefore, the theologian-apologetes made use of internal motives only in a secondary manner and denied the primacy (or priority of value) of the methodology of immanence, admitting that it only has a *temporal priority* inasmuch as it *disposes* the subject to the consideration of the other motives of credibility and inasmuch as it afterwards confirms other arguments.[149]

However, according to the theologian-apologetes, *priority of perfection* belongs to the methodology that comes closest to the end of apologetics—namely, to proving the credibility of the mysteries of faith as being manifestly revealed by God.[150] This methodology is an external one, arguing from mir-

---

[147] Victor Cardinal Dechamps, *Entretiens sur la démonstration catholique* in *Oeuvres* (Malines: Dessain, 1861).

[148] Cardinal Newman, having too little confidence in speculative reason, insisted especially upon psychological, moral, and historical arguments. He shows the harmony of Christianity with natural religion, which conscience bears witness to as being true. Nevertheless, he also makes clear the intervention of divine providence as regards the preservation of monotheism in Jews, the fulfillment of the messianic prophecies in Christ, and the miraculous diffusion of Christianity.

[149] However, this temporal priority is opposed to the priority of perfection, for a disposition is more imperfect than that to which it disposes: nor is it surprising that it confirms it afterwards, since, as Aristotle and St. Thomas frequently show: "Just as the disposition in the way of generation *precedes* the perfection to which it disposes in those things that are successively brought to perfection, so too does it naturally *follow* the perfection that a given thing has already attained, just as the heat that was the disposition to the form of fire is an effect flowing from the form of fire that now exists" (*ST* III, q. 7, a. 13, ad 2). Likewise, the phantasm disposes to the idea and afterwards expresses it sensibly, or an emotion disposes to volition and afterwards follows it as willed.

[150] In many places in this work, we use this expression: "The mysteries of faith are evidently cred-

acles or from the miraculous life of the Church as from a moral miracle.

An internal methodology can have a certain priority from the perspective of the subject (*quoad nos*), inasmuch as it disposes the subject, but not from the perspective of the object (*quoad se*). Such is the common outlook of the theologian-apologetes on this matter.

B. Many philosopher-apologetes in France, such as Léon Ollé-Laprune and Georges Fonsegrive,[151] hold that the aforementioned methodology is not suitably accommodated to contemporary minds, for as they say, arguments from the history of the Church that refer to the miracles performed during the early days of Christianity and that show forth the miraculous life of the Church do not have the power to efficaciously move the souls of contemporary men, who are imbued with prejudices and reject *a priori* everything that is supernatural. Moreover, contemporary men proclaim, with Kant {{117}}, *the autonomy* of reason and hence refuse to admit a religious doctrine that would be *authoritatively* proposed by God and the Church unless its necessity (at least its practical necessity) is first clear on the basis of an intimate consideration of Christianity.

Hence, these philosopher-apologetes, considering unbelievers who still need to be converted rather than the end of apologetics itself, most especially made use of *internal criteria* and *intrinsic-external* criteria. Nevertheless, they do not reject external-extrinsic criteria—namely, miracles—but, rather, proposed them, as it were, secondarily, after prejudices are removed. Therefore, they began by showing the conformity of Christianity with the aspirations of our nature and showing that the cure for our misery is only found in Christianity and Catholicism, so that the necessity (at least the practical necessity) of embracing the doctrine of the Catholic Church may be clear. Ferdinand Brunetière generally proceeded along the same lines.

In these systems, the powers of natural reason are frequently disparaged, just as they are in the writings of Pascal; nevertheless, the ontological value of speculative reason is generally admitted, even without considering the practical requirements of human life. Thus, they say that the existence of God and of miracles can be known certainly by specu-

---

ible, as being *manifestly revealed by God.*" The meaning is clear from the context, for we do not deny the obscurity of these mysteries, which will be manifest to us only in heaven, but we only affirm that fact—namely, that *it is manifest that they have been revealed by God*, which is more briefly stated in the aforementioned formula. These two formulas are related to each other as a modal proposition *de re* and a modal proposition *de dicto*.

[151] See Léon Ollé-Laprune, *De la certitude morale* (1880); *Le prix de la vie*, 4th ed. (1897); *La philosophie et les temps present* (1890); *La vitalité chrétienne* (1901); *La raison et le rationalisme* (1906). Also see George Fonsegrive, *Le catholicisme et la vie de l'esprit* (1899).

lative reason, although, from their outlook, they can only be perceived if one presupposes certain moral dispositions—namely, perfect sincerity and a good will.

According to the theologians, this methodology is useful and suited to contemporary minds, but in order for it to suffice for manifesting true credibility, it not only must show the moral necessity of embracing Catholicism in order to pursue an integral moral life, but also must show the divine origin of the doctrine of Christ and of the Church, since the mysteries of the faith must be believed on account of the authority of God who reveals and not on account of their necessity for right living.

C. HOWEVER, CERTAIN PHILOSOPHER-APOLOGETES, SUCH AS MAURICE BLONDEL[152] AND FR. LUCIEN LABERTHONNIÈRE,[153] indulge in an agnosticism of speculative reason and propose a new methodology of apologetics for showing the truth of the Catholic faith to the agnostics and immanentists of our time. They affirm the primacy of the methodology of immanence in such a way that they hold that were this methodology no longer used, the other methodologies would remain inefficacious.

This new methodology depends on *a twofold foundation*—namely, moderate agnosticism and semi-immanentism. *This moderate agnosticism* consists *in the following*: Speculative reason cannot defend its ontological value except according to the practical requirements of human action. Were we to remove the requirements of action, our speculative knowledge would remain *notional* and *subjective*; it only posits the problem of action and directs action. However, objective reality is reached through action.[154]

---

[152] See Maurice Blondel, "Lettre sur les exigences de la pensée contemporaine en matière d'apologetique," *Annales de philosophie chrétienne* (Jan.-July 1897) [*sic*]; *L'action,* 1893. [Trans. note: See Maurice Blondel, *The Letter on Apologetics & History and Dogma,* trans. Alexander Dru and Illtyd Trethowan (Grand Rapids, MI: Eerdmans, 1995); *Action (1893): Essay on a Critique of Life and a Science of Practice,* trans. Oliva Blanchette (Notre Dame, IN: University of Notre Dame Press, 1984).]

[153] Fr. Lucien Laberthonnière in many places fought against the old methodology of the theologians and scholastic philosophy in the *Annales de philosophie chrétienne,* the collection of which from 1905 to 1913 was condemned by the Sacred Congregation of the Index.

[154] See Maurice Blondel, *L'action* (1893), 463: "*For science,* what difference could one discover between what appears to exist forever and what is? And *how could one distinguish between reality itself and an invincible and permanent illusion* or, so to speak, an eternal appearance? *For practice,* matters are otherwise: only by *in acting AS IF it were,* alone does it possess what is, *if it is truly* [*sic*]." Likewise, see *L'action,* 426–427: "To show that we are inevitably led to affirm (regardless of what the value of this assertion may be) the reality of objects of knowledge and of the ends of action ... *this is not,* in spite of the renewal of perspective, *to leave the determinism of phenomena*; it is to manifest how solely by the fact that we think and that we act it is necessary for us to act *as if* this universal order were real and these obligations were founded." Likewise, *L'action,* 497: "Metaphysics has its substance in the acting will. It has truth only from this expe-

Hence, the ancient definition of truth must be rejected: {{118}} the adequation of the reality and the intellect;[155] it must be said that *truth is the real adequation of mind and life* and that truth is had when our mind knows and affirms the exigencies of our life and action. For example, if proofs[156] for the existence of God are considered merely in a speculative manner, they remain merely notional and do not prove the divine reality. Thus is the primacy of action and practical reason asserted.

In its foundation, this new methodology *does not lack affinity with immanentism.* Indeed, in this principle we find religion (even supernatural religion) cannot be imposed externally; in virtue of reason's autonomy, man wishes to accept nothing externally except what is required for the perfect development of his faculties. Thus, religion (even supernatural religion) must be proposed as an aid somehow postulated *intrinsically* [*ab intrinseco*] for the perfect development of our action.

Blondel's doctrine differs from immanentism, for according to imma-

---

riential and dynamic perspective: it is less a science of what is than of what causes things to be and to become: today's ideal can be tomorrow's reality." Likewise, *L'action,* 437: "*The knowledge which before the exercise of choice [l'option] was simply subjective and propulsive, becomes, after it, privative and constitutive of being.* . . . The second of these knowledges, that which follows upon the determination freely made in the face of this reality necessarily conceived, *is no longer only a subjective disposition;* instead of *posing* the practical problem, it translates its solution into our thought; instead of placing us in the presence of *what is to be done, it gathers from what is done what is.* It is therefore truly an objective knowledge, even though it is reduced to noting the deficit of action." Hermes spoke quite similarly, as was said above.

[155] With regard to the definition of truth, Blondel says, in "Point de depart de la recherche philosophique," *Annales de philosophie chrétienne* (1906): 235: "For the abstract and chimerical *adaequatio rei et intellectus* is substituted . . . the *adaequatio realis mentis et vitae [the real adequation of mind and life.*" But because the life about which one speaks in this new definition of truth is human life, how can one avoid the condemned modernist proposition: "Truth is no more immutable than man himself, since it evolved with him, in him, and through him" (Pius X, *Lamentabile,* prop. 58, Denzinger, no. 3458)?

Concerning this philosophy of action, see the many articles of Fr. Marie-Benoît Schwalm in the *Revue Thomiste*—"L'acte de foi, est-il raissonable?" *Revue Thomiste* 4 (1896): 56[n1]; "Les illusions de l'idéalisme et leurs dangers pour la foi," *Revue Thomiste* 4 (1896): 413–441; "L'apologétique contemporaine: Doit-elle adopter une méthode nouvelle?" *Revue Thomiste* 5 (1897): 62–94; "La crise de l'apologétique," *Revue Thomiste* 5 (1897): 239–270; "La croyance naturelle et la science," *Revue Thomiste* 5 (1897): 627–645; "Le dogmatisme du coeur et celui de l'esprit," *Revue Thomiste* 6 (1898): 578–619.

Likewise, see the review of two works concerning this matter in Réginald Garrigou-Lagrange, "Chronique de métaphysique," *Revue Thomiste* 21 (1913): 351–371. Likewise, see the article of Auguste Valensin [Aug. et Alb Valensin], "Méthode d'Immanence" in the *Dictionnaire apologétique,* vol. 8. Also see Joseph de Tonquédec, *Immanence: Essai critique sur la doctrine de M. Maurice Blondel* (Paris: Beauchesne, 1913).

[156] [Trans. note: Reading *probationes* for *probatione.*]

nentism religion (even the Catholic religion) proceeds from our vital immanence according to the development [*evolutionem*] of religious sentiment. But Blondel's doctrine can be called *semi-immanentism* inasmuch as it affirms that the Catholic religion, although supernatural and revealed by God, is postulated intrinsically by our nature such that it would indeed exceed the powers, but not the demands, of our nature.[157]

{{119}} From this twofold foundation, this new methodology of immanence has a kind of affinity with modernism and with Hermesianism.

Now, on the presupposition of these principles, what do these new apologetes say concerning the various criteria of apologetics?

(a) *With regard to external-extrinsic criteria*, they do not acknowledge the philosophical knowability of the probative force of miracles. For, according to them, if one removes the exigencies of human action, speculative reason cannot know ontological reality with certainty, nor any given separate, extramental fact. Nay, the separation of phenomena, just as the fixity of the laws of nature, pertains only to our manner of conceiving things, not to reality, which is ever changing. Thus, miracles are not exceptions to the laws of nature as they are in reality, but instead are exceptions to the laws of appearances (exceptions "to anthropomorphic appearances," as Blondel says, and "to an illusory order," as Fr. Laberthonnière says[158]). In this, we can quite clearly see a vestige of Kantian agnosticism.

And therefore, [according to Blondel] *the ontological value of miracles*, which is admitted by common sense, can be neither scientifically nor philosophically defended in order for us to hold that miracles are special interventions by God in order to confirm and prove the fact of revelation. Miracles have only a *symbolic value*—namely they manifest to us the presence of God in the world and in our life, hence provoking the soul to an examination of religion, which it symbolically confirms. Nay, this symbolic value of miracles can only be perceived by minds that are already morally aware of the exigencies of human moral action and rightly disposed to admit divine action in ordinary facts.

Hence, according to Blondel,[159] if a miracle is intimately (metaphysically) probed,

---

[157] See Maurice Blondel, "Lettre sur les exigences de la pensée contemporaine en matiére d'apologétique," *Annales de philosophie chrétienne* (Jan.-July 1896): 600: "Modern thought, with jealous sensitivity, considers the notion of *immanence* as the very condition of philosophy; that is, if among the reigning ideas, there is a result to which it attaches itself as to certain progress, it is the ideal that at bottom is very just, namely that *nothing can enter into man that does not come from him* and does not correspond in some manner to a need of expansion, and that, neither as a historical fact, nor as a traditional teaching, nor as an obligation added on from without, is there for him a truth that matters and a precept admissible without being, in some manner, autonomous and native to him."

[158] See *Bulletin de la Société française de philosophie* (June 1911): 144 and (Mar. 1912): 143. Also see Joseph de Tonquédec, *Immanence*, 200–227.

[159] See Blondel, *L'action*, 396: "The idea of fixed laws in nature is only an idol; each phenomenon

there is nothing more found in it than in ordinary facts; but there is nothing less [miraculous] found in utterly ordinary facts than is found in miracles. Indeed, in all facts, the rightly disposed soul will see the presence of the divine action; however, *the miracle does compel one to pay heed and symbolically provokes the human mind to an examination of religion.*

Therefore, having presupposed speculative reason's agnosticism, extrinsic-external criteria can be neither scientifically nor philosophically defended as special interventions on the part of God useful for proving the fact of revelation, but they do have a symbolic value subordinated to the exigencies of our action and incite the soul to an examination of religion that they symbolically confirm. In other words, the probative force of miracles is subordinated to internal criteria (or to the method of immanence), which has primacy.

{{120}} (b) *However,* what value does *an intrinsic-external motive—namely the miraculous life of the Church—*have in this new apologetics? According to the [First] Vatican Council, it is "an irrefutable testimony of the Church's divine mission" as a moral miracle.[160]

Now, having presupposed the principles of this new apologetics—namely, that physical miracles cannot be discerned philosophically and scientifically—how could a moral miracle be discerned? Indeed, it is clear, as the modernists themselves admit, that something "unknown" is hidden in the life of the Church, but how can the fact of God's supernatural intervention be shown within her? Hence, according to this new apologetics, the value of this motive, just as that of miracles, seems to be only symbolic for manifesting the presence of the divine action in the world, in our life, and especially in the Church. However, it is not yet proven that the Church not only is a superior form of religious evolution but moreover is supernaturally founded by God. Nay, the symbolic value of this motive is subordinated to internal criteria and can only appear to minds that are already aware of the exigencies of human moral action.[161]

---

is a singular case and a unique solution. To go to the heart of the matter, there is nothing more, without a doubt, in the miracle than in the least of ordinary facts, but also there is nothing less in the least ordinary of fact than in the miracle. Indeed, behold the meaning of these exceptional brusque events that provoke reflection upon more general conclusions: what they reveal is that the divine is not only in what seems to exceed the customary power of man and of nature, but even is everywhere that we gladly believe that man and nature are [self-]sufficient. Therefore, miracles are miraculous only in the sight of those who are already prepared to recognize the divine action in the most usual of events and acts. These sudden shocks act only inasmuch as one grasps in them, *not the sensibly marvelous,* what this is [*qu'est-ce que cela*], *but the symbolic meaning.*"

[160] [First] Vatican Council, *Dei filius,* ch. 3 (Denzinger, no. 3014).

[161] See Blondel, *L'action,* 395: "Whether or not they be supernatural in their principle, it is not in the sensible signs themselves that *we must look for the origin of our idea of revelation.* It is *by the development of practical activity* and thanks to the effort of the will to make itself equal to its own élan, that there is born, as we have seen, *the need for an exterior correspondence* and

(c) *As regards internal criteria*, these apologetes exaggerate their value, for while they diminish the power of miracles, they too greatly extoll the aspirations and exigencies of our nature.

Blondel and Laberthonnière intend to demonstrate that supernatural religion, even though it is not owed to human nature, is nevertheless required somehow by our nature so that we may arrive at a perfect development [*evolutionem*] of our faculties, such that we are bound to embrace such supernatural religion. Thus, they show that we experience aspirations to something superior, infinite, and divine, which, by a necessity of nature, we desire as [our] ultimate end. However, we cannot reach the Infinite Being without his help. Therefore, God's supernatural aid (that is, revelation) is intrinsically demanded by our nature;[162] according to Blondel, our nature also demands a mediator and savior by whose mediation we are enabled to approach God. Next, it is historically shown that these required divine aids are found only in Christianity and Catholicism. Finally, the divine origin of Catholicism, which is symbolically manifested through miracles and the miraculous life of the Church, becomes *practically certain* in the very *experience* of the Christian religion under the aid of grace.[163] Thus, supernatural religion is in some manner required intrinsically {{121}} by our nature, and the principle of immanence is preserved, just as the method of immanence holds primacy.

A CRITIQUE OF THIS NEW APOLOGETICS. Against this new methodology, theologians commonly raise three objections in particular: (a) It

---

for a necessary complement to our intimate action."—See ibid., 397: "Therefore, it is not from revelation itself (on the hypothesis that revelation exists), nor from natural phenomena (on the hypothesis that revelation does not exist) that there can come to man *the idea of precepts or of revealed dogmas. It is from an internal initiative that this notion springs."*

162 See ibid., 462: "It is impossible that the supernatural order not exist, since the entire natural order guarantees it by demanding it." Likewise, see *Lettre*, 3rd ed. art., p. 603 and 6th ed. art., p. 345. [Tr. note: Perhaps this refers to various editions of Blondel's *Lettre sur les exigences de la pensée contemporaine en matière d'apologétique*, though the further publication citation details are opaque in Fr. Garrigou-Lagrange's citation, thus being directly presented here.]

163 See ibid., 402: "There are offered to man acts that, hypothetically, are purely of faith, acts that he has no natural reason to impose on himself. . . . If he is consistent, *it is necessary that he give an attempt*; and the reason for this *experience* is to bring, in the desired contract, all of man's part, by acting for that which is nothing in man, *so as to see if the whole of God is revealed in it. It is only by an effective experimentation that one can know what is in it.*[. . .] Thus (as strange as this rule of conduct may seem), he who has understood the necessity, *who has felt the need for faith, must, without having it, act as though he already had it*, so that it may gush forth into his awareness from the depths of this heroic action that submits the whole man to the generosity of its *élan*. For it is not from thought that faith passes to the heart; it is from practice that it draws a divine light for the mind [*esprit*]. God acts in this action, and this is why the thought that follows the act is infinitely richer than that which precedes it. It has entered into a new world where no philosophical speculation can lead it nor follow it."

See Lucien Laberthonnière, "Dogme et théologie," *Annales de philosophie chrétienne* (Feb. 1908): 502–508; (Oct. 1908): 70–78; (Jan. 1910): 400.

is founded on a semi-agnosticism that must be rejected; (b) it presupposes semi-immanentism, which is erroneous; and (c) it does not rightly preserve the formal motive of faith.

(a) *It is founded on semi-agnosticism* (or agnosticism in the order of speculative reason), for it alters the definition of truth, which is conceived of only subjectively as the "real adequation of the mind and life." Thus, nothing remains except practical certitude. How can this condemned proposition of the modernists be avoided: "Truth is no more immutable than man himself, since it evolved with him, in him, and through him."[164] Hence, the philosophical knowability of miracles and also of God's existence is destroyed; nay, without the ontological and transcendent value of concepts used in the formation of dogmas, the latter's absolute truth and immutability are destroyed. Moreover, how can those who hold this theory avoid this condemned proposition of the modernists: "The dogmas of faith are to be held only according to their practical sense; that is to say, as preceptive norms of conduct and not as norms of believing."[165] Hence, this semi-agnosticism seems to lead to agnosticism properly so-called.

(b) *It presupposes a semi-immanentism that is equally to be rejected.* Indeed, if the Catholic religion is demanded by our nature, it is owed to us and, hence, is not supernatural. For that which is supernatural is not only above nature's powers but also above its demands. What is demanded by our nature is only the natural beatitude that is found in abstractive knowledge of God and in natural love of God. Thus, this proposition from Baius has been condemned: "The sublimation of human nature and its elevation to participation in the divine nature were due to the integrity of man in his first state and therefore to be called natural, not supernatural."[166]

The new apologetes respond: Our aspiration to the supernatural order is not found in our nature of itself, and abstractly considered, but is established in man *de facto* and concretely with his ordination to the supernatural end. Indeed, man does not now exist in a merely natural state, but even if he has neither habitual grace nor supernatural faith, he is stirred preveniently [*praevenitur et excitatur*] by actual grace to turn unto God the Author of salvation. Nor is it necessary that the aspiration to Christianity be perceived consciously as properly supernatural by its end. It suffices that we be aware of our *inability* to fulfill the superior tendencies of the soul and that we not be aware that the satisfaction of these aspirations is found in Christianity. We can express our disquietude according to that expression of St. Augustine: "Our heart is restless until it rests in thee."

---

[164] Pius X, *Lamentabile*, prop. 58 (Denzinger, no. 3458).

[165] Ibid., prop. 26 (Denzinger, no. 3426).

[166] Pius V, *Ex omnibus afflictionibus*, no. 21 (Denzinger, no. 1921).

The theologians issue a counterpoint, noting that the question is not thereby resolved. The problem is only shoved aside and reappears as regards the first ordering of mankind to the supernatural {{122}} end—namely, whether this ordination was altogether gratuitous, or whether it was demanded intrinsically as the new apologetes wanted to show by virtue of the principle of immanence. Indeed, this principle either is or is not preserved in this first ordination. If it is not preserved, this new apologetics does not prove what it set out to prove, and the objections of naturalism remain without a resolution. If, on the contrary, the principle of immanence is preserved even in this first ordering, how can the error of Baius be avoided? No way of escape remains except perchance by a worse error—namely, in the denial of the ontological value of our reason; thus, the exigencies for the supernatural order would only be subjectively and not objectively necessary.[167]

Hence, the encyclical *Pascendi* notes:

> And here We cannot but deplore once more, and grievously, that there are Catholics who, while rejecting immanence as a doctrine, employ it as a method of apologetics, and who do this so imprudently that they seem to admit that there is in human nature a true and rigorous necessity with regard to the supernatural order . . . and not merely a capacity and a befittingness[168] for the supernatural.[169]

(c) *The formal motive of faith is not rightly preserved.* Indeed, divine faith is established on the authority of God who reveals and not on religious experience. However, according to Blondel, the divine origin of Catholicism is made certain only *practically* in the experience of the Christian religion, under the aid of grace. By contrast, the Church holds that our rational certitude in the fact of revelation must be firmer, so that we may believe with utter surety on account of the authority of God who reveals.[170]

Moreover, the man who does not yet believe but is aware of the need for faith would, as the new apologetes say, need to act as though he already believes so that he may

---

[167] For an examination of this part of Maurice Blondel's doctrine, see Joseph de Tonquédec, *Immanence*, 155.

[168] Catholic theologians admit only a conditional and inefficacious desire to see God through his essence, as must be exposited at greater length later on so as to make manifest our nature's obediential potency or elevability to the supernatural order. See our discussion later on in vol. 1, ch. 12. [Trans. note: Fr. Garrigou-Lagrange is here referring, technically, to the *Thomistic* position on this matter, though to his eyes, as well as those of his translator, it seems to be theologically necessary.]

[169] Pius X, *Pascendi*, no. 27 (Denzinger, 2103, old numbering). [Trans. note: Taken from the official Vatican translation.]

[170] See Pius IX, *Qui pluribus*, against the followers of Georg Hermes (Denzinger, nos. 2778 and 2779).

find certitude concerning revelation in this action or experience of Catholicism. But how can this experience of Catholicism be had without the reception of the sacraments, and how can he who does not yet believe receive the sacraments? Also, how can the teaching of the modernists that was condemned in the encyclical *Pascendi* be avoided: "The aim (the apologist) sets before himself is to make the nonbeliever attain that *experience* of the Catholic religion which, according to the system, is the sole basis of the faith"?[171] "If you ask on what foundation this assertion of the believer rests, they answer: In the experience of the individual. On this head the Modernists differ from the Rationalists only to fall into the opinion of the Protestants and pseudo-mystics."[172]

Thus, what can be proven by the methodology of immanence? In a way, it is clear that man is sufficient unto himself and stands in need of divine aid to attain his end, even his natural end (e.g., for the fulfillment of all the precepts of the natural law).[173] However, this does not prove {{123}} the need for properly supernatural aid. Moreover, this methodology can bring to light a kind of moral need to embrace Christianity in order to live morally and religiously;[174] however, this does not prove that Christianity is not only a more vigorous religion, which the modernists already admit, but also a religion revealed by God and infallibly true in all its dogmas and precepts, to be admitted with utter surety according to the proper and immutable sense of its dogmas unto the end of time. This is made manifest by external criteria that prove the fact of revelation, and the knowability of the probative force of these external criteria presupposes the ontological value of reason, which is denied by agnostics.

Therefore, the new methodology of immanence does not suffice by itself. However, it is useful, especially for contemporary minds, which proclaim the autonomy of reason. It shows them man's insufficiency and need for some superadded aid. Thus, the man who does not yet believe is prepared to consider the external criteria of Catholicism. Therefore, the methodology of immanence can have a kind of *temporal priority but not a primacy of value*. It can be prior relative to us (i.e., as regards the preparation of the

---

[171] Pius X, *Pascendi*, no. 35 (Denzinger, no. 3500). [Trans. note: Translation taken from Denzinger.]

[172] Pius X, *Pascendi*, no. 14 (Denzinger, no. 3484). [Trans. note: Translation taken from the official Vatican translation, as the current edition of Denzinger does not include the full text.]

[173] See *ST*, I-II, q. 109, a. 4 and a. 1.

[174] The [First] Vatican Council acknowledges the moral necessity of the natural truths of religion. See *Dei filius*, ch. 2 (Denzinger, no. 3005): "[It is to be ascribed to this divine revelation] that such truths among things divine that of themselves are not beyond human reason can, even in the present condition of mankind, be known by everyone with facility, with firm certitude, and with no admixture of error. It is, however, not for this reason that revelation is to be called absolutely necessary, but because God in his infinite goodness has ordained man to a supernatural end."

subject who does not yet believe) but not prior in itself and objectively for the rational defense of Catholicism.

We have examined elsewhere more recent works by Blondel, *La pensée, L'être et les êtres*, and a second, completely reworked edition of *L'action*.[175] Indeed, in these works, in order to resolve objections presented to him, the author draws closer to traditional [philosophical] positions. However, he always defines truth and certitude according to the opinions *"of the philosophy of action"* so that he admits *not a primacy of extramental being* to which our intellect must be conformed but, rather, *a primacy of action* and of human action (or of free will).[176]

---

[175] See Réginald Garrigou-Lagrange, "Vérité et option libre selon M. Maurice Blondel," *Acta academiae romae S. Thomae* (Turin: Marietti, 1935), 46–69; "La notion pragmatiste de la vérité et ses consequences en theologie," ibid., (1943), 153–178. Likewise, Réginald Garrigou-Lagrange, "La théologie et la vie de foi," *Revue Thomiste* 40, New Series, 18 (1935): 492ff. Also see F.-X. Maquart, *Elementa philosophiae*, vol. 3, *Critica* (Paris: André Blot, 1938), 174–186 (De doctrina cognitionis iuxta D. Blondel). Also, Joseph de Tonquédec, *Deux études sur "La Pensée" de M. M. Blondel* (Paris: Beauchesne, 1936). [Trans. note: The article from 1935 in *Revue Thomiste* is cited p. 994ff, which is outside the bounds of the issue in question. The article cited above from 1935 is relevant to matters being discussed here. A translation is included as Réginald Garrigou-Lagrange in "Theology and the Life of Faith," *Philosophizing in Faith: Essays on the Beginning and End of Wisdom.*, ed. and trans. Matthew K. Minerd (Providence, RI: Cluny Media, 2019), 421–443.]

[176] Yet Maurice Blondel affirms in his work *L'être et les êtres* (Paris: Félix Alcan, 1935), 415: *"No intellectual evidence, even that of principles*, absolute of themselves and possessing a necessary ontological value, *is imposed upon us with a certitude* that is spontaneously and infallibly constraining; no more than our idea of the Absolute Good acts upon our will, as though we already had the intuitive vision of perfect goodness." In response, we must say: with St. Thomas, I deny the parity of the two, because our adherence to the principle of contradiction as it is the law of being (e.g., a square circle is really impossible outside the soul) is *a necessary adherence*, while, on the contrary, as wayfarers, our love of God is free because God who is not clearly seen does not draw our will infallibly, and inasmuch as He prohibits various acts He can displease us. By contrast, the principle of contradiction is concerned with an object that is true and evident from every perspective: a square circle not only cannot be imagined or conceived but is unrealizable, really impossible outside the soul, and this is an absolute evidence without which every objective certitude is brought to ruin." If the first principles are not evidently certain, they are only very likely probabilities, and so too are the proofs of the existence of God that are founded on them. See *ST* I-II, q. 17, a. 6: "If there are things apprehended to which our intellect naturally assents, such as the first principles, such assent or dissent *is not in our power* but in the order of nature. And therefore, properly speaking, they do not fall under our command." [Trans. note: Following the Leonine edition, I am reading "proprie loquendo nec imperio subiacet" for "proprie loquendo naturae imperio subiacet".]

Hence, *"the philosophy of action"*, if it does not wish to return to the *philosophy of being* (or to traditional metaphysics), does not overcome *probabilism* with regard to the ontological value and necessity of the first principles. Thus also, the last works of Maurice Blondel unhappily still mixed truth with error regarding the very nature of our *adherence* to the first

{{124}} However, as we have shown, in defending the traditional definition of truth (namely, truth is the conformity of our intellect not only with our subjective life but with extramental reality), in order that our judgment be *objectively true* it does not suffice that it be conformed with our life and its exigencies. Beyond this, these requirements must have a foundation in reality through conformity with the very rule of our life and with its true ultimate end—that is, *through conformity to reality*. Certainly, the judgment of prudence (even if it is speculatively erroneous on account of entirely involuntary ignorance) is *practically true through conformity to right appetite* (or right intention), but the very intention of our will is said to be *right* if it tends to a due end, and the judgment in particular about the ultimate end must be *true*, not only in respect to our subjective life and our will but also with respect to extramental reality and to the ultimate reality. Thus, in *ST* I-II, q. 19, a. 3, St. Thomas says, "The object of the will is proposed to it by reason . . . and therefore *the goodness of the will* depends *on reason* in the same way that it depends on its object." Likewise, see ad 1 and 2:[177] "The very desire for the due end presupposes right apprehension concerning the end, an apprehension which is known through reason." Émile Boutroux registers the same criticism of the philosophy of action.[178]

Therefore, like it or not, in order to define [the nature of] a *right* will, "the philosophy of action" must return to the traditional definition of truth, and this definition is not *"the conformity of mind and life"* but *"conformity of the judging mind with extramental reality"* and especially with the primordial laws of being that are expressed in the first principles of contradiction, causality, and finality.

Thus, we can see all the more clearly that apologetics is not a science that is specifically distinct from sacred theology, as though it were a philosophy of religion without a direction that must be established by faith. Indeed, God does not leave the motives of credibility for us to discover but, instead, he himself determined these motives as his seals and has affirmed their rational probative force.

These remarks suffice for providing a historical overview of the methodology of apologetics. However, we will set forth a rational defense of the traditional methodology itself when we come to our discussions of the true notions of the supernatural order, revelation, faith, and credibility.

---

principles. Our teacher Fr. Marie-Benoît Schwalm, O.P., had justly noted this in his first articles on the philosophy of action proposed by Blondel. These articles seemed to many people to be too severe; they were metaphysically and theologically true. See Marie-Benoît Schwalm, "Les illusions de l'idéalisme et leurs dangers pour la foi," *Revue Thomiste* 4 (1896): 413–441; "L'apologétique contemporaine: Doit-elle adopter une méthode nouvelle?" *Revue Thomiste* 5 (1897): 62–94; "La crise de l'apologétique," *Revue Thomiste* 5 (1897): 338–370; "Le dogmatisme du coeur et celui de l'esprit," *Revue Thomiste* 6 (1898): 578–619.

[177] [Trans. note: The text reads "ad 1 ad 2," though the cited text is only ad 2.]
[178] Émile Boutroux, *La science et la religion* (Paris: Flammarion, 1908), 296.

BOOK ONE
INTRODUCTORY REMARKS

On the Notion, Possibility, Necessity, and Discernibility of Revelation

SECTION I

On the Notion of Supernatural Revelation

Prologue and a Preliminary Article concerning the Notion of Revelation
Ch. 4.   The Definition and Division of Revelation
    Art. 1.   The Catholic Notion of Revelation and Heterodox Notions Thereof
    Art. 2.   Theological Explication of the Catholic Notion of Revelation
    Art. 3.   The Division of Revelation
Ch. 5.   On the Notions of Mystery and of Dogma
    Art. 1.   The Catholic Notion of Mystery and of Dogma; Heterodox Notions
    Art. 2.   Theological Explication of the Catholic Notion of Mystery and of Dogma
Ch. 6.   On the Notion of Supernaturality
    Art. 1.   The Catholic Notion of Supernaturality; Heterodox Notions
    Art. 2.   Theological Explication of the Catholic Notion of Supernaturality and the Division of Supernaturality

PROLOGUE

{{125}} *Division of this section*—In order to form a true notion of the revelation of supernatural mysteries, we must determine the exact sense of the terms "revelation," "mystery," and "supernaturality." Hence, three chapters must be distinguished:

1) The definition and division of revelation
2) The definition and division of mystery
3) The definition and division of supernaturality

Thus, we will proceed analytically—that is, by analyzing the complex notion of revelation, so as to discover what belongs to it (1) from the perspective of God who reveals and from the perspective of man to whom it is proposed and (2) from the perspective of its object (namely, that of the mysteries). Finally, (3) the notions of mystery and of revelation will be illustrated synthetically in light of the simpler notion of supernaturality.

It is better to proceed thus, simultaneously analytically and synthetically, than to immediately {{126}} discuss the loftier and simpler notion of supernaturality, for in our treatise we are concerned with the supernatural order only as it is related to revelation. Therefore, one must start from the notion of revelation in general so as to arrive at the notion of strictly supernatural revelation—that is, of formally supernatural mysteries. This was the procedure followed by the [First] Vatican Council in the second chapter (On Revelation) of its Constitution on the Catholic Faith [*Dei filius*]. So too does symbolic positive theology first collect what is taught by the Church about revelation (cf. Denzinger, index). Systematic theology must proceed along similar lines in this treatise.

However, because revelation is the foundation of supernatural religion, a brief article on the notion of religion in general must first be provided.

Preliminary Article concerning the Notion of Religion

We do not wish to linger on this notion, which is proposed differently by various philosophical systems that will be examined later in the question concerning the possibility of revelation. For now, it suffices for us to briefly set forth the heterodox notions of religion that will be judged later, and the traditional notion that is considered true by the Church.

Authors do not agree *concerning the etymology* of the word *religion*. Indeed, some believe it to be from *relegere* [to read again], others from *reeligere* [to choose again] or *religare* [to bind fast]. However, whatever may be the case regarding its origin, this term signifies a given moral bond joining man to God.[1]

(1) *Heterodox notions.* They can be divided inasmuch as they proceed either from empiricism or from idealism, whether pantheistic or agnostic.

According to empiricists or sensualists, religion, like ethics, is reduced to the sensible order of pleasing and useful things. It is a kind of emotion arising either from ignorance of the law of nature, from the subconscious, or from the sense of dependence upon the collective, which the unsophisticated conceive of as a Higher Being to be honored religiously. (This will be taken up in chapter 9 when we come to examine the empiricist agnosticism of Spencer, the positivists, the pragmatists, and so forth, as well as when we come to examine the empiricist evolutionism of Haeckel.)

According to the pantheistic idealists, such as Spinoza, Fichte, Schelling, Hegel, and others, religion is the God-consciousness that men have when they realize that they exist in God. And every religious cognition, they say, remains symbolic, imaginative, and hence inferior to the philosophical conception of God. (This will be taken up below in chapter 8 in our examination of idealistic evolutionism.)

According to Kantian agnostic idealists, religion consists in a way of fulfilling duties toward ourselves and others as though they were established by God; however, there are not special duties that we owe to God. This will be taken up in our examination of idealistic evolutionism.)

Finally, many *deists* admit the necessity of some internal worship; however, they deny the usefulness of prayer and external worship.

{{127}} (2) *The traditional notion of religion.* Religion, like science, can be understood in two ways, either objectively or subjectively.

Objectively, religion is defined as *the complex of truths and precepts by which our life is ordered to God.*

Subjectively understood, religion is not a kind of emotion of sensibility but, rather, *a voluntary disposition of mind—nay, a virtue—*by which man, knowing that some supreme Divinity exists, is inclined toward showing it *worship* on account of its excellence and dominion.[2]

This definition is had from a diligent observation of the facts of religion and is nothing other than an explication of the vague and common notion that is handed on by common sense. Hence, as we will see through our criticism of the aforementioned systems, this notion presupposes the true notions of the soul and of God.

---

[1] See *ST* II-II, q. 81, a. 1.
[2] See *ST* II-II, q. 81, a. 1.

Religion is called *natural* inasmuch as it relies solely upon divine truths and precepts that are known by the natural light [of reason] without supernatural revelation. On the other hand, religion that is founded upon revelation is called *supernatural*.

Later, in the final chapter [of the second volume] of this work, we will take up the duty of professing natural religion, together with that of receiving divine revelation that has been sufficiently proposed.

(3) *The various religions existing today* (in 1937).
A.   Of the 2.048 billion inhabitants of the world:

a)   *Christianity*, which nearly fills Europe and America, and also has spread throughout other parts of the world, numbers 735 million, or 36 percent of the world's inhabitants. Of these, 383 million are Catholic, 195 million Protestants, and 148 million Orthodox. Nine million other Christians exist.

b)   *Confucianism* is found throughout Asia in particular and includes 353 million adherents, or 17 percent of the world's inhabitants.

c)   *Hinduism* is found throughout Asia in particular and numbers 246 million worshippers, or 12.4 percent of the world's inhabitants.

d)   *Islam* is found throughout Asia and Africa in particular and includes 353 million worshippers, or 11.5 percent of the world's inhabitants.

e)   *Buddhism* is found throughout Asia in particular and numbers 212 million, or 10.3 percent of the world's inhabitants.

f)   *Taoists* are in China in particular and number 40 million worshippers, or approximately 2 percent of the world's inhabitants.

g)   *Shintoism* is found particularly in Japan and has 18 million adherents, or 0.85 percent of the world's inhabitants.

h)   *Jews* number 16 million, or 0.75 percent of the world's inhabitants.

i)   {{128}} Finally, *other pagans* number 115 million, or 5.6 percent of the world's population, while 78 million, or 3.8 percent of the world's inhabitants, are said to be without any particular form of religion.[3]

---

[3]   For these numbers, which are to be accepted with moral certitude, see Konrad Algermissen, *Konfessionskunde* (Hannover: Verlag Joseph Giesel, 1939), 70. [Trans. note: In the original, this list-item was not given a letter in the outline. Hence, the next *j* was *i* in the original Latin.]

j) *Modern racism* identifies religion with love of race and the fatherland. On this, see pages 149 and 171 of the AAS [*Acta Apostolicae Sedis*] 29, 1937 edition of Pope Pius XI's encyclical *Mit Brennender Sorge*.[4]

However, rationalists believe that Christianity stands out among all religions either on account of its teaching or its effects, or upon the authority of the faithful among whom there were always many very wise and very educated people so that, if revelation were to exist, it would be sought in Christianity.

A. *In Christianity* itself, there are three historical stages, as it were, distinguished from each other.

a) *Primeval religion*, which was revealed to our first ancestors and the patriarchs, destined for the whole human race, and lasted up to Moses for the Jews, but for the Gentiles, up to the promulgation of the Christian religion, properly speaking.

b) *Mosaic religion*, which was manifested and imposed through Moses for the Israelite people alone, was a kind of renewal of the primeval religion and a preparation for the Church of Christ.

c) *Christian religion*, properly speaking, presents itself as being revealed by God through Christ for all men up to the consummation of the age. Additionally, Christianity is found in the Catholic Church wholly and entirely [*maxime et integralis*] with the notes of apostolicity, unity, catholicity, holiness, and hence is methodically set forth by that authority that claims infallibility for itself. Hence, the first thing that must be considered is the notion of revelation handed on by the Catholic Church.

---

[4] Thus, already Troeltsch (1865–1923) said that the various contemporary religions are "Festwerdungen der grossen Rassengeister." He considered the religions of the various races equally as termini of the awareness of their religious culture, among which religions Christianity would possess at least a relatively outstanding value for the people of Europe. See Ernst Troeltsch, *Der Historismus und seine Uberwindung* (Berlin: Pan Verlag Rolf Heise, 1924), 80–83.

CHAPTER FOUR

The Definition and Division of Revelation

{{130}} There are three articles in this chapter:

Art. 1. The Catholic notion of revelation and heterodox notions thereof

Art. 2. Theological explication of the Catholic notion of revelation

Art. 3. The division of revelation

ART. 1: THE CATHOLIC NOTION OF REVELATION AND HETERODOX NOTIONS THEREOF

§1. The nominal definition of revelation

§2. The more explicit definition proposed by the Catholic Church

§3. Heterodox notions of revelation

Here we are concerned with the notion of revelation (rather than with its nature), for we must begin with the nominal definition, which, as a notion belonging to the first apprehension of the mind and not to judgment, abstracts from the formal truth or falsity of our judgment about the reality in question. From the beginning of one's discussion with rationalists, the notion of revelation that is proposed by the Church must be accepted. That is, it must be accepted after the manner of a *status quaestionis* by those who do not yet believe, so that they may understand what the Catholic Church intends to signify when she speaks of divine revelation and of supernatural mysteries. Otherwise, rationalists deny only what they do not know, for in order to deny or affirm a given predicate about a given subject, we must first know what the subject and predicate signify.

§1. The Nominal Definition of Revelation

This definition is made known through its etymology. Now, etymologically, "revelation" denotes the taking away or removal of a curtain [*veli*], and the term itself signifies the removal of the veil [*velaminis*] of a thing impeding understanding. In Greek, revelation is called ἀποκάλυψις, especially to designate a supernatural manifestation (1 Cor 2:10; Matt 16:17), or φανέρωσις, which is understood as pertaining rather to natural manifestation (Rom 1:19).

Therefore, *revelation* signifies the *manifestation of a thing that was once hidden* or at least obscure. And it is called *divine* or *human* inasmuch as the thing is manifested either by God or {{131}} by man. Now, *divine* revelation is called *natural* or *supernatural*. The first, which is called revelation improperly speaking, is the manifestation of divine truth through naturally knowable creatures according to the natural exercise of our reason. Thus, it is said in Romans 1:19–20 (DR): "Because that which is known of God is manifest in them. For God hath manifested it unto them. For the invisible things of him from the creation of the world are clearly seen, being understood by the things that are made." However, *supernatural* revelation (that is, revelation properly speaking) signifies the manifestation, through an intervention by God, of a truth, beyond the order of nature. Thus is it said in 1 Corinthians 2:9–10 (DR): "That eye hath not seen, nor ear heard: neither hath it entered into the heart of man. . . . But to us God hath revealed them by his Spirit."

This supernatural revelation is called *substantially supernatural* inasmuch as the revealed object of itself exceeds the powers and exigencies of created intelligence (e.g., the revelation of the mystery of the Trinity). It is called *modally supernatural* inasmuch as the way that it is brought about is supernatural, even if the revealed object, of itself, does not exceed the powers of our intellect, such as is the case for the natural truths of religion—for example, the divine goodness and immortality of the soul.[1]

Hence, it is clear that supernatural revelation does not signify the same thing as inspiration, for inspiration does not involve the divine manifestation of any given truth but, rather, only designates a divine instinct or divine motion enabling one to infallibly judge and write down even facts that are already naturally known. Thus, Matthew is said to have written in the Gospel, under God's inspiration, the facts of Christ's life, which he already

---

[1] Certain theologians call this modally supernatural revelation *formal* revelation and the other *material* revelation [*sic*].

knew naturally from sight without revelation.

Thus, we understand the term *supernatural revelation* to mean a divine action manifesting a truth previously hidden from us and beyond the order of nature. In this definition, revelation is considered as a fact, and the nature of this fact is negatively designated in contrast with the natural order.

§2. The More Explicit Definition Proposed by the Catholic Church

The Church hands on a more explicit notion of revelation in which the nature of supernatural revelation appears more clearly, together with the circumstances of the fact of revelation. Hence, (A) the principal declarations of the Church must be gathered together; (B) afterwards, the definition of revelation must be established on their basis.

A. *In the Councils*, this notion is found all throughout, though especially in the [First] Vatican Council's Constitution on the Catholic Faith, chapter 2, *De revelatione*, when it is said:

> The same Holy Mother Church holds and teaches that God, the beginning and end of all things, can be known with certainty from the things that were created through the natural light of human reason.... But it pleased His wisdom and goodness *to reveal Himself and the eternal decrees of His will in another and supernatural way*, as the Apostle says: "In many and various ways God spoke of old to our fathers by the prophets; but in these last days he has spoken to us by a Son." (Heb 1:1–2).[2]

The Council also assigns the *end*, explaining why this supernatural revelation is absolutely necessary:

> It is to be ascribed to this divine revelation that such truths among {{132}} things divine that of themselves are not beyond human reason can, even in the present condition of mankind, be known by everyone with facility, with firm certitude, and with no admixture of error. It is, however, not for this reason that revelation *is to be called absolutely necessary*, but *because* God in his infinite goodness has *ordained man to a supernatural end*, viz., to share in the good things of God that utterly exceed the intelligence of the human mind.

However, the *object* of divine revelation is more explicitly determined in the fourth

---

2   [First] Vatican Council, *Dei filius*, ch. 2 (Denzinger, nos. 3004 and 3005).

chapter of the Council's constitution.[3] On the basis of what is said there, we can say: Beyond truths that are penetrable even by reason, Christian revelation contains both *mysteries broadly speaking*, such as God's eternal decrees, and *mysteries strictly* speaking, which are entirely impenetrable to reason,[4] nay, even transcending angelic intellects.[5] The latter sort of mysteries are those that cannot be demonstrated with the progress of science.[6] Nevertheless, they do not contradict reason[7] but, rather, surpass it, and remain obscure as long as in this life "we are absent from the Lord, for we walk by faith and not by sight," as the Apostle says (2 Cor 5:6–7, DR).

Finally, Christian revelation is *credible through external signs*[8], faithfully guarded *by the Church*, and *infallibly* declared and *proposed* by her.[9] It is *neither* imperfect,[10] nor as such *to be perfected* through progress,[11] *nor in any way changed in some other sense.*[12]

B. *The integral definition of revelation according to the four causes* can be established on the basis of these declarations by the Church. This will illuminate whatever belongs *per se* to revelation, for as St. Thomas says in *In II Phys.*, lect. 5: "Several causes of one thing are assigned *per se*, along with several definitions according to various causes, though, the perfect definition embraces all the causes." Moreover, the nature of Christian revelation spoken of by the Church is illustrated by certain principal circumstances. Hence, it can be defined thus:

> *A free and essentially supernatural divine action by which God*, in order to lead mankind to the supernatural end that consists in the vision of the divine essence, *speaking to us through the prophets and, last of all, through Christ, under a kind of obscurity, manifested supernatural mysteries and the natural truths of religion* so that they might thereafter be infallibly proposed by the Church, without any change in meaning, until the end of the world.

---

[3] See ibid., nos. 3015, 3016, 3020.

[4] See ibid., nos. 3015, 3041.

[5] See Pius IX, *Gravissimas inter*, Denzinger, no. 2856.

[6] See [First] Vatican Council, *Dei filius*, ch. 4, no. 3016 and can. 4.3 (Denzinger, no. 3043).

[7] See ibid., Denzinger, no. 3017.

[8] See ibid., ch. 3 (Denzinger, no. 3009).

[9] See ibid., ch. 4 (Denzinger, no. 3020).

[10] Pius IX, *Syllabus of Errors*, no. 5 (Denzinger, no. 2905).

[11] Pius IX, *Qui pluribus*, Denzinger, no. 2778ff; [First] Vatican Council, *Dei filius*, ch. 4 Denzinger, no. 3020).

[12] [First] Vatican Council, *Dei filius*, can. 3.1 (Denzinger, no. 3031). [Trans. note: He also cites the 10th edition Denzinger index Ia and Ib.]

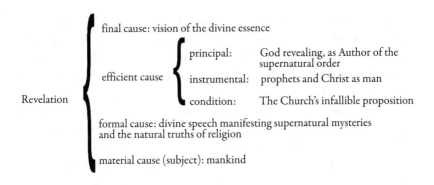

The various parts of this definition are explained according to the four causes.

(1) *The end*, which is the first of the causes: to lead mankind to the supernatural end, which consists in the vision of God.[13] {{133}} The obscure revelation made to us in our wayfaring state [*revelatio viae*] is essentially ordered to this end—namely, to the clear and glorious revelation experienced *in patria* [*revelatio patriae*]. And it is fitting that it at first be obscure, for as St. Thomas says in *ST* II-II, q. 2, a. 3, "Man cannot reach the supernatural vision of God except as a kind of learner taught by God. . . . However, man does not become a participant in this teaching all at once but instead only successively, in accord with the mode of his nature. Now, everyone learning in this manner must believe, so that they may arrive at perfect knowledge—as the Philosopher also says, 'he who wishes to learn must first believe' (*Sophistical refutations*, bk. 1, ch. 2)." Thus, by considering the end of revelation, we can see that the obscurity of the revealed mysteries is something fitting, for just as human faith in the authority of a human teacher is a fitting way to reach full knowledge [*scientiam*], so too divine faith in the authority of the divine teacher is the fitting path to the vision of glory.

(2) *Efficient cause.* Now, regarding efficient causality, we must distinguish (a) the principal cause, (b) the instrumental cause, and (c) the condition.

(a) *The principal cause* is *God who manifests*. But we must diligently note something overlooked by many who later cannot explain how our divine faith is not merely modally supernatural (that is, effectively [i.e., as regards the efficient cause that brings it about]) but in fact is substantially supernatural (that is, on the basis of its formal motive). Given that, as we have said, the end of revelation is essentially supernatural—namely, the glorious

---

[13] See ibid., ch. 2 (Denzinger, no. 3005); Benedict XII, *Benedictus Deus* (Denzinger, no. 1000).

vision [of the Deity]—the efficient cause of revelation must be God not only *qua* Author of the natural order, or *qua* free Author of sensible miracles,[14] but rather *qua the Author of an essentially supernatural order*—namely, of invisible grace and of glory. For the order of agents must correspond to the order of ends.[15]

The Church clearly speaks in this way about God who reveals.[16] Indeed, the [First] Vatican Council[17] cites texts of Sacred Scripture that attribute revelation to the Spirit of God, or the Heavenly Father (that is, to God *according to his intimate life*, by which he is *our Father*[18] and not only the Author of our nature and of any given creature): "But to us God hath revealed them *by his Spirit*. For the *Spirit* searcheth all things, yea, the *deep things of God*" (1 Cor 2:10, DR). And the Council adds that the Only Begotten himself confessed *to the Father* because he hid these things from the learned and prudent and revealed them to the little ones (Matt 11:25, DR). In the same text, Jesus says, "Yea, *Father*: for so hath it seemed good in thy sight. All things are delivered to me by *my Father*. And no one knoweth the Son but the *Father*: {{134}} neither doth anyone know the Father, but the Son, and *he to whom it shall please the Son to reveal him*." Likewise, Jesus said to Peter: "Blessed art thou, Simon Bar-Jonah: because flesh and blood hath not revealed it to thee, but *my Father who is in heaven*" (Matt 16:17, DR). Likewise, in John 5:36–38 (DR): "The works themselves, which I do, give testimony of me (this is

---

[14] For God *qua* free Author of nature can bring about a miracle, for the miraculous effect is not essentially (or entitatively) supernatural but, rather, is only effectively supernatural [(that is, as regards the efficient causality involved)]. For example, in the resurrection of a given corpse, *natural life* is given back to it (but not supernatural life), though this natural life is given back *supernaturally*. By contrast, when God produces grace in us, he *supernaturally* produces an *essentially supernatural life*, likewise doing so when he reveals supernatural mysteries by infusing a light essentially proportioned to these mysteries to be believed, as we will discuss below.

[15] See *ST* I-II, q. 109, a. 6.

[16] See [First] Vatican Council, *Dei filius*, ch. 2 and 4 (Denzinger, nos. 3004, 3015) and Leo XIII, Decree of the Holy Office, *Post obitum*, no. 38 (Denzinger, no. 3238). In the latter, the following proposition of Rosmini has been condemned: "God is the object of the beatific vision insofar as He is the author of works *ad extra*," because it does not distinguish well enough between God the Author of nature and God the Author of grace and glory.

[17] See [First] Vatican Council, *Dei filius*, ch. 4 (Denzinger, no. 3015).

[18] See *ST* I, q. 33, a. 3: "God is called the *Father* of particular beings according to the similitude of grace (which is a participation in the divine nature), who are also called adoptive sons, in accord with which they are ordered to the inheritance of eternal glory through the accepted gift of grace, as is said in *Romans* 8:16 (DR): 'For the Spirit himself giveth testimony to our spirit, that we are the sons of God.' But (God is called the Father) of other beings according to the similitude of glory, inasmuch as they already possess the inheritance of glory, as is said in *Rom.* 5:2 (DR): '[and we] glory in the hope of the glory of the sons of God.'"

a naturally knowable, *sensible* testimony, says St. Thomas),[19] that the Father hath sent me. And the Father himself who hath sent me hath given testimony of me: neither have you heard his voice at any time, nor seen his shape. And you have not his word abiding in you: for whom he hath sent, him you believe not." Thus, not all who see a sensible testimony (i.e., a miracle) hear a spiritual testimony (i.e., the voice of the Heavenly Father).

Indeed, as the free Author of the natural order, God could have revealed solely natural truths of religion and not supernatural mysteries and could have confirmed this revelation with miracles.[20] Then this revelation would have been *only* modally supernatural. And we will say later on that the fact of Christian revelation is naturally known on the basis of miracles, inasmuch as it is *effectively* [i.e., by way of efficient cause] from God (that is [*seu*], inasmuch as it is supernatural with regard to the manner [*quoad modum*] of its production). However, inasmuch as it is essentially supernatural, it is believed by divine faith, which is simultaneously *what* is believed and *that by which* it is believed.[21]

Thus, we are here speaking of God who reveals precisely *qua* Author of an essentially supernatural order.[22]

(b) *The instrumental cause* of revelation is the prophets and Christ *qua* man, for they immediately received revelation from God and, under the illumination of God, handed it on to us as God's instruments or [*seu*] ministers. However, the effect of the instrumental cause that acts in virtue of the principal agent is reduced to the principal agent. Hence, it is said, "God speaking *in* the prophets, lastly . . . has spoken to us *in* the Son" (Heb 1:1–2). Inasmuch as revelation is made to the prophet, it is called immediate. Inasmuch as it is handed on to us by the mediation of the prophet, it is called mediated.

---

[19] See St. Thomas, *In V Ioan.*, lect. 6, no. 9.

[20] Thus, theologians admit that God could have created man in a state of integral (or perfect) nature without supernatural grace.

[21] See Cajetan *In ST* II-II, q. 1, a. 1, no. 11. Also, Salmanticenses, *Cursus theologicus, De gratia*, tr. 14, disp. 3, dub. 3, no. 40.

[22] Even primitive revelation and the Mosaic revelation were, according to the Church, substantially supernatural, for it was always necessary with a necessity of means to salvation "to believe that God exists and that he is a rewarder of those seeking him" (Heb 11:6). However, these first things believed can implicitly contain, as is necessary, other things to be believed (such as the Trinity and the Incarnation) only if it is a question of the existence of God as he is the Author of the supernatural order and of divine providence inasmuch as he has distributed to men the supernatural means for salvation (cf. *ST* II-II, q. 1, a. 7). Hence, this proposition is condemned: "Faith in the broad sense, which is based on the testimony of creatures or on a similar reason, is sufficient for justification" (Innocent XI, Sixty-Five Propositions Condemned in the Decree of the Holy Office, March 2, 1679, Denzinger, no. 2123).

However, it always is the Word of God and not the word of man. He who speaks to us is not the prophet alone but, rather, God *in* the prophet.

(c) *However, the necessary condition* for revealed things to be proposed to us infallibly[23] is the proposal of revelation by the Church, who was divinely founded for this purpose with God's assistance. After the fact of revelation, the Church is related to it as God's minister. However, unlike the prophets and Christ, who handed on a new revelation, {{135}} her role is to preserve and infallibly declare revelation. Hence, she is related to it as a condition rather than as a cause; for a cause flows positively into the effect, whereas the condition (or application of the agent to the patient) is necessary that the cause may flow into the effect but does not of itself flow into it. The Church proposes revealed [truths] but does not indeed instrumentally reveal. Hence, theologians commonly say that the Church's proposing of revelation in no way pertains to the formal motive of faith.[24]

(3) *The formal cause of revelation* (that is [*seu*], its formal constitutive) is expressed thus: the free and supernatural divine action by which supernatural mysteries and natural truths of religion are obscurely manifested by way of speech. Therefore, revelation formally is *a speech* (or *testimony*) *of God*, and this speech is specified by the revealed object. Hence, the object must be considered first, followed by the testimony of God.

The revealed object contains not only the natural truths of religion but also *mysteries*, both *broadly speaking* (e.g., the eternal decrees of God)[25] and *strictly speaking* (i.e., those which transcend every created intellect[26] and indeed cannot be demonstrated after revelation is made).[27] And the [First]

---

[23] [Trans. note: As the Latin reads, the *conditio sine qua non*. Generally, *sine qua non* will be maintained in the translation, although the contemporary reader may consider this broadly as a "necessary condition."]

[24] See Charles Billuart, *Summa sancti Thomae, De fide*, diss. 1, a. 2. And therefore, presupposing knowledge of the motives of credibility, *without a vicious circle*, we can believe supernaturally that the Church is infallible on account of revelation as on account of *the motive* of our faith and believe revelation on account of the authority of the Church, as *applying* revelation itself. Indeed, it is a normal and regular occurrence [*ordinarium est*] that causes are causes to each other but in different genera (thus fire depends upon application as *upon a condition* that it may burn [that thing], and the application [of that thing] depends upon the burning power of fire as upon *an efficient cause*). By contrast, a vicious circle takes place when one [reasons] from one thing to another, and back again, doing so from the same perspective [*sub eadem ratione*]. See again Billuart in the place cited above.

[25] See [First] Vatican Council, *Dei filius*, ch. 2 (Denzinger, no. 3004).

[26] See ibid., ch. 4 (Denzinger, no. 3015).

[27] See ibid., ch. 4 (Denzinger, no. 3016) and can. 4.1 (Denzinger, no. 3041). Pius IX, *Gravissimas inter* (Denzinger, no. 2857).

Vatican Council expressly defined that mysteries strictly so called are *essentially* supernatural (i.e., from the perspective of their essence).

Indeed, it declared:

> The perpetual common belief of the Catholic Church has held and holds also this: there is a twofold order of knowledge, distinct not only in its *principle* but also in its object, because in the one we know by natural reason, in the other by divine faith; in its *object*, because apart from what natural reason can attain, there are proposed to our belief mysteries that are hidden in God that can never be known unless they are revealed by God. . . . For *divine mysteries by their very nature* so *exceed* the created intellect that, even when they have been communicated in revelation and received by faith, they remain covered by the veil of faith itself and shrouded, as it were, in darkness as long as in this mortal life "we are away from the Lord; for we walk by faith, not by sight" (2 Cor 5:6).[28]

These essentially supernatural mysteries are the *per se* object of Christian revelation. The natural truths of religion are called preambles of faith, for they can be known *per se* by the natural light of reason.

On the basis of this essentially supernatural specificative object, it is clear what the *revealing action* formally is:

(a) *It is a free divine action* that altogether surpasses the exigencies of our nature, and the Council states: "But it pleased his (namely, God's) wisdom and goodness to reveal himself and the eternal decrees of his will [to mankind] in another and supernatural way."[29]

{{136}} (b) *It is an essentially supernatural action*: This is clear not only from its end, as was said above, but also from the proper object of revelation, which is the mystery of God's intimate life. Hence, the revealing action is not natural, like the divine concurrence needed so that any given creature may act naturally in its order. Nor is it only modally supernatural, as is the production of a sensible miracle, for such a miracle is only effectively supernatural [(i.e., as regards efficient causality)] but not entitatively supernatural. (For example, the resurrection of a corpse gives back natural life in a supernatural manner but does not give it supernatural life). However, the revelation of supernatural mysteries is an essentially supernatural act, proceeding from God according to his intimate life. Hence, in the Gospel, it is called "the voice of the Heavenly Father." And Christ says to the Pharisees, who see the

---

28 See ibid., ch. 4 (Denzinger, nos. 3015–3016).

29 Ibid., ch. 2 (Denzinger, no. 3004). See also Pius X, *Pascendi dominici gregis*, no. 37 (Denzinger, 2103, old numbering).

miracles, "Neither have you heard his (namely, the Father's) voice at any time ... for whom he hath sent, him you believe not" (John 5:37–38, DR).

(c) *It is a manifestive action after the manner of speech*, according to the expression of the Apostle, cited by the Council: "God ... spoke in times past to the fathers by the prophets, last of all, in these days, hath spoken to us by his Son" (Heb 1:1–2, DR). Thus, revelation differs from the infusion of the light of faith, for all the faithful immediately accept the light of faith from God, but not revelation, which is handed on to us by the mediation of the prophets and Christ.

As St. Thomas notes in *De veritate*, q. 18, a. 3, according to a twofold hearing there corresponds *a twofold speech*. Indeed, there is:

> a kind of *external speech*, by which God speaks to us through preachers and *a kind of internal* speech by which He speaks to us through internal inspiration. However, the internal inspiration itself *is called a kind of speech by way of likeness to external speech*. Indeed, just as in an external speech we bring forward to the hearer himself not the thing itself that we desire to make known but a sign of that thing, namely a significative expression, so too, God in inspiring internally does not present His essence to be seen but, rather, some sign of His essence, which is a kind of spiritual likeness of His wisdom. By both kinds of hearing does faith arise in the hearts of the faithful. It occurred through internal hearing in those who first accepted and taught the faith, such as in the Apostles and the Prophets. Whence, it is said in Psalm 84:9 (DR): "I will hear what the Lord God will speak in me." However, through the second kind of hearing faith is born in the hearts of the other faithful, who accept knowledge of the faith through other men.

However, what it is transmitted instrumentally to us faithful through the prophet or the Church is the spiritual voice of the Heavenly Father (that is, a spiritual testimony), which differs from the sensible testimony of miracles and is confirmed by them as by a sign. Hence, revelation is, properly speaking, an act of God speaking (that is [*seu*], a divine speech); however, the spiritual hearing existing in the prophet is called passive revelation. Later on, in our theological explanation of the notion of revelation, we will see how divine speech can be conceived by way of analogy with a human teacher's speech.

(4) **The material cause**[30] **(that is [*seu*], the subject to whom revelation is made)**, is *mankind*, as was said at the [First] Vatican Council: "It

---

[30] The material cause of revelation, just as that of science, is threefold: the subject in which it is received; the object about which it is concerned; and the parts from which it is composed. However, here it is a question only of the subject in which it is received.

pleased his (namely, God's) wisdom and goodness to reveal himself (to mankind)";[31] indeed, by the mediation of the prophets and Christ, God reveals himself to all men. Thus, it is a question of common, not private, revelation. And {{137}} in virtue of the subject to whom revelation is made, the mode according to which the divine testimony must be expressed is determined so that all men may be able to know it without error, even to the end of the world. Indeed, based on all this, it is clear that revelation *must be expressed in accord with the common and immutable notions of natural reason* (that is [*seu*], the common sense of nature) and not in accord with some variable and incommunicable mystical experience, nor according to the notions properly belonging to a given school of philosophy.

The modernists did not heed this well enough when they reduced revelation to the prophet's religious experience. Indeed, public revelation must be clearly distinguished from private revelation. The latter is *per se* for the advantage of a given person or of a small number of people, and thus can take place mystically so that it would be, as it were, incommunicable. Hence, as theologians say,[32] more often than not, these private revelations are uncertain, dubious, and fluid, and it is quite difficult to discern where revelation ceases and where human interpretation begins. On the other hand, common revelation is for the advantage of the whole Church and can be understood by all. Hence, St. Paul contrasts it to it glossolalia, which is unintelligible to the ears of listeners. Indeed, he says in 1 Corinthians 14:1–5 (DR):

> Follow after charity, be zealous for spiritual gifts; but rather that you may prophesy. For he that speaketh in a tongue speaketh not unto men, but unto God: for no man heareth. Yet by the Spirit he speaketh mysteries. But he that prophesieth speaketh to men unto edification and exhortation and comfort. He that speaketh in a tongue edifieth himself: but he that prophesieth, edifieth the church. . . . For greater is he that prophesieth than he that speaketh with tongues: unless perhaps he interpret, that the church may receive edification.[33]

As regards the expression and communication of revealed [data] to mankind, we must note this important point: Whereas affective emotions can only be communicated through sympathy (and even then only vaguely), common notions, by contrast, can express an objective reality and can be expressed in words. Things of this sort are the notions of being, unity, truth, goodness,

---

[31] Ibid., ch. 2 (Denzinger, no. 3004).

[32] See Vincent Contenson, O.P., *Theologia mentis et cordis*, bk. 7, diss. 2, ch. 1, spec. 2. [Trans. note: One may consult the 1875 edition published in Paris by Vivès.]

[33] See 1 Corinthians 14:1–9, 18–19 (DR).

intelligence, will, justice, and mercy, as well as the notions of nature and of person. And, in fact, dogmas are expressed by means of these notions.

From all of this, we can see what the Catholic notion of revelation is. Before we can set forth the theological explanation of this notion, we must briefly refer to heterodox conceptions of it.

§3. Heterodox Notions of Revelation

These notions can be divided relative to the supernaturality of revelation, inasmuch as they either destroy or diminish it (as is the case in naturalism and semi-naturalism) or, on the other hand, materially[34] exaggerate what is supernatural in revelation—namely, by diminishing the powers of reason (as is the case in forms of pseudo-supernaturalism).
{{138}}

Heterodox notions of Revelation
- The pseudo-supernaturalism of the first Protestants, of Baius, of the Jansenists, and of fideists
- Naturalism
  - *absolute rationalism*
    - absolute evolutionism (Hegel)
    - agnosticism (Kant, modernists, and positivists)
  - *semi-rationalism*

(1) At first sight, PSEUDO-SUPERNATURALISM seems to exalt the supernaturality of revelation, when in reality it diminishes it and paves the way for naturalism.

A. This conception appeared in the writings of *the first Protestants*, both (a) as regards the proposing of revelation and (b) as regards the nature of revelation.

(a) *As regards the proposing of revelation*, the first Protestants replaced the infallible proposition of revelation by the Church,[35] along with the evi-

---

34 Indeed, concerning this, there cannot be a *formal* exaggeration; thus, as St. Thomas says in *ST* I-II, q. 44, a. 4: "Man alone cannot ever love God as much as He should be loved, nor believe or hope in Him as much as one ought. Whence, much less can there be excess in this matter; and thus, the good of *a theological* virtue does not consist *in a mean*, but rather, is all the greater inasmuch as we more closely approach the summit. . . . But from our perspective . . . we must be carried into God in believing, hoping, and loving according to the measure of our state [*nostra conditionis*]. . . . Whence, *per accidens* (and materially) there can be a *mean* and an *extreme* in theological virtue from our perspective"—e.g., these extremes are desperation, presumption, infidelity, and excessive credulity (or fideism).

35 This proposition of Luther is condemned: "It is certain that it is not the power of the Church or the pope to decide upon the articles of faith, and much less concerning the laws for morals or for good works." See Leo X, *Exsurge Domine*, no. 27 [Denzinger, no. 1477].

dence of credibility from external signs, with *the private inspiration of the Holy Spirit* in any given believer.

Indeed, they rejected the infallible authority of the Church for proposing revelation. Hence, as the pre-conciliar schema for the [First] Vatican Council notes: "The pseudo-reformers are accustomed to discern the genuine word of God by way of 'relish' and 'taste', to which end they placed in any believer whatsoever an immediate testimony from the Holy Spirit."[36] According to them, the rule of faith is Sacred Scripture, and indeed that alone. However, whenever difficulties arise regarding the sense of Scripture, they must be resolved by private inspiration. Thus they judge through a private spirit that this or that article is revealed and to be believed. Likewise, through private inspiration they discern between true and false religion, excluding from consideration external signs and notes, as though human reason could not discern miracles. Hence, if one comes to ask how they know and prove that their religion is true, they recur only to private inspiration, which can be contrived by anyone whatsoever and proven by nobody.

Thus, they appear to exalt the supernaturality of revelation when they speak of the immediate communication of any believer whatsoever with the Holy Spirit, whereas in reality, private inspiration leads to the principle of free examination, which is the foundation of rationalism and individualism. Hence, the pre-conciliar schema of the [First] Vatican Council notes this pseudo-supernaturalism led to the naturalism of liberal Protestants:

> However, more recent (Protestants) retain the same method and substitute natural religious sentiment or a natural need felt by the religious soul for this testimony of the Holy Spirit through which sentiment immediately, and without the revealed truth being made credible to us through extrinsic criteria, we embrace the Christian religion as being true and divine.[37]

And the schema cites Schleiermacher, "Doctrina Fidei, §2."

{{139}} (b) *Likewise, with regard to the nature of revelation* does pseudo-supernaturalism appear in the doctrine of the first Protestants, for like Baius and Jansen, they held that the sublimation and exaltation of human nature to a participation in the divine Nature was *owed* to the integrity of its first condition, and hence must be called natural and not supernatural.[38] Therefore, revealed mysteries would not be, properly speaking, supernatural.

---

[36] See Vacant, *Études sur le Concile du Vatican*, vol. 1, 593 (doc. 6, no. 16).

[37] Ibid.

[38] Pius V, *Ex omnibus afflictionibus*, no. 21 (Denzinger, no. 1021). Likewise see nos. 1ff (Denzinger, no. 1901ff) and no. 79 (Denzinger, no. 1079).

B. In a way, this error once more appeared in the writings of the *fideists*, such as Louis Bautain, who held that reason by itself cannot prove the existence of God nor the fact of revelation: These truths can be known certainly only by faith.[39]

Hence, pseudo-supernaturalism only materially exaggerates what is supernatural in revelation. However, it in fact does not exalt grace but, rather, diminishes nature so that grace would be a perfection owed to nature. In this way, it leads to naturalism, just as [the doctrine of] private inspiration leads to free examination.

(2) NATURALISM also frequently retains the term "revelation," but it assigns a new meaning to it.[40]

Now, we must distinguish absolute naturalism (or absolute rationalism), which unqualifiedly denies the supernaturality of revelation, from semi-rationalism, which essentially diminishes it.

A. *The absolute rationalism* held today is subdivided inasmuch as it admits either pantheistic evolutionism (as for the Hegelians) or agnosticism (as for the Kantians, positivists, and modernists). However, in the past, rationalism was proposed in the form of deism, more or less tending to pantheism (e.g., in [Victor] Cousin).

(a) *Pantheistic evolutionism* radically denies even the foundation of the supernatural order inasmuch as it identifies the essence of God with the essence of creative evolution. This was condemned by the [First] Vatican Council: "If anyone says . . . that the divine essence becomes all things by self-manifestation or evolution, or lastly that God is the universal or indefinite being which, by self-determination, constitutes the universality of beings, differentiated in genera, species, and individuals, let him be anathema."[41] This pantheism ultimately implies that our life cannot be elevated to the supernatural order, something condemned by the same Council: "If anyone says that man cannot be called by God to a knowledge and perfection that surpasses the natural but that he can and must by himself, through constant progress, finally arrive at the possession of all that is true and good, let him be anathema."[42] Quite obviously, if human reason does not essentially differ from the divine reason, it can know everything naturally by its

---

[39] Gregory XVI, Response of the Holy Office, Sept. 14, 1842 (Denzinger, no. 2765).

[40] Naturalism and rationalism are commonly understood as being the same thing—namely, a system denying the possibility of the elevation of our nature (naturalism) and hence of our reason (rationalism) to the supernatural order.

[41] [First] Vatican Council, *Dei filius*, can. 1.4 (Denzinger, no. 3024).

[42] Ibid., can. 2.3 (Denzinger, no. 3028).

own natural development [*evolutione*].

Hence, absolute evolutionists, the Hegelians, who retain the *term* "revelation," understand by this term nothing other than *the progressive evolution of our reason and natural religious sentiment.* They hold that the Christian religion is a form or *moment of the evolution of the human spirit*, and they acknowledge that this form is superior to art [in the progression of the historical manifestations of the Absolute]. However, above art and religion, we would find the highest form of evolution—namely, philosophical reason, {{140}} the supreme arbiter of truth and falsity and judge of religious truth. Therefore, as we will discuss later in our exposition of absolute evolution, Hegel interpreted the particular dogmas of Christianity in a merely natural sense. For example, in the Trinity, he saw nothing other than the fundamental law of universal evolution, which takes place by passing through the opposition of theses and antitheses, giving rise to progressive syntheses.[43]

(b) *Agnosticism* does not, properly speaking, deny the existence of a God who is essentially distinct from the world, nor does it formally reject the foundation of the supernatural order. However, it does hold that whatever is found outside the phenomena and laws of phenomena remains unknowable, at least for theoretical reason. Thus, based on these presuppositions, as is noted in the encyclical *Pascendi*: "All will readily perceive what becomes of *Natural Theology, of the motives of credibility, of external revelation.* The Modernists simply make away with them altogether; they include them in *Intellectualism*, which they call a ridiculous and long ago defunct system."[44] Agnosticism, however, leads to immanentism, for as the same encyclical says: "All external revelation absolutely denied, it is clear that this explanation (for the phenomena of religion, whether natural or supernatural) will be sought in vain outside man himself."[45] This explanation "must, therefore, be looked

---

[43] Spinoza too, in the *Theologico-Political Treatise*, ch. 1 (On Prophecy) and ch. 2 (On Prophets) had given a naturalistic definition of prophetic revelation. Chapter 2 begins with these words: "From the previous chapter, as I have already indicated, it follows that prophets were not gifted with more perfect minds, but indeed with *a livelier power of imagining*, which the narrations of Scripture abundantly teach as well."

In the first chapter, he had said, "The phrases of Scripture, 'The Spirit of God was given to the prophet,' and 'God poured his spirit into men,' only mean that the prophets had power that was singular and beyond the common lot, and that they devoted themselves to piety with an extraordinary constancy of soul."

[44] Pius X, *Pascendi dominici gregis*, no. 6 (old Denzinger, no. 2071). [Trans. note: Taken from the official translation.]

[45] Ibid., no. 7. [Trans. note: I have placed in parentheses, following Fr. Garrigou-Lagrange's own practice, a comment that he placed after the quotation, which was possible given the Latin grammar. This enables the official translation to be retained along with his interpretive remark.]

269

for in man; and since religion is a form of life, the explanation must certainly be found in the life of man. Hence the principle of *religious immanence* is formulated." Finally, immanentism leads to *evolutionism*, at least relative evolutionism (or evolutionism *quoad nos*) inasmuch as the multiplicity of religious phenomena cannot proceed from the natural religious sentiment except through a progressive evolution. Thus, we have the notion of revelation ultimately proposed by many liberal Protestants and modernists: *The notion of God speaking to man is a mere metaphor*, for God does not have a mouth: "*Revelation could be nothing else than the consciousness acquired by man of his relation to God.*"[46]

{{141}} And from this it follows, as is said in the Oath against Modernism: "Faith is *a religious sentiment bursting forth from the hidden places of the subconscious* under the pressure of the heart," and not an assent of the intellect to the truth revealed by God on account of the authority of God who reveals.

Likewise, according to the modernists: "The dogmas the Church presents as revealed are not truths fallen from heaven, but a certain interpretation of religious facts that the human mind has acquired by laborious effort."[47] "The divinity of Jesus Christ is not proved from the Gospels. It is a dogma that the Christian conscience has derived

---

[46] Pius X, Decree of the Holy Office, *Lamentabili*, no. 20 (Denzinger, no. 3420). See Auguste Sabatier, *Esquisse d'une philosophie de la religion d'après la psychologie et l'histoire* (Paris: Fischbacher, 1897), bk. 1, ch. 2, "The Mythological Notion of Revelation—The Dogmatic Notion.—The Psychological Notion." Against the Catholic notion of revelation Sabatier wrote, 43: "To make of dogma (that is, of an intellectual datum) the object of revelation is first of all to remove its religious character from it by separating it from piety; next, it is to place it into irreducible conflict with reason, which forever progresses. . . . The faith that in the Bible was an act of confidence and of consecration to God, becomes an intellectual adherence to a historical testimony or to a doctrinal formula. . . . One admits that orthodoxy can exist outside of piety. . . . At its base, this idea of revelation is wholly pagan. . . . Therefore, let us conclude, against all the traditional orthodoxies, that the object of the revelation of God can only be God Himself, that is to say, the *sentiment of* [*His*] *presence in us, awakening the soul to the life of justice and of love.* . . . The scholastic notion is not only irreligious, it is likewise anti-psychological. By entering into human understanding, these supernatural forms of knowledge [*ces connaisances surnaturelles*] introduce into it an irreducible dualism. Sacred sciences stand next to profane sciences without it being possible to organize them all together into a coherent and harmonious body, for they do not have the same nature, nor do they proceed from the same method and do not accept the same control." On 52: "The revelation of God must be interior, evident, and progressive. (*Interior*: it is the sentiment of God's presence in us. *Evident*: with a religious and moral evidence.) Now, it only is recognized through the clarity with which it inundates us and not through miracles. *Progressive*, that is, it develops itself with the progress of the moral and religious life." Liberal Protestants generally speak along these lines.

[47] Pius X, Decree of the Holy Office, *Lamentabili*, no. 22 (Denzinger, no. 3422).

from the notion of the Messiah."[48] "The dogmas of the faith are to be held only according to their practical sense; that is to say, as preceptive norms of conduct and not as norms of believing."[49] For example, in relation to Jesus, we are to behave as though he were God and toward the Eucharist as though it were the Body of Christ.

Below, in our exposition concerning agnosticism's denial of supernatural revelation, we will see how Kant and later on Schleiermacher, Ritschl, and the modernists all interpret the dogmas of Christianity in a natural sense.

B. Finally, *semi-rationalism* (or moderate rationalism), held by thinkers like Hermes, Günther, and Frohschammer, indeed acknowledges external supernatural revelation, handed on to us by Christ, but it reduces the supernaturality of this revelation to a mere modal supernaturality, inasmuch as semi-rationalism holds that all dogmas, even the Trinity, are demonstrable by reason alone after they are revealed.[50]

These are the principal heterodox notions of revelation: The first is reduced to a false supernaturalism that paves the way for naturalism whereas the others are reduced to rationalism, whether absolute or moderate. Now, however, we must pass on to the theological explanation of the Catholic notion of revelation.

ART. 2: THEOLOGICAL EXPLICATION AND DEFENSE OF THE CATHOLIC NOTION OF REVELATION

§1. The formal constitutive of revelation must be determined analogically.

§2. Divine revelation is formally the speech of God to men after the manner of a teaching authority.

§3. Divine speech is performed objectively through a supernatural proposition of the truth, and subjectively through the influence of a supernatural light it proportions [the receiver] to judge infallibly concerning the truth proposed.

§1. The formal constitutive of revelation must be determined analogically

As we have said, according[51] to the Catholic Church, the formal constitutive

---

[48] Ibid., no. 27 (Denzinger, no. 3427).

[49] Ibid., no. 26 (Denzinger, no. 3426).

[50] See [First] Vatican Council, *Dei filius*, ch. 4 (Denzinger, no. 3015), can. 4.1 and 4.3ff (Denzinger, nos. 3041 and 3043ff). Also see Pius IX, *Qui pluribus*, Denzinger nos. 2775ff; and his letter *Gravissimas inter* to the Archbishop of Munich-Freising, Dec. 11, 1862, old Denzinger, no. 1666ff.

[51] [Trans. note: Correcting a mistake that duplicates the heading for section 2 here as well.]

of revelation, strictly speaking, is "a supernatural speech by God to men."[52] And not only is it said that God {{142}} speaks to men through the prophets but also that God speaks immediately to the prophets so that they may teach other men externally. Therefore, the notion of this revelation must be explained inasmuch as it is made immediately to the prophets, before they speak to men.[53]

How can this immediate revelation be called a form of speech? How can speech be attributed to God, who is a pure spirit and does not have a mouth? Obviously, it is attributed to him only *in an analogical manner*, indeed, through *an analogy of proportionality*[54]—namely, just as human speech is related to its own proper effect, so too is divine revelation related to its own proper effect. Now, logicians define the analogy of proportionality as follows: "Those things referred to through the same term, while the notion signified through the term is indeed *simpliciter* diverse, though proportionally the same, that is, similar according to a proportion."[55] Thus, sense

---

[52] See Denzinger [10th ed.], index I, a.

[53] See Ambroise Gardeil, *Le donné révélé et la théologie* (Paris: Lecoffre, 1910), bk. 1, ch. 2, "Revelation" (the Catholic notion of revelation, the mystical (modernist) notion, the Catholic doctrine of revelation and its Thomist explanation); ch. 3, "Dogma" (the case of Theologism, the common [*courante*] response, examination of this response, what renders the common response absolute and definitive); bk. 2, ch. 1, "The metaphysical relativity of dogma"; ch. 2, "The development of dogma."

[54] [Trans. note: On the importance of the analogy of proper proportionality see Tommaso de Vio Cajetan, *The Analogy of Names, and the Concept of Being*, trans. Edward A. Bushinski and Henry J. Koren (Eugene, OR: Wipf and Stock, 2009). For a lengthy defense of Cajetan's as regards theological notions, see Maurílio Teixeira-Leite Penido, *Le role de l'analogie en théologie dogmatique* (Paris: Vrin, 1931). As the reader may know, there are great controversies regarding Cajetan's work on analogy. Although we could cite a number of positions, on the negative register, a forceful account is that found in Bernard Montagnes, *The Doctrine of the Analogy of Being According to Thomas Aquinas*, trans. Edward.M. Macierowski and Pol Vandevelde, ed. Andrew Tallon (Milwaukee: Marquette University Press, 2008).

For a general defense of Cajetan's position, one should consider together the work of Long and Hochschild, who respectively plumb the metaphysical and logical / semantic issues at play here. See Joshua P. Hochschild, *The Semantics of Analogy: Rereading Cajetan's De Nominum Analogia* (Notre Dame, IN: University of Notre Dame Press, 2010). Steven A. Long, *Analogia Entis: On the Analogy of Being, Metaphysics, and the Act of Faith* (Notre Dame, IN: University of Notre Dame Press, 2011). Likewise, see James Anderson, *The Bond of Being: An Essay on Analogy and Existence* (St. Louis: Herder, 1954). Above all, however, see the lucidly clear Yves R. Simon, "On Order in Analogical Sets," in *Philosopher at Work: Essays by Yves R. Simon*, ed. Anthony O. Simon (Lanham, MD: Rowman & Littlefield, 1999), 135–71. Simon very carefully exposits the issue of analogy without becoming enmeshed in the detailed polemics that often obscure these matters.]

[55] See Antoine Goudin, *Philosophia iuxta inconcussa tutissimaque divi Thomae dogmata*, vol. 1 (Paris: Bibliothecae novae, 1851), *Logica maior*, Ia Pars., disp. 2, q. 1, a. 1.

cognition and intellective cognition are not univocally forms of cognition but instead analogically are such, inasmuch as the senses are related to the sensible just as the intellect is related to the intelligible. These two kinds of cognition differ *simpliciter*, even as regards the very notion of cognition,[56] but they are proportionally similar. Hence, we must determine how divine revelation and human speech essentially differ and how they proportionally agree.

Modernists immediately object: Speech can only be attributed to God *metaphorically*; God's speech to the prophets is a mere metaphor. If we wish to conceive of revelation psychologically and philosophically, it must be understood as something immanent [to the prophet]—namely, something proceeding from the prophet's subconscious. In reality, the prophet did not, properly speaking, hear the divine speech. This is said metaphorically. However, he did have a livelier religious experience [than others]. This particularly moving experience was soon thereafter expressed through preaching in an imaginative form, then later on in a conceptual form. However, when these concepts of Christian experience are appropriated by the Church so that they are held as dogmas, they are not truths that have fallen out of heaven. Thus, revelation must be understood psychologically.

To this we must respond that the *analogy of proportionality is twofold*—namely, metaphorical and proper. It is *proper* when the notion signified through the analogous term is found in both analogates formally and truly, just as wisdom is found in man and in God. It is *metaphorical* when the signified notion is found formally in one and by way of likeness through a transfer to the other, just as anger is found formally in man and only metaphorically in God, in whom there are no passions. "Such is the case in all things that are said *symbolically* of God, as when He is called a lion or a sun, or things of this sort, for matter, which cannot be attributed to God, makes up part of these things' definitions."[57]

{{143}} Thus, it is obvious that speech, inasmuch as it is bodily, is only metaphorically attributed to God. However, in human speech, the formal element is something spiritual by which the thought of the speaker is manifested to the intellect of the hearer, and hence, brute animals cannot speak. Why, therefore, cannot speech, inasmuch as it is spiritual, be attributed to God *analogically* and *properly*, just as wisdom is attributed to him? In order to manifest the impossibility of this attribution, we would need to prove that speech, even spiritual [speech], includes some imperfection in its formal notion.

---

[56] Indeed, knowledge is not a genus, for every genus is univocal; knowledge is something analogous that can be attributed to God.

[57] St. Thomas, *De veritate*, q. 2, a. 11.

Therefore, this analogical notion of spiritual speech must be explained so as to show that *no imperfection is contained in it.* This explanation ultimately preserves the doctrine of the Church declared at the Fourth Lateran Council: "Between Creator and creature no similitude can be expressed without implying a greater similitude."[58]

However, since every analogy involves both likeness and unlikeness, we must determine how the divine speech is said to be *like* human speech (and like precisely what kind of human speech) and how it *differs* from it.

This explanation is given by theology and explained by St. Thomas in *ST* II-II, q. 171–174, in the treatise on prophetic revelation.[59]

§2. Divine Revelation Is Formally the Speech of God to Men after the Manner of a Teaching Authority

This is made manifest in a twofold manner: (A) from revelation itself, for according to us the very notion of supernatural revelation has itself been revealed, and (B) from the rational analysis of this notion.

A. *Considering revelation itself*[60] as it is discussed in Sacred Scripture and in the Church's own definitions, as we have already said, we have the idea that revelation is God's *speech*: "God, who, at sundry times and in divers manners, spoke in times past to the fathers by the prophets, last of all, in these days, hath spoken to us by his Son" (Heb 1:1, DR). Likewise, the revelation that is immediately made to the prophets is called speech (cf. Isa 50:4, a text that will be cited immediately below). Also see Psalm 84:9 and Hosea 2:4.

Second, we have the idea that this divine speech is *after the manner of a teaching authority.* Thus, the prophets said, for example, in Isaiah 50:4 (DR): "The Lord hath given me a learned tongue, that I should know how to uphold by word him that is weary: he wakeneth in the morning, in the morning he wakeneth my ear, that I may hear him as a master [or teacher]."

---

[58] Fourth Lateran Council, ch. 3 (Denzinger, no. 806).

[59] Nevertheless, as will be said below, *a bodily voice* can be *effectively* [i.e., by way of efficient causality] attributed to God, though not formally; however, this bodily voice, whenever it is thus produced by God, does not pertain essentially to divine revelation and is not its formal constitutive, which is what we are currently discussing.

[60] Without falling into a vicious circle, Sacred Scripture is cited, as also are the decisions of the Church, in order to explain what the Catholic Church exactly understands by the term "revelation"; however, afterward revelation so-defined must be rationally defended, both with regard to its possibility and with regard to its existence.

Hence, revelation itself can manifest what revelation is, just as light manifests itself, as Cajetan notes in *In ST* II-II, q. 1, a. 1, no. 11.

Likewise, Christ is called a teacher[61]: "The people were in admiration at his doctrine, for he was teaching them as one having power, and not as the scribes and Pharisees" (Matt 7:28–29, DR). And Christ himself said: "You call me Master and Lord. And you say well: for so I am" (John 13:13, DR).[62]

Consequently, the Church defines her *infallible magisterium* for proposing revealed truths[63] and condemns {{144}} the modernists, who say that "Christ did not teach a determined body of doctrine applicable to all times and all men but, rather, inaugurated a religious movement adapted or to be adapted to different times and places."[64]

B. *Through the rational analysis of the notion of revelation*, it is also clear that revelation is rightly said to be (a) a [form of] speech, (b) after the manner of a teaching authority.

(a) It is rightly said to be *speech*, analogically and properly, for this analogical likeness is not taken according to what is bodily in human speech but according to what pertains to the notion of being a sign, whether bodily or spiritual. St. Thomas clearly explains this in the text that has already been cited: "Indeed, just as in an external speech we bring forward to the hearer himself not the thing itself that we desire to make known but a *sign* of that thing, namely a significative *expression*, so too, by inspiring internally, God does not present His essence to be seen but, rather, some *sign* of His essence, which is a kind of *spiritual likeness* of His wisdom."[65]

The Holy Doctor most excellently distinguishes this spiritual expression [*vocem*] from a bodily expression that sometimes is produced in revelation and that, like a miraculous sensible sign, is attributed to God only *effectively* [(i.e., as regards efficient causality)] and not formally. Indeed, he says in *In V Ioan*, lect. 6:

> God bears witness to someone in two ways, namely sensibly and intelligibly. *Sensibly* indeed as through a merely-sensible voice; and in this manner, He bore witness to Moses upon Mount Sinai (Deut 4:12). Likewise, through a sensible appearance, as he appeared to Abraham (Gen 26 and Isa 6:1). However, in those visions neither the bodily voice nor the visible figure of God is like that of some given animal, except according to efficient causality [*effective*], inasmuch as it is formed by God. For, since God is a spirit, He neither emits

---

[61] [Trans. note: *Magister / teacher* is being used here as a translation for the Hebrew term *rabbi*.]

[62] Cf. biblical concordances on the words "teacher" / "master," "I teach," and "teaching" [*magister, doceo, doctrina*].

[63] See [First] Vatican Council, ch. 3 (Denzinger, no. 3011). Also, Pius IX, Letter *Tuas libenter* to the Archbishop of Munich-Freising, Denzinger, no. 2879.

[64] Pius X, Decree of the Holy Office, *Lamentabili*, no. 59 (Denzinger, no. 3459).

[65] St. Thomas, *De veritate*, q. 18, a. 3.

a sensible voice from Himself, nor can be expressed in a figure. However, He bears witness *in an intelligible manner* by inspiring into the hearts of some people what they must believe and hold.—Psalm 84:9 (DR): "I will hear what the Lord God will speak in me"; Hosea 2:14 (DR): "I will lead her into the wilderness: and I will speak to her heart."—Therefore, the Pharisees were able to receive the first form of testimony, and this is not surprising, for they were only from God according to efficient causality [*effective*], as was said, "Those voices and appearances." However, they were not able to receive the witness of *that intelligible voice*: "Nor did you ever hear his voice, etc.," that is, you were not participants in it, that is, you did not have that intelligible witness, and therefore it is added, "And you do not have his word remaining in you," that is: You do not have the interiorly inspired word.

Hence, revelation is legitimately called, analogically and properly, [*a kind of*] *spiritual speech*.

(b) Furthermore, this divine speech is rightly said to take place after the manner *of a teaching authority*. For he who speaks to us as a most wise superior so as to manifest loftier truths is related to us as a teacher. Now, God speaks to us as a most wise superior. Therefore [, he is related to us as a teacher.] Thus, as St. Thomas says in *ST* I, q. 107, a. 2:[66] "Not every kind of speech is an *illumination*." For example, someone who is inferior to us neither teaches nor illuminates us; but "every illumination is a (spiritual) speech." Mere speech occurs through a simple manifestation of a concept; illumination occurs after the manner of a teaching authority and of a teaching, according to a resolution to the truth of the first truth [*ad primam veritatem*].[67]

§3. What Does This Divine Speech Involve?

According to St. Thomas,[68] divine speech takes place objectively *through the supernatural proposing of a truth* {{145}} and subjectively *through the influence of a supernatural light proportioned* to judging infallibly concerning the truth divinely proposed.

This is also manifested in some way through Sacred Scripture, and more

---

[66] "Whether an inferior angel speaks to a superior." He responds affirmatively, but the inferior does not illuminate the superior.

[67] [Trans. note: In the case of divine revelation, one would translate this as "resolution to the First Truth."]

[68] See *ST* II-II, q. 173, a. 2.

explicitly through an analysis of the notion of teaching (that is, of a teaching authority [*magisterii*]).

From Sacred Scripture, the objective proposing of revealed truth is distinguished, in some manner, from the internal light for judging [concerning this truth], for whenever someone, such as Pharaoh,[69] Nebuchadnezzar, or Belshazzar, receives only a representation of some things through imaginary or bodily likenesses, they are not illuminated so as to render a judgment. "And such a person is not to be considered a prophet," says St. Thomas,[70] "but such an apparition is something imperfect in the genus of prophecy. . . . However, he will be a prophet only if his intellect is illuminated so as to likewise judge concerning those things that have been seen by others in their imagination, as is obvious in the case of Joseph, who explained Pharaoh's dream: 'Joseph answered: The king's dream is one: God hath shewn to Pharaoh what he is about to do.'[71]"

An analysis of the notion of teaching [*doctrinae*] can manifest this point as well, for every teaching takes place through the objective proposing of the truth[72] and has its efficacy in virtue of an internal intellectual light proportioned to the truth thus proposed.

We must insist on this point with particular urgency, as much because adversaries (namely, rationalists, liberal Protestants, and modernists) particularly deny *the teaching value* of revelation, as well as because this ultimately undergirds the foundation of the Church's teaching authority. Quite obviously, sacred theology must treat of the true notion of a divine teaching authority, and this falls to the treatise on revelation. Hence, we must ask: What is necessary for accepting truth (1) from a teaching authority[73] in general, and (2) from a divine teaching authority?

(1) **What is required for receiving truth from a teaching authority in general?** The thesis of St. Thomas concerning the general nature of a teaching authority (or [*seu*] of a doctrine) stands as the golden mean and peak between the innatism of Plato and the empiricism of the sensualists.[74]

---

[69] [Trans. note: The text reads Genesis 61:25, though almost certainly is 41:25, which is cited by St. Thomas in the article that Fr. Garrigou-Lagrange will soon cite in the body of the text. However, that text of Genesis belongs to the speech wherein the patriarch Joseph interprets Pharaoh's dream, which is itself communicated at the start of 41.]

[70] *ST* II-II, q. 173, a. 2.

[71] Genesis 41:25 (DR). But if the proposing of the thing is done naturally, even if a supernatural light is given so as to judge infallibly, this is not revelation but instead inspiration.

[72] [Trans. note: Reading *veritates* as *veritatis*.]

[73] [Trans. note: Reading *magisterio* for *magiterio*.]

[74] See *ST* I, q. 117, a.1; *De veritate*, q. 11, a. 1 (On the Teacher).

Empiricists reduce teaching [i.e., doctrine] to the material proposition of phenomena that suffice for sensible knowledge. Plato and the innatists believe not only that the light of reason preexists in us but also that science preexists in us in act, although it is obscured. St. Thomas shows the necessity of an internal light by which the first principles are manifested so that the disciple [i.e., the student / learner] can judge according to this light concerning the truth proposed to him, or at least concerning the authority of the teacher.

Indeed, St. Thomas says in *De veritate*, q. 11, a. 1:

> There are two ways of acquiring science. On the one hand, it is acquired when natural reason through itself (from first naturally known notions or principles) arrives at knowledge of things that were not known, and this way is called *discovery*. On the other, such acquisition occurs when something external supports natural reason, and this way is called *learning by instruction [disciplina]* .... (However, art imitates nature.) Whence, *one person is said to teach another inasmuch as the former sets forth,* {{146}} *through signs, the discourse of reason that he undertakes within himself by means of natural reason.* And thus, through signs of this sort proposed to him as though they were a kind of instrument, the natural reason of the learner arrives at knowledge of things that were unknown. Therefore, just as the doctor is said to cause health in the sick person, along with the action of nature, so too *a man is said to cause science in another by the operation of that person's natural reason; and this is to teach.* .... However, if one person proposes to someone else those things that are not included in *per se nota* principles, or are not manifested to be included in them, he does not cause scientific knowledge in that person but, perhaps opinion or faith, although even this is caused in some way from innate principles, for from these *per se nota* principles he considers that those things that follow from them necessarily are to be held with certitude, whereas those things that are contrary to them are to be entirely rejected. However, he can render assent to others, or not do so. Now, the *light of reason,* by which principles of this sort are known, *is implanted in us by God,* being, as it were, a kind of likeness of the uncreated truth resounding within us. Whence, since every human teaching cannot have efficacy except in virtue of that light, it is obvious that *God alone teaches interiorly and principally,* just as one's own interior nature likewise is what principally brings about healing. Nevertheless, however, both to heal and to teach are said properly concerning the aforementioned way [of teaching and healing, namely, by an external agent].

The doctor heals; but what would he do with all his medicines if a root principle of healing did not remain in the nature of the sick person? Likewise, the teacher teaches;

but what would he accomplish in all of his lectures if a root principle of science (i.e., the natural light of first principles) did not exist in the learner?[75] As St. Thomas says in the same article, "The doctor only ministers to nature, which is the principal agent";[76] such is also the case for the human teacher in relation to natural reason. Hence, to teach is to cause science in another, which was in him only virtually, in the naturally known principles. Thus, "every teaching and every discipline," as Aristotle says, "takes place on the basis of pre-existing knowledge."[77]

Therefore, two things are necessary for receiving truth from a teaching authority in general—namely, *the objective proposition of truth* and the *internal light* for judging concerning the proposed truth (or at least concerning the authority of the teacher—namely, about his scientific knowledge [*scientia*] and trustworthiness). Thus, a proposed truth is either intrinsically evident or at least evidently credible; and in the beginning, as Aristotle said, "He who wishes to learn must first believe,"[78] so that he may gradually arrive at evidential knowledge of reality.

Hence, this notion of teaching[79] stands as a golden mean between the innatism of Plato and the empiricism of the sensualists. Nay, this mean is likewise the peak between opposed extremes, for in this mean the nature of the activity of teaching is determined more formally, purely, and loftily.

According to Plato's innatism, as St. Thomas notes in *ST* I, q. 117, a. 1, "To learn is nothing other than to remember [something which was known before the union of the soul and the body]." Indeed, Plato did not know how to distinguish between science in potency and science in act, thinking that science already preexists in act in the mind of the learner, although, as it were, in an obscured form. Hence, the teacher would do nothing other than, through the Socratic method of maieutic, draw out into recollection or current consideration those things that {{147}} the learner already knew. At first sight, this outlook seems loftier, but it is only an apparent form of loftiness. Indeed, philosophical reflection shows that innatism is unfounded, contrary to experience, and contrary to the true notion of the human composite.[80]

Something similar to Platonism is found in *the theory of the ontologists* concerning

---

75 See Marie-Benoît Schwalm, "L'action intellectuelle d'un maître, d'après S. Thomas," *Revue Thomiste* 8 (July 1900): 251–272.

76 Thus, the doctor who does not consider the nature of the sick person proceeds neither rightly nor vitally, but only offers medicines and forever increases them. Likewise, the teacher who juxtaposes theses and reasons without ordering them under the light of first principles does not proceed vitally.

77 Aristotle, *Posterior analytics*, 1.1; also see lect. 1 of St. Thomas's commentary on this.

78 See *Sophistical refutations*, 1.2, no. 2, which is cited in *ST* II-II, q. 2, a. 3.

79 [Trans. note: Reading *doctrinae* for *doctrine*.]

80 Cf. *ST* I, q. 84, a. 3.

human teaching authority [*magisterio*] (according to the vision of the eternal reasons in God), which was already refuted by St. Thomas in *ST* I, q. 84, a. 5. And, as will be discussed later, this outlook of the ontologists had a kind of influence on their theory concerning the divine teaching authority [*magisterio*], leading to the diminution of the supernaturality of revelation[81]; thus, Rosmini believed that the mystery of the Trinity could be reduced to the principles of natural reason.

By contrast, *empiricists (or [seu] positivists)* do not consider the necessity of the natural light of reason but consider only the external proposing of the object. They reduce intellectual knowledge to sense knowledge and teaching to material information (or [*seu*] an enumeration of phenomena). Likewise, in relation to the divine teaching authority, the Pelagians, considering supernatural things in a material manner, said: External revelation suffices, and the internal light of faith is not necessary. Similarly, as we will discuss later on, the theory of faith that was proposed by Ockham and the medieval nominalists, who were their own era's empiricists, in this regard has affinities with Pelagianism. Thus, it is not surprising that, according to the ways of empiricism, the modernists reduce revelation to religious experience.

Corollary: However, since every kind of teaching takes place through the objective proposing of the truth and has efficacy by virtue of an intellectual light, *that light must be proportioned to the object to be manifested*. The sensible body is manifested by a bodily light, whereas intelligible truth is manifested by an intellectual light.

Based on these two requirements for accepting truth from a teaching authority [magisterium] in general, what can a human teacher give? He cannot give an interior light, which is given only by God, the Author of created intelligence. The human teacher gives the intelligible thing but not intelligence.[82]

Nevertheless, the human teacher [*doctor*] not only materially proposes the truth but also illuminates it, at least objectively—namely, by methodically ordering the ideas of the learner under the proximate principles and, at last, by resolving the proposed truth to higher and more universal principles—and thus, "He strengthens the intellect of the learner inasmuch as he proposes to him the ordering of the principles to the conclusions," for perhaps the student might not have great enough discursive intellectual strength to be able to deduce the conclusions from principles on his own (*ST* I, q. 117, a. 1). Thus, the demonstrative middle [*medium demonstrationis*] (that is [*seu*], the principle) proposed by the human teacher is rightly

---

[81] [Trans. note: Reading *supernaturalitas Revelationis* for *supernaturalitas, Revelationis*.]

[82] This is spiritually set forth in *The Imitation of Christ*, bk. 3, ch. 2: "(Human teachers) can indeed sound forth the words, but do not confer their spirit. They hand on the letters but you open the sense. They shout with words, but you give understanding to the hearer."

called the *objective light* and indeed simultaneously is what is known and *that by which* many other things are known. And to the degree that this principle is simpler and loftier it is all the more universal, for more universal effects are reduced to loftier causes.

Consequently, a teacher is all the more luminous to the degree that he reduces the proposed truth to loftier and more universal principles.[83] Thus, great teachers such as Plato and Aristotle, {{148}} were led to a kind of natural revelation. Plato, coming after philosophers who hardly transcended sensible experience, in a certain way revealed the existence of the intelligible order, and Aristotle ordered the various intelligible things under the first notion of being and the principle of contradiction.

However, if our teacher were of a loftier created nature, like the angels, according to faith, he would know intuitively a number of various regions of the intelligible world through simpler and more universal ideas through a kind of loftier synthesis. Hence, he would more greatly strengthen our intellect than would a human teacher—namely, by adapting to our intellect what he has understood in a superior manner—and his superior light would shine forth in the object so proposed, just as the light of the intellect of a human teacher shines forth in the demonstrative middle that he proposes to us.[84]

Finally, if our teacher is God himself, the source of all intelligibility and of intel-

---

[83] The more luminous a teacher is, to that degree will his material individuality be less apparent, and the greater will his universal understanding exceed his private experience. Indeed, then the master becomes, as it were, an objective light. Thus *classics*, for example St. Thomas whose individuality never appears in his works, is, as it were, a crystal intellectual radiation of spiritual light not impeding but communicating so that he himself is not seen. On the other hand, *romantics* and many philosophers today (or, rather, self-psychologists) propose neither a teaching nor illuminative principles but narrate their experience. They are not related to their students as *lights by which* many are illuminated but as *something known*, perhaps exceptional but ultimately *singular*. So too, in a certain way, for those who reduce theology to religious psychology.

[84] See John of St. Thomas, *Cursus theologicus*, *In ST* I, q. 117, disp. 25, a. 2, no. 8: "The angel who illuminates is akin in some way to the human who teaches, and in some way exceeds him. He is akin indeed inasmuch as he proposes an object that is better disposed for external proposition and not by acting within the intellect (by effectively giving or impressing either a light or a species). He exceeds the human teacher in the fact that the means or object proposed by the illuminating angel, since it is of a superior nature and of a loftier intellect, also elevates the inferior intellect in its manner of operating, so that sometimes the angel that is illuminated is rapt out itself and exercises its operation according to the manner of the superior, illuminating intellect. Whence, sometimes we see that a man is rapt in an excess of mind and acts with abstraction from the senses, which mode of operating arises from the efficacy of the proposition of the object made by a superior power, whether by God or by an angel, who through the efficacy of that proposed object even alters the inferior intellect's manner of operating, which one man cannot do with respect to another when he teaches him because he is not of a superior nature in respect to the other man." Also see Billuart, *Summa sancti Thomae, De angelis*, diss. 2, no. 2.

ligence, could he not manifest to us not only immense regions of the intelligible order, and reduce them to the principles of being inasmuch as it is being, but also manifest the properly divine order that is reduced to the Deity considered precisely as the Deity? Why could he not simultaneously illuminate us subjectively by giving us a light proportioned to a divine object?

(2) *What is required for accepting truth from a divine teaching authority?* This is deduced from the two things required for accepting truth from a teaching authority in general. A divine teacher can propose a truth in two manners: (1) with evidence of the truth, as he manifests his essence immediately to the blessed; (2) without evidence of the proposed truth, which must be believed on account of the authority of him who reveals, as he reveals supernatural mysteries to wayfarers. However, based on what we have said heretofore, it is already obvious to some degree that two things are essentially [*per se*] required for accepting truth from a teaching authority [*magisterium*] on account of its authority, namely: (A) *something on the part of the object*—that is, the supernatural proposing of the truth to be believed—and (B) *something on the part of the subject*—namely, the light proportioned [to that truth]. Each of these must be considered in part.

A. *The supernatural proposal of the truth to be believed, by which such truth is manifested, is objectively required.*

{{149}} However, this involves three [lit. *duo*] things: (a) that something that was previously hidden is proposed by God, (b) to be accepted in a determinate sense, and (c) that the divine origin of the revelation is most certainly made manifest.

(a) *That something that was previously hidden is proposed by God.* In this way, revelation is distinguished from mere inspiration, which does not, of its very essence, involve the supernatural acceptance of an object but, rather, only an infallible judgment concerning something to be narrated or written—that is, concerning something "which man apprehends in the ordinary course of nature."[85]

Thus, Matthew is said to have written infallibly, under divine inspiration, the facts of Christ's life, which he already naturally knew. Thus, the essential character of inspiration only requires a divine elevation of one's judgment (i.e., of the second operation of the mind)—indeed, not only of one's speculative judgment concerning the truth of the thing to be narrated and concerning the aptitude of the words for exactly expressing the reality in question, but also an elevation of one's practical judgement concerning the book to be written and concerning the advantageousness of writing this or that. Thus, God is called the Author of the inspired book, and since formal truth is found in judgment

---

[85] *ST* II-II, q. 173, a. 2c.

and not in our intellect's first apprehension, the whole inspired book is infallibly true. In prophetic revelation, there must be not only the elevation of judgment but also the *acceptance* of some supernatural object that was once hidden, which is properly said to be revealed or manifested. However, this acceptance pertains to the first operation of the mind (i.e., to first apprehension), which precedes judgment. As we will discuss later, this apprehension can come about in three ways—namely, through the supernatural proposal of a given object by the mediation of the senses and the imagination, through the mediation of the imagination by itself, or through the immediate arrangement of ideas by God in the prophet's intellect.

(b) It is also necessary that what was previously hidden be proposed *to be accepted in a determinate sense*. Otherwise, if the prophet in no way understood the sense in which this teaching is to be believed, he could not believe anything determinately, nor propose revelation to other men fittingly so that it may be believed. Nevertheless, in the prophetic instinct by itself, which is something imperfect in the genus of prophetic revelation, "sometimes he whose mind is moved to express certain words does not understand what the Holy Spirit intends through these words, as is obvious in the case of Caiaphas when 'he prophesized that Jesus was to be killed for the people' as is read in John 11:51."[86]

(c) *It is necessary that the divine origin of revelation be manifested in a most certain manner.* Otherwise, the proposed truth could not be believed most firmly and formally on account of the authority of God who reveals but would be only an object of religious opinion, which Protestants often call faith-confidence or religious experience. Indeed, [without such certitude,] the prophet could not distinguish what is said by God from those things that proceed either from the inspiration of a demon or from his own imagination or subconscious; nor, hence, could he divinely believe the revealed mystery, nor propose the divine word,[87] properly so called, to others, nor affirm the connection of an invisible and interior revelation with a miracle to be performed in confirmation of it. However, this manifestation of the divine origin of revelation is brought about for the prophet under the prophetic light, which we will soon discuss below.

{{150}} As regards the fact of this manifestation and certitude, St. Thomas says in *ST* II-II, q. 171, a. 5:

> The prophet has the greatest certitude concerning those things that he expressly knows through *the spirit of prophecy*, holding as certain that these things have

---

[86] *ST* II-II, q. 173, a. 4.

[87] [Trans. note: Reading *verbum* for *verbus*.]

been divinely revealed to him. Whence, it is said in Jeremiah 26:15 (DR): "*In truth* the Lord sent me to you, to speak all these words in your hearing." Otherwise, if he did not have certitude about this, the faith that rests on the words of the prophets would not be certain. And we can take a sign of prophetic certitude from the fact that Abraham, having been admonished in a prophetic vision, prepared himself to sacrifice his only-begotten son, which he in no way would have done had he not been utterly certain of the divine revelation.

Nonetheless, (as St. Thomas adds), the (prophet) is sometimes related to those things that he knows through a (prophetic) *instinct* in such a way that he cannot fully discern whether he knew this by some divine instinct or through his own spirit. However, not everything that we know by a divine instinct is manifested to us with prophetic certitude, for such an instinct is something imperfect in the genus of prophecy.

In other words, this refers to the instinct "which the human mind suffers without knowing it," as St. Augustine says in *The Literal Meaning of Genesis*, bk. 2, ch. 17.

However, in our treatise we are concerned with revelation properly speaking and not with this imperfect instinct. Nay, according to the Church, Christian revelation is something most perfect in the genus of revelation, for Christ was more than a prophet. Hence, theologians commonly say (*ST* III, q. 9, a. 2), that, even as a man, Christ on earth already had *the vision* of the mysteries of the divine essence, which he handed on to the faithful. This was a fitting state of affairs for the divine teacher of all humanity so that he could lead all men to the beatific vision, "because it is always necessary that the cause be more powerful [*potior*] than its effect [*suo causato*]." Thus, Christ spoke with the greatest of authority when he affirmed the divine origin of his doctrine: "Amen, amen, I say to you." This formula is found twenty-five times in the Gospel of John.[88]

Hence, the divine proposing of the truth to be believed is objectively required for prophetic revelation, as divinely manifested. And in this regard, we can see the likeness that exists between the speech of a divine teacher and that of a human teacher. Now, however, we must consider the subjective illumination in which we have the unlikeness that is preserved in every analogy, according to what St. Thomas says: "Man represents to his student certain things through signs of speech; however, he cannot illuminate interiorly, as does God."[89]

B. *Subjectively, a proportionate supernatural light is required* in order *to judge infallibly concerning a divinely proposed truth and concerning its divine origin.*

---

[88] See St. Thomas, *In III Ioan.*, 4, lect. 3.
[89] *ST* II-II, q. 173, a. 2.

Here we are concerned with the prophet's prophetic light, to which proportionally corresponds, afterwards, the assistance of the Holy Spirit given to the Church, as well as the internal light of faith for any given believer, all the while preserving the distinction between immediate revelation and mediate revelation.

Proof: A proportion must exist between the knowing principle, the act of knowing, and the object to be known by which [such] knowledge is specified. Now, without an internal supernatural light, our reason remains disproportioned to knowing infallibly a supernatural object that has been proposed and that is to be believed. Therefore, subjectively, there needs to be {{151}} a proportionate supernatural light. This is explained by St. Thomas:

> Just as the manifestation of bodily vision occurs through bodily light, so too the manifestation of intellectual vision occurs through an intellectual light. Therefore, *a manifestation must be proportioned to the light through which it occurs, just as an effect is proportioned to its cause.* Thus, since, as we have seen, prophecy pertains to a knowledge that exists above natural reason, we must conclude that prophecy requires *some kind of intellectual light exceeding the light of natural reason.*[90]

Otherwise, the prophet would not assent infallibly and supernaturally to the proposed truth.[91]

---

[90] *ST* II-II, q. 171, a. 2.

[91] With regard to this *required proportioning*, two things can be noted, which will become clearer later on (in ch. 4, a. 2, §2, division of supernaturality).

(a) The prophet must adhere to an object supernaturally and infallibly proposed by God with infallible certitude subjectively. Now, human reason is not naturally proportioned to the required *infallible firmness of adherence*. Also, by the light of reason alone, the divine origin of interior revelation is not manifested certainly; therefore, if by the light of reason alone the prophet considers what occurs in himself, he will not be able to discern infallibly whether this arises from God who reveals, or from the illusion of a demon, or from his own exuberance. Then he would have only an opinion, or moral certitude, but not a subjectively infallible adherence. (Cf. *ST* I-II, q. 112, a. 5).

(b) Additionally, if the object proposed by God is not only a future contingent belonging to the natural order but instead is an essentially supernatural mystery, such as the Trinity, since adherence is specified by the object to be believed, it must be of the same order. Hence, this requires *an essentially supernatural light* so that the prophet's intellect may be proportioned not only to the required firmness of adherence but to the supernatural object. Otherwise, he would only materially and not formally attain supernatural mysteries, just as a dog materially hears human speech while not understanding its intelligible meaning, or rather as the student sometimes materially hears the teacher's conclusion while not understanding the power of the

This infused light is "more principal in prophecy than the representation of things, because judgment is what brings knowledge to completion."[92] Thus, Joseph, illuminated in order to interpret the dreams of Pharaoh, is to be reckoned to be a prophet from this very fact. This infused light illuminates and elevates the notions and verb [*verbum*] by which objective proposition is accomplished. Such notions can be naturally acquired ones, like the notions of person and nature. Nonetheless, such notions are supernaturally illuminated in such knowledge. Likewise, *in judgment*, the verb[93] "is" is affirmed not only naturally under the light of reason but also supernaturally under the divine light. Thus, the affirmation is infallible and proportioned to the supernatural object [in question].[94]

St. Thomas also shows that *the prophetic light exists in a passing manner* in the prophet and not as a permanent *habitus*.

Indeed, he says:[95]

However, a light can be in a given person in two ways: in one way, as a permanent form, as bodily light is in the sun and in fire; in another way, as a given passion, or of a passing impression, as light is in the air. {{152}} However, the prophetic light is not in the intellect of the prophet in the manner of a permanent form; otherwise, the prophet would need to always possess the ability to prophecy, which is obviously false (cf. 2 Kgs 4). . . . And the reason for this is because the intellectual light existing in someone as a remaining and perfect form perfects the intellect principally for knowing the principle of those things that are manifested through that light, just as through the light of the agent intellect the intellect especially knows the first principles of all other things, which are naturally known. However, the principle of those things that pertain to supernatural knowledge, which are manifested through prophecy, is God Himself, whom prophets do not see through His essence. However, He is seen by the blessed *in patria*, in whom there is a light of this sort as a kind of per-

---

demonstration on account of the weakness of his intellect.

92 *ST* II-II, q. 173, a. 2.

93 [Trans. note: Reading *verbum* for *verbus*.]

94 See ibid., ad 3: "Man can form whatsoever imaginative forms by his natural power, considering forms of this kind absolutely; however, not so that they be *ordered* to representing intelligible truths that exceed man's intellect; but *this requires the aid of a supernatural light*." Cf. John of St. Thomas, O.P., *Cursus theologicus, De gratia*, disp. 20, a. 1, no. 9; Salmanticenses, *Cursus theologicus, De gratia*, disp. 3, dub. 3, no. 53; Édouard Hugon, *Cursus philosophiae Thomisticae*, vol. 3 *Metaphysica* (Paris: Lethielleux, 1935), pt. 1 (*Metaphysica psychologica*), 136–137 (On the *species* and word required for supernatural knowledge).

95 *ST* II-II, q. 171, a. 2.

manent and perfect form, according to the expression of Psalm 35:10: "In your light, we will see light."

> Therefore (St. Thomas concludes), it follows that the prophetic light is in the prophet's soul as some passion or passing impressions. . . . Just as the air is ever in need of a new illumination, so too the mind of the prophet always is in need of a new revelation, just as the student who has not yet acquired the principles of an art is in need of being instructed in each detail. Whence, too, Isaiah 50:4 (DR) says, "in the morning he wakeneth my ear, that I may hear him as a master [or teacher]."

Similarly, for a simple inspiration, it is subjectively required that "the intellectual light be divinely poured in, not (necessarily) for knowing supernatural things, but rather, for judging with the certitude of the divine truth those things that human reason can know."[96]

Therefore, a supernatural, prophetic light is necessary so that the prophet may have an infallible and proportionate certitude concerning the revealed reality, and concerning the very fact of revelation, so that he may most certainly distinguish the Word of God from those things that he thinks through his own spirit.

Corollaries. Likewise, proportionally, afterwards the Church must have the assistance of the Holy Spirit for proposing revelation; otherwise, she would propose this truth to us only with moral certitude, as historical knowledge is known, and thus fallibly, not infallibly.

Finally, believers must know the fact of revelation and revealed realities not only with moral certitude, inasmuch as this fact and the miracles that confirm it are proposed by history, but most firmly inasmuch as revelation is proposed infallibly by the Church,[97] for otherwise, something false could fall under faith.[98] However, this adherence of faith requires an infused light; otherwise, our faith would be subjectively proportioned neither to the supernaturality of the object to be believed, nor to the required firmness of adherence. The Pelagians did not acknowledge the necessity of this internal light, and the nominalists of the Middle Ages diminished this necessity.[99]

---

[96] *ST* II-II, q. 174, a. 2.

[97] Cf. *ST* II-II, q. 5, a. 3: "The formal object of faith is the First Truth, according to what is manifested in Sacred Scripture and the teaching of the Church, which proceeds from the First Truth," and ad 2: "Those who abandon this means totally fall away from faith," such as a formal heretic, even if he retains historical knowledge of the fact of revelation, as is seen in Luther's followers.

[98] Cf. *ST* II-II, q. 1, a. 3.

[99] The necessity of this light is thus manifested by St. Thomas in *ST* II-II, q. 6, a. 1 (Whether faith is infused into man by God): "Two things are required for faith, one of which is that

{{153}} Thus, we can clearly see what is objectively and subjectively required for receiving the truth from a divine teaching authority [*magisterio*]. And thus, it is clear why divine revelation is analogically called *speech* and also a *teaching authority* [*magisterium*]. It is like the speech of a human teacher as regards the external proposition of the object, but it is unlike it as regards the infusion of an internal light, which can be impressed spiritually onto the human intellect by God alone.

Having thus theologically explained the notion of revelation, we must pass on to the various ways that the notion of revelation may be divided.

---

believable things be proposed to man, which is required so that man may explicitly believe something. However, the other thing required for faith is *the assent of the believer* made to those things that are proposed. Therefore, as regards the *first* of these, it is necessary that faith be from God. For those things that are of faith surpass human reason and hence do not fall into man's knowledge except by God who reveals. But, indeed, they are immediately revealed by God to certain people, such as the prophets. . . . However to others they are proposed by God in sending preachers of the faith. . . .

"As regards *the second*, namely for the assent of man in those things that are of faith, *a twofold cause* can be considered. One such cause is *an external inducement*, like a seen miracle, or the persuasion of a man inducing to faith. Neither of these is a sufficient cause, for of those who see one and the same miracle and those who hear the same preaching, some believe and some do not believe. And, therefore, it is necessary to posit some *interior cause* that moves man interiorly to assent to those things that are of faith. However, *the Pelagians* posited this cause only *in man's free choice*. And for this reason, they said that the beginning of faith is from us, namely inasmuch as it is from ourselves that we are prepared to assent to those things that are of faith; but the consummation of faith is from God, through Whom those things that we must believe are proposed to us.

"However, this is false (and condemned as a heresy); for *since man is elevated above his nature when he assents to those things that are of faith, it is necessary that this be in him from a supernatural principle moving interiorly*, and this principle is God. Therefore, as regards assent, which is the principal act of faith, faith is from God moving in an interior manner through grace."

Thus, it has been defined that even unformed faith (i.e., faith without charity) is a gift of God, bringing with it "an illumination and inspiration of the Holy Spirit." See [First] Vatican Council, *Dei filius*, ch. 3 (Denzinger, no. 3010). Hence, faith thus perfects the intellect "so that the intellect may tend infallibly toward its object" (*ST* II-II, q. 4, a. 5). For this reason, supernatural certitude is higher than any given natural certitude (cf. *ST* II-II, q. 4, a. 8).

But just as empiricists do not see the necessity of an intellectual light for accepting truth from a human teaching authority, so too nominalist theologians, such as Ockham, and later on Molina, did not see *the absolute necessity* of the interior light of faith for believing revealed things on account of the supernatural authority of God who reveals. However, to avoid Pelagianism, they held that the infused *habitus* of faith is *de facto necessary* for believing as is necessary for salvation. And in this nominalistic and Molinist theory of faith, the Thomists and Suarez saw the danger of semi-Pelagianism, which held that the grace of faith was only necessary for believing more easily. [Trans. note: Reading *gratia fidei* for *gratia fide*.] See Billuart, *Summa sancti Thomae, De gratia*, diss. 3, a. 2, §2. Also see Suarez, *De gratia*, bk. 2, ch. 11.

ART. 3: THE DIVISION OF REVELATION

§1. This Division Is to Be Taken according to the Four Causes

Earlier, after providing the nominal definition of revelation, we briefly enumerated its principal divisions. Now, however, we must show the reason why these divisions are not accidental but instead are *per se* and adequate. Now, just as revelation is defined according to the four causes, so too is it divided in like manner.

{{154}} (1) *From the perspective of the formal cause*, the division is twofold:

      A. On account of its *supernatural* object, it is subdivided into:

              revelation that is essentially supernatural;

              revelation that is modally supernatural.

      B. On account of the *manner* in which it is proposed, revelation is divided

          (1) as regards the manner of representation, inasmuch as it is made:

              a) sensibly,

              b) imaginatively,

              c) intellectually;

          (2) as regards the state of the prophet, inasmuch as he is:

              a) awake,

              b) in a state of ecstasy,

              c) asleep.

(2) *From the perspective of the agent*, revelation is divided into:

      active revelation,

      passive revelation.

(3) *From the perspective of the material cause* (that is [or], *subject* in which it is received), it is divided into:

      immediate revelation,

      mediate revelation.

(4) *From the perspective of the end*, revelation is divided into:

      private revelation,

      common revelation.

The classification of these divisions makes clear what is principal—namely, that which is taken formally from the supernaturality of the object. By contrast, that which is taken from the manner or from the perspective of the subject is secondary. Hence, it follows that mediate revelation is not formally and specifically inferior to immediate revelation.

§2. Explanation of This Division

(1) *From the perspective of the formal cause*

A. ON ACCOUNT OF THE SUPERNATURALITY OF THE OBJECT, revelation is divided into revelation that is essentially supernatural and that which is modally supernatural. It is called *essentially supernatural* if its object is supernatural by its very nature, like the mystery of the Trinity. It is called *only modally supernatural revelation* if the object, by its very nature, does not exceed the natural powers of reason—like, for example, the unity of God—even if it is naturally unknowable on account of its contingency or indetermination, as is the case for a future contingent of the natural order, or on account of its hidden state, as is the case for secrets of the heart.[100] (See, later on, chapter 6, where we discuss the division of the supernatural into that which is *essentially supernatural* and that which is *modally supernatural*.)

{{155}} Hence, in the treatise on faith, *ST* II-II, q. 2, a. 3 and a. 4, St. Thomas distinguishes two questions: (1) "Whether salvation requires us to believe something above natural reason," here considering Christian revelation inasmuch as it is objectively and essentially supernatural; and (2) "whether we must believe those things to which natural

---

[100] This division of prophecy is found in St. Thomas. He says in *ST* II-II, q. 174, a. 3: "*The lowest degree* of prophecy is when someone from an interior instinct is moved *to do something externally*, as is said of Samson in Judg. 15:14 (DR): 'the Spirit of the Lord came strongly upon him: and as flax is wont to be consumed at the approach of fire, so the bands with which he was bound were broken and loosed.'—*However, the second degree* is when someone is illuminated by an interior light *to know something that however does not exceed the limits of natural knowledge*, as is said of Solomon in 1 Kgs [3 Kgs, DR] 4:32–33: 'he spoke three thousand parables: and his poems were a thousand and five. And he treated about trees, from the cedar that is in Libanus, unto the hyssop that cometh out of the wall: and he discoursed of beasts, and of fowls, and of creeping things, and of fishes,' and all this was done from a divine inspiration; for it was said, 'And God gave to Solomon wisdom, and understanding exceeding much.' However, these two degrees," St. Thomas adds, "are below *prophecy properly speaking*, because they do not attain *unto a supernatural truth*." Cf. the preceding article, ad 3.

And in the prologue of question 171, he also distinguished prophetic revelation, properly speaking, inasmuch as it extends itself either only to *future human events* or to *supernatural mysteries*. Indeed, he had said: "Prophetic revelation extends not only to future human events, but also to divine realities, both with regard to those things that are proposed to be believed by all, which pertain to faith, and with regard to loftier mysteries which are known by those who have reached perfection and which pertain to wisdom."

reason can arrive," here considering only the natural truths that are contained in Christian revelation.

We must note that in order to accept revelation that is only modally supernatural (e.g., the revelation of a natural future contingent), it suffices to have a light that is modally supernatural. However, in order to accept the revelation of the Trinity, the Incarnation, and so forth, an internal light that is essentially supernatural is required. Otherwise, the light would not be proportioned to the object, nor would the act of faith be proportioned to the supernatural object to be believed, by which this act is specified. Hence, the Thomists say that the light of theological faith is essentially supernatural, like habitual grace, whereas the prophetic light necessary for infallibly knowing natural future contingents is a grace of an inferior order, a freely given grace,[101] which is modally supernatural. (See chapter 6, where we present the division of supernaturality.)[102]

---

[101] See *ST* I-II, q. 111, a. 5.

[102] In other words, the light of theological faith by which the intimate life of God is known pertains reductively to habitual grace—that is, to the participation in the divine Nature as it is divine (or to the participation in the Deity), whereas the prophetic light by which a future contingent of the natural order is known is only a participation in some divine attribute—namely, the divine knowledge [*scientia*] (see Gonet, *Clypeus theologiae Thomisticae, De gratia*, disp. 3, art. 1, §2, no. 11; also see Salmanticenses, *Cursus theologicus, De fide*, tr. 17, disp. 2, dub. 5, no. 124.) Hence, the gift of prophecy, which stands out among all the graces freely given, had been granted to unbelievers and pagans. Indeed, Caiaphas (John 11) prophesied that it is more expedient that one man die for the people, and Balaam, although he was a soothsayer and idolater, received the gift of prophecy (Num 22). Therefore, the Apostle, in 1 Corinthians 12:31 (DR) and 13:8 (DR), after having enumerated the graces freely given, adds: "And I shew unto you yet a more excellent way"—namely, charity—"Charity never falleth away: whether prophecies shall be made void or tongues shall cease or knowledge shall be destroyed." Likewise, in Luke 10, Christ forbids his disciples from rejoicing in the miracles that they perform. These examples make manifest the distance which separates essential supernaturality from what is only modally supernatural.

Therefore, St. Thomas says in *In III Sent.*, dist. 24, a. 1, ad 3: "Although prophecy and faith are concerned with the same thing, such as the passion of Christ, they are nonetheless not the same: because faith *formally looks upon* the passion from the perspective of that by which it is under *something eternal*, namely inasmuch as God has suffered, whereas it *looks upon* that which is *temporal in a material manner*, but matters are *vice-versa* for prophecy."

The Salmanticenses explain this point as follows: "We judge it to be more probable that the certitude of the assent of faith exceeds, speaking without qualification [*simpliciter*], the certitude of prophetic knowledge. We are led to say this because, although we hold that both faith and prophecy rest upon divine revelation, nonetheless, the revelation of God, as specifying faith, in contrast to moving one to prophetic knowledge, exhibits greater certitude and consequently brings with it a greater certitude in the assent of faith. However, this difference arises from the fact that the *specificative formal objectum quod of faith is only God as He is in Himself*; however, the other things that faith attains are secondary objects, nor are they attained by faith in any other way than in relation to and in subordination to that primary object—indeed, this is what gives faith its character as a theological virtue. *However, the*

{{156}} B. On account of the manner according to which revelation is formally made, it is divided into *sensible, imaginative, and intellectual*.[103]

(a) *Revelation is made sensibly* (that is [*seu*], by mediation of the senses) when sensible signs are formed by God. And "a sensible sign is either some bodily thing externally appearing to sight, such as clouds, or an expression [*vox*] externally formed and coming into man's hearing."[104] However, expressions [*voces*] are more expressive signs.

(b) *Revelation made through an imaginary vision*, not by the mediation of the senses. Here we are speaking of revelation made through imaginary likenesses impressed by God in the prophet's imagination, or inasmuch as *species* already taken in by the imagination from sense experience are divinely ordered through a proportion for revealing a truth.

This imaginary prophecy is divided in accord with the *state* of the prophet inasmuch as it happens while *sleeping*, while *awake*, while *in ecstasy*, or while *rapt*.

Concerning the distinction between the first two, St. Thomas says in *ST* II-II, q. 174, a. 3, "*The vision that occurs while awake pertains to a higher degree of prophecy* because the prophetic light that draws the soul toward supernatural things while it is occupied with sensible things while awake would seem to be of greater power than that light which finds the soul of man withdrawn from sensible things while *sleeping*." Imaginative vision can also occur *through ecstasy*, as noted in *ST* II-II, q. 174, a. 1, ad 4, or through being *rapt* when the prophet is drawn away from apprehension of sensible

---

primary object of prophecy is either some temporal thing in particular, for example a future contingent or the secret of the heart, *or at least is not some uncreated thing in particular*, but instead is every revealable thing that abstracts from the temporal and the eternal. Whence, the *motive of theological faith* is the testimony of God as firstly and essentially revealing God Himself; however, *the motive of prophecy* is the testimony of God as revealing something temporal, or as revealing an object abstracting from the temporal and the eternal." Now, essentially supernatural (i.e., effectively and intrinsically supernatural certitude) is loftier than supernatural certitude whose supernaturality is only modal (i.e., effectively but not intrinsically). See St. Thomas, *In* III *Sent.*, d. 24, a. 1, ad 3.

Indeed, faith can exist without charity and sanctifying grace, for a pious affect of belief on the part of the will suffices for [such unformed faith]; but faith so-considered, although it is a supernatural gift of God, is called dead (or unformed) and exists in the sinner as in a preternatural and violent subject. The same is true for unformed hope. Indeed, [strictly speaking] they [i.e., the theological virtues] are properties of grace according to the notion of perfect virtue and as they exist in a connatural subject. Thus, their supernaturality pertains reductively to the supernaturality of sanctifying grace. (See Billuart, *Summa sancti Thomae, De gratia*, diss. 4, a. 4.)

[103] See *ST* II-II, q. 174, a. 1, ad 3.

[104] Cf. Exodus 19, 20:18; 24:9 and 7; and 33:9.

things and elevated to a given imaginary or intellectual vision.[105] And St. Thomas adds: "When prophetic revelation is made in imaginary forms, a withdrawal from the senses is necessary (at least an imperfect withdrawal), so that such an apparition may not be referred to those things that are sensed externally."[106]

{{157}} Imaginary vision is also *objectively* divided "with regard to the expression of imaginable signs by which intelligible truth is expressed"; *these signs* are either *words* or *meaningful things* [*res significativae*]:

> And because words are the signs that most fully express intelligible truth, therefore, a loftier degree of prophecy is found when the prophet hears words expressing an intelligible truth, whether while awake or in sleep, rather than when he sees certain things that meaningfully convey the truth [*res significativas veritatis*], such as seven full ears of grain signifying seven years of plenty. . . . A loftier degree still is found when the prophet not only sees signs of words or of facts, but also sees (either while awake or in sleep) *someone speaking with him* or demonstrating something to him, for through this, the prophet's mind is shown to approach more closely to the revealing cause. And an even loftier degree of prophecy is found if he who speaks or demonstrates is seen (while awake or in sleep) *in the appearance of an angel*, than if he is seen *in the appearance of a man*, and even loftier still if he is seen (while awake or in sleep) *in the appearance of God*, according to the words of Isaiah 6:1 (DR): "I saw the Lord sitting."[107]

(c) *Revelation can be made intellectually*—namely, not through the mediation of the senses nor the imagination but, rather, according to an immediate impression of intelligible *species* by God or according to a divine ordering of naturally acquired *species*.[108]

After his exposition of those things that pertain to prophecy through sensible vision and through imaginative vision, St. Thomas says:

> However, above all these degrees is a third genus of prophecy in which an intelligible and supernatural truth is manifested without any imaginative vision. However, this exceeds the notion of prophecy strictly speaking... for prophecy

---

[105] Cf. *ST* II-II, q. 175, a. 2 ad 2. Also see ad 1: "Being rapt adds something beyond ecstasy, for ecstasy involves being beyond oneself, namely according to which someone is placed outside of his particular order; however, being rapt adds to this a kind of violence," at least from the perspective of the mode of operation, if not from the perspective of the terminus.

[106] *ST* II-II, q. 173, a. 3.

[107] Ibid.

[108] Cf. *ST* II-II, q. 173, a. 2, ad 1, ad 2, and ad 3; also, a. 3.

implies a kind of obscurity and removal from intelligible truth. And therefore, those people who see through an imaginative vision are more properly called prophets, although that prophecy that occurs through an intellectual vision is nobler, so long as the same truth is revealed in both. But if the *intellectual* light be divinely infused into someone, not for knowing some supernatural things, but for judging according to the certitude of the divine truth those things that human reason can know, such an intellectual prophecy is below that which is made with an imaginative vision leading to supernatural truth.[109]

This intellectual revelation can occur *in a rapt [state of soul]*. However, this is not absolutely necessary, as is said in *ST* II-II, q. 173, a. 3: "Removal [*alienatio*] from the senses occurs only when the mind is elevated to contemplate things which are more sublime."[110] And in being rapt "the excess of mind can be such that it contemplates the Divine Essence itself."[111] According to St. Augustine and St. Thomas, "Such was the rapture experienced by St. Paul and by Moses."[112] Concerning Moses, we read in Numbers 12:8 (DR): "plainly, and not by riddles and figures doth he see the Lord." And St. Paul says in 2 Corinthians 12:1–4 (DR):

> If I must glory (it is not expedient indeed) but I will come to visions and revelations of the Lord. I know a man in Christ above fourteen years ago (whether in the body, I know not, or out of the body, I know not: God knoweth), such a one caught up to the third heaven. And I know such a man (whether in the body, or out of the body, I know not: God knoweth): That *he was caught up into paradise* and heard secret words which it is not granted to man to utter.

Along with St. Augustine, St. Thomas held that Moses and St. Paul saw the very essence of God while rapt, and "rightly so," said the Angelic Doctor, "for just as Moses was the first Teacher of the Jews, so too was Paul the first Teacher of the Gentiles."[113] However, {{158}} the prophetic light does not suffice for that vision. Instead, what is needed is "the light of glory after the manner of a transitory passion."[114]

According to the common opinion of theologians, while *Christ* was alive on earth

---

[109] *ST* II-II, q. 174, a. 3c and a. 2 ad 2.

[110] *ST* II-II, q. 173, a. 3, ad 3.

[111] Cf. *ST* II-II q. 175, a. 3, ad 1.

[112] Ibid.

[113] *ST* II-II, q. 175, a. 3.

[114] *ST* II-II, q. 175, a. 3 ad 2. See ibid., ad 3: "Thus Paul in rapture was not beatified in a habitual manner but, instead, only had the act of those who are beatified. It follows that the *act* of faith was not simultaneously present in him; however, the *habitus* of faith was then simultaneously found in him."

as a man, he had the light of glory as an enduring form, without being rapt, though *in a way that was loftier than being in ecstasy and rapt*. For he hinted that he *saw* God when he preached: "We speak what we know and we testify what we have seen" (John 3:11, DR). " Father, I will that *where I am*, they also whom thou hast given me may be with me: *that they may see my glory which thou hast given me*" (John 17:24, DR). "No man hath ascended into heaven, but he that descended from heaven, *the Son of man who is in heaven*" (John 3:13, DR), meaning that, even as a man, he enjoyed the heavenly vision. Indeed, this was a fitting state of affairs for him as the teacher of all humanity, so that he might lead them to the vision of the divine essence.[115] This was also manifested, in a way, in his sublime manner of teaching, which had the greatest authority and loftiest elevation, along with the greatest simplicity.

Based on these divisions of revelation, it is clear how the prophetic revelation could grow with the advance of time up to Christ himself, though no further.[116]

(2) *From the perspective of the agent*, revelation is divided into *active* and *passive*. Indeed, since revelation is the action of God moving man's intellect, it can be understood either *actively*, inasmuch as it is from God as from a cause, or *passively*, inasmuch as it is received in a subject—namely, in a prophet. Active revelation is the very speech, manifestation, or "touch by which the Holy Spirit is said to touch and illuminate the mind" of the prophet. Passive revelation is "the perception of the divine speech by which the Holy Spirit speaks inwardly to the mind."[117]

Note well that *active* revelation is the divine action *formally immanent in God*—namely, the divine essence itself—and likewise it is *virtually transitive* [*transiens*][118] inasmuch as it produces an effect *ad extra*. It itself is the formal motive of divine faith, which is hence called a theological virtue. As Cajetan remarks, "Revelation is specified as the formal object of faith on account of active revelation, and to say or to reveal posits in God an action that is the very substance of God."[119] In other words, active revelation is the First Truth speaking, considered in second act. And this active revelation can be known evidently and immediately only under the light of glory. The prophet knows it from its proper effect—namely, from passive revelation under the prophetic light; thus, it has the evidence of the one bearing witness to this effect. However, others, who accept revelation by the mediation of a prophet, naturally know active revelation from extrinsic and con-

---

[115] See *ST* III, q. 9, a. 3.

[116] See *ST* II-II, q. 174, a. 6.

[117] St. Thomas, *De veritate*, q. 12, a. 1.

[118] A formally transitive [*transiens*] action is one that is from the agent as an accident and is received terminatively in the patient. This implies an imperfection and hence must not be attributed to God.

[119] *In ST* II-II, q. 1, a. 1, no. 9.

comitant signs (e.g., historically certain miracles) and know it supernaturally by divine faith, inasmuch as active revelation proposed by the Church (and not only by {{159}} history) is at once that by which we believe and that which is believed, just as light is that by which we see and that which is seen, as we will need to discuss later.

(3) *From the perspective of the material cause, that is [seu], the subject* in which it is received, revelation is divided into *immediate* and *mediate*. Immediate revelation is that which is received by the prophet himself, whereas mediate revelation is that which is received by other believers through the mediation of a prophet or [*seu*] the Church.

(4) *From the perspective of the end*, revelation is divided into *private* and *common*. Private revelation is that which is made essentially and primarily for the use of a given man or of a few, whereas common revelation is that which is made essentially and primarily for the salvation of the whole human race, as we said above. The end spoken of here is only the end *for whom* revelation is useful. However, the end on account of which [*finis cuius gratia*] (that is [*seu*], the end, properly speaking) [revelation is made] is always the glory of God, to whom all things are subordinated, for the order of agents must correspond to the order of ends, and the action of the First Agent cannot fail to be ordered to the supreme end of the whole universe and of all souls—namely to God himself, who is to be manifested in his glory.

CHAPTER FIVE

On the Notions of Mystery and of Dogma

{{160}}

Art. 1. The Catholic notion and heterodox notions

Art. 2. Theological explanation of the Catholic notion and division of mysteries

ART. 1: THE CATHOLIC NOTIONS OF MYSTERY AND OF DOGMA; HETERODOX NOTIONS

§1. The Catholic Notion of Mystery

From the definitions and declarations of the Church, as we find them set forth in the systematic index of Denzinger's *Enchiridion*, we have the following:

A. *The notion of mystery.* The Church has declared:

Beyond the truths penetrable by reason, Christian revelation contains both *mysteries broadly speaking,* such as the eternal decrees of God,[1] and *mysteries strictly speaking,* which are utterly impenetrable by reason,[2] nay, that even *transcend* angelic intellects (or *every created intellect*),[3] *mysteries that cannot become known except by being divinely revealed, and after this revelation has been handed on, they cannot be demonstrated along with the pro-*

---

[1] See Denzinger, no. 3004 [First Vatican Council, *Dei filius*, ch. 2].

[2] See Denzinger, nos. 2732ff [Gregory XVI, *Mirari vos*], old 1640ff [Pius IX, *Acerbissimum vobiscum*], 2828 [Pius IX, *Eximiam tuam*], 2850ff [Pius IX, *Gravissimas inter*], 2878 [Pius IX, *Tuas libenter*], 2909 [Pius, IX, *Syllabus of Errors*, no. 9], 3015 [First Vatican Council, *Dei filius*, ch. 4], 3041 [First Vatican Council, *Dei filius*, can. 4.1], 3225 [Leo XIII, *Post obitum*, no. 25].

[3] Denzinger, no. 2856 [Pius IX, *Gravissimas inter*].

gress of science.[4] Nevertheless, they do not contradict reason[5] but, rather, exceed it,[6] *forever remaining obscure,*[7] and are not contrivances of men opposed to the common good.[8]

The Church's principal definition concerning this matter is found in canon. 4.1 of the [First] Vatican Council's document *Dei filius*: "If anyone says that in divine revelation no true and properly so-called mysteries are contained but that all dogmas of faith can be understood and demonstrated from natural principles by reason, if it is properly trained, let him be anathema."[9] Likewise in chapter 4 of that document:

> The perpetual common belief of the Catholic Church has held and holds also this: there is a twofold order of knowledge, distinct not only in its *principle* but also in its object, because in the one we know by natural reason, in the other by divine faith; in its *object*, because apart from what natural reason can attain, there are proposed to our belief mysteries that are hidden in God that can never be known unless they are revealed by God. . . . For *divine mysteries by their very nature* so *exceed* the created intellect that, even when they have been communicated in revelation and received by faith, they remain covered by the veil of faith itself and shrouded, as it were, in darkness {{161}} as long as in this mortal life "we are away from the Lord; for we walk by faith, not by sight" (2 Cor 5:6).[10]

Similarly, see Pius IX, *Syllabus of Errors* no. 9[11] and the declarations of Pius IX against the semi-rationalism of Jakob Frohschammer in *Gravissimas inter* to the Archbishop of Munich-Freising.[12]

According to these declarations, three things are required for *a mystery properly speaking,*[13] namely: (1) that there be *a truth hidden in God*, one that by its nature surpasses every created intellect; (2) *that it could not become known without being divinely revealed*, for truths hidden in God can indeed

---

4   See Denzinger, nos. old 1642ff [Pius IX, *Singulari quadam*], 2850ff [Pius IX, *Gravissimas inter*], 2854ff [ibid.], 2904 [Pius IX, *Syllabus of Errors*, no. 4], 2909 [ibid., no. 9], 3016 [First Vatican Council, *Dei filius*, ch. 4], 3041 [ibid., can. 4.1], 3043 [ibid., can. 4.3].

5   See Denzinger, nos. 2775ff [Pius IX, *Qui pluribus*], 2811 [Pius IX, Decree of the Sacred Congregation of the Index, 1855, against Augustine Bonnetty, no. 1], and 2909 [Pius IX, *Syllabus of Errors*, no. 6].

6   See Denzinger, nos. 2854 [Pius IX, *Gravissimas inter*], 3015 [First Vatican Council, ch. 4].

7   See Denzinger, nos. 824 [Gregory IX, *Ab Aegyptiis argentea*], 306 [First Vatican Council, ch. 4].

8   See Denzinger, nos. 2775 [Pius IX, *Qui pluribus*], 2907 [Pius IX, *Syllabus of Errors*, no. 7].

9   Denzinger, no. 3041.

10   Denzinger, nos. 3015–3016.

11   See Denzinger, no. 2909.

12   See Denzinger, nos. 2852, 2854, and 2856.

13   See Vacant, *Études sur le Concile du Vatican*, vol. 2, 187.

be manifested without revelation (e.g., the divine decree concerning the destruction of Jerusalem is knowable after the fact); (3) that *even once revelation is handed on, it remains hidden*, for indeed certain things can be known only by revelation but are easily understood after revelation is made (e.g., that the Church forever must be ruled by Christ's will by one supreme pontiff, whereas, on the contrary, the mystery of the Trinity, even once revelation has been handed on, remains obscure).

B. *The nature of dogma.* According to the [First] Vatican Council, *Dei filius*, ch. 3: *Dogmas are assertions "that are contained in the word of God, written or handed down, and which by the Church, either in solemn judgment or through her ordinary and universal teaching office, are proposed for belief as having to be divinely revealed."*[14] Such an assertion is called a defined dogma if it is proposed by a solemn judgment. It is called a Catholic dogma if proposed by the ordinary and universal magisterium.[15]

Hence, a dogma is related to a mystery as an assertion is related to the thing that is asserted. Thus, it is said: The Church declares the meaning of a dogma, rather than the meaning of a mystery; that is, she declares the meaning of the statement [*enuntiationis*] that expresses the mystery.

However, a dogma is not absolutely the same as a *dogmatic formula*, for there can be many dogmatic formulas for one dogma, such that later ones are more explicit than earlier ones. Thus, the mystery of the Incarnation was expressed first as "the Word of God was made flesh" and then later as "The Word, consubstantial to God the Father, was made man."

Thus, we speak of the history of dogmas and not of the history of mysteries, for the preparation undertaken for a dogmatic formula against heresies, its promulgation, and later on the promulgation of more explicit formulas of the same dogmas are all historical facts, whereas, on the contrary, a mystery of itself is not a historical fact (e.g., consider the mystery of the Trinity).

The Church's principal definitions concerning the nature of dogma are as follows:

---

[14] Denzinger, no. 3011. Likewise, see Denzinger, nos. 2879 [Pius IX, *Tuas libenter*], 2909 [Pius IX, *Syllabus of Errors*, no. 9], 2922 [ibid., no. 22], 3020 [First Vatican Council, *Dei filius*, ch. 4], 3041ff [First Vatican Council, *Dei filius*, can. 41ff], 3483ff [Pius X, *Pascendi dominici gregis*], 3488ff [ibid.]

[15] Dogmas proposed by the solemn judgment of the Church are called *defined* dogmas, or also simply dogmas of faith. Dogmas proposed by the ordinary and universal magisterium of the Church, but not yet solemnly defined, are called *Catholic* or *revealed* dogmas or truths looking toward faith [*veritates ad fidem spectantes*].

If anyone says that, as science progresses, at times a sense is to be given to *dogmas* proposed by the Church different from the one that the Church has understood and understands, let him be anathema.[16]

For the doctrine of faith that God has revealed has not been proposed like a philosophical system to be perfected by human ingenuity; rather, it has been entrusted to the spouse of Christ as a divine trust to be faithfully {{162}} kept and infallibly declared. Hence also that meaning of the sacred *dogmas is perpetually to be retained* which our Holy Mother Church has once declared, and there must never be a deviation from that meaning on the specious ground and title of a more profound understanding. "Therefore, let there be *growth* and abundant progress in *understanding*, knowledge, and wisdom, in each and all, in individuals and in the *whole Church* at all times and in the progress of ages, but only within the proper limits, i.e., *within the same dogma, the same meaning*, the same judgment.[17]

§2. Heterodox Notions of Mystery and of Dogma

These heterodox notions can be reduced to two—namely, to the naturalistic notion and the semi-naturalistic notion. However, the first can be subdivided inasmuch as it is proposed either by rationalists or modernists or [*aut*] liberal Protestants.

A. **Rationalists** either simply reject supernatural mysteries as absurd or unintelligible,[18] or they reduce them to natural mysteries (that is [*seu*], to natural truths that can be known without revelation).[19] Thus Kant, like the modalists before him, reduced the three persons of the Trinity to three naturally knowable attributes of God. Similarly, Hegel saw in the mystery of

---

[16] [First] Vatican Council, *Dei filius*, can. 4.3 (Denzinger, no. 3043).

[17] Ibid., ch. 4 (Denzinger, no. 3020). See Vincent of Lérins, *Commonitorium*, no. 28. Also see [First] Vatican Council, *Pastor aeternus*, nos. 3069–3070: "The Roman pontiffs . . . have defined as having to be held those matters that, with the help of God, they had found consonant with the Holy Scriptures. *For the Holy Spirit was not promised to the successors of Peter that they might disclose a new doctrine by his revelation, but rather that with his assistance they might reverently guard and faithfully explain the revelation or deposit of faith that was handed down through the apostles.*"

[18] [First] Vatican Council, *Dei filius*, can. 2.2 and 2.3 (Denzinger, nos. 3027 and 3028).

[19] See ibid., can. 3.3 (Denzinger, no. 3033).

the Trinity nothing other than three moments of universal evolution: thesis, antithesis, and synthesis. Thus, Pius IX's *Syllabus of Errors* condemned this proposition: "The mysteries of the Christian faith are the outcome of philosophical reflections."[20]

Consequently, rationalists consider *dogma* either as being an empty fabrication by imagination or as *the symbolic expression of a natural truth (or of a natural mystery)*. Hence, the portion of truth that is contained[21] in this symbolic expression ought to be determined by human reason, which rationalism holds is the supreme arbiter of truth and falsity and the chief norm, superior to religion, just as [the latter] is superior to the symbolism of the arts.[22] Hence, for them, the meaning of dogmas *varies* with the progress of the sciences and of philosophy: "Divine revelation is imperfect and hence subject to continual and indefinite progress, which ought to correspond to the progress of human reason."[23]

B. *Modernists, like liberal Protestants as well*, follow the ways of rationalism regarding the notion of mystery and dogma, as is clearly set forth in the encyclical *Pascendi*. According to modernism:

> Therefore the religious sentiment, which through the agency of vital immanence emerges from the lurking places of the subconsciousness, is the germ of all religion, and the explanation of everything that has been or ever will be in any religion (even the Christian religion).... The religious man must *ponder* his faith.... The operation of the intellect in this work is a double one: First by a natural and spontaneous act it expresses its concept *in a simple, ordinary statement*; then, on reflection and deeper consideration, or, as they say, by *elaborating its thought*, it expresses the idea in *secondary propositions*, which are derived from the first, but are more perfect and distinct. These secondary {{163}} propositions, if they finally receive the approval of the supreme magisterium of the Church, constitute *dogma*....
>
> (Whence) these *religious formulas* (or dogmas) have no other purpose than to furnish the believer with a means of giving an

---

[20] Pius IX, *Syllabus of Errors*, no. 7 (Denzinger, no. 2907).

[21] [Trans. note: Reading *continetur* for *continentur*.]

[22] See Pius IX, *Syllabus of Errors*, On absolute rationalism, nos. 3 and 4 (Denzinger, nos. 2903 and 2904).

[23] Ibid., no. 5 (Denzinger, no. 2905).

account of his faith to himself. These formulas therefore stand midway between the believer and his faith; in their relation to the faith, they are the inadequate expression of its object, and are usually called *symbols*; in their relation to the believer, they are mere *instruments*. Hence *it is quite impossible to maintain that they express absolute truth*: for, *in so far as they are symbols, they are the images of truth, and so must be adapted to the religious sentiment* in its relation to man; and as *instruments, they are the vehicles of truth, and must therefore in their turn be adapted to man* in his relation to the religious sentiment. *But the object of the religious sentiment*, since it embraces that *absolute, possesses an infinite variety of aspects* of which now one, now another, may present itself. In like manner, he who believes may pass through different phases. Consequently, the formulae too, which we call *dogmas, must be subject to these vicissitudes*, and are, therefore, liable to change. Thus the way is open to the *intrinsic evolution of dogma*. An immense collection of sophisms this, that ruins and destroys all religion.[24]

The modernists add:

Dogma is not only able, but ought to evolve and to be changed . . . That religious formulas, to be really religious and not merely theological speculations, ought to be living and to live the life of the religious sentiment. . . . In other words, it is necessary *that the primitive formula be accepted* and sanctioned *by the heart*; and similarly the subsequent work from which spring the *secondary formulas* must proceed under the guidance of the heart. Wherefore if for any reason *this adaptation* (to the religious sense) *should cease to exist, they* (the secondary formulas) *lose their first meaning and accordingly must be changed"*[25]

Thus, the modernists judge that the meaning of dogma is variable, and as the encyclical says: "Inflated with a boastful science, they have reached that pitch of folly where they pervert the *eternal concept of truth* and the true nature of the religious sentiment."[26]

See also the modernist propositions condemned in the decree *Lamentabili*, no. 58: "Truth is no more immutable than man himself, since it evolved with him, in him, and

---

[24] Pius X, *Pascendi dominici gregis*, nos. 10–13 (Denzinger nos. 3481–3483). [Trans. note: As above, I have followed the official translation.]

[25] Ibid., no. 13.

[26] Ibid.

through him."[27] Likewise, see nos. 22, 26, 59, and 60.[28] No. 62: "The chief articles of the Apostles' Creed did not have the same sense for the Christians of the first ages as they have for the Christians of our time."[29] No. 64: "Scientific progress demands that the concepts of Christian doctrine concerning God, creation, revelation, the Person of the Incarnate Word, and Redemption be reformed."[30] For example, the [dogmatic] formula expressing the nature of the hypostatic union would indeed have been true at the time of the Council of Nicaea because it was conformed to the state of philosophy in that era; now, however, according to the modernists, following upon the developments that philosophy has undergone, it cannot be admitted, due to the new notion of personality [that philosophy now holds]. Hence, we read in the formula of the Anti-Modernist Oath:

> I sincerely hold that the doctrine of Faith was handed on to us from the Apos-
> tles through the orthodox Fathers in the same sense and always according to the
> same opinion. And therefore I utterly reject the heretical fabrication asserting
> the evolution of dogmas passing from one meaning to another, different from
> that which the Church previously held; and equally, I condemn every error by
> which, in place of the divine deposit, handed on to the Spouse of Christ to be
> cared for by her with fidelity, it suffices that one have a philosophical fabrica-
> tion, or creation of consciousness, gradually developed by the striving of men
> and to be perfected in the future by an indefinite progress.

Thus, clearly, the modernists, like liberal Protestants as well, draw near to absolute rationalism.

{{164}} C. *Semi-rationalists*, however, such as Hermes, Günther, and Frohschammer differ from the rationalists inasmuch as they acknowledge that the mysteries of Christianity were handed on to us by divine revelation that is external, doing so in a properly supernatural manner. However, they agree with the rationalists inasmuch as they reduce the supernatural mysteries to natural mysteries. Indeed, they say that with the progress of philosophy, *mysteries* handed on by revelation *can be demonstrated* through principles of natural reason, at least those mysteries that are intrinsically nec-essary. This supposed demonstrability of the mysteries is condemned as a heresy by Canon 4.1 in *Dei filius* of the [First] Vatican Council.[31] Similarly condemned is the Rosminian proposition holding that the mystery of the

---

27 Pius X, *Lamentabile*, prop. 58 (Denzinger, no. 3458).
28 See Denzinger, nos. 3422, 3426, 3459, and 3460.
29 Denzinger, no. 3462.
30 Denzinger, no. 3464.
31 See Denzinger, no. 3041.

Trinity can be demonstrated, at least indirectly, following upon the revelation of this mystery.

The principle errors of semi-rationalism are condemned in Pius IX's *Syllabus of Errors*, nos. 8 and 14[32] and in the letters of Pius IX *Eximiam tuam* to the Archbishop of Cologne,[33] *Qui pluribus*,[34] and *Gravissimas inter* to the Archbishop of Munich-Freising.[35]

Indeed, this semi-rationalistic notion of supernatural mysteries leads to the conclusions enunciated by Hermes—namely, that the formal motive on account of which the mysteries of faith must be admitted is not necessarily the authority of God who reveals but instead can take on the form of a philosophical demonstration for the philosophers who understand this demonstration. Hence, according to Guenther, the doctrine revealed by God is, as it were, a philosophical discovery to be perfected by human ingenuity; and therefore, *the definitions of the Councils are not absolutely true, but only relative to the state of science and of philosophy at the time of the definition.* This was condemned as a heresy by the [First] Vatican Council in canon 4.3 of *Dei filius*.[36] Likewise, in canon 4.2 of the same document the corollary was condemned: "The human sciences, . . . even if opposed to revealed doctrine, may be held as true and cannot be proscribed by the Church."[37] The principle of rationalism is clear in this semi-rationalistic doctrine, and especially in this proposition condemned in the *Syllabus of Errors*: "As there is a distinction between the philosopher and his philosophy, he has the right and the duty to submit himself to the authority he acknowledges as legitimate; but *philosophy neither can nor must submit to any authority.*"[38] Hence "philosophy is to be treated without any regard to supernatural revelation."[39] Thus, philosophy is not only distinguished from faith and from theology but, moreover, is said to be separated from them, in the end intending to judge, as the supreme arbiter, concerning the value of faith itself and of theology.

ART. 2: Theological Explication of the Catholic Notions of Mystery and of Dogma

§1. Definition of mystery in general and its division
§2. On the intelligibility of the mysteries and on their interconnection
§3. Explanation of the notion of dogma

---

[32] See Denzinger, nos. 2908 and 2914.

[33] See Denzinger, nos. 2828ff.

[34] See Denzinger, nos. 2775ff.

[35] See Denzinger, no. 2850ff. [Trans. note: He also adds Gregory XVI's *Dum acerbissimas*, old Denzinger, nos. 1618ff.]

[36] See Denzinger, no. 3043.

[37] See Denzinger, no. 3042. [Trans. note: He incorrectly cites Denzinger, no. 3044 [1819].]

[38] Pius IX, *Syllabus of Errors*, no. 10 (Denzinger, no. 2910).

[39] Ibid., no. 14 (Denzinger, no. 2914).

§4. On the immutability of dogma and on its progressive understanding

§1. Definition of Mystery in General and Its Division

The theological explanation of the Catholic notion of mystery is drawn from the definition of mystery in general and from its division into natural and supernatural mysteries. Rationalists deny this division; semi-rationalists reduce it to an accidental division.[40] The Church considers it {{165}} to be necessary and essential. And this must be explained before the possibility and existence of revelation may be defended, in order to have an exact notion of mystery.

Mystery in general is defined as a secret and hidden reality (or truth) exceeding our knowledge, although deserving of our knowledge. If it is not in some manner above our knowledge, it would not deserve to be called a mystery. Therefore, the various ways of calling something a mystery are said in accord with how certain things exceed knowledge.

Mystery is essentially and adequately divided into natural and supernatural, for it is called "natural" inasmuch as it can be known without supernatural revelation, at least as regards its existence, and it is called "supernatural" inasmuch as, without supernatural revelation, we cannot know of it, even as regards its existence.

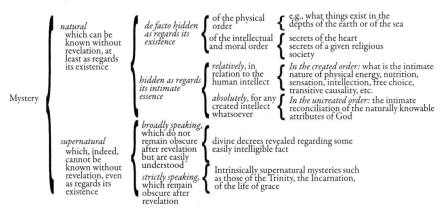

Natural mysteries are hidden things that nevertheless can be known without supernatural revelation, at least as regards their existence.

Natural mystery is subdivided inasmuch as it exceeds our knowledge in two ways: (1) as regards the fact of its *existence*, although this fact, of itself, is

---

40 For, according to the semi-rationalists, mysteries that are called supernatural exceed the discovery of reason but not its demonstrative power after being proposed.

naturally knowable; (2) not as regards the fact of its existence but as regards its *intimate essence* (or [*seu*] as regards its intimate mode).

Natural mysteries that exceed our knowledge *as regards the fact of their existence* are either (a) of the physical order, and then they are inaccessible on account of distance or {{166}}material impediments (e.g., what things exist in the depths of the earth or the sea), but their heretofore-unknown existence is naturally knowable; or (b) they are of the intellectual and moral order, such as secrets of the heart that are only naturally manifested through human revelation. Likewise, the secrets and rites of a given religion are called mysteries inasmuch as they are not known by those who are not initiated into them (e.g., the Eleusian mysteries).

Natural mysteries that exceed natural knowledge, not as regards their existence but *as regards their intimate essence* (or [*seu*] intimate mode) are subdivided inasmuch as they are (a) *relative* natural mysteries (namely, relative to the human intellect qua human) or (b) *absolute* natural mysteries (namely, in relation to every created intellect qua created).

Relative natural mysteries, as regards their intimate essence[41] (or [*seu*] intimate mode), exceed the human intellect because our intellect does not know intelligible and spiritual things intuitively but only in an abstract manner from sensible things. Thus, things that are not mysteries for the angels are mysteries for us. For example, by ascending from material things to spiritual ones, in the physical order, science does not determine the nature of the intimate essences of matter,[42] physical energy, universal attraction, and electricity. In the biological order, there are the intimate essences of nutritive assimilation, intussusception,[43] deassimilation, reproduction, and growth in living things. The intimate character [*modus*] of these vital phenomena remains obscure. In the psychological order, what is the intimate nature of sensation? Indeed, Aristotle most excellently says that

---

[41] We have said, "As regards its *intimate* essence," and not only "as regards its essence," for the agnosticism of the nominalists must be avoided, according to whom the real essences of things are entirely unknown to us, so that the human intellect could not arrive at real definitions but only at nominal definitions. Thus universals would be mere names (as radical nominalists and positivists say) or mere concepts (as Kant says). But traditional philosophy teaches that we do not have *intuitive* notions of real essences (as the angels have) but, rather, have *abstract* notions, which according to a relation to sensible notes are composed from genus and difference. These notions are not *comprehensive* because they do not manifest the essences of things inasmuch as they are knowable.

[42] Prime matter is defined by Aristotle only analogically from common notions (such as passive potency and subject) and as regards what is proper to it *in a negative manner* (neither a what, nor quality, nor a quantity, etc.) or *in a relative manner* (the first subject of substantial mutation and of the substantial form).

[43] [Trans. note: Concerning the meaning of this term in scholastic use, as regards the ontological issue of material assimilation in living organisms, see Jacques Maritain, "The Philosophy of the Organism: Notes on the Function of Nutrition," trans. Matthew K. Minerd, *Nova et Vetera* 19, no. 2 (Spring 2021): 633–651.]

it is a kind of received action [*quoddam pati*] by which the sensing subject becomes the other inasmuch as it is other, and does not merely become other (as already happens in material change). Therefore, sensation requires a change that is not merely material but, rather, is already in some manner spiritual, one that is called intentional or representative. However, what is the intimate nature of this intentional change? We know it *in a positive manner* only *on the basis of common notions*, in which it agrees with material change. Hence, it is called a "change" and "intentional" or tending to an object, which is rendered present in another manner by it. Taken in isolation, these various notions express something that is already found in the merely material order. However, what is proper to this intentional change is known by us *in a negative manner* (thus we say it is not material) and *in a relative manner* (thus we say it is of a higher order than the merely material order). Hence, it remains a natural mystery—namely, the *intimate nature* of sensation and how it is intimately produced. Likewise, what is the intimate nature of intellective abstraction? The illumination of the agent intellect by which the intelligible is actuated in the sensible? The intimate nature of [intellectual] conception? We know these things on the basis of the common notions in which they agree with sensible things, and as regards what is proper to them, we know them only relatively and negatively. They ever remain a mystery. Likewise, what is free choice? What is the intimate and mutual relation of this choice with the final practical judgment in the end of deliberation? A [philosophico-]scientific explanation can indeed be given for these things, one formed from common notions, as well as through expression in negative terms and in way that is relative to sensible things. Nonetheless, the mystery remains. {{167}} Likewise, in the metaphysical order, what is the intimate nature of the way that created existence is limited by created essence? What is the intimate nature of the transitive action that is indeed from the agent and in some manner originatively in the agent, while nonetheless being terminatively in the patient? Indeed, contradiction is avoided, but it remains a mystery for us.

These natural mysteries are relative to our intellect, which does not know intelligible and spiritual things intuitively but instead knows them only on the basis of our knowledge of sensible things and in an abstractive manner. On the other hand, a created pure spirit (i.e., an angel) intuitively knows created spiritual things through proper concepts, as well as the essences of bodily things. Hence, sensation and created intellection do not contain a mystery for it.

However, absolute natural mysteries are those things that as regards their intimate essence (or [*seu*] as regards their intimate mode) transcend every created intellect, even though their existence could be known without revelation. These mysteries pertain to the uncreated order—namely, to the proper and intimate mode of the naturally knowable divine attributes. Indeed, these attributes, as we will discuss later, cannot be naturally known in a positive manner by a created intellect solely *on the basis of the common notions* in which they analogically come together with created things, and their proper mode is naturally known only *in a negative manner* (e.g., a nonfinite good) or *in a relative manner* (e.g., a supreme good). Thus, *the intimate* reconciliation of all these attributes in God (or [*seu*] the intimate mode of this reconciliation) is hidden for every created intellect. Indeed, we naturally know *that* they are reconciled. We even can explain in negative and relative manner *how* they are, but the intimate mode of this reconciliation remains a mystery. For example, how are we to reconcile God's absolute simplicity with the plurality of simply simple perfections that are formally and eminently in the Deity? How are we to reconcile God's absolute immutability with his free act, which nonetheless did not need to exist? Likewise, there is his infinite goodness and his permission of evil; and again, what about the reconciliation of the greatest of mercy with infinite justice? Hence, as we will say later, on account of the imperfection of our natural knowledge concerning God, we have a conditional and inefficacious *natural* desire to see the divine essence, inasmuch as it is the root of the naturally knowable divine attributes (and not, however, of the Trinity or of the order of grace and glory), for only through this vision of the divine essence would we come to positively know the intimate way that these attributes are reconciled.[44]

However, supernatural mysteries are those things that, without divine revelation, cannot be known by any created intellect, even as regards their existence.

These supernatural mysteries are subdivided into mysteries *broadly speaking* and mysteries *strictly speaking*.

Supernatural mysteries broadly speaking are those that, once revelation has been handed on, do not remain obscure and are understood easily. This is so because they exceed the created intellect not on account of their intrinsic supernaturality but, rather, on account of the given mystery's contingency or indetermination.

These mysteries broadly speaking are the divine decrees on which the existence of a given future contingent depends, whether that fact pertains to the natural order or to the supernatural order, because then it is considered as a fact and not in its nature. For example, without revelation, we cannot know when the end of the world will occur, something that is a future contingent of the natural order.[45] Likewise, without revelation we

---

[44] See *ST* I, q. 12, a. 1. Also see *SCG* III, chs. 51, 54, and 57. [Trans. note: For a very clear exposition on the divine names according to Fr. Garrigou-Lagrange's position within the Thomist school, see Réginald Garrigou-Lagrange, "On the Eminence of the Deity: In What Sense the Divine Perfections are 'Formally and Eminently' in God," in *Philosophizing in Faith: Essays on the Beginning and End of Wisdom*, ed. and trans. Matthew K. Minerd (Providence, RI: Cluny Media, 2019), 341–360.]

[45] To this category of mysteries pertains, according to St. Thomas, the creation of the world inasmuch as it was not from eternity but was in time. Indeed, this immediately depends upon the divine freedom and according to St. Thomas cannot be demonstrated *a posteriori*, at least for men. See *ST* I, q. 46.

cannot know that, {{168}} according to the will of God, the Church is to be ruled forever until the end of the world by one supreme Pontiff; this pertains to the supernatural order but is only considered as a fact and is easily understood after having been revealed. The [First] Vatican Council refers to these mysteries broadly speaking when it says: "But it pleased His (namely, God's) wisdom and goodness to reveal Himself and the eternal *decrees of His will* in another and supernatural way."[46]

However, supernatural mysteries properly speaking are those that remain obscure even after revelation has been handed on. The reason for this obscurity is because they exceed the created intellect not because of their contingency and future character [*futuritionem*] but, rather, because of their *intrinsic supernaturality*; or, as the [First] Vatican Council says, because "by their very nature [they] exceed the created intellect"[47] and "cannot be understood and demonstrated from natural principles of reason."[48] They are mysteries that pertain to the intimate life of God—that is, to the Deity according to its most proper formal character [*sub propriissima ratione*] as the Deity, or to the participation in this intimate life (that is, to grace and glory). Indeed, God is naturally knowable according to the common and analogical notions of being, truth, intelligence, will, and so forth, but not according to the most proper and intimate formal character as the Deity.[49]

Things of this sort include the mystery of the Trinity (that is, the intimate life of God), the mystery of our elevation to the order of supernatural life—namely, the mystery of grace and of glory, as well as the mystery of predestination, the mystery of the Incarnation, the mystery of Redemption (that is, the infinite value of the theandric act of Christ dying upon the Cross), the mystery of the dwelling of the Holy Spirit in the souls of the

---

[46] [First] Vatican Council, *Dei filius*, ch. 2 (Denzinger, no. 3004).

[47] Ibid., ch. 4 (Denzinger, no. 3016).

[48] Ibid., can. 4.1 (Denzinger, no. 3041). [Trans. note: Note that Fr. Garrigou-Lagrange makes the statement negative so as to express the Catholic position, in contrast to the anathema that he is citing.]

[49] Hence, in Pope Pius IX's letter (against Jakob Frohschammer) of December 11, 1862, to the Archbishop of Munich-Freising, it is read (Denzinger, no. 2851): "The author (Frohschammer) teaches especially that philosophy, if one has a right notion of it, can perceive and understand not only those Christian dogmas that natural reason has in common with faith (that is, as a common object of perception), but also those that principally and properly constitute Christian religion and faith, namely, the supernatural end of man itself and all that is related to it; and also that the most holy mystery of the Incarnation of the Lord belongs to the province of human reasoning and philosophy; and that reason, when this object is presented [to it], can by its own proper principles arrive at those [dogmas] with understanding." Against this, it is said (Denzinger, no. 2853): To mysteries properly speaking "belong particularly and clearly all those that treat of the supernatural elevation of man and his supernatural fellowship with God and that are known to have been revealed for this purpose."

righteous, the mystery of the intimate life of the Church, and the mystery of the production of grace through the sacraments. In sum, whatever is intrinsically supernatural remains a mystery. Among these mysteries, some are naturally *visible in a qualified sense* but not as regards what is intimate and intrinsically supernatural in them. For example, the Church herself, with all her marks, is visible, but nevertheless, the intimate life of the Church is not naturally visible; so too for religious life. Similarly, the visible facts of Christ's life, which are also called mysteries, can be historically known as regards what is human in Christ but not as regards what is intrinsically supernatural and divine. Similarly, the sacraments are visible, but their supernatural power for producing grace is not. Likewise, the fact of revelation, as confirmed by miracles, is visible, but what is intrinsically supernatural in them remains a mystery.

§2. On the Intelligibility of the Mysteries and on Their Interconnection

{{169}} Since the rationalists deny the intelligibility of supernatural mysteries *a priori* and, hence, do not wish to examine the fact of revelation, we must discuss what the Church teaches concerning the intelligibility of mysteries, strictly speaking.

All these supernatural mysteries, which are *per se* objects of faith, are proposed by the Church as being truths that are obscure, incomprehensible, and indemonstrable, though not unintelligible. Also, they are handed on not as a heap of disparate truths but instead as interconnected and properly "as a determinate body of doctrine."[50]

The [First] Vatican Council says: "We believe that what he has revealed is true, *not because the intrinsic truth of things* is recognized by the natural light of reason, but because of the authority of God himself who reveals them."[51] [Nevertheless, if] "reason illumined by faith inquires in an earnest, pious, and sober manner, it attains by God's grace a *certain [aliquam] understanding of the mysteries,* which is most fruitful, both from the *analogy* with the objects of its natural knowledge and from *the connection of these mysteries with one another and with man's ultimate end.*"[52]

Hence, something must be said (A) about the intelligibility of the mysteries and (B) about their interconnection.

---

[50] See [First] Vatican Council, *Dei filius*, ch. 4 (Denzinger, no. 3016), and Pius X, Decree of the Holy Office, *Lamentabili sane exitu*, no. 59 (Denzinger, no. 3459) against the modernists.

[51] See [First] Vatican Council, *Dei filius*, ch. 3 (Denzinger, no. 3008).

[52] Ibid., ch. 4 (Denzinger, no. 3016).

A. *The supernatural mysteries*[53] *are incomprehensible and indemonstrable, but testimony about them is analogically intelligible.* Indeed, incomprehensibility is not the same thing as unintelligibility.

(1)[54] *The mysteries are not unintelligible.* Something is *incomprehensible* when it cannot be totally comprehended or penetrated by our intellection. For example, the naturally knowable attributes of God, such as omnipotence, are incomprehensible but are nonetheless analogically intelligible. Nay, they are demonstrable.[55] Something is *indemonstrable* when it cannot be deduced in a necessary manner from evident principles (*a priori demonstration*) or from the facts of experience (*a posteriori demonstration*), nor manifested by a *reductio ad absurdum* (*indirect demonstration*). Thus, something that is only probable can in no way be demonstrated, but it nevertheless is intelligible. Something is *unintelligible* when it is opposed to intellection, either because it is obviously absurd (e.g., a square circle) or because it is utterly meaningless, like words that are uttered accidently without interrelation among them.

According to the Church, supernatural mysteries are incomprehensible. Nay, they cannot be demonstrated either *a priori*, or *a posteriori*, or through a *reductio ad absurdum*.[56] Nevertheless, testimony concerning them is not unintelligible. Indeed, it is not evidently absurd. What the predicate signifies is understood, as well as what the subject signifies, and the verb *is* (that is [*seu*], the existence of the mystery) is affirmed by God. The connection of the predicate and the subject remain inevident, and hence it is said: Faith is not of things seen.[57]

Thus, frequently, an unintelligent student affirms the demonstration of some conclusion on account of the authority of his or her teacher and, nonetheless, this proposition is not entirely unintelligible for him or her. Indeed, this is because, just as is the case for the nature of intellection, intelligibility too is predicated analogically (i.e., in various ways) and is more or less perfect, thus giving rise to a number of degrees: divine intellection, angelic intellection, human intellection, and in the last, intellection of principles, of conclusions, and of sufficiently credible testimony.

{{170}} (2) *The mysteries are analogically intelligible.* In the divine testimony, the subject and predicate are analogically intelligible for us. For God, in revealing, in order to express his testimony, makes use of our naturally

---

[53] [Trans. note: Reading *supernaturalia* for *supernaturalis*.]

[54] [Trans. note: Reading "1" for "2."]

[55] Nay, something can be simultaneously *immediately seen* and *incomprehensible*, as is God's essence for the blessed. See *ST* I, q. 12, a. 7.

[56] See Leo XIII, Decree of the Holy Office, *Post obitum*, no. 25 (Denzinger, no. 3225).

[57] See *ST* II-II, q. 1, a. 5.

acquired notions, which directly express something created and analogically express something uncreated. For instance, the notion of *paternity* comes to analogically express the divine paternity; likewise, the natural notion of *filiation* comes to analogically express the divine filiation of the second person of the Trinity; similarly, the notion of *adoptive filiation* comes to analogically express our supernatural filiation. It is a question of *an analogy of proportionality, not a merely metaphorical one* (as when God is called a sun or fire) *but, rather, a proper one.*

This analogy, as we will discuss below, is the golden mean between univocity (from which follows the pantheistic confusion of God and the world, and hence the denial of the supernatural order) and equivocity (from which it follows that God is unknowable, except in an absolutely improper sense— namely, metaphorically or symbolically).[58]

The principles of analogy are indicated by revelation itself inasmuch as God, in revealing supernatural mysteries, makes use of analogical notions that already exist in our mind. Thus, the mystery of the Trinity is expressed by the analogical notions of *nature, person, generation, word, spiration,* and *love.* But afterwards theology explains these notions and brings forth new ones, as St. Augustine and St. Thomas manifested the Trinity in a certain way by way of analogy with the operations of the soul—namely, of intellection and of love.[59] Likewise, the mystery of the Incarnation is expressed by means of the analogical notions of nature, person, and union and is in some way made manifest from an analogy of the union of the soul with the body. The life of grace is illuminated through analogy with a good *habitus,* which is, as it were, a second nature in the natural order. Sin is explained through an analogy with death. The supernatural virtues, which are, like grace itself, a mystery properly speaking and therefore intrinsically supernatural, are made manifest through analogy with the natural virtues. Similarly, the intimate constitution of the Church is made manifested through an analogy with natural society. These analogies, especially those that are not indicated by revelation, must be conveyed carefully, without exaggeration, as the [First] Vatican Council says, "Earnestly, piously, and soberly," and one must always heed what was said at the Fourth Lateran Council: "Between Creator and creature no similitude can be expressed without implying a greater dissimilitude."[60]

(3) *This intelligibility of the mysteries is not* FORMALLY *understood "without the illumination and inspiration of the Holy Spirit."* Indeed, the

---

[58] See *ST* I, q. 13, a. 5.

[59] But analogies proposed by theologians are not certain except inasmuch as they are explanations of analogies revealed by God himself. For reason of itself alone cannot discover the right analogies for knowing supernatural mysteries but only for knowing God qua the Author of nature.

[60] Fourth Lateran Council, ch. 3 (Denzinger, no. 806).

[First] Vatican Council said, "If reason illuminated by faith inquires in an earnest, pious, and sober manner, it attains *by God's grace* a certain [*aliquam*] understanding of the mysteries, which is most fruitful,"[61] and earlier it had said, citing the words of the Council of Orange: "No man can 'assent to the Gospel message,' as is necessary to obtain salvation, 'without the *illumination* and *inspiration* of the Holy Spirit, who gives to all delight in assenting to the truth and believing it.' Wherefore faith itself, even when it is not working through love (Gal 5:6), *is in itself a gift of God*."[62]

Indeed, this intelligibility of the mysteries is supernatural and hence {{171}} can be attained *formally* only under the infused light of faith, by which our intellect is elevated and the dogmatic proposition's notions, as well as the verb *is* [connecting subject and predicate], are illuminated. Otherwise a *proportion* between knowledge and the object to be believed would be lacking, and it would not be most firmly believed; instead, the dogmatic formulas would be known only *materially, solely as regards their letter*. It would be akin to the student who is not yet skilled lacking the *habitus* of metaphysics, whenever he does not understand a given metaphysical principle *in itself* (according to its necessity and absolute universality) but understands it only *materially* in the examples given so as to lead him onward, as it were, hand in hand. (See what we said above in the preceding chapter about the necessity of the prophetic light.)

Hence, it is said in 1 Corinthians 2:14 (DR): "But the sensual [*animalis*] man perceiveth not these things that are of the Spirit of God. For it is foolishness to him: and he cannot understand, because it is spiritually examined." Concerning which St. Thomas in his commentary on this letter says:

> Man is called *animal* on account of the apprehensive power, *which judges concerning God according to a body-bound phantasm*, according to *the letter of the law*, or according to some *philosophical notion*, which are interpreted in accord with the sense powers. . . . Such a man cannot perceive those things that are of the Spirit of God. . . . Indeed, those things about which *the Holy Spirit illuminates the mind* are above the senses and human reason . . and therefore cannot be grasped by him who only relies upon sense cognition.

(And in the same place, the Holy Doctor says:) "Someone is also called *animal* in relation to the appetitive power, namely, inasmuch as it is solely moved by

---

61 [First] Vatican Council, *Dei filius*, ch. 4 (Denzinger, no. 3016).

62 Ibid., ch. 3 (Denzinger, no. 3010). [Trans. note: Fr. Garrigou-Lagrange cites Eph 2:8, not Gal 5:6.]

things that appeal to the sense appetite.

Hence Christ said in Matthew 7:6 (DR): "Give not that which is holy to dogs; neither cast ye your pearls before swine." Now, the mysteries of truth are signified by pearls, says St. Thomas in his commentary on Matthew. Likewise, in Matthew 13:14 (DR), the word of Isaiah is referred to: "By hearing you shall hear, and shall not understand: and *seeing you shall see, and shall not perceive.*" For among those who heard the parables (without the explanation given to the apostles), men of good will saw what was there for them to see; however, others who resisted the grace of faith did not see. Hence, in treating of mental blindness and dullness, St. Thomas says, "*From the subtraction of grace it follows that the mind would not be illuminated divinely for seeing rightly,* and the heart of man would not be softened for living rightly."[63]

See *ST* II-II, q. 6, a. 1, on the necessity of infused faith: "Since, in assenting to those things that are of faith, man *is elevated above his nature,* this must come to him from a supernatural principle moving him interiorly, and this principle is God," and the external proposition of things to be believed, itself confirmed by miracles, does not suffice, as was defined against the Pelagians and semi-Pelagians.[64]

Hence, according to St. Thomas, a demon who has lost supernatural faith but naturally believes attains the first supernatural truth and supernatural mysteries only in a material manner in the letter of the Gospel and through the miracles by which it is sensibly confirmed.[65]

---

[63] *ST* II-II, q. 79, a. 3; q. 15, a. 1.

[64] Second Council of Orange, can. 7 (Denzinger, no. 377).

[65] *What does it mean to materially attain some object?* It is to attain it as regards what is material in it and not what is formal in it; for example: to hear an intelligible locution only with regard to what is sensible in it, or to hear a supernatural locution as regards what is natural in it. This arises from an imperfection of the knowing faculty that is not proportioned to its object and from the inequality of intelligences either of different orders or in the same human species.

For example, the dog hears an intelligible speech in a merely sensible manner; this is to hear materially. Likewise, in a superior order, to hear a symphony from the perspective of juxtaposed sounds, not from the perspective of its harmony. In a more superior order: to understand as something mechanical something that is vital (as mechanists do when they write on biology) or to understand as something empirical something that is intellectual (as empiricists do in treating psychologically about our intellect).

Likewise, to understand a given doctrine according to a mechanical juxtaposition and not the organic subordination of theses. Thus, many understand Thomism *materially* and indeed admit all the parts of Thomism, are neither Scotists, nor Suarezians, nor Molinists, but do not formally perceive the subordination of its theses. For example, when they treat of our natural intellectual knowledge, they insist more upon the material resolution to sensible things than the formal resolution to the intellectual evidence of the first principles. They do not deny this formal resolution, but they do not perceive its importance. On the contrary, *St. Thomas always speaks formally* and hence is the prince of theologians; and not even outstanding Thomists such as Cajetan understand the doctrine of the master as formally and profoundly as the master did; it would have been necessary to have an intellect of the same power and to see this doctrine *not in the letters but in the spirit of the doctor*. His words formally express his conception, but frequently they arouse only vague notions in the minds of disciples, who understand the doctrine from the perspective [Trans.: reading *quoad* for *quod*] of the material letter and not from the perspective of the spirit. Many confuse this material letter with the literal sense. Cajetan often says of Durandus of Saint-Pourçain and Scotus that *they only understood materially* the articles of St. Thomas.

When it is a question not of a given doctrine but of only one proposition, it is less apparent if one knows materially and not formally. Nevertheless, this is, for example, to understand a metaphysically true proposition from only a physical perspective; when it is said, for example, that every agent makes its like [*omne agens agit sibi simile*], certain people see only the examples: man begets a man, an ox begets an ox; they do not perceive that every agent acts inasmuch as it is determined and hence produces a similar determination, whether specifically, generically, or analogically, so that this principle is utterly universal and has value even for God the Creator. Likewise, to understand as probable what is proposed as being apodictic, because the necessary connection of subject and predicate is not perceived, because concerning the subject and the predicate one has highly vague [*confusae*] notions (for example, for conceiving that true freedom is deduced from reason). Hence to understand materially is not of itself to err.

Likewise, in our question: one can assent to a supernatural locution only from the perspective of what is naturally knowable in it—namely, to know *the letter of Sacred Scripture and not its spirit*. "For the letter killeth: but the spirit quickeneth," 2 Corinthians 3:6 (DR), about which St. Thomas says: "The law without the spirit interiorly impressing the law upon the heart is an occasion of death."

This is also clear if we consider just one proposition taken by itself—for example, God is triune. This truth is understood formally and evidently by the blessed in heaven; it is understood *formally according to the testimony of God the Author of grace* by believers; it is understood materially by the demon who lacks infused faith. What does it mean to say this materially? The demon understands analogically what the subject (God) and the predicate (Triune) naturally signify, but *the formal aspect of this proposition* [*formale huiusce propositionis*] is the verb IS *as testified to by God the author of grace and inasmuch as it is referred to supernatural mysteries*. Now, the demon does not attain the verb *is* as testified to by God the Author of grace, but only as confirmed by the miracles by which there is manifested only an extraordinary intervention of *God the Author of nature*. Hence, the demon perceives all these things *as illuminated by a natural light*, and thus a proportion to the formally supernatural things by which such are to be attained is lacking.

See St. Thomas *In III Sent.*, d. 23, q. 3, a. 3: "*Reason leading to things to be believed* can be taken either *from something created*, as when through some sign we are led to something to be believed, whether concerning God or concerning other things, *or it is taken from the Uncreated Truth itself*, as we believe something that has been divinely said to us through ministers. . . . And in the first manner is faith found in the demons, inasmuch as *from natural knowledge itself, together also from miracles*, which they see to be above nature in a much subtler manner than we do, they are compelled to believe those things that exceed their natural knowledge. However, they do not have faith in the second manner." See Capreolus[, *Defensiones*,] *In III Sent.*, d. 23 against Scotus and Peter Auriol. Also see *ST* I, q. 64, a. 1; II-II, q. 5, a. 2; and *De malo*, q. 16, a. 6.

Hence, just as a student sometimes does not understand a metaphysical principle in itself

{{172}} Thus, we have the profound meaning of the declarations of the [First] Vatican Council concerning "the illumination and inspiration of the Holy Spirit" necessary for saving faith and for "a certain understanding of the mysteries by God's grace."[66]

{{173}} B. *However, the interconnection of the mysteries* and their connection with man's ultimate end is in part revealed and in part deduced by sacred theology. Just as in general metaphysics all notions are ordered under the notion of being, the supreme mystery to which all the others are subordinated is the *mystery of the intimate life of the Deity*, which is expressed explicitly in the dogma *of the Trinity. The supernatural life of grace* to which man has been elevated from the beginning of his creation is revealed as being a participation in the intimate life of God (that is [*seu*], in the divine nature). Original *sin*, and mortal sin in general, is a privation of this life of grace; death and the various *punishments*, such as the punishment of hell, are consequences of sin. However, *redemption* through the *Incarnate Word* is the reparation for sin. Finally, the effects of Redemption are *the Church's life, the power of the sacraments, justification, grace* given to us, and *the supernatural virtues* by which man is ordered to *eternal life*, which consists in the vision and enjoyment [*fruitione*] of the divine essence and the *Holy Trinity*.

These connections were revealed and constitute *the doctrine of faith* preached by Christ and the apostles before coming to be arranged by sacred theology. However, this science explains these connections more explicitly and deduces theological conclusions from them, just as metaphysics more explicitly proposes the [inter]connections of the truths of natural reason. Theology thus is "faith seeking understanding" and properly, as St. Thomas said, "a science subalternated to the knowledge [*scientia*] of God and of the blessed" (*ST* I, q. 1, a. 2), and "a kind of impression of the divine knowledge [*scientia*]" in us (*ST* I, q. 8, ad 2). In this way, we come to acquire "a most fruitful understanding" of the mysteries and, in reality, the believer is taught by God, the Teacher, so that he come to the evidence of the divine knowledge [*scientia*] (that is [*seu*], to the vision of God's essence).

As regards the subordination [of these mysteries], the mystery of the Trinity is the loftiest of all, and most obscure from our perspective, but when it will be made evident to us under the light of glory, then by that very fact the other supernatural mysteries that essentially depend upon it will be evident for us. For now, we are disciples believing upon the authority of the [M]aster, progressively being initiated into the divine knowledge, and

---

but only materially in examples chosen for an introduction, so too does the demon attain the first, Uncreated Truth (or the essentially supernatural active revelation) only through the miracles by which it is sensibly confirmed. See what will be said below about credibility.

[66] See Fr. Lacordaire, 17th *Conference*, vol. 2, 333–335 (edition in 8vo). [Trans. note: No further citation details given.]

yet, already in the obscurity of faith, we contemplate the connection of the mysteries with the supreme mystery.

The Holy Trinity

Father

Son	Spirit
Creation and elevation	Eternal Life
Original sin	Communion
	of Saints
Incarnation	*Charity*
Redemption	Hope
Church	Divine Faith
Sacraments	Grace
Body of Christ	Sending of
	Holy Spirit

All things go forth from God and return to him; first, the Father is manifested in the creation and supernatural elevation by which we are his sons. Then the Son is manifested in the Incarnation, the Redemption, and in the Church and the sacraments, especially the Eucharist. Finally, the Holy Spirit is manifested in the progressive sanctification of souls all the way to unitive life with God and to the beatific vision.

§3. Explanation of the Notion of Dogma

As we have said, according to the Church, dogmas are related to revealed mysteries as an assertion is related {{174}} to the thing that is asserted. It is called a defined dogma if it is proposed by a solemn judgment of the Church; it is called a Catholic dogma if it is proposed by the ordinary and universal magisterium of the Church without a solemn definition.

Hence, dogma is related to the judgment of *the teaching Church* (*ecclesia docens*) just as the proposition externally formulated by a human teacher is related to his internal judgment; and dogma is related to the judgment of faith of the *learning Church* (*ecclesia discens*) as a rule or norm as the proposition formulated by the teacher is to the mind of the disciple. Thus, this Catholic notion of dogma differs in an essential manner from the modernist notion holding that the proposition of revelation is not properly a *teaching authority* but only a right expression of Christian experience.

Inasmuch as it is a given proposition to be believed, dogma is something *complex*, whereas, on the other hand, a mystery of the faith—namely, the thing itself believed—is *something incomplex* (for example, the mystery of the intimate life of God). This is explained by St. Thomas in *ST* II-II, q. 1, a. 2 (Whether the object of faith is something complex according to the manner of an enunciable statement?):

I respond that it must be said that known things are in the knower according to the mode of the knower. However, the characteristic mode of the human intellect is to know the truth by composing and dividing, as we said earlier (ST I, q. 85, a. 5). And therefore, the human intellect knows things that are simple of themselves according to a kind of complex expression: just as, on the other hand, the Divine Intellect knows in an incomplex manner those things that of themselves are complex. Therefore, the object of faith can be considered in two ways. In one way, it can be considered *from the perspective of the very thing that is believed.* And thus understood, the object of faith is something *incomplex,* namely the thing itself, about which faith is had. In another way, it can be considered *from the perspective of the believer.* And from this perspective, the object of faith is something *complex according to the manner of an enunciable statement.*

Likewise, in ad 2: "*The believer's act [of faith] is not terminated at the enunciable statement but instead at the reality [thus known].* For we only form enunciable statements so that we may have knowledge of things through them. Just as this holds in science, so too does it hold for faith." And in ad 3: "However, the vision *in patria* will not be akin to an enunciable statement but, rather, to simple understanding." Thus, we have a sufficient explanation for the distinction between a dogmatic proposition and the believed mystery. *What is believed is not the dogmatic formula; instead, what is believed is, by the mediation of this created formula, the mystery itself,* the "depths of God," as St. Paul says. The *uncreated,* absolutely supernatural mystery of God's intimate life is the primary object of our faith, which, hence, is essentially supernatural, although the notions from which dogmatic formulas are composed are natural, such as the notions of nature and of person.[67]

---

[67] And this is not considered enough by nominalists and Molinists who hold that our faith is only modally supernatural, hence holding that natural faith, like that found in the demons, has the same formal specificative object as does our supernatural, infused faith.

In reality, on the contrary, the infused light of faith illuminates and elevates the notions and [intellectual] word by which the dogmatic formula is composed. Indeed, in this formula, the verb *is* can be affirmed in various manners: In the natural faith had by demons it is affirmed naturally, under the natural light [of its intellect] on account of the evidence of signs (ST II-II, q. 5, a. 2, ad 2); in infused supernatural faith it is affirmed supernaturally and infallibly under the infused light [of faith].

Thus, analogically, the same conclusion is affirmed in various manners, either on account of the evidence of a demonstration or on account of the authority of a teacher, and then faith and science concerning the same proposition are specifically diversified as *habitus* [pl.] on account of the diversity of formal motive.

[Trans. note: Earlier on this topic, Fr. Garrigou-Lagrange cites Éduouard Hugon, *Cursus philosophiae Thomisticae,* vol. 3, *Metaphysica* (Paris: Lethielleux, 1935), pt. 1 (*Metaphysica psychologica*), 136–137 (On the *species* and word required for supernatural knowledge).]

However, among dogmas (that is, among things to be believed), *certain ones are called articles of faith; they are the principal things to be believed*, which after the manner of the first principles of reason, involve a special connection to other things to be believed which are contained in them in some manner. Thus, our faith is reduced to twelve (or fourteen, according to some) articles of faith determined in the Apostles' Creed.[68] *The Catechism of the Council of Trent* explains the division of the Creed as follows:

> Christianity proposes to the faithful many truths which, either separately {{175}} or in general, must be held with an assured and firm faith. Among these what must first and necessarily be believed by all is that which God Himself has taught us as the *foundation* and summary *of truth concerning the unity of the Divine Essence, the distinction of Three Persons*, and the actions which are peculiarly attributed to each. The pastor should teach that the Apostles' Creed briefly comprehends the doctrine of this mystery. For, as has been observed by our predecessors in the faith, who have treated this subject with great piety and accuracy, the Creed seems to be divided into *three* principal *parts*: one describing *the First Person of the Divine Nature, and the stupendous work of the creation*; another, the *Second Person, and the mystery of man's redemption*; a third, *the Third Person, the head and source of our sanctification*; the whole being expressed in various and most appropriate propositions.[69]

---

[68] See *ST* II-II, q. 1, a. 6 and 8.

[69] Part 1: 1. I believe in one God, the Father Almighty, creator of heaven and of earth.
Part 2: 2. And in one Lord Jesus Christ, the Only-Begotten Son of God, our Lord.
   3. Who was conceived by the Holy Spirit, born of the Virgin Mary.
   4. Who died under Pontius Pilate, was crucified, died, and buried.
   5. He descended into hell; on the third day, he rose from the dead.
   6. He ascended to heaven, sits at the right of God the Father Almighty.
   7. Thence is he to come to judge the living and the dead.
Part 3: 8. I believe in the Holy Spirit, the Lord and life-giver, who proceeds from the Father and the Son.
   9. I believe in the Holy Catholic Church, the Communion of saints.
   10. The remission of sins.
   11. The resurrection of the flesh.
   12. Life Eternal.

However, these articles correspond to the following mysteries whose connection we indicated above:
   Part 1: The mystery of the divine paternity, and the mystery of Creation.
   Part 2: The mysteries of the divine filiation, the Incarnation, and the Redemption.
   Part 3: The mysteries of the procession of the Holy Spirit, the sanctification of souls, and life eternal.

§4. On the Immutability of Dogma and on Its Progressive Understanding

According to the [First] Vatican Council, as was said above, "The *meaning* of the sacred dogmas *is perpetually to be retained* which our Holy Mother Church has once declared."[70] Nevertheless, as the Council said in the same document, *Dei filius*, citing the words of St. Vincent of Lérins, this is true in such a way that there is "*growth* and abundant progress in *understanding*, knowledge, and wisdom, in each and all, in individuals and in the *whole Church* at all times and in the progress of ages, but only within the proper limits, i.e., *within the same dogma, the same meaning*, the same judgment."[71]

To explain this, we must distinguish the proposition of the doctrine of faith (A) after Christ and the apostles and (B) before Christ.

A. *After Christ and the apostles, the same doctrine of the faith already perfectly revealed is more and more explicitly proposed by the Church.* The [First] Vatican Council speaks of this proposition. Indeed, it says: "For the doctrine of faith that God has revealed has not been proposed like a philosophical system to be perfected by human ingenuity; rather, it has been entrusted to the spouse of Christ as a divine trust to be faithfully kept and infallibly declared."[72]

Hence, after Christ and the apostles, revelation is complete and no new common revelation is made; the only new revelations that are made are private ones, but they do not pertain to the Church's infallible teaching.[73] Moreover, *men cannot perfect, through their own ingenuity, the divine doctrine* {{176}} *handed on to the Church;* they would adulterate it or mix fallible elements into it. Therefore, the Church can neither increase nor decrease the doctrine transmitted to her by Christ and the apostles; and therefore, *the doctrine of faith* IN ITSELF *is immutable, not to be perfected,* for in order for the truth of faith to be believed, there is need of divine revelation by which it is constituted as something to be believed IN ITSELF.

Nonetheless, FROM OUR PERSPECTIVE, the number of things to be

---

[Trans. note: Fr. Garrigou-Lagrange does not cite the text. It is *Roman Catechism*, pt. 1, prol. ("Division of the Creed"). Translation taken from the ecclesiastically approved *Catechism of the Council of Trent*, trans. John A. McHugh and Charles J. Callan (Rockford: TAN, 1982), 13. Emphases are based on Fr. Garrigou-Lagrange's text.]

[70] [First] Vatican Council, *Dei filius*, ch. 4 (Denzinger, no. 3020).

[71] Ibid. See the canons of *Dei filius* (Denzinger, nos. 3021–3043).

[72] Ibid., ch. 4 (Denzinger, no. 3020).

[73] See ibid., ch. 2 (Denzinger, no. 1787) and Pius X, Decree of the Holy Office, *Lamentabili sane exitu*, no. 21 (Denzinger, no. 3421).

believed can be increased inasmuch as revealed doctrine is proposed more explicitly by the *Church's magisterium*; for the doctrine already revealed by Christ is not to be believed, *from our perspective*, except when it is sufficiently proposed by the Church. However, the Church proposes the revealed truths contained in Sacred Scripture or Tradition gradually and successively, first by her ordinary magisterium and afterwards by a solemn judgment through a definition, and there can be many formulas for one and the same dogma, with later formulas being more explicit than the earlier ones. Thus, she proposes *things anew but not new things*.

For example, the primitive formula of the dogma of the Incarnation was "The Word was made flesh." Later on, this was more explicitly defined: "The Word, consubstantial with God the Father, was made man." Likewise, all the faithful of the primitive Church believed that the Blessed Virgin Mary was "full of grace" without restriction. However, later on, this fullness of grace was more explicitly defined as also containing the grace of the Immaculate Conception.[74] Thus, in the natural order, the first principles of reason are expressed more explicitly by philosophy than by natural reason. Likewise, real definitions through genus and difference are more explicit than are nominal or common definitions. (For example, the Thomistic definition of freedom is more explicit than the common definition, but it does not express something else.) And frequently, greater labor is required in the "hunt for a good definition," as Aristotle said,[75] than for deducing the properties from an explicated definition. For instance, Molinists do not yet agree with Thomists with regard to the definition of human freedom.

Hence, after the apostles, in accord with the ongoing explication of dogmas, *understanding of the things increases for the whole Church*, with the assistance of the Holy Spirit, though without there being a new revelation. This is treated at greater length in the treatise on the Church.[76]

---

[74] From the beginning of Christ's Church, all the faithful believed, implicitly and in act, in the Immaculate Conception, whereas they believed without restriction in the fullness of the Blessed Virgin Mary's grace. And those who denied the Immaculate Conception did not know that they believed this truth implicitly and in act. This denial did not proceed from their faith but from their erring reason. Later, the Church explicitly defined what in reality was implicitly in act in the divine faith of all. Likewise, a given philosopher, having the true common notion of the free will, can err when he defines this philosophically, and later find the true philosophical definition of free will; he had that implicitly in the notion held through common sense but did not know that he had it already.

[75] See Aristotle, *Posterior Analytics*, bk. 2. Also see St. Thomas, *In II Post. An.*, lect. 14–20. [Trans. note: See "On the Search for Definitions According to Aristotle and St. Thomas" in *Philosophizing in Faith: Essays on the Beginning and End of Wisdom*, trans. Matthew K. Minerd (Providence, RI: Cluny Media, 2019), 21–34.]

[76] See Johannes Vincentius De Groot, *Summa apologetica de ecclesia catholica ad mentem S. Thomae Aquinatis*, 3rd edition (Ratisbon: Manz, 1906), 309, 373, 374, and 780. Also see

This explication is made in a threefold manner:

(a) *The scientific proposition* of those things that hitherto were indeed *explicitly* believed but *in a popular manner*. Thus, the mystery of the Holy Trinity was first handed on in a general form but later on the consubstantiality of the divine persons was defined.

(b) *The explicit proposition* of those things that are only *implicitly* contained in the sources of revelation. For example, the Immaculate Conception of the Blessed Virgin Mary.

(c) {{177}} *The learned and certain proposition* of those things that have only been taught *incidentally* [*obiter*] or *in practice*. This progress, like the preceding kind, suffices only for secondary truths that do not need to be believed explicitly. Thus, for example, there is the case of the validity of baptism conferred by heretics.

The principal cause of this progress is the invisible assistance of the Holy Spirit; the secondary causes are the studious investigation of theologians and the devotion of the faithful. Among the occasions [for this progress] heresies must be counted, as well as the progress of the natural sciences, especially of philosophy.[77]

B. *Before Christ, the same doctrine of faith was manifested with increasing explicitness through successive revelations.* Thus the number of articles of faith increased while the faith of the first Fathers was in its sub-

---

Vacant, *Études sur le Concile du Vatican*, vol. 2, 281, and his articles "Dogme" and "Explicite" in *Dictionnaire théologie catholique*. [Trans. note: Here, Fr. Garrigou-Lagrange is speaking a bit loosely. As he himself has noted before, the Church can be considered in theology from several perspectives, though always within the unity of the one science of theology. The text of De Groot to which he refers is within the continuation of apologetics. It is not primarily concerned with the inner essence of the Church and her properties in detail, as one would find, for instance, in the magisterial, multiple-volume work of Cardinal Charles Journet on this topic. See Charles Journet, *L'église du verbe incarné, essai de théologie spéculative*, in *Œuvres complètes de Charles Journet*, vols. 1–5, ed. René and Dominique Mougel (Saint-Maurice, CH: Éditions Saint-Augustin, 1998–2005). On the state of scholastic treatise *De ecclesia* in the first half of the twentieth century, see Joseph C. Fenton, "Towards an Adequate Theological Treatise *De Ecclessia*," in *The Church of Christ: A Collection of Essays by Monsignor Joseph C. Fenton*, ed. Christian Washburn (Tacoma, WA: Cluny Media, 2016), 1–19.]

[77] *Regarding the knowledge of the Apostles*, see Vacant, *Études*, vol. 1, 378: "According to the Councils of Trent and the [First] Vatican Council, all the truths that enter into the deposit of Christian revelation were manifested to the Apostles before the death of St. John. Does it follow that the Apostles explicitly knew all the points that the Church has defined or that she will define through the centuries? ... It would be temerarious to think that the infused science of the Apostles was inferior to the acquired science of the Fathers and of later theologians; however, in manifesting to the apostles with an incomparable *clarity*, the *necessary principles* that constitute the *foundation* of Christian doctrine, God was able to allow them to not know the *contingent applications* that would be made of them through the ages."

stance the same as the faith of those coming after them, being supernatural faith with the same primary formal object (the intimate life of God) and the same formal motive (the authority of God who reveals).

This is explained by St. Thomas in *ST* II-II, q. 1, a. 7.[78] In brief, he holds that the first things that are believed [*prima credibilia*] were revealed before Christ's coming, indeed from the beginning of the world, and that they are, as it were, the first principles for the whole of faith, implicitly containing the other things that are believed [*prima credibilia*], which would come to be revealed later. These *first things to be believed* are that *God exists* and *that he repays man according to his deeds* [*remunerator est*]. Later on, the mysteries of the Incarnation, the Redemption, and the Trinity were gradually revealed in an increasingly explicit manner. However, the faith in question is always specifically the same because as St. Thomas says, "Whatever was believed at a later time was contained in the faith of the Fathers who came before, albeit implicitly."[79]

{{178}} Hence, the two first things to be believed—namely, that God exists and that he repays men according to their deeds—are not only con-

---

[78] Whether the articles of faith have increased over the course of time? "I respond that it must be said that the articles of faith stand in relation to the teaching [*doctrina*] of faith just as do *per se nota* principles in the teaching [*doctrina*] that is had by way of natural reason. A particular order is found in these principles, as certain ones are contained in others in a simpler manner—just as all principles are reduced to this as to a first, namely, 'It is impossible to affirm and to deny [i.e., one and the same thing at one and the same time from one and the same [perspective],' as is obvious from Aristotle's discussions in the fourth book of the *Metaphysics*. Similarly, all the articles of faith are implicitly contained in certain first things that are believed [*in aliquibus primis credibilibus*]; as it is believed that God exists and that He has Providence concerning men—as is said in Heb 11:6 (DR), 'For he that cometh to God must believe that he is: and is a rewarder to them that seek him.' For, in the Divine Existence is included all that we believe to exist eternally in God, in which our beatitude consists. However, contained within faith in Providence there are included all those things temporally dispensed of by God for the sake of man's salvation, such things being the way to beatitude. And in this manner also, some of the of the other subsequent articles are contained in others: for example, faith in the redemption of man implicitly contains the Incarnation of Christ, His Passion, and all things of this sort.

"Therefore, it must be said thus, namely, that *with regard to the substance of the articles of faith*, there has not been an increase in them through the passing of time, for whatever was believed at a later time was contained in the faith of the Fathers who came before, although it was so contained in an implicit manner. However, *as regards further explication*, the number of articles did increase, because certain things were explicitly known by those who came later on, which were not explicitly known by those coming before them."

[79] St. Thomas profoundly and precisely wrote *implicitly* and not *virtually*, although this adverb *implicitly* is not understood in the same manner in this question before Christ and after Christ, as we will say in resolving a doubt immediately below.

cerned with God qua Author of nature but, rather, are *concerned with God qua Author of the supernatural order of grace* and with providence and *remuneration* that are *supernatural* and not merely natural. Thus, "The God of Abraham, the God of Isaac, and the God of Jacob," is called, "God our Savior," "the Living God," "God our refuge and our strength" (Ps 45). Likewise, "Thou art my father: my God, and the support of my salvation" (Ps 88:27, DR). It is not a question of God merely qua naturally knowable First Mover and Pure Act, for we cannot say that the supernatural mysteries that we believe were implicitly contained in the natural knowledge that Aristotle had concerning the existence of God drawn from [his knowledge of] sensible things. Natural reason knows God from the formal perspective of *being*, as he is the First Being and the First Cause of natural things. Divine faith knows God from the intimate and most eminent formal perspective of *the Deity*, namely according to his intimate life. See *ST* II-II, q. 174, a. 6: "Inasmuch as it is ordered to faith *in the Deity*, prophetic revelation increased through three distinct eras, namely before the law, under the law, and under grace."

Thus faith, which has always been necessary for salvation, has always been specifically the same faith. Hence, the following proposition has been condemned by the Church: "Faith in the broad sense, which is based upon the testimony of creatures or on a similar reason, is sufficient for justification."[80] Indeed, on the basis of this faith, broadly speaking, God is known as the Author of nature but not as the Heavenly Father, the Author of grace.[81]

Therefore, we must distinguish the time before Christ from the time after Christ and the apostles. Before Christ, the same doctrine of faith is *revealed with increasing explicitness*. After Christ and the apostles, the same doctrine of faith, which was already perfectly revealed, *is proposed with increasing explicitness* by the Church.

A doubt. But why does St. Thomas say that the faith of the Old Testament *implicitly* contains supernatural mysteries that were later revealed by Christ? This transition

---

[80] Sixty-Five Propositions Condemned in the Decree of the Holy Office, March 2, 1679, no. 23 (Denzinger, no. 2123).

[81] The teaching found in this article of St. Thomas perfectly coheres with articles 4 and 5 of the same question in which it is proven that something cannot be simultaneously scientifically known [*scitum*] and believed by the same person in the same respect. For he who scientifically believes in the existence of the Author of nature or that of natural providence cannot believe these truths simultaneously, but he simultaneously can and must believe in the existence of God the Heavenly Father, the Author of grace, and in supernatural providence. Indeed, these are not preambles of faith but are the first to things that are believed [*prima credibilia*], which are to be believed *per se* by all. Cf. *De veritate*, q. 14, a. 9, ad 8.

from implicit to explicit seems [to pertain] only to the progressive knowledge of dogma after Christ. For to contain *implicitly* is to contain *in act and vaguely* [*actu confuse*]. Why didn't St. Thomas say that the faith of the Old Testament *virtually* contained mysteries that were later on revealed? To contain virtually is to contain not in act and vaguely but in potency, just as a principle virtually contains a conclusion and as a genus contains a subordinate species.

Response: Development [*explication*] (or [*seu*] explication [*explicitatio*]) is twofold, and we have an analogy of this twofold development in natural knowledge: (a) A notion is developed in other subordinate notions; (b) one and the same notion (e.g., that of freedom) is first known vaguely but then later on distinctly.

(a) The notion of being contains, *in act and implicitly*, the inferior notions that express the modalities of being and not something outside of being, for outside of being there is nothing. Hence, being is not a genus, for a genus only *virtually* [*virtute*] (not in act and implicitly) contains subordinate specific differences, which are extrinsic to it; thus, rationality is extrinsic to animality.[82]

{{179}} Likewise, the Deity (the intimate life of God) and supernatural providence, which are the first things to be believed, *in act and implicitly* contain the supernatural mysteries to be revealed later on—namely, the Trinity, the Incarnation, and the Redemption. Indeed, these mysteries are not outside the Deity, nor outside of supernatural providence, just as the modalities of being are not outside of being.

Hence, divine faith, in the Old Testament, developed [*evolvitur*], as does a child's natural reason, which first knows being and later on the other notions of common sense—namely, the notions of truth, goodness, life, intelligence, freedom, and so forth. Therefore, this explication is brought about through new and, nevertheless, extrinsic notions. New things are manifested (and not only the same things in a new manner).

(b) One and the same notion can be first known *vaguely* and then afterwards come to be known *distinctly*. For example, the common notion of freedom is vague, whereas the philosophical notion of freedom is distinct, expressing the genus and specific difference. This development [*explicatio*] is brought about through a greater distinction concerning the same notion, not through new notions.[83]

---

[82] See Billuart, *Summa sancti Thomae*, prooem., a. 7. A proposition contained in the deposit of faith *in a virtually connective manner* [*virtualiter connexive*] does not pertain to faith but to theology; a proposition contained *implicitly* or *virtually in an inclusive manner* [*virtualiter inclusive*] in the deposit of faith is revealed *in itself* even if not yet *from our perspective* because it is not yet proposed by the Church.

[83] Most Thomists and many theologians of all the schools hold (against Gabriel Vasquez, Andreas de Vega, Francisco Suarez, and [Juan de] Lugo) that the Church cannot define as *a dogma of faith* a theological conclusion that is revealed only virtually in a connective manner but instead can only infallibly condemn the denial of this certain theological conclusion. Indeed, a dogma of the faith must be contained "in the word of God, written or handed down

Likewise, after Christ, the Incarnation of the Word was first known vaguely and later on came to be distinctly known through the formula of consubstantiality. Or the fullness of the Blessed Virgin Mary's grace was first known vaguely but then afterwards came to be known distinctly through the formula of the Immaculate Conception. Likewise, through many propositions the Church came to explain given complex facts like, [for example,] the administration of the sacraments instituted by Christ.

Thus, both before and after Christ's coming there is only an explication of the first things to be believed, though not in the same way.

What we have said suffices for setting forth the theological explanation of the notions of mystery and of dogma.

... as having been divinely revealed" ([First] Vatican Council, *Dei filius*, ch. 3, Denzinger, no. 3011), and is to be believed *only* on account of the authority of God who reveals. However, what is only connected with revealed things cannot be called revealed simply and properly but is distinguished from revelation. Hence, the Church would not only infallibly care for and explain the deposit of faith but *would perfect the doctrine of the faith and would establish new dogmas*, if through a definition it makes *de fide* what beforehand was not an object of divine faith. Finally, if the aforementioned could be defined as a dogma of faith, why could not certain theological conclusions that are quite remote also be defined? Thus, a great part of the *Summa theologiae* of St. Thomas could become a dogma of faith—which cannot be admitted, since these things were not simply and properly revealed.

Therefore, it is necessary to distinguish accurately between a theological conclusion that is only virtually-connectively revealed and a truth that is implicitly but formally revealed. In reality, it is sometimes very difficult in practice to make this distinction before the Church's definition. See Salmanticenses, *Cursus theologicus, De fide*, disp. 1, no. 124–133; De Groot, *De ecclesia*, q. 9, a. 2; Adolphe Tanquerey, *Synopsis theologiae dogmaticae: ad mentem s. Thomae Aquinatis hodiernis moribus accommodata*, 12th ed., vol. 2, *De fide* (Rome: Desclée et socii, 1921), no. 190. And other texts . . . [Trans. note: Details added for Tanquerey. The citations end with ". . .", which has been translated as "And other texts . . ."]

Concerning this matter, we cannot admit the particular opinion of Fr. Marín-Sola, O.P., exposited in his book *La evolucion homogénea del dogma católico*, 2 vols. (Valencia: La Ciencia Tomista, 1923). [See *The Homogeneous Evolution of Catholic Dogma*, trans. Antonio T. Piñon (Manila: Santo Tomas University Press, 1988).] See what we said above in ch. 1, a. 1, §5 about theological conclusions and also in Réginald Garrigou-Lagrange, *The One God: A Commentary on the First Part of St. Thomas's Summa*, trans. Bede Rose (St. Louis, MO: B. Herder, 1943), 49–56. [Trans. note: At the beginning of this paragraph, reading *corca* as *circa*.]

As regards the contrary opinion, see Andreas de Vega *Tridentini decreti de iustificatione expositio, et defensio libris 15. distincta, totam doctrinam iustificationis complectentibus*, bk. 11, ch. 39; Suarez, *De fide*, disp. 3, sect. 11; De Lugo, *De fide*, disp. 1, nos. 268–277.

CHAPTER SIX

On the Notion of Supernaturality

{{180}} This chapter is divided into two articles:

Art. 1. The Catholic notion and heterodox notions of supernaturality
Art. 2. The theological explication of the Catholic notion of supernaturality

ART. 1: THE CATHOLIC NOTION AND HETERODOX NOTIONS OF SUPERNATURALITY

§1. The state of the question and the nominal definition of supernaturality

§2. The Catholic notion of supernaturality and of the supernatural order

§3. Heterodox notions of supernaturality and of the supernatural order

§1. (A) The State of the Question and (B) the Nominal Definition of Supernaturality

A. *State of the question.* After the notions of revelation, mystery, and dogma, we must set forth the notion of supernaturality and of the supernatural order. Indeed, we intend to prove against naturalists (or [*seu*] rationalists) the possibility and existence of some revelation of supernatural mysteries—that is, that Christianity is not only a superior form of the natural evolution of man's religious sentiment but instead is an essentially supernatural religion that is infallibly true in all its dogmas and precepts.

However, these adversaries—namely, naturalists—simply speaking, either deny the existence of a supernatural order (as with evolutionistic pantheists, who identify the divine nature and intelligence with human intelligence in perpetual progress), or they deny the knowability of a supernatural order (as with agnostics, whether they are empiricists or idealists like the positivists and Kantians).

And therefore, from the beginning of the discussion, we must indicate what the Catholic Church intends to signify by means of these words: "the supernatural order." In other words, we must begin by setting forth the Catholic notion of supernaturality. Naturalists, who deny the existence or knowability of a supernatural order, either admit our definition of this order (and then their denial of it is a contradiction of our affirmation)[1] or they understand something [different] by this term and first must be taught what this term signifies according to the Catholic Church. Otherwise, disputation would be impossible.

B. *The nominal definition of Supernaturality.* Indeed, the *nominal and vague definition* of supernaturality can already be drawn from a mere consideration of this term, for "supernatural" {{181}} signifies *that which is above nature.* However, the term "nature" commonly has a twofold signification: It expresses either the essence of some given thing (e.g., as when we speak of the nature of gold, silver, or of man) or the complex of all the things of the universe, depending on each other in accord with determinate laws. Therefore, "supernatural" commonly signifies "that which is above nature taken as a whole—namely, above the laws of nature." Hence, an effect that cannot be *produced* according to the laws of nature is called supernatural, and a truth that cannot be *known* according to the natural laws of our intellect is called supernatural.

From this nominal definition, the state of the question is clearer, and the solution to this question depends on the notion of nature in general, and in particular on the distinction between created nature and the divine nature. And indeed, *pantheists*, who hold that God and all things in the universe are of one and the same nature,[2] deny the existence of a supernatural order because nothing is above nature, which they hold is identical with God. According to them, God is the immanent principle of the whole of natural evolution. However, those who, like the *deists*, admit that God is essentially distinct from the world, while denying that he can act freely outside the order of nature, reject the possibility of a supernatural effect—namely, of miracles. Finally, certain *theists*, such as semi-rationalists, admit that God is essentially distinct from the world and likewise admit the possibility of miracles, but they do not wish to distinguish in God an order of natural

---

[1]   [Trans. note: The text appears to be corrupted here. Reading "vel admittunt nostrum definitionem huiusce ordinis, et tunc eorum negatio est contradictio nostrae affirmationis, vel . . ." for "vel admittunt nostrum definitionem huiusce ordinis, et tunc eorum negatio contradictio nostrae affirmationem huiusce ordinis, et tunc eorum negatio est contradictio nostrae affirmationis, vel . . ."]

[2]   See [First] Vatican Council, *Dei filius,* can. 1.3 and 1.4 (Denzinger, nos. 3023 and 3024).

mysteries (e.g., the intimate reconciliation of the divine immutability and freedom) in contrast to an order of supernatural mysteries (e.g., the Holy Trinity). Hence, they admit the possibility of supernatural effects but not of supernatural truth. Against all of these various positions, the Catholic Church affirms not only the existence of an order of supernatural effects, but even that of an order of supernatural truths. Therefore, we must consider what the Church exactly understands by the term "supernaturality."

§2. The Catholic Notion of Supernaturality and of the Supernatural Order

The Catholic Church defines the supernatural not only vaguely as "what is above nature" but precisely as "what is above every created nature inasmuch as it exceeds the powers and exigencies of any created nature whatsoever," although it does not exceed the passive perfectible capacity of our nature, as well as that which befits our nature. Hence, supernaturality, according to the Church, is at least twofold, namely: (1) *the supernaturality of miracles, which exceed the efficient powers* (or causality) and exigencies of any created nature whatsoever, but not the knowing powers of human nature; (2) *the supernaturality of the mysteries strictly speaking, and of the life of grace and glory, which exceed* not only the efficient powers and exigencies of any created nature whatsoever, but also *the knowing and appetitive powers* (or [*vel*] natural merit) of any created intellectual nature whatsoever.

(1) This Catholic doctrine can quite clearly be seen, as regards *the supernaturality of miracles*, in the definitions of the [First] Vatican Council, *Dei filius*, canon 4.3,[3] and in the corresponding chapter, wherein it is said that miracles are "divine facts . . . which as they manifestly display the omnipotence [and infinite knowledge] of God, they are the most certain signs of divine revelation adapted to the intelligence of all men."[4] This means that miracles exceed all the effective powers of any created nature whatsoever, though not our reason's knowing power.

(2) As regards *the supernaturality of mysteries strictly speaking, as also for* {{182}} *the supernaturality of grace and of glory,* the doctrine of the Church can be seen in (A) her condemnation of naturalism, semi-naturalism, and Pelagianism, as well as in (B) her condemnation of the pseudo-supernaturalism of Baius and the Jansenists. Indeed, the naturalists and semi-naturalists deny that mysteries are above the *knowing* powers of our reason; the pseudo-supernaturalists deny that the mysteries of Christianity, grace, and glory

---

[3] See Denzinger, no. 3043.
[4] Ibid., ch. 3 (Denzinger, no. 3009).

are above the *exigencies* of our nature.

These declarations by the Church must be treated briefly.

A. *Against naturalism*, we have the definitions that have already been cited from the [First] Vatican Council: "If anyone says that man cannot be called by God to a knowledge and perfection that surpasses the natural but that he can and must by himself, through constant progress, finally arrive at the possession of all that is true and good, let him be anathema."[5] Likewise, in the fourth chapter of *Dei filius*:

> The perpetual common belief of the Catholic Church has held and holds also this: there is a *twofold order of knowledge*, distinct not only in its *principle* but also in its *object*; in its principle, because in the one we know by natural reason, in the other by divine faith; in its object, because apart from what natural reason can attain, there are proposed to our belief *mysteries* that are hidden in God that can never be known unless they are revealed by God.[6]

Nay, as is said in the same text, according to the Church, "Divine mysteries by their very nature exceed the created (and not only the human) intellect."[7]

Before this, the Council condemned pantheism,[8] which is the foundation for naturalism, for from pantheism it follows that God did not freely create the world and cannot act freely *ad extra* outside the determinism of nature (in other words, he cannot perform miracles), nor does he have a supernatural life infinitely exceeding the various degrees of created life. Likewise, see Pius IX's *Syllabus of Errors*,[9] especially the first proposition, from which the second, third, fourth, and fifth propositions follow.

(a) *Against semi-rationalism*, the Church has defined: "Divine mysteries by their very nature so exceed the created intellect that, even when they have been communicated in revelation and received by faith, they remain covered by the veil of faith"[10] "and cannot be understood and demonstrated from natural principles by reason, if it is properly trained."[11]

Hence, according to the Church, the order of supernatural truth *objectively* exceeds every created intellect, so that mysteries of this order cannot be known without supernatural revelation, nor can they be demonstrated after revelation is made.

(b) *Against Pelagianism and semi-Pelagianism*, it has been defined that in order to believe supernatural mysteries with divine faith, we need not only external revelation but

---

[5] Ibid., can. 2.3 (Denzinger, no. 3028).
[6] Ibid., ch. 4 (Denzinger, no. 3015).
[7] See ibid. (Denzinger, no. 3016).
[8] See ibid., can. 1.3 and 1.4 (Denzinger, nos. 3023 and 3024).
[9] See Pius IX, *Syllabus of Errors*, nos. 1–8 (Denzinger, nos. 2901–2908).
[10] [First] Vatican Council, *Dei filius*, ch. 4 (Denzinger, no. 3016).
[11] See ibid., can. 4.1 (Denzinger, no. 3041).

also stand in need of internal grace. This is likewise the case in order that one may love God and act as is necessary for salvation—nay, even "for a pious affect of belief," which represents the beginning of faith. However, according to the Church, this internal grace is above all natural powers, is gratuitously given to us by God, and is indeed not owed to our natural merit, nor even to our prayer.[12]

Hence, according to the Church, the order of supernatural truth and life exceeds the *powers* of our nature not only objectively but also *subjectively*—that is, inasmuch as even after revelation, which objectively proposes supernatural things, we cannot subjectively believe and love them as we ought without an internal supernatural grace, for there needs to be a proportion between the act of knowledge or of love and the object that is known or loved.

B. *Against the pseudo-supernaturalism of Baius*, the Church defines that the supernatural order of truth and of life absolutely exceeds not only the powers but also the *exigencies* of human and angelic nature.[13] It suffices to cite the twenty-first proposition of Baius: {{183}} "The sublimation of human nature and its elevation to participation in the divine nature were *due* to the integrity of man in his first state and are therefore to be called natural, not supernatural." This condemned thesis of Baius was also found in the first Protestants, such as Luther, and later on the Jansenists admitted the same doctrine.[14] Hence, they said: Human nature, deprived of the gift of original justice, "without the grace of the Liberator is not free except for evil."[15]

In our own days, modernists have also denied that the mysteries and life of Christianity exceed the exigencies of our nature.[16]

Thus is the Catholic notion of supernaturality sufficiently determined both from the perspective of causality (miracles) and from the perspective of knowledge (mysteries). But when the Church speaks about the supernatural order, without qualification, it is a question of the order of supernatural truth and life.[17]

---

[12] See the Councils of Carthage (canons 4 and 5, Denzinger, nos. 226 and 227), the Council of Ephesus (canon 1, Denzinger, no. 267), the letters of St. Celestine I (Denzinger, 138 and 141, old numbering), and the Second Council of Orange (canons 3–7 and 25, Denzinger, nos. 373–377 and 395).

[13] See Pius V, *Ex omnibus afflictionibus*, nos. 1–8, 21, 24, 34, 42, 61–64, 69, and 79 (Denzinger, nos. 1901–1908, 1921, 1924, 1934, 1942, 1961–1964, 1969, and 1979).

[14] See papal bull, issued by Pope Clement XI, *Unigenitus Dei filius*, Sept. 8, 1713, against the Jansenistic errors of Pasquier Quesnel, nos. 34 and 35 (Denzinger, nos. 2434 and 2435).

[15] See ibid., no. 38 (Denzinger, no. 2438).

[16] See Pius X, *Pascendi dominici gregis*, no. 37 (Denzinger, 2103, old numbering).

[17] See [First] Vatican Council, *Dei filius*, ch. 4 (Denzinger, no. 3014); Leo XIII, Decree of the Holy Office, *Post obitum*, nos. 36 and 38 (Denzinger, nos. 3236 and 3238); and Pius X, *Pascendi dominici gregis*, no. 37 (Denzinger, 2103, old numbering).

§3. Heterodox Notions of Supernaturality

These heterodox notions are the aforementioned that have been condemned. They can be divided thus: (1) as regards the supernaturality of the mysteries, and (2) as regards the supernaturality of miracles. This must be set forth in order to make clear how errors opposed to each other agree in the confusion of nature and grace.

(1) *As regards the supernaturality of the mysteries and life of Christianity*. In a way, there is an opposition of naturalists and Pelagians on the one hand and pseudo-supernaturalists (i.e., the first Protestants, Baius, and Jansen) on the other, and nevertheless, they agree in the confusion of the natural and supernatural orders. Generally speaking, extreme, erroneous systems arise from the same ignorance of the loftier conception in which the various aspects of truth are reconciled.

A. *Naturalists*, semi-rationalists, and Pelagians openly destroy or diminish the supernaturality of the mysteries and of the Christian life, for naturalism reduces supernatural mysteries to natural mysteries that can be known without revelation, at least as regards their existence, likewise reducing the Christian life to natural morality [*ad honestatem naturalem*]. Semi-rationalists reduce supernatural mysteries to natural mysteries, which can be demonstrated, at least after revelation has been made. Pelagianism reduces the Christian life[18] to the natural moral life, inasmuch as we can live as Christians without internal grace, at least after revelation has been made.

Hence, non-Catholics [*acatholici*], especially rationalists, often use the term "natural" in a kind of knowledge-centric sense to indicate what can be sensed, using the term "supernatural" for whatever goes beyond [sense] experience; or they use the term "natural" for whatever is finite, while using the term "supernatural" for that which is infinite, not distinguishing a twofold order of truth in God.

In these conceptions, something exceeding our natural powers does indeed remain, but it represents a kind of excess of natural mystery, not a supernatural one. This outlook has the tendency to fall into radical optimism concerning the present state of humanity, holding that human nature is absolutely self-sufficient and autonomous [thereby holding] that original sin is something to be denied.[19]

B. On the other hand, *the pseudo-supernaturalism* of the first Protestants, Baius, and the Jansenists exaggerates the befittingness of our elevation to the supernatural order, such that this elevation would be owed to the exigencies of nature and, hence, would not be gratuitous (or supernatural). Thus, they hold that grace exceeds the powers but not the exigencies of nature and was owed to the full integrity of the first

---

[18] [Trans. note: Reading *vitam* for *vitae*.]

[19] See Council of Carthage, can. 2 (Denzinger, no. 223).

man, as was immortality.[20]

{{184}} This outlook tends toward a form of pessimism as regards the present state of humanity—namely, inasmuch as they exaggerate the consequences of original sin, the existence of which is denied by Pelagians and naturalists. According to the Jansenists, man, deprived of the gift of original justice, is now free only to do evil.

C. Notwithstanding this opposition, *naturalism and pseudo-supernaturalism agree in their confusion of the natural and supernatural orders*: Because according to the former outlook, there is not, simply speaking, an order exceeding *the powers* of our nature, which is more or less identified with the divine nature; and according to the other conception, the supernatural order exceeds the powers, though *not the exigencies*, of our nature. And, in fact, the pseudo-supernaturalism of the first Protestants led to the naturalism of contemporary liberal Protestants. True supernaturality is denied by both sides, though in different ways: either in relation to our nature's powers, or in relation to its exigencies.[21]

(2) *As regards the supernaturality of miracles*, there are also two principal heterodox notions. The first pertains to *determinism*, which openly destroys the supernaturality of miracles and denies what exceeds the powers of nature. The other seems to exaggerate the supernaturality of miracles inasmuch as it affirms that miracles exceed even our knowledge (or [*seu*] is unknowable). This conception pertains to *agnosticism*. These two notions, which seem to be opposed to each other, are nonetheless reduced to naturalism.

A. *Determinism* holds that everything arises of necessity, in accord with the determinate laws of nature, so that God himself could not act outside the order of physical laws, just as he cannot act outside of mathematical or metaphysical laws. And therefore, miracles would not be above the powers and laws of created nature (as was held by Nicolas Malebranche, who asserted that miracles are not above the natural laws of the superior world of the angels)—nay, they would not be above the powers and laws of sensible nature (as is held by contemporary determinists). Nevertheless, many liberal Protestants and modernists concede *that a miracle is an extraordinary natural fact*, one that has not yet been scientifically explained, though which religious sentiment can attribute to the divine

---

[20] Pius V, *Ex omnibus afflictionibus*, nos. 21, 78 (Denzinger, nos. 1921, 1978).

[21] Moreover, Luther said that the grace by which we are justified is only an external favor of God but is not a supernatural gift poured out into our hearts through the Holy Spirit. (See Council of Trent, *Decree on Justification*, can. 11, Denzinger, no. 1561.) Likewise, Baius said, "The justice by which the sinner is justified through faith consists formally in the observance of the commandments; it is the justice of works. It does not consist in any sort of grace in the soul by which man . . . is internally renewed and is made a sharer in the divine nature." (Pius V, *Ex omnibus afflictionibus*, no. 42, Denzinger, no. 1942; see also no. 44, Denzinger, no. 1944). This represents the reduction of the Christian life to natural morality [*honestatem naturalem*], as is also found in the Pelagians.

benevolence, such as an answer to a prayer. Hence, miracles would not have an ontological value, as a seal from God for confirming revelation most certainly, but *would have only a symbolic value* for summoning the soul to an examination of religion and of [religion's] conformity with the aspirations and exigencies of our nature.[22]

B. *Agnosticism* holds, by contrast, that the determinism of nature cannot be demonstrated—nay, that utter contingency is more probable, such that *the laws of nature would be fixed and immutable only according to our manner of conceiving and not in reality outside the soul*. And therefore, miracles are not evidently impossible. (Physical science speaks about what is and not about what is possible or impossible). Nevertheless, *a miracle* exceeding all the powers of nature would be *unknowable* for us and would likewise exceed our knowledge, for we know only the phenomena and phenomenal laws, being unable to discern the intervention of a transcendent cause in the world. Indeed, we do not know all the laws of nature and, hence, {{185}} what exceeds them. Nay, [as agnostics would say,] according to our manner of conceiving things, every phenomenon presupposes a prior phenomenon, and a miracle would be a phenomenon without a phenomenal antecedent. That is, it would be contrary to the law or principle of causality. Hence, miracles are unintelligible and cannot have an ontological value for us as a seal from God for confirming revelation in a most certain manner. However, according to certain moderate agnostics, an abrogation of the laws does happen inasmuch as the laws are conceived by us, *an abrogation for our manner of conceiving*, and thus it has a *symbolic value* and summons the soul to an examination of religion and of [religion's] conformity with the aspirations and exigencies of our nature.[23]

C. Hence, agnosticism, although it is opposed to objective determinism, [ultimately] preserves a form of subjective determinism and can be reduced to a form of naturalism.

These are the principal heterodox notions of supernaturality as regards mysteries and as regards miracles. At first glance, some of them appear to increase supernaturality, but in reality, they all diminish supernaturality essentially (as in the case of semi-naturalism) or destroy it (as in the case of naturalism).

ART. 2: THEOLOGICAL EXPLICATION OF THE CATHOLIC NOTION OF SUPERNATURALITY

§1. Definition of supernaturality
§2. Division of supernaturality
§3. What the natural and supernatural orders are
§4. Resolution of objections

---

[22] See our discussion later on in vol. 2, ch. 19 (On the Value of Miracles).
[23] See Blondel, *L'action* (1893), 396.

§1. Definition of Supernaturality

In order to explain the Catholic notion of supernaturality, it is necessary to determine: (A) what "nature" and "natural" signify, for "supernatural" designates what is above nature; (B) precisely what the term "supernatural" signifies; and (C) how the supernatural differs from the connatural, the free, the artificial, and the fortuitous.

A. *What does "nature" signify?* The signification of this term is set forth by St. Thomas in *In* II *Phys*, ch. 1, lect. 1 and 2; *In* V *Meta.*, ch. 4, lect. 5; *ST* I, q. 29, a. 1, ad 4; and *ST* III, q. 2, a. 1. In the last text, the Holy Doctor, following Aristotle, gives the various senses of this term, which is first taken physically but then metaphysically:

"The term 'nature' is designated *from nativity*." Therefore, St. Paul says in Ephesians 2:3 (DR): "We were by nature children of wrath"—that is, from birth.[24] "Whence," says St. Thomas:

At first the term (nature) was imposed (a) to signify *the generation* of living things, {{186}} which is called "birth" or "budding forth," so that the word "nature" designates, as it were, "about to be born." Then, (b) the term "nature" was transferred so as to signify *the principle of this generation*. And because the principle of generation in living things is intrinsic to them, (c) the term "nature" was further employed so as to signify *any intrinsic principle whatsoever of motion*, according to what the Philosopher says in II *Phys.*, (text 3), namely that "nature is the principle of motion in a thing as regards what it is essentially [*per* se] and not according to what is accidental [to it]." (That is, the nature in anything whatsoever is the radical principle of the operations and passions that are *per se* suitable to it. For example, fire of its nature is said to burn, man by his nature desires to know, man by his nature is mortal). (d) However, this principle either is the (substantial) *form* or *matter*. Whence, sometimes nature refers to form, though at other times to matter. (Thus, man is said to be made up of two partial natures.) (e) And because *the end of natural generation* is in that which is generated, namely the essence of the species, which the definition

---

[24] Many rightly note: Since the expression "natural" in this manner denotes the same thing as "original" or that which is connected with the origin, sometimes *in a broad and improper sense* it was employed to designate: (1) *a truly supernatural gift* which, when it is connected with our origin (e.g., the original holiness conveyed to Adam in his creation), is called "natural" in this sense by certain Fathers; (2) *a gratuitous gift* that perfects nature within the limits of its native condition (for example, immunity from concupiscence). However, today, in order to avoid equivocations ([like those committed by] Baius and the Jansenists), such a manner of speaking ought to be carefully avoided.

signifies, *the essence of a species of this sort is also called its "nature."* And this is how Boethius defines nature in the book *De duabus naturis*, saying: "Nature is what informs a thing with its specific difference," that is, what completes the definition of the species. Therefore, we are now speaking about nature as it signifies the essence, or what it is [*quodquid est*], or the quiddity of the species.

Finally, (as Chrysostom Javelli notes in *In* V *Meta.*, lect. 5), nature signifies *"the essential order of things concurring per se and principally for the perfection of the universe."* Thus, it is said that a dead man rising is not in accord with nature. And God pertains to nature so considered as the Author, conserver, first mover moving and directing, and end of the natural order.[25]

However, these various significations of the term "nature" are reduced to one, which is prior, not according to the way of discovery but of itself—namely, *any given thing's nature is its essence, as the radical principle of the operations and passions that are per se suitable to it.* Thus, nature is said analogically of the divine nature and of created natures.

Now, what does the term "natural" signify? For any given being, it designates "That which is suitable to it according to its nature."[26] And this must be considered according to the four causes. In other words, it is:

(a) The very *nature* or essence itself—namely, whatever is required so as to constitute some being in its species; thus, the body and the rational soul constitute man's nature.

(b) *The passivities* that are in a nature in relation to proportionate agents.

(c) *The powers* (or faculties) that flow from the essence itself (e.g., in man, the intellect and the will, as well as the activities to which these faculties are essentially ordered).

(d) *The exigencies* of this nature, or whatever is required so that it may arrive at its natural end (thus, the divine concurrence necessary so that any given second cause may act in its own order); this is called a debt of nature.

(e) Finally, in a rational nature (or, rather, a person) *the merit* coming from its legitimate natural action—namely, a right to a proportionate reward—that is, for achieving the natural end. This is owed to the person naturally.

---

[25] See Aristotle, *Physics,* VIII and *Metaphysics*, XII.
[26] *ST* I-II, q. 10, a. 1.

Thus, whatever is proportioned or determined for any given being according to its nature is natural for it.

B. *What exactly does the term "supernatural" signify?* For any given finite being, "supernatural" designates *that which exceeds the proportion of its nature and can gratuitously perfect it.* And just as the term "natural" is taken according to the four causes, so too the supernatural, exceeding the proportion of any given nature, surpasses its essential predicates, its natural passivities, {{187}} powers, exigencies, and indeed its natural merit. Hence, the supernatural is in no way owed to nature.

Nevertheless, the supernatural can (and indeed does) perfect nature, if the supernatural is, in fact, gratuitously bestowed upon it. And indeed, the supernatural is not something unbefitting to nature (for then it would be contrary to nature), nor is it indifferent to it (for then it would be neither good nor bad), but instead *is befitting to that nature,* not indeed according to the latter's essence, powers, exigencies, or natural passivity (for then it would be natural) but, rather, *according to its obediential (that is, elevable) potency.* St. Thomas says in *ST* I, q. 2, a. 2, ad 1: "Faith presupposes natural knowledge, just as nature presupposes grace, and as *a perfection* presupposes *that which is perfectible.*"

Now, what is an obediential (that is, elevable) potency? This must be explained later at length (in chapter 12, "On the Possibility of Revelation"). However, for the definition being sought right now, it suffices to say that an obediential (that is, elevable) potency is that by which inferior things are naturally constituted such that they can obey agents of a superior order and accept from them a perfection to which they are not [positively] ordered by their own nature.

Thus, as St. Thomas says, "That a stool may be made from wood, or that seeing man be made from a blind one, is not found in a natural power"[27] but, rather, only in an obediential potency [in the wood and the blind man]. Indeed, wood of itself is not ordered to the form of a stool rather than to the loftier form of a statue. Rather, it accepts this from the artificer inasmuch as it is obedient to him. Similarly, clay obeys the potter. This analogy is indicated in many places in Sacred Scripture: "As clay is in the hand of the potter, so are you in my hand, O house of Israel, says the Lord."[28] Likewise, an animal

---

[27] St. Thomas, *Compendium theologiae,* ch. 104. Likewise, see *ST* I, .q 115, a. 2, ad 4; II-II, q. 2, a. 3; III, q. 1, a. 3, ad 3; q. 11, a. 1c. Also see *De veritate,* q. 8, a. 4, ad 13 and a. 12, ad 4; q. 12, a. 3, ad 18; q. 29, a. 3, ad 3. Likewise, see *De potentia.,* q. 1, a. 3, ad 1; q. 6, a. 1, ad 18; *De virtutibus,* q. 1, a. 10, ad 13. Cf. *Tabulam auream,* the word, "Potentia," no. 10.

[28] Jeremiah 18:6 (DR). See Jeremiah 18:1–6 (DR): "The word that came to Jeremias from the Lord, saying: 'Arise, and go down into the potter's house, and there thou shalt hear my words.' And I went down into the potter's house, and behold he was doing a work on the wheel. And

is directed and instructed in an instrumental manner by man to hunt or to some other works that exceed its proper power.

Hence, St. Thomas says: "In the human soul, just as in any given creature, a twofold passive potency can be considered. One indeed exists in comparison to a natural agent, whereas the other exists in comparison to the First Agent, who can reduce any given creature to a higher act than that to which a natural agent can reduce it. And this is usually called the creature's obediential potency [*potentia obedientiae*]."[29]

Hence, relative to a given nature, the supernatural is that which surpasses its essence, natural passivities, powers, exigencies, and natural merit, but not, however, its obediential (or [*seu*] elevable) capacity.

However, the absolute supernatural with which we are concerned in our treatise must be distinguished from the relative supernatural.

{{188}} *The relative supernatural* (or *the supernatural secundum quid*) is that which exceeds the proportion of only *a given created nature* but *not of the whole* of created nature. For example, what is natural and specific for man is supernatural for the dog that obeys man. Or what is natural and specific for an angel is supernatural for man; for example, the divination that is caused by demonic revelation or for their illusions [*praestigia*] that are the simulacra of a miracle.[30]

The absolute supernatural (that is [*seu*], the *supernatural simpliciter*) is that which exceeds the proportion *of the whole* of created and creatable nature—namely, what surpasses the powers and exigencies of any creature whatsoever. This is the kind of supernaturality we are concerned with in our treatise, and it is divided, as we will soon say, into modal supernaturality (which is found in miracles) and essential supernaturality (which is found in mysteries strictly speaking, in grace and glory).

C. *In what way does the supernatural differ from what is contrary to nature* [*contranaturali*], *from the free, from the artificial, and from the fortuitous?* All these in one way or another are distinguished from the natural. As the natural is *determined* by nature, the free, the artificial, and the

---

the vessel was broken which he was making of clay with his hands: and turning he made another vessel, as it seemed good in his eyes to make it. Then the word of the Lord came to me, saying: 'Cannot I do with you, as this potter, O house of Israel, saith the Lord?'" Likewise, *Isaiah* 45:9. And again, *Sirach* 33:13–14 (*Ecclesiasticus*, DR): "As the potter's clay is in his hand, to fashion and order it: All his ways are according to his ordering: so man is in the hand of him that made him, and he will render to him according to his judgment." Likewise, *Romans* 9:21 (DR): "Or hath not the potter power over the clay, of the same lump, to make one vessel unto honour and another unto dishonour?"

29 *ST* III, q. 11, a. 1.

30 See *ST* I, q. 110, a. 4; II-II, q. 95, a. 4.

fortuitous are variously distinguished from it. As the natural is *proportioned* to nature, the supernatural and that which is contrary to nature are variously distinguished from it.

As regards the first difference, it suffices to say: Like acts of art [*actio artificialis*], free actions are not determined by nature but need a new determination, which is brought about through deliberation.[31] A fortuitous or chance occurrence is determined neither by nature nor by deliberation but instead occurs in nature *per accidens* as though it were intended.[32]

However, the supernatural and that which is contrary to nature are distinguished in various ways from the natural, as it is proportioned to nature.

That which is contrary to the inclination of a given nature is said to be contrary to nature; it is the same as that which is violent. And St. Thomas says in *ST* II-II, q. 175, a. 1: "Something is said to be violent when its principle is external, with the thing that undergoes the violence conferring nothing, as is said in *Nicomachean Ethics* 3.1. However, everything concurs with that to which it tends according to its own inclination, whether voluntary or natural." Hence, violence is inflicted by an extrinsic principle and is opposed to the inclination of the thing undergoing it. That is, it turns the thing undergoing it away from those things to which it is naturally ordered [*pronum*] (e.g., a laceration of our body is violent inasmuch as the sensitive nature flees from injury to its body; likewise, it is contrary to nature that a monstrosity [*monstrum*] be born).

{{189}} However, as the term indicates, *the supernatural in no way is contrary to the inclination of nature* but instead surpasses it, and if the supernatural is, in fact, given to that nature, it gratuitously perfects the latter, as

---

[31] Thomists generally say, "*The natural* is that whose principle is within it. *The artificial* is that whose principle is external—namely, in the reason of the one making it. Finally, *the violent* is that whose principle is not only external but also is opposed to its natural inclination. Hence, the violent is opposed to nature. But the artificial as such is not opposed to nature, 'but rather, imitates it.'" See Antoine Goudin, *Philosophia juxta inconcusa tutissimaque Divi Thomae dogmata, Physica*, pt. 1, d. 2, q. 1.

[32] See Aristotle, *Physics*, bk. 2. St. Thomas, *In* II *Phys.*, lect. 9 and 10.

Certain rationalists say that miraculous facts arise by chance (or fortuitously). Thus, Renan said, the tomb of Christ was fortuitously found to be empty. Against this, it must be said that the fortuitous effect requires a *per accidens* cause. For example, the fortuitous discovery of treasure in the ground *per accidens* arises from the fact that the ground is dug for another end. Hence, it would be necessary to assign a *per accidens* cause for which the tomb of Christ was found to be empty, and none are apparent nor can be imagined. Nay, the fortuitous is only said relative to secondary causes and not in relation to the First Cause, who orders all things. See *ST* I, q. 116, a. 1.

we said above.[33]

Naturalists (or [*seu*] rationalists) do not wish to consider the profound opposition that exists between the supernatural and that which is contrary to nature. Nay, they hold that the supernatural, as it is conceived by the Church, is contrary to nature, especially against the autonomy of our reason. Hence, they say, "Human reason is so independent that faith cannot be enjoined upon it by God"[34]

Theologians respond: This represents an adulteration of the notion of supernaturality, as St. Thomas explains in *ST* I, q. 105, a. 6, ad 1 and in *SCG* III, ch. 100 (that those things that God does outside the order of nature are not contrary to nature). In sum, the Holy Doctor says: The motion that God, qua universal agent, impresses upon a created nature, inasmuch as it is something unaccustomed and distinct from that to which it is naturally ordered [*prona*], is not to be called violent (or contrary to nature), for God does not bring about violence when he acts in creatures according to their own particular inclination, which is *to obey* their Creator, to whom they are more connaturally subjected than the body is to the soul or the arm to the will. "*In every creature, there is a certain obediential potency* [*obedientialis potentia*], *inasmuch as every creature obeys God so as to receive into it whatever God may come to will.* . . . (And) by the power of a supernatural agent, there are things that can be done (in it) which cannot be done by the power of a given natural agent."[35] Thus, wood obeys the craftsman so as to receive the form of a statue.

However, if a given miracle is said to be "*contrary to nature,*" this is said *in an improper manner*. For example, when fire miraculously does not burn martyrs in a furnace, this is not, properly speaking, against the nature of fire, which is naturally constituted to obey God so as to receive whatever is not opposed [to its nature]; however, improperly speaking, this is contrary to nature inasmuch as "in the nature (of fire) there remains a disposition contrary to the effect that God brings about," as St. Thomas says in *De potentia*, q. 6, a. 2, ad 3.

Nevertheless, God can, when he wishes, inflict *a punishment contrary to nature* upon a sinner for his sin, and then he in a certain sense inflicts violence, acting not qua universal

---

[33] That which is contrary to nature is also distinguished from *the preternatural*, the signification of which will be determined below in §2 in the division of supernaturality: The praeternatural are said to be miracles inasmuch as their supernaturality is inferior to the supernaturality of grace; and, in particular, miracles of an inferior order are called "beyond [*praeter*] nature" rather than "above [*supra*] nature." See St. Thomas, *De potentia.*, q. 6, a. 2, ad 3.

[34] [First] Vatican Council, *Dei filius*, can. 3.1 (Denzinger, no. 3031).

[35] St. Thomas, *De virtutibus in communi*, q. 1, a. 10, ad 13.

mover but, rather, according to the manner of a particular agent.[36] This divine action is in accord with the order of justice, and punishment is against the nature of the one suffering it.

However, the elevation to the supernatural order, revelation, and miracles are indeed not punishments inflicted by God but, on the contrary, are manifestations of his supreme benevolence and gratuitous love. Therefore, *the supernatural* and *that which contrary to nature* are *radically opposed to each other*, just as supernatural beatitude and the eternal misery of the damned are opposed to each other. Hence, there cannot be a greater or more damnable error and confusion than to say that the elevation to the supernatural life is contrary to nature. From God's perspective, this represents the confusion {{190}} of the most excellent, gratuitous gift with a punishment inflicted by God, and from man's perspective, it represents the confusion of the supernatural and sublime actions of the saints with superstition, which is contrary to religion. However, according to the Catholic faith, to affirm this is to tend to true misery, which is irreparably contrary to nature. The supernatural life is indeed contrary to the corrupt inclinations of our nature arising from sin, such as concupiscence and pride, which, therefore, call for mortification. "For if you live according to the flesh, you shall die: but if by the Spirit you mortify the deeds of the flesh, you shall live" (Rom 8:13, DR). "If any man will come after me, let him deny himself, and take up his cross, and follow me" (Matt 16:24, DR). However, the supernatural life is not contrary to our nature, precisely as a nature. The former gratuitously perfects the latter according to a marvelous harmony that is found especially in the illuminative and unitive life of the saints, and most excellently in Christ.

Nay, the supernatural existing in us according to the manner of a *habitus* is called *connatural*—that is, so to speak, as a second nature. Thus, as St. Thomas often says, through the infused gift of wisdom, we judge concerning divine things according to a kind of connaturality with them, which is had through charity.[37]

§2. *Division of Supernaturality*

(1) This division is proposed. (2) It is proven. (3) It is explained in parts. (4.) Four corollaries to be noted.

(1) *This division is proposed*:

According to the Church, as was said above, there is, however, a twofold supernaturality— namely, (a) the supernaturality of a miracle, which exceeds the efficient powers and exigencies of any given created nature, though not the knowing powers of human nature; and (b) the supernaturality of mys-

---

[36] See John of St. Thomas, *Cursus philosophicus, Philosophia naturalis* (*Physica*), pt. 1, q. 11, a. 3 (How the violent is distinguished from the natural).

[37] See *ST* II-II, q. 45, a. 2.

teries strictly speaking, as well as the life of grace and of glory, which exceeds not only the efficient powers and exigencies of any given created nature but also the knowing powers (and, consequently, the appetitive powers) of a created intellectual nature.

To explain this distinction, theologians commonly divide the supernatural into the essentially supernatural and the modally supernatural.

However, the *essentially supernatural* [*supernaturale quoad substantiam*] does not designate the substantial supernatural (or the supernatural existing as a substance), for it can be either *substantial* and uncreated (as is the intimate life of the Trinity) or *accidental* and created (as is grace). Rather, the essentially supernatural expresses the same thing as the supernatural *quoad essentiam* and signifies that which is *intrinsically (or entitatively) supernatural*—that is, exceeding not only, from the perspective of causality, all the efficiently causal powers and exigencies of any given created nature but also exceeding, by its supernatural essence, every created nature, inasmuch as it is either the divine nature or a participation in the divine nature precisely as divine. This essential supernaturality is likewise cognitionally supernatural [*supernaturale quoad cognoscibilitatem*]—that is, exceeding the natural knowing powers of any given created intellectual nature, for truth and being are convertible. Therefore, supernatural being exceeds the order of natural truth.

By contrast, *that which is solely modally supernatural* is something essentially (or entitatively) natural, though it is either *produced in a supernatural manner* or *ordered in a supernatural manner* to a supernatural end. An example of the former can be seen in the case of natural life being supernaturally given back to a corpse through miraculous resurrection. An example of the latter can be seen in the case of an act performed by an {{191}} acquired natural virtue, such as temperance, which is also ordered through charity to the reward of eternal life.

Several times heretofore, making use of nominal definitions, we have cited this distinction between essential supernaturality and modal supernaturality. For example, we have said that revelation supernaturally manifesting merely natural truths is called solely-modal supernatural revelation (or [*vel*] effectively supernatural revelation), like a miracle of the intellectual order. On the other hand, revelation manifesting supernatural truths is called essentially supernatural revelation.

(2) *This division is proven*:

Now, however, we must show that this division of the supernatural is not merely an accidental division but instead is *necessary, immediate,* and *adequate.* Such an explanation is of use, for equivocations frequently arise from vague conceptions concerning this division, which is fundamental in all of theology and, in particular, in the treatise on revelation.

Nominalist theologians like William of Ockham and Gabriel Biel, as well as Durandus of Saint-Pourçain, John Duns Scotus, Luis de Molina, and in a certain manner Juan de Lugo,[38] did not acknowledge the essential and absolute difference between essential supernaturality and modal supernaturality. Instead, they only acknowledged a *de facto* difference between them, saying that theological faith is modally supernatural.

Our thesis is: *Absolute supernaturality is divided per se and adequately into essential supernaturality and modal supernaturality.*

This thesis is proven as follows.

A necessary, immediate, and adequate division is that which is taken from the formal notion of the whole to be divided, according to differences that are immediately opposed to each other, so that the members thus delineated are perfectly adequate to the whole thus divided.

Now, the division of supernaturality into essential supernaturality and modal supernaturality is a division of this kind.

Therefore, this division is necessary, immediate, and adequate.

The major premise is drawn from [the very rules of] logic.

Indeed, a *necessary* or per se (or [*seu*] essential) division is opposed to an accidental one, which is also customarily called a *per accidens* division. The first is taken from the formal notion of the whole to be divided. The second is taken according to accidents (for example, as when people are divided into white, black, yellow, and copper-colored). An *immediate* division is one that assigns the members into which the whole is immediately divided. If, on the contrary, having neglected the more principal parts, the secondary parts are brought to the fore, great confusion will be born of such a division. An *adequate* division is had when the members, considered all together, perfectly equal the whole— that is, when they do not exceed it or fall short of it. We have such an adequate division if the immediate differences drawn, according to the formal notion of the whole being divided, are themselves opposed to each other by an opposition of contradiction and of contrariety, as when, for example, substance is divided into bodily and non-bodily substance, for there cannot be a third member between these.

Now, the minor premise is proven as follows. The absolute supernatural is that which exceeds the powers and exigencies of any given created nature. Now, *this excess can only have a foundation either in the intrinsic causes* of the thing that is called {{192}} supernatural (and thus we have essential supernaturality—that is, intrinsical / entitative supernaturality) *or in the extrinsic*

---

[38] See Salmanticenses, *Cursus theologicus, De gratia*, tr. 14, disp. 4, dub. 2, §3, no. 34; disp. 3, dub. 3, nos. 40 and 60.

causes of the thing that is said to be supernatural (and thus we have modal supernaturality, whether effectively or from an extrinsic end).

Quite clearly, this division is taken in accord with the formal notion of the whole to be divided (namely, in accord with the *excess* of the thing that is called supernatural precisely on account of this excess). Its differences are immediate inasmuch as such excess is founded immediately either upon the intrinsic causes of the supernatural thing or in its extrinsic causes. Its differences are also opposed contradictorily and contrarily to each other and are perfectly equal to the whole, for something is either intrinsically or only extrinsically (and, hence, not intrinsically) supernatural. Nor can a third member be conceived (between these notions). Hence, this division is necessary, immediate, and adequate, as is the division of causes into intrinsic and extrinsic causes. However, the intrinsic causes of a given thing are the matter and form constitutive of the thing, whereas the extrinsic causes are the efficient cause and the end.

Therefore, it is easy to reduce the common division of supernaturality to the division of the four causes, as the Thomists do. For example, see John of St. Thomas,[39] the Salamanca Carmelites,[40] and Suarez.[41]

John of St. Thomas says:

> It must be noted that *supernaturality* can belong to a thing from the perspective of three principles, namely *from the efficient cause, the final cause,* and *the formal cause.* It cannot belong to it from the perspective of material causality, given that the material cause is the very subject in which such supernatural forms are received, and this is the soul itself or one of its powers, which are natural beings [*entia naturalia*], even though they receive [these supernatural forms] on account of an obediential potency.
>
> *From the perspective of the efficient cause*, something is called supernatural when it is *done in a supernatural manner,* whether the thing thus done is supernatural or natural, just as the resurrection of a dead person or the illumination of a blind person are modally supernatural, though the thing done is natural, namely [the returning of] the [natural] life of a man or the power of sight.
>
> *From the perspective of the final cause*, something is called supernatural when it *is extrinsically* [*ab extrinsico*] *ordered to a supernatural end.* For example, if an

---

[39] John of St. Thomas, *Cursus theologicus, De gratia*, disp. 20, a. 1, solv. arg, no. 4.
[40] Salmanticenses, *Cursus theologicus, De gratia*, tr. 14, disp. 3, dub. 3, no. 24.
[41] Francisco Suarez, *De gratia*, bk. 2, ch. 4.

act of temperance (or some other acquired virtue) is ordered by charity toward the merit of eternal life, it receives in itself a *supernatural mode of ordering* toward such an end. And in this way, the *humanity of Christ* has a supernatural mode of union to the Word to which it is ordered as toward an end and a terminus of union.[42]

From the perspective of formal causality, something is called supernatural *when from this formal, specificative form [ratione] it is oriented to [respicit] a supernatural object.* And this alone is called *essential supernaturality*, which is so with regard to the act's *species* and nature, which is taken from the formal object.

{{193}} Thus, the division of the supernatural must be written:

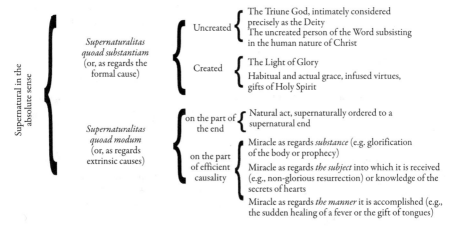

Supernatural in the absolute sense	*Supernaturalitas quoad substantiam* (or, as regards the formal cause)	Uncreated	The Triune God, intimately considered precisely as the Deity / The uncreated person of the Word subsisting in the human nature of Christ
		Created	The Light of Glory / Habitual and actual grace, infused virtues, gifts of Holy Spirit
	Supernaturalitas quoad modum (or, as regards extrinsic causes)	on the part of the end	Natural act, supernaturally ordered to a supernatural end
		on the part of efficient causality	Miracle as regards *substance* (e.g. glorification of the body or prophecy) / Miracle as regards *the subject* into which it is received (e.g., non-glorious resurrection) or knowledge of the secrets of hearts / Miracle as regards *the manner* it is accomplished (e.g., the sudden healing of a fever or the gift of tongues)

(3) *This division, with its subdivisions, is exposited in parts*:

We are here concerned with the division of a given potential whole, which on account of its extension contains several things under it as parts, as a genus contains species under it. However, the supernatural is not univocal, like a genus, but instead is *analogous*, for

---

[42]   Indeed, the humanity of Christ (that is [*seu*], his human nature) is not essentially supernatural like the divine nature or grace; however, it is *supernaturally* united to the divine nature by which they come together in the one person of the Son of God. Hence, Christ's humanity *reductively* pertains to this category of extrinsic supernaturality, so that John of St. Thomas says that it indeed is not intrinsically (or essentially) supernatural but is miraculously and personally united to the Word according to a union that is a real created relation of this nature to the Word (*ST* III, q. 2, a. 7). However, Christ's personality is essentially supernatural and uncreated.

nothing is univocally predicated of God and of something created.[43]

Hence, by priority, supernaturality is said of uncreated essential supernaturality, secondarily of created essentially supernatural gifts, and finally of modal supernaturality.

Moreover, this division is not through opposed realities [*res*] but, rather, through *opposed notions* [*rationes*].[44] Thus, one and the same thing, like grace, can be both essentially supernatural and modally supernatural (as regards the manner of its production). However, something is called modally supernatural without qualification when its supernaturality is solely modal. Thus, we will say: The fact of Christian revelation is at once essentially and modally supernatural and hence, from the first perspective, is known by divine faith but, from the second perspective, is known by reason on the basis of knowledge of miracles.

A. In the first category—namely, *that which is essentially supernatural*—the first member (i.e., *the uncreated supernatural*) alone is *substantially* supernatural—that is, {{194}} existing as a substance.[45] Indeed, theologians commonly reject the intrinsic possibility of any created supernatural substance, as we will discuss below. Hence, *created cases of essential supernaturality* can exist only as an *accident*. Such things include the light of glory or habitual grace and actual grace proportioned to habitual grace, as well as the supernatural virtues that proceed from habitual grace as properties do from an essence (*ST* I-II, q. 110, a. 3 and a. 4), and also the gifts of the Holy Spirit (*ST* I-II, q. 68). These accidents are essentially supernatural because, through habitual grace, we are "made partakers in the divine nature," as 2 Peter 1:4 says (cf. *ST* I-II, q. 112, a. 1).[46] Thus, habitual

---

[43] See *ST* I, q. 13, a. 5.

[44] This is how St. Thomas speaks in *ST* I, q. 5, a. 6, ad 2 concerning the division of the good into the fitting, the useful, and the pleasant: "This division is not through opposed realities [*res*] but through opposed notions; however, it is said properly of pleasant things, which have no other notion of appetibility than pleasure, since they are sometimes hurtful and [morally] unbefitting [*inhonesta*]. But those things are called useful which do not have the source of their desirability in themselves but are desired only so as to lead to something else, as when one takes a bitter medicine [for the sake of achieving health]. However, those things are called fitting that have within themselves the reason for their being desired."

[45] [Trans. note: Fr. Garrigou-Lagrange is being a little loose with the language here. God does not exist in the *category* of substance. Although unable to be defined through proximate genus and specific difference, we can give a quasi-definition of substance as "a thing to whose nature it belongs to exist not in something else." As Aquinas notes in *ST* I, q. 3, a. 5, ad 1, "substance" includes the notion of the given *essence* that *exists* in this particular way (i.e., such as not to be in another). This implies a distinction between essence and existence that is not acceptable for the divine simplicity. Thus, while substance provides the closest analogate in our experience for articulating the divine aseity, we should be careful with our words on this matter. Regarding this definition of substance, see John F. Wippel, *The Metaphysical Thought of Thomas Aquinas* (Washington, DC: Catholic University of America Press, 2000), 228–237.]

[46] See Council of Trent, *Decree on Justification* (Denzinger, nos. 1528ff, 1546ff); Pius V, *Ex omnibus afflictionibus*, no. 21 (Denzinger, no. 1921). Other texts might be cited as well.

grace does not, as is the case for miracles, only exceed all the efficient powers and exigencies of any created nature whatsoever *in an effective manner*, but it exceeds, *in an essential manner*, every created and creatable nature, as well as all the knowing powers (and, hence, all the appetitive powers) of any created intellectual nature. And therefore it is said that "the good of grace in one man is greater than the natural good of the whole universe."[47] The least act of supernatural charity is greater than all the angelic natures that have been created and that could be created, taken together, just as the least act of reason is more perfect than all heavenly and earthly bodies taken together. Just as the spiritual transcends the bodily, so too the essentially supernatural exceeds all created natures *in an essential manner*.

B. In the second category, namely *that which is modally supernatural*, (a) the first member of the division, *that which is modally supernatural on the part of an extrinsic end*, is something essentially natural that is supernaturally ordered to a supernatural end, as for example, when the act of a natural virtue is ordered by charity to eternal life. Hence, theologians,[48] along with St. Thomas, generally say concerning the observation of the commands of the natural law: "The commands of the law can be fulfilled not only with regard to the substance of that given action but also *as regards the mode of acting*, namely, so that they might be done *out of charity*. Thus, neither in the state of integral nature, nor in the state of corrupt (or [*seu*] fallen) nature can man fulfill the commands of the law without grace" (*ST* I-II, q. 109, a. 4). Thus, the following proposition of Baius was condemned by Pius V: "The well-known distinction of the Doctors of a double manner of fulfilling the commandments of the divine law, the one pertaining only to the substance of the works commanded and the other pertaining to a certain way that renders the works capable of leading the one who does the works to the eternal kingdom (that is, the way of merit) is false and should be rejected."[49]—The Nominalists and Molina did not see the difference between this kind of supernaturality and the supernaturality of faith.[50]

(b) Finally, *that which is modally supernatural on the part of the efficient cause* (or the efficiently supernatural [*seu effective*]) is something essentially (i.e. [*seu*], entitatively) natural which, nonetheless, can only be produced by God in a supernatural manner. For example, in the miraculous resurrection of someone who has died, natural life is supernaturally bestowed upon that person, and this is something that is naturally knowable. Thus, *a miracle*, properly speaking, exceeds *in its effecting power* [*effective*] all the efficiently

---

[47] See *ST* I-II, q. 113, a. 9, ad 2.

[48] See Charles René Billuart, *De gratia*, diss. 3, a. 5.

[49] St. Pius V, *Ex omnibus afflictionibus*, no. 61 (Denzinger, no. 1961); also see no. 62 (Denzinger, no. 1962).

[50] See ibid., a. 2, §2. Indeed, they said that man can naturally believe the supernatural mysteries on account of the formal motive of infused faith, but a light is required for the grace of faith so that the act might be performed *in a supernatural manner* as is necessary for salvation— namely, so that it may be ordered to supernatural faith.

causal powers of any created nature whatsoever. Hence, as was said in *Dei filius* at the [First] Vatican Council: "They manifestly display the omnipotence of God."[51]

But sometimes confusions arise regarding the division of supernaturality and the division of miracles. Hence, we must briefly explain this division of miracles on the basis of what St. Thomas says in *ST* I, q. 105, a. 8. This division is taken from within the order of efficient causality, from which the formal notion of the miraculous is drawn.

{{195}} In that text, St. Thomas says:

> Something is said to be a miracle through a comparison to *the natural power* that it exceeds. Therefore, the more that it exceeds the power of nature, so much the more will it be called a miracle. Now, there are three ways that something can exceed the power of nature. In one way, it can do so *as regards the substance of what is done*, as when two bodies simultaneously are in the same place (e.g., if the sun were to go backwards in its course or if a human body were glorified). None of these things can be *done* by nature. These kinds of miracles represent the loftiest kind of miracle.

> Second, something can exceed the power of nature not with regard to what is done but, rather, *as regards that in which it is done*, as in the case of the resuscitation of the dead, the returning of sight to the blind, and other such things. Indeed, nature can cause life, though not in a corpse, and it can furnish the power of sight, but not in the blind. These kinds of miracles hold the second rank among miracles.

> In a third way, something exceeds the power of nature *as regards the mode* and order of its production, as when someone is suddenly cured of a fever by the divine power without any treatment or the normal process of nature in such things. . . . And these represent the lowest sort of miracles.

Miracles of this third category are properly said to be outside the order of nature [*praeter naturam*] rather than *above* [*supra*] it. That which is said to be "preternatural" is reduced to this category of miracles.[52]

---

[51] [First] Vatican Council, *Dei filius*, ch. 3 (Denzinger, no. 3009).

[52] In *De potentia*, q. 6, a. 2, ad 3, St. Thomas calls these categories of miracles: (1) miracles *above* nature, (2) miracles *contrary to* [*contra*] nature, and (3) miracles beyond the order of [*praeter*] nature.

However, the term "contrary to nature" for the second category must be understood *secundum quid* and not *simpliciter*, for these kinds of miracles are not contrary to the creature's obediential potency but, rather, are contrary to a given natural inclination (e.g., a corpse's natural inclination to decompose).

First corollary, *regarding the distinction between that which is essentially supernatural* [*supernaturale quoad substantiam*] *and that which is substantially miraculous* [*miraculum quoad substantiam*]. These two things must not be confused, just as the modally supernatural must not be confused with the modally miraculous. Indeed, the division of supernaturality is drawn on account of the various ways that there can be an excess [in relation to nature] depending upon the three kinds of causality—namely, the formal, efficient, and final cause, whereas by contrast, the division of kinds of miracles is drawn on account of the ways that there can be an excess only within the order of efficient causality. Hence, in the expression "essentially supernatural [*surnaturale quoad substantiam*]," the words "quoad substantiam" are to be taken in their *formal sense*. By contrast, in the expression "that which is substantially miraculous [miraculum *quoad substantiam*]," the words "quoad substantiam" are to be taken *as regards efficient causality* [*effective*]. Hence, that which is substantially miraculous (e.g., the glorification of the body) is only, of itself,[53] something that is modally supernatural (i.e., as regards efficient causality). Therefore, an infinite abyss separates the essential supernaturality of the light of glory or grace from the nonessential, efficiently-causal [*effectivam*] supernaturality of the sensible luminosity of a glorified body. Hence, as St. Thomas says in *ST* III, suppl., q. 85, a. 2, ad 1: "The luminosity of the glorified body will be loftier than the luminosity of nature, *generically in relation to its cause*, but *not as to its species*. Whence, on account of its *species*, the luminosity of nature is proportioned to sight, and so too will the glorious luminosity [of the blessed be so proportioned]." Thus, the apostles were able to see the glorious body of the resurrected Christ (see *ST* III, q. 55, a. 6).

If we diligently reflect on the opposition between the essentially supernatural and that which is substantially miraculous (which is something that of itself is only modally supernatural), St. Thomas's various texts can be explained with {{196}} ease and be reconciled with the aforementioned common division of supernaturality (cf. §4 above where we resolved certain objections).

Likewise, as regards the third category, note well that although a miracle in general is said to be "outside the order of nature," miracles of the third order are more properly called *preternatural* rather than *supernatural*.

Likewise, the term "preternatural" is used to describe the gifts of bodily immortality as well as immunity from pain and concupiscence which were gratuitously bestowed upon Adam in the state of original justice. See *ST* I, q. 97, a. 1: "There were certain supernaturally and divinely given powers in man's soul, by which it was able to preserve the body from all corruption, so long as it remained subject to God." These gifts were entitatively natural and only modally exceed the powers of nature, like a miracle of the third order noted above, for nature can preserve life, avoid pain, and moderate concupiscence, though *not always*.

[53] However, there are some miracles (e.g., St. Paul's conversion), which are formally and essentially supernatural. See *ST* I-II, q. 113, a. 10. Likewise, the Incarnation of the Word, which is placed among miracles of the first order in *De potentia*, q. 6, a. 2, ad 3.

Second corollary, *regarding the division of the modally supernatural knowledge*. This order of knowledge can be divided along the same lines as for the division of miracles, for it is a miracle of the intellectual order. Thus, below knowledge that is formally essentially supernatural (as are the beatific vision and theological faith), we can find *three kinds of knowledge that are modally supernatural (or in relation to efficient causality)* concerning any intrinsically natural object of knowledge. Indeed, natural knowledge of this sort can exceed a natural knowing faculty in an efficiently-causal [*effective*] (or [*seu*] elicitive) manner in three ways:

(1) *Efficiently-causal as regards the substance* [*quoad substantiam*] of knowledge, as certain knowledge effectively exceeds every created intellect, as we will discuss below.

(2) *Efficiently-causal as regards the subject in which it is found*—for example, knowledge of a natural object already existing but off in a distance exceeding the visual capacities of a given man, though not those of all men (*ST* II-II, q. 171, a. 3). Similarly, such knowledge is had as regards the secrets of the heart, which are naturally known by the person in whom they [actually] exist.

(3) *Efficiently-causal quoad modum*, like instantaneous knowledge of some human science or human language that is had without study (i.e. [*sic*], the gift of tongues).

Hence the supernaturality of prophecy is of an inferior order of supernaturality than is the supernaturality of divine faith.[54] Therefore, St. Thomas says, "Although prophecy and

---

[54] However, divine *inspiration* for *infallibly* judging and writing what can now be naturally known and judged without infallibility seems, at first sight, to be only modally supernatural from the perspective of efficient causality [*effective*], like the gift of tongues. Nonetheless, if we consider this inspired knowledge more diligently, infallibility's mode appears to pertain not only to its coming into being [*fieri*] but [also] to its existence [*esse*] and to its essence. Hence, it must be called essentially and *efficiently* [*effective*] supernatural, just as the prophecy by means of which one infallibly knows a natural future contingent that can already be known in a conjectural manner through natural reasoning.

However, like prophecy about a natural future contingent, this kind of inspiration is inferior to knowledge that is *formally and essentially supernatural* (as is, for example, theological faith). Hence, St. Thomas says, "If the intellectual light is divinely infused into someone not for knowing something supernatural but for judging with divine certainty about something that can be known by human reason [alone], such intellectual prophecy is inferior to that which exists with an imaginary vision, leading one to a supernatural truth" (*ST* II-II, q. 174, a. 2, ad 3).

Hence, just like theological faith, prophetic revelation of the supernatural mysteries is *formally and essentially supernatural* and only modally supernatural *from the perspective of efficient causality* [*effective*]. The same holds for the case of inspiration for infallibly writing not only

faith are had about the same thing, for example, Christ's passion, they are nonetheless not had in the same way, for *faith formally looks upon* the passion from a kind of *eternal* perspective (namely, inasmuch as God suffered) while considering its *temporal* aspect only *materially*, whereas the opposite is the case for prophecy" (*In* III *Sent.*, d. 24, a. 1, ad 3).

From this, it is quite clear why the supernaturality of sanctifying grace and of charity is loftier than the supernaturality of graces freely given that are called "the grace of healing, the doing of works of power, the discernment of spirits, various kinds of tongues, and the interpretation of discourses" (see 1 Cor 12:9). However, there are certain loftier freely given graces that are essentially supernatural, for they pertain to knowing divine things— namely, "Faith, words of wisdom, and of knowledge."[55] {{197}} Nonetheless, they are inferior to habitual grace, by means of which we are given a share in the divine nature, for St. Thomas says in *ST* I-II, q. 111, a. 5 (Is freely given grace of greater dignity than sanctifying grace?):

> In 1 Corinthians 12, the Apostle, after enumerating the freely given graces, adds, "And I shew unto you yet a more excellent way" (DR), and as is clear from what follows, he is speaking of charity, which pertains to sanctifying grace. Therefore, sanctifying grace is much more excellent than freely given grace. . . . For the higher the good to which a virtue is ordered, to that degree is it more

---

naturally knowable historical facts but [indeed] Sacred Scripture inasmuch as it is sacred (i.e., as containing matters of faith), as well as for the loftier freely given graces "faith, words of wisdom, and of science," which exist for the sake of instructing others in divine matters.

[Trans. note: This footnote only exists in the footer, though it seems to be associated with the text in the body to which I have connected this particular note.]

[55] These last freely given graces—namely, faith, [words of] wisdom, and [words of] science, which are distinct from theological faith and from the Spirit's gifts of wisdom and science— exist for the sake of instructing men about divine matters, as St. Thomas explains when he interprets St. Paul's words in 1 Corinthians 12 in *ST* I-II, q. 111, a. 4. This article can be summed up in the following division:

Freely-given grace is ordered to the instructing of others in divine matters	in order to bestow full knowledge of divine things	*faith* concerning principles
		words of wisdom concerning principal conclusions
		words of knowledge concerning examples and effects
	in order to confirm divine revelation	by doing . . . . { the grace of healing / the doing works of power
		by knowing . . . . { prophecy / discernment of spirits
	in order to present the divine word to one's listeners in a suitable manner	*various kinds of tongues*
		the interpretation o speeches

excellent. However, the end is always superior to those things that are ordered to the end [i.e., the means]. Now, sanctifying grace orders man immediately to union with his last end, whereas freely given graces order man to a given thing that prepares one for the last end, just as through prophecy, miracles, and other such things men are led to union with the ultimate end. Therefore, *sanctifying grace is much more excellent than freely given grace.*

Hence, St. Paul says in 1 Corinthians 13:1–2 (DR): "If I speak with the tongues of men and of angels, and have not charity, I am become as sounding brass, or a tinkling cymbal. And if I should have prophecy and should know all mysteries, and all knowledge, and if I should have all faith, so that I could remove mountains, and have not charity, I am nothing."

This corollary, as well as the following ones, confirms that the aforementioned division of supernaturality is adequate.

Third corollary, *regarding that which is supernatural in an ordinary sense and that which is supernatural in an extraordinary sense.* Sanctifying grace, the virtues, and gifts of the Holy Spirit, according to the various degrees of the purgative, illuminative, and unitive life, all pertain *to that which is supernatural in an ordinary sense*, for the unitive life is the mature state of the supernatural life. Freely given graces and even the loftier degrees of the gifts of the Holy Spirit (especially of the gift of wisdom, inasmuch as it is joined to the freely given graces called words of wisdom or science) pertain to *that which is supernatural in an extraordinary sense.*[56] This is what St. Thomas seems to say in *ST* II-II, q. 45, a. 5. (When interpreting this text, see *ST* I-II, q. 111, a. 4, ad 4.)

Fourth corollary, *regarding that which is hypostatically supernatural.* This supernaturality does not lay outside the aforementioned division of supernaturality. However, just as the hypostatic union itself {{198}} "is a kind of relation which we consider between the divine and human natures, inasmuch as they come together in the person of the Son of God, . . . this union (or [*seu*] this relation) does not exist in God in a real manner but, instead, only in a rationate manner [=as a '*relatio rationis*']; however, it really exists in the human nature, which is a kind of creature" (*ST* III, q. 2, a. 7). Hence, the hypostatic order is a union, according to person, of uncreated essential supernaturality, with Christ's human nature.[57]

---

[56] This kind of supernaturality is called *extraordinary* inasmuch as it is not ordinarily required for the personal sanctification of the soul, though not so that it would be something rare in the miraculous life of the whole Church. For the miraculous conversion of the world, God frequently gave his Church freely given graces and "does not cease, even in our days, to bring about miracles by the hands of His saints so that the faith might be confirmed" (SCG I, ch. 6).

[57] Thus, Cajetan writes in *In ST* III, q. 1, a. 3, no. 6: "As a matter of fact, there are *three orders* found in the universe, namely, *the order of nature, the order of grace,* and *the order of God and the creature together.* . . . The second presupposes the first, and the third presupposes both of

§3. What the Natural and Supernatural Orders Are

By the division of supernaturality set forth above, we can easily understand what these two orders are according to the Church's teaching.

A. WHAT IS THE NATURAL ORDER?

In general, an order is a disposition according to priority and posteriority relative to some principle (cf. *In* V. *Meta.*, lect. 13 and *ST* II-II, q. 26). The principle of order is its efficient cause and end, whereas the means are ordered to the end according to some kind of law. Therefore, the natural order is the disposition of the various natures of creatures according to priority and posteriority relative to God qua Author and end of such natures. Thus, God pertains to the natural order as the extrinsic efficient and final cause of this order, though obviously not as the intrinsic (or immanent) form, which would represent a pantheistic identification of the world's substance with the divine substance. Hence, creation, conservation, and the divine concurrence necessary for the natural actions of creatures all pertain to the natural order, as regards efficient causality.

For man, the natural order is the suitable disposition of natural means to man's natural end. In this way, we have the following:

(a) *The formal end* is possession of God, not through [direct,] intuitive vision [of the Deity] but, rather, through reason by means of discursive cognition.

---

the prior two. And similarly, foreordaining and foresight of the first is presupposed by the foreordaining and foresight of the second, and likewise, the foreordaining and foresight of the third presupposes the foreordaining and foresight of the first two. Thus, God first ordered the universe according to the order of nature, and given that the universe does not attain the full enjoyment of God [*divinam fruitionem*], the order of grace was added to it. And given that the last order does not reach the highest possible mode of union with God, he foreordained the creature to personal union with God." Likewise, see *In ST* III, q. 1, a. 1, no. 7. Similarly, see Billuart in *De Deo*, diss. 9, a. 6, §2: "Others, indeed perhaps suitably, do not hold that there is a priority in the divine decrees among the three orders of *nature, grace, and the hypostatic union*, for they say, just as the artisan does not first intend the roof or the foundation but, rather, first intends a suitable habitation and, for the sake of that intends the whole house made corresponding to that, made up of all of its parts, so too *God* first willed to manifest His glory *ad extra* and for this end *chose to create this world* as an integral whole, with all of its parts and all of its orders, namely, the orders of nature, grace, and the hypostatic union, *as a single work* most suitably adapted to His end. . . . *But the order of nature was disposed so that it may serve the order of grace, and the order of grace so that it may yield to the glory of Christ.*"

(b) *The supreme agent* is God qua Author of our nature, who moves us to our natural actions; *the secondary agent* is man by his human nature and the faculties proper to it.

(c) *The objective means* are naturally knowable created things; *the subjective means* are the light of reason, naturally acquired ideas, and the exercise of man's faculties, especially his intellect and will under the influence of God's natural concurrence.

(d) Finally, *the law of this order* is the natural law, grafted into the hearts of all; through obedience to this natural law, man may have natural merit (i.e., a right to a natural reward), which is the kind of sanction pertaining to this order.

{{199}}

B. What is the supernatural order?

The supernatural order is the suitable disposition of those things that exceed the proportion of created nature, relative to God as their Author and End.

However, we must distinguish the *essentially* supernatural order, which is called the supernatural order without qualification [*simpliciter*] from that which is supernatural *only in an efficiently-causal way* [*effective*].

The essentially supernatural order is the suitable disposition of those things that are formally and substantially supernatural. In other words, it is the supernatural order of truth and life pertaining to grace and glory. Thus, for the case of man, we have the following:

(a) *The formal end* is the possession of God through intuitive vision and love of the same order [*eiusem generis*], for love follows upon knowledge.

(b) *The primary agent* is God the Author of grace and glory; *the secondary agent* is man inasmuch as his nature is elevated through sanctifying grace, the infused virtues, and the gifts of the Holy Spirit.

(c) *The objective means* are external revelation proposed by the Church, the sacraments, and all the external, supernatural means for salvation; *the subjective means* are the internal light of faith as well as the exercise of the supernatural virtues under the supernatural influence of actual grace.

(d) *The law* is the complex of God's positive precepts for pursuing the supernatural end.

Therefore, God can and must be considered in two ways—namely, qua *Author and End of the natural order* and qua *Author and End of the supernatural order*. From the first perspective, he is known by natural reason and philosophy, being thus attained from the common formal perspective of being. From this perspective, he is called the Author of nature, the First Mover, the First Cause, the Necessary and First Being, and the Orderer of the universe. From the other perspective, he is known through revelation and faith, being thus attained from the intimate formal perspective of the Deity, and he is called our Heavenly Father,[58] especially in the New Testament (Matt 4:9). However, in the Old Testament, he is called the God of Abraham, Isaac, Jacob (Exod 3:6); the living God (Ps 83:3); our God (Ps 67:21); God my salvation (Ps 41:3); the God of my salvation (Ps 37:23); God our refuge and strength (Ps 45:1); God of my heart (Ps 72:26); our God who is gracious and true (Wis 15:1); the hidden God (Isa 45:15); the God of Israel, the Savior (Isa 45:15); my Father, my God, and the support of my salvation (Ps 88:27).[59]

Hence, a condemnation was issued against this proposition of Baius rejecting the distinction between the natural and the supernatural orders: "The distinction of a twofold love of God, namely, a natural love whose object is God as the *author of nature* and a gratuitous love whose object is God *as beatifying* is meaningless and imaginary; it has been devised as a mockery of the Sacred Scriptures and of the numerous testimonies of ancient authors."[60] For the same reason, two propositions of Rosmini which we have already cited were likewise condemned.[61] Similarly, Innocent XI condemned the claim: "Faith, in the broad sense, which is based on the testimony of creatures or on a similar reason, is sufficient for justification."[62] Indeed, when one says, "Salvation requires that one believe that God exists and that he is a just rewarder," {{200}} one is not merely speaking of God qua Author of nature and knowable from the testimony of creatures. Rather, it is a question of God, the Author of the supernatural order, him who is know-

---

[58] See *ST* I, q. 33, a. 3.

[59] The reader may refer to biblical concordances where they list cases for the word "God."

[60] Pius V, *Ex omnibus afflictionibus,* no. 34 (Denzinger, no. 1934).

[61] See Leo XIII, Decree of the Holy Office, *Post obitum* (1887), nos. 36 (Denzinger, no. 3236) and 38 (Denzinger, no. 3238): "*The supernatural order* is established by the manifestation of being in the fullness of its real form; the effect of this communication or manifestation is a deiform sense ('sentiment'), which begun in this life, constitutes the light of faith and of grace and which, completed in the [next] life, constitutes the light of glory"; "*God is the object of the beatific vision* inasmuch as He is the author of works *ad extra.*"

[62] Holy Office Decree, March 2, 1679, no. 23 (Denzinger, no. 2123).

able through revelation. Otherwise, the faith necessary for salvation would merely be a natural faith, which was had by Deists, such as Robespierre, who during the French Revolution worshiped the Supreme Being and Reason, while however rejecting everything supernatural.

C. Could that which is only efficiently supernatural be produced by God inasmuch as he is the Author of nature?

That which is supernatural only from the perspective of efficient causality and not entitatively, such as the miraculous production of natural life in a corpse, does not exceed God's power qua the Author of nature. Indeed, to prove the possibility of miracles, it suffices to consider God inasmuch as he is the *free* Author of nature and its Lord.[63] Hence, already in philosophy we can prove the possibility of miracles. Moreover, it is not incoherent for God to perform a sensible miracle for a natural spiritual end (e.g., to confirm the truth of natural religion or the precepts of the natural law). Thus, miracles do not pertain to the order of supernatural truth and can be known by reason alone. However, as a matter of fact, in our present state of existence, they are ordered to the confirmation of essentially supernatural revelation. Moreover, as we will discuss below, miracles can manifest the fact of revelation inasmuch as this fact is supernatural, at least modally so.

---

[63] Hence, in *De potentia*, q. 6, a. 5, ad 5, St. Thomas speaks of a fact recounted by St. Augustine in *De civitate Dei*, 10.16, where we are told of a certain vestal virgin who, as a sign of her preservation of chastity, carried water from the Tiber in a vase that had holes in it without having any of the water leak from the vessel. In response to the objection citing this example, St. Thomas writes, "It is not unlikely that as a commendation of chastity that the True God, through His good angels, would perform a miracle of this kind, retaining the water in the vessel, for if something good existed in the Gentiles, it came from God. However, if this were done by demons, this does not stand against what we have said, for . . . just as demons can move a body locally, so too can they hold back such movement."

Likewise, Aloïs Van Weddigen says in his *De miraculo* (Louvain: Excudebant Vanlinthout Fratres, 1869), 212, "Nothing would be amiss if, in a state of pure nature, God were to miraculously render health to a man in response to his prayer." Likewise, see [Alexandre] Mercier, O.P., "Le surnaturel: Preuves et éclaircissements," *Revue Thomiste* [Old Series] 10 (1902): 552: "In the same case in which God would not have judged it good to sanctify and deify creation, clearly nothing would have prevented Him from sometimes directly intervening so as to bend the inexorable laws of nature and to substitute Himself for second causes . . . in order to grant the prayer of one of His creatures in distress. He assuredly could have done such a thing in such a state. On this hypothesis, there would have been a (modal) supernatural[ity] in the world, but the supernatural *order* would not have been realized therein." Nonetheless, this possibility never would have been a necessity.

D. ON THE RELATION BETWEEN THE SUPERNATURAL AND NATURAL ORDERS.

(1) The Church has defined that *there cannot be disagreement* between these two orders, "since both arise from the one and same immutable source of truth, the most excellent and great God."[64] (2) Indeed, this relationship is one of *subordination* and *harmony* so that reason and faith "bring mutual help to each other."[65] Therefore, these two orders are *distinct* but *not separated*. On the contrary, they are *united* as that which perfects and that which can be perfected. "Indeed, thus," writes St. Thomas, "faith presupposes natural knowledge, just as grace presupposes nature, and as a perfection presupposes that which can be perfected."[66] Hence, philosophy must be distinguished, though not separated, from sacred theology,[67] and likewise, the state must be distinguished but not separated from the Church.[68]

By contrast, rationalists hold that human reason is autonomous and not subordinated to revelation and faith. According to them, such subordination would not be harmonious but, rather, would be an illegitimate form of external rule [*heteronomia*]. Nay, they even invert the subordination, saying that philosophical reason is the supreme judge of the value of religious faith, {{201}} distinguishing on its own what is merely symbolic in faith from what is true. This rationalist conception presupposes the denial of the supernatural order, as well as the identification of the human intellect with the divine intellect, which would exist in a state of perpetual becoming.

§4. Resolution of Objections against the Division of Supernaturality Discussed Above

This division does not seem to be (1) essential [*per se*] and immediate, nor (2) adequate, nor (3) conformed to St. Thomas's teaching.

(1) *Objection*: An essential and immediate distinction is not made through differences of a subsequent division. Now, this division of supernaturality is made through differences of a subsequent division—namely, the division of miracles into those that are

---

[64] See Pius IX, Decree of the Sacred Congregation of the Index, June 11 (15), 1855 (Denzinger, no. 2811). Moreover, see Pius IX, *Syllabus of Errors*, no. 6 (Denzinger, no. 2906) and [First] Vatican Council, *Dei filius*, can. 4.2 (Denzinger, no. 3042).

[65] Ibid. (Denzinger, no. 2811). Moreover, see Pius IX, *Qui pluribus* (Denzinger, no. 2775) and [First] Vatican Council, *Dei filius*, ch. 4 (Denzinger, no. 3016).

[66] *ST* I, q. 2, a. 2, ad 1.

[67] Pius IX, *Syllabus of Errors*, no. 10 (Denzinger, no. 2910).

[68] Ibid., no. 55 (Denzinger, no. 55).

substantially such [*quoad substantiam*] and those that are modally miraculous. Therefore, this division of supernaturality is not essential and immediate.

Response: I distinguish the major premise, conceding it in the cases where such divisions are made in the same respect, denying it, however, if those divisions are made from different perspectives. Likewise, I contradistinguish the minor premise, denying that they are made in the same respect but conceding that they are indeed so divided if we see that the terms are being understood from different perspectives. Therefore, I deny the inference and the conclusion, for in the division of supernaturality, these differences are taken in their most general sense according to the opposition of an intrinsic cause in relation to extrinsic causes, whereas, on the contrary, in the division of miracles, these differences are taken only within the particular order of efficient causality. Therefore, "quoad substantiam" is taken *formally* in the division of supernaturality, whereas it is taken *efficiently* [*effective*] in the division of miracles. Likewise, "quoad modum" is taken meaning "extrinsically" in the division of supernaturality, whereas it is understood as being "modally efficient" in the division of miracles.

Continued insistence on the point: Even when this division is considered in the most general sense, it is not an essential division. An essential division must be made through members that are opposed to each other. Now, the aforementioned division is not made through members that are opposed to one another, for grace is at once essentially supernatural and also modally supernatural as regards the mode of its production. Therefore, this division is not an essential one.

Response: I distinguish the major premise, conceding it if one means that an essential division must be made through members that are opposed to each other according to opposed formal notions [*rationes*], though denying it if one means that it is through opposed realities [*res*]. Now, as we have said, this division of supernaturality is made through opposed formal notions and not directly through opposed realities [*res*], just like the division of the good into the morally befitting, the useful, and the delightful (*ST* I, q. 5, a. 6, ad 2). Thus, the formal notion of moral befittingness and of being pleasing are opposed to each other even though one and the same thing can be morally befitting and delectable; so too the formal notion of essential supernaturality and the formal notion of modal supernaturality are opposed to each other, even though one and the same thing, such as grace, can simultaneously be essentially supernatural and modally supernatural as regards the mode of its production. However, something is properly called modally supernatural when it is supernatural only from this perspective, just as something is properly called useful when it does not have some other formal character of goodness.

(2) *Objection to the second point above*: However, this division does not seem to be adequate, for a division in which some part of the whole to be divided is omitted is not adequate. Now, in the aforementioned division, prophecy is omitted, as well as knowledge of secrets of the heart and the gift of tongues. Therefore, the aforementioned division is not adequate.

Response: I deny the minor premise, for the gift of tongues is reduced to the category of the modally miraculous, knowledge of secrets of the heart to the category of that which is miraculous regarding the subject in which it is found, and prophecy is either reduced to the category of the substantially miraculous (if it is concerned with a natural future contingent) or (if it is prophetic revelation concerning a supernatural mystery) pertains, like theological faith, to that which is formally essentially supernatural and not to that which is only [modally] supernatural as regards its efficient causality.

(3) *Objection to the third point above*: This division stands in contradiction with St. Thomas's way of speaking, for he says in *ST* II-II, q. 171, a. 2, ad 3: "Every gift of grace elevates man to something which is above human nature. Now, this can happen in two ways. In one way, it can be *as regards the substance* of the act, as in the doing of miracles and the knowing of hidden and uncertain things of divine {{202}} wisdom; and man does not receive the gift of habitual grace for performing these kinds of acts. In another way, it is something above human nature *as regards the mode of his act*, though not according to its substance, such as to love God and know Him in the mirror of His creatures, and for this, man receives the gift of habitual grace."

Response: In this text, "quoad substantiam" is not taken "formally" but, rather, "efficiently" [(that is, as regards efficient causality)] as in the division of miracles in *ST* I, q. 105, a. 8, designating the act even generically considered, inasmuch as it exceeds the power of nature. However, *the mode* of the act is not an accidental modality but, rather, is the *formal and specific modality* that arises from the formal object. This is clear from the context and from *ST* I-II, q. 63, a. 4. As we will discuss below, this is how we must interpret Capreolus, Cajetan, and Soto. John of St. Thomas explains this as follows:

> We respond that St. Thomas does not understand "the substance of the act" as meaning the specific formal character and nature of the act, as we are understanding the expression in our current discussion, nor does he there understand "mode" as something accidentally supervening upon the act. Rather, he speaks of act "quoad modum" to describe an act *quoad elicientiam* (i.e., elicitively or efficiently) from a power according to the proper mode of its power, that is, through some principle and power permanently impressed upon it. However, he speaks of an act "quoad substantiam" regarding the very entity of the act or an effect that is *supernaturally brought about* (i.e., effectively), even if this is not brought about in the same manner in which the power connaturally elicits its acts.[69]

Now, the truth of this interpretation of St. Thomas's text is utterly clear, for in this article he asks whether prophecy is a *habitus*, and in the response to the third objection he

---

[69] John of St. Thomas, *Cursus theologicus, De gratia*, diss. 20, a. 1, solv. arg.

intends to show why our soul is in need of the *habitus* [*pl.*] of faith and charity, whereas prophecy does not need a prophetic *habitus*. The doubt is resolved from a consideration of the supernaturality of those gifts not in themselves but, rather, relative to the *elicitation* (or *production*) of acts, for which a *habitus* is required. Thus, we see that a *habitus* is not necessary for prophetic knowledge, for this knowledge exceeds [all] created power[s] essentially and effectively [*haec cognition exceedit quoad substantiam effective facultatem creatam*]. On the contrary, the habitus of faith and charity are required because acts of faith and charity must be elicited (or produced) when we will to do so.

Most certainly, in this text, St. Thomas does not wish to say that the supernaturality of charity and of theological faith is inferior to the supernaturality of freely given graces of prophecy and the gift of miracles, for he quite clearly teaches the opposite in *ST* I-II, q. 111, a. 5, following what is taught by Scripture and Tradition. Indeed, like grace, charity is a formal participation in the divine nature,[70] whereas miracles are supernatural only *efficiently*, according to the terminology used by St. Thomas in his commentary on St. John's Gospel.[71]

Final objection: The aforementioned division is not admitted, at least in the same manner, by all theologians. Hence, it does not seem to belong to theological science [precisely as science, as expressing certain knowledge and not a mere opinion] but, rather, to some particular theological system. For *the nominalists*[72] did not hold that habitual grace is entitatively supernatural (or a formal participation in the divine nature) but, rather, held that it is only a quality that has *a moral value* for eternal life on account of God's institution or good pleasure, just as money has its value on account of the king's institution. This was what William of Ockham taught. The nominalist Durandus of Saint-Pourçain spoke along the same lines, at least as regards faith. *Scotus*[73] even said that theological faith is not entitatively supernatural but instead only supernatural *quoad modum*. Finally, *Luis de Molina*[74] and *Juan de Lugo*[75] wish for the formal motive of theological faith to be penetrable by a natural faith {{203}} that proceeds from a rational consideration of miracles, even though de Lugo holds that *de facto* theological faith is essentially supernatural. Only the *Thomists* and *Suarez* hold that the formal motive of infused faith exceeds the

---

[70] See *ST* II-II, q. 110, a. 3 and 4; q. 114, a. 3. Also see the general index of St. Thomas's works for the words "grace" and "nature."

[71] See *In V Ioan.*, lect. 6, nos. 8 and 9.

[72] Regarding their theories of supernaturality, see Salmanticenses, *De gratia*, tr. 14, disp. 4, dub. 2, §3; disp. 3, dub. 2 and 3.

[73] See John Duns Scotus, *In I Sent.* prol., and I, d. 17, q. 3, no. 33. Also, *In III Sent.*, dist. 23, q. unica, no. 4–14 and d. 25, q. 2.

[74] See Luis de Molina, *Concordia*, q. 14, a. 13.

[75] Juan de Lugo, *De fide divina*, disp. 9. On this question, see Jean-Michel-Alfred Vacant, *Études théologiques sur les constitutions du Concile du Vatican d'après les actes du concile*, vol. 2 (Paris: Delhomme et Briguet, 1895), 7.

powers of reason. They alone propose this distinction: *Revelation as proceeding from God the Author of nature and of miracles* is knowable by reason [alone], whereas *revelation as proceeding from God the Author of grace is held only upon faith.*

Response: The nominalists' theory of supernaturality is generally rejected today, a theory that paved the way for the theories of Luther and Baius.[76] According to Luther, habitual grace is nothing other than an extrinsic denomination, a position that was condemned as a heresy at the Council of Trent: "If anyone says . . . that the grace that justifies us is only the favor of God, let him be anathema."[77]

As regards Scotus's doctrine concerning the supernaturality of grace, Jean-Baptiste Gonet wrote:

> This opinion is commonly rejected . . . because it does not distinguish between intrinsic (or entitative) supernaturality and extrinsic (or modal) supernaturality, contrary to the common consensus of theologians admitting that there are beings that are intrinsically and entitatively supernatural. Nay, this even stands in contradiction to the faith providing for such gifts.[78]

Likewise, before Gonet we can already find Cajetan saying in *In ST* I, q. 12, a. 5, no. 12:

> From what has been said (in this article), the falsity of Scotus's opinion in *In* I *Sent.*, quaest. prol. is obvious, for there he holds that the natural and supernatural are not distinct *realities* but only *relations to active causes*. However, in line with what we have said here, the light of glory, charity, and the gifts of the Holy Spirit and other such things all are supernatural entities, *not only because they can be caused by a supernatural agent* but [also and more importantly] because they cannot be connatural to any creature that exists or that ever could exist. For this reason, they are called supernatural beings, nay, beings of a divine order.

And even Francisco Lychetus himself, a faithful commentator on Scotus, says in his commentary on *In* III *Sent.*, disp. 25, q. 2, no. 72:

> It was not always something to be held *de fide* that (acts of faith, hope, and charity) are supernatural in their substance. . . . However, from the time of the Council of Vienne up to the time of the Council of Trent, it was only more probable that there might be *habitus* that are essentially [*per se*] infused. And after the Council of Trent that greater certitude was upheld, and it seems more

---

[76] See Pius V, *Ex omnibus afflictionibus*, no. 42 (Denzinger, no. 1942).

[77] Trent, *Decree on Justification,* can. 11 (Denzinger, no. 1561).

[78] Jean Baptiste Gonet, *Clypeus Thomisticus, De gratia*, disp. 2, a. 3.

probable to me that it is a matter of faith, [namely,] that certain ontological aids [*aliqua auxilia physica*] are given as essentially infused aids for the sake of those sorts of acts (of faith, hope, and charity).[79]

As regards the opinion of Molina and de Lugo, who hold that the *habitus* and act of infused faith are *de facto* essentially supernatural and nonetheless do not have a formal motive that is inaccessible to natural faith, we must say:

(1) This opinion disregards the necessary distinction between revelation as proceeding from God the Author of nature and of miracles (this is the motive of natural faith) and revelation as proceeding from God the Author of grace (this is the motive of infused faith).

(2) As the Thomists[80] and Suarez[81] both say, this opinion of Molina and Lugo is opposed to the fundamental principle, "The species of any given *habitus* depends on the formal character of the object, without which the species of that *habitus* cannot remain"[82] Therefore, if natural faith proceeding from a rational consideration of miracles and theological supernatural faith had the same formal motive, they would not be specifically distinct, and the supernaturality of theological faith would be brought to destruction. {{204}} Hence, here in agreement with the Thomists, Suarez says that this opinion, which he attributes to Molina, is contrary to the opinion that is held "in common by Doctors writing about the faith."[83] And he adds:

It comes quite close to the error of Pelagius holding that once revelation has been made, man can believe by his own powers, as I just said above. For if

---

[79] See John Duns Scotus, *Opera omnia*, vol. 15 (Paris: Vivès), p. 200.

[80] See Salmanticenses, *De gratia*, tr. 14, disp. 3, dub. 3, nos. 40 and 60.

[81] Suarez, *De gratia*, bk. 2, ch. 11.

[82] *ST* II-II, q. 5, a. 3. If this fundamental principle is rejected, "Nothing in the true philosophy will remain unscathed regarding the species and distinction of powers and *habitus* [pl.]," as the Salmanticenses say in *De gratia*, tr. 14, disp. 3, dub. 3, no. 60. Suarez likewise says in *De gratia*, bk. 2, ch. 11, no. 23: "Some respond that those acts are formally and essentially distinguished through their entities, though we do not need to seek out something formally distinct in them from the perspective of their objects. However, this means nothing other than overturning the principle of the distinction of acts by their objects. [Indeed,] it means nothing other than overturning the whole of philosophy, which teaches that motion and everything essentially including a relation to something other than itself... receive their *species* from their termini or objects."

[83] Suarez, *De gratia*, bk. 2, ch. 11, no. 8.

that motive is natural, within the order of our intellect's own natural powers, natural faith is sufficiently proportioned to such assent and there is no reason why it would not be sufficient in its own genus for salvation, since it depends on God only as testifying [*cum deo soli tanquam attestani nitatur*] . . . but grace will not be necessary for that, except (externally) on the part of revelation, which Pelagius did not deny. However, to say that a greater grace (or aid) is only required so that the assent may be more perfect in the genus of being, although it would not be necessary by force of the object, comes quite close to what Pelagius said, namely, that grace is required only for enabling our actions to be performed more easily. Likewise, it seems to be a flight invented solely for the sake of escaping the testimony of the Councils and the Fathers.[84]

What would be the character of faith that is only *de facto* (and not essentially) essentially (i.e. *quoad modum*) supernatural? What would be the character of a man who is only *de facto* essentially rational (and not by his essence)? All of these assertions involve contradictions, unless one wishes to preserve the terminology of the Councils through the use of illogical reasoning.

Thus, what we have said provides a sufficient defense for the commonly received notion of supernaturality, as well as its common division into essential supernaturality and modal supernaturality. Now, presupposing what we have said heretofore concerning the notions of revelation, mystery, and supernaturality, we must now consider the possibility of revelation.

---

[84] Ibid., no. 17. Likewise, see Billuart, *De gratia*, diss. 3, a. 2, §2.

On the Possibility of Revelation

{{205}}

Part 1. Negative Defense: An Examination of the Principles of Rationalism

Ch. 7. On Rationalism / Naturalism in General
  Single Article. Definition and Division of Rationalism

Ch. 8. Examination of Pantheistic Evolutionism, Inasmuch as It Denies the Possibility of Supernatural Revelation from the Perspective of the Object

  Art. 1. Exposition of Pantheistic Evolutionism in its Materialistic and Idealistic Forms

  Art. 2. Critique: Pantheistic Evolutionism Ultimately Must Deny the First Principles of Reason

Ch. 9. Examination of Agnosticism, Inasmuch as It Denies the Possibility of Supernatural Revelation from the Perspective of the Subject (i.e., Man)

  Art. 1. Exposition of Empirical Agnosticism and Idealistic Agnosticism

  Art. 2. Criticism of Agnosticism through a *Reductio ad Absurdum*

Part 2. Positive Defense of the Possibility of Revelation

Ch. 10. On the Possibility of Supernatural Revelation in General and Specifically the Possibility of Revelation of the Natural Truths of Religion

  Art. 1. On the Possibility of Immediate Revelation

  Art. 2. On the Possibility of Mediate Revelation

Ch. 11. On the Possibility of the Revelation of Supernatural Mysteries, Considered from the Perspective of the Object

  Single Article. Proof for the Existence of a Supernatural Order of Life and Truth in God (i.e., the Existence of the Order of Supernatural Mysteries)

Ch. 12. On the Possibility of Revelation of Supernatural Mysteries, Considered from the Perspective of the Agent and Subject

Single Article. A Defense Is Offered for This Possibility and Especially for the Existence of the Obediential or Elevable Capacity of Our Nature in Relation to the Supernatural Order

Having considered the notions of revelation, mysteries, and supernaturality, we treat of the possibility of supernatural revelation. Now, because rationalism denies the very possibility of revelation, we must first examine the foundations for this denial and provide at least a negative defense of the possibility of revelation through a rational criticism of the principles of rationalism. This will be our task in the first part of this second section. However, in its second part, we will marshal a positive defense on behalf of the possibility of revelation.

PART ONE

Negative Defense:
An Examination of the Principles
of Rationalism

CHAPTER SEVEN

On Rationalism / Naturalism in General

{{206}}
Single Article: Definition and Division of Rationalism

§1. The definition of rationalism
§2. What the foundation of rationalism (or the claim that reason is absolutely autonomous) is
§3. The consequences of naturalism and rationalism
§4. On the spirit of rationalism, according to the Church
§5. Division of systems of rationalism and naturalism

§1. The Definition of Rationalism

Rationalism[1] can be defined in the words of the third proposition condemned in Pius IX's *Syllabus of Errors*: *The doctrine holding that* "*human reason*, without any consideration at all of God, *is the sole judge of truth and falsehood, of good and evil*; it is a law unto itself, and by its natural powers, it suffices to care for the good of men and nations."[2] This leads to the denial of supernatural revelation, as is clear from the following propositions drawn from the *Syllabus*: "All religious truths originate from the natural power of human reason. Hence, *reason is the principal norm* by which man can and must reach knowledge of any kind of truths whatever." "Faith in Christ is detrimental to human reason; and divine revelation not only is of no use but

---

[1] See Denzinger nos. 1642ff [old numbering, Pius IX, *Singulari quadem*], 2814 [Congregation of the Index, *Theses against Augustine Bonnety*, no. 4], 2828 [Pius IX, *Eximiam tuam*, letter to the Archbishop of Cologne, June 15, 1857], 2910ff [Pius IX, *Syllabus of Errors*, nos. 10ff], 1885 [old numbering, Leo XIII, *Immortale Dei*, no. 47].
[2] Pius IX, *Syllabus of Errors*, no. 3 (Denzinger, no. 2903).

is even harmful to man's perfection." "The prophecies and miracles set forth in the narration of Sacred Scriptures are the inventions of poets; the mysteries of the Christian faith are the outcome of philosophical reflections."[3]

To put the matter more briefly, in the words of the [First] Vatican Council, absolute rationalism is the doctrine holding that "human reason is so *independent* that faith cannot be enjoined upon it by God."[4] Hence, *rationalism is a system of thought {{207}} rejecting the existence and possibility of revelation on the pretext of following the laws and dictates of reason.*[5]

Therefore, what formally constitutes rationalism is *the principle of the absolute autonomy of reason*, the formula of which rationalists seek to find in the words of Descartes: "Nothing is to be called true if it is not such in a clearly evident way." Descartes himself admitted through faith, on account of the authority of God who reveals, inevident, although evidently believable, supernatural mysteries. Rationalists say human reason, that is, "philosophy, neither can nor must submit to any authority."[6] By contrast, it must judge as though it were the supreme arbiter of what is true and false (or at least symbolic) in Sacred Scripture. Such was the position expressed by Spinoza in his *Tractatus theologico-politicus*, which contains the rationalistic solution to questions concerning inspiration, prophecy, miracles, and free inquiry. Modern rationalism historically proceeds from the Lutheran principle of free inquiry. At first, the innovators rejected the authority of the Church for proposing revelation, but later on, rationalists rejected the authority of God himself who reveals.[7]

§2. What the Foundation of Rationalism (or the Claim That Reason Is Absolutely Autonomous) Is

The proximate foundation for rationalism is naturalism;[8] its remote foundation is pantheism and atheism. Indeed, rationalism presupposes that no knowable truth exists above the natural powers of our reason. This is to deny either the existence of a supernatural order of truth and life or at least of the

---

3 Ibid., nos. 4, 6, 7 (Denzinger, nos. 2903, 2906, and 2907).

4 [First] Vatican Council, *Dei filius*, can. 3.1 (Denzinger, no. 3031).

5 According to another definition, rationalism is opposed to empiricism and likewise also designates intellectualism defending the essential distinction between the senses and the intellect.

6 Pius IX, *Syllabus of Errors*, no. 10 (Denzinger, no. 2910).

7 This is affirmed in the [First] Vatican Council, *Dei filius*. On this, see Jean-Michel-Alfred Vacant, *Études théologiques sur les constitutions du Concile du Vatican d'après les actes du concile*, vol.1 (Paris: Delhomme et Briguet, 1895), 99 (Protestantism) and 112 (Rationalism).

8 [Trans. note: Reading *naturalismus* for *raturalismus*.]

knowability of such an order, even through revelation.[9] However, properly speaking, this denial is called *naturalism*. {{208}} Although this term frequently is used as having the same meaning as "rationalism," nonetheless it is more appropriate to say that it designates the foundation of rationalism, for properly speaking, *naturalism* represents the denial of the possibility of the elevation of our *nature* to the supernatural order, and *rationalism* is the application of this doctrine to human *reason*, just as liberalism is its applica-

---

[9]   See Léon Ollé-Laprune, Member of the Institute, *La raison et le rationalisme*, preface by Victor Delbos (Paris: Perrin, 1906), 17th and 18th lessons (Rationalism and its various forms): "*It is a doctrine* (or, at the very least, a tendency) *which suppresses every form of knowledge and even every* [extramental] *thing* or absorbs it into reason. However, the word 'reason' has many acceptions. Hence, there are various forms of rationalism, which we catalogue as follows. (1) *An excessive use of reasoning*. Here, one ignores the sensible, factual order, holding only to *a priori* deductions and constructions. (2) One proclaims the *sovereignty of abstract, theoretical reason* or misunderstands that which is obscure and complex, the living complexity [of existence]. Here, we find the state of mind found in philosophers of the seventeenth century. (3) One proclaims the *sovereignty of (experimental) science* and no longer that of reason. Here, one claims to defend oneself against every form of metaphysical speculation and decides matters as the master. As a kind of dogma, one holds that the world is universally determined, something that seems to be the condition for the possibility of science. Whence, as a corollary, miracles come to be thought to be impossible (4) *An attempt to found scientific pretension upon metaphysical principles*. Here, the background dogma is the idea that everything is intelligible, in the sense that everything can be reduced to (human) thought, given that everything, in the end, is thought of. An example of this can be found in the rationalism of Spinoza. (5) *Critical rationalism*. This holds that everything is explained within universal evolution. Everything comes in its own place. It is a question of understanding everything and of explaining everything. Everything is determinate. (6) *A reaction against intellectualism*. This is marked by a clear and lively awareness of the absurdity of the pretenses of certain intellectuals. Thus, one mocks their self-conceit. Here, the great bent of such rationalism is to place something unconscious at the beginning of everything, . . . a kind of freedom, something we must just rely upon. . . . And hence, we find ourselves faced with a form of fideism, which joins forces with criticism or with this penetrating understanding of all the laws of life. This is a rationalist manner of being a fideist, . . . for while declaring that the transcendent is unknowable, one ever continues to claim that human thought remains the sole master of its judgments, with no superior authority governing over it. The final form of rationalism: all the preceding forms agree in *forbidding God, in the name of reason, to intervene in the world, to reveal Himself,* and to perform miracles. Likewise, they agree in *reducing religious facts to the measure of our thought*. This is the free-thinking sort of rationalism with its infinite nuances. . . . As a kind of master, reason is always that by which one decides all things.

"If one wishes to express the vital core of rationalism, we can reduce it to five propositions: (1) being is reduced to (human) thought; (2) the will is reduced to thought; (3) reason is self-sufficient, so that it cannot claim to be founded upon anything; reason is what is absolute (4) faith is reduced, in the last analysis, to reason and that which would be definitively refractory [to reason] has no worth; (5) reason, deciding all things, in the last accounting, is the sole master and sole judge of truth. Is this true? And if one does not admit the truth of rationalism, are we thus condemned to leave thought in the hands of chance and to renounce reason?"

tion to freedom. Hence, rationalism is proximately founded on naturalism, just as, contrariwise, the virtue of faith is founded on grace, as a property is founded upon its essence.

If naturalism ultimately denies not only the knowability of a supernatural order of truth but even the very existence of this order, then it is itself founded on *pantheism*, for in order for there to be no truth above the powers of our rational nature, it is necessary that our nature be identified with the divine nature. Likewise, if nature itself is identified with God, there will be nothing beyond the efficient powers of nature, meaning that miracles are impossible, for all phenomena thus proceed from the divine nature naturally, without any free decree.

Nay, pantheism (i.e., the identification of the finite and the infinite in the same subject) is so absurd that it cannot, properly speaking, be conceived. However, it is expressed in one of two hypotheses. On the one hand, it is claimed that (a) the world is reduced to God, existing through himself [*per se*], and this is the absorption of the world into God, acosmism. Its principle is found in antiquity in Parmenides, who affirmed the existence of a single, immobile being, while denying every form of multitude and mode as vain appearances. Absolute realism tends toward this outlook, holding that universal being exists formally on the side of reality as something subsistent. The other option for pantheism is (b) to reduce God to the world, and this represents the absorption of God into the world (or *atheism*). This is the form of pantheism found, today, in evolutionistic pantheism, as is noted in Pius X's encyclical *Pascendi*: "Yet it is a fixed and established principle among them that both science and history must be atheistic: and within their boundaries there is room for nothing but phenomena; God and all that is divine are utterly excluded."[10] Thus, the remote foundation for rationalism is pantheism or even atheism.

Hence, as will be even clearer in the course of our discussions, the possibility of supernatural revelation cannot be denied from the perspective of the object, lest one be thereby led to hold a form of atheism.

This series of errors is clearly set forth in Pius IX's *Syllabus of Errors*. The first heading is entitled, "Pantheism, naturalism, and absolute rationalism." However, the first condemned proposition is pantheistic (or, rather, atheistic), with the subsequent propositions necessarily following from the first. Indeed, it states:

There does not exist any supreme, all-wise, all-provident being dis-

---

[10] Pius X, *Pascendi*, no. 6 (Denzinger, no. 2073 [old numbering]).

tinct from this universe of things. God is identical {{209}} with the nature of things and therefore subject to change. God actually becomes himself in man and in the world. All things are God and have the very substance of God. God is one and the same reality with the world and so is spirit with matter, necessity with liberty, truth with falsehood, good with evil, and justice with injustice.[11]

The second proposition follows from the first: "Any action of God on man and the world must be denied."[12] That is, any revelation or miracle must be denied.[13]

§3. The Consequences of Naturalism and Rationalism

These consequences of naturalism and rationalism are spelled out in Pius IX's *Syllabus of Errors*. As we have already said, naturalism is the denial of the possibility of our nature being elevated to the supernatural order, and hence, it simultaneously represents a denial of original sin (i.e., the privation of original justice). In other words, naturalism at once rejects both man's supernatural nobility and human misery. Hence, it also rejects the necessity of redemption.

However, just as, according to the Church, the supernatural virtues follow upon supernatural grace, flowing into the various faculties of our soul (namely, faith, hope, charity, Christian prudence, Christian justice, Christian fortitude, and Christian temperance), so too naturalism itself lies at the root of rationalism as regards our reason, liberalism as regards our will, humanitarianism as regards our love, sensualism as regards our sensibility, and socialism as regards society. For this reason, we can provide this synoptic form for Pius XI's *Syllabus*:[14]

---

[11] Pius IX, *Syllabus of Errors*, no. 1 (Denzinger, no. 2901).

[12] Ibid., no. 2 (Denzinger, no. 2902).

[13] See Dom Paul Benoît, *La cité antichrétienne au XIXe siècle: Les erreurs modernes*, vol. 1 (Paris: Palmé, 1885). The contents of this text are as follows. "*The nature of rationalism* as regards the supernatural order and the natural order: disguised forms of rationalism" (13–113). "*The practical side of rationalism*: the universal secularization of the State, legislation, schooling, philosophy, morality, religion, and the life of the people; the systematic doctrine of the sovereignty of the people; the adoration of man; the unleashing of the masses; anarchy and despotism" (113–485). "*The origin of rationalism*. How it arose from Protestantism.—Its form in the eighteenth century.—Revolution, the law and end of its work: the equality of citizens, the destruction of Christ's rule, especially His social rule.—Rationalism under the Empire. Liberalism from 1815 to 1848.—Free thought" (488–582).

[14] See the works of Cardinal Louis-Édouard Pie, *Oeuvres complètes* (Paris: Oudin, 1878). Espe-

naturalism . . . . {
rationalism
liberalism and humanitarianism
sensualism
socialism
} {
christian faith
charity, hope, and obedience
chastity and mortification
the reign of God in society
} {
Supernatural
grace
}

Indeed, just as naturalism represents the denial of our elevation to the supernatural order and rationalism the denial of revelation, so too does liberalism represent the denial of the duty to accept divine revelation, either for the individual or, at least, for society [as a whole].[15] And thus, {{210}} liberalism, which holds that faith is not necessary for

---

cially, see his *Instructions synodales sur les principals erreurs du temps present*. Also see Juan Donoso Cortés, *Oeuvres*, vol. 2 (Paris: Vaton, 1858), 211ff. [Trans. note: This seems to be the text of Cortés to which Fr. Garrigou-Lagrange is referring as p. 212ff in an unnamed edition. See Donoso Cortés, "On the Generative Principle of the Most Grievous Errors of Our Day" in *Donoso Cortes: Readings in Political Theory*, trans. Vincent McNamara and Michael Schwartz (Ave Maria, FL: Sapientia Press, 2008), 141ff.]

In contrast to his thought, see the works of the rationalist Ferdinand Buisson, the director of primary education and then professor at the Sorbonne, *La foi laïque (extraits de discours et d'écrits 1878–1911)* (Paris: Hachette et Cie, 1912). See immediately below for citations from this work.

[15] See Pius IX, *Syllabus of Errors*, *Indifferentism*, no. 15: "Everyone is free to embrace and profess the religion that by the light of reason he judges to be true" (Denzinger, no. 2915).

Liberalism. Prop. 77: "In our age it is no longer advisable that the Catholic religion be the only State religion, excluding all the other forms of worship" (Denzinger, no. 2977). Prop. 80: "The Roman pontiff can and should reconcile and adapt himself to progress, liberalism, and modern culture." (Denzinger, no. 2980).

Atheism and ethics. Prop. 56: "Moral law needs no divine sanction, and there is not the least need that human laws conform to the natural law or receive their obligatory force from God" (Denzinger, no. 2956).

Atheism and the family. Prop. 66–67: "The sacrament of matrimony is nothing but an appendage to the contract and separable from it, and the sacrament itself consists merely in the nuptial blessing"; "By natural law the bond of matrimony is not indissoluble, and in various cases divorce, properly so-called, can be sanctioned by civil authority" (Denzinger, no. 2966–67). [Trans. note: Fr. Garrigou-Lagrange only has "Matrimony is not a sacrament" for the first quote.]

Atheism in the schools. Prop. 47: "*The best state of civil society demands that the people schools that* are open to all children of any class of people and the public institutions in general that are destined for the teaching of literature and the more exact studies and *for caring for the education of youth should be exempted from all authority, control, and power of the Church* and be subjected to the full authority of the civil and political power, exactly according to the pleasure of the rulers and the standard of current public opinion" (Denzinger, no. 2947). [Trans. note: Fr. Garrigou-Lagrange cites only the sections in italics.]

Atheism and society. Prop. 60: "Authority is nothing else but the sum of the number and forces of matter." (Denzinger, no. 2960) Likewise, see Pius IX, *Quanta cura*, no. 4: "The people's will, manifested by what is called public opinion or in some other way, consti-

salvation, substitutes itself for Christian obedience, just as rationalism substitutes itself for faith. Similarly, humanitarianism (i.e., love of humanity without any relation and subjection to God) substitutes itself for charity, by which we love our neighbors for God's sake. Nay, in humanitarianism, the order of charity is inverted, for as its defenders say, we must revere all human opinions even if they are contrary to the Word of God, which is to scorn God himself. Hence, according to the Church, this human respect, which is often called "modesty," represents the falsest form of humility. Thus, liberalism and humanitarianism are false forms of charity, mere imitations, like glass beads in comparison with a real diamond. Similarly, in humanitarianism, the desire for earthly felicity is substituted for hope in heavenly beatitude.

Likewise, as regards our sense, desires, sensualism, effeminacy [*mollitia*], and the legitimacy of divorce are substituted for mortification, chastity, patience, and Christian fortitude.

Finally, as regards society [as whole], socialism is substituted for the reign of God in society and for Christian justice, as though society itself, not God, had established the particular rights and duties regarding familial and social life and as though man's end were not heavenly beatitude but, rather, a future earthly city.[16] Hence, certain socialists speak of society with a mystical lilt to their voice as though they were speaking of God, for in their eyes, society is indeed God in the very process of his own self-becoming.[17]

---

tutes a supreme law, free from all divine and human control; and that in the political order accomplished [deeds], [precisely because] they are accomplished, have the force of [law]" (Denzinger, no. 2890; see nos. 2890–2896).

[16] *On socialism*, see *Quanta cura*, no. 4, where the error of socialism is explained in this way: "Domestic society or the family derives the whole principle of its existence from the civil law alone; and consequently, that on civil law alone depend all rights of parents over their children, and especially that of providing for education" (Denzinger, no. 2891). Likewise, in his encyclical *Quod apostolici muneris*, Leo XIII states, regarding socialism: "The Church, with much greater wisdom and good sense, *recognizes the inequality among men, who are born with different powers of body and mind, [as well as] inequality in actual possession [of goods]*" (Denzinger, no. 3133). [Trans. note: Fr. Garrigou-Lagrange also cites *Syllabus*, no. 18 (Denzinger, no. 2918), which doesn't make sense in this context.]

[17] See Ferdinand Buisson, *La foi laïque* (cited in *Dictionnaire apologétique*, "Laïcisme"): "To shackle reason and to constrict the intellect represents the commission of a sacrilege. . . . *The only religion capable of regenerating humanity*, held for too long in slavery by dogmatic religions, is freedom of conscience served by intelligence. *It is the cult of human reason*" (198). Now, "is it possible," Buisson adds, "to be *a free thinker* without being *a republican* and to be a republican without being *a socialist*?" (196). As is shown in *Dictionnaire apologétique, loc. cit.* col. 1785, laicism holds: "The laicist spirit = absolute autonomy of the individual.—Autonomy of the individual = popular sovereignty.—Popular sovereignty = a democratic republic, universal suffrage, perfect equality of all goods, and socialism"

Jean Jaurés, in his *Discours à la Chambre des députés* on Feb. 11, 1895 stated: "*What we must safeguard above all else*, what is the inestimable good conquered by man through all of the prejudices, sufferings, and battles that he has undergone, *is the idea that there is no truth* that is

{{211}} *Semi-rationalism* must be noted among the consequences of rationalism. It is *an attempt at reconciling rationalism with the Catholic faith.*[18] It differs from absolute rationalism inasmuch as it admits the fact of divine revelation properly so called. However, it does agree with it, inasmuch as it holds that all revealed mysteries can be demonstrated by means of principles of natural reason and, hence, holds that there is no necessity that we believe on account of the authority of God who reveals. In this way, semi-rationalism preserves the autonomy of reason. Likewise, the semi-rationalists say, "As there is a distinction between the philosopher and his philosophy, he has the right and duty to submit himself to the authority he acknowledges as legitimate; but philosophy neither can nor must submit to any authority."[19]

This kind of semi-rationalism (as well as liberalism) was held by Günther, Hermes, and Frohschammer.[20] In speaking about semi-rationalism, the [First] Vatican Council wrote:

With this impiety (of rationalism) spreading in every direction, it has come about, alas, that many even among the children of the Catholic Church have strayed *from the path of genuine piety*, and as the truth was gradually diluted in them, their Catholic sensibility was weakened. Led away by diverse and strange teachings and *confusing* nature and grace, human knowledge and divine faith, they are found to distort the genuine sense of the dogmas which Holy Mother Church holds and teaches, and to endanger the integrity and *genuineness* of the faith.[21]

Liberalism, which we can find expressed in the thought of Felicité de

---

sacred, that is, one that man is forbidden to fully investigate. The greatest thing in the world is *the sovereign freedom of the mind* [*esprit*]. . . . *It is that every truth that does not come from us is a lie.* . . . It is that if the very ideal of God were made visible, *if God Himself stood before the masses in a tangible form, man's first duty would be to refuse Him obedience and to consider Him as an equal in discourse*, not as a master to whom one would be subject."

18 Cf. Pius IX, *Syllabus of Errors*, §II (Moderate Rationalism).

19 Ibid., no. 10 (Denzinger, no. 2910).

20 See Gregory XVI, *Dum acerbissimas*, Denzinger, no. 1618 (old numbering); Pius IX, *Qui pluribus*, no. 5 (Denzinger, no. 2775); Pius IX, Letter *Eximiam tuam* to the Archbishop of Cologne, June 15, 1857 (Denzinger, no. 1655 [old numbering]); Pius IX, Letter *Gravissimas inter* to the Archbishop of Munich-Freising, Dec. 11, 1862 (Denzinger, no. 1666 [old numbering]).

21 [First] Vatican Council, *Dei filius*, introduction, no. 8. Vacant, *Études théologiques sur les constitutions du Concile du Vatican d'après les actes du concile*, vol. 1, 119. [Trans. note: The translation of this text from *Dei filius* can be found in *Decrees of the Ecumenical Councils*, trans. Norman P. Tanner (Georgetown: Georgetown University Press, 2016).]

Lamennais, was another such attempt at reconciliation. Lamennais[22] confused supernatural faith, which is necessary for salvation, with the common faith of the whole of humanity, which is preserved through tradition in all religions, a faith that he called common sense (or general reason). Liberalism and indifferentism followed from this confusion, holding that any kind of profession of faith suffices for salvation.

Speaking against the liberalism of Lamennais, Pope Gregory XVI wrote, "From an extended and unrestrained desire for novelty, truth is not looked for where it truly is found and holding the holy and apostolic traditions in lower esteem, but instead is looked for in other vain, futile, and uncertain teachings which are not taught as being approved by the Church, all the while such men in their great vanity wrongly believe that the truth is supported upon teachings."[23] Lamennais confused the glory of God and the salvation of souls with the passing breezes [*aura*] of popular favor and thus arrived at a false notion of charity.

More recently, *the modernists* had nearly the same bent of thought, intending (like the semi-rationalists and liberals) to discover a middle point of reconciliation between naturalism and the Catholic faith. Now, a virtuous mean does indeed exist between two vices that are opposed by way of excess and defect. However, between truth and falsity, as well as between good and evil, the only mean that exists {{212}} is mediocrity (i.e., the confusion of good and evil, as well as the perversion of the true norm of judgment and of the will).

Therefore, the Church condemned these attempts to reconcile rationalism with the Catholic faith, for there can be no reconciliation between contradictories (in this case, the affirmation and denial of a supernatural order, and of an essentially supernatural religion). This contradiction does not exist merely in relation to the letter of the teaching of faith but also as regards its spirit.

§4. On the Spirit of Rationalism, according to the Church

This must be briefly discussed for two reasons: (1) so that we may see with greater clarity that it is completely impossible for us to reconcile rationalism with the Catholic faith, contrary to what may be claimed by semi-ration-

---

[22] See Lamennais's work in the journal *L'avenir*. Also see the second volume of his *Essai sur l'indifférence*.

[23] Gregory XVI, *Singulari nos affecerant gaudio* (Letter to the French Bishops, June 25, 1834), Denzinger, no. 1617 (old numbering). [Trans. note: Fr. Garrigou Lagrange cites "Denz., 1623–1617." 1623 correlates to 2752, the second proposition against Bautain issued by Gregory XVI on Sept. 8, 1840.]

alism and modernism; (2) so that the usefulness and necessity of moral arguments in apologetics may be manifested with greater clarity.[24]

---

[24] Even though he does not always sufficiently preserve the gratuity of our elevation to the supernatural order, in his book, *Action* (392 and 368), Maurice Blondel profoundly sets forth the spirit of modern rationalism. Indeed, he says: "Finally, it would be strange to oppose to the supernatural order that which is its sole *raison d'être* and proper definition. What would it be if it were only an object of study, a conquest of human effort, if it came emerged from philosophy itself? What would it be if it did not require of man anything that would exceed, disconcert, and bruise his nature? ... Once more, one would claim that the natural order does not suffice for man. But the ultimate desire of this perspective would be for the supernatural order to be inserted back into the natural order itself. One claims that only the notion of revelation does not endure rational discussion. And one does not endure that this negative conclusion would be discussed: *on the pretext of respect, free examination refuses examination*. One imposes upon oneself, in relation to dogma, a mute reservation which dogma does not require, which dogma condemns. And these respectful people who do not wish for one to critique it are those very people in whose eyes it is a wholly human invention. ... One seems 'ready to die in order to not be able to name Him whom one adores.' And if He is named, one rends one's garments while crying out blasphemy; a singular bulimia, which under the appearance of a devouring appetite, hides a satiety, a disgust, an absence of every generous hunger. *When one loves the truth more than oneself, does it cost to lower one's feeble thought before the infinity of what is to be believed?* Here, we find ourselves faced with the seed of a greater inconsistency, a regular origin of all the others. It seemed that the expansion of the human heart was infinite, that its need for tenderness, dedication, and merited happiness, the only kind that it could savor, was insatiable; it seemed that one was ready to suffer and die from such love. But faced with the sensible or intellectual sacrifices that the egoism of pride or of the will must make to conscience, we thus find ourselves faced with a revolt as though this was tyranny and intolerance" (392).

"If the gravity of the fault is veiled over, ... if *evil* first of all seems to be only a *lesser good*, ... let us not conclude against the sincere confession of conscience: it remains living and ardent only inasmuch as, according to the dictum of Carlyle, it more or less reminds us of what we more or less know. That is, under these approximations of knowledge, *there is an absolutely infinite difference between a good man and a liar.* Doubtlessly, in the middle region of the soul, there are superficial nuances which distinguish the common run of men. How are we to admit a measureless responsibility in a boundless infirmity? How are we to believe in the infinite malice of this man whom I know and whom I love in his weakness, inconsistency, and unfortunate condition? But one must not believe that the role of our human ignorance is indulgence and love because it is not justice. And nonetheless, without judging anyone—for the moral commandment, 'You shall not judge,' is absolute—penetrate a little further and experience the hearts of men. See in your imagination this miserable person who, without having ever dreamt of it, would rather die of hunger than commit an evil deed: by the very apex [*la point de l'âme*] of his soul, this uncouth man clings to eternal life. What portions will be dealt out on the day of justice, and [on that day] there will be nothing arbitrary, nothing external, nor anything excessive in the extremity of the divine reprisals.

"It seems that there is nothing simpler, nothing more natural or more legitimate than to say to one's own will: 'You will not go further on; you will receive nothing from on high; you will give nothing from what you have; you will not go outside of yourself.' But, nonetheless, here we see that this reserved and expectant attitude is locked up within a voluntary denial and a positive privation, στέρησις. *In order to refuse every eminent gift and to be confined within*

{{213}} It is not a question of the spirit of this or that rationalist, who can be oblivious to the gravity of their error. Rather, we are concerned here with the spirit of rationalism itself.

Frequently, in its religious philosophy, rationalism commends, with great emphasis, not only sincerity in the search for truth but also [our] natural religious sentiment. Nay, it admits the mysteries of Christianity, understood in accord with a natural interpretation. Thus, for example, consider the work of Kant and Hegel regarding these matters. However, in Sacred Scripture, it is said, "Test spirits to see whether they are from God" (1 John 4:1). "Take care that nobody deceive you through philosophy" (Col 2:8). "Indeed, the wisdom of this world is foolishness before God" (1 Cor 3:19). "The mystery of iniquity is already at work" (2 Thess 2:7). And Christ, who prayed for all sinners, said, "I do not pray for the world" (John 17:9) in order to thereby express the wickedness of [this] world's spirit.

Indeed, the spirit of rationalism is manifestly clear when it proclaims the principle of the absolute autonomy of reason—namely, "Human reason is so independent that faith cannot be commanded of it by God." According to the Church, this is the very spirit of infidelity, disobedience, rebellion, and of "the pride of life," spoken of in 1 John 2:16. In other words, it is the love of one's own excellence without subjection to God.

Thus, this spirit of rationalism is so radically opposed to the spirit of God that the principle of the absolute autonomy of reason is not only "wicked and perverse" but, as is stated in various encyclicals, the expression of "the most foolish kind of arrogance," nonsense that leads to the freedom of destruction, which "by the deceit of the wicked spreads forth everywhere."[25]

Likewise, in the opening of the constitution *Dei filius*, the [First] Vatican Council stated:

---

oneself, one makes use of the very same thing that one claims to do without. To see it from outside, *sub specie materiae*, the act thus dampened seems without a doubt to be restricted and invalidated. *But man's great fault is to employ his infinite power in an act of self-limitation*: only his will is strong enough to stop his will. And if the route can be blocked off even to God, if man can annihilate Him and make Him no longer exist for man, this is because he makes use of it against Him by first accepting what he needs in order to repel him" (368).

"Moreover, without prejudging any properly religious question—that is of another order— is it necessary to exclude, by philosophy, the obstacles that accumulate, doubtlessly erroneously, a *philosophy that is hostile and biased* not against this or that dogmatic formula but *to the very notion of revelation* and to the possibility and relevance of every form of defined dogma" (393).

25 See Gregory XVI, *Mirari vos* (Denzinger, nos. 2730ff). Likewise, see Pius IX, *Ineffabilis Deus* (Denzinger, no. 1642ff [old numbering; cf. 2800ff]) and *Quanta cura* (Denzinger, no. 1688ff [old. numbering]).

Thereupon there came into being and spread far and wide throughout the world that doctrine of rationalism or naturalism—utterly opposed to the Christian religion, since this is of supernatural origin—*which spares no effort to bring it about that Christ,* who alone is our lord and savior, *is shut out from the minds of people and the moral life of nations. Thus they would establish what they call the rule of simple reason or nature.* The abandonment and rejection of the Christian religion, and the denial of God and his Christ, has plunged the minds of many into the abyss of pantheism, materialism, and atheism, and the consequence is that *they strive to destroy rational nature itself, to deny any criterion of what is right and just,* and to overthrow the very foundations of human society.[26]

In this, we already see the expression of a refutation of rationalism.[27] {{214}} In the pre-conciliar schema, we read:

> Therefore, detesting the portents of these sorts of errors, because of the dut[ies] falling to Our supreme pastoral office as well as from the very sentiments of our own soul, to the greatest degree possible for us [*quo maxime possumus*] and solicitous for the eternal salvation of souls, we simultaneously most strongly admonish and implore those who hold positions of authority and who privately or publicly hold an office in schools for the educating and instruction of youth, that they ward off from the souls of those who are placed in their care this pestilential march of unbelief and fortify them against the dangers of falling under its sway.[28]

> The majority of recent pantheists typically say *that what is taught in pantheistic philosophy is likewise in reality contained in the Christian faith,* saying however, that there is a great distinction in the form of conceiving and understanding the same thing. They say *that faith is the lowest form* of conceiving the truth, whereas *pantheistic speculation is the supreme and most perfect form* [*of wisdom*]. Indeed, they say that the truth is not understood *per se* by the Christian faith but instead is accepted under concepts of particular, sensible things and veiled in symbols, whereas it falls to [philosophical] speculations to understand the pure truth *per se. Hence, they boast that they in no way deny the dogmas of the*

---

[26] [First] Vatican Council, *Dei filius,* introduction, no. 7 (trans. Tanner). See Vacant, *Études sur le Concile du Vatican,* vol. 1, 112 and 572.

[27] Also see *Schema concilii Vaticani,* doc. 6, ch. 2.

[28] *Schema concilii Vat.,* doc. 6, ch. 2. See Vacant, *Études sur le Concile du Vatican,* vol. 1, 572.

Christian creed concerning God, the Trinity, the Incarnation, the Redemption, the Resurrection, etc. but, *quite to the contrary, speculatively understand them*. By this trickery, while they peddle these fictions concerning the evolution of *pure being* in the world and humanity as though they were speculative declarations of Christian dogmas, they eagerly strive to hold these two positions, so that they may once protect themselves from the infamy of atheism and impiety, and yet *assault the Christian religion by deforming its dogmas and abusing its terms with great efficacy*. Hence, in the exposition of pantheistic impiety we have deemed it opportune to mention also this *deceit* and abuse of Christian terms.[29]

In a word, *the spirit of rationalism is*, as the [First] Vatican Council says, *to perversely substitute the kingdom of nature and reason for the kingdom of God*.

Now, concerning this, we must note five points that are admitted by all Catholics, though they are generally expressed by way of rhetoric [*oratorio modo*] rather than theologically.

(1) Encyclicals use the term "perversity" in accord with its proper sense, which indeed is most suitable here, for perversity is *the intention [voluntas] to invert the essential order of things*—namely, so that creatures may no longer be subjected to God but, rather, God to creatures. In this, we see *a spiritual sin* that is much graver than carnal sins, for "it involves a greater turning away from God" (*ST* I-II, q. 73, a. 5). And this perversity of will presupposes a radical overturning of judgment, which is nothing other than something contrary to the gift of wisdom and is called, in Sacred Scripture, spiritual *"foolishness"*[30] or "carnal wisdom."[31] "The sensual man perceiveth not these things that are of the Spirit of God. For it is foolishness to him: and he cannot understand" (1 Cor 2:14, DR). Indeed, wisdom judges all things in relation to God, the First Cause and Ultimate End, whereas spiritual foolishness *judges all things, even those related to God, relative to that which is lowest*—namely, freedom of thought—without any rule.[32] Hence, it is quite clear that, according to the Church, the absolute autonomy of rationalism is nothing other than the false autonomy of the Prodigal Son, which leads to servitude and penury (cf. Luke 15:11). This is something that is not heeded well enough by semi-rationalist theologians such as Günther and Hermes, as well as the modernists coming after his day.

{{215}} (2) Nay, according to the schema of the [First] Vatican Council, the spirit of rationalism proceeds *from a more radical impulse toward perversity*.[33] Indeed, Catho-

---

29 Ibid., doc. 6, no. 4. See Vacant, *Études sur le Concile du Vatican*, vol. 1, 582.
30 1 Corinthians 3:19.
31 2 Corinthians 1:12.
32 See *ST* II-II, q. 46, a. 1.
33 *Schema concilii Vaticani*, doc. 6 (Vacant, *Études sur le concile*, vol. 1, 580): "It cannot be denied that in this more recent era we find men faced with that great temptation, by which the ancient serpent seduces those living in the world, to turn on themselves [*eo dirigi*], so that men would

lic theologians have always discussed the principle of the absolute autonomy of created reason when discussing a graver spiritual sin—namely, that of the demons. In assigning not only the material object of this sin but also its formal character, St. Thomas provided a most profound definition of naturalism. In *ST* I, q. 63, a. 3, he writes:

> In this (the angel) had an undue desire to be like unto God, for *he desired as the ultimate end of beatitude that which he was able to attain* BY THE POWERS OF HIS OWN NATURE, *turning his desire* AWAY FROM SUPERNATURAL BEATI- TUDE WHICH COMES FROM THE GRACE OF GOD. Or, if he desired as his last end that likeness to God which is given by grace, he willed to have this through THE POWER OF HIS OWN NATURE AND NOT [AS SOMETHING RECEIVED] FROM THE DIVINE AID according to God's own ordering of things. . . . In this, he *perversely willed to be like unto God.*

Similarly, rationalism either rejects the supernatural mysteries, as well as our elevation to the supernatural order, or wishes to know the supernatural mysteries by the natural power of reason. Hence, it is not surprising if, in looking upon the rationalistic principle of the autonomy [of nature and of human reason], the Church sees nothing other than the spiritual rebellion whose motto is "I will not serve."

(3) We must also note that *the perversity of the spirit of rationalism* is not always immediately apparent, for *it is not as much found in the object to which it tends as in its mode of tending toward its object.* It proposes to itself a good object—namely, social and intellectual progress—though without God's aid and without obedience to God. St. Thomas also notes this point in relation to the sin of the angels:

> Sin can take place by freely *choosing something that is good in itself, though not according to a due measure or rule.* In this way, the defect leading one to sin exists only on the side of the person's choice, which does not have a due order, and not on the side of the thing that is chosen. For example, someone may choose to pray without heeding the order established by the Church. And a sin of this kind does not presuppose ignorance but instead only presupposes an absence of consideration concerning those things which should be considered. And in this way, the Angel sinned by turning himself toward his own good through a

---

thus, little by little, be turned away from the light of faith or certainly from simplicity and gen- uineness of the obedience of a faith, to which every intellect must be brought into captivity, as well as from goods of the supernatural order in general [*fere*] and thus to take rest in human reason alone and in the natural order of things." Then, immediately a comment is registered regarding semi-rationalism in the same document: "This milder form [of rationalism], whose errors are less manifest, poses an even greater danger."

free choice without ordering this to the rule of the divine will.[34]

This finds a pointed summary in the words of Cajetan: "He pridefully tended to things that were good in themselves." In this case, perversity is not found in the object but, rather, in the mode of tending toward the object.

Likewise, in setting itself in opposition to divine revelation, rationalism says that it intends something good per se—namely, science, social and intellectual progress, as well as peace among men—nay, even sometimes the progress of our very religious sentiment. However, it tends toward these natural goods "by turning itself away from the supernatural beatitude that comes from God's grace" and intends to fulfill all these aims by the power of its own nature, to the exclusion of Christ, so that, as the [First] Vatican Council expresses the matter, it seeks to establish the kingdom of nature and reason.

(4) *Nay, rationalism establishes gatherings of religions so that all of them may be reconciled*, and in these gatherings all religions are represented except for Catholicism. An apparent good is all the more dangerous to the degree that it resembles the true good. According to the words of St. Paul[35] and St. John, the Antichrist will not appear suddenly as a manifest and violent enemy of the Church but will lead people astray through deceitful marvels {{216}} as a false Christ: "Then, if any man shall say to you, 'Lo, here is Christ, or there,' do not believe him. For there shall arise false christs and false prophets and shall shew great signs and wonders, insomuch as to deceive (if possible) even the elect."[36] And similarly, St. John said, "Dearly beloved, believe not every spirit, but try the spirits if they be of God: because many false prophets are gone out into the world. By this is the spirit of God known. Every spirit which confesseth that Jesus Christ is come in the flesh is of God: And every spirit that dissolveth Jesus is not of God. And this is Antichrist, of whom you have heard that he cometh."[37]

Thus, we have a verification of the expression "the corruption of the best is the worst"—namely, the corruption of charity and religious faith under the appearance of tolerance and the reconciliation of all churches and religions.[38]

---

[34] *ST* I, q. 63, a. 1, ad 4.

[35] See 2 Thessalonians 2:3–11 (DR): "the man of sin be revealed, the son of perdition . . . shewing himself as if he were God. . . . For *the mystery of iniquity already worketh*. . . . And then that wicked one shall be revealed . . . in all seduction of iniquity to them that perish: because they receive not the love of the truth, that they might be saved. Therefore God shall send them the operation of error, to believe lying. That all may be judged who have not believed the truth but have consented to iniquity."

[36] Matthew 24:23–24 (DR).

[37] 1 John 4:1–3 (DR).

[38] According to Kant, the Church Triumphant will be nothing other than the union of all churches and religions according to the principles of merely natural and rational religion. (See his work *Religion within the Bounds of Mere Reason*.)

(5) This perversity is indeed rarely fully self-conscious in men. "The sensual man perceiveth not these things that are of the Spirit of God," nor, consequently, the infinite gravity of sin, which is an act of turning away from God. This gravity is better understood by the [blessed] angels, who intuitively see the divine essence, than it is by the demons. Likewise, the perversity of rationalism is better understood by theology than it is by rationalism itself. Theology knows that it itself is "a kind of impression of the divine knowledge" (*ST* I, q. 1, a. 3) and in the same way knows that rationalism is the perverse denial of the divine knowledge and goodness, being as it were the negative theology of another Church, one of denial and of antipathy [*odii*].

Thus, we can see the usefulness and necessity of utilizing moral arguments in apologetics, especially in applied apologetics [*in arte apologetica*], for such arguments dispose the as-yet-unbelieving man to consider other arguments, as well as the revelation, properly speaking.

§5. Division of Systems of Rationalism and Naturalism

This division must be taken from the definition of rationalism. However, as we have said, rationalism is a teaching that denies the possibility of supernatural revelation because it holds that no knowable truth exists above the natural powers of our reason. Hence, rationalistic systems are essentially and adequately divided according to the way that this denial is expressed—namely, either as rejecting the very *existence* of the order of supernatural being and truth or as denying only *the knowability* of this order through revelation. Therefore, the first kinds of systems reject the possibility of supernatural revelation *from the perspective of the object* (e.g., pantheists). The rest deny the same possibility either *from the perspective of the subject* (that is, of man who cannot rationally receive revelation, thus giving us the position held by agnostics) or *from the perspective of God as an agent*, who cannot do something outside of the natural order (thus giving us the position held by deists). Hence, we can propose the following division for the various systems of rationalism:

Rationalism denies the possibility of supernatural revelation	either from the perspective of the object:	*pantheistic evolutionism*	idealistic (e.g., Hegel) empiricist (e.g., Haeckel)
	or from the perspective of the knowing subject:	*Agnosticism*	idealistic (e.g., Kant) empiricist (e.g., positivists)
	or from the perspective of the God as an agent:	*Deism*	(Cherbury, Voltaire, Cousin, J. Simon)

{{217}} (1) Now, systems belonging to the first division can be reduced to pantheism and, today, to *pantheistic evolutionism*, which was condemned in the first proposition of Pius IX's *Syllabus of Errors* and in canon 3.2 of the constitution *Dei filius* promulgated by the [First] Vatican Council.[39]

The latter text states: "If anyone says that man cannot be called by God to a knowledge and perfection that surpasses the natural, but that he can and must by himself, through constant progress, finally arrive at the possession of all that is true and good, let him be anathema." This doctrine presupposes what is said in the first proposition of the *Syllabus of Errors*, namely: "God actually becomes himself in man and in the world; all things are God and have the very substance of God," as the pantheists say, especially Spinoza, Schelling, Fichte, Hegel, and Haeckel, as well as other modern thinkers. These systems deny the existence of supernatural being and truth, as well as the possibility of miracles, because they reject the existence of God the Free Creator, who is really and essentially distinct from the world. They say that the First Cause is immanent within the world. Hence, this doctrine is also called *immanentism*. However, having thus done away with the existence of a transcendent God existing above the world, they still find it necessary to provide an explanation for religious phenomena experienced in man's natural life. Hence, all religions (even the Christian religion) are explained through the evolution of our natural religious sentiment, and the value of this sentiment, as well as its evolution, is judged by reason, which remains the supreme arbiter of truth and falsity, good and evil, and utterly autonomous, according to the very principle at the root of rationalism.

The evolutionistic and pantheistic systems of rationalism are subdivided inasmuch as they take on two forms: *empiricist* and *idealistic*. *Empiricist* (or materialistic) *evolutionism* is defended by people like Haeckel. *Idealistic evolutionism was proposed* by Fichte and Hegel.

(2) However, systems of the second kind—namely, that[40] deny the possibility of supernatural revelation *from the perspective of the subject*—can be reduced to *agnosticism*, which was condemned in particular in Pius X's encyclical *Pascendi*.[41]

Indeed, agnosticism denies the ontological and transcendent value of the first notions and principles of our reason. In other words, it holds that reason can only know phenomena and the phenomenal laws that are the object of external or internal experience but cannot know the substantial being of things, nor *a fortiori* that which transcends finite beings. Hence, it denies the knowability of the existence of a God who is really and essentially distinct from the world, as well as the knowability of the

---

[39] See Pius IX, *Syllabus of Errors*, no. 1 (Denzinger, no. 2901) and [First] Vatican Council, *Dei filius*, can. 2.3 (Denzinger, no. 3028). [Trans. note: Correcting the later citation based on the text that follows. Fr. Garrigou-Lagrange's cited the equivalent of no. 3027.]

[40] [Trans. note: Reading *quae* for *que*.]

[41] See Pius X, *Pascendi*, nos. 6 and 7 (Denzinger, nos. 3475 and 3477).

possibility and existence of miracles. Nay, from this perspective, a miracle cannot even be conceived of, for it would be contrary to the principle of causality, which is here formulated as "Every phenomenon presupposes *an antecedent phenomenon*," for in this system of thought, phenomena are not intelligible in relation to being and to the Supreme Being but, rather, only as regards their inter-relations. Therefore, the idea of a miracle is unthinkable. Consequently, supernatural revelation cannot be conceived of, and even if our mind's notions were supernaturally ordered by God, they most certainly could not analogically express the divine mysteries because they have neither an onto-logical nor a transcendent value but instead only one of the phenomenal order. From this outlook, the expression of the mysteries could only be metaphorical / symbolic, and philosophical reason thereby would remain the supreme arbiter of the value of religious symbolism.

Hence, according to agnosticism, a God who is really and essentially distinct from the world perhaps exists as the foundation of a supernatural order, but from our perspective it is as though this supernatural order did not exist. Consequently, agnostic systems strive to explain all religious phenomena, even Christ's life and Christianity itself, {{218}} by way of a resolution to the primitive phenomena of our natural religious sentiment. Thus, we once again find ourselves faced with a form of immanentism and evolutionism that is not, properly speaking, pantheistic but is instead agnostic. Whatever extramen-tal reality may be in itself, things can only be explained according to phenomenal laws. Therefore, every form of faith and religious experience must be explained according to the laws of the natural evolution of our religious sentiment. However, these laws are sci-entifically known by reason, which ever retains its place as the supreme arbiter.

These agnostic systems are subdivided in the same manner as are evolutionistic ones—namely, as falling under two forms, one being *empiricist* and the other *idealis-tic*. *Empiricist agnosticism* is defended, for example, by David Hume, Herbert Spencer, Auguste Comte, Émile Durkheim, William James, and many modernist thinkers, whereas *idealistic agnosticism* is defended by Immanuel Kant, Albrecht Ritschl, [Louis Auguste] Sabatier, and others.

Therefore, we must undertake an investigation of evolutionism, which denies the possibility of supernatural revelation from the perspective of the object, and, thereafter, an examination of agnosticism, which rejects this possibility from the perspective of the subject.

(3) *Deism* (in thinkers like Voltaire, Victor Cousin, and J[ules] Simon), by contrast, denied the possibility of revelation *from the perspective of God as an agent* inasmuch as this position held that God cannot act outside of the laws of nature. Thus, Robespierre, as a deist, wished to institute a cult of the Supreme Being and rejected everything supernatural.[42] This form of

---

[42] [Trans. note: Reading *omnes supernaturales* for *omnes supernaturale*.]

naturalism will be refuted later on when we undertake the positive defense of the possibility of revelation.[43]

---

[43] See Donoso Cortés, *Oeuvres*, vol. 2 (1862), 212, 228, etc., "On the generative principle of the gravest errors of our days" (a thirty-page letter to Cardinal Fornari to be presented to Pius IX). [Trans. note: See Donoso Cortés, "On the Generative Principle of the Most Grievous Errors of Our Day" in *Donoso Cortes: Readings in Political Theory*, trans. Vincent McNamara and Michael Schwartz (Ave Maria, FL: Sapientia Press, 2008), 141ff.] This text shows that *Deism* is the principle of modern errors, for if God does not care for individuals, *a sin is no longer an offense against God* but, rather, is only an act against reason, which continually evolves. Once upon a time, theft may well have been prohibited. However, socialists now say, "Private property is itself theft." However, if sin no longer is an offense against God, *a fortiori original sin will be denied and, hence, the redemptive Incarnation, regeneration through grace, the sacrifice of the Mass, the sacraments, the priesthood, matrimony as a sacrament, and eternal life*. Thus, we find ourselves brought back to the complete naturalism of paganism.

In this way of regression and descent, which is vaunted as being progress, *liberalism*, says Donoso Cortés, wishes to remain situated at a kind of middle altitude, neither admitting nor denying Christianity. However, this uncertainty does not suffice for action. Therefore, after liberalism there follows *radicalism* as a form of denial, then *socialism*, and finally *materialistic communism*, which denies the rights of property, family, the country as such [*patriam*], and religion. This was written by Donoso Cortés in the year 1852 with the greatest of clarity, and from that time onward we have seen a complete verification of his predictions. Among the writings of this great Catholic writer, one must read, along with the aforementioned letter to Cardinal Fornari, two of his principal writings, *Discours sur la situation générale de l'Europe* 1850 (vol. 1, 399) and *Essay sur le catholicisme* (vol. 3). [Trans. note: For the second text, See Donoso Cortés, *Essays on Catholicism, Liberalism, and Socialism: Considered in their Fundamental Principles*, trans. William McDonald (Dublin: William B. Kelly, 1874).]

Examination of Pantheistic Evolutionism, Inasmuch as It Denies the Possibility of Supernatural Revelation from the Perspective of the Object

{{219}} The thesis of this chapter can be stated thus: *Pantheistic evolutionism denying the possibility of supernatural revelation from the perspective of the object must deny the first principles of reason.*

There are two parts to this chapter:

Art. 1. An exposition of pantheistic evolutionism in general, followed by a consideration of its empiricist and idealistic forms in particular, regarding how this doctrine denies the order of supernatural truth.

Art. 2. A critique of both forms of pantheistic evolutionism: In either form, it finds itself forced to deny the first principles of reason. We will close by providing a resolution to objections, especially those registered against the real value of the supreme principle of reason.

ART. 1: EXPOSITION OF PANTHEISTIC EVOLUTIONISM IN ITS MATERIALISTIC AND IDEALISTIC FORMS

§1. Pantheistic evolutionism in general

§2. Materialistic or empiricist evolutionism

§3. Idealistic evolutionism

§1. What Is Pantheistic Evolutionism in General?

In general, pantheistic evolutionism is the doctrine holding that the principle of all things does not exist from itself and from eternity, constituted in its full perfection as something really and essentially distinct from the world, but, rather, is always in the midst of becoming and is nothing other than this fundamental becoming itself, which by its self-determining constitutes the universe, such that things themselves are merely various moments in this universal flux. God is self-creative evolution.

As we have said already, this doctrine is expressed and condemned in the very first proposition of Pius IX's *Syllabus of Errors*:

> There does not exist any supreme, all-wise, all-provident divine being distinct from this universe of things. God is identical with the nature of things and therefore subject to change. God actually becomes himself in man and in the world. All things are God and have the very substance of God. {{220}} God is one and the same reality with the world and so is spirit with matter, necessity with liberty, truth with falsehood, good with evil, and justice with injustice.[1]

Similarly, the [First] Vatican Council, in *Dei filius*, canon 1.4 condemned three forms of evolutionism:

> If anyone says that finite beings, the corporeal as well as the spiritual, or at least the spiritual ones, have *emanated* from the divine substance; or that the divine essence becomes all things by self-manifestation or self-*evolution*; or lastly that God is the *universal* or *indefinite* being which, [through] self-determination, constitutes the universality of beings, differentiated [into] genera, species, and individuals, let him be anathema.[2]

And we can read in the pre-conciliar schema:

> If some kind of emanation is posited, one should instead say *that all things come into being from a single essence*. However, [such thinkers] once again conceive of this becoming in two ways. There are those who call that essence . . . by the name of God, thus saying *that God becomes the world*; or there are those who assign the name of God only to an already-evolved essence, thus holding

---

1. Pius IX, *Syllabus of Errors*, no. 1 (Denzinger, no. 2901).
2. [First] Vatican Council, *Dei filius*, canon 1.4 (Denzinger, no. 3024).

that *the world becomes God*. Whence, the most common distinction is between Theopantism and Pancosmism.[3]

The first form of evolutionism condemned by the Council is the emanationism, held once upon a time by the Neo-Platonists, the second Schelling's pantheism,[4] and the third the pantheism of Hegel.

There are two parts to absolute evolutionism that must be distinguished from each other—namely, a negative part and a positive one.

A. *Its **negative part*** is (1) *the denial of the existence of the True God, the Creator*. Indeed, it denies the necessity for the intervention of a creative cause in the production of matter, vegetative life, sense life, and the intellective soul. All beings and phenomena would come forth naturally in accord with evolution of the first principle immanent in the world. This is pantheistic immanentism.[5] (2) *Hence, it denies the existence of a supernatural order of truth and life* which is founded on God. Indeed, it already can claim for our natural reason what Catholic theology says about supernatural grace—namely, that it is a formal participation in the divine nature. Nay, [absolute evolutionism ultimately] identifies our reason with the divine reason. This leads to the doctrine that was condemned at the [First] Vatican Council: "If anyone says that man cannot be called by God to a knowledge and perfection that surpasses the natural, but that he can and must by himself, through constant progress, finally arrive at the possession of all that is true and good, let him be anathema."[6] (3) *The denial of the possibility of miracles then follows*, for miracles arise from the free intervention of God who is essentially distinct from the world. Now, according to pantheistic evolutionism, God is neither really nor essentially distinct from the world and likewise cannot act freely within it.

B. With regard to religious philosophy, ***the positive part*** of absolute evolutionism is *its explanation of the various phenomena of religion through the evolution of our religious sentiment*. Thus, it affirms that dogmas came into existence without any revelation, properly so called, likewise holding that the Catholic Church was not divinely instituted.[7] [Hence,] her dogmas are always changeable: "Truth is no more immutable than man himself, since

---

[3] See Jean-Michel-Alfred Vacant, *Études théologiques sur les constitutions du Concile du Vatican d'après les actes du concile*, vol. 1 (Paris: Delhomme et Briguet, 1895), doc. 6 (581).

[4] See ibid., doc. 12 (642 and 212).

[5] See the article "Immanence" [by Fr. Albert Valensin] in the *Dictionnaire apologétique de la foi catholique*.

[6] [First] Vatican Council, *Dei filius*, canon 2.3 (Denzinger, no. 3028).

[7] See Pius X, *Pascendi*, nos. 12, 26, 30 (Denzinger, nos. 3482, 3493, 3494–3497).

it evolved with him, in him, and through him."[8]

So defined, absolute evolutionism essentially differs from *moderate evolutionism*, which admits at least that God the Creator intervened in [the world] to produce matter, vegetative life, sense life, the intellective soul, and the infusion of grace. {{221}} Moderate evolutionism holds only that the species of plants or animals which now exist are not ontological species with indivisible and immutable specific differences but are only empirical classes under which there are certain true yet few [*quibusdam veris ac paucis*] species of living things, from which they arise through successive transformations, somewhat like how the various kinds of dogs come from the dog species. This moderate form of evolutionism has not been condemned by the Church; however, this treatise is not the place to discuss it.[9]

§2. Materialistic or Empiricist Evolutionism

This doctrine, which is often called monism, affirms that the principle of all things is matter itself, which already contains the rudiments of life and of consciousness. Thus, all the phenomena of vegetative, sense, and intellective life mechanistically come forth from matter. Therefore, in this system, reason is a superior form of experience and of the whole of evolution. Nothing lies above it. Therefore, positive reason constituting the positive sciences is absolutely autonomous, the sole arbiter of truth and goodness.

Materialistic or [*vel*] empiricist evolutionism must be distinguished as a general philosophy, on the one hand, and as a religious philosophy on the other. It must be briefly set forth according to the ordinary form in which it is found in our days, as in the writings of Ernst Haeckel.[10]

A. *The general philosophy* of this system teaches there is nothing above the order of physiochemical phenomena as something essentially distinct from it.

Those holding this position intend to prove it both indirectly and directly. Here we will only present their main arguments.

---

[8] Pius X, *Lamentabili*, no. 58 (Denzinger, no. 3458).

[9] [Trans. note: For a very open-minded Thomistic discussion of evolution, indeed in the first pages of the *Revue Thomiste*, see the articles by Ambroise Gardeil, "L'évolutionisme et les principes de S. Thomas," *Revue Thomiste* 1 (1893): 27–45, 316–27, and 725–37; 2 (1894): 29–42; 3 (1895): 61–84 and 607–33; 4 (1896): 64–86 and 215–47.]

[10] Especially as it is found in his work *Die Welträtsel: Aeigmata universi*. See the exposition of Haeckel's doctrine in Émile Boutroux, *La science et la religion* (Paris: Flammarion, 1908), pt. 1, ch. 3. [Trans. note: See Ernst Haeckel, *The Riddle of the Universe*, trans. Joseph McCabe (Amherst, NY: Prometheus Books, 1992). Émile Boutroux, *Science and Religion: In Contemporary Philosophy*, trans. Jonathan Nield (London: Duckworth, 1912).]

(a) *Indirectly*: Otherwise, the principle of the conservation of energy would be brought to ruin, a principle that is, they say, the most certain principle in the whole of modern physics and chemistry.

And indeed, if vegetative, sense, rational, moral, and religious life were essentially above the order of physical energy, the total quantity of energy would be altered by their influence upon the physiochemical order. Thus, the principle of conservation of energy would be brought to ruin, for that principle holds that physical energy always exists with the same total (namely, actual and potential) quantity. The overall sum of energy is constant. Therefore, sense life, intellectual life, and moral life are nothing other than a kind of effect (or result) of physiochemical phenomena. In other words, they are epiphenomena. (See §3 of the next article where we present a resolution to objections.)

(b) *Directly*, materialistic evolutionism is also defined from a consideration of the similarities[11] that exist between material and spiritual phenomena. For example, oxygen atoms have an affinity with hydrogen atoms so as to produce together a water molecule. Thus, we already here find ourselves faced with a rudimentary form of inclination. Love and discord govern all the elements, as Empedocles said. Modern thinkers merely change the words and say, "attraction" and "repulsion." This attraction or affinity, according to the overall structure [*complexionem*] of organisms, leads to the affinities that are found in plants, animals, and men. All the various combinations of atoms are brought about through mechanical forces. However, the psychic element of matter is perfected through mechanical evolution itself.

A religious philosophy is deduced from this general philosophy.

B. *Its religious philosophy* contains two parts—namely, a positive one and a negative one.

{{222}} (a) *Its negative part* is its denial of a supernatural order of truth[12], as well as its denial of the possibility of miracles.

Indeed, this outlook holds that there is nothing above material nature, for it holds that matter is the principle of all things. Likewise, nothing would exist above human reason because positive reason is the supreme form of all evolution. Finally, miracles are impossible, for they would involve the free intervention of the First Cause in the world,[13] whereas this outlook holds that the First Cause is immanent in the world. Indeed, it is there as something material and unfree, meaning that all phenomena necessarily proceed according to physical determinism.

---

[11] [Trans. note: Reading *similitudinum* for *similitudines*.]
[12] [Trans. note: Reading "ordinis veritatis ac supernaturalis" as "ordinis veritatis supernaturalis".]
[13] [Trans. note: Reading *in mundo* for *in mundum*.]

(b) *The positive part* of the religious philosophy of materialistic evolutionists intends to explain religious phenomena and to respond to the
demands made by man's religious sentiment. According to Haeckel, positive science can already satisfy the speculative needs of our reason, though
not yet the exigencies of the heart. However, the practical value of positive
science is not inferior to its speculative value, and therefore religion will
gradually be set aside with the progress of the sciences. Yet, before positive
science can satisfy the needs of the human heart through its evolution, it is
useful for religions to fulfill this office.

Therefore, for this time of transition, positive reason, which is the sole
arbiter of truth and goodness, determines what is to be preserved in religion
and especially in the principal religion, Christianity.

However, *as regards the truth* [i.e., as a transcendental], according to Haeckel, nothing
in Christianity is to be retained because its made-up revelation teaches that another supernatural, spiritual, and future world exists, one that, according to philosophical positivism
is nothing other than a verbal entity and the mere passing breath of one's voice. Hence,
this made-up revelation considers as being vain and lowly phenomena that which in fact
is, according to monism, the only and indeed most important reality—namely, the material world. Dogmas are inventions of the imagination providing consolation for human
suffering. However, they generate dissensions and impede progress.

As regards the beautiful, nothing in Christianity is to be retained, because Christian
art does not truly pertain to Christianity, for it exists within Christianity as something
that is self-contradictory, indeed as a protestation raised by the senses against the immoderate spiritualism of religion.

As regards the good, something in Christianity is to be retained, indeed the greatest
part of primitive Christianity, which especially taught the precepts of charity, tolerance,
and compassion, which are good precepts that are truly human and much more ancient
than Christianity itself. Indeed, these duties do not presuppose dogmas, as they say, and
are just as much fulfilled by unbelievers as they are transgressed by the faithful. Hence,
these good precepts are not proposed with sufficient *moderation* by Christianity but,
rather, with exaltation exceeding the limits of truth. (Thus, under the pretext of moderation, mediocrity is proposed as though it were the mean of virtue between opposed
vices when, in fact, it is the mean between good and all too evident evil. Nay, it is a kind
of amalgamation of them and the perversion of the whole of morality.) Therefore, as
Haeckel concludes, if Christianity is proposed along the lines of how it is proposed by
many liberal Protestants, it can be admitted for the time being as an aid to monism, favoring moral progress, and indeed may last until it becomes useless. Then, positivist religion
will be self-sufficient.

Practically, the following is then necessary: (1) the Church must be separated from the State so that the Church may be deprived of the aid from

the State; (2) lay education must be established, for religion pertains only to education within the family in relation to one's private life, not as a matter falling to social life;[14] {{223}} (3) finally, a course in the history of religions must be established in schools so that religious dogmas may be shown to be what they really are—namely, mere poetic symbols of moral truths.

---

[14] Jules Payot, *La morale à l'école* (Paris: Armand Colin, [no year]), 231: "*Religious beliefs.* §1 *Beliefs do not prove anything; only acts count*; let us judge men according to what they do, never according to what they believe.—§2 *Nobody knows the whole truth.* No belief about God, the origin of the world, or man's origin and destiny is accepted by those who are thinkers. We can only form suppositions about these questions, nothing more. Christians themselves are divided into Protestants, Catholics, Orthodox, etc. Therefore, they are not in agreement about what must be believed. This proves that nobody knows the whole truth. Indeed, it is utterly foolish and indeed criminal to wish to persecute anyone who does not share in our beliefs. Let each person believe in accord with his sentiments. Let each person be free to believe or not believe. (This is indifferent for the moral life.)—§3 *Religion is a private affair.* In France, the State neither financially supports nor recognizes any religion. Each person goes to the church that he has chosen or he may go to no church at all—each according to his pleasure. Religion is a private affair. Nobody can intervene in it. Each person is left to absolute freedom. Nothing is more reasonable nor more just.—§4 *Causes for the slowness of progress.* For centuries upon centuries, the progress of the sciences was slow because men were impulsive, proud, and violent. In their pridefulness, they could not wait for years to seek out some modest truths. Rather, they preferred completely made up beliefs which were accepted without examination, thus giving them the illusion that they knew something, in the greatest of detail, concerning the creation of the world and that of man. Violent, they did not admit the freedom to have beliefs differing from their own, and they persecuted free minds. For many centuries and up to our own days, the mind, freedom of thought, and the virility of independent seekers were all hated and persecuted. . . . Not long ago, it was finally perceived that pride makes people only fools and ignorant. Our scientists know that in order to command the hostile forces [of nature], the laws of nature must be obeyed. In order to do this, we must know them and study them patiently. Therefore, modesty is needed, for one can only discover a few things on one's own. Our discoveries are possible only thanks to the collaboration of hundreds of people seeking the truth at once.—§5 *The raucous and the workers. Galileo.* On the one side, there were always the impulsive, the prideful, and the violent, who made much noise and accomplished very little, who have caused humanity irreparable harm. On the other side, there were modest, patient, and meditative persons, who strove to have clear sight in the fog of prejudices and thoughtless beliefs. Humanity owes all of its progress to their patient work. One of these modest scientists was Galileo, who discovered that the earth revolves around the sun. Thus, for this discovery, the ignorant and prideful condemned him to perpetual prison. . . . Today too we find stubborn and wicked opposing inquiring and free minds.—§6 *Moral progress is slower than scientific progress.* —§7 *The reason to hope for the future*: there is a greatly growing number of people who have a very lively sense of injustice and who suffer on account of it. The number of those who fight against evil, sickness, poverty, . . . and social injustices is growing.—§8 *Let us respect believers and non-believers.* —§9 *Collaborators in the fraternal city.* The peace of minds will be complete on the day when everyone knows that *no man and no group of men do not know the entire truth.* Let us take courage and in our discussions be courteous and respectful of others' conscience.*"

And, afterwards, when Christianity finally becomes useless, the only thing that will remain will be *positivist religion*—that is, *the worship* [*cultus*] *of Truth, Goodness, and Beauty*, which is nothing other than *science, sociology, and art.* This is the real trinity to be substituted for the imaginary Trinity talked about by the theologians.

This doctrine has been disseminated by Masons—indeed, sometimes with apparent tolerance, urbanity, and modesty—in order to show that the virtues do not depend on religious faith but that, rather, religious opinions (just like political ones) are what in fact generate dissensions and quarrels. Nay, even more dangerously, they praise Christianity, which they interpret in a merely natural manner, as though Christ were only a great sage like Socrates. They abhor the Cross and mortification, {{224}} and replace the Cross with a star, which is a symbol of deified humanity.

In this, it is clear how naturalism leads to rationalism, liberalism, humanitarianism, and sensualism and, in relation to society, to socialism. In all places, the kingdom of nature (or of humanity) is substituted for the kingdom of God.[15]

There can be no greater denial of the supernatural order, although this denial can be more perverse in idealistic evolution, which at first sight seems to preserve the lofty character of intellectual and moral life. Nay, it even seems to exalt it.

§3. Idealistic Evolutionism

This kind of system gradually appeared in the doctrine of Spinoza and afterwards in that of Fichte and Schelling. However, it was especially constituted by Hegel and was spread abroad by the school of Right Hegelianism. Indeed, it was held in high esteem (and even now is held in great esteem) in the writings of modern philosophers and in the writings of historians of philosophy such as Eduard Zeller and Kuno Fischer, and especially in the writings of the exegetes of the Tübingen School. Baur applied the *a priori* principles of Hegel to exegesis as did Ewald, Reuss, Knobel, as well as Wellhausen today. In France, Renan and Loisy likewise proceed from Hegelianism.

In this doctrine, all beings and phenomena, even religious ones, come forth naturally through evolution, not indeed from matter, but rather from a kind of ideal principle, which they call the Absolute. Human reason, espe-

---

[15] Concerning the historical materialism of the communists, see the encyclical of Pius XI, *Divini redemptoris* (Mar. 1937) and Benoît Lavaud, "La philosophie du bolchevisme," *Revue Thomiste* 32 (1932): 599–633.

cially philosophical reason, is the loftiest form of the whole of evolution, in which the Absolute becomes self-conscious. Such philosophical reason is superior to religion and is the absolutely autonomous and supreme arbiter of truth, judging the declarations of the Church without itself being judged by anyone. Thus, the words of St. Paul in 1 Corinthians 2:15 (DR), "The spiritual man judgeth all things: and he himself is judged of no man," come to be applied to such philosophical reason, for according to them, it is the Absolute in self-conscious form.

Let us look into the following points: (1) how this doctrine was found in some manner in the writings of the ancient Gnostics; (2) how Spinoza's pantheism paved the way for it; (3) the pantheism of Fichte; (4) the pantheism of Schelling; (5) what specific form it takes in Hegelianism. In relation to the denial of the supernatural order of truth, we must gather together the relevant points which are expressly discussed in histories of philosophy.

(1) *Gnosticism.* The Gnostics called their doctrine γνῶσιν—that is, "true knowledge"—in order to distinguish it from common knowledge to which the common, humble Christians and apostles were devoted.[16] This gnosis was a naturalistic interpretation of Christianity according to principles of emanationism (drawn from Brahmanism) and of Zoroastrian dualism.

The general idea of Gnosticism is *that God never manifests himself, nor acts immediately in the world,17* (i.e., the denial of supernatural revelation and of miracles) because this would diminish the divine perfections *but instead performs such actions by the power of divine spirits* (aeons, αἰῶνες) *born of him* (thus being a form of emanationism). One of these spirits, called the "demiurge," formed the world and men out of eternal matter which the utterly perfect God could not at all create (thus representing a form of dualism). *The human spirit is born of God as well,* through the mediation of superior spirits, {{225}} though weighed down by matter, which is the principle of evil. And therefore, it was necessary that a spirit that was superior to the demiurge would enter into the world in order to free the human spirit and reconcile it with God. This spirit was the eon Christ.

Hence, in this doctrine, *emanation* is substituted for free creation, just as was done by Neo-Platonists, especially in the writings of Plotinus. *This emanation represents the denial of the supernatural order,* for our soul would already be a participation in the divine nature so that what the Catholic faith says about sanctifying grace would be true of our soul [in the natural order]. However, the emanationism of the ancients differs from the evolutionism of modern thinkers inasmuch as the former held that it was a descending form of emanation, not an ascending one, and likewise inasmuch as it was considered to

---

[16] Likewise, today rationalists call their doctrine, "Science," science *par excellence.*

[17] [Trans. note: Reading *in mundo* for *in mundum.*]

be transitive [*transiens*] and not immanent. That is, in its ancient form, such [Neoplatonic] emanationism did not hold the world would become God but, rather, that God would become the world, and the substance that emanated was held to be extrinsic to the substance from which it emanated, just as rays of light exist outside of the sun. Nonetheless, finite things are of the same order as the First Cause, from which they proceed of necessity, for God produces the things of the world just as the sun illuminates. Thus, our soul would emanate from God like a kind of spiritual radiation. (See §3 below in the next article, where we resolve various objections.) This doctrine of emanationism in some form historically passed through the works of Neo-Platonists and Arab philosophers to the pantheists of the fifteenth century (e.g., to Giordano Bruno and then to Spinoza). It was already refuted at length by St. Thomas.[18]

(2) *The pantheism of Spinoza.* Spinoza is the prince of the modern rationalists, both in his philosophical principles and in their application to the exegesis of Sacred Scripture. For in his *Theologico-Political Treatise* he laid the foundations for the rationalistic principles concerning revelation, inspiration, the possibility of miracles, and the interpretation of Sacred Scripture. This hermeneutic is founded on his general philosophical outlook, which is set forth in his *Ethics.*

In Spinoza's *Ethics*, the denial of the supernatural order is clear (A) in his theory of substance, (B) in his theory of knowledge, and (C) in his theory of love (or beatitude).

A. *His theory of substance* is founded on his absolute realism and on his application of the methods of mathematics to philosophy. This theory is reduced to this claim: *Substantial being [ens substantiae] is unique*; there is only one substance.

Spinoza arrived at this conclusion *on the basis of his absolute realism* concerning the simple and adequate notions [which our knowledge forms]—namely, those which, as Descartes said, are clearly and distinctly conceived by us, like the ideas of substance, extension, and thought. These notions are known without the possibility of error, are considered by reason *sub specie aeternitatis*,[19] and in fact express[20] something that is fixed and eternal in the universe. Consequently, the notion of substance expresses universal substance, subsistent from eternity. Thus, substance *in general* is identified with the divine substance, something in line with [his] absolute realism, which holds that the universal exists formally in reality itself [*a parte rei*]. (However, Spinoza becomes a nominalist

---

[18] In the *Summa contra gentiles*, St. Thomas refuted the pantheists of his day, as well as the Averroists. See *SCG* I, chs. 26, 27, 32, 50, 65, 81, 82, and 88; II, chs. 23–27, 31–37, 73, 76, 78, 85, and 87.

[19] See Spinoza, *Ethics*, bk. 2, prop. 44.

[20] [Trans. note: Reading *exprimunt* for *exprimuntur*.]

when it comes to confused notions[21] that cannot be geometrically defined. According to him, these notions designate only collections of phenomena (e.g., animality, humanity, and so forth). Likewise, the intellective faculty designates only a collection of thoughts [*cogitationum*].)[22]

{{226}} Moreover, Spinoza strives to apply the *geometric method* to philosophy because geometry is an exact science and, hence, is the exemplar of the sciences. Now, the geometer posits definitions and then deduces properties from them, considering neither final nor efficient causality. Therefore, one must proceed along these lines in philosophy in order for it to be an exact science. Hence, he denies that God *is the extrinsic efficient* and final *cause* of the world. (Instead, God is conceived as being an *immanent cause*.)[23]

Thus, Spinoza posits a definition of substance, from which the unicity of substance follows (*Ethics* 1), for he conceives of substance as self-subsistent being in the sense of aseity [*a se subsistens*], a definition that befits God alone. However, in *Ethics* 1, prop. 11 he proves the existence of a substance so-defined in an *a priori* manner (by St. Anselm's argument). In this, we see his absolute realism.

Then Spinoza strives to geometrically deduce the *divine attributes* from the divine substance—namely, *infinite knowledge* and *infinite extension*. However, our various individual thoughts and the various forms of extension that constitute bodies are nothing other than a series of phenomena existing from eternity. Thus, an isolated, singular phenomenon cannot be produced directly by the divine substance (here we have a denial of the possibility of miracles) but instead proceeds from preceding phenomena according to an eternal process *ad infinitum* in accord with mechanistic determinism. Thus, the divine freedom and every form of freedom is denied, for a necessary effect follows from a determinate cause, and no effect can follow from an undetermined cause (cf. *Ethics* bk. 2, prop. 48).

As is clear, this theory of substance represents *a denial of the supernatural order*, for without grace our soul is already of the same nature as God. Indeed, it is more than a participation in the divine nature. It is a finite mode of God, existing in God himself. Hence, the divine nature does not transcend our natural knowledge. Likewise, it *denies of*

---

[21] [Trans. note: Reading *notiones* for *notionis*.]

[22] Absolute realism regarding the primary notions of being or substance leads to nominalism regarding the inferior notions of genera and species. Indeed, if universal being or universal substance formally exists *from the perspective of the thing* [/ *reality*] (i.e., outside the soul), by that very fact it is identical with the divine being. Hence, other substances, other species, and faculties are nothing but the mere passing wind of the voice and merely verbal entities, for outside the divine being the only thing that exists are phenomena which proceed from preceding phenomena, themselves proceeding from preceding phenomena and so on eternally *ad infinitum*.

[23] See Léo Michel, "Le système de Spinoza au point de vue de la logique formelle," *Revue Thomiste* 6, old num. (1897): 711–722.

the possibility of miracles, for all phenomena presuppose an antecedent phenomenon, and nothing can be produced immediately and freely by God, for God is an immanent cause, not a transcendent one. Nay, he is a necessary cause, not a free one, even though he is not compelled [to act] (see *Ethics* bk. 1, prop. 18 and 33).

B. *His theory of knowledge* perfects his denial of the supernatural order. See *Ethics* 2, prop. 47: "The human mind has adequate knowledge of God's eternal and infinite essence." This follows from what precedes. The human mind naturally has a vague [*confusam*] intuition of the divine essence because the divine essence is nothing other than substantial being, which is the first thing that falls into our intellectual apprehension and to which we resolve all of our intelligible notions. Hence, what St. Thomas says about universal being which is analogically common to God and creatures, Spinoza says of substantial being, which according to him is not only univocal but is uniquely singular. This is a form of *pantheistic ontologism*: All of our intellectual knowledge depends on the intuition of the first being (which is the divine being). [Thus, according to Spinoza,] the first thing known by our intellect is the first reality ontologically speaking . Something similar can be found in the ontologism of Nicolas Malebranche and also in Antonio Rosmini—namely, the fact that universal being is not sufficiently distinguished from the divine being and, hence, the order of natural truth is not distinguished clearly enough from the order of supernatural truth. This distinction is radically destroyed in Spinoza's pantheistic ontologism, for according to him, our natural intuition is a mode of absolute knowledge (see *Ethics* bk. 1, prop. 31) that differs from God's knowledge [*cogitatione*] as vague knowledge [*confusa cognitio*] and distinct knowledge differ from each other in relation to the same object. However, this distinction does not suffice for constituting two orders of knowledge, for a vague and common [*vulgaris*] notion of being is of the same order as the metaphysical notion of being.

C. *His theory of love and beatitude* applies the same denial of the supernatural order to the will, for according to Spinoza, "The mind's intellectual love {{227}} for God is the very Love of God by which God loves Himself . . . (or, in other words) the mind's intellectual love of God is part of the infinite love by which God loves Himself" (*Ethics*, bk. 5, prop. 36). His denial of personal immortality follows from this, and Spinoza admits only the existence of an impersonal immortality.

All of these conclusions proceed from his pantheistic definition of substance, leading to the radical denial of the supernatural order. Only the distinction between "Nature Naturing" and "Nature Natured" is preserved, which Spinoza explains in *Ethics* 1, prop. 29, scholium as follows: "We must understand 'Nature Naturing' to mean that which exists[24] in itself and is conceived through itself. . . . This is God. . . . However, I understand 'Nature

---

24 [Trans. note: Adding this "est," which exists in the original of Spinoza but not in Fr. Garrigou-Lagrange's text.]

Natured' to be that which necessarily follows from God's nature."

(3) *The pantheism of Fichte*. This form of pantheism proceeds *in part from Spinoza and in part from Kant*. As we said above, Spinoza admitted that there was a natural intuition of the divine being (thus expressing a form of pantheistic ontologism and absolute realism). Kant, by contrast, denied the existence of any form of intellectual intuition whatsoever, likewise denying the first apprehension of universal being abstracted from sensed things, holding that the first categories of our reason are only *a priori* subjective forms used for establishing a classification of phenomena. (This represents a form of agnostic subjectivism or, in other words, subjective conceptualism). However, Fichte discovered a great and insoluble difficulty in Kantianism; namely, the application of the subjective categories to external phenomena remains arbitrary. Why does reason apply the category of causality, instead of the category of substance, to these [given] phenomena? If one responds, "Because reason sees a relation to causality in these phenomena," then we find ourselves back at the scholastics' first apprehension, which is brought about with abstraction. Therefore, in order to preserve the principles of subjectivism and *to avoid the arbitrary application of the categories*, we must say (according to Fichte) that *the phenomena themselves arise from the knowing subject, not from something external to the subject*. Hence, reason is thoroughly autonomous because it is not only the principle of the categories but also of phenomena.

But how does the knowing subject (the ego) produce the phenomena (or the object, the non-ego)? Fichte responds: unconsciously and involuntarily. He explains this by distinguishing, within the knowing subject, the empirical, finite, and individual ego that is self-conscious from the transcendent, infinite, and universal ego. However, what is this *transcendent ego*? It is something at once ideal and real—namely, *the very practical reason of human society* that increasingly comes to know and bring about the moral order. However, this social practical reason has the most vigorous existence in German science and philosophy, gradually constituting the domains of natural, penal, and political law.

Thus, Fichte reconciles Spinoza and Kant in subjective and moral pantheism. The principle of all things is immanent—namely, absolutely autonomous practical reason and the freedom of humanity. Hence, in his work *The Critique of All Religion*, Fichte says *the living God is Humanity itself*. "I have an abhorrence for every religious concept which considers God a personal being. This conception is unworthy of {{228}} mankind." For a personal God, Fichte adds, would be a knowing subject limited by the object of his knowledge and thus would not be the infinite God. However, in this proposition, Schelling found the point on which to articulate a refutation of Fichte's doctrine.

(4) *The pantheism of Schelling*. Schelling rightly refuted Fichte, just as Fichte had refuted Kant. The universal ego, says Schelling, cannot itself produce the non-ego (i.e., the object) because it is its correlative, and they are by nature simultaneous. Furthermore, each is limited by the other. Therefore, neither is Absolute; instead, both presuppose the Absolute. This is how the existence of the Absolute is proven.[25]

What, however, is the Absolute? It is neither object, nor subject, nor nature, nor spirit, nor reality, nor idea. Rather, it is their root and wellspring, or [*seu*] the identity of differences. Thus, Schelling comes back to the Spinozist position, for according to him, *the Absolute* is not truly transcendent, distinct from the world in reality and essence. Instead, *through its manifestation, it becomes all things—namely, becomes the human spirit and nature.* In

---

[25] In *ST* I, q. 3, a. 7, St. Thomas says, "Every composite has a cause, for those things that of themselves are diverse, do not come together in some one thing except through some cause uniting them together. However, God does not have a cause since He is the first efficient cause."

Fichte insists: However, the duality of object and subject is essentially required for knowledge. Therefore, if God is entirely simple, he knows nothing.

In response, drawing on what St. Thomas says in *ST* I, q. 14, a. 2, I concede that this duality is essentially required for the case of created cognition. However, I deny that it is needed for uncreated cognition, for the divine intellect is *pure act*, just like the divine intelligible, "And it is only because the senses or intellect are in potency that they are *other* than their object, be it sensible or intelligible. Therefore, since God has no potentiality but, rather, is pure act, it is necessary that in Him the intellect and the understood thing be one in all respects" (ibid.).

Likewise, what St. Thomas says against Averroes in *ST* I, q. 76, a. 2 also holds good against Fichte. There St. Thomas asks whether the intellective principle would be multiplied according to a multiplication of bodies. In response, he says that if the intellect were one for all men, there would be no reason for assigning a distinction between my intellection and yours in relation to the same object, for there would be no distinction on the part of the subject or of the object.

Similarly, what St. Thomas argues in *ST* I, q. 79, a. 4 in his proof for the existence of a first intelligence from the imperfection and motive nature of our own cognition itself holds good against Fichte: "We must posit above the intellective human soul some superior intellect, from which the human soul would obtain the power of understanding. For it is always the case that that which participates and that which is mobile and imperfect calls for something prior to it which is such through its essence and is immobile and perfect. Now, the intellective human soul has an imperfect form of understanding, both because it does not know all things and because it passes from potency to act in the things that it does know. Therefore, there must be a loftier intellect by which the soul is assisted in its knowing." And because this supreme intellect must be immobile and perfect, it is thus distinct from our mobile and imperfect intellect.

Likewise, see *ST* I, q. 79, a. 2. *Only the divine intellect is in no way passive*: Or "it is related to universal being as the act of all being. . . . However, no created intellect can be related as act to whole of universal being, for then it would need to be an infinite being. . . . *The human intellect is in potency in relation to intelligibles*." Hence, against Fichte, *it is not the principle of all phenomena. Were that so, by that very fact it would be omniscient.* Human knowledge [*scientia*] would be the cause of things, and *no mystery would remain for us*. This is quite obviously a false claim.

his first philosophy, Schelling says that the Absolute is universal reason in which spirit and nature are identified. In his second philosophy, he affirms that the Absolute is the primitive will. This is a form of pantheistic voluntarism, like what will be found later on in Schopenhauer.

{{229}} In this pantheism, we find a form of *descending evolution*, just as we found in the writings of the emanantists—namely, God becomes the world rather than the world God. This was condemned by the [First] Vatican Council immediately after emanationism: "If anyone says that the divine essence becomes all things by self-manifestation or self-evolution, let him be anathema."[26]

This doctrine represents *the denial of a supernatural order* inasmuch as [it claims that] our reason has a natural intuition of the Absolute and cannot be elevated to a loftier form of knowledge, but there can only be a passage from vague knowledge to distinct knowledge within the natural order. Therefore, Schelling proposed a rationalistic interpretation of the Trinity and the Incarnation, holding that there are three moments in the intimate evolution of God in his process of becoming.[27]

These various systems can be summarized as follows:

Spinoza	*Kant*
PANTHEISTIC ONTOLOGISM	SUBJECTIVE AGNOSTICISM
intuition of God	rejection of intellectual intuition

Fichte
PANTHEISTIC SUBJECTIVISM
ego and non-ego

Schelling
THE ABSOLUTE BECOMES THE WORLD

(5) *The pantheism of Hegel*

A. How did it begin as a critique of Schelling?
B. The principles of his logic and metaphysics.
C. Application to the philosophy of nature.
D. Its application to the philosophy of spirit and to religious philosophy.

A. *Hegel begins with a critique of Schelling's system*: A relatively transcendent Absolute explains nothing, for the oppositions that constitute

---

[26] [First] Vatican Council, *Dei filius*, can. 1.4 (Denzinger, no. 3024).
[27] See Alfred Weber, *Histoire de la philosophie européenne*, 5th ed. (Paris: Fischbacher, 1892), 470. In this work, there is a clear exposition of the relations between the systems of Spinoza, Kant, Fichte, Schelling, and Hegel.

the real world cannot be deduced from it, especially the opposition between nature and spirit. In other words, *the passage from the primitive unity of the Absolute to the multiplicity of the phenomena is not explained in Schelling's system.* Hence, such a relatively transcendent Absolute is nothing other than a mere abstraction (that is, a verbal entity).

Something true is expressed here in this critique—namely, the fact that the world indeed cannot be deduced intelligibly from the supreme being if the supreme being is utterly perfect in itself and does not stand in need of being perfected. According to the Christian faith, such a passage is brought about through the utterly free act of creation. However, Hegel rejects this notion of free creation because it is not sufficiently intelligible, leading him to hold that it is an imaginative (or metaphorical) conception.

Therefore, Hegel strove, against Schelling, to show *how the multiplicity of phenomena logically and necessarily proceeds from a kind of primitive unity.* To explain this, he does not admit, as does Schelling, that the Absolute is relatively transcendent, for then it would not need to be perfected. Instead, he posits an Absolute that is entirely immanent within the world. Nay, the Absolute is not {{230}} immobile under its modes (as Spinoza wished), for the appearance of changeable modes in this immutability would thereby remain unexplainable. Rather, *according to Hegel, the Absolute is nothing other than the process itself or universal becoming, being especially an ideal process.*

In this way, arising from a criticism of prior forms of pantheism, idealistic evolutionism came into existence, a position that was condemned at the [First] Vatican Council: "If anyone says that God is the universal or indefinite being which, by self-determination, constitutes the universality of beings, differentiated in genera, species, and individuals, let him be anathema."[28] As the pre-conciliar schema notes, it is evident that in this system God does not become the world (as in the writings of those professing an emanationist outlook and in Schelling) but, rather, the world becomes God through its evolution. Thus, in response to the question, "Does God exist?" Renan blasphemously responded: "He does not exist . . . yet." Likewise, today, many conceive of God as creative, ascending evolution.

B. *Hegel's logic and general metaphysics* strive to explain the [developmental] process of ideas and things. Against the materialists, he establishes that spirit and ideas are something that we know better than matter because we have an immediate knowledge of spirit and not of matter, which is intelligible only through a resolution to the categories of reason. Hence, *in the [developmental] process of spirit and ideas* (but not, however, in the

---

[28] [First] Vatican Council, *Dei filius*, can. 1.4 (Denzinger, no. 3024).

[developmental] process of physical energy) *we find the exemplar and cause of all phenomena.* Thus, from the beginning, Hegel admits *panlogism* as a hypothesis: "Everything that is real is rational," as well as the identity of logic (Denklehre) and metaphysics (Seinslehre). Thus, the [developmental] process of ideas, which is known through logic, is the developmental process of things themselves, for what is most real in things are the very formal notions in them. Hence, the science of reason (or logic) is a universal science (or metaphysics).

Therefore, what is the [developmental] process of ideas? The first idea is the idea of universal being, which suffuses all the other notions—those of quantity, quality, action, and so forth. However, how can universal being, which is somehow things, become something other than itself? By what principle and by what power do the modalities of being come forth? Hegel responds: This internal principle is *contradiction*, which is found in being itself. *For universal being is simultaneously non-being* because it is absolutely undetermined, not yet something, nor qualified in some way, nor quantified. However, that which is merely undetermined is non-being. Thus, being is simultaneously non-being. And this *contradiction is fruitful*, for if being were only being, it would remain immobile (as Parmenides said) and, consequently, would remain sterile. Thus, the appearance of the modes of being would remain inexplicable. Likewise, if being were only non-being, it would remain sterile, for nothing comes into being from nothing. However, being is in fact fruitful, precisely because it simultaneously is non-being. That is, *becoming itself* appears logically and necessarily as *the synthesis* in which the first *thesis* and first *antithesis* (i.e., being and non-being) are reconciled, for becoming itself simultaneously is and is not, for in some way it already is, all the while also not being what it will come to be.

However, a new contradiction comes forth in becoming itself, one that leads to a loftier synthesis. And ever after, the evolution of universal being will establish all things into genera, species, and distinct individuals. *It is the logical developmental process of the Creative Idea.* {{231}} This is no mere critique of Kant, saying that the idea of being has an ontological value. No, Hegel goes further, for according to him, the idea of being is reality itself, and all things that exist are only moments of this evolution of the real idea. *Thus, being becomes nature,* inasmuch as it posits itself outside itself and *will become spirit,* inasmuch as through consciousness it returns to itself and knows itself. Hence, contradiction emerges as something fruitful, and philosophers always have run into insoluble antinomies, though they did not heed the fact that antinomy or contradiction is the fundamental law of the whole of evolution. *Thus, the principle of the identity of contraries is simulta-*

*neously the law of superior reason and of reality, whereas the classical principle
of contradiction is only a law of inferior (or discursive [ratiocinantis]) reason,*
which makes use of abstract and immobile ideas. Therefore, contradiction is
not an impediment to cognition but, rather, is a stimulant for it.

The modernists spoke in a similar manner. See *Pascendi*, no. 36: "They have found
that even its dogma is not exempt from errors and contradictions. . . . (But this is legitimate, [they say] because dogmas are vital truths.) Now, life has its own truth and its own
logic, belonging as they do to a different order" (Denzinger, 2102, old numbering [cf.
no. 3500]). Likewise, see *Lamentabili*, no. 58: "Truth is no more immutable than man
himself, since it evolved with him, in him, and through him" (Denzinger, no. 3458).

C. **The philosophy of nature** strives to explain how universal being
becomes quantity (or space) through its evolution because it is determined
and [yet] remains infinite.

Now, *quantity* is extensive and intensive, from which there arises a *proportion* that
constitutes the essence of various things. This becoming which is not yet self-conscious is
matter in which *attraction* and *repulsion* are opposed to each other. In this way, physical
phenomena appear, then *vegetative* and *sensitive life*, and finally *rational life* when creative evolution becomes self-conscious, at least in a vague manner in man. This rational
life appears on earth because, more than any other place in the entire universe, the earth
provides a more apt climate for sensitive and rational life. This philosophy of nature is
incredibly arbitrary, for one cannot deduce the animal organism or the plant organism
from inferior forms of evolution. Next, Hegel ascends to spirit.

D. **The philosophy of spirit and religious philosophy**. This part also
contains a thesis, an antithesis, and a synthesis—namely, subjective spirit,
objective spirit, and absolute spirit.

Subjective (or individual) spirit is the first appearance of spiritual life in the first men
who have only individual life or family life and hence only know what is individually
useful for themselves.

Objective (or social) spirit gradually proceeds from subjective spirit and is found in
social institutions, which have come into existence through the course of history, especially in law (or legality). This social life is loftier than the merely individual life of the
first men on account of the dignity of the common good. The death penalty is legitimate
for preserving social principles,[29] rather than for correction, and is especially a proclamation of the Idea. Likewise, according to Hegel, matrimony is indissoluble inasmuch as
social life is loftier than individual life and reason loftier than sensibility. War is legitimate when it is undertaken on behalf of the ideal progress of humanity and, by the power
of determinism, rights fall to the State, which in fact happens to be the victor. {{232}}
According to idealistic evolutionism, victory is the voice of God; in the political order,

---

[29] [Trans. note: Reading *principia socialia* for *principia sociaia*.]

facts that have come to completion, by the very fact of their coming into being, have the force of right. (This was condemned by Pius IX in *Quanta cura*.[30]) Among all the states, one comes to stand out and leads evolution, like the Greeks in antiquity and then the Romans. Likewise, in Europe there is some "chosen people of God."

Finally, *morality proceeds from legality* inasmuch as objective spirit (or common legislation) is accepted as a norm by subjective spirit (that is, by individuals). However, we once more find ourselves faced with an opposition, here between individualism and the rights of the State. Thus, a superior synthesis appears—namely, absolute spirit.

Absolute spirit knows how objective spirit (i.e., legislation) proceeds from individual spirit and, along with it, concurs in bringing about a loftier spiritual life, for above a merely individual life and above a social or political life, we find the true form of spiritual life, which knows spirit itself through reflection. However, this spiritual life appeared in three forms: (a) *art*, (b) *religion*, and (c) *philosophy*.

(a) *Art* first appeared and then, gradually, thereafter various kind of arts, inasmuch as the idea found in them increasingly transcends matter—namely, architecture, statuary, painting, and music, which expresses cogitations and the internal senses, and finally, poetry. Artistic inspiration, above all poetic inspiration, is in some way something divine. Eastern art, which is pantheistic, is opposed to Greek art, which is human, whereas Christian art is simultaneously divine and human, as well as more spiritual.

(b) *Religion*, however, is born as the antithesis of art, for art remains all too sensible, identifying spirit and matter, God and the world. In general, art is pantheistic, whereas religion, by contrast, is theistic, separating God from the world in reaction to the pantheism of art. Thus, in the various texts of the Bible, monotheism is defended, and idols are condemned as sensible representations of God. Nonetheless, *religion remains a symbolic (or metaphorical)* representation *of God* and thus conceives of God as a transcendent person like a superior human intelligence governing all things as the King of kings and Lord of lords. The [characteristic] error of religion is anthropomorphism.

However, there is an ascending evolution among various religions. For an inferior form of pantheism is found in Eastern religions, acosmism, as it were, as though only God existed. On the other hand, we find a form of humanism in Greek religion, as though man alone exists, with the gods being made in the image of man,[31] although fate would remain above the gods. Finally, *the Christian religion is the synthesis of the Eastern inspiration and that of the Greeks* inasmuch as the object of Christian worship is simultaneously *the God-man*, not God in the abstract (as in the East), nor an ideal humanity (as in Greece) but, rather, the God-man in the concrete. Therefore, Christianity is the loftiest form of religion, though it remains a symbolic representation of the Absolute

---

[30] See Denzinger, no. 2890.

[31] [Trans. note: Ignoring "da" in "et dii sunt da imaginem hominis."]

(i.e., of the union of the infinite and the finite).

(c) Therefore, *speculative philosophy* is necessary as the superior synthesis above art and religion. It too evolves, according to the opposition of [various philosophical] systems. Thus, in antiquity, with Parmenides, we find the philosophy of being and with Heraclitus, the philosophy of becoming itself. Thereafter, we see various reconciliations (e.g., in the writings of Democritus). A new antithesis arises between the sophists and Socrates, from which Platonism was born. However, Plato and Aristotle were set in opposition to each other, coming to a reconciliation in the emanationism of Plotinus. Now, Greek philosophy and Christianity were at first set in opposition to each other but gradually came to a form of reconciliation in St. Augustine, according to the Platonic outlook, and later, by St. Thomas, according to the Aristotelian outlook. Finally, there arose the opposition between scholastic philosophy and modern philosophy. However, within the latter, {{233}} there was an opposition between British empiricism and the spiritualism of Descartes, Spinoza, and Leibnitz. A synthesis was proposed by Kant. However, the doctrine of Fichte arose from Kantianism, to which Schelling was opposed, and in the end, idealistic evolutionism appeared, in which the evolution of universal being (or becoming itself) became self-conscious not only in a vague way but also philosophically.

Hence, this ascending evolution of the Creative Idea can be written out as follows:

	Idealistic evolutionism	
	Self-conscious becoming	
Materialistic evolutionism		Spiritualism
	Philosophy	
Art		Religion
	Absolute spirit	
Subjective spirit		Objective spirit
	Unconscious becoming	
The unconscious idea of Being		The unconscious idea of non-being

Finally, speculative philosophy, now constituted, judges religion from on high and itself is judged by nobody.

First of all, it represents a denial of the supernatural order,[32] for nothing is above human reason, above absolute spirit—namely, above the loftiest form of the whole of evolution. Therefore, miracles are impossible, for all things proceed of necessity according to logical determinism. Now, something unknown can remain in this history of a given religion such as Christianity,

---

[32] [Trans. note: reading *ordinis* for *ordo*.]

as the modernists will say later on, but this is only the natural mystery of evolution itself.[33]

Philosophy judges what is to be preserved from religion, for both have the same object (i.e., the universal synthesis), but this synthesis is symbolically conceived of by religion, while being scientifically conceived of by philosophy. Among all religions, Christianity is the supreme form because it is not bound to sensible things but instead adores God in spirit and truth. Therefore, Christian dogmas are to be retained, though they must be understood in a more philosophical manner.

Hence, from the dogma of creation, according to Hegel, we must retain the idea that the infinite itself alone exists, though simultaneously with the finite. However, the finite is not outside of the infinite, for the infinite would be limited by the finite. Hence religious theism is an illusion of the imagination, which represents all things in space. (Such was the way that the modernists spoke as well.) And therefore, Hegel contradictorily identifies the finite and the infinite in becoming itself: The power immanent in evolution is infinite, whereas the moments of evolution are finite. (Such things can be found in the modernist Édouard Le Roy.[34]) {{234}} Indeed, given discursive reason's inferiority, when it looks upon this, it sees a contradiction; however, the law of superior reason is "contradiction is fruitful," and outside of contradiction there is only sterility and death. In the words of Heraclitus, war is the mother of all things.

The Trinity is to be retained in the sense that there is a thesis, an antithesis, and a synthesis in absolute spirit: the knowing subject, the object known, and knowledge (or the union of both); a trace of the Trinity is found in all things, for all things proceed according to the opposition of thesis and antithesis, finding a reconciliation in their synthesis. This is the developmental process of the Creative Idea. (Likewise, later on the

---

33 Why, therefore, is Hegelianism called *transcendentalism*? This term seems, rather, to affirm the existence of a supernatural order. It is so called because, in contrast to empirical (or materialistic) evolutionism, it explains all things through the evolution of a given principle transcending sense experience. However, this principle in no way transcends finite beings nor human reason. Nay, it is human reason itself. And thus, this *transcendentalism* is so called in comparison to empiricism but, in reality, is a form of *absolute immanentism* in comparison to theism, for it radically denies (even more than did Schelling) the existence of a God transcending the world.

34 See Édouard Le Roy, "Comment se pose le problème de Dieu (suite et fin)," *Revue de métaphysique et de morale* 15, no. 4 (July 1907): 512: "Our life is incessant creation, and the same is true for the world. This is why *immanence and transcendence* are no longer contradictories. They *correspond to two distinct moments of duration: immanence to what has become, transcendence to becoming*. If we declare God immanent, what we mean is that we know about Him what has come into being in us and in the world; but, for the world and for us, an infinite process of becoming remains, an infinite process which will be creation properly so called, not a mere development. From this perspective, God appears as being transcendent, and it is as transcendent that we must above all discuss Him in our relations with Him, according to what we have recognized with regard to the divine personality."

semi-rationalist Günther, following along the Hegelian ways, will strive to demonstrate the Trinity inasmuch as in God there must be a subject, an object, or the Word), and the union of these two—namely, the Spirit of God.)

Some aspect of the Incarnation also must be preserved—namely, the fact that the most excellent form of spiritual life appeared in Jesus, which is now known scientifically in the speculative philosophy of evolution. (Thus, today, Harnack and many rationalists contend that no supernatural element can be found in Christ's life with certitude and that his miraculous conception, as well as other narratives concerning his infancy, enjoys no authority. The same must be said of his miracles and the fact of the Resurrection. However, it is historically certain that Christ's life and death were influential in forming Christians' behavior [*mores*], and Christ in particular taught that God is to be considered as being the Father. This represents the essence of Christianity.[35] According to Alfred Loisy, Christ did not teach a body of doctrine but, rather, began a kind of religious movement to be adapted to various times and places. He announced the imminent end of the world but did not intend to found the Church.[36])

Likewise, in the Redemption, Hegel found the fundamental law of evolution—namely, God negated and emptied himself when he became man; afterwards, through his Passion and death, he destroyed this self-denial, drawing all things to himself. Likewise, in the Christian soul, the inferior life leads through sorrow and mortification to a loftier form of life. Nay, according to Hegel, certain souls and even certain peoples are chosen by God and predestined as the central moments of universal evolution. Hence, Renan said, in a way, we speak as the theologians do.

Thus, the dogmas of Christianity are symbols of the truths of speculative philosophy. Regarding these pantheists, the pre-conciliar schema for the [First] Vatican Council, doc. 6, ch. 1 notes:

> However, over and above the impiety which they express in their [written] positions add more [impiety] in their words, for they are accustomed to conceal the monstrous opinions [*monstra opinionum*] that they form concerning the most holy names of the mysteries of the Christian religion, and when they speak of the Trinity, the Incarnation, the Redemption, and the Resurrection, they are eager to persuade the heedless that their doctrines still have something Christian animating them, thereby twisting and distorting *the very venerable mysteries of the true religion in the most perverse ways.*[37]

---

[35] See Adolf Harnack, *Das Christenthum und die Geschichte*, published in 1896.

[36] See Denzinger, Decree of the Holy Office *Lamentabili*, July 3, 1907 (the errors of the modernists), nos. 52 and 59 (Denzinger, nos. 3452 and 3459).

[37] Vacant, *Études sur le Concile du Vatican*, vol. 1, 571.

This perversity is an intentional overturning of the essential order of things. Reason is not subordinated to faith but, rather, judges faith from on high. Philosophy is not the hand-maiden of theology, but on the contrary, religion is placed in the service of philosophy.[38] {{235}} Hegelianism is no longer held today as a system of thought. However, its spirit remains in the philosophy of more recent rationalists.

Henri Bergson in his book *Creative Evolution*[39] strives to prove absolute evolutionism through the principle that "there is more in motion than in immobility" and, hence, that immobility can be had from motion but not vice versa. Hence, there is no first Unmoved Mover who is Pure Act but, rather, there is only creative evolution. Thus, Édouard Le Roy, a disciple of Bergson, denies the absolute necessity and universality of the principle of contradiction as if this principle held true only in immobile things and not in becoming itself (i.e., according to what absolute evolutionism holds, not in the fundamental reality).[40] On this, see our discussion in the next article where we resolve objections raised against our position.

Bergsonism is a kind of inverted Hegelianism, for Hegelianism is a form

---

[38] Thus in the human spirit we find verified that which St. Thomas had said with such great profundity in *ST* I, q. 63, a. 3 concerning the pride of the angel who perversely wished to imitate God and be like unto God inasmuch as nothing is supernatural for God: "In this way the demon had an undue desire to be like unto God, for he desired as the ultimate end of beatitude that which He was able to attain by the powers of his own nature, turning away his desire from supernatural beatitude which comes from the grace of God. Or, if he desired as his last end that likeness to God which is given by grace, he willed to have this through the power of his own nature and not as something received from the divine aid according to God's own ordering of things." St. Thomas thus determines the formal constitutive of this sin of the spirit, whatever might be the material object about which it is committed. Thus, rationalism, in order to affirm the absolute autonomy of reason either denies supernatural mysteries or interprets them in a natural way.

However, an erroneous doctrine is all the more perverse and dangerous to the degree that it makes use of the truth in recommending itself. The truth does not exist in it as the soul of the doctrine but rather as the slave of a deceptive spirit in subordination to error. Hence, idealistic evolutionism, which naturally interprets the supernatural mysteries, is more perverse than materialistic evolutionism, which rejects these mysteries full cloth. Nothing is more similar to an angel than a demon transfigured into "an angel of light" (2 Cor 11:14). Nothing is more apparently similar (and, ultimately, more profoundly dissimilar) to a great speculative theology than the expressions of an idealistic sophistry about religion. It makes use of the same terminology, though in the opposite sense. However, contraries have the same formal character, one being known through the other. He who perfectly understands the first principle of reason—namely, the principle of contradiction—perfectly knows the error opposed to it—namely, the [Hegelian] principle of the identity of contraries.

[39] See Henri Bergson, *L'évolution créatrice* (Paris: Félix Alcan, 1907), 341.

[40] See Édouard Le Roy, "Sur la logique de l'invention," *Revue de métaphysique et morale* 13 (1905): 200, 204. This text is cited below in the next article where we take up a resolution of objections.

of panlogism whereas, by contrast, Bergsonism is a form of absolute anti-intellectualism. Hegel reduces that which in fact is to that which ought to be, accomplished fact to the ideal law, and success to morality, for all facts arise by necessity from the evolution of the Idea. Bergsonism, by contrast, like empiricism, reduces that which ought to be the case to that which is, law [or, right] to accomplished fact, and morality to success. However, these two opposed systems admit the identity of contraries in becoming itself. Thus, notwithstanding their differences, they are, in some way, the same in evolution or consider the same evolution in opposed ways.

The *biblical rationalism* of many contemporary thinkers arises from these philosophical systems, as also from Kantian agnosticism,[41] especially that of the modernists, as is set forth in the encyclical *Pascendi.*[42]

The denial of the supernatural order (i.e., *immanentism*) remains: {{236}} Religion cannot be admitted unless it proceeds from our vital immanence, and our reason is so autonomous that God cannot command that it assent to faith.[43] In the eyes of the Church, this immanentism is nothing other than a new philosophical term for spiritual pride (or love of one's own excellence). However, things must be named by their proper names, for otherwise the philosopher becomes the teacher of equivocation[44] and not a teacher of truth. "[But let your speech be] yea, yea: no, no. [And that which is over and above these is of evil]" (Matt 5:37). Thus can we express the principle of contradiction, which is rejected by Hegel. However, once this principle is done away with, systematic and universal confusion is identified with the supreme harmony, "spirit with matter, necessity with liberty, truth with falsehood, good with evil, and justice with injustice," as we read in the first proposition of Pius IX's *Syllabus.*[45] Hence, according to absolute evolutionism, *the absurd is not impossible, but the supernatural* (both in the form of mysteries or of miracles) *is absolutely impossible.* One cannot descend further into error. This is already clear from the perspective of common sense and will soon be confirmed in the light of philosophical reasoning.

---

[41] See Vacant, *Études sur le Concile du Vatican*, vol. 1 ,108–111 ("The rationalism at the heart of Protestantism. §84 The influence of Spinozism and Schleiermacher.—§85 The influence of Hegelianism.—§86. The mythism of Strauss.—§87 The theory of Baur.—§88. Later theories"). Also see Georges Goyau's volumes *L'Allemagne religieuse*.

[42] See Pius X, *Pascendi*, nos. 11ff and 26ff (Denzinger, nos. 3482ff and 3493ff).

[43] [First] Vatican Council, *Dei filius*, can. 3.1 (Denzinger, no. 3031).

[44] [Trans. note: Reading *aequivicationis* for *aequivicationem*.]

[45] Pius IX, *Syllabus of Errors*, no. 1 (Denzinger, no. 2901).

ART. 2: CRITIQUE: PANTHEISTIC EVOLUTIONISM ULTIMATELY MUST DENY THE FIRST PRINCIPLES OF REASON

The thesis that we will be defending is that pantheistic evolutionism, in both its idealistic and materialistic forms, must deny the first principles of reason. And, as we will see in the resolution to objections raised against us, it can only marshal mere sophistical arguments against the supreme principle of reason (i.e., the principle of contradiction).

This is expressly treated in philosophy, but it must be brought to bear here for the defense of the existence of the supernatural order. Thus, in the theological treatises *De Deo*, *De homine*, and *De virtutibus*, St. Thomas gathers together, under the direction of faith, the philosophical truths necessary for explaining and defending the faith.

Hence, we have three tasks in this article:

§1. What are the first principles of reason and how are they subordinated?

§2. Pantheistic evolution must deny these principles.

§3. Resolution of objections.

§1. What Are the First Principles of Reason and How Are They Subordinated?

In book 4 (Γ) of *Metaphysics*, from chapter 3 to the end of that book (lect. 5-17 in St. Thomas), Aristotle shows that the first principle of reason is the principle of contradiction and defends its real value by resolving the objections of Heraclitus and of the Sophists, which have been taken up afresh by Hegel and his disciples. In his commentary on the *Metaphysics* and in the *Summa theologiae*, St. Thomas developed this Aristotelian doctrine by showing the subordination of these principles, which corresponds to the division of the four causes and can be written thus: [see next page]

Principle of contradiction:
Being is not non-being.

Principle of identity:
Being is being; non-being is non-being.

{{237}} *Principle of substance*:
Everything which is is a substance;
a phenomenon is only that by which something appears.

Principle of raison d'être:
Every being has a *raison d'être*, either in itself or in another.

The principle of efficient causality:	*Principle of finality*:
Every contingent being is efficiently	Every agent acts on account of
caused by another.	an end.

Principle of change:
Every change presupposes a changeable subject.

We have explained and defended these principles at greater length in another work of ours that was more philosophical in character.[46] Here we will only undertake a briefer form of exposition.

A. *The supreme principle of reason is the principle of contradiction*, for it is immediately founded on the first notion of reason—namely, the notion of being in its opposition to non-being.[47] Its logical form is: It is impossible

---

[46] See Réginald Garrigou-Lagrange, *God: His Existence and His Nature: A Thomistic Solution of Certain Agnostic Antinomies*, vol. 1, trans. Bede Rose (St. Louis, MO: B. Herder, 1949), 111–241.

[47] See St. Thomas, *In IV Meta.* lect. 6ff. Likewise, see *ST* II-II, q. 1, a. 7, where we read: "Thus, the articles of faith are involved in the doctrine of faith like how self-evident principles are involved in the teaching that can be had through natural reason. *And there is indeed an order found in such principles*, so that some are implicitly contained in others, just as all principles are reduced to this one: It is impossible to simultaneously affirm and deny [one and the same thing from the same perspective], as is clear from *Metaphysics* 4, text. 9." Likewise, *ST* I-II, q. 94, a. 2: "There is a kind of order found in those things that fall into man's apprehension. For that which first falls into man's apprehension is being, the understanding of which is included in everything that someone understands. Therefore, the first indemonstrable principle is that *it is impossible to simultaneously affirm and deny* [one and the same thing from the same perspective], which is founded upon the notion of being and of non-being. And, as the philosopher says in *Metaphysics* IV, text. 9, all the other principles are founded upon this one." And again, see *De veritate*, q. 1, a. 1, regarding the subordination of the first notions of reason and its correlative principles. According to St. Thomas, this subordination is: (1) *being*, (2) *thing*, (3) *one*, (4) *something*, (5) *true*, (6) *good*. These notions transcend the supreme genera

to affirm and deny one and the same thing from the same perspective. Its metaphysical form is: It is impossible that one and the same thing simultaneously be and not be. Or, to express it even more briefly, being is not non-being.

In its logical form, it expresses the fact that the absurd cannot be *thought* (at least that which is obviously absurd, like a square circle), and in its ontological form, it expresses the fact that the absurd cannot *exist*. Through the distinction between the logical formulation and the ontological formulation of this principle, natural reason affirms the real (or extramental) value of the principle of contradiction—namely, that that which is absurd (e.g., a square circle) not only cannot be thought but clearly [*evidenter*] cannot exist outside the soul.[48]

{{238}} B. *The principle of identity*. The supreme principle can also be expressed in a positive form—namely: "Being is being, non-being is non-being." In this case, it is called the *principle of identity*. It is not a tautology but instead is the positive affirmation of the identity of being and of its opposition to non-being. Nay, it is the affirmation of the absolute and immutable value of truth. Hence, men say, "Good is good; evil is evil," or spiritual authors say, "Spirit is spirit; flesh is flesh," in order to affirm their essential difference. Thus, Christ the Lord said: "But let your speech be yea, yea [and] no, no," without equivocation (Matt 5:37, DR).

The principle of identity[49] can be more explicitly formulated: "Every being has a determinate essence," or "every being is a thing." This is not a tautology, for "*being* is taken from the act of existence, whereas the term *thing* expresses the essence of a being."[50] "Res" (thing) is here taken in the sense

---

which are substance, quantity, quality, relation, action, passion, etc. This classification can be perfected through the classic division of the four causes. And *of itself*, the form is prior to the end, the agent, and matter, for of itself being is prior to the good, action follows on being, and matter is subordinate to the form. "However, *in the order of causation* [*in causando*], the good is prior to being, just as the end is to the form.... The causality of the end is first, because the agent does not act except on account of an end, and the matter is moved by the agent to the form" (*ST* I, q. 5, a. 2, ad 1).

48 Descartes, by contrast, inconsiderately said that even though a square circle cannot be conceived by us, perhaps it can be made by the all-powerful God. On this, see the beginning of the *Discourse on Method*. However, if this were true, even the "cogito ergo sum" could fail to be certain, for perhaps thought would simultaneously be non-thought, and I could simultaneously be and not be; perhaps there is no thinking subject but, rather, some kind of becoming in which contradictories would be identified, as Hegel wished.

49 [Trans. note: Reading *identitas* as *identitatis*.]

50 See *De veritate*, q. 1, a. 1, "We do not find something said absolutely which can be said to hold for every being except its *essence* by which it is said to be. Thus, we impose the term *thing*,

of "reality," which holds for all beings, not inasmuch as a being a "thing" is contrasted with being a person.

C. *Principle of substance.* However, if *the unity and identity* of any given being is considered in relation to its various and variable phenomena, then the principle of identity takes on a new determination, and essence is conceived as substance, thus giving us the *principle of substance*: Everything that is is a substance, and a phenomenon (or a phenomenal accident) is only *that by which* something exists and appears in a given way (e.g., that by which something is white, warm, large, and so forth). The principle of substance can be expressed in another form so that its foundation on the principle of identity may be clearer; namely, "every being is one and the same under its various and variable phenomena, if it has phenomena." The phrase "if it has phenomena" is added because the idea of a phenomenon or appearance presupposes a being that appears [*ens apparens*] but not vice versa, for a being existing in itself does not presuppose a phenomenon. (Inseity is constitutive of substance.) Thus, it is not contradictory to say that the divine substance completely transcends the phenomenal order.

These three principles are taken from an intrinsic cause that is constitutive and specificative of any being whatsoever, which is called the formal cause or its formal constitutive principle.

The other principles that we will now discuss are taken from extrinsic causes (namely, the efficient and final causes) and from the material cause. The transition to these principles is made through the principle of *raison d'être*.

D. *The principle of raison d'être* is expressed in a most general manner as "Every being must have a *raison d'être*."[51] In other words, every being

---

which, as Avicenna says in the beginning of his *Metaphysics*, differs from *being* in that the latter is taken from the act of existence, whereas the term *thing* expresses the quiddity or essence of a being." Also see Zigliara, *Summa phil.*, vol. 1 (Paris: Delhomme et Briguet, 1900), 234.

[51] We do not, like Leibnitz, call this principle "the principle of *sufficient reason*," in the quasi-univocal sense that he gives to the notion of "sufficient reason," which ultimately leads to determinism (i.e., the denial of true freedom). We explain this at greater length in our work *God: His Existence and His Nature*, 306–338 ("Freedom and the principle of raison d'être"). There, we discuss St. Thomas's idea of a sufficient motive as differing from how this is conceived of by Leibnitz. [Trans. note: Note, however, the fact that Fr. Rose, in his admirable translation, renders "principe de raison d'être" as "the principle of sufficient reason."]

Moreover, "raison d'être [*ratio essendi*]" is taken objectively as the foundation of *the reason for knowing*, even if as regards the imposition of the term *ratio* first signifies the ability of knowing something from another (*reor*). Thus, *ratio* designated the idea, ordination, exemplar, motive, and appearance of a thing, its definition, essence, mode of existence, and so forth.

Subjectivists, like Kant, hold that the principle of *raison d'être* is known through a reflection

{{239}} must have a reason on account of which it exists rather than not. This principle is self-evident, having immediate evidence, though it can be indirectly demonstrated through a *reductio ad absurdum*, for if some given being did not have a *raison d'être*, the reason why it exists rather than not existing would not be distinguished from nothingness, for it is proper to non-being [*nihili*] to have no *raison d'être*, given that it is opposed to being.[52]

According to this most general acceptation, "raison d'être" abstracts from an intrinsic *raison d'être*, and from an extrinsic one, but implicitly or vaguely contains these divisions, just as an analogue contains its analogates.

However, according to an explicit consideration of the analogates, we can have a more explicit formula for the same principle—namely, "Every being has a *raison d'être* either in itself or in another." Indeed, it has it in itself if it is its own existence by its very essence [*per suam essentiam*], thus meaning that it is its own *raison d'être*. However, it has its *raison d'être* in another if it does not exist from itself. If[53] this *raison d'être* is in another, it is called an extrinsic *raison d'être* or an extrinsic cause.

However, there are two kinds of extrinsic causes—namely, the efficient cause and the final cause. Thus, under the general principle of *raison d'être*, we find the principles of efficient causality and finality.

E. ***The principle of efficient causality*** is expressed as follows: "It is necessary that every contingent thing be efficiently caused by another," or, to put it another way, "It is necessary that that which is not from itself be produced by another." This principle is self-evident, having immediate evidence from the apprehension (or definition) of the terms. Nonetheless, it

---

by reason upon itself, inasmuch as reason always inquires into the reasons for things. However, they do not explain how this intention formed by our reason is of use for the knowing of things, holding that it is a postulate confirmed through action. Thus, speculative certitude is brought to ruin.

However, in reality, the principle of *raison d'être* is known through direct, not reflex, intellection. And, as regards the thing signified, "ratio" ["raison"] is said first of the objective *ratio* (e.g., of the essence that is the reason for the properties); however, as regards the imposition of the name, it may perhaps be first used by us for designating a subjective *ratio*. Similarly, in *ST* I, q. 13, a. 6, St. Thomas speaks of the perfections which are said first of God as regards the thing that is signified, and first of creatures as regards the imposition of the name.

52 An *immediately* evident proposition cannot be demonstrated directly, for direct demonstration is brought about through a *middle term*, which cannot exist between terms that are immediately connected. *Indirect* demonstration (or demonstration through a *reductio ad absurdum* marshalled against those who deny a given principle) only gives extrinsic evidence based on the strength of the absurd conclusion that follows from that denial. This *extrinsic evidence is inferior to intrinsic evidence, which is had in the simple intuition of the self-evident principle.*

53 [Trans. note: Reading *si sit* for *sit sit*.]

can be indirectly demonstrated through a *reductio ad absurdum*, for indeed, contingent being is defined as that which can exist or not exist. Now, if it did not exist from another but was instead uncaused, it would follow that it would simultaneously be from itself and not from itself. For it would be from itself, given that it is uncaused [on such a supposition], and simultaneously would not be from itself, given that it is contingent. However, if it were neither from itself nor from another, then it would have no *raison d'être*, [no] reason why it would exist rather than not. Thus, it would not be distinct from nothingness. Therefore, the denial of the principle of causality not only leads to unintelligibility (as Kant concedes) {{240}} but also leads to an impossible and absurd state of affairs. In other words, the idea of an "uncaused contingent being" implies a contradiction.[54] As St. Thomas says, following Aristotle: "Nothing reduces itself from potency to act; rather, something can be reduced from potency to act only through a being that is in act" (*ST* I, q. 2, a. 3).

F. *The principle of finality* is expressed by Aristotle and St. Thomas in relation to the agent: "Every agent acts on account of an end."[55] In other words, not only does an effect exist as the terminus of an action, but [moreover,] there must be a reason on account of which an agent acts instead of not acting.

(a) This principle is *self-evident* if we attentively consider what is signified by its subject and predicate. Indeed, every agent does not indifferently produce any effect whatsoever but instead produces an effect that is determinate and *per se* suitable to it, although it can simultaneously produce a *per accidens* effect. (For example, we see through sight and do not hear through

---

[54] This proposition, "some uncaused contingent exists," implies a contradiction, for existence cannot belong to such a subject. Indeed, it would not belong to it essentially, for such a subject of itself is contingent (i.e., can exist or not exist). Nor, however, could existence belong to it from the fact that it is uncaused, for there would be no foundation for this belonging and attribution, given that it exists neither from itself nor from another. Hence, to say that "some uncaused contingent exists" is to say, "some subject having no foundation for existence exists," or, in other words, "existence belongs to it and does not belong to it from one and the same perspective," which is absurd.

[55] Some thinkers, such as Paul Janet in his book *Les causes finales*, deny that this principle is evident *a priori* [i.e., *self-evidently per se nota*], because such people have not provided the correct formulation for the principle itself. They say, "Everything has an end," immediately leading them to object, "However, accidental conjunctions do not seem to have an end." In reality, finality must be considered in relation to an agent inasmuch as the final cause and the efficient cause are two extrinsic causes that are relative to each other. Hence, we must say, "Every agent acts on account of an end." Thus, two agents can be accidentally joined together. In that case a *per accidens* effect is produced. However, each of these agents has its own *per se* effect and end.

it. The act of seeing is *per se* suited to the power of sight, just as the act of hearing is to the power of hearing, intellection to the intellect, and the act of willing to the will.) However, this effect, which is *per se* suitable to the agent, properly deserves the name "end," as the perfecting good to which the agent tends and as the *raison d'être* of the action.

Indeed, irrational agents do not know the formal character [*rationem*] of the end, and plants do not consciously tend toward their own proper perfection but, rather, are naturally inclined and ordered to that which is *per se* suitable for them. For example, the sprout coming from an acorn would not produce an oak tree rather than a pear tree if it were not naturally inclined and ordered to this effect.[56]

Now, *to-be-ordered* presupposes *to-order*, or, in other words, passive ordination presupposes active ordination, which belongs to intelligence, for only intelligence[57] knows the *raisons d'être* of things (and hence knows the *raisons d'être* for their means). Thus, the arrow is directed by the archer. Hence, every agent acts on account of an end, at least executively. That is, it tends to an end either on its own or on account of a superior agent providing it with its direction.

Thus, this principle of finality ("Every agent acts on account of an end") is self-evident, a fact that we see even more clearly if we consider Aristotle's formula, "Potency is designated in relation to act," for it pertains to the very notion of an agent's power that it be ordered to an act to be produced (e.g., sight to the act of seeing and hearing {{241}} to the act of hearing) just as the potency of the patient is ordered to something to be received.[58]

(b) Hence, the principle of finality *can be indirectly demonstrated* through a reduction to the principle of *raison d'être* and, hence, to the principle of contradiction. Indeed, as St. Thomas says in *ST* I, q. 44, a. 4, "Every agent acts on account of an end. Otherwise, this would not follow from an agent's action rather than that, except in a chance manner." Likewise, in *ST* I-II, q. 1, a. 2, he says:

---

[56] See *SCG* III, ch. 2: "Every inclination of an agent *tends* toward something certain, for a given action does not proceed from any indiscriminate power whatsoever. Rather, heating comes from heat and cooling from cold. Whence we also can say that actions specifically differ according to a diversity of active powers."

[57] [Trans. note: Reading *intelligentia* for *intelligentiam*.]

[58] "The formal notion of power [*potentia*] holds for God inasmuch as his power is the principle of an effect but not as it is the principle of action (for this is the divine essence), except, perhaps, according to our way of understanding" (*ST* I, q. 25, a. 1, ad 3). Hence, in God power [*potentia*] is not, properly speaking, ordered to act. However, nonetheless, God acts on account of an end,—namely, for the sake of communicating his goodness.

An agent does not move except from the intention of an end. For, if the agent were not determined to some [determinate] effect, it would not do this rather than that. Therefore, in order for it to produce a determinate effect, it must be determined to something certain, which has the character of an end. However, just as this determination is brought about in a rational nature through the rational appetite, which is called the will, so too it is brought about in other beings through the natural inclination that is called a natural appetite.[59]

In this, we can see the *reductio ad absurdum* relative to this point, for if the agent produces not just any particular, indifferent effect but, rather, produces one that is determinate and suitable to it, *while not tending* toward it (or by not intending it), it would follow that *this* essential *befittingness* in relation to the effect itself *would not be intended and* [*therefore*] *would utterly lack a raison d'être*. Indeed, this befittingness and determination actually existing in the effect could not have been produced unless it had already existed in some manner in the productive action. Now, it cannot exist in the productive action actually and formally, as it exists in the effect, but rather can only be there *virtually*, inasmuch as the act tends to the effect and is ordered to it. Hence, if we deny this ordination we likewise deny the *raison d'être* of the determination and goodness essentially and suitably fitted to an effect. An action is essentially tendential [*intentionalis*] (i.e., tending to that which is to be done), for otherwise, it would produce nothing determinately. However, if there is only a passive ordination in it, then there must first be [*praerequiritur*] an active and intelligent ordination, just as the arrow is directed by the archer. Therefore, this *raison d'être* cannot be anything but an intended end, and it does not suffice to have recourse to chance[60] or solely to efficient causality.[61]

---

[59] Also see St. Thomas, *In II Phys.*, ch. 3 and *SCG* III, ch. 2. Also, Tommaso Maria Zigliara, *Summa philosophica*, vol. 1, 517; Édouard Hugon, *Cursus philosophicus Thomisticus*, vols. 5 and 6.

[60] See St. Thomas, *In II Phys*, lect. 7–10. Indeed, *chance is a per accidens cause* and can only explain an accidental befittingness, not an essential one. For example, when a person digging a grave accidentally finds a treasure, this is something arising from chance. However, all effects cannot be *per accidens*, for *that which is per accidens happens to that which is per se*. The person digging a grave essentially [*per se*] intends [the digging of] a grave, and if he did not have any essential intention, nothing accidental would take place. Likewise, *per accidens* being is the accidental conjunction of two things (e.g., musicality and whiteness), but this accidental conjunction presupposes that both of these terms essentially be what they are. Musicality is *per se* musicality, and whiteness *per se* is whiteness. If there is nothing *per se*, there will be nothing *per accidens*.

[61] For were we to reject the existence of final causality, the efficient cause would have no reason

{{242}} G. *Finally, the principle of change* is taken from the perspective of matter and is expressed, "Every change presupposes a changeable subject." This principle is [self-]evident on the basis of the notion of change, "for it is of the very notion of change that one and the same thing now be different from what it previously was."[62]

This principle is likewise demonstrated indirectly, through a *reductio ad absurdum*, for a change without a changeable subject would be a change of nothing. In other words, there would be a change and yet nothing that would have changed, which is absurd. This would be like saying that there is a current without a flowing liquid or fluid subject, or as though there were a breeze without air, a breeze in an absolute vacuum.

The principle of change is expressed by St. Thomas in *ST* I, q. 9, a. 1 (Whether God is altogether immutable): "Everything that is changed in some way is in potency in some way . . . (and) in one respect, something remains in that which is moved, while in another way, something passes away."

Notwithstanding this principle, creation (i.e., production *ex nihilo*) remains possible, for "creation is not change" but, rather, is the production of the whole of [a finite] being, presupposing no subject for this production. Such production requires an infinite active power.[63]

All of these principles correspond to the four causes and, as St. Thomas says, are founded on the supreme [principle], at least inasmuch as those who deny these principles can be reduced to absurdity (i.e., to the denial of the principle of contradiction) or those who doubt these principles can be led to doubt the supreme one. However, such doubt is absurd, for if something perhaps can simultaneously both be and not be (and hence, simultaneously affirmed and denied from the same perspective), then this doubt can be simultaneously a doubt and a non-doubt. In other words, doubt itself vanishes before our eyes and nothing remains, not even the opposition between nothingness and being, which is the peak of absurdities and the very annihilation of nothingness itself, for nothingness cannot be conceived without being opposed to being.

---

for acting rather than not acting, as well as for acting in this manner and not in some other way. Indeed, if an action is not brought about for the achieving of a good proportioned to the inclination of the agent, then the action itself exists without any *raison d'être*. An inclination is essentially ordered to something, just as the imperfect is ordered to the perfect.

[62] *ST* I, q. 45, a. 2, ad 2.

[63] See *ST* I, q. 45, a. 2, ad 2 and III, q. 75, a. 8.

§2. Pantheistic Evolutionism Must Deny the First Principles of Reason

Let us ascend from secondary principles to the supreme one. However, among the secondary principles, let us begin with the principle of efficient causality, given that this causality is clearer.

(1) **Denial of the principle of efficient causality.** To say that the more is produced from the less is to deny the principle of efficient causality. Now, absolute evolutionism must say that the more is produced from the less. Therefore, absolute evolutionism must deny the principle of efficient causality.

Now, we will first prove the minor premise as follows. Indeed, according to absolute evolutionism, the real principle of all things is not from itself and eternally constituted and perfect but, on the contrary, evolves, ever passing from an imperfect state to an increasingly perfect state. This is to affirm that the more perfect arises from the more imperfect (or that the more would be produced from the less).

This affirmation is clear in the case of materialistic evolution, for according to it, the real and initial principle of all things is matter, containing within itself alone the rudiments of life, though lacking sensation and intellection. And to say that sense life and intellective life come forth through evolution from this primitive matter is to say that the more is produced {{243}} from the less. All our intellects, and all of our sciences, would arise from a kind of blind, deaf, imbecilic, and stupid God—that is, from the mud of the earth, which quite obviously is an absurdity invented for the sake of avoiding the supernatural mysteries.

Likewise, in its idealistic form, absolute evolutionism affirms that all things proceed from the idea of universal, indeterminate being, which is not yet self-conscious. This utterly vague and unconscious idea appears as the august and venerable form of nothingness, for it neither actually-formally nor actually-eminently[64] contains the subsequent forms of ascending evolution but, rather, only contains them potentially, as the imperfect contains the perfect to which it is ordered. Therefore, for idealistic evolution as well, the more is produced from the less.

The major premise is proven as follows. However, to say that the more is produced from the less is to deny the principle of efficient causality, for this greater form of being would lack an efficient cause and would arise from nothingness without a creative cause, meaning that being would be produced

---

[64] For it would already be Self-Subsistent Existence (that is, the Transcendent God).

from nothingness. In order to avoid the mystery of creation, they fall into contradiction, for the denial of the principle of efficient causality leads to the denial of the principle of *raison d'être*—nay, to the denial of the principle of contradiction—for if something which does not exist from itself does not exist from another, it would then not have a reason why it would exist rather than not exist and hence could not be distinguished from nothingness.

By contrast, in virtue of the principle of efficient causality, it is clear that if being, life, intelligence, morality, and sanctity exist today, it is necessary that there exist, from eternity, being, life, intelligence, morality, and sanctity—nay, that Being *a se*, Life *a se*, Intelligence *a se* exists. Otherwise, if beings of the same nature as our own (i.e., contingent beings) alone exist from eternity, they would have no *raison d'être*, given that they would not have in themselves a reason for their existence. A given contingent being does not necessarily require another contingent being as a cause, but both of them necessarily require a necessary being. The more is not produced from the less. Therefore, the First Cause must eminently have of itself all the perfections that now exist in the world.[65]

(2) *The denial of the principle of finality*. According to the principle of finality, every agent acts on account of an end (at least executively). Now, absolute evolutionism must deny that every agent acts on account of an end (at least executively). Therefore, absolute evolutionism must deny the principle of finality.

The major premise expressed above is proven as follows. Every agent tends to an end at least executively—namely, to an end intended by itself or by a superior agent, as the arrow is directed by the archer. Indeed, action presupposes the ordination of an agent's power to a given act (e.g., the power of sight to the act of seeing) and passive ordination presupposes active ordination. And only intelligence orders, for it alone knows the reason for the end and the *raison d'être* of the means.[66]

{{244}} The minor premise is proven as follows. Absolute evolutionism must deny that every agent acts on account of an end, at least executively—that is, under the direction of a superior intelligence. Indeed, according to

---

[65] See *ST* I, q. 2, a. 3, where he discusses the five ways for demonstrating God's existence.

[66] See *ST* I, q. 2, a. 3, fifth way. Also see *ST* I-II, q. 1, a. 2: "Those things that lack reason tend to an end on account of a natural inclination, as though moved by another and not, however, by themselves. For they do not know the reasons for the end. (Through sensation, the animal knows *the thing that is the end but not the formal character of the end* [*as such*].) And therefore, they can order nothing to an end but only are ordered to an end by another, for the whole of irrational nature is compared to God as an instrument is to a principal agent, as we discussed above (cf. *ST* I, q. 22, a. 2 and q. 105, a. 5)."

this system, an Ordering Intelligence does not exist *a se* from eternity.

This denial of finality is clearer in materialistic evolutionism, for it strives to explain all things through material causality, which it more or less confuses with efficient causality. However, it formally rejects the final cause and [the existence of] an ordering intelligence. By contrast, idealistic evolutionism sometimes admits an unconscious finality inasmuch as the inferior forms of evolution tend to superior ones unconsciously. However, in this [philosophical] system, such a tendency lacks any *raison d'être*. Indeed, in truth, an active ordination of an ordering intelligence[67] is required, and idealistic evolution denies the existence of an Eternal Intelligence. According to this [philosophical] system, the idea is at first unaware of itself and arrives at consciousness only with the appearance of man. Hence, evolution has no director guiding its action.

Moreover, the denial of the principle of finality leads to the denial of the principle of *raison d'être* and to the denial of the principle of contradiction, as we said above. By contrast, when admitted, the principle of finality enables the demonstration of the existence of a Universal Orderer (cf. St. Thomas's "fifth way").

(3) *The denial of the principle of change.* According to the principle of change, change presupposes a changeable subject that is in some way distinct from the change itself, which exists in that subject. Now, absolute evolutionism mixes together, without any distinction, the subject of evolution and evolution itself (or universal becoming itself). Therefore, absolute evolutionism must deny the principle of change.

As we already discussed above, the major premise is [self-]evident. No change occurs without a changed subject that differs from what it previously was. Otherwise, there would be a change in nothing (i.e., no change).

Turning to the minor premise, absolute evolutionism mixes together, without any distinction, the subject of evolution and evolution itself, for materialistic evolutionism reduces matter to physical energy in order to be able to explain how matter would have within itself the principle of its own motion. According to this position, matter is physical energy itself or, in other words, its very own activity, which is always in motion. Likewise, idealistic evolutionism reduces the whole of reality to ideal becoming itself, and all realities are only moments of this universal becoming. Thus, motion does not need a first extrinsic mover and does not need an explanation, for it itself is the principle for the explanation of all things.

But then the principle of change is denied, and one must confess that

---

[67] [Trans. note: Reading *ordinatio* for *ordinario*.]

there is a flow without any flowing subject, as though there were a flow without liquid or fluid, a vibration without air, flight without a flying bird, and the act of thinking without a thinking subject. Man cannot say, as Descartes wished to say, "I think, therefore I am," but must instead only say in an impersonal manner, "There is thought," as one says in an impersonal manner, "It is raining."[68] And grammar would then need to contain only impersonal verbs. Against theism, evolutionism objects: {{245}} God existing outside the world is nothing other than an abstract being formed by human reasoning [ens rationis], illegitimately conceived of as an actual being (the realization of an abstraction). In reality, the notion of a subject-less, universal becoming is what is only an abstraction. Only *this* motion in this mobile thing exists, not motion in general, for it would be something absurd—namely, the flow of nothing.

By contrast, what is required is a first subject for the changes of sensible things—namely, matter. However, this subject, which is changeable and utterly imperfect of itself, is not its existence through its essence. (That is, it does not include existence in its definition.) Rather, it is conceived only as something capable of existing and, hence, is not being from itself, just as it does not move or act from itself. Therefore, it is contingent. Nor could it be produced from a preceding subject, since it would be the first subject. Therefore, it is produced *ex nihilo*. Finally, this production *ex nihilo* can only be brought about through an infinite creative power. "For if the power of the agent is greater to the degree that the (passive) potency in question is more remote from act, then the power of the agent producing something from no presupposed potency, as we find in a creating agent, must be infinite."[69] Thus, there must be a Creator-Agent outside of evolution, and evolution cannot be self-creative, for then there would be evolution without a cause, without a subject, and without an end.

(4) *The denial of the principle of raison d'être*. Absolute evolutionism cannot avoid this denial, for [according to it,] evolution itself does not have a *raison d'être*, neither in another nor in itself. Indeed, it does not have such a *raison d'être* in another because, according to [such] evolutionism, there is no transcendent cause existing beyond evolution itself. Nor does it have a cause in itself, for evolution is motion (or the transition from non-determination to determination, or, as Aristotle says, from potency to act). Now, this transition does not have its *raison d'être* in itself, for non-determination

---

[68] [Trans. note: This same language is found in other works of Fr. Garrigou-Lagrange, who is playing on the French expression "Il pleut."]

[69] *ST* I, q. 45, a. 5, ad 3.

is not a determination, nor does it contain determination in itself eminently. Potency cannot be reduced by itself to act, for then the more would be produced from the less and being from nothingness.

(5) *The denial of the principle of substance.* According to this principle, everything that is is a substance, or everything that is is one and the same under its various and variable phenomena (if it has phenomena, for a phenomenon is only that by which something is such and appears to the senses). The appearances of a thing presuppose a thing that appears. Now, according to absolute evolutionism, not only are there not diverse substances, but indeed, there is not even one single substance, for there is only a universal becoming without a subject, phenomena (or appearances) without a thing that appears.

(6) *The denial of the principle of contradiction (or of the principle of identity).* From the denial of the preceding principles, the denial of the supreme principle of reason indirectly follows, although this principle is even directly denied by absolute evolutionism.

Indeed, according to the principle of contradiction or identity, being is being and non-being is non-being—in other words, being is not non-being. Hence, every being is a thing (i.e., something having a determinate essence, not many natures) and thus is something one and the same.

Now, absolute evolutionism denies the absolute opposition of being and non-being, saying that being and non-being are identified in becoming itself, consequently denying that any being has a determinate essence. This leads to the conclusion that "God is one and the same reality with the world, and so is spirit {{246}} with matter, necessity with liberty, truth with falsehood, good with evil, and justice with injustice."[70]

Therefore, absolute evolutionism must directly deny the principle of contradiction (or of identity).

The major premise was explained above. The minor is evident from the definition of absolute evolutionism, in which God is said to be nothing other than creative evolution, with God in truth becoming himself in the world and in man. Hence, all natures are said to be the same, just as being and non-being are the same in becoming itself. Consequently, that which is true is not *simpliciter* true but is only true *secundum quid* (or relatively). Likewise, falsity is not *simpliciter* opposed to truth but, rather, is only opposed to it *secundum quid*. In other words, *falsehood is only something that is less true*, and *truth is something that is less false*. Hence, just as physical hypotheses concerning the nature of light or electricity are said to be neither true nor false but instead suitable [*commodae*]

---

[70] Pius IX, *Syllabus of Errors*, no. 1 (Denzinger, no. 2901).

and temporarily useful for the sake of classifying phenomena, so too[71] the relativity of cognition would need to be admitted even for the first principles of reason. In that case, there would be no absolute and immutable truth, and it would not be true to say, "What is is, and what is not is not" (cf. Matt 5:37). Rather, we would need to say, "Perhaps it is; perhaps it is not." Nay, probability itself would not even remain, for it is itself designated in relation to certitude. Finally, a relative falsity would of necessity lead to a relative truth and vice versa, just as a thesis would lead to an antithesis and so on *ad infinitum*. Hence, they say, "Heresy is nothing other than a new dogma in the process of becoming, in accord with the process of dogmatic development." According to us, however, heresy is a dogma in a corrupted form or, rather, the *simpliciter* false denial of a dogma and not merely a less true form. Likewise, *evil would only be a lesser good leading of necessity to a greater good* in accord with the absolute optimism of ascending evolution. No norm would remain fixed. Hence, the Church defends the laws of reason against rationalism when she condemns the modernist definition of truth: "Truth is no more immutable than man himself, since it evolved with him, in him, and through him."[72] Indeed, the modernists do not define truth as "the adequation of reality and the intellect" but, rather, as "the adequation of mind and life." However, this life is human life, which they hold must forever change, as though instability were not a defect but, rather, a perfection, and as though stability, firmness, and constancy were inertia, sterility, and death.

Hence, absolute evolutionism denies all of the first principles of reason, as well as the four causes correlative to these principles, for it holds that there is a universal becoming without any subject, without an efficient cause, without an intended end. Indeed, in this becoming, all contraries and contradictories are one. This is exactly what is expressed in the first proposition condemned by Pius IX in the *Syllabus of Errors*.

By contrast, *by virtue of the principle of contradiction (or identity), we can prove that the First Cause* of all things *is identically and formally Self-Subsistent Existence*, in whom essence, existence action, understanding, and willing are all the same. This is the loftiest verification of the principle of identity. Indeed, if the First Cause were not Unreceived Self-Subsistent Existence, there would be in it a composition of essence and existence, and this composition would presuppose a loftier cause.[73] For by virtue of the principle of identity, "*every composite has a cause*, for those things that of themselves are diverse do not come together in some one thing except through a cause joining them together."[74]

---

[71] [Trans. note: Reading *ita* for *ta*.]

[72] Pius X, *Lamentabili*, no. 58 (Denzinger, no. 3458).

[73] See St. Thomas's fourth way in *ST* I, q. 2, a. 3.

[74] *ST* I, q. 3, a. 7.

{{247}} In other words, things that are diverse *of themselves* are diverse and not that united thing. Therefore, if they are united, this union is brought about by some other thing. Thus, a composite first cause would not be the first cause. Hence, the first cause must be Self-Subsistent Existence (*ST* I, q. 3, a. 4) and consequently completely simple, immutable, and infinite (*ST* I, q. 3, a. 7; q. 7, a. 1; q. 9, a. 1). Therefore, it essentially transcends the world, for the world is essentially composite and mutable (*ST* I, q. 3, a. 8). This refutation of pantheism necessarily follows from the principle of contradiction or identity, whose loftiest verification is found in the "I am Who Am" of Exodus (Exod 3:4). Stated in general: Being is being and cannot be non-being; God, however, says, "I am who I am and cannot not be."

Indeed, if the fundamental law of our reason and of reality is the principle of contradiction (or of identity), the supreme reality must be the very real identity of essence and existence (or Self-Subsistent Existence). Thus, the five ways for proving God's existence are joined together in the opposition of the principle of identity with the mutability[75] and composition[76] of the world so that it is immediately clear in this opposition that the world is not being from itself but that only Self-Subsistent Existence is being from Itself. Nor is it surprising that the *a posteriori* proofs of God's existence are remotely founded on the principle of contradiction (or identity), for they proximately rely on the principle of causality, which has the principle of contradiction as its ultimate foundation.[77] Thus, God is known in the mirror of sensible things through the reflection of the light of the first principles, for in their light we clearly see the contingency of the mutable and composite world and, hence, its dependence upon the Immobile and Simple Being.

Nay, some evolutionist philosophers, like Hegel and a number of modernists,[78] thus "became vain in their thoughts" (Rom 1:21, DR), so that *they confessed that they denied the first principles of reason*. Hence, they say that the supreme principle of reason (i.e., the principle of contradiction) is indeed a law of discursive reason [*rationis ratiocinantis*], which utilizes abstract and immobile ideas. However, it is not a law of our superior reason (or of the intellect), which considers the ever-flowing and living reality itself, in which contradictories are the identified [with each other]. However, in the resolutions to the objections, we will see that this denial of the real value of the principle of contradiction is mere sophistry.

---

[75] This is the first, second, and third way. See *ST* I, q. 2, a. 3.

[76] This is the fourth and fifth way. In the fourth, it is a question of the composition and imperfection of finite things; in the fifth, it is a question of an ordered multitude.

[77] We have discussed this matter at greater length in our book *God: His Existence and His Nature*, trans. Bede Rose (St. Louis, MO: B. Herder, 1949), 139–176; vol. 2, 20–22, 436.

[78] See Pius X, *Pascendi*, no. 37.

But already, absolute evolutionism appears to us as an incontrovertible demonstration through absurdity for the existence of a God who transcends the world, he who is the source of the supernatural order. For, if the truth of the principle of contradiction is granted, the necessity of the other principles of reason is thus preserved, and we thus also have a rigorous demonstration of the existence of God the First Mover, First Creative Cause, and Supreme Intelligence who has ordered all things. Therefore, if Hegelianism did not exist, the theologian would need to invent it as a kind of demonstration through absurdity.

Hence, absolute rationalism could not better demonstrate its own irrationality. It is as if one were to say, "In order to reject the existence of God the Creator, {{248}} we must deny [the existence of] the world itself or else hold that it is the domain of radical absurdity. In order to reject the supernatural order, we must destroy nature itself. In order to reject revelation and the faith owed to it, we must radically overturn the very essence of reason."[79]

§3. Resolution of Objections

A. Objections raised by absolute evolutionism in general
B. Objections raised by materialistic evolutionism specifically
C. Objections raised by idealistic evolutionism specifically
D. Objections raised by emanationism

A. Objections raised by absolute evolutionism in general

1. *Objection*: Absolute evolutionism cannot actually be contrary to the first principles of reason, for it is founded on experience and the principle of causality.

Proof: By force of the principle of causality, the more cannot be produced from the less. Now, there is in fact more in motion than in immobility. Therefore, motion cannot be produced by an immobile being but instead exists from itself and is the principle of all things. Such runs the argument of Bergson in his book *Creative Evolution*.[80]

---

[79] In the great irony of providence, this denial of reason is called "Rationalism." As the Psalmist says (Ps 2:4,1 DR): "He that dwelleth in heaven shall laugh at them [for they have] devised vain things." Just as when a powerless boy fights against a giant the latter laughs at him, so too the derision of the rationalists who deny the supernatural order is laughed at by God. And the evolutionists themselves, through this absurdity, prove the doctrine that they fight against—namely: The real principle of all things is not matter, nor the self-unconscious Idea, but instead is Existence Itself, as well as Infinite Intellection Itself, a brilliant intellectual flash of light and the fire of love that is eternally subsistent, "the light of life," and "the true light, which enlighteneth every man that cometh into this world" (John 1:9, DR).

[80] See Henri Bergson, *L'évolution créatrice* (Paris: Félix Alcan, 1907): "There is *more* in movement than in the successive positions attributed to the mobile, *more* in becoming than in the forms traversed in turn, *more* in the evolution of the form than in the forms realized one after another. Therefore, philosophy will be able to draw terms of the second kind from the first

Response: I concede the major premise but make a distinction concerning the minor. If the argument means that there is more in motion than in *the privative immobility of potency* (or in the *terminus a quo* of motion), I concede the point. However, I deny it if it means that there is more in motion than in *the negative immobility of the act itself* whether of the agent or of the end of the motion. Moreover, I make a distinction with regard to the conclusion, conceding what it says if it means that movement cannot be produced from an immobile being by the immobility of potency. However, I deny it if it means that it cannot be produced by the immobility belonging to act.

Allow me to explain. The immobility of potency (or of the *terminus a quo* of the motion itself) is the privative immobility of something inert (i.e., a privation of motion). By contrast, the immutability [*sic*] of act is a negative immobility of a perfection that is superior to motion and is called not *inertia*, but *stability and constancy*. Motion is superior to instability and inconstancy, just as immobile spiritual contemplation is superior to the roaming activity of the imagination or as the surety of a holy will is loftier than the agitation and tumult of sensibility. Inertia and complete stability of life are opposed to each other as the lowest and loftiest of things. Thus, Aristotle says that matter is incorruptible and ingenerable, but not in the same way God is, for God is above corruptibility, whereas matter is below it (i.e., as the subject at which corruption is terminated, meaning that matter cannot be corrupted but only annihilated).

{{249}} 2. *The point is urged, however*: There is more in motion (or in activity) than in the immobility of act itself. Therefore, the difficulty remains.

Proof: The mover is related to the mobile as act to potency. Now, more is found in the mover itself when it is actually moving than in an immobile mover. Therefore, there is more in movement (or activity) than in the immobility of act itself.

Response: I concede the major premise. However, I make a distinction regarding the minor premise. If it means that there is more found in the actually moving mover (i.e., in *a moved mover*), I concede the point. However, I deny it for the case of the *first Unmoved Mover*. Likewise, I make a distinction regarding the conclusion. I concede that there is more in motion (or activity) than there is in the immobility of any given mover. However, I deny that there is more in [the motion of a finite moved mover] than in the immobility of the act of the supreme Unmoved Mover.

Allow me to explain. There is more in activity than in the immobility of a mover which requires pre-motion in order to act, for from this perspective, this inferior mover is mobile. However, the same does not hold for the Supreme Mover, who requires no

---

but not the first from the second. Speculation must take its point of departure from the first. *However, the intellect reverses the order of the two terms* and on this point ancient philosophy proceeds along the path traveled by the intellect. It installs itself in the immutable. It gives itself Ideas . . . and passes on to becoming by way of attenuation and diminution. At the foundation of ancient philosophy there necessarily lies this postulate: there is more in the immobile than in movement."

pre-motion, for he himself is his own activity, his own action [*suum agere*], through his essence.

3. *Yet the objector continues to urge the point*: Now, there is more in the activity of this First Mover than in its own immobility. Therefore, the difficulty remains.

Proof: When the First Mover begins to move, there is then more in him than before. Now, the First Mover does indeed begin to move; otherwise, he would act in the same manner from eternity, meaning that there would be no new effect in the world. Therefore, there is more found in the activity of the First Mover than in his immobility.

Response: I make a distinction regarding the major premise. I [would] concede it if there were *a newness of action* in the First Mover. However, if there is only *a newness of effect*, I deny it. Moreover, I contradistinguish the minor premise. If it means that the First Mover begins to move such that there would be a newness of action, I deny it. I concede the point if it means that there would be a newness of the effect. Therefore, I deny the consequence and the inference.

Allow me to explain. In *SCG* II, ch. 35, St. Thomas says: "The newness of the divine effect does not demonstrate the newness of an action in God, since His action is His essence, as we showed above in bk. 1, ch. 45." Thus, the action by which God acts *ad extra* is formally immanent and virtually transient (or transitive). As formally immanent, it is the same as the divine essence because Self-Subsistent Existence is its own activity. This action is nevertheless called virtually transitive [*transiens*] because it contains in itself the perfection of a formally transitive act. That is, it can produce an effect *ad extra*.[81]

4. Continuing to insist on the point, however, now, there cannot be newness of effect without there simultaneously being newness of action in the First Mover. Hence, the First Mover is not immobile but instead is creative evolution itself.

Proof: If one posits a cause in act, the effect immediately and necessarily follows. Now, according to the response expressed above, the divine action is eternal. Therefore, the divine effects ought to be all eternal, nor can there be newness of effect.

Response: First, I make a distinction in the major premise. I concede it if it means that an effect immediately and necessarily follows upon the positing of a necessary cause in act existing in time. However, I deny it if it refers to a *free cause existing above time*. Moreover, I contradistinguish the minor. I concede it if it asserts that the divine action is a free cause *ad extra*, existing above time. However, I deny it if it means that it is a necessary cause existing in time. Therefore, I deny the consequence and the inference.

Allow me to explain. God is a free cause because the supreme agent by whom nature is ordered must be an agent acting through intellect and will (*ST* I, q. 19, a. 4), and a will is free in relation to any particular good (*ST* I, q. 19, a. 3). Hence, the divine causality transcends time, is measured by eternity (*ST* I, q. 10), and produces time as well as motion, for time is the "measure of motion according to before and after" (ibid.). Hence,

---

[81] See *ST* I, q. 25, a. 1, ad 3.

God produces created things and new effects in the world whenever he wills, without any change in his will. For, as St. Thomas says in *SCG* II, ch. 35:

> Just as the doing of a thing is determined through the intellect in all of its conditions, so too does it prescribe its time, {{250}} for art does not only determine that something should be such and such, but also so that it is to be at a given time—as the doctor determines that medicine is to be taken at a given time. Whence, if his willing were of itself efficacious for producing the effect, the effect would follow anew from his previous willing, with no new action being needed on his part. Therefore, nothing prevents us from saying that God's action existed from eternity, even though the effect of this action is not eternal but instead comes into existence at the time ordained by Him from eternity.... God simultaneously brought both creation and time into being.

5. *Continued insistence on the point*: Even without newness of action, more would be produced from what is less in the case of creation. Therefore, the difficulty remains.

Proof: When an effect is posited outside of the cause, there is more being than there was before. Now, through creation, created things are posited outside of the First Cause. Therefore, after creation, there would be more being than before. Hence, the more would be produced from the less.

Response: First, I distinguish the major premise, conceding it if it means that there is *more being extensively and improperly speaking*; however, I deny it if it means *intensively and properly speaking*. I concede the minor premise and distinguish the conclusion. I concede that more would be produced from the less if after creation there were more being, intensively speaking—that is, more perfection. However, I deny it if there is only more being extensively speaking (i.e., by participation).

Allow me to explain. Since the First Cause eminently and in a more excellent manner contains in himself all creaturely perfections altogether—nay, since he is infinite, that is, the complete plenitude of existence—God and all creatures taken together are not something more perfect and better than God alone, for the Infinite is not made greater by the addition of the finite. Thus, after creation, there are more beings but not, properly speaking, more being. Hence, St. Augustine said in Tr. 11 on the Gospel of John: "If you are without God, you will be less; if you are with God, God will not be greater. He does not become greater because of you, but you become less without Him." And, in *In* III *Sent.*, d. 6, q. 2, a. 3, ad 1, St. Thomas says: "A created good is related to the Uncreated Good as the point is related to the line, since there is no proportion of the one to the other. Thus, just as the line is not made greater by the addition of a point, so too does the addition of a created good . . . to the Uncreated Good not make the latter better. Or also because the complete formal character of all good things exists in God, . . . whence, no good can be added to Him, for every good is already in Him." Likewise, when students understand the teaching of a given teacher (e.g., St. Thomas), without however perfecting it, more wisdom does not come into existence, even though there are more wise people. The wisdom of the teacher is not perfected thereby but, rather, is extended to others.

6. The objector urges the point further still. Now, after creation, there is more being, intensively speaking.

Proof: More being, *intensively speaking*, is the same as saying *more perfect being*. Now, the creative action in God is a perfection the absence of which would be an imperfection. Therefore, after creation, there is more being, intensively speaking.

Response: I concede the major premise. However, I make a distinction as regards the minor. If it means that the divine freedom would consist in an indifference *of potency* to many acts, like human freedom, I would concede the point. However, in reality, it consists in the indifference *of one utterly simple pure act* in relation to various objects. This act of the divine will is simple in itself and is only virtually multiform. Insofar as it is terminated at the divine goodness, it is necessary; inasmuch as it is terminated at creatures, it is free (see *ST* I, q. 19, a. 3, ad 5). As Cajetan says in his comments on *ST* I, q. 19, a. 2, the free act in God is a free perfection "whose opposite is not imperfection." It is better to say, with other Thomists, the free divine act does not add a perfection [to God] but presupposes the perfection of the utterly pure act and is subject to failure only extrinsically, on account of the willed thing's own ability to fail.[82]

7. *Yet another point is urged*: Indeed, something cannot be added extensively to the Infinite Being. Now, if a new being exists outside of the Infinite Being, something would be added to the infinite. Therefore, there cannot be a new being outside of the infinite.

Response: I make a distinction regarding the major premise. I concede that nothing can be added extensively in the order of quantity *to a quantitatively infinite being on either side* [*a parte ante et a parte post*]. However, I make a sub-distinction if one means {{251}} *nothing can be added to a being of infinite perfection*: I concede the point if one is speaking of the same order of perfection; I deny it if one is speaking *of an inferior order of perfection*. For Infinitely Perfect Being Itself can bring about something outside of Itself (*ST* I, q. 7, a. 1).

Allow me to explain. A quantitative infinity would be unlimited in bodily magnitude but finite as regards its perfection, for it would be material and held within the limits of matter. Spirit, however, transcends these limits and hence abstracts from here and now, from time and space.

Otherwise, *if an infinitely perfect being could not bring about something outside of himself, we would need to deny that he has the power to create*, thus meaning that he would lack a given perfection. *Thus, he would no longer be infinitely perfect*. Likewise, fire has the complete perfection of heat in itself and nonetheless (nay, for this very reason) can heat something (e.g., water or wood).

---

[82] See Billuart, *Summa sancti Thomae, De Deo*, diss. 7, a. 4.

Hence, if the finite is not posited outside of the infinite, it is posited within the infinite itself, as pantheists wish to be the case. Then, something is simultaneously finite and infinite, an assertion that is not a mystery (like creation) but instead is evident absurdity. *And pantheism is so absurd that it cannot be thought, even though atheistic, as well as acosmic, pantheism does indeed exist [sed est vel atheismus vel acosmismus].* That is, one either holds that God is absorbed into the world (as evolutionists do today) or that the world is absorbed into God (as eastern pantheism holds regarding nirvana). Then one is forced to deny either the first principles of reason or the most certain facts of experience.

8. Yet again a response is offered by the objector. Indeed, in an inferior order there cannot be a caused being outside of the infinite.

Proof: Something simple in itself cannot be diversified by itself but, rather, only by something else. Now, being qua being is something simple in itself, and outside of being, nothing exists (as Parmenides once said and then, centuries later, Spinoza). Therefore, being cannot be diversified; hence, being is only one.

Response: I make a distinction regarding the major premise. If this is *univocal*, like a genus, I concede that it can only be diversified through extrinsic differences. However, I deny the point if this is *analogous*, for an analogue contains in act-implicitly [*actu implicite*] a given variety—namely, its analogates. I concede the minor premise but make a distinction regarding the conclusion. I concede that it would indeed be the case if being were univocal. However, I deny it if *being is an analogous term*, for then it contains the modalities of being in act-implicitly [*actu implicite*]. Hence, in *In* I *Meta.*, ch. 5, lect. 9, St. Thomas says, "In this, Parmenides was deceived, for he used being as though it had one formal character [*ratione*] and one nature, as is the case for the nature of a genus. Indeed, this is impossible, for being is not a genus but, rather, is said in many ways about various things."

However, existence is multiplied precisely as it is received in various essences, for act is multiplied and limited by the potency in which it is received (*ST* I, q. 7, a. 1). And being is analogically said of potency and act. Concerning the analogy of being, see our discussion below in ch. 9, §2, where we will critique agnosticism.

9. Still, even if being were an analogue, creation is impossible. Therefore, the difficulty stands.

Proof: What has been made necessarily undergoes becoming at some time. Now, every becoming presupposes a subject. Therefore, it is impossible that something would come into being *ex nihilo*.

Response: In *ST* I, q. 45, a. 2, ad 3, St. Thomas says, "Since creation comes about without motion, a given thing is at once created and has been created," and in ad 2: "*Creation is not change*, except only after the way that we understand things, for it is of the very notion of change that one and the same thing now be different from what it was before."

10. And yet creation at least seems to be contrary to the principle of finality, for to act on account of an end is suitable for an agent that requires an end. Now, God the

Creator stands in need of nothing. Therefore, God the Creator would not act on account of an end.

Response: In *ST* I, q. 44, a. 4, ad 1, St. Thomas says, "*God does not act on account of some need that He has*, or for the sake of something that would profit Him, *but does so only on account of His own goodness.*" Hence, as was said at the [First] Vatican Council: "God," created, "of His own goodness and almighty power, not for the increase of His own happiness or for the acquirement of His perfection, but in order to manifest His perfection through the benefits that {{252}} He bestows upon creatures with absolute freedom of counsel."[83] Hence, creation in no way involves a contradiction, whereas, by contrast, creative evolution is contradictory at least four times over, in relation to the four causes.

11. *A final point of insistence*: Absolute evolutionism does not seem to necessarily imply the denial of the existence of an order of supernatural truth, for even if it were true, many unknowable mysteries would remain, especially the mystery of creative evolution itself.

Response: I will let pass the claim that *natural* mysteries would remain. However, I deny that *supernatural* mysteries would remain. For a supernatural mystery is one whose existence cannot be known without supernatural revelation.

B. Objections raised by materialistic evolutionism specifically

First objection: Materialistic evolutionism is founded on the first principles of modern physics, especially on the principle of the conservation of energy. Therefore, it is not contrary to the first principles of reason.

Proof: According to the principle of the conservation of energy, the total quantity of energy in all of its transformations ever remains the same. Now, were the First Mover distinct from the world to influence the world, the total quantity of energy would be changed (i.e., increased). Therefore, there cannot be a First Mover distinct from the world. Rather, the first principle of motion is the very physical energy of the world, which is either actual or potential.

Response: I make a distinction regarding the major premise. I concede it if it means that the total quantity of energy remains the same inasmuch as *some given motion comes to an end and another equivalent one is produced under the invisible influence of the First Cause.* Otherwise, I deny it. Moreover, I contradistinguish the minor premise. I concede it if the principle of the conservation of energy is incorrectly [*indebite*] understood without any cessation of motion and production of an equivalent energy under the invisible influence of the First Mover. Otherwise, I deny it. Also, I deny the consequence and the inference.

Allow me to explain. The principle of the conservation of energy is approximatively verified only in the inferior order of physio-chemical phenomena inasmuch as experience approximatively bears witness to the equivalence producing and produced energy (e.g., the equivalence of motive power in the form of local motion and of the heat gen-

---

[83] [First] Vatican Council, *Dei filius*, ch. 1 (Denzinger, no. 3002).

erated through this motion). However, sometimes, this equivalence is unduly thought of as though there were no true production of equivalent energy but only the transformation of the same energy which would remain numerically (or individually) the same.[84] This imaginative representation comes from Descartes, who conceived of local motion as though it were something numerically the same passing from one subject into another, akin to how the same water passes from one vessel into another, losing the form of one vessel so that it might receive the form of the other. However, in reality, *motion as a general phenomenon* does not exist. There is only *this motion*, and it is *here* inasmuch as it is in *this* subject. Hence, *this* numerically same motion cannot *pass over* from one mobile thing into another. But the motion of the prior mobile thing *produces* another motion in another mobile, or the motion of the prior mobile being *is not transformed* into heat but instead *generates* or *produces* heat.[85] Now, the prior motion produces the second motion only as a second cause (i.e., under the invisible influence of the First Cause). This influence would indeed not be necessary, and the divine conservation alone would suffice, as Descartes wished, if {{253}} motion ever remained numerically the same, by passing from one subject to another. However, this is impossible. And experimental science cannot prove that the invisible influence of the First Cause does not exist or that it is not necessary. Hence, also, physicists today acknowledge that it was never proven that the world is "*a closed system*" (i.e., separated from every external influence, even an invisible one).[86]

---

[84] Physicists indifferently speak of "transformation" or "production." However, metaphysically speaking, this distinction is not indifferent.

[85] See Adolphe Ganot, *Traité de physique*, 20th ed., ed. Georges Maneuvrier (Paris: Hachette et Cie, 1887), 65: "Transformation of work into a living force and of living force into work. Principle of conservation of energy"; 1024: "Equivalence of work and heat. There is a numerical relation between the quantities of *destroyed* work and the corresponding sensible heat and vice versa. Nonetheless, there is a qualitative degradation of energy, for the heat *begotten* through mechanical work cannot *reproduce* an equal amount of mechanical work."

[86] See Henri Poincaré, *La science et l'hypothèse*, 112–119. There, he discusses the value of the principle of inertia, which holds that "a body separated from every external influence will forever remain at rest if it is immobile and will forever remain in motion if it is moved, at least in a resistance-free vacuum where there is no resistance." This principle of inertia is necessarily connected with the principle of the conservation of energy, which is formulated as stating, "The total energy of any given system of bodies separated from every external influence (i.e., the sum of its actual and potential energies) will remain the same."

Poincaré says, "Has there ever been an experiment undertaken on bodies removed from the action of every force, and if this has been done, how did the experimenter know that these bodies were not submitted to any force?" The principle of inertia is a hypothesis suggested by particular facts ([e.g.,] the movement of projectiles) and "fearlessly extended to the most general of cases (e.g., in astronomy) because we know that in these general cases *experience can neither confirm nor contradict it*" (ibid., 119).

Likewise, it cannot be proven that a given system of bodies (and especially the whole physical world) is a *closed system* (i.e., is separated from every external influence, even one that is invisible like divine premotion). See Émile Boutroux, *De la contingence des lois de la nature*,

In order to reject the necessity of the influence of the First Mover, one must prove that *nothing new* comes into being in the world. However, then energy would forever remain in the same immobile form. In reality, in the energy that is transformed (or, rather, in the energy producing an equivalent [amount of] energy) there is *more* than in energy that is privatively immobile (i.e., through a privation of motion or inertia); hence, the influence of the First Mover is required.

Thus, if the principle of the conservation of energy is reduced to its due limits, it is no more opposed to the influence of the First Mover than is the ancient principle of Aristotle: "The corruption of one thing is the generation of the other," for, in reality, the corruption of one form of energy (e.g., local motion and the motive power) is the generation of the other (e.g., heat), for local motion is not transformed into heat but, rather, generates or produces heat. Indeed, human activity remains relatively the same over the earth, and nonetheless, mankind is continuously renewed through corruption and generation. Similarly, physical activity remains the same in the physiochemical order, and nonetheless, bodies and their activities are renewed. The corruption of one is the generation of the other. Hence, *the conservation of energy would not exclude the influence of the First Mover unless this conservation were absolute immobility and identity, without any newness of effect* {{254}} *in the world*. However, this is contrary to the most certain facts of experience. In other words, the world could not be the same as the First Cause unless the world were completely immobile, by an immobility of perfection, not inertia (i.e., unless it were infinitely perfect and incapable of further perfection).

Second objection: Materialistic evolutionism objects that the phenomena of vegetative, sense, and rational life can all be reduced to physiochemical phenomena inasmuch

---

3rd ed., 78–85. Ernest Naville, *La physique moderne*, 2nd ed., 35–42. Marc de Munnynck, "La conservation de l'énergie et la liberté morale," *Revue Thomiste*, Old Series, 6 (1898): 697–706; "La conservation de l'énergie (Encore)," 413–426. René Hedde, "Les deux principes de la thermodynamique," *Revue Thomiste*, Old Series, 12 / New Series, 4 (1904): 706–727: "The law applies only presupposing a universe as a *system that is closed* to every external action. This hypothesis, which is necessary for establishing the law, cannot be a corollary of it. Therefore, if spiritual substances intervene in the material world, the demonstration of the law will be in default, and we will be incapable of foreseeing, in the name of physics, the consequences of such an intervention. Therefore, it seems that certain spiritualist philosophers have quite wrongly held that the principle of the conservation of energy is a kind of objection against human freedom. Even though human freedom might modify the total quantity of energy in the universe, the physicist would still have the right to proclaim the conservation of the energy of the material universe, the only thing that he is concerned with, for he is not interested in maintaining some unknown sum of energy but rather is concerned with knowing whether the phenomena that he studies are incapable of making it vary. Therefore, the law does not reach either human freedom or the divine freedom. It does not represent an objection against either of them" (726).

We have treated this point concerning the principle of the conservation of energy in our book *God: His Existence and His Nature*, vol. 1, 259–260, 270–282; vol. 2, 447–452.

as these already contain the beginnings of life and the inclinations of affinity, cohesion, attraction, repulsion, and so forth.

Response: A vital act (e.g., nutritive assimilation) cannot be reduced to physiochemical phenomena because this act is *a movement from an intrinsic principle*, whereas by contrast, physiochemical motion is a motion *from an extrinsic principle*.[87] Likewise, sensation is something of a superior order, "For knowing beings are distinguished from non-knowing beings in the fact that non-knowers have nothing but their own form, *whereas the knower of its very nature can have even the form of another thing*, for the species of the known is in the knower." Hence, the nature of a knowing being is less restricted and limited through matter than is a non-knower.[88] Moreover, intellection is *a fortiori* of a superior order, for "sense cognition is concerned with external sense qualities, whereas intellective cognition penetrates to the essence of the thing."[89] And the formal object of the intellect is not color or sound but, rather, *universal being*. Being, however, abstracts from matter. Thus, we know even things that are immaterial, such as truth, goodness, and holiness, which transcend matter, space, and time. If materialism were true, there would be nothing above material things, and erroneous philosophical systems would not need to be refuted by reason but instead destroyed by strength of arms, like material buildings. However, spirit and morality are above material power and are less restricted or limited, transcending matter and space. The drums and torments of war can do nothing against a given philosophical system or against the moral right of a given nation. Likewise, because our bodies are enclosed within the limits of matter, they cannot flee from an earthquake, but our spirits transcend these limits.

C. Objections raised by idealistic evolutionism

Absolute evolutionism, as proposed by Hegel, preserves the principle of contradiction as a law of inferior reasoning (i.e., of discursive reason [*rationis ratiocinantis*]), which uses immutable ideas. However, it denies that this principle is a law of superior reason, which gazes upon ever flowing reality. It argues against the real value of this principle as follows:

1. *First objection*: Pure (or universal) being is absolutely undetermined.

Now, that which is absolutely undetermined is mere non-being.

Therefore, pure being is mere non-being.[90]

---

87 See *ST* I, q. 18, a. 1 and 3.

88 See *ST* I, q. 14, a. 1.

89 *ST* II-II, q. 8, a. 1.

90 Likewise, following the principles of Bergsonian thought we find Édouard Le Roy writing thus in "Sur la logique de l'invention," *Revue de métaphysique et morale* 13 (1905): 200–204: "The principle of non-contradiction [*sic*] is not as universal and necessary as it is believed to be. It has its domain of application and has its restricted, limited meaning. *As the ultimate law of discourse and not of thought in general, it holds only for the static*, the fragmented, the immobile—in brief, it holds for things endowed with an *identity*. However, *there is contradiction in*

Response: This argument is sophistical in nature, for the demonstrative middle—namely, "that which is *absolutely undetermined*"—is not taken with the same extension in {{255}} the major premise as in the minor, for in the major it designates only the denial of generic and specific determination, whereas in the minor it also designates the denial of being [*entitas*] itself, which genera and species presuppose.

However, there would in fact be a contradiction if undetermined being were to exist from itself as the principle of all things.

2. *However, the objector urges on*. Now, undetermined being exists from itself as the principle of all things.

Proof: The real is the same as the ideal, for if the ideal is destroyed from any given thing, nothing remains. Now, the first idea is the universal idea [of being]. Therefore, the first reality is the universal, ideal being.

Response: I make a distinction regarding the major premise. I accept it if it asserts that *the real is the same as the ideal in Pure Act*. However, *outside of Pure Act*, I deny it. Likewise, I contradistinguish the minor premise, conceding it if it means that the first idea is the idea of universal being in us. However, I deny it if it means that this is the case in Pure Act, for God knows himself (namely, Self-Subsistent Existence) before knowing universal, undetermined being. Therefore, I deny the consequence and the inference.

Allow me to explain. In God, the real and the ideal are indeed the same—namely, Self-Subsistent Existence, Truth itself (or the Supreme Intelligibility and Intellection itself).[91] However, outside of God, the real and the ideal are distinct from each other, for according to the testimony of consciousness, the man who conceives of and desires a treasure does not by that very fact possess that treasure. And the idea can only be conceived of as a representation that is essentially relative to the represented being. Thus, it is entitatively distinguished from the latter, even though it may be intentionally and representatively the same as it. Hence, if whatever is intelligible in a given thing is destroyed, it is not surprising that nothing would remain, for that intelligible thing is a being, but not the idea of being.

3. *A continued urging on this point*: Now, even in Pure Act, we find that contradictories are identified as in pantheistic evolution. Therefore, the principle of contradiction is not a law of reality.

---

the world, as there is identity. It is made up of fleeting mobilities—becoming, duration, life—which by themselves are not discursive and are transformed by discourse in order to grasp them in contradictory schemata."

They add: *Being without internal contradiction would be sterile. Contradiction is fruitful.*

Aristotle already responded to this in arguing against Heraclitus in *Metaphysics*, 4.5: *If all contraries were identified, there would be eternal rest, not motion*, for something could not become something else, for the *terminus a quo* of motion would already be identified with its *terminus ad quem*. Therefore, nothing would be able to be moved.

[91] See *ST* I, q. 14, a. 4.

Proof: In Pure Act, Infinite Mercy is identified with Inexorable Justice, as is Absolute Immutability with Utter Freedom. Now, these attributes are contradictory to each other. Therefore, contradictories are identified even in Pure Act.

Response: I concede the major premise but deny the minor. For these *divine attributes are not contradictory* but, rather, *are diverse* simply simple perfections which in virtue of their own natures *demand that they be identified in the eminence of the Deity, radically excluding contrary imperfections or vices.* Thus, Infinite Mercy demands to be identified with Inexorable Justice and radically excludes the vice of cruelty; on the other hand, Justice seeks to be identified with Mercy and excludes criminal indulgence for the impenitent. This identification of the divine attributes is the mystery of the Deity. In this, there is no contradiction, as we will show when we argue against agnosticism. Nay, it absolutely excludes contradiction inasmuch as the Divine Being radically excludes non-being, the Divine Truth completely drives away error, and the Supreme Goodness is essentially opposed to wickedness. Likewise, created holiness unites within itself firmness of faith against heresies with the benevolence of charity toward erring men, just as it excludes fanaticism (i.e., the mere appearance of faith) and liberalism (i.e., the mere appearance of charity).

By contrast, according to Hegel, God and the world are one and the same thing. Thus, spirit is the same as matter, necessity as freedom, truth as falsity, good as evil, and charity as perversity. Hence, Hegelian being is an absurd and perverse imitation of God, a systematic and universal confusion, a mere likeness of the supreme harmony. Indeed, *harmony* is had from the subordination of distinct things to some one thing, whereas *confusion* is the subversion of [any and every] ordering principle. "The corruption of the best is the worst." The corruption of spirit is greater than is the corruption of flesh, and so too is the abuse of reason in rationalism, especially the abuse of the term "charity," using this term for commending the toleration of impiety. There is nothing loftier in this life than charity but nothing worse than *false charity*, for it is a more efficacious instrument of impiety.

D. Objections raised by emanationism

{{256}} [*Objection:*] Even if God were to exist as Self-Subsistent Existence and Intellection Itself, finite things cannot come forth from him through creation *ex nihilo* but, rather, come forth through emanation. Hence, they are of the same nature as God and are participations in the divine nature, meaning that we already see verified of them what the theologians say about supernatural grace. Consequently, the supernatural order does not exist [for there is only one order, that of being].

According to emanationism, finite things flow from the divine substance in nearly the same way as the spider pulls forth its web from its own innards. Emanation is, as it were, a kind of imperfect generation. According to Plotinus and the Gnostics, *emanation* is *transitive* inasmuch as the substance that has emanated is extrinsic to the emanating substance. On the other hand, according to Spinoza and Schelling, emanation is *immanent* inasmuch as the emanating substance expands itself within itself. In emanationism God becomes the world (in contrast to ascending evolutionism, wherein the world becomes God.)

Together [*communiter*], theologians *respond* that transitive emanationism presupposes the divisibility of the divine substance, which is completely simple and indivisible. Immanent emanation presupposes a confusion of the finite and the infinite.

1. *However, the following point is insisted upon as an objection*: God can only produce something outside of himself by emitting something from himself. Now, that which is emitted from God emanates from the divine substance. Therefore, finite things emanate from the divine substance.

Response: First, I make a distinction regarding the major premise. If God were simultaneously the efficient cause and material cause of the produced thing, I [would] concede the point. However, if he is only the efficient cause, I deny it. Likewise, I contradistinguish the minor premise. I concede that something emitted from a cause that is at once efficient and material indeed emanates from it, like the filaments drawn from the spider's innards. However, I deny that this is so for what is produced by a cause that is only an efficient cause. In reality, to create is to produce something *ex nihilo*—that is, from no presupposed subject. *God is not a material cause*. Nay, there is no material cause in the case of creation. Hence, the creative power must be infinite.[92] Hence, creatures are said to be *from God* but not *of* God, nor *out of* God, for the prepositions "of" and "out of" designate a material cause.

Against transitive emanatism, see *ST* I, q. 19, a. 3 and 4, as well as *SCG* II, ch. 23: "God acts through free choice of will, not out of natural necessity," for an agent acting through understanding and will is prior to an agent acting through nature.[93] Likewise, see *ST* I, q. 90, a. 1, "Whether the soul was made or is of the substance of God," as well as *SCG* II, ch. 83. The Holy Doctor argues *from the indivisibility of the divine nature*: Since the divine substance is completely incommunicable [*impartibilis*], the human soul cannot be something of the divine substance unless it is the whole of the divine substance. Now, given that the human soul is finite and mutable, it obviously is not the whole of the divine substance. Therefore, the human soul is not something of the divine substance. Hence, God can be neither the material nor the formal cause of things but instead can only be their efficient and final causes, which are extrinsic causes. Therefore, in *ST* I, q. 3, a. 8, St. Thomas says, "David of Dinant most foolishly said that God is prime matter."

2. *A continued point is urged*: Nonetheless, a transitive action proceeds (or emanates) from the agent into the effect. Now, God is the efficient cause of the world. Therefore, in the production of the world, something emanates from God as the efficient cause.

Response: We must distinguish between a formally transitive action, which is suited

---

92 See *ST* I, q. 45, a. 5, ad 3.

93 For it is necessary that an agent acting through nature be predetermined, by another superior intellect, to the end and means necessary for achieving that end.

to created agents, and *a formally immanent but virtually transitive action that is suited to God*. For the divine action is said to be formally immanent because it is identified with the divine essence, and it is said to be virtually transitive inasmuch as it eminently has the perfection of a formally transitive action, without any of the imperfections involved in the latter. However, a formally transitive action (e.g., heating) is essentially imperfect, for it is an accident proceeding from a created agent {{257}} while being terminatively received in the passive recipient.[94] However, the effect of this action is not the passing of the same accident from the agent into the passive recipient; rather, under the influence of the transitive action, the effect is educed from the passive potency of the patient. This fecund conjunction of the action of the agent and the passivity of the patient is the natural mystery of created causality, which requires the intervention of the First Mover. However, it is not a contradiction, as though some numerically one and the same accident were to migrate from one subject to another. Hence, there is not an emanation even in formally transitive created action (nor, *a fortiori*, in virtually transitive uncreated action).

3. *Yet the objector insists yet more*. Even if God cannot be a material cause, nonetheless he is the formal cause of all things. Therefore, immanent emanationism must be admitted.

Proof: God is existence itself. Now, existence itself is the most formal of all things (as St. Thomas says in *ST* I, q. 7, a. 1). Therefore, God is the formal [cause] of all things.

Response: I first make a distinction regarding the major premise. I concede it if you mean that God is *Self-Subsistent Existence*. However, I deny it if you mean that he is existence actuating whatsoever given finite essence. I contradistinguish the minor premise in the same way. On this, see *ST* I, q. 3, a. 8 and the other texts cited under the title of this article, especially SCG I, ch. 26: "*That God is not the formal existence of all things*." For an informing form is a part of the composite and, hence, is a participated form: "However, just as that which participates is posterior to that which is *through its essence*, so too is the very participated thing itself [posterior in like manner]. . . . However, it has been shown that God is the first being *simpliciter*."[95]

4. *Yet another point can be insisted*. Nonetheless, as Spinoza said, there cannot be two substances.

Proof: For they would either have the same attributes (and then could not be distinct); or they would not have the same attributes, and then they could in no way agree in the formal character of substance. Spinoza developed this argument in *Ethics*, pt. 1, prop. 6. However, he adds nothing essential to it.[96] This objection coincides with Parmenides's doctrine: Being cannot be diversified by something else, for the only thing besides being is nothingness.

---

94 See John of St. Thomas, *Cursus philosophicus,* vol. 2 (*Naturalis philosophiae*), ed. Beatus Reiser (Turin: Marietti, 1933), q. 14, a. 3 and 4.

95 *ST* I, q. 3, a. 8.

96 See Zigliara, *Summa phil.*, vol. 2, 18.

Response: These two substances can have the same attributes, whether they be specific, generic, or analogous, and nonetheless be numerically distinct (e.g., two men). Even the divine substance and created substance agree in the analogical notion of being while, nonetheless, being distinct, for God is being from himself and utterly simple, whereas, on the contrary, [every] creature is being from another, something composed from genus and difference, essence and existence, and having accidents. This response presupposes *that being is analogous and not univocal*, as we have already said against Parmenides.

The pantheism of Spinoza and Schelling was already refuted by St. Thomas in *ST* I, q. 3, a. 6: "*In God, there is no composition of subject and accident*, for a subject is compared to accidents as potency to act. God, by contrast, is Self-Subsistent Existence, with no admixture of potency at all." That is, *God is not susceptible to further perfection.*

This is how all forms of pantheism are refuted, inasmuch as God is required as the First Cause, Self-Subsistent Existence, which is utterly simple and immutable, whereas the world (as well as any finite being whatsoever) is something composed and mutable. In this, we clearly see that the radical principle of distinction between God and the world is found in the fact that *God is Self-Subsistent Existence.*

Indeed, this is *the fundamental truth of Christian philosophy.*[97] Granted, it is not fundamental according to the way of discovery. (In this order, the first truths are the first principles of reason and the facts that are clear based upon experience.) Rather, it is fundamental according to the way {{258}} of judgment, as St. Thomas says in *ST* I, q. 79, a. 9[98]—namely, inasmuch as reason assigns the supreme reasons for things and judges temporal things according to eternal formal notions [*rationes*]. For the five ways of proving God's existence flow together into this terminus: God is Self-Subsistent Existence. *Indeed, the utterly immobile uncaused First Cause* (first, second, and third ways), who is *completely simple and intelligent* (fourth and fifth ways), *must be Self-Subsistent Existence* (*ST* I, q. 3, a. 4). In other words, in God alone are essence and existence identical. This is, as it were, the keystone or ultimate joint at the peak of the edifice. It is the golden key of the whole of the treatise on the one God and of the whole of Christian philosophy. Indeed, all of the attributes of God are deduced from this fact: his absolute simplicity, immobility, eternity, infinity, supreme goodness, omniscience, and so forth. Likewise, it is deduced that God alone is the creator, universal mover, and end of all beings. Nothing can exist unless it be caused by God, nothing can act unless it be moved by God, and all things are ordered to

---

[97] See Norbert del Prado, *De veritate fundamentali philosophiae christianae* (Friburg, CH, 1911). This magisterial work is divided into five books. The four first books treat this truth in the philosophical order, whereas the fifth does so in relation to sacred doctrine—that is, to the mysteries of the Trinity, the Incarnation, the Eucharist, and the beatific vision.

[98] [Trans. note: On this topic, also see Réginald Garrigou-Lagrange, "On the Twofold *Via inventionis* and the Twofold *Via iudicii* According to St. Thomas," *Philosophizing in Faith: Essays on the Beginning and End of Wisdom*, ed. and trans. Matthew K. Minerd (Providence, RI: Cluny Media, 2019), 11–20.]

God and to his goodness so as to manifest his mercy or justice.

Also, this already enables us to prove the existence of an order of supernatural truth inasmuch as the *Deity*, in what is proper to it (i.e., according to its *intimate life*), in its utterly eminent simplicity, exceeds (as we will discuss below) the natural knowledge attainable by any created or creatable intellect whatsoever. (See our discussion in ch. 11 below, where we undertake a refutation of ontologism.)

CHAPTER NINE

Examination of Agnosticism, Inasmuch as It Denies the Possibility of Supernatural Revelation from the Perspective of the Subject (i.e., Man)

{{259}} *The thesis of this chapter can be stated thus: Because agnosticism denies the possibility of supernatural revelation from the perspective of the subject (i.e., man), it can be reduced to absurdity.*

After considering pantheistic evolutionism, which denies the possibility of supernatural revelation from the perspective of the object, we must examine agnosticism, which denies this possibility from the perspective of the subject (i.e., from the perspective of man).

There are two parts to this chapter:

Art. 1. Exposition of empirical agnosticism and idealistic agnosticism: How this doctrine denies the possibility of revelation

Art. 2. Criticism of agnosticism through a *reductio ad absurdum*

ART. 1: EXPOSITION OF EMPIRICAL AGNOSTICISM AND IDEALISTIC AGNOSTICISM

§1. Agnosticism in general

§2. Empiricist agnosticism

§3. Idealist agnosticism

§1. Agnosticism in General

A. *Definition of agnosticism.* Generally speaking, agnosticism is a system of thought holding that *human reason can only know phenomena*, which are or can be the object of our internal or external experience. *Whatever tran-*

scends phenomena remains unknowable—hence the name "agnosticism." It is the opposite of ancient gnosticism, which claimed that it knew all things. Certain agnostics, such as John Stuart Mill, say that only subjective phenomena are knowable, thus meaning that the existence of the external world remains in doubt. Others, like Herbert Spencer, admit the existence of the external world, especially on account of how bodies offer up active resistance, likewise holding that this world is symbolically knowable. However, they hold that things as they are in themselves outside of the mind remain unknowable and that human reason cannot know whether the substance of bodies or of the soul exists, nor what they are, for perhaps there is only one substance or, nay, perhaps not even one but instead only the evolution of phenomena according to determinate laws.

{{260}} However, if human reason cannot know sensible things as they are in themselves in their own substance, *a fortiori* it cannot demonstrate the existence of the First Cause, nor know whether this Supreme Cause would by its very essence transcend the world or whether, on the contrary, it would be immanent within it. Agnosticism confirms its thesis through an exposition of the antinomies (or contradictions) which, according to it, cannot be avoided in our knowledge of the essence of bodies, that of the essence of the soul, or our knowledge of the nature of the First Cause.

As is explained in the encyclical *Pascendi*:

> Modernists place the foundation of religious philosophy in that doctrine which is usually called Agnosticism. According to this teaching human reason is confined entirely within the field of phenomena, that is to say, to things that are perceptible to the senses, and in the manner in which they are perceptible; it has no right and no power to transgress these limits. Hence it is incapable of lifting itself up to God, and of recognizing His existence, even by means of visible things.[1]

B. *The foundation of agnosticism. It denies ontological value of the first notions, as well as of their transcendent value, and hence, denies the first principles of reason.* According to the agnostic outlook, these notions and correlative principles only have a phenomenal value. That is, their only value would be knowing phenomena and their laws, without, however, having an *ontological value*—that is, without use for knowing the substantial being of things existing under the phenomena. For example, the notion of substance

---

[1]   Pius X, *Pascendi*, no. 6 (Denzinger, no. 3475).

would designate only a collection of phenomena. Likewise, the notion of causality would be only the notion of the temporally-successive character of phenomena, meaning that the principle of causality should be expressed as "Every phenomenon presupposes an antecedent one and thus *ad infinitum* into the past." Hence (and *a fortiori*) the first notions of reason and their correlative principles would have no *transcendent value*, namely, for knowing the Supreme Being or transcendent First Cause. (The term "transcendent" is being used here not only for saying that something transcends genera and species [as do the transcendentals] but rather indicates the fact that it transcends the world and every finite being.) This is the general philosophical conclusion reached by agnosticism.

C. *The consequences of agnosticism in religious philosophy.* This outlook has both positive and negative consequences. Negatively speaking, there are three principal consequences:

(a) *The unknowability of the existence of a God* who is essentially distinct from the world, a God who is the principle of the entire supernatural order.

(b) *The unknowability of the miraculous intervention of God* in the world (or, in other words, the unknowability of the fact of revelation confirmed through miracles); nay, miracles cannot be conceived, for this would mean that there would be a phenomenon without some phenomenal antecedent, a claim that stands in contradiction to the principle of causality [(as it is formed by such thinkers)].

(c) Even if the fact of revelation were knowable, *revelation can only be symbolic (or metaphorical)* because it would be expressed in accord with the notions formed by our reason (e.g., the notions of nature or person) which only have a phenomenal value and hence cannot truly express the divine reality, which exists above all phenomena (if it indeed exists at all).[2]

Nonetheless, in the positive part of its religious philosophy, agnosticism strives to explain the religious facts of various religions by way of a resolution to certain primitive phenomena that are the first manifestations of our religious sentiment. Thus, it passes over into a form of *immanentism* (inasmuch as religious sentiment, which they declare to be the source of all religion, is immanent within us) {{261}} and also into a form of *evolutionism*, at least from our own perspective (that is, as regards the explanation of religions), although the existence of a transcendent God is not expressly denied in itself, nor the absolute possibility of miracles, as occurs in pantheistic evolutionism.

---

[2] See ibid., nos. 6 and 12 (Denzinger, nos. 3475 and 3483).

Thus, agnosticism remains *a species of absolute rationalism*, for according to it, human reason, while indeed being quite weak, is thoroughly autonomous and is the supreme arbiter of truth and falsity and of good and evil, judging the value of faith and of the Church's definitions, itself being judged by nobody. It is superior to faith, just as scientific explanation is superior to symbolic cognition.

Hence, the difference is clear between the humility of agnostics, who always speak about the infirmity and limits of human reason, and Christian humility, which acknowledges the sublime mysteries of the divine nature in submission and adoration.

However, agnosticism has taken on two forms: *empiricist* and *idealist*. The empiricist agnostics most especially include positivists such as Herbert Spencer, Auguste Comte, the neo-Comtean [Théodule-Armand] Ribot, William James, and others, as well as many modernists.

The idealist agnostics most especially include Kant, as well as neo-Kantians such as Charles Renouvier, Friedrich Schleiermacher, Albrecht Ritschl, and Louis Auguste Sabatier, as well as many modernists.

We will now turn to a brief exposition of both forms of agnosticism.

§2. Empiricist Agnosticism

(1) *The general philosophy of this system of thought*. In this system, the ontological value of the first notions of reason are denied precisely because *the idea is reduced to a kind of composite or common image produced by the imagination [phantasiae], to which a common name is then connected*. This is a form of absolute nominalism. This composite image is produced quasi-mechanically, according to the laws of imaginative association, inasmuch as individual images which are similar strengthen each other and dissimilar ones weaken each other. In the end, what remains in our memory is a kind of common, vague image (e.g., the image of a dog without a determinate stature or color). On account of its vagueness, this image would indeed be insufficient for thought, but a remedy is found in the common name joined to it (e.g., the term "dog," which belongs to all dogs). Hence, as the nominalist Condillac said, science ultimately is well-constituted language. The universal only exists in [mere] terms [*nominibus*].

And therefore, like images of the imagination [*phantasiae*], *our ideas only represent sensible phenomena*. In other words, *they only have a phenomenal value*. Likewise, judgment is reduced to the association of two images, and reasoning to empirical sequences of representations. Hence, the first principles of reason are nothing other than empirical associations reiterated many times and confirmed by regular succession [*hereditate*].

For example, the notion of substance is nothing other than the notion of a collection of phenomena, and the notion of personality expresses only the collection of internal phenomena under one supreme phenomenon, which is "self-consciousness." The notion of causality signifies the mere succession of phenomena and, hence, the principle of causality is expressed: "Every phenomenon presupposes an antecedent phenomenon, from which it proceeds, and so forth *ad infinitum* into the past."

Nothing is knowable outside of the phenomena and their laws. This conclusion necessarily {{262}} follows from the reduction of intellectual knowledge to sense knowledge. The intellect no longer is a power that "reads the depths of things" [*intus legit*] but, rather, is just like sense knowledge, which, as St. Thomas says, is "occupied with sensible external qualities and does not penetrate any deeper [than do they]."[3] According to positivists and nominalists, whatever is conceived beyond or above the phenomena is only a scholastic or verbal entity, an empty name without any correlative representation.

(2) *The religious philosophy expressed by empiricist agnosticism.* The religious philosophy of this outlook can be explicated with a view to its negative assertions, especially as expressed by Herbert Spencer. After speaking of this, we will then see what is said positively by Spencer, the followers of Comte, William James, and others.

A. **Negative part**

(a) *First, the knowability of the First Cause is denied*, for empiricist agnosticism rejects the transcendent value of the first notions (as well as that of the first principles of reason), for it does not acknowledge their ontological value. Hence, the principle of causality, expressed as "Every phenomenon presupposes an antecedent phenomenon, and so on *ad infinitum* into the past," cannot be the foundation for the demonstration of God's existence. Similarly, reason cannot legitimately attribute to God or the Absolute [notions like] reality, truth, goodness, intelligence, will, freedom, justice, mercy, and so forth, for all of these notions only have a phenomenal value (i.e., relative to experience). Consequently, they cannot express the Absolute. Nay, we are told that the use of these notions in attempting to know God necessarily generates *antinomies* (or contradictions). For example, according to Spencer, an antinomy exists between the divine simplicity and the divine consciousness, inasmuch as consciousness implies the duality of subject and object; likewise, an antinomy exists between God's absolute immutability and freedom because a free act would add something contingent and mutable to God. Similarly, there are antinomies between the supreme goodness and the permission of evil, between infinite justice and infinite mercy, and so forth. According to Spencer, whatever is said about the Absolute not only is mysterious and incomprehensible but [moreover] is contradictory. According to the logic of phenomenalism, especially according to the aforementioned

---

[3] *ST* II-II, q. 8, a. 1.

formulation of the principle of causality, the existence of the Absolute cannot even be proven. However, Spencer admits this existence, though he adds that all hypotheses regarding the nature of the Absolute imply a contradiction. Atheism is absurd, as is pantheism, as well as theism. It is impossible to say whether the Absolute is immanent or transcendent, personal or not, intelligent and free or not.

This unknowability necessarily follows from the empiricist denial of the ontological and transcendent value of the first notions of reason. John Stuart Mill, the positivists, William James, and others all speak along these lines.

(b) *The impossibility of discerning a miraculous intervention by God who reveals also follows*. Perhaps miracles are not intrinsically impossible. However, they cannot be conceived of by us, for contrary to the principle of causality [so conceived], they would be a phenomenon without a phenomenal antecedent.

(c) Nay, even if the fact of revelation were discernable, *revelation would remain merely symbolic and metaphorical*, for it would be expressed in accord with the notions of our reason, which only enjoy a phenomenal value and, hence, cannot truly express a supra-phenomenal reality. For example, our notion of personality designates only a collection of internal phenomena under one supreme one, which is "self-consciousness." Hence, this notion cannot express a divine person which is not phenomenal in any way. We must speak of the notion of nature along the same lines.

{{263}} B. **Positive part**

Nonetheless, empiricist agnosticism intends to provide an explanation for religious phenomena. Let us briefly see what is said about these matters by Herbert Spencer, Auguste Comte, the Neo-Comteans, and William James.[4]

(a) *According to Herbert Spencer*, religions are nothing other than the striving of the human spirit toward acquiring representations of the Unknowable Itself, representations that are indeed conformable to our categories and customs. These conceptions are only symbolic, and although they involve speculative contradictions, they nonetheless excite our religious sentiment. However, in the evolution of this sentiment, its moral element gradually comes to prevail over its cultic and propitiatory elements, making the anthropomorphic characteristics of God (e.g., God's anger and avenging justice) pass away. Thus, religion today cannot be anything other than *an indefinite awareness of the Absolute*. Every science leads to mystery, and religion begins where science leaves off. (Without difficulty, all religions are reconciled in this natural religion. Nay, atheism, pantheism, and theism can all be reconciled in it. This is the harmony to which absolutely autonomous and inde-

---

4   See Georges Michelet, *Dieu et l'agnosticisme contemporain* (Paris: Beauchesne, 1909). [In particular, see the sections:] God according to the sociological school (Comte); God according to religious pragmatism (James); God according to religious immanentism (Blondel and Le Roy). Cf. Émile Boutroux, *Science et religion* (Paris: Flammarion, 1908). See the chapters: A. Comte and the Religion of Humanity; Herbert Spencer and the Unknowable; Haeckel; Ritschl; The Philosophy of Action; William James and Religious Experience.

pendent reason arrives. It is not subject to the Truth, which would free it, but, rather, is subject to all the opposed errors it intends to reconcile.)

(b) *According to Auguste Comte*, religion is reduced to the moral life (or, rather, to social life) and hence is always necessary. Positive science and positive philosophy (which is, [according to him], the coordination of the sciences) can indeed reduce our various forms of knowledge into a sufficient unity. However, they do not efficaciously move people to social action and do not preserve our social bonds well enough. For this, religion is necessary, and without it, science by itself generates egoism and pride.

Therefore, metaphysical dogmas, which are obsolete today, must be eliminated from ancient religions. We must, however, preserve their moral truths which, in reality, are founded on our nature and indeed foster its progress. In other words, we must establish *a positivist religion*.

Therefore, Comte sought after the principal assertions to be preserved from religions, especially from Christianity, reducing them to these two: the existence of God and the immortality of the soul. However, the idea of God, inasmuch as it corresponds to the needs of our nature, is nothing other than the idea of some universal, immense, and eternal being with whom human souls communicate, providing them with the power needed for overcoming egoism so that charity and fraternity may prevail.

Now, for positivist religion, what is that *great and supreme being*, the source of the moral life? It is *Humanity Itself*, as Comte himself says. This Humanity is not only an empty abstraction and not only the collection of men now existing but, rather, is the continuity and solidarity of all generations[5] of men throughout time. It is constituted from all the good thoughts and deeds of our forebears, by whom we are aided in making further progress. This Humanity ever lives in us and is the principle and end of the social and moral order, the receptacle and source of all morality. It is the True God in whom we live, move, and have our being. It is not a fictive God like the one we find in theism but instead is a real being who ever moves us to overcome egoism so that solidarity may prevail.

Likewise, what is immortality according to positivist religion? It is *immortality in Humanity Itself*, which gathers together, preserves, and converts into its own nature whatever good is found in individuals' transitory lives. Indeed, throughout the course of its existence, Humanity is more so composed {{264}} of the dead than of the living. These dead live on morally in the memory of the living. This memory is not sterile but instead is affective and effective. Hence, the dead act in the living and excite a noble imitation of them. This is true immortality. The personal immortality promised by Christianity is only an imaginative fiction.

Therefore, positive religion is *the religion of Humanity*. Its first precept is live for other men—that is, live for one's family, country [*patria*], and for Humanity. Only then does the Great Being live and reign in us, our souls being transformed with fraternity

---

[5]   [Trans. note: Reading *generationum* for *generationem*.]

(i.e., altruism) dominating over egoism. To fulfill these duties, the *worship* established by a new religion will be of use, and this worship will involve the veneration of the *Positivist Trinity*: the Great Being (*Humanity*), the Great Temple (*Earth*), and the Great Medium (*Space*). (This is the religion that is thought up by autonomous reason, which is so independent that faith cannot be commanded of it by God. St. Paul himself said [1 Cor 1:20, DR]: "Hath not God made foolish the wisdom of this world?" Thus, the objection is turned into an argument—"heresies must exist"—so in their folly, the wisdom of faith may appear all the more.)

Likewise, *for contemporary Neo-Comteans* (e.g., Lucien Lévy-Bruhl and Émile Durkheim) religion is a collection of dogmas and precepts imposed upon individuals by human society itself for the sake of social progress. In this sociological explanation of religion, the religious sentiment is only an individual effect of social obligation. One must *believe in the perfectibility of society, hope in society, and love society*. Thus, Humanity is substituted for God. (A great deal of academic reverence is not to be preserved for these authors. This would be to the detriment of the reverence owed to God.)

Do we not here, in this empiricism, find a kind of verification for the parable of the prodigal son? Human reason denies the natural certitude of the existence of God, refuses to be obedient to the infallible God, and hands that over to society in all of its fallibility, rejecting the holy law that leads to freedom of spirit and beatitude, subjecting itself rather to an often-tyrannical law that leads to servitude and misery? It does not wish to adore the infinitely perfect God but adores utterly imperfect and feeble Humanity. This is, in its proper form, *sociolatry*—namely, *the modern form of superstition and flippant credulity*.

(c) *According to many empiricist psychologists*, such as Ribot (psychology of sentiments), religious phenomena are nothing other than *unconscious projections of our affections* and desires onto some imaginary object. They strive to prove this on the basis of an analogy between natural love and mystical love, for in both cases we find a succession of exaltation and depression. Thus, St. Teresa [of Ávila] would have believed that she heard from God himself what she in fact already desired. (Therefore, no distinction remains between true and false mysticism, between the life of St. Teresa [of Ávila] and the religious sensibility of Jeanne-Marie Guyon, notwithstanding the manifest differences in the effects of these two forms of mysticism. According to spiritual authors who specifically treat of the interior life, this represents a confusion of spiritual love with an inferior form of love, indeed, the confusion of spirit with flesh. However, by virtue of the principle of contradiction, or identity, flesh is flesh and spirit, spirit.)

(d) *According to William James* (in his 1902 work, *The Varieties of Religious Experience*), the principal religious fact is prayer and faith-confidence [*fiducia*] (or faith) by which the religious man imagines that he has relations with another, supreme being from whom he can receive help and peace. Only afterwards are dogmas conceived of in order to explain the religious experience. However, in reality, dogmas are adventitious additions that are essentially dependent upon the current state of philosophy and the sciences.

Now, what is the *value of religious experience*? James responds that whatever the origin or genesis of religion may be, this is of little important, for its value is to be judged from its practical usefulness (*pragmatism*). However, the principal fruit of religion is holiness. Indeed, holiness sometimes produces immoderate deprivations, austerity, obedience, and humility. On account of this lack of moderation, these fruits are of dubious value. {{265}} Nonetheless, holiness increases the moral strength, charity, harmony, and peace in the world. Nay, sometimes, religious faith-confidence heals sicknesses. Hence, religion alone thus elevates men above egoism, generates strength of soul and perseverance in adversity. Neither science nor, indeed, sociology suffice for obtaining this end. Hence, religious faith is useful.

Finally, what is the *object of this religious experience*? According to James, the object of religious experience is that which proceeds from our subconscious, where inspiration (whether poetic or religious) is prepared in a vague and hidden way. This subconscious has certain ineffable relations with another inaccessible world, and "prayer implores the aid of the powers of this order."

However, it is impossible to know this order in itself. All *dogmas* are nothing but representations accommodated to the genius of individuals or societies. Their truth cannot be proven, although they are sometimes *useful*, at least for a time, and help in overcoming egoism. Therefore, any given person can and must admit the dogmas that are personally useful for as long as they are useful. Thus, one can admit the existence of a personal God, particular providence, one that does indeed hear our prayers, and the immortality of the soul. These are not absurd, although they cannot be demonstrated. However, if *they are useful, they are practically true.*

Nonetheless, William James *rejects theism*—namely, the existence of one single, infinite God—as being a very improbable hypothesis:

> The vaster vistas which scientific evolutionism has opened, and the rising tide of social democratic ideals, have changed the type of our imagination, and the older monarchical theism is obsolete or obsolescent. The place of the divine in the world must be more organic and intimate. An external Creator and his institutions may still be verbally confessed at Church in formulas that linger by their mere inertia, but the life is out of them, we avoid dwelling on them, the sincere heart of us is elsewhere. . . . Our contemporary mind having once for all grasped the possibility of a more intimate *Weltanschauung*, the only opinions quite worthy of arresting our attention will fall within the general scope of what may roughly be called the pantheistic field of vision, the vision of God as the indwelling divine rather than the external Creator, and of human life as part and parcel of that deep reality[6]

---

[6] William James, *A Pluralistic Universe* (London: Longmans, Green and Co., 1909), 30.

Many modernists proceed along the lines of James's pragmatism. As is said in the encyclical *Pascendi*: "If you ask on what foundation this assertion of the Believer rests, they answer: *In the experience of the individual*. On this head the Modernists differ from the Rationalists only to fall into the opinion of the Protestants and pseudo-mystics."[7] In reality, William James quite often confuses true and false mysticism (that is, flesh and spirit).

These are the principal theories of empiricist agnosticism for explaining religious phenomena. They ever deny the notion of supernatural revelation.

§3. Idealist Agnosticism

(1) General philosophy

In this system, which was given its form by Kant in particular, the ontological value of the first notions and principles of reason is denied inasmuch as these notions are reduced not {{266}} to a mere sensible image but instead to merely subjective rational categories, which are called *a priori forms of the intellect*. However, these subjective categories can only unite phenomena together so that a necessary and universal science of phenomena can be constituted, at least subjectively. Therefore, empiricism must be rejected because it cannot explain the necessity and universality of science, especially of modern physics, as well as general ethics, whose principles must be admitted by everyone.

For example, the notion of substance is a subjective form of the intellect by means of which phenomena attributed to the same subject are united together, and the notion of causality is a subjective form by means of which

---

William James is praised by certain Catholics who do not perceive the infinite distance separating Catholicism from this pragmatism. He wrote in ibid., 29–30: "The theological machinery that spoke so livingly to our ancestors, with its finite age of the world, its creation out of nothing, its juridical morality and eschatology, its relish for rewards and punishments, its treatment of God as an external contriver, an 'intelligent and moral governor,' sounds as odd to most of us as if it were some outlandish savage religion. The vaster vistas which scientific evolutionism has opened, and the rising tide of social democratic ideals, have changed the type of our imagination, and the older monarchical theism is obsolete or obsolescent."

[Trans. note: These quotes are slightly different from the text provided, which is in Latin in the body of the text and French in the footnote. The Latin in the body shortens the passage a little and reorders the beginning slightly. However, to avoid a translation chain from English to French to Latin to English, I have chosen to draw directly from James's text. Note, however, that Fr. Garrigou-Lagrange draws attention to the ultimate conclusion in a very direct manner: "Today, the only opinions deserving consideration pertain to pantheistic doctrines, that is, to immanentism."]

7 Pius X, *Pascendi*, no. 14 (Denzinger, no. 3484).

phenomena that successively appear in time are united. Time and space are *a priori* forms of sensibility. Personality is an *a priori* form of reason by means of which internal phenomena are united together under [the notion of] "self-consciousness." Likewise, the principle of causality is an *a priori* synthetic (not analytic) principle—namely, one by means of which the phenomena that successively appear in time are united necessarily or *a priori* under the category of causality.

Thus, the subjective unity of scientific knowledge is progressively constituted, inasmuch as the forms of sensibility (i.e., time and space) inform phenomena and inasmuch as the categories of the intellect bring about a loftier form of classification and, finally, the subjective synthesis is perfected according to the application of the three ideas of reason—namely, the idea of the world (cosmology), the idea of the soul (psychology), and the idea of God (theodicy).

(2) *Religious philosophy*

A. Negative part

(a) *Idealistic agnosticism rejects the* possibility of *a speculative demonstration of God's existence*, for the first notions of reason lack ontological value and, *a fortiori*, transcendent value. Demonstrations of God's existence, founded on the principle of causality, are illegitimate since this principle would only have a phenomenal value for the subjectively necessary union of phenomena that appear in time.

Nay, according to Kant, when speculative reason wishes to know God, it cannot avoid falling into *antinomies* (i.e., contradictions). The existence of a First Cause transcending the world is simultaneously proven and disproven. The same holds for both divine and human freedom, the infinity of the world in time and space, and the divisibility of matter *ad infinitum*.

(b) Likewise, *it denies the knowability of miracles and the fact of revelation*, for we cannot know whether a given fact would be immediately caused by God, given that the principle of causality is only useful for the union of phenomena in their successive appearance. Every phenomenon presupposes an antecedent phenomenon. A miracle would stand outside of this law of causality.

(c) *Finally, idealistic agnosticism denies the transcendent value of dogmas*, even if they were to come from God, for dogmas are expressed according to the notions formed by our reason, which lack transcendent value. Hence, dogmas can only be metaphoric (or symbolic) expressions.

Therefore, in the third part of his work *Religion within the Bounds of Mere Reason*,[8]

---

8   See Immanuel Kant, *Die Religion innerhalb de Grenzen der blossen Vernunft* (Königsberg, 1793); *Sämtliche werke*, ed. Karl Rosenkranz, vol. 10, 130ff. Likewise, see Victor Delbos, *La philosophie pratique de Kant* [(Paris: Alcan, 1905)], 639ff.

Kant rejects the value of historical or ecclesiastical / liturgical faith. He says: {{267}} "This faith can only be symbolic. Nay, it is the particular faith of a given sect, not that of all men. Finally, it is *servile*, that is, contrary to the legitimate autonomy of reason." On account of this servility, it is the principle of deceit and superstition: "To believe in historical revelation is to confess that one is absolutely certain about the existence of this revelation, and moral conscience forbids us to assert as true that which we cannot know as true."[9]

B. **Positive part**

According to Kant, the existence of a personal God above the phenomenal order is, for speculative reason, a probable hypothesis, for antinomies are not wholly insoluble. Nay, they are resolved through the distinction between the phenomenal and intelligible orders. Hence, practical reason can and must affirm the existence of a personal God through an act *of natural faith*, for it arrives at a subjectively sufficient (although objectively insufficient) certitude concerning the existence of God the [Just] Rewarder, inasmuch as God alone can immutably unite virtue and beatitude in a future life. This union is required by this *a priori*, subjectively necessary, synthetic principle: The virtuous man is worthy of beatitude so perfect that it cannot be lost.

Kant strives to reduce Christian faith to this moral faith founded on the requirements of practical reason. Hence, he proposes a naturalistic interpretation of Christian dogma. Indeed, according to him, practical reason is absolutely autonomous, and it discriminates between what is true and what is merely symbolic in Christian faith.

The dogma of the *Trinity* cannot signify that there are three persons in God but instead only three attributes of the Supreme Rewarder. *The Incarnation* of the Word can

---

[9] Ibid., pt. 4, chs. 5 and 6.

In the same work, Kant hands on principles for a new system of hermeneutics. The first principle of this system is (as is rightly set forth by Cornley in his *Introduction générale à l'étude des livres saints* [on the Old Testament]): namely, that the sacred books are to be explained in such a manner that only the precepts of natural religion may be found in them. If there are texts that contradict these precepts, one need not abstain from a contorted explanation, and context need not matter. Indeed, one need not seek out what the author said but, rather, what he ought to have said. If the author brings forth prophecies, miracles, or deeds performed in order to prove what he says, all such things are to be disregarded.

Cornley adds: "However, the hermeneutic system proposed by Kant is no less absurd than it is impious. We call it 'absurd' because it does not teach what the meaning of the author's own thought is but, rather, how a [new] meaning is to be substituted for the words of the author thus interpreted; likewise, we call it 'absurd' because it denies history, etc. It is impious because it teaches how to abuse the sacred texts so that the Kantian religion may be propagated under the cover of propagating those texts' own meaning. Therefore, it fosters deceit and utterly overthrows its own power."

[Trans. note: Unless otherwise noted, I will be following the text of Kant as presented by Fr. Garrigou-Lagrange. Also, this translation is taken from Fr. Garrigou-Lagrange's citation of p. 748 of Cornley's work.]

be nothing other than the fulfillment of the perfect moral life in Christ. Christ is just and perfect and, in this sense, can be called the Son of God. However, he is not God. *The Redemption* is not the paying of a price of infinite worth on account of an offense committed against God in order to bestow supernatural grace upon men. Rather, Christ's death upon the Cross has a moral meaning and value, as the supreme example of moral courage. Thus, Christ redeems us through his heroic example, morally arousing us to virtue and to fight against the lusts of the flesh and cowardice. *Original sin* is nothing other than the fight that actively occurs in any given man between his sensuality and his will, between flesh and spirit. *Regeneration* (or justification) is not brought about through the infusion of sanctifying grace and the remission of sins but, rather, is found in the fact that the will dominates the flesh. *The Church* is only truly useful as an assembly of those who struggle against sensuality so as to more perfectly obey the categorical imperative. Neither worship nor ministry are required, except as instruments for preserving the moral law. Sacraments do not cause grace but, rather, are only symbols, sensible figures of moral realities. *The Church militant* is only the gathering of sects that fight among themselves. However, through these disputes, ecclesiastical faith progressively passes over to religious (or moral) faith. This is what the coming of the kingdom of God consists in. And the Church Triumphant will be the reconciliation {{268}} of these various sects in natural religion, within the limits of pure reason.[10] Luther had rejected the authority of the Church, thus positing the principle of free examination. Jean-Jacques Rousseau had proposed a naturalistic interpretation of the Gospel.[11] Kant brought the work of the pseudo-reformation to its perfection by rejecting divine revelation itself.

Now, various kinds of agnosticism come forth from Kant. On the one hand, there is (a) that which is found in a number of liberal Protestants such as Friedrich Schleiermacher, Albrecht Ritschl, and Adolf von Harnack. On the other hand, we have (b) that which is

---

[10] See *Religion innerhalb der Grenzen der blossen Vernunft*, 3.7: "The successive passage from ecclesiastical belief to the sovereignty of pure religious belief (i.e., purely rational belief) is the coming of the kingdom of God. . . . Historical belief inevitably gives rise to disputations, thus deserving the name 'church militant.' Nonetheless, there is hope that it will come, in the end, to be the Immutable Church, *the completely-unified Church, the Church Triumphant.*"

[11] See Jean-Jacques Rousseau, *Émile* (*Profession of Faith of the Savoyard Vicar*). Rousseau was born in Geneva to a Protestant family. He converted to Catholicism perhaps for the sake of financial gain and always lived an immoral [*inhonestum*] life, as he himself cynically confesses in his own confessions. Notwithstanding this immorality, Kant, who himself had a kind of austere conscience, highly praised Jean-Jacques Rousseau and was moved by the *French Revolution* with the greatest admiration, inasmuch as he saw therein *the principle of the autonomy of human reason* in the social order: It imposed its own law freely upon itself. This principle, which was enunciated by Rousseau, even held true, according to Kant, in the moral order. The French Revolution is its proclamation. Thus, we can see quite clearly the difference standing between the spirit of the Revolution and the spirit of the Gospel and the Church. See Albert Farges, *La religion de J. J. Rousseau* (Paris: [Maison de la bonne presse], 1917).

found in modernists such as Édouard Le Roy, George Tyrrell, and Alfred Loisy.

(a) *Liberal Protestants.* Friedrich Schleiermacher (1768–1834)[12] is the prince of the liberal Protestants after Kant. With Kant, he denied the possibility of metaphysics. According to him, we do not know whether or not God is truly a person distinct from the world. Nonetheless, religion remains, and it is nothing other than *religious sentiment* or awareness of our reliance upon the Infinite. It matters little that the Infinite is essentially distinct from the world, provided that we perceive It in everything and have some kind of communion with It. Hence, Schleiermacher says that "divine revelation cannot be made credible by outward signs; consequently, men must be moved to faith solely by each one's inner experience or by personal inspiration," something condemned by the [First] Vatican Council.[13] The supernatural life is thus reduced to the moral life, and Christ is the ideal sage.

Albrecht Ritschl[14] spoke along nearly the same lines, believing with Kant that our rational concepts are merely subjective. With Schleiermacher he held that religion relies on religious sentiment without, however, embracing pantheism. He admits that truth is contained in Sacred Scripture. However, in order to distinguish what is merely symbolic in Sacred Scripture from what is true, the supreme criterion (as Kant himself said) is conscience. Hence, Ritschl defended "liberal Christianity," which retains the terms "revelation," "miracle," "Trinity," "the Incarnation," and "Redemption" while, however, denying their reality. Christian religion is said to be revealed inasmuch as God has led and taught the Christian conscience. Miracles are extraordinary events in which the senses perceive a symbol or sign of divine benevolence. However, for science, the same events are something natural that has not yet been explained. Hence, he rejected the ontological value {{269}} of miracles and held that they only have a *symbolic value.* Likewise, as regards dogmas, they do not manifest God himself but, rather, express only our sense of faith-confidence [*fiduciae*], fear, hope, and love for God. In the evolution of dogmas, what remains one and the same through time is the religious emotion and the religious sentiment. However, our concepts perpetually change.

Adolf Harnack[15] rejected miracles and, hence, supernatural revelation, reducing

---

[12] His principal work is *Der christliche Glaube nach den Grundsaetzen der evangelischen Kirche*, ([Reutlingen: Mäcken], 1821). See Lichtenberger's article, "Dogmatique," in *Encyclopédie des science religieuses*. As regards the Catholic judgment concerning Schleiermacher's system, see Jean-Michel-Alfred Vacant, *Études théologiques sur les constitutions du Concile du Vatican d'après les actes du concile*, vol. 1 (Paris: Delhomme et Briguet, 1895), vol. 1 (71, 103, and 108) and vol. 2 (39). And *Schema prosynodale Con. Vatic.*, doc. 6, note 16 (Vacant, vol. 1, 593).

[13] *Dei filius*, can. 3.3 (Denzinger, no. 3033).

[14] Albrecht Ritschl, *Theologie und Metaphysik*, 2nd ed. (Bonn: A. Marcus, 1887); *Unterricht in der christlichen Religion*, 3rd ed. (Bonn: [A. Marcus], 1888). Henri Schoen, *Les origines historiques de la théologie de Ritschl* (Paris: Fischbacher, 1893).

[15] See Adolf Harnack, *Dogmengeschichte*, 2nd ed. (Fribourg im Brisgau: Mohr 1890), vol. 3, 762ff; *Das Christenthum und die Geschichte* ([Leipzig: Hinrich,] 1896). See *L'essence du chris-*

Christianity to a loftier form of natural religion. Nay, he eliminated from theology whatever has the appearance of speculative philosophy or dogma. According to him, *practical reason* and *history* suffice for rightly explaining religion. Christ's life and death had the greatest influence for shaping Christian conduct. The essence of Christianity is reduced to this: God is our Father, and we should hope in him, loving him like our neighbors. Provided that this essence is preserved, Christianity can be changed in accord with contemporary fashion.

Louis Auguste Sabatier[16] disseminated within France the rationalist theories of the Germans. He proceeded from Kant's agnosticism, rejected miracles and supernatural revelation, and hence rejected the idea of religion founded on authority.[17] *In place of the method of authority, he substituted historical methodology and psychological methodology,* on account of the autonomy of reason.[18] He retained the terms "revelation" and "dogma." However, he dissolved their very realities, in accord with the principles of agnosticism.

---

tianisme, French translation, ([Paris: Fischbacher], 1900), 41.

[16] See Louis Auguste Sabatier, *Esquisse d'une philosophie de la religion d'après la psychologie et l'histoire*, 7th ed. (Paris: Fischbacher, 1903); *Les religions d'autorité et la religion de l'esprit* (Paris: Fischbacher, 1903).

[17] See Louis Auguste Sabatier, *Les religions d'autorité et la religion de l'esprit*, 3: "The evidence extracted by rational criticism remains the foundation of historical certitude. Things are entirely different for the methodology of authority. The testimony by means of which one argues is properly speaking the testimony of God. The foundation here is the axiom that it is reasonable and just for human reason to be subordinate to the divine reason and even to remain silent and humble before it. Every argumentation of this kind, whether one admits it or not, in reality implies that the thinking subject in fact *declares his incompetence* and, consequently, *performs a conscious or unconscious act of abdication.*"

[18] See ibid.: "We find ourselves stunned when we see how up until the seventeenth century the ancients held such authority in the schools. Nonetheless, this childish method was overcome on the day when Galileo and Bacon opposed against it, in physics, the law of observation and experience, and when Descartes, in philosophy, submitting all traditional ideas to a provisional doubt, resolved to accept as true only those truths that seemed to be true in an evident manner. This represented an intellectual revolution of an incalculable scope which brought the long tutelage of the human mind to an end by affirming its autonomy.

"*To say that the mind is autonomous* does not mean that it is absolutely lawless. *Rather, it is to say that the* SUPREME *norm of its ideas and acts is found in itself, in its own proper constitution, and not outside of itself.* . . . Such is the principle of the character, independence, and marvelous development of modern culture for these past three hundred years. By insisting upon remaining subject to an old method, from which all the other disciplines have freed themselves, theology would find itself not only in sterile isolation but would be exposed to mortal contradictions and the conclusive condemnations of an ever more independent and self-assured reason."

The authority of God who reveals would constitute a heteronomous [norm] opposed to reason's autonomy. By contrast, according to Catholic theology, even in the natural order, the eternal law is the *supreme* rule of our activity. Our reason is a *proximate* rule such that one rule is ordered under the other. (See *ST* I-II, q. 19, a. 4.)

Let us briefly see what he held to be the revelation, origin, and development [*evolutio*] of dogmas.

What is revelation? It is the progressive knowledge of God manifesting himself *within the consciousness of any given individual.* Therefore, the fact of revelation does not need proof, for it is a fact of religious consciousness in all men, although it was livelier in the prophets and in Christ.

Whence arises this progressive knowledge of God? *It arises from a kind of emotion* of reverence, fear, and worship. {{270}} This emotion is born in our soul from an intimate contact with the Divine Being. From this emotion, there proceeds the prayer of the heart by which we seek out light, courage, and peace from God. Revelation is nothing other than a favorable answer to our prayer. In this way, religious knowledge is progressively perfected in any given honest consciousness [*conscientia recta*].[19]

Whence do dogmas arise?[20] A religious emotion is at first expressed in an imaginative form but then comes to be expressed in a conceptual form. However, when these concepts of Christian consciousness are approved by the Church, they are held as being dogmas. For example, from the emotion of fear there arises an imaginative representation of the divine wrath; then a notion of the divine justice is formed. Likewise, from the emotion of love and adoration there arises a religious concept of the divine goodness and paternity. Thus, *dogmas do not directly express* the divine reality, which remains unknowable. Rather, they [merely] express *our emotions* and are symbols expressing religious experience. Religious faith and theology cannot transcend *symbolism.*[21]

---

[19] See his *Esquisse d'une philosophie de religion.* Ch. 1, On the psychological origin of religion and its nature. Religion is the prayer of the heart.—Ch. 2, Religion and revelation. §1 The mystery of religious life. §2 The mythological notion of revelation. §3 The dogmatic notion [of revelation]. §4 The psychological notion [of revelation].—Ch. 3, On miracles and inspiration. §1 In antiquity. §2 In the Middle Ages. §3 In the face of science and of piety.

[20] See ibid., bk. 3, ch. 1, What is a dogma? (Catholic notion and Protestant notion [of dogma]).—Ch. 2, The life of dogmas and their historical evolution.—Ch. 3, The science of dogmas (its relations with the Church and philosophy).—Ch. 5[*sic*], The critical theory of religious consciousness. (Outdated theories of knowledge, the Kantian theory, subjectivity, symbolism.)

[21] Ibid., 398 (Symbolism): "Many good minds stiffen up against these ineluctable conclusions arising from a rigorous analysis of religious knowledge and its psychological genesis. Supposing that you are right, they say, and indeed the mental constitution of our spiritual nature thus condemns religious thought to symbolic forms, cannot a supernatural divine revelation make us break through this limit and bring to us religious ideas that are indeed adequate to their object (and, consequently, having a pure and absolutely veridical character)?

"To our eyes, it seems like a rather strange complaint to wish for a revelation from God that would be brought about outside of the conditions of knowledge, that is, outside of those forms [of expression] in which it could alone be accessible to us. Is it not clear that this immediately means that the very idea of revelation would become contradictory? If God willed to give us a gift that we could receive, must he not appropriate its form to that of our mind, *thus meaning that it would make use of our ideas* and of our language in order to explain the nature of the

What, therefore, is the immutability of dogmas? He responds: Religious emotion and the prayer of the heart remain. God is always conceived as the heavenly Father, conversion will always be a new birth, and religious consciousness cannot not desire the kingdom of God. In this sense, Christ said, "Heaven and earth will pass away, but my words will not pass away" (Matt 24:35). However, *the intellectual meaning of dogmas develops [evolvitur] and is transformed* with the progress of human reason and of the sciences. Now, this *development* especially occurs in three ways:

1. Certain dogmas pass away *by falling out of use* (e.g., faith in the existence of demons or in the eternity of hell).

2. *Through digestion [intussusceptionem]*, certain formulas take on {{271}} an entirely new meaning, as happens for the terms "the Trinity," "satisfaction," "inspiration," "miracles," and "revelation."

3. *Through renewal,* some formulas that have fallen into oblivion are brought back to life or are sometimes created anew (e.g., justification through faith and the universal priesthood of believers).

Through this theory of "symbolic criticism," Sabatier intended to relieve the concerns and scruples of the religious conscience and thus to reconcile orthodoxy with rationalism so that all religious souls could work together on behalf of moral unity. (Peace is indeed desirable, but it must be peace in truth. In error, there is nothing but a mere simulacrum of peace, as liberalism is a [mere] simulacrum of charity. Hence, Jesus said in Matthew 10:34: "I did not come to send peace but, rather, the sword. . . . He who loves his father or mother more than me is not worthy of me," and afterwards in John 14:27 (DR), "My peace I give unto you: not as the world giveth, do I give unto you." See lect. 7 of St. Thomas's commentary on John 14: "The peace of the world is counterfeit, for it is only external and for the enjoyment of temporal things. Christ's peace is true, bringing internal and external rest, and is ordered to eternal goods.")

This fictitious reconciliation, according to the same spirit, was proposed in an almost identical manner by modernism, and as a theory of revelation, modernism added nearly nothing new [to the discussion]. It reiterates the theories of Kant and of liberal Protestantism. Modernism continually speaks of renewal while itself lacking originality. It would be tiresome for us to exposit its theories at length. Therefore, it suffices to note its principles.

---

benefits that He bestows? *Now, it is certain that as soon as our ideas are transported outside of time and space, they contradict each other and destroy themselves* and that we are reduced to conceiving and expressing invisible and eternal things through contemporary, earthly images. If in order to speak to us about His mysteries, God made use of anything other than human means, we could not understand them at all, thus meaning that His revelation would no longer be a form of revelation. Is this not the reason why, when God willed to reveal Himself to men, He only made use of men as His instruments and why He whom we call his Son only spoke of the things of the kingdom of God in images and parables?"

(b) *Among the modernists*, the agnostic theory of revelation was proposed to the philosophical world by Édouard Le Roy,[22] in a spiritual and mystical manner by George Tyrrell,[23] and in a critical and historical manner by Alfred Loisy.[24]

According to Édouard Le Roy, the existence of God cannot be demonstrated because the principle of causality, upon critical examination, implies nothing more than the interconnection of phenomena. Nonetheless, religious experience witnesses to God's existence. However, God is not transcendent, at least in the way that theologians say that he is. Rather, he is the active principle of evolution. God comes into being in man and in the world.[25]

Miracles, and hence miraculous revelation, cannot be known with certitude. Nay, this would involve a phenomenon existing without the existence of a prior phenomenon, which would stand in contradiction with the principle of causality. In reality, *a miracle is an extraordinary effect of living faith* (or of religious experience) so that the prior phenomenon is religious faith itself, which produces the miracle. Therefore, there is a kind of law of miracles ruled by the universal law of causality.

What then are dogmas? If we take the term intellectually (or *speculatively*), *dogmas cannot have a positive meaning*, for the notions used for expressing them do not have an ontological and transcendent value and, hence, give rise to antinomies. Nonetheless, dogmas can have *a negative sense* and a *positive-practical* sense. In a negative sense, they exclude heresies, whereas in a positive-practical sense they are norms of action. For example, the expression {{272}} "a personal God" negatively manifests that God is not a body and not a mere idea, while positively and practically declaring: *Act in relation to God just as though you were acting in relation to a person.* Likewise, "Jesus is God" means: *Act in relation to Jesus as though you were acting in relation to God.* Similarly, the Resurrection of Christ does not signify the reanimation of a corpse but, rather, expresses a kind of spiritual influence by Christ in souls after his death. This theory is condemned in

---

[22] See Édouard Le Roy, *Dogme et critique* (Paris: Bloud, 1907).

[23] George Tyrrell, *Through Scylla and Charybdis* (London: Longmans, 1907), ch. 12. See "Theologisme" in *Revue pratique d'apologétique*, [no. 4] (July 1907): 501, 537–541. For a criticism of this theory of revelation, see Ambroise Gardeil, *Le donné révélé et la théologie*, chs. 2 (Revelation) and 3 (Dogma).

[24] See Alfred Loisy, *L'evangile et l'eglise* (Paris: Picard et Fils, 1902). *Autour d'un petit livre* (Paris: Alphonse Picard et Fils, 1903), 193. *Simples réflexions sur le décret du Saint-Office Lamentabili sane exitu et sur l'encyclique Pascendi dominici gregis* (Ceffonds, 1908), 57.

[25] Édouard Le Roy, "Comment se pose le problème de Dieu (suite et fin)," *Revue de métaphysique et de morale* 15, no. 4 (July 1907): 512: "Immanence and transcendence are no longer contradictories. They correspond to two distinct moments of duration: *immanence to what has become, transcendence to becoming.* If we declare God immanent, what we mean is that we know about Him what has come into being in us and in the world; but, for the world and for us, an infinite process of becoming remains, an infinite process which will be creation properly so called, not a simple development. From this perspective, God appears as being transcendent."

the decree *Lamentabili*: "The dogmas of the faith are to be held only according to their practical sense; that is to say, as preceptive norms of conduct and not as norms of believing."[26] The same holds for the Resurrection of Christ concerning which the following is condemned: "The Resurrection of the Savior is not property a fact of the historical order. It is a fact of merely the supernatural order (neither demonstrated nor demonstrable) that Christian (consciousness) gradually derived from other facts."[27]

In England, George Tyrrell spoke about revelation and dogmas in nearly the same way as did Sabatier. First, according to him, *revelation is a kind of emotion,* or religious experience of the presence of God, his providence, and his fatherhood. He held that this experience is found in all believers. Thus, he identified revelation with faith and faith with experience proceeding from religious sentiment.

However, he held that this experience *is first expressed in an imaginative manner.* Thus, Christ is conceived by Peter as the Messiah, by Paul as the second Adam, by John as the Word, and by the first believers as the Son of God.

Finally, there appears the intellectual expression of religious experience, for example, at the Council of Nicaea: the Word who is consubstantial with the Father. These dogmatic formulas are useful for rejecting heresies, but they are not always absolutely true. *The Church can sometimes err* and, in fact, has erred with regard to dogmatic formulas.

Indeed, [Tyrrell held that] the Church is necessary for arousing and directing man's religious sentiment, and one must obey her as a kind of social authority. However, *the first and ultimate rule of faith is each person's conscience*, inasmuch as each person is illuminated by the Holy Spirit. Sometimes, men who are more spiritual see things more clearly than does the Christian community and are excommunicated by the Church on account of their new way of speaking, though they remain in the Church. And what had been at first rejected soon comes to be received by the Christian community, whereas by contrast, not a few of those things that were once held as dogmas have now fallen into disuse.

Likewise, in Germany, Hermann Schell taught that the Church's authority is necessary only on account of people's limited insight, which commonly prevails. Hence, there is no obligation for the learned to accept this authority unconditionally.

Loisy, a modernist exegete, defended nearly the same doctrine through exegesis of Sacred Scripture. It would be tedious for us to refer to Loisy's theses, which make up nearly all of the propositions condemned in the decree *Lamentabili*.[28] The following summary suffices for our purposes: *Modernist exegetes* hold that Sacred Scripture is to be interpreted in the same way as are other merely human documents, and gradually reject everything supernatural by allegorical and psychological interpretations. They hardly [*parum*] consider the sense of the Church, the authority of the Fathers, or the analogy

---

26 Pius X, *Lamentabili*, no. 26 (Denzinger, no. 3426).

27 Ibid., no. 36 (Denzinger, no. 3436).

28 Ibid., no. 1[ff] (Denzinger, nos. 3401[ff]).

of faith but instead interpret the sacred books *through a resolution to an innate character*—that is, *to the religious experience of the human author*, to the psychology of Jeremiah, Isaiah, or St. Paul, rather than according to a resolution to the First Truth who reveals, which is the formal motive of faith. Nay, often, exegetes who are more or less modernists unconsciously substitute their own more familiar psychology for the psychology of the sacred author, which remains rather hidden. In this way, they greatly diminish the supernatural elevation of mind of someone like St. Paul, more or less reducing it to proportions that are akin to our own religious life. Thus, they also gravely diminish the unity and supernatural character of Sacred Scripture.[29] {{273}} Therefore, God's book becomes a collection of books written by various men. The abuse of this psychological method in exegesis is already a form of *relativism and the path to naturalism.*[30]

---

[29] See Vincenz Zapletal, *Hermeneutica biblica* (Friburg, CH: Bibliopolae Universitatis, 1908), 140: *On certain false principles for interpreting Sacred Scripture. Heterodox systems of exegesis* deny that Sacred Scripture must be interpreted in accord with the Church's sense, the unanimous consent of the Fathers, and according to the analogy of faith (i.e., Catholic doctrine). Moreover, they reject the authority of Catholic interpreters. (See Leo XIII, *Providentissimus Deus*, nos. 14ff; Denzinger, nos. 3283ff.)

These heterodox systems are especially the following: *Systems of internal light* ([e.g.,] Pietists and Quakers), holding that the internal light of the Holy Spirit suffices for knowing the meaning of Sacred Scripture. *Systems of accommodation* ([e.g.,] in Semler), holding that the Lord Jesus Christ and the apostles conformed themselves to Jewish errors in order to accommodate their doctrine to the comprehension of their listeners. *Systems of moral interpretation* ([e.g.,] in Kant), holding that Sacred Scripture is true inasmuch as it proposes the moral precepts of natural religion, although dogmas and miracles can only be admitted as symbols of moral truths. *Systems of mythical interpretation* ([e.g.,] Strauss and Renan), holding that the accounts of miracles contained in Sacred Scripture must be set aside as myths and fables. *Finally, systems of psychological interpretation* ([e.g.,] [Heinrich] Paulus), holding that the supernatural elements of Sacred Scripture are to be psychologically explained according to a kind of evolution of religious consciousness.

[30] We can clearly see the great distance separating this subjective method from the method followed by the Doctors of the Church by considering, for example, St. Thomas's commentaries on St. Paul's letters. Nay, St. Thomas writes of the human author of the sacred text in the prologue of his commentary on the *Song of Songs* (Parma ed., vol. 14, 388): "However, we do not care about the instrumental cause because this kind of cause is related to the teaching like an instrument, like the quill of the writer, according to the words of Ps 44:2: 'My tongue is the pen of a scribe writing quickly.' Therefore, just as it would be superstitious, when asking about the author of a given book, to seek out what pen he wrote the book with, so too in a certain way it seems superstitious for someone to inquire with great solicitude about the instrumental causes of Sacred Scripture, for *if it indeed is true that the book comes from the Holy Spirit, one need not expend great care in seeking after another author.* However, if we need to care about this, we say that Solomon was the cause of this book." However, if the book is considered precisely as being written by the human author, abstracting from its divine origin, then it is quite useful to know who wrote this book in order to determine its historical value, for example, whether John wrote the Fourth Gospel.

[Trans. note: The commentary on the *Song of Songs* mentioned above was once purported

As is clear, *modernism* proceeds from empiricist or idealistic agnosticism to imma-nentism[31] and evolutionism, as though the entire Catholic religion were to proceed from the natural development of religious sentiment.[32] In this reconciliation of the Catholic faith with rationalism, reason or human consciousness remains thoroughly autonomous, and supernatural faith is destroyed. How great is the distance separating this apologet-ics from that of St. Paul, who said: "*Even so we speak, not as pleasing men but God*, who proveth our hearts" (1 Thess 2:4, DR); "For there shall be a time when they will not endure sound doctrine but, according to their own desires, they will heap to themselves teachers having itching ears; and will indeed turn away their hearing from the truth, but will be turned unto fables" (2 Tim 4:3–4, DR). Concerning this latter text, St Thomas wrote:

> A fable is something composed from marvels which are lacking in truth. And such men, having itching ears, wished to hear. . . . *Indeed, [they] always wished to hear new, unheard of, and curious things*, indeed even sometimes harmful things, as is said in Acts 17:21, "The Athenians occupied themselves with nothing other than telling or hearing something new."

And thus, St. Thomas concludes, heretical doctrines come to be multiplied. Such also was the case in the time of modernism, which can be defined as: "Weariness in belief disguis-ing itself as the perfection of faith."

ART. 2: CRITICISM OF AGNOSTICISM THROUGH A *REDUCTIO AD ABSURDUM*

{{274}} §1. Defense of the ontological value of the first notions and principles of reason
§2. Defense of the transcendent value of the same notions and principles
§3. Resolution of objections

Agnosticism rejects the possibility of supernatural revelation from the per-spective of the subject (i.e., from man's perspective) inasmuch as it denies

---

to have been from St. Thomas's hand. It is now ascribed to Giles of Rome.]

[31] The teaching of Maurice Blondel does not distance itself far enough from modernism. (See *L'action;* "Lettres sur les exigences de la pensée contemporaine en matière d'apologetique," *Annales de philosophie chrétienne* (Jan.-July, 1896). See what we discussed in the Prologue con-cerning the methodology of apologetics. ['Trans. note: See Maurice Blondel, *The Letter on Apologetics & History and Dogma*, trans. Alexander Dru and Illtyd Trethowan (Grand Rapids, MI: Eerdmans, 1995); *Action (1893): Essay on a Critique of Life and a Science of Practice*, trans. Oliva Blanchette (Notre Dame, IN: University of Notre Dame Press, 1984).]

[32] See Pius X, *Pascendi*, no. 7 (Denzinger, no. 3477).

the ontological and, *a fortiori*, the transcendent value of the first notions and principles of reason. Therefore, we must look into how strong this denial really is. Technically, this topic finds its proper treatment in philosophy. However, here in the theological treatise on revelation, we must of necessity gather together the things said in philosophy concerning the value of our natural intellectual knowledge so that we may defend *the objective value of the very supernatural knowledge of faith*, which presupposes natural knowledge as grace presupposes nature and perfection presupposes that which is perfectible. Thus, as we said in the beginning of our criticism of pantheistic evolutionism, St. Thomas, in the theological treatises on God, man, and the virtues, gathers together those things that are proven in philosophy concerning these matters. Were he not to do so, no analogy could then be formed for knowing supernatural things. However, this process of gathering together is theological, inasmuch as it is performed under the direction of faith and is ordered to the defense and explanation of the faith.

§1. Defense of the Ontological Value of the First Notions and Principles of Reason

We will discuss the following claims in this section:

A. This ontological value of the first notions and principles of reason cannot be directly demonstrated.

B. However, it can be directly defended through an explanation of the terms [making up the principles in question].

C. And they are indirectly demonstrated through a reduction to absurdity and illogicality.

A. ***There cannot be a direct demonstration of these principles.*** That which is naturally and immediately evident is not directly demonstrated, for a direct demonstration uses an ostensive[33] middle term between the subject and the predicate of the conclusion, and there cannot be a middle term between two terms that are immediately connected. Now, the ontological value of the first notions and principles of reason is naturally and immediately evident. Every man naturally sees that the principle of contradiction is not only a logical law of reason but [indeed is] an ontological law of reality. In other words, *it is immediately evident that something absurd not only cannot be thought but also cannot exist.* For example, a square circle is not only unthinkable but [also] is impossible outside the soul. It is not something capable of being represented or of existing. Yes, indeed, Descartes feigned doubt concerning this matter.

---

[33] [Trans. note: Reading *ostensivum* for *estensivum*.]

He thought that perhaps God could make a square circle through his infinite power.[34] However, this doubt is contrary to natural reason and contrary to the first and primary evidence, the absolute opposition between being and non-being. Hence, this doubt does not truly exist in the intellect but, rather, is an illusion of the imagination and an empty misuse of language.[35] Hence, at the end of *Metaphysics* 4.3, Aristotle says, "For it is impossible for anyone to think the same thing is and is not, as some think Heraclitus says. For what a man says, he does not necessarily believe."[36]

{{275}} Likewise, whatever the empiricists may say, every man naturally has this evidence, which is intellectual, not sensible, in nature. *Even outside of the limits of experience, something cannot occur without a cause.* In other words, contingent being depends on necessary being. This principle cannot be directly demonstrated, but it can be indirectly demonstrated through a reduction to absurdity, as we said concerning absolute evolutionism. Thus it is founded on the primary evidence of the principle of contradiction.

The reason for this primary evidence is that the intellect's object is being. Thus, we see the being (of sensible things) and the first principle of being before we reflexively know our reason and the idea of being. Hence, when they stop considering their own system, agnostics themselves admit the ontological value of the first principle of reason. Nay, they admit it even when they exposit their own system of thought, for they hold that what they set forth in their books is conformed to their thoughts and that these books cannot simultaneously exist and not exist.

On account of this immediate evidence, the ontological value of the first principles cannot be directly demonstrated. Such a demonstration would always be a begging of the question [*petitio principii*] or a vicious circle. The principles are more evident [in themselves] than if they were demonstrated. Thus, the light of the sun is not illuminated but, rather, illuminates, just as the First Cause cannot be caused but can cause.

B. **Direct defense.** The ontological value of the first notions and principles of reason is defended directly *through an explanation of their terms.* This explanation manifests the essential distinction of the intellect from the senses, inasmuch as St. Thomas says, "Sense knowledge is occupied with the

---

34 See the beginning of René Descartes, *Discours de la méthode.* [Trans. note: Fr. Garrigou-Lagrange also cites "*Rep.* 5 mes. obj," which perhaps refers to the objections responded to by Descartes related to his *Meditations.*]

35 [Trans. note: Reading *abusus verborum* for *Iudus verborum.*]

36 Aristotle, *Metaphysics*, trans. William D. Ross, in *The Complete Works of Aristotle*, vol. 2, edited by Jonathan Barnes, (Princeton, NJ: Princeton University Press, 1995), 4.3.

external sensible qualities of a thing, whereas intellective knowledge penetrates all the way to a thing's essence,"[37] and first of all to being, for "*being is the proper object of the intellect,* and thus is the first intelligible [thing], just as sound is the first audible [thing]."[38] In other words, precisely because it is oriented around being (τὸ ὄν) intellective knowledge has a value that is ontological and not merely phenomenal.[39]

This direct defense of the ontological value of the first notions of reason can be proposed in the form of a syllogism that is not, properly speaking, demonstrative (or illative) but, rather, is explicative,[40] so as to make the meaning of the terms clearer.

(1) It does not suffice to show that these notions arise from the senses, for this is true also for our notions of phenomena (e.g., of heat) that have an objective value but not a properly ontological one (i.e., for expressing being existing under the phenomena).[41]

(2) Nor does it suffice to show that the first notions of reason are something representative, for this is also true of our notion of rationate being [*ens rationis*], which belongs to the logical, not the ontological, order. In the argument, the following two things must be joined together: the origin in sensation and the intellectual representation of being, for it is a question of the ontological order, inasmuch as it first appears to us in sensible things, though exceeding the merely phenomenal and logical orders.

{{276}} The notions and principles by which we express not sensible phenomena but, rather, things that are *per accidens sensible and per se intelligible, which we resolve into intelligible being,* have a value that is ontological and not only phenomenal.

Now, the first notions and principles of reason do not express sensible

---

[37] *ST* II-II, q. 8, a. 1.

[38] *ST* I, q. 5, a. 2.

[39] See *De veritate*, q. 1, a. 1.

[40] [Trans. note: As Fr. Garrigou-Lagrange explains in "Theology and the Life of Faith," in *Philosophizing in Faith: Essays on the Beginning and End of Wisdom,* trans. Matthew K. Minerd (Providence, RI: Cluny Media, 2019), 431n19: "We use the expression '*Objectively illative* reasoning' for that form of reasoning which leads *to another* [*objectively new*] *truth.* For example, from the Divine Intelligence, we can deduce the Divine Freedom through this major: every intelligent being is free. On the contrary, a reasoning is only *explicative* (or at most *subjectively illative*) when it establishes the *equivalence* of two propositions in enunciating the *same truth.* For example, there is the *equivalence* of these two propositions: 'You are Peter and upon this rock I will build my Church; and the gates of hell will not prevail over it' = 'The successor of Peter, when he speaks *ex cathedra* to the universal Church, in a matter of faith and morals, cannot be deceived.'" Also see Réginald Garrigou-Lagrange, *The Sense of Mystery: Clarity and Obscurity in the Intellectual Life,* trans. Matthew K. Minerd (Steubenville, OH: Emmaus Academic, 2017), 28n41.]

[41] For being is primarily said of substance, and the senses do not *per se* grasp the external accidents of bodies inasmuch as they are beings ("of being") but, rather, inasmuch as they are sensible.

phenomena but, rather, express something that is *per accidens* sensible and *per se* intelligible and is resolved into intelligible being.

Therefore, the first notions and principles of reason have a value that is ontological and not only phenomenal.

(a) *The major premise is explained* from the Aristotelian distinction between a "per se sensible" and a "*per accidens* sensible" that *per se* is intelligible. Indeed, a phenomenon (or appearance) of a thing is *per se* sensible. That is, it is a *per se* and immediate object of the external or internal senses. For example, sensible qualities (e.g., heat, color, and sound) are *per se* sensible. Thus, the notion of heat only has a phenomenal value, and the law "heat expands iron" is only a phenomenal law, even if it is verified outside of the soul in the external phenomena. However, besides such phenomena (or *per se* sensibles), man grasps through his intellect something that is more profound still, something that is "*per accidens* sensible" and "*per se* intelligible" (e.g., substance and, especially, the being of sensible things). For being abstracts from every sensible quality and nonetheless is said to be *per accidens* sensible on two heads:

> (1) because it belongs to that which is *per se* sensible, just as white[-ness] happens to belong to a man . . . and (2) because it is grasped by the intellect (and thus by the sensing person, without any discursive thought) immediately upon the presence of the sensed thing, just as, for example, immediately upon seeing someone talking or moving, I apprehend his life through my intellect and, hence, can say that I see that he lives,[42]

even though life is not *per se* sensible, like color. Therefore, notions that express *per accidens* sensibles that are *per se* intelligible not only have a phenomenal value but also have a superior value which is called ontological, referring to the very being existing under the phenomena. Indeed, all of the first notions of our reason are reduced, as we will soon discuss, to being [qua being] (ὄν ἡ ὄν), which is the first intelligible [thing], just as color is the first visible [thing]. We must speak likewise about the first principles founded on these notions.

(b) *The minor premise is explained as follows.* The first notions of reason indeed do not express sensible phenomena but, rather, *per se* intelligible phenomena which are resolved into intelligible being. Indeed, these notions are the notions of being, essence (or reality), existence, unity, truth, goodness,

---

[42] St. Thomas, *In* II *De anima*, lect. 13.

substance, efficient causality, finality, and so forth, all of which abstract from every sensible quality and from all matter. That is, they transcend the order of [mere] phenomena.

This is obvious, first of all, for the case of *being*, for being is not something *per se* sensible (e.g., as are color or sound) but instead is something deeper and more universal, by its very formal notion abstracting from all matter. It is not a phenomenon but instead is the *raison d'être* for phenomena. This intimate *raison d'être* is not something extended, colored, sounding, hot, or cold. It is not perceived by the senses but instead is immediately grasped by the intellect upon the presence of the sensed thing, without any intervening discursive thought. Nay, the intellect neither grasps nor {{277}} judges anything except in relation to being, just as sight perceives nothing except by reason of color. Indeed, every notion is resolved into the first notion of being. In every judgment, the verb is reduced to the verb "is," the copula of any given judgment (Peter runs = Peter is running). Finally, every process of reasoning assigns the *raison d'être* for the conclusion.[43] Thus, judgment differs essentially from an association of images and reasoning from an empirical sequence of events [*a consecutione empirica*].

The same must be said of the transcendental properties of being, which are *one, true,* and *good.* Indeed, they do not express phenomena but, rather, something deeper, for the *one* is indivisible being,[44] the *true* is being conformed to the divine intellect or the conformity of our judgment with extramental being,[45] and the good is being [qua] desirable (in other words, the good is that which all things seek).[46] These notions express something intelligible whose formal notion involves no phenomena. Thus, truth is not quantitatively great or extended, nor is it hot or cold.

Likewise, *substance* is something deeper than phenomena, for it is being that subsists in itself and not in another.[47] The intellect first grasps being under the phenomena and considers that these phenomena are various and variable, whereas, by contrast, the being in question remains one and the

---

[43] Thus, we can see quite clearly in all three operations of the intellect that the object of the intellect is being.

[44] See *ST* I, q. 11.

[45] See *ST* I, q. 16.

[46] See *ST* I, q. 5.

[47] See *ST* I, q. 3, a. 5, ad 1; III, q. 76, a. 7: "*Substance* as such *is not visible* to the bodily eye; *nor does it fall under any sense,* nor under the imagination but, rather, *falls only under the intellect,* whose object is 'that which is,' as is said in *De anima 3,* text 26." Hence the body of Christ, as it exists in the Eucharist, cannot be seen by any bodily eye, for it is in this sacrament according to the mode of substance.

same. This one and the same being subsisting in itself is called a substance. Hence, this notion is only a new determination of the notion of being, just as the principle of substance, "everything *that* is is a substance," is a new determination of the principle of identity, "being is being, non-being is non-being."

Similarly, the notions *of efficient causality* and *finality* do not express things that are sensible *per se* (or phenomena), for the senses do not perceive efficiency or finality, as they perceive color. Efficiency and finality are *per se* intelligible and are only sensible *per accidens*, for they are extrinsic *raisons d'être* for the thing produced. Efficiency is the production of an effect, whereas finality is the *raison d'être* for the means ordered to an end. However, these *raisons d'être* can be *per se* perceived only by a faculty whose formal object is being, not by a faculty that is properly concerned with color or sound. Hence, in *ST* I-II, q. 1, a. 2, St. Thomas says: "Those things that lack reason, like animals, tend to an end on account of a natural inclination, as though moved by another and not, however by themselves. For they do not know the reasons for the end." The swallow that collects straw for its nest sensibly knows its nest (or the thing that is the end). However, it does not know the formal character of the end [precisely as such], for the end is not something that is *per se* sensible, but, instead, is *per se* intelligible. Therefore, the first notions of reason and their correlative principles enjoy an ontological value.

Confirmation:

(a) *Application of this defense against empiricist agnosticism.*

These per se intelligibles, which are the primary object of our reason, *cannot be expressed in some sensible image, even a composite one* or a common one, {{278}} as empiricists wish. For this sensible representation only manifests *juxtaposed phenomena*, not their *intimate raison d'être*, by which the phenomena become intelligible. Hence, empiricists must reduce substance to a mere collection of phenomena. However, substance signifies something else—namely, being existing in itself. Likewise, they reduce causality to a succession of phenomena, whereas causality signifies the effective production (or realization) of a given thing, not the succession of things. Thus, day follows upon night without being caused by night. Likewise, a composite image of a clock differs from the notion of a clock. In the first representation, which a parrot can have, only the juxtaposed phenomena of a clock is manifested (i.e., a machine that regularly makes a sound). By contrast, the notion of a clock manifests the *raison d'être* for these phenomena (e.g., a machine whose uniform motion is measured in relation to the sun's apparent movement, for the sake of telling time). The parrot can indeed have a common (or vague and mixed) image of a clock with a name connected to it and can even utter the words aloud, "The clock is making a sound." However, it does not know the *raison d'être* (i.e., the efficient and final cause) of the motion of this machine. Nay, it is unaware of the *raison d'être* of the name that it unconsciously uses, for the name is a sign whose formal content [*ratio*] is in the thing signified. This makes it clear that it is impossible to reduce an idea to a confused image, combined with a common term. Radical nominalism would reduce human speech to mere unintelligent parroting, for the *raison d'être* of words is only perceived by a faculty whose object is being.

Nominalists will object: The substantial being under the phenomena is a *verbal entity*, for it does not fall under experience. To this we must respond by conceding that it does not fall under *per se sensible* experience. However, we deny that it does not fall under it *per accidens*. For immediately upon the presence of the sensed thing, substantial being is grasped by the intellect. And this intellectual apprehension, which precedes induction and deduction, belongs to experience in which sense knowledge and the first intellectual apprehension of the subject of phenomena are united, for the object of experience is not heat or color in general but, rather, this hot or colored subject, so that the colored is known by sight and substance by the intellect. Hence, the *raison d'être*, which is the *font of intelligibility for all of the phenomena, cannot be a verbal entity, for much rather, it has a greater, more stable, and more profound reality than the phenomena.* Hence, it cannot *per se* be perceived by the senses, "which are concerned with the external, sensible qualities of things." Thus, *substance is hidden from the senses not because it falls short in reality but, rather, because it has an excess of reality,* just as the shining sun remains hidden from an owl on account of its excessive brilliance. Therefore, when the agnostic empiricist doubts that substances exist, he is like an owl, which cannot see the brilliance of the sun. Its bright light is like shadow to him, and he can only know the shadow of phenomena, not being able to see into the depths of things [*non intus legit*] and is "like the horse and the mule, who have no understanding" (Ps 31:9, DR).

(b) *Against idealistic agnosticism: Per se intelligibles*, which are simultaneously *per accidens* sensible, *cannot be expressed through merely subjective forms or ideas.* Indeed, then, they would be conceived of as something merely subjective, meaning that there would not be a distinction between rationate being [*ens rationis*] and real being [*ens reale*], between the conceived notion of substance and real substance itself,[48] between the logical formula of the principle of contradiction (one and the same thing cannot be affirmed and denied of the same thing from the same perspective) and the ontological formula of the same principle (the same thing cannot simultaneously be and not be). One must at least say: The absurd is indeed unthinkable, but perhaps it is not really impossible outside of the soul. This is contrary to the primary evidence graspable by any intellect whatsoever, and as we will soon say in our indirect defense of these principles, a doubt concerning the impossibility of a given absurd thing is itself absurd and impossible. He who truly doubts

---

[48] [Trans. note: This is slightly reworked, as the original reads "inter ideam substantiam et substantiae conceptam."]

the real value of the principle of contradiction would be akin to brute animals, which do not have the light of the intellect. In other words, such doubt is only sophistical wordplay in the imagination {{279}} and cannot exist in the intellect. Thus, once man opens his eyes, his sight cannot fail to see the brilliance of the sun present before him, and he who cannot see the sun in its brilliance lacks sight and is blind.

C. *Indirect defense.* The ontological value of the first notions of reason is defended indirectly by reducing agnostics to unresolvable difficulties and, finally, to absurdity (or illogicality).

(a) *There are at least four* UNRESOLVABLE DIFFICULTIES *for empiricist agnosticism.* (1) *It cannot explain the absolute necessity and universality of the first principles of reason,* for according to this system of thought, the principle of causality is only an experiential law. Thus, it holds that it would not be absolutely contradictory to think that outside of the limits of experience something might come about without a cause. Therefore, how can [empiricist agnosticism] explain our natural certitude about the absolute impossibility of any becoming occurring without a cause? (2) Empiricist agnosticism cannot explain our natural certitude about *the objective value of our intellect.*[49] Indeed, it responds: This certitude is "a natural illusion." However, this does not resolve the difficulty, for illusion is *per accidens* and not *per se,* whereas nature is something that has a *per se* determination. (3) *Empiricist agnosticism cannot explain the value or inferential* [*illativum*] *strength of* [*valid*] *syllogisms.* For, according to empiricism, as John Stuart Mill thought, the syllogism is a tautology inasmuch as the major premise is [merely] a simple collection of singular things. Hence, it already contains, in act, the singular with which the conclusion is concerned. Consequently, it is a tautology. Otherwise, it does not contain that singular in any way, and in that case, nothing is concluded. In order for a syllogism to have the power needed to reach a conclusion, the major premise must not be a mere collection of particulars but, rather, must be the expression of a truly universal truth that transcends singulars, as species transcend individuals and virtually contain them. (4) *Empiricist agnosticism cannot assign a foundation for induction*—that is, for ascending from knowledge of singular cases to a universal law. This foundation must transcend [mere] experience and rely upon intellectual abstraction as well as upon first, necessary principles. Thus, the principle of induction finds its foundation in the principle of *raison d'être*: The same determinate cause in the same circumstances always produces the same effect; otherwise, there would be a variation in the effect without a

---

[49] [Trans. note: Interpreting *intelligentiae* like the French *intelligence*, which often can be translated as *intellect* in Fr. Garrigou-Lagrange.]

raison d'être. However, according to empiricism, there are no necessary principles. Thus, every form of science is brought to ruin, as well as every inductive or deductive method.

(b) *Likewise, at least three* UNRESOLVABLE DIFFICULTIES *remain for idealist agnosticism.* (1) *It cannot explain* why all men have *natural certitude concerning the objective character of our principles.* (2) *One must admit the existence of a priori synthetic judgments.* However, these judgments are *inexplicable* and, indeed, lack an objective rational motive. The evidential character of such judgments is neither *a priori* nor experiential. Therefore, they are blind and irrational. (3) *The application of the categories* to a given set of phenomena rather than to others *remains arbitrary* and without motive, for if a relation to the category of substance were to appear in these phenomena rather than to the category of causality, this would be because our intellect would grasp substance in these phenomena rather than causality. Thus, the subjective category is useless. However, if the intellect grasps nothing, the application of the categories is thereby rendered arbitrary. Why then could we not say night is the cause of day since it precedes day? And why do we condemn a murderer if he himself is not really the cause of death {{280}} but, rather, is so only according to our subjective manner of thinking? As Fichte rightly said, in order to avoid the arbitrary application of the categories, while preserving the principles of subjectivism, we must say that the phenomena themselves arise from our own consciousness according to an unconscious projection. And Fichte admitted this conclusion. However, then our knowledge [*scientia*], like God's knowledge [*scientia*], would be the cause of things, meaning that no mystery would remain for us, which is contrary to the evident fact that our knowledge is imperfect.[50]

Thus, agnosticism, whether in its empiricist form or its idealistic form, runs into unresolvable difficulties.

(c) NAY, *agnosticism ultimately is reduced* TO ABSURDITY. Indeed, a fourfold absurdity follows from the denial of the ontological value of the first notions of reason—namely, as regards all aspects of intellectual knowledge: (1) as regards the object, (2) as regards the idea and principles, (3) as regards the act of understanding, and (4) as regards the intellect itself. Having suppressed the essence of a given thing, it is not surprising that everything pertaining to it would become absurd.

(1) *As regards the object.* If the intellect knew only its ideas and not things [in themselves], the object of direct intellection (e.g., causality) could no longer be distinguished from an object of reflexive intellection (e.g., the

---

[50] See *ST* I, q. 79, a. 2.

idea of causality). Now, it is clear that our notion of causality is distinguished from our notion of the idea of causality, and a reflex-act necessarily presupposes a direct act and therefore cannot be identified with it without formal contradiction.[51]

(2) *As regards the idea and principles.* Indeed, if, [as idealists hold,] in direct intellection, the idea is not that *by which* we know but, rather, *is that which we know*, then the idea (or representation) is not essentially relative to the represented thing. Therefore, the idea is not the idea of something but, rather, is *the idea of nothing.* In other words, it would simultaneously and in the same respect be and not be an idea, which is absurd. Therefore, *the idea*—whether it be impressed in the mind or expressed by it (i.e., the mental word)—*is essentially relative to the intelligible thing.* (Granted, we can *accidentally* [*per accidens*] construct an erroneous definition that does not correspond to any essence or intelligible. However, this happens only as regards composite things "from the perspective of the composition occurring in the definition . . . For example, when a given definition is false in itself, implying a composition of things that cannot be combined . . . . Whence, {{281}} we cannot be deceived regarding simple things whose definitions cannot involve any composition . . . as is said in *Metaphysics* 9.10.")[52]

Indeed, nothing prohibits a rationate being [*ens rationis*] or the idea itself from being the object of reflex intellection. However, this reflex intellection presupposes direct intellection, which terminates at the intelligible reality and not at the idea.

Likewise, if the notion of being were lacking in ontological value, *the principle of contradiction would only be a subjective law of reason and not a*

---

[51] See *ST* I, q. 85, a. 2 ("Whether the intelligible species abstracted from the phantasms are related to our intellect as *that which* is known or as *that by which* it is known"). Here, the subjectivism (or relativism) of the Sophists, against whom Aristotle wrote in the 4th book of the *Metaphysics*, is refuted. There, he treats the value of the principle of contradiction. Here, St. Thomas says: "The likeness of the visible thing is that according to which sight sees, and the likeness of the understood thing, the intelligible *species*, is the form by which the intellect understands. However, *because the intellect reflects upon itself*, by means of such a reflection it understands both its own act of understanding and the species by means of which it understands. Thus, *the species understood in a secondary manner is that which is understood. However, that which is understood first is the thing, whose likeness is the intelligible species.*" Likewise, see his responses to the three objections to the article above.

Cf. Cardinal Tommaso Maria Zigliara, *Summa philosophica*, vol. 2, 264 and 266: "The idea is essentially representative (that is, essentially objective), for it essentially expresses, in an ideal manner, the object whose intelligible likeness it is. It is intrinsically contradictory to say that the idea is the object of our direct intellection; . . . otherwise, intellection could exist without an understood object, something which is clearly contradictory."

[52] *ST* I, q. 85, a. 6.

certain law of reality. Indeed, perhaps a square-circle would be possible outside of the intellect. Then one could be in doubt concerning the extramental impossibility of any given absurd thing. Now, such a doubt is absurd, for that simultaneously existing and not-existing thing would, at once, correspond and not correspond in the same respect to our idea of being. However, this supposition is likewise *subjectively* unthinkable and is nothing other than sophistical wordplay. For the idea of being is utterly simple, and something cannot correspond to it only partially. If something is conformed to it, then it is a being. If it is not conformed to it, then it is non-being. Likewise, becoming itself is a not-yet-determined and imperfect being, and even there we do not find being and non-being identified in the same respect. Hence, agnostics cannot deny the ontological value of the principle of contradiction without denying its logical value (which is posterior to its ontological value).

(3) *As regards the act of intellection,* the same absurdity would follow as for the idea, for the act of intellection (like act of sensation as well) is intentional. In other words, it is essentially relative to something known. To deny this essential relation is to deny the act of intellection, for this intellection would be *an intellection of nothing.* Moreover, if the agnostic really doubted the ontological value of the principle of contradiction, he would also doubt the existence of his own thought and could not say, "I think," but rather, *"Perhaps I simultaneously think and do not think."*

(4) *As regards the intellect[53] itself,* the same absurdity follows if one doubts its essential relation to being. *Without a relation to being, the intellect itself becomes absolutely unintelligible.* Now, it is absurd and subjectively unthinkable that the intellect, the principle of intellection, would be unintelligible. In reality, empiricist agnosticism destroys the intellect inasmuch as it reduces it to sense cognition. However, in idealistic agnosticism, insofar as the intellect lacks a relation to being, it becomes unintelligible and posits that it forms synthetic *a priori* judgments which, as we said above, are judgments lacking in motive, blind and irrational. Thus, irrationality is asserted in the intimate depths of the life of reason. Therefore, [the notion of] an intellect without an essential relation to being, which is its formal object, is an absurdity. In order to avoid this absurdity, Fichte posited that our knowledge is identical with the universal intelligible being. Thus, our intellect would not be passive in any way but, rather, would be the principle of all

---

[53] [Trans. note: Fr. Garrigou-Lagrange seems to be using "intelligentiam" here in a way akin to "l'intelligence" in French, which for him can be rendered variously as "intelligence," "intellect," and "understanding." Because he mostly is speaking of the faculty here, I have chosen "intellect."]

phenomena. However, then no mystery would remain for us, and our intellect would be omniscient like the divine intellect, a claim that is patently false. (See *ST* I, q. 79, a. 2. In contrast to the divine intellect, our intellect is not intelligible being, the source of all intelligibility and reality, but instead is passively related to being.)

Thus, we have a sufficient direct and indirect defense for the ontological value of the first notions of reason. (However, also see the resolution of objections below.) Now, we must turn to the question of their transcendent value.

§2. Defense of the Transcendent Value of the Same Notions and Principles of Reason

{{282}} We speak of the *transcendent value* of these same notions and principles in order to indicate that they are of use for knowing not only the substantial being that exists under the phenomena but, even more, for knowing God himself, the First and Transcendent Cause, expressing what he is *in a proper manner* and not in a merely metaphorical or *symbolic* manner. Indeed, agnostics admit that God can be known symbolically and that dogmatic formulas have a metaphorical value, so that the proposition "God is wise" or[54] "God is triune" would be only metaphorical utterances like "God is angry." Hence, in reality, dogmas would not express what God himself is but, rather, our emotions relative to God, meaning that God would be called Father inasmuch as we can have faith-confidence in him as in a father. Hence, [one will be forced to say, along the lines of the twenty-sixth proposition condemned in the decree *Lamentabili*,] "The dogmas of the faith are to be held only according to their practical sense; that is to say, as preceptive norms of conduct and not as norms of believing."[55] One would need to act in relation to Jesus *as though* he were God, but one could not in reality affirm that Christ is God. Nay, one could not in reality affirm that God is intelligent or free. This question is treated by St. Thomas in the twelve articles contained in *ST* I, q. 13, especially in article 3, where he asks whether some names are said of God *properly* or whether all are attributed to him *metaphorically*.

Thus defined, the transcendent value of the first notions of reason can be defended in two ways, either (A) directly or (B) indirectly, through a reduction to absurdity.

---

54 [Trans. note: Reading *vel* for *ve*.]

55 Pius X, *Lamentabili*, no. 26 (Denzinger, no. 3426).

A. *Direct defense*. The direct defense [of the transcendent value of these notions and principles], which is also a direct demonstration,[56] is set forth by St. Thomas in *ST* I, q. 13, a. 2, and 3c and ad 1; likewise in *ST* I, q. 4, a. 2 and 3; *De potentia*, q. 7, a. 5; and *SCG* I, ch. 30. It can be reduced to the following syllogistic form.

The notions of simply simple and analogous perfections are not unfitting for expressing [something concerning] the Most Perfect Being analogically but *properly* and, in fact, thus do express [this Being], if the world indeed requires an Infinite Cause having these perfections.

Now, the first notions of being, one, truth, goodness, efficient cause, and end, as well as the notions of intellect and will, along with their properties (such as wisdom, justice, and mercy) all express simply simple, analogous perfections.

Therefore, these first notions are not unfitting for expressing the Most Perfect Being analogically but *properly*, and in fact thus do express [this being], if the world requires an Infinite Cause having these perfections.

In other words, therefore, these notions have a value that is transcendent and not merely symbolic. They are what we could call the precious pearls or diamonds adorning our reason.

This demonstration is founded on the Aristotelian and Thomistic doctrine of analogy, which is essentially opposed to symbolism or the equivocity held by agnostic nominalists and to the univocity of immoderate, pantheistic realism.[57]

{{283}} (1) **The major premise** of this demonstration needs to be explained. What is the meaning of its terms? A SIMPLY SIMPLE PERFECTION is that which implies no imperfection in its formal notion,[58] although it may

---

[56] Indeed, now, presupposing the ontological value of these notions, we can demonstrate their transcendent value by means of a demonstrative middle term.

[57] Just as the realism of Aristotle and St. Thomas stands like a golden mean and summit between the immoderate realism of Plato and of the pantheists, on the one hand, and the agnosticism of the nominalists, on the other, so too the Thomistic doctrine of analogy, which is a consequence of its moderate realism (the universal exists foundationally on the side of the thing), it also stands as a golden mean and summit between, on the one hand, univocity of being, which leads to pantheism, and on the other, equivocity of being, which leads to the agnosticism of the nominalists. I have set forth this doctrine of analogy at greater length in Réginald Garrigou-Lagrange, *God: His Existence and His Nature*, trans. Bede Rose (St. Louis, MO: B. Herder, 1949), 203–267; also, in a four-article series, "La valeur transcendante et analogique des notions premières. Thomisme et agnosticisme," *Revue Thomiste* 20 / New Series, 12 (1912): 628–648 and 721–742; 21 / New Series, 13 (1913): 17–48 and 159–188.

[58] We can add to the perfect definition of a simply simple perfection: "Which it is better for a given being to have, inasmuch as it is being, than for it not to have it." Thus, even though the

exist in an imperfect manner in a creature. For example, being, wisdom, and life involve no imperfection in their formal characters and nonetheless exist in a finite manner in creatures. By contrast, a *secundum quid* (or mixed) perfection also involves imperfection in its formal character—e.g., as animality implies bodiliness, as does reason (or imperfect intelligence, which is discursive—that is, passing from potency to act, not immediately understanding all things in a comprehensive manner). However, a simply simple perfection, even as in its participated form in created beings, is something pure, like a vein of diamonds in the earth.

AN ANALOGICAL PERFECTION is said in opposition to a univocal one and to those that are equivocal.[59] *Univocal* [terms] (in Greek, συνώνυμα) are those whose term is shared in common and whose formal character signified through the term is *simpliciter the same*. Thus, "animal" is univocally said of a worm, a horse, and of man, for the generic formal character signified through the term "animal" (i.e., a body living a sensate life) is *simpliciter* the same in them, notwithstanding the inequality of the specific differences that are extrinsic to the genus (for worms have sensation according to a formal character that is *simpliciter* the same as that which holds for man). *Equivocal* [terms] (in Greek, ὁμώνυμα) are those having a common term but whose formal characters signified through that term *are totally (or from every perspective) diverse*. Hence equivocal [terms] only agree in the vocal utterance [*vox*] used. There is no real likeness [among the things to which the term is applied] but instead only a verbal likeness. Thus, with respect to the term "dog," the domestic animal, a kind of fish, and the constellation *canis major* are by chance all designated in the same manner. *Analogous* [terms] (which Aristotle calls terms that are equivocal, not through chance but, rather, through counsel, or proportionally similar—in Greek, κατ᾽ ἀναλογίαν)[60] are, according to St. Thomas, those whose term is common but for whom the formal character [*ratio*] signified through that name is *simpliciter diverse* in those things thus signified,[61] while *nonetheless being secundum quid the same*

---

divine relations involve no imperfection, they are not simply simple perfections. Otherwise, the Father, to whom the relation of filiation does not belong, would lack some simply simple perfection. Likewise, the free act of creating in God is not a simply simple perfection.

59 See John of St. Thomas, *The Material Logic of John of St. Thomas*, trans. Yves R. Simon, John J. Glanville, and G. Donald Hollenhorst (Chicago: University of Chicago Press, 1955), q. 13. Also see Antoine Goudin, *Philosophia iuxta inconcussa tutissimaque divi Thomae dogmae, logical major*, pt. 1, diss. 2.

60 Aristotle, *Categories*, 1; *Posterior Analytics*, 2.13 and 14; *Metaphysics*, 4.1, 10.1, 12.4; *Nicomachean Ethics*, 1.6.

61 Thus, for example, *sensation* and *intellection* are analogically called *forms of knowledge* [*cog-*

(i.e., through some proportion or relation). For example, we analogically use the term "health" in speaking of pulse, air, medicine, food, and animals. {{284}}.

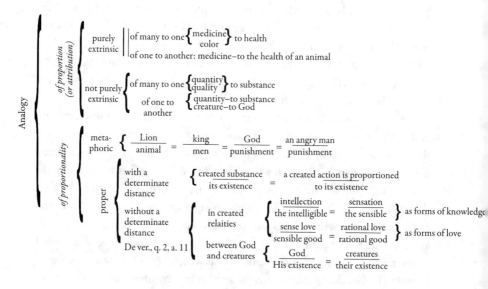

nitiones], and knowledge is not found in them in *simpliciter* the same way but instead is only *secundum quid* the same, inasmuch as sensation is related to that which is sensible as intellection is related to the intelligible. Thus, these two forms of knowledge, even as forms of knowledge, are *simpliciter* different from each other and only *secundum quid* the same.

Certain scholastics, like *Scotus* and *Suarez* (*Metaphysical Disputations*, disp. 2, sect. 2, no. 35) hold that analogous [terms] are those that have a common name, with a formal character signified through the name being *simpliciter* the same and only *secundum quid* diverse. This is rejected by the Thomists, for *this definition is found even for the case of univocal* [terms] (e.g., in the animality which is *simpliciter* the same and *secundum quid* diverse in man and worm). Hence, *Scotus* (in I, dist., 3, q. 1 and 3, as well as dist. 8, q. 3) even defends the univocity of being. This univocity is refuted by *Cajetan* in his comments on *ST* I, q. 13, a. 5 and in his treatise *On the Analogy of Names*. In reality, if being were univocal, its differences would be extrinsic to it and, thus, would be nothing, from which pantheism would follow, for creatures would no longer be able to be distinguished from the Divine Being. Moreover, if simply simple perfections were univocal, they would need to be distinct in God as they are in creatures. Hence, Scotus held that there is a formal-real distinction found among the divine attributes, a claim which the Thomists hold cannot be reconciled with the absolute simplicity of the divine essence. On this, see Garrigou-Lagrange, *God: His Existence and His Nature*, 246–267.

Finally, certain eclectic authors, not wishing to determine whether Thomist, Scotistic, or Suarezian metaphysics is true, say that analogous terms are those which have a common term while signifying through this name a formal character that is *secundum quid the same* and *secundum quid diverse*. However, this does not indicate what this formal character *simpliciter* is, and a definition must say what the defined thing *simpliciter* is.

Analogy is twofold—namely, *analogy of proportion, or* [*seu*] *attribution* (according to a proportion to one principal [analogate]), and *analogy of proportionality* (according to a similitude of proportions).[62]

An analogy of proportion (or of attribution) is drawn according to *the proportion* of one or many [analogates] to another principal one and of itself implies only *an attribution (or extrinsic denomination)* in the inferior analogates.[63] For example, medicine is said to be healthy just as is an animal's color relative to the animal's health, which the medicine causes, whereas its color is a sign of that health. As St. Thomas notes in *ST* I, q. 13, a. 2, some people in the Middle Ages said that names that are absolutely and affirmatively said of God, such as "good" and "wise," "are imposed to signify His relationship [*habitudinem*] to created things. Thus, when we say, 'God is good,' we would thereby mean, 'God is the cause of goodness in things.'" Rabbi Moses (Maimonides), to whom St. Thomas refers in the same article and in *De potentia*, q. 7, a. 5, more or less spoke this way. According to his opinion, God would be called good according to an analogy of attribution relative to creatures and only according to an extrinsic denomination. However, as St. Thomas says, why could we not say, "God is a body, given that He is the cause of bodies"? Thus, all knowledge of God would come to ruin if we accepted this position.

{{285}} The analogy of attribution that is formed according to an extrinsic denomination does not exclude an intrinsic denomination. Hence, it sometimes exists as *excluding* an analogy of proper proportionality and *sometimes is conjoined with it*, as we will discuss at greater length below. Thus, quantity and quality are said to be beings relative to substance, inasmuch as they are accidents of substance and depend upon it, even though being is found in them intrinsically.

The analogy of attribution is subdivided from the perspective of its matter into an analogy *of many to one superior* [*analogate*] or *of one to another*. It has already been made clear God and creatures cannot analogically agree according to a relation to something prior to them both, for nothing is prior to God according to the truth of reality [*secundum rei veritatem*]. Some, like Rosmini, unduly have said that being in general is in some way prior to God and creatures.[64] However, there can only be a logical priority in this matter, due to our imperfect manner of knowing. Nevertheless, nothing forbids us from saying that creatures are beings according to a relation to God, from whom creatures receive their existence.

However, the analogy of proportionality is formed *according to a similitude of pro-*

---

62 See *De veritate*, q. 11, a. 1 and John of St. Thomas, *Material Logic*, q. 13

63 Hence, St. Thomas calls analogy of attribution *analogy only according to intention* (i.e., through an extrinsic denomination) *and not according to existence*. See *In* I *Sent.*, dist. 19, q. 5, a. 2, ad 1 and *Quodlibet* 9, q. 2, a 2.

64 See Leo XIII, Decree of the Holy Office *Post obitum* (Dec. 14, 1887), nos. 6 and 7 (Denzinger, nos. 3206 and 3207).

portions that are variously related to each other, not according to a proportion of one or many to another principal [analogate]. Hence, the analogy of proportionality is generally defined by Thomists as "Those things that have a common term, while the formal character or essence signified through that name is *simpliciter* diverse, although proportionally the same, that is, according to a likeness of proportions." However, there always is a principal analogate, as we will soon see.

This analogy of proportionality is subdivided into metaphorical analogy and proper analogy. It is *metaphorical* if the analogous term is found properly and intrinsically in only one, as "king" is properly said of a king ruling over men and only metaphorically of a lion, in respect to [lesser] animals, according to a proportion:

$$\frac{\text{king}}{\text{men}} = \frac{\text{lion}}{\text{animals}}$$

Thus too, we properly speak of animals having feet, while only metaphorically speak of the "foot of a mountain." In general, theologians say certain names that formally imply an imperfection are said only metaphorically or symbolically of God, as when God is said to be a sun or fire; so too do we only metaphorically say that God is angry, given that anger formally is a passion and cannot formally exist in a pure spirit.[65] Already, this shows the error of Maimonides and modern agnostics, who hold that all names said of God are only metaphorically or symbolically said of him. They do not distinguish between simply simple perfections (e.g., justice) and mixed perfections (e.g., anger). Hence, in *De potentia*, q. 7, a. 5, St. Thomas says against Maimonides:

> There would be no difference between saying, "God is Wise," and "God is angry," or "God is a burning fire." For he is said to be angry because he acts after the manner of an angry man when he punishes, for angry men are accustomed to act this way. He is also called a [burning] fire because he acts like a fire when he cleanses, something that fire does in its own way.

An analogy of proper proportionality holds [*verificatur*] when *something analogically common is found intrinsically and properly in the various analogates, even if it exists in a more perfect manner in the principal analogate.*[66] For example, being is thus said of sub-

---

[65] See *De veritate*, q. 2, a.11 and *De potentia*, q. 7, a. 5.

[66] Therefore, this analogy is not constituted through an extrinsic denomination according to a relation to a principal analogate. However, there does exist a principal analogate in which the analogical formal notion is found more perfectly [than in the others]. Indeed, this perfection is derived in the others from this principal analogate. For many things cannot be analogically similar except through a relation to one cause, as is shown in St. Thomas's fourth way for proving God's existence (*ST* I, q. 2, a. 3). For "those things that are diverse among themselves

stance and accident because substance is related {{286}} to its own existence as an accident is to its own existence. An accident intrinsically and properly is a being, even though it depends on substance. Thus, between substance and accident there is simultaneously an analogy of proper proportionality and one of attribution.

However, this analogy of proper proportionality is subdivided, at least materially, depending on whether there is or is not a determinate distance among the analogates in question.

If there is a *determinate distance,* this analogy exists together with an analogy of proportion. This is found between created substance and the accidents proportioned to it (e.g., between bodily substance and bodily accidents, between created spiritual substance, and the spiritual accidents proportioned to it):

$$\frac{\text{created substance}}{\text{its existence}} = \frac{\text{accident}}{\text{its existence}}$$

In that case, there is a determinate distance between the analogates, just as there is between the numbers one and two. And, as St. Thomas says in the aforementioned passage from *De veritate*: "It is impossible for something to be said of God and creatures according to this mode of analogy, for no creature has such a relation (or determinate distance) to God through which the divine perfection could be determined." To admit this kind of analogy between God and creatures would presuppose the truth of Spinozist pantheism, according to which creatures are modes of the divine nature or emanations of the same order as God.

An analogy of proper proportionality *without a determinate distance* is found within the created order. Thus, sensation and intellection are analogically and properly called forms of knowledge, without there being a determinate distance between them, for sensation is related to the sensible as intellection is to the intelligible. So too, sense love and spiritual love are analogically and properly called forms of love without a determinate distance existing between them, for sense love is related to the sensible good as rational love is to a rational good.

According to the latter kind of analogy of proper proportionality (i.e., without a determinate distance), it does not seem contradictory to say that something is *intrinsically* and *properly* (i.e., *not merely metaphorically*) said of God and of creatures. Nay, the evidence for our major premise is had in this way; namely, the notions that express simply simple and analogous per-

---

do not agree in some one thing except through some cause uniting them" (*ST* I, q. 3, a. 7). And those things that participate in one and the same analogical perfection do not have that perfection from themselves but, rather, accept it from a superior cause. For multitude does not render the meaning of unity but instead itself arises from unity (see *ST* I, q. 11, a. 1 and 2).

fections are not unfit for expressing the Most Perfect Being analogically but properly.

Indeed, having explained the terms of this proposition, the following two points are evident. (1) The notions of simply simple perfections—namely, those that involve *no imperfection* in their formal notion—are not opposed to expressing the Most Perfect Being (at least in some manner, though indeed properly), for *nothing is opposed to the Most Perfect Being except on account of imperfection.*

(2) It is evident that the notions that express perfections that are simply simple and already *analogous* in the created order are not unfit for expressing the Most Perfect Being analogically and properly—namely, *according to some non-metaphoric proportionality*—for as we have said, proportionality does not require a determinate distance between the analogates involved. (This proportionality is metaphysical, not mathematical. It is founded on being, not on quantity.)

{{287}} However, the second part of the major premise is: In fact, these notions thus express the Most Perfect Being if the world *requires* an infinite First Cause having these perfections. This is evident, and this requirement was proven in our preceding thesis regarding absolute evolutionism, for in virtue of the principle of causality, whose ontological value we have already defended, the world requires a First, Uncaused Cause, which would be a necessary, supreme, and most perfect being governing all things, Self-Subsistent Existence without any limit of essence. However, all of the simply simple perfections can be deduced from pure [*per essentiam*] Being [or that which exists through its very essence].[67] Hence, a priori, from a simple analysis of the notions of simply simple and analogous perfections, we negatively manifest their transcendent value. That is, these notions are not opposed to expressing God properly. And we can positively see this value *a posteriori* inasmuch as the world requires a most perfect First Cause.[68]

(2) **Now, the minor premise** of our demonstration is: The first notions of being, one, truth, goodness, efficient cause, and end, as well as the notions of intellect and will, along with their properties (e.g., wisdom, justice, and mercy) all express simply simple, analogous perfections.

This must be proven first for being, one, truth, and goodness, abstracting from the application of these notions to God, for otherwise, there would

---

[67] See *ST* I, q. 2, a. 3; q. 3, a. 4; q. 7; and so forth.

[68] Hence, according to St. Thomas, the proposition "God is" is not self-evident *quoad nos* but instead requires an *a posteriori* demonstration, even if it is self-evident *quoad se* (see *ST* I, q. 2, a. 1).

be a vicious circle in our argumentation.

Already in the finite order, BEING is said according to an analogy of proper proportionality for created substance and accidents. Moreover, the formal notion of being involves no imperfection, for it abstracts from all matter and from every limit of genus and species (for it transcends [all] genera), and also from every finite mode. Therefore, this notion is not opposed to expressing the Most Perfect Being according to an analogy of proper proportionality without a determinate distance. Hence, as finite substance is related to its own existence so that it is *being* existing *in itself,* and accidents are related to their own existence as *existing in another,* the Most Perfect Being is not opposed [*non repugnat ad*] to being related to his own existence in such a way that he would be called a *being a se* and even a substance.[69]

The same must be said concerning [the transcendental] *one* (undivided being), as well as *the true,* which is being conformed to the intellect, and *the good* (perfect and desirable being). Indeed, already in the finite order, "good" is said according to an analogy of proper proportionality of both material and spiritual goods. Moreover, it involves no imperfection in its formal character, for it abstracts from [any] finite mode [of realization]. Therefore, this notion is not opposed to expressing the Most Perfect Being according to an analogy of proper proportionality without a determinate distance being found between the analogates. Hence, just as a *fruit* is said to be *good* on account of the perfection that is befitting to it, or a *horse* on account of an analogous perfection, or a *moral act* on account of a perfection of another order, so too the Most Perfect Being is not opposed to being called *the Infinite Good.* A fruit is only physically good, whereas a virtue is morally good. {{288}} The Most Perfect Being is called good absolutely and infinitely by means of the formal notion of goodness, which involves no imperfection and is not opposed to this infinite mode [of realization].

Likewise, [the notions of] *efficient* and *final cause* involve no imperfection and are analogical. Indeed, they immediately designate an order to being inasmuch as they are extrinsic *raisons d'être of a caused being.* Hence, to cause (or produce) being involves no imperfection, whereas, by contrast, *to heat* does not formally designate an order to being but, rather, to a particular modality of being—namely, to heat. Hence, that which is formally heated

---

[69] See *ST* I, q. 3, a. 5, ad 1. However, God is not in the genus [or category] of substance, for the substance which is in a genus is a being to which it is fitting that it exist in itself [thus implying a distinction between subsistence, essence, and existence]. God, however, is his own existence, and existence transcends [all] genera.

is something limited. However, the agent qua agent involves no limitation.

Moreover, [the notion of] cause is already designated analogically in the finite order concerning the four causes, and within the order of efficient causality, it is analogically said of a principal [efficient] cause and an instrumental [efficient] cause (e.g., of an artisan and his instrument).[70] Hence, as an instrument is related to its effect so that it is said to be a cause in virtue of another, so too a finite principal cause is related to its limited effect so that it is said to be its proper cause. Thus, the Most Perfect Being is not opposed to being related to some utterly universal effect (namely, to the existence [*esse*] of things precisely inasmuch as it is existence) and is analogically and properly said to be a cause, though the transcendent, First Cause.

The same must be said of the [notion of an] end, which involves no imperfection and already in the finite order is analogically said of the ultimate end in a given genus and of intermediate subordinate ends.

Finally, *knowledge* and *love*, as well as *intellect* and *will*, are simply simple, analogical perfections, for the intellect immediately designates an order to being, which is its adequate formal object. So too the will designates an immediate order to the good. Therefore, according to their formal characters, they are not in some genus but, rather, are analogical, like being and the good.[71] Moreover, already in the finite order, knowledge is said of sensation and intellection according to an analogy of proper proportionality. Therefore, since it involves no imperfection, the Most Perfect Being is not opposed to being so designated. Thus, we can write the following proportionalities:

Forms of Knowledge

sense		created intellect		uncreated intellect
-----	=	-----	=	-----
sensible		created intelligible		uncreated intelligible

---

[70] [Trans. note: Here, efficient causality is used for the example, though there also can be, for example, instrumental causality in the domain of extrinsic formal causality.]

[71] Therefore, if, in us, these perfections are found in some genus and in some species (namely, in the genus of quality and the species of power or of faculty or habitus, or activity [*operationis*]), this is according to their *created mode* [of realization] and not according to their *formal, analogical notion*. For example, in us, wisdom is a *habitus*. However, it formally abstracts from this mode [of realization and designates only knowledge through the highest causes, and this involves no imperfection.

Forms of Love

sense love		rational love		uncreated love
-----	=	-----	=	-----
sensible good		rational good		uncreated good

Hence, science is *properly* said of both God and man. However, in man, science exists as a quality in the species of *habitus*, and as measured by things, in accord with its *created mode* [of realization in him]. However, these imperfections do not pertain to the *formal notion* of science, just as the imperfections of a hard stone in the earth do not pertain to the nature of hardness. However, in God, {{289}} wisdom [*sic*] is not an acquired *habitus* but instead is the divine essence. Moreover, it is not measured by things but, rather, causes them.[72] Thus, love is also *properly* said of both God and of man but, nonetheless, "our will and our love are not the cause of the goodness of things but, rather, are moved by them as by their object, ... (whereas, in contrast,) God's love infuses and creates the goodness found in things."[73]

However, the transcendent value of the first notions of reason are demonstrated inasmuch as these notions express simply simple, analogous perfections. Thus, too, is the transcendent value of their correlative principles proven—namely, the principles of contradiction, identity, *raison d'être*, substance, efficient causality, and finality—in virtue of which we ascend from the finite order to the Infinite Cause [of all things].

B. *Indirect demonstration of the transcendent value of the first notions and principles of reason.* This indirect proof is performed through a reduction to absurdity. Indeed, having denied the transcendent value of the first notions and principles of reason, we will find ourselves doubting the very existence of God the First Cause. However, if the existence of the First Cause is dubious, then the principle of causality will [itself] be cast into doubt, for if the First Cause perhaps does not exist, then perhaps something can come into being without a cause, or perhaps the collection of all contingent beings is causeless. However, if the principle of causality is in doubt, the same must be said about the principle of contradiction, for then, perhaps, there will be something existing neither from itself nor from another. Hence, it would be indistinguishable from nothingness. However, doubt concerning the principle of contradiction is absurd, inasmuch as, as we have said, it is absurd to doubt the opposition between nothingness and being. Indeed, doubt itself

---

[72] See *ST* I, q. 14, a. 8.
[73] *ST* I, q. 20, a. 2.

would disappear, for it would be simultaneously doubt and non-doubt (or certitude). Man could not be certain of his doubt, for perhaps he would simultaneously be in doubt and not in doubt.

Conclusion. In this way, agnostics are reduced to absurdity since they deny the ontological and transcendent value of the first notions and principles of reason. And the ontological value of these notions is thus directly made clear inasmuch as these notions do not express *per se* sensible things (i.e., phenomena) but, rather, *per se intelligible* and *per accidens* sensible ones. However, their transcendent value is directly manifested inasmuch as these notions express *analogous perfections that imply no imperfection.*

Hence, revelation is not impossible, but rather, as we will discuss below, God can order the notions of our reason and form from them propositions that analogically and properly can express the transcendent divine reality. Granted, the transcendent value of the notions by which strictly supernatural mysteries (such as the divine paternity, filiation, and spiration) are expressed cannot be demonstrated prior to revelation. However, following upon revelation, they can be defended against those who deny them, and one can likewise urge that such terms do not posit any imperfection in God.

§3. Resolution of Objections Raised by Agnostics against the Ontological and Transcendent Value of the First Notions and Principles of Our Reason

A. *Objections against their ontological value*

{{290}} These objections were already proposed by the ancient sophists and skeptics, such as Protagoras, and were refuted by Aristotle in *Metaphysics*, bk. 4, as well as by St. Thomas in *ST* I, q. 85, a. 2 (whether the intelligible *species* is *that which* is known or *that by which* we know).

1. *The main objection runs as follows*: Nothing is known except inasmuch as it is in the knower. Now, something extramental cannot exist in a knower. Therefore, something extramental cannot be that which is known.

Response: I make a distinction regarding the major premise. I concede that nothing is known except inasmuch as it is in the knower, either *per se* or through a likeness that represents it. However, I deny this if it means only *per se*. Likewise, I contradistinguish the minor, conceding that something extramental cannot be in the knower *per se*. However, I deny that it cannot be there through a likeness representing it. I deny the conclusion and the inference.

2. *However, it will be insisted*: In that case, the representative likeness will be what is known and not the extramental thing. Therefore, the difficulty remains.

Proof: That which is known in act is in the knower, for it itself is the intellect in act.

However, only the likeness of the object is in the intellect. Therefore, that which is known in act is only the likeness of the object and not the extramental thing.

Response: I will begin by distinguishing the major premise, conceding that that which is known in act is in the knower according to its *representative* or intentional *existence*. However, I deny that it is there according *to its physical existence*. Moreover, I contradistinguish the minor premise, conceding that that which is in the intellect is only the likeness of the object according to its physical existence. However, I deny that it is a likeness of the object according to its intentional existence. Therefore, I deny the conclusion and the inference. Allow me to explain. Intentional (or representative) existence is essentially relative to the existence of the thing. Hence, the representative idea is not first known but, rather, is that *by which* the extramental object is known. In other words, the idea is not the representation closed in on itself, like a picture or a statue, but instead is essentially open, so to speak, and immediately refers the intellect to the thing so that the idea can itself only be known through a reflection following on direct intellection.

3. *However, it will be further insisted*: At least the expressed idea (or the mental word) is what is known. Therefore, the difficulty remains.

Proof: We only know the extramental thing in the internal word. Now, that word is not the means by which knowledge happens but, rather, is the terminus of knowledge. Therefore, the extramental thing is not the terminus (or *that which is*) known.[74]

Response: I concede the major premise. However, I make a distinction regarding the minor premise. I concede that the mental word is the terminus as *that in which* the thing is known. However, I deny that it is that which is known. I make a distinction regarding the conclusion. I concede that the extramental thing is not the *terminus in quo*, the terminus in which the extramental thing is known. However, I deny that it is not the *id quod*, that which is known. Allow me to explain. The mental word is the expression of the intelligible thing, and as the expression, it is essentially relative (or intentional) to that which is expressed. Hence, intellection, according to its physical or entitative existence (i.e., as an accident immanent in the soul), is terminated at the word. However, according to its intentional existence and properly as intellection, it is terminated at the known thing. This is befitting to it inasmuch as it is something spiritual and essentially ordered to something else.[75] As St. Thomas says in *De veritate*, q. 2, a. 2:

---

[74] Such was the position of Édouard Le Roy in his *Dogme et critique*, as well as in "Comment se pose le problème de Dieu (suite et fin)," *Revue de métaphysique et de morale* 15 (July 1907): 488 and 495: "Something outside or beyond thought is, by its very definition, unthinkable."

[75] [Trans. note: For an excellent summary of this topic, see Réginald Garrigou-Lagrange, "*Cognoscens quodammodo est vel est aliud a se* (On the Nature of Knowledge as Union with the Other as Other)," in *Philosophizing in Faith: Essays on the Beginning and End of Wisdom*, trans. Matthew K. Minerd (Providence, RI: Cluny Media, 2019), 63–78.]

This is the perfection of the knower inasmuch as he is a knower, for something is known by a knower inasmuch as the known itself is in some way in the presence of the knower. Therefore, in *De anima* 3 (comm. 15) it is said that the soul is, in some way, all things because by its very nature it can know all things. {{291}} And in this way, it is possible that the perfection of the entire universe would [be able to] exist in a single thing.

Hence, subjective idealism, which conceives of the idea as something self-enclosed, like a kind of picture, has a quasi-quantitative and material notion of the idea [or mental word][76] but not a qualitative, spiritual notion of it. From this perspective, idealism does not transcend the spatialized conceptions formed by materialists. However, spirit, qua spirit, transcends space.

4. *And yet it will be insisted*: However, the representative value of the idea remains doubtful.

Proof: In order to know the representative value of an idea, one would need to compare it with the thing itself. Now, this comparison is impossible, for we can only know the thing itself through an idea. Therefore, the value of the idea itself remains doubtful.

Response: A distinction must be made regarding the major premise. I would concede the point if an idea were *that which* is known (like a picture or statue). However, I deny it if [, as is the case,] an idea is essentially *relative to the reality in question* [*ad rem*]. I will let the minor premise pass. I distinguish the conclusion in the same way. Here, see what St. Thomas says in *De veritate*, q. 1, a. 9:

> Truth exists in the intellect as a consequence of the intellect's act and as something known by the intellect. It *follows* the act of the intellect inasmuch as the intellect's judgment is concerned with reality [*re*] as it is. However, *it is known* by the intellect inasmuch as the intellect reflects upon its act, not only in knowing its own act but inasmuch as it knows its proportion to reality [*rem*]. Now, this cannot be known without the nature of this act itself being known, and this cannot be known without knowing the nature of its active principle, namely, the intellect itself, which by its very nature is ordered to conformity with reality [*rebus*].

That is, the nature of intellection and of the intellect is essentially relative to intelligible being.

---

[76] [Trans. note: Here Fr. Garrigou-Lagrange is using the term "idea" loosely, for in strict Thomist vocabulary, the term "idea" designates the creative idea of the artist, which, properly speaking, belongs to the practical order of making. Other Thomists of his own line occasionally do this, likely under the general pressure of modern philosophical vocabulary, which often uses "idea" in this sense. However, he certainly is not unaware of the distinctions required by more formal vocabulary.]

5. *Still, the objector will insist*: However, an idea does not represent the extramental object as it is in itself. Therefore, the difficulty remains.

Proof: The idea is formally universal. Now, the extramental thing [*res*] is singular. Therefore, an idea does not represent the thing as it is in itself.

Response: First, I make a distinction regarding the major premise, conceding that the idea is formally universal *as regards its manner of representing*. However, I deny that it is so *as regards the nature represented*. Moreover, I contradistinguish the minor, conceding that indeed the extramental thing is singular, as regards its manner of existence, while, however, denying that it is so as regards its nature. Therefore, the idea represents the nature of the thing, although it does not represent the singular mode of this thing's existence. See *ST* I, q. 85, a. 2, ad 2: "The nature itself which happens to be subject to being understood, or to being abstract, or to the intention of universality, only exists in singular things. However, this very thing which is understood, or abstracted, or subject to the intention of universality, exists in the intellect." The mode of universality befalls this nature[77] in the intellect and does not stand in the way of objectivity, for the intellect does not know the nature (e.g., of a stone) as something *separate* but, rather, does so *separately* from its individuating conditions. Thus, sight sees the color of an apple without its smell and, nonetheless, color does not exist in the apple without its smell.[78]

6. *And yet it will still be insisted*: The notions of reason express in a universal manner only that which is perceived by the senses in the particular thing. Now, the senses only perceive the phenomena in the particular thing. Therefore, the notions of reason only express the phenomena in the universal but, however, lack ontological value.

{{292}} *Response*: I make a distinction regarding the major premise, conceding that the notions of reason express in a universal manner only that which is perceived by the senses in the singular as *either sensible per se or per accidens*. However, if one is referring only to that which is sensible *per se*, then I deny it. I contradistinguish the minor premise. I concede that the senses only perceive phenomena as things that are *per se* sensible. However, I deny this if one means that they are so limited as regards *per accidens* sensibles. The senses do not only perceive the phenomenon of color but also perceive *the colored*, which is known qua colored by sight and qua substance and being by the intellect.

---

[77] [Trans. note: Reading *naturale* as *naturae*.]

[78] In ch. 4 of *De ente et essentia*, St. Thomas states: "*Nature* or essence can be considered in three ways: (1) *absolutely*, and in this way the only thing that can truly be said of it is that which falls to it on account of its definition; (2) *inasmuch as it exists in individuals*, in a singular manner; (3) *inasmuch as it is in the intellect*, in an abstract and universal manner.

"Therefore, if it is asked whether this *nature, absolutely considered,* (e.g., the nature of humanity) can be called *one* or *many*, neither is to be conceded, for both are outside of the understanding (or definition) of humanity and can both befall it."

It is multiplied in individuals and is considered by the intellect as one thing able to exist in many. This represents the most profound solution to the problem of universals.

7. *It will be urged, however*: The ontological value of the first notions and principles of reason is founded on the value of sensation. Now the value of sensation is not metaphysically certain but is only physically certain. Therefore, the ontological value of the first notions of reason is not metaphysically certain.

Response: I make a distinction regarding the major premise. I deny that the ontological value of the first notions and principles of reason is *formally and intrinsically* founded on the value of sensation. However, I concede that it is so founded *materially and extrinsically*. I will let the minor premise pass. Moreover, I contradistinguish the conclusion, conceding that the ontological value of the first notions and principles of reason would not be metaphysically certain if it were formally and intrinsically founded on sensation. However, I deny it if it were materially and extrinsically founded on sensation.

Allow me to explain. The ontological value, as well as the necessity, of the first principles is [self-]evident, not with sensible evidentiary strength but with that of the intellectual order, not under the sun's light but, rather, under that of the intellect. However, it presupposes sensation, from which it acquires such notions. This metaphysical certitude is loftier than the physical certitude of sensation. Nay, the value of sensation can be defended without a vicious circle by the principles of reason and thus can be made metaphysically certain, at least in an extrinsic manner. For example, sensation without a present sensed thing would be a violation of the principle of contradiction. A sense faculty not ordered to sensing something would be a violation of the principle of finality. A sensation not caused by a sensed object would be a violation of the principle of causality. Hence, we have allowed the minor to pass, for the value of sensation is metaphysically certain in an extrinsic manner—that is, through a resolution to metaphysical principles.[79]

Thus, causes are causes of each other, though in different genera of causality, without there being a vicious circle.[80] See *ST* I, q. 84, a. 6 (fine) and ad 1: "We cannot say that sense knowledge is the complete and perfect cause of intellectual cognition but, rather, is in some way the matter of the cause. . . . For the light of the agent intellect is required, through which we immutably know the truth [found] in mutable things and distinguish

---

[79] [Trans. note: For a more detailed treatment on this point, see Yves Simon, *An Introduction to the Metaphysics of Knowledge*, trans. Vukan Kuic and Richard J. Thompson (New York: Fordham University Press, 1990), 89–91n9. The topic of precisely understanding the nature of sensation has been repeatedly emphasized by John Deely in, e.g., *Intentionality and Semiotics: A Story of Mutual Fecundation* (Scranton, PA: University of Scranton Press, 2007), 159–63. One should see also Réginald Garrigou-Lagrange, "There Cannot Be Genuine Sensation without a Real Sensed Thing," trans. Thomas De Pauw, ed. Edward M. Macierowski in *Philosophizing in Faith: Essays on the Beginning and End of Wisdom*, ed. and trans. Matthew K. Minerd (Providence, RI: Cluny Media, 2019), 101–119.]

[80] [Trans. note: For further discussion of this important principle, see Réginald Garrigou-Lagrange, *The Order of Things: The Realism of the Principle of Finality*, trans. Matthew K. Minerd (Steubenville, OH: Emmaus Academic, 2020), 319–347.]

things themselves from the likenesses of things." Likewise, in *In De Trinitate Boetii*, q. 3, a. 1, ad 4 (*fine*): "Knowledge of principles is drawn from the senses and, nonetheless, the light by which the principles are known is inborn. Thus, faith is from hearing and nonetheless the *habitus* of faith is infused." Likewise, in *De veritate*, q. 11, a. 1:

> The light of such reason, by which first principles are known by us, has been imparted to us by God, as a kind of likeness of the uncreated truth resounding within us. Whence, since all human teaching can only have efficacy in virtue of that light, it is clear that God alone is the one who internally and principally teaches, just as nature principally and interiorly heals.

Similarly, see *ST* I, q. 84, a. 5 and *Posterior Analytics*, bk. 2, lect. 20.

8. Nonetheless, agnosticism is not absurd. Indeed, that which is absurd cannot be thought, but agnosticism is something that can be thought. Therefore, it is not absurd.

Response: I make a distinction regarding the major premise. I concede that the absurd cannot be thought inasmuch as it implies a contradiction immediately and in a completely obvious way, such as in the notion of a square circle. Otherwise, I deny it. Indeed, since a contradiction may not be so evident, the mind can sophistically or inadvertently combine impossible things in a single proposition, at least in words. And the objections raised by sophistical thinkers are frequently only word games. Thus, we witness a kind of radical nominalism therein: They are speciously arranged words with a kind of appearance of truth, nothing else. On this topic, see Plato's dialogue, *The Sophist*; the object of sophistics [i.e., sophistical reasoning] is not being but, rather, non-being.

9. At least we can say that agnosticism cannot be reduced to absurdity. Indeed, this reduction would presuppose the value of the principle of contradiction. Now, the agnostic doubts this value. Therefore, he cannot be reduced to absurdity.

{{293}} *Response*: I distinguish the major premise, conceding that this reduction would presuppose the *logical value* of the principle of contradiction. However, I deny that it would presuppose its *real value*, at least for arguments where an interlocutor will not concede it [*saltem in casu ad hominem*]. I contradistinguish the minor premise. I will let pass the claim that the agnostic doubts the real value of the principle of contradiction (for he, in fact, only feigns such doubt). However, I deny that he doubts its subjective, logical value. Thus, he is reduced to absurdity inasmuch as, even according to its subjective consideration, as we said above, a fourfold absurdity is clear: as regards the object of direct intellection, an idea, intellection, and the intellect itself.[81] An idea that is not relative to the intelligible would be the idea of nothing (or, in other words,

---

[81] [Trans. note: As in several other places, reading "intelligentiam" here in a more restricted sense, along the lines of Fr. Garrigou-Lagrange's own French, which often uses "intelligence" for "intellect."]

would be both an idea and a non-idea). Nay, the agnostic wishes at least to affirm his own thought process, and therefore, [if he does indeed deny the principle of contradiction,] he should also doubt his own thinking, saying, "Perhaps I am simultaneously thinking and not thinking." Thus, like Cratylus, he would find himself reduced to absolute silence like a plant.[82]

B. *Objections against the transcendent value of the first notions and principles of reason*[83]

1. *Objection*: The transcendent value of more universal notions is illegitimately founded on the transcendent value of a less universal notion. Now, the transcendent value of the notions of being, one, good, and so forth is founded on the transcendent value of the notion of cause, which is less universal. Therefore, the transcendent value of the more universal notions lacks a legitimate foundation. In other words, it cannot be said that God exists, or is a being, except because God is required as a First Cause. However, the transcendent value of the notion of cause presupposes the transcendent value of the notion of being and not vice versa.[84]

Response: I make a distinction regarding the major premise. I concede it if one means that the transcendent value of more universal notions is illegitimately founded on the transcendent value of less universal notions *in itself* [*quoad se*] and from the perspective of the *non-repugnancy* of the attribution [*quoad non repugnantiam attributionis*]. However, I deny the claim *from our own perspective of knowing* [*quoad nos*] and from the perspective of *actual attribution*, provided that the less universal notion is essentially *relative* (as is the notion of *cause*) and enables one to ascend *a posteriori* from knowledge of the world to knowledge of the First Cause. Hence, I contradistinguish the minor premise in the same way.

Allow me to explain. *In itself*, the transcendent value of the notion of being is prior to the transcendent value of the notion of cause, but not *from our own perspective of knowing*. Hence, in *ST* I, q. 2, a. 1, St. Thomas says:

> Considered *in itself*, the proposition, "God is," is self-evident, for the predicate is the same as the subject because God is His own existence. However, because we do not know God quidditatively, this is not self-evident *for us*. Instead, it needs to be demonstrated through those things that are more known from

---

[82] See Aristotle, *Metaphysics*, 4, 4 and 5.

[83] Regarding the resolution of these objections, the exposition of anti-nominalists, and a comparison of the Thomist resolution of the matter in relation to the Scotistic and Suarezian solutions, see our discussion in *God: His Existence and His Nature*, vol. 1, 232[–241], 245[–251]; vol. 2, 190–267.

[84] This agnostic sort of objection is exposited in Marcel Hébert, "Anonyme et polyonyme: Second étude sur la 'personnalité divine,'" *Revue de la métaphysique et de la morale* 11, no. 2 (March 1903): 231-247 (esp. 241).

our own perspective, though less known as regards their very nature, namely through [His] effects.

Hence, from the perspective of *non-repugnance of the attribution* [*quoad non repugnatiam attributionis*], the transcendent value of being appears (even from our perspective) before the transcendent value of the notion of cause precisely because being is a simply simple and analogous perfection. Hence, to cause (or to produce being) is also analogous and involves no imperfection. However, if it is a question of *the actual attribution* of these perfections to God, then this actual attribution, made from our own perspective as knowers, is founded on the fact that the world requires a First Cause having these perfections. And inasmuch as the notion of cause is relative and not absolute, it enables us to ascend from knowledge of the world to knowledge of the First Cause. Nay, the world requires a First Cause in virtue of the principle of causality, which is founded on the principle of contradiction (or identity) and ultimately on the notion of being, which forever retains its place of primacy.

{{294}} 2. *It will be urged*: However, causality is not legitimately attributed to God, as explained in Kant's fourth antinomy. Indeed, God is required [according to your account] as the absolutely immutable First Cause. Now, an immobile cause, which would produce a new effect without a newness of activity, is something unthinkable. Therefore, the divine causality cannot be conceived.

Response: I concede the major premise. However, I make a distinction regarding the minor premise, denying it if you mean that an immobile cause producing a new effect without newness of activity is unthinkable *as regards the formal notion of what a cause is*. However, if you mean this *as regards the divine mode of causing*, allow me to make a sub-distinction. I concede that such a divine mode of causing cannot be *positively* conceived of on the basis of our knowledge of creatures. However, I deny that it cannot be conceived of *negatively* and *relatively*. Likewise, I distinguish the conclusion in the same manner. On account of the imperfection of this knowledge, the divine causality remains a natural mystery. Nonetheless, this causality can be known without contradiction in a negative manner (an uncaused, non-premoved cause) and relatively (and eminent causality, above time, which is produced by it, as is motion, which is measured by time).[85]

3. *A further point of insistence*: Even if the notion of cause would provide a sufficient foundation for attributing simply simple perfections to God, nonetheless, these perfections, considered in themselves, do not seem to be befitting to God.

Indeed, no proportion exists between the finite and the infinite, intrinsically considered. Now, without this proportion, the perfections of creatures cannot be attributed to God analogically and formally. Therefore, this analogical and formal attribution is impossible.

---

[85] See *SCG* II, ch. 35.

Response: I make a distinction regarding the major premise. I concede it if it means that there is *no quantitative proportion, properly speaking,* between the finite and the infinite. However, I deny it if it means that there is no proportion in the sense of a *proportionality*. I contradistinguish the minor premise in the same way.

Allow me to explain. In reality, a sufficient proportionality exists between the relationship of the sense [power] to the sensible and the intellect to the intelligible, meaning that sensation and intellection can be called forms of knowledge analogically, though properly and formally, and even that intellection and knowledge may also be attributed to God in a formal manner. Similarly, being is said to be related [*se habet*] of itself to existence, whether in another (accident), in itself (substance), or from itself (God).[86] Therefore, *a proportionality* is found here, though it is not *mathematical* or quantitative in nature but instead *is ontological (or metaphysical)*.

4. *Still, the objector will urge*: However, given that proper (and not metaphorical) knowledge arises from some proportionality, at least three of the terms of the proportionality must be foreknown so that one may infer the fourth member. Now, in the aforementioned proportionality between God and creatures, two terms of the proportionality remain unknown. Therefore, no proper, nonmetaphorical knowledge arises from this proportionality.[87]

Response: First, I make a distinction regarding the major premise. I concede that three members must be known [either] immediately or in a mediate matter. However, I deny that [all] three must be immediately known. I also make a distinction regarding the minor premise. I concede that two created terms in the aforementioned proportionality are *immediately* known and that the third is known *in a mediate manner*. However, I deny that the two other terms of the proportionality remain unknown. Therefore, I deny the consequence and the inference.

Allow me to explain. Consider this proportionality:

$$\frac{\text{First Cause}}{X} = \frac{\text{contingent being}}{\text{its existence}}$$

In this proportionality, the First Cause is related to its existence as contingent being is related to its existence. There are two created terms that are immediately known. The third term (namely, the First Cause) is known in a mediated manner inasmuch as the world requires a cause. The fourth term (the divine existence) is inferred according to the analogical likeness of being, for being is that which is related to existence, either from

---

[86] See *De veritate*, q. 23, a. 7, ad 9.
[87] This argument can be found in many modernists. See the index entry "analogique" in Édouard Le Roy's *Dogme et critique*.

itself or from another. This fourth member is known *positively* inasmuch as it analogically is in agreement [*analogice convenit*] with creatures. However, it is known *negatively* and *relatively* as regards its own proper divine modality.

5. *Yet, in response, it is urged*: Then the notion of being is a notion of some relation, or relationship [*habitudinis*], to existence. Relativism follows from this assertion, for if the first notion is relative, there can be no absolute knowledge.

{{295}} *Response*: The notion of being is not a notion of some accidental relation like paternity or filiation. Rather, being involves *an essential* (or transcendental[88]) *relation* to existence. Hence, we don't say that being is a relation [*habitudo*] to existence but, rather, is that which is related to [*se habet*] existence, that whose act is existence inasmuch as its essence is essentially ordered to existence, whether it were to have its existence from another or from itself (in which case it is existence itself, [that is, God]). Every contingent being has an essence that is distinct from its existence. He who is being from himself is existence itself by his very essence. Thus, the intellect is not a mere relation but instead is something relative to intelligible being.

6. *Continuing to insist in objection, however*: Nonetheless, those things that are in the same genus are univocal and not analogical. Now, the intellect and will are in the genus of quality as faculties. Therefore, they are not analogical notions and hence are not analogically befitting of God.

Response: I make a distinction regarding the major premise. I concede that those things which are in a given genus according to their *formal character* are univocal. However, I deny that they are univocal if they are only in a genus as regards *their created modality*. I contradistinguish the minor premise. I concede that the intellect and the will are in one genus according to their created modality. However, I deny that this is so according to their formal character.

7. *And yet*, certainly, no proportionality exists between God and creatures. Indeed, God differs more from creatures than creatures do from nothingness. Now, there is no analogy of proportionality between creatures and nothingness. Therefore, *a fortiori*, there is no analogy of proportionality between God and creatures.

Response: I make a distinction regarding the major premise. I concede that God differs from creatures more than creatures do from nothingness, *as regards their mode of existence*. However, I deny that this holds *as regards their formal character of their being*. I concede the minor but make a distinction regarding the conclusion. I concede that there is not an analogy between God and creatures as regards the finite mode and an infinite

---

[88] [Trans. note: For an explanation of this point of doctrine, see the brief but clear text drawn from the works of Austin Woodbury in appendix included in Réginald Garrigou-Lagrange, "There Cannot Be Genuine Sensation without a Real Sensed Thing," trans. Thomas De Pauw, ed. Edward M. Macierowski in *Philosophizing in Faith: Essays on the Beginning and End of Wisdom*, ed. and trans. Matthew K. Minerd (Providence, RI: Cluny Media, 2019), 116–119.]

mode of the analogates [*quoad modum finitum et modum infinitum*]. However, I deny this as regards the formal notion of being [*rationem formalem entis*], for being can exist according to various modalities, in a finite mode and in an infinite mode.[89] Hence, it was said at Lateran IV: "Between Creator and creature no similitude can be expressed without implying a greater dissimilitude."[90]

8. *However, it is urged*: Then, the notion of being would be something prior to God. Now, nothing is prior to God. Therefore, the response is false.

Response: I make a distinction regarding the major premise. I concede that the notion of being is prior to God logically, *according to our manner of conceiving things*. However, I deny that this is so *according to the truth of reality*. Our intellect, which abstracts its concepts from sense data, knows abstract and analogous being prior to knowing Self-Subsistent Existence. And when we know Self-Subsistent Existence, that appears to us as being the very fullness of being, the cause of all being. Hence, it is really prior to being which is abstracted from sensible things.

9. *Yet it is urged*: Nonetheless, simply simple perfections cannot at once be found in God analogically and formally. Rather, they must be found in him only virtually [i.e., only inasmuch as it is within the scope of his causality], as are bodiliness and animality.

Indeed, the various perfections whose formal notions are distinct cannot be identified, lest they be destroyed. Now, the various divine perfections must be formally identified in the Deity; otherwise, there will be a formal-actual distinction in God, and this is opposed to God's utter simplicity. Therefore, these various perfections cannot be analogically and formally in God but, rather, must be found in him only virtually, as are bodiliness and animality. Hence, God is only knowable metaphorically.

First response: I make a distinction regarding the major premise. I will let pass the assertion that they cannot be identified *in reality and in their formal notion* without being destroyed. However, they can be identified *in reality though not in reason* [*re et non ratione*]. I contradistinguish the minor premise in the same manner.

Allow me to explain. On account of its eminence, *the Deity* is *virtually multiform* [*multiplex*]. Hence, it offers *a real foundation* for a virtual distinction among the [divine] attributes. This distinction is not formal-actual. In other words, it does not exist before the mind's own consideration, as Scotus wished to be the case, {{296}} but it is indeed founded on reality. And this suffices for saying, for example, that God punishes through his justice and not through his mercy, for the reality in question, which in itself is unified while being virtually manifold, is equal to many things.

Nonetheless, agnostic thinkers will urge: From the fact that the Deity is virtually multiform, it only follows that intellect and will are in it *virtually* but not formally, just as animality or bodiliness are virtually in God (or as the colors of the rainbow are

---

[89] See *De potentia*, q. 3, a. 4, ad 2.

[90] Denzinger, no. 806.

virtually but not formally in white light). Hence, the objection remains.

In resolution of this sub-objection, we have a second response insisting upon the eminence of the Deity.

Second response: I make a distinction regarding the major premise. I concede that the various perfections in question cannot be identified in a formal notion *of the same order* without being destroyed. However, I deny that they cannot be identified in a formal notion *of a loftier order*. I contradistinguish the minor premise, denying that then they would need to be identified in the Deity as though it were a formal notion of the same order, but conceding that they are indeed so identified in it as in a formal notion of a loftier order. I deny the consequence and the inference.

The Deity is loftier than being, one, goodness, intelligence, love, and so forth. Thus, "all of the perfections that are found in [created] things in a divided and manifold manner preexist in God in a united and simple manner."[91] Indeed, to exist, live, and understand can be naturally participated in stones, plants, and men. By contrast, the *Deity* as such (that is, the intimate life of God) can only be participated in supernaturally through grace. Hence, it is said that the object of natural theology is God *considered under the formal character of being* (or as the Author of nature), whereas the object of supernatural theology is God *considered under the formal character of the Deity* (that is, as the Author of grace and glory).

Regarding this matter, in order to make clear the eminence of the intimate life of God (or of the Trinity), Cajetan writes in nos. 7 and 8 of his comments on *ST* I, q. 39, a.1:

> In the formal order—that is, the order of formal notions considered in themselves and not speaking from the perspective of our knowledge of them—there is a single formal notion in God, one that is not purely absolute nor purely relative, not purely communicable, nor purely incommunicable, but instead, one that most eminently and formally contains both whatever absolute perfection there is [in Him] and whatever the relational nature of the Trinity [*Trinitas respectiva*] requires. . . . However, we err if in proceeding from absolute and relational things [in the created order] to God we then imagine that the distinction between the absolute and the relational is somehow prior to the divine reality. . . . Indeed, the complete opposite is the case, for *the divine reality is prior to being* and to all of its differences, for it is *above being, above one*, and so forth.

It is always the case that those things that are found in a divided manner in inferior things are found in a united manner in superior ones. For example, in one and simple act of sight, all the visible things in a given region are marvelously gathered together in a single glance.

10. *Yet it will be insisted*: However, perfections whose formal characters are distinct

---

[91] *ST* I, q. 13, a. 5.

from the loftier formal notion of the Deity cannot indeed be identified in it without being destroyed. Now, according to what was just said, such an identification does exist in the Deity. Therefore, [the distinct perfections] are destroyed [in God] just as the colors [of the rainbow] are destroyed in white light on account of such light's excessively great perfection.

Response: I make a distinction regarding the major premise. I deny the claim *if these perfections, through their own proper characters, demand to be identified when they are purified from all potentiality*. Otherwise, I concede it. I contradistinguish the minor premise in the same manner while denying the consequent and the inference.

Allow me to explain. When simply simple perfections are purified of all potentiality, they demand to be identified with each other in the Deity. Therefore, they are not destroyed in this identification, for no reality, by what is proper to it, tends to its own destruction. *On the contrary, these perfections only exist in their purest state by being so identified*. An analogy for this identification can be found in created holiness, which is, like grace, a participation in the divine nature, for utterly different virtues are united in holiness, and in this union these virtues are not diminished but, rather, are most fully strengthened. Thus, in Christ's death upon the Cross, we find at once the most profound of humility along with the loftiest majesty, the apex of courage, the heights of meekness, the most perfect manifestation of justice, and the most excellent {{297}} charity and mercy. "Mercy and truth have met each other; justice and peace have kissed" (Ps 84 [85]:11, DR) This is the sublime harmony of the Cross, the manifestation of the reconciliation of the various divine perfections.

In virtue of their own proper characters, these divine perfections demand to be identified when they are purified of all potentiality. This identification can be easily shown for those perfections that are distinct in creatures *solely in virtue of creaturely potentiality*, as we see in intellect and intellection. Indeed, these latter perfections are not even virtually distinct in God.[92] However, it follows from this that even other perfections that are distinct in creatures, *of their own formal character* (e.g., intellect and will) also demand to be identified in Pure Act, where they are found in their utterly pure state. On this, see our

---

[92] See John of St. Thomas, *Cursus theologicus*, In *ST* I, q. 14, disp. 16, a. 2, solv. arg., nos. 19, 20, 28, and 33. Charles René Billuart, *Summa sancti Thomae, In ST* I, diss. 2, a. 1; diss., 5, a. 1, dico 2°. Cf. *ST* I, q. 25, a. 1, ad 3.

The reason for this is because if existence and essence (or even essence, intellect, and intellection) were virtually distinct in God, then *something in God would be conceived of as being potential, with a foundation in reality*. Now, since God is the height of actuality, we cannot conceive of him as having some distinction with a [virtual] foundation in reality in potency to existence, operation, or to something else.

Nonetheless, we can admit that there is an *extrinsic virtual distinction* between these divine perfections—namely, one that has a foundation in creatures, not in God, inasmuch as Pure Act has in itself that which in creatures pertains to potency and to act.

discussion in *God: His Existence and His Nature*, vol. 2, 243–246. Also, see the schema presented below in ch. 11, a. 1, §2.

Hence essence, existence, intellect, intellection, and the understood essence (or the First Truth) are not virtually distinct in God (*ST* I, q. 14, a. 4). Likewise, there is not a virtual distinction between the divine essence, existence, will, and necessary love of the infinite goodness. However, intellection and will are virtually distinct from each other, and in intellection, there is a virtual distinction between God's science of simple understanding regarding creatures, his science of vision, and providence relative to creatures. Similarly, there is a virtual distinction in God's love between his necessary love, his free love of creatures, mercy, and justice. Nonetheless, all these perfections are identified in the Deity, and they remain formally therein, indeed, in their utterly pure state. However, *the divine modality of this identification remains hidden from us* and can be naturally known only in a negative and relative manner as something undivided and eminent. This is the *supreme mystery of the natural order,* for we naturally conclude that the divine perfections are identified in God, while the intimate mode of this identification remains hidden from us. And because the highest part of a lower order touches the borders of the lowest of a higher order, this supreme natural mystery is in some way joined with the supernatural mysteries in the Deity, as will be discussed in chapter 11.[93]

---

[93] Particular pseudo-antinomies are resolved in the treatise *De Deo uno*, in which a defense, and in some way an explanation, is provided concerning the reconciliation of the divine perfections taken individually.

(a) Divine *knowledge* and God's utter simplicity are reconciled inasmuch as the knowing subject and the known object are distinct in created realities only on account of each of their potentiality [i.e., the known's potentiality, of itself, for being known, and the knower's potentiality, of itself, for knowing]. See *ST* I, q. 14, aa. 2 and 4. In this way, we have a refutation for the objections raised by Fichte and Spencer asserting that the divine science would presuppose duality, which is opposed to the divine simplicity.

(b) Intellectual *life* and the *life* of love are not opposed to utter immutability, for this immobility is not an inert immobility but instead an immobility of perfection, and of fullness of existence, which essentially has whatever it can have. On the contrary, movement in life is an imperfection, for progress presupposes a privation of the good to which we tend (see *ST* I, q. 18). The highest form of life is found in the tranquil contemplation of the infinite truth. However, such rest is not a privation of motion. Rather, the possession of the good (i.e., beatitude) is above motion (see *ST* I, q. 26).

(c) *The free act* is not something contingent in God but instead is the necessary love of God inasmuch as it has a non-necessary relationship [*habitudem*] with created things. See *SCG* I, ch. 82: "By one and the same act, God's will wills Himself and other things. However, its relationship to Himself is necessary and natural, whereas its relation to other things is according to a kind of . . . voluntary befittingness." Also see *ST* I, q. 19, a. 3, ad 4. Likewise, God's *good will* is simultaneously entirely free and utterly suited to [His] Being according to the judgment of Wisdom (See Cajetan, *In ST* I, q. 19, a. 2).

(d) *The permission of evil* is not irreconcilable with God's utter goodness and omnipotence, for as St. Thomas says, following St. Augustine: "Since God is utterly good, nothing evil can

{{298}} Thus, we have a sufficient refutation of agnosticism in its denial of the onto-logical and transcendent value of the first notions and principles of reason (and, hence, also, in its rejection of the possibility of divine revelation). We at least have an indirect resolution to the pseudo-antinomies presented to us by agnostics. The mystery remains, yet without contradiction. *By contrast, agnosticism is what leads to unresolvable antino-mies*; namely, perhaps God, the First Cause, does not exist; hence, perhaps the principle of causality and even the principle of contradiction are false; perhaps God is simultaneously a cause and an effect, the means and the ultimate end, flesh and spirit, finite and infinite, the best of things and evil [*perversus*]. In this case, no truth would remain. The various perfections would not be reconciled in the Deity, but rather, truth and falsity would be identified with each other, as well as justice and injustice, all in the uncertain flow of evolution. *In order to avoid the divine mystery,* [*agnosticism*] thus *posits utterly open contra-diction*, thereby giving us a proof through absurdity for the divine Mystery itself.[94]

---

insinuate itself into His works, unless He were so omnipotent that he could draw good even out of evil" (see *ST* I, q. 2, a. 3, ad 1; q. 48, a. 2, ad 3). This is how the problem of evil is resolved. Evil is permitted as ordered to a greater good, which is the manifestation of mercy and justice (see *ST* I, q. 23, a. 5, ad 3).

(e) Finally, *mercy and justice* are not opposed as contradictories but, rather, are two proper-ties of the Divine Love inasmuch as the Divine Good is self-diffusive (this is the principle of mercy) and is to be loved above all things, having an utterly strict right to this (hence being the principle of justice). Nay, mercy demands to be identified with justice, as it excludes cruelty, and conversely, justice seeks to be identified with mercy, as it excludes pusillanimity. However, "the work of divine justice always presupposes the work of His mercy and is founded on it." Thus, in a certain manner, mercy has the upper hand over justice (see *ST* I, q. 21, a. 4).

[94] We read in Sacred Scripture, "Woe to you that call evil good, and good evil: that put darkness for light, and light for darkness: that put bitter for sweet, and sweet for bitter. Woe to you that are wise in your own eyes, and prudent in your own conceits" (Isa 5:20-21, DR). Hence, the Lord says, "I confess to thee, O Father, Lord of Heaven and earth, because thou hast hid these things from the wise and prudent, and hast revealed them to little ones" (Matt 11:25, DR). And St. Paul: "If any man among you seem to be wise in this world, let him become a fool, that he may be wise" (1 Cor 3:18, DR), so that he may receive the light of divine revelation from on high. "God, who commanded the light to shine out of darkness, hath shined in our hearts, to give the light of the knowledge of the glory of God, in the face of Christ Jesus" (2 Cor 4:6, DR).

PART TWO

Positive Defense of the Possibility of Revelation

PROLOGUE

{{299}} *State of the Question and Its Division*—Already in our critique of naturalism / rationalism in its dual pantheistic and agnostic forms, we defended, at least negatively and on the basis of common characteristics, the possibility of supernatural revelation. However, we must now turn to a positive defense of supernatural revelation on account of what is proper to it.

The state of this question, as well as its division, is made clear from the specific objections of rationalists that remain (1) against the possibility of revelation in general, (2) against the possibility of revelation of the natural truths[1] of religion, (3) against the possibility of the revelation of supernatural mysteries, and (4) against the possibility of mediate revelation—that is, a revelation proposed to men by the mediation of prophets and of the Church.

Indeed, thus presupposing the refutation of absolute evolutionism and agnosticism, many difficulties remain, first and especially those proposed by the deists, who admitted the possibility of demonstrating the existence of God, who is essentially distinct from the world, while rejecting, however, the possibility of God freely and supernaturally intervening in the world.

(1) *Against the possibility of supernatural revelation in general*, at least three sorts of arguments are presented:

(a) This revelation would be *a miracle* and hence contrary to the immutability of God and of natural laws.

(b) It would be *contrary to the vitality* of our intellect, for it would

---

[1] [Trans. note: Reading *veritatem* as *veritatum*.]

require a supernatural assent and, hence, an assent that is violent, not vital, for a supernatural assent cannot come forth from the natural spontaneity of our powers.

(c) *A fortiori*, this revelation would be *contrary to the autonomy* of our reason, for autonomy is perfect spontaneity and vitality. However, through revelation, our intellect would be, as it were, "driven into captivity" and would need to accept not only the phenomena to be observed and coordinated but also a doctrine already constituted and imposed externally by way of authority.[2]

As the rationalist [Otto] Pfleiderer said, "The intellect would be no more than a lifeless vessel, receiving what someone pours into it."

{{300}} (2) *Against the possibility of the revelation of the natural truths of religion*, rationalists object: *Reason does not need* revelation of these truths, which do not exceed the natural powers [of the intellect]. Otherwise, reason, according to its own nature, would be maimed, wounded, and as it were, corrupted. However, this is unintelligible, for there can indeed be a wound in the body but not in the very nature of a spiritual faculty like reason.

(3) *Against the possibility of the revelation of supernatural mysteries*, semi-rationalists register many and sundry objections:

(a) Even if it is proven against pantheism that God is essentially distinct from the world, it does not follow that there would be an order of *supernatural* mysteries but only that there is an order of natural mysteries, like creation, providence, foreknowledge, and so forth.

(b) Even if there are supernatural mysteries in God, *how could they be expressed* in the natural notions of reason, which have a value only for natural knowledge of God?

(c) Hence, this revelation would require an essentially supernatural assent of the same order as the revealed mysteries. However, such

---

[2]   See Édouard Le Roy, *Dogme et critique* (Paris: Bloud, 1907), 9 and 15: "If we must hold the practical and moral meaning of dogma is something secondary and derived, placing its intellectual meaning in the most prominent place, . . . any given dogma will then appear as being a *subjugation, a limitation to the rights of thought*, like a menace of intellectual tyranny, like an obstacle and a restriction externally imposed upon freedom of inquiry. All these things are radically contrary to the very life of the mind, to its need for autonomy and honesty, to its generative and fundamental principle, namely, the principle of immanence." Also, on 7: "From the time of Descartes, is it not doubtlessly true that the first principle of method is that one must not hold as being true something that one has not clearly seen to be so?"

an assent would be entirely above the *vitality* of our intellect and hence would be violent, not vital.

(d) Finally, this revelation would be utterly opposed to the *autonomy* of our reason. Indeed, it would be necessary to admit, with utterly firm certitude, dogmas that are utterly unintelligible for us and that even would be beyond the limits of our religious experience, such as the Trinity, an eternity of punishments, and so forth, thus remaining empty words for us, utterly useless and lacking any determinate meaning. This would represent an abdication of our reason, which God cannot demand of us. Therefore, the incomprehensible mysteries of Christianity, like the Trinity, the Incarnation, and so forth, are only symbols of natural truths,[3] especially moral ones, thus only being practically useful in character.

(4) Various kinds of objections are registered *against the notion of mediate revelation*—namely, that which is proposed to believers by the mediation of prophets and the Church, especially the objection stating that if God is intimately present to all things and souls, it is more befitting that he immediately reveal himself to each person. Such is the position of liberal Protestants and modernists, who reduce revelation to each person's religious experience, although such experience was livelier in the prophets. Thus, revelation would be proposed more easily, as they say, even to those who cannot hear evangelical preaching.

We will devote three chapters in this section to the resolution of these difficulties:

- Chapter 10: On the possibility of supernatural revelation in general and specifically the possibility of the revelation of the natural truths of religion (immediate revelation and mediate revelation).
- Chapter 11: On the possibility of the revelation of supernatural mysteries, considered from the perspective of the object. Here we will defend the *existence of a supernatural order of truth in God*.
- Chapter 12: On the possibility of the revelation of supernatural mysteries, considered from the perspective of the subject (i.e., from man's perspective). Here we will defend *the existence of our nature's obediential or elevable capacity to the supernatural order*.

---

3   [Trans. note: Reading *veritatem* as *veritatum*.]

On the Possibility of Supernatural Revelation in General and Specifically the Possibility of Revelation of the Natural Truths of Religion

Art. 1.   On immediate revelation—namely, that which is made immediately to the prophets{{301}}

Art. 2.   On mediate revelation—namely, that which is proposed to other men by mediation of prophets

ART. 1: ON THE POSSIBILITY OF IMMEDIATE REVELATION

§1. Reason alone can prove this possibility.

§2. Resolution of objections.

§1. Reason Alone Can Prove the Possibility of Immediate Revelation of the Natural Truths of Religion

In our earlier chapter on the notion of revelation, we set forth what the Church holds the nature of revelation to be.

There, we said that as the term denotes, revelation is the removal of a veil impeding our understanding of a thing or, in other words, the manifestation of a thing that heretofore was hidden. Divine revelation properly so called is revelation made by God, not through the creation of natural things but, rather, beyond the order of nature. If the natural truths of religion were all that was revealed in this manner, revelation would only be modally supernatural, as regards the manner of its production, like a miracle. However, if supernatural mysteries are also revealed, revelation is thus essentially supernatural or essentially, like sanctifying grace.

Hence, as was said above, *revelation is formally a divine act of speech, after the manner of a teaching authority*, which is made objectively *through the supernatural proposition of the truth* and subjectively *through the influence of a supernatural light proportioning the intellect* to infallibly judge concerning the truth that has been divinely proposed.

Now, in our current discussions we must prove the *intrinsic possibility* of the revelation of the natural truths of religion (that is, its non-opposition to existence), as well as its *extrinsic possibility* (that is, its possibility relative to an agent capable of producing that which is not intrinsically opposed to existence). In this thesis, the extrinsic possibility of supernatural revelation is relative to *God's ordinate, though extraordinary, power*. It is not only a question of God's merely absolute power without dependence upon the divine wisdom, for by his merely absolute power, God can do many things that are extrinsically opposed to the end of creation. (For example, as regards such merely absolute power, he can annihilate all creatures.[1])

{{302}} Our demonstration is reduced to this syllogism:

The possibility of an action that obviously is not opposed to the possibility of being realized (neither from the perspective of its object, nor from the perspective of the subject, nor from that of the agent) can be demonstrated by reason alone.

Now, supernatural revelation of the natural truths of religion obviously is not opposed to the possibility of being realized (neither from the perspective of its object, nor from the perspective of the subject, nor from that of the agent).

Therefore, the possibility of the supernatural revelation of the natural truths of religion can be demonstrated by reason alone.

The major premise is obvious, especially if this non-opposition is also obvious in relation to the end of the agent and of the patient, for then this action is obviously possible according to its four essential [*per se*] causes, whether intrinsic or extrinsic.

The minor premise is proven from the following three perspectives.

(1) **From the perspective of the object**. The natural truths of religion can be revealed, (a) because presupposing the proof of God's existence, they obviously can be known as something received from God, and (b) they are not opposed to being known from other [sources], whether by way of demonstration or authoritatively from testimony, for these truths, of themselves, are indifferent to these various manners of being known, which hold from the perspective of the knower.

(2) **From the perspective of the subject (i.e., from man's perspective)**

A. *In general*, this revelation is not opposed [to natural human pos-

---

[1] See *ST* I, q. 101, a. 3 and 4.

sibilities], for if man can be legitimately taught by a human teacher, who can deceive and be deceived, why could he not be taught by God, who can neither deceive nor be deceived?

B. *In particular*, this revelation is not opposed [to natural human possibilities], neither (a) from the perspective of our ideas, nor (b) from the perspective of its objective motive, nor (c) from the perspective of subjective certitude, nor (d) from the perspective of man's end.

(a) *It is not opposed to them from the perspective of our ideas*, which quite certainly (given the preceding thesis) can express the natural truths of religion; and they are not opposed to being ordered by God so that they might express such truths immediately, just as they are ordered by us or by a human teacher.

(b) *Neither is such revelation opposed* [*to human possibilities*] *from the perspective of* [*our*] *objective motive of adherence*, for it is not opposed to our legitimate autonomy, which is subordinated to God, that we believe God on account of his authority, since God clearly can neither deceive nor be deceived. Hence, the [First] Vatican Council said against the rationalists: "Since man is totally dependent upon God, as upon his Creator and Lord, and since created reason is absolutely subject to uncreated truth, we are bound to yield . . . the full homage of the intellect and will to God who reveals."[2] Hence, the principle of the absolute autonomy of reason is condemned: "If anyone says that human reason is so independent that faith cannot be enjoined upon it by God, let him be anathema."[3]

Indeed, the autonomy of our reason, as well as that of our will, *is not absolute but instead is relative*—that is, subordinated to the Uncreated Truth and to divine authority. Moreover (and this is[4] our glory):

> Only the created rational nature has an immediate ordering to God, for other creatures do not attain something universal but only something particular (as is such for inanimate things, plants, and animals). However, the rational nature, inasmuch as it knows {{303}} the universal notion of the good and being, has *an immediate* order to the universal principle of being.[5]

Nay, this immediate subordination to God is the very foundation of our relative autonomy, and it frees us from subjugation to inferior things. Indeed, because our intellect is

---

2   [First] Vatican Council, *Dei filius*, ch. 3 (Denzinger, no. 3008).
3   Ibid., can. 3.1 (Denzinger, no. 3031).
4   [Trans. note: Reading *est* for *et*.]
5   *ST* II-II, q. 2, a. 3.

immediately subordinated to being and truth (and, above all, to the First Truth), *it is not contained within the phenomena* as though in a prison, nor does it need to subject itself to the false inventions of men. Thus, precisely because they deny the ordering [*ordinatio*] of our intellect to God, rationalists, and especially agnostics, do not liberate reason but, rather, drive it into captivity. Similarly, our will, because it is essentially ordered to the universal good and is immediately subordinated to God, the supreme good, remains indifferent (or free) before particular goods, which do not have a practically obvious necessary connection here and now with beatitude in general. Because it is ordered to the universal and supreme good, the will cannot be satisfied by a particular good. It is free in relation to such goods.[6]

By contrast, if the authority of the truth is done away with, especially that of the First Truth, we will see the establishment of the tyrannical kingdom of often-false human opinions and superstitious reverence toward human teachers, as well as false science. Likewise, once the authority of the Highest Good and of the divine will is rejected, true freedom (i.e., an elective faculty ordered to the means *preserving an order to the end*[7]) will no longer exist but will be replaced by license, which leads to oppression of the good by the evil (that is, to tyranny). Thus, we find a confirmation of the parable of the prodigal son, not only for individuals but likewise for nations. By contrast, Christ said, "If you continue in my word . . . *the truth shall make you free*" (John 8:31–32, DR; also, 8:32–59). This whole chapter of John's Gospel sets forth the nature of true freedom of spirit: The divine truth handed on by tradition frees us from our passions, errors, and the prejudices of false wisdom. This has never been practically understood by liberals, who hold that divine revelation and immutability of dogmas would impede the free progress of science.[8] Nonetheless, the truth alone sets us free.

(c) *Likewise, revelation is not opposed* [*to human possibilities*] *as regards the subjective certitude we can have concerning the fact of a divine act of speaking.* Indeed, the intellect of the prophet is not opposed *to being illuminated* subjectively by God so that he may be made certain regarding the origin of revelation, which afterwards is confirmed by visible signs. For in general, inferior agents are not opposed to being moved and perfected by superior ones, to which they are naturally subject, as St. Thomas shows in the treatise on faith, in *ST* II-II, q. 2, a. 3:

> In all ordered natures, we find that two things concur to the perfection of the inferior nature: one in accord with *its own, proper*

---

[6] See *ST* I, q. 83, a. 1; II-II, q. 10.

[7] See *ST* I, q. 62, a. 8, ad 3.

[8] Pius IX, *Syllabus of Errors*, nos. 77ff (Denzinger, 2977ff); [First] Vatican Council, *Dei filius*, ch. 3 (Denzinger, no. 3008); ibid., can. 3.1 (Denzinger, no. 3031).

movement, whereas the other is in accord with *the movement of a superior nature*. For example, the water (of the sea) by its own movement is moved to the center of the earth, whereas by the movement of the moon it is moved around the center of the earth by way of ebb and flow.[9]

Similarly, in us, physiochemical movement is subordinated to vital motion in nutrition or respiration,[10] and our vital movements are subject to our sense life in sensation. Likewise, sensation and imagination are subject to reason and receive direction from it. Similarly, the animal is directed by man. Why would human reason, which is essentially subordinated to the Divine Intelligence, be opposed *to being illuminated* by it so that it may be certain about the divine origin of revelation? Why couldn't the prophet's intellect accept this spiritual illumination and be instrumentally moved by God, as our imagination is instrumentally moved by reason? On the contrary, this fact is completely in conformity with the universal law of the subordination of causes.

{{304}} (d) *From the perspective of man's end*, this revelation is not opposed [to natural human possibilities], for man is naturally ordered to knowledge of the truth (and especially the Supreme Truth—namely, God—inasmuch as he is the Author of our nature) as well as to natural love of the Highest Good above all things. Nay, man is naturally inclined to love God more than himself, "for any given part naturally loves the common good of the whole more than its own, proper particular good."[11] Now, revelation of the natural truths of religion manifests to us the perfections of God, especially his infinite goodness toward us. Thus, it reveals to us, free from error or doubt, the ultimate end to which all of our acts already must be directed in the natural order.

(3) *From the perspective of God*, supernatural revelation of the natural truths of religion is not opposed [to the domain of possibilities] (a) in general inasmuch as it is a miracle, nor (b) in particular as it is a miracle

---

9   [Trans. note: The example limps slightly, though it would have seemed correct on the Aristotelian model of natural movement, whereby the water of the sea would have naturally moved toward the center of the earth, though not seeing that the ebb and flow of the tides is just another effect of a something formally and naturally falling to water. In St. Thomas's eyes, here, the example is intended to show that the water could undergo an instrumental causality under the moon's influence. Fr. Garrigou-Lagrange's further examples draw this out.]

10 [Trans. note: Precisely because the part *as a part* falls under the higher influence of the substantial form of the living organism.]

11 *ST* II-II, q. 26, a. 3.

belonging to the intellectual order.

(a) *It is not opposed* [*to the domain of possibilities*] *inasmuch as it is a miracle*, for as we will discuss at greater length below,[12] God can[13] act outside of hypothetically necessary laws, which do not place a limitation upon the divine freedom. Now, physical laws (and even psychological ones) are things of this sort. For example, it is hypothetically necessary that fire burns, that the dead do not rise again, and that man knows freely willed future events only in a conjectural manner. That is, fire left to itself, if it acts, burns, but this does not exclude the possibility that a superior agent might impede the action of fire. Likewise, the dead corpse, left to itself, will not arise by its own power. However, this law does not exclude the possibility that it could arise by the divine power. Likewise, by his natural powers, man can know free future events only in a conjectural manner. Nonetheless, this law does not exclude the possibility of him accepting, through a divine illumination, utterly certain knowledge of free future events. The laws that God cannot act in contravention to are absolutely necessary ones, such as, for example, mathematical or metaphysical laws. He cannot act outside of the bounds set by the principles of contradiction, causality, or finality. For example, he cannot move the intellect of a prophet to an absurd or impious thought.

God's miraculous intervention in us is not violent in character, for it is in accord with the creature's deepest and most profound inclination—namely, the inclination to obey its Creator, to whom it is more connaturally subjected than the body is to the soul or the arm to the will.[14]

(b) *Revelation is not opposed* [*to the domain of possibilities*] *inasmuch as it represents a miracle of the intellectual order*—that is, one by which God supernaturally moves the prophet's intellect objectively (by ordering his ideas) and subjectively (by illuminating his intellect so that he may infallibly judge [concerning those ideas]).

Indeed, God can move our intellect *objectively* by ordering our ideas not only by means of the senses and the imagination (as also happens in the case of a human teacher) but also immediately, for God is the First Intellect, preserving every intellect in existence. Indeed, he is intimately present to the intellect and is the First Intelligible Being from whom every form of intelligibility found in things and ideas is derived.[15]

Likewise, God can *subjectively* move the prophet's intellect by illumi-

---

[12] See ch. 19 of this work, concerning the notion and possibility of miracles.

[13] [Trans. note: Reading *potet* as *potest*.]

[14] See *ST* I, q. 105, a. 6; *SCG*, III, ch. 100.

[15] See *ST* I, q. 105, a. 3 (whether God moves the created intellect immediately).

nating him, in a transitory manner, by means of a prophetic light so that the prophet may infallibly {{305}} judge concerning the truth divinely proposed to him and concerning the divine origin of revelation. The reason for this is that God is the source of the whole of one's intellective power and of intellectual illumination. And for the revelation of the natural truths of religion, it suffices that there be a proportionate light that is modally supernatural, from the perspective of its manner of production. Such a form of revelation does not require a light that is essentially supernatural, like the light of our faith, the possibility of which cannot be demonstrated by reason alone. (On this point, see our resolution of the last objection presented in the next section.)

Finally, this revelation is not opposed to the end intended by God the Creator. Nay, it is well suited to it, for it manifests the divine goodness and is ordered to God's glory.

Thus, by reason alone, supernatural revelation of the natural truths of religion can be demonstrated as being possible, in line with God's extraordinary (though ordinate—that is, in line with the divine wisdom) power. It is not opposed [to the order of things], neither in itself, nor in relation to God, nor to our own capacities [*nec nobis*].

§2. Resolution of Objections

Presupposing, for now, the possibility of miracles and, hence, the possibility that God can supernaturally and immediately order the ideas of a prophet to express divine testimony, we find that there are two particular series of objections raised in this matter in particular. One series argues on the basis of claims related to *the autonomy* of our reason, as though this divine doctrine could not be *objectively* imposed upon us on the basis of the authority of God who reveals. The other series argues on the basis of claims related to *the vitality* of our knowledge, as though God could not *subjectively* move the prophet's intellect to infallibly adhere to a divinely proposed truth.

A. *Objections based on the autonomy of reason*

1. *Objection*: God cannot demand the abdication of reason. Now, reason would abdicate its own rights by adhering with utter certitude to non-evident assertions upon the mere authority of someone speaking. Therefore, God cannot demand the adherence of faith to revealed truths, at least in the case of the wise and of philosophers.

Response: I make a distinction regarding the major premise. I concede that God cannot demand the absolute abdication of reason. However, I deny that he cannot demand *the subordination* of reason to an infallible divine authority. I contradistinguish the minor in the same way and deny the consequence as well as the inference.

2. *It will be insisted*: However, at least speculative reason cannot be bound to furnish

this kind of adherence. Indeed, speculative reason assents only on account of the intrinsic evidence of the reality [known], whereas practical reason also assents on account of the practical befittingness of an action. Now, revealed truths are not proposed for our adherence on account of their intrinsic truth. Therefore, revealed truths must be admitted only by practical reason "as preceptive norms of conduct and not as norms of believing," as the modernists say.[16] For example, we must act in relation to Jesus as though he were God, just as in practice we walk upon a bridge as though we were utterly certain that it is sufficiently solid. Thus, the certitude of faith is inferior to scientific certitude.

Response: I make a distinction regarding the major premise. I concede that speculative reason assents only on account of the intrinsic evidence of the reality [known] *in scientific assent*, indeed, in virtue of a direct demonstration. However, I deny that this is the case for *an assent of faith*. I concede the minor premise and distinguish the sense of the conclusion along the same lines as what I said for the major premise.

"For faith is in the speculative intellect as in its subject, as is utterly clear from what the object of faith is."[17] For the primary object of faith is the First Uncreated Truth and not some work to be done, depending on our practical reason.[18]

{{306}} 3. *Nonetheless, it is urged*: However, the authority of God who reveals cannot be the formal motive for our adherence but, rather, only a condition for it, just as the proposal of a truth expressed by a human teacher is only a condition for a student's adherence, not its motive.

Indeed, those things that are revealed by God must be admitted on account of their own truth. Now, they have this truth in themselves and not as something derived from the authority of God who reveals. Therefore, these assertions must not be admitted on account of the authority of God who reveals. Such was the position of semi-rationalist thinkers like Frohschammer, aiming to preserve the absolute autonomy of reason.[19] Indeed, in this way reason would remain the arbiter of truth and falsehood, and would not offer obedience to God.

Response: I make a distinction regarding the major premise. I concede that truths revealed by God must be admitted on account of their intrinsic truth—if they are revealed scientifically, "by the persuasive words of human wisdom," as St. Paul says in 1 Corinthians 2:4. However, I deny this if they are proposed, as the Apostle says in the same text: "in shewing of the Spirit and power, that your faith might not stand on the wisdom of men, but on the power of God" (1 Cor 2:4–5, DR).

4. *A further insistence, however*: At least you must say that God cannot diminish the

---

[16] Pius X, *Lamentabili*, no. 26 (Denzinger, no. 3426).

[17] *ST* II-II, q. 4, a. 3, ad 3.

[18] See *De veritate*, q. 14, a. 4.

[19] See the letter of Pius IX, *Gravissimas inter*, sent to the Archbishop of Munich-Freising on December 11, 1862 (Denzinger, 1666, old numbering).

freedom of science. Now, revelation imposed by way of authority would diminish the freedom of science. Therefore, God cannot reveal [in this way] and command faith of us.

Response: I make a distinction regarding the major premise, conceding that God cannot diminish true freedom of science (i.e., freedom of inquiring into the truth). However, I deny the claim that he cannot diminish the freedom of wandering about upon the winding paths of error. Now, divine revelation does not diminish freedom of inquiring into the truth, for the revealed truth is not contrary to the true notion of discovery. Much to the contrary, revelation frees reason from doubts, from the false prejudices of worldly wisdom, and from the spirit of error, opening to our contemplation the truths of the kingdom of God, which are above the kingdom of nature and reason. However, the autonomy and insubordination of rationalism rejects divine mysteries in order to embrace the radical absurdity of absolute evolutionism (or the blindness of agnosticism). Likewise, when men of great genius reject revelation, they ultimately arrive at foolish theories, and this provides us with a new sign of the truth of revelation. Hegel proclaimed that radical absurdity is the supreme law of superior reason, and this law is admitted by free reason with docility. We cannot conceive of a more wretched form of intellectual servitude. In reality, we here see the intellect driven into the narrow confines of captivity, closed up within phenomena—nay, not even able to escape from contradiction.[20]

---

[20] See Jacques Maritain, "L'esprit de la philosophie scolastique: La liberté intellectuelle," *Revue Thomiste* 22 / New Series, 14 (1914): 517–542, esp. 535–536: "An impassable abyss separates Christian thought from the *spirit* of modern philosophy: *inter nos et vos magnum chaos firmatum est*. On the one side, we have submission of the mind to God and to the truth, as well as freedom of the mind [*esprit*]. On the other side, the claim of absolute independence alongside servitude of the mind [*esprit*], the elevation of man and of human science above all else alongside the inevitable dissolution of thought into atheism and absurdity. Specifically modern philosophy does not know the things of God, *non sapit ea quae Dei sunt, sed ea quae hominum*.

"Thus, it seems far too hard to say that we must, in this way, reject the immense effort of three centuries. Hear us aright. We do not reject everything that modern philosophers have been able to say or think. Such a rejection would be foolish. However, what is important is not this or that theory, or this or that partial view of things, but rather, the intellectual direction taken and its principles. We reject the spirit of modern philosophy, its specific principles, its overall orientation, and the final terminus toward which it tends. None of this is to be retained. Philosophy, being the science of first causes, is indeed of such a character that if a philosopher is mistaken upon principles, he is utterly mistaken."

Similarly, see ibid., 532 and 523–524: "*The mind* [*esprit*] *has its full spontaneity in the fecundity of contact with the divine truth, in being ruled and measured by God, not in the misery and solitude of naturalism.* . . . *Enslavement to what is relative* is one of the most prominent characteristics of modern philosophy in opposition to scholastic philosophy."

Likewise, many modern thinkers conceive of positive science according to the spirit of positivism (i.e., empiricism). Hence, they explain particular phenomena *through a subordination of particular laws to the more universal laws of material phenomena*. Thus, there arises a tendency to reduce religious facts to psychological facts, then to reduce these to biological phenomena which themselves are finally reduced to physiochemical phenomena, as though all things were

{{307}} This opposition between true freedom of spirit and the false autonomy of disbelief is not a new affair. Rather, it is expressed in the ancient antithesis between "I will not serve" and "to serve God is to reign"—that is, to reign over the passions of the flesh and over the spirit of error and evil. On this matter, one must read the words found in 8:31–59 of St. John's Gospel.[21]

5. *It will be urged*: Human reason cannot be merely passive in the reception of doctrine that is imposed by way of authority.

Response: Reason need not stand in a merely receptive posture in these matters but, rather, should inquire into the motives of credibility for this doctrine and afterwards, "illuminated by faith inquire in an earnest, *pious*, and sober manner, [thus attaining] *by God's grace* [*Deo dante*] a certain understanding of the mysteries."[22]

6. *Objection*: Revelation of the natural truths of religion is not necessary, since reason can know these truths by its own power. Therefore, this revelation is not something befitting.

---

founded on the principle of the conservation of energy.

By contrast, according to Christian philosophy, phenomena must be explained *through a subordination of particular causes to the most universal cause, which is supreme and highest—namely, God.* Hence, the subordination of laws, as it is conceived of by empiricists, inverts the order of causes, tending thus toward materialism.

[21] Jesus said to those Jews who believed in him: "If you continue in my word . . . you shall know the truth: and *the truth shall make you free.* They answered him: 'We are the seed of Abraham: and *we have never been slaves to any man.* How sayest thou: *You shall be free?*' Jesus answered them: 'Amen, amen, I say unto you that whosoever committeth sin *is the servant of sin.* Now the servant abideth not in the house for ever: but the son abideth for ever. If therefore the son shall make you free, you shall be free indeed. I know that you are the children of Abraham: but you seek to kill me, because my word hath no place in you. . . . Which of you shall convince me of sin? If I say the truth to you, why do you not believe me? He that is of God heareth the words of God. Therefore you hear them not, because you are not of God.' The Jews therefore answered and said to him: 'Do not we say well that thou art a Samaritan and hast a devil? . . . Art thou greater than our father Abraham who is dead?' . . . Jesus said to them: 'Amen, amen, I say to you, before Abraham was made, I AM.' They took up stones therefore to cast at him. But Jesus hid himself and went out of the temple" (John 8:31–59, DR).

The same opposition exists today between the Church and rationalism. To reject the authority of God who reveals leads to the most wretched form of dejection and servitude. The truth is openly fought against and falsity is tyrannically imposed, a falsity that utterly oppresses and blinds the very deceptive people who impose it. This is permitted by God, and in this sense are we to understand Sacred Scripture: "(The Lord) hath blinded their eyes and hardened their heart, that they should not see with their eyes, nor understand with their heart" (John 12:40, DR). Whereas, in contrast, the obedience of faith is the source of the true freedom of spirit of the children of God. Indeed, it is so great a freedom over errors, carnal wisdom, and the passions that St. Paul could write: "The sensual man perceiveth not these things that are of the Spirit of God. . . . But the spiritual man judgeth all things: and he himself is judged of no man" (1 Cor 2:14–15, DR).

[22] [First] Vatican Council, *Dei filius*, ch. 4 (Denzinger, no. 3016).

Response: I concede that revelation of the natural truths of religion is not necessary, strictly speaking. However, it is morally necessary—namely, so that the most important of these truths "may be known by everyone with facility, firm certitude, and no admixture of error."[23] Although the principal natural truths of religion (e.g., the existence of God the Supreme Lawgiver) can be easily known by reason, this is not the case for all of these truths. (See our discussion later on in the chapter devoted to the necessity of revelation.)

7. *Yet the objector will insist*: Those truths that must be naturally known in order for us to accept revelation cannot themselves become known through revelation. Now, the fundamental truths {{308}} of natural religion [*sic*], such as the existence of God and his trustworthiness, should be naturally known in order to accept revelation. Therefore, these truths cannot be made known through revelation.

Response: I make a distinction regarding the major premise. I concede that these truths cannot be made known through revelation so that they would be known *simpliciter*. However, I deny that such revelation is impossible in order that they may be known more firmly and more explicitly. Indeed, all men naturally have at least vague knowledge of the existence of God the Lawgiver and Universal Governor of all things. However, if, on account of prejudices and the objections of false philosophy (e.g., those raised by materialism), they doubt the existence of God, this truth can be manifested to them through revelation confirmed by miracles, for miracles themselves brilliantly declare God's omnipotence and freedom over nature. Thus, certain materialists, holding that the laws of nature are absolutely deterministic, have experienced manifest miracles and were thereby led to acknowledge God's existence and freedom, thus accepting Christian revelation.

B. *Objections based on the vitality of our knowledge*

These objections are raised as though God could not *subjectively* move the prophet's intellect so that he would infallibly adhere to the divinely proposed truth.

1. *Objection*: A vital action cannot be subjectively external to the person eliciting it. Now, intellection, of its very essence, is a vital action. Therefore, intellection cannot subjectively come to man externally from God who reveals.

Response: I make a distinction regarding the major premise. I concede that vital action cannot be subjectively external to the person eliciting it as from a proximate cause. However, I deny that it cannot thus be extrinsic as regards its origin from a superior and principal cause. I concede the minor premise and distinguish the conclusion in the same manner. Indeed, already in the natural order, God premoves all living things as the First, Extrinsic Cause.

2. *However, it will be insisted*: Neither can human intellection be moved by God as by a superior and principal cause. Indeed, a vital action must not only be elicited from an intrinsic principle but must also be elicited from the living thing's own power. Now, an act of intellection that would instrumentally come into existence by the power of God would

---

[23] Ibid., ch. 2 (Denzinger, no. 3005).

not be from the intellect's own power. Therefore, intellection cannot come into existence instrumentally by God's power.

Response: I make a distinction regarding the major premise. I concede that a vital action must be elicited from the living being's own power, whether in its own bare power or as elevated. However, I deny that it needs to be from its own power alone, thus excluding the possibility of elevation. I contradistinguish the minor premise in the same way. We have an example for this in man inasmuch as the intellect makes use of the imagination, as well as the eyes, as instruments. And under the influence of the intellect, the eyes not only are capable of sight but, in some way, are intelligent, which is not the case in brute animals.[24] Thus too, the musician, as it were, gives life to the harp, elevating its own proper power so that it may come to produce an artistic effect. Thus, why could God not make use of the prophet's intellect just as our intellect makes use of our imagination?

3. *It will be urged, however*: Now, the elevation of vitality (or the notion of a superadded vitality) cannot be conceived of after the manner of an instrumental power. Therefore, the difficulty remains.

Moreover, vital activity is, of its very essence, something coming forth from within the agent. Now, a superadded vitality would come from outside of the agent. Therefore, a superadded vitality is intrinsically opposed [to the very possibility imposed on us by the immanent character of vital action].

Response: I make a distinction regarding the major premise. I concede that vital activity, considered as *that which* is vitally produced, of its very essence comes from within the agent. (Hence, God cannot produce a vital act in a stone, thus, for example, making the stone see.) However, I make a sub-distinction regarding the claim that vital activity, understood as *that by which* the vital act is produced, cannot come from outside of the agent. I deny this claim if one means that it cannot come from the extrinsic Author of life itself. However, I will let the matter pass regarding another external agent. I contradistinguish the minor premise in the same manner, while denying the consequent and the inference.

Indeed, God, as the First Cause, already in the natural order moves all created agents from within by applying their power to the works of life.[25] Likewise, he can move the created intellect to a vital act exceeding the creature's own proper power. The leader of an army in some way communicates his own vitality to his soldiers. Why would it be

---

[24] [Trans. note: Maritain took up this issue in his aesthetic theory in *Art and Scholasticism*, where he discusses "intelligentiated sensation." Fr. Garrigou-Lagrange cites this text approvingly regarding the nature of *Habitus* in his relatively-late-life *De beatitudine*. On this topic, see John Trapani, *Poetry, Beauty, and Contemplation: The Complete Aesthetics of Jacques Maritain* (Washington, DC: The Catholic University of America Press, 2011); "'Radiance': The Metaphysical Foundation of Maritain's Aesthetics," *Beauty, Art, and the Polis*, ed. Alice Ramos (Washington, DC: The Catholic University of America Press, 2000), 11–19.]

[25] See *ST* I, q. 105, a. 5.

impossible that God, the source of life, would not enliven and illuminate man's intellect? {{309}} As is said in the Psalms, "God, my light, ... enliven me in accord with Your word."[26]

4. *The objector will insist, however*: Still, the possibility of this new vitality supernaturally produced by God cannot be proven but, at best, can only be urged persuasively.

Indeed, this supernaturally produced vitality would be supernatural life. Now, the possibility of participated supernatural life cannot be demonstrated by reason alone. Therefore, the possibility of a superadded vitality for infallibly receiving revelation cannot be proven.

Response: I make a distinction regarding the major premise. I concede that it would be a vitality that is essentially supernatural for receiving the revelation of strictly supernatural mysteries. However, I deny that it would be a vitality that is essentially supernatural for receiving only the revelation of the natural truths of religion. Also, I contradistinguish the minor premise. I concede that the possibility of life that is essentially supernatural and participated in by us indeed cannot be demonstrated by reason alone. However, I deny that reason alone is incapable of demonstrating the possibility of a light that is modally supernatural from the perspective of its production. And, in fact, it suffices that there be a light proportioned to the object to be revealed and believed in.[27] However, in this

---

26 Sometimes (e.g., in *Cursus theologicus, In ST* III, q. 9, disp. 11, a. 2, no. 27), John of St. Thomas says: "The light of prophecy is also a quality establishing the intellect as a principal cause of prophetic knowledge." This is properly true of the infused light of faith and is found in some way in the case of prophecy inasmuch as prophetic knowledge is vital. However, John of St. Thomas does not deny that the prophet is God's instrument for handing on revelation to us. Much to the contrary, he often affirms this point, following St. Thomas. He only holds that the prophet "is not an instrument in the sense in which purely inanimate things, which purely serve ministerially, are instruments, not having an elicitive principle principally in themselves," as he says in *Cursus theologicus, In ST* I-II, q. 68, disp. 18, a. 2, no. 32. Indeed, it is rather the case that the prophet, just like the sacred author, has his own proper activities of intellect and will, which are instrumentally elevated by God so that he may know and announce or write in an infallible manner and not in a merely conjectural one.

27 See *ST* II-II, q. 171, a. 3: "The manifestation that is brought about through some light can extend to all those things that are placed under that light, just as *bodily sight* extends to all colors and the soul's natural knowledge extends to all those things coming under the *light of the agent intellect*. Now, prophetic knowledge is had *through a divine light* by which all things can be known, divine ones as much as spiritual ones, the spiritual as much as the bodily."

Likewise, *ST* II-II, q. 174, a. 2, ad 3: "However, if the intellectual light is divinely infused into someone, not for knowing certain supernatural things but, rather, for judging with the certitude of the divine truth those things that can be known by human reason, it is thus the case that such intellectual prophecy is below that which is had with an imaginary vision leading one to [knowledge of] supernatural truth. Prophecy of this latter kind is what was had by all of those who are numbered among the Prophets."

Cf. Salmanticenses, *Cursus theologicus, De fide*, disp. 2, dub. 5, §4, no. 124: "Although both faith and prophecy rely upon divine revelation, nonetheless, the revelation of God as specifying faith has a greater certitude than that which moves to prophetic knowledge. Now, this

thesis, we are only concerned with the revelation of the natural truths of religion. By itself, reason defends objections against the possibility of a light that is essentially supernatural. However, it can neither prove nor disprove it. (We will discuss this below.)

Regarding the distinction between what is modally supernatural and what is essentially supernatural, see our discussion above in ch. 6. (There too, we respond to objections drawn from the terminology used by St. Thomas in *ST* II-II, q. 171, a. 2, ad 3.) According to the Holy Doctor, it is certain that:

> Sanctifying grace is much more excellent than is freely-given grace, for sanctifying grace immediately orders man to union with his last end, whereas freely-given graces order man to a given thing that prepares one for the last end, just as through prophecy, miracles, and {{310}} other such things men are led to their being united with the ultimate end.[28]

Hence, it is not surprising that *the possibility of miracles and prophecy* are philosophically demonstrable, although *the possibility of sanctifying grace and of the theological virtues* is not.

Indeed, revelation (whether primitive, Mosaic, or Christian) simultaneously manifested natural truths of religion along with supernatural truths of religion. However, right now, we are only considering the possibility of revelation in general and, in particular, that of the natural truths of religion. We are not yet concerned with the question of supernatural mysteries.

5. *Still, it will be urged*: But, even for revelation that is modally supernatural, the prophet must have evident awareness of the divine speech (i.e., of the divine origin of revelation itself) before he may perform miracles in confirmation of it. Now, this evidence cannot exist outside of the vision of the divine essence, for the divine speech is identical with the divine essence. However, this vision is essentially supernatural, and its possibility cannot be demonstrated. Therefore, the possibility of revelation that is modally supernatural cannot be demonstrated.

Response: I make a distinction. I deny that a prophet must have *evident knowledge of the divine speech in itself*. I concede that the prophet must have such evident knowledge of it *in its proper effect*—namely, in passive revelation [i.e., revelation considered from the perspective of *being received*]. However, this effect can be known outside of the beatific vision under the light of prophecy. But those who have never received immediate revelation do not have experience of this entirely unique certitude. In *Cursus theologicus, De*

---

difference arises from the fact that the formal specificative *obiectum quod* of faith is God alone, as He is in Himself. . . . By contrast, the primary object of prophecy is either some determinate temporal thing or at least is not determinately something uncreated."

[28] *ST* I-II, q. 111, a. 5.

fide, tr. 17, disp. 3, dub. 1, no. 5, the Salmanticenses teach:

> In order for someone to know with evidential knowledge that the divine testimony exists, or *precisely that there is* [*quoad an est*] a speech coming from God, it suffices that one have evidential, quidditative knowledge of a given effect connected with a given testimony (or act of speech) specifically and according to its own proper formal character. . . . However, although God's speech, in itself, is something uncreated and *ad intra* ["within" the Deity], it nonetheless places a given, specific effect in the intellect of the hearer, an effect that necessarily implies [its origin] at least obliquely, though this [alone] does not imply that someone knows this created effect of the divine speech in an evident manner and through its proper species.

This is brought about under the light of prophecy,[29] as St. Thomas says in *ST* II-II, q. 171, a. 5:

> About those things that the prophet expressly knows through *the spirit of prophecy*, he has the greatest of certitude, and holds it to be certain that these things have been divinely revealed to him. Whence, it is said in Jeremiah 26:15 (DR): "*In truth* the Lord sent me to you, to speak all these words in your hearing." Otherwise, if he did not have certitude about this, the faith that rests upon the words of the prophets would not be certain. And we can take a sign of prophetic certitude from the fact that Abraham, having been admonished in a prophetic vision, prepared himself to sacrifice his only-begotten son, something he in no way would have done had he not been utterly certain of divine revelation.

---

[29] This evidential knowledge of the proper effect of divine revelation, under the light of prophecy, presents the prophet with *evidential knowledge* of the revealed mysteries not in themselves but *as bearing witness to them* [*in attestante*]. And, properly speaking, "evidential knowledge for bearing witness" [*evidentia in attestante*] is had only under the light of prophecy. Nonetheless, certain theologians say that such evidence is also had through natural and immediate knowledge of the miracles that confirm revelation. However, because miracles are not the more proper effect of active revelation but, rather, a divine sign connected with revelation, this evidential knowledge is only improperly said to be "evidential knowledge for bearing witness" but, properly speaking, is "evident knowledge of credibility," as we will discuss below. Now, this evident knowledge of credibility can be had either from immediate knowledge of the signs of God or mediately through the testimony of men referring to these signs.

Art. 2: On the Possibility of Mediate Revelation

§1. The possibility of mediate revelation can be proven by reason alone. {{311}}

§2. Resolution of objections.

§1. The Possibility of Mediate Revelation Can Be Proven by Reason Alone

[Our] adversaries say: If God provides for all things and is present in all souls, it would be befitting that he immediately reveal himself to each person through religious experience. Hence, men would need to adhere to revelation with utter firmness and in an infallible manner. However, revelation transmitted through a prophet or the Church would no longer be the word of God but instead would be the mere word of man. Thus, men could not infallibly adhere to it. Finally, if divine faith is necessary for salvation, it would be more easily proposed to all through immediate revelation, for many cannot hear the preaching of the Gospel.[30]

Nonetheless, the possibility of mediate revelation, together with its befittingness, can be proven by reason alone in two ways: (A) from the perspective of God and (B) from the perspective of man.

A. *From the perspective of God.* In general, divine providence governs inferior things through superior ones and inferior men through greater ones, who are God's ministers. Now, divine revelation fittingly is brought about according to the general disposition of divine providence. Therefore, it is befitting that divine revelation would be transmitted to men through God's ministers.

The major premise is explained by St. Thomas in *ST* I, q. 22, a. 3:

> Two things pertain to divine providence: the *reason* for the ordering of foreseen things to the end and the *execution* of this order, which is called "governance." Therefore, as regarding the first of these, *God immediately provides for all things*, for He has in His intellect the reason for all things, even the least of them. And in assigning whatsoever causes to their effects, He gives those causes the power to produce those effects. . . . However, as regards the latter, there are certain means of divine providence, for *He governs the inferior through the superior*, not on account of a lack of power on His part

---

[30] We find such an argument in the profession of faith of the Savoyard vicar in Jean Jacques Rousseau's *Émile*.

but, rather, on account of the abundance of His goodness, *so that He might communicate the dignity of causality even to creatures.*

And in ad 1: "The dignity of the king involves having ministers in the execution of his providence. However, the fact that he does not form the detailed plan [*non habeat rationem*] for those things that are to be done by them arises from a shortcoming on his part."

The minor premise is explained in *ST* II-II, q. 172, a. 2 and in *ST* I-II, q. 111, a. 1 and 4: "The order of things consists in the fact that certain ones are led back to God through others and that man works with others so as to lead them back to God. However, man cannot bring this about by moving others interiorly (for this falls only to God) but can only do so through externally teaching and persuading." Therefore, it is possible and suitable that revelation would be brought about mediately—namely, through the mediation of ministers of God, that is, prophets.[31]

Likewise, as regards how faith must be explicated following on revelation, "for the same reason {{312}} the explanation of the faith must come to lower men through higher ones, . . . and superior men, to whom it falls to teach others, are bound to have a fuller knowledge of things to be believed and to believe [them] in a more explicit manner."[32]

And nonetheless, divine revelation transmitted through the prophets remains the word of God, for the prophet is only a minister and instrument. "However, the activity of the instrument is attributed to the principal agent, under whose power the instrument acts," just as a written book is attributed to the author and not to his pen.[33]

The same argument can be proposed in a negative manner as follows: We cannot deny that God has a power and right that belongs to all superior humans. Now, superior humans can command their subordinates through ministers whose words are to be accepted formally as being the very words of their superiors. Therefore, God can reveal truths of religion through prophets whose words are to be received formally as God's own words.

B. *From the perspective of man.* The same conclusion can be proven from man's perspective as follows.[34]

It is natural for man to learn from men in society. Now, grace perfects nature by preserving nature's own inclination. Therefore, it is befitting that

---

[31]   Likewise, see *ST* III, q. 55, a. 1.

[32]   *ST* II-II, q. 2, a. 6.

[33]   *ST* II-II, q. 172, a. 2, ad 3.

[34]   See Cajetan, *In ST* II-II, q. 171, a. 5, no. 5.

men would be instructed about divine things through ministers of God who propose his freely given revelation.

The major premise is obvious and contains the fundamental reason why man is social, for socialness is deduced from man's rational character. Human reason, which is the lowest of intellects, arrives at knowledge of those things that are necessary for human life only in a gradual manner through successive discursive reasoning. Therefore, it is natural for man to learn from men. Very few would discover the elementary truths of geometry and the other sciences without a teacher. This is why Pascal is cited as being an extraordinary genius [because of his native abilities in contrast to this general state of affairs].

The minor premise is obvious as well, inasmuch as that which is perfective must be conformed to that which is perfectible.

Confirmation:

It is not suitable that revelation would be brought about immediately in all people,

> for prophecy requires an utterly great elevation of the mind to spiritual contemplation. This is impeded by the vehemence of the passions and through inordinate occupation with external things. Whence, we also read concerning the sons of the Prophets in 2 Kings 4:38 that "they lived together with Elisha," leading a kind of solitary life, lest they be impeded in the gift of prophecy through worldly occupations.[35]

§2. Resolution of Objections

1. *Objection*: God immediately provides for all things. Now, revelation depends on providence. Therefore, revelation should be made to all immediately.

Response: I make a distinction regarding the major premise. I concede that God immediately provides for all things *as regards the ordering* of things. However, I deny that this holds *for the execution of this order* (cf. *ST* I, q. 22, a. 3). I concede the minor premise while making a distinction regarding the conclusion. I concede that God immediately provides for revelation to reach all men. However, I deny that he immediately reveals himself to all men.

2. *Objection*: God is intimately present in all souls and can act by himself in them. Now, properly speaking, revelation is a divine action for the illumination of souls. Therefore, revelation ought to be brought about in all souls in an immediate manner.

---

[35] *ST* II-II, q. 172, a. 4.

{{313}} *Response*: I make a distinction regarding the major premise. I concede that God alone can operate *subjectively* in souls and make an impression upon their wills. However, I deny that God alone can *objectively* move man's intellect. I contradistinguish the minor premise. I concede that revelation exists for the illumination of souls objectively. However, as regards the claim that it exists for the illumination of them subjectively, allow me to make a sub-distinction. I concede this for the prophet who accepts the prophetic light. However, I deny it for others who accept the light of faith.[36]

3. *Objection*: However, revelation transmitted through a prophet is no longer the word of God but, rather, is the word of man. Hence, we cannot infallibly adhere to it.

Response: The prophet is God's minister (or *instrument*). Now, the activity and effect of an instrument are attributed to the principal agent in virtue of which the agent acts.

4. *Objection*: Yet the minister can consciously or unconsciously change the words of God.

Response: A divine motion specifically prevents this kind of change. In virtue of this, the words of God are *infallibly* transmitted, just as the writer moves his pen in order for the written work to be a true expression of his thought. Hence, the Psalmist says: "My tongue is the pen of a scrivener that writeth swiftly" (Ps 44:2, DR).

5. *Objection*: Then, under this motion, the prophet is not free. This is not a befitting state of affairs.

Response: Our response is drawn from *ST* I, q. 83, a. 1, ad 3, where St. Thomas writes:

> Free choice of the will is a cause of its own motion . . . though not its first cause. Therefore, God is the First Cause moving both natural and voluntary causes. And just as in moving natural causes He does not thereby remove the natural character of their activity, so too in moving voluntary causes He does not thereby remove their voluntary character. Rather, He is the very cause of this free character, for He acts in each thing according to its own proper character.

6. *Objection*: However, a minister of God cannot be infallibly known as being such by other men and be distinguished from a false prophet.

Response: His prophetic mission is confirmed *by visible divine signs* and "is proven through an argument drawn from the divine power so that when he performs some work that God alone can do, it is believed that those things which he speaks of come from God, just as when letters sealed by the signet ring of the king but carried by someone else are believed to have contents expressing his will."[37] (Also, see our discussion below about the motives of credibility.)

7. *Objection*: However, other men cannot infallibly discern true miracles [from false

---

[36] See *ST* II-II, q. 172, a. 2, ad 1.

[37] See *ST* III, q. 43, a. 1.

ones], for reason can err. Hence, mediated revelation cannot infallibly be accepted as being the word of God.

Response: From rational knowledge of miracles, we can have sufficient rational credibility, and from the light of infused faith, we can have the infallible certitude of faith. Thus, even mediate revelation is infallibly received as being the word of God. (See our discussion below concerning credibility in general.)

8. *Objection*: Nonetheless, then, the testimony of God is believed on account of the lower testimony of the prophet. Thus, the formal motive of our faith is no longer something divine.

Response: The human and sensible testimony of the prophet is not the *formal motive* of our faith but, rather, is only a [necessary] *condition* for it. Thus, the sensation that is required for knowing the terms of the first principles of reason is not the formal motive of our adherence to the truth of the first principles but, rather, is only [a necessary] condition for it.

9. *Objection*: Mediate revelation does not ultimately come to all men, for many in remote regions cannot hear the preaching of the Gospel. Therefore, this is an unbefitting situation if faith is necessary for salvation.

Response: St. Thomas responds in *De veritate*, q. 14, a. 11, ad 1:

> Granting that everyone is bound to explicitly believe something, an unbefitting state of affairs does not follow if someone is reared in the forests or among brute animals, for it falls to divine providence to provide each person with those things that are necessary for salvation, provided that there is no impediment placed before it on the part of such a person. Indeed, if someone reared in this way follows the lead of his natural reason in desiring the good and fleeing what is evil, {{314}} it most certainly must be held that God would reveal to him through an internal inspiration those things that must be believed or would direct some preacher of the faith to him, just as He sent Peter to Cornelius (cf. Acts 10:20).

Concerning this matter, see what was taught by Pope Pius IX: "The gifts of heavenly grace are by no means to be lacking for those who by this light desire and seek with sincerity of soul to be recreated."[38] Likewise:

> We know as well as you that those who suffer from invincible ignorance with regard to our most holy religion, by carefully keeping the natural law and its precepts, which have been written by God in the hearts of all, by being disposed to obey God and to lead a virtuous and correct life, can, by the power

---

[38] Pius IX, *Singulari quadam* (Denzinger, 1648, old numbering).

of divine light and grace, attain eternal life. For God, who sees, examines, and knows completely the minds and souls, the thoughts and qualities of all, will not permit, in His infinite goodness and mercy, anyone who is not guilty of a voluntary fault to suffer eternal punishment.[39]

Hence, *per accidens*, immediate revelation can be bestowed upon the soul, when one does what is in one's power, even while one is invincibly ignorant of the preaching of the Gospel. However, *we must not judge those things that are per se by means of those that are per accidens*. Nevertheless, as we have said, *per se*, mediate revelation is well suited to mankind, both from the perspective of God and from our own perspective [as finite, rational knowers].[40]

---

[39] Pius IX, *Quanto conficiamur moerore* (Denzinger, no. 2866). [Trans. note: For a study of this matter explicitly in light of magisterial statements, see Joseph C. Fenton, *The Catholic Church and Salvation* (Westminster, MD: The Newman Press, 1958). For a more recent study of related questions, see Ralph Martin, *Will Many Be Saved?: What Vatican II Actually Teaches and Its Implications for the New Evangelization* (Grand Rapids, MI: Eerdmans, 2012). Likewise, for a perspective nearly identical to Fr. Garrigou-Lagrange's, see Édouard Hugon, *Hors de l'Eglise point de salut*, 4th ed. (Paris: Téqui, 1927).]

[40] See the end of the resolution of objections in chapter 13 (on the necessity of revelation) below. In *Cursus theologicus*, *De fide*, disp. 6, dub. 1, no. 89, the Salmanticenses note, concerning immediate revelation that is made *per accidens* to those who are invincibly ignorant of the gospel and who under the influence of actual grace do what lies in their power to do: "This does not mean to posit a connection between mere nature and (the) grace (of illumination) but, rather, between this grace and preceding supernatural aids. . . . Such a manner of instruction in the faith is rare and extraordinary, but it is not miraculous, for the current state of God's providence calls for it [quia illum exposcit praesens Dei providentia], as well as man's elevation to the supernatural end, presupposing that every form of external preaching is lacking."

Likewise, see Jean-Michel-Alfred Vacant, *Études théologiques sur les constitutions du Concile du Vatican d'après les actes du concile*, vol.1 (Paris: Delhomme et Briguet, 1895), 141–143.

Nay, in *ST* I-II, q. 89, a. 6, St. Thomas says: "When a (non-baptized) man begins to have use of his reason, he is not entirely excused from the guilt of venial and mortal sin. However, the first thing that occurs to a man is *to deliberate about himself*. And if someone orders himself to a due end, the remission of original sin will follow through grace." On this topic, along with many other Thomists, Billuart says in his comments on this passage: "This first aid (bestowed upon the child at the first moment of reason) is not strictly speaking from explicit faith but, rather, from a kind of illumination concerning the first things to be believed which does not prevent negative disbelief concerning others. And before this in his *Summa sancti Thomae*, in *De Deo*, diss. 7, art. 8, solv. obj., ad obj. 4a: "According to this . . . manner of speaking, man will be justified either immediately or after the passage of time. If immediately, it will happen as soon as he consents to this aid, if God then instructs him explicitly through an internal revelation concerning the things to be believed and confers upon him efficacious graces for a perfect conversion. This seems to be what is said in *ST* I-II, q. 89, a. 6. On the other hand, such a person may be justified later on when and however God sees fit to provide this man with explicit faith and efficacious graces. And this is what is indicated by St. Thomas in *De veritate*, q. 14, a. 11, ad 1, as well as in *In X Rom.*, lect. 3."

On the Possibility of the Revelation of Supernatural Mysteries, Considered from the Perspective of the Object

{{315}} This chapter's thesis can be stated thus: *The possibility of the revelation of supernatural mysteries is proven from the perspective of the object inasmuch as we can demonstrate the existence of a supernatural order of life and truth in God.*

Single Article: Proof for the Existence of a Supernatural Order of Life and Truth in God (i.e., the Existence of the Order of Supernatural Mysteries)

§1. Heterodox doctrines and the Church's doctrine.

§2. On the demonstrability of the existence of a supernatural order of truth and life in God.

§3. Demonstration of the existence of a supernatural order *objectively* exceeding the natural powers of the created intellect.

§4. First corollary: The supernatural order even *subjectively* exceeds the power of any created intellect whatsoever.

§5. Second corollary: Moreover, the supernatural order exceeds *the exigencies* of any created intellect whatsoever.

§6. Third corollary: There cannot be disagreement nor confusion between natural truths and supernatural truths; rather, they exist in *harmony*.

§7. Resolution of objections raised by semi-rationalists and those coming from Scotus.

§8. Examination of ontologism, as well as a resolution of the objections raised by ontologists.

§1. Heterodox Doctrines and the Doctrine of the Church

A. *Heterodox doctrines concerning the possibility of the revelation of supernatural mysteries, considered from the perspective of the object.* Already above (ch. 6), we set forth heterodox notions of supernaturality. In relation to the present question, they can be divided into three categories.

(1) *Pantheistic rationalists* as well as *semi-rationalists* deny the existence of an order *objectively* exceeding the powers of our reason. (2) *Pelagians and semi-Pelagians* deny that the supernatural order *subjectively* exceeds the powers of our nature, or at least what can be merited naturally. Thus, according to them, presupposing external revelation, internal grace would not be necessary for believing, or at least for the beginnings of faith. {{316}} (3) *The first Protestants, Michael Baius,* and *Cornelius Jansen* deny that the natural order exceeds the *exigencies* of our nature. Thus, grace would be something owed to nature.[1]

B. *The doctrine of the Church.* As regards our current question, it suffices to refer to the condemnations expressed by the Church against pantheistic rationalism, semi-rationalism, and the errors that are commonly rejected today by theologians concerning the transcendence of the supernatural order.

(1) *Against pantheistic evolutionism* (e.g., as it is found in Hegel), the [First] Vatican Council declared: "If anyone says that man cannot be *called by God to a knowledge and perfection that surpasses the natural* but that he can and must by himself, through constant progress, finally arrive at the possession of all that is true and good, let him be anathema."[2] Consequently, the order of supernatural truth objectively exceeds the powers of our nature, and even its natural perfectibility, however great it may progressively develop through the course of countless centuries.

(2) *Against semi-rationalists,* especially against Frohschammer,[3] the Church has been even more determinate about the nature of the order of supernatural truth. Semi-rationalists admitted the essential distinction of God from the world, as well as the fact of revelation. However, they held that all revealed mysteries that necessarily pertain to God (e.g., the Trinity), at least after being revealed, can be demonstrated from natural principles and by the powers of our reason.

---

[1] See Pius V, *Ex omnibus afflictionibus,* no. 21 (Denzinger, no. 1921).

[2] [First] Vatican Council, *Dei filius,* can. 2.3 (Denzinger, no. 3028).

[3] Pius IX, Letter *Gravissimas inter* to the Archbishop of Munich-Freising, Dec. 11, 1862 (Denzinger, no. 2851).

As we said above, this doctrine was condemned by Pius IX,[4] as well as by the [First] Vatican Council, which defined: "If anyone says that in divine revelation no true and properly so-called mysteries are contained but *that all dogmas of faith can be understood and demonstrated from natural principles by reason*, if it is properly trained, let him be anathema."[5]

Likewise, in the chapter corresponding to this canon, the same Council defined:

> The perpetual common belief of the Catholic Church has held and holds also this: *there is a twofold order of knowledge, distinct not only in its principle but also in its object*; indeed, in its *principle*, because in the one we know by natural reason, in the other by divine faith; in its *object*, because apart from what natural reason can attain, there are proposed to our belief mysteries that are hidden in God that can never be known unless they are revealed by God . . . . For *divine mysteries by their very nature* so *exceed* the created intellect that, even when they have been communicated in revelation and received by faith, *they remain covered by the veil of faith itself and shrouded, as it were, in darkness* as long as in this mortal life "we are away from the Lord; for we walk by faith, not by sight" (2 Cor 5:6).[6]

This means that these supernatural mysteries are indeed not contrary to reason but, rather, above reason and above the virtuality of natural principles of reason. Nay, "by their very nature, they exceed the created intellect," and hence any intellect that could be created, for of their very nature they exceed the nature of the created intellect and not only the contingent state wherein this intellect finds itself. In *Gravissimas inter*, Pius IX said: "They even transcend the natural intelligence of the angels."[7] And therefore, supernatural knowledge of these mysteries is not something that completes nature [precisely as nature] (as, for example, in the state of original justice, the freely given privilege of immunity from inordinate concupiscence was only a gift pertaining to the integrity of nature). Rather, it transcends the integrity of our nature as well as the order of gifts that are modally supernatural from the perspective of efficient causality [*dona solum effective supernaturalia*], for such supernatural knowledge is *essentially* supernatural and not only modally supernatural, as regards its manner of production.

{{317}} (3) *Likewise, Rosmini was condemned*[8] on account of a kind of

---

4   See ibid. (Denzinger, nos. 2851 and 2854); Letter *Tuas libenter* to the Archbishop of Munich-Freising, Dec. 21, 1863 (Denzinger, no. 2878); *Syllabus of Errors*, no. 9 (Denzinger, no. 2909).

5   [First] Vatican Council, *Dei filius*, can. 4.1 (Denzinger, no. 3041).

6   Ibid., ch. 4 (Denzinger, nos. 3015–3016).

7   Pius IX, *Gravissimas inter* (Denzinger, no. 2857).

8   [Trans. note: Bl. Antonio Rosmini-Serbati (1797–1855) had his work *Delle cinque piaghe*

confusion of the order of natural truth with that of supernatural truth.

Regarding the errors of *Rosmini*, see no. 36 of the Holy Office's decree *Post obitum*, from 1887, condemning the following proposition: "*The supernatural order* is established by the manifestation of being in the fullness of its real form; the effect of this communication or manifestation is a deiform sense ('sentiment'), which begun in this life, constitutes the light of faith and of grace and which, completed in the [next] life, constitutes the light of glory."[9] Likewise, no. 38: "*God is the object of the Beatific Vision* inasmuch as He is the author of works *ad extra*."[10] Also, see no. 25: "*When the mystery of the Most Blessed Trinity has been revealed, its existence can be demonstrated* by merely speculative arguments, negative indeed, and indirect; yet such that through them the truth is brought to philosophical studies and the proposition becomes scientific like the rest."[11]

These errors of Rosmini are founded on a kind of *univocity of being* in relation to God and creatures.[12]

(4) *Likewise, the errors of the ontologists* were condemned in the Decree of the Holy Office on September 18, 1861, especially concerning the fact that they insufficiently distinguished the natural order from the supernatural order.

Thus, consider the following three condemned propositions:[13] "*The immediate knowledge of God*, habitual at least, is essential to the human intellect, so much so that, without it, it [the intellect] can know nothing, since indeed it is itself the light of understanding"; "that *being* which we know in all things and without which [we know] nothing is the divine being"; "*universals*, considered in their reality, are not really distinct from God."

(5) *Finally, Catholic theologians commonly teach today*: (a) even through his absolute power, God *cannot create an intellect that through its own proper, natural powers could see God as he is in himself*; (b) *nor can he create a super-*

---

della santa Chiesa placed on the index during his lifetime. After his death, forty propositions taken from his works were condemned. He was later rehabilitated and beatified for his heroic virtue in 2007. Details on his rehabilitation should be interpreted in light of the 2001 decree by then-Cardinal Ratzinger, "Note on the Force of the Doctrinal Decrees concerning the Thought and Work of Fr Antonio Rosmini Serbati," promulgated July 1, 2001. *Rosmini* was rehabilitated, not the conclusions that might be drawn from his works by those who are not careful.]

9   Leo XIII, Decree of the Holy Office, *Post obitum* (Dec. 14, 1887), no. 36 (Denzinger, no. 3236).
10 Ibid., no. 38 (Denzinger, no. 3238).
11 Ibid., no. 25 (Denzinger, no. 3225).
12 See ibid., nos. 1–16 (Denzinger, nos. 3201–3216).
13 Pius IX, Decree of the Holy Office, September 18, 1861, nos. 1–3 (Denzinger, nos. 2841–2843).

natural substance to which the light of glory would be connatural.[14]

These two conclusions are commonly held, as Gonet writes, "Against *Durandus of Saint-Pourçain, Luis de Molina, Juan Martínez de Ripalda*, and *Rodrigo de Arriaga . . .* whose opinion Gabriel Vasquez calls foolish, [John Paul] Nazarius rash, and Domingo Bañez manifest ignorance."[15] *Scotus and the nominalists* before Molina had defended a similar opinion, denying the absolute necessity of a supernatural light of glory for seeing God.[16] Cajetan,[17] however, says, after the Council of Vienne:

> Note well that the position of Scotus and his followers can no longer be held concerning this matter, for Pope Clement V's *Ad nostrum, De haereticis* expressly condemned errors which hold that the soul does not need the light of glory elevating it to the vision of God. In this you see that the Church, having embraced St. Thomas's teaching, determined not only the need for this light but also the cause for this necessity, namely, so that *the soul may be elevated* to such a vision, as St. Thomas says in this article.

Gonet speaks in a similar manner against Scotus.[18]

{{318}} *According to Scotus and the nominalists, the natural order is not necessarily distinct from the supernatural order precisely because the very essence of God* transcends every created intellect but instead *is only distinct from it in a contingent manner, on the basis of the divine freedom,* which has *de facto* established angels and wayfaring men in such a *state* that they do not intuitively see the divine essence.[19] Scotus's opinion here is consistent with two theses of his overall system: *Being is univocal to God and creatures* (hence, there is not an essential and necessary distinction between the natural and supernatural orders), and *God's will is higher than his intellect* (thus, the distinction between the two orders is freely constituted).

This conclusion is also consistent with the principles of nominalism,[20] according to

---

[14] On the proof of these conclusions, see Salmanticenses, *Cursus theologicus, In ST* I, q. 12, disp. 3, dub. 1 and 2.

[15] Gonet, *Clypeus Thomisticus*, tr. 2 (*De possibilitate visionis Dei*), disp. 1, a. 1, §3.

[16] See Scotus, *In III Sent.*, dist. 14, q. 1; *In IV Sent.*, dist. 49, q. 11.

[17] See Cajetan, *In ST* I, q. 12, a. 5, no. 9.

[18] See Gonet, *Clypeus Thomisticus, De gratia*, disp. 2, a. 3 ("Whether habitual grace is an entitatively supernatural form"): "Scotus's opinion is commonly rejected, because it does not distinguish between what is intrinsically supernatural (that is, *quoad entitatem*) from what is *extrinsically* supernatural (that is, *quoad modum*). This is contrary to the common consent of theologians who admit that there are beings that are supernatural intrinsically and entitatively. Nay, this is even contrary to the faith providing for such gifts."

[19] See Scotus, *In I Sent.*, dist. 3, q. 3, no. 24–25.

[20] See Tommaso Maria Zigliara, *Summa philosophica*, Ontologia, bk. 2, ch. 1, a. 4 (Properties of essences, against the nominalists).

which the common term "humanity" designates a collection of men and not a necessary and immutable nature.

However, this merely contingent distinction seems to be irreconcilable with the doctrine defined at the [First] Vatican Council: "There is a twofold order of knowledge, distinct not only in its *principle* but also in its *object.* . . . For divine mysteries *by their very nature* so exceed the created intellect that, even when they have been communicated in revelation and received by faith," they cannot be demonstrated.[21]

Hence, this excess is founded on the very nature of God, not on the divine freedom.

§2. On the Demonstrability of the Existence of a Supernatural Order of Truth and Life in God

In defense of revelation, it is not entirely necessary that we demonstrate the existence of an order of supernatural truth in God. Indeed, it suffices that we show that those opposed to this cannot efficaciously disprove the existence of this order, just as they cannot disprove the possibility of the mystery of the Holy Trinity.

Nonetheless, in order for our refutation of naturalism to be more profound, we must ask (1) whether it is possible to demonstrate the existence of a supernatural order of truth; (2) how this would be argued on behalf of from the perspective of man; (3) how this would be argued on behalf of from the perspective of God.

(1) *Is demonstration of the existence of a supernatural order of truth possible?*

The difficulty in this matter lies in the following question: How could we show that there exists in God not only an order of natural mysteries (such as foreknowledge of future free acts, the reconciliation of the divine freedom with his divine immutability, etc.) but, rather, an order of strictly supernatural mysteries, which cannot be known unless they are revealed and which, after such revelation is bestowed, remain indemonstrable (such as the mystery of the Most Holy Trinity)?

Certain theologians seem to suppose that this demonstration is impossible[22] because the proposed demonstration is generally taken from God's infinity, on the basis of which

---

[21] [First] Vatican Council, *Dei filius*, ch. 4 (Denzinger, nos. 3015–3016). [Trans. note: Fr. Garrigou-Lagrange includes the final words in the quote itself, though that's not exactly what is said in the document, as can be seen from the lengthier citation of this section above.]

On this matter, see Jean-Michel-Alfred Vacant, *Études comparées sur la philosophie de S. Thomas d'Aquin et sur celle de Duns Scot* (Paris: Beauchesne, 1891), 12–20. Likewise, see Matthias Joseph Scheeben, *Dogmatik*, Treatise on God, no. 278.

[22] See Ignatius Ottinger, *De revelatione supernaturali* [(Freiburg: Herder, 1897)], 54.

we can only know of the existence of natural mysteries in God (e.g., the mystery of the reconciliation of {{319}} his infinite knowledge [*scientiae*] with both divine and human freedom). At first sight, this opinion concerning the impossibility of demonstrating the existence of the supernatural order seems to preserve the transcendence of this order. However, upon more careful reflection, such a denial seems, on the contrary, to have an affinity with the thesis of Scotus, Molina, and Ripalda holding that by his absolute power, God can perhaps create an intellect that through its own proper powers would see God's essence in itself. For, in fact, these theologians, doubting the demonstrability of the existence of a supernatural order in God, by the same token find themselves in doubt about whether God, according to his intimate life, completely transcends any natural, created knowledge whatsoever.

Now, there indeed cannot be a direct and ostensive demonstration that would lead to a positive, natural knowledge of the order of supernatural truth, for this order, by its very definition, exceeds every form of natural knowledge. Nor can there be a demonstration of the existence of this order from any naturally known effect without revelation, for such an effect would need to be intrinsically supernatural, like grace, and therefore would already transcend natural knowledge.[23] However, it is not *a priori* contradictory to speak of an *indirect demonstration relative to the natural limits of whatsoever created intellect*, for according to this kind of demonstration, the order of supernatural truth can be known *not positively and in itself* but, rather, only *negatively and relatively*. That is, it is not contradictory to say that we can prove the existence of a given order that is naturally unknowable with regard to its essence as well as with regard to the existence of any one of its particular mysteries. This is the same as proving that there is in God an order of truth and life exceeding the limits of natural, created knowledge.

However, because *this proof*, like the distinction between supernatural mysteries and natural ones, *is established only following upon revelation* as a form of defense [in apologetic theology], we must say: By reason alone we can efficaciously *defend* the claim that there is in God an order of mysteries that are not only natural but one that, indeed, is supernatural.[24] Very soon, we will prove this claim, thus providing an even more profound refutation of naturalism (or pantheism).

(2) *How are we to argue for this from the perspective of the created*

---

[23] See *ST* I-II, q. 112, a. 5.

[24] See Cardinal Tommaso Maria Zigliara, in *Propaedeutica ad sacram theologiam in usum scholarum seu tractatus de ordine supernaturali*, 5th ed. (Rome, 1903), bk. 1, ch. 9, [no.] 3: "The Catholic doctrine that, from our perspective, there is a twofold order of divine truths in God (one natural and the other supernatural) is not only held by faith but also by reason."

intellect? What is the basis for the limits of its natural knowledge?
These limits must be considered from two perspectives—namely, as regards the *extension* of our knowledge and as regards its *intension* (or penetration). This distinction is commonly admitted. For example, future free actions exceed the extension of our natural knowledge. However, after their appearance, they do not exceed our intellect's penetration if their cause can be easily known. By contrast, the metaphysical doctrine of Aristotle, even if it is clearly set forth to young students, sometimes exceeds their mind's penetration, for their intellects are not yet sufficiently disposed and proportioned to this object, having not yet acquired the *habitus* of science.[25]

What is the basis for the limits of our knowledge's extension, as well as the limits of its intention (or penetration)?

{{320}} The limits of the extension of a given form of knowledge are drawn from its objective medium whereas, by contrast, the limits of its intension or penetration are drawn from the power of the knowing faculty or from its *habitus*. These points can be proven both *a posteriori* and *a priori*.

(a) *The limits of the extension of knowledge are drawn from its objective medium.* The objective medium [of knowledge] is that in which knowledge attains the various objects to which it is extended. For example, for sense knowledge, the mirror in which many objects are seen is an objective medium. For intellective knowledge, *the principle in which conclusions are known* has the role of being an objective medium. Hence, a simply objective medium is simultaneously *what* is known and *that in which* some other thing or things are known. By contrast, a subjective medium is only *that by which* something is known, and it is the representative idea[26] or the *habitus* (or light) strengthening the intellect. Sometimes, an idea, in contrast to a *habitus*, is said to be an objective medium in a qualified sense [*secundum quid*], for it is an objective medium *quo* though not a *medium quod* or a *medium in quo*.

Having so defined what an objective medium is, we thus can prove *a priori* that the limits of knowledge's extension are drawn from it. Indeed, it is a question either of disparate [*disparata*] knowledge or connected knowledge. Disparate extension (or knowledge of disparate things, for example,

---

[25] [Trans. note: Or, better yet, metaphysical wisdom, *sapientia*. On this topic, see Matthew K. Minerd, "Wisdom Be Attentive: The Noetic Structure of Sapiential Knowledge," *Nova et Vetera* 18, no. 4 (Fall 2020): 1103–1146.]

[26] [Trans. note: From the context, Fr. Garrigou-Lagrange is referring here to the intellectual *species impressa*, which is only a *quo*. By contrast the *species expressa*, according to the later Thomist school, is a *medium in quo*. Fr. Garrigou-Lagrange admits this doctrine in other places.]

of various individuals) can only exist if these various things are objectively proposed. However, this disparate extension is of little importance, for it does not constitute an order of truths. However, if it is a question of connected extension, obviously this extension of knowledge is all the greater to the degree that the extension of the objective medium taken up by the intellect is greater. This proposition is self-evident, *for from principles and in them, we can only see the truths that are virtually contained therein.*

This is also confirmed *a posteriori* by way of examples. The order of plant life cannot be known solely from principles of the order of inorganic mechanistic action or chemical action. It is above their extension. Hence, materialists labor in vain when they wish to explain vital phenomena in a merely mechanistic way. Likewise, the order of sense life exceeds the virtuality of the principles of biology. Similarly, the order of intellective and moral life cannot be known solely by the principles of sense life, and sensualists and empiricists labor in vain, wishing to explain [intellectual] ideas in terms of a composite image, judgment as a form of association of images, and reasoning through merely empirical sequences. Likewise, from mathematical principles that pertain to the order of quantity, we cannot deduce a metaphysical conclusion (e.g., concerning God's existence), for this conclusion pertains to a more universal and superior order—namely, the order of being inasmuch as it is being. Thus, it is sufficiently clear that the limits of the extension of knowledge are taken from its objective medium (or from the virtuality of its principles). Therefore, we are faced with the question of whether there is in God an order of truth exceeding the virtuality of the natural principles of reason (or of metaphysics). Semi-rationalists and Rosmini deny this, intending to reduce the mystery of the Trinity to the philosophical (or metaphysical) order.[27] By contrast, according to the Church, God's *intimate* life transcends the order of natural reason, just as plant life transcends the mechanistic order. *The kingdom of God* surpasses the kingdom of nature and of reason.

{{321}} (b) *The limits for the intension (or penetration) of knowledge are drawn from the vigor of the knowing power or from a habitus of this power.* This second conclusion can likewise be proven *a priori* and *a posteriori*.

In fact, one and the same doctrine, proposed in the same manner to a number of listeners is penetrated (or understood more deeply [*intus legitur*]) by one listener more than another. Those people who have already been trained in such matters clearly and distinctly understand this doctrine,

---

27 Leo XIII, Decree of the Holy Office, *Post obitum* (Dec. 14, 1887), no. 25 (Denzinger, no. 3225).

whereas others understand it only obscurely and in a vague manner. This is an obvious fact of experience. Thus, *a posteriori*, it is clear that with the growth of a scientific *habitus* acquired through exercise, the penetration (or intension) of knowledge grows.

This can also be proven *a priori*, for knowledge is brought about inasmuch as the known exists in the knower and is received into the knower according to the mode (or capacity) of the knowing faculty or *habitus* of the knower. Hence, presupposing the identity of the objective medium, greater or lesser penetration cannot arise from anything but the faculty of understanding proper to individual men, who are more or less naturally disposed for intellectual knowledge and have trained themselves more or less through study. Thus, in the sense order, the night owl cannot see the sun, whereas the eagle, on account of the vigor of its sight, gazes upon the sun without blinking.

Therefore, *we must ask* (1) whether there exists in God an order of truth exceeding the *objective medium* of the knowledge that is naturally possible for a created intellect (and, indeed, for any intellect that could be created)—namely, an order of truths that cannot be known from the natural principles of reason and that remains indemonstrable even after revelation; (2) whether there exists in God an order of truth exceeding the *vigor* of the created intellect so that even if this truth were objectively proposed to us, our intellect, by its own natural power, could not formally know it but would instead stand before it like an owl staring at the sun.

As is already evident, if the first question is to receive an affirmative answer, the second will also be affirmed as a kind of corollary to the first. For that which exceeds the natural objective medium of a given faculty likewise exceeds the natural power of this faculty, which is specified by its natural objective medium—just as a metaphysical conclusion (e.g., concerning God's existence) exceeds the objective medium of mathematics (namely, the order of quantity) and, therefore, exceeds the power of the *habitus* of mathematics. Thus, mathematicians frequently understand metaphysical demonstrations only with great difficulty, understanding in a quantitative manner that which must be understood qualitatively.

(3) *How are we to argue for this from the perspective of God?*
Many argue from God's infinity, saying the order of supernatural truth is an order exceeding the natural knowledge of whatsoever created intellect; now, on account of his infinity, God exceeds every form of natural knowledge had by whatsoever created (or finite) intellect. Therefore, an order of supernatural truth exists in God.

Indeed, from this, we have an apodictic proof that there is in God an order of natural (or philosophical) mysteries, whose intimate essence exceeds every created intellect, although their existence is naturally knowable (that is, without revelation). Thus, for example, the mystery of God's infallible foreknowledge of free future actions is founded on his infinity, especially on the infinity of the divine knowledge [*scientiae*] which of itself and from eternity extends to all knowable things, even free future actions. {{322}} From God's infinity, it indeed follows that all the naturally knowable divine attributes have an eminent and infinite mode [of reality]. And this mode cannot be naturally known *in a positive manner* but, rather, only *negatively* (nonfinite wisdom) and *relatively* (the supreme wisdom). On account of the imperfection of this natural knowledge, any divine attribute is a natural mystery for us, and indeed, it is especially true that the intimate reconciliation of his attributes remains hidden, even though we may hold most certainly from revelation that all of these attributes are reconciled and identical in God. (For example, utter immutability and complete freedom most certainly are reconciled, although the intimate mode of this reconciliation remains hidden from us.)

Hence, from God's infinity, we can indeed prove that in God there is an order of natural (or philosophical) mysteries. However, against the semi-rationalists, the existence of a supernatural order of mysteries (i.e., one that cannot be known without being divinely revealed and that remains indemonstrable even once revelation has been made) is not immediately clear.

Regarding this matter, we must note that if there were only natural (or philosophical) mysteries found in God, the formal object of natural reason would be no more distinct from the formal object of infused faith than this latter would be from the formal object of the beatific vision. There would only be a distinction as between what is obscure and what is clear or between the vague and the distinct (e.g., like the distinction found between the natural reason of a given uneducated man and a metaphysician). Hence, the natural light of reason would not be of another order than the light of infused faith or the light of glory. Indeed, semi-rationalists, along the lines of Rosmini,[28] erred by not distinguishing between these formal objects, as though natural reason already would vaguely see the formal object seen by the blessed in heaven.

Therefore, how are we to argue, from the perspective of God [*ex parte Dei*], in order to prove that an order of supernatural mysteries exists in God? *We must argue to this conclusion on the basis of the intimate life of God (or God considered under the intimate and utterly eminent formal character [ratione] of the Deity)* inasmuch as, in the words of Cajetan, "the formal notion of the *Deity* is prior to being and to all of its differences, for it is *above being*,

---

[28] See ibid., nos. 1, 36–38 (Denzinger, nos. 3201, 3236–3238).

unity, and so forth."[29] In its utterly simple eminence, all the simply simple perfections are identical, perfections that are attributed of God by natural reason alone. Thus, we have a confirmation for St. Thomas's own words: "All the perfections of things which are found dividedly and multiplied in created things preexist in God in a unified and simple manner,"[30] as will be even clearer on the basis of the exposition we provide below. Therefore, if we wish to argue from God's infinity, such infinity must be taken not as the mode of any given divine attribute but, rather, as a negative expression for the Deity as such.

Hence, Thomists commonly say *God sub ratione Deitatis* is the subject of sacred theology, just as he is the primary object that is supernaturally believed *in via* and seen in heaven.[31] St. Thomas had said in *ST* I, q. 1, a. 6: {{323}} "*Sacra doctrina most properly* makes determinations *concerning God* . . . not only as regards what can be known about Him through crea-

---

[29] See Cajetan, *In ST* I, q. 39, a. 1, nos. 7 and 8.

[30] *ST* I, q. 13, a. 5. (Also see no. 7 of Cajetan's comments on this article as well as nos. 10ff for his resolution of the objections raised by Scotus.)

[31] See Cajetan, *In ST* I, q. 1, a. 7, no. 1: "The formal subject of Sacred Theology is *God inasmuch as He is God*. . . . And, in order to maintain the integrity of this doctrine, you must penetrate well what is conveyed by this expression 'inasmuch as He is God.' . . . Man can be understood in four ways: (1) as a rational animal and, hence, is understood quidditatively, inasmuch as he is man; (2) as a substance, and so he is conceived of *in communi*; (3) as naturally tame, and so he is conceived *per accidens*; . . . (4) as the noblest of animals, and thus he is conceived in relation to something else. So, in the aforementioned proposition, proceeding in reverse order, God can be considered as: (4) the Highest Cause and universally according to something predicated in relation to something extrinsic [*ad extra*], and in this way, He is considered *in relation to something extrinsic* [*relative ad extra*]; (3) He can also be considered as wise, good, just, and universally according to notions that can be attributed to Him, and thus He is considered *quasi per accidens*; (2) He can also be considered *as being, act*, etc., and thus He is considered *in communi*. And to these three modes that are quasi-simple are reduced composite considerations such as *pure act, first being*, etc. For, in such things, God is considered as He stands under a *common concept*, as well as *relative* or *negative* ones, as is obvious. However, before all of these modes, God can be considered *according to His own quiddity*, for, according to the order of nature, this is the first notion of all and is the foundation of the others: and we circumlocute [*circumloquimur*] around this quiddity by means of the term *Deity*. And thus, in asking whether *God sub ratione Deitatis* (as distinct from the notion of goodness, and so forth) is the subject of this science, we are really asking whether God is the subject of this science precisely from the perspective of the formal character of His own proper quiddity. Thus, the quiddity of God is the formal character of this subject precisely according to His reality [*ut res est*]."

On this, also see John of St. Thomas, *Cursus theologicus*, disp. 2 (On sacred doctrine), a. 10. Likewise, see Gonet, Billuart, and other commentators on St. Thomas in this same place.

Scotus, however (in *In* I *Sent*, prol. q. 3, a. 4, no. 7), teaches: "There does not need to be a first object of our theology, *as it is ours*, except one that is first known, and it is about this first known thing that the first truths are known. That first known thing is infinite being."

tures but also *as regards that which He alone knows about Himself* and has communicated to others through revelation." Likewise, see *ST* I, q. 13, a. 8 (Whether the name "God" is a name of nature [as opposed to activity / operation]).[32] By contrast, metaphysics treats of God not from the perspective of the intimate, most proper, and eminent formal character of the Deity but, rather, under the completely common notion of *being*. This is so because the object of metaphysics is being inasmuch as it is being, and therefore this science extends to God as the First Being, as knowable on the basis of [our knowledge of] creatures.[33] Moreover, as theologians commonly teach, the metaphysical constitutive of the divine nature (which, according to the majority of them, is Self-Subsistent Existence) contains the divine attributes only *actu implicite*, whereas the Deity contains them *actu explicite*.[34]

Finally, all preachers of the faith call the supernatural mysteries hidden in God *the mysteries of the intimate life of God* (or of the Deity itself).[35] Indeed, through infused faith, even if we do not know God *as he is in himself* (this will be the case only in our heaven homeland),[36] we do nonetheless obscurely know God according to his intimate life (i.e., *the Deity*) and are not limited to knowing God as he is knowable on the basis of our knowledge of creatures.

{{324}} All simply simple perfections are identified in the *Deity* so that they are in it

---

32 See *ST* I, q. 13, a. 11, ad 1: "As regards that for which the name is imposed for the sake of signifying, the name "God" is more proper than is the name 'He who is' because the former is imposed for the sake of signifying the Divine Nature."

33 See Gonet, *Clypeus Thomisticus*, disputatio proemialis, art. 4 (in fine): "*Metaphysics does not consider God sub ratione Deitatis*, like theology, *but rather, considers Him as He [can be considered from the perspective of] being abstracting from intelligible matter.*"

34 See Billuart, *De Deo*, diss. 2, a. 1 and 3.

35 See St. Francis de Sales, *Treatise on the Love of God*, bk. 2, chs. 1 and 2: "That the divine perfections are nothing but one single, though infinite, perfection"; "That in God there is only one single act, which is His own Divinity."

36 Hence, in this thesis we must speak of God *sub ratione Deitatis* rather than *of God as he is in himself*. This distinction, which is necessary for expressing the difference between infused faith and the beatific vision, is not given by St. Thomas in *ST* I, q. 12, because in this question he is only concerned with the possibility of the beatific vision. Likewise, in this question, he does not distinguish in God natural mysteries from supernatural mysteries, for the intrinsic evidence of all these mysteries is had through one and the same beatific vision. Indeed, in order to know the intimate reconciliation of God's utter immutability and his complete freedom, we need to see God's very essence, although for us wayfarers, this mystery is natural—that is, knowable as regards its existence—not requiring revelation (in this, it differs from the mystery of the Trinity, cf. *ST* II-II, q. 2, a. 3 and 4). However, this distinction between natural mysteries and supernatural mysteries is utterly necessary in our treatise as something standing against the positions of the rationalists and semi-rationalists who both deny it.

actu explicite, whereas by contrast, God *sub ratione entis* contains them only *actu implicite*. They can be progressively deduced from God the First Being, whereas, by contrast, they are seen without any deduction in the Deity clearly seen.

We have examined this at greater length in another work.[37] St. Thomas himself says in *SCG* I, ch. 3: "It is *most evidently apparent* that there are certain truths about divine matters that totally exceed the capacities of human reason (as well as the capacities of angelic intellects)."

The Deity is[38] above being inasmuch as it contains in its *eminence* the simply simple perfections of aseity [*entis a se*], unity, truth, goodness, intelligence, love, justice, and mercy, somewhat as white light contains the seven colors of the rainbow, though with one important difference—namely, that white light only contains these colors *virtually-eminently* and thus is neither blue nor green, whereas by contrast, God contains simply simple perfections *formally-eminently* and therefore is one, good, and so forth.

An intellect that has not been elevated to the supernatural order is somewhat like the eye that would not be able to see white light, not even in a vague manner, but was limited only to seeing the seven colors of the rainbow.

It remains that "the Deity as such is above being and above one," and whereas *being* can be *participated in naturally* by a stone, plant, animal, man, or angel, *the Deity* cannot be *participated in* except *supernaturally* through grace, which indeed is defined as a participation in the divine nature as the radical principle of strictly divine activities [*operationum*], especially the immediate vision of the Deity.

However, if the divine essence did not of itself have a single, most eminent formal notion that is utterly proper to itself, one in which all simply simple perfections would be identified but, rather, were only *an aggregate heap of perfections* that are naturally knowable (as seems to be what Scotus thought, positing *a formal-real distinction between the divine perfections*[39]), then *there would not be a necessary distinction* between the order of supernatural mysteries and the order of natural mysteries. Rather, these two orders would only be distinguished *in a contingent manner by God's will*, as Scotus in fact thought (here joining the nominalists). Then, the Most Holy Trinity would not be a supernatural mystery on account of its utterly eminent nature but, rather, would be so only because God did not wish for us to know the Trinity naturally.

The same unbefitting conclusion is found in *ontologism*, which does not draw a careful enough distinction between supernatural mysteries and natural divine mysteries,

---

37 See Réginald Garrigou-Lagrange, *God: His Existence and His Nature: A Thomistic Solution of Certain Agnostic Antinomies*, vol. 1, trans. Bede Rose (St. Louis, MO: B. Herder, 1949), 33–42.

38 [Trans. note: Reading *est* for *et*.]

39 Against Scotus, see Cajetan, *In ST* I, q. 13, a. 5 and q. 39, a. 1; John of St. Thomas, *Cursus theologicus, De Deo*, disp. 4, a. 6; Billuart, *De Deo*, diss. 2, a. 3.

even if it does not deny the divine infinity.

This suffices regarding the demonstrability of the existence of a supernatural order. Thus, we know how we are to argue both from the perspective of the limits of natural created knowledge as well as from the perspective of God.

§3. Demonstration of the Existence of a Supernatural Order *Objectively Exceeding the Natural Powers of the Created Intellect*

As we have said, this demonstration presupposes our earlier {{325}} refutation of pantheistic evolutionism and agnosticism, proving that God exists as really and essentially distinct from the world.

Our argument is established at once from the perspective of the created intellect and from that of God, as we said in the previous section. Hence, it can thus be written in syllogistic form, ascending from easier things to more difficult ones:

On the basis of our knowledge of creatures [*ex creaturis*], we cannot positively know God from the perspective of the intimate formal notion of the Deity.

Now, the natural objective medium of any given created intellect can only be a creature.

Therefore, by means of its own natural objective medium, no created intellect can positively know those things that immediately[40] pertain to God considered from the intimate formal notion of the Deity. Hence, this constitutes an order of supernatural truth.

(1) **Proof of the major premise. On the basis of our knowledge of creatures [*ex creaturis*], we cannot positively know God from the perspective of the intimate formal notion of the Deity.**
On the basis of our knowledge of creatures [*ex creaturis*], God is only known according to the perfections that are *analogically and evidently common* to him and creatures and is only known *negatively* and *relatively* as regards that which is *proper* to him. Now, as we have already said, *God considered from the perspective of the intimate formal notion of the Deity* is God according to what is most proper to him. Therefore, on the basis of our knowledge of creatures, we cannot positively know God from the perspective of the intimate formal character of the Deity.

We will explain this in parts.

---

[40] The term *immediately* is the same as *per se primo*, just as man is *per se primo* rational and *per se non primo* living or [*seu*] animal, and *per accidens* white or musical.

A. God can *only be known analogically* on the basis of our knowledge of creatures, for creatures are so inferior to God that they cannot have either a specific or generic likeness with him but, rather, can only have an analogical likeness with him, for God transcends the limits of any species or genus.

This is proven by St. Thomas in *ST* I, q. 4, a. 3 and q. 13, a. 5. In the latter article, he argues thus:

> It is impossible that something would be predicated univocally of God and creatures. *For every effect that does not equal the power of its efficient cause falls short of having a likeness of the agent and thus is not of the same formal character as it.* Thus, what is found in effects in a divided and multiplied manner is found in the cause simply and in the same manner—just as the sun, according to its one and unified power, produces the manifold and various forms in those things inferior to it. In the same way, as we said above (in a. 4), all the perfections of things found in a divided and manifold manner in created things preexist in God in a unified manner.
>
> Therefore, when a given term pertaining to a perfection is said of a creature, it signifies that perfection as something distinct from the others, according to the formal character of the definition. For example, when the term "wisdom" is said of man, we are thus signifying some perfection distinct from man's essence, as well as from his power and existence, as well as from all other such things. However, when we apply this term to God, we do not intend to signify something distinct from His essence, power, or existence. Thus, when the term "wisdom" is said of man it in some way circumscribes and embraces the thing signified. However, this is not so when it is said of God. In that case, it leaves behind the thing signified as something not fully embraced, exceeding the signification of the term. Thus, it is clear {{326}} that the term "wisdom" is not said of God and man according to the same formal character.[41] The same holds for the others. Hence, no term is univocally predicated of God and creatures.

Thus, on the basis of our knowledge of creatures, God is only known *analogically*, according to perfections that are *evidently*[42] analogically common

---

[41] From this, it is clear that according to St. Thomas, an analogue is defined as "those things having a common term while the *ratio* signified by that name is *simpliciter diverse* and *secundum quid* (that is, proportionally) the same." This definition differs from the Suarezian definition of analogy, which holds that the analogical *ratio* is *simpliciter the same* and *secundum quid* diverse.

[42] I say "evidently," for as we will discuss below in the following thesis, before the intimate life of God is known through intuitive vision, it can be revealed to us *obscurely, and for this* revela-

to himself and to creatures, as is explained at length in *De veritate*, q. 2, a. 1 and 11: "Just as the term 'sight' is said of both bodily sight and intellectual sight because as sight is in the eye so is understanding in the mind." In other words, sensation and intellection are analogically (or proportionally) called *forms of knowledge* [*cognitiones*], yet they are indeed properly such, inasmuch as sensation is related to the sensible as intellection is related to the intelligible. So too, knowledge or intellection are attributed to God inasmuch as the uncreated intellection is related to the uncreated intelligible as created intellection is related to the created intelligible. Similarly, God is analogically said to be being, good, and so forth.

B. Hence, that which is *proper to God* can be known on the basis of our knowledge of creatures only *negatively* or *relatively*. We negatively say God is not finite, not mutable, not temporal, not in potency in any way, and so forth. And this is said about any given divine attribute. In a relative manner, we say that God is the supreme, first, most perfect, maximally eminent being, and we speak about his supreme wisdom or goodness in a similar manner.[43]

Therefore, on the basis of our knowledge of creatures, we cannot *positively* know God from the completely proper perspective of the *Deity*. Just as we cannot positively know the nature of plant life on the basis of knowledge of mechanistic motions, nor the nature of sensation on the basis of our knowledge of vegetative life's motion, nor the nature of what intellection properly is by our imagination, so too God's intimate nature cannot be known on the basis of knowledge of creatures.

Hence, St. Thomas says in *ST* I, q. 13, a. 8, ad 2:

> On the basis of our knowledge of divine effects we cannot know *the divine nature* according to what it is in itself so that we would know it quidditatively. Instead, as we said above, in this way we know it by way of eminence, causal-

---

tion, God uses naturally acquired notions of our reason that can *analogically but not evidently* express the mystery of the intimate life of the Deity (or of the Trinity). Nay, in dogmatic formulas, the verb "is" can only be affirmed on account of God who reveals. Thus, "it attains by God's grace a certain understanding of the (supernatural) mysteries . . . from the analogy with the objects of its natural knowledge" ([First] Vatican Council, *Dei filius*, ch. 4, Denzinger, no. 3016). However, *these analogies between the intimate life of God and created natures* are not naturally known by us and *can be revealed by God alone, who alone naturally knows his own intimate life*. See *ST* I, q. 32, a. 1 and *De veritate*, q. 10, a. 13.

43 Hence, in general, it is said that man naturally knows God *through the way of causality* (by attributing to the First Cause the simply simple perfections that are participated in by creatures) and *by the way of negation and eminence* (by negatively and relatively determining the infinite and eminent *mode* according to which the simply simple perfections exist in God). See *ST* I, q. 12, a. 12.

ity, and negation. Thus, the name "God" signifies the divine nature. Indeed, this name is imposed in order to signify {{327}} something existing above all things, something that is their principle and is separate from all of them.

Likewise, in a. 9c and ad 3: "This name 'God' is incommunicable according to reality. . . . By contrast, the names 'good,' 'wise,' and so forth can in reality be communicated to many beings." Also see a. 11, ad 1. The Deity as such cannot be participated in by creatures naturally (but, rather, can only be participated in supernaturally through grace) and hence is not naturally knowable on the basis of one's knowledge of creatures.

We now must consider the minor premise of our argument.

(2) *Minor premise: Now, the natural objective medium of any given created intellect can only be a creature.*

This minor premise can be proven both (A) indirectly and (B) directly.

A. *Indirectly*. If the natural objective medium of a created intellect were not a creature but, rather, the divine essence immediately seen, *then a created intellect would be specified by the same formal object as is the divine intellect*. Now, those things that are specified by the same formal object are of the same nature. Therefore, in this case, a created intellect would be of the same nature as God and thus would be a [kind of] created God. In other words, the nature of our soul would be a created divine nature, and this is a pantheistic contradiction of terms that cannot be affirmed without, like Hegel, denying the principle of contradiction (or identity). On the contrary, by virtue of this principle, God is God and the creature is a creature, just as one says that spirit is spirit and flesh is flesh in order to affirm the fact that their natures are distinct.

St. Thomas sets forth this indirect argument in *SCG* III, ch. 52.[44]

B. *Directly*. In *ST* I, q. 12, a. 4, St. Thomas sets forth and develops this proof.[45] The Holy Doctor's proof can be reduced to the following syllogistic form.

A spiritual essence whose mode of immateriality exceeds the mode of

---

[44] *SCG* III, ch. 52: "However, it is not possible that some created substance by its own proper power could reach this mode of vision (i.e., vision of the divine essence). Indeed, an inferior nature can attain that which is proper to a superior nature only through the action of the superior nature having that property, just as water can only be warm through the action of fire. However, to see God through the divine essence itself is proper to the divine nature, for it is proper to any given agent to act through its own proper form. Therefore, no intellectual substance can see God through the divine essence itself unless God renders this possible." Concerning this matter, see Gonet, *Clypeus Thomisticus, In ST* I, q. 12, disp. 3, a. 3

[45] See Cajetan's commentary on this article, as well as the remarks made relative to it by John of St. Thomas in his *Cursus theologicus*. A compendium of the points made there can be found in Billuart, *Summa sancti Thomae, In ST* I, q. 14, a. 1 and q. 12, a. 4.

immateriality of the nature of a given knower cannot be known by it naturally and immediately. Now, *the divine essence has a mode of immateriality infinitely exceeding the mode of immateriality of any given created or creatable intellect*. Therefore, the divine essence cannot be naturally and immediately known by any creatable intellect. (Hence, only a creature can be the natural objective medium of a creatable intellect.)

Now, this argument is founded on the very definition of knowledge. As Aristotle had profoundly said, followed by St. Thomas (*ST* I, q. 14, a. 1):

> Knowers are distinguished from non-knowers in the fact that non-knowers only have their own form, whereas *knowers are naturally apt also to have the form of another thing*, for the *species* of the known is in the knower.[46] {{328}} (For example, plants become hot under the sun's rays but in no way become the sun, whereas, by contrast, when the animal sees the sun, it in some way becomes the sun, namely, intentionally, representatively having in itself the form of the sun. It accepts into itself the form of the other, not as its own form but, rather, inasmuch as it is the form of the other, for it does not appropriate this form to itself, placing its limits upon it, as though it would become warm. Rather, it receives it as the form of the other. The knower becomes the other inasmuch as it is other.)[47]

> Whence (St. Thomas continues), it is clear that the nature of a non-knowing thing is much more restricted and limited than that of a knower, and the nature of knowing beings has a greater amplitude and extension than that of non-knowers. For this reason, the Philosopher says in *De anima* 3.8 that "the

---

[46] Aristotle, *De anima*, 2.12, no. 4 (lect. 24 of St. Thomas), 3.4, no. 3 (lect. 7 of St. Thomas), 3.8, no. 1 (lect. 13 of St. Thomas).

[47] See John of St. Thomas, *Cursus philosophicus*, de Anima, q. 4, a. 1: "Note that St. Thomas did not say that knowers are able to have *another form* but, rather, said that they can have *the form of another thing*, for any being whatsoever can have another form, receiving into itself some perfection or form coming extrinsically to it (e.g., when a plant becomes warm). . . . *Knowers*, however, are elevated above non-knowers in the fact that they can receive into themselves what is other, precisely as other (or inasmuch as it remains distinct in the other) so that they are not only what they themselves are in themselves but *can also become that which is other than themselves*. For example, *when I see a color, the eye does not become colored in itself but, rather, color, which is really in the other is intentionally and visually placed in the eye*." And for this, immateriality is required in the potency that is receptive in this manner, as St. Thomas proves in *ST* I, q. 14, a. 1 and *De veritate*, q. 2, a. 2.

However, the objections of Scotus against the reasons exposited by St. Thomas in *ST* I, q. 12, a. 4 (Whether some created intellect through its own natural powers can see the divine essence) arise from his insufficient understanding of this principle: Knowledge occurs inasmuch as the known immaterially exists in the knower according to the mode of the knower.

soul is in some way all things."

Now, a form is restricted through matter. . . . Therefore, it is clear that *the immateriality of any given thing is the reason that it is knowing by nature [cognoscitive]*, and the *mode of knowledge is found in knowers according to the modes of their immateriality*. Whence, in *De anima* 2.12, it is said that plants do not know on account of their materiality. The senses, however, are knowing powers [*cognoscitivus*] because they receive the species of things without their matter. And the intellect is even more so a knowing power [*cognoscitivus*] because it is more separated from matter and unmixed, as Aristotle says in *De anima* 3.4. Whence, since God exists at the highest degree of immateriality, it follows that the highest degree of knowledge is found in Him.[48]

Now, these general principles are easily applied to our question, as is explained in *ST* I, q. 12, a. 4: "For knowledge occurs inasmuch as the known is (immaterially) in the knower. *Now, the known is in the knower according to the mode (of immateriality) of the nature of the knower. Therefore, if the mode of existence of a given known thing exceeds the mode (of immateriality) of the knowing nature in question, knowledge of that thing necessarily* {{329}} *is above the nature of that knower.*" Hence, the senses only know singular sensible things, while intelligible things are above the power of the senses. Otherwise, if, for example, the

---

[48] This profound notion of knowledge itself is set forth at length in *De veritate*, q. 2, a. 2: "The perfection of one thing cannot be in another according to the determinate existence that it has in that thing. . . . And because the forms of things are determined through determinate matter, hence a given thing is knowable inasmuch as it is separated from matter. Whence, that into which such a perfection of the thing is received must itself also be immaterial."

As St. Thomas notes in the same place, *materialists* therefore do not understand what knowledge is, failing to see the difference between "becoming other as other" and "becoming other (e.g., becoming hot)." Hence, materialists aim at reducing knowledge to some physical (and not psychological) impression within the organism. By contrast, *idealists* exaggerate the immanence of knowledge and conceive of the representation as something merely internal but closed in on itself, like a picture, not something essentially relative to an extramental object. Thus, neither materialists nor idealists understand what knowledge properly is, for it requires something beyond the conditions of matter in its particular kind of reception and activity. Hence, already, the sense soul is spiritual in some way, although it is not independent from matter, for it receives the *species* in a representative manner without any alteration of it, as vision is not elicited through the mediation of warmth and moisture.

[Trans. note: To be sure to understand the intricacies involved in this doctrine of sensation, which are somewhat skimmed over here by Fr. Garrigou-Lagrange because of the difficulties involved in the matter, the reader should consult Yves R. Simon, "An Essay on Sensation," in *Philosopher at Work: Essays by Yves R. Simon*, ed. Anthony O. Simon (Lanham, MD: Rowman and Littlefield, 1999), 57–111.]

senses were to know the first principles of reason, this knowledge would occur according to two opposed modes of immateriality simultaneously. Subjectively, it would be intrinsically dependent on the organism and objectively would be intrinsically independent from the organism, which is contradictory, for it is specified by its object.

Now the divine essence has a mode of immateriality infinitely exceeding the mode of immateriality of any given created and creatable intellect, for God alone is Self-Subsistent Existence and *is pure act not only in the order of being but also in the order of intelligibility*. Indeed, he is intelligibility (or truth) itself through his essence [*per essentiam*], as well as *Self-Subsistent Intellection*, as it were, an infinitely bright flash of intellectuality, surpassing, by his pure spirituality, the spirituality of any given created intellect or created idea (even any infused one).[49] Therefore, no created or creatable intellect can naturally see God through his essence. Rather, it stands before God in his glory like a night owl before the sun.[50]

Hence, the natural objective medium of a created intellect can only be a creature, whether concretely received or abstractly, like genera, species, and the transcendentals (e.g., the notions of being and one in which the first principles of reason are founded). Therefore, in general, it is said that *man cannot naturally know God immediately but, rather, only in the mirror of creatures*—nay, in the mirror of sensible things inasmuch as the proper object of our intellect is being as it is found in sensible things (i.e., the essence of sensible things). Thus, in accord with such a relation to sensible things

---

[49] An infused, created idea would only be intelligible in a participated manner and, hence, could not express the infinitely luminous Self-Subsistent Intellection as It is in Itself (see *ST* I, q. 12, a. 2).

[50] This is set forth with clarity by Billuart in *Summa sancti Thomae, De Deo*, diss. 4, a. 2, when he says: "Knowledge takes place inasmuch as the known is in the knower. Now, the known is in the knower according to the mode of the knower, for that which is in another is in it according to its own mode. Thus, if the knowing nature has *existence in matter*, as is the case for the rational soul, naturally, it knows all things, according to the mode of having a material quiddity through *species* that are abstracted from sensible things [*a sensibus*]. If it *does not* have *existence in matter but is in potency to existence*, as is the case for the angels, it knows other things according to its own mode, that is, according to the mode of a nature that is in potency to existence. However, when God is known according to the mode of a material quiddity or one that is potential, He is not known quidditatively as He is in Himself, since He Himself is *His own existence* and *utterly pure act*. Therefore, an object whose mode of existence exceeds the mode of existence of the nature of a knower cannot be naturally known by that knower quidditatively and as it is in itself." Likewise, see Billuart's resolution of Scotistic objections.

[*secundum habitudinem ad sensibilia*], we know the first principles of being and of reason and God himself (or the First Being).[51]

> Even the angels cannot naturally know God immediately but, rather, do so in a kind of mirror, "for the angelic nature is a kind of mirror representing the divine likeness."[52] "In the intellects of men and of angels, there is a kind of natural obscurity inasmuch as *every creature exists in the shadows in comparison with the immensity of the divine light.*"[53] Hence, the proportionate object of a created intellect is an intelligible that is obscure. For us humans, it is the intelligible existing in the shadows of sensible things, for the human soul exists at the lowest rank of intellectual substances.[54] However, as we said, God can only be known in the mirror of creatures *analogically*, with what is proper to him being known only *relatively and negatively*.

{{330}} Thus, our conclusion stands: Therefore, by its own natural objective medium, no created intellect can positively know what pertains immediately to God precisely from the perspective of the Deity. Hence, this constitutes an order of supernatural truth.

As Job said: "Behold, God is great, exceeding our knowledge" (Job 36:26, DR), as well as St. Paul to Timothy: "The King of kings and Lord of lords, who. . . . inhabiteth light inaccessible" (1 Tim 6:15–16, DR).

Confirmation:

In order to better understand this conclusion, we can illustrate it through an analogy drawn from St. Paul, conveyed in 1 Corinthians 2:9–15 (DR), where, in order to show the nature of the supernatural object of faith and the beatific vision, he wrote:

> Eye hath not seen, nor ear heard: neither hath it entered into the heart of man, what things God hath prepared for them that love him. But to us God hath revealed them by his Spirit. For the Spirit searcheth all things, yea, the deep things of God (τὰ βάθη τοῦ Θεοῦ —that is, God considered from his intimate and utterly proper formal character as the Deity). *For what man knoweth the things of a man, but the spirit of a man that is in him? So the things also that are of God no man knoweth, but the Spirit of God.* Now we have

---

[51] See *ST* I, q. 12, a. 12; q. 55, a. 2; q. 76, a. 5; q. 88, a. 3; q. 89, a. 1.

[52] *ST* I, q. 56, a. 3.

[53] *ST* II-II, q. 5, a. 1, ad 2.

[54] See *ST* I, q. 76, a. 5.

received not the spirit of this world, but the Spirit that is of God: that we may know the things that are given us from God. . . . But the sensual man perceiveth not these things that are of the Spirit of God. For it is foolishness to him: and he cannot understand. . . . But the spiritual man judgeth all things: and he himself is judged of no man.

Indeed, we can naturally know the external life of other men but not the intimate life of the secrets of their hearts, unless they reveal them to us. Thus, we can naturally know God only in a kind of surface-level way, in the mirror of creatures. However, his intimate depths, which remain hidden within him, can only be known if God himself supernaturally reveals them.

Hence, just as we cannot deny that God has an intimate life, so too we cannot deny that supernatural mysteries exist in God.

Conclusion: Our entire demonstration can be summarized in the fact that the notion of what an intellect is itself is, like being, analogous. Therefore, the created intellect and the divine intellect are akin to each other [*convenit*] only according to an analogy of proper proportionality, inasmuch as each is related to its proper object, and these diverse objects are only analogically akin to each other [*analogice convenient*] as intelligible beings precisely in being, which is the adequate object of our intellect inasmuch as it is an intellect.

Hence, we can schematically write:

$$\text{Intellect} \begin{cases} \text{divine proper object} \ldots\ldots\ldots \text{the divine essence} \\ \text{angelic} \ldots\ldots\ldots\ldots\ldots\ldots\ldots \text{essence of the angel} \\ \text{human} \ldots\ldots\ldots\ldots\ldots\ldots\ldots \text{essence of a sensible thing} \end{cases} \Bigg\} \text{being}$$

Thus, it is clear why no created intellect can, by its own natural objective medium, positively know what pertains essentially and primarily (i.e., immediately) to God considered from the perspective of the intimate notion of the Deity. Hence, without revelation, the intimate life of God constitutes a supernatural order of mysteries that cannot be analogically known on the basis of our knowledge of creatures. In this, mysteries, strictly so called, differ from the natural mysteries that are treated in natural theology. This will all be quite clear in the course of our resolution to objections below after we set forth the corollaries to what we have said thus far.

§4. First Corollary: The Supernatural Order Even Subjectively Exceeds the Power of Whatsoever Created Intellect

{{331}} On this matter, see *ST* I, q. 12, a. 5 on the necessity of the light of glory for seeing God. Also, see *ST* II-II, q. 6, a. 1, on the necessity of the light of faith for believing supernatural mysteries already revealed and sufficiently proposed through the preaching of the Gospel.

This stands in opposition to the positions held by the *Pelagians* and *semi-Pelagians* who said that in order to believe the mysteries of faith, or at least in order to have the beginnings of faith, it suffices that we have external revelation through the preaching of the Gospel. Thus, the internal light of faith strengthening the intellect would not be necessary.[55] Likewise, it is opposed to the Beghards, who said: "The soul does not need the light of glory raising it to see God and to enjoy him beatifically"[56]

This corollary is deduced from the preceding thesis. Indeed, *the natural vigor of any given knowing power is specified by its natural objective medium and is proportioned to it*, for potency is said in relation to act, which itself is specified by its object.[57] Now, as we have proven, an order of supernatural mysteries exists in God, mysteries that exceed the natural objective medium of any intellect that could ever be created. Therefore, these mysteries exceed even the natural power of any given created intellect. Hence, in order for a created intellect to be able to see God, it stands in need not only of objective manifestation but also of subjective strengthening, for it intrinsically lacks the power needed to see God in this manner. Without this strengthening, it would stand before God in his glory like the owl before the sun, whose splendor is too great for its gaze.

Hence, the Thomists unanimously hold against Scotus and Molina that, even by God's absolute power, the created intellect cannot see God through his essence without the light of glory, for the intellect, which is *intrinsically impotent in these matters*, needs to be intrinsically elevated (or strengthened) so that it may be intrinsically able to know

---

[55] The Second Council of Orange, can. 5 and 6 (Denzinger, nos. 375–376).

[56] Council of Vienne, *Ad nostrum qui*, no. 5 (Denzinger, no. 895).

[57] In *ST* I, q. 89, a. 1, St. Thomas says: "Indeed, in all intellectual substances we find an intellective power through the influence of the divine light. Indeed, this is one and simple in the first principle, and to the degree that intellectual creatures are more distant from the first principle, to that same degree is that light divided and diversified, like lines further away from the center of a circle. Hence, God knows all things through His One Essence. However, even though superior intellectual substances know through many forms, nonetheless, they do so through fewer and more universal ones that have a greater power enabling a greater comprehension of things *precisely because of the efficacy of the intellective power* found in them. However, in inferior knowers there are many less universal forms, having less efficacy in comprehending things, inasmuch as they fall short of the intellective power of superior beings."

God in this way.[58] Likewise, the internal light of faith is needed in order to formally assent to the mysteries of faith.

§5. Second Corollary: Moreover, the Supernatural Order Exceeds the Exigencies of Whatsoever Created Intellect

This corollary is stated *against Baius*, whose following proposition was condemned by Pope St. Pius V: "The sublimation of human nature and its elevation to participation in the divine nature were due to the integrity of man in his first state and therefore to be called natural, not supernatural."[59] The same doctrine is found in the writings of the first Protestants[60] and in the writings {{332}} of the Jansenists,[61] and in turn appeared in the writings of the modernists, who held that human nature contained a true demand for the supernatural order and not only a befittingness for such elevation.[62]

The falsity of this doctrine is clear in light of our own thesis, as was also already made clear by St. Thomas, for example in *ST* I-II, q. 109, a. 5 and 6; q. 112, a. 3; q. 114, a. 2 and 5. Likewise, see *ST* I, q. 62, a. 2; *De veritate*, q. 27, a. 2; q. 14, a. 2, and so forth.

Indeed, that which absolutely exceeds the natural objective medium of any given creatable intellect simultaneously exceeds its natural end (or its natural perfection). Now, that which exceeds the natural end (or perfection) of something exceeds the exigencies of that nature. Therefore, the order of supernatural truth and life exceeds the natural exigencies of any creatable intellect precisely because it exceeds its natural objective medium.

Proof of the major premise: A natural perfection (or end) is proportioned to natural powers and, hence, to the natural objective medium by which these powers are specified.

The minor is quite clear, for otherwise the exigencies of nature would extend beyond a natural end, and God as the Author of nature would have given us a natural tendency and exigency that he could not satisfy as a natural end. Thus, the order of agents would not correspond to the order of ends, bringing the principle of finality, "Every agent acts for an end," to ruin.

Hence, our elevation to the supernatural order is in no way owed to us but,

---

58 See John of St. Thomas, *Cursus theologicus, In ST* I, q. 12 (On the light of glory). Also see Gonet on this.

59 Pius V, *Ex omnibus afflictionibus*, no. 21 (Denzinger, no. 1921). Also see nos. 23 and 26 (Denzinger nos. 1923 and 1926).

60 See Luther's remarks on the third chapter of Genesis in his *Commentary on Genesis*; John Calvin, *Institutes of the Christian Religion*, bk. 1, ch. 15.

61 See Clement XI, *Unigenitus Dei filius*, no. 35 (Denzinger, no. 2435); Pius VI, *Auctorem fidei*, nos. 16 and 18 (Denzinger, nos. 2616 and 2618).

62 Pius X, *Pascendi*, no. 37 (Denzinger, 2103, old numbering).

rather, is bestowed in a completely gratuitous manner as an effect of God's mere good pleasure and benevolence.[63]

By contrast, the general motion by which God, qua universal mover in the order of nature, moves all creatures to their activity is in some way owed to created natures according to the common laws of providence. This does not mean that God would have an obligation in relation to a creature but, rather, that he moves each agent according to the mode of its nature. Thus, God himself must not annihilate human souls, which are immortal of their very nature.

In this way, we have a sufficient proof for our thesis concerning the existence in God of an order of supernatural truth and, hence, concerning the possibility of revelation of supernatural mysteries from the perspective of the object.

---

[63] If man were created in a state of pure nature, his ultimate end (or beatitude) would have been natural, commensurate to the conditions of nature. This *natural ultimate end* consists in a perfect union [*coninctione*] with God through the *abstractive* knowledge and affection that are possible through natural powers and aids. In contrast, supernatural beatitude is found in clear vision of God with beatific love.

Certain theologians say that in the state of pure nature there would not have been a bodily resurrection. Others say that there would have been one, for the resurrection is only modally supernatural and not as regards the nature of the resurrection so effected [*non quoad terminum*], depending upon God, the author of nature. Others, however, say that the righteous to be beatified in that state would not die but that God would transfer him living into the place of beatitude. These three opinions are probable in their character, though perhaps the second is more probable.

For the resolution of the objections raised by Baius and Jansen, see Billuart, *Summa sancti Thomae, De gratia*, diss. 2, praeambula, a. 2 (Whether the state of pure nature was possible).

See *De veritate*, q. 14, a. 2 ("There is a twofold ultimate end for man"). One of these ends is proportioned to human nature, because natural powers suffice for obtaining it, and this is the felicity spoken of by the philosophers, whether the contemplative [life] consisting in the act of wisdom, or the active life, which primarily [*primo*] consists in the act of prudence and by consequence [*consequenter*] in the acts of these moral virtues. However, man's end that exceeds the proportion of human nature is a different affair, for man's natural powers do not suffice for obtaining it, *nor for knowing about it nor for desiring it. Rather, it can only be promised to man through the divine liberality*. Isaiah 64:4 (DR): "the eye hath not seen, O God, besides thee, what things thou hast prepared for them that wait for thee," and this is eternal life.

Likewise, in *De veritate*, q. 27, a. 2: "According to his nature, man is proportioned to a given end for which he has a natural appetite, and according to his natural powers, he can act so as to attain this end, which is the contemplation of divine things in a way that is possible to man according to the powers of his nature. Philosophers have placed man's ultimate felicity in this. However, God has prepared another end for man, one exceeding the proportion of human nature, namely, eternal life, which consists in the vision of God through His essence, which exceeds the proportion of any given created nature, being connatural to God alone."

§6. Third Corollary: There Cannot Be Disagreement nor Confusion between Natural Truths and Supernatural Truths. Rather, They Exist in Harmony

(1) There cannot be disagreement between these two orders of truth.

This is said against certain *Averroists* of the thirteenth century, as well as against Pietro Pomponazzi in the fifteenth century, who was afraid to directly deny the truth of the Catholic faith and said: "At least according to philosophy, it is true that the rational soul is mortal or one in all men." These claims were condemned at the Fifth Lateran Council in 1513: {{333}} "And since truth cannot contradict truth in any way, we define every statement contrary to the truth of the enlightened faith to be entirely false; and so we strictly forbid that teaching any other doctrine be allowed."[64]

In the nineteenth century, *semi-rationalists* like Günther said that philosophy not only can demonstrate the mysteries of faith but, moreover, can, by its own natural progress, know God and the soul more profoundly and truly than does faith, whose mode of expression remains too symbolic or metaphorical. Hence, according to them, a legitimate opposition between faith and philosophy can exist.

At the same time, certain *fideists*, like Augustin Bonnetty, fell into the same error, though for the opposite reason. According to them, human reason is so weak that it leads in a quasi-natural manner to doctrines opposed to the truth of faith. Hence, Bonnetty had to subscribe to this proposition: "Although faith is above reason, nevertheless no true dissension, no disagreement can ever be found between them, since both arise from the one same immutable source of truth, the most excellent and great God, and thus bring mutual help to each other."[65]

Against the semi-rationalists, and simultaneously against the fideists, the [First] Vatican Council took up the definition of the Fifth Lateran Council and assigned the reason for it:

> However, though faith is above reason, there can never be a real discrepancy between faith and reason, since the same God who reveals mysteries and infuses faith has bestowed the light of reason on the human mind, and *God cannot deny Himself, nor can truth ever contradict truth.* The deceptive appearance of such a contradiction is mainly due to the fact that either the dogmas of faith have not been understood and expounded according to the mind of the Church or fanciful conjectures are taken for verdicts of reason.

---

[64] Leo X, *Apostolici regiminis* (Denzinger, no. 1441).

[65] Pius IX, Decree of the Sacred Congregation of the Index, June 11 (15), 1855 (Denzinger, no. 2811).

Thus, "we define that every assertion that is opposed to Enlighted faith is utterly false."[66]

This follows as a kind of corollary of our thesis, for as we said, supernatural truths are founded on the intimate life of God, whereas natural truths are founded on God the Author of nature and on creatures. Now, God cannot deny himself, nor can there be a contradiction in God.[67] {{334}} For the same reason, there cannot be disagreement between the light of faith and the light of reason.

Likewise, in general, truth can never contradict truth. For truth is a judgment inasmuch as it affirms that what is is and that what is not is not. Now, something cannot simultaneously be and not be. This is the principle of contradiction, the foundation of logic and metaphysics, dogmatically confirmed in the aforementioned definitions of the Fifth Lateran Council and the [First] Vatican Council.

In order for truth to be able to contradict truth, as certain relativist modernists wish, *being would need to be equivocal.* That is, it would need to signify things that are completely different (and not analogically similar), as the term "dog" equivocally designates the domestic animal as well as a certain constellation. Then truth could contradict truth, meaning that the principle of contradiction would not have a real value, as Hegel taught. There would be no absolute truth, and nothing would be absolutely true. Instead, contradictories would be simultaneously true.[68]

Certain *modernists* admitted this kind of relativism, as is obvious from the condemned modernist proposition: "Truth is no more immutable than man himself, since it evolved with him, in him, and through him."[69] Hence, they said: "Nay, they admit openly, and with ill-concealed satisfaction, that they have found that even its dogma is not exempt from errors and contradictions. They add also that this is not only excusable but—curiously enough—even right and proper."[70] However, then nothing would remain true. It would be no truer to say that God transcends the world than that he is immanent within it as the soul of the world.[71] Likewise, it would be no truer to say that God is Pure

---

[66] [First] Vatican Council, *Dei filius*, ch. 4 (Denzinger, no. 3017). See Vacant, *Études théologiques sur les constitutions du Concile du Vatican d'après les actes du concile*, vol. 2, 235.

[67] See *SCG* I, ch. 7.

[68] Against this sophistical position, see the fourth book of Aristotle's *Metaphysics*.

[69] Pius X, *Lamentabili*, prop. 58 (Denzinger, no. 3458).

[70] Pius X, *Pascendi*, no. 36 (Denzinger, 2102, old numbering). [Trans. note: Drawn from the official Vatican text. I have removed ellipses for the sake of clarity.]

[71] See ibid., no. 39 (in fine) (Denzinger, 2109, old numbering): "The same conclusion follows from the distinction." Hence, in the formula for the Anti-Modernist Oath (*Motu proprio*, Sept.

Act than that he is universal evolution itself; and it would be no truer to say that God is the highest good and he who is most powerful than it would be to say that he is evil and weak. Hence, in *De potentia*, q. 7, a. 7, St. Thomas had said against Maimonides: "If nothing were predicated of God and creatures except by way of pure equivocation, . . . since all of our knowledge about God is drawn from creatures, we would know nothing about God except empty names corresponding to nothing in reality, . . . and all demonstrations given by philosophers concerning God would be sophistical." Thus, therefore, so long as the principle of contradiction stands, there cannot be disagreement between natural truths and supernatural truths.

(2) *And there cannot be a pantheistic confusion of these two orders*, for *being is not said univocally* but, rather, analogically, of the necessary being and contingent being. Indeed, this confusion would follow from univocity of being, and there could not be an essential diversity of being, for something univocal like as a genus is only diversified through extrinsic differences. As St. Thomas says:

> It cannot be thought that something would be added to being in order to diversify it, for that which is added to being would need to be extraneous to it. However, something of this kind would have to be nothing. Whence, it does not seem that being can be diversified. . . . However, in this, Parmenides was deceived, for he used [the notion] "being" as though it were a single formal character and a single nature, like the nature of a genus. {{335}} And this is impossible, for being is not a genus but, rather is said in different ways (that is, analogically) of different things.[72]

Hence, just as equivocity of being would lead to a contradiction between the natural and supernatural orders, the claim that being is univocal leads to the pantheistic confusion of these orders. Thus, it is clear that Scotus recklessly affirmed that being is univocally said of God and creatures. The first consequence of this affirmation seems to be the condemned proposition of Antonio Rosmini: "In the being that prescinds from creatures and from God, which is indeterminate being, and in God, non-indeterminate but

---

1, 1910), we read: "Likewise, I condemn and reject the opinion of those who say that erudite Christian men have a kind of twofold personality—one a believer and the other a historian— as though the historian could retain those things that contradict the faith of the believer or, so long as he would not directly deny any dogmas, could build upon premises which would lead to the conclusion that the dogmas are false or something doubtful."

[72] See St. Thomas, *In I Meta.*, lect. 9.

absolute being, the essence is the same"[73] However, these propositions imply semi-rationalism—that is, the confusion of the two orders. Hence, Rosmini tried to philosophically demonstrate the mystery of the Holy Trinity.[74]

(3) *There is harmony (or subordination) between the order of natural truth and the order of supernatural truth*, as between created and uncreated. Hence, *even if philosophy is specifically distinct from sacred theology, it cannot be separated from it but, rather, is subordinated to revelation*, just as "created reason is absolutely subject to the Uncreated Truth."[75] Hence, these semi-rationalist propositions have been condemned: "As there is a distinction between the philosopher and his philosophy, he has the right and the duty to submit himself to the authority he acknowledges as legitimate; but *philosophy neither can nor must submit to any authority*"; "philosophy is to be treated without any regard to supernatural revelation."[76]

This harmony was set forth in ch. 4 on faith and reason (on the mutual relation between revelation and reason) in the [First] Vatican Council constitution, *Dei filius*.[77] See index Ic in [the older versions of] Denzinger. These matters are of central importance throughout this treatise on revelation, especially in the next two theses and in book 2, where we will discuss the motives of credibility taken from the sublimity of Christ's doctrine and from the miraculous life of the Church, in which all of the aspirations of our nature find their fulfillment.

However, we must now resolve objections raised against the demonstration of the existence of an order of supernatural truth.

§7. Resolution of Objections Raised by Semi-rationalists and Those Coming from Scotus

There are three series of difficulties to be considered:

A. Objections drawn from St. Thomas's own principles (as though our thesis proves too much)

B. The objections of semi-rationalists (as though it did not sufficiently prove its claims)

C. The objections of Scotus

---

[73] Leo XIII, Decree of the Holy Office, *Post obitum* (Dec. 14, 1887), no. 6 (Denzinger, no. 3206). Likewise see nos. 1–5 (Denzinger, nos. 3201–3205).

[74] See ibid., no. 25 (Denzinger, no. 3225).

[75] [First] Vatican Council, *Dei filius*, ch. 3 (Denzinger, no. 3008).

[76] Pius IX, *Syllabus of Errors*, no. 10 (Denzinger, nos. 2910 and 2914).

[77] See Vacant, *Études théologiques sur les constitutions du Concile du Vatican d'après les actes du concile*, vol. 2, 241 (The rights of the Church in scientific question).

A. *From the principles of St. Thomas*, it seems that our thesis proves too much.

First objection: One and the same thing cannot simultaneously be the object of demonstration and the *per se* object of faith (*ST* II-II, q. 1, a. 5). Now, the order of supernatural mysteries is the *per se* object of faith. Therefore, the order of supernatural mysteries cannot be demonstrated.

Response: I make a distinction regarding the major premise. I concede that it cannot be the same from one and the same perspective. However, I deny that this is true if the truth is known from different perspectives. Moreover, I sub-distinguish the minor premise. I concede that an order of supernatural mysteries considered *positively* and *in itself* is the *per se* object of faith. However, I deny that this is so if it is considered *negatively* and *relative to the limits of our intellect*. I sub-distinguish the conclusion in the same way.

{{336}} Thus, what the supernatural order is in itself and what its mysteries are both are matters held by faith alone. However, the existence of this order, *negatively* considered, can be proven through reason as the existence of an order of naturally unknowable truths.

Second objection: Now this response stands in contrast to the common opinion of Thomists. Therefore, it seems false.

Response: I make a distinction regarding the major premise. I concede that the existence of God, inasmuch as he positively is the Author of the order of grace and glory, is something held by faith alone. However, I deny that the existence of God, inasmuch as his essence transcends the limits of our natural knowledge, is something so held. Indeed, the order of grace and glory are positively known only through faith or through the beatific vision.[78]

Third objection: However, as was defined at the [First] Vatican Council against semi-rationalists, without revelation, man would not have an explicit notion of any strictly supernatural mystery. Therefore, the existence of the order of these mysteries cannot be demonstrated by reason alone.

Response: Already above, in asking whether this demonstration would be possible, we discussed this. The proof that we set forth, just like the distinction between supernatural divine mysteries and natural divine mysteries, is established only following on the giving of revelation, being offered after the manner of a defense. Nonetheless, by reason alone, from a right notion of God, we can *efficaciously* defend that an order of properly supernatural truth and life are found in God. Similarly, the fact of revelation is only known after revelation, and nonetheless, by reason alone, it is proven from the miracles by which it is confirmed.

---

[78] See Billuart, *Summa sancti Thomae, De fide*, diss. 1, a. 6, solv. obj.: "Although the natural light of our reason cannot by its own power know the possibility of supernatural faith in particular, that is, inasmuch as it is a formal participation in the divine intellect infused by God, nonetheless it can know it in a general manner [*in communi*], inasmuch as it is superior to human faith, just as it can know that God is the supernatural author in general, that is, as able to do something that would be above all of nature. Though, in so doing, it does not determine what it is in its specific character [*in particulari*]. Such was the position of our Gonet [*noster Gonet*]."

B. *The objections of the semi-rationalists (or at least ones that are akin to their way of thinking)*

First objection: When considered negative and relatively, we do not have a demonstration that the supernatural order exists. Indeed, God exceeds the created intellect on account of his infinity. Now, from the divine infinity, we only have a proof of the existence of natural mysteries in God, not supernatural ones. Therefore, the demonstration of the existence of a supernatural order (even when negatively considered) remains impossible.

Response: I make a distinction regarding the major premise. I concede that, *absolutely speaking*, God exceeds the created intellect on account of his infinity, inasmuch as his infinity is a negative expression of the Deity as such. However, I deny this inasmuch as infinity is only the mode of any given divine attribute. I contradistinguish the minor premise as well. I will let pass the claim that only the existence of natural mysteries is all that is proven from the divine infinity inasmuch as it is the mode of any given divine attribute. I deny it, however, inasmuch as it is a negative expression of the Deity as such.

I said I will let the minor premise pass under the aforementioned form because any given infinite attribute, as we will discuss below, can be considered in two ways—namely, from creatures or as an expression of the intimate life of God. Now, the Deity constitutes a supernatural order, for it is not only an aggregate heap of naturally knowable perfections but, rather, is the eminent formal notion constituting the intimate life of God.

2. *It will be insisted, however*: The existence of a supernatural order cannot be demonstrated from the Deity as such. Indeed, the Deity qua Deity is the immediate foundation for the intimate reconciliation of the divine attributes. Now, this intimate reconciliation of God's attributes is only {{337}} a natural mystery, for its existence is known without revelation. Therefore, the Deity qua Deity does not constitute an order of supernatural mysteries.

Response: I make a distinction regarding the major premise. I concede that, relative to his naturally knowable attributes, the Deity is the immediate foundation for their reconciliation. However, I deny that the Deity is such intimately in itself and not in relation to these attributes. I concede the minor premise. I make a distinction regarding the conclusion as well. I concede that *relative to naturally knowable attributes, the Deity* does not constitute an order of supernatural mysteries. However, I deny this *as it is in itself and intimately*.

However, it is obvious that in itself and intimately considered, the Deity must have its own formal constitutive, for otherwise it would be nothing more than an *aggregate heap* of naturally knowable divine perfections. This would be akin to how empiricists (or [seu] nominalists) say that the substance of a bodily thing is nothing more than a collection of accidents (or [seu] phenomena). Our intellective life would be reduced to the empirical association of the representations of our imagination [*phantasiae*]. However, in reality, just as substance exceeds phenomena and intellective life exceeds sense life, so too the Deity transcends all of the perfections that are common to God and creatures.

Moreover, it is not only superior to the reconciliation of the inferior [attributes] but also exists in itself and for itself. Nay, the inferior ones exist on account of it (e.g., as our senses exist on account of our intellect). Hence, the Deity does not merely exist for the sake of the reconciliation of the naturally knowable divine attributes but, indeed, exists *in itself for itself*, and all other [things] exist for its sake.

However, in some way, we even find that the common expression, "The highest of a lower order touches upon the lowest of a higher order," is confirmed in God, for the supreme natural mystery—namely, the intimate reconciliation of the naturally knowable divine attributes—touches upon the Deity itself, which is the principle of strictly supernatural mysteries, especially that of the Holy Trinity. Thus, in a lower domain of things, notwithstanding the absolute distinction of different orders, the highest function of the imagination [*imaginationis*] touches upon the lowest function of reason, the highest form of plant life touches upon the lowest degree of sense life, and the highest order of inorganic mechanistic beings touches upon the lowest degree of life.

3. *It will, however, be urged*: Still, the Deity as such is even positively knowable through the first principles of reason.

Indeed, the first principles of reason are principles of being inasmuch as it is being. Now, the Deity qua Deity is not outside of being inasmuch as it is being. Therefore, the Deity qua Deity can be positively known through the first principles of reason and hence is only a natural mystery.

Response: I make a distinction regarding the major premise. I concede that the first principles are principles of being that analogically belong to both God and creatures. However, I deny that they univocally belong to God and creatures. I contradistinguish the minor premise as well. I concede that the Deity is being analogically. However, I deny that it is univocally such. Therefore, through the first principles of reason the Deity can be known positively under the analogical notions of being, one, good, and so forth—however, not under the utterly proper formal notion of the Deity.

4. *It will be insisted*: Even if being is analogous, there cannot be essentially supernatural mysteries.

Proof: That which is above the virtuality of the principle of contradiction would be absurd. Now, supernatural mysteries would be above the virtuality of the principle of contradiction and that of the other principles of reason, for they would be indemonstrable. Therefore, these mysteries would be absurd (that is, not only above but contrary to reason).

Response: I make a distinction. That which is above the virtuality of the principle of contradiction not *in itself* but *from our perspective*, as something indemonstrable for us, is not absurd. Nay, it can even appear to us as being something that is probable. Now, supernatural mysteries are not *in themselves* above the virtuality of the principle of contradiction. This principle is confirmed in them, but *from our perspective*, they cannot be demonstrated from principles [known by natural reason]. Nonetheless their truth can be defended against the objections and argued for on the basis of persuasive arguments. Thus, in *ST* I, q. 2, a. 1, St. Thomas says that the proposition, "God exists," is something self-evident [*per se nota*] in itself, though not from our perspective.

More explicitly, we must also respond that supernatural mysteries are above {{338}} the virtuality of the principle of contradiction considered *according to the created mode* of being, but not above the virtuality of the principle of contradiction considered *according to its uncreated modality*. And because they positively belong in an essential and primary manner to this *intimate* mode of the divine essence and not to that which is evidently common to God and created natures in an analogical way, these mysteries cannot be naturally known and cannot be demonstrated even after revelation is extended to us. See *ST* I, q. 32, a. 1 and *De veritate*, q. 10, a. 13. Hence, in order to manifest the Trinity, we can bring forth reasons that are probable, not demonstrative.

5. *It will yet be urged*: This does not prove the existence of an order of supernatural mysteries but only of one supernatural truth—that is, the intimate life of God.

Response: It is not a contradiction to say that this intimate life of God contains many truths, as we know to be the case according to revelation (e.g., the mystery of the divine paternity, of the generation of the Son, and the spiration of the Holy Spirit). And even if there were only one supernatural truth, our thesis would remain true in what is essential to it. Nay, the supernatural order is maximally one on account of its utter purity and simplicity. And as it is known more fully, it is known in a more unified manner, as it will be in the life of beatitude.

6. *Still, it is insisted*: But then, as regards the divine attributes, there would be only natural mysteries, not supernatural ones. Hence, we must not admit, beyond the natural providence proven from the order of the world, that there is a supernatural providence that would dispose supernatural means to salvation and would contain the supernatural mystery of predestination.

Response: I concede that God's attributes, as they are naturally knowable from creatures, contain only natural mysteries. However, I deny that as expressions of the intimate life these attributes are so limited. Thus, in the *Summa theologiae*, the treatise *De Deo uno* not only speaks about God as the Author of the natural order but, moreover, speaks theologically about God as the Author of the supernatural order. Therefore, when he comes to speak of providence, his concern is not merely with natural providence but also with supernatural providence. The same holds for the divine will and knowledge [*scientia*]. Thus, through the senses alone, the merely sensible aspects of a man's face are known, but the expression of his intimate life is known in its physiognomy only through the intellect.

7. *Yet*, at least according to the aforementioned demonstration, there would be supernatural mysteries only in the intimate life of God but none when he acts *ad extra*. Hence, the Incarnation, Redemption, sending of the Holy Spirit, and so forth are not essentially supernatural mysteries.

Response: If God acts *ad extra* according to his intimate life, this activity *ad extra* is essentially supernatural, as is the case, for example, for the justification of souls and their beatification. However, if God acts *ad extra* in a way that is not according to his intimate life, this *ad extra* activity is not essentially supernatural, as is the case, for example, for the general divine concurrence in virtue of which all creatures (even inanimate ones) act.

8. *Yet it will be urged*: Nonetheless, according to the aforementioned demonstration, there cannot be some created thing that is essentially supernatural. Therefore, sanctifying grace is not something essentially supernatural.

Response: Some created thing can be essentially supernatural so long as it is essentially relative to the Deity as such. However, grace is a participation in the divine nature as it is divine and is essentially ordered to glory (or to the immediate vision of the divine essence as it is in itself). Grace itself, like faith, hope, and charity, as well as all of the *per se* infused virtues are supernatural mysteries, whose possibility cannot be demonstrated but only can be persuasively argued on behalf of and defended against objections. However, in virtue of our demonstration, there cannot be a supernatural substance that would be created, for substance is being in itself and to [*sic*] itself, having its specification in itself, whereas by contrast, some created thing that is entitatively supernatural [(e.g., created grace)] must be essentially relative to something, that is, to the Deity by which it is specified. Hence, it can only be an accident.

{{339}} 9. *Then it is insisted*: In that case, the intimate life of God, whether in itself or as participated, if it is supernatural in that way, cannot be revealed to us by the mediation of the natural notions of our reason (e.g., by means of our notions of paternity and filiation), for as was said, no analogy exists between the intimate life of God and created natures.

Response: I concede that there is not an *evident* analogy between them, one that would be knowable by reason alone. However, it is not excluded that there is an analogy that can be revealed by God alone, who alone naturally knows his own intimate life.[79] On this, see the next thesis below.

C. **The objections of Scotus.** See Scotus *In IV Sent.*, d. 49, q. 11; *In I Sent.*, d. 3, q. 3.[80] Also see Cajetan's responses in his commentary on *ST* I, q. 12, a. 4.

1. *Objection*: From the fact that the known is in the knower according to the mode of the knower, it only follows that the knower can naturally know an object of a superior order only in an inferior way. However, it does not follow that this knower would be absolutely incapable of knowing the object naturally. Therefore, the Deity (or the intimate life of God) can perhaps be naturally known vaguely in a finite manner.

---

[79] See *ST* I, q. 32, a. 1. *De veritate*, q. 10, a. 13.

[80] [Trans. note: As has been the case throughout, Fr. Garrigou-Lagrange does not adequately refer to the various redactions and editions of Scotus, whose works were not in critical edition when the early editions of *De revelatione* were being penned.]

Response: I make a distinction regarding the antecedent. I concede that a knower can naturally know an object of a superior order only in an inferior manner—that is, only in relation to a formal object of an inferior order, namely, *in an inferior mirror*. However, I deny that it can naturally know that object immediately, according to the formal character of a superior order, even if only in a vague way. And I deny the consequent. Indeed, we naturally know God in the mirror of creatures, according to the common notions of being, goodness, and so forth, though not immediately according to the proper and intimate formal character of the Deity. Otherwise, our knowledge would at once exist according to two opposed modes of immateriality—namely, according to a human mode and according to a divine mode. This superior mode cannot be participated in except through the infusion of a supernatural light, which is a kind of participation in the divine nature. In reality, to know God in a vague manner is to know him from the perspective of the common formal character of being and not from the perspective of the utterly proper formal notion of the Deity. Scotus only materially understood St. Thomas's proposition, "The known is in the knower according to the mode of the knower," and failed to understand it formally.

2. *Objection*: There does not need to be a proportion between the intellect and its natural objective medium. Indeed, for the human intellect, this medium is of an inferior order—namely, the essence of sensible things. Therefore, similarly, the natural objective medium can be of a superior order.

Response: I deny the supposed parity, for the superior can naturally elevate the lower to its own proper mode, but it cannot be elevated according to its own mode (i.e., naturally) to the superior mode.

3. *Objection*: Then an inferior angel could not naturally know a superior angel. Now, this is false.

Response: Two angels are of the same order of immateriality. Hence, the lower angel can naturally know the superior one, though not as distinctly as the superior one knows himself.

4. *Objection*: Being is univocal to God and creatures. Therefore, the Deity itself can be naturally known from the first principles of being, at least vaguely and indistinctly.[81]

Response: Being is not univocal but, rather, is analogous, for the univocal is diversified through extrinsic differences. However, being cannot have extrinsic differences, for there is nothing outside of being. (See *ST* I, q. 3, a. 5.)

5. *Objection*: Likewise, someone can object that perhaps an infused idea, which is naturally suitable for angels, can, in a vague manner, represent the Deity as it is in itself.

Response: Even if it is infused, a created idea is intelligible through participation,

---

[81] [Trans. note: For a recent study of the Scotist doctrine of being, see Garret R. Smith, "The Analogy of Being in the Scotist Tradition," *American Catholic Philosophical Quarterly* 93, no. 4 (2019): 633–673.]

{{340}} according to a created mode of immateriality. Hence, it cannot vaguely represent Self-Subsistent Intellection in Itself, which is a kind of bright flash of intellectuality having an intention or radiance that is infinite. (See *ST* I, q. 12, a. 2).

6. *Objection*: Perhaps it would not be contradictory to speak of a created substance that would have the vision of the divine essence as something naturally befitting to it.

Response: On the contrary, the contradictory character of such a claim can be proven (1) from the perspective of the object and (2) from the perspective of the knowing subject.

(1) This substance would then have an intellect of the same nature as the divine intellect, for it would be specified by the same *formal object*. Hence, it would be a kind of created divine nature, which mixes terms together [*implicat in terminis*], just as it implies pantheism.

(2) This substance would be supernatural, but it is intrinsically contradictory to speak of a created supernatural substance. Indeed, something created cannot be essentially supernatural unless it is essentially relative to the Deity as such and thus specified by it, for only the essence of God is above every created nature. Now, no created substance can be essentially relative to the Deity and specified by it, given that *substance* is *being in itself* and *to itself* [*ad se*]. In other words, it has its specification in itself and cannot be defined through an order to something else. By contrast, some accident, like a power or *habitus*, can be essentially relative to something else. Thus, grace, which is the seed of glory, is specified by the essence of God, for it is a participation in it and orders us to full sight of it.[82]

7. *Objection*: Nonetheless, if the divine essence absolutely exceeds our intellect, our supernatural elevation to the vision of the divine essence will be impossible, just as a sense power cannot be elevated to intellection.

We will respond in the next thesis, following *ST* I, q. 12, a. 4, ad 3, that the essence of God clearly seen is outside of the latitude of *the proper object* of our intellect. That is, it is not manifested in the mirror of creatures. However, it is not outside of the latitude of our intellect's *adequate object*, which is being in general and anything whatsoever that is intelligible. Hence, it is not evidently contradictory to speak of our supernatural elevation to the vision of God. By contrast, whatsoever intelligible is outside of the latitude of both the proper and common sensibles. Hence, the sense cannot be supernaturally elevated to intellection.

8. *Objection*: It suffices that between the natural order and the supernatural order there be a contingent distinction dependent upon the divine freedom. Thus writes Scotus.[83]

---

[82] See Gonet, *Clypeus Thomisticus, De gratia*, disp. 2, a. 3. Billuart, *Summa sancti Thomae, De Deo*, diss. 4, a. 5, §4.

[83] See Scotus *In* I *Sent.*, d. 3, q. 3, nos. 24 and 25: "Nothing can be rendered adequate to our intellect from the nature of the power in the formal character of a first object except in an utterly general fashion. However, *in this state*, the *quiddity of sensible things* is adequate to it as the formal character of its motive. Therefore, in this state, it does not understand anything

Response: As we said above, this opinion of Scotus is in harmony with the two theses of his system—namely, (a) that being is univocal to God and creatures {{341}} (and hence there is no essential distinction between the natural order and the supernatural order) and (b) God's will is higher than his intellect (thus the distinction between the two orders [of nature and grace] is freely constituted).

However, this merely contingent distinction seems to be completely irreconcilable with the doctrine defined at the [First] Vatican Council: "There is a twofold order of knowledge, distinct not only in its *principle* but also in its *object*. . . . For divine mysteries *by their very nature* so exceed the created intellect."[84] Hence, they exceed it *per se*, from the very nature of God, and not only on account of a free divine decree.

Moreover, if this distinction were contingent, God, by his absolute power, could create an intellectual substance that would have the immediate vision of the divine essence as something natural. However, as we said above, this created substance would be supernatural, which is intrinsically contradictory. Thus, it is contradictory to speak of a created divine nature, just as the pantheism naturally following from the univocity of being is contradictory. However, the divine freedom cannot bring about that which is intrinsically absurd. Hence, Scotus's doctrine concerning the contingent distinction between the natural and supernatural orders[85] is false and leads to pantheism, as well as to

---

that is not contained under that first motive.

"However, if one asks what the reason for this state is [*quae est ratio istius status*], I respond as follows. A state seems to be nothing other than the stable permanence formed by the laws of divine wisdom. Now, it is established according to those laws of wisdom that in this state our intellect would understand only those things whose *species* shine forth in the phantasms. And this is the case either as a penalty for original sin or on account of a natural harmony among the powers of the soul in their operation. . . . However, that harmony, which in fact holds in this state, is not from the nature of our intellect inasmuch as it is an intellect, nor even as it is in a body, for then when in the glorified body it would necessarily have similar harmony, which is false. *Therefore, as far as this state is concerned, either from the mere will of God or from merely punitive justice, or from infirmity* (falling from original sin) . . . I say whether this is the total cause, or something else, the quiddity of material things is not, in any case, the first object of the intellect but, rather, is something common to all intelligible things."

[84] [First] Vatican Council, *Dei filius*, ch. 4 (Denzinger, nos. 3015–3016).

[85] See Vacant, *Études comparées sur la philosophie de S. Thomas d'Aquin et sur celle de Duns Scot*, 14: "St. Thomas's conception closely traces the limits that separate the world of nature from the world of grace, whereas that of Scotus tends to mix them. Likewise, while that of the Angel of the School was, as it were, the citadel on high from which the Church has victoriously pushed back all the attacks which have been taken up anew since the fifteenth century against the dogma of grace, we see that of the Scotists gradually abandoned an important position to the enemy. . . .

"The Thomist doctrine affirms that the natural order constituted by God in virtue of the creative act is in no way confused with the order of grace. . . . Thus, St. Thomas retains philosophy's own character as a science that is entirely distinct from theology. Thus, it is from his writings that, six centuries after his death, the [First] Vatican Council drew the formulas that it set in opposition to contemporary traditionalists and the rationalists. And everything leads

the denial of the principle of contradiction.

Now, however, we must examine how this distinction is elaborated by ontologists.

§8. Examination of Ontologism, as well as a Resolution of the Objections Raised by Ontologists

{{342}} Ontologism seems to be opposed, in no small way, to our thesis: The divine essence, precisely as it is in itself, absolutely surpasses the natural knowledge of any given created intellect. Indeed, according to ontologism, *God is the first object that our mind sees from the first moment of its creation.* Hence, in the ontologistic system of thought, this formula holds strong: The first thing ontologically speaking (God) is also the first thing logically speaking (i.e., the first thing known by us).

However, whereas all ontologists allege that there is this kind of immediate intuition of God, nonetheless, they do not all explain this intuition in the same way.

Beyond the properly pantheistic ontologism of Spinoza, which we examined above,[86] three species of ontologism can be distinguished from each other: (1) the ontologism of Nicolas Malebranche, (2) moderate ontol-

---

one to believe that it is the armory that will forever furnish the most toughened weapons for resisting the errors that diminish or exaggerate the value and rights of human reason.

"By contrast, the Scotist theory affirms that the natural order cannot be perfect without a supernatural complement. The consequence flowing from this claim is that it is impossible to fix the limits where the natural order ends and where the supernatural order begins.... As Scotus made grace into a kind of complement of nature and, on the other hand, given that, according to Catholic dogma, grace is a gratuitous gift, logic forces Scotus to conclude . . . that the natural or supernatural character of God's gifts depends, for each, upon an arbitrary determination by God.... He was thus led to place the most legitimate conclusions of reason into doubt." According to him, it is perhaps accidentally the case and miraculously that the human soul is immortal; perhaps its immortality is a gratuitous gift (*In IV Sent.*, d. 43, q. 1, no. 23); likewise, our first duties toward our neighbor do not derive necessarily from our nature, but rather, their determination arises from the divine freedom, which would have been able to determine them in a completely different manner (*In III Sent.* d. 37).

Likewise, see Scheeben, *Dogmatik*, Treatise on God, no. 278: "Set next to the profound explanation of God's invisibility provided by St. Thomas, that of Scotus combatting him seems quite superficial and mechanical. Scotus limits himself to saying that God is naturally invisible to the creature because his absolute independence requires that he not spread out his light around himself, except *when he wishes to do so* through his condescension toward the creature. To reason thus is not only to explain nothing. Moreover, it is to significantly weaken the explanation on an essential point, namely the fact that God, because of his natural invisibility, can render himself visible *not through his will alone* but through *a supernatural influence* that transfigures the created spirit's power of sight."

[86] See our discussion in ch. 8 (examination of pantheism).

ogism, (3) the ontologism of ideal being proposed by Antonio Rosmini.

(1) *The ontologism of Nicolas Malebranche.* Malebranche (1638–1715) thought that we immediately see necessary and universal truths in God through an intellectual intuition. Nay, he held that God is the immediate cause of our sensations, for which external things only play the role of being occasions for his actions. (Hence, his causal system is a form of occasionalism.) Nonetheless, according to Malebranche, we do not see the divine essence as it is in itself but, rather, in a relative sense. That is, we see the divine essence as it is the archetype of those things that fall under the knowledge we have through our senses[87] and our intellect (e.g., the divine ideas of man, substance, spirit, quantity, mathematics, and so forth, as well as the divine attributes relative to the same things). These divine ideas and these attributes are indeed really the same as the divine essence. However, they are virtually (or rationately) distinct, and this distinction suffices, according to Malebranche, so that the divine ideas and divine attributes would be seen without God's essence thereby being seen.[88]

His system intends to have probative strength, for according to him the notion that our ideas would be abstracted from sensible things cannot be admitted. Bodily things cannot act upon the sensitive soul (for the superior does not suffer action from the inferior) and therefore are only occasions for sensation, which has God for its cause. *A fortiori*, that which is necessary, universal, and eternal in our intellectual knowledge cannot arise from singular contingent things. Hence, the clearer and simpler explanation for our thoughts is to say that we see all things in God, for all intelligible things exist in a necessary, universal, and eternal manner in God, and God himself is intimately present to us. Moreover, God must be the first thing willed and loved above all things. Therefore, he must also be the first thing known.

Criticism of Malebranche. This doctrine already made its appearance in the Middle Ages,[89] and St. Thomas examined it in *ST* I, q. 88, a. 3 (whether God is that which is first known by us) as well as in {{343}} *ST* I, q. 85, a. 5 (whether our soul sees everything that it understands in the eternal reasons).[90] Likewise, the Angelic Doctor offered refutations against occasionalism. See *ST* I, q. 105, a. 5 and *De potentia*, q. 3, a. 7.

---

[87] [Trans. note: Reading *cognitioni sensum* as *cognitioni sensuum*.]

[88] See Nicolas Malebranche, *Recherche de la vérité*, ch. 3.

[89] Nay, in the fourteenth century, among the Beguines and Beghards, the Council of Vienne condemned this proposition: "Any intellectual nature in its own self is naturally blessed, and the soul does not need the light of glory raising it to see God and to enjoy Him beatifically" (Council of Vienne, *Ad nostrum qui*, no. 5; Denzinger, no. 895).

[90] Also, see St. Thomas, *In De Trinitate Boetii*, q. 1, a. 3; q. 6, a. 3; *De veritate*, q. 18, a. 1.

According to St. Thomas's thought, we must say that Malebranche's ontologism is devoid of solid arguments. Indeed, it is not impossible that our universal intellectual ideas would be abstracted from singulars (*ST* I, q. 85, a. 1). Nor does it follow from the fact that God is intimately present in us *as a cause* that he would be intimately present in us *as an object* (*ST* I, q. 84, a. 5). Finally, nor does it follow from the fact that he is our ultimate end that he would be the first thing known, for we first desire beatitude in general, just as we first know being in general (*ST* I, q. 2, a. 1, ad 1).

Moreover, Malebranche's ontologism stands in contradiction to the facts of human sense knowledge, for [were his account true] our sense organs would be useless. Likewise, it stands in contradiction to the facts of our intellectual knowledge, for our intellect would need to see all intelligible things in God, making no use of phantasms, and thus would also know spiritual substances. Thus, he who is born blind would have knowledge [*haberet scientiam*] of colors.

Finally, in order to preserve the distinction between the natural and supernatural orders, Malebranche alleges that we see the divine ideas immediately and in themselves but do not, however, see the divine essence in itself. Now, this is contradictory, for a divine idea taken in itself really is the divine essence. Therefore, the former cannot be seen without the latter being seen. Indeed, as St. Thomas says in *ST* II-II, q. 173, a. 1:

> *It is not possible that someone would see the reasons for creatures in the divine essence itself without thereby also seeing the divine essence,* both because the divine essence itself is the formal source [*ratio*] for all of the things that are made (although this ideal formal content adds nothing to the divine essence except a [rationate] relation to the creature) and also because knowledge of something in itself (which is to know God as the object of beatitude) comes before knowing that same thing through a comparison to something else (which is to know God according to the reasons for things existing in Him).

Hence, neither the divine ideas nor the divine attributes can be immediately seen in themselves without the divine essence itself being seen.

Thus, contrary to its author's intention, Malebranche's ontologism leads to *the confusion of the natural order and the supernatural order*. Nay, properly speaking, it leads *to pantheism*, for indeed, if the divine ideas are universals not only in representation but also in the order of existence [*in essendo*],[91]

---

[91] Among the errors of ontologists, this proposition was condemned: "*Universals*, considered in

the divine ideas exist in things as constituting their specific nature. Thus, we find ourselves faced with pantheism.[92] In particular, in ontologism, as in absolute realism, being in general is confused with the divine being. However, by contrast, we must say that being is analogically said of God and creatures. Likewise, in the order of acting, occasionalism leads to pantheism, for if God alone acts, God alone exists, for activity follows upon being. The fundamental error of Malebranche seems to be the confusion of the divine being with being in general, which in reality {{344}} is the adequate object of our intellect—namely, the object in which the first principles are known.

Cardinal Hyacinthe Sigismond Gerdil (1718–1802) defended Malebranche's system, and Vincenzo Gioberti (1801–1852) gave a kind of poetic amplification to this doctrine.

(2) *Moderate ontologism* distinguishes two things in our objective perception, —namely, that which is singular and that which is universal. The singular, which is the immediate object of a sense power, is seen in itself, contrary to what Malebranche asserted in this matter. However, the universal, which is necessary, eternal, and immutable, can only exist in God. Hence, it can only be seen immediately in God through an intellective intuition. The arguments adduced in defense of this claim more or less are the same as Malebranche's. This opinion was held by Casimir Ubaghs (1800–1875), Louis Branchereau (1819–1913), [Flavien] Hugonin, [Jules] Fabre, and others.

The same difficulties remain here as what we found in Malebranche's system. Hence, in 1861, the Sacred Congregation of the Holy Office declared that the following propositions cannot be safely taught:

1) Immediate knowledge of God, at least habitually had, is essential to the human intellect, such that it cannot know anything without that knowledge since, indeed, it is the intellectual light itself.

2) That being that is found in all things, and without which we understand nothing, is the divine being.

3) Universals considered from the perspective of reality are not really distinct from God.[93]

(3) *The ontologism of Antonio Rosmini*.[94] What earlier ontologists said

---

their reality, are not really distinct from God" (Pius IX, Decree of the Holy Office, September 18, 1861, no. 3; Denzinger, nos. 2843).

[92] See Cardinal Tommaso Maria Zigliara, *Summa philosophica*, vol. 1 (Paris: Delhomme et Briguet, 1900), Ontologia (4); theologia naturalis (1).

[93] See Pius IX, Decree of the Holy Office, September 18, 1861, nos. 1–7 (Denzinger, nos. 2841–2847).

[94] See Antonio Rosmini, *Nuovo saggio sull'originale delle idee*, 5th ed. (1852). *Teosofia*, vol. 4 (Del

about universals Rosmini taught concerning transcendental *being*, which first falls under the apprehension of our intellect and is predicated of all things and of each thing in particular. He taught that this being [ens] or "being [*esse*] which man contemplates, must be something of the necessary and eternal being, the creating cause, the determining and final cause of all contingent beings, and this is God."[95]

Criticism. This new form of ontologism confuses being in general with the divine being. It proceeds from an immoderate form of realism: Universal being exists formally from the perspective of reality and thus is identical with the divine being. Hence, being is not said analogically of God and creatures but, rather, univocally. Nay, it is the same in God and in creatures. However, this doctrine leads to pantheism, as is obvious from Rosmini's own propositions: "There is no finite reality, but God causes it to exist by adding limitation to infinite reality.—Initial being becomes the essence of every real being.—Being that actuates finite natures and is joined with them is cut off from God."[96]

{{345}} Against this system of thought, we merely need to refer to what we already proved above—namely, that being is said analogically of necessary being and contingent being, for it does not designate in them a notion that is *simpliciter* the same but, rather, designates a notion that is only proportionally the same, inasmuch as necessary being is related to its uncaused existence as contingent being is related to its own caused existence.[97]

However, having rejected the true notion of analogy, it is not surprising that Rosmini did not preserve the necessary and essential distinction between the natural order and the supernatural order, as is clear in a number of his condemned propositions. Thus, he intended to philosophically demonstrate the Divine Trinity (prop. 25), and the thirty-sixth condemned proposition thus says: "The supernatural order is established by the

---

divino nella natura), sect. 1, ch. 1, no. 2ff. For a criticism of this system, see Cardinal Tommaso Maria Zigliara, *Propaedeutica ad sacram theologiam*, bk. 1, ch. 12; *Summa philosophica*, Psychologia, bk. 4, ch. 2, nos. 9–10.

95 See Leo XIII, Decree of the Holy Office, *Post obitum* (Dec. 14, 1887), no. 5 (Denzinger, no. 3205). This document contains the forty condemned propositions of Rosmini, promulgated after the death of their author. They were excerpted from his own works, especially from his *Teosofia*, as Cardinal Zigliara shows (in the location in *Propaedeutica* cited above). Antonio Francesco Davide Ambrogio Rosmini-Serbati was born March 25, 1797, in the town of Rovereto, in Tyrol. He was ordained in 1821 and founded the "Istituto della Carita," a congregation of priests, in 1828. He died on July 1, 1855, having rejected his errors.

96 See Leo XIII, Decree of the Holy Office, *Post obitum* (Dec. 14, 1887), no. 12 (Denzinger, no. 3212). See in the same place the other propositions to be cited below.

97 See *ST* I, q. 13, a. 5.

manifestation of being in the fullness of its real form; the effect of this communication or manifestation is a deiform sense ('sentimento') which begun in this life, constitutes the light of faith and of grace and which, completed in the next [*altera*] life, constitutes the light of glory."[98] Thus, supernatural faith does not seem to be, in this system, something of a loftier order than natural reason.

The thesis concerning the univocity of being leads to this conclusion. By contrast, on the basis of the analogy of being between God and creatures, there follows the essential and absolute distinction of the natural order from the supernatural order, and hence the possibility of supernatural revelation from the perspective of the object. Now, however, we must turn to a consideration of this possibility from the perspective of the subject—that is, from the perspective of man to whom this revelation is proposed.

---

[98] Leo XIII, Decree of the Holy Office, *Post obitum* (Dec. 14, 1887), no. 36 (Denzinger, no. 3236).

On the Possibility of Revelation of Supernatural Mysteries, Considered from the Perspective of the Agent and Subject

{{346}} The thesis of this chapter can be stated thus: *The possibility of the revelation of supernatural mysteries, considered from the perspective of the subject and agent, cannot be disproven. Nay, we can persuasively argue that our nature has an obediential or [vel] elevable capacity for the supernatural order.*

Single Article: A Defense Is Offered for This Possibility and Especially for the Existence of the Obediential or Elevable Capacity of Our Nature in Relation to the Supernatural Order

§1. State of the question.

§2. This possibility cannot be disproven.

§3. We can persuasively argue that our nature has an obediential capacity to be elevated to the supernatural order, arguing from a consideration of the adequate object of our intellect.

§4. The existence of the same capacity can be persuasively argued for from a consideration of our natural desire to see God through his essence.

§5. Resolution of objections.

§1. State of the Question

This thesis intends to respond to the objection that is often proposed against the preceding conclusion. This objection is found in *ST* I, q. 12, a. 4, obj. 3, was later developed by Scotus, and finally reappeared in the writings of the modernists. In the aforementioned text, St. Thomas placed before himself the following objection: "A bodily sense cannot be elevated to understand an incorporeal substance, for that is above its nature. Therefore, if to see God through His Essence is above the nature of any created intellect, it seems that no created intellect can arrive at seeing the essence of God," even supernaturally.

Likewise, Scotus said:[1] If knowledge of the divine essence were above the nature of our intellect, the blessed will never see God, for no power can be elevated above its specificative object, just as sight {{347}} cannot be elevated to intellection. Otherwise, this power would pass beyond the limits of its essence and would not remain specifically the same.

Modernists have their own objections here as well. (1) If the supernatural order were to infinitely exceed the powers and exigencies of our nature objectively and subjectively, then our elevation to this order would be contrary to the inclination of our nature and thereby would be *violent*. For our adherence to supernatural mysteries ought to be essentially supernatural and, hence, would not proceed from our own natural vitality. Therefore, it would be a kind of non-vital knowledge, imposed externally in by way of mere authority [*auctoritative*], contrary to the autonomy (or perfect vitality) of our reason. This revelation would be a "principle of death" for us rather than a principle of life, like eating a stone, which does not nourish but, rather, brings about death. Nay, this revelation would be, they say, like a stone falling out of heaven upon our head.

Hence, according to the modernists, we must change our notion of nature and conceive it not as something fixed and stable but, rather, as something flowing, ever in the midst of evolution and containing supernatural life within itself in a germinal form.[2] Thus, the modernists return to the

---

[1]   *In IV Sent.*, d. 49, a. 11; *I Sent.*, d. 3, q. 3; *Quod.*, q. 14, a. 2. See Cajetan's response to Scotus in *In ST* I, q. 12, a. 4.

[2]   Édouard Le Roy wrote in "Sur la notion de dogme. Réponse à M. l'abbé Wehrlé," *Revue biblique* 3 (Jan. 1906): 7–38 (esp. 21): "For our part, we do not preserve untouched in its specific meaning this traditional notion of *nature*, which is the cause of all the evil [in this matter], rendering the conflict radically unresolvable. This is why we cannot reconcile the principle of immanence and the affirmation of the supernatural. Human nature is more a progress and a becoming than it is *a thing*. It is not expressible by a concept constituted once and for all. It is not definable in atemporal terms. Experience and development are integral parts of it. It is open and dynamic. It is, by its very essence, life, duration, and invention. Nothing can be defined *statically* and *separately* (at least if one wishes to touch upon the very foundation of things)—and human nature least of all. . . .

"This being granted, what are we exactly saying when we formulate this famous principle of immanence? Merely something quite simple and certain. It is not at all a question of I know

error of Baius: The supernatural order would not absolutely and infinitely surpass the natural order.[3]

(2) The modernists add that this revelation of essentially supernatural mysteries would be useless, for these mysteries would be unintelligible for us like empty words. Indeed, they would infinitely exceed the natural objective medium of our intellect as well as its natural notions and principles. {{348}} Hence, they could not be understood, nor expressed, in a truthful way by means of the natural notions of our reason. The conceptual expression of these mysteries would only be *metaphorical* and symbolic, leaving natural reason as the supreme arbiter for judging the sense in which these formulas ought to be accepted, just as it judges concerning the merely metaphoric value of the expression "God is angry," for anger is a passion and hence does not properly exist in God. Thus, the formulas of supernatural mysteries would be merely metaphorical.

§2. This Possibility Cannot Be Disproven

I do not say that it is demonstrated, for this possibility cannot be proven, as is clear from what we said in our preceding thesis. Also, any mystery that is essentially supernatural [in its very being] is likewise supernatural from the perspective of its knowability [*quoad cognoscibilitatem*], inasmuch as truth and being are convertible. Now, revelation of supernatural mysteries (or our elevation to the supernatural order) is itself a mystery that is essentially supernatural. Therefore, this revelation and elevation is supernatural from the perspective of its knowability. Hence, its possibility cannot be demonstrated by reason alone.

---

not what *naturalist* doctrine, according to which man would be self-sufficient for fulfilling his destiny. Who holding such a doctrine has ever had the naivety and audacity to call himself a Catholic? However, who does not also see that a doctrine of this kind necessarily presupposes the static and closed-up concept of 'nature' that I recalled above? No, the principle of immanence does not present a kind of summary of a *doctrine*, above all a doctrine involving exclusion and the cutting up of things. Rather, it describes a *method* and is related less to the truth in itself than to our manner of entering into relation with it. What it says is that a truth that would come to us purely *from without*, like something radically external, foreign, and heterogenous to our mind, without prior preparations in us and without preexisting dispositions, without any postulates (even be they latent) on our own part, I say that such a truth is *a principle of spiritual death*—if we can indeed use the word 'truth,' for it would be inadmissible, ungraspable, a pure non-being for us, and yet, one nonetheless accepts it by *being subjected* to it as a kind of [merely] verbal instruction. Such a stone within the organism does not provide nourishment but, rather, kills. Such an aerolite falling from the heaven either will not reach you or will split open your head. . . . The religious problem must inexorably arise *in us* if we wish for it to exist *for us*. In order to be living, every truth must have its roots in us, must be inserted in us, and must respond to a need that is more or less felt by us."

[3] See Pius X, *Pascendi*, no. 37 (Denzinger, 2103, old numbering).

We did indeed demonstrate the existence of an utterly supernatural order, considered in general and negatively, as exceeding our reason. However, any mystery pertaining to this order remains indemonstrable.[4]

Nonetheless, this possibility cannot be disproven, and reason can marshal a defense of it against the objections of those who deny it.

Indeed, in order to disprove the possibility of the revelation of supernatural mysteries from the perspective of the agent and subject, one must demonstrate the contradictory nature of at least one of the four things required for this revelation. That is, one would need to prove:

(a) either that it is contradictory to say that God acts freely *ad extra* according to his intimate life;

(b) or that no idea of our mind can analogically and properly express supernatural mysteries as things to be believed;

(c) or that it is contradictory to speak of [an intellectual] light that is essentially supernatural, elevating the vitality of our intellect to assent supernaturally to these mysteries;

(d) or, finally, that our nature does not contain an obediential or elevable potency for the supernatural order.

Now, none of these four positions can be proven.

Therefore, the possibility of the revelation of supernatural mysteries cannot be disproven from the perspective of the subject and agent.

To explain this argument, many very difficult matters must be set forth, which are understood more clearly in the particular treatises of theology [*in theologia speciali*]. However, they must be borne in mind here [*iam sunt scitu necessaria*] if we wish to resolve the objections of modernists down to the roots of their arguments.

{{349}} (1) *The major premise is obvious.* Indeed, it provides a complete enumeration because, as we said above, revelation is a supernatural act of God that requires three things from man's perspective—namely, the ordering of our intelligible *species* or ideas to the manifestation of a truth that heretofore was hidden; a supernatural light for adhering infallibly and supernaturally to the divinely proposed truth; and finally, this elevating light presupposes that we have an elevable potency, which is called an obediential potency, for the receiving of this elevation from God.

---

[4] See Billuart, *Summa sancti Thomae, De Deo*, diss. 4, a. 3, appendix (Whether the possibility of the beatific vision can be demonstrated or known of through the light of reason alone). His response is negative. Such is also the case for other Thomists commenting on the same points in the treatise *De deo* [*in eodem loco*]—for example, Gonet, the Salmanticenses, and others. Likewise, in ibid., *De fide*, diss. 1, a. 6, ad obiectionem 2: "Natural reason cannot by its own power know the possibility of supernatural faith in a particularized manner [*in paritculari*]."

However, if the divinely proposed truth is essentially supernatural, then the [intellectual] light [for knowing this truth] must be proportioned to this object inasmuch as *habitus* and acts are specified by their objects. In order to essentially and formally believe a supernatural mystery, we must have an infused faith that is essentially supernatural. Natural, acquired faith, such as is found, for example, in demons, reaches supernatural mysteries only in a material manner, just as (all proportions maintained) a dog materially hears human speech in its sensible sound without grasping its intelligible meaning. Hence, it is said, "But the sensual man perceiveth not these things that are of the Spirit of God. For it is foolishness to him" (1 Cor 2:14, DR).

(2) *The minor premise* will be explained in parts. There can be no demonstration of these four claims.

A. One cannot prove that it is contradictory to say that *God freely acts ad extra according to his intimate life*—namely, by communicating to us a participation in the Divine Nature qua divine (i.e., a participation in his intimate life). Indeed, we are to deny nothing of God, he who is the Most Perfect Being, except on account of some imperfection. Now, the idea that God would act freely *ad extra* according to his intimate life does not imply any imperfection in God, for every agent acts inasmuch as it is in act and is self-diffusive inasmuch as it is good. However, such self-diffusivity takes place freely if he already has infinite goodness in himself, having no need to act *ad extra* for the seeking of his own beatitude. Finally, "to the degree that a given nature is loftier, it is equally the case that what emanates from it is all the more intimate," as is excellently explained in *SCG* IV, ch. 11. Indeed, the living being acts in a more intimate way than inorganic bodies, animals more than plants, man more than brute animals, and the greater a man is in knowledge [*scientia*] or virtue, to that degree does that which emanates from him more intimately exist within him.

God, however, is pure act and the highest good. Hence, it cannot be proven that it is contradictory to speak of God communicating to us some kind of participation in his intimate life. Just as fire can ignite things, why could not God in some way "deify [us] by communicating a share in the divine nature through a kind of participation in His likeness"?[5]

B. Nor can one prove the claim that *no idea of our mind is able to analogically and properly express supernatural things like things that are believed* [*credibilia*]. Indeed, as we already said above against the semi-rationalists, the natural notions and principles of our reason cannot express the mysteries of God's intimate life as *things that are scientifically known* [*scibilia*] (that is,

---

[5] *ST* I-II, q. 112, a. 1.

things that can be demonstrated); however, for revelation, it suffices that they be expressed analogically and properly,[6] as *things that are believed*, according to the testimony of God who reveals them obscurely and not according to intrinsic evidence. Now, our mind's incapacity for expressing {{350}} such things cannot be proven. Indeed, as we said, the only reason that something can be denied of God, he who is the Most Perfect Being, is on account of such a thing's imperfection. Now, one cannot demonstrate the imperfection that would follow in God from the expression of the Deity through the notions of procession, paternity, filiation, spiration, relation, and so forth, by which the supreme supernatural mystery (namely, the mystery of the Holy Trinity) is obscurely manifested to us. Likewise, one cannot prove the imperfection that would follow for God from the expression of the mysteries of the Incarnation, Redemption, Eucharist, and so forth.

Indeed, it is true that before revelation we cannot prove the transcendent and analogical value of these notions for expressing God's intimate life in a true manner. However, God has made use of these notions, and after revelation of them, theology can defend their transcendent value against the objections of those who deny them. Thus, theology makes use of philosophy "in order to resist those things *that are said against faith*, either by showing that they *are false* or by showing *that they are not necessary*."

Nay, one can manifest the fact that there is a kind of befittingness regarding the supernatural mysteries. For example, St. Thomas manifests the befittingness of the mysteries of the Holy Trinity, the Incarnation, the elevation of our nature to the supernatural order, the Eucharist, and so forth, on the basis of the aforementioned principle, "to the degree that a given nature is loftier, it is equally the case that what emanates from it is all the more intimate," or, "it pertains to the very character of the good that it communicate itself to others. Whence, it pertains to the notion of the highest good that it would communicate itself in the highest manner."[7]

Hence, one cannot prove that it is contradictory to speak of the revelation of supernatural mysteries from the perspective of our ideas. What is quite clearly contradictory, as we already have said, is that some created idea (even an infused one) would represent Self-Subsistent Existence and Intellection as he is in himself, or that supernatural mysteries would be demonstrated on the basis of the notions and principles of our reason. Indeed, they are above the virtuality of our principles, although not contrary to them, for they pertain positively to the Deity as such—that is, to the proper and intimate mode of a superior analogate of being, although this mode cannot be known naturally except in a negative and relative manner.

---

6 *Properly* is said here in opposition to *metaphorically* or *symbolically*.

7 *ST* III, q. 1, a. 1.

C. One cannot prove that it is contradictory to speak of *an [intellectual] light that is essentially supernatural*, necessary for adhering infallibly and supernaturally to the mysteries of the intimate life of God. Indeed, it is contradictory to speak of a created supernatural substance, as well as of a created idea representing God as he is in himself. However, a supernatural light elevating the created intellect is an accident and not a substance. Hence, it is an accident playing its role on the side of the subject, strengthening his intellect, and does not play its role on the side of the object as representing God actually as he is in himself.

Now, just as an accident is a being in another, it can also be a *being ordered to another [ens ad aliud]*, like a power or *habitus*, which are specified by the object to which they are essentially ordered. Hence, one cannot prove that it is contradictory to speak of a given created accident specified by God, reduplicatively precisely as he is God (i.e., one essentially ordered to knowing and loving the intimate life of God). Already in the natural order, our intellect is a created and finite power that nonetheless {{351}} is essentially ordered to analogous being—that is, to knowing all beings, at least in the mirror of sensible things. Hence, Aristotle said, "The soul is, in some way, all things."

That supernatural light cannot indeed *actually* represent the essence of God as it is in itself. However, it is not obviously contradictory to say that it has an essential *tendency* toward God precisely as he is God and, in this way, elevates our intellect. (This is explained at length by the Thomists when they speak of the question of the beatific vision.)[8]

D. Finally, one cannot disprove *that our nature has an obediential capacity to be elevated to the supernatural order*. As St. Thomas says on this matter:

Indeed, because a sense power is completely material, it can in no way be elevated to something immaterial. However, given that our intellect—or also that of an angel—of its own nature is elevated above matter, it can be elevated above its own nature through grace to something higher. And a sign of this is that sense vision cannot in any way know abstractly what it knows concretely, for it can in

---

8 See Billuart, *Summa sancti Thomae, De Deo*, diss. 4, a. 5 (on the light of glory); a. 6 (why there cannot be *species* representing God as he is in himself). "The difference between the light of glory and a *species* is the fact that the *light* of glory holds *on the side of the power* which it elevates to the supernatural order, and this suffices so that it be proportioned to attaining God in a finite way. However, *the species* holds *on the part of the object* as its formal likeness, representing it as it is in itself. Now, nothing can represent God as He is in Himself unless it be immaterial and infinite like God Himself" (ibid., a. 6, solv. obi., 1st obj.).

no way perceive a nature except as this particular one. However, our intellect can consider abstractly what it knows concretely . . . for it considers the very form of things in itself, nay, . . . *it separates out existence itself [esse ipsum] through abstraction.*[9] And therefore, since the created intellect by its very nature is able to apprehend a concrete form and a concrete existence in abstraction by way of a kind of resolution, *it can be elevated by grace to know the Separate, Subsistent Existence.*[10]

This elevation at least cannot be disproven.

However, this last point stands in need of explanation, for the true notion of our nature's obediential or elevable potency for the supernatural order provides the key for resolving objections drawn from the vitality and autonomy of our reason: How can our vitality be elevated to elicit essentially supernatural acts? Now, this capacity is made manifest in two ways: (1) from the perspective of *our intellect's natural object*; and (2) subjectively, from the perspective of our *natural desire to see God through his essence.*

§3. We Can Persuasively Argue That Our Nature Has an Obediential Capacity to Be Elevated to the Supernatural Order, Arguing from a Consideration of the Adequate Object of Our Intellect

St. Thomas makes this argument in *ST* I, q. 12, a. 4, ad 3, and it underwent

---

[9] [Trans. note: Fr. Garrigou-Lagrange has "ipsum esse secernit per abstractionem", whereas the original reads, "tamen potest ipsum esse secernere per intellectum, dum cognoscit quod aliud est ipse, et aliud est suum esse": however, it can separate off existence itself by the intellect when it knows that the thing itself is one thing and that its existence is another. There, St. Thomas is referring to the angelic intellect, though the point is applicable to the human intellect as well. There are dangers in speaking of "abstraction" here as though the human intellect grasps being through the psychological act of quidditative abstraction (though one may broadly speak of an imperfect abstraction here in a logical sense, though it would be consequent to the initial act of judgment).

On this topic, though coming at St. Thomas's texts from a different direction than Fr. Garrigou-Lagrange, see John Wippel in "Metaphysics and 'Separatio' According to Thomas Aquinas," *The Review of Metaphysics* 31, no. 3 (Mar. 1978): 431–70. Fr. Garrigou-Lagrange was not unaware of these issues. See Réginald Garrigou-Lagrange, "De intelligentia naturali et de primo obiecto ab ipsa cognito," in *Acta Pontificiae Academiae Romanae sancti Thomae Aquinatis et religionis catholicae* 6 (1939–1940): 137–54. Also see Jacques Maritain, *Existence and the Existent*, trans. Gerald Phelan and Lewis Galantière (New York: Pantheon, 1948), 10–46 (esp. 26–28n13 and 28–30n14).]

[10] *ST* I, q. 12, a. 4, ad 3.

development by later Thomists in their comments on the same article.[11] It can be reduced to the following syllogism.

There is in us an obediental or elevable capacity for knowledge of a reality that exceeds the proper object of our intellect, though not its adequate object.

{{352}} Now, God, known from the intimate perspective of the Deity [*sub ratione intima Deitatis*], does not exceed the *adequate* object of our intellect—namely, *being its full latitude*—although it does exceed its proper object, namely, the essence of sensible things.

Therefore, we have in ourselves an obediential or elevable capacity for knowledge of God's intimate life—that is, knowledge of supernatural mysteries.

In order to explain the major premise, three things must be discussed: (1) what an obediential potency is; (2) what the proper object of our intellect is; (3) what its adequate object is. (4) Finally, we must defend the minor premise.

(1) ***What an obediential potency is.*** St. Thomas discusses this matter in *ST* III, q. 11, a. 1; q. 1, a. 3, ad 3; *De virtutibus in communi*, a. 10, ad 2 and ad 13; *Compendium theologiae*, ch. 104. Also, see the *Tabula aurea* at the word "potentia," no. 10.

In order to understand this notion, we must consider the division of potency itself, according to St. Thomas.[12] [The following diagram summarizes the various senses of the term "potentia" or "potency" according to St. Thomas and the Thomist school:]

potency
- *objective potency* (i.c. possibility): non-opposition to existence
- *subjective potency*
  - *active*
  - *passive*
    - *natural*
    - *obediential* relative to...
      - a created agent of a superior order (e.g., wood in relation to a carpenter)
      - God
        - the Author and master of nature
        - the Author of supernatural life

---

[11] See John of St. Thomas, Domingo Bañez, the Salmanticenses, and Billuart, *Summa sancti Thomae, De Deo*, diss. 4, a. 3, obj. 4.

[12] See John of St. Thomas, *Cursus philosophicus, Physica*, q. 4, a. 2 (*in fine*).

With Aristotle, St. Thomas[13] first distinguishes possibility (which is also called "objective potency") from subjective potency. *Possibility* is non-opposition to existence. *Subjective potency* is some subject's aptitude or real principle for acting or undergoing something. For example, man has the ability [*potentiam*] to understand.

Aristotle[14] divides *subjective potency* into active and passive potency. *Active* potency is a principle of action (e.g., the will). *Passive* potency is the aptitude for undergoing or receiving something from another. Thus, the human intellect is said to be a passive potency inasmuch as it is an aptitude to receive an impression from the intelligible object, although it also is active in another respect—namely, for eliciting an act of understanding.

Passive potency either is natural or obediential, as St. Thomas says in *ST* III, q. 11, a. 3:

> In the human soul, just as in any given creature, we can consider two kinds of passive potency. On the one hand, there is that which is related to a natural agent and, on the other, there is that potency that is related to the First Agent, who can reduce any creature to some act that is higher than what it can be reduced to by a natural agent, and this is usually called an obediential potency in the creature.[15]

A natural passive potency is immediately ordered to an act or object proportioned to nature. For example, the intellect is naturally and immediately ordered {{353}} to the receiving of intelligible species abstracted from sensible things.

By contrast, *an obediential potency* is not naturally ordered to some act or object but, rather, *designates an order to an agent of a superior nature, which it obeys.* And this can be considered in two ways:

(a) It can be considered in relation *to a relatively supernatural agent.* Such is the case for wood in relation to the carpenter from which it can receive the form of a stool or a table, for wood is not naturally ordered to the first form any more than it is ordered to the latter but, rather, receives this ordination from the craftsman. However, the wood does prerequire determinate natural passive potencies for being made into a table, something that is not found, for example, in water.

---

[13] See *In V Meta.*, lect. 14; *In IX Meta.*, lect. 1.

[14] See In V *Meta.*, lect. 14.

[15] Likewise, see *De potentia*, q. 6, a. 1, ad 18.

(b) Secondly, obediential potency can be considered in relation *to an absolutely supernatural agent*—namely, in relation to God. Thus, as St. Thomas writes, "In every creature, there is a kind of obediential potency inasmuch as every creature obeys God so that it may receive in itself whatever God wills."[16] However, the divine will and omnipotence are limited only with regard to that which involves contradiction in relation to existence, for an infinite active power can make something from no presupposed real passive power, as happens in the case of creation. Indeed, the less the passive potency, the greater is the perfection of the active power [involved in reducing it to act].[17] And therefore, an obediential potency in the creature relative to God is not an active faculty but, rather, is a passive aptitude. Nay, this aptitude is nothing other than a mere non-opposition to receiving from God what God wills.

However, this obediential potency in relation to God can be considered in two ways. (a) It can be considered in relation *to God the Author and Lord of nature* (e.g., as in a corpse in relation to God who is the Author of bodily life and of the resurrection [of such natural bodily life]). Thus, all creatures are naturally suited to obey God without any violence being done to them, just as the arm is naturally suited to be moved by the will. And this obediential potency is prerequired for any miracle whatsoever to occur. Thus, a miraculous effect is [modally] super-natural, not contrary to the natural order.

(b) In another way, "obediential potency" is said in relation *to God the Author of supernatural life.* This potency does not exist in every creature, for brute animals are by their nature unable [*repugnant*] to be elevated to supernatural life. Indeed, our question here can be stated as follows: Is this passive obediential (or "elevable") potency (i.e., this non-opposition) found in man?

(2) *What the proper object of our intellect is.* Following Aristotle, St. Thomas teaches that the proper object of our intellect is the essence of sensible things (or *intelligible being existing in sensible things*).[18]

This can be proven in two ways: (A) *a posteriori* and (B) *a priori*.

---

[16] *De virtutibus in communi*, q. 1, a. 10, ad 13.

[17] See *ST* I, q. 45, a. 5, ad 3.

[18] See *ST* I, q. 12, a.4; q. 85, a. 1; q. 84, a. 7; q. 87, a. 3; II-II, q. 8, a. 1. In Aristotle see *De anima* 3.6 and 3.7 (lect. 11 and 12); *Metaphysics*, 1.1; *Post. Anal.*, 2.15. Also see Zigliara, *Summa philosophiae*, Psychologia, bk. 4, ch. 1, no. 3.

A. *A posteriori.* The proper object of any knowing faculty is that which is first and essentially known by it so that all other things known by this faculty are known in relation to its formal character [*ratione illius et ad modum illius*].[19]

{{354}} Now, our intellect first and essentially knows the intelligible being of sensible things, as well as the essences of these things, knowing all other things (namely, the intellective soul and God) in relation to them.

Therefore, the proper object of our intellect is the intelligible being of sensible things (or the essence of sensible things).

The major premise is the definition of a proper (or proportionate) object, by which we can distinguish the human intellect, the angelic intellect, and the divine intellect from each other.

The minor premise is *inductively* obvious, for our intellect naturally first knows the intelligible (or universal) abstracted from sensible things—namely, the being of sensible thing—and, with increasing distinctness, the various essences of sensible things.[20] For our intellectual knowledge is not through infused species but, rather, through ones that are abstracted from our sense knowledge, which is clear *a posteriori* "from the fact that if we lack some sense, we also will lack the knowledge [*scientia*] of those things that are grasped by that sense. Thus, the person born blind cannot have knowledge of colors. And this would not be the case if our intellect had ideas [*rationes*] of all intelligible things naturally infused into it."[21]

Afterwards, our intellect knows the intellective soul and God in relation to sensible things, in the mirror of sensible things. Thus, we positively know created spirits and God according to predicates that are analogically *common* to them and sensible things (e.g., being, essence, unity, goodness, action, and so forth). However, we only negatively and relatively know what *properly* belongs to created spirits and God. Thus, we conceive of spirituality negatively as immateriality and intellectual activity relative to physical light (thus speaking of "the light of the intellect"). Nay, we know nothing naturally without turning toward the phantasms, at least to the phantasm of a word corresponding to an idea.[22]

Hence, *a posteriori*, it is clear that the proper object of our intellect is "not any being and truth whatsoever but, rather, being and truth considered in material things. We come to know all other things on the basis of our knowledge thereof."[23]

B. Likewise, this point is made manifest *a priori* from the fact that our

---

[19] See *ST* I, q. 1, a. 7.
[20] See *ST* I, q. 85, a. 3.
[21] *ST* I, q. 84, a. 3 and 6.
[22] See *ST* I, q. 84, a. 7; q. 87, a. 1–4, and q. 88.
[23] See *ST* I, q. 87, a. 3, ad 1.

intellect is a faculty of the soul, which is naturally united to the body. Indeed, knowledge occurs inasmuch as the known is in the knower, indeed being in the knower according to the knower's mode of being. Now, the human intellect is naturally joined to the body (and, thus, to the senses). Therefore, the proper (or proportionate) object of the human intellect is the intelligible that exists in sensible things.[24]

In other words, "a knowing power is proportioned to that which is knowable. Whence, the proper object of the angel's intellect, which is completely separated from a body, is an intelligible substance separated from a body. Thus, it knows material things through an intelligible of this sort. However, the proper object of the human intellect which is joined to a body, is a quiddity or nature existing in bodily matter. Through these kinds of natures of visible things, it even can arrive at some knowledge of invisible things."[25] "Indeed, inferior spiritual substances, namely [human] souls, have their being as connected to the body inasmuch as they are forms of bodies. Therefore, on account of their very mode of existence, it falls to them to seek out their intelligible perfection through bodies, for otherwise, they would be united to bodies for no reason."[26] Hence, on account of its natural *weakness*, our intellect is ordered to knowing the intelligible existing in the shade of sensible things.[27]

{{355}} From this, it is also clear *a priori* (that is, from the cause that explains the conclusion) that the proper object of the human intellect is the essence of sensible things, just as the proper object of the angelic intellect is the essence of a created spiritual thing, and the proper object of the divine intellect is the divine essence. The supreme intellect is proportioned to the supreme intelligible, and the lowest intellect to the lowest intelligible.

(3) *What the adequate or extensive object of our intellect is.* St. Thomas responds[28] that it is *being according to the full latitude of being and not only inasmuch as it is knowable in the mirror of sensible things.*

The Holy Doctor says in *ST* I, q. 79, a. 7:

> Powers of the soul are distinguished according to the various formal characters of their objects.... We already said above (q. 59, a. 4) that if a given power were ordered according to its proper formal character to a given object according to the common formal character of that object, that power would not be differentiated according to the particular differences of that object—just as the power

---

[24] See *ST* I, q. 12, a. 4.

[25] *ST* I, q. 84, a. 7.

[26] *ST* I, q. 55, a. 2.

[27] See *ST* I, q. 76, a. 5.

[28] See *ST* I, q. 12, a. 4, ad 3; q. 79, a. 7; q. 5, a. 2; I-II, q. 94, a. 2; *De veritate*, q. 1, a. 1; *Compendium theologiae*, q. 104.

of sight which considers its object according to the formal character of being colored is not diversified according to the formal character of white or black. Now, the intellect considers its object *according to the common notion of being*, for the possible intellect is "that by which we can become all things" [*quo est omnia fieri*]. Whence, the power of the possible intellect is not diversified by any difference of beings.

Indeed, on the basis of this we can easily prove that our intellect extends to every being inasmuch as every being is at least *analogically* knowable in the mirror of sensible things. Thus, we know our spiritual soul and God himself in this way. Nay, quasi-*a priori*, it is clear that the adequate formal object of our intellect is *being* inasmuch as nothing is intelligible for us except according to a resolution to being and to the first principles of being. Indeed, every notion is resolved into the very first notion of being;[29] likewise, every judgment has as its formal element the verb "is," which is, as it were, the soul of the judgment; finally, every reasoning assigns the *raison d'être* [that is, the reason for *the existence*] of the thing asserted in the conclusion, or at least of the assertion of this thing. Thus, nothing is intelligible in the three activities of our intellect [*mentis*] (conception, judgment, and reasoning) except through a resolution to being. And this makes it clear that the formal and adequate object of the intellect is *being*. Hence, God is knowable, at least analogically, under the formal notion of being and in the mirror of sensible things, contrary to what agnostics assert.

However, it is more difficult to prove that the adequate and extensive object of our intellect is being according to the full latitude of being—that is, also as exceeding what is knowable in the mirror of sensible or even spiritual creatures.

St. Thomas argues persuasively on behalf of this on the basis of a sign—namely, from the distinction between the senses and our intellect. See the aforementioned text, *ST* I, q. 12, a. 4, ad 3:

> Given that the sense of sight is completely material, it cannot in any way be elevated to [knowledge of] something immaterial. However, *our intellect* (or that of the angels), given that it is in some way *elevated above matter* by its nature, can through grace be raised above its nature to something higher. And a *sign* of this is that sense vision cannot in any way know in abstraction {{356}} that which it knows concretely, for it cannot perceive nature except as being this particular thing. However, our intellect can consider in abstraction what it knows concretely. Indeed, even if it knows things having a form in matter, nonetheless it resolves the composite into both of these and considers the *form* separately by itself. Similarly, although it is connatural to the angel's intellect

---

[29] See *De veritate*, q. 1, a. 2.

that it know that the concrete thing exists in a given nature, nonetheless, it can separate that very *existence* through its intellect when it knows that the thing itself is different from its existence. Therefore, *since the created intellect by its very nature is able to grasp* the concrete *form* and concrete *existence through abstraction* by way of a kind of resolution, *it can be elevated through grace so that it might know* the separate subsisting substance and *separate subsisting existence.*

Likewise, he says in *ST* I-II, q. 113, a. 10: "*The soul* is naturally capable of grace, *for from the very fact that it is made in the Image of God, it is capable of* [*being united to God*] *through grace,* as St. Augustine says in the aforementioned text (*De Trinitate,* bk. 14, ch. 8)." However, the soul is made in the image of God inasmuch as it is made like unto it not only inasmuch as it exists, nor only inasmuch as it lives (like plants and animals) but, rather, *inasmuch as it understands,* as is explained in *ST* I, q. 93, a. 2.[30]

On the basis of these texts, the Thomists came to form the following argument, which they proposed as something probable, though not apodictic:

In our intellect, we must distinguish the active power of understanding, which is specific to us, from the passive capacity that belongs to every created intellect (and according to which our soul is made in the image of God).[31]

Now, this passive capacity of our intellect is greater than its active power and of itself is not limited to some order of intelligibles, whereas, by contrast, our intellect's active capacity extends only to those things that are knowable on the basis of our knowledge of sensible things.[32]

Therefore, this passive capacity is not opposed to being elevated to

---

[30] This whole question 93 must be carefully read in order to have a deep understanding of the present problem. Much concerning this matter can be found in Joachim Sestili, *De naturali intelligentis animae capacitate atque appetitu intuendi divinam essentiam* (Rome: Festa, 1899), pt. 2 (on the nature of the Image and its exigencies—on the natural capacity of the Image), 41–92. However, Sestili admits that we have an *innate* inefficacious natural desire to see God through his essence (though not after the manner of a weight inclining our nature [*non per modum ponderis naturae*]). As will be discussed below, we hold that this desire is elicited.

[31] Indeed, as Aristotle and St. Thomas explain in *De anima,* bk. 3, lect. 10: "In every nature that is sometimes in potency and sometimes in act, we must hold that there is something that is in (passive) potency to all things which are of that kind and something that is like an active and productive cause. . . . However, the soul in its intellective part is sometimes in potency and sometimes in act. Therefore, it is necessary that these different [principles] be found in the intellective soul."

[32] Also, in general, *for every creature its passive capacity has a greater amplitude than its active power,* for it operates inasmuch as it itself is in act but can undergo action under the influence of more universal superior agents. Thus, any creature can receive more than it can do.

knowledge of the most perfect intelligible being, surpassing the mirror of creatures.

Indeed, the mode of informing the intellective power from the perspective of the intelligible object, however utterly perfect it may be, is nothing other than a spiritual mode [of existence] excluding all matter and hence does not seem to exceed our "elevable" or obediential capacity.[33]

{{357}} Therefore, this passive obediential capacity belongs to the human intellect not properly inasmuch as it is *human* but, instead, inasmuch as it is *an intellect*[34]—that is, not properly as it is united to a body but, rather, inasmuch as it is purely immaterial and transcends the body, which is made clear in the following division:

---

[33] Domingo Bañez and John of St. Thomas disagree here regarding a secondary matter, at least in their terminology. John of St. Thomas says that the capacity of the intellect, which is ordered to being according to its full latitude, is univocal, not in the formal character of being and of itself, but in the manner in which the intellect is passively actualizeable and elevable to understanding. Indeed, he says that this constitutes the generic formal character of created intellects. (Cf. John of St. Thomas, *De anima*, q. 10, a. 3). Bañez, in contrast, says in his comments on *ST* I, q. 12, a. 1 (and here seems to speak more correctly on this matter): This capacity is specified by an analogous and not a univocal object, for *a threefold capacity* can be considered in our intellect: (1) *the specific capacity* by which we know sensible things or [other things] in the mirror of sensible things, (2) *the generic capacity* on account of which we come together with angels and on account of which the separated soul sees the angels, and (3) *the analogous capacity* on account of which we have a unique likeness to God [*qua convenimus cum Deo*] who is to be known supernaturally, by which we are made in God's image. Bañez's thought in this matter better agrees with St. Thomas's doctrine about the soul being analogically made in the image of God, for the intellect as intellect is analogous, like the being by which it is specified.

Moreover, it is utterly certain that natural being and supernatural being only analogically agree in the formal character of being, and thus too in the formal character of their knowability, for truth and being are convertible.

Likewise, see Billuart, *Summa sancti Thomae, De Deo*, diss. 4, a. 3, solv. obj.

[34] See St. Thomas's comments on Hebrews 4:12 (DR): "The word of God . . . is more piercing than any two edged sword; and reaching unto *the division of the soul and the spirit*." He says: "Our spirit is that by which we have something in common with spiritual substances. However, in speaking of our soul, we refer to what we hold in common with brute animals . . . . The essence of the soul is one and the same thing which through its essence enlivens the body and through its power, which is called the intellect, is the principle of understanding." Likewise, see his comments on 1 *Thessalonians* 5:23.

Similarly, see Johannes Tauler's sermon for the Monday after Easter (trans. Noël, vol. 2, 306): "Certainly we do not hold converse with the heavens by our bodies, nor by our soul inasmuch as it bestows life upon the body, but rather, only by our spirit, 'Indeed, God is spirit and he who adores God must adore Him in spirit' (John 4:24), that is, from the deepest place within himself, in truth, in knowledge—all things that belong to the spirit. Therefore, outside of the spirit, we have no access or entry to God. It is by the spirit, says St. Augustine, that we have a greater resemblance to God. It is by the spirit that we are *capable*, that we have the *capacity for God*." Likewise, see vol. 4, 69.

Intellect $\begin{cases} \text{divine proper object} \ldots\ldots\ldots \text{the divine essence} \\ \text{angelic} \ldots\ldots\ldots\ldots\ldots\ldots\ldots \text{essence of the angel} \\ \text{human} \ldots\ldots\ldots\ldots\ldots\ldots\ldots \text{essence of a sensible thing} \end{cases}$ being

By contrast, a distinction between the proper and adequate objects cannot be drawn for the senses and, hence, neither can we speak of there being an elevable capacity in the senses for knowledge of immaterial things.

Thus, our major premise is persuasively argued: We have an obediential capacity for being elevated to knowledge of a reality exceeding the proper object of our intellect, though not its adequate object. Now, this [adequate] object is being according to the full latitude of being—namely, being even as exceeding the mirror of sensible and spiritual creatures. Now, however, we must defend this minor premise.

(4) *God, even considered from the intimate perspective of the Deity [sub intima ratione Deitatis], does not exceed the adequate object of our intellect,* which is being according to {{358}} its full latitude, although he exceeds its proper object, which is the essence of sensible things or the mirror of sensible things.

This minor premise is made manifest as follows.

The supreme [*superius*] analogate is contained within the latitude of the common analogue itself. Now, God, even considered from the intimate perspective of the Deity, is the supreme analogate of being in general [*in communi*]. Therefore, God, even considered from the intimate perspective of the Deity, is contained within the [full] latitude of being in general [*in communi*], which is our intellect's adequate object.

The major premise is clear. The supreme [*superius*] analogate is contained within the latitude of the common analogue itself, for otherwise this common analogue would not truly be common to all of its analogates. Thus, the divine wisdom and human wisdom are within the latitude of wisdom in general.

The minor premise can easily be made clear. God, formally considered as the first *being*, is the supreme analogate of being in general. However, from the perspective of this general formal character, God is known by us even naturally in the mirror of sensible things and more perfectly by the angels in the mirror of intelligible things.

However, presupposing (as was urged earlier) that the adequate object of our intellect is being according to its full latitude (namely, being even as exceeding the mirror of sensible and intelligible creatures), it is quite clear that God, considered from the intimate perspective of the Deity, does not exceed being understood in this sense.

Indeed, the formal and utterly proper notion of the Deity is loftier than all simply simple perfections, which are identified in its eminence, and thus is *above being* and *above unity* [*unum*].[35]

Nonetheless, the Deity *formally*-eminently contains the formal character of being, whereas it only *virtually* contains mixed perfections such as animality. Therefore, God in himself is formally being and is not outside of [the formal character] of being. Nay, it is only in the Deity that *being* and the other simply simple perfections exist in their utterly pure state—that is, without any admixture with potentiality. Therefore, presupposing that the adequate object of our intellect is being according to its full latitude and without restriction, the Deity (i.e., the intimate life of God) is found within this latitude. In this way, we have a defense for the possibility of our intellect being elevated to supernatural knowledge *of the intimate nature of utterly pure being*, first according to the obscurity of faith and afterwards according to the clarity of immediate vision.

{{359}} *The value of this argument.* As the Thomists commonly say,[36] this argument is not apodictic in character but, rather, is very probable. As the Salmanticenses say:

> It is not evident, by the natural light of reason, that the adequate object of the intellect is being inasmuch as it abstracts from natural and supernatural [being]. Whence, he who asserts that its object is only natural being (namely, being as naturally known in the mirror of creatures) cannot be convinced that this is evidently false by the light of natural reason alone.—Moreover, although we freely grant that it is evident that the object of the intellect is being according to

---

[35] Indeed, in *ST* I, q. 13, a. 5, St. Thomas says: "What is found in effects in a divided and mani-fold form is found simply and in the same mode [*in eodem modo*] in the cause, just as the sun according to a single power produces many and sundry forms in inferior things. In the same way, all the perfections of things that are found in created things in a divided and multiplied manner preexist in God in a united fashion." Now, Cajetan explains this in no. 7 of his com-mentary on this article: "The formal notion of wisdom and the formal notion of justice are elevated to a single formal notion of a superior order, namely, the proper notion of the Deity, and are one single formal notion, *eminently* containing both of them, not only virtually (like light containing the notion of heat) but *formally* (as light contains the formal character of being a heating power)." Likewise, in *In ST* I, q. 39, a. 1, no. 7, Cajetan says: "The deity (or the divine reality) is prior to being and all of its differences, for it is *above being, above unity* [*unum*], and so forth. . . . And hence, in the Trinity the notions of being absolute and relative are elevated to a single divine reality and formal character."

[36] See Salmanticenses, *Cursus theologicus, In ST* I, q. 12, disp. 1, dub. 2, §§2 and 3, nos. 44–47; Billuart, *Summa sancti Thomae, De Deo*, diss. 4, art. 3, appendix.

its common, analogical formal character, nonetheless, one cannot thence conclude with evidence through the natural light of reason that it can see God in an utterly perfect manner—and, hence, quidditatively as He is in Himself—for it would suffice that He be knowable in some other, more imperfect manner.[37]

Nor is the possibility of the light of glory demonstrable by the powers of reason since such a light itself would be essentially supernatural, like the beatific vision itself.

And therefore, this argument is presented by St. Thomas as being a "sign"[38] that we have an obediential potency to being elevated to supernatural life; however, he does not present it as a demonstrative argument.[39] Now, this suffices against adversaries who deny the possibility of the revelation of strictly supernatural mysteries, for they cannot disprove this possibility, and their objections can be resolved as being false or at least as not being necessary.[40]

§4. The Existence of an Obediential or Elevable Capacity for Supernatural Life Can Be Persuasively Argued for from a Consideration of Our Natural Desire to See God through His Essence

At first sight, this question seems to be purely theological and not to pertain to apologetics. Nonetheless, it needs to receive *an apologetic treatment*, especially if apologetics is able to be reduced to fundamental (or critical) theology. Otherwise, the apologete will not rightly argue from our natural aspirations to divine and supernatural things.

Many modern apologetes exaggerate these aspirations and draw close to Baius's errors, as was noted in the encyclical *Pascendi* in a text that we have already cited on several occasions:

And here We cannot but deplore once more, and grievously, that there are Catholics who, while rejecting *immanence* as a doctrine, employ it as a method of apologetics, and who do this so imprudently that they seem to admit that there is in human nature a true and rigorous necessity with regard to the super-

---

[37] Salmanticenses, *Cursus theologicus, In ST* I, q. 12, disp. 1, dub. 2, §§2 and 3, nos. 47.

[38] See *ST* I, q. 12, a. 4, ad 3: "Et huius signum est."

[39] See *ST* III, q. 55, a. 5 on the difference between a demonstrative reason and an argument from a sign. Also, *ST* I, q. 32, a. 1, ad 2.

[40] See St. Thomas, *In De Trinitate Boetii*, q. 2, a. 3.

natural order and not merely a *capacity* and a *befittingness* for the supernatural, such as has at all times been emphasized by Catholic apologists. Truth to tell it is only the moderate Modernists who make this appeal to an *exigency* for the Catholic religion. As for the others, who might be called intergralists, they would show to the nonbeliever, hidden away in the very depths of his being, the very *germ* which Christ Himself bore in His conscience, and which He bequeathed to the world.[41]

{{360}} Thus, this question must be treated in fundamental theology or apologetics. *We here find ourselves faced with the question of the insertion point of supernatural life into our nature.* Therefore, let us see what the traditional doctrine is in this matter.

We will propose (1) St. Thomas's argument, (2) the error of Baius and the Jansenists concerning this matter, and (3) the various opinions [*sententias*] of theologians.

(1) *St. Thomas's argument and a doubt concerning its interpretation.* On this issue, see *ST* I, q. 12, a. 1: "Man has in himself a natural desire *for knowing the cause* when its effect is known; thence arises wonder in men. Therefore, if the intellect of the rational creature could not reach the First Cause of things, *one of its nature's desires* will remain void."

Even more explicitly, he says in *ST* I-II, q. 3, a. 8:

The object of the intellect is that which is, that is, the essence of things, as is said in *De anima* 3.6. Whence, the perfection of the intellect grows to the degree that it knows the essence of something. Therefore, when man knows an effect and knows that it has a cause, he *naturally* has a desire *to also know the "what it is"* [, that is, the essence] *of the cause.* [. . .] And this desire is one of wonder, causing him to look into such matters. . . . Therefore, if the human intellect, knowing the essence of some created effect, knows only the fact of God's existence, its perfection does not yet, without qualification, reach the First Cause, thus meaning that a *natural desire* to inquire into the First Cause remains in him. Whence, he is not yet perfectly blessed. Therefore, for this perfect beatitude, the intellect must reach the very essence of the First Cause.

In *SCG* III, ch. 50, the same thing is made manifest as regards separate substances (i.e., angels), inasmuch as "the angels' *natural* desire does not come

---

[41] Pius X, *Pascendi*, no. 37 (Denzinger, 2103, old numbering).

to a rest in the natural and *imperfect* knowledge that they have about God but, rather, is even more aroused to see the divine substance."

Now, this argument can be expressed formally: A natural desire cannot be in vain (i.e., tend toward something impossible);[42] now, man has a natural desire to know not only whether there is a First Cause but, moreover, *what this First Cause is in itself*; therefore, to know the essence of the First Cause as he is in himself does not seem to be impossible for man; that is, it does not seem to be above man's elevable capacities.

A doubt. Many object *this argument either proves too much or too little.*

Indeed, it proves too much if it is a question of an absolute and efficacious desire for intuitive [i.e., unmediated, direct] vision of God, for this efficacious desire or exigency cannot be frustrated. Hence, our elevation to the supernatural would not only be possible but would be owed to our nature (and hence natural). This was Baius's error and represents the confusion of the two orders, in contradiction with our preceding thesis. Nay, Baius and Jansen brought forth this very argument from St. Thomas in defense of their own positions.

However, this argument *proves too little if it holds that such a desire is only conditional and inefficacious* (i.e., a vellity), for this vellity not only can be *de facto* frustrated but even perhaps would tend to something impossible (e.g., if someone were {{361}} to conditionally and inefficaciously desire the vision of God not only intuitively but also in a comprehensive manner, something that in fact is incommunicable [and pertains only to God, who alone has comprehensive knowledge of his essence]). To desire conditionally is to desire under the condition of the possibility of the thing desired [*sub conditione possibilitatis rei desideratae*] and therefore can be concerned with something that is impossible [for this impossibility might not be known when such a thing is conditionally desired]. This difficulty pertains to St. Thomas's major premise.

A similar objection has been proposed *regarding the minor premise. Too much* is proven if its sense is that *the explanation of natural things demands intuitive knowledge of the essence of the First Cause.* For then there would be a natural, efficacious desire for supernatural vision, which hence would be owed to nature as something natural, as Baius thought.

However, it *proves too little* if it means that *the explanation of natural things requires only perfect abstractive knowledge of the essence of the First Cause.* Indeed, it seems that this solely abstractive knowledge is desired naturally, for God is the cause of natural things not through his nature (for he does not act *ad extra* through a natural necessity) but through his intellect and will, according to his ideas. Therefore, in order to have an explanation

---

[42] Indeed, St. Thomas intends for this argument to defend the *possibility* of the beatific vision, rather than the fact of this vision, for our elevation to the supernatural order, according to the Church's own teaching, depends upon God's freedom.

of natural things, it suffices to know that God is the First Being who is intellectual and volitional in his activity [*est primum ens, inteligens et volens*]. In this way, we preserve the conclusion of our preceding thesis concerning the absolute distinction between the order of natural truth and the order of supernatural truth.

However, the resolution of this difficulty will become clear by looking at the condemnation of Baius's error in this matter, as well as from an examination of the various opinions of theologians.

(2) *The error of Baius and the Jansenists.* Baius and the Jansenists held that there is a natural and *efficacious* desire for the beatific vision, meaning that this vision would be *owed* our nature and, hence, would be natural. They spoke in like manner about the grace by which we are ordered to the vision of glory.

See the propositions of Baius, which have been condemned: "The sublimation of human nature and *its elevation to participation in the divine nature were due* to the integrity of man in his first state and are therefore to be called natural, not supernatural."[43] "It is absurd to hold that from the beginning man was raised above his own natural condition through a certain *supernatural* and *gratuitous* gift so that he might worship God supernaturally with faith, hope, and charity."[44] "The integrity of the first creation was not the undeserved exaltation of human nature but *its natural condition*."[45]

Likewise, this proposition of Pasquier Quesnel was condemned: "The grace of Adam produced nothing except human merit."[46] Likewise, see the errors of the Synod of Pistoia.[47]

The Jansenists invoked St. Augustine and St. Thomas in defense of their position. They argued on the basis of (1) St. Augustine's *Confessions*, bk. 1, ch. 1, where he says, "You made us, O Lord, for Yourself, and our hearts will be restless until they rest in You"; and [(2)] *De Trinitate*, bk. 3, ch. 3, where he wrote, "Nature impels us to desire beatitude, and the Immortal Creator instilled this in it." (3) They likewise argued from St. Thomas, who defends the claim that intellectual substances can see God through his essence because a natural desire to see God cannot be vain (see *ST* I, q. 12, a. 1 and *SCG* III, chs. 50–52).

Theologians commonly respond to this[48] by saying that St. Augustine in

---

[43] Pius V, *Ex omnibus afflictionibus*, no. 21 (Denzinger, no. 1921).

[44] Ibid., no. 23 (Denzinger, no. 1923).

[45] Ibid., no. 26 (Denzinger, no. 1926).

[46] Clement XI, *Unigenitus Dei filius*, no. 35 (Denzinger, no. 2435).

[47] See Pius VI, *Auctorem fidei*, nos. 16 and 18 (Denzinger, nos. 2616 and 2618).

[48] See Billuart, *Summa sancti Thomae, De gratia*, diss. 2, a. 2 (Whether the state of pure nature was possible), resolution of objections (Lyon, 1857), 285 and 339.

the first text is speaking of the heart elevated through grace and illuminated by faith.

{{362}} The same can be said of the second text, though it is more likely a question of beatitude in general, not in particular as the clear vision of God. St. Thomas does not speak of a natural efficacious desire but, rather, an inefficacious one, for according to him a natural, efficacious desire must be related to a good proportioned to nature and owed to it.

See *ST* I-II, q. 114, a. 2: "*Eternal life is a kind of good exceeding the proportion of created nature, for it even exceeds its knowledge and desire*, according to the words of 1 Cor 2:9 (DR): 'That eye hath not seen, nor ear heard: neither hath it entered into the heart of man, what things God hath prepared for them that love Him.'" Likewise, see *ST* I-II, q. 109, a. 5 (Whether man can merit eternal life without grace); a. 6 (Whether man can be prepared for grace without the aid of grace); q. 112, a. 3; q. 114, a. 5. He always argues from the surpassing character of supernatural life. Likewise, in *ST* I-II, q. 62, a. 1, ad 1 and ad 3, he argues from the necessity of the theological virtues and, in q. 68, a. 2, concerning the necessity of the gifts of the Holy Spirit. In *ST* I, q. 62, a. 2, on the necessity of grace for the angels, he says, "To see God through His essence is above the nature of any created intellect whatsoever. Whence, *no rational creature can have a movement of the will ordered to that beatitude except by being moved by a supernatural agent. This is what we call the aid of grace*." Likewise, in *ST* I, q. 23, a. 1, while defining beatitude, he says, "The end to which the creature is ordered is twofold. One exceeds the proportion and powers of created nature, and this end is eternal life, which consists in the divine vision. This is above the nature of any given creature, as we discussed above. However, there is another end that is proportioned to nature, namely, one that a created thing can attain according to the power of its nature." Likewise, see *De veritate*, q. 14, a. 2: "Man has a twofold ultimate good. One such good is proportioned to human nature (the felicity spoken of by the philosophers), *and the other is a good beyond any proportion with human nature.*"

Hence, according to St. Thomas, the natural desire to see God *is not efficacious* and is not a desire arising from an exigency of nature. Nor is it an *innate* desire like the weight of nature directed toward its proper perfection, coming before every elicited act, but, rather, is a question of an act *elicited* by the will and proceeding from knowledge of the First Cause's effects, as is explicitly said in *De veritate*, q. 22, a. 7: "Man has within himself a desire for his ultimate end in general, namely, so that he naturally desires to be complete in goodness. However, what this completeness consists in (whether in the virtues, in the knowledge of the sciences, or in pleasures, or other such things) has not been determined for him by nature."[49] See the resolution of the objections of the Jansenists discussed below.

---

[49] See the other texts of St. Thomas cited in Billuart in the text cited in the previous footnote.

(3) *Examination of the various opinions of theologians.* Five things must be dealt with in this section: (A) terminology: the division of [the notion of] appetite; (B) a presentation of the opinion of Augustinians; (C) the opinion of Scotus; (D) Cajetan's opinion; and (E) the more common position held by Thomists.

A. *Terminology*: *The division of [the notion of appetite or love].*

The commonly accepted division can be written clearly as follows:[50]

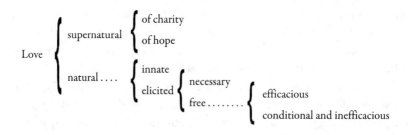

{{363}} Love is called *natural* when it proceeds from a natural principle and is borne toward an object proportioned to nature.[51] By contrast, it is called *supernatural* when it proceeds from a supernatural principle—namely, from grace, charity, or hope—and is borne toward an object exceeding the proportion of nature. Thus, the Church condemned Baius's proposition rejecting this distinction of a twofold love of God (namely, a natural and supernatural love, the first being that by which God, known through the natural light of reason, is loved as the Author of natural goods and the second being that by which God, known through faith, is loved as the Author of grace and glory.[52]

---

[50] See Billuart, *Summa sancti Thomae, De gratia*, diss. 3, a. 4 against Baius and Janus. Also see Gardeil's article "Appétit" in the *Dictionnaire de théologie catholique*. Also see Sestili, *De naturali intelligentis animae capacitate atque appetitu intuendi divinam essentiam*, 92–217. Sestili holds that there is an *innate* inefficacious natural desire [to see God]. We hold that this desire is *elicited*. However, Sestili's opinion comes close to ours when he holds that this desire does not exist as a weight inclining our nature and presupposes some knowledge. Likewise, see his *Disputatam quaetionem de possibilitatem desiderioque primae causae substantiam videndi* in the appendix to the third volume of the new edition of the *Commentarium Ferrariensis in Contra Gentes*, (Rome, 1900).

[51] I say, "the proportion of nature" inasmuch as it does not exceed the powers or exigencies of nature or, at least, a natural vellity.

[52] See Pius V, *Ex omnibus afflictionibus*, no. 34 (Denzinger, no. 1934): "The distinction of a *twofold love* of God, namely, a *natural* love whose object is God *as the author of nature* and a *gratuitous* love whose object is God *as beatifying* is meaningless and imaginary; it has been devised as a mockery of the Sacred Scriptures and of the numerous testimonies of ancient authors."

Natural love is itself twofold—namely, innate and elicited.[53] It is *innate* as a natural weight directed toward a good proper to each (that is, an inclination of nature preceding the apprehension of the good). Thus, without knowledge, the plant desires the light of the sun as something necessary for it. That is, it is inclined toward it. See *ST* I, q. 19, a. 1. We can similarly speak of the sense appetite (both concupiscible and irascible) and of the rational appetite, all of which are faculties. Now, as is explained in *ST* I, q. 60, a. 5, all creatures thus naturally love God, the Author of nature, for any given creature is more strongly inclined to the divine good than to its own proper good, just as the natural part of some whole is more inclined to the preservation of the whole than to its own good. (Thus, the hand naturally exposes itself to physical harm in order to preserve the head; otherwise the inclination of nature would be perverse.) "Man *has within himself* an appetite for his final end in general."[54] Likewise, see *ST* II-II, q. 26, a. 3.

Elicited love is that by which, on the basis of the apprehension of the good, a knower moves itself to pursue it. And just as the knowledge by which it is directed is an act elicited from a knowing faculty, so too this love is an act elicited by an appetitive faculty.

Now, elicited appetite itself is also twofold in nature—namely, necessary or free (that is, elective). A *necessary* elicited appetite is that which proceeds from the apprehension of the good without any deliberation, somewhat as is even found in brute animals. Likewise, men thus love God above all, as it were, in a vague way and from the formal perspective of being the highest good and beatitude as such, which they seek in all things. *Free or elective* love is that by which the rational nature, on the basis of deliberation and having weighed out the merits of the issue at hand, inclines itself to that.

{{364}} Moreover, this deliberated love can be efficacious or, by contrast, conditional and inefficacious. *An efficacious, deliberated, elicited desire* presupposes a judgment concerning the goodness and natural achievability of the desired object. *A conditional and inefficacious deliberated elicited desire* presupposes a judgment about the goodness as well as the natural non-achievability of the desired object.[55]

---

[53] See *ST* I, q. 19, a. 1 and 9; q. 59, a. 1; q. 80, a. 1.

[54] See *De veritate*, q. 22, a. 7.

[55] Billuart says in *Summa sancti Thomae, De gratia*, diss. 2, a. 2, solv. obiectiones: "It is called 'inefficacious' because it is conditioned so that I would will this if it were possible; or, if it were absolute, it nonetheless is not ultimately efficacious in the execution of the thing [*non tamen sortitur efficaciam ad rei executionem*]. The other [kind of desire] is called efficacious because it is both absolute and can apply means proportioned to the achieving of the end."

This subdistinction thus posited within efficacious love or desire itself is explained by

This final form of appetite is only a velleity: This good is utterly desirable but naturally unattainable—I would wish for it, if God were to gratuitously bestow me with the means for obtaining it; indeed, how great would such felicity be! Finally, this velleity is either *explicit* or *implicit*, inasmuch as the desired object is known vaguely [*confuse*] or distinctly.

This suffices for setting our terminology in order. Let us now pass over to an examination of the various opinions of theologians.

B. *Opinion of Augustinians.* Certain theologians in the eighteenth century, such as [Enrico] Noris and [Giovanni Lorenzo] Berti, called themselves Augustinians, teaching a particular doctrine about grace that they claimed to have drawn from the works of St. Augustine. In short, they contended that grace and the other privileges conceded to Adam in his innocence were owed to him not out of justice but from a kind of propriety on the part of the Creator.

Hence, they said we have in ourselves *an innate, natural appetite* for the intuitive vision of God, *indeed one that is in some way efficacious*, though not in Baius's sense, for the intuitive vision of God is our natural end as regards desire [*quoad appetitionem*], though it is supernatural from the perspective of its actual achievement and as regards the means for attaining it. Although these means are supernatural and not strictly owed to us, nonetheless, they are indeed in some way owed to us on account of the goodness of providence, which does not deny the means that are necessary for [reaching this] end. Hence, these Augustinians said that the state of pure nature was possible only for the absolute power of God, though not for his ordered [*ordinaria*] power.[56]

Criticism. This opinion has too great an affinity with Baianism, for it does not preserve the absolute distinction between the natural and supernatural orders. And in order to preserve some distinction, the principle of finality (namely, *every agent acts on account of a proportionate end*) must be denied, for according to this position, God as the Author of nature would have given us an innate desire for an end to which he could not lead us as the Author of nature.[57] This will be even clearer in our critique of the opinion of Scotus.

Billuart as follows (*De gratia*, diss. 3, a. 4): One is efficacious as regards the effect alone, whereas the other is efficacious as regards the effect and the affect. However, this subdistinction of *affectively efficacious* and *effectively efficacious* love does not properly pertain to our question but to another—namely, whether fallen man can efficaciously, by his natural powers without grace, love God above all things *as the Author of nature* solely. The Thomists respond negatively: Neither by an effective efficacious love nor by an affective efficacious love can fallen man love God above all things without grace healing his nature. Instead, he can only love God by an inefficacious love, which is a simple taking of pleasure in God's goodness.

[56] See Berti, *Opera*, vol. 5, diss. 2, ch. 1, nos. 1 and 8; Eugène Portalié, "Augustinianisme," in *Dictionnaire de théologie catholique*; Hugo Hurter, *Nomenclator litterarius theologiae catholicae*, 3rd ed., vol. IV, 885 and III2, 1–5.

[57] See Billuart, *Summa sancti Thomae, De gratia*, diss. 2, a. 2 (*in fine*).

C. *Scotus's opinion* (see Scotus, *In Sent.*, prol., q. 1 and *In IV Sent.*, dist. 49, q. 10). According to Scotus, we have *an innate, but nonetheless inefficacious, natural desire* for intuitive vision of God. This is so because this highest beatitude is befitting to all, and also their end, {{365}} therefore founding an innate appetite. However, it is not known by all and hence is not efficaciously desired. This opinion is also attributed to Durandus of Saint Pourçain and D[omingo de] Soto (*De natura et gratia*, bk. 1, ch. 4). [Gregory of] Valencia likewise seems to be inclined to the same position,[58] as well as certain authors in recent days.

Critique. From the argument given by Scotus, it only follows that we only have in ourselves an innate natural appetite for beatitude in general, though not for the beatific vision, for this vision is not suited to our nature as something proportioned to it.[59] Moreover, the Thomists[60] in general note that *if this desire*, spoken of by Scotus, *were innate, it should be efficacious.* And this is clear for three reasons: (a) from the perspective of our nature; (b) from the perspective of God as the Author of nature; and (c) from the perspective of the object of this desire.

(a) *From the perspective of our nature.* Indeed, as John of St. Thomas says:

> An innate appetite, as distinct from an elicited one, implies a relationship that is founded on the nature itself, not as a knower but, [rather, precisely] as it is a given entity to which something is befitting according to its reality. Now, *there is no relationship* between natural entity and a supernatural form, *nor a positive and natural befittingness* [for the supernatural order] arising from the nature itself, for a supernatural form surpasses it and is not proportioned to it, meaning that nature by itself is only in obediential potency in relation to such a supernatural form. Therefore, we do not have in our nature an innate appetite for the supernatural vision of God.

Moreover, this innate appetite must be efficacious, for a desire is inefficacious inasmuch as it proceeds from a conditional judgment (e.g., "I would will this naturally unattainable good if God were to freely elevate me to it"). Now, an innate appetite does not proceed from knowledge but, rather, proceeds from nature itself and [therefore] corresponds to the powers or exigencies of nature.

(b) *From the perspective of God.* God as the Author of nature cannot cause an inclination that he cannot satisfy as the Author of nature and the natural end, for the order of agents must correspond to the order of ends. Otherwise, *God would somehow be able to*

---

[58] Concerning Domingo de Soto's opinion, see what Bañez says in his comments on *ST* I, q. 12, a. 1.

[59] See *De veritate*, q. 22, a. 7; q. 14, a. 2. Also see the resolution of objections in the current article.

[60] See John of St. Thomas, *Cursus theologicus*, *In ST* I, q. 12, disp. 12, a. 3.

be greater inasmuch as he is the Author of nature than he is as the natural end. Now, God as the Author of nature cannot lead [intellectual agents] to clear vision of God, for this vision is a supernatural effect. Therefore, it does not fall to the Author of nature to give an innate desire of this sort.

(c) *From the perspective of the object.* Something cannot be at once essentially natural and essentially supernatural. Now, *this innate appetite would be at once essentially natural* (as a property of [our] nature) *and essentially supernatural* (*as being specified by a formally supernatural object*). Therefore [such a desire cannot exist.] Nor can it be said that it is specified by an object that is entitatively supernatural but known naturally, for this innate appetite would not proceed from knowledge of God in the mirror of sensible things, but rather, independent from any kind of knowledge, it would tend to God as he is in himself.

Note well: On account of this last difficulty, *Thomists in general reject the active obediential potency* defended by Suarez, who in this question (as in many others) seeks to find a middle way between St. Thomas and Scotus. Along with other Thomists, Billuart says:

> This active obediential potency implies a contradiction, for it would be at once natural and supernatural. It would be natural because it would be inborn to all natural agents, following their nature as a property, while being supernatural because it would be immediately ordered to supernatural effects. Secondly, this active obediential potency would destroy the entire order of grace, for having posited its existence, grace would be superfluous, since all supernatural effects, which are attributed to grace and the other supernatural *habitus* [pl.], {{366}} could come into being through this active obediential potency.[61]

However, Suarez only holds that we have an elicited and inefficacious natural desire for the beatific vision and in this point draws back from Scotus's position.

D. **Cajetan's opinion.** Cajetan's opinion on this matter was radically opposed to Scotus. In *In ST* I, q. 12, a. 1, no. 10, Cajetan says:

> In proof of this, note well that the *rational creature* can be considered in two ways: in one way *absolutely* and in another way *as ordered to felicity.* If it is considered *in the first way,* then *nature and its desire does not extend beyond the powers of nature,* and thus I concede that it does not naturally desire the vision of God in Himself absolutely. However, if it is considered *in the second*

---

[61] See Billuart, *De Deo,* diss. 4, a. 5, §3. Likewise, John of St. Thomas in *ST* I, q. 12, disp. 14, a. 2, no. 11 adds: "From such a position holding that there is an active obediential potency [to the supernatural order], as explained by these authors on account of *a partial concursus* [of agents], there arise all those unsuitable conclusions that are validly refuted when discussing the topic of grace"—namely, the differences separating Suarezianism from St. Thomas.

way, then *it naturally desires the vision of God, for as such, it knows certain effects (namely, of grace and glory)* whose cause is God inasmuch as He is God in Himself absolutely (and not as the agent who exercises universal causality). Now, once these effects are known, any intellect naturally desires knowledge of the cause of these effects. Hence, even if desire for the divine vision is not natural to the created intellect, absolutely speaking, it nonetheless is natural to it, presupposing the revelation of such effects. And thus, both the reason alleged here and the further reasons for the same thing gathered in *SCG* III, ch. 50, lead to the conclusion that a created intellectual nature would still experience an open desire if it could not see God.—However, we must say that this would be discussing the intellectual creature as ordered to felicity, not as considered absolutely in itself, for it is common to any given science that the terms would always be understood as they fall under that science, as is clear concerning quantity in physics. However, it is clear from *SCG* II, ch. 4 that creatures fall under theological consideration only inasmuch as they are ordered, governed, and predestined by God to God as the supreme end of all things. Otherwise, as is clear, theological topics would not be considered by the theologian as being ordered to the highest and proper cause.

Cajetan wrote this against Scotus, as in *In ST* I, q. 1, a. 1, no[s]. 9[–10], and perhaps, not proceeding with great enough moderation, tended to the opposite extreme. Indeed, in sum he denies the existence of some natural desire to see God proceeding from the knowledge of natural effects and admits only the existence of some connatural desire to see God based upon knowledge of the effects of grace and glory (and by "connatural" he means to indicate conformity even with nature, once supernatural effects have been experienced). This is also how Cajetan explained himself in *Opuculum*, vol. 3, tract. 7.

Critique. Sylvester of Ferrara and many other Thomists wrote against this opinion of Cajetan. *Sylvester* says in his commentary on *SCG* III, ch. 51, after citing Cajetan's opinion:

> But this *does not seem to be in agreement with St. Thomas's thought on this matter.* (1) Because he showed above in ch. 49 that separated substances know something about God through their own essences, and in ch. 50 he proves that their natural desire does not find rest in such knowledge by which they know about God through their own essences but, rather, is incited even more to desire to see the divine substance. . . . (2) Because the reason adduced by St. Thomas in *ST* I, q. 12, a. 1 . . . is not limited to knowledge of the effects of grace and glory but, rather, extends *to knowledge of any effect whatsoever* and to every knowledge of a cause. . . . (3) Because then, such a desire would only exist in those who know supernatural effects of grace and glory, and this is false for,

as St. Thomas says in *SCG* III, ch. 51,[62] "this desire is found in every intellect."

[The conclusion is clear:] Therefore[, Cajetan's interpretation is wrong here]. This is the position of Ferrara, who is joined by many {{367}} Thomists like Bañez, John of St. Thomas, the Salmanticences, Gonet, Billuart, Gotti, and others.[63]

In addition, *the desire spoken of by Cajetan cannot be called simpliciter natural but, rather, is only natural secundum quid*—namely, as conformed to nature—for in reality, this desire, like the desire of infused hope or charity, proceeds from supernatural knowledge of the effects of grace and glory, thus being *simpliciter supernatural and efficacious*. Now, much to the contrary, St. Thomas speaks of a *simpliciter* natural desire proceeding from knowledge of natural effects.

Nay, in fact, *we find in Plato's writing a marvelous expression of this natural desire proceeding from knowledge of natural effects*. Indeed, in the *Symposium*, Plato teaches that, according to the ascending dialectic of love, we must first love the beauty of bodies, sounds, and colors. Then, one must ascend upward, and because the beauty of the human body depends upon the soul, from which the body receives its motion and life, we must love beauty of soul. However, since this dignity of the soul consists in noble deeds, which are founded on the best precepts and commandments, we must love the excellent doctrines that measure human actions. However, the excellence of these doctrines depends on the extraordinary perfection of the supreme knowledge [*scientiae*], whose object is Beauty itself and the Good subsisting in itself. And then Plato expressly says:

> [When someone arrives at that supreme doctrine,] *drawing towards and contemplating the vast sea of beauty*, he will create many fair and noble thoughts and notions in boundless love of wisdom; until on that shore he grows and waxes strong, and at last the vision is revealed to him of a single science, which is the science of beauty everywhere. To this I will proceed; please to give me your very best attention:

> He who has been instructed thus far in the things of love, and who has learned to see the beautiful in due order and succession, when he comes toward the end will suddenly perceive a nature of wondrous beauty (*and this* [*beauty*], Socrates, *is the final cause of all our former toils*)—a nature which in the first place is everlasting, not growing and decaying, or waxing and waning; secondly, not fair in one point of view and foul in another, or at one time or in one relation or at one place fair, at another time or in another relation or at another place foul, as if

---

[62] [Trans. note: lit. "cap. 51 et 51".]

[63] In their commentaries on *ST* I, q. 12, a. 1 and in the treatise *De gratia* when they consider the question, "Whether the state of pure nature was possible."

fair to some and foul to others, or in the likeness of a face or hands or any other part of the bodily frame, or in any form of speech or knowledge, or existing in any other being, as for example, in an animal, or in heaven, or in earth, or in any other place; but beauty *absolute, separate, simple, and everlasting*, which without diminution and without increase, or any change, is imparted to the ever-growing and perishing beauties of all other things. . . .

But what if man had eyes to see the true beauty—the divine beauty, I mean, pure and clear and unalloyed, not clogged with the pollutions of mortality and all the colours and vanities of human life—thither looking, and holding converse with *the true beauty simple and divine* (ἀλλ᾽ αὐτὸ τὸ θεῖον καλὸν δύναιτο μονοειδὲς κατιδεῖν)? Remember how in that communion only, beholding beauty with the eye of the mind, he will be enabled to bring forth, not images of beauty, but realities (for he has hold not of an image but of a reality), and bringing forth and nourishing true virtue to become the friend of God and be immortal, if mortal man may.[64]

{{368}} Hence, Plato ascended from natural effects to knowledge of the existence of the Highest Good and Beauty, and expressing this velleity, said: "But what if man had eyes to see the true beauty!"

Likewise, in speaking of Plato and the Platonists, St. Augustine said in *The City of God*, bk. 8, ch. 8: "They did not call blessed the man who enjoys the body, nor him who has enjoyment of the soul, but rather, him who has enjoyment of God: not as the soul enjoys the body or itself, nor as one friend enjoys his friend, but rather, as the eye enjoys light." In this latter text, perhaps it is not a question of God intuitively known but, rather, God inasmuch as his light manifests other things to us. Nonetheless, the Platonists could have had probable knowledge that the vision of God is not absolutely impossible.[65] And they were aided in reaching such conjectural knowledge of beatitude through their trade with the Hebrews and their reading of Sacred Scripture.[66]

---

[64] [Trans. note: This was written in Latin in the original. Taken from Plato, *Symposium*, trans. Benjamin Jowett (Project Gutenberg, 2008), http://www.gutenberg.org/files/1600/1600-h/1600-h.htm.]

[65] Nay, on account of Plato's immoderate realism, he exaggerated the natural power of our reason, like the ontologists would come to do later on. Nonetheless, having already rejected Plato's immoderate realism, we still can retain the value of the ascending dialectic leading to the velleity to see God.

[66] See Billuart, *Summa sancti Thomae, De gratia*, diss. 2, art. 2, solv. obi. However, knowledge of Sacred Scripture was not necessary for this desire expressed by Plato, for as is clear in his own exposition of the matter, the ascending dialectic of love, proceeding from knowledge of *natural* effects, leads to this velleity of its very essence and in a sufficient manner.

Therefore, we must say with Sylvester of Ferrara: According to St. Thomas, as well as according to the truth itself, we have a natural desire to see God, and this desire does not necessarily presuppose knowledge of the effects of grace and glory but, rather, merely requires knowledge of natural effects, on the basis of which we desire to know what the First Cause is in Itself.

Nay, *Cajetan* seems to hold this in his comments on *ST* I-II, q. 3, a. 8, for after he reiterates the response cited above from his commentary on *ST* I, q. 12, a. 1, he says:

> However, in particular, descending into the matter of this article, we can say that the human intellect, knowing *that God exists* and having knowledge of Him *in a general way*, naturally desires to know God in His essence [*scire de Deo quid est*] inasmuch as He is included among the ascending rank of causes [*in quantum sub numero causarum comprehenditur*] and not absolutely, except as a kind of consequence. And this is true, for it is natural for us, after seeing an effect, to desire to know what its cause is, whatever it may be.—Hence, note well, novice reader, that it is one and the same thing to know God quidditatively [*cognoscere quod quid est Dei*] and to see God through His essence. Indeed, you can see well that this is manifestly proclaimed in the proof presented in this last article of this question.

E. *The more common opinion of the Thomists.* At the time of Michael Baius and the Jansenists, this question was greatly disputed in the various theological schools. This led the Thomists to reach greater terminological precision in order to avoid equivocations, as well as to avoid falling into the errors committed by Baius. Thus, they came into agreement about how to speak in interpreting St. Thomas's doctrine. Already before this, Sylvester of Ferrara and Domingo Bañez conveyed the best distinctions.[67]

Sylvester of Ferrara had said: "We naturally desire to see God in terms of a *vision of the First Cause*, not a vision of the object of supernatural beatitude. For we can naturally know that (God) is the cause of other things. However, we cannot naturally know that He is the object of supernatural beatitude."[68] {{369}} And this agrees with what Cajetan concedes in *ST* I-II, q. 3, a. 8. However, Sylvester did not sufficiently determine the nature of this desire from the perspective of the subject.

Bañez, however, explained this, saying:

---

[67] Chronologically speaking, this progress took place from Cajetan to Billuart: Cajetan (1469–1534), Bañez (1528–1604), John of St. Thomas (1589–1644), Gonet (†1681), the Salmanticenses (1631–1679), Vincenzo Gotti (1664–1742), and Billuart (1685–1792). The errors of Baius were condemned in 1567 and the Jansenists in 1653–1664.

[68] Sylvester of Ferrara, *In SCG* III, ch. 51.

Man can have a natural appetite, that is, one that is elicited from the powers of nature, namely, *a kind of conditional and inefficacious desire to see God.* . . . However, to say that St. Thomas does not speak of an *elicited* act but, rather, of that kind of weight, which Soto imagines, such reasoning would itself have no weight [*nihil ponderis haberet ratio ista*]. For to what end would he say man has a natural desire to see the cause after having seen an effect? And if he were to say that the source of this desire was that aforementioned weight [i.e., a natural, unelicited inclination], it would even incline one [toward such knowledge] independent of any need to experience some effect. . . . I said that it is *conditional* because, through his natural powers, man cannot be certain that such a good is possible. Therefore, such a desire is conditional: if it were possible. For example, a man can desire or will to not die, if this is possible. And although such a condition would not be explicit in his mind, nonetheless, it is implicitly contained in the object which is represented as good and not as possible.[69]

Later on, *the majority of Thomists* came to admit this position: *By a desire that is not innate but, rather, elicited, conditional, and inefficacious, man naturally desires to see the essence of God the Author of nature.*[70] The Thomists generally add that this desire is also *free*—namely, not necessary from the perspective of its specification.[71]

We will now prove what this desire is (a) subjectively and (b) objectively.

(a) *Subjectively*, it is an *elicited, non-innate* desire because it proceeds from knowledge of the First Cause's effects and is not the weight of our nature [inclining us] prior to [any act of] knowledge.[72]

It is *conditional*—that is, following a hypothetical judgment: I would will to see God's essence, if this were possible, and if God were to will to

---

[69] See Bañez, *In ST* I, q. 12, a. 1.

[70] Such is the position of John of St. Thomas, Gonet, the Salmanticenses, Gotti, Billuart, and others, and many others outside of the Thomist school agree on this point, like even Suarez in a way, even though he admits the existence of an active obediential potency. See these authors in their commentaries on *ST* I, q. 12, a. 1 and the treatise *De gratia* (Whether the state of pure nature was possible).

[71] See Salmanticenses, *Cursus theologicus*, tr. 2, disp. 1, dub. 4, §3. And this is somewhat contrary to Sylvester of Ferrara and in line with Cajetan's tendency. It is also contrary to Suarez (bk. 2, On the negative divine attributes, ch. 7, nos. 10 and 11), Vasquez, and Valentia, who admit that in our nature, considered in itself, there is a non-innate, though elicited, conditioned, and inefficacious desire (although they say it is necessary from the perspective of its specification) to see God as he is one and triune in himself, or inasmuch as he is the Author of both grace and of nature. Here, as in many other things, Suarez seeks to find a middle way between Scotism and Thomism.

[72] See *ST* I, q. 12, a. 1; *De veritate*, q. 22, a. 7; *In* IV *Sent.*, dist. 49, q. 1, a. 3, quaest. 3.

elevate me to this vision, which exceeds [my] natural powers and exigencies.[73] Hence, it is *inefficacious* because it is conditional. That is, it is concerned with a good that exceeds [our] natural powers and exigencies.[74]

Finally, though this is of little importance, it is *free* (or elective), not only as regards exercise but also as regards specification, for the will is necessitated regarding specification only by its adequate object considered in itself. Now, clear vision of God is not the essential (or adequate) object of the will *in via*. Indeed, *in via*, the will sometimes desires many things other than beatitude in particular, indeed, things that are opposed, not ordered, to it. Certainly, we are naturally inclined to the aforementioned velleity, but it can be impeded in particular people on account of their perversity of will.

{{370}} (b) *Objectively, vision of the essence of God* is naturally desired, not inasmuch as he is triune and one, as the Author of grace, but rather only inasmuch as he is one and *the Author of nature*. This is said in contrast to the positions of Suarez, Vasquez, and Valencia and is proven by Sylvester of Ferrara and the Salmanticenses.[75]

Indeed, this natural, elicited desire follows upon natural knowledge. Now, we naturally know God as the Author of nature, not as the Author of grace. And this natural knowledge remains very imperfect, especially *regarding the intimate reconciliation of the naturally knowable divine attributes*. Indeed, the antinomies expressed by agnostics can be resolved, and this reconciliation of the divine attributes does not involve contradiction. However, we remain faced with the obscure mystery of the intimate reconciliation of, for example, complete immutability with utter freedom, infinite and omnipotent goodness with the permission of evil, or even infinite mercy and infinite justice. "Therefore, this (very imperfect) knowledge does not quiet the natural desire but, rather, drives it on toward vision of the divine substance,"[76] namely so that the divine essence may be known as the root of the naturally knowable divine attributes—that is, the essence of God, the Author of nature.[77] However, we do not naturally know that the vision of the essence of God, he who is triune and the Author of grace, is some-

---

[73] See *ST* I, q. 12, a. 4.
[74] See *ST* I, q. 23, a. 1; q. 62, aa. 1 and 2; I-II, q. 114, a. 2.
[75] See Salmanticenses, *Cursus theologicus, De Deo*, tr. [2], disp. 1, dub. 5, nos. 73, 75, and 77.
[76] See *SCG* III, ch. 50.
[77] From this perspective, the divine essence is the supreme natural mystery, for the existence of this mystery is known without revelation. However, its intimate mode [of existence] remains hidden. Thus, we find ourselves faced with a verification for the principle, "The supreme degree of a lower order reaches the lowest of the higher order," and notwithstanding the absolute difference of the various orders, a kind of continuity is preserved within their hierarchy.

thing desirable. Therefore, the object of this natural desire is not formally supernatural but instead is only materially so, for this object is known to be desirable under the light of natural reason. Or, as the Salmanticenses say: "The reality [*res*] desired is *materially supernatural*, though, not the reason for desiring . . . for it is desired from the formal perspective of being maximally good."[78] Such is the abyss existing between this natural desire and infused faith or charity.

St. Thomas himself said: "Charity loves God above all things more eminently than nature, for nature loves Him above all inasmuch as He is the principle and end of natural good[ness], whereas charity loves Him as the object of beatitude and inasmuch as man has a kind of spiritual fellowship with God."[79] Moreover, Pius V condemned Baius's proposition denying this essential distinction between natural love for *God the Author of nature* and supernatural love for *God the Author of grace*.[80]

It is completely contradictory to say that an essentially natural *desire* tends toward a formally supernatural object, for acts and *habitus* are specified by their formal objects. Now, just as a single thing (entitatively) can be, from two different {{371}} formal-objective perspectives, the object of a sense power (as it is sensible) and the object of the intellect (as it is an intelligible being), so too, and for the same reason, God considered solely as a reality and not as an object [*eadem res divina*] can be,[81] from two different formal-objective perspectives, both the object of a natural desire and the object of a supernatural desire, inasmuch as he is known either in an external manner by reason or intimately through revelation and faith.

However, it is indeed *de facto* and *de iure* true that there cannot be intuitive *vision* of the essence of God the Author of nature, without one having vision of the essence of the Triune God, the Author of grace. Indeed, there is only one and the same vision because it is *immediate*, with no mediating creature, whereas on the contrary, the desire for this vision is natural

---

[78] See Salmanticenses, *Cursus theologicus, De Deo*, tr. 2, disp. 2, dub. 5, nos. 75 and 77. Likewise, see John of St. Thomas, *Cursus theologicus, De gratia*, disp. 20, a. 1, solv. obi., no. 5: "A natural act can be concerned with *a supernatural object materially considered*, from a natural motive and formal perspective. In that case, it specifically differs from the act that is concerned with the same object from a supernatural motive and formal perspective."

[79] *ST* I-II, q. 109, a. 3, ad 2. Likewise see *ST* II-II, q. 26, a. 3; *De veritate*, q. 14, a. 2; *In I Cor*, ch. 13, lect. 4.

[80] See Pius V, *Ex omnibus afflictionibus*, no. 34 (Denzinger, no. 1934).

[81] [Trans. note: Concerning the distinction between considering God *ut res est* and *ut obiectum est*, see Réginald Garrigou-Lagrange, *The Sense of Mystery: Clarity and Obscurity in the Intellectual Life*, trans. Matthew K. Minerd (Steubenville, OH: Emmaus Academic, 2017), 126n9.]

or supernatural, depending on whether it proceeds from knowledge of the effects of God the Author of nature or from knowledge of the effects of God the Author of grace.

The value of this argument. The Thomists[82] commonly hold that this argument, as well as the preceding one taken from the adequate object of our intellect, is not apodictic but only very probable for manifesting our nature's potency for being elevated to the supernatural order. Indeed, we argue from a natural, conditioned, inefficacious desire: How good it would be for me to see God, if God were to elevate me to this vision!

Granted, since such a desire could, absolutely speaking, be frustrated, we cannot demonstratively prove the possibility of the beatific vision on the basis of us having such a desire.[83] However, the argument is persuasively probable, for it does not seem true to say that a *natural* (and non-fantastical) desire, one that is found in all men, even the wise and prudent, tends toward something impossible. It is theologically certain that the beatific vision, no less than the other supernatural mysteries of the Trinity, the Incarnation, and so forth, cannot be proven demonstratively by natural reason. However, reasons from befittingness can be brought forth in order to manifest its possibility in some way.[84]

Thus, we can see how St. Thomas's argument neither proves too much nor too little. It would prove too much if it were a question of an efficacious desire. It would prove too little if St. Thomas wished to convey an apodictic demonstration.

And therefore, on the basis of two arguments—namely, from a consideration of this natural desire and of the adequate object of our intellect—we can manifest our nature's obediential or elevable potency for the supernatural order to knowledge of supernatural mysteries, first grasped obscurely, then, ultimately, in clear vision.

Conclusion of this thesis concerning the possibility of revelation. Based on this thesis, as well as the preceding ones, we can see that the

---

[82] See Billuart, *Summa sancti Thomae, De Deo,* diss. 4, a. 3, appendix; *De gratia,* diss. 2, art. 2, solv. obj.

[83] Someone could hyperbolically say: Even if this supernatural vision were impossible, this velleity would not be entirely *in vain* but, rather, would be a sign of the essential imperfection of the creature and an occasion for adoration of the essentially hidden divine mystery. This is akin to desiring not only intuitive but comprehensive vision of God, something that is impossible for us to have.

[84] See *SCG* I, ch. 8. We have examined this problem in our work, *The Sense of Mystery,* trans. Matthew K. Minerd (Steubenville, OH: Emmaus Academic, 2017), 123–170; also Garrigou-Lagrange, *On the One God,* trans. Bede Rose (St. Louis, MO: B. Herder, 1943), 332–339.

Catholic teaching on these matters is a kind of *peak of truth* standing above opposed forms of naturalism (namely, pantheistic evolutionism and agnosticism) and also above semi-rationalism and the pseudo-supernaturalism of the Protestants, Baius, and the Jansenists. Thus, in general, in the most difficult questions, there are two radically opposed and erroneous solutions, one sinning by excess and the other by defect. {{372}} Afterwards, there then appear mediocre, eclectic opinions, opportunistically attenuating and juxtaposing the extremes in a kind of mechanical, nonorganic way. However, truth is found in the peak, where there is an organic and positive reconciliation of the various aspects of the truth that are obscured in the opposed errors.[85]

Thus, for these theses, we must write the peak of truth over the opposed errors:

Catholic doctrine
concerning the supernatural order

| Semi-rationalism | Pseudo-supernaturalism |
| Pantheistic evolutionism | Naturalistic agnosticism |

Indeed, evolutionism says that through its natural development, human reason can reach knowledge of the highest truth; nothing is above it; therefore, it cannot be elevated to the supernatural order.

By contrast, agnosticism says human reason is so weak that it can know only phenomena and their laws; it does not know substances, causes, and ends; certainly, it cannot accept supernatural revelation and cannot discern it.

Semi-rationalism holds that reason can receive revelation. Nay, it even holds that after such revelation is received, reason can demonstrate all revealed mysteries. Hence, they are not properly supernatural.

Pseudo-supernaturalism teaches that reason is so weak that it necessarily needs revelation, which, hence, is not supernatural, properly speaking.

The Catholic doctrine [on these matters] holds that reason can receive revelation of properly supernatural mysteries that cannot be demonstrated after that revelation. However, in no way can there be a demand for this elevation to the supernatural order, which nonetheless is greatly befitting to

---

[85] Thus, above the oppositions of nominalism and exaggerated realism, as well as above subjective conceptualism, we find the realism of St. Thomas. Likewise, above the oppositions of mechanism and dynamism, as well as the false reconciliations of them, we find hylomorphism. And in the moral order, the right notion of moral conscience stands above laxism and rigorism, as well as their overly empirical reconciliation.

our nature. Only this doctrine preserves at once the transcendence of God's intimate life as well as the dignity of human reason, showing us that God alone can reconcile in his supernatural gifts their *absolute gratuity*, on the one hand, and their *perfect befittingness* in line with the aspirations with our nature, on the other. This will be even clearer in light of the resolution of objections.

§5. Resolution of Objections

There are two opposed series of objections. (A) The first contains objections of rationalists: We cannot have an elevable potency to the supernatural order. (B) The second consists in pseudo-supernaturalism: Our nature does not have only an elevable potency to the supernatural order but, rather, has a positive ordination to this and demands that it be so.

{{373}} A. *Objections against the existence of our elevable potency to the supernatural order*, presupposing the absolute transcendence of this order.

1. *Objection*: An obediential potency must be either natural or supernatural. Now, it is not natural, since it is ordered to supernatural things, and it is not supernatural, since it is a property of our nature. Therefore, it does not exist.

Response: This potency is not supernatural, for it is not an infused gift and does not *immediately* designate an ordering *to a supernatural object* to be known and loved. Rather, it is subjectively natural inasmuch as it is identical with our nature and is properly called "obediential" inasmuch as it is turned toward a *supernatural agent* whom it obeys. In other words, it is our nature's elevable potency for supernatural things.

2. *It is urged*: The created intellect is more distant from God than the senses are from our intellect. Now, a sense power cannot be elevated to knowing intelligible things. Therefore, our intellect cannot be elevated to knowing the supernatural mysteries of God's intimate life.

Response: I make a distinction regarding the major premise. I concede it as a comparison of their manners of existing. However, I deny it as regards the formal character of the intellect. I concede the minor premise. I make a distinction regarding the conclusion, conceding it only if our intellect somehow did not analogically share with God the formal character of intelligence [*si non conveniret cum Deo in ratione intelligentiae*]. Otherwise, I deny it.

3. *A continued insistence*: Elevation is not possible in this way, for our intellect cannot be elevated beyond its adequate object. Now, its adequate object is being. Therefore, our intellect cannot be elevated beyond metaphysical knowledge of God inasmuch as he is a being.

Response: I concede the major premise. I make a distinction regarding the minor premise. I deny that its adequate object is being inasmuch as it is knowable in the mirror of sensible things. I concede that it is being according to its full latitude. I similarly distinguish the conclusion.

4. *It is urged*: Elevation is not possible in this way, for the Deity is above being and above unity. Now, supernatural knowledge must reach God according to the formal character of the Deity and not only according to the formal character of being. Therefore, such elevation is impossible.

Response: I make a distinction regarding the major premise. I concede that the Deity is above being inasmuch as it *formally*-eminently contains being as a simply simple perfection. However, I deny it as though it virtually-eminently contained being as a kind of mixed perfection. I concede the minor premise. I distinguish the conclusion just like the major premise.

5. *Another objection*: There is no natural desire for a supernatural object, for we desire to know the essence of the First Cause in order to explain natural things. Now, an explanation of natural things is had through abstractive knowledge of the essence of the First Cause. Therefore, we do not desire intuitive vision of God.

Response: I make a distinction regarding the major premise. I deny we desire it only to explain natural things. However, I concede that we have such a desire in order to explain even how the attributes of God are reconciled. I distinguish the minor premise in the same way.

6. *It will be urged*: This intuitive vision is not desired for explaining the intimate reconciliation of God's attributes, for in that case such vision would be owed to our nature and, hence, would not be gratuitous.

Response: I make a distinction regarding the antecedent. I concede that it is not desired by an efficacious desire. I deny, however, that it would not be desired by an inefficacious desire.

7. *It is insisted*: Moreover, it is not desired by an inefficacious desire. Even an inefficacious desire cannot be at once substantially natural and objectively supernatural. Now, this is what a natural desire for seeing the essence of God would be. Therefore, such a desire implies a contradiction.

Response: I make a distinction regarding the major premise. I concede that this is true if the desire is *formally speaking* objectively supernatural. However, I deny it if it is so *materially speaking*. I concede the minor premise if one is speaking of a natural desire to see the essence of God the Author of grace. However, I deny it if one is speaking of a natural desire to see God the Author of nature.

8. And yet *the objector insists*: However, in the preceding thesis, it was said that reason by itself can demonstrate that there is an order of mysteries in God, ones that are not only natural but also supernatural. Therefore, {{374}} we can naturally desire vision of God, even as he is the Author of the supernatural order.

Response: We already said in the preceding thesis that this demonstration of the existence of an order of supernatural truth and life is only brought forth after revelation as a kind of defense, for prior to receiving revelation, we do not have an explicit notion of this order. Moreover, by this demonstration, we do not know God positively as the Author of grace and glory but, rather, know him as containing in himself truth and life, which transcend any natural knowledge whatsoever.

9. *It is insisted*: There is no distinction of two formalities in an utterly simple formal notion. Now, the Deity is an utterly simple formal notion. Therefore, God the Author of nature cannot be distinguished from God the Author of grace.

Response: I make a distinction regarding the major premise. I concede that there is no real distinction. However, there can be a distinction according to our way of conceiving things. And this suffices for specifying the natural desire that follows natural knowledge concerning God.

10. *It is insisted*: Then the possibility of vision of the essence of God the Author of nature is persuasively argued on behalf of, though not the possibility of vision of the essence of God the Author of grace, except *per accidens*.

Response: I deny [this], for this distinction indeed holds for the *desire* for the vision of the divine essence but not for *the act of this vision*. For that desire is twofold inasmuch as it proceeds either from knowledge of the effects of God the Author of nature or from knowledge of the effects of God the Author of grace, whereas by contrast, *immediate* [knowledge] of the divine essence is specified by the divine essence itself, with no mediating natural or supernatural effects. Hence, not even by God's absolute power can there be vision of the essence of God the Author of nature without vision of the essence of God the Author of grace, for one and the same essence is seen *immediately* according to the same formal motive.

11. *Another objection*: Such an elevation would at least involve a contradiction because supernatural knowledge would not be vital. For vital knowledge is that which proceeds from the natural vitality of our intellect. Now, supernatural knowledge could not proceed from this natural vitality but instead would exceed it.

Response: I make a distinction regarding the major premise. I concede that such an act must proceed from its natural vitality either as bare [i.e., without grace and the light of faith] or as elevated. However, I deny it if one means that it can only proceed from the natural vitality of our intellect. Our intellect's vitality must be elevated by grace, which is *a new life*. And according to the Thomists, the intellect and supernatural *habitus* concur as *two complete causes*, though from different perspectives. The supernatural *habitus* concur as the complete proximate formal character by which the intellect is elevated and proportioned to the supernatural act, whereas the intellect is the total elicitive principle. By contrast, Molina and Suarez conceive of the intellect and supernatural *habitus* as two *partial causes*, like two people dragging a ship along. Hence, Suarez holds that man has an *active* obediential potency, which we hold to be contradictory, as was said above.[86]

12. *Another objection*: At least to our eyes, a contradiction is involved in speaking of an obscure revelation of supernatural mysteries. For these mysteries would be unintelligible for us and could only be expressed metaphorically through natural notions.

Response: I concede that they could only be metaphorically expressed through natural notions if these kinds of notions, properly understood, always involved an imperfection in God. Otherwise, I deny the claim. Now, notions such as paternity, filiation, spiration, and so forth do not always involve imperfection, as is shown in the particular treatises of theology. Therefore, even if supernatural mysteries are incomprehensible, they are intelligible not only metaphorically but even properly and analogically. For, as the [First] Vatican Council said: "Nevertheless, if reason illumined by faith inquires in an earnest, pious, and sober manner, it attains by God's grace a certain understanding of the mysteries, which is most fruitful, {{375}} both from the analogy with the objects of its natural knowledge and from the connection of these mysteries with one another and with man's ultimate end."[87]

13. *Certain modernists object*: It is better to change the notion of nature and conceive of it as something flowing, progressing, and containing the seed of supernatural life.

Response: This would represent the revivification of Baius's heresy. Nay, it would involve a pantheistic confusion of the divine nature with the created nature, as happens in the absurd hypothesis concerning the idea of a created, supernatural substance. Properly speaking, this would be a form of evolutionistic pantheism.

B. *The other series of objections: Our nature has in itself a positive inclination to the supernatural order and not only an obediential potency.*

1. *Objection*: A potency not positively ordered to some act does not found a relation of befittingness to that act but instead is either opposed to it or neutral in relation to it. Now, according to the Thomists, an obediential potency is not ordered to supernatural knowledge. Therefore, this obediential potency does not suffice for supernatural knowledge to be befitting for us.[88]

Response: I make a distinction regarding the major premise. I concede that it does not found a relation of *immediate* befittingness to that act. However, I deny that it does not found a relation of befittingness *by means of a possible elevation*. I concede the minor premise and distinguish the conclusion just like the major premise.

Indeed, an obediential potency is immediately relative *to a superior agent* that the inferior nature obeys. For example, wood does not have a positive ordination to the form of a stool rather than to the form of a statue. However, wood has an obediential potency in relation to the artisan from whom it receives a positive ordination to the

---

[86] See John of St. Thomas, *Cursus theologicus, In ST I*, q. 12, disp. 14, a. 2, no. 11.

[87] [First] Vatican Council, *Dei filius*, ch. 4 (Denzinger, no. 3016).

[88] This objection is found in Scotus, *In Sent.*, prol. Cajetan response to Scotus in *In ST I*, q. 1, a. 1.

form of a statue rather than to the form of a stool. Similarly, the obediential potency of our intellect immediately designates an order to God as he is an agent and receives from God a positive ordination to vision of the divine essence. This positive ordination in us is the infused light of faith, the beginning of eternal life (or sanctifying grace, the seed of glory).[89]

2. *Objection*: Now, there must be an immediate befittingness. Therefore, the difficulty remains. For that which we naturally desire is immediately fitted to our nature. Now, we naturally desire the very vision of the divine essence and not only some gift to be gratuitously determined by God. Therefore, vision of the divine essence is immediately fitted to our nature.

Response: I make a distinction regarding the major premise. I concede it for an innate and absolute desire. However, I deny it for an elicited and conditional desire. I distinguish the minor premise in the same way. Allow me to explain. It would always be mediated by a condition; namely, I desire to see God's essence, if this were possible, if God would will to bestow upon me the supernatural means for this vision. Nay, this vision is not known naturally except in a general manner, as something superior to our abstractive knowledge. However, we do not naturally know what this supernatural vision would formally be. Hence, it is desired only implicitly and conditionally.

3. *Objection*: That which has the greatest befittingness should be absolute and opposed to gratuity. Now, the beatific vision is suited to us in the highest degree. Therefore, it is absolutely suited to our nature and is not something given gratuitously. This was the argument of Baius, as well as certain more recent authors.

Response: I make a distinction regarding the major premise, conceding it for that which has the greatest natural befittingness, while denying it for supernatural befittingness. I distinguish the minor premise and conclusion in the same way. Allow me to explain. Supernatural befittingness, notwithstanding its gratuity—nay, by virtue of this gratuity—exceeds natural befittingness and thus is the greatest and most profound form of befittingness. And this is quite marvelous. Here we see how supernatural gifts differ both from natural ones (in which there is no gratuity) and from the delusions of false mysticism (wherein there is not conformity with our nature). *For God alone can join together in his supernatural gifts these apparently* {{376}} *opposed extremes—namely, utter befittingness and utter gratuity*—inasmuch as these gifts *not only satisfy* our natural desire *but also exceed it*. Supernatural gifts perfect us more than natural ones, and from this perspective, they are more fitted to us [*nobis magis conveniunt*], with an exceptional and supernatural befittingness [*convenientia*]. They perfect that which is deepest within our soul—that is, the insertion point for the supernatural life, namely, our obediential potency. *Nothing more intimate* is found within the nature of our soul, for here, within ourselves, we find something corresponding to God's infinite power and benef-

---

[89] See *De veritate*, q. 14, a. 2.

icence, for our obediential potency is nothing other than the entire essence of our soul inasmuch as it is apt for receiving from God whatever he might will. This is the ultimate root for our resolution to this issue. Some would like to discover some contradiction in it whereas, on the contrary, it represents the sublime reconciliation of extremes that can only be united by God.

4. *Objection*: Cornelius Jansen argued along the following lines. Man could not be created in a merely natural state, wherein his natural appetite could not have been satisfied. Now, without the vision of God's essence, man's natural appetite cannot be satisfied, as St. Augustine and St. Thomas both teach. Therefore, man could not have been created without an ordination to the vision of God's essence, which, therefore, is something owed to his nature and not supernatural.

Response: This would be true if it were a question of an efficacious natural appetite. However, otherwise, if it is a question of a *velleity*, it does not hold. Jansen unjustly takes up St. Augustine's texts, for in these texts it is either a question of the heart's desire already elevated through grace or the natural desire of beatitude in general.[90] However, in St. Thomas's texts, it is a question of an inefficacious natural desire on the basis of which we can conjecturally but not apodictically prove the possibility of the beatific vision. And it would not be unsuitable if a conditional, inefficacious desire were not satisfied, just as it would not be unsuitable if the appetite of a man conditionally desiring to rule the whole world, if he could, were not satisfied. It is possible that the disappointment of this kind of desire would not be a serious penalty and punishment without sin, as Jansen said. However, after the gratuitous elevation to the supernatural order, to be deprived of the vision of the essence of God after death is indeed a serious penalty and punishment, but in such a case this deprivation is indeed on account of a sin. Thus, one may consider a kind of analogy in the case of a man who is gratuitously elevated to the rank of nobility who perhaps later on comes to be deprived of his title because of the infamy of his character.

5. *Objection*: Finally, certain more recent authors, like Maurice Blondel, object that, at least in our present state, after the ordering of mankind to the supernatural end, even he who has not yet been regenerated by grace—nay, even an unbeliever who has never heard the preaching of the faith—has an efficacious desire for supernatural life. Now, such a desire does not proceed from grace but from nature. Therefore, such a desire is at once efficacious and natural.

Response: Regarding the major premise, I deny that this man has an intrinsically efficacious desire by virtue of his nature. However, I will let pass the claim that he would have one that is unconsciously efficacious by virtue of an extrinsic divine ordination under the influence of prevenient grace. Regarding the minor premise, this desire does not proceed from nature considered in itself but, rather, already presupposing the ordination of man to the supernatural end, it arises under the influence of

---

[90] See Billuart, *Summa sancti Thomae, De gratia*, diss. 2, a. 2. Solv. obj. iansenistarum.

actual prevenient grace soliciting man to faith. In this way, it is not contradictory to say that this desire would be at once efficacious and in some way natural (or connatural). It is a kind of restlessness, in accord with the words of St. Augustine in *Confessions*, bk. 1, ch. 1: "You made us, O Lord, for Yourself, and our hearts will remain restless until they rest in You." However, we do not naturally know that this restlessness arises from a privation of properly supernatural life such that it could not be satisfied in perfect natural religion.

In this way, we have a resolution for the objections opposed to the claim that our nature has an obediential or elevable potency for the supernatural order. Thus, we have made manifest the possibility of the revelation of supernatural mysteries from the perspective of man and from the perspective of God who reveals.

On the Befittingness and Necessity of Revelation

On the Befittingness and Necessity of Revelation

{{377}} *State of the Question*—Presupposing the possibility of supernatural revelation, either of the natural truths of religion or of supernatural mysteries, we now must ask about the befittingness and necessity of this revelation. For not everything that is possible is befitting, and even though certain rationalists do not deny the possibility of religion, they reject its befittingness. By contrast, traditionalists and fideists have said that supernatural revelation would be so befitting for us that we would, absolutely speaking, need it in order to know natural truths of religion.

Therefore, we must now consider whether supernatural revelation is suitable and necessary, and if it is, in what way. In the first article of this chapter, we will set forth heterodox doctrines concerning this matter as well as the Church's doctrine, and then, in the second article, will take up a rational defense of the latter.

ART. 1: HETERODOX DOCTRINES AND THE CHURCH'S DOCTRINE ON THE BEFITTINGNESS AND NECESSITY OF REVELATION

§1. Heterodox Doctrines

Concerning this question, we find ourselves faced with two heterodox theses that are opposed to each other. (1) On the one hand, there are the rationalists and the semi-rationalists. (2) On the other, there are the traditionalists and the fideists.

(1) *Rationalists* deny the befittingness of supernatural revelation, for as they say, even if it were possible, it would be unsuitable for a number of reasons.

A. *As regards the natural truths of religion, it would be superfluous,* given that reason alone can know these truths. Nay, it would impede the progress of science by imposing an immutable doctrine limited to the conceptual expression of a given era [*temporis*].

B. *As regards supernatural truths,* this revelation *would require a kind of abdication by reason* in order to believe unintelligible mysteries. This faith would be useless and likewise could not be had by men who are unable to hear the preaching of the Gospel.

Semi-rationalists indeed do admit the befittingness of the revelation of natural truths of religion. However, they reject the befittingness of the revelation {{378}} of supernatural mysteries for nearly the same reasons as the rationalists.

(2) *Traditionalists and fideists*, like *Hugues Felicité Robert de Lamennais*,[1] *Louis-Eugène-Marie Bautain*,[2] and *Augustin Bonnetty*[3] have a kind of affinity with the fideism and pseudo-supernaturalism of the first Protestants, Baius, and Jansen. Indeed, according to them, *supernatural revelation of the natural truths of religion is absolutely necessary* so that human reason may be able to know these truths. In other words, without faith, *reason is psychologically* [*psychice*] *unable* to arrive at certain knowledge of these truths. Hence, we describe this by using the term "fideism."[4] Moreover, because primitive revelation is transmitted to various peoples and preserved through tradition, fideists are also called "traditionalists."

A. *According to rigid traditionalism,* man would have no *intellectual* notion without a tradition coming from our first father Adam because without primitive revelation man would not have discovered speech. Such was the position held by *Louis-Gabriel-Ambroise de Bonald* under the influence of nominalism. Étienne Bonnot de Condillac thought that speech is entirely necessary for intellectual knowledge. (In reality, nominalism holds that the universal only exists in terms, with the concept being reduced to an image connected

---

1   See Gregory XVI, *Mirari vos arbitramur* (Denzinger, no. 2730).

2   See Gregory XVI, Response of the Holy Office, Sept. 14, 1842 (On the Demonstrability of the Christian Religion), no. 1[ff] (Denzinger, no. 2765[ff]).

3   See Pius IX, Decree of the Sacred Congregation of the Index, June 11 (15), 1855, no. 1[ff] (Denzinger, no. 2811[ff]).

4   See Jean-Michel-Alfred Vacant, *Études théologiques sur les constitutions du Concile du Vatican d'après les actes du concile*, vol. 1 (Paris: Delhomme et Briguet, 1895), 139. Already, the nominalist Nicholas of Autrecourt, a disciple of Ockham, was condemned in 1348 on account of a similar error, for he said, "Apart from the certitude of faith, there was no other certitude except the certitude of the first principle or what can be reduced to the first principle" (Clement VI, Retraction of Nicholas of Autrecourt, Nov. 25, 1347, no. 11 / Denzinger, no. 1033). Also see the subsequent propositions. Fideism passed from the nominalists to Luther and later on to Baius and Jansen. It was even found in the apologetic works of Pierre-Daniel Huet (1630–1721).

with the common term associated with that [averaged-out image].)

According to *Lamennais*, individual reason cannot arrive at absolute certitude and therefore needs recourse to *common sense*, which is preserved in the traditions of peoples and comes from primitive revelation, as does speech.[5]

{{379}} B. *However, according to mitigated traditionalism*, man would arrive at no *moral* and *religious* notion without primitive tradition proceeding from revelation. Such was the position of *Gioacchino* Ventura (179[2]–1861). Nonetheless, he conceded that once the principal truths (like the existence of God, the immortality of the soul, and the first moral principles) are accepted through tradition, they can be defended and demonstrated by reason.

The fideists *Bautain* and *Bonnetty* also proposed a form of mitigated traditionalism, though in a slightly different form.[6]

As they themselves intended, the traditionalism of the fideists is radically opposed to rationalism. Nonetheless, just as the pseudo-supernaturalism and fideism of the first Protestants led to the rationalism of liberal Protestantism (inasmuch as the latter substitutes religious sentiment for private

---

[5] See Vacant, *Études*, 142: "Traditionalism, like ontologism, was prepared for remotely by Descartes' theory of innate ideas. It had more proximate preparations in the thought of the sensualists (or *nominalists*) of the eighteenth century, ... who placed their attention on language's relationship with thought. Condillac said, 'Science is [merely] a well constructed language.'— *Joseph de Maistre* (1753–1821) is commonly regarded as the precursor of traditionalism and, indeed, his works contain it in seed. ... However, the true father of traditionalism is Viscount *de Bonald* (1753–1840). The insights developed by him were suggested in particular by Gerdil, the disciple of Malebranche and Descartes, as well as by Condillac, the disciple of Locke. The generative idea of his system is the claim that man 'thinks his speech before speaking his thought' and that words are what produce our ideas. ... If this were true, man was absolutely incapable of inventing language and, along with language, all of the absolute and necessary truths that form the basis of metaphysics and morality: the existence of God and His perfections, the spirituality and immortality of the soul, and the nature of good and evil. According to Viscount de Bonald, primitive revelation manifested these truths to us, truths that we then transmit with language, with God's infallibility being the sole guarantor that its certitude has a foundation.

"Abbé *Hugues Felicité Robert de Lamennais* (1782–1854) took up the same theme, placing it upon a broader foundation. He made it into a complete system, which he developed in his *Essai sur l'indifférence en matière de religion*, vol. 2, ch. 20. He draws a distinction between individual reason, which exists in each man, and *common sense*, which is manifested in the common beliefs of all humanity. According to him, common sense is transmitted in all peoples through tradition, which, like language, goes back to God, the Creator and Father of the human race. Individual reason would be unable to arrive at truth and *de iure*, absolute certitude and could only provide a *de facto*, instinctive certitude. Common sense alone would give *de iure* certitude, for in the final analysis it rests upon the very authority of God, whose teachings are maintained by mankind."

[6] See ibid., 143.

inspiration), so too in the writings of Lamennais, traditionalism led to indifferentism and liberalism. Indeed, Lamennais said that in order to be saved, it suffices to have common sense's knowledge of God and that one only needs to believe the natural truths of religion, which are infallibly transmitted by various peoples through tradition and have been manifested by primitive revelation. The principle of liberalism follows from such claims: "Man can attain the eternal salvation of his soul by any profession of faith, provided his moral conduct conforms to the norms of right and good."[7]

§2. Doctrine of the Church

The [First] Vatican Council defined:

> The same Holy Mother Church holds and teaches that God, the beginning and end of all things, can be known with certainty from the things that were created through the natural light of human reason. . . . But it pleased his wisdom and goodness to reveal Himself and the eternal decrees of His will in another and supernatural way . . . — It is to be ascribed to this divine revelation that such truths among things divine that of themselves are not beyond human reason can, even in the present condition of mankind, be known by everyone with facility, with firm certitude, and with no admixture of error. It is, however, not for this reason that revelation *is to be called absolutely necessary*, but *because* God in his infinite goodness has *ordained man to a supernatural end*, viz., to share in the good things of God that utterly exceed the intelligence of the human mind.[8]

Likewise, see the canon corresponding to this[: "If anyone says that the one true God, our Creator and Lord, cannot be known with certainty [by] the natural light of human reason through the things that are created, let him be anathema."][9]

From this solemn definition, we have three propositions, which are

---

[7] See Gregory XVI, *Mirari vos arbitramur* (Denzinger, no. 1613). Also, see Gregory XVI, *Singulari nos affecerant gaudio* (Denzinger, 1617, old numbering); Pius IX, *Syllabus of Errors*, nos. 15 and 77 (Denzinger, nos. 2915 and 2977).

[8] [First] Vatican Council, *Dei filius*, ch. 2 (Denzinger, nos. 3004 and 3005).

[9] Ibid., can. 2.1 (Denzinger, no. 3026).

explained in the pre-conciliar *relatio*.[10]

(1) *Revelation of the natural truths of religion is not absolutely necessary*, for reason can by itself alone, on the basis of created things, certainly know the existence of God, the principle and end of all things. It is to a matter to be held on divine faith that reason can do this, on account of its physical potency—that is, in due proportion to its object.[11] {{380}} And it is closely connected to faith [lit. *proximum fidei*] that reason can prove the existence of God, even in accord with man's moral potency—that, is without any great difficulty—for Sacred Scripture declares that those who do not know God are foolish, mad, and inexcusable.[12] Moreover, theologians commonly deny the possibility of invincible (i.e., inculpable) ignorance or error about the existence of God, the Author of nature.[13]

Thus, traditionalism and fideism are heresies inasmuch as they deny the possibility of demonstrating by reason alone the existence of God on the basis of [our knowledge of] created things. The same must be said of Kantianism and positivism.

(2) *The revelation of the natural truths of religion is morally necessary* (that is, maximally useful) so that all may easily, with firm certitude and with no admixture of error, know not only certain natural truths of religion (e.g., the existence of God) but also *the sum of the natural truths of religion*. The Council speaks of this sum (or collection) of truths when it says, "such truths among things divine that of themselves are not beyond human reason." While all of these truths taken together do not exceed reason's physical potency, they do exceed its moral potency, for reason is encumbered by many impediments to attaining perfect knowledge concerning such matters.[14]

---

[10] See Vacant, *Études*, vol. 1, 660 (*Relatio* and vote on the amendments to the second paragraph, *relatio* by Vinzenz Gasser, Bishop of Brixen [Bressanone], Italy).

[11] See Billuart, *Summa sancti Thomae, De gratia*, diss. 3, a. 2, §1: "*A physical potency* is that which holds from itself a due proportion with its object, abstracting from the impediments to attaining that; and *a moral potency* is that which, beyond a due proportion with its object, is also not entangled or held up by any impediments, lest otherwise it would not be able to pass into act and attain its object."

[12] Thus, Scripture says, "The fool hath said in his heart: There is no God" (Ps 13:1, DR). " But all men are vain, in whom there is not the knowledge of God: and who by these good things that are seen, could not understand him that is, neither by attending to the works have acknowledged who was the workman" (Wis 13:1, DR). "For the invisible things of him, from the creation of the world, are clearly seen, being understood by the things that are made. His eternal power also and divinity: so that they are inexcusable" (Rom 1:20, DR).

[13] See Billuart, *Summa sancti Thomae, De Deo*, diss. 1, a. 4: "There cannot be either positive or negative invincible ignorance about the existence of God the Author of nature."

[14] In the pre-conciliar *relatio* the following was said about this matter: "Therefore, if we do not

(3) *The revelation of supernatural mysteries is simpliciter (or strictly) necessary, supposing the gratuitous ordination of man to the supernatural end.*

ART. 2: RATIONAL DEFENSE OF THE CHURCH'S DOCTRINE CONCERNING THE BEFITTINGNESS AND NECESSITY OF REVELATION

§1. Revelation is indeed morally necessary so that men may know certain natural truths about God.

§2. Revelation of the full array [*complexus*] of the natural truths of religion is morally necessary.

§3. Revelation of supernatural mysteries is hypothetically, though strictly, necessary.

§4. A persuasive argument can be made for the befittingness of the gratuitous ordering of mankind to the supernatural end.

§5. A doubt: Whether in the state of pure nature the revelation of the full array of natural truths of religion would have been morally necessary.

§6. Resolution of objections.

{{381}} Thus, the Church's resolution of these matters will stand forth like a *golden mean* and *peak of truth* between and above the opposed excesses of rationalism and traditionalism, as well as above the mediocrity of either moderate rationalism or moderate traditionalism.

§1. Revelation Is Indeed Morally Necessary So That Men May Know Certain Natural Truths about God

In order to understand this proposition as well as the following ones, we must recall the philosophical definition and division of necessity:

---

teach that it is absolute necessity in this matter, nonetheless, we do teach that there is *a kind of moral,* that is, relative, *necessity.* . . . That is, there is a necessity that *does not hold from the perspective of the object*, for from the perspective of the object it is a question of those divine truths that are not, of themselves, beyond human reason. Rather, it is a question of a necessity which holds *from the perspective of the subject*, that is, man in the present condition in which mankind finds itself."

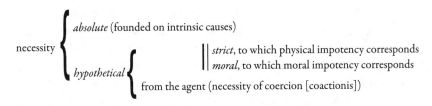

Indeed, taking up Aristotle's doctrine[15] and perfecting it, St. Thomas says in *ST* I, q. 82, a. 1:

> Necessity is said in many ways, for *that which cannot not be* is *necessary*. Now, this can belong to something in one way *from an intrinsic principle*, either *a material one*, as when we say that everything composed of contraries must be corrupted (or is corruptible), or *a formal principle*, as when we say that a triangle necessarily has three angles which are equal to two right ones. This kind of necessity is *natural and absolute*.—In another manner, it can belong to something which cannot not be *on account of something extrinsic*, either *its end* or *its efficient cause* [*agente*]. Regarding the end, this is akin to how someone *cannot attain* a given end or *cannot attain it well* without *this given thing*, as food is necessary for life and a horse for a journey. This is called "necessity of the end," which is sometimes called "utility." However, on the part of the agent, necessity belongs to something when someone is forced by another agent, so that he cannot act in a contrary manner. This is called "necessity of coercion [*coactionis*]."

Hence, *absolute* necessity is founded on a thing's intrinsic principles, and it corresponds to metaphysical or mathematical impossibility. For example, a triangle must have three angles that are equal to two right angles, and man must be a rational animal.[16]

Hypothetical necessity is founded on extrinsic causes. If it depends on an extrinsic agent, it is called "necessity of coercion [*coactionis*]" and corresponds to physical, not metaphysical, impossibility. For example, it is physically necessary that flesh burn under the influence of fire. However, if it is founded on the end and is *strict*,[17] then it also at least corresponds to

---

15 See Aristotle, *Metaphysics* 5.5 (lect. 6 of St. Thomas's commentary).

16 Nonetheless, man can naturally lose the use of reason, for we must distinguish the faculty that necessarily belongs to a given subject from the exercise of this faculty. Likewise, man is corruptible by his nature, but his body can be preserved from corruption by an extraordinary divine action.

17 This *strict hypothetical necessity* is sometimes called *absolute necessity*, but this is not a proper use of terminology, for that which is absolute and that which is hypothetical are opposed to

physical impossibility. For example, it is physically impossible to live without food. However, if there is not strict necessity but only *the greatest usefulness* for achieving an end, it is called {{382}} moral necessity and corresponds to moral impossibility, which is nothing other than great difficulty that is *de facto* insuperable according to the ordinary conditions of our life.

With this terminology in place, our first proposition is proven as follows.

The first principles of reason are naturally known without a teaching office coming from tradition [*magisterio traditionis*] and without revelation. Now, *on the basis of these principles, natural reason is easily led to knowledge of the existence of God, the First Cause and Supreme Lawgiver.* Therefore, without the aid of revelation, human reason can likewise know certain natural truths about God.[18]

The major premise is clear. "Just as sight naturally and immediately knows its formal object (i.e., color), so too the intellect naturally and immediately knows its formal and adequate object, namely *"being* and *those things that essentially belong to being* precisely as such. Our knowledge of the first principles, such as the fact that we cannot affirm and deny the same thing [of the same subject], and other such principles, is founded on this knowledge of being."[19] Therefore, these principles are not acquired through a human teaching office but, rather, as Aristotle says, "All teaching and every discipline is brought about from preexisting knowledge."[20] That is, it presupposes natural knowledge of the first principles. Not from the teaching of a master but from the impulse of nature do all men desire to know. And because science is knowledge through causes, there is in us a natural desire to know the cause when we know its effects.[21] And therefore, prior to any teaching, children express their questions: "What is the cause of this? Why is this so?" And from a natural impulse, they will continue to ask questions until they receive a response expressing an identity between the predicate and the subject. Indeed, one asks why man is wise, not why wisdom is wisdom. Likewise, one asks why man exists, not why existence itself exists.

---

each other. Properly speaking, one says, *"simpliciter* necessary" in opposition to "necessary *secundum quid*" (or *"ad bene"*).

[18] See *ST* I-II, q. 109, a.1. The Thomists commonly teach, as does Billuart in *Summa sancti Thomae, De gratia,* diss. 3, a. 2: "I say, first, that fallen man, without a special grace superadded to nature, but solely with the general prevenient concourse [of the First Cause] can know given natural truths." This position is articulated against certain older thinkers as well as Vasquez.

[19] *SCG* II, ch. 83.

[20] Aristotle, *Posterior Analytics,* 1.1. See *ST* I, q. 117, a. 1; *De veritate,* q. 11, a. 1.

[21] See *ST* I, q. 12, a. 1.

The minor premise, however, receives a lengthy proof in philosophy. From the principle of causality, "everything that comes about has a cause," and from the things that indeed do come about, common sense (i.e., natural reason) easily arrives at knowledge of some Cause that never came into being and is being from itself [*ens a se*]. Likewise, from a consideration of the order found in the world, it is led to knowledge of the Supreme Governor. Similarly, from the precept of conscience and from moral obligation, whose strength is superior to circumstances of place and time, individuals, society, and so forth, natural reason rises up to knowledge of the Supreme Lawgiver, inasmuch as moral obligation, which has its proximate foundation in the principles of our reason,[22] requires a supreme foundation in God. There is no law without a legislator. And therefore, just as theologians commonly do not admit that there is invincible ignorance concerning the first principles of the natural law, so too they do not admit that there is such ignorance regarding God's existence.[23]

{{383}} However, other naturally knowable attributes of God do fall into oblivion or are corrupted, as are the secondary principles of the natural law, "either on account of wicked persuasions or even on account of corrupt customs."[24]

Similarly, natural reason is naturally certain *about the existence of free choice of the will* and responsibility. Indeed, immediately upon deliberation, our natural intellectual insight perceives, at least vaguely, the absolute disproportion existing between the universal good specifying the will and the particular good about which it is deliberating. Hence, man naturally knows that he holds lordship over his acts and is certain about his dominating indifference concerning particular goods, even if he does not know how to formulate a demonstration proving the existence of free choice of the will, nor how to resolve the objections registered against it by determinists.

Likewise, we have a kind of natural certitude *concerning the immortality of the soul,* for as St. Thomas says, "The intellect differs from the senses inas-

---

[22] See *ST* I-II, q. 94, a. 2. The first principle of practical reason: the good is to be done and evil avoided.

[23] See St. Thomas's commentary on Romans 1:21: "Then ignorance excuses from sin when it thus proceeds and causes a sin without that ignorance itself having been caused by sin; just as when someone having employed all due diligence strikes his father thinking that he strikes a foe. But if the ignorance is caused by a sin, such ignorance cannot excuse the subsequent sin.... Therefore, St. Paul first proposes what he intends by saying: Thus, what is known of God is in them (i.e., in the Gentiles) *such that they may be inexcusable,* that is, such that they could not be excused on account of their ignorance." Likewise, see *SCG* III, ch. 38.

[24] *ST* I-II, q. 94, a. 6.

much as it grasps being [*esse*] not only as limited to here and now but, rather, being [*esse*] absolutely and according to all time. Whence, everything having an intellect naturally desires to exist [*esse*] forever."[25] *However, on the basis of such a desire, we do not know what the conditions of the future life might be.*

Philosophical reason explains and defends these first certitudes of natural reason through a scientific reduction to the first principles—that is, through a resolution to *being*. However, common sense (that is, natural reason) spontaneously and in a vague manner resolves its certitudes to being precisely because being is its formal object, just as color is the formal object of sight.

And therefore, revelation is indeed not morally necessary in order for men to know certain natural truths about God. Hence, the fideist Bautain had to subscribe to this proposition: "However weak and obscure reason became through original sin, there remained in it sufficient clarity and power to guide us with certitude to the existence of God, to the revelation made to the Jews by Moses, and to Christians by our adorable Man-God."[26]

§2. Revelation of the Full Array of the Natural Truths of Religion Is Morally Necessary

This revelation is not strictly (or *simpliciter*) necessary, for on its own, our reason is not physically unable to know all the natural truths of religion. Indeed, these truths do not exceed the natural objective medium of our intellect, and we can arrive at knowledge of them through [knowledge of] sensible things.[27]

Nonetheless, revelation of the full array of natural truths of religion is morally necessary for firm, easy, and errorless knowledge of all these speculative and practical truths *collectively*.[28] {{384}} This is proven as follows:

---

[25] See *ST* I, q. 75, a. 6.

[26] Theses subscribed to by Louis-Eugène Bautain by Order of His Bishop, Nov. 18, 1835 and Sept. 8, 1840, no. 6 (Denzinger, no. 2756).

[27] Many theologians hold, without improbability, that *fallen* man without any special grace can, by the physical power [of his intellect], know all truths that are knowable on the basis of [his knowledge of] sensible things not only *separately* but also *collectively* because, they say, they do not exceed man's capacity in view of the acuity of his inborn powers [*ingenio acuto pollentis*].

[28] St. Thomas, all Thomists, and the majority of theologians, consent to the truth of this thesis when it is understood in this manner. However, a dispute does exist even among the Thomists —namely, whether fallen man can morally know *all* natural truths *separately* or only *many* of them.—Because he did not hold that the wound of ignorance is in the speculative intellect but only is in the practical intellect, Cajetan seems to hold that fallen man can even morally know, without revelation, all natural *speculative* truths, even collectively considered. (See Cajetan, *In*

Something is morally necessary when we cannot *de facto* overcome a great difficulty in the ordinary conditions of our life without having that morally necessary thing. Now, without revelation, in the ordinary conditions of our life, men cannot *de facto* overcome the difficulties involved in knowing the sum of the natural truths of religion firmly and without error. Therefore, to this end, the revelation of these truths is morally necessary.

The major premise is the definition of moral necessity explained above.

The minor premise is proven by St. Thomas in three ways, taken up by the [First] Vatican Council: "Because the truth discovered about God by reason would be arrived at only by few, after a long time, and mixed together with errors. Nonetheless, man's entire salvation, which is found in God, depends upon knowledge of such truth."[29]

The Holy Doctor unfolds this threefold reasoning in greater detail in *ST* II-II, q. 2, a. 4:

Man must accept by way of faith not only those things that are above reason but also those which can be known through reason, doing so for three reasons.

First, indeed, [he must do so] *in order that man may more quickly arrive at knowledge of the divine truth,* for the science to which the proof of God's existence belongs, as well as other such things, is the last thing proposed to man in his investigations, given that it presupposes many other sciences. And thus, man would arrive at knowledge of God only after much of his life had passed.

Second, [he must do so] *in order for knowledge of God to be something held more widely,* for many cannot undertake scientific study, either for lack of mental abilities or on account of other occupations and necessities falling to our temporal life, or even on account

---

ST I-II, q. 109, a. 1).—Gonet says in *De gratia*, disp. 1, a. 1, §4: "In the state of fallen nature, man can without grace (or a special help) know both speculative and practical natural truths *in particular*" (and he even speaks about moral possibility).—"In the state of fallen nature, man cannot (morally) attain the complete *collection* of speculative and practical truths of the natural order."—What Billuart teaches in *De gratia*, diss. 3, a. 2, §1 seems more probable to us: "Without any superadded special grace, fallen man cannot, at least by his moral potency, know *either collectively or in particular* all natural truths, whether speculative or speculatively practical.... For among natural truths, some are so arduous and difficult that hitherto no man would have been able to arrive at them."

[29] *ST* I, q. 1, a. 1.

of laziness in learning. All such people would be entirely cheated of knowledge of God if divine things were not proposed to them after the manner of faith.

Third, [he must do so] *on account of certitude,* for human reason is very deficient when it comes to divine matters. A sign of this can be seen in the fact that Philosophers who, through their natural investigations, have deeply looked into human things have fallen into many errors and mutual contradictions. Therefore, in order for men to have knowledge of God that is free of doubt and error, it was necessary that divine things be handed on to them by way of faith, as though they were said by God, who cannot deceive.

These reasons receive even ampler development in *SCG* I, ch. 4,[30] and {{385}} are summed up by the [First] Vatican Council when it says, "[So that such truths might] be known by everyone with facility, with firm certitude, and with no admixture of error." All other reasons [for such moral necessity] can be reduced to these three, since they are taken (1) from the object, (2) from the subject, and (3) from the subject and object together.

(1) *Confirmation based on the history of philosophy*
Nearly all philosophers who did not acknowledge or accept revelation,

---

[30] In this chapter of the *Summa contra gentiles,* we find the following order for the three unsuitable things that would follow were the natural truths of religion abandoned to the research of reason alone.

"The first such unsuitable thing would be the fact that *few men* would have knowledge of God. (Some would be hindered on account of a poor physical makeup, on account of which many are not disposed to having scientific knowledge.... But some are hindered on account of the necessities of life.... However, some are hindered by laziness...).

"The second unsuitable thing would be the fact that those who could succeed at knowing or discovering the aforementioned truth *would barely reach it after a long period of time,* both on account of the profundity of this truth, which the human intellect is suited to reach through human inquiry only after undergoing a long period of training, and also on account of the many things that it requires as prerequisites, as was discussed above, and finally during the time of youth, when the soul is agitated by various motions of the passions, one is not suited for attaining knowledge of such lofty truth.

"The third unsuitable thing would be the fact that, on account of our intellect's weakness in judging, as well as the intermingling of our phantasms, *much falsity would be mixed* into human reason's investigations. And therefore, even those things which are very truly demonstrated would remain doubtful for many when they are not aware of the strength of the demonstration, especially when they see the various men who are reputed to be wise teach different doctrines. Even among many true things that are demonstrated, there is sometimes mixed something false, which ... is asserted for a sophistical reason, though it sometimes is reputed to be a demonstration."

indeed even the greatest among them, committed grave errors concerning God, his distinction from the world, his providence, his foreknowledge, the freedom of God and man, the spirituality of the soul, and the future life.

In the Greeks, who greatly cultivated philosophy, we first find the polytheism that was fought against by Xenophanes, and the first philosophers, like the Ionians, Heraclitus, and Democritus, were materialists. Parmenides and the Pythagoreans, along with Anaxagoras, posited certain principles of spiritualism but did so imperfectly and with the admixture of grave errors. After a long time—namely, after two hundred years of speculation among this people, who were endowed with great speculative gifts—there appeared, with Socrates, the true method of the perennial philosophy, along with its essential lineaments, which Plato developed and Aristotle composed into a scientific system, though not without a number of errors regarding providence and free creation properly so called, nor did these philosophers firmly assert the immortality of the soul. As regards morals, Plato commended the idea of sharing wives—nay, also the exposing of infants if they were deformed. Likewise, Aristotle made excuses for the wanton images of the gods depicted in the temples. However, immediately after Aristotle, Greek philosophy fell anew into materialism with the Epicureans and Stoics, or into skepticism with the Pyrrhonists. Neoplatonic philosophy imitated Christianity, though, doing so while denying the freedom of creation, teaching the pantheistic emanation of things from God and explaining evil through matter.

In the Middle Ages, with the exception of certain pantheists and the Averroists, philosophy in the schools was rightly subordinated to the truths of the faith and was thus preserved from error.

In modern thinkers, who not only distinguished philosophy from faith but, going further, separated them, we find the immediate appearance of sensualism and materialism in the British empiricists or the immoderate idealism of Descartes alone with many {{386}} errors leading to voluntarism [*libertismum*][31] and to subjectivism.[32] There are many errors even in Leibnitz's writings, especially psychological determinism, both in God and in us. Finally, with Kant, we arrive at agnosticism and with Fichte, Schelling, and Hegel at pantheistic evolutionism. Today, countless philosophers are positivists. Hence, they deny the necessity of the principles of reason, God's

---

[31] According to Descartes, the necessity of the principle of contradiction depends on the divine freedom.

[32] The utterly first principle, according to Descartes, is "I think, therefore I am"; however, the truth of this would not remain if we rejected the absolute truth of the principle of contradiction.

knowability, and the foundation of moral obligation, and they acknowledge only an obligation that is externally imposed by society for preserving what is useful for life in common. Thus, a practical materialism grows in strength, holding that "authority is nothing else than the sum of the number and forces of matter."[33]

All of this provides us with a confirmation concerning the moral necessity of the revelation of the natural truths of religion. Hence, the Church, who is the guardian of the deposit of revelation, is also called the guardian of reason, as is clear in Pius X's encyclical *Pascendi*, which defends the powers of reason against agnosticism.

(2) *Confirmation based upon the history of peoples and religions*

There is no people, whether uncivilized or cultured, who without divine revelation would find the sum of the natural truths of religion and would avoid falling into the most shameful errors concerning religious matters. Indeed, history clearly bears witness to the fact that among the pagans the greatest errors grew in strength regarding religion even among the Greeks and Romans, who nonetheless cultivated arts, sciences, and philosophy.

The notion of God is shamefully corrupted for many: Polytheism or dualism (i.e., the doctrine that there are two principles [of reality]) or idolatry flourished through nearly everywhere, and still does among the uncivilized tribes of Africa and Oceania. However, those who acknowledged some supreme divinity numbered among their gods said that said divinity was subject *to fate*. Nay, they attributed many vices and lustful desires to the gods.

However, *worship* offered to the gods often fell into license, as in the feasts of Saturnalia. Nearly nobody reflected on the internal worship owed to God. Hence, Cotta says, in Cicero's writing: "Who has ever thanked the gods for the fact that he is a good man?"[34] Before Seneca and Marcus Aurelius, we hardly find an author who teaches that God is to be loved.

The immortality of the soul was denied by man or called into doubt. Others, however, judged that a future life would be quite unfortunate even for good men.[35]

Finally, *regarding morals*, enemies and slaves were often treated with cruelty, fornication was not counted among vices, and the sin against nature

---

[33] Pius IX, *Syllabus of Errors*, no. 60 (Denzinger, no. 2960).

[34] Cicero, *De natura deorum*, 3.36.

[35] See Fustel de Coulanges, *La cité antique* [(Paris: Hachette, 1927)], 1.1.

was rather common, as is testified by Cicero,[36] Plutarch,[37] Sallust,[38] and Epictetus,[39] all of whose testimony is confirmed by the Apostle himself, who said: "For their women have changed the natural use into that use {{387}} which is against nature. And, in like manner, the men also, leaving the natural use of the women, have burned in their lusts one towards another... Being filled with all iniquity, malice, fornication, avarice, wickedness: full of envy, murder, contention, deceit, malignity, whisperers."[40]

However, *even the most illustrious philosophers were not strong enough to lead the people to true worship of God and the practice of the natural virtues.* They were not able to do so on account of a lack of knowledge [*scientiae*] and authority, for they ever quarreled with each other about everything, and their own lives were not in harmony with their moral opinions. Nay, many philosophers looked down on the profane masses and did not wish to teach the people, and therefore they at least privately mocked the gods, while publicly worshiping them.

However, we too, looking upon peoples who are drawing away from the truth of faith, see the reappearance of the shameless errors of materialism and depraved morals along these same lines.

From all of these points, we can clearly see the moral necessity of the revelation of the natural truths of religion.

§3. Revelation of Supernatural Mysteries Is Hypothetically, but Strictly, Necessary

(1) We will show this necessity. (2) Then, we will show why it is befitting for this revelation to be obscure at first.

(1) **This necessity is proven** in *ST* I, q. 1, a. 1 by St. Thomas, whose argument can be proposed in logical form as follows: It is *simpliciter* (or strictly) *necessary that the end be pre-known* by men who must order their intentions and actions to the end; now, *the supernatural end* to which men must order their intentions and actions *cannot be known without revelation*; therefore, the revelation of this supernatural end, as well as the means proportioned to it, is *simpliciter* (or strictly) necessary, presupposing the gratuitous ordering of man to this end.

---

[36] *De natura deorum*, 1.28.

[37] *De liberis educandis* (*in fine*).

[38] *Bellum Catilinae*, 12–13.

[39] *Enchiridion*, ch. 47.

[40] Romans 1:26, 27, and 29 (DR).

The major premise is clear, for everything that is willed must first be known.

The minor premise, however, is the conclusion of our earlier thesis: The order of supernatural truth infinitely exceeds the objective medium of our natural reason. Moreover, for lack of a proportionate medium [of knowing], knowledge of supernatural mysteries is not only physically but also metaphysically impossible.[41]

(2) *It is suitable that this revelation is at first obscure.* Rationalists object that if this revelation remains obscure, it is not suitable, because it proposes to us mysteries that are unintelligible and useless for directing our life.

We must respond to this objection: If God were to reveal his essence to us in full clarity, as he does to the blessed in heaven, we would not meritoriously incline ourselves toward the supernatural end by our own exertion. Now, man must *meritoriously* incline himself to this end, for by his nature he is rational and free, and grace is conformed to nature.

Moreover, even if supernatural mysteries are obscure, they nonetheless are in some way analogically intelligible, not as seen but as believed.

This argument is proposed by St. Thomas in *ST* II-II, q. 2, a. 3, when he says:

> {{388}} Man's ultimate beatitude consists in a kind of supernatural vision of God. Now, man cannot reach such vision except by being taught by God, according to those words of St. John (John 6:45, DR): "Everyone that hath heard of the Father and hath learned cometh to me." However, *man does not become a participant in such learning all at once but, rather, does so gradually and over time, in accord with the mode of his nature.* Now, everyone learning in this way must believe in order to arrive at perfect knowledge, as the Philosopher says, "He who is to learn must believe."

Nay, in a befitting manner, this obscure revelation was indeed gradually proposed in the Old Testament before being given in its fullness through Christ.

This reason is unfolded in detail in *SCG* I, ch. 5, and many others can be added to it [*et plures aliae adduntur*].[42]

---

[41] That is, even by his absolute power, God cannot provide us with knowledge of supernatural mysteries without means proportioned to this object (i.e., without objective manifestation and the [subjective] elevation of our intellect).

[42] See *SCG* I, ch. 5: "It is also necessary that this kind of (supernatural) truth be proposed to man

§4. A Persuasive Argument Can Be Made for the Befittingness of the Gratuitous Ordering of Mankind to the Supernatural End

As we discussed above, this gratuitous ordination was defined against Baius[43] and at the [First] Vatican Council.[44]

However, the befittingness of this ordering is persuasively argued for (1) from the perspective of God and (2) from the perspective of man.

(1) *From the perspective of God, out of his infinite goodness*

It is befitting [*convenit*] to the Highest Good—namely, God—that he would communicate himself to creatures according to what is most *intimate* in himself. Now, what is most intimate to God is his divine nature, precisely qua divine. Therefore, it is befitting to God that he would communicate to us a participation in his divine nature (i.e., in his supernatural, intimate life).

The major premise is explained by St. Thomas in *ST* III, q. 1, a. 1: "It belongs to the very character [*ratio*] of the good that it communicate itself

---

for belief *so that he may have truer knowledge of God*. For we truly know God only when we believe that He is above everything that can be thought about God by man on account of the fact that the divine substance surpasses man's natural knowledge. Therefore, on account of the fact that certain things surpassing reason are proposed to man about God, man has a firmer opinion that God is something above what can be thought of [by man].

"Another benefit thence arises, namely, *the repression of presumption*, which is the mother of error. Indeed, there are certain men who have such a great estimation of their own genius that they believe that they can measure out the whole divine nature by their own intellect. In other words, they judge that what seems to them to be true is what is indeed true and that what does not seem true to them is, in reality, false. Therefore, in order to free the human soul from presumption so that it may come to a modest inquiry into the truth, it was necessary that certain things completely surpassing man's intellect be divinely proposed to man."

Note that in defining this presumption St. Thomas exactly expresses *the principle of rationalism*: the absolute autonomy of reason—namely, that human reason should place itself as the measure of all truth and reality in that "they believe that they can measure out the whole divine nature by their own intellect. In other words, they judge that what seems to them to be true is what is indeed true and that what does not seem true to them is, in reality, false." According to this principle, human reason would be identical with the divine reason, as the pantheists Spinoza, Fichte, and Hegel thought.

In the same place, St. Thomas adds: "Another benefit appears from what the Philosopher says in *Nicomachean Ethics* 10.7. When Simonides persuaded a certain man to put aside knowledge of divine matters and to apply their skills to human affairs saying that humans should understand human things and morals mortal things. Against him, the Philosophers said that *man should draw himself toward what is immortal and divine to the degree that such is possible*. Whence, in the first book of *On the Parts of Animals*, he says that, although we perceive very little about superior substances, nonetheless, *that little bit that we can know must be loved and desired more than all knowledge that we have of lesser substances*."

43   See Pius V, *Ex omnibus afflictionibus*, no. 21 (Denzinger, no. 1921).

44   See [First] Vatican Council, *Dei filius*, ch. 2 (Denzinger, nos. 3004 and 3005).

to others. Whence, it belongs to the character of the highest good that it would communicate itself to the creature in the highest way." {{389}} And in *SCG* IV, ch. 11 it is added: "To the degree that a given nature is higher, what emanates from it is all the more intimate." Indeed, when plants and animals are perfect, they materially generate. Man, however, communicates something even more intimate and spiritual through teaching, education, and friendship. However, he does fall short in such intimate communication on account of his limited goodness. God, however, is utterly good. Thus, it is befitting that he would communicate himself in the highest degree, according to what is most intimately his.

The minor is clear. Indeed, already in acting as the Author of nature, God communicates to his creature some analogical participation of his perfections—namely, to exist, to live, and to understand. Inanimate bodies are analogically related to God inasmuch as they are *beings*, plants and animals inasmuch as they are *living*, and men inasmuch as they are *intelligent*. However, no creature naturally has a participation in the *Deity* (i.e., the divine nature precisely inasmuch as it is divine). Hence, in order for God to communicate himself according to what is most intimately his, he must offer us a participation in his divine nature precisely inasmuch as he is divine— that is, a participation in his intimate, supernatural life. And this is befitting for him to do on account of his infinite goodness, which is [self-]diffusive in the highest manner. This argument is probable in character, for human reason by itself cannot know God's intimate life, nor, as we said above, can it demonstrate the possibility of the communication of this intimate life *ad extra*, nor hence can it prove the befittingness of its communication. Moreover, even if the highest good is essentially self-diffusive, he nonetheless is diffusive freely, not necessarily, for "God's goodness is perfect and can exist without others, since there is nothing that He could receive from others that would increase His own goodness."[45]

(2) *From the perspective of man*

The elevation required for our natural, conditional, inefficacious desire [to see God] to be satisfied is simultaneously befitting to us and gratuitous. Now, without our elevation to the supernatural end, our *natural, conditional, inefficacious desire to see God as he is in himself* cannot be satisfied. Therefore, man's elevation to the supernatural end is at once befitting and gratuitous.

The major premise is persuasively argued: Befittingness is involved because this desire is natural; gratuity is involved because this desire is not efficacious and does not imply an exigency [postulated by our nature].

---

[45] See *ST* I, q. 19, a. 3.

The minor premise is clear from the previous thesis.

Hence, this elevation remains completely *gratuitous* inasmuch as it exceeds the exigencies of our nature, as we said above. Nonetheless, it is simultaneously very *befitting*, by a befittingness founded not on a positive inclination or ordination of our nature to the supernatural end but, rather, on an obediential potency related to a supernatural, elevating agent. Therefore, only after this elevation do we have a positive ordination and inclination to the supernatural end. This inclination is found in the infused theological virtues of faith, hope, and charity. See *De veritate*, q. 14, a. 2:

> In nature itself there is a kind of beginning of the very good that is proportioned to nature.... Whence, it is also necessary that, in order for man to be ordered to the good of eternal life, there must be a kind of beginning of it in him to whom it is promised.... And this beginning exists through faith, which holds, from an infused light, those things that naturally exceed our knowledge.

Thus, God marvelously joins together in his supernatural gifts {{390}} two things that at first glance seem to be irreconcilable—namely, *utter gratuity* and *utter befittingness*. Indeed, nothing is more gratuitous for us than the elevation to the beatific vision (or the Incarnation or the Eucharist), and nonetheless, nothing is more befitting. For what perfects us more greatly from this perspective is more befitting. Now, natural felicity would be found in abstractive knowledge of God and in natural love of God above all things. However, the beatific vision, which is absolutely gratuitous, perfects us more greatly than this. Likewise, God's friendship is not owed to us, but what could be more befitting? This intimate reconciliation of gratuity with befittingness is a profound note of true supernaturality, which is all the clearer to the degree that nature is increasingly rectified through mortification and passive purification, as happens in the saints. By contrast, false mysticism separates or confuses them [i.e., such gratuity and befittingness]. Either it speaks, arrogant in its delusions, about an imaginary perfection contrary to nature (like the Montanists and Jansenists) or, by contrast, falls into naturalism through the confusion of grace and nature, as well as into neglect of mortification. The more nature is purified from sensuality and pride, the more does supernatural life appear befitting to it.

§5. A Doubt: Whether in the State of Pure Nature the Revelation of the Full Array of Natural Truths of Religion Would Have Been Morally Necessary

This question was not formally resolved by the [First] Vatican Council, which speaks of "the present condition of mankind," presupposing man's ordination to the supernatural end.

Gioacchino Ventura, along with the moderate traditionalists, said that this revelation would be morally necessary, even in a state of pure nature, and hence must be called natural, as something owed to nature.[46] However, this doctrine is generally rejected by theologians, for what proceeds from God outside of the order of nature cannot be called natural, even if it is befitting that our nature would receive it.[47]

Therefore, theologians respond to this question in a different way. We will present (1) the opinion of Cardinal Franzelin and (2) the distinction offered by Cardinal Zigliara and the Thomists, by which this response is perfected.

(1) **Cardinal Franzelin**, in accord with the teachings of Francisco Suarez and Juan de Ripalda, says:

> In creating man as ordered to his natural end, God, who is infinitely wise and infinitely good, hating nothing that He makes, by an antecedent will would have willed that all men arrive at their end, and for that reason would have prepared sufficient means by which the achievement of this end would be rendered *morally possible*. Because this natural end would have been quite different from our end in the current, supernatural order, the means would also have a different relationship to that end, meaning that there would thus be a different order of providence. All the means would have corresponded to the innate character of man's formal end (natural knowledge and love) and to the connected character of the composite human nature (rational animal). *There would have been many external aids for an apt proposition of objects* and for the removing of insuperable difficulties, as well as *internal aids through morally right thoughts and affects* excited by the proposed objects themselves, and *sufficient knowledge of God and the natural law, thus rendering the fulfillment of the law morally possible*, so that men could achieve their natural end. And this would not have been a supernatural gift. . . . For although this would have been a gratuitous benefit bestowed these particular persons, it nonetheless would not have exceeded, for the whole of nature, God's natural providence directing

---

[46] See Gioacchino Ventura, *La tradition et les semi-pélagiens de la philosophie, ou le semi-rationalisme dévoilé* [Paris: Gaume, 1856], ch. 6, §44.

[47] See Vacant, *Études*, vol. 1, 350; *ST* III Suppl., q. 75, a. 3 (Whether the resurrection is natural).

man to their natural end . . . and nor could it have been thought to be modally [*sic*] supernatural in the strict sense.[48]

{{391}} Hence, according to Franzelin, these aids, which would be morally owed to human nature in a purely natural state, would not have been an external, miraculous revelation, which is at least modally supernatural, but instead would have been good natural inspirations, like those received by Plato and Aristotle to speak correctly of God. But because God in fact revealed supernatural mysteries to us, he manifested to us the whole array of the natural truths of religion in the same supernatural manner.

(2) *Cardinal Zigliara perfected Franzelin's response by distinguishing*, along with the Thomists, the state of pure nature from the state of integral nature (that is, the state of perfect nature that nonetheless has not been elevated to supernatural life).[49]

A. *In the state of pure nature, men would not have been able to morally know the entire array of the natural truths of religion* but only the principal truths among these, such as the existence of God the highest Lawgiver and [utterly just] Rewarder. Hence, in *De veritate*, q. 18, a. 2, St. Thomas says about Adam: "According to his natural perfection, man could only know God from creatures." And the Thomists generally hold that the grace that is morally necessary for firmly knowing, without error, the entire collection of the natural truths of religion is modally supernatural and exceeds the state of pure nature.[50]

Nonetheless, in this state, men would have been able to arrive at their natural end through knowledge of the principal natural truths of religion, and they would not have had in themselves an aversion to God the Author of nature, as well as the other wounds of ignorance and concupiscence that arise from original sin. Indeed, nature would not have had supernatural gifts. It would have been liable to ignorance and concupiscence but not, properly speaking, wounded in its natural powers [*in naturalibus*].[51]

B. *In the state of integral nature*, even if not elevated to supernatural life, man would have immediately accepted from God the complete perfection of his nature with regard to knowledge and his powers and even modally supernatural privileges such as freedom from ignorance, concupiscence, death, and the fluctuating passions. In this state, *there would have been a revelation that was only modally supernatural*, by which men would have known easily, firmly, and without error the full array of the natural truths of reli-

---

[48] See Franzelin, *De divina traditione*, appendix, ch. 3, §4, 558. Also see the citations of Suarez and Ripalda in the same place.

[49] See Tommaso Maria Zigliara, *Oeuvres philosophiques*, trans. A. Murgue, vol. 1, *Essai sur les principe du traditionalisme* [Lyon: Vite et Perrussel, 1880], nos. 34 and 97.

[50] See Billuart, *Summa sancti Thomae, De gratia*, diss., 2, praeambula, a. 1 "On the various states of human nature"; diss. 3, a. 2, §1 (*in fine*). Likewise, see Gonet, *Clypeus theologiae Thomisticae, De gratia*, dips. 1, a. 1, §4.

[51] See Billuart, *Summa sancti Thomae, De gratia*, diss. 2, a. 3; Gonet, *Clypeus theologiae Thomisticae, De gratia*, dips. 1, a. 1, §4.

gion. "Nothing would have prevented God from creating man in a state of integral nature without original justice, that is, grace."[52] However, in fact, Adam was born with the gift of integrity received from supernatural sanctifying grace, for as long as [his] superior reason was obedient to God through grace, the body was perfectly obedient to the soul and the sense appetite to reason.

Therefore, in our thesis, we affirm that the revelation of the full array of the natural truths of religion is morally necessary not in the state of pure nature but, rather, in our current state, presupposing man's ordination to the supernatural end.

§6. Resolution of Objections

A. Objections from the perspective of rationalism. B. Objections from the perspective of traditionalism and fideism.

A. Objections from the perspective of rationalism

(a) *Objections against the befittingness of the revelation of the natural truths of religion*

{{392}} 1. *Objection*: Truths that can be known by reason alone are superfluously revealed. Now, the truths of natural religion can be known by reason alone. Therefore, they would be revealed superfluously—that is, without any necessity.

Response: I concede that they would be revealed superfluously if reason could not only physically but also morally know all of these truths without trouble, firmly, and without error. Otherwise, I deny the claim.

2. *Objection*: This revelation would restrict the freedom of science. Therefore, it is not befitting. Such is the claim made by many modernists.

Response: I concede that it would restrict the freedom of wondering around outside the paths of truth. However, I deny that it would restrict true freedom of inquiry. For God can only reveal the truth, and freedom of scientific investigation is freedom in the application of principles and the apt method for discovering truth and not error. Hence, Christ said, "If you continue in my word, you shall be my disciples indeed. And you shall know the truth: and the truth shall make you free" (John 8:31–32, DR). Not only does revealed truth free us from wicked passions and sins inasmuch as it presents us with true goods, but it also frees our intellect from errors, doubts, hesitation, and fluctuation, showing us the principle for the synthesis of all truths. For this principle can be nothing other than the First Truth, and he who rejects the First Truth cannot reconcile particular truths. He will hold that there are antinomies between them and gradually will slide toward relativism, as though all opinions were relatively true, finally coming to deny the value of the first principle of reason, thereby joining Hegel in such denial. Hence, the [First] Vatican Council said: "Faith frees and protects reason from errors and provides it with manifold

---

[52] Billuart, *Summa sancti Thomae, De gratia*, diss. 2, a. 1, §3 (*in fine*).

insights."[53] Man does not have an unbounded freedom to think, say, and write anything whatsoever, without qualification, but, rather, has a freedom that is limited through just laws.[54] See our discussion below [at the end of the second volume] concerning liberalism and the obligation to receive religion that has been sufficiently proposed.

3. *Objection*: Even if this revelation were of great use for us, it would not follow that it would need to be bestowed, for in the physical order, God does not always bestow what is morally necessary (that is, maximally useful) to us. Therefore, nor does he do so in the moral order.

Response: I will let pass the claim that in the physical order God does not always bestow what is morally necessary for this or that individual. I deny it as it regards mankind in general. For God in his justice and providence distributes to plants, animals, and men those things that are necessary for life, in order that they might arrive at their natural end, and if he permits any evil to be done, he does this for the sake of a greater good. Hence, and for all the more reason, in the moral order, God always gives what is morally necessary for mankind in general. Moreover, no parity exists between the physical order and the moral order, for any given man, whose soul is immortal and whose end is God, is worth more than any species of animals. Christ said in Matthew 6:25: "And is not the soul more than food?" Therefore, God provides in a specific way for any given man and gives to whomever has arrived at the use of reason aids that are morally necessary and sufficient for salvation. However, if man does not resist these gifts, he will receive more and will arrive at his ultimate end.[55]

4. *Objection*: But then revelation of the natural truths of religion would be morally necessary, even if God were to have created man in a state of pure nature. Now, this involves a contradiction, for no supernatural gift is owed to human nature precisely as natural.

Response: Here we repeat what we said above—namely, that in the state of pure nature men would not have easily known the sum of the natural truths of religion but instead only the principal ones. Therefore, it remains the case that revelation is morally necessary for knowing the full array of these truths, and this knowledge is of the greatest

---

53 [First] Vatican Council, *Dei filius*, ch. 4 (Denzinger, no. 3019). Likewise see Pius IX, *Singulari quadam* (Denzinger, nos. old 1642[ff]); Pius IX, Brief *Eximiam tuam* to the Archbishop of Cologne, June 15, 1857 (Denzinger, no. 2829); Pius IX, Letter *Tuas libenter* to the Archbishop of Munich-Freising, Dec. 21, 1863 (Denzinger, no. 2877); Pius IX, *Syllabus of Errors*, no. 14 (Denzinger, no. 2914); [First] Vatican Council, *Dei filius*, can. 2.2 (Denzinger, no. 3027).

54 Gregory XVI, *Mirari vos* (Denzinger, nos. 2730ff); Pius IX, Letter *Gravissimas inter* to the Archbishop of Munich-Freising, Dec. 11, 1862 (Denzinger, old no. 1666ff, new no. 2858–2859); Pius IX, *Quanta cura*, no. 3 (Denzinger, 1690, old numbering); Pius IX, *Syllabus of Errors*, no. 79 (Denzinger, no. 2979); Leo XIII, *Immortale Dei*, no. 38 (Denzinger, no. 3179); [First] Vatican Council, *Dei filius*, can. 2.2 (Denzinger, no. 3027).

55 Pius IX, *Singulari quadam* (Denzinger, 1647, old numbering); Pius IX, *Quanto conficiamur moerore* (Denzinger, no. 2866).

use, especially after original sin, {{393}} for avoiding numberless errors and, notwithstanding the great difficulties involved, for arriving at our supernatural end.

(b) *Objections from rationalists against the befittingness of the revelation of supernatural mysteries*

1. *Objection*: It is not fitting for us to receive revelation of those things that are not conformed to reason. Now, supernatural mysteries are not conformed to reason. [Therefore, it is not fitting that they be revealed to us.]

Response: I concede that they are not conformed to reason as demonstrable things. However, I deny that this means that they are necessarily contrary to reason. Indeed, as we said above, supernatural mysteries are above reason, incomprehensible, and indemonstrable. However, they are neither irrational nor unintelligible. That which is incomprehensible is that which cannot be understood comprehensively. That which is unintelligible is that which stands in contradiction with our understanding. Those things that are probable are intelligible and not demonstrated. As St. Thomas says, supernatural mysteries "exceed the comprehension of reason and therefore seem to contradict reason, although they do not, just as an uneducated man holds that it seems to be wrong to say that the sun is larger than the earth and that the diagonal is incommensurable with the side [of a square], things which nonetheless appear as rational to the learned."[56]

2. *Objection*: Whatever is above the virtuality of the first principles of reason and being, even above the virtuality of the principle of contradiction, is absurd. Now, given the fact that supernatural mysteries are indemonstrable, they are above the virtuality of the principles of reason. Therefore, they are absurd.

Response: As we said in the question concerned with the possibility of revelation, these mysteries are above the virtuality of the principles of reason and of being from our perspective, not in themselves, for they are not above the virtuality of these principles according to the mode of Uncreated Being. However, this eminent mode [of being] is not known naturally, except in a negative and relative manner, and is known obscurely through faith. Hence, these mysteries are not absurd. Indeed, much to the contrary, the Trinity will appear in full evidence in the beatific vision.

3. *Objection*: Even if they are not absurd, these mysteries are unintelligible like meaningless words.

Response: I concede that these incomprehensible and indemonstrable mysteries are not intelligible as concerns their intrinsic truth. However, I deny that they are not intelligible as being testified to by God. Indeed, the testimony of God is not unintelligible. We understand what is to be believed when we hear it said, "The Word was made flesh." In any given dogma, we know, at least analogically, what is signified by the subject and by the predicate (the nominal definition [*quid nominis*]). The existence of the mystery is affirmed by God, though what this mystery is (its real definition [*quid rei*]) remains

---

[56] *De veritate*, q. 14, a. 10, ad 7.

obscure and is known as an enigma. For this reason, the [First] Vatican Council said: "We believe what He has revealed is true, not because the intrinsic truth of things is recognized by the natural light of reason, but because of the authority of God who reveals them."[57] Also see what we said above in ch. 5, a. 2, §2 regarding the intelligibility of the mysteries.

4. *Objection*: However, it is imprudent to assent to those things that reason cannot resolve into its own principles.

Response: I concede this if they are not evidently believable. Otherwise, I deny it. Indeed, we believe many things in a non-imprudent way, on account of the proven authority of human testimony. *A fortiori*, without falling into imprudence, mysteries can be believed on account of the authority of God, whose intervention is confirmed by miracles. Indeed, we thus have, by means of the divine testimony, confirmed by these signs, an extrinsic resolution to the first principles: It is rational to believe God.

5. *Objection*: Even if the fact of revelation could be proven, supernatural mysteries would have remained obscure and thus would have been useless for us (for example, like the mystery of the Trinity).

Response: I will let pass the claim that they would have been useless for our merely natural life. I deny this in relation to our supernatural end.

6. *It will be urged, however*: Indeed, they would not be useful in relation to our supernatural end either, for they would remain far too obscure.

Response: With the [First] Vatican Council, we can say: "If reason illuminated by faith inquires in an earnest, pious, and sober manner, it attains *by God's grace* a certain [*aliquam*] understanding of the mysteries, which is most fruitful, {{394}} both from analogy with the objects of its natural knowledge and from the connection of these mysteries with one another and with man's ultimate end."[58] And, as St. Thomas remarks in *SCG* I, ch. 5, "Aristotle says in *Nicomachean Ethics* bk. 10, ch. 7 that man should draw himself toward immortal and divine things to the degree that this is possible," and the tiniest amount of knowledge that we can have about the loftiest things is more desirable than clear knowledge about lesser things. However, in order to have the most fruitful understanding of the mysteries, we must experience the supernatural contemplation that comes from the gifts of the Holy Spirit.[59]

7. *Objection*: It is unbefitting that someone be bound to that which is impossible. Now, those who cannot hear the preaching of the Gospel would thus be bound to something impossible if they had to assent to supernatural mysteries. Therefore, this revelation is not befitting for mankind.

Response: We respond along with the words of St. Thomas found in *De veritate*, q. 14, a. 11, ad 1:

---

[57] [First] Vatican Council, *Dei filius*, ch. 3 (Denzinger, no. 3008).
[58] [First] Vatican Council, *Dei filius*, ch. 4 (Denzinger, no. 3016).
[59] See *ST* I-II, q. 68, a. 2.

While indeed everyone is bound to believe something explicitly, an untenable situation does not follow in the case of someone who is reared in the forests or among brute animals, for it falls to divine providence to provide each person with those things that are necessary for salvation, provided that such a person places no impediment before it. Indeed, if someone reared in this way follows the lead of his natural reason in desiring the good and fleeing what is evil, it most certainly must be held that God would reveal to him, through an inward inspiration, those things that must be believed or would direct some preacher of the faith to him, just as He sent Peter to Cornelius (cf. Acts 10:20)

Likewise, see ad 2.

This cannot be denied without denying the divine goodness or providence, which is naturally knowable. Hence, Christ said (Matt 6:25–26, DR), "Behold the birds of the air, for they neither sow, nor do they reap, nor gather into barns: and your heavenly Father feedeth them. Are not you of much more value than they? Is not the [soul] more than the [food]?" Hence, Pius IX said:

> We know as well as you that those who suffer from invincible ignorance with regard to our most holy religion, by carefully keeping the natural law and its precepts, which have been written by God in the hearts of all, by being disposed to obey God and to lead a virtuous and correct life, can, by the power of divine light and grace, attain eternal life. For God, who sees, examines, and knows completely the minds and souls, the thoughts and qualities of all, will not permit, in His infinite goodness and mercy, anyone who is not guilty of a voluntary fault to suffer eternal punishment. However, also well-known is the Catholic dogma that no one can be saved outside the Catholic Church and that those who obstinately oppose the authority of the Church . . . *and stubbornly remain separated* . . . cannot obtain salvation.[60]

---

[60] Pius IX, *Quanto conficiamur moerore* (Denzinger, no. 2866–2867). Also see Pius IX, *Singulari quadam* (Denzinger, 1647, old numbering).

As regards the various explanations offered by theologians in this matter, see Vacant, *Études*, vol. 1, 135; vol. 2, 136–149; vol. 2, 140: "On the good faith in certain unbelievers and heretics." He discusses in 141–149 ("In the absence of the preaching of the Gospel, are private revelations the only means for arriving at supernatural faith?"): "God will make use of inspirations of grace when they can lead to His ends. In general, it is only when these inspirations are powerless that He has recourse to new revelations and miracles." Likewise, see Édouard Hugon, O.P. *Hors de l'Église, pas de salut*, 2nd ed. (1914). Also see immediately below in this section where we respond to the objections of traditionalists.

[Trans. note: For a study of this matter explicitly in light of magisterial statements, see Joseph C. Fenton, *The Catholic Church and Salvation* (Westminster, MD: The Newman Press, 1958). For a more recent study of related questions, see Ralph Martin, *Will Many*

B. Objections from the perspective of traditionalism and fideism

1. *Objection*: It seems that without primitive revelation transmitted through the traditions held by [various] peoples, human reason could not know, with certitude, God's existence, for a greater distance separates God and human reason than the distance that separates our senses from sensible things existing outside of our field of sensation.

Response: There is no parity here, for the senses know sensible objects only if they are objectively present and acting upon the organ of sensation. Reason, by contrast, can know some cause from an effect that is first known, without the objective presence of this cause.

{{395}} 2. *It is insisted*: There is no proportion between God and creatures. Therefore, creatures do not lead to knowledge of God.

Response: I concede that there is no proportion of perfection regarding their manner of existence. However, there is a proportion of causality. For just as heating proceeds from fire or illumination from light, so too is the very existence of creatures caused by the First [Self-]Subsistent Existence, as well as the motion of all things by the First Mover, and the ordination of things by the First Orderer. And this suffices for us to know, with certitude, God, not as he is in himself but, rather, analogically and in the mirror of creatures.

3. *It will be urged, however*: Nonetheless, tradition notwithstanding, human reason has fallen into the shadows. *For all the more reason* would this be the case if there were no tradition and primitive revelation.

Response: This does not prove the physical impossibility, nor even the moral impossibility, of knowing something about God, but only the moral impossibility of knowing easily, firmly, and without error the full array of natural truths of religion. Moreover, as St. Thomas notes, regarding the truths and "secondary precepts [of the natural law], the natural law can be blotted out of men's hearts either on account of wicked persuasions or even on account of corrupt customs."[61]

4. *It is urged*: However, as de Bonald says,[62] man knows his speech after speaking his thoughts, and man cannot think before speaking his thought without expressing it in words. Hence, he was not able to invent speech but, rather, had to accept it from God who reveals. Thus, revelation was necessary for us to have intellectual and social life.

Response: This theory ultimately arises from the nominalism of Condillac, who as a sensist philosopher reduced the intellectual idea to the image produced by the imagination, to which a term is joined. Thus, he said that sciences are merely well-constructed language. Hence, for sensists or nominalists, man must be defined not as a rational animal but as the speaking animal, for all of his properties are deduced from the fact that he

---

Be Saved?: What Vatican II Actually Teaches and Its Implications for the New Evangelization (Grand Rapids, MI: Eerdmans, 2012).]

[61] *ST* I-II, q. 94, a. 6.

[62] See Louis-Gabriel-Ambroise de Bonald, *Recherches philosophiques* (Paris: Librairie d'Adrien le Clere et Cie, 1826), vol. 1, 144. See Vacant, *Études*, vol. 1, 142, 302, 330; vol. 2, 136.

speaks. On the contrary, speech is only a property of man, one that can be deduced from reason, for the intelligible meaning of words and the relation of words to notions and to things signified can be known only by reason. Nor is it true to say man could not speak without words. Of course, he does not have intellection without turning to the phantasms [*sine conversione ad phantasmata*]. However, primitive phantasms are natural signs, not conventional ones (like words). Hence, if man had been created in a purely natural state, he would have naturally come to speech by employing signs for expressing his thoughts and by gradually perfecting these signs, as is clear in linguistic history.

5. *Objection*: The salvation of unbelievers who are invincibly ignorant of the Gospel can only be explained through tradition—that is, the preservation of primitive revelation in various peoples. In order to be saved, it suffices to believe the fundamental truths of the intellectual and moral order that were revealed to us at the beginning of the world by God, being infallibly preserved in the traditions of all peoples. They constitute the common sense or common faith of humanity founded on the authority of mankind and, at their origin, in the authority of God. Such is the position expressed by traditionalists, especially Lamennais in his *Essai sur l'indifférence*, vol. 2, ch. 20.

Response: As Vacant has shown,[63] this theory must be theologically rejected for three reasons in particular. (1) It confuses common sense with supernatural faith, for it fails to preserve the essential difference between the natural knowledge, assisted by common speech, that men have concerning the existence of God with supernatural faith, which is, properly speaking, founded on the authority of God who reveals.[64] (2) Without any foundation, it holds that all religions are infallibly true with regard to dogmas that are necessary for salvation. Thus, the Catholic Church would only be more perfect in the same genus because it would represent {{396}} the progress of common reason or of the faith of mankind. This represents a denial of the essential supernaturality of the Church's doctrine and life. (3) The liberalism or indifferentism of Lamennais follows from this theory. These were condemned by Gregory XVI in the encyclical *Mirari vos* on Aug. 15, 1832:

> We now come to another important cause of the evils with which we regret to see the Church afflicted, namely, indifferentism, or that wrong opinion according to which . . . man can attain the eternal salvation of his soul by any profession of faith, provided his moral conduct conforms to the norms of right and good. . . . From this foulest source of indifferentism there flows the absurd

---

[63] See Vacant, *Études*, vol. 2, 137.

[64] Hence, this proposition has been condemned: "Faith in the broad sense, which is based on the testimony of creatures or on a similar reason, is sufficient for justification" (Innocent XI, Sixty-Five Propositions Condemned by the Holy Office, Mar. 2, 1679, no. 23, Denzinger, no. 2123).

and wrong view, or rather, insanity, according to which freedom of conscience must be asserted and vindicated for everyone. . . . But "What worse death is there for the soul than the liberty of error?" as Augustine said.[65]

The moral truths that are contained in false religions can indeed help men of good will, who are equipped to obey God and to live a morally upright life; however, "they can only attain eternal life by the power of divine light and grace,"[66] as was said above against the objections of rationalists.

6. *Objection*: But then one must have recourse to private revelations and miracles, which must not be multiplied needlessly.

Response: As the Salmanticenses say on this matter:

> God bestows each and every man with sufficient aids for salvation, at least aids that are remotely sufficient. Whence, neither a man reared in the woods, nor a child arriving at the use of reason, may do all that he can as ordered to salvation unless he makes use of the aforementioned aids. Indeed, if he so acts, he will receive further, more proximate aids, and if he is not lacking in the grace of God, he will at last be illuminated by faith and achieve righteousness. Whence, we do not posit that there is a connection between solely natural things and grace but, rather, between the latter and the preceding supernatural aids. . . . This manner of instruction in the faith is rare and extraordinary, but it is not miraculous, for the current providence of God demands it, as well as the elevation of man to the supernatural end, supposing that external preaching is lacking.[67]

As regards *implicit faith*, see Billuart.[68]

7. *Objection*: More recent partisans of the method of immanence, more or less following the pathways of fideism, say that the proofs of God's existence are inefficacious if they are considered in a merely speculative manner, without love for God. True and certain knowledge of God's existence is essentially practical, vital, and active, presupposing free love, by which our entire life is ordered to God. Now, this love and, consequently, this practical certitude presuppose the supernatural grace of faith. Thus, our elevation to the supernatural life is demanded by our very nature.

---

[65] Gregory XVI, *Mirari vos* (Denzinger, nos. 2730 and 2731). See Denzinger, nos. 2730–2732 (old nos. 1613–1617).

[66] See Pius IX, *Quanto conficiamur moerore*, no. 7 (Denzinger, nos. 2866).

[67] Salmanticenses, *Cursus theologicus, De fide*, disp. 6, dub. 1, no. 89. See Vacant, *Études*, vol. 2, 149.

[68] Billuart, *Summa sancti Thomae, De Deo*, diss. 7, a. 7, solv. obj., obj 5, inst. (ed. in 8°, vol. 1, p. 315); *De peccatis*, diss., 8, a. 7, §1 (*in fine*) (vol. 4, 441).

Response: This objection proceeds from Kant's agnosticism, holding that speculative [*theoreticae*] reason's proofs concerning God's existence do not have sufficient objective certitude. However, this Kantian doctrine has been rejected both by the [First] Vatican Council and by sound philosophy, as we have proven elsewhere at length.[69] Moreover, if human reason of itself, without supernatural grace, could not certainly know God the Author of nature, then our elevation to the supernatural order would be owed to our nature and would not be something supernatural. However, this represents Baius's error,[70] as well as that of more recent semi-immanentists.[71]

According to the Thomistic doctrine, *natural* divine aid suffices for natural knowledge of God's existence,[72] for the order of agents must correspond to the order of ends.

What we have said suffices with regard to the befittingness of revelation. Now we must turn to a consideration of the discernibility of the fact of revelation—that is, the [rational] credibility of the mysteries.

---

[69] See Réginald Garrigou-Lagrange, *God: His Existence and His Nature: A Thomistic Solution of Certain Agnostic Antinomies* (St. Louis, MO: B. Herder, 1949), 40–60 (Does the teaching of the Church permit us to maintain that the method of immanence is indispensable and that it precedes all others) and the remainder of the volume as well (ch. 2, The Possibility of Proving the Existence of God). [Trans. note: Fr. Garrigou-Lagrange's self-citation is a bit cryptic, reading "I, c. I, P., n. 6, c. II". Therefore, I have fleshed this out as meaning no. 6 in pt. 1, ch. 1, as well as the whole of ch. 2, which makes up the remainder of the first volume in English.]

[70] See Pius V, *Ex omnibus afflictionibus*, no. 21 (Denzinger, no. 1921).

[71] Pius X, *Pascendi*, no. 37 (Denzinger, 2103, old numbering).

[72] Cf. *ST* I-II, q. 109, a. 1, as well as Gonet's commentary against Vasquez.

SECTION IV

On the Credibility of the Mysteries of the Faith: The Knowability of the Fact of Revelation

{{397}} Prologue: The State of the Question and Its Division

Ch. 14. On the Act of Faith in Relation to Credibility

Art. 1.   The Catholic Notion of Faith and Heterodox Notions of It

Art. 2.   Theological Explanation of the Catholic Notion of Faith, Considered from the Perspective of Its Object and from the Perspective of the Subject

Art. 3.   How Revelation Must Be Known Precisely as the Formal Motive of Infused Faith

Ch. 15. On the Notion of Rational Credibility and Its Necessity for the Act of Faith

Art. 1.   The Nature of Rational Credibility

Art. 2.   The Necessity of Certain Rational Credibility, at Least with Moral Certitude

Art. 3.   On the Office of the Judgment of Credibility in the Genesis of the Act of Faith

Art. 4.   Resolution of Objections (The Reconciliation of the Rational Obedience of Faith with the Obscurity, Freedom, and Supernaturality of Faith)

Ch. 16. On the Demonstrability of Credibility on the Basis of the Motives of Credibility

Single Article.

PROLOGUE: STATE OF THE QUESTION AND ITS DIVISION

§1. The State of the Question and Its Difficulty

Having already treated of the notion of revelation, as well as its possibility and befittingness, following the logical order of our inquiry, as well as the order followed by the [First] Vatican Council, we now must treat the question of the possibility *of the acceptance* of this revelation by believers through faith. We already have said that the prophet himself, who immediately receives revelation from God, must, under the prophetic light, have certitude concerning the very fact of revelation so that he might infallibly propose the divine doctrine to men as something revealed by God. The question now facing us is the following: *How can the mysteries of faith be rationally credible for believers who accept revelation, though not immediately from God?* Indeed, if the mysteries of faith cannot be rationally credible for the faithful, their faith would be nothing but flippant credulity, for prudence dictates that nothing is to be believed {{398}} unless it is credible: "He who believes quickly (that is, rashly), is flippant of heart," as is said in the book of Sirach (19:4).

Now, in this question concerning the rational credibility of the mysteries of faith, just as in the preceding questions, we find ourselves in opposition to rationalists and, in particular, liberal Protestants. *Indeed, rationalists simply deny* that the mysteries of the Christian faith are rationally credible, whereas *Protestants (especially liberal Protestants) do not understand the rational credibility of Christianity in the same sense as does the Catholic Church.* Neither of them have the same notion of credibility and hence neither have the same proof of credibility, given that they differ concerning the very notion of faith, for the notion of credibility ultimately depends on one's notion of faith. According to the Catholic Church, divine faith is founded on the authority of God who reveals, whereas by contrast, Protestants (especially liberal Protestants) hold that religious faith is nothing other than religious experience proceeding from religious sentiment. Hence, they are radically opposed to each other regarding the notion of credibility.

However, there cannot be great disagreement among Catholic theologians regarding the notion of credibility and how it is proven, for this has been explicitly determined by the magisterium. However, not all theologians agree concerning the essential supernaturality of faith and, hence, concerning the relation of faith to rational credibility.[1] This must be briefly discussed after the manner of a *status quaestionis*, the state of the question, so that the true difficulty to be resolved may be clearer for us.

The difficulty of this question is expressed as follows in the objection raised by the rationalist Victor Cousin in the first chapter of his *Introduction à l'histoire de la philosophie*:

> Philosophy is the light of all lights, the authority of all authorities. Those who wish *to impose an alien authority upon philosophy and upon thought* do not realize that only one of two things is possible: *either thought does not understand this authority*—and thus, it is as though such authority didn't really exist—*or it does understand it*, forming an idea of it, and accepting it on this score, *thus taking itself as the ultimate measure, rule, and authority.*

In other words, that which absolutely stands above all other forms of knowledge neither can, nor should, be subject to another form of knowledge. Now, philosophy stands absolutely above all other forms of knowledge, even above faith. In fact, when a Christian believes surely, does he not use his reason as a measure, rule, and ultimate and supreme authority [in this act of faith]? Indeed, if the Christian believes the mysteries of faith because God revealed them, he believes that God revealed such mysteries precisely because of the motives of credibility. Hence, the first motive of faith is found in the motives of credibility. However, it is a property of the natural power of reason to know and weigh out those motives, and it moves itself to assent to them. Therefore, it is proper to the natural power of reason to command the act of faith. Therefore, reason—and, hence, philosophy—truly is the measure as well as the ultimate and supreme authority of all things to be known, even when the Christian believes. All of this summarizes Fr. Lepidi's own exposition of Victor Cousin's objection, which Lepidi himself already admirably resolved in accord with St. Thomas's thought on these matters.[2]

{{{399}}} As regards the resolution of this difficulty, the various theological schools do not agree with each other at all.

According to Scotus, Molina, and many modern thinkers, *theological faith is not essentially supernatural, on account of its formal motive,* because *according to them, this formal*

---

[1] See Ambroise Gardeil, *La crédibilité et l'apologétique,* 2nd ed. (Paris: Lecoffre, 1912). This illustrious work deserves to be read in full.

[2] See Alberto Lepidi, *Elementa philosophiae Christianae* (Paris: Lethielleux, 1875), vol. 1, 31–34.

motive is knowable by reason alone, for on the basis of miracles, anyone can know, by reason alone, that the mysteries of faith are revealed by God and can believe them naturally, just as the demons believe. However, in order to have theological faith, there must be an added supernatural modality. Thus, [according to them,] theological faith is only modally supernatural, resting upon a naturally knowable [formal] motive.

In contrast, *the Thomists and Suarez* say that [merely] preserving the rationality of the obedience of faith is not enough. Beyond this, *faith's essential supernaturality must be preserved, a supernatural certitude that cannot be formally resolved into the prerequisite inferior rational certitude [coming from motives of credibility]*. Hence, according to them, the formal motive of faith is essentially supernatural and cannot be known formally as such by reason alone, although reason can know the fact of revelation with certitude from an inferior and external perspective. Therefore, for the Thomists, *the essential supernaturality of faith must be reconciled with the rational obedience owed to it*. This is the principal difficulty involved in this issue.

§2. Division of the Question concerning Credibility

This division is taken from the nominal definition of credibility, which must serve as our starting point. Now, the word "credible" signifies that which can be believed, just as "scientifically knowable" [*scibile*][3] is that which can be known scientifically and the probable or opinable that which can be the object of opinion. Now, something is called rationally credible if it is not imprudent for one to believe it, because it is in accord with right reason. Hence, "rational credibility" signifies nothing other than the aptitude of a given assertion for being rationally believable. In a word, that which is deserving of faith is called "credible."

And *the credible is subdivided* inasmuch as something appears *worthy of* either *human and mutable faith* or *divine and irrevocable faith*.

From this nominal signification, it is clear that the real definition of credibility depends on the notion of faith. Hence, *if there are two opposed notions of divine faith*—namely, one that is Catholic and the other Protestant (especially liberal Protestant)—there will consequently be *two opposed notions of credibility* and, hence, two methods for proving credibility.

---

3   [Trans. note: One might translate this "knowable," but there are reasons for rendering this as "scientifically knowable." On this, see Ioannis a Sancto Thoma, *Ars Logica*, p.2, q.27, a.1 (823a:15–22): "*Scientific knowability* [*esse scibile*] adds over and above mere intelligible existence [*esse intelligibile*] such mode of knowing, namely that something is understood not merely in a simple manner but, rather, illatively, from causes (or premises) proceeding to conclusions, for to know scientifically [*scire*] is to know [*cognoscere*] the cause on account of which something is, etc."]

Thus, from this nominal definition of credibility, it is already clear that the rational credibility of the mysteries of faith is *a necessary condition for a prudent act of faith*. Nay, if the act of divine faith must be not only prudent but also utterly firm and irrevocable, to the point of being ready to suffer martyrdom rather than call our faith in doubt, it is already clear *that firmer credibility is required for believing in an irrevocable manner* by divine faith than for believing by human faith. In other words, the true notion of the rational credibility of the mysteries of faith must be determined not only according to the requirements of our reason but also according to the requirements of faith, "lest it be deceived and err in a matter of so great importance," as Pope Pius IX said in his encyclical *Qui pluribus* against the followers of Georg Hermes.[4]

Therefore, in order to determine *the real definition of credibility* and to distinguish it from the definitions proposed by liberal Protestants, {{400}} semi-rationalists, or even by fideists, we must ask what divine faith and the act of faith are, according to the Catholic Church's own understanding, and rationally defend this Catholic notion on the basis of our preceding theses. Then we must determine the real definition of rational credibility itself, its necessity for faith, the distinction and relationship between the judgment of credibility and the act of faith, and finally the manner in which this rational credibility can and must be proven.

Hence, here in *Section IV: On Credibility in General*, there are three chapters:

- Ch. 14: On the Act of Faith in Relation to Credibility
- Ch. 15: On the Notion of Rational Credibility and Its Necessity for the Act of Faith
- Ch. 16: On the Demonstrability of Credibility on the Basis of the Motives of Credibility

In *Section V: On the Value of the Motives of Credibility Considered Each in Particular*, we will discuss [in the next volume]:

- Ch. 17: On the Value of the Motives of Credibility That Are Internal to Us
- Ch. 18: On the Value of External Motives That are Intrinsic to Religion
- Ch. 19: On the Value of Miracles
- Ch. 20: On the Value of Prophecy

---

4   See Pius IX, *Qui pluribus*, against the followers of Georg Hermes, no. 7 (Denzinger, no. 2778).

CHAPTER FOURTEEN

On the Act of Faith
in Relation to Credibility

{{{401}}} There are three articles in this chapter:

Art. 1. The Catholic notion of faith and heterodox notions thereof

Art. 2. The theological explanation of the Catholic notion of the act of faith, considered from the perspective of both the object and the subject

Art. 3. How revelation must be known precisely as the formal motive of faith

ART. 1: THE CATHOLIC NOTION OF FAITH AND HETERODOX NOTIONS THEREOF

§1. The Catholic Notion of Faith and of the Act of Faith

The [First] Vatican Council defined both the virtue of divine faith and the act of faith.

Logically, we must discuss the act before the virtue. However, for the sake of brevity, we will bring together what has been defined concerning the virtue of faith before the particular things declared regarding the act of faith.

A. The virtue of faith

The virtue of faith is a supernatural virtue by which we believe truths revealed by God because of the authority of God who reveals. Indeed, the Council says:

This faith, which is the beginning of man's salvation, is a supernatural virtue[1] whereby, inspired and {{402}} assisted by the grace

---

[1] At least at the time of the Council of Trent, it was certain that divine faith is an *entitatively* supernatural virtue and not only one that has its supernaturality *effectively*—that is, as a natural

of God, we believe that what He has revealed is true, not because the intrinsic truth of things is recognized by the natural light of reason, but because of the authority of God Himself who reveals them, who can neither err nor deceive. For faith, as the apostle testifies, is 'the substance of things hoped for, the proof of things not seen' (*Heb* 11:1).[2]

Likewise, in the corresponding canon, we read: "If anyone says that divine faith is not distinct from the natural knowledge of God and of moral truths; that, therefore, for divine faith, it is not necessary that the revealed truth be believed on the authority of God who reveals it, let him be anathema."[3]

The Council adds that this definition holds even for unformed or dead faith—namely, that which exists without charity: "Wherefore, faith itself, even when it is not working through love (Gal. 5:6), is in itself a gift of God, and the act of faith is a work appertaining to salvation by which man yields voluntary obedience to God Himself by assenting to and cooperating with grace which he could resist."[4] Likewise, the corresponding canon states: "If anyone says that . . . the grace of God is necessary only for living faith which works by love (Gal. 5:6), let him be anathema."[5]

This definition is stated against rationalists, semi-rationalists, and liberal Protestants.

Now, rationalists (e.g., like Kant) admit only a moral faith that in itself is natural and has the requirements of practical reason as its formal motive. However, liberal Protestants like Schleiermacher and the modernists reduce religious faith to religious experience, the

---

effect that is supernaturally produced (like the healing of a man born blind).

See Salmanticenses, *Cursus theologicus, De gratia*, tr 14, disp. 3, dub. 3, §1, no. 25: "We presuppose that the *habitus* of theological faith is *per se* infused, having a supernatural formal object [*speciem*]. All theologians agree in this. And rightly so on two heads. First of all, this seems to be defined by the Council of Trent, sess. 6, ch. 7, can. 11 and 12, and therefore there are not lacking weighty Doctors who teach that this is certain *De fide*. Moreover, they agree because theological faith is of the same order as sanctifying grace, which certainly is entitatively supernatural."

Scotus, indeed (*In* I *Sent.*, prol. and d. 17, q. 3, no. 33) did not admit that faith is entitatively supernatural but only is causally (or effectively) so. However, the Scotist Francesco Lychetus (ca. 1465–1520), wrote: "From the time of the Council of Vienne up to the time of the Council of Trent, it was only more probable that there might be *habitus* that are *essentially* [*per se*] infused. And after the Council of Trent that greater certitude was upheld, and more truly seems to me that it is a matter of faith itself, [namely,] that certain ontological aids [*aliqua auxilia physica*] are given as *essentially* infused aids for the sake of those sorts of acts" (*In Scot.* III *Sent.*, disp. 25, q. 2, no. 72, Vivès, vol. 15, 200).

[2] [First] Vatican Council, *Dei filius*, ch. 3 (Denzinger, no. 3008).
[3] Ibid., can. 3.2 (Denzinger, no. 3032).
[4] Ibid., ch. 3 (Denzinger, no. 3010).
[5] Ibid., can. 3.5 (Denzinger, no. 3035).

motive of which is conformity of the truths[6] of religion with our higher aspirations. Finally, semi-rationalists like Hermes deny that the formal motive of faith is necessarily the authority of God who reveals. According to them, a sufficient motive is found in the practical necessity of believing, which is made manifest by reason alone. Thus, grace would be necessary only for living faith. Hence, for all of these, religious truth would be credible inasmuch as it appears to be conformed to the aspirations or exigencies of our nature.

B. The act of faith

Many things have been declared by the Catholic Church concerning the act of faith—namely, that it is *a supernatural assent of the intellect, at once utterly certain and free,* by which we believe the truth revealed by God *on account of the authority of God who reveals.* Hence, it presupposes a certain judgment concerning the rational credibility of the mysteries of faith.

Let us briefly see what the Church says concerning: (a) its intellectuality; (b) its supernaturality; (c) its certitude; (d) the prerequisite certain judgment regarding its credibility; and (e) the freedom of the act of faith.

(a) *It is an intellectual assent* and not a kind of religious sentiment.[7] However, this assent is intellectual under the command of the will and, hence, is said to be free. Indeed, the [First] Vatican Council says: "We are bound to yield by faith the full homage of intellect and will to the God who reveals."[8]

(b) *The assent of faith is supernatural.* The [First] Vatican Council says: "No man can 'assent to the Gospel message,' as is necessary to obtain salvation, 'without the illumination and inspiration of the Holy Spirit, who gives to all delight in assenting to the truth and believing in it.'"[9] The Council of Orange said the same.[10] The supernatural illumination is for the intellect, whereas the inspiration is for the will.

{{403}} Nay, against the semi-Pelagians, the Council of Orange defined: "Moreover, *the beginning of faith* and the very desire of faith [*affectum credulitatis*] is a gift given through grace, that is, through the inspiration of the Holy Spirit reforming our will from unbelief to faith and from impiety to piety."[11]

(c) *Regarding the certitude* of the assent of faith, it is said to be certain, infallible, and immutable on account of its motive—namely, God who reveals[12]—and firm above all

---

6 [Trans. note: Reading *veritatem* as *veritatum*.]
7 See Pius X, *Pascendi,* no. 7 (Denzinger, no. 3477) as well as the Anti-Modernist Oath.
8 [First] Vatican Council, *Dei filius,* ch. 3 (Denzinger, no. 3008).
9 Ibid. (Denzinger, no. 3010).
10 See Denzinger, no. 375.
11 See ibid. [The text slightly differs from the form found in Denzinger. I have translated this directly from Fr. Garrigou-Lagrange's Latin.]
12 See Pius IX, *Qui pluribus,* no. 7 (Denzinger, 2778); [First] Vatican Council, *Dei filius,* ch. 3 (Denzinger, nos. 3008 and 3013); ibid., can. 3.6 (Denzinger, no. 3036); Pius X, *Lamentabili,* no. 25 (Denzinger, no. 3425).

other judgments [*super omnia firmus*] on account of its adherence in virtue of the will's motion[13] under the illumination and inspiration of the Holy Spirit.[14] As was said at the [First] Vatican Council: "For the merciful Lord stirs up and aids with His grace those who are wandering astray, that they be able to 'come to the knowledge of the truth' (1 Tim 2:4) and those whom 'he has called out of darkness into His marvelous light' (1 Pet 2:9; Col 1:13), He confirms with His grace that they may persevere in this faith, for He deserts none who do not desert Him."[15]

It has also been declared that the assent of faith is more certain than the judgment of credibility prerequisite [for the act of faith itself], for the following propositions have been condemned: "The will cannot effect that assent to faith in itself be stronger than the weight of reasons impelling toward assent"; "hence, anyone can prudently repudiate the supernatural assent that he had."[16]

Finally, it has been defined that the assent of faith is irrevocable in the sense that "those who have received the faith under the teaching authority of the Church can never have a just reason to change this same faith or to call it into question."[17]

(d) *As regards the certain judgment of credibility as a prerequisite* [for the act of faith], we must note what Pius IX said against the followers of Georg Hermes:

> Indeed, human reason, lest it be deceived and err in a matter of so great importance, ought to investigate diligently the fact of divine revelation so that it can know with certainty that God has spoken. . . . [And so, human reason,] knowing clearly and distinctly [from these most splendid and equally most strong proofs] that God is the Author of this faith, can proceed no further; but rejecting and dispelling every difficulty and doubt, it must render all obedience to this faith.[18]

Merely probable certitude concerning the fact of revelation does not suffice,[19] nor merely subjective pseudo-mysticism,[20] nor only internal [psychological] experience or private

---

13   See Innocent XI, Condemnation by the Sacred Office, Mar. 2, 1679, no. 19 (Denzinger, no. 2119).

14   See [First] Vatican Council, *Dei filius*, ch. 3 (Denzinger, nos. 3010 and 3013–3014).

15   Ibid. (Denzinger, no. 3014).

16   See Innocent XI, Condemnation by the Sacred Office, Mar. 2, 1679, nos. 19 and 20 (Denzinger, nos. 2119 and 2120).

17   [First] Vatican Council, *Dei filius*, ch. 3 (Denzinger, no. 3014); also see ibid., can. 3.6 (Denzinger, no. 3036).

18   Pius IX, *Qui pluribus*, nos. 7 and 9 (Denzinger, nos. 2778 and 2780).

19   See Innocent XI, Condemnation by the Sacred Office, Mar. 2, 1679, no. 21 (Denzinger, no. 2121); Pius X, *Lamentabili*, no. 25 (Denzinger, no. 3425).

20   See Innocent XI, Condemnation by the Sacred Office, Aug. 28, 1687 (and in *Caelestis pastor*), no. 53 (Denzinger, no. 2253).

inspiration,[21] but instead one must have certain knowledge about this fact of revelation.[22] As regards this kind of knowledge, "reason *precedes* faith."[23]

(e) *Finally, the act of faith is free.* The [First] Vatican Council defined: "If anyone says that the assent to the Christian faith is not free but is produced with necessity by arguments of human reason . . . let him be anathema."[24] In other words, the assent of faith is free even after certain knowledge of the motives of credibility. Hence, the error of Pico della Mirandola was condemned: "It is not in the free power of man to believe that an article of faith is true when it pleases him and to believe that it is false when it pleases him."[25] Thus, the assent of faith is free, not only with a freedom of exercise[26] (to believe or not believe) but likewise with a freedom of specification (to believe or disbelieve). Indeed, already in scientific knowledge we have a freedom of exercise,[27] for "the actual consideration of a thing that is known scientifically falls under the free will, for it is in man's own power to consider or not consider it."[28]

Thus, we have before us the necessary details concerning the Catholic notion of the act of divine faith.

§2. Heterodox Notions of Faith

Heterodox notions of faith			
	Pseudo-supernaturalism.........		of the first Protestants, of Baius, and of the fideists
	Naturalism	Absolute naturalism	the Kantian theory of faith / theory held by many liberal Protestants
		Semi-naturalism	the pelagian and semi-pelagian theory / the theory held by semi-rationalists / the theory held by semi-immanentists

{{404}} Heterodox notions of faith, like heterodox notions of revelation,

---

[21] [First] Vatican Council, *Dei filius*, can. 3.3 (Denzinger, no. 3033).

[22] Theses Subscribed to by Louis-Eugène Bautain by Order of His Bishop, Nov. 18, 1835 and Sept. 8, 1840, no. 2 (Denzinger, no. 2752); Pius IX, *Qui pluribus*, no. 7 (Denzinger, no. 2778); [First] Vatican Council, *Dei filius*, can. 3.3 (Denzinger, no. 3033); Pius X, *Pascendi*, no. 39ff (Denzinger, 2106ff, old numbering).

[23] See Theses Subscribed to by Louis-Eugène Bautain by Order of His Bishop, Sept. 8, 1840, no. 5 (Denzinger no. 2756); Theses against the Traditionalism of Augustin Bonnetty, no. 3 (Denzinger, no. 2813).

[24] [First] Vatican Council, *Dei filius*, can. 3.5 (Denzinger, no. 3035).

[25] See Denzinger, 737, old numbering.

[26] Indeed, the followers of Georg Hermes admitted this freedom of exercise in the act of faith and, nonetheless, were condemned by the [First] Vatican Council.

[27] See *ST* I-II, q. 17, a. 6; II-II, q. 2, a. 1, ad 3.

[28] *ST* II-II, q. 2, a. 9.

can be divided in relation to what they hold regarding the supernaturality of faith, inasmuch as they either destroy or diminish it (as happens in naturalism, semi-rationalism, liberal Protestantism, and modernism) or, on the contrary, materially exaggerate what is supernatural in faith by diminishing the powers of reason (as happens in the pseudo-supernaturalism of the first Protestants and of the fideists).[29]

Let us begin with the pseudo-supernaturalism of the first Protestants, for it appeared chronologically first and then afterwards (by means of the principle of private inspiration and of free inquiry) led to semi-naturalism and the naturalism of the liberal Protestants.

We already set forth these heterodox notions in the historical overview of apologetic methodology[30] and afterwards in treating of the various heterodox notions of revelation. Therefore, we can be brief in recalling the details of these positions.

(1) Pseudo-supernaturalism

{{405}} Here we will go over (A) the pseudo-supernaturalism of the first Protestants and (B) that of the fideists.

A. *The first Protestants*, like Luther and Calvin, argued on behalf of a notion of faith that is more subjective than is the Catholic notion. They did so for four reasons:

(a) They rejected the infallible external authority of the Church for proposing revelation[31] and therefore posited in each believing person *an immediate inspiration of the Holy Spirit* for discerning in Sacred Scripture the authentic *Word of God*, as well as its true meaning, by means of a [kind of so-called spiritual] savor and taste. Together with

---

[29] These various theories can be written according to their more or less radical opposition [to each other] as follows so that we can represent the superiority of the Thomistic doctrine and, below it, the place held by the Molinist theory of faith that is only modally supernatural, which we will discuss below.

Thomism
Essentially supernatural faith
Molinism
Modally supernatural faith

Semi-Pelagianism		*Fideism*
Pelagianism		*Baianism*
Naturalism		*Protestant pseudo-supernaturalism*

[30] See above our Prolegomena, ch. 3, On the Methodology of Apologetics, art. 3 and what we there said regarding the *Lutheran* notion of faith, the *Kantian* notion of it, that of Hermes, and that expressed by *liberal Protestants*, as well as the notion of faith expressed by Catholic thinkers who hold to *the philosophy of action*.

[31] See Leo X, *Exsurge Domine*, no. 27 (Denzinger, no. 1477).

private inspiration, which is supernatural, they admit private inquiry [i.e., private inter-pretation], which ultimately leads to rationalism and individualism, given their rejection of the authority of the Church.

(b) Beyond (historical) faith, by which they believe in the truths contained in Sacred Scripture, the first Protestants admit an even more subjective form of faith—namely, that by which any given believer believes that his sins have been forgiven and that he is justified without any works at all. This faith, which Protestants call "faith-trust" [*fiducia*], paved the way for the conception of faith held by liberal Protestants, who identify the act of faith with natural religious experience.

(c) Finally, Luther was a nominalist and an adversary of Aristotelian and scholastic philosophy.[32] On account of his philosophical skepticism, he could not attribute a great value to extrinsic motives of credibility like miracles but could only give such value to internal motives. This philosophical skepticism leads to *fideism*: The truths that tran-scend experience are certain only by faith. This also leads to naturalism, for if reason is so weak, Christian faith and grace are owed to our nature and hence are not supernatural.

(d) Nay, [the first] Protestants, in a way that is akin to the thought of Michael Baius and the Jansenists, said that the exaltation of human nature to a sharing in the divine nature was *owed* to the full integrity of man's first condition and hence must be called natural, not supernatural.[33] From this it follows that revealed mysteries are not essentially supernatural.

Therefore, pseudo-supernaturalism does not exalt grace but, rather, diminishes nature. Thus, grace is owed [to man] and, thus, would be natural. Moreover, the notion of private inspiration leads to private inquiry [or "private interpretation"], exalting the right of individual reason, and thus prepares for the naturalism of liberal Protestantism.

B. *Fideists* like Bautain and Bonnetty, as well as the traditionalists, also diminish the powers of reason.

According to them,[34] human reason cannot prove with certitude the existence of God, nor the infinity of his perfections, nor the spiritual reality and freedom of the

---

[32] [Trans. note: There are some more recent scholars who nuance some of the classic connections drawn between Luther and late-scholastic nominalists. For instance, see Heiko A. Oberman, *The Harvest of Medieval Theology: Gabriel Biel and Late Medieval Nominalism* (Grand Rapids, MI: Baker Academic, 2000); *The Dawn of the Reformation: Essays in Late Medieval and Early Reformation Thought* (Grand Rapids, MI: Eerdmans, 1992). One should, however, also see the important study by Paul Hacker, *Faith in Luther: Martin Luther and the Origin of Anthropocentric Religion* (Steubenville, OH: Emmaus Academic, 2017).]

[33] Pius V, *Ex omnibus afflictionibus*, no. 21 (Denzinger, no. 1921).

[34] See Theses Subscribed to by Louis-Eugène Bautain by Order of His Bishop, Nov. 18, 1835 and Sept. 8, 1840, nos. 1ff (Denzinger, nos. 2751ff); Sacred Congregation of the Index, June 11 (15), 1855, Theses against the Traditionalism of Augustin Bonnetty, nos. 1ff (Denzinger, nos. 2811ff).

rational soul. Likewise, they hold that *the fact of revelation cannot be proven*. As regards these various questions, reason does not precede faith. In order to have certain knowledge of these truths, one needs at least common faith founded on traditions and primitive revelation. This has been condemned by the Church, who holds that "right reason demonstrates the foundations of faith."[35] Fideism leads to naturalism inasmuch as divine revelation is said to be owed to our nature if reason is thus deficient.

(2) Naturalism and semi-naturalism

{{406}} The following outlooks belong to absolute *naturalism*: (A) the Kantian theory of faith; (B) the theory held by many liberal Protestants; and (C) the theory of the modernists. The following outlooks belong to *semi-naturalism*: (A) the Pelagian and semi-Pelagian theories of faith; (B) the theory of the semi-rationalists, especially of Georg Hermes; and (C) the theory of semi-immanentists. These various theories were set forth at greater length in our historical overview of apologetics. Therefore, they can be briefly summarized here.

NATURALISM

A. *The Kantian theory of faith* has a twofold foundation:

(a)   On the one hand, there is his speculative agnosticism. According to Kant, speculative [*theoretica*] reason cannot know with certitude what exists beyond the phenomenal order (e.g., the existence of God the First Cause) and hence cannot discern revelation or miracles.

(b)   On the other, there is his position concerning the autonomy of the will and of practical reason, which imposes the categorical imperative (or the moral law) upon itself.

Based on this twofold foundation, we can only have *moral faith by which we believe the postulates of practical reason* deduced from the categorical imperative—namely, the existence of free will, the future life, and God the one who justly rewards. This moral faith has subjectively sufficient certitude, although it is objectively insufficient. Its [formal] motive is not the authority of God who reveals but, rather, the exigencies of practical reason inasmuch as the categorical imperative (or the moral law) would not be preserved if these postulates were rejected.

B. *The theory of liberal Protestants* like Schleiermacher, Ritschl, Sabatier, and Harnack reduces faith to *a natural religious sentiment* and the act of faith to religious experience, which is livelier in Christianity than in other religions. Hence, the *credibilia* are mysteries of Christianity inasmuch as it appears to us to be conformed to the aspirations and exigencies of our religious sentiment. The first Protestants rejected the infallible proposition of divine truth by the Church, which proposition is a [necessary] condition for faith. Now liberal Protestants reject not only the [necessary] condition but the formal

---

[35] [First] Vatican Council, *Dei filius*, ch. 4 (Denzinger, no. 3019).

motive of faith—namely, the authority of God who reveals—conceiving of religious faith as being something that is, simply speaking, natural.

C. *The theory of the modernists.* Like the liberal Protestants, the modernists reduce faith to a religious sentiment and the act of faith to *religious experience.* The foundation of this theory is twofold: agnosticism and immanentism, as is shown in the encyclical *Pascendi.*[36] In virtue of the modernists' agnosticism, they hold that human reason can know with certitude only phenomena and phenomenal laws. Hence, even the religious phenomena of Catholicism must be explained not through God's supernatural intervention but, rather, in accord with the development [*evolutionem*] of the religious sentiment immanent within us. Therefore, Catholic faith is nothing other than the religious experience of the truths proposed by the Church. However, the credibility of the mysteries is had inasmuch as something "unknown" appears to be hidden in the history of the Church, and this "unknown" is the best thing for us and responds to the requirements of our religious awareness.[37] However, this ultimately leads to the denial of the immutability and absolute truth of dogmas.[38] Nay, faith is subject to science and philosophy inasmuch as the value of the concepts of dogmatic formulas is determined by philosophy; however, according to the modernists, this value is only phenomenal in character and not ontological.[39]

SEMINATURALISTS differ from naturalists inasmuch as they admit at least the external fact of supernatural revelation. However, they diminish the supernaturality of faith on the side of both the subject and the object.

{{407}} A. *The Pelagians* said, presupposing external revelation, *internal grace is not necessary for one to believe* as is necessary for salvation. One only needs natural knowledge of the signs of revelation and natural good will.

The *semi-Pelagians* said that internal grace is not required at least *for the beginning of faith* but is given, however, so that one may believe more easily and more firmly.[40]

B. *The theory of the semi-rationalists,* especially of Georg Hermes. According to the semi-rationalists, all the *mysteries* of the Christian faith *can be demonstrated* by reason, at least after revelation. In this way, the essential supernaturality of faith is destroyed; faith would be only modally supernatural, as regards the first proposition of the object [which then could be demonstrated].[41]

---

[36] Pius X, *Pascendi*, nos. 6 and 7 (Denzinger, nos. 3475 and 3477).

[37] See ibid., no. 35 (Denzinger, nos. 3499–3500).

[38] See ibid., nos. 12, 13, and 26 (Denzinger, nos. 3483 and 3493).

[39] See ibid., no. 17 (Denzinger, no. 3486).

[40] See the Synod of Orange, can. 5 (Denzinger, no. 375).

[41] See Pius IX, *Syllabus of Errors*, can. 8–14 (Denzinger nos. 2908–2914); [First] Vatican Council, *Dei filius*, can. 4.1 (Denzinger, no. 3041); Gregory XVI, *Dum acerbissimas* (Denzinger, old nos. 1618[ff] / cf. new no. 2738[ff]); Pius IX, *Qui pluribus* (Denzinger, nos. 2775ff); Pius IX, *Eximiam tuam*, Letter to the Archbishop of Cologne, June 15, 1857

Among the semi-rationalists, *Hermes* especially developed a theory concerning faith. This Hermesian theory found its basis in Kantianism, relying on a twofold foundation:

(a) Speculative agnosticism: Theoretical reason can arrive only at merely subjective persuasion regarding objective reality, which in actual fact can only be apparent and phenomenal.

(b) The autonomy of reason: Practical reason imposes the moral law on itself, and sometimes there arises an obligation to admit as being true something that really is theoretically doubtful (e.g., the testimony of the external senses or the truth of history).

If these positions are presupposed, the external motives of credibility, such as miracles, are only speculatively probable, and *the formal motive of faith is not the authority of God who reveals but a kind of exigency of practical reason*. The simple faithful must believe the mysteries on account of revelation, and revelation itself on account of a kind of practical necessity, for without revelation, they cannot arrive at certain knowledge of moral and religious truths. Philosophers, however, can demonstrate the mysteries of Christianity, though they nonetheless must admit that revelation is necessary for the simple faithful and as a condition for the first proposition of the mysteries, which could then afterwards be demonstrated [by reason alone]. Hence, the credibility of the mysteries is had not so much from the manifestation of the fact of revelation as it is from the exposition of the exigencies of our moral life.

C. *The theory of semi-immanentists.* Certain Catholic philosophers, like Maurice Blondel and Lucien Laberthonnière, who defend the primacy of action and of practical reason and, hence, also defended the primacy of the method of immanence, can be called semi-immanentists. Failing to take due care concerning these matters, they seem to hold that our nature makes a true demand for the supernatural order. Indeed, they concede to the agnostics that, by itself, speculative reason cannot defend its own ontological value. According to them, if we remove the requirements asserted by human action, our speculative knowledge remains notional and subjective and can only posit the problem of action and direct action, whereas action itself is what reaches objective reality. Nay, truth is nothing other than the real adequation of mind and life inasmuch as a judgment is conformed to the requirements of our life.

Hence—and in this we can see their semi-immanentism—religion, indeed even supernatural religion, must be proposed as an aid postulated in some way intrinsically on the basis of the exigencies of our action, for by virtue of the autonomy of reason, man wishes to accept nothing extrinsically unless it is required for the perfect development of his faculties. Immanentism says that Catholicism arises from the development of the religious sentiment that is immanent within our nature. These philosophers say that

(Denzinger, no. 2828); Pius IX, *Gravissimas inter*, Letter to the Archbishop of Munich-Freising, Dec. 11, 1862 (Denzinger, old no. 1666).

Catholicism is revealed by God, but it responds to the exigencies of our nature. Thus, they draw close to Baianism,[42] for something owed to our nature is neither gratuitous nor supernatural.[43]

As discussed above, on account of their speculative agnosticism, these philosophers do not admit the ontological value of miracles but instead only admit their symbolic value. Moreover, in other respects, they excessively extol the value of internal motives, as though the mysteries of Christianity (e.g., the Incarnation and Redemption) were demanded by our nature. Finally, *they hold that the divine origin* {{408}} *of Christianity becomes certain only in Christian experience itself under the aid of grace, and that divine faith is identified with this experience.* This is not lacking in some affinity with modernism.[44] It does not sufficiently preserve the formal motive of faith—namely, the authority of God who reveals—nor the rational knowability of the fact of revelation. Hence, this theory is far too akin to semi-naturalism.

These are the principal heterodox notions of faith. If the final form is not itself heterodox, it is at least proposed in far too incautious a manner, seeming to hold that human nature expresses true demand for the supernatural order, and this is the error of Baius, as was noted in the encyclical *Pascendi*.[45]

ART. 2: THEOLOGICAL EXPLANATION OF THE CATHOLIC NOTION OF FAITH (I.E., AN ANALYSIS OF THE ACT OF FAITH CONSIDERED FROM THE PERSPECTIVE OF THE OBJECT AND FROM THE PERSPECTIVE OF THE SUBJECT)

1. *From the perspective of the object*: (1) the formal object *quod*; (2) the objective formal motive; (3) whether revelation as an uncreated divine action belongs to the formal motive of faith; and (4) whether proposal by the Church belongs to the formal motive of faith.

2. *From the perspective of its subject* [*of inherence*]: (1) what it means to believe, as well as to believe in God; (2) on the supernaturality of the act of faith; and (3) on the reconciliation of freedom with the surpassing certitude of faith.

First, we must note that the virtue of faith and the act of faith itself, inasmuch as they are essentially supernatural, are *mysteries* strictly speaking.[46] They must *not* be thought of *univocally* according to a resolution to inferior notions—namely, to acquired natural faith (for this would in reality be a material explanation of the act of divine faith)—but, rather,

---

[42] See Pius X, *Pascendi*, no. 37 (Denzinger, 2103, old numbering).

[43] See Pius V, *Ex omnibus afflictionibus*, no. 21 (Denzinger, no. 1921).

[44] See Pius X, *Pascendi*, no 35 (Denzinger, nos. 3499–3500).

[45] See Pius X, *Pascendi*, no. 37 (Denzinger, 2103, old numbering).

[46] See ch. 5, a. 2 of this work (on the division of mysteries).

must be *analogically* explained,[47] indeed materially in comparison to acquired natural faith but formally through a resolution to something superior (namely, to the uncreated intellectual light of God who reveals).

In this article, we will see how these two explanations of the act of faith are opposed to each other.

§1. Explanation of the Act of Faith from the Perspective of the Object

The object of faith can be considered in two ways—namely, (1) the object that [*quod*] is believed and (2) the formal object by which [*quo*] it is believed (or the formal objective motive for why we believe).[48]

(1) *The object that* is believed is [either] material or formal. The *material* object of faith is everything that can be believed (namely, *everything revealed by God*). This material object is subdivided into *the per se object* of faith (namely, everything revealed that cannot be known without revelation) and *the preambles of faith* (namely, those revealed things that can be known {{409}} even without revelation but are prerequisites for [knowing] the supernatural mysteries—namely, God's existence and other such natural truths of religion that can be demonstratively proven [by reason alone]).[49]

---

[47] See *De veritate*, q. 14, a. 9, ad 4: "'To believe' is said *equivocally* of the faith of men and that of demons, who do not have in themselves a kind of infused light of grace as is found in the faithful."

[48] See *ST* II-II, q. 1, a. 1 and *De veritate*, q. 14, a. 8.

[49] See *ST* II-II, q. 1, a. 5, a. 3: "Those things that can be demonstratively proven are numbered among things to be believed not because they themselves would *simpliciter* be held by faith in all people but, rather, because they are prerequired for those things that are of faith and must be presupposed by those who do not have demonstrative knowledge of them."—*ST* I, q. 2, a. 2, ad 1: "*That God exists* and other such things which can be known about God through natural reason, as is said in Rom 1:20, are not articles of faith, but rather, are preambles to the articles."

Objection. St. Thomas seems to contradict himself, for he says in *ST* II-II, q. 1, a. 7: "All the articles are implicitly contained in two particular *credibilia*, namely, that it is believed *that God exists* and that He providentially cares for the salvation of men, as is said in Heb 11:6 (DR): 'For he that cometh to God must believe that He is and is a rewarder to them that seek Him.' For in the divine existence are included all things that we believe to exist eternally in God, and our beatitude lies in such things. However, faith in His providence includes all those things that are temporally dispensed by God for the salvation of men, such things being the way toward our beatitude." Therefore, on the one hand, St. Thomas says that "God exists" is not an article of faith and is not believed by the faithful who have demonstrative knowledge of it, and on the other hand, he says that "God exists and is a just rewarder" are two principal articles of faith that implicitly contain the others and must be believed in by all the faithful, according to the authority of St. Paul.

The Thomists respond (cf. Gonet, *Clypeus theologicae Thomisticae*, De fidei, disp. 1, a. 6, §2), when it is said that "God exists" is not an article of faith but, rather, a preamble of faith, it

Hence, the preambles of faith "pertain to faith *per accidens* and not *per se*," as St. Thomas says in *In* III *Sent.*, d. 24, a. 2, ad 2 quaest.

However, the *per se* object of faith is either primary and formal or secondary. The *primary* and *formal* object of faith is *God sub ratione Deitatis*, from the perspective of the Deity—that is, according to his intimate life. In other words, it is *the First Truth in the order of existence*, as exceeding the natural knowledge of any intellect that could ever be created, for from this perspective, God can be known by a created intellect through supernatural revelation alone. This object is called formal because, as St. Thomas says, "Nothing falls under faith except as ordered to God, just as the object of medicine is health, for the art of medicine considers nothing except as ordered to health."[50]

However, the *secondary per se* object of faith includes all those things outside of God's intimate life that can be known by revelation alone, like the mysteries of the Incarnation, the Redemption, grace, the Eucharist, the other sacraments, the supernatural virtues, and the beatific vision. All of these things proceed from God's intimate life and are ordered to it.

{{410}} To sum this up, therefore, we can schematically present what we have said as follows: [see next page]

---

is a question of *the existence of God the Author of nature*. By contrast, when it is said that "God exists" is the first article of faith, implicitly containing the others, it is a question of *the existence of God the Author of the supernatural order*. From this latter, loftier perspective—namely, as the First Cause of the supernatural order—God's existence is not proven philosophically, and it is only under this loftier perspective that this implicitly contains the mystery of the Trinity. The same distinction must be made regarding the divine unity, providence, and so forth. The unity of God the Author of nature is demonstrated, but not the most eminent unity, which notwithstanding remains in the Trinity. Even providence in general is demonstrated but not inasmuch as it orders and disposes supernatural means for our salvation. Hence, St. Thomas says in *De veritate*, q. 14, a. 9, ad 8: "Inasmuch as knowledge of God's unity is demonstrated, it is not an article of faith but, instead, is presupposed for the articles of faith, for the knowledge of faith presupposes natural knowledge, just as nature presupposes grace. However, the unity of the divine essence, such as it is held by believers, namely with omnipotence and providence over all things, and other such things (e.g., the Trinity), which cannot be proven, constitutes an article of faith." In this latter text, the words "providence over all things" refers to providence even over supernatural means.

[50] See *ST* II-II, q. 1, a. 1.

The material object of faith	per se object	primary and formal	: God *sub ratione Deitatis*, i.e., from the formal perspective of His intimate life
		secondary	: The supernatural mysteries that are ordered to God
	preambles of faith		: The natural truths of religion

(2) **The formal object *quo* (or the formal motive) of faith** is "the authority of God who reveals," as is defined by the [First] Vatican Council.

Now, the term "authority" contains two things: trustworthiness and the knowledge required for teaching. These two are required in order for one to recognize, for example, the authority of a given teacher or witness. Hence, to say with the [First] Vatican Council that the formal motive of faith is the authority of God who reveals is the same as saying, along with the common expression of the Thomists: "*Faith's formal object quo is the First Truth expressing itself* [*in dicendo*] (or the divine *trustworthiness* [*veracitas*] revealing), inasmuch as it connotes the First Truth in the order of knowledge, that is, *the infallible wisdom of God*."[51]

The first part of this proposition is proven as follows. The motive of faith in general is the *trustworthiness* of the one who teaches. Now, divine faith is said to be that by which we believe in God. Therefore, the motive of divine faith is the trustworthiness of God who reveals. The major premise is clear, for this is what distinguishes the assent of faith from the assent of experience, whether of science or of opinion. The motive of the assent of faith is the trustworthiness of the one who speaks to us, whereas the motive of the assent of experience is sensible evidence. The motive of scientific assent is the truth of the principle from which a [given] scientific conclusion is drawn. The motive of the understanding of principles is their intellectual self-evidence. Finally, the motive of opinion is a probable reason on account of which we assent with uncertainty and fear of error. By contrast, faith is a certain form of adherence to a non-evident object [known from] someone's testimony. Hence it cannot rest on any other motive than the trustworthiness of the one testifying to it—namely, that trustworthiness by which the witness speaks the truth and cannot deceive. Thus, I believe what my father tells me. Hence, the motive of divine faith is the trustworthiness of God who speaks [to us through revelation].

The second part of the proposition is proven as follows. In order for faith to be certain, it must rest upon an indubitable motive. Now, the trustworthiness of a speaker is not indubitable *unless it connotes knowledge*

---

[51] See the commentators on *ST* II-II, q. 1, a. 1. For example, John of St. Thomas, Gonet, and Billuart.

required in the speaker. Therefore, the trustworthiness of God who reveals is the [formal] motive of infallible [and] divine faith only if it connotes *the infallible wisdom of God*—namely, inasmuch as God can neither deceive nor be deceived. Indeed, it does not suffice that the witness could not deceive out of wickedness. Beyond this, it is also required that he cannot deceive even out of ignorance, and it is indeed the case that God himself cannot be deceived in his knowledge.

These points suffice for the formal motive of faith: It is the trustworthiness of God who speaks, connoting infallibility. In a word, it can be expressed thus: the authority of God who reveals.

Objection: The reason why God can neither deceive nor be deceived also pertains to the motive of faith. Now, this reason is because God is the First Truth in the order of existence [*in esssendo*], for this {{411}} is why he cannot fall short in the orders of understanding and speaking. Therefore, the First Truth in the order of existence also pertains to the formal motive of faith.

Response: I deny the major premise, concede the minor, and deny the inference. For *to ask why God can neither be deceived nor deceive is not to ask about the reason for the assent of faith but, rather, about the reason for these divine attributes*—namely, the divine trustworthiness and infallibility. Hence, the First Truth in the order of existence does not enter into the motive of faith. Belief is established upon the authority of God who reveals, just as sight is established upon the colored inasmuch as it is visible, although knowledge of the reason why a body happens to be colored does not pertain to external sight but, rather, to discursive reasoning. Likewise, if it is asked why God is veracious and infallible, we do not respond qua believers but, rather, qua theologians, for God is the truth itself in the order of existence (that is, the Deity). *Indeed* (and this must be carefully noted), *the assent* of faith *is not discursive* but, rather, is simple, being established solely on the testimony of him who speaks. Otherwise, it would no longer be an assent of faith. Nay, the supernatural certitude of faith would be formally resolved into the inferior certitude of discursive reason and would be in line with this lesser order, which would thereby serve as the basis of our certitude of faith [*peiorem partem sequeretur*].[52] (See our discussion below

---

[52] See John of St. Thomas, *Cursus theologicus, De fide*, q. 1, disp. 1, a. 2, §2: "Certain (nominalist) authors believe that faith depends upon some acquired knowledge not only as a condition or remote disposition but as a *per se* reason concurring with faith, such that they would resolve faith into this proposition known *by the natural* light [of reason], namely 'God is trustworthy,' [*verax*] and 'God has spoken,' inasmuch as these propositions are attained through human knowledge. However, this reasoning must be completely excluded, for the assent of faith is more certain than every form of natural (or acquired) knowledge since it has the highest, supernatural infallibility. . . . Others, like Durandus of Saint Pourçain and Gabriel Vasquez held that to believe on account of revelation is to believe on account of that as something previously known and believed, so that faith would thus include two acts of assent, with the

in §3 on how revelation is known and whether it is the formal motive of faith.)

{{412}} (3) *First doubt*: *Does revelation itself, as an uncreated and free action of God who reveals, pertain to the formal motive of faith, or is it only a necessary condition for it?*

---

second being deduced from the first. However, in that case, the second assent of faith would depend upon the natural light [of reason] (on account of such a deduction)."

In his remarks on *ST* II-II, q. 1, a. 1, Domingo Bañez writes: "A second conclusion: The assent of our faith cannot be reduced to the acquired faith by which we believe that the Church is trustworthy, as in the rule or formal reason for believing. This conclusion is so certain that the opposite position seems in our eyes not only to be rash but even an error against faith. It is proven as follows. It is erroneous to say that human faith is as certain as divine faith. Now, if the certitude of divine faith is reduced to the human faith by which we believe that the Church is trustworthy as in a medium and formal rule of believing, it obviously follows that human faith is not only equally certain but, rather, is more certain than divine faith."

Vincenzo Gotti writes in [*Theologia scholastico-dogmatica juxta mentem Divi Thomae Aquinatis*], *De Fide*, tr. 9, dub. 4, §2: "Since faith is a theological virtue, the adequate formal motive of belief must be divine, namely, the divine testimony, so that someone would be moved to believe adequately on account of this and not on account of some other reason. Now, if belief were to be brought about through discourse, the adequate motive for believing would no longer be the divine testimony but, rather, the connection between the divine testimony and the existence of the thing believed in, which is at least inadequately distinguished from the divine testimony. (For example: whatever God has revealed truly exists; now, God has revealed the Incarnation; therefore, the Incarnation truly exists.) Therefore, belief does not come about through discursive reasoning."

Objection: He who believes on account of the testimony of God should reduce his faith in the end to this *naturally* known principle: "The First Truth can neither deceive nor be deceived."

Response (following Gotti's remarks in the same text): I make a distinction regarding the antecedent. I concede that this would be the ultimate judgment as a preamble of faith. However, I deny that it would be such as something constitutive of the very assent of faith. The aforementioned discursive argument is indeed something to be admitted as a preamble of faith, but not as something that is completely a formal aspect of the assent of faith. Indeed, in the act of assent, every process of discursive reasoning comes to a halt, and he who believes only believes because God speaks and on account of his testimony. On this alone does he rely and not upon human discursive reflection. The Church herself acts in like manner in her decisions regarding the faith. Indeed, before resolving a matter, she calls together her teachers and discusses and examines the matters at hand, undertaking a truly discursive project at that time. However, in her formal definition, setting aside this discourse, she declares this truth as being revealed by the Holy Spirit, according to the form of the decree that we see in Acts 15:28 (DR): "For it hath seemed good to the Holy Ghost and to us."

"Thus, he who believes does not first know the divine dictum and then pass on to believe. Instead, by one and the same act he attains it *as that which it is* [*ut quod*], a revealed mystery, and *that by which* [*he believes, ut quo*], namely revelation itself.... Revelation is, as it were, the light under which he knows the revealed reality."

St. Thomas,[53] Thomists (e.g., Capreolus, Cajetan, John of St. Thomas,[54] the Salmanticenses,[55] Gonet, and others) and even Suarez, de Lugo, [Camillus] Mazzella, Cardinal Billot, and others, believe that active revelation belongs to the motive of faith. Scotus[56] and the Scotists, on the contrary, with St. Alphonsus de Liguori and certain others, say that active revelation is only a necessary condition for faith.

The first opinion, as [Camillus] Mazzella notes,[57] seems to be more conformed to the [First] Vatican Council's definition of faith as "the virtue by which we believe on account of the authority of God who reveals," for these words offer an explanation for the formal motive of faith without making any distinction. Nay, a definition does not include the prerequisite conditions for the thing in question but, rather, includes [only] those things that pertain to the very essence of the thing. Nonetheless, according to Vacant,[58] the Council did not resolve this question and did not condemn the other opinion.

Thomists defend their position on the basis of Sacred Scripture and theological reasoning. Indeed, *Sacred Scripture* does not distinguish the motive and necessary condition of faith but, rather, says *that the divine testimony is the reason why we believe*. For example, see 1 John 5:9–10 (DR): "If we receive the testimony of men, the testimony of God is greater. . . . He that believeth in the Son of God hath the testimony of God in himself. He that believeth not the Son maketh him a liar: because he believeth not in the testimony which God hath testified of his Son." Likewise, see John 5:36–38 (DR): "But I have a greater testimony than that of John. . . . And the Father himself who hath sent me hath given testimony of me: neither have you heard his voice at any time, nor seen his shape. And you have not his word abiding in you: for whom he hath sent, him you believe not." (Also see St. Thomas's commentary on this verse.) See also Matthew 16:17 (DR): "Blessed art thou, Simon Bar-Jona: because flesh and blood hath not revealed it to thee, but my Father who is in heaven." And see St. Paul, 1 Corinthians 2:5, 10 (DR): "That your faith might not stand on the wisdom of men, but on the power of God. . . . But to us God hath revealed them by his Spirit. For the Spirit searcheth all things, yea, the deep things of God." Likewise, in his letter to the Galatians 1:12 (DR): "For neither did I receive it of man: nor did I learn it but by the revelation of Jesus Christ."

---

[53] See *De veritate*, q. 14, a. 8 (ad ult.): "In matters of faith, the very testimony of the First Truth holds the same place as that which is held by principle[s] in demonstrative sciences."

[54] See John of St. Thomas, *Cursus theologicus, De fide*, disp. 1, a. 1, no. 19.

[55] Salmanticenses, *Cursus theologicus, De fide*, disp. 1, dub. 3, no. 89 and later on dub. 2, no. 57.

[56] Scotus, *In III Sent.*, dist. 23, quaestio unia, § "Aliter."

[57] See Mazzella, *De virtutibus infusis*, no. 341.

[58] See Vacant, *Études théologiques sur les constitutions du Concile du Vatican d'après les actes du concile*, vol. 2, 32.

Theological reasoning also proves that active revelation pertains to the formal motive of faith as its constitutive form. This proof is had from the distinction between a motive and a condition. *A motive or cause positively influences its effect.* For example, by its action, fire burns wood. *By contrast, a condition* neither positively moves nor influences but, rather, is necessary so that the cause may have influence and only applies the already-in-act cause to the patient [i.e., that which is acted upon], for example, by touching the fire to the wood. Hence, the argument runs as follows: *That which formally constitutes the formal character of a testimony, rendering authority itself formally motivating, itself pertains to the formal motive of faith and is not only* {{413}} *a condition applying a cause to its effect.* Now, active revelation formally constitutes the formal character of the testimony and renders the divine authority formally moving, for divine authority that does not speak does not formally bear witness, nor is it something that moves hearers [to belief]. Therefore, the single formal motive of faith is the First Truth actually bearing witness—that is, the authority of God actually speaking.

If the motive were the authority of God, in first act, independent of active revelation, by virtue of this motive, our faith would be hypothetically infallible but not categorically so. We would always implicitly think: *If* this is in fact revealed by God, then it is infallibly true.

The Thomists hold that nothing created can pertain to the formal motive of a theological virtue. However, active revelation guarantees that it is a question of an uncreated action of God who reveals.

(4) **Second doubt:** *Does the proposition (or testimony) of the Church pertain to the formal motive of faith, or is it only a necessary condition?*

The Thomists commonly respond, against Durandus of Saint Pourçain, Cardinal de Lugo, and [Miguel] de Medina, that the Church's proposing does not pertain to the formal motive of faith in any way but instead is *only a necessary condition for it. For this proposing does not formally influence* the intellect and will of the believer *but, rather, only applies already-existing revelation to us.* The only thing that moves us to believe is the authority of God actually revealing. Likewise, a professor proposing St. Thomas's teaching to his students is only a necessary condition. St. Thomas's authority is the formal motive for their acceptance of this teaching, not the authority of this professor. Likewise, the intellect gazes upon the truth of the first principles on account of their [self-]evidence, and the explanation of the terms in which these principles are expressed was only a [necessary] condition [for grasping their self-evidence]. Likewise, the will is moved by the good itself, but the will can only love the good if the latter is proposed by the intellect, although this proposing is only a [necessary] condition for its love.[59]

---

[59] Thus, presupposing knowledge of the motives of credibility, without a vicious circle, we can

Moreover, the testimony of the Church is something created. However, nothing created can enter into the formal motive of faith, nor into hope and charity. Otherwise, they would not be purely divine theological virtues.[60]

Nonetheless, against the Protestants, we must hold that the Church's proposing of the truth of revelation is a necessary condition [*conditio sine qua non*] for our faith. Protestants posit private inspiration in place of this proposing by the Church divinely established by Christ. However, as is shown in the treatise on the Church,[61] this rule is not divinely instituted, nor certain, nor sufficient for settling controversies.

These points suffice for explaining the act of faith from the perspective of its object and formal motive.

---

supernaturally believe in the infallible authority of the Church *on account of* revelation as upon the motive for our faith, and believe in revelation *on account of* the authority of the Church as applying revelation itself. The expression "on account of" has a different meaning in each of these two cases. In the first proposition, it is taken formally, though not in the second. A vicious circle, by contrast, would only exist if we passed between these two claims while understanding this expression in the same manner in each of them. It is quite ordinary for causes to be causes of each other, though in different genera of causality. Thus, the intellect objectively moves the will and is itself moved by the will as regards exercise. Likewise, the senses provide the matter for intellection while being judged by the intellect.

    [Trans. note: On the topic of the mutual dependence of causes, see Réginald Garrigou-Lagrange, *The Order of Things: The Realism of the Principle of Finality*, trans. Matthew Minerd (Steubenville, OH: Emmaus Academic, 2020), 319–347.]

[60] See Gonet, *Clypeus theologicae Thomisticae, De fide*, disp. 1, a. 2.

[61] [Trans. note: By which Fr. Garrigou-Lagrange seems to mean texts like that of his confrere Fr. Reginald Schultes, whose course was a continuation of Fr. Garrigou-Lagrange's course *De revelatione*. As Fr. Garrigou-Lagrange noted above, this perspective should not be confused with a theology of the Church in its own mystery (like what one finds in Journet's multi-tome *L'église du verbe incarné*. Rather, Schultes's *De ecclesia* (and, likewise, I would suspect the *Tractatus de ecclesia* spoken of by Fr. Garrigou-Lagrange here) is primarily concerned with the Church's divine institution and authority, not her inner mystery. It thus remains part of apologetics as one integral part of the unified science of theology. As Schultes himself explains in Reginald Schultes, *De ecclesia catholica praelectiones apologeticae* (Paris: Lethielleux, 1925), 2: "The proper object of our treatise is the institution and divine authority of the Catholic Church. The Catholic Church can be considered from various formal perspectives: we can consider either [1] its historical development and influence in the past (church history), [2] its intimate nature as the Mystical Body of Christ having the sacraments as its means of conferring grace, along with other such matters (dogmatic theology), or [3] it can be considered as being divinely instituted and endowed with divine authority. This last perspective will be that which is taken in our treatise on the Catholic Church." For some reflections on the issue of the *Tractatus de ecclesia*, see Joseph Clifford Fenton, "Toward an Adequate Theological Treatise *De Ecclesia*," in *The Church of Christ: A Collection of Essays by Monsignor Joseph C. Fenton*, ed. Christian D. Washburn (Tacoma, WA: Cluny Media, 2016), 1–19.]

§2. Explanation of Faith and the Act of Faith from the Perspective of the Subject

{{414}} On this point, three things must be discussed: (1) what, in general, it means to believe and to believe in God, and how the intellect and will are involved in the act of faith; (2) why divine faith, its act, and the beginning of faith must be intrinsically supernatural; and (3) how the freedom and the utter certitude of the act of faith are reconciled.

(1) **What belief is [*quid sit credere*].** We must discuss (A) what faith in general is and (B) what it means to believe in God.

A. St. Thomas treats this question in *ST* I-II, q. 2, a. 1 and 2, and at greater length in *De veritate*, q. 14, a. 1. He intends to justify the definition given by St. Augustine—namely, "to believe is to think with assent"[62]—or as St. Thomas himself says: "To believe is an act of the intellect inasmuch as it is moved by the will to assent."

We read at length in *De veritate*, q. 14, a. 1:

> St. Augustine sufficiently describes belief since its nature is demonstrated through this kind of definition, as well as its distinction from all other acts of the intellect, as is clear from the following observations. . . .

> *We do not find faith in the first act of the intellect*, namely in *simple apprehension*, in which there is neither truth nor falsity essentially, just as they are not found in non-complex terms, for we believe what is true and do not believe what is false. Instead, *belief pertains to the second act of the intellect* according to which it composes and divides *by affirming* and *denying*.

> Now, in this second act, our intellect is related to each side of a given set of contradictory enunciations in different ways.

> *In doubt*, the intellect is not inclined more to one side than to the other but, instead, fluctuates between the two sides of the contradiction.

> *In opinion*, the intellect is inclined more to one side than to the other, though without being completely determined, holding one side of the contradiction with fear that the other may be true [*cum formidine alterius*].

> *In certitude*, the intellect is determined such that it adheres completely to one

---

[62] St. Augustine, *De praedestinatione sanctorum*, ch. 11.

side [of the contradiction in question]. However, this sometimes comes *from the intellect* and sometimes *from the will.*

The intellect is determined by the intelligible either immediately (intuition [*intuitio*][63] of the first principles) or mediately (science).

However, sometimes, the intellect cannot be determined to one side of a contradiction neither immediately through the definitions of the terms, as in our knowledge of principles, nor even by virtue of the principles, as happens in demonstrative conclusions, but, instead, is determined *through the will* which chooses to assent to one side determinately and precisely on account of something that is sufficient for moving the will, though not for moving the intellect, namely, because it seems good or befitting to assent to this side. And this is *the disposition of the believer.* This is the case when someone believes the words of some man because it seems fitting or useful to do so. Thus, too we are moved to believe in the things said by God[64] inasmuch as the reward of eternal life is promised to us if we believe. And this reward moves the will to assent in those things that are said, even though the intellect would not be moved by something understood. Therefore, St. Augustine says (*In Ioann.*, tr. 26) that "man can do other things unwillingly, but he can believe only willingly."

{{415}} This can be schematically summarized as follows:

judgement
- *doubt*: the intellect *is not more inclined* to one side of a contradiction than to the other
- *opinion*: the intellect is *more inclined to* one side of a contradiction, with fear of erring, thus and is not determined to it
- *certitude*: the intellect is determined to one thing
  - *by the evidence of the object*
    - immediately (intuition of principles)
    - mediately (science)
  - *by the will* (faith) because the object is non-evident; however, it is good to assent to the words of some witness, on account of his authority

From this, we have a justification for St. Augustine's definition: "To believe is to think with assent" or to assent with reflection [*cogitatione*].

For, as St. Thomas shows in the text of *De veritate*, q. 14, a. 1 cited above,

---

[63] [Trans. note: For the sense of intuition being referred to here, see R. M. Jolivet, "L'intuition intellectuelle," *Revue Thomiste* 15 (Jan. 1932): 52–71. The point is not that it is a hazy intuition but instead that *intellectus* is a direct, non-discursive form of knowledge.]

[64] [Trans. note: Following Leonine with "dictis Dei." Fr. Garrigou-Lagrange seems to have accidentally forgotten *Dei*, though the context clearly demands it.]

precisely because *assent* is involved, belief is distinguished from the activity by which the intellect considers simple forms—namely, quiddities—as well as from doubt and opinion (for the person who opines does not have assent, given that he is not firmly established in his acceptance of one side of a contradiction). However, precisely because *discursive reflection [cogitatio]* is involved, belief is distinct from understanding (of principles), though because it involves discursive reflection and assent, as it were, equally, it is distinct from science. For discursive reflection is the movement of the intellect that has not yet come to rest because its object is not yet evident and does not sufficiently move and determine it. [As St. Thomas continues in *De veritate*, q. 14, a. 1]:

> In science, discursive reflection leads to assent and assent to the resting of the intellect. However, *in faith, assent and discursive reflection are both involved, as it were, equally, for in the case of faith, assent is not caused by discursive reflection, but rather by the will,* as we said above. However, because the intellect is not terminated at one thing in this way such that it would be led to its own proper terminus, namely, sight of a given intelligible thing, its motion does not yet come to rest but instead still has discursive reflection and inquiry about the things that it believes, though it assents to them in an utterly firm manner. For inasmuch as it depends only upon itself, it does not find satisfaction and is not terminated at one thing but, rather, is only terminated by from without. Thus, the intellect of the believer is said to be "captive" because it is bound upon terms that are foreign to it and not its own, as is said in 2 Corinthians 10:5 (DR): "Bringing into captivity every understanding." Thus too, the believer can experience within himself an upsurging that is opposed to what he holds with utter firmness, although this cannot happen in him who understands [principles through *intellectus*] or has scientific knowledge.[65]

Hence, *to believe is to assent, with discursive reflection, to the testimony of another person on account of the authority of the person testifying [to the*

---

[65] [Trans. note: That is, the believer can remain faithfully assenting to something while a kind of questioning comes forth, nonetheless not overthrowing his or her faith. However, the person who doubts something known through *intellectus* or *scientia* (or also *sapientia*) in fact does not have those forms of knowledge, which are known precisely as being evident either in themselves (*intellectus*) or through a middle term (*scientia* and *sapientia*).]

truth in question]. Therefore, belief is essentially *distinct from opining*, for in opinion we do not have certitude (that is, firm adherence). For example, I believe that my father is dead because this is testified to me by my brother, and while I do not actually see this fact, I nonetheless most firmly assent to it, not merely opining in this matter.

St. Thomas notes (in *De veritate*, q. 14, a. 1, ad 3) that to believe rightly is called "to assent" and not "to consent," for "assent properly belongs to the intellect because it implies an absolute adherence to what is assented to. However, properly speaking, to consent is an act of the will, because to consent is to perceive something [*sentire*] along with something else [*simul cum alio*]." Therefore, in the act of faith, the intellect concurs through its assent in adherence to the truth of faith and the will through consent to the intellect's adherence. Hence, as St. Thomas says, "To believe is an act of the intellect assenting to the truth, doing so {{416}} from a command by the will."[66] For the will does not only apply the intellect to consideration [of the truth in question], as happens in science but, rather, determines it to one side of the contradiction. "The intellect of the believer is determined to one thing through the will, not through reason. Therefore, assent is here understood as referring to the act of the intellect inasmuch as it is determined to one thing by the will."[67] It is an act elicited by the intellect but commanded by the will.

---

[66] See *ST* II-II, q. 2, a. 2 and 3; q. 4, a. 1.

[67] *ST* II-II, q. 2, a. 1, ad 3. Also see *ST* I-II, q. 17, a. 6 (*Whether the act of reason is commanded*): "The act of reason can be considered in two ways. In one way, *it can be considered as regards the exercise of its act*. In this case, the act of reason can always be commanded, as when someone is told to pay attention and use his reason.

"In another way, *it can be considered as regards its object*. In this regard, we can note two kinds of acts by reason. One such kind of act involves the *apprehending* the truth about something, and this does not lie in our power, for this happens through some light, be it natural or supernatural. Therefore, this kind of act of reason is not in our power and cannot be commanded.

"The other kind of act of reason is that by which it *assents* to the things that it grasps. Therefore, if it is a case of things *naturally* assented to by the intellect when they are grasped, such as the first principles, such an assent or dissent does not lie in our power but in the order of nature. Therefore, such things, properly speaking fall under the command of nature.

"However, there are *certain things that are grasped without yet convincing the intellect, such that it can neither assent or non-assent*, or at least must suspend its assent or dissent for some reason. And in such things, assent itself or non-assent *lies in our power and falls under our command*."

Likewise, see *ST* II-II, q. 2, a. 1: "The act of *belief* has *firm adherence* to one side of a contradiction, and in this, the believer has something in common with the scientific knower or the one who understands. However, his knowledge is *not* perfect *through manifest vision*. In this, he holds something in common with the person who doubts, suspects, or who opines. Thus, it is proper to the believer to reflect [or think] with assent."

Thus, believing is a *free act* in our power because the object of belief is not evident and does not suffice for moving or determining [the intellect]. However, a sufficient motive is needed so that the will can rationally and firmly move and determine the intellect to assent rather than dissent, and this motive is found in this: It is good to believe in a witness who deserves faith (namely, who has due science and trustworthiness), especially if an excellent reward is promised to the believer. Thus, I believe the testimony presented to me by my father.

B. From this definition of faith in general, we can easily deduce what belief in God is and what divine faith is.

To believe God is to assent to those things that are revealed by God, by the command of the will on account of the authority of God who reveals.[68] Moreover, as we will soon discuss, because grace is required for this, St. Thomas says, "To believe (God) [*credere (Deo)*] is an act of the intellect assenting to the divine truth from a command of the will, moved by God through grace."[69] Likewise:

> *Divine faith* is a *habitus* of the mind by which eternal life begins within us, making the intellect assent not to things that are apparent, or, as the Apostle says in Heb 11:1 (DR), "Faith is the substance of things to be hoped for, the evidence [*argumentum*] of things that appear not," for the first beginning of something is customarily called its substance. . . . {{417}} However, here "evidence" [*argumentum*] is understood as meaning "the effect of argument" [or "conviction"] namely, because the believer's intellect is convinced by the divine authority to assent to those things that it does not see.[70]

And because "belief is immediately an act of the intellect, . . . it is necessary that faith be in the intellect as in a subject and is in the speculative intellect, as is clear from the object of faith (for it is not an operable truth but instead

---

[68] See *ST* II-II, q. 2, a. 2: "Thus, the act of faith is also *to believe God* [*credere Deo*] because the formal object (or motive) of faith is the First Truth, to whom man adheres, as that on account of which he assents in his belief." The act of faith is called "belief in a God" [*credere Deum*] inasmuch as what is believed in is God himself or something pertaining to God and is called "belief in God" [*credere in Deum*] inasmuch as the intellect is moved by the will, which is referred to the First Truth as to its end (cf. ibid.).

[69] *ST* II-II, q. 2, a. 9.

[70] *ST* II-II, q. 4, a. 1.

is the Uncreated Truth).[71] Nonetheless, the First Truth, which is the object of faith, is the end of all our desires and actions. Hence, faith acts through love [*dilectionem*].[72] However, charity is called the form of faith inasmuch as through charity the act of faith is perfected and given its full form [*formatur*]. One and the same *habitus* of faith is formed and unformed, for the distinction of formed and unformed faith is drawn according to what pertains to the will and not to the intellect. Thus, it does not *per se* pertain to faith.[73]

(2) *Why divine faith, its act, and the beginning of faith must be intrinsically supernatural.* This is treated by St. Thomas in *ST* II-II, q. 6, a. 1 and 2, where he discusses the *habitus* of faith as regards its cause (*Whether faith is infused into man by God* and *Whether unformed faith is a gift of God*) and in *De virtutibus in communi*, a. 10, as well as in *De veritate*, q. 14, a. 2.

Let us now see what we must say as regards (A) the virtue of faith, (B) the act of faith, (C) the beginning of faith, and (D) how the Thomists disagree with the Scotists and Molinists regarding the supernaturality of faith.

A. *Why the virtue of faith must be supernatural and infused.*
St. Thomas responds in ST II-II, q. 6, a. 1:

Two things are required for faith. First, *credibilia* must be proposed to man; second, the believer must assent to the things proposed to him. Regarding the first, it is necessary that faith come from God, for those things that are of faith exceed human reason and hence do not fall into man's thought, unless God reveals them[. . . .]

However, as regards the second thing required, namely, man's assent to those things that are of faith, we can consider a twofold cause here. One indeed is something external inducing him to belief, such as seeing a miracle or by someone's persuasive argument leading to faith. Neither of these is a sufficient cause for faith, however, for when multiple people see one and the same miracle or hear one and the same preaching, some believe and others do not. Therefore, we must hold that there is another, interior cause which inwardly moves man to assent to those things that are of faith.

Now, the Pelagians held that this cause was only man's free will, and for this

---

[71] [However,] see *De veritate*, q. 14, a. 5: "It must be known, however, that it is not in the speculative intellect absolutely but, rather, is there inasmuch as it undergoes the command of the will."

[72] *ST* II-II, q. 4, a. 2. Also see *De veritate*, q. 14, a. 5.

[73] *ST* II-II, q. 4, a. 3, and 4.

reason they said that the beginning of faith comes from us alone, namely inasmuch the preparation prepared for assent to the things of faith comes from us, though we receive the consummation of faith from God, who proposes to us the things that we must believe.

However, this is false, for *since man, in assenting to those things that are of faith is elevated above his nature*, he must have within himself a supernatural principle inwardly moving him, namely, God. Therefore, faith, as regards assent, which is the principal act of faith, comes from God who inwardly moves us through grace.

{{418}} In other words, since the primary object to be believed in is essentially supernatural (for it is God, according to his intimate life), the intellect of the believer must be proportioned to this object through an essentially supernatural power, infused into man by God and not acquired by man. *Otherwise, no proportion would exist between the intellect of the believer and the object to be believed.* However, this proportion is absolutely necessary, *for virtues are specified by their formal objects and must be of the same order as those objects.* Hence, just as the senses cannot know intelligible things because they are not proportioned to the latter, so too the intellect, by its own natural powers, cannot believe in formally supernatural things as such, even if they are proposed to it externally through preaching. Hence, the external light of revelation does not suffice. [Beyond this,] the internal light of faith is needed.[74] And this is true not only for living faith, which acts through charity, but also for unformed faith. This faith, which exists without charity, is itself a gift of God.

By contrast, the faith of the demons is natural and acquired. Therefore, it does not attain supernatural mysteries formally as such but only reaches them *materially* as regards the natural meaning of their words. Thus, the dog hears human speech materially—that is, as regards its sensible sound—without hearing its intelligible meaning. So too, he who does not have an ear for music *materially* hears a symphony by Beethoven. He hears its sounds without formally perceiving the inner soul animating the symphony. Similarly, a student sometimes only materially hears a metaphysical principle (namely, in examples provided to him) without grasping its absolute necessity in itself. The natural faith of the demons reaches the *letter of the Gospel but not its spirit*; it gnaws upon the outer bone

---

[74] See *De veritate*, q. 14, a. 1, ad 5: "What pertains to the perfection [in question], namely, to assent, is caused by a simple light, namely, that of faith. However, inasmuch as this light is not perfectly participated in, the imperfection of the intellect is not completely done away with. Thus, the movement of reflection remains restless within it."

without tasting the marrow.[75] They stand before Sacred Scripture like the dog before a syllogism written out with pieces of meat [*ante syllogismum cum carne scriptum*]. However, by the supernatural light of faith, we have some understanding of supernatural things, as St. Paul says in 2 Corinthians 3:6 (DR), "For the letter killeth, but the spirit quickeneth," and in Romans 7:6 (DR), "But now we are loosed from the law of death wherein we were detained; so that we should serve in newness of spirit, and not in the oldness of the letter." Likewise, in 1 Corinthians 2:12, 14–16 (DR):

> Now, we have received not the spirit of this world, but the Spirit that is of God: that we may know the things that are given us from God. . . . But the sensual man perceiveth not these things that are of the Spirit of God. For it is foolishness to him: *and he cannot understand*, because it is spiritually examined. But the spiritual man judgeth all things: and he himself is judged of no man. For who hath known the mind of the Lord, that he may instruct him? But we have the mind of Christ.

(Likewise, see St. Thomas's commentary on this text.)[76]

---

[75] As we will discuss in the next article, the formal motive of the demons' faith is an evident miracle or *the authority of God the Author and Lord of nature*, but not the authority of God the Author of the order of grace and glory, *the voice of the Heavenly Father*, which only Christ's sheep can hear, as is said in John 10:26.

[76] See *ST* I-II, q. 106, a. 1 (*Whether the new law is a written law*). St. Thomas responds by arguing on the basis of Hebrews 8:8, 10 (DR): "Behold the days shall come, saith the Lord. . . . For this is the testament which I will make to the house of Israel after those days, saith the Lord: I will give my laws into their mind: and in their heart will I write them." "Therefore," concludes St. Thomas, "the new law is a law that is instilled into our hearts." He immediately goes on to explain this, saying, "I respond that it must be said that each thing seems to be what is most powerfully found within it, as the Philosopher says in *Nicomachean Ethics* 9.5. However, that which is most powerfully found in the law of the New Testament—indeed that wherein its entire power is found—is the grace of the Holy Spirit, which is given through faith in Christ. And therefore, *the New Law is principally the very grace of the Holy Spirit, which is given to those who believe in Christ*. And this is quite clear from the words of the Apostle, who says in Rom 3:27 (DR): 'Where is then thy boasting? It is excluded. By what law? Of works? No, but by the law of faith.' Indeed, he calls the very *grace of faith* a law. And he says even more expressly in Rom 8:2 (DR): 'For the law of the spirit of life, in Christ Jesus, hath delivered me from the law of sin and of death.' Hence too, St. Augustine says in chs. 17 and 26 of *De spiritu et littera* that just as the law of deeds was written upon stone tablets, so too *the law of faith was written in the hearts of the faithful*. And elsewhere in the same book (ch. 21), he says, 'What are the laws of God written by God Himself in our hearts if not the very presence of the Holy Spirit?' However, the New Law has certain things that are *dispositive* in relation to the grace of the Holy Spirit, and pertaining to the use of this grace, which are, *as it were, secondary matters* in the new law. These are the kinds of things that must be taught to the faithful, both in words and in writings, as much regarding things to be believed as regarding things to be done." Also

{{419}} B. *As regards the act of faith, actual grace is required for the same reason.* According to the Council of Orange[77] and the [First] Vatican Council,[78] as we already cited above: "No man can 'assent to the Gospel message,' as is necessary to obtain salvation, 'without the illumination and inspiration of the Holy Spirit, who gives to all delight in assenting to the truth and believing in it." *The reason for the necessity of grace is the proportion that must exist between the act of faith and the supernatural object believed in, for acts are specified by their objects* and hence must be of the same order [as their objects].

Hence, St. Thomas says in *ST* I-II, q. 109, a. 1 (*Whether man can know any truth without faith*):

> The human intellect does have a given form, namely the intellectual light itself, which is of itself sufficient for knowing certain intelligible things, namely those things that we can arrive at through knowledge of sensible things. However, the human intellect cannot know higher intelligible things except by being perfected by a more powerful light, like the light of faith or prophecy, which is called the light of grace inasmuch as it is something super-added to nature.... (In order to have this kind of knowledge) man stands in need of a new illumination super-added to the natural illumination [of his intellect].

C. *Why grace is required for the beginning of faith—namely, for the pious affect of belief,* as defined at the Council of Orange against the semi-Pelagians.[79] It is required because we cannot, without supernatural aid, *will something that is essentially supernatural.* That is, [without grace,] we cannot will to believe in supernatural mysteries and desire the good promised to believers. Otherwise, our volition would be disproportioned to the object willed. However, volition is specified by the object willed and, hence, must be of the same order as it.[80] This affect of belief [*credulitatis*] is a kind of resting in the utter

---

see ad 1 regarding the Gospel writings.

77 See Council of Orange, can. 5 (Denzinger, no. 375).

78 See [First] Vatican Council, *Dei filius*, ch. 3 (Denzinger, no. 3010).

79 See Council of Orange, can. 5 (Denzinger, no. 375).

80 See *De veritate*, q. 14, a. 2: "Man has a twofold ultimate end.... One of them is the felicity that the philosophers spoke of.... Man's other good is one that exceeds the proportion of human nature because man's natural powers do not suffice for obtaining it, nor for thinking of it or desiring it... and this is eternal life. Now, precisely on account of this good, the will is inclined to assent to those things that it holds through faith.... However, nothing can be ordered to a given end unless it first has some kind of proportion to the end from which the desire for the end arises within him.... Now, the will moved by the aforementioned good proposes some-

trustworthiness of God (and not in the divine goodness in itself, which is required for the love of charity),[81] and in the good promised to believers.[82] {{420}} This pious affect of belief can be expressed in the words of St. Peter: "Lord, to whom shall we go? Thou hast the words of eternal life, and we have believed" (John 6:69–70, DR).

D. *How do the Thomists differ from the Scotists and Molinists regarding the supernaturality of faith?*

Not all theologians agree about the supernaturality of faith. *St. Thomas*,[83] *the Thomists*, and *even Suarez*[84] hold *that man cannot believe in supernatural truths from the formally supernatural motive of divine revelation without [receiving] a special internal grace*, both on the part of the intellect

---

thing that is not apparent to the intellect as being something worth of assent. Thus, it gives the intellect a determination to that which is not apparent, namely so that it may assent to it."

[81] St. Francis de Sales says (in his *Traité de l'amour de Dieu*, vol. 2, ch. 14): "Pious discourses and arguments, miracles and other advantages of the Christian religion do indeed make it extremely believable and worthy of knowledge. However, only faith makes it believed in and recognized as such, *making one love the beauty of its truth* and *believe in the truth of its beauty*, through the gentle sweetness that spreads forth from it over the will and the certitude that it gives to the understanding. . . . The act of faith consists in this assent given by our mind, which having received the delightful light of the truth, adheres to it in a sweet manner, though one that is powerful and full of assurance as it takes in the authority of the revelation that is made to it." In this chapter, as in chs. 17, 22, and others, St. Francis de Sales sets forth with the greatest of luminosity the same doctrine as does St. Thomas concerning the difference between the pious affect of belief, the love of hope, and the love of charity. Likewise, in ch. 14 of the same work, he most excellently shows that supernatural faith is not discursive but, rather, has a loftier certitude than any given natural form of knowledge: "Now that this obscure light of faith has entered into our mind, not by the power of discourse, nor through arguments that have been presented to us, but solely through the sweetness of its presence, it makes one believe and obey what is thus understood with such authority that the certitude that it gives us concerning the truth exceeds all worldly forms of certitude." The reader should read this entire chapter.

[82] This pious affect of belief and pious motion of the will to believe is not the love of charity, as certain contemporary thinkers [*Neoterici*] contend. Otherwise, the sinner could not elicit an act of faith, something condemned by Alexander VIII in this proposition: "When in great sinners all love is lacking, faith also is lacking; and even if they seem to believe, their faith is not divine but human" (Denzinger, no. 2312). Also in propositions 51 and 52 of Quesnel: "Faith does not act except through charity" and "Faith does not exist without love and confidence." Indeed, what prevents me from believing an enemy whom I otherwise hold to be truthful?

[83] See *ST* I-II, q. 109 (*De gratia*), a. 1; *In II Sent.* d. 28, a. 5; *In Jn.* 5, bk. 6, §9 [*sic*]. Likewise, see Salmanticenses, *Cursus theologicus, De gratia*, tr. 14, disp. 3, dub. 3 (Whether grace is necessary for eliciting the assent of faith, considered in its substance); John of St. Thomas, *Cursus theologicus, De gratia*, disp. 20, a. 1; Tomas de Lemos, *Panoplia gratia*, bk. 4, tr. 1, a. 1; Billuart, *Summa sancti Thomae, De gratia*, diss. 3, a. 2, §2. Also see Cajetan's comments against Scotus in *In ST* II-II, q. 1, a. 1, no. 11; q. 17, a. 5; and I-II, q. 63.

[84] Suarez, *De gratia*, bk. 2, ch. 11.

and on the part of the will. Nonetheless, they concede that once man hears preaching (that is, once he has received external revelation), he can, solely with prevenient natural concurrence [from God] and without any special superadded grace, know and embrace supernatural truths through an imperfect assent *out of some human motive* (as do heretics).

By contrast, *Scotus*[85] *the nominalists, Molina,*[86] *and many others maintain that the assent of faith, even from the motive of divine revelation, is essentially natural and only modally supernatural.* Hence, grace would not be necessary for believing the supernatural mysteries on account of the authority of God who reveals, but only for believing with a pious affect as is needed for salvation. Thus, the necessity of grace would not depend on a supernatural object to be believed in, nor upon the formal motive of faith, but rather, on an extrinsic end to {{421}} which the act of faith must be ordered. Hence, according to Scotus, faith is not entitatively supernatural.[87]

The Thomists and Suarez respond: This represents the destruction of the essential supernaturality of faith, for the act of faith would not be subjectively and entitatively more supernatural than an act of acquired temperance ordered by charity to our supernatural end. In other words, the act of faith would be extrinsically supernatural, not intrinsically so. However, the Thomists say, with one voice:

> The object of the assent of faith is formally supernatural on account of the formal character of its object. Indeed, this is so for its object *quod*, namely, the First Truth itself (the intimate life of God), which is supernatural in itself. It is also so for the object *quo*, namely, the motive or formal reason under which

---

85 See Scotus, *In I Sent.*, d. 17, q. 3, no. 33.

86 See Molina, *Concordia*, q. 14, a. 13.

87 After the Council of Trent, many Scotists did indeed concede that habitual grace and faith are *entitatively* (or essentially) supernatural, though not on account of its formal specifying motive. See the text of Lychetus cited above in note 1. Thus, *infused faith* would be entitatively supernatural, as a property of grace, and nonetheless its formal object and formal motive would not exceed *acquired faith*, which proceeds from natural knowledge of the miracles that confirm revelation. This Scotistic conclusion stands in contradiction to the principle, "The species of a habitus depend upon the formal character of their objects" (*ST* II-II, q. 5, a. 3). Hence, if the formal object of infused faith did not exceed acquired natural faith, infused faith would not be *essentially* and *intrinsically* supernatural but, rather, would only be *extrinsically* supernatural—that is, supernatural *only as regards the efficient causality involved* (like natural sight that is supernaturally given to a man born blind) or supernatural *as regards the final causality involved* (like a natural act ordered by charity to a supernatural end). Nay, it would not even be supernaturally ordered because, according to this theory, the ultimate end could be known without any infused *habitus* and hence can be desired [in this way as well]. Hence, these theologians admit the supernaturality of faith because it is declared in the Councils, but they do not explain the reason for it. Nay, they overturn such a reason that would explain it.

we attain this knowledge, for this too is supernatural, namely, divine revelation (God the Author of the order of grace and not only of the order of nature). Now, a supernatural object formally as such can only be attained by a supernatural act. Therefore, the intellect can only elicit this assent substantially if it receives supernatural aid to do so.[88]

However, if heretics believe certain supernatural mysteries, they do so out of a human motive, not from the supernatural motive of divine revelation. Likewise, the demons naturally believe on account of the natural evidence of signs (namely, of miracles) and not on account of a supernatural motive.

In general, Suarez does not require much regarding the distinction between the natural and supernatural orders, for he holds that our nature has an *active* obediential potency [in relation to the supernatural order], a position that, as we discussed above, the Thomists hold virtually contains a confusion of the two orders. Nonetheless, like the Thomists, Suarez judges that the opinion of Scotus, the nominalists, and Molina does not avoid the danger of falling into Pelagianism. Indeed, he writes:

> If the motive of faith is natural and placed in the order of our intellect's natural powers, natural faith would be sufficiently proportioned to it, and there would be no reason why it would not be sufficient in its own *genus* for salvation, since it would rely upon God alone as testifying... Nor will grace be necessary for that, except on the part of revelation (that is, external grace), which Pelagius himself did not deny. However, to say that a greater grace or aid is only required so that the assent may be more perfect in its being [*in genere entis*], although it would not be necessary by virtue of its object, draws rather close to what Pelagius said, namely that grace is required only for enabling the act of faith to be performed more easily. Likewise, it seems to be a flight invented solely for the sake of escaping the testimony of the Councils and the Fathers.[89]

Faith would be supernatural *de facto*, not *de iure*. Indeed, the nominalists do deny the necessity of essences, reducing them to contingent collections of facts. The supernaturality of faith would not be essential but instead would be a kind of surface-level covering, {{422}} a kind of supernatural plating.[90] This theory considers what is material in faith rather than its formal character and does not heed well enough the fact that the

---

88 Billuart, *Summa sancti Thomae, De gratia*, diss, 3, a. 2, §2.
89 Suarez, *De gratia*, bk. 2, ch. 11, no. 17; likewise, nos. 11, 12, 13, 21, 22, 23, and 24.
90 See Réginald Garrigou-Lagrange, "La surnaturalité de la foi," *Revue Thomiste*, New Series, 14 (Jan. 1914): 17–38.

act of faith is a supernatural mystery that must be explained analogically and must not be known in a univocal manner through a resolution to inferior notions. Otherwise, one should use the same methods in biology as one does in mechanistic physics, merely considering vital processes as though they were the physiochemical phenomena that serve as material dispositions for vital acts. Thus, life would be conceived only as an epiphenomenon of physiochemical powers. In like manner, one would be led to say that psychology should use the same methods as those recommended by empiricists and nominalists when they reduce intellectual knowledge [*intelligentiam*] to internal and external sense experience. Likewise, in the theological order, Pelagianism and semi-Pelagianism, as well as the nominalism of the fourteenth century, provide material explanations for the faith, justification, and the entire Christian life.

This question concerning the essential supernaturality of faith is necessarily connected to another question that we will soon examine—namely, whether the formal motive of supernatural faith can be naturally known. After Scotus, Molina and the Molinists respond affirmatively. By contrast, the Thomists and Suarez respond negatively on account of the essential distinction between natural knowledge and supernatural knowledge.

(3) *How the freedom and utter certitude of the act of faith are reconciled.* We will consider (A) the difficulty of the question itself; (B) St. Thomas's solution; (C) Cardinal de Lugo's solution; and (D) Suarez's solution.

A. *The difficulty of the question*

Already in our discussion of the Church's declarations concerning the freedom of the act of believing, we saw that this is not only a freedom *as regards exercise* (namely, to assent or not to assent) but also is a freedom *as regards specification* (namely, to assent or dissent, for example, by ridicule). Thus, when St. Paul preached the future resurrection of men to the Athenians, "some indeed mocked. But others said: We will hear thee again concerning this matter. . . . But certain men, adhering to him, did believe" (Acts 17:32, 34, DR). The [First] Vatican Council also declared, against Georg Hermes,[91] that this freedom of specification remains even after we have certain knowledge of the motives of credibility. Hermes held that there was only a freedom of exercise, which is already present in scientific assent.

On the other hand, according to the Church, regarding the examination of the motives of credibility, "Indeed, human reason, lest it be deceived and err in a matter of so great importance, ought to investigate diligently the fact of divine revelation so that it can know with certainty that God has

---

[91] [First] Vatican Council, *Dei Filius*, can. 3.5 (Denzinger, no. 3035).

spoken and so render to Him a rational obedience."[92]

Finally, it has been defined that the assent of faith is utterly certain—that is, *infallible* on account of its motive (on account of the authority of God who reveals)—and *utterly firm*, on account of its adherence, in virtue of the motion of the will under the illumination and inspiration of the Holy Spirit.[93]

Having posited these points, a twofold difficulty arises concerning (a) how freedom to dissent from revelation can remain once one has rational certitude concerning the fact of revelation; and (b) how the act of faith, if it is free and not necessary, could be utterly certain (that is, excluding every deliberate fear {{423}} of error). Freedom and opinion are easily reconciled, but there is no small difficulty involved in reconciling freedom with utterly firm certitude.

B. *St. Thomas's solution*

Without any restriction, St. Thomas admits all of the things that must be reconciled here. That is, he acknowledges that the act of faith is free, even as regards its specification: "The act of faith can be meritorious inasmuch as it is placed under the will not only as regards its exercise but also as regards assent."[94] Likewise, he admits that before receiving faith, reason can know the fact of revelation with certainty: "Just as if some Prophet were to announce in advance in a word from God some future thing and bring forth a sign, raising a dead man, leading the intellect of the person who sees this to be convinced so that he would manifestly know that this is said by God, who does not deceive, although that future thing that has been preached is not evident in itself."[95] Finally, St. Thomas acknowledges the act of faith is "*simpliciter* more certain" than the natural intuition of first principles, "because faith rests on the divine truth" and not on human reason.[96]

Having posited these points, St. Thomas resolved the difficulty by saying: (a) *freedom of specification remains in the assent of faith on account of the non-evidence of the object to be believed in*; (b) *the assent of faith is simpliciter more certain than any form of natural assent, even necessary assent, although it is less certain secundum quid.*

(a) *The assent of faith is free, even as regards its specification, on account of the non-ev-*

---

[92] Pius IX, *Qui pluribus*, no. 7 (Denzinger, no. 2778).

[93] Innocent XI, Propositions Condemned by the Decree of the Holy Office, Mar. 2, 1679, no. 19 (Denzinger, no. 2119); [First] Vatican Council, *Dei Filius*, ch. 3 (Denzinger, nos. 3010–3014).

[94] *ST* II-II, q. 2, a. 10.

[95] *ST* II-II, q. 5, a. 2.

[96] See *ST* II-II, q. 4, a. 8.

idence of the mysteries to be believed in. For the Holy Doctor says in *ST* II-II, q. 2, a. 9: "Belief itself is an act of the intellect assenting to the divine truth from a command of the will moved by God through grace. Thus, it falls under free choice as ordered to God." However, why is it an assent from the command of the will? Because the object to be believed does not sufficiently move the intellect, as is said in *ST* II-II, q. 1, a. 4:

> The intellect assents to something in two ways. In one way, it does so because it is moved to such assent by the object itself (as is clear in first principles and in conclusions [drawn through scientific inference]). In another way, the intellect assents to something, *not because it is sufficiently moved by its proper object, but rather, through a kind of choice* voluntarily turning toward one side rather than to another. And if this indeed exists with doubt and fear that the other side might be true, it will be an opinion. However, if such assent is made with certitude, without any such fear, then it will be faith.

And St. Thomas concludes in the same text: "Now, those things are said to be seen which by themselves move our intellect or senses to knowledge of them. Thus, it is clear that *we can have neither faith nor opinion concerning things that are seen*, either by the senses or by the intellect."

Likewise, "it is not possible for one and the same thing to be scientifically known [*scitum*] and believed in" (a. 5), for the intellect of someone who has scientific knowledge about something [*intellectus scientis*] is sufficiently moved by the known object through principles, whereas the intellect of the believer is not sufficiently moved by the object, which remains non-evident. Hence, the believer stands in need of a free command from the will in order to believe. The mysteries of the Trinity, the Incarnation, the Passion, the Eucharist, predestination, eternal punishment, and future beatitude remain *obscure* in themselves and can displease a man of evil will.

Nay, as we will discuss below, according to St. Thomas, although the external fact of revelation can be naturally known from evident miracles, nonetheless, the formal motive of faith (namely, the First Uncreated Truth who reveals) is something essentially supernatural and not seen but, rather, is believed. Indeed, as is said in *ST* II-II, q. 4, a. 1: "*The First Truth* is the object of faith inasmuch as it is *not seen*, as well as those things that we hold on account of it."

{{424}} This Thomistic position [*sententia*] is confirmed by the existence of the non-deliberate doubt that is experienced by believers. Nay, certain holy souls, in the passive purification of the spirit, must vehemently repress these non-deliberate doubts, and their faith indeed will grow in the midst of these temptations against faith. This helps to make clear that, notwithstanding the evidence of credibility, faith remains free, on account of the obscurity of the mysteries. However, sometimes, in the midst of these temptations, the very evidence of credibility diminishes, though the soul is strengthened in a hidden manner by the gifts of the Holy Spirit.

Hence, the freedom of faith remains even after one has certitude regarding the fact of revelation. However, in the case of an evident miracle performed in confirmation of revelation, deliberate dissent can only arise from an utterly perverse freedom.[97] Thus, Christ said: "If I had not come and spoken to them, they would not have sin: but now they have no excuse for their sin. He that hateth me hateth my Father also. If I had not done among them the works that no other man hath done, they would not have sin: but now they have both seen and hated both me and my Father." (John 15:22–24, DR). Likewise, after Christ healed the man with a withered hand, as well as the blind and deaf demoniac, "the Pharisees hearing it, said, 'This man casteth not out devils but by Beelzebub the prince of the devils'" (Matt 12:24, DR). Likewise, after the miracle performed by SS. Peter and John, the leaders of the priests and the scribes "could say nothing against it . . . and they conferred among themselves, saying, 'What shall we do to these men? For indeed a miracle hath been done by them, known to all the inhabitants of Jerusalem. It is manifest: and we cannot deny it.' But that it may be no farther spread among the people, let us threaten them that they speak no more in this name to any man" (Acts 4:14–17, DR). Therefore, even when faced with a manifest miracle, freedom to not believe remains, for man not only can choose not to will to believe but can *refuse to believe*, ridiculing or denying it as madness, for the mysteries (e.g., the mysteries of predestination or eternal punishment) remain *non-evident* and can be *displeasing* to a man of bad will.

Nonetheless, as St. Thomas says, "The demons are more greatly compelled to believe on account of the perspicacity of their natural intellectual power. Thus, *the faith of demons is in a way compelled* by the evidence of the signs. . . . And it is displeasing to the demons that the signs of faith are so evident that they would be compelled to believe through them."[98] This faith is not unqualifiedly compelled but, rather, only in some way. A small amount of freedom of specification is found in it because the mysteries remain obscure. However, it would be *incredibly foolish* for the demon to deny their truth, and he does not wish himself to be foolish. Likewise, as the Thomists note, the throwing of goods off a ship out of fear during a shipwreck is said to be a compelled action, though not unqualifiedly so but, rather, only in some way.[99]

(b) *Although the assent of faith is free, it is simpliciter more certain than necessary assent*

---

[97] See Jacques-Bénigne Lignel Bossuet, *Elévations* [*sur les mystères*], 18th sem., 20th elevation (The contradictions of Jesus Christ lay bare the secrets of the heart): "We must connect the words, 'This child will be subject to contradiction,' to these ones, 'The thoughts that many hide in their hearts will be laid bare.' If Jesus Christ had not appeared upon the earth, we would not know the profound malice, the profound pride, the profound corruption, the profound dissimulation and hypocrisy of man's heart."

[98] *ST* II-II, q. 5, a. 2.

[99] See Billuart, *Summa sancti Thomae, De fide*, diss. 4, a. 2.

in the natural order, though it is less certain in a qualified way [secundum quid].[100]

It is *unqualifiedly [simpliciter] more certain, "because it has a more certain cause. . . .* For faith rests on the divine truth. . . . And man is much more certain about those things that he *hears from God,* who cannot be deceived, than about those things that he sees on account of his reason which can."[101] Indeed, the formal motive of faith is the authority of God who infallibly reveals. Moreover, the firmness of adherence subjectively depends not only on the will, presupposing a certain judgment of credibility, but also on the internal inspiration and illumination of the Holy Spirit. Hence, according to its nature, supernatural faith is more certain than every form of natural assent.

{{425}} However, *in a qualified sense [secundum quid],* the assent of faith is less certain than necessary natural assent. The term "secundum quid" here denotes "from our perspective" or according to the disposition that exists on the side of the subject, for "from our perspective, that which man's intellect more readily pursues is more certain" and we more readily pursue a truth that is evident than one that is not. That is, although the obscure knowledge of faith is of itself loftier than natural knowledge, it is *less proportioned to our intellect* and less satisfying for it. Thus, the possibility remains that one may have "doubt, not on the side of faith's cause but on our side, inasmuch as our intellect is not able to fully reach those things that are of faith."[102] Hence, it is said in 2 Corinthians 4:6–7 (DR): "God . . . hath shined in our hearts. . . . But we have this treasure in earthen vessels, that the excellency may be of the power of God and not of us."

This doctrine can be illustrated by an example—namely, by comparison of metaphysical certitude with physical certitude. *Metaphysical certitude,* which is had from intellectual evidence, according to a necessary resolution to intelligible being is *simpliciter* and *of itself firmer than physical certitude,* which is had from sensible evidence, by the mediation of the senses. Nonetheless, *sensible things* that are obvious to the senses are *more knowable from our perspective* than are intelligible things that are separated or abstracted from matter. For example, the principle of finality, "every agent acts on account of an end," is metaphysically certain, indeed as certain as the formal existence of colors outside the soul, and nonetheless, certain people doubt the necessity of the principle of finality but not the formal existence of colors. Aristotle often said (e.g., in *Metaphysics*

---

[100] See *ST* II-II, q. 4, a. 8.

[101] Ibid.

[102] *ST* II-II, q. 4, a. 8, ad 1. Commonly, it is said, "Exclusion of *deliberate* fear of error pertains to every form of certitude, and holds together as an undivided whole [*consitere in indivisibili*]. Nonetheless, from this perspective, divine faith is firmer than natural certitude, inasmuch as the believer is prepared to have greater fear about a given form of natural evidence than about the object of faith.

"However, *non-deliberate* fear is more greatly excluded by naturally certain assent coming from evidence than by the assent of faith. For the exclusion of this non-deliberate fear is an effect of evidence."

1.1) purely intelligible things are more knowable in themselves, though not from our perspective, because they are utterly remote from the senses, and by contrast sensible things are barely intelligible in themselves (because they exist in matter and in motion), even though they are more so from our perspective. Likewise, supernatural things believed by divine faith are more certain in themselves than are the first principles of reason, though less so from our perspective.

Objection: Then faith is only more certain abstractly speaking. However, as it is found *in us*, it is less certain than natural knowledge. Therefore, our faith, inasmuch as it is [actually] ours, is *simpliciter* less certain than natural scientific knowledge.

In response, following Gonet,[103] *faith is more certain intrinsically [quoad se] and in us, though not from our perspective [quoad nos]*:

> For it is one thing to say that some *habitus* or science would be more certain inasmuch as it is in us and another to say that it would be more certain from our perspective. For the first, it suffices that a given *habitus* or science, as received in our intellect and to the degree it informs it, bestows upon it a greater certitude and adherence to the truth. However, for the second, it is moreover required that such certitude be more connatural and proportioned to our intellect, satisfying it and bringing it to rest, and more fully removing the motion of hesitation and doubt from it.

Hence, the light of faith infused into us by God produces its formal effect in our mind such that the assent of faith is more certain in itself and in us, though less certain from our perspective than is natural certitude. "We have this treasure in earthen vessels" (2 Cor 4:7). On account of this imperfection of faith from our perspective, man needs the gifts of the Holy Spirit, especially the gifts of understanding and wisdom, which have a certitude that presupposes infused charity, giving rise to a certitude that comes from a kind of *connaturality* with divine realities.[104]

{{426}} Thus, St. Thomas reconciles the freedom of faith with its infallible certitude. The act of faith is free, even from the perspective of specification, on account of the non-evidential character of the mysteries to be believed, and is utterly certain in virtue of its formal objective motive, as well as in virtue of the internal illumination and inspiration of the Holy Spirit.

C. Cardinal Juan de Lugo's opinion in this matter

Cardinal Juan de Lugo explained[105] this in a different way, *holding that the assent of faith is free on account of the non-evidence of the existence of revelation*. He explains this

---

[103] See Gonet, *Clypeus theologiae Thomisticae*, disp. Proemialis, a. 5.

[104] See *ST* I-II, q. 68, a. 2; II-II, 8; q. 45, a. 2.

[105] See de Lugo, *De fide*, disp. 2, no. 2ff.

claim as follows. Faith first requires the judgment of credibility. However, that judgment, "the existence of revelation can and ought to be prudently believed," is indeed evident, for it excludes any fear whatsoever, even imprudent fear. However, the very existence of revelation is not for that reason evident, for the judgment "revelation exists" is certain insofar as it excludes prudent fear, but it is not evident, inasmuch as it admits imprudent fear. Now, as long as revelation is not evident, whereas its authority is evident, we do not have evident knowledge of the truth of the revealed object. And for as long as this remains non-evident, there is nothing that necessitates the assent of the intellect (that is, the assent of faith).

Critique: According to this opinion, the freedom of faith would be destroyed if human reason could know the fact of revelation without even imprudent fear. However, this knowledge does not seem impossible, for as St. Thomas says, "This would be as if some Prophet were to announce in advance in a word from God some future thing and bring forth a sign by raising a dead man, leading the intellect of the person who sees this [sign] to be convinced so that it would manifestly know that this is said by God, who does not deceive, although that future thing that has been preached is not evident in itself. Thus, the formal character of faith would not be done away with."[106] And Pius IX said, "Indeed, human reason, lest it be deceived and err in a matter of so great importance, ought to investigate diligently the fact of divine revelation so that it can know with certainty that God has spoken and so render to Him, a rational obedience." And after the enumeration of the motives of credibility, Pope Pius IX continues: "And so, human reason, knowing clearly and distinctly from these most splendid and equally most strong proofs that God is the Author of this faith, can proceed no farther; but, rejecting and dispelling every difficulty and doubt, it must render all obedience to this faith, since it holds as certain that all which faith itself proposes to men to be believed or to be done has been transmitted by God."[107]

Thus, reason can be certain about the fact of revelation without any fear of erring, and nonetheless supernatural mysteries remain obscure, for difficulties are not lacking concerning the Holy Trinity, eternal punishment, the mystery of predestination, the mystery of the Eucharist, and so forth. Hence, the intervention of human freedom, under the influence of God's grace, is needed, "in order to inwardly cast aside and remove whatsoever difficulty or doubt and produce the obedience of faith," if I may use the words of Pope Pius IX. Hence, the Thomistic solution must be preferred to that of Cardinal de Lugo.[108]

---

[106] See *ST* II-II, q. 5, a. 2.

[107] Pius IX, *Qui pluribus*, no. 9 (Denzinger, no. 2780); see nos. 7–9 (Denzinger, nos. 2778–2780).

[108] The more common opinion in the Thomist school is that faith can be had even alongside [*compossibilis sit*] the evidential knowledge of revelation that the prophet has under the prophetic light, or which the angels had *in via*, so long as the revealed mystery remains obscure.

D. Suarez's resolution of this issue

Suarez[109] draws back from St. Thomas in this matter, inasmuch as he admits that the same object, considered from the same perspective can simultaneously be seen and believed by the same person. Hence, the freedom of the act of faith cannot be explained from the non-evidence of the object believed in because sometimes, {{427}} according to Suarez, the object believed in is evident. (For example, someone can simultaneously scientifically know [*scire*] and believe in the unity of God from the same perspective.[110])

Nonetheless, Suarez concedes what Cardinal de Lugo denies—namely, the possibility of having evidential knowledge of the very existence of revelation.

Therefore, how can the freedom of faith be preserved? Mazzella explains Suarez's response as follows: "With these points in place, there can be a twofold assent in a revealed truth. One tends toward it on account of evidently known authority and revelation. Hence, it is determined by the very presence of the object and is necessary. The other kind is borne to that truth on account of the authority itself and the revelation that is not seen (but instead is believed). Hence, it is determined by the command of the will and is free."[111] Thus, the freedom of faith would remain, for *man can choose between natural, scientific faith* (as is found in the demons) *and the supernatural faith of authority.*

Critique: It is not clear how the authority of God who reveals could be simultaneously seen and not seen by the same person, unless the authority of God the Author of nature and miracles, an authority that is naturally known [*scita*], were distinct from the authority of God the Author of grace and glory, an authority that is revealed and believed in. However, Suarez does not present this distinction, and were he to use it, he would thus return to the Thomistic doctrine: One and the same thing, considered from the same perspective cannot simultaneously be seen and believed (i.e., cannot simultaneously be

---

This is a question of *evidence in attestation* [*evidentia in attestante*]. This opinion is defended by Cajetan, Sylvester of Ferrara, [Diego] Alvarez, the Salmanticenses, Gonet, Billuart, and others, although Bañez draws back from it. John of St. Thomas defends the position as being at least probable. See Gonet, *Clypeus theologiae Thomisticae, De fide*, disp. 1, a. 7.

[109] See Suarez, *De fide*, disp. 3, sect. 9, nos. 1 and 7.

[110] The Thomists say that one and the same man can simultaneously believe and scientifically know the same divine attribute, though from different perspectives. Namely, he can *scientifically know it inasmuch as it pertains to God the Author of nature* and *believe in it inasmuch as it pertains to God the Author of the order of grace and glory*. In this way, providence is demonstrated as an attribute of the Author of nature but not as an ordering of supernatural means to the supernatural end. From this loftier perspective, it contains the mystery of predestination. Likewise, as St. Thomas says (*De veritate*, q. 14, a. 9, ad 8): "Inasmuch as knowledge of God's unity is demonstrated, it is not an article of faith but, instead, is presupposed for the articles of faith, for the knowledge of faith presupposes natural knowledge, just as nature presupposes grace. However, the unity of the divine essence such as it is held by believers, namely with omnipotence and providence over all things, and other such things (e.g., the Trinity), which cannot be proven, constitutes an article of faith."

[111] Camillus Mazzella, *De virtutibus infusis*, 3rd ed. (Rome, 1884), 354 (no. 668).

evident and non-evident) for the same man. Moreover, Suarez does not seem to explain the *intrinsic* freedom of the act of supernatural faith but only an extrinsic freedom—namely, that of choosing between natural faith and supernatural faith. And such a form of freedom does not imply that the act of supernatural faith would be intrinsically free.

Thus, the Thomistic solution concerning the reconciliation of freedom and the certitude of faith remains.

Art. 3: How Revelation Must Be Known Precisely as the Formal Motive of Infused Faith (That Is, on Supernatural or [*Vel*] Intrinsic Credibility)

§1. The state of the question and the difficulty involved in it.

§2. What do Sacred Scripture and Tradition say about this matter?

§3. What did the medieval theologians before St. Thomas teach?

§4. What does St. Thomas teach in these matters?

§5. Historical exposition of the opposition between the Thomists and Suarez on the one hand and the Scotists, nominalists, Molina, Lugo, and a number of modern thinkers on the other.

§6. Proof of the Thomist opinion.

§7. Resolution of objections.

§8. Appendix: Corollaries of the Thomistic thesis concerning the supernaturality of faith and our manner of knowing the formal motive of faith.

§1. The State of the Question and the Difficulty Involved in It

We have already exposited the act of faith from the perspective of its object and motive, as well as from the perspective of the subject. Now, however, {{428}} we must consider the conjunction of the believing subject with the object to be believed in knowledge of the motive on account of which it is believed. As we said above, this motive is the authority of God who actually reveals—that is, the active revelation of the mysteries of faith. However, already solely by the light of reason, it is evident that God can neither deceive nor be deceived, and as we will discuss below, from a consideration of miracles, we can have rational certitude concerning the fact of revelation. Thus, we find ourselves faced with the question: In order to have supernatural faith, *does it suffice to have natural knowledge* of the authority of God who actually reveals, *or rather, do we need to have supernatural knowledge* of the formal motive of faith? Nay, the question facing us is whether this motive exceeds the powers of reason.

Already, in the prologue of this fourth section, we set forth this difficulty in the words of Victor Cousin, who, himself a rationalist, said *the ultimate resolution of the certitude of faith* is brought about in *the rational evidence of credibility, thus meaning* [according to him] *that philosophical reason is superior to faith.*

In other words, the problem can be expressed thus: Without the internal light of faith does the soul remain blind regarding the formal motive of faith, or deaf to God's voice? Or, on the contrary, do we already see and hear it in a vague manner—thus meaning that grace would only be necessary for more firmly knowing this motive of faith, in order to better hear the voice of God and believe the mysteries with a pious affect, as is needed for salvation.

According to the Thomists, to raise this question is already to resolve it, for the formal motive of an infused theological virtue specifies it and, hence, it can be formally attained by it alone. And based on the preceding theses, it is already clear what our response will be; namely, *the trustworthiness* [*Veracitas*] *of God the Author of nature, as well as the fact of revelation, can be naturally known as something modally supernatural, externally manifested, and confirmed by miracles; however, active revelation, as something essentially supernatural, proceeding from God the Author of grace, is attained by faith alone, being something formally of faith, as that which is believed, as well as that by which it is believed.*

However, we must show that this solution is in conformity with the teaching of Christ set forth in the Gospel, Tradition, and the theology of St. Thomas. In this matter, the Thomists gradually came to perfect their terminology by resolving the objections raised by Scotus, the nominalists, Molina, and others.

This lengthy article, which can be skipped over by beginning students, is nothing other than the history of this fundamental problem and a defense of the Thomistic thesis.

In order for the difficulty of the question to be clearer, let us first see (A) what the Church has and has not defined and (B) the points on which theologians disagree in this matter.

A. *The Church* has not defined whether the formal motive of infused faith is inaccessible to our reason without an infused light on account of its supernaturality.[112]

However, there is something certain in the Church's teaching on this matter—namely, that *the faithful must hold the fact of revelation* not only as something proposed with moral certitude by history, referring to the miracles of Christ, but also *with utter firmness as being proposed infallibly by the Church herself with the assistance of the Holy Spirit.* Therefore, the Church

---

[112] See Vacant, *Études*, vol. 2, 74–75; also see Vacant, *De certitudine iudicii quo assentimur existentiae revelationis* (Pictavii, 1878).

has defined not only her own infallibility[113] but also that God has in fact revealed to us himself and the eternal decrees of his will,[114] *that this revelation was* {{429}} *properly supernatural,* that it did not come forth through the development [*evolutionem*] of the religious sentiment from the subconsciousness of the prophets,[115] *being in fact confirmed* not by wonders to be dismissed as myths but, rather, *by miracles properly so called, over which the Church ultimately judges* with a certitude superior to natural certitude.[116] All of these points have been solemnly defined and must be believed in by all believers with utter firmness.[117]

B. **Nonetheless, theologians disagree** regarding something that is not explicitly defined in this matter. On the one hand, the *Thomists and Suarez* say that revelation, as the formal motive of infused faith, exceeds the powers of reason and must be supernaturally known, simultaneously being *that by which and that which is supernaturally believed in* [i.e., at once the means and object of our faith.] Otherwise, divine faith would be neither essentially supernatural nor infallible and *simpliciter* more certain than any form of natural knowledge but, rather, would be resolved into natural certitude.

On the other hand, *the Scotists, nominalists, Molina,* and a number of modern authors say that the formal motive of infused faith does not exceed the natural powers of reason, and it suffices that one *naturally* knows the infallibility and trustworthiness of God as well as the fact of revelation. This knowledge is essentially natural, but it is confirmed both through the Church's declarations and through the infused light of faith. Indeed, these theologians sufficiently preserve in this the rationality of the obedience of faith, but we must ask whether they sufficiently acknowledge its essential supernaturality and infallible certitude. They conceive of faith as a discursive form of knowledge.

This question is commonly called *the problem concerning the ultimate resolution of faith.* Precisely stated, it can be expressed thus: What is the source of the Catholic believer's formal and firm belief that God has revealed the articles of faith, which he infallibly believes, such that he would be prepared to suffer martyrdom for the sake of their truth?

---

[113] See [First] Vatican Council, *Dei filius*, chs. 3 and 4 (Denzinger, nos. 3012, 3017, 3020).

[114] Ibid., ch. 2 (Denzinger, no. 3004).

[115] Pius X, *Pascendi*, nos. 11–26 (Denzinger, nos. 3482–3493).

[116] See [First] Vatican Council, *Dei filius*, can. 3.4 (Denzinger, no. 3034).

[117] Nor is it impossible, according to St. Thomas, to simultaneously naturally know the fact of revelation from historically certain signs and to believe in it on account of the infallible testimony of the Church, for as he says in *ST* III, q. 55, a. 5c and ad 2 and 3, the apostles simultaneously knew Christ's resurrection from sensible signs and believed in it from a loftier perspective on account of the infallible testimony of Christ and the Scriptures.

If one responds that the fact of revelation is *naturally* known from historically certain miracles so that the ultimate resolution of faith is made into this natural certitude, how can our faith relying on this properly natural knowledge be essentially supernatural and infallible, being more certain, without qualification, than any natural knowledge whatsoever?

However, on the other hand, if one responds that the First Truth who reveals is *supernaturally* believed "under the illumination and inspiration of the Holy Spirit" spoken of by the [First] Vatican Council, then, as Scotus asks, how can we avoid an infinite regress in revelations or a vicious circle: Do I believe in revelation on its own account or on account of something else?

Nor does it suffice to say that the fact of revelation is infallibly known through the authority of Sacred Scripture or of the Church, for this infallible authority is either believed in *supernaturally* on account of revelation or is admitted *naturally* on account of miraculous evidence. Thus, the difficulty remains: What is our faith *ultimately* resolved into?

This problem is of the greatest importance in the topics discussed in the treatise on faith, for its correct resolution is necessary in order for one to preserve a correct understanding of the essential supernaturality of faith and of the other infused virtues.[118]

{{430}} In this part of fundamental theology devoted to the study of revelation, we cannot pass over this debate: *How should revelation itself be known as the formal motive of faith?*

From this perspective, many Thomists call this problem *the question concerning supernatural and intrinsic credibility*[119] in opposition to rational and extrinsic credibility, inasmuch as the former is had immediately from knowledge of the formal motive of faith, whereas the other is had from knowledge of the motives of credibility, especially miracles.

Therefore, the problem facing us here is of great importance *for reconciling the essential supernaturality of faith with the rational obedience that it calls for* and for showing how the assent of faith is infallible and *simpliciter* more certain than the rational conclusion of apologetics concerning the fact of revelation. The true conception of the relation between the rational judgment of credibility and the act of faith (and, hence, between apologetics and

---

[118] Hence, the Thomists discuss this question both in the treatise on grace and in the treatise on faith. We will see this below in the citations from the Salmanticenses, John of St. Thomas, Gonet, Gotti, Billuart, and even Suarez (*De gratia*, bk. 2, ch. 11; *De fide*, pt. 1, disp. 3, sect. 6).

[119] See Ambroise Gardeil, *La crédibilité et l'apologetique*, 2nd ed. (Paris: Gabalda, 1912), 63: "*Supernatural credibility* is the transcendental [*sic*] property possessed by the object of revelation in relation to the intellect perfected by the virtue of supernatural faith. *Rational credibility* is the transcendental property possessed by the objective divine revelation in relation to natural understanding." Likewise, see his article "Crédibilité" in the *Dictionnaire de théologie catholique*, col. 2210.

faith) depends on the resolution of this question. Nay, *in this, we are faced not merely with the question of the letter of apologetics [i.e., its literal sense] but, rather, with its spirit*—namely, with the question of the end of the rational defense of faith: whether this rational defense can be *the essential [per se] foundation* for the supernatural certitude of faith or, rather, whether it only *takes one by the hand and leads him in the direction of faith [manuductio ad fidem]*. In other words, our question can be stated thus: Is faith so precious and sublime that it can only be essentially *[per se]* founded on the uncreated divine light? Hence, we are asking *whether we should attribute the greatest of importance to divine grace and prayer in practical apologetics for the conversion of unbelievers.*[120]

This problem is similar to the fundamental question of critical metaphysics; namely, how is the formal motive of natural intellectual certitude known? Whereas empiricists (or nominalists) reduce the certitude of the first principles of reason to the certitude of experience (i.e., of sense experience), thus bringing to ruin the absolute necessity of these principles, traditional philosophy by contrast holds that the motive for the certitude of the principles is their intellectual evidence, although sensation is a prerequisite for knowledge of the terms from which those principles are composed.

Regarding the method for resolving this problem, we must recall that inasmuch as the virtue of faith and the very act of faith are essentially supernatural, they are *mysteries* strictly speaking. Thus, they are *not* to be thought of *in a univocal manner* through a resolution *to inferior realities*—namely, to natural, acquired faith. Such a resolution would be a material explanation of the act of divine faith. Instead, they must be explained *analogically*,[121] indeed materially comparing them to natural acquired faith, though formally resolving them in light of something *superior* (namely, the uncreated light of God who reveals).

{{431}} We must historically set forth the two opposed solutions. However, before that, let us see what can be drawn from Sacred Scripture and Tradition. Likewise, let us consider what was taught by theologians prior to St. Thomas. Following on this, we will see more clearly the opposition that exists between the Thomistic position [*sententiam*] and that of the nominalists and Molina.[122]

---

[120] Regarding the perspective of this question, see Henri-Dominique Lacordaire, *Conférences*, ed. in 8°, 334–337 and 344–347.

[121] See *De veritate*, q. 14, a. 9, ad 3: "'To believe' is said *equivocally* of the faith of men and that of demons, who do not have in themselves a kind of infused light of grace as is found in the faithful."

[122] In this question concerning the necessity of the grace of faith, Thomism and Molinism cannot agree with each other, since they are opposed concerning grace in general, the divine concur-

§2. What Do Sacred Scripture and Tradition Say about This Matter?

A. *In Sacred Scripture*

The solution to this question is not found in Sacred Scripture in theological terms. However, as Melchior Cano showed,[123] we can nonetheless find something explicit enough in it.

Indeed, Sacred Scripture calls faith "the substance of things to be hoped in" or, in other words, the foundation of the spiritual edifice and the beginning of eternal life. Hence, it is essentially supernatural, like eternal life itself.

Moreover, on many occasions, the New Testament calls the formal motive of faith "the voice of the heavenly Father," "the voice of the Son," and "the testimony of the Holy Spirit," who spoke through the prophets. And it is explicitly affirmed that men who resist the grace of faith cannot hear this voice of the Father, or that of the Son, or that of the Holy Spirit, even if they materially hear the words of the Gospel and see miracles. Therefore, according to Sacred Scripture, the formal motive of faith cannot be known without grace. This doctrine is in particularly found in the following texts of Sacred Scripture:

> Hebrews 11:1 (DR): "Now, faith is the substance of things to be hoped for, the evidence of things that appear not." ("The substance"—that is, the beginning of eternal life, which is essentially supernatural.)

> John 5:36 (DR): "The works which the Father hath given me to perfect, the works themselves which I do, give testimony of me, that the Father hath sent me (these testimonies are sensible)," but Christ adds in v. 37 (DR): "And the Father himself who hath sent me hath given testimony of me: *neither have you heard his voice at any time.*" (Indeed, the Pharisees see the miracles but they do not hear the voice of the Father.)

---

rence [in all our activity], [God's] foreknowledge, and predestination. Hence, Billuart rightly sets forth the Thomistic opinion in *Summa sancti Thomae, De gratia*, diss. 3, a. 2, §2: "Against certain (Molinist) theologians who say that fallen man can by his own powers assent with a natural assent to supernatural revelation on the basis of the motive of divine revelation, ... and thus *making of the powers of nature in themselves dispose one to supernatural things and infallibly seek after them*, not indeed out of the merits of those natural actions but, rather, relying on a covenant between God and Christ, making it be the case that grace is always given on the basis of what the powers of nature are in themselves. To our eyes, this opinion does not seem to sufficiently distance itself from Semi-Pelagianism, for they did not say that supernatural assent can be elicited by the powers of nature, though it was implied in their terms; nor did they say that this natural assent, properly speaking, would merit the gift of grace but that it would only be the occasion seized upon by God for conferring grace, as I have already discussed elsewhere."

[123] See Melchior Cano, *De locis theologicis*, bk. 2, ch. 8.

John 10:25–27 (DR): "The works that I do in the name of my Father, they give testimony of me. But you do not believe, because you are not of my sheep. *My sheep hear my voice.*"[124]

Matthew 13:9 (DR): "He that hath ears to hear, let him hear."

Matthew 16:17 (DR): "Blessed art thou, Simon Bar-Jona: because flesh and blood hath not revealed it to thee, but my Father who is in heaven."

Matthew 11:25 (DR): "I confess to thee, O Father, Lord of Heaven and earth, because thou hast hid these things from the wise and prudent, and *hast revealed them to the little ones.* Yea, Father: for so hath it seemed good in thy sight. All things are delivered to me by my Father. And no one knoweth the Son but the Father: neither doth any one know the Father, but the Son, and he to whom it shall please the Son to reveal him." (Neither the letters {{432}} of the Gospel nor miracles are hidden from the wise and the prudent; rather, what is hidden is the Word of God, which is spirit and life.)

John 6:64–66 (DR): "'The words that I have spoken to you are spirit and life. But there are some of you that believe not.' For Jesus knew from the beginning who they were that did not believe and who he was that would betray him. And he said: 'Therefore did I say to you that no man can come to me, unless it be given him by my Father.'"

John 6:44–45 (DR): "No man can come to me, except the Father, who hath sent me, draw him. And I will raise him up in the last day. It is written in the prophets: 'And they shall all be taught of God.' *Everyone that hath heard of the Father and hath learned cometh to me.*"

John 12:44 (DR): "He that believeth in me doth not believe in me, but in him that sent me."

John 15:21 (DR): Jesus says, concerning the Pharisees, "*they know not him who sent me*"; and immediately afterwards, while speaking about miracles, he says, "But now they have both seen and hated both me and my Father."

---

[124] See St. Thomas's commentary where he discusses John 5:36 and 10:26. There, following SS. John Chrysostom and Augustine, he speaks of "those predestined to belief," to the grace of faith: "My sheep hear my voice"; others see the miracles and read the words of the Gospel but do not believe.

John 14:17 (DR): "*The Spirit of truth, whom the world cannot receive, because it seeth him not, nor knoweth him. But you shall know him*; because he shall abide with you and shall be in you."

John 18:37 (DR): "For this was I born, and for this came I into the world; that I should give testimony to the truth. *Everyone that is of the truth heareth my voice.*"

Philippians 1:29 (DR): "For unto you it is given . . . to believe in him."

1 Corinthians 12:3 (DR): "And no man can say the Lord Jesus, but by the Holy Ghost."

2 Corinthians 3:5 (DR): "Not that we are sufficient to think anything of ourselves, as of ourselves: but our sufficiency is from God."

Galatians 1:8 (DR): "But though we, or an angel from heaven, preach a gospel to you besides that which we have preached to you, let him be anathema." (Therefore, faith is utterly certain and essentially divine.)

1 John 5:10 (DR): "He that believeth in the Son of God hath the testimony of God in himself."

Romans 8:15–16 (DR): "You have received the spirit of adoption. . . . For the *Spirit himself giveth testimony* to our spirit that we are the sons of God."

1 Corinthians 2:7–16 (DR): "We speak [of a] wisdom . . . which none of the princes of this world knew. For if they had known it, they would never have crucified the Lord of glory. . . . *But to us God hath revealed them by his Spirit.* For the Spirit searcheth all things, yea, the deep things of God. For what man knoweth the things of a man, but the spirit of a man that is in him? So the things also that are of God, no man knoweth, but the Spirit of God. *Now we have received not the spirit of this world, but the Spirit that is of God: that we may know the things that are given us from God. . . . But the sensual man perceiveth not these things that are of the Spirit of God. For it is foolishness to him: and he cannot understand,* because it is spiritually examined. . . . *But we have the mind of Christ.*"

In these texts of Sacred Scripture, the formal motive of faith is called "the voice of the Father," "the voice of the Son," and "the testimony of the Holy Spirit." Moreover, it is explicitly affirmed that men who resist the grace of faith cannot hear the Father's voice, even though they may see miracles and hear the words of the Gospel. Therefore, according to Sacred Scripture, the formal motive of faith cannot be known without the grace of faith. The voice of the Father comes to us through the Son, is accepted through supernatural faith, and finally [is perfected] through the gifts of the Holy Spirit: "His unction teacheth you all things" (1 John 2:27, DR). (Below, we will discuss what St. Thomas said about these texts. Likewise, see what Melchior Cano[125] and Bossuet[126] say concerning them.)

{{433}} B. *Tradition*

Especially in their explanation of the aforementioned texts from Sacred Scripture, the Fathers of the Church affirm quite often that divine faith is essentially supernatural and more certain than every natural form of knowledge. They defended this in particular against the Pelagians and the semi-Pelagians. Nay, many, including St. Augustine, explicitly hold that man cannot without the internal grace of faith know the light—that is, the Divine Truth, which is the formal motive on account of which the revealed mysteries must be believed.

Among the Fathers of the Church, we must especially cite *Clement of Alexandria*[127] and *St. Basil*, who, after brilliantly showing the power of credibility, admonishes his reader: "Nobody can think about the Son without first being *illuminated by the Spirit*."[128]

---

[125] Melchior Cano, *De locis*, bk. 2, ch. 8.

[126] Bossuet, *Elevations sur les mystères*, 18th week, 17th elevation (Humility resolves all difficulties): "Your pride places you into rebellion against God. Humility must be your true sacrifice. And why did He spread out in His Scriptures these mysterious shadows if not in order to refer us to the Church's authority, where the spirit of tradition, which is that of the Holy Spirit, decides all things? Forget yourself, you who complain of the *obscurity of the Scriptures*, so that *its exceedingly bright light would dazzle you more than its holy shadows confuse you*. Have you not seen the Jews ask Jesus to explain Himself, as well as Jesus explaining Himself such as He wished, so that there no longer was ambiguity in His discourses? And what happened? Nothing whatsoever. The very light blinded them with its dazzling light. The more it was made manifest, the more they revolted against it, and if someone wanted to hear it, *the light was obscure and more shadowy for their stricken eyes than the very shadows themselves.*

"Finally, above all, you need to believe that those who believe owe everything to God, that they are, as the Savior said, 'Taught by Him'—*docibiles Dei*, in a word, *docti a Deo* (John 6:45)—that He must speak within us and pass into the hearts of those to whom He comes in a special way in order to make Himself heard. Therefore, stop your reasoning about these things: humble yourselves. 'Let him who has ears to hear, hear' (Matt 11:15 and 13:9). However, let him know that *these ears that hear are themselves given by God*: 'aurem audientem et oculum videntem Dominus fecit utrumque [The hearing ear, and the seeing eye, the Lord hath made them both],' Prov 20:12 (DR)."

[127] See St. Clement of Alexandria, *Stromata*, bk. 2, ch. 2, PG 8, col. 937.

[128] St. Basil the Great, *Letters*, PG 32, cols. 329–330.

Likewise, *St. John Chrysostom*, in speaking about the grace needed for faith, says: "If it is from God, how do they who do not believe sin, since the Holy Spirit does not give them His help. . . . nor the Son lead them into the way[?] . . . If the Father draws, the Son leads, and the Spirit illuminates, how do they sin who neither are drawn, nor led, nor illuminated? Because they do not render themselves worthy *to receive that illumination*."[129]

St. Cyril of Alexandria profoundly said: "But since it was the work of no common wisdom to acknowledge that He Who was veiled in human form is God, *He saith that he cannot come to Him (i.e., Christ) who has not yet received, i.e., understanding from God the Father*, and with reason. For if every good gift and every perfect gift is from above and cometh down from the Father of lights, how much more will not the acknowledgement of Christ be a gift of the Father's Right Hand."[130]

And later on, in the same commentary on John 4, he writes: "Therefore in that God is Father, and is so conceived of and proclaimed, He implants the knowledge of His Own Son in His hearers. . . . *God the Father will be conceived of as having implanted in us the knowledge of His Own Offspring not by a voice breaking forth from above*, and resounding round the earth like thunder, *but by the Divine Illumination shining forth as it were in us, to the understanding of the Divinely inspired Scripture* . . . for it is written of the holy disciples, that then *opened He their eyes*, to the understanding, that is, the holy Scriptures."[131]

Hence, St. Cyril greatly commends the methodology of a certain apologist thus:

> Then shewing that the Mystery concerning Himself was a God-taught good in men, and the knowledge of Him a work of the grace from above, He says that they cannot attain unto Him, save drawn by the teaching of the Father. But this is the plan of one whose only aim is to persuade them to consider, that they ought, weeping and sorrowing for those things wherein they had already grieved Him, to seek to be made free, and to be drawn unto salvation through faith in Him, through the Counsel of the Father, and the aid from above which lighteneth to them the way and maketh it smooth, which when they sinned, had become exceedingly rugged.[132]

However, above all others, we must here read *St. Augustine* against the Pelagians and the semi-Pelagians. {{434}} In particular in his text *On the Predestination of the Saints*, he makes clear the supernaturality of the beginnings of faith. Now, if you object that you

---

[129] St. John Chrysostom, *Expos. in ps.*, 115, PG 44, col. 322.

[130] St. Cyril of Alexandria, *Commentary on John's Gospel*, PG 73, cols. 605–606. [Trans. note: Taken from Cyril of Alexandria, *Commentary on John*, vol. 1, trans. and ed. P. E. Pusey et al. (Oxford: James Parker & Co., 1874), 438–439.]

[131] Ibid., cols. 555–556 (trans. Pusey et al., 402–403).

[132] Ibid., cols. 551–552 (trans. Pusey et al., 399–400).

do not sense this grace within yourself, he responds: "*Far removed from the senses of the flesh is this teaching in which the Father is heard, and teaches to come to the Son.* . . . We see that many come to the Son because we see that many believe in Christ, *but when and how they have heard this from the Father, and have learned, we see not. It is true that that grace is exceedingly secret,* but who doubts that it is grace?"[133]

But why, according to St. Augustine, is this faith supernatural? Because the light of the divine testimony, manifesting the mysteries to us, cannot be received by natural powers but, rather, presupposes that we have eyes that are adapted to it. Thus, this light of divine testimony is *that which and that by which* we believe, as St. Augustine shows outstandingly in *In Ioann. Evang.*, ch. 8, v. 14, tract. 35,[134] there explaining the Lord's words to the Pharisees: "I am the light of the world. . . . Although I give testimony of myself, my testimony is true" (John 8:12–14, DR).

St. Augustine explains this as follows:

"*Our mind,* which is the eye of the soul, *unless it be irradiated by the light of truth,* and *wondrously shone upon by Him who enlightens* and is not enlightened, *will not be able to come to wisdom* nor to righteousness. . . . The Jews then answered, "You bear witness of yourself; your witness is not true." Let us see what they hear; let us also hear, yet not as they did: they despising, we believing; they wishing to slay Christ, we desiring to live through Christ. Let this difference distinguish our ears and minds from theirs, and let us hear what the Lord answers to the Jews. "Jesus answered and said to them, Though I bear witness of myself, my witness is true; because I know whence I came and whither I go." *The light shows both other things and also itself.* Thou lightest a lamp, for instance, to look for your coat, and the burning lamp affords you light to find your coat; *do you light the lamp to see itself when it burns?* A burning lamp is indeed capable at the same time of exposing to view other things which the darkness covered, and also of showing itself to your eyes. So also the Lord Christ distinguished between His faithful ones and His Jewish enemies, as

---

[133] Augustine, *De praedestinatione sanctorum*, PL 44, ch. 13, col. 970. Likewise, *De dono perseverantiae*, PL 45, col. 1019. [Trans. note: Taken from Augustine, *On the Predestination of the Saints*, trans. Peter Holmes and Robert Ernest Wallis, revised by Benjamin B. Warfield, Nicene and Post-Nicene Fathers, First Series, vol. 5, ed. Philip Schaff (Buffalo, NY: Christian Literature Publishing Co., 1887), edited for online use by Kevin Knight and available at http://www.newadvent.org/fathers/15121.htm.]

[134] PL 35, co. 1658[ff]. Also, on this matter, see the other testimonies of the Fathers found in Roüet de Journel, *Enchiridion patristicum*, p. 855 and nos. 417, 418, 846, 963, 1223, 1248, 1303, 1503, 1970, and 2144. Likewise, see cols. 2239–2258 in Fr. Gardeil's aforementioned article "Crédibilité" ("La crédibilité chez les Saints Pères") in the *Dictionnaire de théologie catholique*.

between light and darkness: as between those whom He *illuminated with the ray of faith*, and those on whose closed eyes He shed His light. So, too, the sun shines on the face of the sighted and of the blind; both alike standing and facing the sun are *shone upon in the flesh, but both are not enlightened in the eyesight.* The one sees, the other sees not: the sun is present to both, but one is absent from the present sun. So likewise the Wisdom of God, the Word of God, the Lord Jesus Christ, is everywhere present, because the truth is everywhere, wisdom is everywhere. One man in the east understands justice, another man in the west understands justice; is justice which the one understands a different thing from that which the other understands? In body they are far apart, and yet they have the eyes of their minds on one object. The justice which I, placed here, see, if justice it is, is the same which the just man, separated from me in the flesh by ever so many days' journey, also sees, and is united to me in the light of that justice. *Therefore the light bears witness to itself; it opens the sound eyes and is its own witness, that it may be known as the light.* But how about the unbelievers? Is it not present to them? It is present also to them, but *they have not eyes of the heart* with which to see it. Hear the sentence fetched from the Gospel itself concerning them: "And the light shines in darkness, and the darkness comprehended it not." . . . *The witness of the light then is true, whether it be manifesting itself or other things; for without light you cannot see light,* and without light you cannot see any other thing whatever that is not {{435}} light. If light is capable of showing other things which are not lights, is it not capable of showing itself? Does not that discover itself, without which other things cannot be made manifest? . . . Therefore our Lord Jesus Christ is worthy to bear witness to Himself.[135]

The Augustinian comparison between the blind man and the unbelieving Pharisees contains the solution to our problem. St. Augustine says: "So, too, the (bodily) sun shines on the face of the sighted and of the blind; *both alike standing and facing the sun are shone upon in the flesh, but both are not enlightened in the eyesight*"[136] because the blind man is deprived of sight. Likewise, the True Light of spirits [*spirituum*] illuminates the understanding of the believer and the unbeliever; *both are illuminated in reason* (on account of miracles that are evident to all), but *both are not illuminated in their mind's eye* [*acie animi*], for the unbeliever "does not have the eyes of the heart." Hence, the unbeliever

---

135 [Trans. note: Taken from Augustine, *Tractates (Lectures) on the Gospel of John*, trans. John Gibb, Nicene and Post-Nicene Fathers, First Series, vol. 7, ed. Philip Schaff (Buffalo, NY: Christian Literature Publishing Co., 1888), edited for online use by Kevin Knight and available at http://www.newadvent.org/fathers/1701035.htm]

136 Ibid.

does not perceive the true light, which is the motive of our faith: "Without the light you cannot see the light." In other words, the First Truth who reveals, the motive of our faith, is not known by the unfaithful Pharisee, even though he may know miracles. In order to know him, internal grace is needed. Then, the First Truth revealing (or the divine light) manifests himself without implying a vicious circle, and without a regression *ad infinitum*, for no other revelation is needed in order to make revelation manifest. "Do you light the lamp in order to see that very lamp when it burns?" This is the response that is to be made to Scotus.[137]

Therefore, according to St. Augustine, without interior grace, the formal motive of faith cannot be known.

Hence, the Council of Orange defined against the semi-Pelagians:

> If anyone asserts that to be able by one's natural strength to think as is required or choose anything good pertaining to one's eternal salvation or to assent to the saving message of the Gospel without the illumination and inspiration of the Holy Spirit, who gives to all ease and joy in assenting to the truth and believing it, one is deceived by the heretical spirit and does not understand the word said by God in the Gospel: "Apart from me you can do nothing" (John 15:5) or the [word] of the apostle, "Not that we are sufficient

---

[137] Nonetheless, this text of St. Augustine does not imply that a miracle requires grace in order to be known with certainty, as some wish to interpret it. (See Maurice Blondel, "Lettre sur l'apologétique," *Annales de philosophie chrétienne* (Jan. 1896): 345. Also, Lucien Laberthonnière, "Le problème religieux," *Annales de philosophie chrétienne* (Mar. 1897): 623 (note). And in others as well.) Indeed, in this text, St. Augustine contrasts the believer to the Pharisee and presupposes that the Pharisee knows the miracles of Christ and cannot deny these signs, as is seen in Acts 4:14 and 4:16.

Hence, as Fr. Gardeil notes in col. 2255 of the article "Crédibilité" cited above, in many places St. Augustine affirms that a miracle is proposed "to the one who is unable to see the truth so that he may be made fit to see it" (*De utilitate credenda*, ch. 16, no. 34, PL 42, col. 591). "He who calls you so that you may believe will not desert you; even though He may order you to believe what you cannot see, nonetheless He does not send you away seeing nothing, hence you would be able to believe what you do not see. . . . He also came and performed miracles" (*Serm.* 126, PL 38, col. 700). And according to St. Augustine, miracles can be known by the light of natural reason and the senses: "Every man has eyes by which he can see the dead arise" (*Serm.* 98, no. 1, PL 38, col. 591).

Hence, according to St. Augustine, there is a great difference between seeing miracles and hearing the voice of the Heavenly Father. Hence, the Lord had said in John 10:25–27 (DR): "The works that I do in the name of my Father, they give testimony of me. *But you do not believe, because you are not of my sheep. My sheep hear my voice.*" And St. Paul, in Ephesians 1:17–18 (DR), prays, saying: "That God . . . may give unto you the spirit of wisdom and of revelation, in the knowledge of him: *the eyes of your heart enlightened*, that you may know what the hope is of the glory of his inheritance in the saints."

of ourselves to claim anything as coming from us; our sufficiency is from God" (2 Cor 3:5).[138]

{{436}} The [First] Vatican Council said the same thing.[139]

Molina objects: The Council only asserts that grace is necessary for believing *as is necessary for salvation*, but not for the substance of the act of believing, not for knowing the formal motive of faith.

The Thomists respond:[140] According to the Council, grace is necessary for believing as is necessary for salvation. Now, *he who believes* not on account of the natural evidence of miracles but, rather, *on account of the formal motive of infused theological faith* already *believes as is necessary for salvation*, for he hears the voice of the Father. Therefore, grace is necessary in order to believe on account of the very formal motive of infused faith and in order to know this motive formally as such.

§3. What Did the Medieval Theologians before St. Thomas Teach?

In the twelfth century, regarding this question, Abelard, whose thought on these matters destroyed the supernaturality of faith, stood in opposition to the School of St. Victor, which defended it.

ABELARD (†1142) drew close to semi-rationalism, which later on in the nineteenth century was defended by Georg Hermes. For Abelard thought that the formal motive of faith is not the authority of God who reveals but, rather, something rational. He expressly said, "And it is not believed because God had said it but, rather, it is received because one is convinced that it is thus."[141] And because we have only probable reasons regarding the mysteries, faith, according to Abelard, is only a rational opinion, "an opinion [*existimatio*] of things that are not apparent."[142] However, grace is necessary not for faith but for charity, which perfects faith. In the nineteenth century, Hermes would come to embrace a similar doctrine.

HUGH OF ST. VICTOR (†1141), by contrast, defended the supernaturality of faith, affirmed the obscurity of the mysteries of faith, and upheld their credibility on account of the probative strength of miracles. However, he insisted on the necessity of the Holy Spirit's internal inspiration and illumination for belief. Concerning this inspiration, he said, "For *He has internally taught* our human ignorance *through an illuminating inspiration*

---

138 Second Synod of Orange, can. 7 (Denzinger, no. 377).

139 See [First] Vatican Council, *Dei filius*, ch. 3 (Denzinger, no. 3010).

140 See, for example, Billuart, *Summa sancti Thomae, De gratia*, diss. 3, a.2, §2.

141 PL 178, col. 1050.

142 Ibid., col. 1051.

inwardly, although He may have instructed it outwardly through doctrinal erudition or have confirmed it through the presentation of miracles."[143] Hugh of St. Victor places belief in our affect: "Belief exists in our affect, but what is believed exists in our knowledge."[144]

St. Bernard (†1153) also defended, against Abelard, the absolute certitude and supernaturality of faith. "However, far be it from us that we think that there is something legitimately uncertain in our faith or hope, as he [Abelard] thinks, and that the whole of it is not founded *on certain and solid truth* (this is the formal motive of faith), divinely *persuaded* by oracles and miracles (this is rational credibility). . . . That testimony was made with great trustworthiness."[145] Likewise, regarding the influence of grace: "If [there were] not [such an abundance of such proofs], finally, the *Spirit renders testimony to our spirit* that we are Sons of God. Therefore, how could someone dare to call faith an opinion [*aestimationem*] unless he is someone who has not yet accepted that Spirit or who does not know the Gospel or thinks it is a fable? 'I know whom I believe in and am certain,' shouts the Apostle, and you come hiss the words, 'Faith is an opinion.'"[146]

Likewise, William of Auxerre (†1231) distinguished two kinds of faith, one concerned {{437}} with revealed mysteries but that is natural, arising from the evidence of miracles, and another kind that is "gratuitous" or supernatural coming "through an illumination." However, this gratuitous faith "says in the heart of man: I now believe not on account of a natural reason but on account of what I see. . . . Thus, when faith is present, man is not now made fit to believe through the reasons which he at first had [through the other sort of faith]. Those reasons do not generate faith in him but they do confirm and increase gratuitous [faith]."[147]

Likewise, William of Auvergne (†1249) vehemently fought against Abelard's semi-rationalism, admitting the probative strength of miracles and the absolute certitude of our faith founded on God's testimony.[148]

Alexander of Hales (†1245) clearly distinguished acquired faith from infused faith. "The[149] former is gathered from testimony and reason and does not suffice for salvation." This acquired faith disposes for gratuitous faith. "Nevertheless, we must note," he says, "that reason and the faith that comes from reason are related to gratuitous faith as a prior disposition is related to a given [substantial] form. *For it disposes the soul to receive the light by which it assents to the first truth for its own sake*, but in the mode of nature, not

---

[143] PL 176, 217.

[144] Ibid., col. 331.

[145] PL 182, 1061–1062. These texts are cited by Ambroise Gardeil in the aforementioned article "Crédibilité" in the *Dictionnaire de théologie catholique*, col. 2259ff.

[146] PL 182, col. 1061–1062.

[147] *In IV Sent.*, bk. 3, tr. 3, ch. 1, q. 4.

[148] *Opera omnia, De fide*, art. 1, p. 2, 4, 8, 15.

[149] [Trans. note: An opening quote is placed here without any correlative closing quote. Only this first sentence is found in Alexander of Hales's text.]

of grace. And it is said to lead it along as a loom shuttle leads a thread [*sicut tela filum*]. Then, human reason ceases when the faith thus led does not rely on it."[150] This gratuitous faith is not resolved into acquired faith, for it is loftier and of a superior certitude: "Natural reasons are a motive for having faith by way of *arousing* one to assent to the first truth for its own sake, though such faith does not rest on them."[151]

ALBERT THE GREAT likewise defended the supernaturality of faith. Indeed, in speaking of rational arguments from miracles, he said: "They do not cause the consent of faith but, instead, only bring about reflection concerning the thing that is believable. And because they are not sufficiently probative, they therefore at best serve faith in a material manner, which is a tenuous form of knowledge. Formally, it is perfected on the side of our affect."[152] "Given that faith is a simple light similar to the first truth, it produces simple science [*scientiam*] of the truth of things believed."[153] As we sometimes find in Sacred Scripture, the term "science" here denotes certain knowledge.

ST. BONAVENTURE also defended the absolute supernaturality of infused faith with utter clarity. Indeed, he said, "Certain people assent to the truth that has been heard, being moved by human persuasion, for example, on account of . . . miracles, . . . and such faith is *simpliciter* acquired. However, others *assent to the truth of faith on account of a divine illumination.*"[154]

> Therefore, if someone asks, "What moves one to believe this? Namely, is it Scripture, or miracles, or grace, or eternal life itself?" We must say *that what principally moves to this is the very illumination* that begins in the infused light which indeed enables us to think about God, not only in a lofty manner but also piously. And this is so because this illumination comes forth from the eternal light itself, to which our intellect is held captive in obedience and . . . it renders it apt to believe whatever {{438}} pertains to the divine honor and worship, even if these things are above our reason. However, there are a number of things that move us like *little supports* and that are, in some way, induce-

---

[150] *Summa universae theologiae*, pt. 3, q. 68, m. 2.

[151] Ibid., m. 7, a. 3, § Sent. propria.

[152] *In* [IV] *Sent.*, l. 3 [*sic*], d. 23, litt. A, a. 1, ad 4 (Paris, 1894), 406.

[153] *In IV Sent.*, l. 3 [*sic*], dist. 23, litt. B, a. 3, ad 1 (410).

[154] *In IV Sent.*, d. 23, a. 2, q. 2, concl. The full text is: "However, certain people assent to the truth of faith *on account of divine illumination*, just as those *who are united to the first truth above all and for its own sake* and many Christians who do not [*sic*] have charity. Such people have faith through an infusion, for they freely assent in conjunction with the divine illumination, an illumination, I say, that elevates reason to things that are above itself. Thus, *just as we say that an illumination enabling us to know future things* is infused because it elevates the soul above those things that are natural to it, so too must we understand the matters before us in our discussion here." Ibid., ad 2: "*Nobody assents to the divine authority for its own sake and above all else except through a divine illumination*, and such belief is infused, not acquired."

ments, for the authentic testimony of Scripture moves, the martyrs and the examples of the saints move, the arguments of the learned and the judgment of the universal Church herself move, as do undeniable miracles.[155]

"Therefore, although it is [not][156] believable from reason on its own that God is triune, it nonetheless is believable on the basis of reason aided by grace and the light that is infused from on high. And what is credible in this manner is not believed irrationally, for grace and the light infused from on high directs reason rather than corrupting it."[157]

Hence, before St. Thomas, the theologians who fought Abelard's semi-rationalism held that the formal motive of faith is *"the first Truth" known in the supernatural light*. Indeed, if this first truth could be known by reason alone, it would be *a natural truth* and hence *would not be the first truth*, for a supernatural truth would be found above it, just as supernatural providence is found above natural providence, although they are the same act in God. Hence, Suarez rightly said:

> In *In* III *Sent.*, d. 23, a. 2, St. Bonaventure distinguishes acquired faith from infused faith concerning the same things through the formal reasons for believing. This is also held by Richard here in a. 7, q. 2. Alexander of Hales [*Alens.*] also wrote of this in pt. 3, q. 64, a. 2 of his *Summa universae theologiae*, and this distinction is commonly held by Doctors writing on faith. However, it is made particularly clear by St. Thomas in *ST* II-II, q. 1, a. 1 and q. 5, a. 2 and 3, especially in ad 1, and in *In* III *Sent.*, d. 24, a. 1, q. 1, as well as in countless other texts where he places the essential reasons for infused faith, both as an act and as a *habitus*, in the formal reason upon which it relies, which he calls the "First Truth who reveals," always distinguishing this assent of Christian faith from every other form of faith concerning the same truths on the basis of the formal object involved, likewise denying that the faith that demons and heretics have in the things they believe is founded on this same formal object.[158]

---

[155] *Quaest. disp. de Trinitate*, q. 1, a. 2, sol.
[156] [Trans. note: Added, based on the text of the Quaracchi edition of St. Bonaventure's works.]
[157] Ibid., ad 3, vol. 5 (56–57).
[158] Suarez, *De gratia*, bk. 2, ch. 11, no. 8.

§4. What Does St. Thomas Teach in These Matters?

We will consider St. Thomas's doctrine chronologically: (A) *his commentary on Peter Lombard's Sentences* (1253ff); (B) *De veritate* (ca. 1261); (C) *his commentaries on Matthew, John, and Paul*; and (D) *ST* II-II (1270).

In general, St. Thomas distinguishes the supernatural order from the natural order more clearly than do earlier theologians because, following the methods he drew from Aristotle, he determines with greater metaphysical precision what human nature is in itself, as well as its properties, and does not consider it [solely] as it factually happens to be concretely and as it is psychologically experienced. Likewise, he considers God in himself before considering him as the Supreme Good and our ultimate end. Hence, better than his predecessors, St. Thomas distinguished what pertains to the light of reason in the judgment of credibility and what pertains to the light of faith in the act of faith.

Commentary on The Sentences

From this commentary, we can gather two conclusions related to our question. *The first conclusion is that the light of faith is per se required for infallibly believing the revealed mysteries and for discretely rejecting things that must not be believed.*

In III *Sent.*, d. 23, q. 2, a. 1, ad 4: "The infused light, which is the *habitus* of faith, manifests the articles [of faith], just as the light of the agent intellect manifests naturally known principles."

Ibid., q. 3, a. 2: "No power, according to its very nature, is determined to those things which are {{439}} above the nature of our reason, among which is numbered faith. Therefore, for this act, we stand in need of a *habitus* that is not acquired, one that will aid us[159] in two ways, namely by making the intellect apt to believe things to be believed, thus strengthening it against difficulty, and by giving it discernment for refuting things that must not be believed, thus strengthening it against error."[160] And he likewise adds in a. 3, q.la 2a: "Man can believe (those things that must be believed) from a general opinion without an infused *habitus*. However, he is inclined discretely to this and not that only through an infused *habitus*. Such discernment is what enables us to avoid believing every spirit. Because such discernment is not found in heretics, it is clear that the *habitus* of faith does not remain in him. And if he believes given *credenda*, he does so on the basis of human reason."

---

[159] [Trans. note: Reading *nos* for *non*.]

[160] However, the Church's infallible proposition of the truth is also needed, for otherwise the faithful could believe something false, not by divine faith but by human faith—namely, through an error by which they would think that something is revealed by God that in fact has been invented by men and is false.

The second conclusion: The formal motive of faith is the First Uncreated Truth, believed in and not seen.

See *In* III *Sent.*, d. 23, q. 3, a. 3: "Reason inducing us to believe can be taken either *from something created,* as when we are led through some sign to believe something, either concerning God or concerning other things, or it is taken *from the Uncreated Truth Itself,* as when we believe certain things that are said to us divinely through [God's] servants. . . . And faith in the first sense is found in the demons inasmuch as, on the basis of natural knowledge itself together with miracles as well, which they see to be above nature much more subtly than we do, they are compelled to believe those things that exceed their natural knowledge. However, they do not have the second kind of faith." Ad 2: "The faith that is found in the demons is not an infused *habitus* but, rather, proceeds from natural knowledge."

By contrast, in *In* III *Sent.*, d. 24, q. 1, a. 1, the following is said about supernatural faith: "Powers and *habitus* receive their *species* from the formal character of their objects . . . . *Indeed, since faith does not assent to something except on account of the First Truth who is worthy of belief,* something is actually worthy of belief only in the light of the First Truth, just as color is visible in physical light. Therefore, the First Truth is formal in the object of faith, which derives the formal character of its object from It." In this text, the First Truth is said to be "worthy of belief" and therefore is believed, not seen. Moreover, it is said to specify the supernatural *habitus* of faith. Therefore, it is the supernatural truth and, hence, is not known by the demons. And if this truth were not supernatural, it would not be the First Truth, for we could find some supernatural truth above it, just as the supernatural providence of God the Author of grace is above natural providence (namely, the providence of God the Author of nature). Likewise, in a. 1, qc. 3: "Faith rests on the First Truth. Thus, since that Truth is infallible, faith cannot be false." By contrast, natural knowledge of miracles is not infallible. In ibid., a. 2, it is said that the First Truth is not seen: "That intelligible form, which will principally be the object of faith, namely God, cannot itself inform our intellect [*formationem intellectus nostri subterfugit*], and is not penetrable by it so long as we are wayfarers, as Augustine says. Once again, we cannot, through demonstration, reduce those things that are of faith (namely, the mysteries) to principles that are seen."

De veritate, q. 14. This question in the *Disputed Questions De veritate* clearly affirms three things: (1) The formal motive of faith is the First Uncreated Truth; (2) this First Uncreated Truth is believed, not seen; and (3) this Truth specifies the supernatural *habitus* of faith and, hence, is supernatural.

(1) *The formal motive of faith is the Uncreated First Truth existing in the divine knowledge.* See *De veritate*, q. 14, a. 8:

Every created truth is subject to failure unless it is rectified by the Uncreated Truth. Thus, assenting to the testimony of a man or an angel would not lead infallibly to the truth except insofar as the testimony of God speaking in them is taken into consideration. Hence, faith which is said to be a virtue must make man's intellect *adhere to the truth which consists in divine knowledge by transcending the truth proper to the human intellect as such* [*transcendendo proprii intellectus veritatem*]. Thus, the believer "is freed from the instability and multiplicity of error through the simple and ever-unchanging Truth," as [Ps.-] Dionysius says in *De divinis nominibus*, ch. 7, ... and thus {{440}} faith, which joins men to the divine knowledge through assent, has God as its principal object and whatsoever other things as things that are then joined to that.

(2) *The formal motive of faith is believed in, not seen. De veritate*, q. 14, a. 8, ad 2: "Although we must believe on the divine testimony everything that we believe, nonetheless, like [God's own] knowledge it is first and principally concerned with itself and then, subsequently, with other things." And in ad 3: "The first truth is the object of vision *in patria* as appearing in its own proper *species*; however, it is the object of faith inasmuch as it is something that does not appear [in its full manifestation]." In ad 4, St. Thomas explains how divine revelation is *at once that which is believed and that by which we believe*, just as light is that which we see and that by which we see:

> In a way, light is the object of sight, though in a way it is not. For inasmuch as light is seen by our vision only by being joined to some determinate body through reflection or in some other way, not light but, rather, color, which always exists in a body having a surface, is said to be the *per se* object of sight. However, inasmuch as things can be seen only insofar as they are illuminated, light itself is said to be visible, as the Philosopher says in the same place (*De anima* 2, com. 67). Thus, the First Truth is the object of faith *per se*.

In other words, just as light is that by which we see and that which we see, so too the First Uncreated Truth who reveals is that by which we believe and that which we believe. Likewise, in ad 9: "The First Truth is involved in faith as both the means [or objective medium] and the object." Similarly, in ad 16: "However, the very testimony of the First Truth is involved in faith as principles are in demonstrative sciences." However, in the sciences, the principle is more certain than the conclusion; therefore, in faith [the First Truth] cannot be less certain. Therefore, he is infallibly believed.

All the same, "Although the divinely infused light is more efficacious than the natural light, nonetheless, in our current state as wayfarers, it is not participated in perfectly by us, but only imperfectly, and therefore ... it does not lead us to the vision of those things for the knowledge of which it is given to us. However, we will have such vision *in patria*, where we will perfectly participate in that light, and in God's light, we will see light" (*De veritate*, q. 14, a. 9, ad 2). Hence, St. Thomas does not say that the believer *perceives* or *intuits* the First Truth but, rather, that he *clings* to the First Truth by his intellect and his will.

In a. 9, ad 4, St. Thomas says that the demons do not believe on account of the Uncreated First Truth but, rather, "are compelled by the evidence of signs. . . . Thus, the term 'belief' is said equivocally of the faithful and the demons, and they do not have faith from some infused light of grace, as is found in believers."

(3) *The formal motive of faith specifies essentially supernatural faith and, therefore, is essentially supernatural.* See *De veritate*, q. 14, a. 2: "Eternal life consists in the full knowledge of God. Therefore, we must have some beginning of this supernatural knowledge in ourselves here below. Now, we do indeed have such a beginning through faith, which through its infused light holds those things that exceed the natural light of reason." Otherwise, if the First Truth were not supernatural, there would be a loftier truth found above it.

Against the errors of the Greeks, ch. 30: "Our faith has its authority neither from the angels, nor from any miracles performed, but rather, from the revelation of the Father through the Son and the Holy Spirit, although angels also revealed things belonging to our faith to certain people, such as to Zechariah, Mary, and Joseph as well, and many miracles have been performed for the strengthening of the faith." Likewise see *SCG* III, ch. 153.

Commentaries on Matthew, John, and Paul
Matthew 11:15 (DR) and 13:13–16 (DR):

He that hath ears to hear, let him hear. . . . Therefore do I speak to them in parables: because seeing they see not, and hearing they hear not, neither do they understand. And the prophecy of Isaias is fulfilled in them, who saith: By hearing you shall hear, and shall not understand: and seeing you shall see, and shall not perceive. For the heart of this people is grown gross, and with their ears they have been dull of hearing, and their eyes they have shut. . . . But blessed are your eyes, because they see, and your ears, because they hear.

Following St. Jerome, St. Thomas says, "We must understand that there are two kinds of eyes. On the one hand, yes, there are our external eyes, by which all men in general see, and this is not what is spoken of here. On the other hand, there are the eyes that are found within us, {{441}} by which the apostles alone saw things. In Ephesians 1:17–18 (DR), it is said, 'May (God) give unto you the spirit of wisdom and of revelation, in the knowledge of Him, the eyes of your heart enlightened.' Whence too, there are external and internal ears by which we hear." And in Proverbs 20:12 (DR): "The hearing ear, and the seeing eye, the Lord hath made them both." Likewise, see Mark 4:12; Luke 8:10; Romans 11:8; and Acts 28:26.

Matthew 11:25–27 (DR): "I confess to thee, O Father, . . . because thou hast hid these things from the wise and prudent, and hast revealed them to little ones . . . neither doth anyone know the Father, but the Son, and he to whom it shall please the Son to reveal him." St. Thomas explains this, saying: "He hides wisdom from the wise by not supplying grace." Hence, although these worldly-wise men may see miracles and hear the words of the Gospel, they do not hear the Father's voice through the Son and the Holy Spirit—that is, the First Truth who reveals.

Matthew 16:17 (DR): "Blessed art thou, Simon Bar-Jona: because flesh and blood hath not revealed it to thee, but my Father who is in heaven." Flesh and blood see miracles and hear the words of the Gospel. What, therefore, is the voice of the Father? St. Thomas notes, "And He says, 'Blessed art thou,' because you do not judge according to what flesh and blood reveal but according to what my Father reveals. Or you do not have this from your own natural exertion but, rather, from my Father. 'For nobody knows the Son except the Father.' Indeed, manifestation falls to him who knows. Thus, it is said in Matthew 11:27: 'Nobody knows except him to whom the Father has willed to reveal [Himself].' And in Daniel we read: "But there is a God in heaven that revealeth mysteries."[161]

John 3:3 (DR): "Jesus answered and said to (Nicodemus): 'Amen, amen, I say to thee, unless a man be born again, he cannot see the kingdom of God.'" St. Thomas writes in lect. 1, no. 2:

> Nicodemus, having an imperfect opinion about Christ, confessed that He was a teacher and performed these signs as a mere man. Therefore, the Lord wished to show him how he could come to a loftier form of knowledge concerning Him. . . . It is as though He said: "It is not surprising if you believe me to be a mere man, for someone cannot know those secrets of the Deity unless he is made fit for it through spiritual regeneration." And this is what He said: "Unless a man be born again, he cannot see the kingdom of God," . . . as though to say, "It is not surprising if you do not see the kingdom of God, for nobody can see it unless he receives the Holy Spirit through whom one is reborn as a Son of God."

Likewise, in lect. 2, no. 1, he says: "It must be said that, according to Augustine, there is a *twofold voice* of the Holy Spirit. By one voice, He speaks inwardly in man's heart, and only believers hear this voice. . . . The other voice is that by which the Holy Spirit speaks in the Scriptures or through preachers. And even nonbelievers and sinners hear this voice."

John 4:42 (DR): "And they said to the (Samaritan) woman: 'We now believe, not

---

[161] [Trans. note: The text cites "ibid.," though the text broadly comes from Matthew 11:27 (DR), which reads: "All things are delivered to me by my Father. And no one knoweth the Son but the Father: neither doth any one know the Father, but the Son, and he to whom it shall please the Son to reveal him."]

for thy saying, for we ourselves have heard him and know that this is indeed the Saviour of the world.'" St. Thomas says in lect. 5, no. 2:

> Three things induce us to faith in Christ. First, there is natural reason. . . . Second, there are the testimonies of the Law and the Prophets. . . . And third, there is the preaching of the Apostles and others. . . . However, when the man who has thus been led along [manducatus] comes to believe, he then can say that he does not believe for any of these reasons—neither on account of natural reason, nor on account of the law's testimony, nor on account of the preaching of others, but on account of the (First) Truth alone. . . . The certitude of faith rests on the divine reason . . . and faith has certitude from the divinely infused light. . . . The principles of faith are known on the basis of the divinely infused light.

John 5:24 (DR): "Amen, amen, I say unto you, that he who *heareth my word* and believeth him that sent me hath life everlasting." Concerning this, St. Thomas says: "'He who hears my word,' that is, me the Word of God, has eternal life, as the reward of faith." Hence, this hearing is essentially supernatural.

John 5:36–38 (DR): "The works which the Father hath given me to perfect, the works themselves which I do, give testimony of me, that the Father hath sent me. And the Father himself who hath sent me hath given testimony of me: neither have you heard his voice at any time, nor {{442}} seen his shape. And you have not his word abiding in you: for whom he hath sent, him you believe not." St. Thomas says in lect. 6, no. 9:

> I respond, in accord with St. John Chrysostom, that the Lord wishes to show to those established in a philosophical outlook that *God gives testimony* to someone in two ways, namely, *in a sensible manner* and *in an intelligible manner*. Sensibly, He does so as solely through a sensible voice. . . . However, He intelligibly testifies by inspiring into the hearts of certain people those things that they should believe and hold. . . . Therefore, (the Pharisees) could receive the first kind of testimony. And this is not surprising, for those voices and sights [species] (and miracles as well) came from God only *effectively* [i.e., as efficiently caused and hence only modally supernatural], as was said. However, they were not able to receive the intelligible testimony of that voice: "neither have you heard His voice at any time, etc." In other words: "You did not partake in it." And further on in John 6:45 (DR), he says, "Every one that hath heard of the Father and hath learned cometh [to] me." However, you do not come to me. Therefore, "neither have you heard His voice at any time, nor seen His shape [speciem]." In other words: *you did not have that intelligible testimony*. Hence, he adds: "And you have not His word abiding in you." That is, you do not have His inwardly inspired word. The reason for this is "Because you do not believe in Him whom He," namely, the Father, "has sent." For the Word of God leads to Christ, since Christ Himself is the natural Word of God. However, every

word inspired by God is a kind of participated likeness of Him. . . . His words, "Neither have you heard His voice," show the threefold manner in which God reveals something to someone. Because He does so either through a sensible voice, as He testified to Christ in the Jordan and on Mount [Tabor] . . . or through a vision of His essence, which He reveals to the blessed, . . . or through an interior word given through inspiration; and (the Jews [confronting Jesus]) did not have this either.

John 6:44–45 (DR): "No man can come to me, except the Father, who hath sent me, draw him. . . . Everyone that hath heard of the Father and hath learned cometh to me." St. Thomas writes in lect. 5, no. 4: "For he who comes through knowledge of the truth must hear Him through God's inspiration, as is said in Psalm 84:9 (DR): 'I will hear what the Lord God will speak in me.'"

John 6:64–66 (DR): "The words that I have spoken to you are spirit and life. . . . Therefore, did I say to you that no man can come to me, unless it be given him by my Father." St. Thomas: "Consequently, according to Augustine, 'It is a great thing to believe; rejoice because you have believed.'"

John 10:25–27 (DR): "The works that I do in the name of my Father, they give testimony of me. But you do not believe, because you are not of my sheep. *My sheep hear my voice.*" St. Thomas, lect. 5, no. 4: "*The works* . . . bear witness to me, namely, because they can only be performed by God. Thus, *they make it quite clear that I come from God.* . . . And therefore, (the Jews [confronting Jesus]) are inexcusable. . . . However, the reason for their lack of faith is their separation from Christ's sheep. . . . 'You are not of my sheep,' namely predestined to believe (at least to the things to be believed at that time). . . . For the very fact that we believe comes from God, as is said in Ephesians 2:8 (DR): 'For by grace you are saved through faith: and that not of yourselves, for it is the gift of God.'" (The Pharisees, however, resisted the grace of faith.)

John 12:36–40 (DR): "Whilst you have the light, *believe in the light*, that you may be the children of light. . . . And whereas he had done so many miracles before them, they believed not in him. . . . He hath blinded their eyes and hardened their heart, that they should not see with their eyes, nor understand with their heart." St. Thomas: "In order that they may not see with their eyes, that is, their spiritual eyes, by understanding Christ's divinity. . . . When it is said that God blinds, this is not to be understood as though it meant that God would impel one to sin but, rather that he does not infuse grace . . . inasmuch as there is something in us opposed to divine grace."

John 14:6 (DR): "*I am* the way, and *the truth*, and the life." St. Thomas: "Indeed, the Truth belongs to Him because He is the Word. . . . And anyone who desires to know the truth must adhere to this Word." This is the motive of faith: the First Truth, who is supernatural, just like the supernatural life being discussed in the text. And in St. John's Gospel, when the First Truth speaks to us, he first manifests himself in these words: "Amen,

Amen, I say to you." Regarding this, St. Thomas notes (*In Ioan*, 3:2):

> This expression, "Amen," {{443}} is from Hebrew, and Christ frequently makes
> use of it. Thus, out of reverence, no translator, neither among the Greeks nor
> Latins, wished to change. . . . However, John the Evangelist is alone among the
> Evangelists in doubling this expression. The reason for this is that the other
> evangelists are principally concerned with handing on those things that pertain
> to Christ's humanity, which do not need to be asserted as strongly, given that
> they are easier to believe. John, however, primarily treats of those things that
> pertain to Christ's divinity, which stand in need of a greater emphasis because
> they are hidden and more remote from man's knowledge.

In other words, essentially supernatural mysteries can only be revealed by the supernatural First Truth, who transcends our reason and who affirms himself, together with
the infusion of the light of faith, when he says, "Amen, amen, I say to you." Then God's
trustworthiness [*veracitas*] is attained by faith itself in a much loftier way than it is by
reason alone.

John 14:26 (DR): "The Holy Ghost, whom the Father will send in my name, He
will teach you all things and bring all things to your mind, whatsoever I shall have said to
you." St. Thomas:

> Just as the effect of the sending of the Son was to lead [men] to the Father, so
> too the effect of the sending of the Holy Spirit is to lead the faithful to the Son
> . . . . Therefore, the Son hands on to us His doctrine since He is the Word, but
> the Holy Spirit makes us capable of receiving that doctrine. Therefore, He says,
> "He will teach you all things." Because whatever man may teach, unless the
> Holy Spirit gives understanding inwardly, such a man works in vain, for unless
> the Spirit is present in the heart of him who hears, the words of the teacher will
> be of no use. Thus, it is said in Job 32:8 (DR): "Inspiration of the Almighty
> giveth understanding." This is even true of the Son Himself, speaking in a
> human manner [*organo humanitatis loquens*], for He too cannot be truly heard
> unless He himself works inwardly through the Holy Spirit.

This text from the Gospel of John also holds for the gifts of the Holy Spirit, although,
according to St. Thomas, theological faith is not inferior to the gifts but, rather, is loftier
because it rules them.[162]

John 15:21–24 (DR): Here, Christ says of the Pharisees, "*They know not him who
sent me*," and then immediately, "If I had not come and spoken to them, they would not

---

[162] See *ST* I-II, q. 68, a. 8.

have sin . . . *but now they have both seen* and hated both me and my Father." St. Thomas, in lect. 4, remarks on the words "they know not Him that sent me," saying: "Here, he is speaking of perfect knowledge, which consists in faith perfecting our understanding and joining our affect to God."

John 18:37 (DR): "For this came I into the world; that I should give testimony to the truth. Every one that is of the truth heareth my voice." St. Thomas remarks: "Therefore, we believe because we are from the truth, namely, inasmuch as we have received the gift of God through which we believe and love the truth."

1 Corinthians 2:10–16 (DR): "But to us God hath revealed them by his Spirit. . . . Now, we have received not the spirit of this world, but the Spirit that is of God: that we may know the things that are given us from God. . . . But the sensual man perceiveth not these things that are of the Spirit of God. For it is foolishness to him: and he cannot understand. . . . But we have the mind of Christ." St. Thomas says in lect. 3: "Just as the senses cannot examine those things that are of the intellect, so too neither the senses nor human reason can judge those things that are of the Spirit of God, thus meaning that such things are examined solely by the Holy Spirit. . . . The Holy Spirit intellectually illuminates the spiritual man and also affectively and volitionally enflames him. . . . Therefore, the spiritual man cannot be judged by the unspiritual man, just as he who is awake cannot be judged by the man who is asleep."

2 Corinthians 4:3–6 (DR): "And if our gospel be also hid, it is hid to them that are lost, in whom the god of this world hath blinded the minds of unbelievers, that the light of the gospel of the glory of Christ, who is the image of God, . . . God . . . hath shined in our hearts, to give the light of the knowledge of the glory of God, in the face of Christ Jesus." See St. Thomas's comments. Likewise, see Hebrews 8:10: "[Thus] saith the Lord: I will give my laws into their mind: and in their heart will I write them." St. Thomas: And this is {{444}} the letter concerning which he adds: "[written] not in ink but by the Spirit of the Living God, not upon stone tablets but upon human hearts."

1 Thessalonians 2:13 (DR): "Therefore, we also give thanks to God without ceasing: because, that when you had received of us the word of the hearing of God, you received it not as the word of men, but (as it is indeed) the word of God, who worketh in you that have believed." St. Thomas: "The very thing that you have believed was brought about in you by God."

Galatians 1:8 (DR): "But though we, or an angel from heaven, preach a gospel to you besides that which we have preached to you, let him be anathema." St. Thomas: "The teaching that is immediately given by God can be nullified neither by man, nor an angel."

Ephesians 1:16–19 (DR, slightly altered): "I ceaselessly give thanks for you (and pray . . . that God . . . may give . . .) you the spirit of wisdom and of revelation, in the knowledge of him: *The eyes of your heart enlightened* that you may know . . . what is the exceeding greatness of his power towards us, who believe." St. Thomas: "He prays for the gift of understanding . . . and the gift of wisdom." However, according to St. Thomas, "the theological virtues are preferred to the gifts of the Holy Spirit and rule them."[163]

Ephesians 2:8–9 (DR): "For by grace you are saved through faith: and that not of yourselves, for it is the gift of God. Not of works, that no man may glory." St. Thomas (lect. 3):

> Indeed, free choice of the will does not suffice for believing, for the things of faith are above reason, as is said in Sirach 3:25 (DR), "For many things are shewn to thee above the understanding of men," and 1 Corinthians 2:11 (DR), "The things also that are of God, no man knoweth, but the Spirit of God," and so forth. Therefore, the fact that man believes cannot come from himself unless God gives it to him, as is said in Wisdom 9:17 (DR): "And who shall know thy thought, except thou give wisdom, and send thy Holy Spirit from above?" Second, he excludes another error, for someone could think that faith would be given to us by God on the merit of our preceding works. To exclude this, he adds: "Not from your works," . . . for this is from grace, as is said in Romans 11:6 (DR): "And if by grace, it is not now by works: otherwise grace is no more grace." . . . "So that nobody may glory" in himself but rather may refer all glory to God.

Likewise, in the Old Testament there are similar texts that are cited by St. Thomas. See Deuteronomy 29:3 (DR): "(Moses said,) 'Thy eyes have seen those mighty signs and wonders, and the Lord hath not given you a heart to understand, and eyes to see, and ears that may hear, unto this present day.'" Likewise, Ezekiel 3:7 (DR), where the Lord says to the prophet: "But the house of Israel will not hearken to thee because they will not hearken to me." Likewise, see Isaiah 6:9–10. Also, Psalm 84:9 (DR), "I will hear what the Lord God will speak in me: for he will speak peace unto his people: And unto his saints: and unto them that are converted to the heart." Also, Psalm 12:4 (DR), "Enlighten my eyes, that I never sleep in death."

In De Trinitate Boetii, q. 3, a. 1, ad 4:

> In the faith by which we believe, there is not only an acceptance of the things to which we assent but also something that inclines us to assent, and this is a kind of light, namely, the *habitus* of faith, divinely infused into the human mind. Indeed, it is more capable of inducing assent than any demonstration, for even though demonstration never leads to a false conclusion, nonetheless, man is often deceived in thinking that something is demonstrated when it in fact is not. Moreover, it is more capable of inducing assent than is the natural light of the intellect, by which we assent to principles, since that light is often

---

[163] Ibid.

impeded by bodily weakness, as is clear in those who are insane. *The light of faith, however, which is, as it were, a kind of seal of the First Truth upon the mind, cannot deceive,* just as God can neither deceive or be deceived. Thus, this light suffices for judging. However, this *habitus* does not move by way of the intellect but, rather, by way of the will. Hence, it does not make us see those things that we believe, nor does it force our assent, but rather, makes us assent freely. Thus, faith clearly comes from God in two ways. On the one hand, it comes from Him from the perspective of the interior light which induces us to assent. On the other, it comes from Him from *those things that are externally proposed,* which took their beginning in divine revelation, {{445}} and these things *are related to the knowledge of faith as things known through the senses are related to our knowledge of principles* because both give us a kind of determination for our knowledge. Thus, just as our knowledge of principles is taken from our senses, while the light by which those principles are known is innate, so too faith comes from hearing, even though the *habitus* of faith is infused.

From this text, we see quite clearly that, according to St. Thomas, the formal motive of faith cannot be known by the light of reason alone (e.g., from a rational consideration of miracles). Indeed, just as the formal motive of the intuition of first principles is their intellectual evidence, which transcends sense knowledge and can be known by the light of the intellect alone, so too the formal motive of faith is the supernatural First Truth, who transcends rational knowledge and can be known by the supernatural light alone.

Finally, in the Summa theologiae, regarding the formal motive of faith, St. Thomas expressly teaches the following: (1) this formal motive is the First Truth; (2) this First Truth is not seen and is essentially supernatural; (3) it is the First Truth in accord with what is manifested in Sacred Scripture and the Church's teaching, which proceeds from the First Truth; (4) heretics do not adhere to this First Truth even if they hold a number of the mysteries of faith; and (5) supernatural faith is specified by this formal motive (hence, this motive cannot be known without supernatural faith, thus meaning that it cannot be known by the demons).

(1) *The formal motive of faith is the First Truth.*

ST II-II, q. 1, a. 1: "If we consider the formal character of the object of faith, it is nothing other than the First Truth, for the faith we are speaking of does not assent to anything unless it has been revealed by God. Thus, faith rests upon the Divine Truth itself as upon its means." He says in a. 2, ad 3: "The vision had by the blessed in heaven will be of the First Truth as He is in Himself . . . but through faith, we do not grasp the First Truth as He is in Himself."

In his commentary on the first article, Bañez objects to himself: "The formal object of any given *habitus* is that with which that *habitus's* act is concerned *per se primo*. But . . . the believer knows in an evident manner that God is the First Truth, since this can be naturally and metaphysically demonstrated: 'God is pure act. Therefore, He is infinitely perfect, the highest truth, the highest goodness, and so forth.' Therefore, the First Truth is not the formal object of the act of belief, since faith and evident scientific knowledge do not exist concerning the same thing." And Bañez responds: "The First Truth is not said to be the formal object of faith such that faith would assent to this: 'God is the first Truth, or God is Trustworthy [*verax*], or what is revealed by God is true.' For all these things are evident. Rather, we say that the formal object of faith is the First Truth inasmuch as It testifies to something that pertains to God as exceeding every natural form of knowledge." And this is explicitly affirmed by St. Thomas in *ST* II-II, q. 5, a. 1, as we will discuss soon below.

(2) *The First Truth who reveals is not seen and is essentially supernatural.*

ST II-II, q. 4, a. 1: "The First Truth is the object of faith inasmuch as it is not seen, as well as those other things that we hold on account of It." Indeed, it is not immediately seen because it is the Uncreated Truth which cannot be seen immediately outside the beatific vision. Nor is it seen from a demonstration *a posteriori*, like a divine attribute demonstrated by reason. Rather, it is believed in, for it exceeds reason.

Hence, in *ST* II-II, q. 5, a. 1 (Whether the angel in his first condition had faith), the Holy Doctor says: "In the object of faith, there is something that is, as it were, *formal*, namely *the First Truth existing above every natural knowledge that a creature can have*, and something material, that to which we assent while adhering to the First Truth." In ad 2, he says: "There was a kind of natural obscurity in the angelic intellect inasmuch as every creature is darkness in comparison with the immensity of *the divine light*, and such obscurity suffices for the formal character of faith." And in a. 4: "Faith can be said to be greater in someone in one way from the perspective of the intellect on account of its {{446}} greater certitude and firmness. In another way, it can be greater from the perspective of the will, on account of a greater promptness, or devotion, or confidence." The reason for this is given in ad 3: "For faith results as *a gift of grace*, which is not equally found in all." Hence, the Lord said to Peter in Matthew 14:31 (DR), "O thou of little faith, why didst thou doubt?" and to the Canaanite woman in Matthew 15:28 (DR), "O woman, great is thy faith."

The next three conclusions are found in *ST* II-II, q. 5, a. 3:

(3) *The formal motive of faith is the First Truth, as is manifested in Sacred Scripture and the teaching of the Church.* In other words, it is revelation inasmuch as it is infallibly proposed to the faithful by the Church and not inasmuch as it is rationally demonstrated from miracles.

(4) *Hence, a heretic does not adhere to this First Truth, even if he holds a number of the mysteries of faith, which in his judgment are revealed and confirmed by miracles.*

(5) *Nay, the heretic rejects the true formal motive that specifies supernatural faith, which hence cannot be known without supernatural faith.*

See *ST* II-II, q. 5, a. 3 (Whether he who disbelieves one article of faith can have unformed faith concerning the other articles):

I respond that neither formed nor unformed faith remains in the heretic who disbelieves one article of faith. The reason for this is that the *species* of any *habitus* depends upon the formal character of its object, without which the species of that *habitus* cannot remain. Now, the formal object of faith is the First Truth, as manifested in Sacred Scripture and the teaching of the Church, which proceeds from the First Truth. Therefore, whoever does not adhere as to a divine and infallible rule to the Church's teaching, which proceeds from the First Truth manifested in the Sacred Scripture, does not have the *habitus* of faith. Rather he holds those things that are of faith in a different manner than through faith. For example, someone may hold some conclusion in his mind without knowing the middle term used for demonstrating this conclusion, thus clearly not having scientific knowledge but, rather, only an opinion. However, it is quite clear that he who adheres to the Church's teaching as to an infallible rule assents to everything that the Church teaches. Otherwise, if he were to pick and choose the things that he wishes to hold and not hold from among the Church's teachings, he would no longer adhere to the Church's teaching as to an infallible rule but, rather, adheres to his own will. . . . Thus, it is clear that he who is an (obstinate) heretic concerning one article does not have faith concerning the other articles but, rather, only a kind of opinion in accord with his own will.

He says in ad 1: "The heretic does not hold the other articles of faith, which he is not in error about, in the same way as the believer holds them, namely, *by unqualifiedly adhering to the First Truth*, for which man *stands in need* of being aided through the *habitus* of faith. Rather, he holds those things that are of faith on account of his own will and his own judgment." And in ad 2: "Faith adheres to all the articles of faith on account of a single mean, namely, the First Truth proposed to us in the Scriptures as rightly understood by the Church in her teaching. Therefore, whoever departs from this mean completely lacks faith." Likewise, in *ST* II-II, q. 6, a. 1: "Since man is elevated above his nature when he assents to those things that are of faith, he must have this within himself from a supernatural principle that inwardly moves him."

Hence, when we speak of the First Truth who reveals, we must say what St. Augustine said about the Gospel: "I would not believe in the Gospel were the authority of the Church not to admonish me to do so."[164] For the Church infallibly proposes that God has supernaturally revealed [what we must believe], just as she proposes the revealed mysteries. Indeed, the Church's proposing so understood is not the formal *motive* of faith but, rather, is the [*necessary*] *condition* infallibly applying revelation to us. Therefore, no vicious circle is involved in this proposing [of supernatural revela-

---

[164] Augustine, *Cont. Epist. Manic.*, ch. 5. See Cajetan, *In ST* II-II, q. 1, a. 1, nos. 3 and 10.

tion]. Rather, causes are causes of each other, though in different *genera* of causality. The motive asserts the condition and is applied by it.[165]

Therefore, the motive of faith is essentially supernatural. Otherwise, it could not specify {{447}} supernatural faith, and thus, as is said in *ST* II-II, q. 5, a. 3, ad 1, man cannot cling to this motive without grace. Hence, the demon who believes "out of the keenness of his natural intellectual abilities" on account of the evidence of miracles (as is said in *ST* II-II, q. 5, a. 2c and ad 2–3) does not believe on account of the formal motive of faith, because he does not adhere to the First Truth who is essentially supernatural and transcends any natural knowledge whatsoever. Therefore, St. Thomas had said in lect. 3 of his commentary on 1 Corinthians 2:

> The sensual man does not perceive those things that are of the spirit of God. Just as the senses cannot examine those things that are of the intellect, so too neither the senses nor human reason can judge those things that are of the Spirit of God, thus meaning that such things are examined solely by the Holy Spirit, according to the words of Psalm 17:31 (DR): "The words of the Lord are fire-tried," that is, proven by the Holy Spirit. Therefore, because the sensual man lacks the Holy Spirit, he cannot examine spiritual things and, consequently, does not understand them.

Nay, indeed, he does not hear the voice of the Father or of the Son, because he is not (or is not yet) one of Christ's sheep: "My sheep hear my voice" (John 10:27).

Hence, based on a complete examination of St. Thomas's works, it is quite clear that he held that the *formal motive of faith* (i.e., *the First Supernatural Truth who reveals*) cannot be known by reason alone but, rather, *is that by which, as well as that which, we supernaturally believe*, as the Thomists have always said.[166]

---

[165] See Billuart, *Summa sancti Thomae, De fide*, diss. 1, a. 2, Resp. ad obiect.

[166] This makes it quite clear that Emmerich David greatly errs in his interpretation of St. Thomas when he writes, in his brief work, *De objecto formali actus salutaris* (Bonn: Hanstein, 1913), 28, after citing *ST* I-II, q. 109, a.1 and others like those that we related above: "We have said that such assertions by the Holy Doctor do not pertain to our question, because, according to the mind of Aquinas himself, *those texts teach that the grace of the supernatural light of faith* required for knowing the truths of faith (even though, at first sight, these very words seem more so to signify internal grace) *is nothing other than the external grace of revelation* and its transmission to individual men through the preaching of the Gospel. It is utterly clear that this is St. Thomas's thought on this matter, as we can see in his own, express words teaching that heretics and demons deprived of every supernatural, internal grace know revealed teachings and can retain them as true." If this were true, what difference would there be between St. Thomas's teaching *on the light of faith* and the doctrine held by the Pelagians?

The opposed and right interpretation of St. Thomas is set forth in Constantin von

Confirmation:

(1) Nay, St. Thomas teaches in *ST* I-II, q. 63, a. 4: "Infused and acquired temperance differ in species, and the same holds true for the other (moral) virtues." Likewise, in ad 1: "*Infused and acquired virtue* not only *differ* as regards their ordering to the ultimate end, but also *as regards their ordering to their proper objects*."[167] Therefore, *a fortiori*, acquired faith and infused faith are distinct not only as regards their order to the ultimate end (so that infused faith would only exist as giving what is necessary for salvation) but also as regards its order to their proper objects, for "*habitus* are distinguished specifically as regards the specific, formal characters of their objects," as he says in this text, *ST* I-II, q. 54, a. 2, and innumerable other texts.[168]

{{448}} (2) Also see regarding hope and charity *ST* II-II, q. 17, a. 5; q. 23, a. 4; q. 24, a. 2; I-II, q. 109, a. 3 (Whether man can love God above all things solely by his natural powers without grace). There, St. Thomas responds in ad 1: "*Charity loves God above all things in a more eminent way than does nature.* Indeed, nature loves God above all things inasmuch as He is the principle and end of the *natural* good, whereas charity loves Him as He is the object of beatitude and inasmuch as man has a kind of *spiritual* fellowship with God." Baius, however, was condemned because he rejected this distinction, saying, "The distinction of a twofold love of God, namely, a *natural* love whose object is God as *the Author of nature* and a gratuitous love whose object is God as *beatifying* is meaningless and imaginary; it has been devised as a mockery of the Sacred Scriptures and of the numerous testimonies of ancient authors."[169]

(3) Likewise, theologians generally distinguish *the natural providence* of the Author of nature, which is demonstrated by reason alone on the basis of the order of the sensible world, from *supernatural providence*, which orders supernatural means to salvation and to which the mystery of predestination pertains.[170] Hence, the Thomists say that the divine trustworthiness can likewise be considered in two ways: as *the trustworthiness of the Author of nature* (and in this way it can be demonstrated) and as *the trustworthiness of the Author of grace and glory* (in this way it is the trustworthiness or *voice of the Heavenly Father through the Son and the Holy Spirit*). From this loftier perspective it is

---

Schäzler, *Neue Untersuchungen über das Dogma von der Gnade und das Wesen des christlichen Glaubens* (Mainz, 1867), 527ff (Wodurch ist der Glaube ein übernatürlicher?). Likewise, see Scheeben, *Dogmatik*, vol. 1, §40, nos. 681 and 689ff, as well as §44, nos. 779–805 against Kuhn and Hermes, as well as against Cardinal de Lugo and Kleutgen.

[167] This difference is utterly clear if we read, on the one hand, what is written about temperance by Aristotle in the *Nicomachean Ethics* and, on the other hand, what St. Thomas writes in the *Summa theologiae* about mortification, fasting, chastity, virginity, modesty, and humility.

[168] Adversaries [to the Thomist position] draw an objection from the last article cited above. This objection will be resolved in §7 below.

[169] Pius V, *Ex omnibus afflictionibus*, no. 34 (Denzinger, no. 1934).

[170] See *ST* I, q. 23.

held by supernatural faith alone and is "trusted in" [*concreditur*] by one and the same act together with the revealed mysteries. Thus, *our faith* is not a mechanical discourse founded upon natural truth but, rather, *is intimately united with the eternal Word of God*, with his intimate life, for *the First Truth who reveals is not something laying in the temporal past but instead remains forever above time in eternity*. Thus, "he that believeth in the Son of God hath the testimony of God in himself" (1 John 5:10, DR). Such a person does not merely rationally know the past and the external fact of revelation confirmed by miracles, as he would know by reference to the historical accounts of Christ's preaching. Therefore, in its essential supernaturality, our faith is much more certain than the most certain of history.[171]

Thus, in order for us to hear the voice of the First Truth, a dwelling place for Christ must be prepared in our hearts. With St. Augustine, St. Thomas admonishes us, "Let us build and fashion a dwelling in our hearts, whither He may come and teach us."[172] Surely, is it not true that "God is intimately within all things,"[173] preserving them in existence? Surely the whole Trinity dwells in just souls?[174] Surely the Holy Spirit gives us the gifts of wisdom and understanding? Nonetheless, divine faith is loftier than {{449}} these gifts and rules them,[175] although the inspiration of the Holy Spirit adds a new perfection to them.[176] Faith indeed can remain without charity and sanctifying grace, but then it finds itself in a state contrary to its nature [*statu violento*] and not in a connatural subject, for as an infused virtue, it is a property of grace.

Thus, the theses of St. Thomas are utterly consistent with this doctrine: The formal motive of faith cannot be known without the internal light of

---

[171] See Scheeben, *Dogmatik*, vol. 1, §40, no. 681: "The motive of faith is purely and immediately divine and, consequently, it is absolutely one and simple, firm and subsistent, identical with the first and immutable source of every truth (*veritas prima*). On the other hand, faith presents itself as a *direct commerce and intimate union with the internal word of God* and, consequently, with His interior life. And given that this internal word did not only exist at the time of the manifestation of the external word but rather subsists in an *eternal* present inasmuch as it is *the eternal word of God*, it elevates our mind to participation in His immortal truth and immortal life and makes us take our rest there. (See Reding, *De fide*, q. 1, a. 1, contr. 2).

"The opposite opinion, holding that the external act of revelation would be a partial motive of faith, can be found in Lugo and Kleutgen (*Theol. der Vorz.*, vol. 4, nos. 110ff). As we have noted, this outlook remains within a *mechanical conception* wherein faith takes on the appearance of a *deductive process*, which would help us discover the truth of its content. It diminishes the transcendental [*sic*, or transcendent] character of faith, which is essentially an élan toward God." Likewise, see Scheeben's remarks later in §44, nos. 778–805.

[172] *In I Ioann.*, ch. 1, lect. 15. See C. von Schaezler, *Introductio in s. theologiam dogmaticam ad mentem S. Thomae*, 353–356 (*De magisterio interiore primae veritatis*).

[173] *ST* I, q. 8, a. 1.

[174] See *ST* I, q. 43, a. 3.

[175] See *ST* I-II, q. 68, a. 8.

[176] See *ST* I-II, q. 68, a. 2.

faith and simultaneously is that *by which* and *that which* we believe. As we will soon see, all the Thomists defend this doctrine.

§5. Historical Exposition of the Opposition between the Thomists and Suarez on the One Hand and the Scotists, Nominalists, Molina, Lugo, and a Number of Modern Thinkers on the Other

In the history of this problem, we can detect, so to speak, reverberations[177] of the principal oppositions found between theological systems on a number of points:

1) Regarding the value of our intellectual knowledge[178] (*nominalism and moderate realism*).

2) Regarding the *distinction between the natural order and the supernatural order*. (Thomism holds that this is a *necessary* distinction, whereas Scotism holds that it is a *contingent* distinction depending on the divine freedom.[179])

3) Regarding *the concurrence* of grace. (Molinism says that actual or habitual grace and our faculty are two *partial, coordinated causes*, whereas Thomism holds that they are *two complete causes*, with the inferior cause being subordinated to the higher [inferior subordinator *priori*].[180])

4) Regarding *the preparation for grace*. (Thomism holds that God does not deny a further grace to those who do what lies in their power with actual grace. Molinism holds that on account of a covenant arranged with Christ the Redeemer, God does not deny grace to him who does that which lies within the powers of his nature. Thus, when man does that which lies within his power, he disposes himself to supernatural things, and they infallibly follow upon this not indeed in virtue of the merits of those natural actions

---

[177] [Trans. note: Reading *repercussio* for *repescussio*.]

[178] For nominalism, the universal is reduced to a collection of facts. Hence, they consider discrete facts above all else, not the formal characters of things. Therefore, in the issue facing us, they do not see the distinction between the formal object of acquired faith and the formal object of infused faith.

[179] See ch. 11 above, concerning the existence of the supernatural order.

[180] See Molina, who teaches that God and creatures are related to each other as two partial causes, like two persons dragging a ship [to shore]. You can see this outlook by consulting his comments on *ST* I, q. 14, a. 13, disp. 26 (Paris, 1876), 158. For a refutation of Molinism on this point, see John of St. Thomas, *Cursus philosophicus Thomisticus, Philosophia naturalis*, q. 25, a. 1 (On the subordination of a second cause to a first cause).

but, rather, in virtue of the covenant established between God and Christ.)[181]

5) Finally, our current problem appeared in a new way *after the condemnation of Protestantism and of Baianism*, so that this historical exposition can be divided into two parts: (A) before the Council of Trent and (B) after the Council of Trent.

A. *Before the Council of Trent*

Before the Council of Trent, Scotus, Durandus, and the nominalists were opposed to the early Thomists like Capreolus and Cajetan.

Scotus (†1308) differs from St. Thomas regarding the essential distinction between the natural order and the order of supernatural truth and life. According to St. Thomas, this distinction is absolutely necessary and is immediately founded on the divine nature, which absolutely exceeds {{450}} the natural powers of any created and creatable intellect, such that God cannot create a substance for whom the intuitive vision of the divine essence would be natural.[182]

By contrast, Scotus held that the distinction between the natural and supernatural is not immediately founded on the divine being, for he admitted the univocity of being. Rather, according to him, this distinction is founded on the divine freedom. In other words, God freely made man such that our intellect knows only through a relation to sensible things, though this does not depend upon the nature of our intellect. Here we have an example of Scotus's voluntarism.[183] Nay, according to Scotus, we have in ourselves an *innate* natural appetite to see God through his essence.

---

[181] See Billuart, *Summa sancti Thomae, De gratia*, diss. 3, a. 7 and a. 2, §2; also see John of St. Thomas, *Cursus theologicus, De Deo*, d. 14, a. 2, no. 11.

[182] See *ST* I, q. 12, a. 4.

[183] See Scotus, *In* I *Sent.*, d. 3, q. 3, nos. 24 and 25. See Vacant, *Études comparées sur la philosophie de S. Thomas d'Aquin et sur celle de Duns Scot*, 12–20: "St. Thomas carefully determines the boundaries of the natural order and the supernatural order. By contrast, according to Scotus, our natural faculties possess, like a *weak seed*, the power of acting supernaturally and of enjoying the intuitive vision of God. This power cannot develop itself without grace. However, it nonetheless constitutes a kind of *toothing stone*. Thus, it follows that we bear within ourselves a natural tendency (*appetitus naturalis innatus*) for seeing God supernaturally. . . . Therefore, the Subtle Doctor was led to make the distinction between nature and grace depend upon God's free will, which can, consequently, change the character of His gifts. . . . The natural or supernatural character of each of these gifts depends upon an arbitrary determination by God." [Trans. note: In architecture, a "pierre d'attente" or "toothing stone" is a projection from a wall that allows future construction to be built in continuity with the foundation of the older construction. Interestingly, Fr. Ambroise Gardeil will use the image himself for the Thomist position. Also, as noted in an earlier chapter, Fr. Garrigou-Lagrange uses a dated and quite inexact method of citing Scotus.]

Consequently, according to Scotus,[184] the natural and the supernatural do not distinguish things but, rather, [indicate distinct] relations to active causes. In other words, the supernatural is that which can be caused only by a supernatural agent—namely, God. According to St. Thomas, by contrast, the supernatural so defined is only modally supernatural, from the perspective of efficient causality (or "effectively supernatural"). Thus, it would be like the resurrection of a dead person, which is supernatural inasmuch as it supernaturally returns the dead person to natural life. By contrast, grace is supernatural not only effectively but also entitatively inasmuch as it is as supernatural life.

Given these points regarding supernaturality in general, it is not surprising that Scotus disagrees with St. Thomas regarding the supernaturality of faith. And in this, Scotus's doctrine can be reduced to three conclusions.

(1) A natural act and a supernatural act can have the same formal object. See Scotus, *In III Sent.*, d. 31, no. 4, § "I say that with respect to the same object and under the same formal character there can be multiple acts . . . that differ like various species related to each other [*se habent*] in the same genus."[185] Likewise, see Scotus, *In I Sent.*, disp. 17, q. 3, no. 33; also see Lychetus's commentary on Scotus, *In III Sent.*, d. 25, q. 1, no. 47.

(2) Infused faith is not necessary on account of the supernaturality of the object, for the formal object of theological faith does not exceed acquired faith.[186]

(3) Infused faith is resolved into the acquired faith by which we believe that the Church is truthful, on account of signs. Otherwise, there would be an infinite regress.[187] However, Scotus speaks in a somewhat obscure manner, and it is not always easy to determine what he teaches and what he says merely in objection to others.[188]

DURANDUS OF SAINT-POURÇAIN (†1334) speaks in almost the same manner as does Scotus. According to him, infused faith is resolved into the acquired faith by which we believe that the Church is {{451}} ruled by the Holy Spirit, and naturally knowable signs are the motives for this acquired faith.[189]

THE NOMINALISTS followed the same opinion.[190] It is not surprising that the nominalists—and Durandus was already a nominalist—hold this opinion. For according to them the essences of things are nothing more than a collection of individuals or deeds.

---

[184] See *In I Sent.*, prol.

[185] See Ripalda, *De ente supernaturali*, bk. 3, disp. 45, no. 3; *De fide*, disp. 3, sect. 3, no. 28.

[186] See Scotus, *In III Sent.*, d. 23, q. 1, no. 8.

[187] See ibid.

[188] As Bañez notes in his comments on *ST* II-II, q. 1, a. 1, dub. 4, Scotus concedes that there is another way for faith to be resolved, a path by which faith is resolved immediately into itself, not into the First Truth who reveals. However, this represents a resolution from the perspective of the subject and not from the perspective of the objective motive, and our concern here is with the latter.

[189] See *In III Sent.*, dist. 24, q. 1, no. 8 and q. 3, no. 8; likewise, see d. 25, q. 3.

[190] For example, see Gabriel Biel, *In III Sent.*, dist. 23, q. 2.

Hence, they do not consider the formal character of infused faith and the formal character of acquired faith in relation to a formal object but, rather, only consider the concrete fact of belief. Thus, [according to them] it suffices that the act of believing as is needed for salvation be *de facto* supernatural, and it matters little that it be *essentially* supernatural in virtue of its formal object.

For the nominalists, the specific distinction between infused faith and acquired faith can be understood solely from the principles of efficient causality involved. They would say to the Thomists: Merely because infused faith could be produced by God alone, it does not follow that it would be essentially supernatural; rather, it only follows that it is something supernatural through efficient causality [*effective*], like the miracle healing a man born blind, who supernaturally receives natural sight, not supernatural sight.[191] Moreover, nominalists like Ockham[192] already are more or less skeptics in the philosophical order, as though all truths transcending experience could be certain only through faith. Thus, they came to diminish the probative strength of miracles and paved the way for the fideism of Luther, who himself was a disciple of the nominalists.

THE FIRST THOMISTS defended St. Thomas's doctrine against Scotus, Durandus, and nominalists like Peter Auriol. Let us consider Capreolus, Cajetan, and Sylvester of Ferrara in particular. According to them, the formal motive of faith is that by which and that which we supernaturally believe. Gradually, [the Thomist school's] terminology was perfected, ultimately explaining matters by distinguishing between the trustworthiness of God the Author of nature and miracles and the trustworthiness of God the Author of grace.

---

[191] See Salmanticenses, *Cursus theologicus, De gratia*, disp. 4, dub. 2, §3, no. 34: "The nominalists assert, in the same manner, that we must philosophize about the quality inhering in us, which we call grace, as we do about money and its value. For just as metal, considered in its very nature, does not have monetary value before the king makes such a designation, so too that quality (they say) from its intrinsic predicates and prior to God's designation is only a kind of entity that lacks sufficient value for man to be rendered acceptable to God. However, just as the addition of the king's extrinsic designation makes metal into money and thus have a moral value without any change in the metal, so too *the addition of God's ordering and favor, that quality receives a moral value and is made into grace without any change occurring in its entity*. This is what was taught by Ockham in *In I Sent.*, d. 17, q. 1. Likewise, Gregory [of Rimini?] in q. 1, a. 2; Gabriel [Biel?], q. 1, a. 1, and a. 3, dub. 4; Peter d'Ailly [*Aliacensis*]. . . . And Durandus seems to agree with these thinkers on this point in *In I Sent.*, d. 17, q. 1 nos. 7 and 8; so too does Scotus in q. 2 of the same distinction."

Luther, a disciple of the nominalists, said, "The grace by which we are justified is only a favor bestowed by God" and is only an extrinsic denomination in us. See the Council of Trent, sess. 6, can. 11. Also see Pius V's bull *Ex omnibus afflictionibus* no. 42, Denzinger, no. 1942 (against Baius's error on this). Moreover, Luther goes forward toward fideism as regards the motives of credibility, thus paving the way for liberal Protestantism, which holds that faith is only natural religious experience.

[192] See Ockham, *In IV Sent.*, bk. 3, q. 8. He seems to admit that probable rational credibility suffices.

Thus, CAPREOLUS (†1444) said in *In* III *Sent.*, dist. 24, q. 1, a. 3, §2 ("To the argument of Scotus"):[193]

> I assent to this article, "God is three and one," because God revealed it and not because John or some other man says that this was revealed to him. This is how we must speak of the assent caused by the *habitus* of faith. And one must not imagine, as the one arguing here imagines, that two or three assents would be necessary in such an assent, namely, one by which I assent to, "God is three and one," and another by which I assent to, "God revealed this," and yet another by which I assent to, "John says that this is revealed by Him," and so forth. No, by a single act, I assent that God is three and one and that God revealed this, just as by one and the same act I believe God, believe in a God, and believe in God.[194]

{{452}} Later on, in §4 of the same text, responding to Scotus's objection, Capreolus adds:

> It does not follow from our conclusion that assent to the article, "God is three and one," will, as the one arguing imagines, depend on an infinite number of prior assents (as though to believe in revelation it would be necessary to have another revelation, and another, and another, *ad infinitum*). . . . For through faith, I primarily and directly assent to "God revealed that He is three and one," just as sight first is objectively oriented [*fertur*] to light; and I secondarily assent to "God is three and one," just as sight is secondarily objectively oriented [*fertur*] to color, although by one and the same act [as that by which it assents in a primary and direct manner].—And when it is asked in addition, "How do I assent to 'God revealed this,' etc. . . . ," we must say that faith assents to it for its own sake and not on account of some other proposition, as though the assent to "God revealed this" would be dependent upon such another proposition, for this is the first thing believed: God or the First Truth revealed whatever is contained in Sacred Scripture and in the Church's teaching. And assent to this proposition is not *efficiently* [*effective*] caused by another preceding assent but, rather, by God moving the intellect internally through the *habitus* of faith to this assent. Nonetheless, this first assent of faith first requires the presentation of this complex expression through an interior or exterior locution either through the reading of Sacred Scripture or through preaching.

---

[193] See John Capreolus, *Defensiones theologiae Divi Thomae Aquinatis*, ed. Paban and Pègues, vol. 5, 317.

[194] And Capreolus uses St. Thomas's words from *In* III *Sent*, d. 23, q. 2, a. 2, q.la 2 and *ST* II-II, q. 3, a. 2.

Thus, we have Capreolus's position.

This point was explained even more clearly a little earlier, at the end of §2: "However, external persuasion or preaching is required to determine the things to be believed . . . but not, however, to cause one's assent. See *ST* II-II, q. 6, a. 1, ad 1." Therefore, Capreolus concludes against Scotus: "Thus, clearly, infused faith, neither as a *habitus*, nor as regards its principal act (namely, to assent to things to be believed), depends *efficiently* [*effective*] upon acquired faith. Nor does its certitude depend upon the certitude of acquired faith as the certitude of a conclusion depends on the certitude of a principle."[195] Nothing clearer can be said against the notion of discursive faith whose certitude would be resolved into inferior natural certitude.

Nonetheless, Capreolus did not at all reject the probative strength of miracles.

CAJETAN (†1534), in his comments on *ST* II-II, q. 1, a. 1, likewise shows against Scotus and Durandus that infused faith is not discursively resolved into acquired faith. In no. 10, he says:

> Since two things concur in faith, namely assent and proposition, as well as the explanation of things to be believed, from the perspective of its *assent*, faith depends upon God alone as upon its agent, object, end, and rule. However, from the perspective of *the proposition* of things to be believed, it can depend upon mediating angels and men by whom God proposes that these or those things must be believed. . . . And hence . . . the Holy Spirit provides for an infallible created rule [of faith], namely the thought and teaching of the Church . . . . Thus, given the two concurrent, infallible rules for faith, there is so great a difference between them that divine revelation is the formal character of the object of faith, whereas the authority of the Church is the minister of the object of faith . . . . Revelation actively considered is the formal character [of faith], namely, the very action and essence of God.

However, how is this formal motive of faith known without there being a vicious circle or an infinite regress? Cajetan responds in no. 11:

> There is neither an infinite regress in revelations, nor a resolution to the truth or testimony of the Church or to acquired faith. Rather, the resolution is made to divine revelation as such, so that it comes to a halt there. In evidence of this, note well that belief that God is the Revealer of the articles of the faith comes about in three ways: in one way, as *what* is purely believed; in another way, as that *by which* it is purely believed; and thirdly, *simultaneously as what is believed and that by which it is believed*. And if faith were to

---

[195] John Capreolus, *Defensiones theologiae*, ed. Paban and Pègues, vol. 5, 318.

consider this fact that I assert, namely, that God has revealed the articles of faith, *solely qua what is believed* (e.g., as it believes in the resurrection of the flesh), we would need to assign some other formal character to the object of faith by which we would believe (and thus there would be an infinite regress). . . . However, if this same thing is believed *only as that by which* the rest are believed, Scotus's question then arises (namely, faith infused is resolved into acquired faith). . . . The true response is that, just as among the transcendentals, {{453}} unity is one and goodness is good, so too the divine revelation is at once *what* we believe and *that by which* we believe. Thus, as unity is one of itself and there stops [in our conceptual resolution], so too *divine revelation, by which other things are believed, is itself believed and not through another revelation.*[196] For one and the same act of faith believes God and believes in God, as is clear below in q. 2, a. 2. . . . And just as it is not possible to form another, further question in faith as to why we believe God, so too it is not possible to seek out another resolution in faith for why you believe in God who reveals. For the act of believing God [*credere Deo*] and belief in God who reveals are one and the same [act].

Do not be poisoned by error when you read our words, "to believe in God who reveals," for this claim implies two things. The first is common even among nonbelievers [*gentilibus*], whereas the second is proper to the faithful. . . . For even those who mock our religion say that they [would] believe in God [*credere Deo*], if He were to have said something, much more than they [would] believe any given good man. However, the second is proper to believers, and we rely upon God as the Revealer of the articles of faith, so that *the act of faith adheres to God as the one who reveals the articles of faith.* . . .

---

[196] See *De veritate*, q. 21, a. 4, ad 4: "In the case of specific forms, what is concrete cannot be predicated of what is abstract, as though to say, 'Whiteness is white,' or 'Hotness is hot,' as is clear from what [Ps.-]Dionysius says (*De div. nom.*, ch. 2). However, in general forms this kind of predication is acceptable, for we say that '*essentia* is being,' 'goodness is good,' 'unity is one,' and so forth. The reason for this is that being is the first thing that falls into the intellect's apprehension. Thus, it is necessary that the intellect attribute being to whatever it apprehends . . . . And because there are certain things that communicate inseparably in the formal character of being, such as one, good, and other such things, it is necessary that these be predicated of whatever is apprehended for the same reason that this so for being." Thus, evidence is evident, of itself.

Hence, Scotus's objection that there would be an infinite regress in revelations is similar to the objection raised by the sophists against the possibility of a supreme criterion for natural certitude, for they said that we would forever need to find *a new criterion for judging the value of any given criterion*. However, much to the contrary, *evidence is evident, of itself.*

Hence, what we have said is clear, namely, that believers ultimately resolve their faith into this adherence to the First Truth who reveals, and not into the acquired faith by which I believe in John the Evangelist, Paul the Apostle, or the community of the Church. . . . Therefore, the *habitus* of infused faith [makes] man adhere to God qua testifying, so to speak, in the formal character of all that is believed, as is said in 1 John 5:10 (DR): "He that believeth in the Son of God hath the testimony of God in himself."

And if Durandus would have kept this mind in *In* III *Sent.*, d. 24, a. 1, he would not have said, "The first reason for believing other things, and to which the ultimate resolution of faith is made, is belief that the Church is ruled by the Holy Spirit," . . . (for) faith in us, in the Apostles, and in the prophets has the same formal character and, consequently, is resolved into the same thing (namely, into revelation and not into proposal by the Church). . . . Moreover, we believe the Church is ruled by the Holy Spirit because this is one of the things that God has said.

And Cajetan adds that there is not a vicious circle involved here, for the formal motive of faith (i.e., divine revelation) and its [necessary] condition (i.e., being proposed by the Church) do not move [our assent] from the same perspective. Causes are causes of each other in different genera of causality. According to Cajetan's teaching, faith is not discursive, and the First Truth who reveals is not the past, external fact of revelation [*externum factum praeteritum revelationis*], confirmed by miracles but, rather, is active revelation, "which is the very action and essence of God" (no. 10) who exists above time, in accord with what is said in 1 John 5:10 (DR): "He that believeth in the Son of God hath the testimony of God in himself."

Nonetheless, Cajetan does not deny the probative strength of miracles, nor the possibility of knowing the fact of revelation naturally and with certitude on the basis of miracles. However, this rational certitude is inferior to the certitude of faith and cannot be its foundation. On this, see his remarks in *In ST* II-II, q. 1, a. 4, nos. 5–6.[197]

---

[197] Certain Molinists object that Cajetan wrote in *In ST* I-II, q. 109, a. 5, no. 6, "Man can believe, hope in, and love God, as well as confess Jesus Christ Himself, through his own natural powers as regards the substance of works to be fulfilled and not inasmuch as they are fulfilled by hope, faith, and charity."

However, as is clear from the context, Cajetan's manner of speaking here does not lead to the idea that the natural act of faith is specified by the same formal motive as is the supernatural act, for Cajetan here explains the distinction presented by St. Thomas between natural love for God and supernatural love of God, and according to the Holy Doctor, they are specifically distinct as two different acts of love (*ST* I-II, q. 109, a. 3, ad 1). Hence, in this place, Cajetan uses the expression "quoad substantiam" generically, not specifically. Moreover, see

SYLVESTER OF FERRARA (†1528) did not speak differently on this matter. See his comments on *SCG* III, ch. 40, §3 and I, ch. 6.

{{454}} B. *After the Council of Trent: After the condemnation of the first Protestants*

Our problem appeared in a new light at the time of the first Protestants and Baius. Indeed, the pseudo-reformers were condemned because they rejected the proximate rule of faith—that is, the infallible proposition of the Church, which they replaced with the unmediated testimony of the Holy Spirit in any given believer.[198] Hence, they diminished the necessity and value of the motives of credibility (e.g., of the marks of the true Church), replacing them with private inspiration. From this perspective, the first Protestants, like Baius[199] and Quesnel[200] after them, seem to exaggerate the supernaturality of faith. However, they in fact fell into pseudo-supernaturalism and fideism, for on the other hand, they destroy the supernaturality of habitual grace and faith. For them, justifying grace is only an extrinsic denomination—namely, the external favor of God[201]—and justifying faith is nothing other than faith-confidence [*fiducia*] in the divine mercy.[202] Likewise, after Baius, it will come to be said that justification does not come about through habitual grace infused into our soul, by which man is renewed and made into a sharer in the divine nature.[203] The nominalist Ockham (in *In* I *Sent.*, d. 17, a. 1) had himself already said that created supernatural [grace] is only a moral [, extrinsic] denomination.

The Council of Trent, in session 6, ch. 7, defined: "'God's love is poured through the Holy Spirit into the hearts' (Rom 5:5) of those who are being justified and inheres in them. Hence, in the very act of justification, together with the remission of sins, man receives through Jesus Christ, into whom he is inserted, the gifts of *faith, hope, and charity, all infused at the same time.*"[204] Also in ch. 8 : "We are said to be justified through faith because 'faith is the beginning of salvation,' the foundation and root of all justification."[205]

In these conciliar texts, the supernaturality of infused faith is presented as being in the same order as the supernaturality of sanctifying grace. Hence, after the Council of Trent, Catholic theologians generally affirm that faith is *entitatively supernatural—that is, essen-*

---

what Cajetan says against Scotus and Durandus in *In ST* II-II, q. 17, a. 5, no. 1. He defends the idea that without infused virtue we would not have an act "proportioned to a supernatural object," nor to the supernatural end.

[198] See Leo X, *Exsurge Domine*, no. 27 (Denzinger, no. 1477).

[199] See Pius V, *Ex omnibus afflictionibus*, no. 22 (Denzinger, no. 1922).

[200] See Clement XI, *Unigenitus Dei filius*, no. 41 (Denzinger, no. 2441).

[201] See Council of Trent, *Canons concerning Justification*, can. 10 (Denzinger, no. 1560).

[202] See Council of Trent, *Canons concerning Justification*, can. 11 (Denzinger, no. 1561).

[203] See Pius V, *Ex omnibus afflictionibus*, no. 42 (Denzinger, no. 1942).

[204] Council of Trent, *Decree on Justification*, ch. 7 (Denzinger, no. 1530).

[205] Ibid., ch. 8 (Denzinger, no. 1532).

tially supernatural.[206] Even the Scotist Francisco Lychetus acknowledged this as being *De fide.*[207]

{{455}} What did the Thomists do at this time? They simultaneously defended the signs of the Church's infallibility and the reasonability of the obedience of faith on the one hand and, on the other, the essential supernaturality of faith. Along these lines, we can consider Melchior Cano against the Protestants. By contrast, Molina and Juan de Lugo defended the notion of discursive faith, as well as its rationality, but they upheld its entitative supernaturality only from the perspective of its active principle, not that of its formal object.

Melchior Cano (†1560), in *De locis theologicis*, bk. 2, ch. 8, simultaneously refuted the Protestants, who substituted the Holy Spirit's private inspiration for the Church's infallible proposition and the testimony of motives of credibility, as well as Scotus, Durandus, and Gabriel [Biel], who substituted the resolution into acquired faith concerning the trustworthiness of the Church for resolution of faith into the common testimony of the Holy Spirit.

In § "Quarto prius . . ." of the aforementioned text, Cano says:

> Therefore, we take it as established fact that, according to a common law, certain external and human incitements are necessary, by which we are induced

---

[206] See Salmanticenses, *Cursus theologicus, De gratia*, tr. 14, disp. 3, dub. 3, §1, no. 25: "It is is to be presupposed that the *habitus* of theological faith is *essentially [per se] infused* and *supernatural as regards its species*. Indeed, all theologians agree on this today. And rightly so, on the one hand, because it seems thus to have been defined by the Council of Trent in sess. 6, ch. 7, canons 11 and 12. And therefore, weighty doctors are not lacking who teach that it is certain with a certitude of faith. Moreover, on the other hand, [they rightly hold this] because theological faith is of the same order as sanctifying grace, which certainly is entitatively supernatural."

See Suarez, *De gratia*, bk. 2, ch. 11, no. 12, where he speaks in a similar manner.

Likewise, see Gonet, *Clypeus theologicae Thomisticae, De gratia*, disp., 2, a. 3 (Whether habitual grace is an entitatively supernatural form): "Scotus's opinion (Prolog. Q.1—and IV dist., 10, q. 8) is commonly rejected, because it does not distinguish between what is intrinsically supernatural (that is, *quoad entitatem*) from what is *extrinsically* supernatural (that is, *quoad modum*). This is contrary to the common consent of theologians who admit that there are beings that are supernatural intrinsically and entitatively. Nay, this is even contrary to the faith providing for such gifts."

[207] See Lychetus, *In* III *Sent.*, disp. 25, q. 2, no. 72 (Vivès, vol. 15, 200): "However, from the time of the Council of Vienne up to the time of the Council of Trent, it was only more probable that there might be *habitus* that are essentially [*per se*] infused. And after the Council of Trent that greater certitude was upheld, and more truly seems to me that it is a matter of faith itself, [namely,] that certain ontological aids [*aliqua auxilia physica*] are given as essentially infused aids for the sake of those sorts of acts (of faith, hope, and charity)." [Trans. note: I have provided slightly more of Lychetus's text at the end of the citation, based on Fr. Garrigou-Lagrange's citation earlier.]

to faith: "How shall they believe him of whom they have not heard? And how shall they hear without a preacher?" (Rom 10:14, DR) Therefore, it is said, "They going forth preached everywhere: the Lord working withal, and confirming the word with signs that followed" (Mark 16:20, DR). . . . Thus, the Church, confirmed by divine signs, proposes revealed truths. (Against the Protestants, a point that he proves through Scripture.)

Then, we must also establish that the aforementioned human authority and all forms of incitements . . . are not sufficient causes of belief. Hence, there is need of an interior efficient cause, namely, the special help of God moving us to belief. (He goes on to prove this through Scripture against the Pelagians).

Thirdly, we must add[208] that the formal character of our faith is not the authority of the Church. In other words, the ultimate resolution of faith is not made into the testimony of the Church. . . . And here, I cannot ignore the error of those who assert (citing here in a note Scotus, Durandus, and Gabriel) that our faith must be reduced thereto as to the ultimate cause of belief, so that we would believe that the Church is truthful, to whom (as they say) we would first assent through acquired faith rather than through infused faith. But *if this were true, the primary formal character of infused faith would not be the Uncreated Truth but, rather, would be a created truth.* Thus, our faith would not rest on the divine truth as its foundation but, rather, on a human truth. Then too, since the assent to a conclusion is not more certain than assent to the principles [in light of which that conclusion is drawn] (*Post. Anal.* 1), if infused faith rested on acquired faith, then when we assent through infused faith to the fact that God is Triune, we will not hold this more firmly or more certainly than the fact that the Church is veracious, which, according to them, would be assented to through acquired faith and through incitements of human causes. . . . *If the assent of Catholic faith were to depend on acquired faith, it could not be altogether[209] firm.* . . .

Now, to these three certain and steadfast opinions, the following likewise connected: *the ultimate resolution of our faith is brought about in an internal efficient cause, that is, in God who moves us to believe.* For example, I assent to the articles, "God is Three," "The Church cannot err," and other universal principles of Christian doctrine, through infused faith, not because John

---

[208] [Trans. note: Reading *sublicendum* as *subiiciendum*, following the original full text here, "Cui et tertium subiiciendum est . . ."]

[209] [Trans. note: Reading *omnio* as *omnino*.]

said it, or any other man, but because God revealed it. However, I immediately *believe* "God has revealed," *being moved by God through a special instinct*. And thus, from the perspective of the formal character of the object [of faith], the mover is the Divine Truth who reveals. However, that does not suffice to move [us] unless an interior cause is present, namely God who also moves through a gratuitous and special concurrence (*ST* II-II, q. 2, a. 9, ad 3; St. Augustine, *Confessions*, 11, ch. 3). . . .

{{456}} Thus, the proposing of things to be believed, the making of persuasive arguments, and the performance of miracles indeed determine the intellect so that it may believe, as [necessary] *conditions* without which the intellect would hardly ever be determined. Nonetheless, *the formal character* of the assent is the light of faith, which God infuses into the believer.

(And immediately before this, Cano had said:) Accordingly, in our assent to the principles of geometry or arithmetic there are many things that are involved as kinds of antecedent preambles, such as sense knowledge, explanation, and the persuasion of the instructor . . . who explains the principles through examples that are manifest to the senses. However, the formal reason for assent is not any of these but, rather . . . is the innate natural light of the intellect by which that evident assent brought about, just as [physical] light is the external formal character that makes colors evident.

And therefore, Cano concedes to the Protestants that the authority of the Church is not the formal motive for our faith. However, he defends the fact that it is the necessary condition without which revealed mysteries would not be infallibly proposed to us.

Thus, we have a solution to the objection raised by the Protestants, which Scotus and Durandus would have found more difficult to resolve; namely, our faith formally rests not upon the testimony of men or the Church but, rather, on the testimony of God himself who moves us through grace, as is said in the first Letter of St. John: "He that believeth in the Son of God hath the testimony of God in himself." Hence, Protestants unjustly say that Catholics do not conceive of faith as being an intimate union of our soul with God who reveals but, rather, as external obedience to the human authority of the Church, which forever stands between the soul and God. This objection confuses the formal motive of faith with its necessary condition, as though one were to confuse the intellectual evidence of the principles of reason with the sensation that they presuppose.

Luis de Molina (§1600) expressly examined our problem in his *Concordia liberi arbitrii cum gratia*, q. 14, a. 13, a. disp. 38 [*sic*].[210] He responded that the supernaturality

---

[210] See Molina, *Concordia liberi arbitrii cum gratia* (Paris: Lethielleux, 1876), 212–233.

of the act of theological faith does not arise from a formal object that cannot be attained by acquired faith but, rather, solely arises from its efficient principle—namely, from God supernaturally moving [the soul].[211] Likewise, he says that the *habitus* of faith is essentially supernatural inasmuch as it is *per se* infused by God. However, its formal object does not exceed acquired faith.[212] "This doctrine," wrote Fr. Wlodimir Ledóchowski, the Superior General of the Jesuits [from 1915 to 1942], "is among those found in Molina's *Concordia*, which no small number of men said ought to be condemned."[213] The same was acknowledged by Gerhard Schneemann.[214]

JUAN DE RIPALDA (1594–1668), who followed the same opinion, explained it thus: "Intrinsically supernatural acts can rightly be admitted, although as regards their formal objects, they do not differ entitatively from natural acts."[215] Also, he writes elsewhere: "Fallible natural assent and infallible supernatural assent can be moved *by the same formal object*, which have distinct *modes of tending to their objects.*"[216]

GILES DE CONINCK, S.J. (1571–1633) also defended Molina's doctrine on this point, and as we will come to discuss, it was perfected by Juan de Lugo.

It is immediately clear that Molina's doctrine in this matter stands in contradiction with the principle of Aristotle and St. Thomas: *Habitus* and acts are specified by the formal object to which they are essentially ordered. {{457}} And this is not surprising, for this opinion proceeds from two Molinist principles that are essentially opposed to the principles of St. Thomas.

Indeed, (a) according to Molina,[217] God and creatures are related to each other as *coordinated partial causes*, like two men dragging a ship [to shore]. In the natural order, God, by his simultaneous concurrence, causes *the existence* [*esse*] of our act, and the

---

[211] See ibid., 213.

[212] See ibid., ad 3.

[213] Fr. Wlodimir Ledóchowski, S.J. [1866–1942, Superior General of the Jesuits from 1915 to 1942], *De doctrina S. Thomae magis magisque in societate fovenda* (1917), 41. Fr. Ledóchowski, thus speaking about Molina's opinion "concerning the identity of the formal object in natural and supernatural acts," does not hold that it is conformed to St. Thomas's doctrine but, rather, believes that the Angelic Doctor's thesis on this matter (just as with his teaching concerning the real distinction between essence and existence in created beings) must be numbered among those propositions "from which, he says, we are permitted to draw back from for truly grave reasons" (ibid., 39).

[Trans. note: Ledóchowski's letter can be found in Wlodimir Ledóchowski, "Epistola A. R. P. Wlodimiri Ledóchowski: Praepositi Generalis Societatis Jesu: De Doctrina S. Thomae magis magisque in Societate fovenda," *Zeitschrift für katholische Theologie* 42, no. 2 (1918): 205–253.]

[214] See Gerard Schneemann, *Controversiarum de divinae gratiae liberique arbitrii concordia: Initia et progressus* (Friburg: Herder, 1881), 265 (note).

[215] See Ripalda, *De ente supernaturali*, bk. 3, disp. 44, no. 2; disp. 45, no. 37.

[216] *De fide*, disp. 3, sect. 6, no. 71.

[217] See Molina, *Concordia*, pt. 1, q. 14, a. 13, disp. 26, fine.

second cause reduces itself from potency to act all by itself without any previous motion from God. Likewise, in the supernatural order, actual grace is only a partial cause, bringing a supernatural modality to the act of faith. Our intellect, however, by its own natural powers, brings the vitality of this act. Hence, in *Concordia*, q. 14, a. 13, disp. 37 (fine)[218] Molina admits that God, by his absolute power, can make our intellect elicit an act of theological faith without the supernatural light of faith. Nay, according to him, we could even be able to see God without the light of glory. God's special assistance would suffice for such acts through his simultaneous concurrence.

By contrast, for the Thomists, in the natural order, the divine premotion and second causes are two *total causes*, the latter of which *is subordinated* to the former and premoved by it. And they hold the same for supernatural motions as well. And as regards supernatural *habitus*, whether it is a question of the light of faith or the light of glory, all Thomists say that the intellect and the supernatural *habitus* concur as two complete causes, though from different perspectives. The supernatural *habitus* concurs as the complete proximate formal character by which the intellect is elevated and proportioned to the supernatural act, whereas the intellect concurs as the total elicitive principle of the act. The same is true for the will and the *habitus* of charity with respect to [supernatural] love.[219]

(b) From the Molinistic notion of the divine concurrence, another principle follows, from which Molina's conclusion follows, as Billuart notes,[220] one that is related to the preparation for grace, in short: "God does not deny grace to him who does that which lies within the powers of his nature." Indeed, according to Molina, he who does that which lies within the powers of his nature thus disposes himself for grace, and such grace follows infallibly not indeed by the merit of those natural acts (for this would be to fall into the Pelagian heresy) but, rather, from a covenant entered into between God and Christ the Redeemer.

"This opinion," as Billuart says, as well as other Thomists,[221] "does not seem, in our eyes, to draw back sufficiently from the error of the semi-Pelagians, for they did not say that the natural assent, properly speaking, merits the gift of grace but is only an occasion that God would take up so that He may then confer grace."

Hence, Molina's opinion, in itself and in its principles, is radically opposed to the Thomist opinion. The same must be said about the Jesuit theologians who followed Molina, like Coninck, Ripalda,[222] Granadas, and others.

BAÑEZ (†1604) defended the same opinion as Cajetan regarding the ultimate reso-

---

[218] See ibid., p. 216 and 220.

[219] See John of St. Thomas, *Cursus theologicus, In ST* I, q. 12 (On the necessity of the light of glory.) Likewise, see Billuart on the same text.

[220] See Billuart, *Summa sancti Thomae, De gratia,* diss. 3, a. 2, §2.

[221] Ibid.

[222] See Ripalda, *De ente supernaturali,* disp. 45, no. 3.

lution of faith. See *In ST* [II]-II, q. 1, a. 1, dub. 4, p. 14:

> First conclusion: According to the ordinary law [of things], certain external motives are necessary, by which men are induced in a pleasing manner [*suaviter*] to receive *de novo* infused faith or even to believe distinctly the various *credenda*.

> Second conclusion: The assent of our faith cannot be resolved into the acquired faith by which we believe that the Church is trustworthy [*veracem*], as to a rule or the formal reason for believing. This conclusion, says Bañez, is so certain that opposition to it seems to us not only to be rash but even erroneous and against what we must hold on faith.

> Third conclusion: The testimony of the Church, inasmuch as she is ruled by the Holy Spirit and inasmuch as {{458}} one of the articles of faith is to believe in the Holy and Catholic Church, is that in which our faith is resolved, in the end, for the distinction and explanation of things to be believed in.

> Fourth conclusion: "That the Church is the infallible rule for proposing and explaining the truths of the faith cannot be reduced to the authority of the Church herself. For this would be a self-referential confirmation. Rather, we must reduce this assent *to the testimony of the Holy Spirit*[223] *inclining us through the light of faith* to this thing to be believed: The Church cannot err. . . . Thus, *the ultimate resolution of faith and of the act of faith is made to the Holy Spirit who reveals.*"

Moreover, in treating of the object of sacred theology in *ST* I, q. 1, a. 7, Bañez clearly says that by the natural light of reason alone God is known as the Author of nature, not as the Author of grace.

SUAREZ (†1617) follows St. Thomas, Capreolus, and Cajetan against the nominalists, Scotus, and Molina, refuting the theory of discursive faith. Indeed, he asserts that divine revelation is *that which* we supernaturally believe as well as *that by which* we believe,[224] likewise asserting that the formal motive of infused faith is essentially distinct from the formal motive of acquired faith.[225] Nay, as regards the necessity of the internal grace of faith, he adds that to say that this grace "is only required so that the assent may be

---

[223] [Trans. note: Reading "ad testimonium Spiritus Sancti inclinantis" for "ad testimonium Spiritu Sancti inclinantis."]

[224] Suarez, *De fide*, pt. 1, disp. 3, sect. 6, 8, and 12, nos. 7–14; disp. 6, sect. 4.

[225] Suarez, *De gratia*, bk. 2, ch. 11, nos. 11–13, 17, 21–23.

more perfect in its being [*in genere entis*], although it would not be necessary by virtue of its object, draws rather close to what Pelagius said, namely that grace is required only for enabling us to perform our actions more easily. Likewise, it seems to be a kind of evasion devised solely for the sake of escaping the testimony of the Councils and the Fathers."[226]

And later on:

> Certain people respond that those acts (acquired faith and infused faith) are formally and essentially distinct through their entities and do not require us to seek out anything formally distinct on the side of the object. However, this represents nothing else than the complete overturning of the principle of the distinction of acts on the basis of their objects, as well as the whole of the philosophy that teaches that motions and everything else that essentially includes a relationship to something else, whether predicamentally or transcendentally, has its *species*—and hence, its distinction—from the *termini* or objects that they are concerned with.[227]

Later on, the Würzburg Jesuits[228] and many other theologians followed Suarez on this matter.

This thesis concerning the essential supernaturality of the formal object of faith was not invented by Suarez, as many say today. It is the Thomistic thesis, as Suarez himself said. However, in his eclectic spirit, he did not explain how this thesis is to be reconciled with the notion of simultaneous concurrence [in causality] and that of [man's] active obediential potency [for the supernatural order],[229] which do agree with Molinism. Moreover, Suarez seems to say that three acts of faith are necessary: First the trustworthiness of God is believed in, then revelation, and third the Trinity. However, it is impossible to believe, by divine faith, in the trustworthiness of God before revelation is believed in. In reality, as Capreolus had said, by one and the same act,[230] we believe in revelation and in the mysteries.[231]

---

[226] Ibid., no. 17.

[227] Ibid., no. 22–23.

[228] Wirceburgenses, *De virtutibus theologicis*, disp. 2, ch. 3, a. 3.

[229] According to the Thomists, as Billuart says in *Summa sancti Thomae, De deo*, diss. 4, a. 5, §3: "This active obediential potency implies a contradiction, for it would be natural and supernatural at one and the same time. It is natural because it would be congenital to all natural agents and follows upon their nature as a property. It is supernatural because it is immediately ordered to a supernatural effect. Moreover, this active obediential potency would destroy the entire order of grace, for having posited this potency, grace would be superfluous, given that all the supernatural effects that are attributed to grace and the other supernatural habitus could possibly be done through this active obediential potency."

[230] [Trans. note: Reading *actu* for *actum*.]

[231] See *ST* II-II, q. 2, a.2, ad 1.

TOMÁS DE LEMOS, O.P. (1555–1629), in the famed discussions of the *Congregatio de Auxiliis*, on May 7 and 28, 1604, before Pope Clement VIII, as is related by Serry,[232] fought against {{459}} Molina's opinion: "This system overturns faith just as it does philosophy. It overturns faith because God is loved and feared by the powers of nature as the supernatural end, and it overturns philosophy because from this agreement, the formal object of a superior *habitus* is attained by inferior powers."[233] And, on May 29, 1604, the fifty-fourth congregation resolved the proposed doubt in accord with the Thomists' interpretation as exposited by Lemos.[234]

At the beginning of the fourth book of his *Panoplia gratiae*, Lemos shows that "the acts of the infused virtues are essentially supernatural, so that such acts can attain supernatural objects and be of the same order as them."[235]

And, in the same place, he says against Molina:

> The utter impossibility of (Molina's) position is clear from the fact that they say that in one and the same act of the will *the entire substance and species of the act,* as proceeding from the will, *is natural.* However, they assert that as immediately flowing through grace from God into that action, as it were, it is *clothed or plastered over with such supernaturality* and thus constitutes a *per accidens* composition in the very act of the will, much more than one thing would be brought about *per accidens* from a wall and whiteness. *Such a per accidens composition is opposed to* [*repugnat*] *a simple act of faith and charity....*[236] Moreover, *grace would not be simpliciter necessary but would only be needed in order to make* (belief) *easier, as Pelagius contended once upon a time.*

This would bring all of philosophy to ruin, for if natural reason could attain a formally supernatural object, then the senses could attain an intelligible object, thus destroying all of the proofs of the spirituality[237] of the soul.

In the end, Lemos approved the interpretation of the Councils' words, "As is needed for salvation," proposed by Suarez and St. Robert Bellarmine.

DIEGO ALVAREZ, O.P., (1550–1635) in 1610 in *De auxiliis divinae gratiae*

---

[232] See Jacques-Hyacinthe Serry, *Historia congregationem de auxiliis* (Louvain, 1699), bk. 3, chs. 35–36.

[233] See ibid., 406.

[234] See ibid., 410.

[235] Ibid., nos. 24 and 25.

[236] Certain other theologians, fighting against Molina's theory, say: "It is a supernatural plating, as something is called "gold plated" in order to designate an object made of copper or white metal covered over with a laminated sheet of gold."

[237] [Trans. note: Following what he says elsewhere, I am reading *spiritualitatis* for *supernaturalitatis*.]

defended the same opinion as Lemos and provided a most excellent treatment of the vitality of supernatural faith.[238] Hence, Alvarez concludes in disp. 63, no. 7: "When it has an equally strong *habitus* of faith, a stronger intellect does not, however, more deeply penetrate the mysteries of faith."[239] Also, in disp. 56, no. 18: "The mysteries of faith are known through *natural species as elevated by the aid of grace*, for just as nature itself is presupposed materially for grace as its receptive subject that is perfected and elevated by grace, so too we can say, all due proportions maintained [*proportionaliter*], intelligible species in nature are, as it were, *materially* presupposed though elevated through the aid of grace so that they may be of service to faith."

Antonin Regnault, O.P. (†1676), In his *De mente Concilii Tridentini circa gratiam efficacem*, 1674, speaks in the same way. See pt. 2, ch. 28 and pt. 1, ch. 19 against Molina, who wrongly [*sinister*] interprets the Council of Orange's words, "as is necessary for salvation."

John of St. Thomas (†1664) in general defends the idea that the formal motive of the infused virtues cannot be attained without supernatural grace. See *Cursus theologicus, De gratia*, vol. 5, disp. 20, a. 1, no. 7. Also, see ibid., solv. arg, no. 4: "Something is only called supernatural *quoad substantiam* when it is supernatural *quoad speciem*, which is taken from the formal object." And see no. 7: "The very vitality is supernatural in these acts (of the infused virtues) because they proceed from a vital power, as elevated [by grace]." Likewise, see no. 9:

> Objection. The act of faith does not only proceed from the intellect as from its radical principle but also proceeds from *species* of the natural order, for supernatural *species* are not infused into us for the act of faith. Therefore, likewise, on the side of its proximate principle, that act will be natural.

> Response: This makes even more manifest the supernaturality of acts in the Beatific Vision which will proceed from supernatural principles as regards

---

[238] See the index of this work at the words "supernaturale" and "fides".

[239] [Trans. note: This text is presented in the original in a very terse format: "intellectus melior, cum aequali habitu fidei, non melius penetrat mysteria fidei." The full text found in the 1610 Roman edition published by Stephen Paulinus (available at https://babel.hathitrust.org/cgi/pt?id=ucm.531909450x) is as follows (p. 456): "Ad tertium respondetur, meliorem intellectum, cum aequali habitu fidei, non melius penetrare ea, quae per se pertinent ad fidem, quam alium habentem intellectum minus perfectum, si uterque utatur habitu secundum ultimum potentiae. [To the third, we must respond that a more powerful intellect, having an equally strong *habitus* of faith, does not more deeply penetrate those things that *per se* pertain to faith than does someone having a less perfect intellect, if both make us of the *habitus* of faith to the full extent of its power.]" Marginally, the text explains this: "Intellectus melior cum aequali auxilio non melius penetrat quae sunt fidei. [A more powerful intellect with equal aid (i.e., of grace) does not more deeply penetrate those things which are of faith.]"]

{{460}} both the light [i.e., of glory] and the *species* [i.e., the divine essence seen in itself]. Nonetheless, to this point, *the entire substance of the act of faith is supernatural* because *even though those species, of themselves, belong to the natural order, nonetheless they are coordinated and combined* in order to form a judgment or propositions of faith. And this coordination is brought about by the supernatural light of faith. Thus, said representation is complex and is *supernatural* through the mode of a truth that is handed on [*per modum veritatis traditae*]. Hence, the light of prophecy and of faith do not only elevate the power to elicit the act of assent but also *order the species* to represent revealed truths in a complex manner [i.e., in enunciations formed by the second operation of the intellect]. And therefore, in *ST* II-II, q. 173, a. 2, ad 3, St. Thomas says, "In order for the *species* or forms to be ordered to represent intelligible truths that exceed man's intellect, the aid of a supernatural light is needed," and in *ST* II-II, q. 1, a. 2, ad 2: "The act of the believer does not terminate at the enunciable proposition but, rather, at reality (i.e., at the supernatural mystery). For we form enunciations only so that we may have knowledge about things through them, both in science and in faith."[240]

Likewise, in the treatise on faith, q. 1, disp. 1, a. 2, no. 1, John of St. Thomas says:

> Is it clear that God has spoken to us infallibly? The whole difficulty lies in this question, for if it is clear that the Church speaks, we still must ask how we are certain that the Church cannot be deceived. And we reduce this again to the fact that God said that the Church cannot be deceived, which involves us in a vicious circle. But if we reduce this to the motives of credibility or to the *miracles* and *signs* by which we are moved to believe we therefore also reduce the whole of belief's infallibility to *something created*, as are miracles and the other signs and motives of credibility which are deduced *through human discourse*.

Then, in no. 6,[241] he responds to this issue, saying:

> *The divine testimony is the formal reason for believing the content of the testimony, as well as for believing the testimony itself.* Now, the Church is the instrument for infallibly proposing, with the assistance of the Holy Spirit, believable things[242] and herself, because *on account of their universality these causes reflect on themselves*, and we do not need to seek out another reason why we believe in the

---

[240] See John of St. Thomas in the same text where he resolves the arguments presented by Molina.

[241] [Trans. note: The original reads 4. In the Vivès edition (vol. 7), this is no. 6.]

[242] [Trans. note: Reading *credibiles* for *credibilis*.]

Church, who thus infallibly proposes, except because she herself says, indeed by the divine testimony, that God speaks thus.

(Immediately before this he had said:) Both of these causes are from God and both have infallibility in different genera [of causality]: the Church as proposing and applying [the revealed truth] like an instrument of God who speaks, and the divine testimony as the formal reason and first authority proposing. Thus, when a king makes a law, he both gives authority to the law so that it may be valid and also gives it to his ministers so that it may be believed [by the people] as proposing a just law. In such a case, the relationship between the two *is not circular because there are different genera of casuality involved in the relationship from the one proposing to the one revealing and vice-versa*,[243] for causes are mutually causes of each other, without involving a vicious circle, as we taught at length in our discussion of Aristotle's *Posterior Analytics* I and *Physics* II, by showing how *causes are causes of each other*,[244] and because they are universal causes that are supreme in their own genera [of causality], each is the formal reason for manifesting itself and the object [manifested] and through itself stands of itself in the line of belief.

Likewise, in art. 3, no. 7:

Just as light is not only the formal character [*ratio*] for seeing colors but also is something seen, so too *the very testimony of God* as from the First Truth is *simultaneously something believed in itself and the reason for believing other things* . . . ; divine faith cannot take its firmness from any knowledge had through the natural light [of reason], since its certitude is of a much more superior kind, namely, supernatural certitude.

Thus, *although by the natural light* [*of reason*] *God is known to be trustworthy*, and by that experience {{461}} see that the Church proposes some things to us to be believed by faith, nonetheless, *faith does not take a kind of firmness* or credibility *from those things, as being known by the natural light* [of reason] or that of experience, but rather, *has its firmness solely from the divine testimony*,

---

[243] [Trans. note: Following the Vivès edition, reading "a proponente ad revelationem et a revelante ad proportionem [*sic*]" as "a proponente ad revelantem, et a revelante ad proponentem."]

[244] The end in intention moves the agent, whereas the agent produces or pursues the end in execution. Matter sustains the form and is contained by the form. Likewise, the will moves the intellect as regards execution but is moved by the intellect as regards specification. Similarly, a principal cause moves an instrument and the instrument disposes for the effect of the principal cause. Thus, the Church is the instrument of God who reveals.

even though those things that are known by the natural light [of reason] can be presupposed for faith as certain remote dispositions or [*seu*] something removing an impediment [to faith].

Likewise, in no. 7 of the same text, John of Saint Thomas notes, against Suarez, that we do not believe "God has spoken," "God is trustworthy [*verax*]," and "God is Triune," by three distinct acts but, rather, believe these [three] together by a single act.[245]

CARDINAL JUAN DE LUGO, S.J., (†1660) says that he holds a middle place between contrary opinions. On the one hand, he teaches, "When speaking *about possibility*, it is not contradictory to say that the acts of a natural virtue and an infused virtue are not distinct from the perspective of their material or formal object,"[246] and thus in this matter speaks along the lines of Molina. However, on the other hand, he admits that supernatural acts are always *de facto* distinct from natural acts as regards[247] their formal object, because God in fact [*de facto*] always concurs with supernatural grace in salvific acts. Indeed, Cardinal de Lugo says, "I respond that: Although the motive object of faith could *of itself* terminate a natural act, *in fact* the intellect as a rule elicits only a supernatural assent. Now, the reason for this is that *God in fact has willed* that faith be the principle of supernatural merit, as we will see below. Therefore, with a sufficient proposition of the motive of faith, God does not concur with a natural act but, instead with a supernatural one, which is proportioned to meriting eternal life."[248]

Hence, according to de Lugo, God's authority is self-evidently known from the apprehension of the terms [of the given proposition], and the fact of revelation is known, at least obscurely, from miracles, which in a certain sense, are the voice of God.[249] And this twofold knowledge, which *of itself* can be merely natural, would always *de facto* bring about supernatural faith in believers on account of God's supernatural help. Thus, the Church's proposing [of revelation], confirmed by miracles, according to Cardinal de Lugo, pertains to the formal motive of faith, and in this respect, he returned to Durandus's doctrine. In the nineteenth century, Cardinal Franzelin[250] followed de Lugo against Suarez.

However, a great difficulty remains: How could some act be *essentially* supernatural in a way that is merely *de facto*? Essences abstract from contingent facts, [at least] according to sound philosophy. This makes it clear that de Lugo's doctrine contains a kind of *contingentism*, like the doctrine of Molina and Scotus. If this were so, the senses could *of themselves* attain the object of the intellect, even though *de facto* they do not. This would

---

[245] See John of St. Thomas, *Cursus theologicus, In ST* I, q. 1, disp. 1, a. 1, nos. 24 and 25.

[246] Juan de Lugo, *De fide*, disp. 9, sect. 1, no. 3 and disp. 1, sec. 1, no. 77; sect. 7, no. 116.

[247] [Trans. note: Reading *quod* as *quoad*.]

[248] Ibid., disp. 9, sect. 1, no. 20. See Vacant, *Études*, vol. 2, 75.

[249] See ibid., disp., 1, sect. 1, no. 77, 100, and 104; disp. 1, sect. 7, no. 116, 123, and 129.

[250] See Franzelin, *De divina traditione*, 602 and 616.

bring to ruin the necessity of the proof of the spirituality of our soul, and we would need to say what Scotus in fact did say: The immortality of the soul is certain by faith alone, for we cannot prove that the soul is incorruptible "naturally and without a miracle."[251]

The SALMANTICENSES, O.C.D., (1631–1679) finally examined all of the theories about the supernaturality of saving acts, infused virtues, and in particular the act of faith, judging these theories according to the most certain principles of St. Thomas, especially refuting Scotus, the nominalists, Molina, and de Lugo.[252]

Their first conclusion is: "Man by his own powers cannot elicit the assent of theological faith considered in its species or substance."

Their second conclusion is: "It is not possible for there to be an act that is entitatively natural and specifically distinct from the assent of theological faith, with the former sort of act attaining the object of the latter under the same motive."[253] {{462}} This is asserted against Scotus, the nominalists, Molina, de Lugo, Coninck, Granados, [Juan de] Dicastillo, and Ripalda.

The first conclusion is proven (1) from the authority of the Doctors, especially of St. Thomas, and (2) by this principal argument: "By his natural powers, man cannot elicit the assent of faith as is needed for salvation (Synod of Orange and the Council of Trent). However, the assent of theological faith, considered in its species and substance and understood independently of other circumstances [*circumscriptis*], must be of such a character that it be needed for salvation. Therefore, through his natural powers alone, man cannot elicit the aforementioned assent in its substance and species."[254]

The second conclusion is also proven, first, on the basis of St. Thomas's authority: "When it is a question of the specification of acts, for he always teaches that their formal distinction is taken from their formal objects or motives" (cf. *ST* I, q. 77, a. 3; I-II, q. 109, a. 1; q. 63, a. 4, etc.). And it is proven, secondly, on the basis of this fundamental reason: "Acts having the same material and formal objects, or [the same] objects *quod* and *quo*, are of the same species. However, the assent of infused faith and the assent of natural faith cannot be of the same species. Thus, they cannot have the same material and formal objects, or [the same] object *quod* and *quo*. Therefore, natural assent cannot attain the same object of supernatural assent under the same motive."[255]

What therefore must be said about de Lugo's doctrine: "By God's absolute power, a natural act can attain the formal motive of infused faith, though this never *de facto* happens"?

---

[251] Scotus, *In* IV *Sent.*, d. 43, q. 2, no. 23.

[252] See Salmanticenses, *Cursus theologicus*, *De gratia*, disp. 3, dub. and 3; *De fide*, disp. 1, dub. 4 and 5.

[253] See ibid., *De gratia*, vol. 14, disp. 3, dub. 3, nos. 28, 37, 40, 45, 48, 49, 52, 60, 61.

[254] Ibid., disp. 3, dub. 3, no. 28.

[255] Ibid., no. 48.

We must respond with the Salmanticenses: "Specification leaves out of consideration any given disposition of things, whether absolute or ordinate [*ordinaria*], and only is concerned with what belongs to quidditative predicates considered in themselves, inasmuch as they take precedence over any executive disposition [that may come to them thereafter]. . . . And therefore, we must firmly hold that acts are specified in any species and distinct through their formal objects and, consequently, specifically distinct acts cannot attain through some power the same formal object."[256]

Immediately before this, the Salmanticenses set forth Molina and de Lugo's objection that "in order for acts to be distinct in species, it suffices that there be a diversity of active principles, although they attain the same formal object." They respond to this

> by denying the antecedent, for if this were true, as our adversaries contend, then nothing in true philosophy would remain unwavering concerning the species and the distinction of powers and *habitus*. Likewise, we would be compelled to establish a new foundation that was not taught by Aristotle, St. Thomas, and the other leaders of the school. And while younger theologians may admit this with ease, we would have no leader from among the ancients. This would fall immediately into the greatest loss of true wisdom; Thus, with regard to this matter, it is necessary to hinder them with all our strength.[257]

Therefore, the Salmanticenses conclude, like all the preceding Thomists: The formal motive of faith—that is, the First Truth who reveals—cannot be naturally known but is simultaneously *that which* and *that by which* we supernaturally believe.[258]

However, [our] adversaries *object*: The formal motive of faith is nothing other than the authority of God actually revealing. Now, the authority of God—that is, his infallibility and utter trustworthiness—is evident solely to the [natural] light of reason, and the fact of revelation is manifested through utterly certain signs—that is, through naturally knowable miracles. Therefore, the formal motive of faith can be known by reason alone. Nay, if it were only believed, belief would involve a vicious circle because evident credibility would be lacking.

The Salmanticenses *respond*:

> {{463}} The proper motive of theological faith is the testimony of God as the supernatural Author and End insofar as He founds supernatural certitude. *However, even though man through his natural powers can rely upon the*

---

[256] Ibid., no. 60.

[257] Ibid.

[258] See ibid., tr. 14, disp. 3, dub. 3, §4, no. 45; likewise, see no. 4; *De fide*, disp. 1, dub. 5, nos. 163 and 193.

testimony of God the natural Author and End, inasmuch as it founds natural certitude, *nonetheless, precisely through those powers he cannot believe by relying on the aforementioned [natural] testimony in order to know the testimony of God the supernatural Author and End* founding supernatural certitude. . . . And thus, the testimony of God can be considered from two perspectives. In one respect, it can be considered as coming from God as the supernatural principle directing man to his supernatural end, by which means it founds the infallibility of the supernatural order. From another perspective, it can be considered as coming from God as the natural principle directing creatures to their natural end, on account of which it founds infallibility of the natural order.[259]

(And they add:) We are taught that the aforementioned distinction is admitted and explained on the basis of those things that theologians commonly teach in a similar difficulty. For the supreme goodness of God in Himself has no less indivisibility than does the utter and infallible certitude of the divine testimony, and this no less holds for God in Himself and for Himself [*nec minus ac ista convenit Deo in se et ad se*]. And nonetheless, *God's twofold love for all things is commonly admitted,* . . . one being natural, the other supernatural. Of course, that indivisible goodness of God . . . inasmuch as it founds a communication in natural goods with creatures is thus the motive specifying the natural love of God. . . . And inasmuch as it founds a communication in supernatural goods with the rational creature, it is thus a motive specifying the supernatural love of charity . . . (*ST* I-II, q. 109, a. 3, ad 1). Nearly the same thing happens in religion. . . . A twofold religion is commonly and necessarily distinguished, one being natural, which man would have had if he were created in a purely natural state[260] and even much more so if he were to exist in the state of natural integrity, and the other being infused, which is found in those who have grace.[261]

Nay, as was said above, Baius was condemned on account of his denial of this distinction, saying: "The distinction of a twofold love of God, namely, a *natural* love whose object is God *as the Author of nature* and a gratuitous love whose object is God *as beatifying* is meaningless and imaginary; it has been devised as a mockery of the Sacred Scriptures and

---

[259] Ibid., *De gratia*, vol. 14, disp. 3, dub. 3, no. 40. These points make it quite clear how greatly certain historians err in confusing the doctrine of the Salmanticenses with that of de Lugo and his disciples. The author of the article "Foi" in the *Dictionnaire de théologie catholique* (col. 491) fell into this error.

[260] [Trans. note: In Fr. Garrigou-Lagrange's text, this is "si concedetur in putis naturalibus"; in the 1878 edition of the Salmanticenses, this is "si conderetur in puris."]

[261] Ibid., no. 42.

of the numerous testimonies of ancient authors."[262]

This classical distinction can be found in St. Thomas's writings as well as those of the later Thomists, and Suarez does not heed it well enough in this question. Also, all theologians admit that *providence* can be considered in two ways. On the one hand, there is *the providence of God, the Author of nature*, which is proven by reason alone from the order of the world and from the fact that God the Author of intelligences is himself intelligent. However, by faith alone we know of *the supernatural providence of God the Author of grace and glory*, which orders supernatural means to salvation.

Likewise, the First Truth who reveals can be considered in two ways, and although according to St. Thomas, one and the same thing cannot be scientifically known and believed by one and the same person from the same perspective, nonetheless, the First Truth who reveals can be known with certainty and believed in supernaturally. This is explained by St. Thomas himself in particular in his commentary on John, ch. 5, lect. 6, no. 9:

> *God testifies to something in a twofold* manner, namely sensibly and intelligibly. He does so sensibly just as through a sensible voice (and miracles). . . . However, He testifies intelligibly by inspiring in the hearts of some what they ought to believe and hold. . . . Therefore, you (i.e., the Pharisees) were able to receive the first kind of testimony, and no wonder, for those voices (and miracles) were from God only *effectively*. However, [you were not able to receive] the intelligible meaning of that voice: "Neither have you heard His voice at any time. . . . And you have not His word abiding in you" (John 5:36–37, DR), that is, you did not have the interiorly inspired word.

{{464}} Likewise, St. Thomas had said in his commentary on John, ch. 3, lect. 2, no. 1:

> It must be said that, according to St. Augustine, *the Holy Spirit is a twofold voice*. One is that by which He speaks *inwardly* within man's heart. And this voice is heard only by *believers* and the saints, as is said in Psalm 84:9 (DR): "I will hear what the Lord God will speak in me." The other voice is that by which the Holy Spirit speaks in the Scriptures or *through preachers*, as is said in Matthew 10:20 (DR): "For it is not you that speak, but the spirit of your Father that speaketh in you." And even *nonbelievers* and sinners hear this voice.

Therefore, the unbelieving Pharisees saw the miracles and heard *the letter of the Gospel*, but they did not hear *the voice of the Heavenly Father*.

Hence, Jesus said in John 5:36–37 (DR): "The works which the Father hath given me to perfect . . . give testimony of me . . . and the Father himself who hath sent me hath

---

[262] Pius V, *Ex omnibus afflictionibus*, no. 34 (Denzinger, no. 1934).

given testimony of me: *neither have you heard his voice at any time.*" John 10:26–27 (DR): "But you do not believe, because you are not of my sheep. *My sheep hear my voice.*" John 6:45 (DR): "Everyone that hath *heard [from] the Father* and hath learned cometh to me." John 18:37 (DR): "Every one that is of the truth *heareth my voice.*" And 1 John 5:10 (DR): "He that believeth in the Son of God hath the testimony of God in himself."

Hence, in conveying this distinction between God the Author of nature and God the Author of grace, the Salmanticenses do not propose a new doctrine but instead, arguing against the changes expressed by Molina and de Lugo, set forth, with utter clarity and profundity, St. Thomas's genuine teaching. Indeed, an infinite distance separates naturally knowing the divine origin of Christianity on the basis of miracles—that is, seeing in miracles *the seal of the Author of nature*—and on the other hand, *supernaturally hearing the voice of the Heavenly Father through the Son and the Holy Spirit.* Hence, St. Thomas had said excellently and with a loftiness of spirit, affirming the sublimity of our faith: "Our faith has its authority neither from angels, nor from any miracles, but rather, from the revelation of the Father through the Son and the Holy Spirit, although . . . many miracles were performed to strengthen the faith."[263] "But we have this treasure in earthen vessels, that the excellency may be of the power of God and not of us" (2 Cor 4:7, DR).

After the Salmanticenses, the same doctrine was set forth by the Thomists *Goudin, Gonet,*[264] *Billuart,*[265] *Gotti,*[266] *Lepidi,*[267] *Zigliara,*[268] *de Groot,*[269] *Gardeil,*[270] *del Prado,*[271] and *de Poulpiquet.*[272] Also, it was set forth quite excellently, as we said above, by *Schaezler*[273] and *Scheeben.*[274] Likewise, more recently, see {{465}} *Guido Mattiussi, S.J.,*[275]

---

[263] St. Thomas, *Contra errores Graecorum*, ch. 30.

[264] Goudin, *Tract. theol. de Gratia*, q. 3, a. 2, §2, concl. 2nd fin. (ed. Louvain, p. 157). This text clearly employs against Molina the distinction between God the Author of nature and God the Author of Grace. Gonet, O.P., *Clypeus Thomisticus*, De gratia, disp. 1, a. 2, nos. 78, 79, and 83; *De fide*, disp. 1, a. 2, no. 55.

[265] Billuart, O.P., *Summa sancti Thomae, De gratia*, diss. 3, a. 2, §2; *De fide*, diss. 1, a. 1, obj. 3, inst. 1.

[266] Gotti, O.P., *De fide*, tr. 9, dub. 4, §2 (against the theory of discursive faith).

[267] Lepidi, O.P., *Elementa philosophiae Christianae*, vol. 1, p. 31–34.

[268] Cardinal Zigliara, O.P., *Propaedeutica ad sacred theologiam*, bk. 1, ch. 16, no. 10, p. 105.

[269] De Groot, O.P., *De ecclesia*, q. 22, a. 3, 836 and 837.

[270] Gardeil, *La crédibilité et l'apologétique*, 2nd ed. (Paris: Lecoffre, 1912), 61–92, 96, etc. Also, his article, "Crédibilité" in the *Dictionnaire de théologie catholique*. Likewise, throughout *Le donné revélé et la théologie*.

[271] Del Prado, O.P., *De gratia* (Fribourg, CH: 1907), vol. 1, 12; vol. 2, 41–45.

[272] De Poulpiquet, O.P., *L'objet intégrale de l'apologétique* (1912), 433–498.

[273] Schaezler, *Neue Untersuchungen über das Dogma von der Ganod und das Wesen des christlichen Glaubens*, 527ff.

[274] Scheeben, *Dogmatik*, vol. 1, §40, nos. 681, 689ff and §44, nos. 779–805.

[275] *Rivista di filosofia neo-scolastica* (Dec. 1918): 416–419.

and Giuseppe *Petazzi*.[276] Suarez's teaching has been defended by *Wilmers*[277] and, with some modification, by *Mazzela*[278] and *Christian Pesch*.[279]

By contrast, the opinion of Molina and de Lugo has been defended by *Franzelin*,[280] *van der Meersch*,[281] *Francisco Schmid*,[282] *Müllendorff*,[283] and a number of others.[284]

Jean-Baptiste-Henri Dominique Lacordaire most excellently developed the Thomistic opinion in an apologetic language.[285]

§6. Proof of the Thomist Position

Based on the preceding historical exposition, the Thomistic position [*sententia*] on this matter is clear; namely, *divine revelation, as proceeding from God the Author of grace and constituting the formal motive of faith, is both that which we believe and that by which we believe*, although, as we will say below, the fact of revelation, as something modally supernatural and confirmed

---

[276] See the series of articles, "Crediblità e fede" in *Scuola cattolica* (1909).

[277] *De fide divina* (1902), 352, 358, and 375.

[278] *De gratia*, d. 1, a. 2; *De virt. infusis*, 3rd ed., 13 and 429.

[279] *De gratia*, nos. 69, 71, and 410.

[280] *De divina traditione*, 4th ed., 602–628.

[281] *De gratia*, 219; *De fide*, 62.

[282] *Innsbrucker Zeitschrift* (1888): 435–459.

[283] Ibid., (1893): 44ff; (1894): 203–335.

[284] Cardinal Billot, *De virtutibus infuses* (1905), 291ff. He partially draws back from de Lugo and partially follows him. See 72–84.

[285] See *Jean-Baptiste-Henri Dominique Lacordaire*, 17th conference, 343–347 (ed. in 8°): "What takes place within us when we believe is a phenomenon of intimate and superhuman light. I do not, of course, mean that external things do not act upon us as rational motives of certitude. Rather, the very act of this *supreme certitude* of which I speak directly affects us like a luminous phenomenon. No, let us go further: it affects us like a *transluminous phenomenon*. . . . We are affected by a transluminous light. . . . If something else happened, how could there be a *proportion* between our adherence, which would be natural and rational, and an object that surpasses nature and reason?" (p. 335)

"The supernatural certitude of faith is an illiterate, transluminous conviction which excludes doubt" (p. 336).

"(Thus), in a single moment, a sympathetic intuition places between two men something that logic could not have placed there after many years. Thus, on occasion, a sudden illumination lights upon the mind of a genius" (p. 346).

"A convert will tell you: 'I read, I reasoned, I willed, and I did not arrive at belief. Then, one day, in a way that I cannot explain, at the corner of a road, next to my fireplace, I cannot recall where, I was no longer the same. I believed. Then I read anew, I meditated, I confirmed my faith through reason. However, what took place within me at the final moment when I reached this conviction is something of a completely different nature than what had preceded that. . . .' Remember well the two disciples who walked upon the road to Emmaus" (p. 353). This entire conference deserves to be read, especially regarding *humble prayer* for obtaining grace.

by miracles, can be naturally known, just as the trustworthiness of God the Author of nature is naturally known.

This position is proven in three ways: (1) on account of the objective infallibility required in faith's knowledge, (2) on account of its infallibility (or subjective firmness), and (3) on account of its essential supernaturality.

(1) *On account of the objective infallibility of faith*

The fact of revelation is not only proposed with moral certitude based upon history that tells of the miracles of Christ but, rather, is infallibly proposed by the Church, who also defines that this revelation was properly supernatural and did not proceed naturally from the subconscious of the prophets, and was confirmed not by marvels, which ought to be rejected as myths, but, rather, by miracles {{466}} properly so called, which are judged in the end by the Church with a certitude that is superior to natural certitude.[286] Now, that which is handed on by the Church infallibly must be believed by all supernaturally. Therefore, the faithful must supernaturally believe the fact of revelation on which the whole of faith is founded; otherwise they would not have *objectively infallible certitude* concerning this fact and, hence, about the revealed mysteries, a certitude that is essentially superior to every form of natural certitude.[287] The formal motive of faith moves only *as known*, and it does not infallibly move unless it is infallibly united to our intellect.

Allow me to explain. Human reason can, of course, be mistaken, not in natural knowledge of the first principles but with regard to conclusions, indeed all the more so to the degree that such conclusions are more remote from the principles. It is not always easy to distinguish a true miracle from a diabolic illusion, or to verify the historical value of the narratives by which miracles are spoken of to us. Moreover, this verification is not possible for many believers who know the signs of revelation only on the testimony of their pastors or their parents. By contrast, the Church, like the prophets before her, judges infallibly concerning the existence of revelation and proposes it as a dogma, just as she proposes her own infallibility.

According to St. Thomas, it is not contradictory to naturally believe the fact of revelation on the basis of historically certain signs and, simultaneously, to believe in it in accord with the Church's infallible proposition, for he himself said in *ST* III, q. 55, a. 5c and ad 2–3 that the apostles simultaneously knew of Christ's Resurrection from sensible signs and believed in it on account of the infallible testimony of Christ and the Scriptures. Indeed,

---

[286] See [First] Vatican Council, *Dei filius*, ch. 2 (Denzinger, no. 3004); ibid., can. 3.4 (Denzinger, no. 3034); Pius X, *Pascendi*, nos. 11 (Denzinger, no. 3482).

[287] See *ST* II-II, q. 4, a. 8.

proof by signs does not give intrinsically evidential knowledge of the reality in question and thus does not prevent us from having faith concerning the same object. Moreover, as we will soon discuss, the fact of revelation is attained by faith as something essentially supernatural and not merely modally supernatural.

(2) *On account of the required subjective firmness in knowledge of the motive of faith*

Indeed, believers must adhere to the Church's proposal of the fact of revelation with *certitude (or subjectively infallible firmness)*. Otherwise, they would lack subjective infallibility in their adherence to the revealed mysteries. Now, this firmness, which must exclude every form of deliberate doubt, even to the point of suffering martyrdom for it, essentially transcends natural reason. Therefore, this adherence must essentially proceed from the infused *habitus* of faith, which perfects the intellect "so that it may tend infallibly to its object."[288]

(3) *On account of the essential supernaturality required for this knowledge*

Adherence to the formal motive of faith must be essentially supernatural (or *proportioned to the motive for believing and to the supernatural mysteries*). Therefore, it essentially proceeds from the infused *habitus* of faith.[289]

In order to understand this third reason, we must consider divine revelation from two perspectives: From its loftier and intimate perspective, it is only known by faith, whereas from an inferior and external perspective, it can be naturally known on the basis of [knowledge of] evident miracles. In the first way, it is considered as being *essentially supernatural*—that is, as a *mystery*. In the second way, it is considered as *modally supernatural*—that is, *as a miracle*. {{467}} A similar distinction is commonly given for the fact of Christ's Resurrection or even for Christ's Passion—nay, even for the Church's infallibility and for the divine attributes.[290]

---

[288] *ST* II-II, q. 4, a. 5.

[289] See *ST* II-II, q. 6, a. 1; q. 5, a. 1 and 3.

[290] See ch. 6, a. 2 above, where we discuss how *the supernatural* is divided into the essential supernaturality and the modal supernaturality.

  This distinction is of great use in explaining the Lord's words to the apostle Thomas in John 20:29 (DR): "*Because thou hast seen me, Thomas, thou hast believed*: blessed are they that have not seen and have believed." In his commentary on this text in John, St. Thomas says, "He sees one thing and believes something else. He sees the man and the scars and on the basis of this believes in the divinity of Him who has resurrected." Likewise, see *ST* II-II, q. 1, a. 4, ad 1 and III, q. 55, a. 5, ad 3. In other words, Thomas naturally knew on the basis of the scars the *miracle* of the Resurrection but believed *the mystery* of the Resurrection of the very Son of God. The external facts of Christ's life were visible inasmuch as they pertained to Christ as a man but were mysteries inasmuch as they pertained to the

This distinction holds as much for *active* revelation as for *passive* revelation,[291] for God could have chosen to reveal only the natural truths of religion, in which case both active and passive revelation would have been *only modally* supernatural. However, he has, in fact, revealed supernatural mysteries, meaning that both active and passive revelation are essentially supernatural, though it can be naturally considered solely as being modally supernatural in its production—namely, as being confirmed by miracles,[292] just as supernatural revelation of solely natural truths of religion would have been confirmed.

With these distinctions in place, the third argument is set forth as follows:

Revelation, qua formal motive of essentially supernatural faith, must itself be essentially supernatural.

Now, that which is essentially supernatural can only, as such, be known supernaturally—that is, through supernatural faith while we do not have the

---

Incarnate Word of God.

For example, *Christ's death upon the cross* was a sensible fact. However, the infinite value of this death is an essentially supernatural mystery. Even many rationalists affirm that Christ loved men in a heroic manner and gave them the ultimate example of courage. However, it is only by supernatural faith that we formally hold that Christ's love in dying upon the Cross was essentially supernatural, nay, theandric. Indeed, the demon believes this by natural faith but only in a material way, like the dog materially hearing the sensible sound of speech without understanding its intelligible meaning.

Likewise, the *Church's infallibility* in some way is made manifest to reason through the notes of the Church. However, considered in its intimate nature, it is essentially a dogma of faith.

Similarly, according to St. Thomas, *the unity of God the* Author of nature is demonstrated [by reason alone], but his unity as a Trinity [of Persons] is held by faith alone. See *De veritate*, q. 14, a. 9, ad 8.

Likewise, the *goodness* of God the Author of nature specifies our natural love of God, whereas the goodness of God the Author of grace and glory specifies charity. See *ST* I-II, q. 109, a. 3, ad 1. Also see Pius V, *Ex omnibus afflictionibus*, no. 34 (Denzinger, no. 1934).

Likewise, *the excellence of God* the Author of nature founds natural religion, whereas the excellence of God the Author of grace and glory founds supernatural religion.

[291] As we said above, *active revelation* is the eternal divine action itself, which is identical with the divine essence. It is the First Truth in [the act of] speaking. However, this uncreated action is made manifest *ad extra* inasmuch as it produces an effect first in the mind of the prophet and inasmuch as God speaks to us through the prophet. However, *passive revelation* is the hearing of the divine testimony, either by an immediate, interior hearing by the prophet himself or by a mediated hearing by believers.

If God had revealed only the natural truths of religion, both active and passive revelation would have been only *effectively* supernatural (that is, modally supernatural, through efficient causality, in action and passion) like the miracles by which it would have been confirmed. However, since God has revealed supernatural mysteries, both active and passive revelation are *formally* supernatural as is the mystery thus revealed.

[292] [Trans. note: Reading *miraculis* for *miraculi*.]

light of glory.

{{468}} Therefore, revelation, as the formal motive of faith, is simultaneously that which we believe as well as that by which we believe.

(1) *The major premise* is proven in two ways: (A) from the perspective of the object and of God who reveals and (B) from the perspective of our faith.

A. *From the perspective of the object and of God who reveals.* For in order to reveal not only natural truths but also supernatural mysteries, God must act not [only] as the free Author of nature but [also] as the Author of the supernatural order of grace and glory. In other words, he must act according to his intimate life. Otherwise, the order of agents would not correspond to the order of ends, and the divine action would be of an inferior order in relation to the object revealed. Hence, Sacred Scripture calls revelation, which manifests to us the supernatural mysteries of the heavenly kingdom, the voice of the Heavenly Father through the Son and the Holy Spirit, for it is not a merely miraculous intervention by God the Author of Nature.

B. *From the perspective of our faith.* The formal motive of faith cannot be of an inferior order in relation to the virtue specified by it. Now, our faith, by which we believe in the supernatural mysteries, is essentially supernatural, and this has been conceded by all theologians from the time of the Council of Trent. Therefore, the formal motive of faith is essentially supernatural.

(2) *The minor premise is*: Now, that which is essentially supernatural cannot, as such, be known except supernaturally—that is, through supernatural faith—while we do not have the light of glory.

This minor premise is likewise proven in two ways: (A) from the perspective of the object and (B) from that of the subject.

A. *From the perspective of the object.* Truth and being are [transcendentally] convertible. Hence, that which is entitatively supernatural (or essentially supernatural) is also supernatural from the perspective of its knowability. Hence, it cannot be naturally known formally as such.

B. *From the perspective of the subject.* Were this not the case, the supernatural certitude of infallible faith would rest formally and intrinsically upon the natural certitude of natural, fallible reason and could not be of a higher order.

Certain people immediately object, however: It is not important that knowledge of the formal motive of faith be infallible and supernatural. It suffices that this motive be infallible.

Response: The formal motive of faith does not move as an unknown efficient cause but, rather, moves objectively inasmuch as it is known, doing so infallibly inasmuch as we adhere infallibly to it through grace. Otherwise, our faith would be only hypothetically infallible, that is, upon the supposition that the mysteries were in fact revealed by God

Himself and not invented by man.

Consequently, our conclusion remains: Therefore, revelation, as the formal motive of faith, is simultaneously that which we believe as well as that by which we supernaturally believe.

In this way, the essential supernaturality of faith is preserved, as well as its infallible certitude, which is superior to metaphysical certitude.

However, this proof can be reduced to this: There must be a proportion between the knowing principle (or the faculty elevated through an infused *habitus*), the objective motive (or the formal object *quo*), and the formal object that [*quod*] is manifested and known. Hence, St. Thomas says:

> As the manifestation of bodily vision is brought about through bodily light, so too the manifestation of intellectual vision is brought about through an intellectual light. {{469}} Therefore, it is necessary that manifestation be proportioned to the light by means of which it is effected, just as an effect is proportioned to its cause .... Thus, for knowledge that exists above natural reason, we stand in need of an intellectual light exceeding the natural light of reason.[293]

This is how St. Thomas proves the necessity of the light of prophecy as well as the light of faith.

Hence, just as the sense [of sight] cannot, by sensible light, know of the existence of God or of man's power of free choice, so too reason, by its natural light alone, cannot know that which exceeds reason. For example, in order to infallibly know some given natural future contingent, we stand in need of revelation that is modally supernatural, though not revelation that is essentially supernatural, because such a natural future contingent exceeds our knowledge on account of its contingency but not on account of some kind of intrinsic supernaturality. By contrast, knowledge of the Trinity requires revelation that is essentially supernatural, as well as an internal light proportioned to it.

Thus, we can write the following proportionalities: [see next page]

---

[293] *ST* II-II, q. 171, a. 2.

Knowing principle	Act	Medium (or objective motive)	Object
Habitus of faith	Act of faith	*Essentially* supernatural revelation	Essentially supernatural mystery
Mind of the prophet	Act of prophecy	*Effectively* supernatural revelation	Natural future contingent
Reason	Act of reason	Principles of reason	Conclusion
Sense	Sensation	Sensible light	Color

Supernatural mysteries formally as such can only be known through an essentially supernatural medium. However, if they are known through natural, acquired faith founded on the evidence of miracles, they would thus only be known *materially*, like the dog materially hearing the sound of human speech without understanding its intelligible meaning, or like the student materially hearing some metaphysical principle on account of sensible examples presented to him without thereby perceiving the absolute necessity and universality of the principle, thus physically or empirically hearing that which is *per se* metaphysical. Thus, he who naturally believes the revealed mysteries on account of the evidence of miracles hears in a natural (and, hence, *material*) manner that which is supernatural. He hears the letter, not the spirit.[294]

{{470}} *Thus, we have a resolution for Victor Cousin's objection*, which we set forth in the prologue of this fourth section. Cousin said:

> Philosophy is the light of all lights, the authority of all authorities. Those who wish *to impose a foreign authority upon philosophy and upon thought* do not realize that only one of two things is possible: *Either thought does not under-*

---

[294] See John of St. Thomas, *Cursus theologicus, De gratia*, disp. 20, a. 1, solv. second. arg., no. 5: "A natural act can be concerned with *a supernatural object materially considered*, doing so *from a natural motive and formal reason*. Then it specifically differs from an act that is concerned with the same object *from a supernatural motive and formal reason*." Such has been the common position of the Thomists, as we saw in the history of this problem discussed in the preceding sections. Thus, a solution to the problem has been at hand after the explanations offered by Tomas de Lemos in the *Congregations de auxiliis*, congregation 44, May 29, 1604. See Jacques-Hyacinthe Serry, *Historia congregationem de auxiliis*, bk. 3, ch. 36, 410.

Nay, on the topic of prophecy, St. Thomas says that it is inferior to infused faith: "Although prophecy and faith may be concerned with the same thing, such as Christ's passion, nonetheless, they are not the same, for *faith formally looks* upon the Passion as having *something eternal* in it, that is, inasmuch as God has died, while *looking upon that which is temporal in a material manner, whereas the opposite is the case for prophecy*" (*In III Sent.*, d. 24, q. 1, a. 1, ad 3).

stand this authority—and thus, it is as though such authority did not really exist—*or it does understand it*, forming an idea of it, and accepting it on this score, *thus taking itself as the ultimate measure, rule, and authority.*

We must respond with Fr. Alberto Lepidi, O.P.:

> We must make a distinction regarding the claim that the Christian makes use of reason as a measure, rule, and ultimate authority when he believes. We concede that he does so when he believes *in an entirely natural manner* according to some purely human opinion. However, we deny that this is true when he believes as is necessary [for salvation] *in an entirely supernatural manner....*

> If it is a question of the latter kind of adherence, then neither does the mind adhere to God who reveals on account of the motives of credibility nor is it proper to reason to command the act of faith. For even though the motives of credibility in some way *prepare* the mind for receiving faith, nonetheless, as was said above, *if the Christian believes as is necessary* [for salvation], namely, under a supernatural motion from God, *then having been made forgetful of himself and elevated above himself*, he thus adheres to God, who reveals the truth, so that the first, ultimate, proximate, and sole principle into which faith is resolved is, from the perspective of the *object, the First Truth as revealing* and, from the perspective of the subject, the motion of the Holy Spirit.[295]

Therefore, this certitude is resolved, *not in the light of the first principles of reason* (under whose light the divine trustworthiness and miracles confirming preaching of the Gospel are naturally known) but, rather, objectively *in the uncreated light of active revelation*[296] and subjectively *in the infused light of faith*, by which our intellect is elevated.

Confirmation:

According to the Council of Orange, the Council of Trent, and the [First] Vatican Council, without internal grace, man cannot believe as necessary for salvation. Now, to believe on account of the formal motive of faith is already to believe as is necessary for salvation. Therefore, this formal motive is unattainable without internal grace—that is, without the inspiration and illumination of the Holy Spirit.

---

[295] Lepidi, *Elementa philosophiae christianae*, vol. 1, 33–34.
[296] [Trans. note: Reading *activae* for *active*.]

§7. Resolution of Objections

There are three series of objections: (A) It is not necessary that the motive of faith be believed; (B) it cannot be believed; and (C) it is, in fact, not believed.

A. **First objection series:** *It is not necessary that the formal motive of faith be believed.*

Initial objection: The formal motive of faith is the authority of God who reveals.

Now, the authority of God who reveals is knowable by reason alone and is naturally known by the demons. Therefore, it is not necessary that the motive of faith be believed.

Response: I make a distinction regarding the major premise. I deny that it is the authority of God *the Author of nature*. However, I concede that it is the authority of God *the Author of grace*. I contradistinguish the minor premise, conceding that the authority of God the Author of nature is knowable by reason alone, though denying that the authority of God the Author of the supernatural order is thus knowable.

1. *First urging*: The infallible authority of the divine testimony is founded on the wisdom and goodness of God. Now, God does not have a twofold wisdom in himself, one natural and the other supernatural. Therefore, we cannot distinguish a twofold authority in the divine testimony.

{{471}} *Response*: There is not a twofold goodness in God. Instead, the divine goodness is related to us in two ways—namely, either as being a natural end and the object of our natural love for God or as the supernatural end and the object of charity.[297] Likewise, divine wisdom can be considered in two ways. Hence, it is said in 1 Corinthians 2:7–10 (DR): "We speak the wisdom of God in a mystery, a wisdom which is hidden . . . which none of the princes of this world knew. . . . But to us God hath revealed them by his Spirit. For the Spirit searcheth all things, yea, the deep things of God."[298]

2. *Second urging*: Even the authority of God the Author of the supernatural order can be known by reason alone.

Indeed, the authority of God confirmed through miracles belongs to God as the Author of the supernatural order. Now, miracles are naturally knowable. Therefore, the authority of God the author of the supernatural order is naturally knowable.

Response: I make a distinction regarding the major premise. I concede that miracles manifest God as the free Author and Lord of nature. However, I deny that they reveal him as the Author of the order of grace and glory. I concede the minor premise. I make a distinction regarding the conclusion, conceding it if miracles were to manifest God as the Author of grace and glory, but otherwise, I deny it. Indeed, miracles are entitatively natural, only being modally supernatural *as regards their manner of production*.

---

[297] See *ST* I-II, q. 109, a. 3, ad 1.
[298] See *De veritate*, q. 14, a. 9, ad 8.

3. *Third urging*: However, the literal sense of the preaching of the Gospel sufficiently manifests that Christian revelation proceeds from God, the Author of grace. Now, this literal sense is naturally knowable. Therefore, the authority of God who reveals can be known in a solely natural manner, even if it pertains to God the Author of grace. Thus, the demons who naturally believe know quite well that the Christian revelation proceeds from God inasmuch as he is the Author of grace.

Response: When naturally known, the letter of the Gospel manifests supernatural mysteries *only materially* but not formally as they are supernatural. "But the sensual man perceiveth not these things that are of the Spirit of God. For it is foolishness to him: and he cannot understand" (1 Cor 2:14, DR). Thus, as we have said many times, the dog only hears human speech in a material way, hearing its sensible sound and not its intelligible meaning. Likewise, he who has absolutely no ear for music, even though he is not deaf, only materially hears a symphony by Beethoven without perceiving the spirit that animates the symphony. Likewise, by a less deficient analogy, on account of the weakness of his intellect, the student only materially hears a metaphysical principle, attaining it only in sensible examples given to him to help in his learning, not perceiving the principle's absolute necessity and universality. This student indeed does know the subject, predicate, and the copula "is" used in this principle, but he does not affirm the verb "is" as is necessary, on account of its true formal motive—namely, on account of metaphysical evidence. Likewise, the demon only materially assents to revelation and the supernatural mysteries, indeed knowing the trustworthiness of God the Author of nature, the fact of revelation on the basis of the evidence of miracles, and the natural meaning of the subject and predicate of a dogma. Nonetheless, he affirms the verb "is" under the natural light by which the signs of revelation and the divine trustworthiness are made manifest. Thus, his faith is resolved into natural certitude.

By contrast, a believer, under the internal, supernatural light, infallibly attains revelation not only as it is manifested in signs but, moreover, as it proceeds from God, the Author of grace, and as it is proposed by the Church with the Holy Spirit's assistance. And on account of revelation that is known in this way, the believer affirms the verb "is" in any given dogma that is to be believed while the infused light of faith illuminates the notion of the subject and the notion of the predicate in the dogma. This is to assent formally to the revealed mysteries, not according to a resolution to the evidence of the first principles of reason but, rather, according to a resolution to the uncreated light of God.[299]

{{472}} So too, those who, through the exaltation of their imagination, speak of the

---

[299] As St. Thomas says somewhere, the elderly person who, like the Cannanite woman, does not know theology can have a firmer and greater faith than certain theologians on account of the greater intensity of his or her infused light of faith and greater devotion. Also see Salmanticenses, *Cursus theologicus, De gratia*, disp. 3, dub. 3, no. 54 and what we said above about the intelligibility of the mysteries in ch. 5, a. 2, §2, note.

phenomena of the mystical life differ from those who are, in reality, mystically united to God in the silence of prayer.

4. *It will be insisted, however,* that it doesn't matter that knowledge of the formal motive of faith be infallible and supernatural, for it is related to it only as a [necessary] condition; and it suffices that the motive itself be infallible.

Response: As we said, the formal motive of faith does not move like an unknown efficient cause but, rather, moves objectively inasmuch as it is *known*. And it infallibly moves inasmuch as we adhere to it infallibly through grace. Thus, the Church's proposition, which is only a [necessary] condition for faith and not its motive, must be infallible.

5. *Objection*: But, for faith to be supernatural, it suffices that natural knowledge of the fact of revelation be elevated through grace. Such is the position of de Lugo.

Response: In that case, faith would be only modally *supernatural* and not essentially supernatural, just as an act of acquired temperance ordered by charity to the supernatural end becomes modally and accidentally (or, in other words, extrinsically) supernatural.[300]

6. *Objection*: However, in order for the act of faith to be essentially supernatural, it suffices that it arise from a supernatural active principle—that is, from the *habitus* of faith—for acts are specified through their active principles. So says Cardinal de Lugo.

Response: An act is not specified by the *habitus* from which it proceeds but, by contrast, a *habitus* indicates an ordering to act (just as potency does), and acts indicate an ordering to their objects. Hence, *habitus and acts are specified by their formal objects.* Therefore, they are essentially supernatural only if their specifying objects are essentially supernatural and unattainable by the powers of nature.[301] If St. Thomas sometimes says,

---

[300] See ibid., disp. 3, dub. 3, no. 31.

[301] See ibid., disp. 3, dub. 3, no. 49.

In countless places, St. Thomas expressly teaches that powers, *habitus*, and acts are specified by their formal objects. See *ST* I, q. 77, a. 3; I-II, q. 9, a. 1; q. 18., a. 2 and 6; q. 49, a. 3; q. 54, a. 1, ad 1; q. 54, a. 2.

Indeed, in *ST* I-II, q. 54, a. 2, St. Thomas says: "*Habitus* are distinguished in three ways: in one way, according to the *active principles* of such dispositions; in another way according to [their] *nature*, and in a third way, according to *specifically different objects*, as will be clear from what follows." And he explains in ad 2: "Different (cognoscitive) middle terms are like the various active principles by which scientific *habitus* [pl.] are diversified." Hence, the active principle specifies as the objectively moving principle, like the principles of the sciences. This is explained at greater length in *ST* I-II , q. 51, a. 3, in which it is said that reason is the active principle of the moral virtues and the understanding of principles is the active principle of scientific knowledge. And in q. 54, a. 3, St. Thomas shows that as ordered to nature [*in ordine ad naturam*] *habitus* are distinguished according to good and evil.

Indeed, in this last article, he says: "Human virtue disposing to acts that are suited to human nature is distinguished from divine virtue or heroic virtue which disposes to an act that is suited to some superior nature." However, as he explains in *ST* I-II, q. 68, a. 1, ad 3, the gifts of the Holy Spirit and the infused virtues differ not only from the perspective of their efficient and purely motive causes but also from the perspective of their objectively *ruling* and

"Acts are specified through their principles," he does not mean through their elicitive principle but, rather, through their objective principle.[302]

7. *Objection*: In order to preserve the specific distinction between infused and acquired faith, it suffices that they specifically differ in moral existence [*in esse moris*]— namely, according to the end to which they are ordered and not according to their formal object. (Such is the position of a number of Molinists.)

{{473}} *Response*: In that case, the act of *infused faith* would only be *extrinsically* supernatural on account of its end, like acquired temperance, which is ordered by charity to our supernatural end. The end does not specify unless it is simultaneously the object. Thus, the supernatural end intrinsically specifies charity.[303]

8. *Objection*: Even if the formal motive of faith were essentially supernatural, it can be attained by a natural act, even though it could not be produced by a natural act.

Response: Just as a supernatural effect cannot be produced through a natural virtue, so too an essentially supernatural object cannot be formally attained by a natural act. Otherwise, objective supernaturality would be destroyed and, similarly, a sense power could attain intelligible things.

9. *Objection*: The only thing that follows from the supernaturality of the object is the fact that it cannot be attained or known proportionately through a natural act, but not that it could not be attained improportionately [*improportionate*]. Such is the position of Granados and Ripalda.

Response: If supernaturality were only something excelling in the natural order, like loftier metaphysical conceptions, I would concede the point. However, I deny it if supernaturality is essentially of a loftier order. In that case, it is in no way attained improportionately by a natural act.

10. *Objection*: Nonetheless, the certitude of faith arises from the command of the will. Therefore, in order for this certitude to be supernatural, it suffices that the movement of the will be supernatural. However, the formal motive of faith does not need to be essentially supernatural and believed.

Response: I deny that the certitude of faith arises from a command of the will as regards its objective infallibility (for this arises from divine revelation). However, I concede that it does arise from the will as regards its subjective firmness, provided that one not exclude the internal "illumination of the Holy Spirit" spoken of by the Coun-

---

measuring causes. Likewise, see *ST* I-II, q. 63, a. 4 (Acquired virtue and infused virtue are specifically distinct according to their formal object.)

[Trans. note: For a treatment of the universality of the principle that acts and *habitus* are specified by their formal objects, see Réginald Garrigou-Lagrange, *Grace*, trans. Dominican Nuns of Corpus Christi Monastery (St. Louis: Herder, 1952), 467–80.]

302 See Salmanticenses, *De gratia*, disp. 3, dub. 3, no. 50.

303 See *ST* I-II, q. 18, a. 6; q. 54, a. 2, ad 3.

cils.[304] Moreover, a supernatural motion would not be needed for the will if the object to which the will was borne could be naturally known and desired through the literal sense of the Gospel confirmed by miracles. The supernaturality of acts always depends[305] on the supernaturality of the object to be believed or desired.

B. Second objection series: *The formal motive of faith cannot be believed.*

1. *Objection*: According to St. Thomas, one and the same thing cannot be simultaneously scientifically known [*scitum*] and believed by the same person. Now, the formal motive of faith—that is, the Authority of God who reveals—is something scientifically known by many. Therefore, at least in their case, it is not believed.

Response: The proof or confirmation of revelation through signs does not give intrinsic evidence of its reality nor scientific knowledge, properly speaking, of the fact of revelation. Hence, it is compossible with faith.[306] Moreover, it is not scientifically known and believed by the same person from the same perspective. Rather, the authority of God who reveals, inasmuch as it formally pertains to *God the Author of grace*, is not demonstrated, and this loftier perspective is that of the formal motive of faith. However, from another inferior and external perspective it is in some way demonstrated from miracles, which are the seal of *the Author of nature*. Hence, St. Thomas says: "Because those things that are of faith exceed human reason, they cannot be proven through human reasoning but, rather, must be proven through the argument of the divine power, so that when someone performs miracles that God alone can do, we may *believe* that the things that he says *come from God*."[307]

2. *Objection*: If the authority of God who reveals is believed, it is either believed on account of another revelation and so forth *ad infinitum*, or it is believed on its own account, and then there is a vicious circle as well as a deficiency in rational credibility.

Response: The authority of God who reveals is believed *on its own account* without a vicious circle, just as light is visible through itself, evidence is evident of itself, and unity is one of itself.[308] And even though divine revelation thus believed may be obscure, it is not lacking in rational credibility, for the act of faith presupposes {{474}} the rational judgment of credibility, founded on divine signs.[309]

3. *Objection*: Nonetheless, if the formal motive of faith is believed, the analysis of the act of faith becomes quite obscure and is not understood by the faithful.

Response: The act of faith must remain obscure, for it is essentially supernatural.

---

[304] See Synod of Orange, can. 5 (Denzinger, no. 375); [First] Vatican Council, *Dei filius*, ch. 3 (Denzinger, no. 3010).

[305] [Trans. note: Reading *pendet* for *pendent*.]

[306] See *ST* III, q. 55, a. 5, ad 2.

[307] *ST* III, q. 43, a. 1.

[308] See Cajetan, *In ST* II-II, q. 1, a. 1, no. 11; Salmanticenses, *Cursus theologicus, De fide*, disp. 1, nos. 163 and 193, as well as all the Thomists cited above.

[309] See the text from St. Augustine's *In Ev. Joann.*, tr. 35 cited above.

Hence, strictly speaking, it constitutes a mystery that is analogically knowable from human faith, not univocally. The infused light of faith is loftier than the natural light of the angelic intellect, and in order to know this mystery as it is in itself, we would need to have the beatific vision. And this mystery is in some way understood by the faithful when they read of the Pharisees in the Gospel: "You do not believe, because you are not of my sheep. My sheep hear my voice" (John 10:26–27, DR). The Pharisees indeed heard the letter of Christ's preaching, confirmed by miracles. However, they did not hear the voice of the Heavenly Father through the Son, for this voice is essentially supernatural.

Hence, St. Augustine said, as we noted above: "*Far removed from the senses of the flesh is this teaching in which the Father is heard, and teaches to come to the Son. . . .* We see that many come to the Son because we see that many believe in Christ, but *when and how they have heard this from the Father, and have learned, we see not.* It is true that that grace is exceedingly secret."[310]

4. *Objection*: The analogy with human faith is not preserved at all, for when we believe someone speaking to us, we do not believe that he is worthy of faith and that he said this, but rather, we know it certainly [*sed scimus*].

Response: A true analogy does exist between divine faith and human faith, although as in every analogy, perfect likeness is lacking. And in this case, likeness is lacking in the fact that generally we see the speaking man whom we believe, whereas we do not see God speaking, and not even the prophet sees God but, rather, only hears him.

Hence, *a perfect analogy is preserved between the faith of the prophet and human faith on the testimony of some man who is immediately heard but not seen*. And, indeed, sometimes the man whom we believe is immediately heard but not seen, perhaps because he knocks on a closed door at night. Then, we recognize his voice, but seeking greater certitude, we ask, "Who are you, knocking on my door?" And he responds, "I am your father." Then, we believe that he who is speaking truly is our father and not someone else. Nay, if afterwards he alleges to us something quite extraordinary and we doubt whether he is speaking seriously or jokingly, we will seek some confirmation from him, and he will respond, "I tell you this in truth and am not speaking in jest." Then we believe that he is trustworthy not only habitually but also in this present case.

Likewise, the prophet, under the light of prophecy, already has certitude that he who speaks is God, at least as the Author of the natural order and the Lord of nature. Nonetheless, he can believe in such revelation as proceeding from God, the author of grace. God speaks to him inwardly, saying, "I am your Father who speaks with you. This is not an illusion."

Likewise, the analogy is perfect between our divine faith ruled by the Church's magisterium and human faith upon the testimony of some man whom we neither see nor immediately hear but only hear through the mediation of an envoy sent from him, as is clear in the example

---

[310] Augustine, *De praedestinatione sanctorum*, PL 44, col. 970 (trans. Holmes and Wallis).

of the messenger bringing the letter of the king.[311] Indeed, "When the trustworthiness of the messenger is not certain, we inquire into his credentials. When this is clear, the letter of the king is accepted on account of the trustworthiness of the messenger. However, the contents of the king's letter are not believed on account of the messenger's trustworthiness but, rather, on account of the king's own trustworthiness. And if the trustworthiness of the messenger is asserted in the king's letters, it is strengthened and more greatly believed on account of the king's own trustworthiness." Let us apply this to the case [at hand]. The Church proposes to us the Word of God: The Church's[312] trustworthiness is believable on the basis of her marks and divine signs. We accept from the Church the Word of God in which the Church's own infallibility is contained. Thus, presupposing the motives of credibility, we believe in revelation on account of the {{475}} Church's authority, as the [necessary] *condition applying* revelation itself, and we believe in the authority of the Church on account of revelation as *on account of the formal motive* of assent. It is a general truth [*ordinarium est*] that causes are causes of each other. Thus, these two reasons are found in different genera of causality. Hence, without a vicious circle, the [necessary] condition and the [formal] motive mutually manifest each other.

Hence, there is a true analogy between divine faith and human faith. Nonetheless, likeness is lacking in the fact that we generally see speaking to us the man whom we believe, though we do not see God speaking to us.

C. **Third objection series:** *At least de facto, the formal motive of faith is not believed in.*

1. *Objection*: If acquired faith and infused faith had different formal motives, man could experience when he elicits an act of acquired faith and when he elicits an act of infused faith, for the intellect cannot be unaware of the reason by which it is moved to belief. Now, nobody can experience the fact that his act [of infused faith] is supernatural. For example, the heretic who believes in the article of the Trinity quite assuredly thinks that he believes [in the Trinity] by infused faith and clearly is plainly deceived. Therefore, acquired and infused faith do not have different formal motives, and hence, at least *de facto*, natural knowledge of the motive of faith suffices.

Response: We must recall the words of St. Augustine: "Far removed from the senses of the flesh is this teaching in which the Father is heard and teaches. . . . It is true that grace is exceedingly secret." The formal motive of infused faith is not seen by a kind of supernatural vision but, rather, is believed. Therefore, it remains obscure, and our intellect adheres to it under the influence of the will. Hence, natural knowledge of the motives of credibility are prerequisites for the supernatural act of faith, and therefore, Suarez rightly notes: "Never does man discern with sufficient evidence whether he is moved and acts from a purely supernatural reason, and this indicates well enough that he can never be

---

[311] See Billuart, *Summa sancti Thomae, De fide*, diss. 1, a. 2.

[312] [Trans. note: Reading *Ecclesiae* for *Ecclesia*.]

completely certain of the supernaturality of his faith, even though he can have a strong hunch concerning it."[313] Nay, concerning prophecy, St. Thomas says, "Those things that the prophet knows through an instinct (and not through perfect prophecy) are sometimes such that *he cannot fully discern whether he thought this through a divine instinct or through his own spirit.*"[314]

Moreover, this question is not to be resolved on the basis of religious experience but, rather, on that of a metaphysical[315] analysis of the revealed doctrine regarding the motive of faith, just as theological conclusions are deduced. Nominalists and empiricists indeed wish solely to resolve on the basis of experience questions that transcend experience. Hence, mechanistic determinists do not wish to admit the essential distinction separating vital phenomena and mechanistic [physical] phenomena, for they do not experientially see the vital principle [of that which lives]. Likewise, sensists do not wish to admit the essential distinction that exists between spiritual knowledge and the senses, for they do not experientially see a pure spirit. Indeed, there is no intellection in this life without the intellect turning to sensible things. Similarly, there is not usually a supernatural act without a corresponding natural act, and it is not easy to distinguish these acts by experience alone. Nonetheless, according to the Councils, it is certain that nobody can believe as is necessary for salvation "without the Holy Spirit's illumination and inspiration," with the illumination for the intellect and the inspiration for the will. Now, certainly, this supernatural illumination produces some formal effect in our intellect, for otherwise it would be utterly in vain. In our adversaries' theory, the necessity of this illumination is not clear but is only affirmed because it is declared by the Councils. In reality, that illumination and the habitual, internal light of faith itself are loftier than the angel's natural intellectual light and are so sublime that in order to have quidditative {{476}} knowledge of them we would need to have the beatific vision, for they are participations in the intimate life of God. Who *knows* [*scit*] the loftiness of our faith and its infinite distance from heretics' acquired faith? God and the blessed know it.[316]

2. *Objection*: However, in order for the act of infused faith to be vital, it must proceed from our faculties, which flow into our natural activity. Therefore, the act of infused faith has something natural about it—namely, its vitality and freedom—and it is supernatural through an adjoined modality.

Response: The act of infused faith proceeds from a vital power as elevated so that the elevation is the reason for the activity, just as the power itself is its root principle. "The light of life" brings new life with it. "He that followeth me walketh not in darkness, but

---

[313] Suarez, *De gratia*, bk. 2, ch. 11, no. 35. Also see Salmanticenses, *De gratia*, disp. 9, no. 17.

[314] *ST* II-II, q. 171, a. 5. Likewise, see St. Augustine's text cited by St. Thomas here.

[315] [Trans. note: Broadly speaking, meaning something like "doing causal analysis in light of the principles at play."]

[316] See *ST* I-II, q. 112, a. 5 (Whether man can know [*scire*] that he has grace).

shall have the light of life" (John 8:12, DR). These two principles are not two partial, coordinated causes, like two men dragging a ship [to shore], but rather are two complete, subordinated causes.

3. *Objection*: Nonetheless, the act of infused faith does not attain the First Truth who reveals, as well as supernatural mysteries, except through the mediation of *species* or ideas of the natural order, for faith does not involve the infusion of supernatural *species*. Now, acquired faith mediated by similar *species* attains the First Truth who reveals, as well as the supernatural mysteries. Therefore, both have the same formal object.

Response: For this reason, we can more manifestly see the supernaturality of the beatific vision, which is immediately terminated at the divine essence, without the mediation of any species. However, as St. Thomas notes in *ST* II-II, q. 1,a. 2, ad 1: "*The act of the believer does not terminate at the enunciable proposition but, rather, at reality*. For we form enunciations only so that through them we may have knowledge about things, both in science and in faith." Indeed, we say, [with] all scholastics against subjectivists: The idea is not what is known but only that by which we know. Hence, we do not believe in dogmatic formulas but, rather, in the very mysteries hidden in God, and faith becomes all the more profound to the degree that it penetrates more deeply into "the depths of God" and does come to a halt at the formulas [*non sistit in formulis*].

Moreover, as John of St. Thomas says:

> Even though those species are themselves of the natural order per se, nonetheless they are coordinated and combined in order to form a judgment or propositions of faith. And *this coordination is brought about by the supernatural light of faith*. Thus, that representation is complex and is *supernatural* through the mode of a truth that is handed on [*per modum veritatis traditae*]. Hence, the lights of prophecy and of faith do not only elevate the power to elicit the act of assent but also order the *species* to represent revealed truths in a complex manner [i.e., in enunciations formed by the second operation of the intellect].[317]

Moreover, the Salmanticenses say: "Insofar as they are entitatively natural, intelligible *species* do not immediately concur in the assent of faith but only do so remotely, inasmuch as they are of service in the apprehension of the terms [of what is believed]. And, in turn, they influence the assent of faith inasmuch as they are ordered and corroborated through the supernatural light."[318] Finally, St. Thomas himself had said in *ST* II-II, q. 173, a. 2, ad 3: "It must be said that, by his natural powers, man can form all sorts of images in his imagination, simply by considering such images. However, he cannot order them so that they may represent intelligible truths that exceed man's intellect. For this, the aid of

---

[317] John of St. Thomas, *Cursus theologicus, De gratia*, disp. 20, a. 1, no. 9.
[318] Salmanticenses, *Cursus theologicus, De gratia*, disp. 3, du. 4, no. 53.

a supernatural light is needed." Also see Cajetan's comments on this article. Hence, just as the natural light of the agent intellect not only abstracts *species* but also illuminates them for the formation of a judgment (that is, so that we can have evidence of the truth), so too the light of faith illuminates the *species* of the dogmatic formula so that we may formally believe "the depths of God." Without this illumination, acquired faith, through the mediation of dogmatic formulas, only attains the supernatural mysteries in a material manner just as, all proportions preserved, the dog materially hears the sound of human speech without understanding its intelligible meaning. Hence, it is said in 1 Corinthians 2:14 (DR): "But the sensual man perceiveth not these things that are of the Spirit of God. For it is foolishness to him: and he cannot understand."

4. *Objection*: If the testimony of God who reveals is attained under the illumination of the Holy Spirit by any given believer, it seems that they do not need the Church's authority {{477}} as applying divine revelation by means of various dogmatic propositions. However, this is the Protestant heresy [in these matters].

Response: To this, we must respond with Cajetan, who says in *In ST* II-II, q. 1, a. 1, no. 10, ad 3rd dub.:

> Since two things concur in faith, namely assent and proposition, as well as the explanation of things to be believed, from the perspective of its *assent, faith depends upon God alone* as upon its agent, object, end, and rule. *However, from the perspective of the proposition of things to be believed, it can depend upon angels or men* by whose mediation God proposes this or that thing to be believed. . . . And hence . . . the Holy Spirit provides for an infallible created rule [of faith], namely the sense and teaching of the Church.

Thus, the Church's proposition is not the motive of faith but, rather, a prerequisite [necessary] condition for it, just as sensation is a prerequisite [necessary] condition for intellectual knowledge of principles, but not the formal motive of this knowledge.[319]

5. Given that the motive of faith is believed on its own account, previous inquiry into credibility is not required so that this assent of faith may be prudent, for this assent of itself has its own legitimacy, just as it has its own certitude [*quippe qui (assensus) ex seipso suam legitimitatem sicut suam certitudinem habet*]. Now, prior inquiry into credibility is needed, as is clear, for example, from the words of Pius IX.[320]

Response: The fact that a judgment of credibility is required so that the act by which the motive of faith is believed on account of itself may be prudent is hardly different from what is true for other acts. For the motive of faith, supernaturally believed in, founds the supernatural certitude of any given assent of faith, but [the motive of faith] does not provide the

---

[319] Likewise, see Billuart, *Summa sancti Thomae, De fide*, diss. 1, a. 1 (in fine).
[320] Pius IX, *Qui pluribus*, no. 7 (Denzinger, no. 2778).

reasonability that arises from the fact that reason judges that the mysteries are evidently credible insofar as [the mysteries] appear to be revealed by God on the basis of evident signs. Hence, evident credibility is a prior [necessary] condition for the act of faith but does not constitute its formal motive.

6. At least this explanation of faith's supernaturality seems to be contrary to St. Thomas's words in *ST* II-II, q. 171, a. 2, ad 3:

> Every gift of grace elevates man to something above human nature. Now, this can be so in two ways. In one way, *as regards the substance of the act*, such as to perform miracles and to know the hidden and uncertain things of divine wisdom. And for these acts, man is not given a habitual gift of grace. In another mode, something is above human nature *as regards the mode* of the act but not as regards its substance, such as to love God and know him in the mirror of creatures. And for this a habitual gift of grace is indeed given.

Response: Already above (in ch. 6 on the division of supernaturality), we explained this text, following John of St. Thomas,[321] and we said that in this response St. Thomas is speaking of supernaturality relative to the efficient cause, just as in the division of miracles,[322] and not relative to the formal cause. Indeed, according to St. Thomas, it is certain that the supernaturality of charity and of faith is loftier than the supernaturality of miracles or of freely given graces,[323] for sanctifying grace and the infused virtues are entitatively and *formally* supernatural, whereas a miracle is only *effectively* supernatural [i.e., only modally supernatural, from the perspective of efficient causality]. However, something can be *effectively* supernatural as regards its substance or *effectively* supernatural as regards its mode. Thus, the text cited in the objection can easily be explained as not causing an issue in this matter.

Nay, comparing the infused virtues and the gifts of the Holy Spirit, St. Thomas says in *In* III *Sent.*, d. 34, q. 1, a. 1, ad 2: "The mode of operation that exists in the virtues is in accord with the human condition whereas *the substance of the habitus* is from a divine gift." Hence, faith, as well as charity and sanctifying grace, are *essentially* supernatural.

§8. Appendix: Corollaries of the Thomistic Thesis concerning the Supernaturality of Faith and Our Manner of Knowing the Formal Motive of Faith

{{478}} These corollaries are distinguished into those related to faith itself, those concerning the other infused virtues and gifts, and those concerning

---

[321] See John of St. Thomas, *Cursus theologicus, De gratia*, disp. 20, a. 1, solv. arg. no. 1.

[322] See *ST* I, q. 105, a. 8.

[323] See *ST* I-II, q. 11, a. 5.

science connected with faith.

I. Corollaries concerning faith itself

(1) *The Thomist theory here preserves the essential supernaturality of faith, which presupposes an intimate union between the believer's intellect and God who reveals,* according to the words of 1 John 5:10 (DR): "He that believeth in the Son of God hath the testimony of God in himself."

Thus, a response is also at hand to the objection raised by the Protestants. They say that Catholics hold that faith is a kind of external act of obedience to the Church, lacking an intimate union between the believer and God who reveals, for it is always mediated by the Church's magisterium and miracles. To this we can respond: Miracles or other motives of credibility are only prerequisite [necessary] conditions for the rational obedience of faith. The Church's act of proposal is only a [necessary] condition that proposes [the truth to be believed in through faith]. Only the uncreated action of God who reveals is the motive of faith. Hence, an intimate union exists between the believer and God, notwithstanding the Church's mediation, just as an intimate union exists between the intellect and the truth of the first principles, notwithstanding the mediation of the sensation that is prerequisite for intellection.

By contrast, the theory of discursive faith does not preserve the supernaturality of faith as well [as does the Thomist position]. Nor does it preserve the vital union of the believer with the First Uncreated Truth who exists above time. Nay, this theory does not provide a clear explanation for the *absolute* necessity of the supernatural light of faith (or the illumination of the Holy Spirit) for adhering to the preaching of the Gospel.

(2) *In no way does the Thomist position diminish the rational duty of faith but, rather, reconciles it with the essential supernaturality of faith.* This reconciliation is founded on the distinction of the two aspects of the fact of revelation, for that fact is modally supernatural inasmuch as it is a miraculous intervention by God and thus can be known by reason alone. However, inasmuch as it is the voice of the Heavenly Father through the Son and the Holy Spirit (i.e., inasmuch as it is a mystery that is essentially supernatural), it is believed [by supernatural faith]. Similarly, as was said of St. Thomas the Apostle: "He saw one thing and believed something else. He saw the man and the scars and on the basis of this believed in the divinity of Him who had arisen from the dead."

(3) *In no way does it diminish the infallible authority of the Church.* Nay, on the contrary, this authority not only appears as being rationally credible on the basis of the marks of the Church but also is supernaturally believed in on account of the First Uncreated Truth.

II. Corollaries concerning the other infused virtues and gifts

(1) *The Thomist position most excellently preserves the essential supernaturality of hope and charity from the perspective of their formal objects,* for this supernaturality presupposes the essential supernaturality of faith. If, {{479}} on the contrary, acquired faith could attain the formal object of infused faith, why couldn't our natural love of God attain the

formal object of charity?

(2) *It most excellently explains the intimate relation that living faith has with the gifts of the Holy Spirit*, especially with the gifts of wisdom and understanding—in a word, with the contemplative life. Indeed, the act of faith is already not discursive knowledge but, rather, a simple and essentially supernatural act by which we adhere to the First Truth and believe in the depths of God. Therefore, faith is a beginning of eternal life ordered to contemplation of divine realities. And although the gifts of wisdom and understanding exceed faith in some way [*secundum quid*]—namely, as regards the manner of operation—nonetheless, living faith is *simpliciter* loftier than the gifts of the Holy Spirit, for it is their rule.[324] Thus, it is clear why the purgative life and the illuminative life under the direction of faith are essentially ordered to the unitive life, and the ascetical life to the mystical life, as is said in the traditional doctrine of spiritual authors.[325] On this, see St. Thomas,[326] Johannes Tauler,[327] St. John of the Cross,[328] and St. Francis de Sales.[329] By

---

[324] See *ST* I-II, q. 68, a. 8; a. 2, ad 1.

[325] As regards the traditional teaching concerning this matter, see the testimony of the Fathers, theologians, and spiritual authors gathered in Auguste Saudreau, *La vie d'union à Dieu d'après les grands maîtres de la spiritualité* (Paris, 1909). This work is a kind of compendium of the history of mystical theology.

[326] See *ST* I-II, q. 68, a. 2 (The gifts of the Holy Spirit are necessary for salvation) and II-II, q. 180 (on the contemplative life). Also see *ST* II-II, q. 161, a. 5, ad 2 (Faith is the foundation of the spiritual edifice). Bossuet, *Instruction sur les états d'orasion*, ed. E. Lévesque ([Paris: Didot,] 1897), ch. 15.

[327] Johannes Tauler, *Institutiones*, ch. 8 (On bare faith).—*Sermons*, trad. Noël, vol. 2, 211, 212—351-352 (at the words "He who is from God, hears God's words")—"My sheep hear my voice—vol. 1, 321, 329, 338-405.—vol. 3, 119-127—vol. 4, 348-354.

[328] St. John of the Cross, *The Ascent of Mount Carmel*, bk. 2, ch. 9 (How faith is the proximate and best proportioned means for acquiring union with God); *The Dark Night*, bk. 2, ch. 9, ch. 17 (How obscure contemplation is secret).

[329] See St. Francis de Sales, *Traité de l'amour de Dieu*, bk. 2, ch. 14: "When God gives us faith, He enters into our soul and speaks with our spirit, not by way of open discourse but by way of inspiration. He proposes what the understanding must believe, doing so in such an agreeable manner that the will receives it with great complacency and such that it incites the understanding to consent and acquiesce to the truth with neither doubt nor defiance of any kind. And this is the true marvel. For God proposes the mysteries of the faith to our soul in darkness and obscurity. . . . And nonetheless, now that *this obscure light of faith has entered into our mind, not by the power of discourse, nor through arguments that have been presented to us, but solely through the sweetness of its presence*, it makes one believe and obey what is thus understood with such authority that *the certitude that it gives us concerning the truth exceeds all worldly forms of certitude*. . . . Faith is the great friend of our spirit, and it can indeed say to the human sciences, which haughtily boast that they are *more evident* and clear than it, as the sacred spouse said to the shepherds: 'I am dark but beautiful.' Oh, human discourses! Oh, acquired sciences! *I am dark*, for I exist among the obscurities of simple revelations which lack apparent evidence, making me appear *black*, making me nearly unrecognizable. *However, I am nonetheless* beautiful in myself on account of my *infinite certitude*, and if mortal eyes could see

contrast, those who conceive of faith as discursive and only modally supernatural consider infused contemplation as something that is merely extraordinary and not necessary for holiness, and this departs from traditional doctrine.[330] In reality, the mystical life is rooted in faith, by which God is united to our mind, and it tends toward an ever livelier and more fruitful manifestation of itself, for "faith is the substance of things to be hoped for" (Heb 11:1, DR).

{{480}} **III. Corollaries concerning science connected with faith**

(1) [*The Thomist position*] *enables us to clearly determine what apologetics (or the defense of the faith) must do.* It must present the motives of credibility but not the formal motive of faith. It leads one by the hand to faith, but it is not the foundation of faith. Hence, in practical apologetics directed to unbelievers, the greatest importance must be attached to divine grace and prayer.

(2) *It also makes clearer the dignity of sacred theology*, which is rooted in infused faith. Hence, it is not surprising that the Thomists hold that a formal heretic cannot have the *habitus* of theology. The only thing that can exist in such a person is the corpse of theology—that is, theological notions lacking their formal connection, which depends essentially upon the light of faith. If, by contrast, infused faith had the same formal object as acquired faith, it seems that a heretic could have the habitus of theology, as Durandus and certain others concede.

(3) *As regards the exegesis of Sacred Scripture, it follows that the rationalist or heretic can only materially know the letter of Sacred Scripture, but not its supernatural spirit*, which is the formal principle of the literal sense. For in order to rightly understand the literal sense of Sacred Scripture, it does not suffice that one have knowledge of grammar, vocabulary, and *merely rational rules of exegesis*. Beyond this, one must bear in mind *Christian and Catholic rules of exegesis*, which proceeds under the light of infused faith in order to rightly understand the expression of the mysteries of faith contained in Sacred Scripture.[331] Just as the philologist does not correctly understand the literal sense of Aristotle's *Metaphysis* if he does not have a philosophical spirit, so too the biblical critic who does not have

---

me such as I am in my nature, they would find me utterly beautiful."

[330] See Saudreau, *La vie d'union avec Dieu*, 483 (on deviation from the traditional doctrine, with certain critiques addressed to Rodriguez) and *Revue du clergé français*, 1st ed. (August 1917).

[331] See Leo XIII, *Providentissimus Deus*, no. 15: "For although the studies of non-Catholics, used with prudence, may sometimes be of use to the Catholic student, he should, nevertheless, bear well in mind—as the Fathers also teach in numerous passages—*that the sense of Holy Scripture can nowhere be found incorrupt outside of the Church, and cannot be expected to be found in writers who, being without the true faith, only gnaw the bark of the Sacred Scripture, and never attain its pith*." Pope Leo XIII here cites St. Gregory the Great, *Moralia in Iob*, 20.9 (al. 22); Clement of Alexandria, *Stromata*, vii., 16; Origen, *De principiis*, iv., 8, and *Homilies on Leviticus*, 4.8; Tertullian, *De praescriptione haereticorum*, 15ff.; St. Hilary of Poitiers, *Commentary on Matthew*, 13.1. See Vacant, *Études*, vol. 1, 710. Also see Vincenz Zapletal, *Hermeneutica biblica*, 113–120, 137ff.

the Christian spirit does not understand the literal sense of the Gospel: "But the sensual man perceiveth not these things that are of the Spirit of God. . . . But we have the mind of Christ" (1 Cor 2:14–16, DR).[332]

Likewise, the Thomistic thesis [on the resolution of faith] makes clear how Sacred Scripture is to be formally interpreted—namely, through a resolution to the First Truth who reveals, to the intimate life of God, and not according to a resolution to the psychological or religious experience of the sacred author (that is, of Jeremiah, Isaiah, or St. Paul). This psychological method, which is especially used by contemporary Protestants, is indeed useful if kept within due bounds. However, it often leads to relativism and naturalism, for gradually that which was only an instrumental cause of Sacred Scripture [namely, this psychological experience] becomes a kind of principal cause, leading one to no longer consider Scripture as being God's Book but, rather, to think of it as being [merely] a collection of human books.

(4) *As regards the history of the Church*, on the basis of our thesis, it is certain that the rationalist or heretic cannot write Church history in an appropriate manner, for the Church is an essentially supernatural society [*institutio*] that is ruled by the Holy Spirit. Of itself, human reason can only materially gather together many facts about the Church's life. However, in order to know the true relationship among these facts, recourse must formally be had to the Church's intimate life, to the supernatural and special providence of God, and not only, as is done by rationalists or heretics, to human causes, the influence of Greek philosophy, {{481}} Roman politics, the natural character of St. Paul, St. Athanasius, St. Cyprian, or of their adversaries. These causes remain secondary.

All of these consequences are of the greatest importance and proceed from the fact that *our faith is essentially supernatural, not only as regards the pious affect of belief but also as regards that which is intellectual in it.* Hence, in theology, exegesis, and Church history, one must essentially proceed not only under the *objective* direction of revealed doctrine but also under the *subjective* influence of the internal light of faith, under the illumination of the Holy Spirit. Only in this way are the words of the Lord confirmed: "He that followeth me walketh not in darkness, but shall have the light of life" (John 8:12, DR). This light of life, already inchoately existing in believers like a seed of glory, is not only necessary for [personal] piety but also for sacred science. Hence, theology is called "sacred," as being distinct from the sciences of the natural order.

This suffices as regards the act of faith in relation to credibility. Now we must discuss rational credibility itself.

---

[332] See St. Thomas's comments on 1 Cor 2:14. Also see Melchor Cano, *De locis theologicis*, bk. 2, ch. 14, no. 13: "Great is the error of those who believe that they can either understand or interpret Sacred Scripture without the particular gift of the Holy Spirit." He proves this from many testimonies drawn from St. Jerome.

CHAPTER FIFTEEN

On the Notion of Rational Credibility and Its Necessity for the Act of Faith

{{482}} Our discussion in this chapter is divided into four articles:

Art. 1. The nature of rational credibility

Art. 2. The necessity of certain, rational credibility, at least with moral certitude

Art. 3. On the office of the judgment of credibility in the genesis of the act of faith

Art. 4. Resolution of objections (the reconciliation of the rational obedience of faith with the obscurity, freedom, and supernaturality of faith)

In the preceding chapter, especially in its final article, we showed the essential supernaturality of faith. Now, however, we must present the rationality of the obedience of faith and how this rationality is reconciled with the aforementioned supernaturality, for some people so vigorously defend this rationality that the absolute necessity of the supernatural light of faith is no longer clear, whereas others insist so much on this necessity that the obedience of faith does not seem to be sufficiently reasonable.

ART. 1: THE NATURE OF RATIONAL CREDIBILITY

§1. The Catholic notion of credibility

§2. Heterodox notions of credibility

§3. Theological explanation of the Catholic notion of credibility

§1. The Catholic Notion of Credibility

This[1] notion finds a particularly clear expression in the documents of the

---

[1]   See Ambroise Gardeil, "Crédibilité," in the *Dictionnaire de théologie catholique*, "IX. Décisions canoniques," cols. 223[0]–2236.

[First] Vatican Council:

> If anyone says *that divine revelation cannot be made credible by outward signs* and that, therefore, men ought to be moved to faith solely by one's inner experience or by personal inspiration, let him be anathema.[2]

And in the next canon:

> If anyone says that *no miracles are possible* and that, therefore, all accounts of them, even those contained in {{483}} Holy Scripture, are to be dismissed as fables and myths; or that *miracles can never be recognized with certainty* and that *the divine origin of the Christian religion cannot be legitimately proven by them,* let him be anathema.[3]

This is explained in the corresponding chapter in the conciliar constitution *Dei filius*:

> (Even if faith is above reason,) however, in order that the *obedience of our faith* be nevertheless in harmony *with reason* [cf. Rom. 12:1], God willed that exterior *proofs* of His revelation, viz., divine facts, especially miracles and prophesies, should be joined to the interior helps of the Holy Spirit; as they manifestly display the omnipotence of and infinite knowledge of God, they are *the most certain signs of the divine revelation* adapted to the intelligence of all men.[4]

> (And the Council adds:) In fact, it is to the Catholic Church alone that belong all those signs that are so numerous and so wonderfully arranged by God to make *evident* the *credibility* of the Christian faith. In fact, the Church *by herself,* with her marvelous propagation, eminent holiness, and inexhaustible fruitfulness in everything that is good, with her catholic unity and invincible stability, is a great and *perpetual motive of credibility and an irrefutable testimony of her divine mission.*[5]

Likewise, see no. 7 of the *Syllabus of Errors* of Pius IX.[6]

---

[2]   [First] Vatican Council, can. 3.3 (Denzinger, no. 3033).
[3]   Ibid., can. 3.4 (Denzinger, no. 3034).
[4]   Ibid., ch. 3 (Denzinger, no. 3009).
[5]   Ibid. (Denzinger, no. 3013).
[6]   See Denzinger, no. 2907.

Moreover, in the Anti-Modernist Oath: "I profess. . . . Second, I accept and acknowledge external arguments of revelation, that is, divine deeds, in particular miracles and prophecies *as utterly certain signs of the divine origin of the Christian religion*, and I hold that they are most excellently adapted to the understanding of all eras and men, even of our own days."[7]

The Church's teaching concerning the notion of the rational credibility of the mysteries of faith can be reduced to four propositions:

(1) Objectively, *the mysteries of the faith are rationally credible inasmuch as the divine origin of the Christian religion can be legitimately proven on the basis of utterly certain signs.*

(2) Subjectively, *before receiving faith, human reason can know this credibility (or divine origin) of the Christian religion with certitude.*

(3) *Indeed, a scientific demonstration of [this] credibility is not required for any given believer.*

(4) *However, merely probable knowledge does not suffice, nor merely subjective knowledge, nor solely internal experience or private inspiration.*

The first proposition is expressly found in the aforementioned definitions from the [First] Vatican Council.

The second proposition is found in the same definitions, inasmuch as the utterly certain signs of revelation are said to be "adapted to the understanding of all." And against fideism, the Church declares that these signs can be known with certainty by human reason before the reception of faith. [Against the fideism of men like Louis-Eugène Bautain, the Church has declared:] "As regards these various questions (the existence of God, the divinity of the Mosaic and Christian revelation), reason can precede faith and should lead us to it."[8] "However weak and obscure reason became through original sin, there remained in it sufficient clarity and power to guide us with certitude to [know] the existence of God, to the revelation made to the Jews by Moses, and to Christians by our adorable Man-God."[9] Likewise, against the followers of Hermes, Pius IX declared:

Indeed, *human reason*, lest it be deceived and err in a matter of so great importance, ought to investigate diligently the fact of divine revelation *so that it can know with certainty that God has spoken* and so render to Him, a rational obedience. . . . But, how many, how wonderful, how splendid are the proofs at hand by which human reason ought to be entirely and most clearly convinced {{484}}

---

7   Also see Pius X, *Pascendi*, no. 39 (Denzinger, 2106, old numbering).

8   See Theses Subscribed to by Louis-Eugène Bautain by Order of His Bishop, Nov. 18, 1835, and Sept. 8, 1840, nos. 1ff (Denzinger nos. 2751).

9   Ibid., no. 6 (Denzinger, no. 2756).

that the religion of Christ is divine.... (Then he enumerates various signs.) All of this certainly shines in every way with so great a glory of divine wisdom and power that the mind and intelligence of each one clearly understands that the Christian faith is the work of God. And so, human reason, knowing clearly and distinctly from these most splendid and equally most strong proofs that God is the author of this faith, can proceed no farther; but, rejecting and dispelling every difficulty and doubt, it must render all obedience to this faith.[10]

This is explained at greater length in the pre-conciliar schemata for the [First] Vatican Council.[11]

The third proposition—namely, "A scientific demonstration of [this] credibility is indeed not required for any given believer in particular"—is found in the text of the [First] Vatican Council itself, where it condemns those who say: "Catholics could have a just reason for suspending their judgment and calling into question the faith that they have already received under the teaching authority of the Church until they have completed a *scientific demonstration* of the credibility and truth of their faith."[12] As we will come to explain, the moral certitude had through common sense suffices, and it can be

---

[10] Pius IX, *Qui pluribus*, no. 7–9 (Denzinger, nos. 2778–2780).

[11] See *Collectio lacensis*, vol. 7, col. 528 and 529 and Vacant, *Études théologiques sur les constitutions du Concile du Vatican d'après les actes du concile*, vol. 1, 575 and 593: "Nor are those lacking who would teach that those supernatural facts (i.e., miracles) cannot be known as motives of credibility unless faith is already presupposed and, hence, *that the very fact of revelation cannot be demonstrated to a man who has not yet received faith* and, hence too, that certain persuasion concerning the truth of the fact of revelation, that is concerning the existence of revelation, cannot precede the reception of the Christian faith. Rather, it would be the case that faith would be produced through divine grace without persuasion of this kind so that such faith would be a spontaneous and immediate act of reason.—Moreover, the Holy See has already found it necessary to proscribe errors of this sort" (referring to the proposition condemned by Innocent XI, Condemnation by the Sacred Office on Mar. 2, 1679, no. 21, Denzinger, no. 2121) and the condemnation of fideism and Hermesianism by Pius IX).

Immediately thereafter, it is added: "However, of itself, it is manifestly clear that the very error against which this article in the schema is proposed is full of danger. *For having rejected or stripped of their value the extrinsic criteria by which God renders His revelation knowable by way of these divine seals*, everything is left to 'internal experience' and 'one's internal sentiment,' *meaning that there is no longer a certain mode for discerning true revelation from fictitious revelation*. Indeed, that [internal] sense, according to ordinary providence, does not have a *supernatural* formal character, and if it is separated from extrinsic criteria is open to the gravest of delusions. Whence, we even see that, on behalf of false religion and manifest errors, men call upon 'experience and internal sentiment,' which they attribute to the Holy Spirit. (Likewise, they say): It is sometimes God's will that one fall away from the Catholic religion to another, if that is found not to satisfy internal experience and one's religions sentiment."

[12] [First] Vatican Council, *Dei filius*, can. 3.6 (Denzinger, no. 3036). Likewise, see ibid., ch. 3 (Denzinger, no. 3010).

had commonly, on the basis of the certain testimony of men (e.g., of one's parents).

The fourth proposition—namely, "Nonetheless, probable certitude of credibility does not suffice"—is had from the condemnation of certain probabilists who said, "The assent of faith, supernatural and useful to salvation, is based on only a probable knowledge of revelation and even on the fear with which one fears that God has not spoken."[13] Similarly, this modernist proposition was condemned: "The assent of faith ultimately rests on an assembly of probabilities."[14] Likewise, see the anti-modernist encyclical *Pascendi*, nos. 6 and 35ff.[15] Nor does merely subjective knowledge of credibility suffice (against the claims of pseudo-mystics).[16] Nor does merely internal experience or private revelation suffice (against the claims of the Protestants).[17] Therefore, certain knowledge of the fact of revelation is necessary.[18]

§2. Heterodox Notions of Credibility

{{485}} As was the case for the heterodox notions of revelation and faith, these heterodox notions of credibility can be divided inasmuch as they either diminish the duties of reason and materially exaggerate the supernaturality

---

[13] Innocent XI, Condemnation by the Sacred Office, Mar. 2, 1679, no. 21 (Denzinger, no. 2121). Concerning this proposition, which was condemned by Pope Innocent XI, see Gardeil, "Crédibilité," col. 2233.

[14] Pius X, *Lamentabili*, no. 25 (Denzinger, no. 3425).

[15] See Denzinger, nos. 3475 and 3499ff.

[16] See Innocent XI, Condemnation by the Sacred Office, Mar. 2, 1679, no. 53 (Denzinger, no. 2253).

[17] See [First] Vatican Council, *Dei filius*, can. 3.3 (Denzinger, no. 3033).

[18] See Pius IX, *Qui pluribus*, no. 7 (Denzinger, no. 2778). In the annotations to the *pre-Conciliar schema for the [First] Vatican Council* in *Collectio lacensis*, vol. 7, col. 1622–1623, we read: "Hence, it is not true that men must be moved to faith solely by internal experience according to the present providence [in the natural order], but rather, human reason before coming to faith must diligently inquire into the fact of revelation so that it may be certain that God has spoken. It is not said what form *this inquiry* and diligence must take on, nor can it be defined in general, for it *is utterly diverse for the various conditions and dispositions of men*. Nonetheless, it is beyond doubt that nobody, not even the uneducated man, can believe by the act of faith without being simultaneously certain (whatever in the end may be the motive accommodated to his capacities) that God has revealed this and that he believes on account of the authority of God who reveals. Therefore, it is not, however, necessary that he be able to *reflexively* consider this authority of God who reveals, much less be able to analytically explain his faith. Moreover, we must hold *that God's internal grace can supply such men with what is lacking in the external proposition of the faith*. However, this does not mean that the proposition of the faith *through motives accommodated to one's capacities* and necessary diligence can be denied and left wholly to internal experience and to a kind of internal instinct." This pre-conciliar disquisition was had before twenty-four deputed Council Fathers by Johann Baptist Franzelin, S.J., consultator for the Theological Commission.

of faith or, on the contrary, exaggerate the duties of reason and essentially diminish or destroy the supernaturality of faith. The first category, which can be called pseudo-supernaturalism, includes the notions of credibility proposed by the first Protestants and, afterwards, by the fideists, whereas the second, which is nothing other than naturalism or semi-naturalism, includes the notions proposed by Kant, many liberal Protestants, semi-rationalists, and modernists.

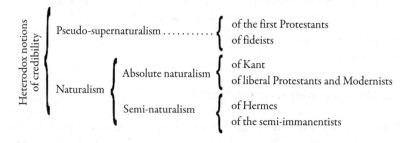

(1) **Pseudo-supernaturalism** of (A) the first Protestants and of (B) fideists.

A. *The first Protestants*, like Luther and Calvin, by rejecting the Church's infallible authority for proposing revelation,[19] were accustomed to discern the genuine word of God on the basis of a "taste" or "savor," which each believer supposedly had in himself or herself through the immediate testimony of the Holy Spirit.[20] Thus, the pseudo-reformers and their disciples judged through a private spirit whether this or that article was revealed and to be believed in, and that this is the true Church. Hence, they [held that] they did not need miracles and external notes for proving the divine origin of their sects. Hence, they held that the *credibility of the mysteries of faith* must be defined as *their aptitude to being believed inasmuch as, under private inspiration, they appear to be revealed by God*. This definition does not preserve the notion of rational credibility, for how can we rationally discern private inspiration from personal delusions? Liberal Protestants would come to substitute natural religious sentiment for this private inspiration, and thus pseudo-supernaturalism led to naturalism.

B. *Fideists and traditionalists*, like Bautain and Bonnetty, did not have recourse to private inspiration to discern the true religion revealed by God but, rather, to the common faith of humanity founded on its traditions and primitive revelation. The fideists reduced common sense to this common faith. According to them, {{486}} human reason was rendered so weak and darkened by original sin that it cannot by itself prove God's existence,

---

[19] See Leo X, *Exsurge Domine*, no. 27 (Denzinger, no. 1477).

[20] See Vacant, *Études sur le Concile du Vatican*, vol. 1, 593 (annotations for the pre-conciliar schemata).

his infinite perfection, nor the fact of revelation from miracles.[21] Hence, according to fideism, *the credibility* of the mysteries of faith is their aptitude to be believed *inasmuch as, according to the common faith of humanity, they are reputed as being revealed by God.*

This notion of credibility does not preserve its rationality, for how can we rationally distinguish common faith founded on traditions and primitive revelation from erroneous inventions made up by men, by which [these] traditions are corrupted?

Fideism is a species of pseudo-supernaturalism inasmuch as it holds that the supernatural is something owed to nature. Thus, it includes the first Protestants and Baius. However, that which is owed to nature must in fact be called natural. Thus, pseudo-supernaturalism leads to naturalism.

(2) **Naturalism and semi-naturalism** essentially destroy or diminish the supernaturality of faith, and if they retain the term "faith," they deny that its formal motive is the authority of God who reveals. Hence, they propose a new notion of credibility, exaggerating the duties of reason, although in fact many of them, such as agnostic thinkers, simultaneously diminish its power.

A. *Kant* admitted only the existence of a moral faith founded on the requirements of practical reason. Hence, according to him, *the credibility* of ethical and (merely natural) religious truths is their aptitude for being believed, *inasmuch as they appear to be conformed to the requirements of practical reason.* Miracles cannot be discerned with certitude.

B. *Liberal Protestants*, like Schleiermacher, under the influence of Kantianism, "generally substitute for the private inspiration of the first Protestants natural *religious sentiment* or the needs of the religious mined. Immediately through this sentiment, without the revealed truth being made credible for us on the basis of extrinsic criteria, the Christian religion would, [according to them,] be embraced as true and divine."[22] Hence, for them, the *credibility* of the truths of religion is their aptitude to being believed *inasmuch as they appear to be conformed to the aspirations and requirements of our religious sentiment.* According to Schleiermacher (*The doctrine of faith*, §11), for men who are not yet inclined to the Christian religion, miracles are particular incomprehensible facts but not signs of a higher power. Hence, the Roman Church's presumption that it can demonstrate its own truth on the basis of miracles must be rejected. This claim was condemned as a heresy by the [First] Vatican Council [which clearly stated][23] the divine origin of the Christian religion can be legitimately proven on the basis of miracles. Moreover, on the basis of its conformity with our reason's aspirations, a given assertion is *worthy of love* or

---

[21] See Gregory XVI, Decree of the Holy Office, Sept. 14, 1842 (Denzinger, no. 2765 [1622 and 1627, old numbering]); Theses against the Traditionalism of Augustin Bonnetty, no. 2 (Denzinger, no. 1650).

[22] See the [First] Vatican Council document annotations (*adnotationes in schemata Concilii Vaticani*) in *Collectio lacensis*, vol. 7, col. 528. Also see Vacant, *Études sur le Concile du Vatican*, vol. 1, 593.

[23] See [First] Vatican Council, *Dei filius*, can. 3.4 (Denzinger, no. 3034).

probable, but not *credible* by divine faith.

C. *Modernists*, as is said in the Anti-Modernist Oath, reduce faith "to a blind religious sentiment arising from the depths of the subconscious under the pressure of the heart and the bending of a morally informed will." In other words, they identify infused faith with a natural religious sentiment. Hence, *the credibility* of the mysteries of faith is only their aptitude for being believed inasmuch as they appear to us as being *conformed to the aspirations and exigencies of our religious sentiment*. Miracles cannot be discerned:[24] "The assent of faith ultimately rests on an assembly of probabilities."[25] Nonetheless, a number of modernists differ from liberal Protestants inasmuch as they acknowledge the influence of a kind of supernatural grace.

D. *Hermes* and a number of semi-rationalists said that the formal motive of divine faith is not necessarily the authority of God who reveals, for following upon revelation, essential {{487}} dogmas can be demonstrated and admitted on account of their intrinsic necessity, at least by practical reason.[26] Nay, the fact of revelation has not been confirmed by miracles except as being *practically* and *subjectively* certain. Hence, according to them, *the credibility* of the mysteries of faith is their aptitude to be believed *inasmuch as they appear to be conformed to the exigencies of our practical reason*. In this way, the absolute autonomy of practical reason remains preserved, as the Kantians wish.[27] Nonetheless, the semi-rationalists did not deny, like Kant, the fact of revelation and the influence of grace.

E. Certain people who promote the *method of immanence*, like Lucien Laberthonnière and Maurice Blondel,[28] do not distance themselves sufficiently from this last notion of credibility, because they make use of this method so incautiously "that they seem to admit that there is in human nature a true and rigorous necessity with regard to the supernatural order and not merely a capacity and a befittingness for it."[29] Hence, their periodical, *Annales de philosophie chrétienne*, was condemned by the Sacred Congregation of the Index from 1905 to 1913.

From this classification of errors, we can see the false notions of credibility in general proceed from a false notion of faith, substituting for the

---

[24] See Pius X, *Pascendi*, nos. 6, 35, and 37 (Denzinger, nos. 3475, 3500 and old no. 2103). Also see the second proposition of the Anti-Modernist Oath.

[25] Pius X, *Lamentabili*, no. 25 (Denzinger, no. 3425).

[26] See the [First] Vatican Council document annotations (*adnotationes in schemata Concilii Vaticani*) in *Collectio lacensis*, vol. 7, col. 527. Also see Vacant, *Études sur le Concile du Vatican*, vol. 1, 591; vol. 2, 31.

[27] See Pius IX, *Qui pluribus*, against the followers of Georg Hermes, no. 7 (Denzinger, no. 2778). Also see our prologue above concerning the historical overview of apologetics from the perspective of methodology, as well as Vacant, *Études sur le Concile du Vatican*, vol. 1, 125–126.

[28] See Joseph de Tonquedec, *Immanence* (Paris: Beauchesne, 1913), 148–149. Also see our prologue above concerning the historical overview of apologetics, considered from the perspective of methodology.

[29] Pius X, *Pascendi*, no. 37 (Denzinger, 2103, old numbering).

true formal motive of faith—namely, the authority of God who reveals—a human and subjective motive so that a new notion of credibility is thus had, as well as a new method for proving this credibility.

§3. Theological Explanation of the Catholic Notion of Credibility

The credibility of the mysteries of faith is theologically defined as the following: *the aptitude of things to be believed inasmuch as they appear to our reason, on the basis of utterly certain signs, to have been revealed by God.*[30]

This definition (A) is illustrated through a comparison with the prerequisite credibility needed for human faith, (B) is simultaneously founded on the preceding theses, and (C) is also confirmed by the insufficiency of the other definitions.

A. Indeed, something is rationally credible by human faith inasmuch as we assent to it on account of suitable witnesses who are worthy of faith—namely, because (a) these witnesses are reputed as knowing what they affirm, (b) they are trustworthy, and (c) they in reality affirm this.

Thus, something is likewise rationally credible by divine and immutable faith inasmuch as, on the basis of certain signs, it appears that this has been revealed by God who can neither deceive nor be deceived.

B. Hence, this notion of credibility is founded on the preceding theses concerning the true notion of revelation and faith. Indeed, if revelation does not proceed from our subconscious but, rather, from God who is essentially distinct from the world and {{488}} our soul, and if the act of faith is not a kind of religious experience but, rather, is the intellect's assent to things revealed by God on account of the authority of God who reveals, something cannot be rationally credible by divine faith unless it seems to our reason to be something revealed by God.

C. Finally, every other definition of credibility is insufficient, as will become quite clear in the next article concerning the necessity of certain credibility. It is already clear that a given assertion, on the basis of its conformity with our aspirations, is not worthy of belief through divine faith but, rather, is only something that is lovable.

Objection: But then, *the evidence of the credibility* of the mysteries, which all believ-

---

[30] In col. 2202 of his article "Crédibilité," Ambroise Gardeil rightly distinguishes, like many Thomist theologians, *rational and extrinsic credibility from supernatural and intrinsic credibility,* inasmuch as the former is known by reason and is the remote aptitude of the mysteries to being believed, whereas the second is known through faith and is the proximate aptitude of the mysteries to being believed, inasmuch as already in act they exist under the supernatural light of revelation by which we supernaturally adhere to them.

ers must have, is not distinct from *evidence* of the mysteries through testimony [*in attestante*]—that is, from evidence of revelation, which theologians hold to be very rare, indeed, as something had only by the prophets and apostles.

I respond with the Salmanticenses by saying that these two forms of evidence differ:

> In order for someone to have evidential knowledge of the mysteries by way of testimony [*in attestante*] (or evidence of divine revelation) he must evidently know that God Himself has spoken and proposes things to be believed. However, in order to have evidence of credibility, it suffices that one judge that evidently, here and now, there are at hand sufficient motives for believing that something has been said by God, even though one may not now see the object, nor [hear] a locution from God. For credibility does not consist either in the proposed object or in the testimony of God but, rather, in things' relationship or disposition, as an object evidently appearing as worthy of faith.[31]

Hence, evidence of the divine testimony, in the proper sense, is evidence of divine revelation from its proper effect—namely, on the basis of passive revelation in the mind of the prophet. However, this effect is known as something at least modally supernatural, under the light of prophecy. Hence, St. Thomas says in *ST* II-II, q. 171, a. 5: "The prophet has the greatest certitude as regards those things that he knows through the spirit of prophecy, and holds it for certain that these things have been divinely revealed to him."[32]

However, in a broad sense, evidence by way of testimony [*in attestante*] also signifies evidence of revelation on the basis of miracles immediately confirming revelation and immediately known by sight.

Now, evidence of credibility is had by a simple retelling of the signs that confirm revelation; however, the certitude coming from this retelling is a moral certitude founded in the testimony of men.

The properties of rational credibility. We can enumerate four properties of rational credibility.

1. *Credibility is something common to all revealed truths.* In *ST* II-II, q. 1, a. 4, ad 2, St. Thomas says:

---

[31] See Salmanticenses, *Cursus theologicus, De fide*, disp. 3, dub. 1, no. 3. Also see John of St. Thomas, *Cursus theologicus, De fide*, disp. 2, art. 3; Gonet, *Clypeus theologiae Thomisticae, De fide*, disp. 1, a. 7.

[32] See Cajetan's comments on this article. Also see Salmanticenses, *Cursus theologicus, De fide*, disp. 1, dub. 5, §3, no. 169: "The Apostles and prophets from whom we receive the faith themselves evidently knew *through the very light of prophecy* that God spoke to them and revealed to them the *credibilia* that they handed on to us." Likewise, see Gonet, *Clypeus theologiae Thomisticae, De fide*, disp. 1, a. 7.

Those things that fall under faith can be considered in two ways. In one way, they can be thought of individually, and in this way, they cannot be simultaneously seen and believed, as was said. However, they can also be considered in general, namely, under the common character of being credible. And in this way, they are seen by those who believe, for they would not be believed unless the necessity of believing them were seen, either on account of the evidence of signs or on account of something else of this sort.

Therefore, credibility belongs to all revealed things {{489}} indiscriminately in accordance with their relation to the signs by which revelation is confirmed.

2. *The truth of credibility is extrinsic to the revealed truths.* Indeed, the evidence of the credibility of the mysteries is not their intrinsic evidence, for the mysteries remain obscure in themselves. Rather, they are extrinsically said to be evidently credible, inasmuch as they appear to be revealed by God on the basis of certain [*certis*] signs.[33]

3. *Credibility is a speculatively practical form of truth.* It is not merely speculative, for it indicates an ordering to the act of faith to be performed— namely, inasmuch as this assertion is evidently suitable for being believed. However, this suitability is only evident if the fact of revelation is speculatively certain, at least with moral certitude, just as historical facts are known. Indeed, moral certitude can be speculative and not only practical, if it is concerned with the existence of a fact and not only with an action to be performed. This point will be made clearer in the next article.

4. *Evident credibility is a necessary condition* [*conditio sine qua non*] *of the act of faith*, as will be proven immediately in the next article.

ART. 2: The Necessity of Certain, Rational Credibility, at Least with Moral Certitude

The thesis of this article is the following: *In order for the mysteries of faith to be rationally credible for us, reason must know, at least with moral certitude, the fact of revelation inasmuch as it is something modally supernatural.* Nonetheless, inasmuch as it is the uncreated and essentially supernatural action of God, revelation is believed in supernaturally and infallibly as the formal motive of faith; namely, it is that *which* and that *by which* we believe, as was shown above.

---

[33] See Cajetan, *In ST* II-II, q. 1, a. 4.

[In this article, we will discuss:]

§1. The difficulty of this question.

§2. What do Sacred Scripture and the Doctors of the Church say?

§3. We stand in need of certain rational knowledge of the fact of revelation.

§4. Moral certitude is sufficient.

§5. This moral certitude can be had by all men, at least with the aid of grace, although grace is not absolutely necessary for having it.

§1. The Difficulty of This Question

The difficulty involved in this question above all consists in the reconciliation of the essential supernaturality of faith with the reasonableness of the obedience of faith. Indeed, in order for this obedience to be rational, reason must know that the mysteries are revealed by God, who can neither deceive nor be deceived. But then it seems that reason alone, by a consideration of miracles, can know the formal motive of faith. Hence, that motive would not be essentially supernatural, nor would the infused faith specified by it be essentially supernatural and more certain than acquired, natural faith founded on the evidence of miracles.

If, by contrast, reason alone cannot know the fact of revelation with certitude, the reasonable obedience of faith perishes.

As we will see, this difficulty cannot be resolved unless we admit the distinction proposed in an earlier chapter—namely, that between the fact of revelation qua {{490}} modally supernatural, like miracles, and revelation as the uncreated and essentially supernatural action of God, properly pertaining to God the Author of grace and not only the Author and Lord of nature. Revelation is known by reason under its lower and external aspect, whereas it is known in its loftier and intimate aspect through faith.

§2. What Do Sacred Scripture and the Doctors of the Church Say?

A. Already in the prologue [of this volume], we historically treated of the methodology employed in apologetics and saw how the prophets, Christ, and the apostles manifested the credibility of the mysteries of faith, especially through miracles and prophecies.

Now it suffices to cite the principal texts that affirm the necessity of rational credibility. Nor do we need to linger at great length on this point, for this doctrine is clearly affirmed by the Church's magisterium, as we saw in the previous article.

[We can gather the following texts from Scripture:]

Sirach 19:4 (DR): "He that is hasty to give credit is light of heart."

John 20:30–31 (DR): "Many other signs also did Jesus. . . . But these are written, that you may believe that Jesus is the Christ, the Son of God."

1 Corinthians 15:17 (DR): "And if Christ be not risen again, your faith is vain."

1 Peter 3:15 (DR): "Being ready always to satisfy every one that asketh you a reason of that hope which is in you."

2 Peter 1:16 (DR): "For we have not by following artificial fables made known to you the power and presence of our Lord Jesus Christ: but we were eyewitnesses of his greatness." (And then St. Peter invokes the testimony of the prophets.)

B. Among the Fathers, as regards the necessity of a certain, rational credibility, we can cite in particular St. Justin St. Clement of Alexandria, Eusebius, St. John Chrysostom, and St. Augustine.[34] However, St. Augustine and St. John Chrysostom, like St. Hilary, St. Ambrose, and others, say that the supernatural certitude of faith is loftier and much firmer than the rational certitude of credibility. Hence, they hold that the formal motive of faith is known with utter firmness under the internal illumination and inspiration of the Holy Spirit.[35]

C. Moreover, [later] theologians generally require certain knowledge of credibility[36] and say with St. Thomas: "The things that are of faith can be considered . . . in general, namely, under the common character of being credible, and in this way, they are seen by those who believe, for they would not believe unless they saw the necessity of believing them, either on account of the evidence of signs or on account of something else of this sort."[37] None-

---

[34] See Gardeil, "Crédibilité," cols. 2239–2258 ("La crédibilité chez les Saints Pères").

[35] See ibid. Also see art. 3, §2 of the preceding chapter.

[36] See ibid., cols. 2258–2299 ("La crédibilité dans la théologie scolastique").

[37] *ST* II-II, q. 1, a. 4, ad 2. Also see *SCG* III, ch. 155: "It was necessary for something to be provided, by means of which the words of the preachers of the faith might be confirmed. However, they could not be confirmed by any principles of reason by way of demonstration since the things of faith exceed reason. Therefore, the words of preaching needed to be con-

theless, as we said above,[38] Hugh of St. Victor, {{491}} St. Bernard, Alexander of Hales, Albert the Great, St. Bonaventure, St. Thomas, all the Thomists, and Suarez hold that the formal motive of infused faith can only be known under the inspiration and illumination of the Holy Spirit. The Thomists in particular defend this teaching against Molina, Ripalda, and certain more recent thinkers.

§3. We Stand in Need of Certain Rational Knowledge of the Fact of Revelation

This can be proven in a strictly formal argument.

Nothing is *rationally credible* by divine and immutable faith unless it is *evidently and only probably credible* by this immutable faith.

Now, nothing is evidently such unless it appears [so] to reason, on the basis of certain signs, to be supernaturally revealed by God.

Therefore, in order for the mysteries of faith to be rationally credible, reason must, on the basis of certain signs, know the fact of revelation as something at least qua modally supernatural.

The major premise is proven as follows. We suppose as something evident the fact that the obedience of faith must be consonant with reason, for otherwise, grace would not be conformed to reason but, rather, would be contrary to right reason, meaning that our faith would be flippant credulity. However, what is needed for something to be rationally credible, (1) as regards faith in general and (2) as regards divine faith in particular?

(1) *As regards faith in general*, nothing is rationally credible unless it is *evidently credible*. Indeed, as Gonet says:

> Without some evidence, nothing is knowable through a determinate judgment, for something that is thoroughly obscure is something that is thoroughly unknowable. Therefore, just as nothing is scientifically knowable [*scibile*] without evidence of scientific knowability [*scibilitatis*] and nothing is deserving of opinion [*opinabile*] without evidence of probability, so too nothing is cred-

---

firmed by certain signs so that they may make manifest that such words came from God. Thus, said preachers performed such kinds of works, healing the sick and doing other such powerful works which God alone could do." Also see *ST* II-II, q. 178 (On the grace of miracles), a. 1 and *ST* III, q. 43, a. 1 (Whether Christ should have performed miracles).

[38] See art. 3, §§3–6 in the preceding chapter.

ible without evidence of credibility.[39]

Hence, in order for something to be rationally believed, *it does not suffice that it be probably credible*. Indeed, in that case *faith would not be distinguished from opinion*, for opinion, which implies fear of error, presupposes evidence of probability (or of likeliness). So long as such evidence remains, an opinion is reasonable and not imprudent, though only as an opinion without firm adherence.

Faith, by contrast, even when considered in general, even if it is merely human faith, exists without fear of erring, for we firmly believe what is seriously asserted to us (e.g., by our father or by our friend). This firmness of adherence does not arise from the evidence of the object but, rather, from a special motion of the will, which determines the intellect to that which is to be believed. However, this motion of the will firmly determining the intellect would be *imprudent* if there were only probability of credibility. That is, a will without a sufficient reason would move the intellect not only to form an opinion but to believe it firmly. Hence, faith would be irrational (or flippant credulity).

Therefore, faith in general requires not only probability of credibility but, [beyond that,] evidence thereof.

(2) *Proportionate evident credibility* is required *for divine faith*, namely, as is expressed in the major premise: Nothing is rationally credible by divine and *immutable* faith unless it appears evidently credible to this immutable faith.

Indeed, an infinite abyss separates these two judgments: "This is credible by human faith because it is said, for example, by Aristotle," and "This is credible by divine faith because it is testified to by God." Divine faith differs essentially from {{492}} human faith as regards the firmness of its adherence, for even if human faith is prudent, it is not founded on an infallible testimony. Divine faith, by contrast, relies on infallible testimony. Hence, it can never be legitimately called into doubt such that we must undergo martyrdom rather than deny the faith or deliberately be in doubt concerning it.[40]

However, this firmness and irrevocability of divine faith, which is founded objectively on the infallible testimony of God, subjectively arises from the will "under the inspiration and illumination of the Holy Spirit."[41] Now, *the will*, even under the influence of grace, *cannot thus rationally and*

---

[39] Gonet, *Clypeus theologiae Thomisticae, De fide*, disp. 1, a. 8, §1.

[40] See [First] Vatican Council, *Dei filius*, can. 3.6 (Denzinger, no. 3036).

[41] See ibid., ch. 3 (Denzinger, nos. 3010 and 3014).

irrevocably move the intellect to believe unless there be a sufficient and legitimate reason for this motion. Nothing is willed without first being known, and this sufficient reason can be nothing other than *evident credibility*. In other words, something is not rationally believable by divine and immutable faith unless it appears as being evidently credible by this immutable faith. Thus, we have sufficiently proven our major premise.[42]

It is manifest that credibility must be proportioned not only to the requirements of reason but also to those of faith.

The minor premise. Now, nothing is evidently credible unless it appears, on the basis of certain signs, to be supernaturally revealed by God.

This is proven on the basis of the notion of credibility. Indeed, in general, even for merely human faith, that which is credible is that which can be believed. Now, to believe is to know something on the basis of testimony, without evidence of the thing testified to. Hence, nothing is evidently credible in general unless three things are certain for reason—namely, (1) *the fact of the testifying*, (2) *the trustworthiness of him who testifies*,[43] and (3) *the (scientific) knowledge [scientia] required to testify*. If any doubt or only probable knowledge arises from any of these three things, we do not have evident credibility but instead only probable credibility, which is nothing other than evident probability.[44]

Thus, all proportions maintained [*proportionaliter*], in order for something to be evidently credible not by any human-religious faith whatsoever but by divine and irrevocable faith, three things are required: (1) that this is *in fact revealed by God*, (2) that God is absolutely *trustworthy*, and (3) that God is *infallible*.

Therefore, in order for the mysteries of faith to be rationally credible, reason must know, on the basis of utterly certain signs, the fact of revelation qua modally supernatural.[45]

---

[42] See Gardeil, "Crédibilité," col. 2212.

[43] [Trans. note: Reading *testis* for *textis*.]

[44] The probability of credibility is had, for example, if the witness only probably has knowledge [*scientiam*] needed in order to testify on its behalf. Hence, his assertion is not evidently credible but instead is only evidently probable according to the degree of the probability of his knowledge [*scientiae*] or authority.

Why would *certitude of credibility* not suffice without *evidence of credibility*? Because every certitude ultimately must be resolved, at least extrinsically, into some evidence, as we said above. However, *evidence of credibility can be* merely *mediate* in character, as we will say below in §4, and in fact, it is such for those who do not see miracles or similar signs but instead admit of them on the basis of human testimony.

[45] See *ST* II-II, q. 2, a. 1, ad 1: "Faith does not have an inquiry of natural reason demonstrating that which is believed. Nonetheless, it has a kind of inquiry concerning those things by which

{{493}} *Why does this conclusion say, "Qua modally supernatural"?*

That is to say, *as regards the mode of its production*, as opposed to being essentially supernatural. For reason, solely by itself, can know[46] the fact of revelation by considering miracles qua miraculous interventions by God in the mind of a prophet [*sic*]. However, reason, solely by itself, cannot know divine revelation as something essentially supernatural proceeding from God, the Author of grace and glory. From this latter, loftier and intimate perspective, divine revelation is held only by divine faith and is the formal motive of infused faith—namely, that which and by which we believe. Thus, considered in its intimate reality, Sacred Scripture calls it the voice of the Heavenly Father, the voice of the Son, or the testimony of the Holy Spirit.

Even if it seems fastidious to reiterate this point, we must insist upon this distinction, which is omitted by many authors even though it is of the greatest importance, as was said in article 3 of the previous chapter. It is brought forth commonly for the divine attributes (e.g., for providence and for the facts of Christ's life). The providence of God the Author of nature is demonstrated by reason alone on the basis of the world's order or *a priori* from [what reason can know concerning] the divine intelligence. However, the providence of God the Author of grace and glory—namely, the supernatural means ordered to salvation—is known by faith alone. Likewise, the unity of God the Author of nature is demonstrated [by reason], whereas his unity as it is preserved in the loftiest way in the Trinity is believed [through supernatural faith.] The goodness of God the Author of nature, which specifies our natural love for God, is demonstrated [by reason alone], but not the goodness of God the Author of grace, which specifies [infused] charity. And the proposition of Baius, who rejected this distinction, has been condemned.[47] Therefore, likewise, this distinction is valid for the divine truthfulness. As the Salmanticenses show: "The testimony of God can be considered from two perspectives. On the one hand, it can be considered qua coming from God as the supernatural principle . . . thereby founding the infallibility of the supernatural order. On the other hand, it can be considered as coming from God qua the principle of nature . . . on account of which it founds infalli-

---

man is led to believe, for example, that they are said by God and are confirmed by miracles." Likewise, in q. 8, a. 4, ad 2: "Even though not all who have faith fully believe those things that are proposed to them to be believed, nonetheless, they understand that they are to be believed and that they must not turn away from them in any way."

Also see *In III Sent.*, d. 23, q. 2, a. 2, q.la 2: "Indeed, the reason by which the will is inclined to assent to those things that it does not see is that God says them, just as man, in those things that he does not see, believes the testimony of some good man who sees those things that he himself does not see." And ibid., q. 3, a. 2, ad 2: "As regards the reason that leads the will to believe, (faith) is said to be from the vision of someone who shows that God is the one who speaks in him who announces the faith."

[46] [Trans. note: Reading *cognoscere* for *cognoscese*.]

[47] See Pius V, *Ex omnibus afflictionibus*, no. 34 (Denzinger, no. 1934).

bility of the natural order."[48] As we said above,[49] this distinction is explicitly used by St. Thomas in his *commentary on John* 5, lect. 6, no. 9.

Likewise, the facts of Christ's life can be considered from two perspectives: (1) as sensible things and thus as kinds of *miracles* (e.g., his Resurrection), and (2) as *mysteries* (namely, inasmuch as they pertain to the Incarnate Word of God). Thus, the Apostle Thomas naturally knew the miracle of Christ's Resurrection by experiencing Christ's scars, whereas he believed in the mystery of the Resurrection of the Incarnate Word of God: "He saw the man and the scars and thereby believed in the divinity of Him who had resurrected."[50] Likewise, Christ's Passion upon the Cross is an {{494}} externally sensible fact but, considered in its intimate nature, is an essentially supernatural mystery of infinite worth. In the same way, the Church's infallibility is manifested externally to reason through her visible marks, though considered in her intimate reality, she is a mystery and dogma of faith.

Likewise, the fact of revelation (God speaking in the prophets) is naturally knowable as *a miracle*, as the miraculous intervention in the world by God the Author and Lord of nature. However, as *a mystery* proceeding from God the Author of grace, it is believed supernaturally and infallibly as the formal motive of infused faith. Thus, the Pharisees, seeing the miracles and materially hearing the letter of the Gospel, did not hear "the voice of the Father" (John 5:37). "But you do not believe, because you are not of my sheep. My sheep hear my voice" (John 10:26–27, DR).

Even if this distinction, which is proposed by the Thomists, is utterly evident according to St. Thomas's principles, it is rarely found in contemporary authors. Indeed, they do not fight it, but many writers omit it and seem to be unaware of it. Consequently, no small confusion remains in the difficult problem of reconciling the supernaturality and rationality of faith.

By this, we have a confirmation of the necessity of certain rational credibility. They who hold that the probability of credibility suffices have only *a religious opinion* concerning the divine origin of Christianity but not utterly firm faith. Such is the position held by liberal Protestants and modernists. Likewise, if there is an error in the judgment of credibility, divine faith does

---

[48] Salmanticenses, *Cursus theologicus, De gratia,* tr. 14, disp. 3, dub. 3, no. 40. Likewise, see Vacant, *Études sur le Concile du Vatican,* vol. 2, 75.

[49] See art. 3, §4 in the preceding chapter.

[50] See St. Thomas, *In XX Jn.,* v. 29, lect. 6 (*fine*). Also see *ST* II-II, q. 1, a. 4 (*Whether the object of faith could be something seen*), ad 1: "Thomas saw one thing and believed another: he saw the man and believing in God confessed [his belief] when he said, 'My Lord and my God.'" Nay, in *ST* III, q. 55, a. 5c and ad 3: "The fact that someone believes those things that he does not see, doing so on the basis of certain visible signs, does not completely deprive him of faith, nor of his merit." Hence, St. Thomas here teaches that the apostles *believed* in Christ's Resurrection on account of testimony of it confirmed by evident signs.

not follow but, rather, [merely] the appearance of faith,[51] like that found in heretics who believe on account of their own judgment and their own will the dogmas that please them, rejecting what does not please them. Thus, they sometimes think that they hold some assertion on divine faith, when in fact, it is false and is held by them only on the basis of human opinion.

§4. Moral Certitude Suffices

Although it is utterly befitting for the faith of the Church as a whole that there be a scientific demonstration of credibility (or a scientific proof of the divine origin of Christianity),[52] this is not required *per se* in any given man. Instead, it suffices that he have moral certitude in the order of common sense, in accord with the various conditions and abilities of persons.[53]

This is proven both because neither scientific certitude nor common physical certitude of the fact of revelation is possible for all the faithful and also because divine faith does not require more than moral certitude of credibility.

{{495}} (1) *Scientific certitude is not possible for all.* This is clear for children and the uneducated who[54] cannot distinctly or scientifically reduce the value of the motives of credibility to the first principles of reason, nor know of their existence in accord with the rules of historical criticism by resolving the objections brought forth by rationalists. However, the certitude of common sense (or natural reason) suffices, like that which men

---

[51] However, certain people do not know how to formulate the judgment of credibility [in explicit terms], though they make use of it in their act of faith. Hence, this judgment can be certain and sufficient in them even though its external formulation is mixed with error or expresses other insufficient motives by which they are at best concomitantly moved. And this especially happens for non-formal heretics—that is, those who remain in good faith—for they believe by divine faith the dogmas that are revealed by God and by human opinion the errors of their sect. They are invincibly unaware that their errors are indeed errors.

[52] However, a scientific demonstration of credibility, founded on metaphysics and history, is maximally befitting for the faith of the Church as a whole, for in general, the faithful invoke the scientific knowledge of the Doctors who scientifically know the motives of credibility and know how to resolve the objections of opponents of the faith. Hence, St. Thomas says in *ST* II-II, q. 2, a. 6: "Men of greater abilities who have the office of teaching others are bound to have fuller knowledge of things to be believed and to believe them more explicitly." For equal reason, the apologete should scientifically know the motives by which faith is rationally defended (cf. 1 Pet. 3:15).

[53] See [First] Vatican Council, *Dei filius*, can. 3.6 (Denzinger, no. 3036).

[54] [Trans. note: There is no comma prior to this clause in the original. Fr. Garrigou-Lagrange is generally very careful with his use of commas for non-restrictive clauses when writing in French. In general, his Latin style is quite in line with his French prose.]

generally have concerning the existence of God the Supreme Lawgiver and concerning the existence of free choice of the will. Indeed, as we will discuss below, the value of the particular signs of Christianity's divine origin can be known with certitude without any scientific training, by natural reason, especially when it is aided by actual grace.

Hence, theologians commonly [speak like John of St. Thomas on this matter]:

> In order to believe by means of infused faith, it is not necessary that one deduce in particular through [inferential] consequence the reasons and motives of evident credibility, for that pertains to the wise and to theologians. However, it is necessary that they at least attain some motive of credibility inasmuch as this is needed for them to believe prudently, for he who believes without some motive of credibility believes imprudently and fickly.[55]

Hence, St. Thomas says that men would have needed to believe Christ even if he did not perform visible miracles, for there were other signs of credibility [available to them],[56] though miracles are the most suitable kind of sign.[57]

(2) *Nor is common physical certitude possible for all.* As will be discussed below, we can sometimes have [evidence] from witnesses of evident miracles that have been performed directly in confirmation of revelation. For example, they who saw the resurrection of Lazarus could have this kind of certitude [namely, physical certitude] concerning Christ's divine mission in this most evident and sensible sign. However, other men, who know divine signs only on the basis of human testimony, only have moral certitude of the fact of revelation confirmed by these signs. For moral certitude differs from metaphysical certitude and from physical certitude inasmuch as the connection between the predicate and the subject in [a morally certain proposition] does not depend on the very nature of one's ideas [as is the case for self-evident, metaphysically certain first principles], nor on the [physical] laws of nature, but rather, on human *mores*, for example, on the basis of human testimony.[58]

---

[55] John of St. Thomas, *Cursus theologicus, De fide*, disp. 2, a. 3, no. 5.

[56] See *Quod.* II, q. 4, a. 1; *ST* III, q. 43, a. 1, ad 3.

[57] See *ST* III, q. 43, a. 1; II-II, q. 178, a. 1.

[58] See what is said later on [in vol. 2] concerning the moral certitude involved in the discerning of miracles in ch. 19, a. 3. For now, however, it suffices to note the following. *Metaphysical certitude* is founded *per se* on *the metaphysical necessity* of what is asserted and on the metaphysical impossibility of the contradictory proposition. *Physical certitude* is founded on physical neces-

{{496}} Hence, Christ said to the Apostle Thomas: "Blessed are those who have not seen and have believed." In other words, blessed are those who were not slow to believe and who even believed without seeing such signs.[59]

Indeed, in the marvelous life of the Church, we always have at hand what the [First] Vatican Council calls "a great and perpetual motive of credibility."[60] However, unbelievers who do not know of the Church, and are converted on account of the words of some preacher, know of this marvelous life of the Church only on the basis of human testimony. Therefore, they only have moral certitude in the order of reason (i.e., before the grace of faith) concerning this motive of credibility.

However, natural reason (or common sense) can have absolute certitude concerning the utter trustworthiness of God as something naturally knowable, in fact, a certitude superior to both moral and physical certitude. Indeed, for all men, it is completely absurd to say that God can err or deceive.

(3) *Divine faith does not require anything more than moral certitude concerning its credibility.* This claim is proven as follows: In order to morally act in the weightiest things of the natural order, moral certitude suffices. Now, divine faith requires a judgment of credibility as something certain in the natural order in order to act morally in [this] grave matter. Therefore, divine faith requires only a morally certain judgment of credibility.

The major premise is proven as follows. The testimony of proven men

---

sity. *Speculative moral certitude* is founded on moral necessity and in the moral impossibility of the opposite being the case. For example, it is morally impossible that a given witness is lying in these circumstances, or it is morally impossible for man to naturally arrive at perfect knowledge of all the truths of natural religion; thus, it is morally certain that this knowledge comes from God.

This common terminology is departed from by those who, with Léon Ollé-Laprune (*De la certitude morale*, 413–414), define moral certitude as: "The firm adherence of the mind to historical or metaphysical truths influencing the moral life, an adherence that exists under the influence of moral dispositions with the concurrence of the will, even if an objective proof would *per se* suffice." This definition of moral certitude is the cause of equivocations because it is not taken from the *per se* motive of this certitude but, rather, from dispositions that *do not per se* concur to this kind of certitude. It would follow that the existence of God, as proven by valid metaphysical arguments, would be only morally certain and that, without the necessary moral dispositions, a very insightful but perverse philosopher could not arrive at certitude regarding God's existence. However, this is false. Nonetheless, the aforementioned definition is useful *ad hominem* against agnostics.

59 See *ST* III, q. 43, a. 1, ad 1: "Miracles diminish the merit of faith to the degree that people are shown to be hard of heart by wishing to believe in those things that are proven divinely by the Scriptures only on the basis of such miracles. And nonetheless, it is better that they be converted to faith through miracles than for them to remain completely unbelieving."

60 [First] Vatican Council, *Dei filius*, ch. 4 (Denzinger, no. 3014).

suffices for condemning a guilty man to death or for believing that a given medicine is not poisonous.

The minor premise is proven as follows. Divine faith does not require a judgment of credibility as a formal motive on which it would be formally and intrinsically founded but, rather, only as a [necessary] condition of an inferior order so that the act of faith may be prudent, with the prudence needed in a weighty matter. Evident credibility is only a kind of guidance leading one to belief.

Hence, there is a twofold resolution for the assent of faith. *The formal and intrinsic resolution* of the certitude of supernatural faith is made into divine revelation itself, which is infallibly and supernaturally believed as the formal motive of faith (that which is believed and that by which it is believed).[61] *However, the material and extrinsic resolution* from the perspective of the [knowing] subject is made into evidence of credibility as in a necessary condition required from the perspective of the subject. And another necessary condition exists from the perspective of the object—namely, the infallible proposition {{497}} of things revealed by the Church, for this proposition is not a formal motive of faith but only a [necessary objective] condition [for it], as we discussed in the previous chapter.

> Thus, in the natural order, metaphysical certitude concerning the truth of the first principles has a twofold resolution. Its formal and intrinsic resolution is made into the intellectual evidence of these principles under the natural light of our intellect. (This evidence is that which is seen and that by which it is seen.) However, they also are materially and extrinsically resolved into sensation and the sense evidence, which is a prerequisite condition for intellectual knowledge of the terms that make up these principles. Hence, metaphysical certitude concerning the truth of these principles is loftier than the certitude of sensation.

---

[61] See Salmanticenses, *Cursus theologicus, De fide*, disp. 1, dub. 5, §1, no. 156: "The assent of faith is *ultimately resolved from the perspective of its motive* or its formal cause into the first truth obscurely revealing." In §3, no. 169: "The Apostles and prophets from whom we receive the faith themselves evidently knew *through the very light of prophecy* that God spoke to them and revealed to them the *credibilia* that they handed on to us." In §3, no. 172: "Other Catholics in the Church know that God has revealed all those things that she proposes to them to believe in through the formal evidence of the divine credibility of the aforementioned object. Whence, the assent of faith in us *is resolved from the perspective of the subject*, or that of the acts which precede it, into the aforementioned evidence of credibility, as *into the* [necessary] *condition* upon which it *per se* depends."

In like manner, the certitude of faith is loftier than the natural certitude of credibility, even if this is itself already utterly firm.[62]

Hence, the moral certitude of credibility would not suffice if the certitude of faith were formally based on it. By contrast, however, it does suffice if faith presupposes it only as a necessary condition belonging to an inferior order so that the act of faith may be prudent, with the prudence needed in a grave matter.

Nonetheless, against the position held by Georg Hermes,[63] this moral certitude is speculative and not merely practical, because it is concerned with some existing or past fact and not only with the moral befittingness [*honestate*] of an action to be performed here and now, as though it were a question of an act of mercy toward the poor or an act of humility. Therefore, what is needed is common speculative moral certitude concerning the fact of revelation.[64]

---

[62] St. Thomas himself sets out this analogy in *In De Trinitate Boetii*, q. 3, a. 1, ad 4: "Just as knowledge of principles is taken from the sense and nonetheless the light by which the principles is known is itself innate, so too, faith is from hearing, even though the *habitus* of faith is infused." Likewise, in *ST* II-II, q. 4, a. 8: "Faith is, simply speaking, more certain than the natural intellectual virtues, namely wisdom, science, and understanding." Therefore, it is more certain than the judgment of credibility. And Innocent XI condemned this proposition: "The will cannot effect that assent to faith in itself be stronger than the weight of reasons impelling toward assent" (Denzinger, no. 2119).

[Trans. note: This footnote has no correlative in the body of the text. This seems to be an appropriate textual correlate.]

[63] See the end of our historical overview of apologetics from the perspective of methodology where we discuss the Hermesian notion of faith. Also see Vacant, *Études sur le Concile du Vatican*, vol. 1, 125–126.

[64] Someone could object: "This moral certitude is not sufficient, for it can *per accidens* be false if the witness invincibly errs in relating a false miracle as being true."

Response: Moral certitude *per se* suffices. Indeed, *per accidens* it is indeed an illegitimate persuasion that is very like moral certitude but, in fact, is not certitude, for one can afterwards discover that this persuasion is unfounded, which never happens for true certitude. Therefore, if one only has this kind of erroneous persuasion, then it follows that one does not have divine faith but, rather, only the appearance of faith. Thus, material heretics, who are in good faith, hold false dogmas by human opinion whereas, by contrast, they assent to certain truths of faith through supernatural faith. And he who thus believes something false can later on acknowledge the falseness of his judgment of credibility concerning this. By contrast, he who believes by divine faith never can later on see that he believed with insufficient or false credibility. If he has many motives of credibility, at least one was sufficient, even if perhaps it was not rightly formulated in its logical expression. See John of St. Thomas, *Cursus theologicus, De fide*, disp. 2, a. 3, no. 14. Likewise, see Édouard Hugon, *Cursus philosophiae Thomisticae*, vol. 1, *Logica* (Paris: Lethielleux, 1927), 256[ff], regarding the difference between moral certitude and firm but erroneous persuasion, which is only apparent moral certitude.

§5. This Moral Certitude Can Be Had by All Men, at Least with the Aid of Grace, Although Grace Is Not Absolutely Necessary for Having It

{{498}} This is certain (A) for all to whom revelation is proposed through Catholic preaching, and (B) it is also true for all others who do what is in their power for achieving salvation.

A. *Regarding all those who hear Catholic preaching*

Indeed, the mysteries of Christianity are proposed to all such people as being revealed by God according to the judgment of the universal Church, which is the most distinguished [*amplissima*] society in which are contained numberless exceptional men, holy doctors, and martyrs. Now, the divine origin of Christianity thus proposed is morally certain in the order of reason. Therefore, moral certitude concerning the fact of revelation is possible for all those to whom revelation is proposed through Catholic preaching.

John of St. Thomas explains this as follows:

> The principal motive for persuading someone of the credibility of our faith is the fact that the universal Church proposes it thus, which is the most distinguished [*amplissima*] gathering of people, containing within her bounds so many excellent men, as well as so many Saints, Doctors, and Martyrs. He who believes the proposition and teaching of such people does not imprudently do so, and the intention of the believer should always be concerned with what the universal and Catholic Church proposes and not this or that particular [person]. However, this motive is lacking for no one, however uneducated he may be, for whoever believes the creed or its articles says that he believes what the Holy Church believes.... Whence, lest this motive be lacking for someone, the Creed speaks of the "One, Holy, Catholic, and Apostolic Church," that is, the universal Church, not this or that [person] in particular. However, all men, however uneducated they may be, are bound to know the Creed.[65]

Objection: However, heretical children [*pueri*][66] already believe what they hear from their parents and pastors and nonetheless do not have sufficient credibility nor divine faith concerning the false doctrines that they confess. Therefore, for equal reason, Catholic children [*pueri*] have insufficient credibility on the basis of the testimony of their parents or pastors.

---

[65] John of St. Thomas, *Cursus theologicus, De fide*, disp. 2, a. 3, no. 5. Likewise, see Salmanticenses, *Cursus theologicus, De fide*, disp. 1, dub. 4, no. 198.

[66] [Trans. note: Reading *heretic* as *heretici*, following the later expression *puer hereticus*.]

Response: There is no parity here, for *the testimony of Catholic pastors expresses the judgment of the universal Church, whereas by contrast, the testimony of heretical pastors expresses the judgment of some particular sect.* Later, the child heretic, examining his sect, can acknowledge its falsity. However, the credibility proposed by the Catholic Church is never found to be false.

Hence, John of St. Thomas says:

> Although they who from childhood are raised among heretics . . . believe what is proposed to them by their ministers and do not have others who may teach them concerning the true faith, nonetheless they do fall short inasmuch as their intention in believing those things is not oriented toward believing what the holy, universal, and catholic Church believes since, rather, they deny the Catholic Church; instead, their intention is only oriented to what they are told to believe by their particular minister or their particular church.[67]

Nonetheless, non-obstinate heretics who are in good faith can supernaturally believe true dogmas, which are proposed to them among various errors.[68] However, they admit false dogmas through human and not divine faith—namely, on the basis of the error by which they believe that God has revealed what he in fact has not revealed. Hence, they believe this false thing not "because God has revealed it" but because they fancy that God has revealed it.

Therefore, speaking *per se*, the testimony of parents and pastors is a sufficient condition for knowing the true motives of credibility. However, *per accidens*, such testimony can fall short; {{499}} that is, *per accidens* it proposes insufficient credibility, in which case true, divine faith does not follow but, rather, the appearance of faith.

Thus, the heretic, examining the credibility of his faith, can acknowledge its falsity. By contrast, the Catholic always finds a confirmation of his judgment of credibility in the miraculous life of the Church, for in her outstanding holiness, inexhaustible fecundity, Catholic unity, and unconquered stability we find ourselves faced with, as the [First] Vatican Council itself said, "an irrefutable testimony of her divine mission."

Therefore, this motive, already known by the mediation of human testimony, can be verified through firsthand [*immediatam*] knowledge of the Church's life. In this way, as will be discussed below, we can have the greatest moral certitude, which approaches physical and metaphysical certitude extrinsically, from a consideration of the laws of psychology and the naturally knowable attributes of God. Indeed, universal error in the Church regarding the fact of revelation would be without a *raison d'être*, contrary

---

[67] John of St. Thomas, *Cursus theologicus, De fide*, disp. 2, a. 3, no. 5.

[68] And concerning these true dogmas, they have sufficient credibility from divine signs that their pastors refer to, though alongside errors as well.

to the principal laws of [philosophical] psychology, and it is metaphysically certain that God cannot permit a false revelation to be intimately joined with the great fecundity of spiritual goods in the Church. "For by the fruit the tree is known" (Matt 12:33, DR).

Finally, we must add that *although grace is not absolutely necessary for this rational certitude of credibility, nonetheless, frequently (and, according to some, ordinarily) it aids the intellect in attaining it.* As Billuart says:[69]

> With respect to believers, nothing prevents it from being the case that the *habitus* of faith which they have would concur in their knowledge of credibility, and St. Thomas seems to assert this as well.[70]—However, as regards those who are disposed to faith and do not yet have the *habitus* of faith, there is a twofold response. Some think that they know credibility only through their natural intellectual powers.... Such is the position held, within our own school, by Jean-Baptiste Gonet [*Ita noster Gonet*].[71]—The other response is that he who approaches faith knows the credibility of the mysteries of faith, aided by a kind of supernatural light, namely, by the actual illuminations by which God illuminates his intellect so that he may perceive and judge those things that are of God, thereby making him *harken to those things that are said and preached*, as it is said in Acts 16 that *the Lord opened Lydia's heart to harken to those things that St. Paul said*, as well as to observe and judge that there is divine credibility in those things that they immediately come to have faith in. The reason for this is that although *absolutely speaking*, the intellect can grasp, by its own natural power, the motives of credibility, nonetheless, these are preambles and dispositions to faith as to an end. ... Whence, although God could absolutely and immediately move our will and elevate our intellect so that it would elicit the act of faith after grasping these natural things, nonetheless that is less in harmony with the natural and common way that things happen, as well as with God's agreeable [*suavi*] manner of

---

[69] Billuart, *Summa sancti Thomae, De fide*, diss. 1, a. 6, resp. to obj. 2.

[70] See *ST* II-II, q. 1, a. 4, ad 3: "The light of faith makes one see those things that are believed, or just as through other virtuous *habitus* man sees that which is suited to that *habitus*, so too through the *habitus* of faith is man's mind inclined to assent to those things that are suited to right faith and not to others." Likewise, see a. 5, ad 1: "Those things that are of faith . . . are known by the faithful not in a kind of demonstrative way, but rather, inasmuch as they see, through the light of faith, that they should be believed." Likewise, see *Quod.* II, q. 4, a. 1; *ST* II-II, q. 2, a. 9, ad 3.

[71] See Gonet, *Clypeus theologiae Thomisticae, De fide*, disp. 1, a. 8.

acting. Therefore, that is at least not the way that things happen ordinarily.[72] Thus, Wiggers, whom we cited earlier [*iam laudatus Wiggers*], held this, and {{500}} this seems to be St. Thomas's own opinion in *ST* II-II, q. 2, a. 9, ad 3, where he says, "He who believes has a sufficient inducement [*inductivum*] for believing, for he is led [*inducitur*] by the authority of the divine teaching confirmed by miracles and, what is more, by the interior instinct of God inviting him [to faith]."[73]

This is a probable explanation for those who arrive at faith. However, those who, like the Pharisees, commit the sin of infidelity with full awareness can themselves also *de facto* grasp the credibility [of faith] with certainty without interior grace, as we will soon discuss.

According to this explanation, by thus ordinarily *aiding* those who arrive at faith so that they may know its credibility, God's interior grace does not supply for any deficiency in the external proposition of the faith but,

---

[72] See Henri-Dominique Lacordaire, *17th Conference*, 333: "He is such a learned man who has studied Catholic doctrine, who does not drive it back with bitterness and even who ceaselessly says: 'You are quite fortunate to have faith; I would like to have it like you but cannot.' And he is speaking truly. He wishes to have it and cannot, for study and good faith do not always suffice for conquering the truth, so that it would be clear that *rational certitude* is not the *primary certitude* on which Catholic doctrine rests. Therefore, this learned man knows the Catholic doctrine. He admits its facts. He feels its power. It is fitting that a man who was called Jesus Christ existed, who lived and died in a prodigious manner. He is moved by the blood of the martyrs, by the constitution of the Church. He will readily say that it is the greatest phenomenon that has traversed the world. He will nearly say, 'It is true!' However, he does not draw this conclusion. *He feels oppressed by the truth*, as one is in a dream in which one sees without seeing. However, one day, this learned man is brought to his knees. He feels the misery of the human condition. He lifts his hands to heaven and says, 'From the depths of my misery, O my God, I have cried to you!' At this moment, something happens inside of him. The scales fall from his eyes. A mystery is accomplished—he is changed! He is a man who is sweet and humble of heart. He can die; he has conquered the truth."

[Trans. note: Fr. Garrigou-Lagrange does not directly cite the edition. See Henri-Dominique Lacordaire, *Conférences de Notre-Dame de Paris*, vol. 1 (Paris: Librairie Garnier Frères, 1921), 297–298.]

[73] This explanation thus set forth by Billuart is found already in John of St Thomas, *Cursus theologicus, De fide*, disp. 2, art. 3, no. 13, and in many other Thomists.

Likewise, De Groot, O.P., *De ecclesia*, q. 22, a. 3: "He who is led to faith, can see the evidence of credibility by the natural light of reason, since human reason considers the external arguments for revelation. However, some supernatural light, like a kind of luminous dawning of the light of faith, is not completely excluded from the judgment of credibility." Also see Ambroise de Poulpiquet, *Le miracle et ses suppléances* (Paris: Beauchesne, 1914), 21–32, as well as the critical review of this work by Fr. Cathala in *Revue Thomiste* (July 1914): 487ff.

rather, only *inclines the attention* of the hearer to the true motives of credibility that are preached with the mysteries and *corrects his intention* so that he may judge aright and not according to the inordinate inclinations of egoism or pride.[74]

Nonetheless, *sometimes "the internal grace of God supplies for that which is lacking in the external proposition of the faith."*[75] As Billuart puts the matter:[76]

> For sometimes only the voice of the preacher suffices, along with the interior light urging on behalf of the credibility of what is said, as is clear in children and uneducated men {{501}} who believe in the words of their pastors whom they know to speak in the name of the Church, in the Indians, who believed the missionaries preaching to them without miracles, and in the Apostles, who followed Christ solely at His calling before they saw any of His miracles.—And nonetheless, it does not follow that the motives of credibility were superfluous to the preaching of the Gospel.... For the mode of arriving at faith that is suited to human nature is that which takes place through the motives of credibility.

And *grace* does not supply [for what is missing here] so that the mysteries might be believed in without evidence of credibility but, rather, *manifests this evidence to us*, for example, in the extraordinary and holy conviction of the preacher of the faith, in the sublimity of this doctrine, in the profound peace that we come to have from it: "Was not our heart burning within us, whilst he spoke in this way?" (Luke 24:32, DR).[77]

---

[74] *Many modern thinkers, filled with philosophical prejudices, seem to stand in need of grace's aid in order to form a right judgment in their knowledge of the value of the signs of revelation.* See Jacques Maritain, "Les deux Bergsonismes," *Revue Thomiste*, New Series, 12 (1912), 448: "The most general cause of philosophical errors consists in, it seems, a kind of inversion of the order of the intellect's ordering to its end, an inversion through which the intellect, instead of tending toward conformity with reality, rather, tends to the degree that it is possible, to conform reality to itself ... as though human science were the measure of being.... Whence comes the absurd *a priori* persuasion that the supernatural order is impossible. Hence, every demonstration of the fact of revelation will be shattered against the brazen wall of this prejudice, and it is only when grace comes to free reason that the latter will find itself in a state to recognize the full scope of the apologetic demonstration."

[75] This is affirmed in the annotations in the *Schemata prosynodalia Concilii Vaticani* (*Collectio lacensis*, vol. 7, col. 1623).

[76] Billuart, *Summa sancti Thomae*, diss. 1, a. 6 (*in fine*).

[77] See Salmanticenses, *Cursus theologicus, De fide*, tr. 17, disp. 1, dub. 4, no. 198: "But if someone is converted to faith without sufficient external calling leading to the aforementioned evidence (of credibility) such that this does not seem to have happened even once [*ut non semel contigisse videtur*], it therefore does not exist, for they lack that evidence; *indeed, they are internally illuminated by a supernatural light by God, upon which the aforementioned evidence follows* .... And if this instinct is from God, it must subject man to the Catholic Church, as to the

"But," as Billuart adds, "if it happens that certain people believe without any motive of credibility, this extraordinary occurrence is miraculous." It is better to say: Then, one has evidence of credibility miraculously, just as the prophet, under the light of prophecy, has evidence of the divine testifying, as happens in private revelations and as took place in St. Paul's conversion. Hence, *internal grace does not totally supply for the external proposition of the motives of credibility, except in extraordinary cases.* This is said against Protestants who would like the judgment concerning the credibility of the mysteries solely on the basis of internal inspiration and thus even to be able to discern between revealed and non-revealed things.[78]

Hence, all those to whom revelation is proposed through Catholic preaching can have moral certitude concerning the fact of revelation.

B. *As regards those who are invincibly unaware of Catholic preaching*

We must hold on faith that those who have the use of reason do [from time to time] accept sufficient grace, at least remotely, for arriving at salvation. Hence, if they do what is in their power, they can, "by the efficacious power of divine light and grace," arrive at sufficient credibility of the mysteries of salvation.[79]

Indeed, if they are numbered among heretics, they can know certain principal mysteries and sufficient motives of credibility through the preaching of their sect, which frequently retains certain truths mixed alongside with error. Thus, they hold the error through human opinion and can believe certain mysteries of salvation through divine faith.

However, if "someone reared in the forests" and invincibly unaware of every form of Christian preaching "were to follow the lead of natural reason in {{502}} seeking the good and fleeing what is evil, we must hold with utter certainty that God would either reveal to him through an internal inspira-

---

infallible rule of things to be believed; otherwise, it will not be from God but, rather, will be a demonic illusion. However, according to St. Thomas, this is found in all Catholics. Whence, since sufficient evidence of the credibility of the mysteries of faith is founded on it, nobody believes without having the aforementioned evidence, although it is not equally present in all, nor equally sensed by them."

Hence, *when grace supplies* for what is lacking in the external proposition of faith, *it does not* supply in such a way that the mysteries would be believed *without evidence of credibility but, rather, makes this evidence manifest to us* (e.g., in the excellence and holy conviction of a preacher of the faith, in the sublimity of the doctrine, or in the profound peace that comes from it). The hearer says to himself, "Only God can know and stir man's heart in so profound a manner." Thus, the disciples on the road to Emmaus said to each other, concerning Christ: "Was not our heart burning within us, whilst he spoke in this way and opened to us the scriptures?" (Luke 24:32, DR).

[78] See Vacant, *Études sur le Concile du Vatican*, vol. 2, 39 and vol. 1, 594.

[79] See Pius IX, *Quanto confiamur moerore* (Denzinger, no. 2865[ff]).

tion those things that must be believed or would direct some preacher to him, as He sent Peter to Cornelius, as we read in Acts 10."[80]

Hence, moral certitude concerning the fact of revelation can be had by all men, at least with the aid of internal grace.

C. *Why is internal grace not absolutely necessary for a certain judgment of credibility?*

This grace is not absolutely necessary because, as we will discuss below, the motives for this judgment are naturally knowable divine signs such as miracles. Hence, as theologians say in general: "It remains quite possible that someone can evidently judge concerning the credibility of a miracle that he has seen while nonetheless not believing on account of his perversity."[81] Thus, many of the Pharisees who saw Christ's miracles resisted grace disposing them to faith. Hence, Jesus said, "If I had not done among them the works that no other man hath done, they would not have sin: but now they have both seen and hated both me and my Father" (John 15:24, DR). Nay,

---

[80] *De veritate*, q. 14, a. 11, ad 1. See Édouard Hugon, *Hors de l'Eglise pas de salut*, 2nd ed. (1914), ch. 4 (The salvation of pagans), 105: "It is not difficult for the first Master of souls to exercise a secret, omnipotent, and irresistible magisterium within the intimate depths of our intellects. As He never does anything useless, He can make use of the religious knowledge of the pagan— all the while correcting and completing them.

"Indeed, our apologists note, as an ordinary means utilized by Providence, either forgotten evangelization which has nonetheless left its traces or also primitive tradition [that such people have]. . . .

"These hypotheses could be acceptable for the theologian as for the apologist on the condition that one always makes appeal to the supernatural action of an infinitely merciful Providence which, sincerely wishing that all men be saved, owes to itself to illuminate each of them according to his or her condition.

"Let us not try to resolve the problem by using responses that would be too satisfying to rationalist eyes. It is always God's side of things that St. Thomas considers, only ever accepting solutions that are worthy of God and of His grace.

"Since the faith required for salvation is *essentially* supernatural, it is necessary, in any hypothesis, that the revelation on which it is supported be supernatural in its *object*, that its *motive* be supernatural, and that *the principle* of the assent be supernatural. God will know how to intervene, in His sublime manner, to arrange the graces of illumination and inspiration, to take, if necessary to correct, and to transform the elements of paganism that can be used, placing them in the service of the conceiving of supernatural truths needed for salvation." Likewise, see 332. Also see Edmond Dublanchy, *De axiomate: Extra ecclesiam nulla salus* (Bar-le-Duc: Contant-Laguerre, 1895), 273–281.

In this matter, Lamennais and certain *liberals* err in saying that the truths necessary for salvation are only the first natural truths of the intellectual and moral order, arising from primitive revelation. On this matter, see Vacant, *Études sur le Concile du Vatican*, vol. 2, 137ff. (On p. 145, Vacant rightly explains the opposition between Suarez and Cardinal de Lugo in this matter.)

[81] John of St. Thomas, *Cursus theologicus, De fide*, disp. 3, a. 2, no. 10.

as is said in Acts 4:16–17 (DR), after the miracle performed by St. Peter and St. John, the priests of the synagogue said: "What shall we do to these men? For indeed a miracle hath been done by them, known to all the inhabitants of Jerusalem. It is manifest: and we cannot deny it. But that it may be no farther spread among the people, let us threaten them that they speak no more in this name to any man."

Likewise, the adversaries of the Catholic Church sometimes acknowledge to themselves[82] that her miraculous life is divine and nonetheless fight against her with greater impiety.[83] {{503}} Moreover, according to theologians, demons can know the fact of revelation with certitude without, however, having interior grace.

Therefore, evident credibility can be known without grace, not only absolutely speaking but also *de facto*.[84] Nay, it can be known alongside obstinate resistance to grace.

Hence, Pius IX says, after the enumeration of the principal motives of credibility: "All of this certainly shines in every way with so great a glory of divine wisdom and power that the mind and intelligence of each one clearly understand that the Christian faith is the work of God."[85]

ART. 3: ON THE OFFICE OF THE JUDGMENT OF CREDIBILITY IN THE GENESIS OF THE ACT OF FAITH

§1. The acts that dispose to the act of faith

§2. The distinction between the judgment of credibility and the judgment of credentity

§1. The Acts That Dispose to the Act of Faith

In order to understand the relation of the judgment of credibility to the act of faith exactly, we must consider the genesis of the act of faith itself.

---

[82] [Trans. note: Reading *Sibi* for *eis*.]

[83] See Prouhon, *De la justice dans la revolution et dans l'église*, vol. 1, 27: "The Revolution believes in humanity, whereas the Church believes in God. She believes in Him better than any sect. She is the purest, most complete, and most brilliant manifestation of the Divine Essence, and only she knew how to worship it."

[84] Indeed, it would be marvelous if reason could *of itself* arrive at this knowledge and never *de facto* do so by its natural powers alone.

[85] Pius IX, *Qui pluribus*, no. 9 (Denzinger, no. 2779). Also see Garrigou-Lagrange, "La grâce de la foi et le miracle: Trois theories, a propos des travaux récents," *Revue Thomiste*, New Series, 18 (Oct. 1918): 289–320.

Now, the act of faith is a deliberate human act elicited by the intellect and commanded by the will under the inspiration and illumination of the Holy Spirit. Hence, we must call to mind the succession of the acts that concur in the deliberation and execution of any given proposed [course of action]. These acts are enumerated and explained by St. Thomas in *ST* I-II, q. 8–18.[86]

I. Acts Concerned with the End
Order of intention

Acts of the intellect	Acts of the will
(1) *Judgment*: This end is *desirable*.	(2) *Desire* (simple willing that is not yet efficacious).
(3) *Judgment*: This end is *attainable and is to be attained*.	(4) Efficacious *intention*: I will this end.

II. Acts Concerned with the Means
A. *Order of choice*

(5) *Counsel*: These means appear to me *in globo* to be suited to the intended end.	(6) *Consent* to these various means.
(7) *Practico-practical judgment* concerning this means that is quite apt and to be chosen.	(8) *Choice* of this means.

B. *Order of execution*

(9) *Command*: the ordering and declaring of the execution[87] of the chosen means.	(10) *Active use* of the will, which moves the other powers to execution.
(11) *Attainment* of the desired end.	(12) *Enjoyment* of the will in the attained end.

---

[86] In this explanation, we follow Ambroise Gardeil, *La crédibilité et l'apologétique*, 2nd ed. (Paris: Lecoffre, 1912), 4–64 and his article "Crédibilité," in the *Dictionnaire de théologie catholique*, col. 2206.

[87] [Trans. note: Reading "*executio*" for "*esecutio*".]

{{504}} *Acts concurring in the act of faith*

I. ACTS CONCERNED WITH THE END
Order of intention

Acts of the intellect	Acts of the will
(1) *Judgment*: The ultimate end is at least implicitly known as a *desirable* good.	(2) *Desire* for the ultimate end—that is, for beatitude or salvation.
(3) *Judgment*: The end can and *ought* to be pursued: I ought to know, serve obey, and love God above all things.	(4) *Intention*: To the degree that it lays within my power, I sincerely will the ultimate end, salvation, and hence will to obey God.

(N.B. In men who arrive at faith, acts 3 and 4 already are performed under the illumination and arousal of interior grace.)
Hearing of faith: Revelation of the saving truth is proposed and confirmed by divine signs.

II. ACTS CONCERNED WITH THE MEANS
A. *Order of choice*

(5) *Counsel* concerning the proposed revelation: *a)* speculative, remotely practical judgment of credibility: *This is credible.* *b)* speculatively-practical judgment of credentity: *This is to be believed by men.*	(6) *Consent* to this credibility. This consent is not yet, of itself, efficacious.
(7) *Practico-practical judgment* of credentity: *This must be believed by me here and now.*	(8) Supernatural *choice* of the act of belief (pious affect of belief).

B. *Order of execution*

(9) *Command*: "Believe."	(10) *Active use* of the will (pious motion).
(11) *Act of faith*: "I believe."	(12) *Enjoyment* of the surety of faith.

§2. The Distinction between the Judgment of Credibility and the Judgment of Credentity

The principal difference [between the judgment of credibility and that of credentity] is found in the fact that the judgment of credibility and even the speculatively-practical judgment of credentity are found not only in those who arrive at faith but also in those who with full awareness commit the sin of infidelity. By contrast, the practically-practical judgment of credentity is found only in those who arrive at faith, and it essentially [*per se*] requires some aid of grace.

Indeed, when the preaching of the Gospel, confirmed by miracles, is proposed to certain people like the Pharisees, they resist internal grace and do not sincerely intend salvation. Hence, they can, having seen such miracles, judge evidently concerning the credibility of the proposed preaching. Nay, they can know the obligation of believing and nonetheless can refuse to believe on account of their perversity. Then the evidence of credibility and of the obligation to believe constitutes full {{505}} awareness in this sin of infidelity. Thus, he who knowingly commits injustice sees that justice must be kept by all and can say, "I see the better thing to do (speculative judgment), and I approve of it (speculatively-practical judgment), and yet I follow the worse path (practically-practical judgment and evil choice)." Hence, Christ said: "If I had not done among them the works that no other man hath done, they would not have sin: but now they have both seen and hated both me and my Father" (John 15:24, DR).

By contrast, when other men like the apostles, Zacchaeus, and Nicodemus had the preaching of the Gospel proposed to them, they were already at least incipiently men "of good will." That is, they did not resist the actual grace coming to them preveniently to arouse them [to faith], and they sincerely intended the ultimate end, which they at least implicitly knew. They did what was in their power and therefore did not only speculatively know credibility and the general obligation of believing but even arrived at a practically-practical judgment of credentity; namely, "This must be believed *by me, here and now.* I see what is better, approve it, and indeed follow it."

However, such a practically-practical judgment of credentity cannot exist in those who resist the grace of the beginning faith and indeed is only made with the aid of actual grace. This is theologically proven from the Council of Orange's definition against the semi-Pelagians: "If anyone says . . . that the beginning of faith and the very desire of faith [*credulitatis affectum*] . . . proceeds from our own nature and not from a gift of grace, namely, from an inspiration of the Holy Spirit changing our will from unbelief to belief and from Godlessness to piety, such a one reveals himself to be in contradiction with the apostolic doctrine."[88] This pious affect of belief is the supernatural choice of the act of believing. Now, however, the practical-ly-practical judgment immediately ruling this supernatural choice must be supernatural, for it proposes things to be believed not only as credible or to be believed in general but, rather, as being good and befitting *for me here and now, according to the actual disposition of* my *will*.

Hence, St. Thomas says: "The beginning of faith is in the affect inasmuch as the will determines the intellect to assent to those things that are of faith, but that willing is not the act of charity, nor that of hope, but rather, a kind of *desire for a good that is promised*."[89] "Therefore," as John of St. Thomas adds, "if it is a desire for a promised good, it is neces-sary that it proceed from some judgment representing the befittingness of the promised good,"[90] and such befittingness [must] not merely [be represented] in the abstract but, rather, concretely for me here and now, something that presupposes that my will is already incipiently moved to things to be believed under the influence of actual grace. For in general, choice *secundum quid* precedes the practico-practical judgment in the order of efficient causality, even though it *simpliciter* follows it in the order of directive formal causality, according to [this] common principle: causes are causes of each other, though in different genera [of causality].[91] Thus, choice makes the ultimate practical judgment truly be the ultimate judgment.

{{506}} According to the Thomists, the practically-practical judg-ment of credentity and the pious affect of belief are essentially supernatural because they are specified by a promised good that is essentially supernatural, to which the will is already moved.[92] Thus, St. Peter says: "Lord, to whom

---

[88] Council of Orange, can. 5 (Denzinger, no. 375).

[89] See *De veritate*, q. 14, a. 2, ad 10.

[90] John of St. Thomas, *Cursus theologicus, De fidei*, disp. 3, a. 2, no. 9.

[91] See Salmanticenses, *Cursus theologicus, De angelis*, disp. 10, dub. 8, no. 270: "Judgment in the order of extrinsic formal causality directs the will so that it may thus determinately render a choice; in the order of efficient causality, the will applies the intellect as regards its exercise so that it may thus determinately judge things."

[92] Someone could object: "A judgment that is essentially supernatural cannot exist before faith. Now, the practico-practical judgment of credentity precedes faith. Therefore, it cannot be essentially supernatural."

Response: I concede that an essentially supernatural and speculative judgment concerning the mysteries of faith in themselves cannot exist before the act of faith. However, by contrast, I deny that this is so for an essentially supernatural and practical judgment concerning the obligation and befittingness for me here and now to believe. For this obligation is founded on naturally known principles, and the affect for things to be believed is produced under the influence of the incitements of grace.

However, if the speculative judgment of credibility prior to faith sometimes may be super-natural, it is only modally supernatural and not *per se* essentially so, for its object can be known

shall we go? Thou hast the words of eternal life?" (John 6:69, DR).

From this, it is clear what office is filled by the judgment of credibility. It is the [necessary] condition[93] for the act of faith inasmuch as its obscure assent must be resolved at least materially and extrinsically into some kind of evidence. Hence, the rational credibility of the mysteries of faith, which can be known by reason alone and which is a remote condition for the act of faith, must be distinguished from the supernatural credibility of these mysteries, which is attained under the light of faith inasmuch as the authority of God revealing in act is that which is believed and that by which the mysteries are believed. Therefore, the act of faith is not the conclusion of the apologetic syllogism. Instead, this syllogism is terminated at the judgment of credibility. In short: "Whatever God reveals is rationally credible; now, God revealed the Christian doctrine, as is clear from the signs by which it is confirmed; therefore, this doctrine is rationally credible."

Art. 4: Resolution of Objections (the Reconciliation of the Rational Obedience of Faith with the Obscurity, Freedom, and Supernaturality of Faith)

There are four classes of objections: (1) probability of the fact of revelation suffices, (2) otherwise the freedom of faith would not be preserved, (3) nor its obscurity, (4) nor its supernaturality.

We must respond to these objections point by point.

§1 Objection: Probability of the Fact of Revelation Suffices for Having Rational Credibility

Objection: In order to act prudently, it suffices that we have speculative probability and practical certitude concerning the moral befittingness of an action. Now, the judgment of credibility is speculative and only remotely practical. Therefore, in order to prudently believe, it suffices that we have a probable judgment of credibility.

{{507}} *Response*: I make a distinction regarding the major premise. I concede it if there is no *danger of grave error and sin*. Otherwise, I deny it. I concede the minor and draw a distinction regarding the conclusion. I concede the latter if one means that in order to prudently believe, a probable judgment of credibility would suffice if there were no danger of grave error as well as of superstition and idolatry. Otherwise, I deny it.

---

by reason alone.

93 [Trans. note: Reading "sine qua non" for "si qua non".]

Allow me to explain. If there is no danger of grave error and sin, speculative probability and practical certitude concerning the moral befittingness of an action is sufficient.[94] For example, for giving alms, we do not require speculative moral certitude concerning the true poverty of the person asking for money and about his intention to use it well. Likewise, the soldier in doubt concerning the justice of a given war is nonetheless morally permitted to take part in it under the order of his leader [*principis*] on account of the reflex principle stating that the leader has a certain right to be obeyed so long as there is no widespread agreement concerning [the war's] injustice. In that case, one is lacking in speculative certitude, which is taken in accord with the conformity of the judgment to the thing itself [or to reality in itself], though one does have practically-practical certitude concerning the moral befittingness of the action, for such certitude is taken "according to conformity with right appetite" (or to intention that is virtuously rectified [*ad intentionem rectam*]).[95]

By contrast, sometimes there is a danger of grave error and sin depending on the very nature of the reality at hand, and it is not removed through an opposed persuasion by one's conscience. For example, in order to give some medicine to a sick person, a doctor must know not only probably but also certainly that this medicine is not poisonous, for otherwise he would risk committing murder, and that risk is not removed by the opposite persuasion of his conscience since it depends upon the very nature of the medicine. Hence, "right reason declares that to the degree that a matter is weightier, and to the degree that error connected to it is potentially more, to that same degree must greater care be taken in order to guard against such an error."[96]

Likewise, in the case of faith, the danger of error is morally grave, for if the revelation at hand is fictitious and not true, the whole of our faith would be founded on error and superstition, meaning that we firmly hold as the Word of God that which is only an invention of men or of demons.[97] If one had only probable credibility, "the intellect would imprudently restrain its fear, given that it could indeed prudently fear [in this case]." Hence, Pius IX said: "Indeed, human reason, lest it be deceived and err in a matter of so great importance, ought to investigate diligently the fact of divine revelation so that it can know with certainty that God has spoken."[98]

1. *It will be urged*: A certain speculative judgment is not needed even in grave danger of error. Indeed, in doubt concerning things needed for salvation (necessity of means), the safer path is to be taken. Now, faith is proposed as being necessary with a necessity as a means for salvation: "He who does not believe shall be condemned." Therefore, even

---

94 See Clément Marc, *Institutiones morales Alphonsianae seu S. Alphonsi Mariae de Ligorio Doctrina moralis ad usum scholarum accommodata*, De conscientia certa, no. 55; De conscientia dubia, no. 41.

95 See *ST* I-II, q. 57, a. 5, ad 3.

96 Salmanticenses, *Cursus theologicus, De fide*, disp. 1, dub. 4, no. 185.

97 Superstition is the vice that is opposed to religion by way of excess. *ST* II-II, q. 92, 94, and 95.

98 Pius IX, *Qui pluribus*, against the followers of Georg Hermes, no. 7 (Denzinger, no. 2778).

while doubt or probability remains concerning the fact of revelation, it is safer to believe.[99]

Response: I concede the major and the minor premises but deny the consequence. For the true consequence is: Therefore, so long as doubt or probability remains concerning the fact of revelation, the safer path is to be followed. However, it remains to determine what the safer path is in this case. Now, one must not believe immediately, because the necessary condition required for faith is lacking (namely, sufficient credibility). Therefore, in such a case one would have only a religious opinion and not theological faith. {{508}} *The safer path is to inquire further into the matter and to pray*, inasmuch as the befittingness of prayer is known by such a person.[100]

Allow me to explain. In general, the safer path is that which favors our obligation, whereas the less safe one is that which favors freedom. Hence, in danger of grave harm [to oneself or another person] or of sin, one is not permitted to follow a probable opinion, setting aside a safer one: "No security is too great where eternity is possibly endangered."

For example, to some Muslim, Catholicism may seem to be more probably instituted by God and safer, while it seems less probable that Islam comes from God. In that case, this man cannot remain a Muslim in good conscience; however, he cannot suddenly and firmly believe in the truth of Catholicism but, rather, is bound to inquire further into the matter and even to pray inasmuch as he knows the necessity of prayer. St. Alphonsus of Liguori says:

> For as long as the heretic judges that his sect is more credible or at least equally credible, he is not bound to believe, for faith has not yet been sufficiently pro-

---

[99] Billuart, in *Summa sancti Thomae, De fide*, diss. 3, a. 3, §2, does not sufficiently consider this distinction to be made in this case concerning the safer path. However, he rightly says, concerning the nonbeliever in doubt between his own sect and the Catholic faith, that even if neither seems safer to him, "he is bound under pain of mortal sin to diligently inquire into the truth, for otherwise ignorance of the true faith would become voluntary and culpable for him. Nor do I doubt that many heretics are in this state, especially those who are found among Catholics."

[100] This objection has a great affinity with the argument proposed by Pascal in his famed wager. Indeed, in this, we can see the fideism and tutiorism of the Jansenists. See Pascal, *Pensées*, ed. Ernest Havet [Paris: Delagrave, 1928], art. 10, p. 174: "Therefore, let us examine this point and say: God exists or does not. But to what side shall we incline? Reason cannot determine in either direction here. . . . Yes, but it is necessary to wager: this is not an optional matter; you have already embarked. Therefore, which will you choose? . . . If you win, you win everything. If you lose, you lose nothing. Therefore, wager without hesitation that He exists. . . . In truth, you will not have those reeking pleasures, glory, and luxury; however, will not others be yours? I tell you that you will have gains in this life and that with every step that you take upon this path you will see so much certitude of gain and so much the nothingness of what you risk that you will in the end recognize that you have made your wager for an infinite and certain thing for which you have given nothing." This argument makes manifest at least the obligation of *diligently inquiring into* revelation by him who already knows that revelation is probable.

posed to him and therefore he would act imprudently. . . . If some doubt arises in him about his given sect, he is bound to inquire further into the matter and to seek light from God. If he neglects to do this, he sins against faith since he would not thus employ the means needed for fulfilling the precept of faith. Finally, if our faith is sufficiently proposed to him, he is bound to embrace it.[101]

Indeed, God does not deny further grace to him who does what is in his power (under the influence of actual grace), including the illumination needed for judging with certainty concerning credibility. Hence, this proposition of certain probabilists is condemned: "An infidel who does not believe will be excused of infidelity since he is guided by a less probable opinion."[102]

However, if it is a question of a believer tempted against faith, the safer part is not only to pray but also to believe—that is, to persevere in faith, which can never be legitimately put into doubt.[103]

2. *It is urged, further, however*: Nonetheless, the uneducated and children admit the fact of revelation on account of the authority of their parents or pastor. Now, this authority gives only probability, for in false religions or sects, pastors and parents teach falsehoods as though they were divinely revealed. Therefore, the uneducated and children can only have probable knowledge concerning the fact of revelation.

Response: To the major premise, *the authority of one's pastor or parents is not a motive of credibility but, rather, is a condition* for knowledge of the motives of credibility, for they refer to signs by which revelation is confirmed. And this condition is *per se* sufficient for moral certitude, even though it may *per accidens* lead to error. As we said in the thesis above, it suffices *per se* inasmuch as the testimony of one's pastor or parents does not differ from the universal testimony of the Church, which is never false. However, *per accidens* pastors and parents refer only to the testimony of a given particular sect, and then this testimony is afterwards set aside as false.

{{509}} Thus, especially under the internal illumination of the Holy Spirit, uneducated people and children can know the fact of revelation with moral certitude through the mediation of the testimony offered on its behalf by their pastor and parents. Moreover, baptized children already have the infused *habitus* of faith, which corroborates the judgment of credibility, and *they who cannot yet judge by themselves concerning credibility admit it on account of the authority of their parents*.

3. *Yet it is insisted*: However, the majority of children and uneducated do not seem to believe on account of the authority of God who reveals and on account of the Church's proposition [of *credibilia*], but the great majority of them believe on the word of their

---

[101] See St. Alphonsus, *Theologia moralis*, bk. 2, ch. 2, no. 9.

[102] Innocent XI, Condemnation by the Sacred Office, Mar. 2, 1679, no. 4 (Denzinger, no. 2104).

[103] See [First] Vatican Council, can. 3.6 (Denzinger, no. 3036).

pastor or parents or because others believe, though they are prepared to believe something else if others were to believe something else.

Response: With Billuart, we say:

> If this were so, their faith is not divine, and pastors and confessors should give attentive care to it. . . . Nonetheless, we must not immediately condemn as lacking true faith people who, upon being asked about the motives for their faith, on account of the slowness of their abilities do not readily and explicitly respond that they believe on account of the authority of God who reveals and that they know that God has revealed this and because the Church who is infallible thus proposes it. Indeed, if he responds with something that virtually and implicitly contains [this fact], namely, that he believes so that he may be saved, because this is the true faith, because God commands it to be believed, and that he knows this because pastors, qua ministers of the Church, so teach this, and that other believers hold it so, or something similar . . . such a person seems to have divine faith.[104]

4. *It will be urged, however*: Unbelievers, hearing some missionary, do not know with certitude whether he is a minister of the universal Church or of a particular sect. Now, many of them seem to come to supernatural faith before perceiving signs. Therefore, probable credibility suffices for supernatural faith.

Response: Then, as was said in the thesis above, *God supplies through an internal illumination* those things that are lacking from the perspective of the internal proposition [of credibility], as Billuart explains in the same text, cited above.

5. *It will be insisted, however*: Certain people are led to faith on account of aesthetic motives—for example, on account of the beauty of Catholic worship, religious music, or chanting. Now, these motives are not morally certain signs of the divine origin of Christianity or of the fact of revelation. Therefore, moral certitude concerning the fact of revelation is not required in order to believe.

Response: If these men arrived at true faith and not mere religious opinion, these motives were only secondary and occasions for inquiring into the true religion; they had a symbolic value for arousing their attention and intention to arrive at the saving truth. Afterwards, under the influence of grace, these men found sufficient motives of credibility that, nonetheless, they perhaps do not know how to set forth explicitly, for such motives are less sensibly [experiential in nature].

6. *Still, it will be urged*, at least when grace supplies, it suffices to have a motive of credibility that, of itself, is probable but which then afterward can be set aside as false.

Response: I deny this, for as we said in the thesis above, *grace does not supply so that the*

---

[104] See Billuart, *Summa sancti Thomae, De fide*, diss. 1, a. 2.

mysteries would be believed without evidence of credibility but, rather, makes this evidence manifest to us, for example, in the sublimity of the teaching, the holy conviction of the preacher of the faith, [or] in the profound peace that the hearer experiences in himself according to the word of the Lord: "My peace I give unto you: not as the world giveth, do I give unto you" (John 14:27, DR). Also see below [and in the next volume] concerning the value of internal motives as well as that of external motives intrinsic to religion.

7. *Still*, nonetheless, in the gravest temptations against faith, evidence of credibility disappears, and nonetheless faith can remain. Therefore, faith does not require certain credibility.

Response: In the midst of such temptations, with the aid of grace, not only does the very act of faith remain but also the certain judgment of credibility. Although ordinary motives may be overshadowed, {{510}} nonetheless, some sufficient motive remains that perhaps cannot be easily and explicitly expressed, and grace supplies in a hidden way for what is lacking on the part of reasoning, the soul being aided through the gifts of the Holy Spirit.[105]

Indeed, souls thus tempted always know the grave obligation of believing[106] and, hence, flee from deliberate doubt, resisting it and praying.[107] In such a case, we must apply the principle that in those things that are necessary with a necessity of means for salvation, the safer path must be taken, and in this case, the safer path is to persevere in faith. Indeed, the following position held by Georg Hermes is condemned: "Catholics could have a just reason for suspending their judgment and calling into question the faith that they have already received under the teaching authority of the Church until they have completed a scientific demonstration of the credibility and truth of their faith."[108]

Faith is not lost except through a mortal and formal sin against [the virtue of] faith, at least through culpable negligence of necessary instruction in the faith or through a grave imprudence in incautious reading of heretics or rationalists.[109]

---

[105] See *ST* II-II, q. 8, a. 2.

[106] See *ST* II-II, q. 8, a. 4, ad 2: "Even if not everyone having faith fully understands those things that are proposed to be believed, nonetheless they understand that they are to be believed and *that they must not deviate from them in any way.*"

[107] Sometimes, holy souls suffer these grave temptations through which they arrive at heroic faith. Indeed, in this way, their faith is fully purified, for with the overshadowing of secondary motives and the growing obscurity of the mysteries, they come to believe on account of the only formal motive of faith—namely, on account of the authority of God who reveals.

[108] [First] Vatican Council, *Dei filius*, can. 3.6 (Denzinger, no. 3036).

[109] See Vacant, *Études sur le Concile du Vatican*, vol. 2, 179 (art. 117): "Is it defined that Catholics cannot ever place their faith in doubt without thereby formally sinning? No, but it is defined that one cannot have an objectively valid reason for placing one's Catholic faith in doubt and that one at least materially sins in so doing. (Art. 118) Nonetheless, the majority of theologians hold that all those who abandon the religious beliefs of their childhood have not been able to do so without committing formal mortal sins either by neglecting the duty of allowing

§2. Evident Credibility Is Reconciled with the Freedom of the Act of Faith

Objection: That which appears to be evidently true is not freely affirmed. Now, if the mysteries of faith are evidently credible, they are evidently true. Therefore, the mysteries are not freely believed.

Response: I make a distinction in the major premise, conceding that what appears as being evidently true with intrinsic evidence [is indeed not freely affirmed], though denying that this is so for *extrinsic evidence*. I contradistinguish the minor premise: I deny that the evidence of credibility is intrinsic evidence of the mysteries, though I concede that it is extrinsic evidence of them.

Indeed, the mysteries are evidently credible, inasmuch as on the basis of certain signs they appear to be revealed by God while remaining intrinsically obscure and indeed cannot in any way be demonstrated after revelation. Such mysteries include those of the Trinity, the Incarnation, Redemption, predestination, and eternal punishment. And the freedom of faith remains on account of this obscurity. "The only manifestation that excludes faith is that which renders what principally belongs to faith to be apparent or seen."[110]

1. *It will be urged, however*: At least evidence of credibility on the basis of immediately seen miracles removes the freedom of faith, for "the faith of the demons is, in some way, compelled by the evidence of signs."[111]

{{511}} *Response*: Demons see miracles far better than we do, and nonetheless their faith is not, simply speaking, compelled, but, as the Thomists explain: "It is only in some way and morally compelled, in nearly the same way that someone throwing his goods out of fear of shipwreck is said to be compelled, for since he does not have evidence of revealed things but only evidence by way of attestation [*in attestante*], this does not simply speaking compel his assent to the revealed reality, which always remains obscure in itself."[112] However, the demon chooses assent rather than utterly foolish denial.

2. *It is urged, however*: This kind of extrinsic evidence indeed does not exist for things held by faith, for otherwise all would believe after the consideration of the motives of credibility, given that denial would be utterly foolish.

Response: It is not the case that everyone believes, and this is so for two reasons—namely, either (1) because they do not sufficiently consider the motives of credibility on

---

themselves to be instructed, or by exposing themselves to the dangers of wicked conversations or wicked texts, or by poorly responding to God's graces. This manner of thinking is best in agreement with the various teachings of our Council."

[110] *ST* II-II, q. 5, a. 1.

[111] *ST* II-II, q. 5, a. 2, ad 1.

[112] See Billuart, *Summa sancti Thomae, De fide*, diss. 4, a. 2.

account of their indifference to salvation, or (2) also because of the wickedness of their affect. Upon seeing the motives of credibility, they still can place some obstacle before faith, like the priests of the synagogue [*sic*] after the manifest miracle performed by SS. Peter and John (Acts 4:16).

3. *It is insisted*: Nonetheless, those who have never seen Rome necessarily admit its existence on account of the evident authority of witnesses. Therefore, likewise, once we are presented with evidence of credibility, we must necessarily admit the revealed mysteries.

Response: Those who have never seen Rome admit of its existence either on account of the authority of witnesses (that is, through human faith) or on account of a necessary proof based upon its effects, for if this city did not exist, many utterly certain facts would be lacking in *raisons d'être* [and] without cause. Then, in such a case, this adherence is necessary just like a proof from effects. By contrast, motives of credibility are not effects of the revealed mysteries but, rather, only extrinsically confirm that they have been revealed.

4. *Still, it is urged*: However, there are certain motives of credibility intrinsic to religion, like the sublimity of revealed doctrine or the marvelous life of the Church. Therefore, evidence of credibility can be intrinsic.

Response: Supernatural mysteries like the Trinity, the Incarnation, predestination, and eternal punishment always remain intrinsically obscure for us as wayfarers. The sublimity of the revealed doctrine is only taken from a kind of befittingness of the mysteries, from their interconnection with each other, and from their analogy with natural truths. Likewise, the life of the Church is not made evident according to its intrinsic supernaturality, nor do we see the Holy Spirit enlivening souls. However, certain external signs manifest this life inasmuch as the Church excels every natural society in her holiness, her Catholic unity, and her unconquered stability. These various signs denote a special intervention by God and thus confirm revelation. However, this is something extrinsic to the revealed mysteries.

5. *It is urged*: Evidence of credibility at least diminishes the merit of faith, for Jesus said disapprovingly: "Unless you see signs and wonders, you believe not" (John 4:48, DR). Likewise, in another place, while speaking of the miracle of his Resurrection, he said: "Because thou hast seen me, Thomas, thou hast believed. Blessed are they that have not seen and have believed" (John 20:29, DR). Therefore, evidence of credibility is not necessary.

Response: I concede that Jesus disapproved of those who sought after signs unnecessarily or who do not believe without immediately seeing miracles with their own eyes. However, I deny that Jesus disapproved of those who say, "I would not believe the mysteries of faith unless I see that they are to be believed rationally." See St. Thomas's words in *ST* III, q. 55, a. 5, ad 3: "Those who are so ready in their soul to believe God even without seeing signs are blessed in comparison with those who do not believe unless they see such signs."

§3. Evident Credibility Can Be Reconciled with the Obscurity of Faith

{{512}} *Objection*: That which is evidently credible is evidently true. Now, the mysteries of faith are not evidently true but, rather, remain obscure. Therefore, the mysteries of faith are evidently credible.

Response: I deny the major premise, for truth is sought intrinsically (or from what a reality [*res*] is), whereas credibility is taken from testimony and *extrinsic* motives. Thus, an evidently credible reality is one that is testified to by a qualified witness.

1. *It is urged*: On the basis of evidence of the divine trustworthiness, and on the basis of the evidence of revelation, confirmed by the most certain of signs, we have evidence that a mystery exists. Therefore, the mystery would not be essentially obscure.

Response: I make a distinction regarding the major premise. I concede that we thus have evidence for [*the existence of a given*] *mystery in the deposit of revelation* to be believed (or that it is something revealed). However, I deny that we have evidence *concerning what it is in itself*, independent of obscure revelation. We only have evidence of the revealed reality according to the formal character common to all revealed things, not as regards its specific predicates (or the connection of its predicates with it as a subject [*seu connectionem cum subiecto*]). For example, the evident credibility of the mystery of the Incarnation neither explains nor constitutes the Incarnate Word, since it is something extrinsic to it. Hence, even though the proposition, "The Word is Incarnate," is evidently credible, it forever remains obscure in itself and consequently remains an object of faith.

2. *It will be insisted*, nonetheless: He who evidently knows the existence of God from his effects does not have faith concerning him. Now, created effects are extrinsic to God. Therefore, similarly, he who knows the mysteries on the basis of the evidence of the signs of revelation does not have faith concerning them.

Response: I concede the major premise and make a distinction regarding the minor. I concede that created effects are extrinsic to God formally speaking but deny that they are virtually [extrinsic to him]. Indeed, an effect virtually exists in the cause from which it proceeds, and therefore the existence of a cause can be evidently known from its effects. By contrast, revelation is completely, both formally and virtually, *extrinsic* to the revealed reality, for it is not its cause regarding its intrinsic existence but only as regards its extrinsic existence—namely, that it has been revealed [*esse revelatum*].

3. *It will be urged, however*: At least that which is evidently credible by divine faith is evidently possible. Now, in divine necessary realities, the possible and the true are one and the same thing. Therefore, the necessary mysteries would be evidently true.

Response: I deny the major premise, for possibility, like truth, is sought from something intrinsic, whereas credibility, by contrast, [is sought] from something extrinsic. Hence, even if we presuppose the evident credibility of the mystery of the Trinity, the intrinsic possibility of this mystery remains obscure.

4. *And yet*, nonetheless, that which is evidently impossible is evidently unbelievable. Therefore, that which is evidently credible is evidently possible.

Response: The consequence does not hold, for one of two opposed statements must be negative and the other affirmative. Hence, the true consequence is: Therefore, that which is not evidently non-believable is not evidently impossible, which we admit.

§4 Evident Credibility Is Reconciled with the Supernaturality of Faith

Objection: Certitude of a superior order cannot be resolved into evidence of an inferior order. Now, evidence of credibility is essentially natural (or rational). Therefore, the supernatural certitude of faith cannot be resolved into it, for such supernatural certitude is essentially loftier than the metaphysical certitude of the first principles.[113]

Response: I make a distinction regarding the major premise. I concede that the certitude of a superior order cannot be *formally and intrinsically resolved* into an inferior order. However, I deny that it cannot be *materially and extrinsically* resolved. Thus, the metaphysical certitude of the first principles materially and extrinsically presupposes {{513}} sensation, while nonetheless being loftier than sensation. The same is the case for supernatural certitude in relation to the evidence of credibility, which is only a necessary condition for the act of faith so that said act can be prudent with the prudence required in a weighty matter.

1. *It will be urged*: A natural judgment cannot be the necessary condition for the supernatural act of faith. Now the judgment of credibility is essentially natural (or rational). Therefore [, the judgment of credibility cannot be the necessary condition for the supernatural act of faith.]

Response: I concede that a natural judgment cannot be the proximate condition for a supernatural act. However, I deny that it cannot be a remote condition for it. In any case, the proximate condition for the act of faith is the practically-practical judgment of credentity, which is essentially supernatural, as we said above.

2. *Yet the objector will insist*: However, nothing can be simultaneously scientifically known [*scitum*] and believed or, in other words, evident and obscure for the same person. Now, revelation is that which is believed as well as that by which we believe. Therefore, the fact of revelation cannot be scientifically known.

Response: I make a distinction regarding the major premise. I concede that one and the same thing cannot be simultaneously scientifically known and believed by the same person from the same perspective. However, I deny that this cannot be so from different perspectives. Now, the fact of revelation is believed inasmuch as it is an *essentially supernatural* mystery, proceeding from God the Author of grace and glory, and is imperfectly known [*scitum*] on the basis of signs, inasmuch it is a miraculous intervention by God,

---

[113] See *ST* II-II, q. 4, a. 8.

one that is *at least modally supernatural*, for from this lower perspective, it can be naturally known on the basis of sensible miracles. Thus, as we said above, at the end of chapter 14, the resurrection of Christ, qua miracle, is naturally knowable on the basis of signs. However, as something attributed to the Word of God, it is held by faith alone. Thus, Christ's death upon the Cross was a visible fact, whereas its infinite value is a mystery. The same can be said of all of the facts of Christ's life.

Hence, as we have already said, on the basis of signs, the fact of revelation is not, properly speaking, known through perfect scientific knowledge, for science is properly had either from a [proper] cause or a proper effect, whereas the fact of revelation is only known on the basis of an extrinsic sign—namely, on the basis of the miracles by which it is confirmed.

3. *It will still be insisted, however*: That which is essentially supernatural, like sanctifying grace, is naturally unknowable, even as regards its mode of production and as regards its existence. Now, divine revelation is essentially supernatural. Therefore, divine revelation is naturally unknowable, even as regards the way it is produced and as regards its existence.

Response: I make a distinction regarding the major premise, conceding that it is *directly* unknowable, but denying that it is unknowable *on the basis of signs*. In itself, the fact of revelation is a supernatural, invisible locution of God to the prophet. It is also the invisible instrumental motion by which the prophet infallibly speaks in the name of the Lord. Hence, this revelation is not naturally knowable directly, not even as regards the way it is produced and as regards its existence. Nonetheless, it is confirmed by signs, especially miracles, and can be known on the basis of them. However, in this way, it is known only qua modally supernatural, for the same miracles could confirm revelation that is *solely modally* supernatural, if God had revealed only the natural truths of religion.

Thus, based upon this resolution of objections, we have a confirmation for our thesis concerning credibility, and it also is clear against Protestant claims that the Catholic faith is not, as they say, a kind of external faith had in accord with a servile obedience to the external magisterium of the Church and in dependence upon miraculous signs. [This claim is wrong,] for the Church's proposition [of revealed truth] is only a[n objective] condition for faith considered from the perspective of its object, and the judgment of credibility founded on divine signs is only a [necessary] condition for faith considered from the perspective of the subject. However, the formal motive of faith is the authority of God who reveals, and infused faith is much loftier and more intimate than the natural religious experience that Protestants substitute for it. This experience often is a kind of sensible piety, whereas infused faith, by contrast, proceeds from sanctifying grace, which exists in the essence of the soul,[114] elevating [and] strengthening it, illuminating the intellect, immediately uniting it with the First Truth who exists above time and dwells within

---

[114] [Trans. note: Reading "quae est in essentia animae" for "quae est essentia animae".]

the righteous. Thus, with St. John, we can truly say: "He that believeth in the Son of God hath the testimony of God in himself" (1 John 5:10, DR).

On the Demonstrability of Credibility on the Basis of the Motives of Credibility

SINGLE ARTICLE

{{514}} §1. The necessity of this demonstration for the faith of the Church as a whole
    §2. The possibility of this demonstration
    §3. The notion of a motive of credibility
    §4. The division of the motives of credibility

§1. The Necessity of This Demonstration for the Faith of the Church as a Whole

In the preceding chapter, it was said that a scientific demonstration of credibility is not required for any particular believer but, rather, that moral certitude of common sense suffices [*sufficere certitudinem sensus communis et moralem*] as something that is within the grasp of all, at least with the aid of grace.

However, for the faith of the Church as a whole, it is utterly befitting that there be a scientific demonstration of credibility—that is, one that is metaphysically well-founded as regards the probative strength of the motives of credibility and historically as regards their existence. This scientific demonstration is not, strictly speaking, necessary for the faith of the Church as a whole, because strictly speaking, the certitude of common sense suffices. Nay, divine grace can at least partially supply for what is lacking in the objective proposition of credibility. Nonetheless, the utter befittingness of this demonstration can be proven *a posteriori* and *a priori*.

(A) *A posteriori*. For in general, believers invoke the scientific knowledge of teachers of the faith [*Doctores*], who know the motives of credibility well enough, so that they can resolve the objections of nonbelievers against the faith and credibility. Now, objections of this kind are proposed in the name of philosophical or historical science. Therefore, teachers who have the duty of instructing others must have a scientific demonstration of credibility that is metaphysically and historically well-founded. Thus, it is especially fitting that this demonstration exist. Likewise, St. Thomas says in *ST* II-II, q. 2, a. 6, "Men of greater abilities who have the office of teaching others are bound to have fuller knowledge of things to be believed and [therefore are bound] to believe them more explicitly."

{{515}} (B) *A priori*. It is utterly befitting that the Church be able to defend the value of the signs of revelation irrefutably if these signs are, of themselves, irrefutable. Now, the Church accepts signs of this kind as coming from God, as she herself affirms.[1] Therefore, it is utterly befitting that the Church be able to irrefutably defend the existence and value of these signs, for otherwise, they would be irrefutable in themselves and not for us precisely qua signs.

However, the utter befittingness of miracles themselves is proven by St. Thomas in *ST* II-II, q. 178, a. 1:

> The Holy Spirit sufficiently provides for the Church in those things that are useful for salvation. . . . (However,) it is necessary that the spoken word (i.e., the preaching of the faith) be confirmed in order for it to become credible. Now, this is brought about through the performing of miracles, according to the words that close the gospel of Mark (DR): "confirming the word with signs that followed." And this is quite reasonable, for it is natural to man that he grasp intelligible truth through sensible effects. Thus, just as man, led along by natural reason, can arrive at some knowledge of God through natural effects, so too through certain supernatural effects, which are called miracles, man is led to some supernatural knowledge of what he is to believe.

If miracles are befitting in this way, the defense of the value of miracles is likewise maximally befitting.

§2. The Possibility of This Demonstration

We must consider two points: (A) the doctrine of the Church in this matter;

---

1   See [First] Vatican Council, *Dei filius*, ch. 3 and can. 3.4 (Denzinger, nos. 3013 and 3034).

(B) the rational defense of this doctrine.

(A) *The doctrine of the Church*

According to the [First] Vatican Council, this demonstration is not only possible but indeed exists, for it is defined: "If anyone says that no miracles are possible . . . or that miracles can never be recognized with certainty and that the divine origin of the Christian religion cannot be *legitimately proven* by them, let him be anathema."[2] Likewise, in the corresponding chapter: "Right reason demonstrates the foundations of faith."[3] Bautain had to subscribe to this proposition: "Proof drawn from the miracles of Jesus Christ, sensible and striking for the eyewitnesses, has lost none of its force with its brilliance with regard to subsequent generations. We find this proof with all certitude in the authenticity of the New Testament, in the oral and written tradition of all Christians."[4] Likewise, see Pius IX's remarks against the followers of Georg Hermes in the encyclical *Qui pluribus*.[5] Finally, in the Anti-Modernist Oath, it is said: "Second, I accept and acknowledge external proofs of revelation, that is, divine deeds, in particular miracles and prophecies *as utterly certain signs of the divine origin of the Christian religion*, and I hold that they are most excellently adapted to the understanding of all eras and men, even of our own days."

In the pre-conciliar schema for the [First] Vatican Council,[6] in order to explain the aforementioned canon concerning the probative strength of miracles, the following is said:

> Among those Protestants who profess to hold Christian revelation, there are many who either entirely deny the value or necessity of the motives of credibility which would be set forth from miracles, the fulfillment of prophecies, etc., or hold that they play a kind of secondary role in reinforcing the faith that one already has, for (as they say) such facts can only be known by him who already has faith. . . . Nor are there lacking those who teach that those supernatural facts cannot {{516}} be understood as motives of credibility unless faith is already presupposed and, hence, that *the very fact of revelation* cannot be *demonstrated* to the man who has not yet received faith. . . . Moreover, the Holy See has already on a number of occasions deemed it necessary to condemn errors of this kind.

---

[2] Ibid. can. 3.4 (Denzinger, no. 3034).

[3] [First] Vatican Council, *Dei filius*, ch. 4 (Denzinger, no. 3019).

[4] Theses subscribed to by Louis-Eugène Bautain by Order of His Bishop, Nov. 18, 1835 and Sept. 8, 1840, no. 3 (Denzinger no. 2753).

[5] See Pius IX, *Qui pluribus*, no. 7 (Denzinger, no. 2778).

[6] *Acta et decreta SS. Concilii Vaticani* in *Collectio lacensis*, vol. 7, 528. Also see Vacant, *Études*, vol. 1, 593.

And the pre-conciliar schema refers to the twenty-first proposition condemned by Innocent XI on March 2, 1679, the [aforementioned] proposition to which Bautain had to subscribe, and Pius IX's declaration against the followers of Georg Hermes.[7]

(B) *The rational defense of this Church teaching*

Someone could object as follows: Even presupposing the discernibility of miracles and its connection with revelation to be confirmed, there cannot be a scientific demonstration of credibility (i.e., of the divine origin of the Christian religion). Indeed, scientific demonstration is had either *a priori* from a proper cause or *a posteriori* from a proper effect. Now, the fact of divine revelation cannot be naturally known either on the basis of its proper supernatural cause or on the basis of its proper supernatural effects, which are also supernatural, like grace, and thus transcend reason. Therefore, the fact of revelation cannot be scientifically demonstrated.

To this, we must respond as follows. It is not necessary that the fact of revelation be proven by a proper and ostensive scientific demonstration, which is had from a proper cause or from a proper effect. *An indirect, broadly speaking scientific demonstration from an extrinsic, though divinely produced, sign* in confirmation of revelation suffices. Thus, as will be said below, a miracle directly manifests the intervention of the divine omnipotence and indirectly manifests the divine origin of the preaching of faith confirmed by it.

As logicians say,[8] direct demonstration, which is also called an ostensive demonstration, is stronger because it manifests the existence of the thing [*quia manifestat rem esse*] on the basis of positive principles and offers to our mind intrinsic evidence concerning this thing. *Indirect* demonstration or demonstration *per absurdum* concludes that the reality in question is such precisely because, otherwise, something absurd would follow. (For example, in the case we are considering, this must be so because otherwise God the Author of miracles would be false witness.)[9] Hence, this demonstration does

---

[7] See Innocent XI, Condemnation by the Sacred Office, Mar. 2, 1679, no. 21 (Denzinger, no. 2121); Theses subscribed to by Louis-Eugène Bautain by Order of His Bishop, Nov. 18, 1835 and Sept. 8, 1840, no. 3 (Denzinger no. 2753); Pius IX, *Qui pluribus*, no. 7 (Denzinger, no. 2778).

[8] See Aristotle, *Post. Anal.*, 1.26 (St. Thomas's comments, lect. 3). Tommaso Maria Zigliara, *Summa philosophica*, vol. 1, *Logica*, 156. Édouard Hugon, *Logica*, 379ff.

[9] See St. Thomas, *Quod.* II, q. 4, a. 1, ad 4: "It cannot happen that someone announcing a false doctrine would perform true miracles for they can only be performed by the divine power, for thus, God would be the witness to falsehood, which is impossible." Likewise, see *ST* II-II, q. 5, a. 2; III, q. 43, a. 1 and 3; *In II Thess.*, ch. 2, lect. 2. Also see *SCG* III, ch. 155 and I, ch. 6; *In IX Jn.*, lect. 3, no. 8.

not offer intrinsic evidence of the reality in question but, rather, excludes fear of error on account of the absurdities that would follow upon its denial. Thus, it is scientific, at least in a broad sense, and is employed in many sciences, even in mathematics.

Hence, St. Thomas says in *ST* III, q. 55, a. 5:

> The term "argument" can be used in two ways. Sometimes, something is called an argument when it is any kind of *reason* making one have faith concerning something that is in doubt. However, it sometimes is said of a given *sensible sign* leading to the manifestation of some truth, a sense that we can find Aristotle himself using sometimes in his own works (cf. *Prior Anal.*, 2.29). *Considering the term "argument" in the first sense,* Christ did not prove His resurrection to His disciples through arguments (the same can be said concerning the divine origin of His doctrine), for such an argumentative proof would have proceeded from certain principles which could only manifest something to His disciples if they knew them, for something cannot be made known on the basis of unknown things. However, if they already knew them, they would not transcend {{517}} human reason and thus would not be efficacious for establishing faith in the resurrection, which exceeds human reason, for it is necessary that principles be drawn from the same order [as the conclusions drawn from them]. However, he proved his resurrection to them through the authority of Sacred Scripture, which is the foundation of faith[10] by saying: "It was necessary that everything that was written about me in the Law, the Psalms, and the Prophets be fulfilled" (cf. Luke 24:44).—However, if the term "argument" is understood *in the second sense,* thus, it is said that Christ declared His resurrection by arguments inasmuch as He showed through certain *evident signs* that He truly had risen. Whence, in the Greek of Acts 1:3, where we have "in multis argumentis" in Latin, the term "argumentum" is in fact τεκμήριον, namely, *an evident sign enabling proof.*

Therefore, if certain Thomists[11] have said that men cannot have scientific knowledge concerning the fact of revelation, this is to be understood as referring to a demonstrative reason through the proper cause of the thing or

---

[10] Thus, too, revelation, as the voice of the Father through the Son and the Holy Spirit, is believed supernaturally, as has been said above.

[11] Cajetan says in *In ST* III, q. 55, a. 6 (on the sufficiency of the signs of Christ's Resurrection): "Understand 'sufficiency' in relation to the ability to cause the certitude of faith, not the certitude of science." That is, the certitude of science properly so called, which is knowledge through the cause on account of which a thing is what it is and cannot be otherwise. Likewise, see Cajetan, *In ST* II-II, q. 1, a. 4, no. 5.

through a proper effect. However, this does not exclude [the possibility of] a rigorous demonstration on the basis of an evident divine sign, reducing the opposite positions to absurdity or to impossibility.[12] Indeed, as we will come to discuss, metaphysics can determine the probative strength of miracles in an apodictic manner.

Moreover, as we will see, the fact of revelation is clear in certain effects that it has, for example, in the miraculous life of the Church inasmuch as this life, which is visible by its external notes, manifestly transcends the natural powers of humanity. Nonetheless, this argument, drawn from these notes as things that are *naturally* knowable, forever remains an argument from a sign.

§3. The Notion of a Motive of Credibility

According to the Catholic Church, the motives of credibility are *the signs or notes by which revealed religion is made evidently credible to divine faith*.[13] They are called *signs* or *notes* inasmuch as they manifest the divine origin of revealed religion (or inasmuch as they are "arguments for divine revelation"[14]). They are called *motives* in relation to the judgment of credibility, which is founded on them.[15]

Therefore, we must carefully distinguish the motives of credibility from the motive of faith and even from motives of credentity. For *the motive of faith* is not founded on {{518}} the signs of divine revelation but, rather, is

---

[12] See Ambroise Gardeil, *La crédibilité et l'apologétique*, 2nd ed. (Paris: Lecoffre, 1912), 78–126 (The rigorous demonstration of credibility). Also see his article "Crédibilité" in the *Dictionnaire de théologie catholique*, cols. 2215–2220. Likewise, see Robert-Constant Lagae, "La certitude rationnelle du fait de la révélation," *Revue Thomiste*, New Series, 10 (1910): 478–489, 618–641, and 791–799.

[13] See [First] Vatican Council, *Dei filius*, can. 3.3 (Denzinger, no. 3303): "If anyone says that divine revelation cannot be made credible by outward signs, . . . let him be anathema." In this text, revelation is taken in its objective sense—that is, meaning revealed mysteries. Also see ibid., ch. 3 (Denzinger, no. 3012): "God has instituted the Church through His only begotten Son and has endowed her with *manifest marks* [*notis*] of His institution so that she may be recognized by all men."

[14] See ibid., ch. 3 (Denzinger, no. 3009): "However, in order that the obedience of our faith be nevertheless in harmony with reason [cf. Rom 12:1], God willed that exterior proofs of his revelation, viz. divine facts, especially miracles and prophecies, should be joined to the interior helps of the Holy Spirit." Here, the term "revelation" is used as referring to the fact of revelation.

[15] See ibid. (Denzinger, no. 3013): "In fact, it is to the Catholic Church alone that belong all those signs that are so numerous and so wonderfully arranged by God to make *evident* the credibility of the Christian faith. In fact, the Church by herself . . . is a great and perpetual motive of credibility and an irrefutable testimony of her divine mission."

the very authority of God who reveals, and the motive of credentity is the divine right founding the obligation to believe.

The motive of credibility also differs from the object "of a pious affect of belief,"[16] for that object is "the good promised to believers,"[17] as well as the goodness of this doctrine thus proposed as divine and confirmed by divine signs. Thus, as we said above, in treating of the judgment of credibility, we can see (1) that revealed religion is credible on account of the divine signs that manifest its divine origin, (2) that it is to be believed on account of the obedience we owe to God and for the sake of our salvation, and (3) that we believe it supernaturally on account of the authority of God who reveals.

Hence, *three* things are required so that a given fact may be *a sufficient motive of credibility*: (1) *that it be certain in itself*, (2) *that it certainly be from a special intervention by God*, and (3) *that its meaning for confirming revelation be certain.*

§4. The Division of the Motives of Credibility

We must consider two points: (A) the Church's manner of speaking about the motives of credibility, and (B) the division itself.

A. *The Church's manner of speaking about the motives of credibility*

At the [First] Vatican Council, the Catholic Church proposed the following:

1) "God willed that *exterior* proofs [*argumenta*] of His revelation, viz., divine facts, *especially miracles* and *prophesies*, should be joined to the interior helps of the Holy Spirit; as they manifestly display the omnipotence of and infinite knowledge of God, they are the most certain signs of the divine revelation adapted to the intelligence of all men."[18]

2) She also proposes [as a motive of credibility] the *miraculous life of the Church herself:* "In fact, the Church by herself, with her marvelous propagation, eminent holiness, and inexhaustible fruitfulness in everything that is good, with her catholic unity and invincible stability, is a great and perpetual motive of credibility and an irrefutable testimony of her divine mission."[19]

3) The Church does not exclude internal motives. Nay, she even says:

---

[16] See Synod of Orange, can. 5 (Denzinger, no. 375).
[17] See *De veritate*, q. 14, a. 2, ad 10.
[18] [First] Vatican Council, *Dei filius*, ch. 3 (Denzinger, no. 3009).
[19] Ibid. (Denzinger, no. 3013).

"God willed that exterior proofs of his revelation . . . should be joined to the *interior helps of the Holy Spirit*."[20] Moreover, Pius IX argued on the basis of [revelation's] miraculous fulfillment of the aspirations of the human heart.[21] However, the Church condemns the Protestant doctrine holding that "men ought to be moved to faith solely by each one's inner experience or personal inspiration."[22] And as was said in the pre-conciliar schema: "Indeed, that internal sentiment, according to ordinary providence [in the order of nature], does not have a *supernatural* formal character, and if it is separated from extrinsic criteria is open to the gravest of delusions."[23]

Therefore, provided that internal motives not be separated from the others, they are indeed admitted by the Church, and the annotations in the pre-conciliar schema from the [First] Vatican Council[24] cite St. Thomas's text in *ST* I-II, q. 2, a. 9, ad 3: "He who believes {{519}} has a sufficient motive for believing, for he is moved by the authority of divine teaching confirmed through miracles and, what is more, by the interior instinct of God's invitation to belief. Whence, he does not believe flippantly."[25]

B. *Division of motives of credibility*

These various motives can be thus ordered, according to a necessary and

---

[20] Ibid. (Denzinger, no. 3009).

[21] See Pius IX, *Qui pluribus*, no. 8 (Denzinger, no. 2779): "For, in truth, this faith is the teacher of life, the guide to salvation, expelling all faults, and in fruitfulness giving birth to and nurturing the virtues . . . [it has illuminated with the light of divine knowledge] all peoples, races, nations, however savagely barbarous and diverse in disposition, customs, laws, and institutions; and has subjected them to the most sweet yoke of Christ Himself, 'Announcing peace' to all, 'announcing good' [Isa 52:7]."

[22] [First] Vatican Council, *Dei filius*, can. 3.3 (Denzinger, no. 3033).

[23] See *Schema prosynodale Conc. Vatic.*, Adnotationes (XVI), *Collectio lacensis*, vol. 7, 529; Vacant, *Études sur le Concile du Vatican*, vol. 1, 594.

[24] See *Collectio lacensis*, vol. 7, 532.

[25] In *Quod.* II, q. 4, a. 1 (Whether men ought to have believed in Christ if He did not perform miracles), St. Thomas had said, "If Christ did not perform visible miracles, other means for drawing men to faith would have remained, by which men would have been bound to submit to faith, for men were bound to believe in the authority of the Law and the Prophets. They were also bound not to resist the interior calling of God [in their souls]." And "to the first, therefore, we must say that among those works which Christ performed among men, we must also count the interior calling by which He drew certain men [to Himself]. As Gregory said in some homily, Christ interiorly drew Mary Magdalene through his mercy, while also receiving [her] through external clemency. Likewise, we must count His doctrine among such reasons, since He Himself likewise said: 'If I had not come and spoken to them, they would not have sin' (John 15:22, DR)."

adequate division through members opposed to each other.[26]

The motives of credibility are either external or internal. They are *external* if they exist outside of the consciousness of the man who believes or who is looking into faith. However, they are *internal* if they are within the consciousness of the man who believes or who is looking into faith.

Now, *external* motives are either *extrinsic* to revealed religion (e.g., miracles and prophecies[27]) or *intrinsic* to revealed religion (e.g., the sublimity of its doctrine and the miraculous life of the Church).

However, *internal* motives are taken from the miraculous fulfillment of our aspirations. They are either *universal* (e.g., the miraculous satisfaction of all of the aspirations of humanity, as is clear from the history of Christianity) or *individual* (e.g., the individual experience of profound peace, which seems to come from God alone—for example, when the disciples on the road to Emmaus said to each other, "Was not our heart burning within us, whilst he spoke in this way and opened to us the scriptures" [Luke 24:32, DR]).

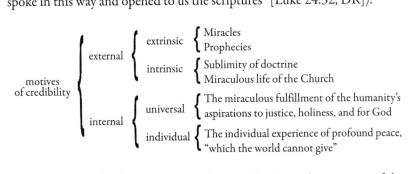

In the second volume of this work, we will take up the question of the value of these motives of credibility, especially the value of miracles, as well as the question of the existence of Christian revelation (that is, the question of the divine origin of Christ's teaching confirmed by these various signs).[28]

---

26 See Vacant, *Études sur le Concile du Vatican*, vol. 2, 37.

27 However, certain miracles and prophecies intrinsically pertain to religion, such as the preaching and fulfillment of Christ's Resurrection, which at once is a mystery of faith and pledge of future glory.

28 Certain people speak of *negative motives*, which, properly speaking, are not motives but, rather, only show that nothing opposes the idea that a given doctrine is revealed. As regards their value, they can be distinguished into *primary motives* that are sufficient in themselves and *secondary motives* that are insufficient in themselves but nonetheless confirm the value of primary motives.